ROUTLEDGE HANDBOOK OF ETHICS AND INTERNATIONAL RELATIONS

Ethics and international relations (IR), once considered along the margins of the IR field, has emerged as one of the most eclectic and interdisciplinary research areas today. Yet the same diversity that enriches this field also makes it a difficult one to characterize. Is it, or should it only be, the social-scientific pursuit of explaining and understanding how ethics influences the behaviors of actors in international relations? Or, should it be a field characterized by what the world should be like, based on philosophical, normative and policy-based arguments? This Handbook suggests that it can actually be both, as the contributions contained therein demonstrate how those two conceptions of ethics and international relations are inherently linked.

Seeking to both provide an overview of the field and to drive debates forward, this Handbook is framed by an opening chapter providing a concise and accessible overview of the complex history of the field of ethics and IR, and a conclusion that discusses how the field may progress in the future and which subjects are likely to rise to prominence. Within are forty-four distinct and original contributions from scholars teaching and researching in the field, which are structured around eight key thematic sections:

- philosophical foundations
- international relations theory
- international security and just war
- justice, rights and global governance
- international intervention
- environment, health and migration
- global economics
- religion and ethics

Drawing together a diverse range of scholars, the *Routledge Handbook of Ethics and International Relations* provides a cutting-edge overview of the field by bringing together these eclectic, albeit dynamic, themes and topics. It will be an essential resource for students and scholars alike.

Brent J. Steele is Professor and Francis D. Wormuth Presidential Chair in the Department of Political Science at the University of Utah, USA.

Eric A. Heinze is Professor in the Department of International and Area Studies at the University of Oklahoma, USA.

"This is a comprehensive and wide-ranging collection which without neglecting traditional subjects such as just war and global justice also covers more recent concerns such as post-colonialism, the emotions and environmentalism. It will be an invaluable teaching resource."

– Chris Brown, Emeritus Professor of International Relations, London School of Economics and Political Science

"Steele and Heinze have assembled an indispensable resource. Scholars, teachers, students, and general interest readers will find this to be the best one-stop reference for the field of ethics and international relations. Comprehensive in scope, rich in detail, and masterful in interpretation, the Handbook gives voice to a wide range of contributors, all of whom share their expertise with clarity and spirit."

– Joel H. Rosenthal, President, Carnegie Council for Ethics in International Affairs

ROUTLEDGE HANDBOOK OF ETHICS AND INTERNATIONAL RELATIONS

Edited by Brent J. Steele and Eric A. Heinze

LONDON AND NEW YORK

First published 2018
by Routledge
2 Park Square, Milton Park, Abingdon, Oxon OX14 4RN

and by Routledge
711 Third Avenue, New York, NY 10017

Routledge is an imprint of the Taylor & Francis Group, an informa business

British Library Cataloguing-in-Publication Data
A catalogue record for this book is available from the British Library

Library of Congress Cataloging-in-Publication Data
Names: Steele, Brent J., editor. | Heinze, Eric A., editor.
Title: Routledge handbook of ethics and international relations / edited by Brent J. Steele and Eric A. Heinze.
Other titles: Handbook of ethics and international relations
Description: Abingdon, Oxon ; New York, NY : Routledge, 2018. | Includes bibliographical references and index.
Identifiers: LCCN 2018000578| ISBN 9781138840201 (hardback) | ISBN 9781315725932 (ebook)
Subjects: LCSH: International relations—Moral and ethical aspects.
Classification: LCC JZ1306 .R68 2018 | DDC 172/.4—dc23
LC record available at https://lccn.loc.gov/2018000578

ISBN: 978-1-138-84020-1 (hbk)
ISBN: 978-1-315-72593-2 (ebk)

Typeset in Bembo Std
by Swales & Willis Ltd, Exeter, Devon, UK

CONTENTS

FIGURES AND TABLES

Figure

Tables

CONTRIBUTORS

Handbook editors:

Brent J. Steele, Professor and Francis D. Wormuth Presidential Chair, Department of Political Science, University of Utah, USA.

Eric A. Heinze, Professor, Department of International and Area Studies, University of Oklahoma, USA.

Thematic editors/contributors:

James Brassett, Reader, Department of Politics and International Studies, University of Warwick, UK.

Debra L. DeLaet, Professor, Department of Political Science, Drake University, USA.

Joy Gordon, Ignacio Ellacuría, S. J. Professor of Social Ethics, Department of Philosophy, Loyola University Chicago, USA.

Anthony F. Lang, Jr, Professor, School of International Relations, University of St. Andrews, UK.

Cecelia M. Lynch, Professor, Department of Political Science, University of California, Irvine, USA.

Cian O'Driscoll, Senior Lecturer of Politics, School of Social and Political Sciences, University of Glasgow, UK.

James Pattison, Professor of Politics, School of Social Sciences, University of Manchester, UK.

Fiona Robinson, Professor, Department of Political Science, Carleton University, Canada.

Contributors:

William Ackah, Lecturer, Department of Geography, Birkbeck, University of London, UK.

David Atenasio, Ph.D. candidate, Department of Philosophy, Loyola University, Chicago, USA.

Tabitha M. Benney, Assistant Professor, Department of Political Science, University of Utah, USA.

Andrea Birdsall, Lecturer, Politics and International Relations, University of Edinburgh, UK.

David L. Blaney, G. Theodore Mitau Professor, Department of Political Science, Macalester College, USA.

Dan Bulley, Reader in International Relations, Department of Social Sciences, Oxford Brookes University, UK.

Chris D. Clarke, Assistant Professor, Department of Politics and International Studies, University of Warwick, UK.

Damian Cox, Associate Professor, Department of Philosophy, Bond University, Australia.

Puneet Dhaliwal, D.Phil. candidate, Department of Politics and International Relations, St. Cross College, University of Oxford, UK.

Amy E. Eckert, Professor, Department of Political Science, Metropolitan State University of Denver, USA.

Carol Farbotko, Honorary Research Fellow, School of Land and Food, Geography and Environmental Studies, University of Tasmania, Australia.

Antonio Franceschet, Professor, Department of Political Science, University of Calgary, Canada.

Caron E. Gentry, Senior Lecturer, School of International Relations, University of St. Andrews, UK.

Luke Glanville, Fellow (Senior Lecturer), Department of International Relations, Australian National University, Australia.

Penny Griffin, Senior Lecturer, Politics and International Relations, University of New South Wales, Australia.

Jonathan Havercroft, Associate Professor, Politics and International Relations, University of Southampton, UK.

Patrick Hayden, Professor, School of International Relations, University of St. Andrews, UK.

Aidan Hehir, Reader, Department of Politics and International Relations, University of Westminster, UK.

Andrew R. Hom, Lecturer, Politics and International Relations, University of Edinburgh, UK.

Kimberly Hutchings, Professor, Politics and International Relations, Queen Mary, University of London, UK.

Beate Jahn, Professor, Department of International Relations, University of Sussex, UK.

Rosemary B. Kellison, Assistant Professor, Department of Philosophy, University of West Georgia, USA.

John W. Lango, Professor Emeritus, Department of Philosophy, Hunter College, City University of New York, USA.

Michael Levine, Professor, Department of Philosophy, University of Western Australia.

Matthew Lindauer, Assistant Professor, Department of Philosophy, Brooklyn College, City University of New York, USA.

Matt McDonald, Associate Professor, School of Political Science and International Studies, University of Queensland, Australia.

Elizabeth Mills, Lecturer, Department of Social Anthropology, University of Sussex, UK.

Seán Molloy, Reader, Politics and International Relations, University of Kent, UK.

Ajay Parasram, Assistant Professor, Department of International Development Studies and Department of History, Dalhousie University, Canada.

Mustapha Kamal Pasha, Professor and Chair in International Politics, Aberystwyth University, UK.

Elisabeth Porter, Professor, School of Communication, International Studies and Languages, University of South Australia.

Ben Richardson, Associate Professor, Department of Politics and International Studies, University of Warwick, UK.

Raúl Salgado Espinoza, Professor Investigador, Departamento de Estudios Internacionales y Comunicación, Facultad Latinoamericana de Ciencias Sociales, Ecuador.

Kate Schick, Senior Lecturer, School of History, Philosophy, Political Science and International Relations, Victoria University of Wellington, New Zealand.

Mona Kanwal Sheikh, Senior Researcher, International Security, Danish Institute for International Studies, Denmark.

Hugo Slim, Head of Policy and Humanitarian Diplomacy Division, International Committee of the Red Cross, Switzerland.

William Smith, Associate Professor, Government and Public Administration, Chinese University of Hong Kong.

Michele L. Statz, Postdoctoral Researcher, Department of Family Medicine and Biobehavioral Health, University of Minnesota Medical School, Duluth, USA.

Kok-Chor Tan, Professor, Department of Philosophy, University of Pennsylvania, USA.

Fernando R. Tesón, Tobias Simon Eminent Scholar, College of Law, Florida State University, USA.

Erin K. Wilson, Associate Professor of Politics and Religion, Faculty of Theology and Religious Studies, University of Groningen, the Netherlands.

Nahed Artoul Zehr, Executive Director, Faith and Culture Center, Nashville, Tennessee, USA.

ACKNOWLEDGMENTS

The editors would like to thank a number of people who helped make this volume possible. We have enjoyed and appreciated working with Nicola Parkin, Lydia de Cruz and Lucy Frederick, and the entire Routledge team, throughout the process of getting this Handbook towards publication. We thank our thematic editors, who have not only been easy to work with but especially impressive in recruiting a talented group of contributors for each theme of the Handbook. The Handbook was kick-started by a symposium held at the University of Utah in the Fall of 2015. We thank the Wormuth Presidential Chair, the Daniels Fund Ethics Initiative and Abe Bakhsheshy, the College of Social and Behavior Sciences and Dean Cynthia Berg, the Tanner Center for Human Rights and Tom Maloney, for their generous support in making that symposium possible. D. Porter Morgan provided logistical and administrative support that was also invaluable for that symposium. For helpful comments at that symposium, we also extend our thanks to Mark Button, Steve Johnston, Anthony Anghie, Deen Chatterjee, John Francis and Lina Svedin. Thanks especially to the University of Oklahoma's Department of International and Area Studies and Mitchell Smith for facilitating and funding a follow-up meeting in Norman in the Fall of 2016. Financial support was also provided by the Office of the Vice President for Research, University of Oklahoma. We thank S. Michael Christian for his tireless copyediting of the entire Handbook, and Nancy Peterson for writing the index. And the co-editors would like to thank one another, not only for the many hours of labor that went into editing this volume, but for the many years of friendship they have shared, and the many more to follow.

INTRODUCTION

Ethics and international relations

An evolving conversation

Brent J. Steele and Eric A. Heinze

Questions about the interplay of ethics and state foreign policy were at the heart of the field of international relations (IR) when it emerged in the early 20th century. While 'international ethics' was largely banished to the periphery of the field during the Cold War years, recent decades have witnessed its re-emergence as one of the most eclectic and interdisciplinary research fields today. This 're-emergence' of ethics and international relations occurred during the latter stages of the Cold War, with scholars again considering the ways in which ethical issues impacted the behaviors of international actors.[1] Similarly inspired research gained momentum in the 1990s, when a host of 'normative' issues – such as genocide, non-violent resistance, human rights, intervention, environmental security, to name just a few – emerged during the end of the Cold War and the beginning of the post-Cold War era. Those working on ethics also began to find a variety of outlets for their work, most especially when the Carnegie Council for Ethics in International Affairs began publishing their journal, *Ethics and International Affairs*, in 1987 and re-issued several key articles from that journal as collected chapters in 'readers'.[2] Indeed, beginning in the 1990s, up to and through the millennium, one could find an increasingly significant collection of works that self-consciously examined international relations using approaches, concepts, and the vocabulary of ethics and normative theory.[3]

Yet there was also a sense throughout its early development as a field, that as a *topic*, ethics would have difficulty breaking into the broader field of IR. For instance, as Mervyn Frost pointed out in 1998, much 'normative' research in the 1990s that was purposed by a social scientific endeavor was still grappling with the age-old concerns of how ethical perspectives, frameworks, or traditions influence, shape, and pattern the behaviors of international actors. Yet for Frost, the broader movement on ethics represented instead a 'turn not taken', with theorists and scholars failing to articulate their own normative views and judgments on the world.[4] There were other challenges for those working on ethics, especially in the United States academy. In this more positivist-oriented field of international relations (within the discipline and departments of political science), because ethics was shaped by less quantifiable or even identifiable entities – such as arguments, ideas, emotions – there seemed to be a built-in limit to how much ethics could be incorporated into 'good' IR research. Furthermore, approaching the world 'normatively' and ethically seemed in tension with the objective purpose of especially US social science. A normative stance, in other words, seemed to be, if not polemical, then prone towards formulating 'biased' results that slip into the realm of opinion and belief, as E. H. Carr famously accused the inter-war 'utopians' of doing.

During the 2000s, the 9/11 attacks and the resulting US-led 'war on terror', a global financial crisis (2007–2008), and further dislocation fueled by globalization and technological advances were all developments examined by an increasing number of scholars from an 'ethical' perspective. Major publications in the field of IR followed suit, as evidenced by the 2008 edition of the *Oxford Handbook of International Relations*, which included in its 'Major Theoretical Perspectives' section nine contributions dealing solely with the 'ethics' of each major perspective of IR theory.[5] Taken together, and for whichever set of reasons one wishes to foreground, ethics is now at the very least *confronted by* most (if not all) scholars of international relations.

The field of ethics and IR

Ethics and international relations is a broad field that approaches the pantheon of topics in international affairs and world relations with a wide array of philosophical, ethical, and normative theoretical resources. Because of its diversity and interdisciplinarity, there are a number of ways to organize the field of ethics and IR. One overlapping categorization has already been intimated above, which is that it involves the distinction between the 'is' versus the 'ought' of international relations.[6] That is, one of the purposes animating scholarship within the field of ethics and IR involves seeing ethics as yet another variable in global politics that both shapes, and is shaped by, the actions of states and other international actors. This strand of research involves addressing the 'why and how' questions of the field – as in, 'why and how do certain factors (such as moral norms) contribute to the strategy/action/behavior of a particular state'? The 'ought' category of research, of course, has been deemed a more 'normative' purpose, involving arguments about the way the world could or should be, as well as providing us the tools to judge the world and its actors, now and going forward. [7]

Even if these two categories of ethics research are anything but mutually exclusive (as evidenced by the contributions to this volume), they have provided one way to characterize and critique the field ever since (at least) Mervyn Frost's iconic 1998 study on a 'turn not taken'.[8] Frost's point then was that, while much research in the 1990s centralized the importance of norms and ethics in shaping the behavior of international actors – including especially states – scholars had yet to fully realize and put forth their own views of what not only was happening (then) but what type of ethics *should* be shaping international relations going forward.

This categorization remains salient, if not preferred, and not least because it recalls the geographic disciplinary differences that characterize the entry points to the field of IR itself. Most scholars and students working in the United States acquired their training in the field of political science, and within that, the subfields of international relations or political theory. Although not averse to the ways in which their research questions themselves are normatively conditioned, this entry point tends to be shaped by the social scientific purpose of ethics and IR – using ethical considerations and principles to explain 'why' actors pursued certain behaviors and policies. Other work, produced by scholars trained in academic contexts perhaps outside of the US and with more interdisciplinary influences akin to the 'classical' approach once delineated by Hedley Bull (1966), have been less shy about proposing normative arguments to grapple with ongoing and/or emerging dilemmas of international politics.

Thus, the same diversity that enriches the field of ethics and IR also makes it a difficult one to characterize. Is it, or should it only be, the social-scientific pursuit of explaining and understanding how ethics influences the behaviors of actors in international relations? Or, might it be a field characterized by what the world *should* be like, based on philosophical and policy-based arguments? Or, finally – and the approach we plan to take in this comprehensive Handbook – can it be both, and further involve the field in an appraisal of how those two conceptions of ethics and IR are inherently linked? This Handbook hopes to provide an inventory of the field of ethics in international relations by bringing together these eclectic, albeit dynamic, themes and topics.

Audiences and goals of the Handbook

The contributions to this Handbook collectively consider both sets of purposes, but also suggest that the two purposes are intertwined now more than ever. Ethical and normative arguments, in order to have power, have to be presented in ways that will resonate with how international actors (individuals, groups, states, and the like) currently approach and view the world. And, social-scientific studies, in order to be more legitimate and transparent, need to foreground the 'ethics' involved in the types of questions that are answered, the methods being utilized, and the answers or (at the very least) policy implications that follow otherwise benign analytical investigations.

In addition to the aforementioned foci of the field, this Handbook is both an inventory of the field of ethics in IR, as well as an investigation into where the field currently is and where it perhaps may be going in the future. So, in addition to the 'is' versus 'ought' foci of the field, the Handbook's contributions can be characterized as 'looking back' as well as 'forward-looking'. Therefore, its contributions were written with at least three sets of audiences and readers in mind.

First, the Handbook provides undergraduate and graduate students with an overview of the topics that constitute the field of ethics and IR, while the chapters provide examples of how to 'do' ethics and IR research. Each of the themes of the Handbook is introduced by a thematic overview essay that provides quick and accessible reference to the important subjects of ethics and IR that fall within that theme. Many contributions provide tangible illustrations of the particular concerns permeating these themes and the field as a whole. As such, the Handbook can be used as a text for courses on ethics and IR but also for more focused ones on any of the topical themes covered here.

Second, as the contributions provide both new ways to characterize the stakes of ethics in IR, as well as new avenues for thinking about ethics going forward, scholars working in the field will find the contributions to this Handbook useful for helping to shape their ongoing research concerns, questions, and investigations. Contributors thus do more than simply re-state the past, but delineate ways to grapple with the topics of ethics and IR that serve to provoke further scholarly debates and discussions.

Third, and finally, the Handbook proves accessible for the educated 'layperson' who may not be familiar with the scholarly debates or topics of ethics in IR, but nevertheless 'practices' ethics and is shaped by ethical considerations in their everyday lives. Mervyn Frost put it succinctly in the opening pages of his most recent characterization of global ethics:

> The ethical dimension of our involvement in international relations is not merely confined to instances . . . where we confront problems that present themselves to us as *overtly* ethical. There is an ethical dimension to even the most run-of-the-mill instances of our engagement with international affairs . . . In our everyday conduct we simply take it for granted, without a thought, that in participating in these spheres of activity we are doing the right thing from an ethical point of view. But were we to be challenged, we would be ready with an answer to justify our actions on ethical grounds.[9]

The arguments, overviews, and characterizations that follow throughout this Handbook provide us with ways to reflect upon our own 'run-of-the-mill' instances of our engagements with international affairs and how, and whether, we really can justify those actions on ethical grounds. We all know that if and when we *are* challenged to do so, whatever justifications we provide themselves can be further challenged. This Handbook can thus offer readers a way of thinking and talking, and even acting, according to what they find 'ethical' – as well as avenues to change those ways should they feel uncomfortable about whether their run-of-the-mill practices continue to be 'ethical'.

Overview and structure

This Handbook is organized around eight 'themes': philosophical foundations; IR theory; security and the ethics of war; ethics and institutions; international intervention; ethics and vulnerability (e.g., migration, health, and climate); the ethics of a global economy; and religious ethics in international politics. The chapters constituting each theme have been shaped, edited, and organized by thematic editors, who provide tangible overview essays introducing readers to each theme. The Handbook also includes two 'bookend' chapters – an historical overview of the field written by Kimberly Hutchings, and a discussion of the 'futures' of ethics and international relations written by Dan Bulley. We think that this structure provides a useful combination of both breadth and depth that is integral to knowing not only where the field has been, but where it is now, and where it may be headed in the future.

Ethics and IR has been shaped and informed by comprehensive, and historical, debates in the field of philosophy. The first theme, on philosophical foundations, examines how the field of ethics and IR has drawn from a variety of philosophers and approaches. As Joy Gordon notes in her thematic overview chapter, scholars working in this genre of ethics have examined the rights, duties, responsibilities, and agency that individuals, groups, and (eventually) nation-states have to themselves and one another. While the list of notable historical figures, philosophers, and theoretical traditions that have made enduring contributions to ethics and IR is extensive, the consultation and engagement that scholars of ethics and IR have had with these philosophical resources is impressive. This theme thus explores the distillation of philosophy in ethics in IR through four contributions covering the philosophical foundations of Kantian approaches to ethics, global justice, the topic of collective responsibility, and constructivism in international ethics.

Scholars have also used international relations (as a field) and its theories to address the role ethics plays in international politics. Fiona Robinson, whose work on the ethics of care has transformed international relations and the role of ethics within it,[10] introduces this theme and discusses the role of care ethics in the 'isms' that follow. With contributions covering realism, critical theory, constructivism, feminism, and postcolonialism, this theme reviews how the major and emerging perspectives of international relations both inform and have been utilized for ethics and IR.

There is arguably no other topic within international relations that has been treated more comprehensively, and historically, by the field of ethics and international affairs than war and security. The framework of 'just war theory', for instance, has witnessed a renaissance of interest in the past two decades. One of the major figures for that re-emergence of just war theory, and the relationship between security and ethics, Cian O'Driscoll,[11] introduces this theme. O'Driscoll provides a comprehensive overview of the contemporary concerns regarding the permissibility of conflict and the morality of certain means and methods of conflict in contemporary global politics. This theme includes three additional contributions on the ethics of war, dealing with analytical approaches, historical and religious approaches, and critical approaches. Security is foregrounded in two additional contributions dealing with the so-called 'traditional' focus of security versus more 'critical security studies' that have emerged in the past two decades.

Ethics has also been characterized by a variety of debates over the institutional contexts for the development and practice of justice, law, rights, and responsibility. These sets of debates ask what roles conceptions of justice, and their embodiment (qualified or not) in international law, play in international politics when it comes to seeking out ethical (re)solutions of international disputes and conflicts? What are the ethical bases for the proliferation of human rights standards throughout the globe in the post-World War II order? Having explored these issues for over a decade in his own work,[12] Anthony F. Lang introduces this theme, which he sees as an engagement of the normative perspectives, mechanisms, and history of justice in international politics. Chapters in this theme include discussions of the historical context of institutions and ethics in IR, the 'constitution' of global justice, human rights, and the ethics of international law.

In light of events such as those in Kosovo in 1999 and the development of the principle known as the 'Responsibility to Protect' (R2P), one of the more salient debates for decades in the field of ethics and IR has been the over the legitimacy of international intervention. When, how, where, and in what form should actors (states or otherwise) intervene into the affairs of other states, and for what purposes is such intervention justified? James Pattison, whose works are major statements for this renewed interest in intervention,[13] introduces this theme with not only a characterization, but also a historicization, of intervention as a chief but evolving concern for the field of ethics in IR over time. Contributions that follow cover the topics of the history of intervention versus sovereignty, the ethics of humanitarian intervention, the Responsibility to Protect, and the ethics of humanitarian aid.

Renewed interest in the field on the vulnerable in international relations intersects front and center with the questions that have been asked within the broader field of ethics and IR for decades. And yet, the vulnerabilities to environmental degradation, migration, and health crises have, as within the overall field of IR, been overlooked. Debra L. DeLaet, a leading scholar focusing on the vulnerable in her own work,[14] introduces this theme with special focus on the ways in which vulnerability is conditioned by ethical dilemmas over the environment, health, and migration. Contributions to this theme include chapters on climate change, transnational migration, global health, and climate refugees.

The recent global financial crisis exposed not only the interdependence of a globalized world, but also the manner in which different conceptions of ethics are involved in responding to such crises globally, nationally, and locally. Economic issues have always been shot through with ethical considerations, with the construction of global financial institutions such as the World Bank and the IMF purposed by the need to prevent the types of economic instability that led (in part) to World War II. Further, how should we respond to increasing inequality and economic deprivation? James Brassett, a scholar who has centralized questions of ethics in work on global political economy,[15] introduces this theme. Contributions that follow cover a variety of salient topics, including gendered discourses of finance, the ethics of alternative finance, postcolonial perspectives on global justice, and the political economy and ethics of biofuels.

When scholars seek out understandings for broader trends in international politics, they may sometimes consider the ways in which 'ethical frameworks' provide agents (from individuals to groups to states) reasons and principles for action. Religion has historically been an important resource for such frameworks. Cecelia M. Lynch, whose most recent work has turned to questions of religion, ethics, and methods,[16] provides an overview for this theme, examining how various religious resources – and attendant texts, histories, and philosophies – have served as significant contexts and resources for those working on ethics and IR.

Overall, the chapters that follow should not be understood as definitive statements about the field of ethics and IR, but rather, contributions to the ongoing conversation on a wide variety of topics, and using a wide variety of approaches, relevant to ethics and IR. As with any scholarly undertaking of this magnitude, there is simply no way to cover every theoretical approach, historical figure, or even substantive topic associated with the field of ethics and IR. What we can do, however, is provide a snapshot of where we perceive the field has been, where it currently is, and where it may be headed in the future. Our hope is that by doing this, readers will gain a sense of the types of concerns addressed by the field, how students and scholars can usefully investigate them, and how we might think about international relations in ways that highlight its 'ethical' dimension in the hope of achieving more 'ethical' outcomes in international affairs.

Notes

1 For example, Robert W. McElroy, *Morality and American Foreign Policy: The Role of Ethics in International Affairs*, Princeton: Princeton University Press, 1992.
2 Joel Rosenthal, *Ethics and International Affairs: A Reader*, second and third editions, Washington, DC: Georgetown University Press, 1999, 2009.
3 A small sampling includes: Mervyn Frost, *Ethics in International Relations*, Cambridge: Cambridge University Press, 1996; A turn not taken: ethics in IR at the millennium, *Review of International Studies*, 24, 5 (1998), 119–132; *Global Ethics*, London: Routledge, 2009. Terry Nardin and David R. Mapel, *Traditions of International Ethics*, Vol. 17, Cambridge: Cambridge University Press, 1992; Frances V. Harbour, *Thinking about International Ethics: Moral Theory and Cases from American Foreign Policy*, Boulder, CO: Westview Press, 1999; Andrew Valls and David Held, *Ethics in International Affairs: Theories and Cases*, New York: Rowman and Littlefield, 2000; J. Coicaud and Daniel Warner, *Ethics and International Affairs*, New York: United Nations Press, 2000.
4 Frost, A turn not taken: ethics in IR at the millennium, *Review of International Studies*, 24, 5 (1998), 119–132.
5 Christian Reus-Smit and Duncan Snidal, *The Oxford Handbook on International Relations*, Oxford: Oxford University Press, 2008.
6 Frost, *Towards a Normative Theory of International Relations: A Critical Analysis of the Philosophical and Methodological Assumptions in the Discipline with Proposals towards a Substantive Normative Theory*, Cambridge: Cambridge University Press, 1986.
7 Steve Smith, The forty years' detour: the resurgence of normative theory in international relations, *Millennium*, 21, 3 (1992), 489–506.
8 Frost, 'A turn not taken'.
9 Frost, *Global Ethics*, p. 10, emphasis original.
10 Fiona Robinson, Globalizing care: ethics, feminist theory, and international relations, *Alternatives*, 22, 1 (1997), 113–133.
11 Cian O'Driscoll, *The Renegotiation of the Just War Tradition and the Right to War in the Twenty-First Century*, London: Palgrave, 2008; Cian O'Driscoll, From Versailles to 9/11: non-state actors and just war in the twentieth century, in *Ethics, Authority, and War: Non-State Actors and the Just War Tradition*, ed. Eric A. Heinze and Brent J. Steele, London: Palgrave, 2009, 21–45.
12 Anthony F. Lang, Jr, *Punishment, Justice and International Relations: Ethics and Order after the Cold War*, Routledge, 2009; *International Political Theory: An Introduction*, London: Palgrave, 2015.
13 James Pattison, *Humanitarian Intervention and the Responsibility to Protect: Who Should Intervene?* Oxford: Oxford University Press, 2010; James Pattison, The ethics of humanitarian intervention in Libya, *Ethics and International Affairs*, 25, 3 (2011), 271–277.
14 Debra L. DeLaet, *US Immigration Policy in an Age of Rights*, New York: Praeger, 2000; Debra L. DeLaet and David E. DeLaet, *Global Health in the 21st Century: The Globalization of Disease and Wellness*, London: Routledge, 2015.
15 James Brassett and Christopher Holmes, International political economy and the question of ethics, *Review of International Political Economy*, 17, 3 (2010), 425–453; James Brassett and Chris D. Clarke, Performing the sub-prime crisis: trauma and the financial event, *International Political Sociology*, 6, 1 (2012), 4–20.
16 C. Lynch, A neo-Weberian approach to religion in international politics, *International Theory*, 1, 3 (2009), 381–408.

1
A HISTORY OF ETHICS IN INTERNATIONAL RELATIONS

Kimberly Hutchings

Introduction

The term 'ethics' refers to practices and ideas relating to issues of what is right or wrong, legitimate or illegitimate, just or unjust to do, as well as a reflection on those practices and ideas. It is often used synonymously with 'morality' and overlaps with the broad category of the 'normative', encompassing not only the rights and wrongs of interactions between individuals and collectives but also the structures that enable and constrain action. If we think of the term 'international relations' as referring to interactions between various sorts of actors from distinct political or cultural communities, then it seems reasonable to assume that ethics in international relations is coextensive with international relations itself. In the same way that ethical values, norms, and conventions are embedded within all human communities, so they are embedded in relations to outsiders, whether as guests to be welcomed, traders to be bargained with, barbarians to be despised, or enemies to be defeated. How then do we set about writing a history of ethics in international relations? If history is a comprehensive account of the past of a particular phenomenon, then a full history of ethics in international relations would require encyclopaedic knowledge of world history, languages, and archaeology and is far beyond my scope as a scholar. But of course, no history is of this kind; history is always a selective interpretation of the past in the light of the present, the availability of evidence, the expertise and capacities of the historian. What follows, therefore, is *a*, not *the*, history of ethics in international relations.

This chapter examines the history of ethics as it has been identified as relevant to the discipline of international relations (IR) during the twentieth and into the twenty-first century. Part of this process has been the setting up of canonical reference points for contemporary debate, so we will begin with a brief account of how classical sources have been treated as historical precursors of contemporary thinking on international ethics. We will then move on to consider the history of ethics in the study of international relations in three parts, which reflect standard periodisation in the history of the discipline. First, we will examine the place of ethics in IR from the early twentieth century to World War Two (WW2). Second, we will then look at international ethics in the Cold War period. Third, we will outline how ethics has become institutionalised as a growing subfield in IR in the post-Cold War period.

The canon of ethics in international relations

There are standard histories of ethics in philosophy and political theory that identify canonical thinkers and perspectives, usually traced from the ancient Greeks to twentieth-century European thought.[1] Scholars working specifically in international ethics have drawn on these histories selectively in constructing their own canon. Edward Keene warns against the tendency within IR to construct 'traditions' that impose a false historical unity on international thought across time. Keene argues that such work may not only distort the meaning of past ideas but may also mean that we miss the key international concerns of thinkers, whether in ancient Greece or nineteenth-century Europe.[2] Nevertheless, it is common for scholars in international ethics to invoke an earlier history of ethical thought that can directly or indirectly contribute to contemporary international ethics. Sometimes this is done through the idea of distinct traditions that develop over time; at other times, historical thinkers are treated much more abstractly as sources of ideas that we can use, as if they were our contemporary interlocutors. We can see this in metatheoretical debates about *approaches* to thinking about international ethics as well as in *substantive* areas of concern such as the ethics of war and the ethics of cross-border distributive justice.

Some histories of international relations and of its discipline stress a sceptical relation between the practices of international relations and ethics, and argue that what distinguishes international relations is the overarching importance of struggles for power, regardless of ethical values (see below). However, recent work in IR suggests that this is an oversimplification, even when it comes to canonical figures within realism such as Thucydides (460/55–411/400 BCE), Machiavelli (1469–1527), or Hobbes (1588–1679). Even where the focus is on flaws in human nature and the impossibility of eradicating war and conflict, there are still ethical values and commitments assumed and pursued in these thinkers' arguments, and contemporary scholars have developed readings of classical realism as a fundamentally ethical enterprise.[3] Having rejected the idea that international relations are inherently amoral, one influential way in which the history of *approaches* to international ethics has been told has been that we can trace back two broad tendencies in international ethical thinking: universalism and contextualism. Ancient Greek and Roman Stoicism has been identified as the origin of universalist ethical thinking. Stoics identified themselves as citizens of the world, rather than of the state, and did not attach ethical relevance to specific cultural/political identities or loyalties. They endorsed the idea that ethical values and principles were universal in scope across humankind. Later Christian and then Enlightenment thinking has been argued to carry through this legacy of universalism, culminating in the cosmopolitan ethical and political theory of Kant (1724–1804), which is identified as linking directly to contemporary cosmopolitan theorisations of global justice, democracy, and human rights. In parallel, Aristotelian (384–322 BCE) ethical thinking, with its emphasis on practical reason and the relation of ethical values to the role played in Greek society has been seen as the origin of contextual approaches to international ethics, in which ethical judgement is assumed to be relative to some aspect of context, whether state, culture, or role. This Aristotelian legacy has been seen as being carried through the incorporation of Aristotle into scholastic thought and culminating in the contextualist ethics of Hegel (1730–1831), which is identified as linking directly to contemporary contractualist and communitarian approaches to global justice, democracy, and human rights. But this is not the only way in which the history of approaches to international ethical thinking have been told. In some cases, the standard categories of international theory, such as realism, liberalism, Marxism, or constructivism, are used; others draw on the distinctions of philosophical ethics, using terms such as 'deontological', 'contractualist', 'utilitarian', or some mixture of the above.[4] In all cases, however, what is set up is an historical connection between the ideas (as interpreted by contemporary scholars) of classical thinkers and modes of ethical reasoning that people are using in arguments today.

In the case of the ethics of war, theorists routinely situate their arguments in relation to a tradition of just war traced back to ancient times. The most significant canonical reference points in the predominant version of the history of just war thinking are Roman law, Christian philosophy, notably the thinkers Augustine (354–430) and Aquinas (1225–1274), and scholars of international law such as Grotius (1583–1645) and Vattel (1714–1767). The history of just war thinking is told as the development of a set of ethical constraints on starting wars (*ad bellum*) and on conduct within war (*in bello*). Within this history of ethics in international relations, the eighteenth and nineteenth centuries tend to figure as a period in which the anarchic state system took hold and *ad bellum* ethical constraints on war were minimised, with just war thinking going into decline until revived by debates following WW2. Debates around international distributive justice tend not to claim such a longstanding genealogy. In their case, it is canonical thinkers from the sixteenth to the nineteenth centuries in Europe who are claimed as progenitors. In particular, Hobbes, Kant, Hegel, and John Stuart Mill (1806–1873) are cited as sources of opposing positions when it comes to the question of what rich states owe to poor states, and whether, if they exist at all, these obligations should be seen as humanitarian obligations or duties of justice.[5] Here, rather than a history of different stages in ethical thinking, we find a history of ongoing opposition between universal and contextual positions.

Whatever the problems inherent in claiming continuity across the history of ethical ideas, predominant histories of ethical thought about international relations testify to two things. First, they demonstrate that surviving texts and debates over the interpretation of classical thinkers are highly significant resources for contemporary scholars. These texts and interpretations provide common discursive reference points and tools through which ongoing ethical questions about war, distributive justice, migration, development, environmental issues, and so on can be framed and addressed. Second, they show that the canonical history of ethics in international thought is a highly selective one. This is pretty much an exclusively Graeco-Roman, Judaeo-Christian, and European history. Moreover, it is one that has focused on only certain elements and dimensions even of this history. For example, students are commonly taught that there is a pathway connecting classical just war thinking in Augustine or Grotius about just cause or the immunity of innocents to contemporary international law and notions of human rights. But their attention is less often drawn to pathways that connect Augustine's or Grotius's claims to the ethical valorisation of civilisational or gendered hierarchies in warfare in the contemporary world.[6] This is something that has begun to change over the past decade, as historians of international ethical thought have started to consider the work of classical thinkers more holistically and contextually.[7] At the same time, alternative standpoints in world history have been introduced as resources for contemporary ethical thought, including canonical figures and ideas from other religious and cultural traditions.[8] And there has begun to be a call for greater dialogue between different historical traditions—e.g., Confucian, Islamic, Hindu, African, and Native American—for thinking about ethical issues in international relations.[9]

Ethics in the founding of the discipline of IR

Recognition of the geographical and cultural specificity of canonical histories of international ethical thought is helpful in grasping the role of ethics in the decades during which the discipline of IR was founded. As a great deal of work in disciplinary history has shown us, the beginnings of IR as the systematic study of international relations were fundamentally intertwined with the geopolitical concerns of policymakers and citizens of the great powers, in particular Germany, Britain, and the United States, in the early twentieth century: imperialism, race, militarism, the effects of a globalising economic order, international law, nationalism, and war. It is also important to note that contributors to this nascent discipline were writing before the sharp division between fact and value, 'is' and 'ought', had taken hold of either social-scientific thinking or philosophical ethics. Moreover, many of those involved in developing categories for thinking about international relations were not academics; they were public intellectuals and practitioners, speaking to public and policy audiences. On all sides of ideological boundaries, from those aiming to save white civilisation from the threat posed by other races, to those engaged in elaborating an economic explanation for imperialism, to those arguing for and against the utility of war, it was taken for granted that international relations were inherently bound up with ethics. Rather than being defined as a separate subfield of investigation, ethical values were integral to the ways in which people argued about the nature of world politics, how relations between states should or should not be regulated, and the pros and cons of colonialism and imperialism.

Ethical ideas were integrated into these arguments in ways that often do not fit well with our contemporary classifications of different ethical viewpoints. Acceptance of some form of philosophy of history in which Western civilisation was the most advanced and had the right to set the rules for the world as a whole was widely accepted by liberals and geopolitical thinkers alike, though not necessarily in the same way or for the same reasons. Traces of social Darwinist, utilitarian, pragmatist, and natural law strands of ethical thinking can be found at work in early twentieth-century liberal arguments for national self-determination and in critiques and defences of imperialism. Although we would now consider liberalism and racism as incompatible doctrines, back then it was common for liberal and even socialist thinkers to accept ideas of racial hierarchy and defend imperialism on the principle of a pedagogic trusteeship in which the civilised had a duty to educate backward races in the arts of self-determination.[10]

Although the 1919 Versailles settlement is often taken to mark the victory of liberal internationalism as an ethical project, its outcomes were vastly different for peoples in different parts of the world, in some cases confirming the ethical value of individual and collective rights and in other cases denying them. It also, of course, failed to unify even the victors of the war in the common enterprise of the League of Nations, let alone those who were defeated. From the point of view of tracing the history of ethics in IR, however, it is important to note that both the public discourse of the post-1919 international order and the growing literature on international relations in the Anglophone world continued to be saturated with ethical values and goals.[11] During this time, the idea became more prominent (though by no means hegemonic) both that international politics needs to be conducted to further ends of peace and prosperity, and equally that the analysis of international politics, whether in the form of the study of colonial administration, foreign policy or trade, the management of international crises—such as the refugee and food crises that followed World War One (WW1)—should also conduce to these good ends. Significantly also, this period saw an increased role for international law, the growth of international regimes and institutions, and a larger and more vocal element of public opinion in support of pacifism across the victor states in WWI than had been seen before.

The work of the League of Nations extended the range of issues seen as relevant to international relations, including as it led initiatives on global health, mass movement of peoples, the status of women, and the status of colonised peoples. Many of the issues with which international ethics now grapples came explicitly onto the international agenda in the inter-war period. Yet in the history of the League that has come to dominate IR's disciplinary history and to shape the place of ethics in IR, it was the question of war and peace that was determinate. As Japan,

Italy, and Germany expanded militarily, a key ethical issue for international relations scholars in the 1930s became the question of the rights and wrongs of war and preparation for war. In retrospect, from the perspective of WW2 and its aftermath, this became identified by IR scholars as *the* key ethical issue. This well-known story is important for the history of ethics in IR because 'ethics' became associated with what were later judged to be mistaken policies of disarmament and appeasement. This is in spite of the fact that positions both pro and contra disarmament and appeasement in the inter-war period made moral claims on both sides, and were often premised on shared ethical values.[12]

Ethics in IR in the Cold War

This new distrust of international ethics took different forms. In E. H. Carr's *Twenty Years' Crisis*, he lambasts 'utopian' approaches to international relations, for either fundamentally misunderstanding the workings of power in politics, or for hypocrisy, that is to say, presenting as 'ethical' what is actually a reflection of partial interests.[13] For Hans Morgenthau, attempts to bring ethics into international politics are premised on a misunderstanding of the dynamics of the anarchic international order and end up backfiring by undermining the capacity of states to protect and preserve ethical values through the manipulation of power.[14] At the same time as these ideas come to prominence in the two countries where the study of international relations was already most institutionalised, the United States and Britain, another set of ideas, pioneered in philosophical ethics and social theory in the early twentieth century, were also becoming established. G. E. Moore's famous statement of the 'naturalistic fallacy' and Max Weber's argument for the separation of the roles of facts and values in social science gained widespread acceptance across Anglophone philosophy and social science.[15]

The 'naturalistic fallacy' refers to a logical mistake that Moore argues was common to most ethical theory at the turn of the nineteenth into the twentieth century. This is the mistake of thinking that you can derive ethical conclusions about what *ought* to be done from factual premises (i.e., about what *is* the case). For example, on Moore's account, the fact that people are dying of starvation does not in itself imply either than this is wrong or that we should do anything about it. It is only if one adds an additional ethical premise, perhaps along the lines of 'all people have a right to food', that it follows that there is any ethical imperative to address the starvation. This idea became the starting point for claims, which gained increasing traction in the 1950s and 1960s, that ethical language makes sense in a different way to factual language, and that we need to be careful not to confuse the two. In relation to a different set of concerns, Weber's well-known insistence on the distinction between facts and values was intended to support the possibility of an objective social science conducted in a way that was as scrupulous and unbiased as possible. This, in turn, encouraged the idea that the emergent social science of international relations during the Cold War period should be as value-free as possible and focus on explaining how things are rather than how they ought to be. Along with scepticism about the effects of overtly ethically engaged research and argument in IR, the above factors helped to shape IR in the Cold War period, in particular in the United States, as a discipline that effectively excluded ethics.[16] Of course, this did not mean that ethics disappeared entirely from the concerns of IR scholars; however, it did mean that it had to be studied either as separate from the social science of IR, often under the umbrellas of other disciplines such as international law, history of political thought, political theory, theology, or philosophy. Alternatively, it meant that integrating ethics into mainstream IR would have to challenge the predominant ways in which the discipline had come to be defined. We find examples of both of these ways of doing international ethics during the Cold War period.

Much of the scholarly debate about ethical issues in international relations throughout this period was focused on the ethics of war. At the end of WW2, in the wake of the Nuremburg and Tokyo trials and as the world moved into the age of a superpower nuclear standoff, new debates opened up about just war *ad bellum* and *in bello*, including specifically the ethics of nuclear deterrence. Some of this work brought IR scholars together with moral philosophers and political theorists.[17] Much of it, however, went on in philosophy and theology departments. Michael Walzer's classic re-articulation of just war theory has become a landmark text for IR scholars, but Walzer was a political theorist and structured his argument in firm contrast to the realist position that was currently dominant in IR circles.[18] As the 1970s progressed, philosophers were reacting against the marginalisation of ethics within analytic philosophy, and a literature in 'applied' ethics, in which ethical principles were applied to empirical problems and cases—including in relation to international politics—began to develop. It is at this time that works in the ethics of development, the ethics of borders, and environmental ethics begin to appear. Peter Singer's famous argument on 'Famine, Affluence and Morality' is published in 1972 and is followed by a series of arguments relating to international humanitarian aid, famine, and the global redistribution of wealth.[19] John Rawls's *A Theory of Justice* had a massive impact on the agenda of Anglophone political philosophy and theory.[20] At the time, Rawls's own observations about interstate relations in the text were not given a great deal of attention, but his philosophical method, the use of the 'original position' in which people arrive at a theory of justice through being detached from the specificities of their identity under the 'veil of ignorance' sparked off a range of responses and debates.[21] Some of these engaged with the question of justice beyond the state. Charles Beitz argues that one should treat the original position as a global one and that Rawls's theory therefore has important implications for global distributive justice.[22] Theorists such as Brian Barry and Joseph Carens address questions about the distinctions between global humanitarianism and global justice and about the ethics of migration.[23] Theorists such as Alasdair MacIntyre and Michael Walzer argue against the abstraction of Rawls's method and in favour of more contextual and communitarian approaches to thinking about justice, and began to elaborate the implications of this for international ethics.[24] By the late 1980s, a whole series of debates about the universality or otherwise of the requirements of justice (as well about what those requirements actually were) was captured as a fundamental opposition between 'liberal' and 'communitarian' thinking.[25] This debate was largely external to disciplinary IR, but clearly raised significant issues for international ethics.

In the meantime, some work going on within IR challenged the mainstream opposition between ethics and social science. In the UK context, the international society approach to studying international relations (sometimes known as the English School), which had roots going back to the pre-WW2 period, argues for the importance of normative standards within international society.[26] Scholars working within this framework are particularly interested in the development of international law and convention, including the laws of war and the idea of international human rights expressed in the Universal Declaration of Human Rights (UDHR) in 1948.[27] For these scholars, ethical issues and arguments were integral to the analysis of international order. They make connections between their arguments and canonical thinkers such as Grotius and are instrumental in identifying international ethics as a distinctive subfield of IR, with its own specific traditions.[28] Another alternative could be found in Neo-Marxist work within IR which rejected the fact/value distinction as untenable, as in Robert Cox's famous distinction between 'problem-solving' and 'critical' theory.[29] During the 1980s, the work of both Antonio Gramsci and Jürgen Habermas became inspirations for the assertion of a critical approach to IR which self-consciously committed itself to ethical values of emancipation. Some of this work combined insights from Marxism with an international society approach.[30]

Some of it overlapped with that of scholars involved in the World Order Models Project, which explicitly focuses on bringing scholars together, in a world of mutually assured destruction, to imagine better ways in which the world could be ordered.[31] Scholars working in all of the above frameworks saw ethics, not just as part of international politics, but also as an appropriate field for reflection within IR.

Ethics was also central to another wave of critical theorising that emerged in IR in the 1980s, in part in response to the apparent hegemony of a narrow, value-free conception of social science within the field. Postmodernist and poststructuralist arguments, as with Marxist arguments, rejected the fact/value distinction. In opposition to Marxism, however, they were also suspicious of claims about emancipatory theory. Following the arguments of Foucault and Derrida, they identified epistemic certainty, whether from the point of view of hegemonic, value-free social science, or from the point of view of a revolutionary subject, as totalising assertions of power.[32] Rather than seeing ethics as about establishing and then realising justice, postmodernist theorists argue that ethics was about the acknowledgement of limitation, about deconstructing apparent certainties, about the need to pluralise perspectives and ideas and to democratise the process of knowledge production.[33] As with international society and Neo-Marxist approaches, however, ethics was assumed to be an irreducible aspect both of international relations and of the ways in which we study it.

Ethics in IR after the Cold War

By the end of the Cold War, although ethics was still marginal to IR as a field of study, there were nevertheless substantial international ethics literatures in existence. This included work (e.g., on war, distributive justice, borders, migration, human rights, development, and the environment) from philosophy and political theory, in which there are also well-established metatheoretical debates about the foundation and scope of ethical judgement. In addition, it included work in which ethical issues and reflection on ethical issues were seen as integral to international relations, including metatheoretical debates about the relation of facts and values in social reality and the foundations and scope of ethical judgement. In 1987, the journal *Ethics and International Affairs*, which sought to be a cross-disciplinary forum for the discussion of ethical issues in international relations, was set up. This is also around the point in time when a seemingly intractable structure of world politics, the superpower rivalry of the USA and USSR, unexpectedly disappears. The dismantling of the Soviet Union challenged preconceived wisdom in IR and extended the space for alternative perspectives to be heard within the discipline. Within this context, a window of possibility opened for greater cross-disciplinary engagement and for ethics to become fully recognised as a subfield of IR, rather than as marking the margins of that in which IR scholars could be interested. It is notable that it is in the early 1990s that we find texts by IR scholars that start to bridge divides between ethical theorising that had gone on in theology, philosophy, and political theory and the categories of international relations theory. Two volumes here stand out, both published in 1992: Terry Nardin and David Mapel's edited volume *Traditions of International Ethics* and Chris Brown's *International Relations Theory: New Normative Approaches*. The former volume seeks to systematise a range of ways in which ethics in international relations can be studied, and includes chapters based on utilitarianism, natural law, biblical approaches, Kantian deontology, as well as chapters on realism, liberalism, and Marxism.[34] The second volume, building on the 'liberalism'/'communitarian' debate from political theory, argues that we can identify two key traditions in international normative theory: cosmopolitan and communitarian.[35] Both books offer ways into the study of international ethics that relate to the theoretical traditions and canonical sources of disciplinary IR and maintain the distinctiveness of *international* ethics, whilst at the same time integrating it into a broader history of ethics. Brown's categorisation was particularly influential, and in the 1990s and 2000s much work in international ethics used the cosmopolitan/communitarian distinction to make sense of debates on distributive justice, human rights, nationality, transnational democracy, environmental justice.[36] In the meantime, an increasing amount of work on international distributive justice, democracy, rights, and war in philosophy and political theory utilised the label of cosmopolitanism to explain and situate their arguments.[37]

Relaxation in the disciplinary politics of IR is one reason why international ethics really begins to flower as a subfield of IR in the 1990s, and the other reason is the shift in the international agenda, from the perspective of a US-dominated IR academy, which followed the end of the Cold War. Within this agenda, not only did the language of ethics become more central to the way in which the foreign policy of the US and its allies was framed, but priorities for international economic and military action were also transformed. Some of this transformation harked back to themes in the philosophy of history that characterised debates in the first half of the twentieth century, in which the victors of the Cold War were identified with what was morally progressive. Within the ethics of war, nuclear deterrence, which had been a major focus of ethical argument during the Cold War, was no longer centre stage. Within a decade, military humanitarian intervention emerged as a vital issue for the ethics of war, and almost three decades on, questions of responsibility to protect, terrorism, torture, and the privatisation of warfare and technology, for obvious reasons, have come to much greater prominence within the field than formerly.[38] In addition, reflecting the rise of international post-conflict settlements, the setting up of the International Criminal Court and various reparative justice commissions and tribunals, issues of *post-bellum* justice have reappeared as a significant element of just war theory.[39] With the collapse of socialist economies and the globalisation of a liberal economic order in the 1990s, ethical theorists become much more focused on issues of distributive justice at the transnational level. Following the pioneering work of Beitz, a more substantial literature emerged on international questions of distributive justice, and Rawls developed his arguments about justice beyond borders in *A Theory of Justice* in his *Law of the Peoples*, a text that supported a contractualist/communitarian approach to the question of global justice.[40] The debate over international distributive justice has become a major subliterature, centred on cosmopolitan arguments and a variety of different kinds of critiques of cosmopolitanism.[41]

Other literatures in international ethics, tracking other developments in international politics, have emerged or been consolidated over the past three decades. One such example is the literature on cosmopolitan democracy, which points to transnational structures and institutions beyond the jurisdiction of the state, from the global economy to the UN and EU, and argues for the need for democratic accountability and control to and by the populations affected by them.[42] Another, related literature is that on the ethics of borders and migration, which from a very small base in Cold War philosophical discussion has become a major focus of concern.[43] Yet another is environmental ethics, which is now standardly included in the agenda of the ethics of international relations in textbooks and surveys.[44] However, perhaps the topic that has come most obviously to the forefront of the concerns of international ethics is that of international human rights. In contrast to the stalemate over the UDHR that characterised the Cold War, the post-Cold War period has been one in which the discourse of human rights has become increasingly hegemonic in international law and institutions, as well as in the work on international nongovernmental institutions. This has been echoed by the development of an international ethics literature on human rights, which addresses metaethical questions about the nature and status of the concept, constructivist questions about how human rights can become internalised norms, and uses the idea of human rights to ground particular policy positions in relation to war, distributive justice, migration, and so on.[45]

Arguments that rely on the idea of there being certain inalienable human rights fall mainly into the category of cosmopolitan ethical theory, since they assume that moral value inheres directly in each human individual and only indirectly in collective entities such as states or cultures.[46] It is certainly the case that within philosophy and political theory in the 1990s and 2000s, cosmopolitan approaches to international ethics have been predominant. However, this has been less the case within IR, even given its increasing engagement with philosophy and political theory. This reflects differences in disciplinary orientation. Philosophers and political theorists take perspectives from moral philosophy and apply them to issues. They will often use the same set of, for example, utilitarian or deontological theories, and apply them to both interpersonal and international issues at a high level of abstraction. They are also more likely to be firmly methodologically individualist. In contrast, IR scholars, even when drawing on the same ethical theories, are usually more focused on the specificity of the international issues with which they are engaging, tend to be resistant to overly high levels of abstraction, and are interested in collective actors and transnational structures as irreducible aspects of international relations. For example, when it comes to the ethics of war, cosmopolitan just war theory, which argues that the same moral intuitions that govern interpersonal killing apply equally to killing in war has not dominated the field in IR.[47] Instead, in IR we find a very large variety of approaches to just war theory, often utilising more pragmatic modes of moral reasoning than those of analytical philosophy and invoking canonical authorities such as Augustine as well as more critical philosophical traditions.[48] In addition, humanitarian intervention and the war on terror (so called) have inspired ethical arguments from critical IR scholars who reject the usefulness of a cosmopolitan/communitarian distinction, but use the work of thinkers such as Derrida, Foucault, Levinas, and Agamben to formulate their ethical critique.[49] Such work seeks to open up questions about the relation between ethics and politics, and about the affective and aesthetic dimensions of ethical judgement, often drawing on poststructuralist ethical arguments previously explored within IR.[50]

Critical perspectives that are very much the product of the post-Cold War period of international ethical thinking are feminist and decolonial arguments, which, in common with poststructuralist approaches, reject the framing of cosmopolitanism and communitarianism as exhausting the possibilities for thought. Feminist work has drawn on the distinctive moral theory of care ethics in order to develop a feminist international ethics of war, security, and gender justice.[51] Decolonial arguments point to the colonial origins and colonising effects of apparently universal discourses, such as the discourse of human rights. And they have drawn on concepts from traditions outside of the Graeco-Roman and Judaeo-Christian to address issues in the ethics of development and distributive justice.[52]

This variety of perspectives has meant that the metaethical, self-reflexive foundations and scope of ethical judgement have become integral to the study of ethics in IR. There are debates between universalism and contextualism about whether there are universal values or principles on which international ethics can be grounded, and, if so, how we are able to know. There are also debates about what are the epistemic status and objectivity of ethical claims and about whether ethical thinking about issues such as international justice should be in the form of ideal theory, in which you construct your theory as if in a context of full compliance with moral principles, or in the form of nonideal theory, in which you construct your theory with the constraints of the real world in mind.[53] There are debates about the moral status or otherwise of individuals as opposed to various kind of collective actors (e.g., states, cultures, and international institutions). Do collective entities ever have any intrinsic, as opposed to derivative (from individuals), ethical value?[54] And there are increasingly debates about the relation between ethics and politics in ethical argument and theorising. Can or should ethics be separated from politics? Are ethical claims also always political, even when they present themselves as rational and objective? Self-reflexivity has most recently extended to the ethics of research itself, paradoxically bringing ethics into the heart of ethical argument in work in which researchers open up questions about the ethical integrity of their own practice.[55]

Conclusion

The recent history of ethics in international relations is complex and plural. As in previous phases of its history, it reflects the dynamics of international politics, responding to events and trends from the end of the Cold War itself, to instances of humanitarian intervention, to global financial crises, the setting up of international development goals, the increase in international peacekeeping and conflict-resolution operations, the wars in Iraq and Afghanistan, the international mass migration of populations, and so on. But this history also revolves around the meanings to be attributed to the two key terms *international* and *ethics*. When Nardin and Mapel, and Brown attempted to systematise the study of ethics in IR in the early 1990s, they were operating with the assumption that the object of inquiry in international ethics—the *international*—was distinctive and that its distinctiveness lay in the fact of separation between communities and cultures, an inside/outside relation. But if we examine the range of approaches that I have attempted to delineate above, other terms have crept into the account in this section, such as 'global' and 'transnational'. If the world is becoming increasingly globalised, then does anything change for ethical theorising about international relations? One thing that does seem to have changed is the extent and scope of what can come under the heading of international ethics; it is certainly not simply focused on the ethics of interstate relations, for it also encompasses various entities from individuals through to trans-state organisations, and the range of questions with which it is concerned, as is testified to by the content of this volume, goes far beyond the questions about war and distributive justice addressed in the international ethics literatures of the 1970s and 1980s.[56]

And what about the term *ethics*? At the beginning of this chapter, I defined ethics as 'practices and ideas relating to issues of what it is right or wrong, legitimate or illegitimate, just or unjust to do, as well as to reflection on those practices and ideas'. As we have seen, this working definition masks deep differences between those who study ethical questions in IR. But these differences should not be interpreted solely as philosophical differences about the foundations and scope of ethical judgement. Ideas about ethics have a history just as much as ideas about the international do. At the beginning of the twentieth century, thinkers concerned with questions about justice and injustice in interstate, intercultural, and interracial relations worked with a toolbox of ethical ideas that many of us would now reject. But it is clear that those tools were integral to the experience of European and US elites during an unprecedented period of capitalist and imperialist expansion. The notion that ethics and politics, and ethics and social science, must be rigidly separated became established within the academy in the mid-twentieth century for reasons that were not wholly philosophical, but reflected the experiences and interests of the dominant academies in the wake of WW2. That assumption shifted as the Cold War ended, reopening the question of the relation between ethics and international relations and creating much more space for work focused on ethical issues in international politics. The vocabularies, concerns, and divisions of contemporary international ethics, explored within this volume, are part of the international context for which they provide diagnoses and prescriptions. In 1987, as noted, a journal devoted to the connection between ethics and international relations was set up—*Ethics and International Affairs*. Since the end of the Cold War, two further journals largely concerned with ethical issues in international politics have been created—*Journal of International Political Theory* and *Journal of Global Ethics*—as well as others relating to human rights, humanitarianism, conflict resolution, and terrorism, which all include material related to ethics. In addition, questions about international justice have become central to much work that appears in philosophy and political theory journals. The major professional associations of IR scholars have also established 'ethics' sections, and there has been a proliferation of guides and textbooks on international ethical themes. In some respects, current work in international ethics reflects longstanding debates that can be traced back at least to the Cold War period. But there is also much that is new, and quite how and why IR scholars are thinking about international ethics in the present, in these diverse and plural ways, may only become clear in retrospect.

Notes

1 E.g., Alasdair MacIntyre, *A Short History of Ethics: A History of Moral Philosophy from the Homeric Age to the Twentieth Century* (London: Routledge and Kegan Paul, 1967); Richard Norman, *The Moral Philosophers: An Introduction to Ethics* (Oxford: Clarendon Press, 1983).

2 Edward Keene, *International Political Thought: A Historical Introduction* (Cambridge: Polity, 2005).

3 Michael C. Williams, *The Realist Tradition and the Limits of IR* (Cambridge: Cambridge University Press, 2005).

4 Terry Nardin and David R. Mapel, eds., *Traditions of International Ethics* (Cambridge: Cambridge University Press, 1992); Chris Brown, *International Relations Theory: New Normative Approaches* (Hemel Hempstead: Harvester Wheatsheaf, 1992); Ian Clark and Iver B. Neumann, eds., *Classical Theories of International Relations* (Basingstoke: Palgrave, 1996); Duncan Bell, *Ethics and World Politics* (Oxford: Oxford University Press, 2010); Kimberly Hutchings, *Global Ethics: An Introduction* (Cambridge: Polity, 2010).

5 Thomas Nagel, 'The Problem of Global Justice', *Philosophy and Public Affairs*, 33, 2 (2005): 113–147; Simon Caney, *Justice beyond Borders: A Global Political Theory* (Oxford: Oxford University Press, 2005).

6 Helen Kinsella, *The Image before the Weapon: A Critical History of the Distinction between Combatant and Civilian* (Ithaca: Cornell University Press, 2011).

7 Edward Keene, *Beyond the Anarchical Society: Grotius, Colonialism and Order in World Politics* (Cambridge: Cambridge University Press, 2002); Keene, *International Political Thought*.

8 David Miller and Sohail H. Hashmi, eds., *Boundaries of Justice: Diverse Ethical Perspectives* (Princeton: Princeton University Press, 2001); William M. Sullivan and Will Kymlika, eds., *The Globalization of Ethics: Religious and Secular Perspectives* (Cambridge: Cambridge University Press, 2007); Marshall J. Beier, *International Relations in Uncommon Places: Indigeneity, Cosmology and the Limits of International Theory* (New York: Palgrave Macmillan, 2005); Leonard T. Chuwa, *African Indigenous Ethics in Global Bioethics: Interpreting Ubuntu* (New York: Springer, 2014).

9 Hans Küng, *Global Responsibility: In Search of a New World Ethic* (Eugene, OR: Wipf and Stock, 1990); Bikhu Parekh, 'Principles of a Global Ethic', in *Global Ethics and Civil Society*, ed. J. Eade and D. O'Byrne (Aldershot: Ashgate, 2005); Kwame Anthony Appiah, *Cosmopolitanism: Ethics in a World of Strangers* (London: Penguin Books, 2007); Fred Dallmayr, *Being in the World: Dialogue and Cosmopolis* (Lexington: Kentucky University Press, 2013).

10 Brian C. Schmidt, *International Relations and the First Great Debate* (Abingdon: Routledge, 2012); Keene, *Beyond the Anarchical Society*; David Long and Brian C. Schmidt, eds., *Imperialism and Internationalism in the Discipline of International Relations* (Albany: State University of New York Press, 2005); Robert Vitalis, *White World Order, Black Power Politics: The Birth of American International Relations* (Ithaca: Cornell University Press, 2015).

11 Lucian M. Ashworth, 'Did the Realist–Idealist Great Debate Really Happen? A Revisionist History of International Relations', *International Relations*, 16, 1 (2002): 33–51; Schmidt, *International Relations and the First Great Debate*.

12 Ashworth, 'Did the Realist–Idealist Great Debate Really Happen?'

13 E. H. Carr, *The Twenty Years' Crisis* (Basingstoke: Palgrave, 2001).
14 Hans Morgenthau, *Politics among Nations: The Struggle for Power and Peace*, 6th edn. (New York: Arnold Kopf, 1985).
15 George E. Moore, *Principia Ethica* (Cambridge: Cambridge University Press, 1993); Max Weber, *Methodology of the Social Sciences*, ed. Edward A. Shils and Henry A. Finch (Abingdon: Routledge, 2017).
16 Nicolas Guilhot, ed., *The Invention of International Relations: Realism, the Rockefeller Foundation and the 1954 Conference on Theory* (New York: Columbia University Press, 2011).
17 Russell Hardin et al., eds., *Nuclear Deterrence: Ethics and Strategy* (Chicago: Chicago University Press, 1985).
18 Michael Walzer, *Just and Unjust Wars: A Moral Argument with Historical Illustrations* (New York: Basic Books, 1977). See also: Charles Beitz et al., eds., *International Ethics* (Princeton: Princeton University Press, 1985); James T. Johnson, *Can Modern War Be Just?* (New Haven: York University Press, 1986); Anthony Ellis, ed., *Ethics and International Relations* (Manchester: Manchester University Press, 1986); Paul Ramsey, *The Essential Paul Ramsey: A Collection*, ed. William Werpehowski and Stephen D. Crocco (New Haven: Yale University Press, 1994).
19 Peter Singer, 'Famine, Affluence and Morality', *Philosophy and Public Affairs*, 1, 3 (1972): 229–243; Onora O'Neill, 'Lifeboat Earth', *Philosophy and Public Affairs*, 4, 3 (1975): 273–292; Henry Shue, *Basic Rights: Subsistence, Affluence and US Foreign Policy* (Princeton: Princeton University Press, 1980).
20 John Rawls, *A Theory of Justice* (Oxford: Oxford University Press, 1971).
21 Ibid.
22 Charles Beitz, *Political Theory and International Relations* (Princeton: Princeton University Press, 1979).
23 Brian Barry, 'Humanity and Justice in Global Perspective', in *Nomos XXIV: Ethics, Economics and the Law*, ed. J. R. Pennock and J. W. Chapman (New York: New York University Press, 1982); Joseph Carens, 'Aliens and Citizens: The Case for Open Borders', *The Review of Politics*, 49, 2 (1987): 251–273.
24 Alasdair MacIntyre, *After Virtue: A Study in Moral Theory* (London: Duckworth, 1981); Michael Walzer, *Spheres of Justice: A Defence of Pluralism and Equality* (New York: Basic Books, 1983); Michael Walzer, 'The Distribution of Membership', in *Boundaries: National Autonomy and Its Limits*, ed. P. G. Brown and H. Shue (Totowa, NJ: Rowman and Littlefield, 1981); David Miller, 'The Ethical Significance of Nationality', *Ethics*, 94, 4 (1988): 647–662.
25 Steven Mulhall and Adam Swift, *Liberals and Communitarians* (Oxford: Oxford University Press, 1992).
26 Charles A. W. Manning, *The Nature of International Society* (London: G. Bell, 1962); Hedley J. Bull, *The Anarchical Society* (New York: Columbia University Press, 1977).
27 Terry Nardin, *Law, Morality and the Relations of States* (Princeton, NJ: Princeton University Press, 1983); R. J. Vincent, *Human Rights and International Relations* (Cambridge: Cambridge University Press, 1986); Mervyn Frost, *Towards a Normative Theory of International Relations* (Cambridge: Cambridge University Press, 1986).
28 Nardin and Mapel, *Traditions of International Ethics.*
29 'Social Forces, States and World Orders: Beyond International Relations Theory', *Millennium: Journal of International Studies*, 10, 2 (1981): 128–130.
30 Andrew Linklater, *Men and Citizens* (London: Macmillan, 1982).
31 Richard Falk, Robert C. Johansen, and Samuel S. Kim, *The Constitutional Foundations of World Peace* (Albany: State University of New York Press, 1993).
32 James Der Derian and Michael Shapiro, eds., *International/Intertextual Relations: Postmodern Readings of World Politics* (Lexington, MA: Lexington Books, 1989).
33 Robert B. J. Walker, *One World/Many Worlds: Struggles for Just World Peace* (Boulder, CO: Lynne Riener, 1988); Richard Ashley and Robert B. J. Walker, 'Reading Dissidence/Writing the Discipline: Crisis and the Question of Sovereignty in International Studies', *International Studies Quarterly*, 34, 3 (1990): 367–416.
34 Nardin and Mapel, *Traditions of International Ethics.*
35 Brown, *International Relations Theory.*
36 E.g., Molly Cochran, *Normative Theory in International Relations: A Pragmatic Approach* (Cambridge: Cambridge University Press, 1999); Kimberly Hutchings, *International Political Theory: Rethinking Ethics in a Global Era* (London: Sage, 1999); Toni Erskine, *Embedded Cosmopolitanism: Duties to Strangers and Enemies in a World of 'Dislocated Communities'* (Oxford: Oxford University Press, 2008).
37 Daniele Archibugi and David Held, *Cosmopolitan Democracy* (Cambridge: Cambridge University Press, 1995); Darrel Moellendorf, *Cosmopolitan Justice* (Boulder, CO: Westview Press, 2002); Gillian Brock,

Global Justice: A Cosmopolitan Account (Oxford: Oxford University Press, 2009); Cecile Fabre, *Cosmopolitan War* (Oxford: Oxford University Press, 2012).

38 Nicholas Wheeler, *Saving Strangers: Humanitarian Intervention in International Society* (Oxford: Oxford University Press, 2000); Uwe Steinhoff, *On the Ethics of War and Terrorism* (Oxford: Oxford University Press, 2007); Alexander Bellamy, *Just Wars: From Cicero to Iraq* (Cambridge: Polity, 2006); Susan Killmister, 'Remote Weaponry: The Ethical Implications', *Journal of Applied Philosophy*, 24, 1 (2008): 121–133; Neta C. Crawford, *Accountability for Killing: Moral Responsibility for Collateral Damage in America's post-9/11 Wars* (Oxford: Oxford University Press, 2013); James Pattison, *The Morality of Private War: The Challenge of Private Military and Security Companies* (Oxford: Oxford University Press, 2014); Alan Buchanan and Robert Keohane, 'Toward a Drone Accountability Regime', *Ethics and International Affairs*, 29, 1 (2015): 15–37.

39 David Crocker, 'Reckoning with Past Wrongs: A Normative Framework', *Ethics and International Affairs*, 13 (1999): 43–64; Brian Orend, 'Justice after War', *Ethics and International Affairs*, 16, 1 (2002): 43–56; Alexander Bellamy, 'The Responsibilities of Victory: *jus post bellum* and Just War', *Review of International Studies*, 34, 4 (2008): 601–625; Daniel Philpott, *Just and Unjust Peace: An Ethic of Political Reconciliation* (Oxford: Oxford University Press, 2015).

40 Thomas Pogge, ed., *Global Justice* (Oxford: Blackwell, 2001); Thomas Pogge, *World Poverty and Human Rights*, 2nd edn. (Cambridge: Polity, 2008); G. Brock and H. Brighouse, eds., *The Political Philosophy of Cosmopolitanism* (Cambridge: Cambridge University Press, 2005); Caney, *Justice beyond Borders*; John Rawls, *The Law of Peoples* (Cambridge, MA: Harvard University Press, 1999).

41 Brock, *Global Justice*; Laura Valentini, *Justice in a Globalized World: A Normative Framework* (Oxford: Oxford University Press, 2011).

42 Archibugi and Held, *Cosmopolitan Democracy*; Raffaele Marchetti, *Global Democracy: Ethical Theory, Institutional Design and Social Struggles* (London: Routledge, 2008); Daniele Archibugi, Mathias Koenig-Archibugi, and Raffaele Marchetti, eds., *Global Democracy: Normative and Empirical Perspectives* (Cambridge: Cambridge University Press, 2012).

43 Brian Barry and Robert E. Goodin, eds., *Free Movement: Ethical Issues in the Transmigration of People and Money* (Hertfordshire: Harvester Wheatsheaf, 1992); Seyla Benhabib, *The Rights of Others: Aliens, Residents and Citizens* (Cambridge: Cambridge University Press, 2004); Christopher Heath Wellman and Philip Cole, *Debating the Ethics of Immigration: Is There a Right to Exclude?* (Oxford: Oxford University Press, 2011); Joseph Carens, *Ethics of Immigration* (Oxford: Oxford University Press, 2013); Dan Bulley, *Migration, Ethics and Power: Spaces of Hospitality in International Politics* (London: Sage, 2017).

44 Bell, *Ethics and World Politics*; Jean-Marc Coicaud and Daniel Warner, eds., *Ethics and International Affairs: Extent and Limits*, 2nd edn. (Tokyo: United Nations University Press, 2013).

45 Thomas Risse, Stephen C. Ropp, and Kathryn Sikkink, *The Power of Human Rights: International Norms and Domestic Change* (Cambridge: Cambridge University Press, 1999); Brooke A. Ackerly, *Universal Human Rights in a World of Difference* (Cambridge: Cambridge University Press, 2008); David Forsythe, *Human Rights in International Relations*, 3rd edn. (Cambridge: Cambridge University Press, 2012); Joseph Hoover, *Reconstructing Human Rights: A Pragmatist and Pluralist Inquiry in Global Ethics* (Oxford: Oxford University Press, 2016).

46 Charles Beitz, *The Idea of Human Rights* (Oxford: Oxford University Press, 2009).

47 E.g., Jeff McMahan, *Killing in War* (Oxford: Oxford University Press, 2009); Farbre, *Cosmopolitan War*.

48 Eric A. Heinze and Brent J. Steele, eds., *Ethics, Authority and War: Non-State Actors and the Just War Tradition* (Basingstoke: Palgrave Macmillan, 2009); Anthony F. Lang, Jr, Cian O'Driscoll, and John Williams, eds., *Just War: Authority, Tradition and Practice* (Washington, D.C.: Georgetown University Press, 2013).

49 Vivienne Jabri, *War and the Transformation of Global Politics* (Basingstoke: Palgrave Macmillan, 2007); Annika Bergman-Rosaond and Mark Phythian, eds., *War, Ethics and Justice: New Perspectives on a post-9/11 World* (London: Routledge, 2011).

50 David Campbell and Michael Shapiro, eds., *Moral Spaces: Rethinking Ethics in World Politics* (Minneapolis: University of Minnesota Press, 1999).

51 Fiona Robinson, *Globalizing Care: Ethics, Feminist Theory and International Relations* (Boulder, CO: Westview Press, 1999); Fiona Robinson, *The Ethics of Care: A Feminist Approach to Human Security* (Philadelphia: Temple University Press, 2011); Laura Sjoberg, *Gender, Justice and the Wars in Iraq: A Feminist Reformulation of Just War Theory* (Lanham, MD: Lexington Books, 2006).

52 Makau Mutua, *Human Rights: A Political and Cultural Critique* (Philadelphia: University of Pennsylvania Press, 2002); Margaret Kohn, 'Postcolonialism and Global Justice', *Journal of Global Ethics*, 9, 2 (2013):

187–200; A. Graness, 'Is the Debate on "Global Justice" a Global One? Some Considerations in View of Modern Philosophy in Africa', *Journal of Global Ethics*, 11, 1 (2015): 126–140.

53 Laura Valentini, 'Ideal vs. Non-Ideal Theory: A Conceptual Map', *Philosophy Compass*, 7, 9 (2012): 654–664.

54 Erskine, *Embedded Cosmopolitanism*.

55 Elizabeth Dauphinee, *The Ethics of Researching War: Looking for Bosnia* (Manchester: Manchester University Press, 2007).

56 Beitz et al., *International Ethics*; Ellis, *Ethics and International Relations*.

PART I

Philosophical Foundations

PHILOSOPHICAL FOUNDATIONS OF INTERNATIONAL ETHICS

Joy Gordon

The field of international ethics (IE) has long involved a philosophical dimension. This has certainly been most apparent in the ways in which IE addresses ethical concerns, such as harm to the innocent, or meta-questions, such as the realist argument that ethics have no role in international politics. Within IE, it is perhaps most common to see reference, explicitly or implicitly, to Mill's utilitarianism, or Kant's categorical imperative that we treat persons as ends in themselves, or principles from the just war tradition, such as discrimination and proportionality. We might say that philosophical approaches to IE can take place on different levels. First, IE may draw on broad ethical frameworks, such as utilitarianism, deontological ethics, or just war doctrine. Next, somewhat less commonly, IE may address more fine-grained ethical questions, such as consent, moral agency, intent, or volition. Last, we may want to consider whether there are interesting ways to push the boundaries, by drawing on disciplines less commonly used in IE, such as epistemology, hermeneutics, and psychoanalysis; and seeking to incorporate critical perspectives, such as post-modern approaches, feminism, and perspectives from the Global South.

It may be the case that the earliest ethical questions of international relations emerged in the context of warfare. Long before Augustine, we see the emergence of the question: what are the moral ties, and consequent duties, we have, not only to compatriots, but to strangers, and even to enemies, in wartime? In writings such as Euripides' *Women of Troy*, the brutality against women, children, and the elderly, none of whom present the least threat to the victorious Greeks, is presented as deeply disturbing. There is a sense that, even in the barbarity of war, there is something wrong about doing gratuitous harm to those who are quite helpless. The principles of just war emerge more formally later on. But the moral intuitions they embody come into play time and again in response to issues in international relations as they emerge. This is certainly true of *jus in bello*, which holds there is a duty to discriminate between combatants and non-combatants, and that no harm should be done that is disproportionate to the military advantage to be gained. We have seen these principles brought to bear as a means of articulating a moral response to gratuitous human damage done in many circumstances outside of war, including economic sanctions. However, it is also true of *jus ad bellum*, the requirements for engaging in warfare, which include just cause, legitimate authority, and right intent. These notions are often invoked in contexts other than warfare, such as the responsibility to protect.

There are a number of other frameworks that have also informed the development of international ethics.

One such framework is the tension between cosmopolitanism and communitarianism. Michael Sandel, Amitai Etzioni, and others suggest that we define ourselves in significant measure by our membership and participation in communities, such as the family and workplace, as well as political communities, such as nations.[1] It is this identification with the particular community that provides a grounding and motivation for the civic contributions of citizens. The nationalism implied by a communitarian approach is reinforced by the centrality of national sovereignty in the post-Westphalian international order, and under contemporary international law.

This stands in contrast with cosmopolitanism, which implies relationships and duties across borders. We see a cosmopolitan agenda, for example, in Marx's project for unity among the working class across national boundaries. But the most influential philosophical justification for cosmopolitanism is found in Kant's essay *Toward Perpetual Peace*.[2] In *Perpetual Peace*, Kant proposes a set of measures intended to reduce the occasions for conflicts among nations, such as prohibiting interference in internal affairs of other nations, the maintenance of standing armies, and the use of tactics that undermine the possibility of future trust. He envisions a global federation of nations, a "league of peace," which will implement the agreement among nations. He proposes as well that, domestically, the nations should have republican constitutions; in this context, the purpose is to avoid despotism not only for the sake of the citizens, but because a ruler who is unlimited in his power can more easily expend the cost, in money and in lives, of pursuing warfare against another state.

Kant's cosmopolitanism is also grounded in his claim that there is a duty of "universal hospitality"—not as an unlimited obligation to take in all strangers under all conditions, nor as a right of strangers to remain permanently. Rather, when Kant speaks of hospitality, he means:

> the right of a stranger not to be treated as an enemy when he arrives in the land of another. One may refuse to receive him when this can be done without causing his destruction; but, so long as he peacefully occupies his place, one may not treat him with hostility.[3]

In part, this reflects Kant's moral philosophy, with its emphasis on universal law that is applicable to all rational beings, entailing the duty to treat all as ends in themselves. In *Perpetual Peace*, he also suggests that the right of universal hospitality is derived from humanity's "common possession of the surface of the earth": "Originally, no one had more right than another to a particular part of the earth." Human beings "cannot infinitely disperse and hence must finally tolerate the presence of each other"; thus, the obligation of universal hospitality. But this is not the final aim; that would be that humanity would move towards world citizenship.[4]

Contemporary developments in cosmopolitanism include, for example, Thomas Pogge's work on global justice, where he holds that "every human being has a global stature as the ultimate unit of moral concern."[5] Pogge articulates the implications of this for, among other things, the global distribution of wealth, international trade regimes, access to pharmaceuticals, corporate taxation, and intellectual property. Seyla Benhabib addresses the rights of the immigrant in the context of cosmopolitanism, arguing for more porous borders in response to transnational migration.[6] And, arguably, the norm of the responsibility to protect that has emerged over the last two decades in part reflects the sense that there is a duty to provide human protection across boundaries, regardless of citizenship or even state sovereignty.[7]

We also see utilitarian arguments for moral duties across boundaries, in the work of Peter Singer and others. In his influential essay "Famine, Affluence, and Morality,"[8] Singer starts "with the assumption that suffering and death from lack of food, shelter, and medical care are bad,"[9] and that "if it is in our power to prevent something bad from happening, without thereby sacrificing anything of comparable moral importance, we ought, morally, to do it."[10] In this essay, Singer appeals to our intuitive view that, if we were walking by a shallow pond and saw a child drowning, we should certainly wade in and save the child, even if it means getting our clothes muddy.[11] Why would we not have an equal duty to those who are displaced or impoverished, and are at risk of death or great suffering, on the other side of the world? Why should something as arbitrary as geographical proximity determine that we have no moral ties, if there exist the logistical means to provide assistance to those in distant lands, who are as much in need as the child drowning in the pond? While Singer is writing about refugees in East Bengal in 1971, the argument obliges us to look more generally at global poverty, at the maldistribution of global wealth and resources, and at the personal and institutional choices that are made which serve to perpetuate this maldistribution.

We see utilitarian arguments in many other domains of international ethics as well. For example, the ethical legitimacy of using nuclear weapons was often challenged on the grounds that the damage would be so great as to outweigh any possible good achieved from military victory. And we can see utilitarian arguments in the context of global governance: in responding to a threat to global security or a violation of international law, is it permissible to use a form of intervention that could do greater harm than that caused by the violation itself?

We also see the influence of Aristotle on the field of international ethics; particularly his notion of *eudaimonia*, or human flourishing. We see this, for example, as it informs the conception of development. We are accustomed to thinking of the development of a nation or a region in terms of economic growth, modern infrastructure, and industrialization. Amartya Sen proposed that economic development might be framed differently, as incorporating not only economic productivity but as entailing greater freedom; and that freedom in turn depends on capabilities. Freedom is compromised by political oppression, but also, in Sen's view, severe poverty, lack of opportunity for expression, and dysfunctional social institutions. Sen's work marked a shift in how development is conceptualized, to include not only economic growth but also human development. This approach has been influential in many domains, including the Human Development Report, issued annually since 1990 by the United Nations. The Human Development Index, on which it is based, looks at life expectancy, adult literacy, and standard of living.[12] Martha Nussbaum developed this approach further, elaborating a specific list of "central human capabilities": life; bodily health; bodily integrity; senses, imagination, and thought; emotions; practical reason; affiliation; other species; play; and control over one's environment.[13] She also addresses the particular ways that development, understood in this context, is gendered, looking at the higher mortality rate of women and girls, the greater risks of assault within the home, the diminished opportunities for political participation, and so forth; which in turn compromise central human capabilities, such as life, bodily integrity, and control over one's environment.[14]

Feminist approaches regarding international relations come into play on many levels. There are feminist explorations of the gender dynamic in warfare, and in the ways that security and warfare are understood. We see this, for example, in studies that document the use of rape as an intentional weapon of war, rather than an incidental outcome of violent conflict. We also see feminist critiques of entire domains within the international arena, such as human rights. Hilary Charlesworth and others have argued that the overarching structure of international human rights serves to reproduce the political exclusion and economic marginalization of women, while obscuring many of the ways their rights are violated.[15] Additionally, feminist approaches to international issues include an ethic of care. Drawing on the tradition of Carol Gilligan, Fiona Robinson criticizes traditional approaches to problems such as global poverty as being too abstract. What is required, she suggests, is a deeper level of consciousness and concern on the part of the privileged, on which to ground a commitment to structural change.[16]

Another core philosophical tension in international ethics involves the question of whether a collective entity—a nation, a people, a multinational corporation, an army, an institution of global governance—can properly be considered a moral agent. If so, then it may be appropriate to speak of such an entity as having not only legal responsibility for its acts and decisions, but moral responsibility as well. It may then be appropriate to impose punishment on such an entity for the wrongful acts attributable to it. However, if a collective entity does not have, or cannot have, moral agency, then punishment (whether for deterrence or retribution), as well as moral judgment, seem not only ineffectual or wrong, but unintelligible as well. In the aftermath of the Second World War, H. D. Lewis argued that the notion of collective responsibility simply makes no sense: a collective body consists of the individuals who comprise it, and while *they* are responsible for *their* acts and choices, the collective entity itself cannot be said to have acted or made choices.[17] By contrast, D. E. Cooper notes that, in fact, we do routinely ascribe moral agency to collective bodies, and we do so in ways that treat these bodies as irreducible to the individuals who may be members or employees or participants in them.[18] While this seems like a rather abstract ontological question, the implications for international ethics are enormous; if collective bodies are ultimately reducible to their members, then collective punishment is then not punishment at all, but rather is "sheer injury."[19] But at the same time, leaders who perpetrate atrocities do not operate in a vacuum. There may be active support from the broader population, not to mention passivity, which helps to make atrocities possible; in the words of Jaspers, "Passivity knows itself morally guilty of every failure, every neglect to act whenever possible, to shield the imperiled, to relieve wrong, to counter-vail."[20]

There are many other ways that philosophical issues in international ethics might play out. For example:

- In warfare, where there are civilian casualties that are viewed as excessive, one response of the party that inflicted the damage is to say "We had no choice." There is an extensive literature on choice, duress, and voluntariness that may be brought to bear in considering the validity of such a claim. In Book 3 of the *Nichomachean Ethics*, Aristotle writes with deep ambivalence about duress, in situations where people fear for their lives or for the lives of their loved ones, and engage in acts that would otherwise be considered destructive and indefensible. In these cases, Aristotle suggests, the person is acting voluntarily in that his actions are within his power to do or not do, "but in the abstract perhaps involuntary; for no one would choose any such act in itself." How might the analysis of voluntariness, by Aristotle and others, deepen the conversation about whether actors in warfare "had a choice"?
- In discussing the "right intention" component of *jus ad bellum*, we may ask about what exactly is meant by the "intent" of a state, and how that might be ascertained. If Congress authorizes the president to go to war, whose intent counts—that of Congress, or that of the president? What if there are multiple actors, and their intentions are different? Can we even speak coherently of the intent of a collective or institutional entity? If not, then what does this imply for the "right intention" requirement of *jus ad bellum*?

- The Doctrine of Double Effect (DDE) arguably provides the explicit philosophical foundation for the notion of collateral damage that is commonly invoked in conflicts. DDE, at its core, rests on a distinction between direct intent and oblique intent. Yet this distinction in turn rests on the view that it is possible for an agent to somehow withdraw her intention from some aspects of her consciously chosen act, but not others. The distinction comes from Aquinas, and there are also extensive writings on this by Anscombe, Bratman, and many others. What are the philosophical arguments for the distinction between direct intent and oblique intent? What are the implications of these for the Doctrine of Double Effect, and for the notion of collateral damage?
- Questions of consent arise in many contexts. In the case of individual persons, we would say that consent is valid only if it is freely given. Consent that is coerced by threats, or consent that occurs where there are no alternatives, would be compromised, or invalid altogether. Is the same true of relations among nations? If a small nation is pressured by a wealthy, powerful nation to sign a treaty that is deeply disadvantageous, can we say that there is consent? What if the larger nation threatens to cut off economic support, leaving the smaller country's economy in a shambles? Does this vitiate consent? Are the notions of consent and coercion used in the contexts of individual persons also applicable to states?
- What does hermeneutics have to offer that might be of use in thinking about, for example, the interpretation of UN Security Council resolutions? "Consensus resolutions," that are adopted by all or most members of the Council, may be deliberately drafted to be vague or innocuous, in order to obtain the widest support possible. Or they may contain provisions that are clearly contradictory, as a result of political concessions. In these cases, what might hermeneutics have to offer us to in thinking about the interpretation of deliberate ambiguity or intentional inconsistencies?

The collection of articles in this section is by no means comprehensive. They are intended rather to give the reader a sense of some of the central questions that may emerge in the field, given the breadth and variation of the philosophical landscape in this area.

The first two articles, by Matthew Lindauer and Kok-Chor Tan, explore the application of broad ethical frameworks in international affairs. The third, by David Atenasio, looks at a specific ethical problem—is collective responsibility coherent and defensible?—then applies that in the context of international criminal law. The fourth, by Raúl Salgado, looks at the responsibility to protect, arguing first for a constructivist approach, then within that, laying out a critical perspective from the Global South. Finally, Michael Levine and Damian Cox explore the problem of moral agency, and in doing so, bring to bear the perspective of psychoanalysis.

In Chapter 2, "Kantian themes in ethics and international relations," Lindauer explores some of the many contributions of the Kantian tradition to international ethics. Looking at *Perpetual Peace*, *Idea for a Universal History with a Cosmopolitan Intent*, and *The Metaphysics of Morals*, Lindauer considers the ways that Kant challenges the realist perspective by arguing for the necessity of moral constraints in resolving practical problems of international stability and security. Further, a just order within domestic society and a just order among nations are interrelated: in *Perpetual Peace*, Kant argues that international stability is dependent upon the domestic constitution of republics; while in *Universal History*, he maintains that a domestically just society is dependent upon just relations among states. Thus, Lindauer argues, Kant offers a challenge to the realist view that moral considerations are irrelevant to the political considerations that shape relations among nations.

In Chapter 3, Tan applies two broad approaches—cosmopolitanism and statism—in looking at global egalitarianism. A core question of the field of global justice concerns the global distribution of wealth. Does global justice require an egalitarian distribution of resources? If so, then what form of egalitarianism should come into play? If there is a duty to rectify global economic equality, then that clearly entails addressing poverty, but also has implications distinct from it as well. In any case, if we are committed to egalitarianism, then how should we conceive of that in this context? Tan discusses two approaches to the argument for egalitarianism: the first is based on the status of persons as equal moral agents; and the second on their associational relations.

Tan then considers a cosmopolitan approach that entails an "individualistic and transnational ideal of distributive justice," looking at arguments such as those offered by Charles Beitz. Statism, by contrast, may be consistent with domestic egalitarianism, and may be consistent with a duty of assistance or cooperation. But statism would deny a global right of individual persons to distributive equality. While statism and cosmopolitanism obviously come into play in many arenas, in the context of global justice Tan suggests that they lead us to consider the very nature of justice itself.

Atenasio, in Chapter 4, looks at the moral and philosophical questions raised by collective responsibility, particularly in the context of collective punishment. Collective punishment has been practiced in warfare since biblical times. But in modern times, it is prohibited under international law, and seems clearly problematic: to exterminate a village because there is one combatant living there seems deeply offensive to our moral intuitions. Atenasio looks closely at different approaches to collective responsibility that reveal its complexities. Are there collective entities that genuinely have a distinct existence, apart from the individuals who comprise them? Or are all collective entities ultimately reducible to their constituent members? In that case, are there situations where it is reasonable to impute liability to the members of a group, such that it is legitimate to punish all members for the acts of a few? Atenasio then explores how these questions might be brought to bear in considering the role of collective punishment under international law. He looks closely the charge of "joint criminal enterprise" used in the International Criminal Tribunal for the former Yugoslavia, and the different forms it has taken.

In Chapter 5, Salgado discusses the constructivist approach to international ethics, applying it in his examination of the principle of the responsibility to protect (R2P). He first reviews the constructivist approach to international norms, then provides an overview of the diplomatic and institutional contexts in which R2P was formulated. He describes the means by which Latin America nations were marginalized from the formative discussions. There was a good deal of variation among Latin American nations in the degree to which they were willing to support the new norm. However, among their responses were sharp critiques, as well as a counter-proposal for a different model, responsibility while protecting (RwP). RwP reflected their concern that R2P granted excessive authority to the nations wielding the greatest military power, and the greatest influence over institutions of international governance; and the sense that these might result in indiscriminate or disproportionate harm, imposed in the name of global governance or international norms.

Cox and Levine, in Chapter 6, look at the question of moral agency in the context of international actors. Can we even talk about moral agency in a landscape consisting of entities such as governments, nations, institutions of global governance, and transnational organizations? They begin by considering four approaches to moral agency: consequentialist accounts of moral responsibility; attribution accounts; accountability accounts; and answerability accounts. With these in mind, they consider whether we can say that "institutions and groups operate as genuine agents." They consider the role of reasons in agent explanation, where these can be seen in the decisions of international actors; and they also consider the acts that are driven by other factors, such as anger or resentment, rather than reasons. They then introduce psychoanalytic theory as a means of exploring situations where an international actor is not transparent to itself in regard to its reasons and motivations. We might see this in dysfunctional institutions, as well as situations where a government, for example, is not transparent to itself (let alone others) regarding its actual reasons for acting.

Overall, these five articles illustrate some of the ways that philosophical frameworks (including but not limited to ethics) might be brought to bear in taking a closer look at the conceptual foundations of issues in international ethics.

Notes

1 Michael Sandel, *Liberalism and the Limits of Justice* (Cambridge: Cambridge University Press, 1981); Michael Sandel, *Democracy's Discontent* (Cambridge, MA: Harvard University Press, 1996).
2 Immanuel Kant, *Perpetual Peace: A Philosophical Sketch*, 1795.
3 *Perpetual Peace*, Third Definitive Article for a Perpetual Peace.
4 *Perpetual Peace*, Third Definitive Article for a Perpetual Peace.
5 Thomas W. Pogge, *World Poverty and Human Rights* (Cambridge: Polity Press, 2002), p. 169.
6 Seyla Benhabib, *The Rights of Others: Aliens, Residents, and Citizens* (Cambridge: Cambridge University Press, 2004).
7 International Commission on Intervention and State Sovereignty, "The Responsibility to Protect," International Development Research Centre, Ottawa Canada, December 2001.
8 *Philosophy and Public Affairs*, vol. 1, no. 3 (Spring 1972).
9 Singer, p. 231.
10 Singer, p. 231.
11 Singer, p. 231.
12 United Nations Development Programme, "Human Development Report 2016" (New York, 2016).
13 Martha Nussbaum, *Creating Capabilities: The Human Development Approach* (Cambridge, MA: Harvard University Press, 2011), pp. 33–34.
14 Martha Nussbaum, *Women and Human Development: The Capabilities Approach* (New York: Cambridge University Press, 2000).
15 See, e.g., Hilary Charlesworth, "What are 'Women's International Human Rights'?", in Rebecca Cook, ed., *Human Rights of Women: National and International Perspectives* (Philadelphia, PA: University of Pennsylvania Press, 1994), pp. 58–84.
16 Fiona Robinson, *Globalizing Care: Toward a Politics of Peace* (Boston, MA: Beacon Press, 1999).
17 H. D. Lewis, "Collective Responsibility," *Philosophy*, vol. 23, no. 84 (1948).
18 D. E. Cooper, *Philosophy*, vol. 43, no. 165 (1968).
19 Lewis, p. 9.
20 Mark R. Reiff, *Social Theory and Practice*, vol. 34, no. 2 (April 2008), p. 217.

2

KANTIAN THEMES IN ETHICS AND INTERNATIONAL RELATIONS[1]

Matthew Lindauer

Introduction

Immanuel Kant's writings on international relations have been extremely influential, spurring the development of idealism,[2] democratic peace theory,[3] and other important traditions in the field. There is something of a disconnect, however, between moral and political philosophy in what is a recognizably Kantian tradition and Kant's mark on the field of international relations. As a result, the strength of the Kantian tradition in international relations and the resources available to theories within this tradition have yet to be fully appreciated.

This chapter has two modest goals relating to two interlocking themes in moral and political philosophy in the Kantian tradition. First, I will bring some of the philosophical issues raised in interpreting Kant's ethics to bear on how we think about a Kantian understanding of international relations. In particular, I will focus on Kantian constructivism[4] and how a constructivist interpretation can inform an understanding of Kant's *Perpetual Peace*[5] and passages in other texts that deal with international relations. Second, drawing on this constructivist account in international relations, I will examine Kant's remarks in *Idea for a Universal History with a Cosmopolitan Intent*,[6] *Perpetual Peace*, and *The Metaphysics of Morals*[7] about the dependency of domestic justice on international justice. By putting these two goals of the chapter together, we can see how a Kantian view of international relations can (1) emphasize the role of morality in international relations while remaining grounded in the resolution of practical problems and (2) offer an important lesson on the requirement that problems of international and global justice be addressed because doing so is a precondition for the resolution of important problems of domestic justice. Each of these points provides a response to, and the second puts pressure on, realist views in international relations.

Kantian constructivism and international relations

I will begin with a distinction drawn by Christine Korsgaard[8] between realist and constructivist approaches in moral and political philosophy.[9] A strand in philosophy that finds some expression in Aristotle's views about the difference between ethics and other areas of inquiry can be put in contrast with a view more closely associated with Plato.[10] For Aristotle, ethics is different from other areas of inquiry because when we examine the virtues through philosophical analysis, "the purpose of our examination is not to know what virtue is, but to become good."[11] Rather than attempting to grasp the Form of Virtue or Goodness, the study of ethics has a point for Aristotle – helping us to figure out how to live our lives in the best way. The idea of a "point" for morality is in direct contrast with the view that the study of morality is just another area of theoretical inquiry. The question of whether or not morality has a point or purpose is the issue that Korsgaard identifies as separating constructivist and realist moral theorists.

Korsgaard holds that morality has a practical purpose. She identifies constructivism as the view that normative concepts are solutions to practical problems. In interpreting Kant's ethics, she describes him as offering the moral law, the "categorical imperative," as the solution to a problem of practical reason. An individual will that is free needs to be governed by principles – a will that operated randomly would hardly be free in the sense of being autonomous and, relatedly, self-guiding. But the presence of those principles also must not be incompatible with freedom of the will – the will must choose them for itself. The relevant principle for Kant that solves this practical problem is the categorical imperative, which tells the will to choose a law without imposing any external constraints on the will's activity. Of course, I cannot go into the details of the argument for this conclusion here. The point, rather, is that the categorical imperative is supposed to solve a practical problem, in this case the problem of practical reason. Now, it may seem that the problem of a free will requiring a principle is not the kind of practical problem that we encounter in politics. Indeed, some have doubted that it really should be thought of as a problem.[12] But it is worth noting that the tradition of interpreting Kant as a constructivist, as characterized by Korsgaard, carries along the idea that normative theorizing is aimed at certain practical problems.

Korsgaard takes this same characterization of constructivism in moral and political philosophy to appropriately describe the work of John Rawls, who named the tradition.[13] For Rawls, we need a conception of justice – a specification of the shared concept 'justice' – that can guide the development and reform of a democratic society. As Rawls' corpus develops over the course of further works, it becomes clear that he was increasingly concerned with the real-world practical problem that his conception was meant to solve. With the move from *A Theory of Justice*[14] to "Kantian Constructivism in Moral Theory" and then to *Political Liberalism*,[15] the practical problem becomes not merely the need for principles in a democratic society that can be implemented, that provide the ability to prioritize among competing principles and goods, and so on. The problem becomes the predicament of a liberal society in which people of diverse faiths and worldviews must coexist and find terms of social cooperation that they can all accept for the right kind of stability, a morally acceptable stability, to be achieved. As Rawls moves into the international sphere with *The Law of Peoples*, he also endorses a conception of his enterprise that has a practical emphasis, emphasizing the achievement of a stable agreement on principles of international justice between liberal and non-liberal but decent societies. Conceptions of justice in both the domestic and international spheres, for Rawls, are assessed in part by their ability to solve practical problems, and do so in the *right way*, not merely by achieving a *modus vivendi* but by establishing terms of cooperation that are fully acceptable to the relevant participants agreeing upon them. Such an approach is labeled that of a "realistic Utopia," and borrowing Rousseau's dictum, Rawls says that his theory of justice involves "men being taken as they are and laws as they might be."[16]

It is in this light that I want to first urge the examination of Kant's work in international relations and views concerning the normative evaluation of interactions between political societies that bear Kant's influence. I am not a Kant scholar, and for the purposes of this chapter, the relevant issue isn't whether Kant was a constructivist or a realist in ethics,[17] or how pervasive any constructivist elements of his philosophy were across his works in moral and political philosophy. Rather than focusing only on ascertaining what Kant the individual might have thought, my goal here is to explore what a constructivist approach of the kind described by Korsgaard can offer to theorists working in international relations.[18] This type of constructivist approach differs from views that are currently described as "constructivist" in international relations,[19] which tend to emphasize the ways in which important aspects of relations between states are constructed through ongoing practices and interactions. However, my view is that the Kantian constructivist approach characterized by Korsgaard is importantly absent from existing debates in international relations, and this label is worth retaining when entering into such debates for reasons of continuity with the philosophical literature.

Why adopt this approach? First, doing so has the potential to unseat some assumptions about Kantian theories that tend to support the kinds of objections typically raised by realists in international relations. Realists are skeptical about the role that morality can play in relations between states.[20] While this skepticism takes different forms for different theorists in the realist tradition,[21] realism is typically contrasted with "idealism," of which Kant is thought of as a key progenitor. As noted by Peter Wilson,[22] idealism is generally characterized as the perspective on international relations that emphasizes the role of international norms, interdependence, and cooperation among states.[23] Further, the term "idealism" is often employed by realists in a rhetorical way, with the purpose of discrediting radical or reformist ideas with which they disagree.[24] For this reason, the association of Realism with *realistic* assessments of what interactions between states really are like and Idealism with *idealistic* and thereby less realistic conceptions is perhaps unavoidable.

While it is clearly true, for instance, that states are often not driven by normative principles in their interactions with other states, Kant and political philosophers working in the Kantian tradition are well aware of this. When paired with a constructivist understanding of normative concepts as solutions to practical problems, idealism can serve as a pragmatic, but still morally constrained, approach to international relations. The separation between a global scheme of relationships between states and persons governed by rules they all could reasonably accept and one that they merely accept because of their current interests and bargaining power is not one between principle-based and fact-based theories. Rather, the former involves a commitment both to practicality and moral constraints (it is questionable that the latter is practically useful, for reasons that I discuss in the next section). These moral constraints (i) inform the kind of solution that we seek for a given practical problem in international relations (not one inconsistent with plausibly moral values), (ii) set a moral goal for the task of doing philosophical work on these questions, that is, helping to solve practical problems, and (iii) provide reasons to revise our conceptions in so far as they cease to satisfy requirements (i) and (ii).

Notably, many of Kant's remarks on international relations support the claim that he has practical constraints in mind when he offers at least some of his views on international relations. His objections to the possibility of world government, for instance, are empirically grounded and based on assessments of what would actually occur in the real world. If "laws invariably lose their impact with the expansion of their domain of governance,"[25] a world government could not effectively legislate. Kant adds that a world government would be a "soulless despotism" bound to devolve into anarchy.[26] In place of a world state, the "*negative* surrogate" of an enduring and expanding federation must be introduced to solve the problem of international relations.

While Kant offers somewhat different conceptions of what would suffice as an appropriate arrangement of international power across his works, these conceptions are also, in part, tailored to empirical conditions that societies actually face when interacting with one another. Indeed, many of the articles of perpetual peace, which provide the blueprint for Kant's *foedus pacificum*, are justified on the basis of practical considerations.[27] Standing armies should be gradually abolished (Preliminary Article 3), not because they are morally wrong in themselves, but because they threaten other nations with the appearance of being ready for war, producing arms races that become more costly for states than going to war itself. National debts in the service of foreign affairs are prohibited (Preliminary Article 4) because they make it too easy for nations to amass a large war chest and jeopardize innocent nations that would be harmed by the bankruptcy of a nation that could not repay its debt. One nation interfering with the constitution and government of another is prohibited (Preliminary Article 5), except in some circumstances where there is an internal conflict in it, not only because doing so violates the rights of an independent people, but also because it "renders the autonomy of every nation insecure."[28] Similarly practical reasons are given in favor of the sixth Preliminary Article, which prohibits acts of war that "shall make mutual trust impossible during some future time of peace."[29] Kant refers to the use of assassins or poisoners, breach of surrender, and the instigation of treason in an opposing nation as "intrinsically despicable," but doesn't stop there. He states that once these means of war that are *mala in se* are used, they "cannot long be confined to war alone."[30] In virtue of carrying over into peacetime, Kant thinks these means threaten to bring about "a war of extermination" where perpetual peace would occur "only in the vast graveyard of humanity as a whole."[31]

In addition to the practical justifications that he gives for most of the preliminary articles of perpetual peace, Kant includes claims about practical consequences in justifying the first of his definitive articles that allow for a state of peace between nations to be actively established. Kant argues that "in addition to the purity of its origin, a purity whose sources is the pure concept of right,"[32] the republican mode of government is less likely than alternatives to resort to war. Kant describes republicanism as the separation of executive and legislative power – the power that executes the law is distinct from the power that decides on the law. Whereas "the easiest thing in the world to do is to declare war" when a ruler is not a fellow citizen, citizens who bear the costs of war, including fighting the war themselves, will be very cautious about deciding to enter into it. It is because citizens and not a ruler or rulers decide on laws to be enacted, including decisions to go to war, that Kant believes a republican government will tend not to resort to war. This is an important part of Kant's justification for the first definitive article's contention that every nation should have a republican civil constitution. The republican form of government is more conducive to solving the practical problem of overcoming tendencies to engage in war than other forms of government, according to Kant, and this is presented both as a strike in its favor and a reason for its presence within the first definitive article of perpetual peace.

Given these points, it is hard not to read *Perpetual Peace* as a work that aims to use moral concepts and principles to solve the practical problem of war. It embodies the idealist commitments to the importance of norms, interdependence, and cooperation among states while remaining practically oriented and responsive to evidence about how individuals and states actually are.

Taking a constructivist approach to international relations also allows for a Kantian view to be flexible in light of the fact that the problems of war and achieving peace are not the only pressing problems currently facing the international order. Other threats, environmental, epidemiological, and so on, could also be part of a Kantian constructivist approach to designing international institutions that emphasizes moral considerations but takes empirical facts into account.

Solving pressing moral problems at the international level requires cooperation not only between liberal societies but also with some non-liberal societies. It is therefore important to note that a practically oriented Kantian approach can embrace the Rawlsian view that non-liberal states of certain kinds must be treated as equal participants in international society.[33] Michael Doyle, while generally embracing Kant's views about the importance of liberal societies to international peace, criticizes the Kantian legacy in international relations for its failures to engage constructively with non-liberal powers.[34] Kant himself was not appropriately sensitive to diversity between different types of societies. While he had some qualms with colonialism, he also embraced what we now recognize as morally problematic views about the causes of differences between peoples and cultures. The requirements to work across lines of different types of political arrangements and not try to stamp out political diversity at the international level are ones that contemporary philosophers working in the Kantian tradition generally accept.

Lastly, Kant may have revised his strong commitments to state sovereignty and the general impermissibility of rebellion if he had observed the changing practical circumstances that the world would face after his death. Kant never witnessed the horrors of the 20th century and the now well-recognized dangers of authoritarianism and obedience to power, dangers that arise from well-known aspects of human psychology.[35] In light of the prominent dangers of state power, Kant may have come to embrace the permissibility of humanitarian intervention, as contemporary Kantian thinkers have.[36] In the case of the right to rebel, Kant notably does not argue that rebellion is wrong in states without the right kind of domestic structure.[37] We may be more or less capacious in our view of which states are ones where we should recognize or perhaps aid rebellions, in keeping with what we've learned about the risks of unchecked state power and the dangers of many humanitarian interventions.[38] However, a Kantian approach need not be hostage to Kant's own views on the topics of state sovereignty or rebellion, as they are peripheral to Kant's own core commitments and not central in any way to a Kantian constructivist approach to theorizing about international relations.

The relationship between domestic and international justice

With the Kantian constructivist approach in mind, I now wish to draw the reader's attention to a passage from Kant's 1784 *The Idea for a Universal History with a Cosmopolitan Intent* that will be important for much of the rest of what I have to say here:

> The problem of establishing a perfect civil constitution depends on the problem of law-governed external relations among nations and cannot be solved unless the latter is.[39]

In this often overlooked passage that opens the "Seventh Thesis" of *Universal History*, Kant seems to be suggesting that solving one problem, a problem of domestic justice, is contingent on another problem being solved, a problem of international justice. In the language of this passage itself, of course, Kant doesn't say anything about normative requirements on the shape that a solution to the international problem must take, whereas the domestic civil constitution needing to be established is described as "perfect." But Kant clearly is not interested in a mere *modus vivendi* in international relations, and also recognizes the imperfection of interactions between persons in even the best liberal republics. He holds that nearly all of our rights are only fully realized within a constitutional republic, and also that perpetual peace is "the supreme political good" in the very last line of the "Doctrine of Right," the first part of *The Metaphysics of Morals*.[40] What is the relation between the two?

In moving to this broader question, we may begin by asking in what ways the problem of securing a domestically just society can be said to be contingent on securing a law-governed, just relationship among states. While this is an interesting way of proceeding, I also want to think about this relationship as a transitive one. That is to say, certain features of human social life can only be secured by solving the problem of a domestically just state and, if we take Kant's suggestion above, securing them will also require solving the problem of a just international order. To express this formally:

Domestic Principle (DP): For certain features of human social life to be secured, the problem of a domestically just state must be solved.

International Principle (IP): For the problem of a domestically just state to be solved, the problem of a just international order must be solved.

Transitivity of the Domestic and International Principle (TDIP): For certain features of human social life to be secured, the problem of a just international order must be solved.

Put this way, in terms of transitivity, the claim is more striking. In some sense, the world has never seen a fully just international order, which is part of what has led realists to posit that international relations are a state of anarchy. However, not many theorists other than thoroughgoing anarchists have been inclined to say that there have never been, even for brief periods of time, states that were just. Further, depending on which features of human social life the existence of a domestically just society is supposed to secure, it is quite a radical conclusion to say that these features have not yet been secured or cannot be in so far as the international order is not just. Rather than eschewing this more radical conclusion, however, I want to pursue it, because it strikes me that good sense can be made of it that is compatible with a Kantian perspective on international relations. Further, if TDIP holds, a problem arises for theorists who wish to view domestic relations in terms of justice and international relations in terms of anarchy, because the lawlessness of the latter jeopardizes the lawfulness of the former.

When Kant expresses what I'm calling the TDIP in *Universal History*, he doesn't explicitly draw the connection between this principle and the more specific aspects of his domestic justice theory. Indeed, *The Metaphysics of Morals* was published in 1797, thirteen years after *Universal History*, which also precedes the *Groundwork*[41] by one year, although the *Groundwork* doesn't give sustained attention to issues of political justice. Instead, Kant is providing a theory of history as driven towards the establishment of a "universal cosmopolitan state."[42] The "theses" provided in this work are propositions that are supposed to show that history is developing in this direction, and that the self-interested motives of human beings progressively give way to moral motivations and expanding, just political institutions. So far this allows us to see why a universal cosmopolitan state might be, as Kant says, "the inevitable outcome of the distress that men cause one another."[43] Just as pre-political individuals eventually had to give up their unconstrained freedom and seek the calm and security of political society, societies will be led to "leave the lawless state of savagery and enter into a federation of peoples."[44] But what about this makes solving the problem of a just international order *necessary* for the solution of the domestic problem, as opposed to an inevitable further development?

Kant states that the consequences of war and the threat of war for states are devastation, upheaval, and the "complete exhaustion of their inner powers,"[45] and hence states must move towards a law-governed relationship with other states. So here we have our first interpretation of the TDIP, one that is fully compatible with the realist's skepticism about the role of morality in international relations. The *stability* of domestic societies, on this interpretation, depends on there being a solution to the problem of anarchy on the world stage, and the only way to get rid of this problem is to develop a law-governed relationship between states. Where a rightful civil constitution enables human tendencies, both to help others and to help ourselves, to contribute to establishing a social order in which we progress as individuals, a just international order will manage the selfish (and perhaps other-regarding) tendencies of states and support such progress. Without law-governed external relationships – relationships with other states, in this case – a domestic state is subject to the destabilizing effects of war and conflict. Hence the aspect of human social life that the domestic state makes possible, progress in line with the development of reason, is contingent upon a just international order being put in place. Such a picture is largely amoral, except in so far as we take the term "progress" to have unavoidable moral connotations. A truly value-neutral version of this argument, of course, can be given solely in terms of the requirements for the stability of a domestic society. Except for the emphasis on progress here, there is little for realists to disagree with in their skepticism about the role of morality in international relations. Maintaining a stable international order is simply in states' interests because they wish to avoid the destabilizing effects of war and conflict.

If we pivot from *Universal History* to *The Metaphysics of Morals*, the TDIP yields a different conclusion about the dependence of domestic justice on international justice, one that centers on the political morality of property rights. Kant's view of the nature of property differs greatly from the well-known Lockean alternative, as well as those of most other deontologists.[46] Obviously, it is also not a utilitarian view, which would reduce the moral significance of property rights to the contributions that property rights conventions make to overall utility. But unlike Locke, Kant doesn't take property rights, at least non-provisional property rights, to be pre-institutional. In the state of nature, prior to the establishment of a constitutional republic, Kant argues that we can only acquire property provisionally. Kant states the Universal Principle of Right (UPR) as follows: "an action is *right* if it can coexist with everyone's freedom in accordance with a universal law, or if on its maxim the freedom of choice of each can coexist with everyone's freedom in accordance with a universal law."[47] Kant holds that the UPR is a "postulate incapable of further proof,"[48] although he does give arguments for the UPR and for the implications he draws from it. The UPR gives rise to the "one innate right" that we each have, which is the right to "*Freedom* (independence from being constrained by another's choice), insofar as it can coexist with the freedom of every other in accordance with a universal law."[49] This is "the only original right belonging to every man by virtue of his humanity."[50] If we think carefully about the conditions of this freedom, according to Kant, we will see that the ability to securely acquire property in ways that we recognize, which place others under obligations to regulate their conduct in relation to our property, cannot be exercised unilaterally. In the state of nature, we can provisionally acquire objects that we are in physical contact with and keep on our persons. But our ability to have a "perfected"[51] right to those objects, a right that includes security of our possession of the object, a clear boundary between what is ours and what is owned by others, and the ability to coerce others who seek to use our property in ways that we do not approve, requires a public authority. The Lockean view, for Kant, wrongly assumes that by acquiring and mixing our labor with an object, we can acquire a secure property right in that object in the state of nature. But where, on such a picture, does the authorization to coerce others who also wish to use that object come from? There must be some justification for the permissibility of preventing others who wish to use your property that is compatible with their innate right to freedom if such coercion would be morally justified.

There are three gaps in the state of nature for Kant that make it the case that a government is required to perfect our property rights.[52] The first I just mentioned – the fact that the unilateral judgment of one individual cannot justify limits on the freedom of other individuals. This includes restrictions on their freedom to use physical matter in the external world, including property that other people have a provisional right to. Second, we must have assurance from others that if we respect their property, they will do the same for us. Otherwise, we are not under an obligation to leave other people's property alone – respect for property rights must be reciprocal. And third, our property rights are indeterminate in the state of nature "with respect to quality as well as quantity."[53] According to Kant, the problem of indeterminacy is the "hardest to solve," and even if it is solved "through the original contract," acquisition remains provisional "unless this contract extends to the entire human race."[54] In Kant's discussions of property in *The Metaphysics of Morals*, he includes both individual property and the property of nations, in each case including rights to territory. The problems of assurance and determinacy, he holds, are subsumed under the problem of acquiring property, and the acquisition of property gives rise to the problem of how unilateral judgment and action of an individual that acquires an object or territory can, by their very discretion, possibly put others under an obligation to treat their property in particular ways. Kant's answer is that unilaterality cannot do so – political authority is required to make such interference with the freedom of others legitimate.

These gaps are not mere "inconveniences" of the state of nature in Locke's sense,[55] but rather features that make the perfection of property rights contingent on the establishment of a constitutional political order. Three branches of government each serve the function of dealing with one of these gaps. The legislative branch solves the problem of unilateral judgment because it is capable of making laws from the standpoint of an "omnilateral will" which makes its determinations on behalf of the citizens as a collective body.[56] The executive branch solves the problem of assurance by enforcing the laws made by the legislative branch. And the problem of indeterminacy is solved by the judiciary, which applies the law to particular cases.

We have seen, then, that one of the features of human social life, for Kant, that requires a just domestic state to be secured is property, and property rights in particular. As Lea Ypi has recently discussed, the territories of states should be treated similarly.[57] Any unilateral act of settlement or acquisition of territory, Kantian reasoning implies, is only provisional unless it is coupled with an obligation to enter into "*universally* inclusive political relations."[58] And because individual property exists within the territorial confines of states, by the TDIP, individual property rights can only be secured when a just international order is present.[59] Ypi points to a key passage[60] where Kant emphasizes this moral dependence of domestic relations on international and cosmopolitan relations: "if the principle of outer freedom limited by law is lacking in any one of these three possible forms of rightful condition, the framework of all the others is unavoidably undetermined and must finally collapse."[61] Here again, the principal problem is that of political authority being needed to move from a unilateral act of acquisition or settlement to a justified state of affairs.

This view of the relationship between domestic property holdings and international justice not only accords with an interesting and plausible theory of property. It is also deeply intuitive, when spelled out in terms of our own entitlements. If the territory that I hold was recently stolen by my nation from another people and nothing has been done to address this fact, it seems indefensible for me to have the right to coerce the original owners if they attempt to recover their holdings. This situation wouldn't be made more acceptable by the mere fact that my nation was relatively just to insiders. And even in the case of historical injustices, there is something odd about claiming an unqualified right to continue using land that was stolen from indigenous peoples. It may also seem wrong to demand that innocent beneficiaries of such injustice give up all such benefits.[62] What seems most appropriate is a solution that balances the fact of historical injustice with the state of things as they are, meaning that current people are not put in dire circumstances for the sake of righting the historical wrong. But in the absence of such a resolution, there is something very tempting about the thought that a nation such as the United States cannot, for instance, justifiably coerce descendants of indigenous peoples or other owners of historical lands to keep them out of its territory (Mexican people seeking to live in California or Texas, for instance). This accords well with the Kantian line of reasoning that, unless the demands of justice between nations are satisfied, holdings within a nation that has perpetuated injustice against another are only provisional.

There are at least three more reasons why the TDIP holds. These also are not reasons that Kant himself affirmed, but they are compatible with Kantian deontology. First, there are *relationships* between citizens and non-citizens of a state which make it the case that the state's treating the non-citizens justly along some dimensions is required for it to treat citizens justly.[63] The clearest illustration of this fact can be given in terms of immigration policy. In the ethics of immigration literature, Michael Walzer[64] and Christopher Heath Wellman[65] have held that immigration policies that use race or ethnicity as selection criteria are not morally impermissible for societies to implement even if it is morally regrettable when societies do so. But in a diverse, modern liberal state, there will typically be at least some citizens who are present that are members of races and ethnicities that states would keep out. Such policies thus treat those insiders as "second-class citizens."[66] This doesn't show, of course, that a state cannot exclude persons who don't share the relevant qualities with citizens. Nor does it imply that the only reasons to treat outsiders respectfully as reducible to reasons of respect for citizens. However, when we see that similar reasoning extends to nationality, religion, gender, gender identity, sexual orientation, and disability, the extent to which societies are constrained in how they treat non-citizens if they are to meet the demands of domestic justice clearly supports the TDIP. The principle of equal respect for members, a core demand of liberal domestic justice,[67] requires the state not to implement policies that exclude or give less than equal treatment outsiders on the basis of such qualities in a wide range of cases.[68] Meeting the demands of domestic justice therefore requires treating non-citizens in ways that many, but not all, of us think are required by the demands of international justice. Given other pre-existing "external relationships" that citizens are parties to, such as relationships with non-citizen family members, it may also be the case that states can only give sufficient weight to the interests of their citizens if they constrain their conduct towards these non-citizens living elsewhere. A law-governed relationship with other states is required in light of the external relationships of a liberal society's own citizens. Fully making the case for this point is beyond the bounds of this chapter, but I have shown at least one way in which attention to the relationships of citizens of liberal societies provides support for the TDIP.

Second, the TDIP may be supported by considerations involving a liberal polity's integrity[69] which make it the case that it must uphold standards of international justice to maintain its domestic justice commitments. By trading with dictators or engaging in unjust wars, liberal democracies act in ways that contradict the commitments that they are supposed to uphold domestically – the commitment to the view that dictatorship is not a legitimate form of government, that unjust aggression is wrong, and so on. In order to act in ways that are consistent with its own commitments at home, a liberal state must carry its moral commitments over to its interactions with outsiders. Hence, the tie between domestic and international justice put forward by the TDIP is also supported by considerations grounded in the notion of a liberal state's political integrity.

Lastly, the TDIP is supported by the fact that in order to take actions that promote domestic security, liberal states must be taken seriously in their efforts to promote international justice. To be viewed as legitimate arbiters of international peace, which benefits the domestic polity, a liberal democracy cannot engage in acts of aggression or wars fought for suspect premises. The possibility of securing the conditions of a domestically just society, across many domains, will require that liberal societies participate on the international stage in ways that engender mutual trust and reciprocity. To tackle the shared threats that societies face, not only in terms of military threats but also to coordinate action on issues such as climate change and the global nature of disease epidemiology, liberal societies must be shown to be trustworthy to other nations. Hence their preventing threats to the domestic policy and maintaining the conditions of domestic justice depend in part on meeting demands of justice in their interactions with other states.

The first, stability-based point that I raised in favor of the TDIP is, again, one that realists can concede. The fact that it is often in states' interests to seek international stability for the sake of promoting their own stability at home does not put pressure on the realist who is skeptical about the role of moral considerations in international relations. However, the four additional points raised in this section point to a stronger connection between domestic justice and international justice that puts pressure on such skepticism. A state whose conduct on the international stage is not constrained by moral requirements threatens to jeopardize its domestic property (including territorial entitlements), to violate demands of domestic justice, to harm its own political integrity, and to lose its legitimacy in taking actions that are required to maintain a just domestic order. Each of these points presuppose that morality must play an important role in international relations – the price of an unjust international order includes the inability to secure domestic justice and many of its morally desirable features.

Conclusion

In this chapter, I have shown that two interlocking themes in Kantian moral and political philosophy can inform our understanding of the Kantian perspective on international relations. A Kantian view can give a central role to moral considerations in theorizing international relations while holding that this role involves solving practical problems that arise at the international level. Further, Kant's view that solving the problem of a domestically just state is contingent on solving the problem of law-governed relations among nations can be shown to generate plausible and challenging claims about the relationship between domestic and international justice. These claims put pressure on realists in international relations who hold that moral considerations are generally unimportant to our theorizing about interactions among states. Insofar as such theorists do not wish to deny the relevance of moral considerations to domestic justice theory, which would be a significant cost and argumentative burden for them to take on, it seems that they must grant a significant role to moral considerations in international relations. It remains for later work to examine each of the two main themes presented in this chapter in greater detail. Nonetheless, I hope to have shown that there is significant further material in Kantian moral and political philosophy for theorists to draw on in advancing and defending Kantian views in international relations.

Notes

1 I am grateful to Joy Gordon, Serene Khader, and Shmuel Nili for helpful discussion on the points raised in this chapter.

2 Pitman Potter, *An Introduction to the Study of International Organization* (New York: The Century Company, 1925); James T. Shotwell, "Plans and Protocols to End War," *International Conciliation*, 208 (1925); Philip Noel-Baker, *The League of Nations at Work* (London: Nisbet, 1926); Alfred Zimmern, *The League of Nations and the Rule of Law, 1918–1935* (London: Macmillan, 1936); Hedley Bull, *The Anarchical Society: A Study of Order in World Politics* (New York: Columbia University Press, 1977); Peter Wilson, "Idealism in International Relations," in *Encyclopedia of Power*, ed. Keith Dowding (Thousand Oaks: Sage Publications, 2011), 332–333.

3 Michael W. Doyle, "Kant, Liberal Legacies, and Foreign Affairs," *Philosophy and Public Affairs*, 12, 3 (1983a): 205–235; Michael W. Doyle, "Kant, Liberal Legacies, and Foreign Affairs," *Philosophy and Public Affairs*, 12, 4 (1983b): 323–353; Andrew Hurrell, "Kant and the Kantian Paradigm in International Relations," *Review of International Studies*, 16, 3 (1990): 183–205; Steven Pinker, *The Better Angels of Our Nature: Why Violence Has Declined* (New York: Viking Books, 2011); Luigi Caranti, "Kantian Peace and Liberal Peace: Three Concerns," *Journal of Political Philosophy*, 24, 4 (2016): 446–469.

4 The Kantian constructivist tradition in contemporary moral and political philosophy begins with John Rawls (see especially his "Kantian Constructivism in Moral Theory," *Journal of Philosophy* 77, 9

(September 1980): 515–572). However, as I explain below, my account draws more closely from the characterization of the constructivist tradition provided by Christine Korsgaard ("Realism and Constructivism in Twentieth-Century Moral Philosophy," *Journal of Philosophical Research*, APA Centennial Supplement: Philosophy in America at the Turn of the Century (2003): 99–122).

5 Immanuel Kant, "To Perpetual Peace: A Philosophical Sketch," in *Immanuel Kant: Perpetual Peace and Other Essays*, trans. Ted Humphrey (Indianapolis: Hackett Publishing Company, 1795/1983b), 107–143.

6 Immanuel Kant, "Idea for a Universal History with a Cosmopolitan Intent," in *Immanuel Kant: Perpetual Peace and Other Essays*, trans. Ted Humphrey (Indianapolis: Hackett Publishing Company, 1784/1983a), 29–40. Hereafter "*Universal History*."

7 Immanuel Kant, *The Metaphysics of Morals*, trans. Mary Gregor (Cambridge: Cambridge University Press, 1797/1996).

8 Korsgaard, "Realism and Constructivism in Twentieth-Century Moral Philosophy."

9 I won't discuss other uses of the term "constructivism" at any length here. There are, of course, many other ways philosophers have employed the term in both ethics and political philosophy. My use of the term also should not be taken to overlap with constructivism in international relations as understood by Nicholas Onuf or Alexander Wendt's "social constructivism." See Nicholas Greenwood Onuf, *World of Our Making: Rules and Rule in Social Theory and International Relations* (Columbia, SC: University of South Carolina Press, 1989) and Alexander Wendt, "Anarchy is What States Make of It: The Social Construction of Power Politics," *International Organization*, 46, 2 (Spring 1992): 391–425.

10 Korsgaard doesn't mention Plato in this article, but the contrast between Plato's approach to ethical thought and Aristotle's is useful here. For her discussion of Platonic realism, see Christine Korsgaard, *Sources of Normativity* (Cambridge: Cambridge University Press, 1996), 37–48.

11 Aristotle, *Nicomachean Ethics*, second edition, trans. Terence Irwin (Indianapolis: Hackett Publishing Company, 350 BC/1999), Book II.2, 19. Aristotle adds "since otherwise the inquiry would be of no benefit to us."

12 Sharon Street, "Coming to Terms with Contingency: Humean Constructivism about Practical Reason," in *Constructivism in Practical Philosophy*, eds. Jimmy Lenman and Yonatan Shemmer (Oxford: Oxford University Press, 2012).

13 See Rawls, "Kantian Constructivism in Moral Theory." Korsgaard takes herself to be offering an understanding of constructivism that is compatible with Rawls's Kantian constructivism, although their descriptions differ in important ways that I do not have the space to discuss here.

14 John Rawls, *A Theory of Justice* (Cambridge, MA: Harvard University Press, 1971/revised edition 1999).

15 John Rawls, *Political Liberalism* (New York: Columbia University Press, 1993).

16 Jean-Jacques Rousseau, *The Social Contract, or Principles of Political Right*, Book I, (1762), trans. G. D. H. Cole, public domain; John Rawls, *The Law of Peoples* (Cambridge, MA: Harvard University Press, 1999), 7.

17 For realist interpretations of Kant, see Allen Wood, *Kant's Ethical Thought* (Cambridge: Cambridge University Press, 1999) and Karl Ameriks, "On Two Non-Realist Interpretations of Kant's Ethics," in *Interpreting Kant's Critiques* (Oxford: Oxford University Press, 2003), 263–282.

18 It is not uncommon for philosophers examining or advancing Kantian themes in moral or political philosophy to separate what Kant himself thought from the Kantian tradition or even Kantian ideas. Onora O'Neill writes: "Much contemporary work on justice is seen, both by protagonists and by critics, as Kantian. Evidently not all its conclusions accord with Kant's views on obligation, rights or justice; but this in itself is not surprising since its aim is to develop Kant's basic insights, even to improve on his conclusions" (Onora O'Neill, *Bounds of Justice* (Cambridge: Cambridge University Press, 2000), 65). Shelly Kagan draws a distinction between "Kantianism" (what Kant himself thought) and "kantianism" (the type of approach to moral theory that Kant represents) when working on a reconciliation of Kantianism and consequentialism (Shelly Kagan, "Kantianism for Consequentialists," in *Immanuel Kant, Groundwork for the Metaphysics of Morals*, trans. Allen W. Wood (New Haven: Yale University Press, 2002), 111–156). Pablo Gilabert also separates Kant's own views on duties of justice and global poverty from views that bear Kant's influence (Pablo Gilabert, "Kant and the Claims of the Poor," *Philosophy and Phenomenological Research*, 81, 2 (September 2010): 382–418).

19 Onuf, *World of Our Making: Rules and Rule in Social Theory and International Relations* and Wendt, "Anarchy is What States Make of It: The Social Construction of Power Politics."

20 W. Julian Korab-Karpowicz, "Political Realism in International Relations," in *The Stanford Encyclopedia of Philosophy*, Summer 2013 Edition, ed. Edward N. Zalta, <https://plato.stanford.edu/archives/sum2013/entries/realism-intl-relations/>.

21 See, e.g., Hans J. Morgenthau, *Scientific Man versus Power Politics* (Chicago: Chicago University Press, 1946) and Kenneth Waltz, *Theory of International Politics* (Boston, MA: McGraw-Hill, 1979).
22 Peter Wilson, "Idealism in International Relations," 332–333.
23 In following Wilson's characterization of idealism, I intend for the term to apply broadly to a perspective in international relations theory, rather than being limited only to the idealist theories put forward by liberal internationalists during the interwar period (see, e.g., Potter, *An Introduction to the Study of International Organization*; Shotwell, "Plans and Protocols to End War;" Noel-Baker, *The League of Nations at Work*; and Zimmern, *The League of Nations and the Rule of Law, 1918–1935*. I am grateful to Eric Heinze and Brent Steele for suggesting that I clarify this point.
24 Ibid., 331.
25 Kant, *To Perpetual Peace: A Philosophical Sketch*, 125.
26 Ibid.
27 I am grateful to Joy Gordon for discussion on this point.
28 Ibid., 109.
29 Ibid., 109–110.
30 Ibid., 110.
31 Ibid.
32 Ibid., 113.
33 Rawls, *The Law of Peoples.*
34 Doyle, "Kant, Liberal Legacies, and Foreign Affairs" (1983b).
35 Stanley Milgram, "Behavioral Study of Obedience," *Journal of Abnormal and Social Psychology*, 67, 4 (1963): 371–378.
36 See, e.g., Carla Bagnoli, "Humanitarian Intervention as a Perfect Duty: A Kantian Argument," *Nomos*, 47 (2004).
37 Arthur Ripstein, *Force and Freedom: Kant's Legal and Political Philosophy* (Cambridge, MA: Harvard University Press, 2009).
38 Michael Walzer, *Spheres of Justice: A Defense of Pluralism and Equality* (New York: Basic Books, 1983).
39 Kant, "Idea for a Universal History with a Cosmopolitan Intent," 34.
40 Kant, *The Metaphysics of Morals*, 6: 355, 124.
41 Immanuel Kant, *Groundwork of the Metaphysics of Morals*, trans. Mary Gregor (Cambridge: Cambridge University Press, 1785/1997).
42 Kant, "Idea for a Universal History with a Cosmopolitan Intent," 38.
43 Ibid., 35.
44 Ibid., 34.
45 Ibid.
46 This discussion borrows from Arthur Ripstein's masterful treatment of these issues. See Ripstein, *Force and Freedom: Kant's Legal and Political Philosophy*.
47 Kant, *The Metaphysics of Morals*, 6: 230, 24.
48 Ibid., 6: 230, 25.
49 Ibid., 30.
50 Ibid.
51 Kant rejects the distinction between perfect and imperfect rights, but Gregor in her editor's notes (58, note 21) and Ripstein use it in describing Kant's view. Gregor attributes the distinction to Pufendorf, who used it as an emendation of Grotius's distinction between faculties and aptitudes. Perfected rights involve the right to use coercion, whereas imperfect rights involve the right to request or petition.
52 Ripstein, *Force and Freedom: Kant's Legal and Political Philosophy*, 24.
53 Kant, *The Metaphyiscs of Morals*, 6: 266, 53.
54 Ibid.
55 John Locke, *Second Treatise of Government*, ed. C. B. Macpherson (Indianapolis: Hackett Publishing Company, 1690/1980), 54.
56 Ripstein, *Force and Freedom: Kant's Legal and Political Philosophy*, 196.
57 Lea Ypi, "A Permissive Theory of Territorial Rights," *European Journal of Philosophy*, 22, 2 (June 2014): 288–312.
58 Ibid., 19.
59 Cf. Ypi, "A Permissive Theory of Territorial Rights."
60 Ibid., 20.
61 Kant, *The Metaphysics of Morals*, 6: 311, 89.

62 Jeremy Waldron, "Superseding Historic Injustice," *Ethics, 103*, no. 1 (October 1992): 4–28.
63 Matthew Lindauer, "External Relationships in Political Philosophy," Doctoral dissertation, Yale University, 2015.
64 Walzer, *Spheres of Justice: A Defense of Pluralism and Equality*.
65 Wellman seems to have changed his views on such policies over time. See Christopher Heath Wellman, "Immigration and Freedom of Association," *Ethics*, 119, 1 (October 2008): 109–141 at 139–141 and Phillip Cole and Christopher Heath Wellman, *Debating the Ethics of Immigration: Is There a Right to Exclude?* (New York: Oxford University Press, 2011) at 149–150.
66 Michael Blake, "Immigration," in *A Companion to Applied Ethics*, eds. R. G. Frey and Christopher Heath Wellman (Malden, MA: Blackwell Publishing, 2003), 224–237 at 233–234.
67 Elizabeth S. Anderson, "What is the Point of Equality?" *Ethics*, 109 (1999): 287–337; Ronald Dworkin, *Taking Rights Seriously* (Cambridge, MA: Harvard University Press, 1977).
68 Matthew Lindauer, "Immigration Policy and Identification Across Borders," *Journal of Ethics and Social Philosophy*, 12, no. 3 (2017): 280–303.
69 Shmuel Nili, "Liberal Integrity and Foreign Entanglement," *American Political Science Review*, 110 (2016): 148–159.

3

GLOBAL EGALITARIANISM

Cosmopolitanism and statism[1]

Kok-Chor Tan

Introduction

Global justice as a philosophical inquiry has excited much interest over the past two decades. If it appears to some observers to be less of a "hot" topic at the moment, it is nonetheless also true that it is now established as an area of specialization in its own right. In any case, under this inquiry, various topics or problems of justice are contested, including the problems of human rights and the limits of state sovereignty, international toleration and liberal internationalism, world poverty and social justice, just war and intervention and terrorism, and climate change justice.

But one topic that has garnered a large share of attention is that of global egalitarianism. The basic question this topic raises is whether global justice ought to include an *egalitarian distributive* commitment or principle. This question has prompted different theories and substantive positions on both sides. As a result, the literature on global egalitarianism has become rather crowded and can appear rather chaotic to someone who is coming to it anew. My aim in this introduction is to identify and clarify what I take to be some of the main contending views on this issue.

While there can be different ways of defending or opposing global egalitarianism, one significant fault-line between proponents and opponents of global egalitarianism is the opposition between "cosmopolitan egalitarians" and "statists".[2] Cosmopolitan egalitarianism, as its name suggests, favors global egalitarianism, whereas statism, as is also hinted by its name, denies that egalitarianism has scope beyond the borders of the domestic state. While I will focus on cosmopolitanism and statism as they pertain to the special question of global egalitarianism, I will note in closing that the cosmopolitanism/statism divide provides two competing philosophical starting points or perspectives on global justice more broadly.

What is global egalitarianism?

To start, a few remarks on "global egalitarianism" to define the parameters of this debate. The substantive question is whether global justice includes some duty of justice to *regulate global economic inequality* between individuals across state borders. Still, three points of clarification are important.

First, the debate is not whether there is a moral duty or duty of justice to *redistribute* resources to persons or countries in need to alleviate extreme poverty or to provide humanitarian relief against natural disasters. Indeed, many of the main positions against global egalitarianism in the literature accept that global morality would include a duty of assistance or humanitarian aid to countries or persons in severe straits. The debate, rather, is whether *global economic inequality* is a concern of justice; that is, whether an injustice remains when there is a certain economic inequality even when no one is suffering from extreme or absolute deprivation. The point of contention, in short, is whether there is a distributive obligation that is attuned to the *relative* economic standing of agents. It is true that concerns of poverty and economic equality can come together, as when excessive inequality results in the impoverishing of the less advantaged. But poverty and economic inequality are nonetheless conceptually and normatively distinct categories, and the question remains whether economic inequality independently of the problem of poverty is a concern of justice. Global egalitarianism is a commitment that goes beyond poverty mitigation.

Second, the debate on egalitarian justice is not a quarrel over the moral equality of persons. To the contrary, the plausible and interesting objections to global egalitarianism do not deny the moral equality of persons. The dispute is whether equal moral respect for agents translates into a duty to regulate economic inequality among them.

This is a familiar point in the domestic discussions. Most libertarians, if any, for example, do not deny that persons are entitled to equal moral consideration by the state. Their view, rather, is that equal moral consideration does not entail egalitarian distributive justice. To the contrary, their basic position, rightly or wrongly, is that respect for the moral equality of persons must rule out state-enforced egalitarian obligations among individuals. Thus, at issue is not whether persons are moral equals. Rather, the engaging issue is whether the presumption of the moral equality of persons entails some form of egalitarian distributive justice. Hence the distinction between *egalitarianism* (as a technical term) and *moral equality* is a useful one to keep in mind. In contemporary political philosophy, it is not unusual to reserve the term "egalitarianism" for the ideal that economic and social equality among agents matters, as distinct from the term "equality" which is used to refer to the more general and formal ideal of the moral equality of persons.

Third and finally, egalitarianism does not mean that there must be actual equality of outcome. This may be a rather obvious point to us, but it is worth clarifying because it will help illuminate what makes a principle an *egalitarian* principle.

Whatever the economic good is that an egalitarian principle aims to distribute more equally, it is not the case that egalitarian justice requires an end state in which the good is *equally allocated* among the relevant agents. What makes an egalitarian distributive principle egalitarian is that it takes an equal distribution to be a benchmark from which departures have to be justified. An egalitarian principle is egalitarian in that it specifies and limits the conditions under which an unequal distribution is admissible.

Thus, a distributive principle is *egalitarian* if it takes persons' (or some moral agents') relative standing to be of interest, and if it takes equal distribution to be the default from which departures have to be justified. To take a famous example, John Rawls calls his "difference principle" an egalitarian principle because it takes an equal distribution among cooperating actors to be the benchmark from which departures have to be justified. As we know, Rawls takes a deviation from the benchmark of equal distribution to be justified when the inequality accrues under an arrangement that benefits the worst-off class of individual most.[3]

In summary, the debate on global egalitarianism is not about our moral duty to respond to poverty or other forms of absolute deprivation; it is not about the moral equality of persons (which is taken for granted); and it is not about whether we should aim at distributive equal outcome as an ideal, but the extent to which unequal distribution ought to be allowed. What the debate engages is the question of whether global justice includes some principle for regulating or controlling economic inequality in the world.

Cosmopolitan egalitarianism

One may defend global egalitarianism in the form of a literal *international* egalitarianism. That is, one could propose that the global egalitarian requirement primarily applies between countries. How *individuals per se* fare under this arrangement of egalitarianism among states is a different matter. While this internationalist position is technically egalitarian, it is not the form of global egalitarianism that is typically defended, if at all. The global egalitarian position most frequently proposed takes the individual to be the basic unit of concern with respect to distributive justice. Specifically, it holds that individuals stand in a relationship of distributive justice to each other beyond the limits presented by the facts of political boundaries and membership or citizenship. It is this normative *individualistic* and *transnational* ideal of distributive justice that distinguishes the label "*cosmopolitan* egalitarianism".

But cosmopolitan egalitarianism is still subject to misunderstanding. Indeed, its modifier "cosmopolitan" itself can mean different things. So it is worth defining what the position normally stands for in order to better locate the opposition between the cosmopolitan egalitarians and their critics.

First, cosmopolitanism does not imply "world statism". The disagreement between cosmopolitan egalitarians and their opponents is rarely, if ever, a debate about the ideal of a world state. The debate, in the first instance, concerns the reach of egalitarian justice, and if issues about a world state should enter the scene, they do so only secondarily.

Second, the individualism of cosmopolitanism does not imply that global distributive justice *cannot* by way of implementation focus on distribution among countries. So long as the distribution among countries is regarded as a means towards realizing the ultimate goal of achieving egalitarian justice for individuals, treating states as the basic distributive unit for administrative purposes is compatible with the cosmopolitan egalitarian ideal. (Thus, the distinction between the ideal or objective, on the one side, and strategy and implementation, on the other.)

Finally, cosmopolitan egalitarianism does not mean that there is no space within global justice for national projects and expressions of collective self-determination. Cosmopolitan egalitarianism need not be cast as the only global end or value, such that all other commitments and principles must be justified or understood by reference to it.

Rather, just as we allow that, within the bounds of domestic justice, persons may do as they wish so long as the requirements of justice are respected and maintained, so within the bounds of global justice, there can be space for national pursuits and other collective projects so long as the requirements of cosmopolitan justice are upheld. Thus, cosmopolitan egalitarianism does not rule out non-cosmopolitan, that is, nationalistic, pursuits; what it does is specify the normative space for such pursuits.

Arguing for cosmopolitan egalitarianism

So how does one make the case for cosmopolitan egalitarianism? For our purpose, we need not get into the details of any particular cosmopolitan egalitarian argument or theory. It will suffice, in order to have a clearer target for the statist opposition, for us to outline one representative strategy in support of cosmopolitan egalitarianism.

First, cosmopolitan egalitarians typically do not reinvent the egalitarian wheel. Rather, they begin from some widely accepted or influential theory of egalitarian justice (conceived for domestic society), and from this starting point, attempt to show that the favored egalitarian theory logically extends to the global domain.

In this respect, Charles Beitz's *Political Theory and International Relations*, published over thirty years ago, has paved the way.[4] To simplify, Beitz takes Rawls's theory of justice as his starting point, and seeks to demonstrate that there is no good reason to limit Rawls's basic commitments and methodology to the state domain. To the contrary, Beitz argues, consistency in reasoning and methodology would require extending Rawls's conclusions to the global domain as well. That is, we must arrive at a globalized version of Rawls's two principles of justice, including his egalitarian distributive principle.[5] Thus, according to Beitz, we have reasons to apply Rawls's own theory of justice to the global context, his own reluctance briefly hinted at in *A Theory of Justice* notwithstanding. What is especially interesting is that in his own more worked out theory of international justice, Rawls confirms and elaborates on his resistance to global egalitarianism. But more on this later.

The details of Rawls's theory of justice and Beitz's interpretation of it need not detain us at the moment. What I want to draw attention to is the form of the argument that we can call "the argument by extension". The extension argument seeks to show that a favored set of arguments for egalitarian justice for the domestic state ought not to be confined to the context of the state, but should extend outwards to the global arena. The normative core of the extension argument is that state and national borders are morally irrelevant and therefore ought not to obstruct the logical outward flow of arguments for egalitarianism to the world as a whole.

The way an extension argument unfolds will depend on the egalitarian theory it begins with. In general, in the contemporary egalitarianism literature, there are two basic approaches to defending egalitarianism. One approach takes it that egalitarian obligations exist between individuals as such given their status as equal moral agents. The other takes egalitarian obligations to apply not between moral agents as such but only between persons who enjoy or ought to enjoy some kind of associational relationship or ties. We can label the former the moral approach to egalitarianism, and the latter the relational approach.

The moral approach can take a variety of forms. "Luck egalitarianism" is just one version of the moral approach to egalitarianism, but it is an illustrative example.[6] Luck egalitarianism, briefly, is the ideal that economic inequality among persons due to their misfortunes and bad luck is the common fate of society to be shared by all and not by the unfortunate alone. Therefore, justice would require some distributive mechanism to mitigate inequality among persons as a result of their luck. This is what follows from the equal moral regard for persons. Globalizing this approach, since the place of one's birth or one's country of residence is in general a matter of luck rather than personal choice, differences in persons' life chances due to such matters ought not to stand uncorrected. To the contrary, there must be some global egalitarian distributive principles to counteract the unequalizing effects of state borders and citizenships on persons' opportunities.[7]

The relational approach likewise can take different forms. But one account holds that the relationship that is necessary for generating egalitarian commitments is that of fair social cooperation. That is, egalitarian duties are activated only when the relevant actors are also participating (or ought to be participating) under some shared cooperative arrangement. Some global egalitarians, adopting this cooperative ideal of egalitarianism, accordingly try to make the case that the global order is a cooperative arrangement of the sort that should trigger global egalitarian commitments. They point to features of the world order, such as trade relations and regulations, and international law and legal norms, as evidence of a global cooperative institutional order, and conclude that if the ideal of social cooperation entails egalitarianism in the domestic context, there is a case as well for global egalitarianism. Indeed, Beitz's proposal for a global difference principle turns on his claim that there is global cooperation of the relevant sort.[8]

Statism

Let us turn to the statist challenge to cosmopolitanism. But as with "cosmopolitanism", it is useful to identify the parameters of the statist position to understand what it claims and does not claim with respect to global egalitarianism.

First, statism is not globalized libertarianism. Libertarians will unsurprisingly reject global egalitarianism because they reject egalitarianism across the board. To be sure, a complete defense of global egalitarian will have to content with libertarianism. But the libertarian challenge is a debate within political philosophy more broadly and not an issue that is unique to global justice. Statism presents special challenge *within* the discourse of global justice because it does not deny that there are egalitarian commitments domestically. Statism is a powerful challenge because it specifically targets *global* egalitarianism rather than egalitarianism at large. So, while egalitarianism within political philosophy must confront the libertarian objection, global egalitarians have a very different (and special) opponent in the statist.

As an aside, as we will see, what makes the statist position especially interesting *philosophically* is that it attempts to show why there are egalitarian obligations at home but none globally. One of the things the statist literature has done is to put forward for our consideration different reasons why egalitarianism matters. If nothing else, this has enriched contemporary political philosophy considerably.

Second, statism does not deny that there are global duties of assistance or humanitarian relief in response to extreme poverty or famine or natural calamities. (So statism is also not a libertarian view in this other sense.) What statism rejects is that there are duties of distributive equality in addition to our moral duties to make sure that basic needs of persons are met.

Basic needs can be defined more robustly or less by different statist theorists, but nonetheless, for each, what we owe to foreigners is not comparative and there is a cut-off point in principle to our obligations. In contrast, egalitarian duties are comparative and ongoing, and therefore belong to a different class of duties from the duty to provide for basic needs.

Third, to reiterate a point made earlier, there is no implication in statist views that persons in the world aren't moral equals. To the contrary, the most interesting statist arguments affirm that persons are moral equals. What they deny is that this moral equality of persons translates into an egalitarian ideal in the global setting. Thus, statism consequently does not deny that individuals are the ultimate units of moral concern. In fact, the most plausible and interesting statist positions affirm the moral primacy of the individual. But even though individuals are the ultimate units of moral concern, statism holds that international justice must be understood in terms of the relationship between state associations in light of the special moral status of the state.

So statism is a carefully circumscribed, and thus a forceful, position. It does not reject egalitarianism across the board; it supports certain global duties of humanitarian aid or duties of assistance; and it does not flippantly deny the moral equality of persons.

Two statist arguments

In its basic form, statism relies on two substantive claims. First, it denies that egalitarianism applies between moral persons as such. Rather, it holds that egalitarianism takes hold only under special social conditions, in particular within special kinds of associations. That is, it supports the relational view of egalitarianism. More specifically, it holds that egalitarian duties are triggered by the unique circumstances of political association. Hence the label "statism." Second, and this is the clincher, it claims that since the relevant egalitarian-triggering association does not exist at the global level (given that it is unique to the state), there is no basis for global egalitarian duties.

Just as some influential global egalitarian arguments are inspired by Rawls's theory of justice, the statist arguments we will discuss below are self-consciously efforts at interpreting and defending Rawls's own objection to global egalitarian as outlined in *The Law of Peoples*.[9] Rawls formulates different objections to global egalitarianism in *The Law of Peoples*. But of special interest is his claim that, while the criterion of reciprocity within the democratic state will require that the gap between the rich and poor be regulated, reciprocity among *peoples* in the international context does not require a similar regulation of economic inequality.[10] Reciprocity in the latter would require only some form of duty of assistance, to help ensure that all peoples are capable of establishing and maintaining well-ordered domestic institutions of their own. Rawls's point is thus quintessentially statist in form. That is, on his view, there is something special or unique about the (liberal) state that generates egalitarian obligations of justice; but no similar grounding condition exists in the global context. The statist arguments we will examine below are in fact attempts at trying to make sense of this special egalitarian triggering feature of the state, and as mentioned, each of the statists we will discuss regard themselves to be developing Rawls's anti-global egalitarian thesis. Different statist theories provide different accounts of what this special egalitarian-triggering feature of political association is. We will look at two different statist arguments in turn.

The coercion argument

The coercion argument claims that egalitarianism matters among persons within a political association because of the special fact of state coercion. On one version of this argument, due to Michael Blake, state coercion is in the first instance problematic because it involves a violation of individual autonomy.[11] When individuals are coerced, their choices are restrained. Yet the state has to be necessarily coercive because this is how the state can best protect and enforce individual freedom.

So how do we reconcile the problem of coercion and the necessity of coercion? How do we resolve this paradox? For Blake, we do this by ensuring that the coercive state takes an interest in the relative standing of individuals. That is, so to speak, the sting of coercion is blunted, indeed made legitimate in the eyes of members of the association, if the institutions the coercive state supports are institutions that include egalitarian values.

This is why egalitarianism matters domestically, namely, to help make legitimate the fact of state coercion. But, and this is the key point, there is no functionally equivalent coercive political authority at the global level, Blake observes. Accordingly, there is no analogous issue of legitimacy at the global plane as in the domestic. Thus, while there is the precondition for egalitarianism in the domestic case (state coercion could not be legitimate otherwise), there is none for egalitarianism in the global case (since there is no global coercion to legitimize).

Thomas Nagel has a slightly different argument from coercion.[12] For Nagel, coercion is a problem that needs to be justified or made legitimate in the eyes of those being coerced, but only in the case where those being coerced are also seen as joint-authors of the system of coercion. (This circumscribing of the set of persons who are in standing to demand justification for coercion against them has significance, as we will see below.) Nagel thus limits the set of individuals to whom justification for coercion is owed. The rest of Nagel's arguments then follow roughly the same track as Blake's: since there is no global coercive system that ought to be regarded as the joint venture of individuals in the world as a whole, there is no need to introduce egalitarian obligations in the global setting.

The cooperation argument

The second influential statist argument focuses on a different and supposedly unique feature of the state or political association. Instead of coercion, the cooperation argument focuses on the ideal of the state as a system based on social cooperation.[13] The state is a cooperative system of a particular kind: it supports and enforces a complex economic structure that determines persons' entitlements, responsibilities, wages, contractual rights, rights of ownership, and the like. It also supports a common market for goods and services, and provides the infrastructure – roads, postal service, education, research support – that allows for the realization and delivery of services and goods.

Because of this intimate economic cooperation, citizens stand in some ideal of reciprocity to each other. This means that none can impose joint arrangements on others that they may reasonably oppose. The steps towards egalitarianism have to be filled in, but essentially, the criterion of reciprocity with respect to institutional arrangements will take us towards some egalitarian commitments to each other.

However, when we turn our gaze to the world, say the statists, we don't find a similar kind of cooperative order. Contra global egalitarians, these statists insist that the global order does not exhibit the kind of economic relationships to generate the same reciprocity requirement. Yes, there are rules governing trade relations, treaties, and economic pacts among countries. But these do not amount to a common economic system in which people's basic ownership rights, entitlements, and opportunities are fixed. Rather than a single economic structure, the international order is more like a minimally regulated stage in which different economic systems interact. Thus, although there is a reason for egalitarianism on account of the ideal of social cooperation, there is no similar basis globally.

Statism versus cosmopolitanism

Both the coercion and cooperation arguments share this basic argumentative form: they present a normative premise or claim about the basis/ground of egalitarianism, and they make an empirical claim about the absence of this ground in the global domain.

Thus, in response to these arguments, the cosmopolitan can target either the empirical or normative premises. Consider, first, the empirical premise of the coercion argument. Is it true that the global order is not a coercive one in the relevant sense? After all, one could point, for just one example, to the fact of immigration restriction. Individuals wanting entry into a (richer) foreign country can be barred, and coercively repelled. So can't one say that the global order is at least coercive in this case, in the sense that persons aren't free to move around? So, isn't there some coercive order that stands in need of justification in the same way that the domestic order needs to be justified? Along these lines, some commentators have countered that the global order can be described as coercive in a normatively relevant sense as per the coercion argument.[14] On the coercion argument's reasoning, the global egalitarian might thus press, would this not lead us to global egalitarianism?

Nagel's coercion argument, however, can evade this first challenge as stated. Recall that, for Nagel, it is not coercion that immediately needs to be justified (to the one being coerced). What needs justification is the coercion against those *who are* supposedly joint authors of the coercive system. That is, only citizens who are supposed to have a say in the construction of their institutional structure are entitled to demand justification for any institutional coercion directed at them. So, Nagel's version of the argument can accept that the outsider who is being kept out by our immigration laws is being coerced, but still maintain that we owe her no explanation because she is not regarded as participant and joint author of our system of laws.

Nonetheless, it seems that Nagel's move cannot evade this objection altogether. If a country's right to enact immigration rules, and to enforce them, is in fact a right grounded in and sanctioned by the international order, then does this not raise the question as to the authorship of the coercive *international order*? So even if one needs to be a joint author of an institutional order before one can have standing to demand reasons for her coercion, immigration rules enacted by individual countries aren't enacted in an international vacuum but are domestic laws *given standing* by an international order. This then raises the question of how we should understand the authorship of this international order that sanctions the authority of states to make laws that have global implications. Should we regard it as the joint creation of all individuals in the world if it is to be legitimate? If so, then individuals in the world at large have the standing to demand justification for any coercion they experience that is sanctioned ultimately by that international order. Would this not put us consequently on the path towards egalitarianism, analogous to the domestic case?

So I think some pressure can be put on the empirical premise of the coercion argument. Similarly, some pressure can be put on the empirical premise of the cooperation argument. The cooperation argument points to economic institutional facts and laws like property rights, contract laws, laws regulating transfers and transactions, and the like, to show why egalitarianism applies within the state. Are there not similar economic institutions in the global arena that can count as arrangements of cooperation? For instance, are there not international laws and norms regulating territorial rights, ownership of natural resources, and international intellectual property rights that are examples of global institutions and laws that ultimately establish and define the terms of ownership? Is the economic success of one country really so detached from and independent of a background international economic structure?

The above are complex issues and involve conceptual as well as empirical interpretations and research. My remarks are in no way meant as decisive or definitive. My point is that the jury is still out on the empirical claims underlying both the coercion and cooperative arguments.

At any rate, closer to the expertise of normative philosophy, even if the empirical premises of both the coercion and cooperation arguments survive scrutiny, their respective normative premises may not. Consider the claim that coercion is the *sine qua non* of egalitarianism. But is it true that coercion is a necessary condition for egalitarianism? One might allow that coercion is a sufficient condition for egalitarianism such that, should there be systematic institutional coercion, egalitarian duties are activated; but to say that it is also necessary is a much stronger claim.

The same question can be posed for the cooperation argument. The ideal of cooperation might very well generate egalitarian obligations; but couldn't there be other reasons? Indeed, there is a lively internal dispute among statists themselves between the coercion side and the cooperation side as to which feature of the state is the triggering feature of egalitarianism. This internal disagreement fuels the suspicion that there is not just *one* necessary motivating reason for egalitarianism.[15]

More fundamentally, why take it as settled that egalitarian duties are "relational" in the sense described above? As mentioned, statists deny that egalitarian duties can arise between moral agents as such. But how decisive and secure is this assumption that egalitarian duties are necessarily "relational" duties? Couldn't egalitarian obligations (also) arise straight away between persons as such, in virtue of their moral standing and relationship to each other, as the moral approach would have it?

Consider that there are non-relational approaches to egalitarianism on the table, notably luck egalitarianism. To be sure, these moral approaches have their legion of forceful critics. But this is not unusual for any complex philosophical account, and the disagreement between luck egalitarianism and its opponents is far from settled to my mind.[16] To the extent, then, that non-relational approaches to egalitarianism remain serious contenders as grounds of egalitarian justice, the statist position turns crucially on a normative premise that is still open to argument.

Conclusion

Statists deny that egalitarian obligations obtain between equal moral agents as such. What activates egalitarian obligations are additional commitments or facts about associative relations among persons. These associative ideals or facts are, according to statists, peculiar to the circumstance of the state and thus absent in the global arena. Some argue, for example, that the coercive character of the state is the distinguishing feature that triggers egalitarian commitments among citizens; others prefer to highlight the cooperative character of the state, in particular in its economic institutions. These attempts can be seen also as ways of explaining why there is a special requirement of reciprocity among citizens that ought to control economic inequality among them, and that why there is no similar requirement of reciprocity among persons at the global level.

These statist arguments rely on various claims that the global egalitarian can try to resist. For example, the global egalitarian can ask whether it is really the case that egalitarianism is an associative obligation and not an obligation that could take hold between persons (in the world as a whole) as such. Or, if she grants the associative approach to egalitarianism, she can try to show that the relevant egalitarian triggering features in fact obtain at the global level as well.

The problem of global egalitarianism has perhaps received more attention in the current literature on global justice than other questions since it engages the staple issues of analytic political philosophy, that of distributive justice and economic equality. While there is as yet no resolution to the global dispute, the statist response has inspired investigations into the conditions under which egalitarianism matters. As a result, a global justice debate has enriched and enlivened the well- traversed topic of egalitarian justice. It re-opens with important motivation a closer study of the question: Why does and should egalitarianism matter? The topic of global egalitarianism is a good illustration of how political philosophy makes progress when it confronts new problem areas.

But statism and cosmopolitanism have implications beyond global egalitarian justice. In fact, the statism versus cosmopolitanism opposition provides two general contrasting philosophical approaches to global justice more broadly. The statist approach to global justice takes it that global justice ought to be essentially understood in terms of justice between states (or some analogous collective agent, such as a people). Statism, therefore, understands global justice as a distinctive domain of justice from that of domestic justice, where justice is primarily that of justice between individuals (even if that relationship is mediated via shared institutions). The cosmopolitan approach, on the other hand, treats global justice to be basically concerned with justice between persons (even if their relationship has to be mediated by complex international and state institutions). Thus, there is no fundamental difference between domestic justice and global justice. Unlike statism, cosmopolitanism does not take global justice to be a distinctive realm of justice. It basically has a single tiered approach to justice.

To reiterate, the statist positions need not deny that the individual is the basic unit of moral concern. It is just that when it comes to global justice, we have to conceive of justice as justice *between states* rather than as justice *between individuals* given the moral significance of the state.

This difference in orientation between statism and cosmopolitanism can account for a range of substantive disagreements in global justice besides that of global egalitarianism. For example, with regard to the problems or questions of the ethics of immigration control, the balance between human rights and state sovereignty, and the tension between international justice and international toleration, our substantive positions on these matters can differ depending on whether we embrace a statist or cosmopolitan orientation. If we begin from a statist perspective, and treat global justice as a distinctive realm of justice, and as essentially a realm of justice that is concerned with the *relationship between (just) states*, we will be more inclined to favor giving states more rights over immigration control, regard state sovereignty as a value that is not reducible to individual rights, and opt for an understanding of international toleration that favors state rights. In contrast, if our orientation is cosmopolitan, then we will be more likely to prioritize the right of individuals to free movement over the right of states to restrict movement, to understand state sovereignty only in relation to individual rights, and to support an account of international toleration that defers to individual (as opposed to state) rights.

The statist versus cosmopolitan dispute is thus the philosophical core in the debate on global justice. Should we conceive of global justice essentially in terms of justice among free and equal persons or in terms of justice among free and independent states or peoples? Is there essentially just one domain of justice, within which each person is entitled to equal respect or concern? Or are there different domains of justice, with different primary subjects depending on the domain? Is justice universally uniform, or is justice necessarily pluralistic and contextual and must take different shapes (with different basic subjects) depending on the social realm in question? The subject of global justice thus instigates inquiry into the very character of justice itself.

Notes

1 I thank participants at a seminar in the Department of Bioethics, the National Institutes of Health, and especially David DeGrazia, for helpful comments and suggestions.
2 These terms have been used, for example, to capture these two general positions on global egalitarianism in Pablo Gilabert, *From Global Poverty to Global Equality* (Oxford: Oxford University Press, 2011); and Laura Valentini, *Justice in a Globalized World: A Normative Framework* (Oxford: Oxford University Press, 2012).
3 John Rawls, *A Theory of Justice* (Cambridge, MA: Harvard University Press, 1971). Thus Rawls calls the "difference principle" a "strongly egalitarian conception"; *Theory*, p. 76.
4 Charles Beitz, *Political Theory and International Relations* (Princeton: Princeton University Press, 1979), Part III.
5 See also Thomas Pogge, *Realizing Rawls* (Ithaca, NY: Cornell University Press, 1989), Part III.
6 For a recent thesis on luck egalitarianism, see Kasper Lippert-Rasmussen, *Luck Egalitarianism* (New York: Bloomsbury Publishing, 2015).
7 See Simon Caney for a developed luck egalitarian account of global egalitarian justice: Caney, *Justice Beyond Border* (Oxford: Oxford University Press, 2005).
8 Beitz, 1979. See also Pogge, 1989; and Darrel Moellendorf, *Cosmopolitan Justice* (Boulder, CO: Westview Press, 2001).
9 John Rawls, *The Law of Peoples* (Cambridge, MA: Harvard University Press, 1999).
10 Rawls, *The Law of Peoples*, p. 114.
11 Michael Blake, "Distributive Justice, State Coercion, and Autonomy", *Philosophy and Public Affairs*, 30 (2001): 257–296; also Blake, *Justice and Foreign Policy* (Oxford: Oxford University Press, 2013).
12 Thomas Nagel, "The Problem of Global Justice", *Philosophy and Public Affairs*, 33 (2005): 113–147.
13 Andrea Sangiovanni, 'Global Justice, Reciprocity and the State', *Philosophy and Public Affairs*, 35 (2007): 3–31; and Samuel Freeman, *Justice and the Social Contract: Essays on Rawlsian Political Philosophy* (New York: Oxford University Press, 2007).

14 See Nicole Hassoun, *Globalization and Global Justice* (Cambridge: Cambridge University Press, 2012); Laura Valentini, *Justice in a Globalized World: A Normative Framework* (Oxford: Oxford University Press, 2011).
15 See, for example, Sangiovanni's criticisms of Blake's (2001) coercion argument in favor of the cooperation argument; and see Blake's reply (2013).
16 See, e.g., Rasmussen (2015). I also discuss some of these attempts in K. C. Tan, *Justice, Institutions and Luck* (Oxford: Oxford University Press, 2012), and "Luck, Institutions and Global Distributive Justice", *European Journal of Political Theory*, 10/3 (2011): 394–421.

4

COLLECTIVE RESPONSIBILITY AND JOINT CRIMINAL ENTERPRISE

David Atenasio

Introduction

It is not unusual to hold a person to blame for wrongful or improper conduct. When wrongdoing occurs at a communal, national or global level, attributions of blame become more difficult and controversial. Collective wrongdoing appears to merit collective responsibility, but many find such a concept difficult to accept. Opponents of collective responsibility argue that the concept is incoherent, harmful and intrinsically unfair.

Despite the best efforts of opponents of collective responsibility, the language of collective responsibility pervades discussions of international relations and global affairs. It feels natural enough to utter such statements as "Britain intentionally sank the *Belgrano*" (Copp, 2006, p. 195). When one country invades another, we might declare an entire nation to be in the wrong (Kelsen, 1943, pp. 533–534). People sometimes speak of Assad, Fidel or Khomeini as if their words and actions implicate the citizens of Syria, Cuba or Iran, respectively. In the darkest of times, some have found it perfectly acceptable to ascribe fault to entire races or religions, such as the Jews, Kurds or Tutsi (Cooper, 2003, p. 17).

The application of collective responsibility has in the past led to measures of collective punishment, most frequently in times of war. The Lieber Code of 1863 permitted Union generals to starve armed and unarmed belligerents to expedite the end of the American Civil War (Darcy, 2007a, p. 10). After the Civil War, Chief of Staff Henry W. Halleck argued that "it is a general law of war, that communities are accountable for the acts of their individual members" (as cited in Darcy, 2007a, p. 9). Terrorists sometimes justify their indiscriminate destruction by appeal to the collective responsibility of whole populations (Reiff, 2008, p. 211). Separatist and national liberation movements feel justified in taking hostages from groups they consider oppressive (Darcy, 2007a, p. 82; 2010, p. 30).

Collective punishment is now outlawed by the Geneva Convention (Darcy, 2010, p. 32). It is against international law to punish innocent individuals for the actions of their fellow group members. While this prohibition stands, as Shane Darcy has noted, the notion of collective responsibility persists in international law (2007a, p. 198). A demand for justice and full accountability has pressured international courts to adopt a legal norm called "joint criminal enterprise." Prosecutors appeal to joint criminal enterprise to hold contributing members of a common plan responsible for the actions of their accomplices and co-conspirators. Joint criminal enterprise functions as a form of collective liability; if one meets certain standards of participation in a wrongful common plan, one is liable for the actions one's fellow group members take to further the common plan.

Collective liability remains controversial among legal theorists and ethicists. Opponents of collective liability argue that it strains against the basic principles of contemporary law and justice (Ainley, 2011, p. 415; Darcy, 2007a, pp. 359–366; 2007b, pp. 397–399; Lewis, 1948, pp. 11–12; Narveson, 2002, p. 186; Osiel, 2005, pp. 798–800; Schabas, 2003, pp. 1034–1036). Consistency demands that if the concept of collective liability is illegitimate when utilized as a justification for collective punishment in times of war, it ought to be illegitimate when employed by international courts as well.

The moral legitimacy of collective liability depends on whether there exists a defensible theory of collective moral responsibility that fairly distributes blame to some group members for the actions of other group members. If no distributive theory of collective moral responsibility turns out to be correct or defensible, then charges of collective liability (and therefore joint criminal enterprise) will be shown to be morally objectionable.

Theorists have proposed a number of different models of collective responsibility. I first survey three popular methods for distributing (or not distributing) responsibility for collective wrongdoing: a narrow individualist model, an intention model and a collectivist model. Once I have articulated these theories of collective moral responsibility, I apply the theories to precedents of joint criminal enterprise in international law. Each theory comes to different conclusions about the justifiability of joint criminal enterprise. One general trend emerges in this analysis. The more expansive a theory of collective moral responsibility becomes, the more it strains against basic ideals of fairness and justice. The narrower and more individualist a theory, the more it may let individuals off the hook for their contributions to collective wrongdoing.

Collective responsibility

Reflecting on the individualistic development of Western moral thought, H. Gomperz (1939) writes:

> Individual responsibility is not the only known form of responsibility; to consider it as such is characteristic of an individualistic age; in earlier stages of civilization archaic forms of collective responsibility were held to be even more significant; and in future stages some form of social responsibility seems likely, to a considerable degree, to supersede it.
>
> *(p. 332)*

In response to Gomperz's controversial claims, H. D. Lewis (1948) doubles down on an individualist notion of morality; he firmly states that "Responsibility belongs essentially to the individual" (p. 3). Lewis's position has come to be known as "methodological individualism" (Copp, 1984, p. 251). Methodological individualism posits that moral responsibility, by definition, attaches only to individuals for their own intentional actions and never to substantial collectives or groups. One is to blame for intentionally transgressing a moral rule, while one is morally praiseworthy for intentionally doing something right or beneficial. Lewis further argues that responsibility only applies to individuals in proportion to their contribution to wrongdoing (p. 13). He believes that we cannot rightfully blame an individual for the full consequences of a group action. Rather, we can only blame the individual for his or her role in bringing about the relevant outcome.

I will refer to Lewis's brand of individualism as "narrow individualism." I call it "narrow" because other methodological individualists after Lewis allow that sometimes individuals may be rightly blamed for the conduct of others. The initial benefits of narrow individualism should be clear. No other theory of collective responsibility stays as safely within the bounds of justice or fairness. Because individuals are only ever blamed or praised for the extent of their contribution to some outcome, there is no worry that they will be blamed disproportionately for what they have done. There is also no worry that narrow individualism will hold some to blame for actions that they did not themselves author or authorize.

The downside of narrow individualism is that it is not always clear how to assess the magnitude of fault for individual contributions to collective harms. The problem is mitigated in unstructured, aggregate group harms. Consider a collection of individuals engaged in a spontaneous riot. Let us suppose that every individual engaged in the riot smashes a window, steals an appliance, sets fire to a building, slashes the tires of an automobile, etc. The collective result of the rioters' actions is the destruction of a city block. The resulting harm is not the result of any coordination or common plan. Rather, each individual contributes one or more harmful actions to the aggregate. Narrow individualism runs into no difficulties of judgment here, for each individual is to blame for his or her own individual act of destruction. We can easily distribute the resulting harm as an aggregate of lesser harms caused by the individuals.

Judgments become more difficult when aggregate harms are coordinated. Consider a group of soldiers who intentionally attack and beat a resident of an enemy village. Let us stipulate that each soldier is alone too weak to kill the resident quickly and efficiently. However, when the soldiers coordinate, their strength is collectively sufficient to expediently inflict mortal harm on the unfortunate villager. Let us suppose that each soldier contributes one or two solid blows to the attack. The aggregate of strikes become too much for the villager, and she succumbs to her injuries. This case is similar to the example of the riot, in that the resulting harm is an aggregate of lesser harms. However, it differs because there is a common plan of coordination to bring about a shared aim among the soldiers. Given narrow individualism, judgments become difficult. Is each soldier responsible only for his or her own individual strikes on the villager, or is each soldier responsible for the resulting murder?

Determinations become murkier when a coordinated set of seemingly harmless actions lead to a collective harm. Consider a group of scientists, engineers and military generals coordinating to build and deploy a powerful new weapon. Each member of the group is jointly necessary but not sufficient to create and utilize this weapon. The scientists spend months testing the theoretical aspects of the weapon, the engineers spend months designing the hardware and software, and the military generals spend months planning on where best to use it. Eventually, a single military private in a plane presses a button to activate the weapon, which kills thousands of civilians. Here, we have one extremely harmful act that is brought about as a systematic coordination of many smaller contributions that are not on their face harmful. Assuming that the use of this weapon violates some moral prohibition, how are we to determine, given narrow individualism, who is to blame for which result? Are the individual scientists responsible for, say, 15% of the resulting harm? Can we attribute a certain number of wrongful deaths to each contributing group member? These questions do not admit of easy answers.

Many individualists now allow that there are certain situations in which individuals may be to blame for the contributions of their fellow group members. One popular theory posits that individuals become morally responsible for collective harms by having a collective intention (or goal) to do wrong (Sadler, 2006; Kutz, 2000a, pp. 137–145, 2000b; Sverdlik, 1986, p. 66; Miller, 2006, p. 177). I will call this theory an intention theory of collective moral responsibility. Intention theories are methodologically individualist; they stipulate that responsibility attaches only to individuals and never to corporate entities. However, they allow that individuals may become responsible for collective actions by intending or aiming at collective ends or outcomes. Sverdlik (1986, p. 66) presents the example of a group of individuals who push a car over a ledge, thereby destroying it. He argues that, while every individual is responsible for his or her own part in pushing the car, nonetheless "each of the people who pushes the car off the ledge is responsible for its destruction if that is what each intended" (p. 66). So, by intending a collective harm, one can be rightfully blamed for the full resulting harm, even if that harm required the causal contribution of other agents.

An intention theory has advantages over narrow individualism. An intention theory is still methodologically individualist. It does not need to posit the existence of corporate entities, but it is capable of distributing blame for large, collective harms. Consider the example of the soldiers attacking the villager. An intention theory stipulates that all those who intentionally participate in bringing about the murder of the villager are to blame for the murder. Similarly, any scientists, engineers and military generals who intentionally participate in creating and utilizing a new weapon are responsible for the devastation caused by the use of the weapon, assuming its use was unjustified. While there may be practical or epistemic difficulties in ascertaining who has a collective intention and who does not, the theoretical lines are clear: those who intentionally participate in collective wrongdoing are to blame or at fault for the outcome of the collective act, if that outcome is what they jointly intended.

The primary weakness of an intention theory is that it risks distributing collective responsibly too liberally. Consider a janitor who scrubs the floors at a multinational corporation responsible for causing tremendous ecological devastation in developing nations. Let us also stipulate that the janitor knows full well about the devastation and intentionally participates in cleaning the offices so that business can go on as usual. From the standpoint of mental states alone, the janitor has a participatory intention to contribute to the collective ecological devastation identical to the participatory intentions of the corporation's executives. So, according to an intention theory, we should *prima facie* distribute collective responsibility for the devastation to the corporation's executives and janitor equally. But this seems to violate basic norms of justice and fairness. To hold the executives and the janitor equally to blame would be disproportionate, as the executives' causal contribution to the ecological harm far outstrips the causal contribution of the janitor. Doing so also holds the janitor to blame for actions she did not intentionally author, authorize or have any control over.

Intention theorists have proposed different mechanisms to mitigate worries of unfairness. Kutz (2000a) suggests that an intention theory should be supplemented with a theory of principals and accomplices, or "direct action and complicit participation" (p. 146). This additional distinction would separate those who intentionally cause a harm directly and those who cause a harm indirectly through complicit participation. In the case of the janitor and the executives at the multinational corporation, the executives would be principals in the wrongdoing, while the janitor would merely be aiding and abetting as an accomplice.

Gadirov (2011) proposes that we augment a basic intention theory of collective moral responsibility with further qualifications. He suggests that it is only those who participate in collective wrongdoing who also have "meshed goals or a web of interlocked intentions" who are responsible for collective wrongdoing (p. 15). This stipulation would prevent an intention theory from holding marginal contributors to a group harm morally responsible. A meshed goals or interlocked intentions provision would narrow down group responsibility to those who are most integrally connected to the common criminal plan. Consider again the case of the janitor and the executives. The executives all have meshed plans that depend upon each other's contributions. The orders of the CEO depend upon the financial coordination of the CFO, for instance. The janitor merely plans to clean the offices. The janitor's plans do not involve strong coordination with the executives. For this reason, Gadirov's theory would rule out the janitor as liable to the distribution of collective responsibility for the firm's ecological wrongdoing.

The third theory of collective moral responsibility differs somewhat from its individualist peers. This theory stipulates that there are two levels of collective moral responsibility: individual and corporate or collective. Individual responsibility attaches to individuals who intentionally do wrong, while collective or corporate responsibility attaches to corporations and groups that intentionally deliberate on and carry out collective actions. An individual con artist might be responsible for fooling someone and taking her money, but a large corporation might as a whole be morally responsible for wrongful corporate actions that defraud others. This theory of collective moral responsibility is typically called a "collectivist" account.

Contemporary interest in collectivist theories of corporate responsibility begins with Cooper (1968, pp. 260–262) defending the assertion that statements about collective responsibility differ categorically from statements about individual responsibility. French (1979, pp. 211–215, 1984, pp. 31–47) develops these ideas further and argues that corporations with articulated decision procedures count as autonomous moral agents.

More recently, Pettit (2004, pp. 170–175, 2007, pp. 181–182) has argued that the existence of certain "discursive dilemmas" entails the moral autonomy of collectives that engage in group deliberations. A discursive dilemma arises when group members come to conflicting decisions when voting on the premises and conclusion of an argument. Consider a parole board of five individuals who must vote on giving parole to a prisoner (Copp, pp. 377–382). The prisoner will be given parole if he successfully meets three of the five criteria. The board members vote on the individual criteria. According to this vote, the prisoner is not given parole, because there is little agreement on which criteria the prisoner meets. However, each member believes that the prisoner meets three of the five criteria, they just all choose differing criteria. If voting on whether to give the prisoner parole, the majority would vote in favor; however, when the members vote on the premises and use a procedure to generate a decision, the prisoner would be denied parole. This conflict in decision methods purportedly demonstrates that the collective itself is an autonomous agent distinct from its members in some way.

The strength of a collectivist theory of collective moral responsibility is that it explains why we sometimes hold groups to blame for collective wrongdoing. If a rogue state unjustly invades and occupies a city in a sovereign nation, many believe it makes sense to say that the rogue state did something wrong and should be held accountable. Some also suggest that, without getting a picture of the social groups to which a person belongs, we cannot properly assess that person's moral character (Isaacs, 2006, p. 60, 2011, pp. 55–56). There is a moral difference between a murderer and one who takes part in genocide, and a collectivist account of collective responsibility acknowledges this difference. One could argue that any theory that does not take account of the moral salience of group membership is therefore deficient in some way.

Collectivists are normally cautious when articulating how a group's corporate fault distributes to its members. Most collectivist theorists stipulate that there is no way to infer individual fault from one's membership in an offending collective (Cooper, 1968, pp. 262–263; French, 1984, p. 14; Copp, pp. 215–216; Pettit, 2007, pp. 180–184; Shockley, 2007, p. 451). It may be true that the corporation BP is to blame for the oil spill in the Gulf of Mexico. But saying that BP is responsible for the oil spill does not entail that a janitor, accountant or executive working for BP is also responsible for the oil spill. These theorists suggest that theories of individual fault and collective fault ought to remain separate and distinct.

Some more ambitious theorists have attempted to articulate the way in which responsibility distributes from an offending collective to its members (see Ohlin, 2008). However, this path is fraught with moral dangers. Without limits as to who counts as a group member, collectivist models that distribute collective responsibility quickly become unfair and unjust. Collectivist accounts that distribute blame evenly risk holding a military general and a mess hall cook equally responsible for an army's misconduct, for example. This violates standards of proportion, as the cook's contribution to the military campaign is inconsequential by comparison to the general's contribution. Similarly, if we hold the mess hall cook responsible for decisions and conduct over which she exercises no influence or control, we unfairly blame the cook for actions she has not personally authored or authorized.

Just as with intention accounts, proponents of distributive collectivist accounts add stipulations or provisions to narrow the scope of who may properly be held responsible for a collective action. For instance, Ohlin (2008, pp. 196–197) argues that only smaller, cohesive organizations qualify for distributive collective responsibility. The sorts of organizations liable to collective responsibility are those that pool information and adopt shared decision procedures (p. 194). This stipulation serves to prevent Ohlin's collectivist account from unfairly distributing responsibility for group actions to marginal contributors. Marginal contributors are usually not a party to a group's decision apparatus, and they frequently know only enough about the common plan to play their individual roles.

Collective liability and joint criminal enterprise

Having surveyed a few of the current theories of collective moral responsibility, let us turn to the developments in distributive collective sanctions in international law. Contemporary precedents of collective sanctioning in international law begin with the International Military Tribunal (IMT) charter of 1945. The Allied nations established the IMT to hold members of Axis countries responsible for the atrocities committed in World War II (Hale & Cline, 2014, p. 265). Achieving justice for crimes committed during World War II was no simple task. A year earlier, Lieutenant Colonel Bernays of the United States War Department noted a "general problem": it would be a challenge to locate and prosecute the thousands of war criminals in Europe, considering how difficult it would be to gather evidence given that many witnesses were dead (Darcy, 2007a, p. 199). As a possible legal solution, Bernays suggested that international courts charge members of the Nazi Government with conspiracy to commit war crimes (p. 200).

The drafters of the IMT charter accepted the validity of conspiracy charges (p. 267). Article 6 of the IMT charter states that:

> Leaders, organizers, instigators and accomplices participating in the formulation or execution of a common plan or conspiracy to commit any of the foregoing crimes are responsible for all acts performed by any persons in execution of such plans.

While the language of participation is admittedly vague, chief prosecutor Robert H. Jackson voiced his support of "the principle of conspiracy by which one who joins in a common plan to commit crimes becomes responsible for the acts of any other conspirator in executing the plan" (quoted in Darcy, 2007a, p. 216).

While the prosecutors at Nuremberg were permitted to utilize charges of conspiracy, few did so, as they found the concept of inchoate conspiracy controversial (p. 225). Prosecutions based on conspiracy were inevitably abandoned or dropped due to a lack of evidence or worries about a lack of jurisdiction (pp. 225–226, n. 191). Years later, the drafters of the Rome Statute decided not to include liability for the formation of a common criminal plan when establishing the ICC (p. 226).

Charges of conspiracy have been unpopular in international law, but they have not been non-existent. The 1948 Genocide Convention criminalizes conspiracy to commit genocide, and individuals were successfully charged with conspiracy to commit genocide in the *ad hoc* tribunal established to deal with the massacres in Rwanda (p. 226, n. 195).

While conspiracy charges are utilized sparingly, the ICTY, an *ad hoc* tribunal established to deal with crimes in the former Yugoslavia, has made significant use of joint criminal enterprise (JCE), another form of common plan liability. Whereas conspiracy criminalizes the formation of a common criminal plan, joint criminal enterprise criminalizes contribution to a common plan involving the commission of a crime (Hale & Cline, p. 268). Joint criminal enterprise precedents first emerged from the ICTY's Tadić ruling. Prosecutors charged Tadić with a crime against humanity for his purported involvement in the killing of five men in the Bosnian village of Jaskici (Ainley, p. 416). The Trial Chamber initially found Tadić innocent of the murders; although Tadić had been in the village, there was no indication he had participated in the murders (p. 416). The Appeals Chamber overturned the ruling. They convicted Tadić on the basis that he had gone to Jaskici with the intention of furthering the common criminal plan of ethnic cleansing by expulsion (p. 416). Since the five murders were a "natural and foreseeable" consequence of the common plan, Tadić's participation made him criminally liable for the five murders (p. 416).

The Appeals Chamber outlined three different forms of joint criminal enterprise in the Tadić ruling, now known as JCE I, JCE II and JCE III. JCE I involves "cases where all co-defendants, acting pursuant to a common design, possess the same criminal intention" (*Prosecutor v. Tadić*, para. 196). According to JCE I, criminal liability distributes to all those who jointly intend to bring about a criminal end together. JCE I deals most effectively with small-scale and coordinated group actions that aim at harmful ends (Ainley, p. 417). All those who intentionally participate in a plan to murder a government official, for instance, become liable for the murder according to JCE I.

JCE II extends to cover "concentration camp" cases (*Prosecutor v. Tadić*, para. 202). JCE II distributes criminal liability to all those who knowingly work to perpetuate a system which produces ill-treatment (Ainley, p. 417). Any participant in a criminal system who is aware of the character of the criminal system and intentionally furthers it becomes liable for the crimes that are committed as a result of the common plan (Hale & Cline, p. 268). This differs somewhat from JCE I. JCE I requires intentional participation in the specific plan to commit a criminal act. JCE II requires no such specific intent. JCE II requires only that an individual intentionally further a criminal system. JCE II holds those bureaucrats and functionaries responsible who freely and intentionally participate in criminal organizations, but who do not themselves intend or aim at causing wrongful deaths (Ainley, p. 417).

JCE III is known as the "extended" form of joint criminal enterprise (Ainley, p. 417; Hale & Cline, p. 268). JCE III extends criminal liability to all participants in a common plan not only for the actions of group members that are part of the common plan, but also for those that are "natural and foreseeable consequence[s]" of the common plan (*Prosecutor v. Tadić*, para. 204). For example, consider a group of militants who enter a village to forcibly remove members of one ethnicity. Let us suppose that the leader of the militant group orders the militia members to carry out the operation without killing anyone. However, a rogue militia member ends up killing a few members of the ethnic group who refuse to leave. In this case, JCE III extends liability for the murder to the leader of the militant group. It is a natural and foreseeable consequence of forcibly removing citizens at gunpoint that wrongful deaths will likely occur (*Prosecutor v. Tadić*, para. 204).

The *actus reus* requirement for all three forms of joint criminal enterprise are identical. Each mode of JCE requires a plurality of persons to participate in some way in a common design that aims at wrongful ends (Darcy, 2007b, p. 382). What differentiates the three is the *mens rea* component. The mental requirement for JCE I is an intention to jointly commit a specific crime. The mental requirement for JCE II is knowledge of a criminal design and an intention to further it. The mental requirement for JCE III is trickier, for JCE III holds individuals liable for actions that they did not intend or know about. It is not an intention that makes one liable under JCE III, but the lack of due care or diligence.

Justifying joint criminal enterprise

Let us first look at the least controversial of the collective liability measures, JCE I. JCE I criminalizes joint intentional participation in an activity that leads to a prohibited outcome. Proponents of collectivist accounts that distribute responsibility will, for the most part, find little morally objectionable about JCE I. If a group may be at fault for the production of an outcome, and an individual knowingly and intentionally participates in the offending group action, then a distributive collectivist model of collective responsibility will distribute blame from the group to the participating individual, assuming the individual's contribution was sufficient. Distributive collectivist theorists may argue over the criteria for blame distribution in collective action, but if blame distributes to any group member for collective wrongdoing, it will surely distribute to those who intentionally play a substantial role in jointly bringing about a criminal end.

Intention theorists will also find JCE I morally acceptable. According to an intention model of collective responsibility, one becomes responsible for a collectively produced outcome if one intentionally participates in the production of that outcome. If soldier A intentionally participates with B, C and D in the liquidation of the members of a small village, then A is to blame for the murders that B, C and D commit. Assuming the truth of an intention theory of collective moral responsibility, it would not be immoral or unjust to hold an individual liable for the contributions of her fellow group members towards a collective end they all share. Since this is what JCE I criminalizes, the intention theorist should have no problem with JCE I.

A narrow individualist may raise some worries about JCE I. If one is only ever responsible for one's own contribution to a collective endeavor, then there might be something unfair about assessing criminal liability to an individual for the full outcome of a collective act. If A, B, C and D collectively kill the members of a village, a narrow individualist would claim that A is only responsible for the murders she individually commits. She (A) would not, according to the narrow individualist, be responsible for the murders that B, C and D commit, even if she wished or believed they would occur.

While JCE I may be acceptable given two of the theories of collective responsibility, JCE II proves to be more controversial. JCE II stipulates that individuals who intentionally further and support a criminal system become responsible for the unjust harm that system causes.

Proponents of a distributive collectivist model of collective responsibility will likely not find JCE II too objectionable. If a system may itself be to blame for wrongdoing, then it is plausible to posit that anyone who intentionally furthers the system inherits some (if not all) of the system's blame. More conservative collectivist theorists will stipulate that fault only distributes to members of smaller, organized collectives. They will perhaps have reservations about how far JCE II should extend. More ambitious collectivist theorists who allow that blame distributes to individuals who participate in larger, global systemic injustices will be more comfortable with a wide application of JCE II.

Intention theorists may not be as sympathetic to JCE II. JCE II does not merely assign liability for those crimes one intentionally commits, but also some crimes one does not intentionally commit. Consider a guard at a concentration camp. The guard intentionally commits a crime by murdering a prisoner in the camp. The murder supports the functioning of the camp, allowing it to run more efficiently. Other camp guards also commit murders in support of the concentration camp. Let us stipulate that the first guard knows about the wrongful general ends or goals of the concentration camp, but knows nothing of the other specific murders. Would an intention theorist say that the first guard intentionally participates in the murders of the other camp guards? Because it is unclear whether the first guard intends that the other murders occur, it is also unclear whether or not an intention theory will hold the first camp guard responsible for the other murders. But JCE II will hold one guard responsible for the murders of the other guards, simply because he supports and furthers the systemic functioning of the camp.

A lot depends on how intentions actually work. JCE II stipulates that one need not have a specific intention to commit an individual crime to be at fault for the crime; it is sufficient that one have a general intention to promote a wrongful system. JCE II therefore transfers specific intent for individual crimes to those who have a general intent to promote the ends of a wrongful collective. Intention theorists who believe it is just to infer specific intent from general intent will accept JCE II as legitimate. Intention theorists who think we cannot infer specific intent from general intent will find JCE II questionable (see Kutz, 2000a, p. 162 and Ohlin, 2011, pp. 744–5).

A narrow individualist model of collective moral responsibility would condemn JCE II as unfair. Narrow individualism assigns responsibility based on individual contribution towards a specific aim. But JCE II holds some responsible for actions that they did not contribute to in any clear way. While the camp guard in the previous example may contribute to the functioning of a criminal system, he did not contribute in any discernible way to the individual murders that the other guards carry out. The first guard did not even know about those murders. So it would be implausible to stipulate that the first guard makes a blameworthy intentional contribution to the murders of his fellow guards. But if this is so, a narrow individualist model will not hold the first guard responsible for the murders of the other guards.[1]

JCE III holds individual group members responsible for any actions that are a natural and foreseeable result of a group action. JCE III differs somewhat from JCE I, JCE II and conspiracy charges. JCE III stipulates that anyone who intentionally participates in a collective action must accept the risks of participation. One of the risks of participation in a criminal enterprise is that wrongdoing will occur. Because one accepts the risks of collective wrongdoing by participating in a collective action, one is liable for any unjust harm that results from one's participation. Like negligence or recklessness, JCE III could be interpreted as a form of liability for failing to take due precaution. For this reason, it is not really a form of collective liability. Being responsible for the natural and foreseeable consequences of participating in a group venture is no different from being responsible for the natural and foreseeable consequences of tossing a lit cigarette in a pile of dry brush. The viability of JCE III turns more on the viability of liability for recklessness than on any considerations of collective liability. I will therefore pass over JCE III, although it is worth noting that many find it objectionable (Ohlin, 2011).

Despite worries about the essential unfairness of collective liability, there are moral theories that justify the application of joint criminal enterprise. While narrow individualism brings into question the legitimacy of JCE I, II and III, collectivist and intention theories are more permissive of some forms of collective sanctioning.

The legal theorist who wishes to demonstrate that the precedents of joint criminal enterprise are in accord with peremptory moral norms must therefore accomplish the following. First, proponents of either distributive collectivist or intention theories of collective responsibilities must address the metaphysical and conceptual challenges that either model raises. Second, they must address the normative worries that distributive collectivist or intention theories are themselves somehow intrinsically unfair or unjust. Next, they must argue why either theory is preferable to any competing theory of collective moral responsibility. Finally, once either a distributive collectivist or intention theory is vindicated, proponents of these theories must demonstrate that legal mechanisms of collective liability will not come with prohibitive social costs. In other words, legal theorists must demonstrate that collective liability successfully furthers the ends of international justice (Darcy, 2007a, pp. 363–366; Osiel, 2005).

The task of morally justifying practices such as joint criminal enterprise is daunting, but this is as it should be. The elimination of more ruthless practices of collective sanctioning (in times of war and peace) is a tremendously important moral and legal development. Before we take Gomperz's (1939) advice and promote norms of collective and social responsibility in our legal and moral practices, we ought to have a really good reason for doing so.

Conclusion

On March 24th 2016, the ICTY found Radovan Karadžić guilty of participating in four joint criminal enterprises (*Prosecutor v. Karadžić*, Judgment Summary). These joint criminal enterprises included a plan to extirpate Bosnian Muslims and Croats from Bosnian Serb-claimed territory, a campaign of shelling civilians living in Sarajevo, the taking of UN peacekeepers and observers as hostages and a conspiracy to eliminate the Bosnian Muslims in Srebenica. For his criminal participation, Karadžić, the wartime leader of Bosnian Serbs during the conflict in the former Yugoslavia, was sentenced to 40 years in jail. At his age, 40 years was effectively a life sentence (*Prosecutor v. Karadžić*, para. 6070).

The ICTY convicted Karadžić on ten of the eleven charges brought against him. Every successful charge brought against Karadžić appealed to his participation in one of the four joint criminal enterprises (*Prosecutor v. Karadžić*, para. 6001–6010). Far from being utilized sparingly, the language of joint criminal enterprise is thus increasingly a major part of our international legal vocabulary. As the Karadžić ruling demonstrates, jurists have shown a strong willingness to use collective liability to advance the cause of international justice.

But we should not mistake ubiquity for legitimacy. Karadžić may deserve little sympathy, but we must not allow our feelings of disgust at what he has done blind us to the conceptual and moral complications lurking in joint criminal enterprise. If some of the more controversial measures of JCE cannot be justified, then jurists should consider replacing them with more defensible legal doctrines (Ohlin, 2011).

The need for a rigorous defense of the principles of collective liability goes beyond joint criminal enterprise. It is very easy to slip into the language of collective responsibility when discussing international affairs. For this reason, we should continue to be vigilant in making sure that our charges of collective responsibility are grounded in principle and not in prejudice. Too often, claims of collective responsibility emerge from our baser and more vindictive tribal instincts. We must continue to remind ourselves that hiding behind the abstract collectivities we blame are human beings with interests, fears, hopes and interpersonal relationships. If we allow claims of collective responsibility to violate their fundamental rights, we make no real progress in the advancement of international justice.

Note

1 A narrow individualist could stipulate that the first guard has been negligent or reckless in working for an organization that he knows will cause a tremendous amount of harm; see May, 1992, p. 48.

Bibliography

Ainley, K. (2011). Excesses of responsibility: The limits of law and the possibilities of politics. *Ethics and International Affairs, 25*(4), 407–431.

Cooper, D. E. (1968). Collective responsibility. *Philosophy, 43*, 258–268.

Cooper, D. E. (2003). "Ideology, moral complicity and the Holocaust." In E. Garrard and G. Scarre (Eds.), *Moral Philosophy and the Holocaust* (pp. 9–24). Burlington, VT: Ashgate.

Copp, D. (1984). What collectives are: Agency, individualism and legal theory. *Dialogue, 23*, 253–268.

Copp, D. (2006). On the agency of certain collective entities: An argument from 'normative autonomy'. *Midwest Studies in Philosophy, 30*(1), 194–221.

Darcy, S. (2007a). *Collective Responsibility and Accountability under International Law*. Ardsley, NY: Transnational.

Darcy, S. (2007b). Imputed criminal liability and the goals of international justice. *Leiden Journal of International Law, 20*, 377–404.

Darcy, S. (2010). Prosecuting the war crime of collective punishment. *Journal of International Criminal Justice, 8*, 29–51.

French, P. (1979). The corporation as a moral person. *American Philosophical Quarterly, 16*(3), 207–215.

French, P. (1984). *Collective and Corporate Responsibility*. New York: Columbia University Press.

Gadirov, J. (2011). Collective intentions and individual criminal responsibility. *Eyes on the ICC, 8*(1), 1–24.

Gomperz, H. (1939). Individual, collective and social responsibility. *Ethics, 49*, 329–342.

Hale, K. & Cline, D. (2014). Holding collectives accountable. *Criminal Law Forum, 25*, 261–290.

Isaacs, T. (2006). Collective moral responsibility and collective intention. *Midwest Studies in Philosophy, 30*, 59–73.

Isaacs, T. (2011). *Moral Responsibility in Collective Contexts*. New York: Oxford University Press.

Kelsen, H. (1943). Collective and individual responsibility in international law with particular regard to the punishment of war criminals. *California Law Review, 31*(5), 530–571.

Kutz, C. (2000a). *Complicity: Ethics and Law for a Collective Age*. New York: Cambridge University Press.

Kutz, C. (2000b). Acting together. *Philosophy and Phenomenological Research, 61*(1), 1–31.

Lewis, H. D. (1948). Collective responsibility. *Philosophy, 24*, 3–18.

May, L. (1992). *Sharing Responsibility*. Chicago: University of Chicago Press.

Miller, S. (2006). Collective moral responsibility: An individualist account. *Midwest Studies in Philosophy, 30*(1), 176–193.

Narveson, J. (2002). Collective responsibility. *The Journal of Ethics, 6*(2), 179–198.

Ohlin, J. D. (2008). Group think: The law of conspiracy and collective reason. *The Journal of Criminal Law and Criminology, 98*(1), 147–206.

Ohlin, J. D. (2011). Joint intentions to commit international crimes. *Chicago Journal of International Law, 11*(2), 693–753.

Osiel, M. (2005). Modes of participation in mass atrocity. *Cornell International Law Journal, 38*, 793–822.

Pettit, P. (2004). Groups with minds of their own. In Schmitt, F. (Ed.), *Socializing Metaphysics* (pp. 167–193). New York: Rowman and Littlefield.

Pettit, P. (2007). Responsibility incorporated. *Ethics, 117*, 171–201.

Reiff, M. (2008). Terrorism, retribution, and collective responsibility. *Social Theory and Practice, 28*(3), 442–455.

Sadler, B. J. (2006). Shared intentions and shared responsibility. *Midwest Studies in Philosophy, 30*, 115–144.

Schabas, W. A. (2003). Mens rea and the International Criminal Tribunal for the Former Yugoslavia. *New England Law Review, 37*(4), 1015–1036.

Shockley, K. (2007). Programming collective control. *Journal of Social Philosophy, 38*(3), 442–455.

Sverdlik, S. (1986). Collective responsibility. *Philosophical Studies, 51*, 61–76.

5

CONSTRUCTING REALITIES IN INTERNATIONAL POLITICS

Latin American views on the construction and implementation of the international norm Responsibility to Protect (R2P)

Raúl Salgado Espinoza[1]

Norms, ethics, and constructivism in IR: introduction

Despite their fundamental role for the construction and maintenance of peace, international norms have been and continue to be violated by international actors. As a result, this study departs from a point of view that norms are not considered as a fundamental instrument of authority and/or medium for the construction and maintenance of peace and order for those who have understood, internalized and accepted them. On this account, norms are viewed as "a broad class of prescriptive statements—rules, standards and so forth—both procedural and substantive" that, following a process of construction, are "prescriptions for action in situation of choice, carrying a sense of obligation, a sense that they *ought* to be followed."[2]

This account of norms is contested by an historical awareness of international relations as norms can contain elements of justice (and injustice). Therefore, international norms are entwined with ethical principles that compel us to behave in certain ways. They motivate international actors to reflect on what ought to be done and what they can expect from others. In the context of international politics, a focus on ethics in international relations (IR) did not become a major area of research until the 1980s.[3] Similarly, the emphasis on norms and normative theory in IR, which had lost its importance when rationalist theories started dominating the discipline, was revived at the end of the 1980s and beginning of the 1990s due to debates positioning constructivism as a new approach to international politics.

Norms and ethics in IR can be studied from three different perspectives. One focuses on the role played by normative ideas and answers the question, "How have ideas about what should be done influenced political behavior?" Another perspective centers its attention on the rationality of ethical behavior, responding to the question, "What ought we to do?" Finally, a third perspective analyzes the impact of moral behavior in political life and the constraints that morality imposes on the decision-maker in his role of international actor. This perspective responds to the question, "Given the realities of political life, what can be done?"[4] This study positions itself within the first perspective and puts emphasis on the role of constructivism in the study of norms and ethics in IR. Constructivism is an approach to international relations that falls under the postmodern approach to interpretative understanding.[5]

Constructivism as an approach to studying international phenomena has its roots in the 1980s and early 1990s through the works of Friedrich Kratochwil, Nicholas Onuf and Alexander Wendt. In the late 1990s, Anthony Giddens contributed to the development of constructivism as a "middle ground," or *via media*, between rationalists and reflectivists.[6] Social constructivism as an approach in IR can be clearly distinguished from the previously dominant theoretical perspectives of realism and liberalism, first, by its ontological assumption about reality. Whereas both realism and liberalism view the object of study as a phenomenon existing independently of the researcher, constructivism holds that the objects of IR—actors, institutions and international events—are socially constructed. Norms, identities and the interests of international actors play a fundamental role in determining the outcome of any international event. Yet norms, for example, are constructed through a process of social interaction (intersubjectivity) and reflect "values that define standards of appropriate behavior for the actors."[7] Hence, ideas, ethics and norms, such as human rights and warfare norms, matter in international politics. These influences also extend to the researcher, whose subjectivity cannot be excluded from the process of knowledge construction.

Constructivism also differs from the realist and liberal approaches in IR in its assumptions about the role played by national interest in the decision-making process. While realist and liberal approaches suggest that the basis for the actor's interest is her rationality (weighing gains against losses), constructivist approaches do not assume that interests are pre-given, fixed, or even straightforward. The actors of international relations—e.g., states, international organizations, international corporations and individuals—are represented and led by people who bear a variety of social roles, identities and cultures, all of which affect their deliberation and behavior.[8] Constructivism holds that national interest, as much as the ethical ideas that seemingly constrain the behavior of a state, are constructed through social interaction, challenging the basic assumptions of realism and liberalism.

Therefore, constructivism can have various and sometimes contentious perspectives on international relations due to its flexibility in epistemological and methodological approaches. These diverse and contentious views of what constructivism entails can be seen as a consequence of a certain alignment of the original reflexive constructivism with the dominant methodological and epistemological views of the 1990s with the intention of occupying the *via media*.[9] At one extreme, constructivism could be closer to some rational, positivist approaches, such as the English School, as well as with realist views, such as classical realist theory as suggested by Barkin.[10] At the other extreme, it could be close to postmodern and poststructural philosophical approaches due to its reflectivist tendency. However, the IR constructivist perspective can be distinguished from the philosophical approaches due to the former's more empirical, analytical approach to international phenomena.[11] It is indeed this analytical "thick" constructivist approach that has been considered as "compatible" with the classical realist theory of IR and which was proposed by Barkin as a "realist constructivism" that enables a dialogue within constructivism and between constructivism and realism.[12]

Constructivism's philosophical roots can be traced back to philosophers and sociologists such as Immanuel Kant, John Locke, Émile Durkheim and Max Weber.[13] Their analyses of society and explanations about how knowledge is constructed describe how norms and rules influence the behavior of international actors, as well as how the national interest is embedded in the creation and application of international norms.

Until the beginning of the 1990s, the main approaches that included international norms in their studies were regime theory and neoliberal institutionalism. In that sense, constructivism, if it were not dominated, was very much enclosed by idealism and liberal approaches.[14] However, international norms were viewed from a rationalist perspective, whereby other important elements of agency such as culture and identity were not relevant in the analysis of the decision-making process.[15] Constructivism has made it possible to analyze the behavior and actions of international actors in terms of norms, rules, culture and identity. Hence, the constructivist analysis of international politics takes into account the context within which actions take place as well as the context of the interpretation and construction of knowledge. This study focuses on the international norm Responsibility to Protect (R2P) to highlight the importance of looking at who participates, as well as how and when. It applies the constructivist framework to describe and interpret from a Latin American perspective how norms are constructed.

This investigation begins with the understanding that there are divergent views on R2P in the Latin American region. While some countries identify with the norm, others do not. While some reject the norm entirely, others are skeptical about the norm's construction and implementation.[16] Hence, this study searches for answers to the questions: Why are there divergent views on R2P in Latin America? Why do some Latin American countries identify more with the norm than others? Why do some reject it, and how do those others believe R2P should be implemented?

In order to develop answers to these questions, this investigation analyzes documents from the United Nations General Assembly and Security Council describing the positions of Latin American countries on R2P. Specifically, this study focuses on the main documents that establish R2P as an international norm: the Report of the International Commission on Intervention and State Sovereignty (ICISS) of 2001, the Report of the Secretary-General's High-Level Panel on Threats, Challenges, and Change of 2004, and the World Summit Outcome Document of 2005. A qualitative content analysis, employed to interpret these documents, was complemented by an interpretation of the statements made by decision-makers in the following three case studies: Brazil, Colombia and Ecuador. Official press releases and newspaper articles were also interpreted and contrasted in order to infer more accurate answers to the proposed questions. This study addresses three important aspects of norm construction and implementation from a Latin American perspective. Firstly, it focuses on the historical context of norm construction and implementation. Secondly, it addresses the role played by the Latin American states in the construction of R2P, and, finally, it describes the views of Brazil, Colombia and Ecuador on the application of R2P in the Libyan conflict.

Norms construction in an international historical context

The construction, destruction and (mis-)use of rules, norms and ideas to create and validate the national interest can be traced back to the Greek civilizations. Historically, international norms and related regulations have been created as a consequence of a major event that transformed or intended to transform the existing international system. For example, the modern European state system followed the Thirty Years' War. The regulations and international norms regulating the members of the League of Nations followed the First World War. The reconstruction and reform of the international system followed the Second World War, whereby the fundamental principles of human rights were introduced in the Charter of the United Nations.

The creation and adaptation of such rules and norms has been accomplished primarily by the dominant political actor in order to judge the less powerful states, which are viewed as the other, the rebellious, the faithless, the sinners, the barbarians, the underdeveloped, and so on. This is a repeating historical phenomenon that has its roots in one of the earliest sociopolitical organizations, the Greek *polis*. It was not until the 1990s that international norms were first invoked to protect weaker states and populations from infringements of international norms, violations of human rights, and outright destruction by stronger powers or one's own governments.

In *History of the Peloponnesian War*, Thucydides chronicles the transformation of the existing international system while contrasting the norms and values of the Athenians with their neighbors. Thucydides shows how the Athenians viewed the system of rules governing their neighbors as less modern than their own. Hence, the others—the barbarians, the underdeveloped and the weak—were obligated to submit to the powerful and developed Athenians, as this was reasonable for the survival of the former. The argument that the weaker must submit to the stronger was developed by the Athenians and shared by their emissaries with the weaker states. This is most clear in *History*'s "Melian Dialogue," where the Athenian representatives tell the Melians that "the strong do what they can and the weak suffer what they must."[17]

This kind of justification for the behavior of the dominant political actor was not so foreign in medieval times either. In the sixteenth century, the Spanish lawyer Francisco de Vitoria focused on universal laws governing political communities and establishing the rights of sovereigns. In his work *On the American Indians*, de Vitoria extended this analysis to the rights of the Native American population, offering an argument that became influential within the Spanish Empire. De Vitoria argued that because Native Americans did not understand or reflect upon the salvation of their souls by believing in the Christian God as the "civilized" Spaniards did, the Native Americans lacked the rational faculties to self-govern.[18] Hence, Catholic beliefs needed to be imposed upon them to save their souls. At the same time, since the Native Americans were not able to govern themselves, they could legitimately be enslaved according to the Europeans' understanding of natural law.[19] However, this account of natural law was not known by the Native Americans; it was as foreign as the invaders. Instead, the diverse indigenous peoples each had their own understanding of natural law which reflected *their* ancestral perspective.

In contrast to the Athenians, who deliberated their intentions *with* their neighbors or enemies and asked them to submit, the Spanish lawyers and erudite "civilized people" constructed an argument primarily on the basis of their beliefs and ethical principles and imposed them on the "barbarians" and "uncivilized" Native Americans. And yet what justifies the "saviors" saving those who appeared to be in danger? If they do accept the offer, how should they be saved? These are the fundamental questions that continue to entertain philosophical and academic debates to the present day. Realities, norms and rules have often been created, and, in many cases, the receiver was not aware of them until the application of the "consensus" affected them. This can be seen in the division of Africa by the European empires in the nineteenth century, as well as the creation of the state of Israel in the heart Palestinian territory following the Second World War.

The creation of IR as a field of inquiry in the last century, and within it the study of ethics, has motivated scholars to explain the reasons underlying such states' behavior. However, the dominant theoretical perspectives for studying international politics provide little opportunity for normative theory to contribute to the understanding of such events, nor do they allow further approaches to develop.

The two examples above have shown that there have always been moral rules regulating the behaviors of individuals, states and political organizations. In many of such cases, however, these rules have not simply been created to avoid war, facilitate peace or improve the life of the community of states, as was the intention of the League of Nations. They have also been created to punish the rebellious, the other, the "barbarians," and they have been misused by powerful states to discursively justify their actions, as they were in the recent invasions of Iraq and Libya. The insertion of constructivism into the debates about knowledge construction within the social sciences, and particularly the use of constructivism to explain international phenomena, such as the fall of the Soviet Union and the end of the Cold War, enabled IR once again to consider norms, rules and culture as fundamental elements of analysis.

The relationship between international norms and national identity also became a fundamental element of investigation for IR. The history of the twentieth century shows us that norms created without the debate and approval of the states affected by their application are more likely to be contested and violated. If these norms are not internalized as part of a state's culture and identity, they can become a motive for new international conflicts. This can be seen in the negotiations surrounding the creation of the League of Nations in the 1920s. The losers of the First World War were not invited to the table for deliberation and negotiations on the norms that were to govern the international community. Consequently, among the defeated there was alienation, lack of recognition, and low self-identification with the norms surrounding the League of Nations. Only fifteen years later, the reviving powers, particularly Germany and Japan, initiated the Second World War and violated all of the recently created international norms.

In contrast, Latin American states welcomed and widely supported the set of international rules created within the League of Nations since many of these states were involved in the shaping and implementation of the norms. In addition, these states believed that a regulation of international behavior would persuade and limit the aggressive, imperialist behavior of their major neighbor, the United States of America.[20] This was also one of the main arguments the Latin American states invoked following the Second World War to support the recreation of international norms and their incorporation into the Charter of the United Nations (UN). Another argument was based on the idea of a Latin American appropriation of the general principles of human rights, which had grown and further developed within a new consciousness of Latin American humanism. All Latin American countries, but particularly the small Latin American states of Costa Rica, Uruguay and Ecuador, supported the construction of the United Nations. These states made relevant contributions to the basic principles of human rights incorporated in the UN Charter.[21] Because Latin American states have self-identified with the fundamental norms underpinning the UN Charter, their support has been unquestionable.

However, the international norm Responsibility to Protect (R2P), which was constructed in the twenty-first century within the new ideas of humanitarian intervention, lacks the unquestionable acceptance in the Latin American region that the UN Charter enjoys. Although R2P still appears to be under construction, Latin American states have divergent views on what it is, as well as when and how it should be applied.[22] This process of construction and the divergent views of it by the Latin American states are discussed in the following section.

The process of construction of R2P and its divergent views in the Latin American region

Humanitarian interventions in order to prevent violations of fundamental human rights were rarely carried out until the early 1990s, despite the signature and confirmation of the main human rights conventions and covenants by the majority of states. Although the set of rules comprising human rights grant protection on the basis of one's identity as a human being, during the Cold War these principles were rarely respected. The Latin American military dictatorships lasting from the 1960s to the beginning of the 1990s were responsible for large-scale violations of human rights. The democratization process and the active promotion of human rights particularly by non-governmental organizations in the region has brought back discussion about human rights norms and the new ideas of humanitarian intervention. Humanitarian intervention permits external actors to intervene in the internal affairs of a state, including through the use of force, to prevent genocide, war crimes and crimes against humanity. Thus, discussions regarding humanitarian intervention make possible the revival of debates about just war and the role of international norms in international politics.

However, most Latin American states are skeptical of humanitarian intervention, particularly in the context of R2P. One reason is that the great powers and dominating states looked away when the region suffered from military regimes that terrorized their populations.[23] Consequently, states in the region have divergent views on R2P that reflect their histories. Another reason is that human rights norms may conflict with and prevail over other established international norms that are of fundamental importance for these states. For instance, both humanitarian intervention and R2P may conflict with two fundamental norms of the international state system, the principle of sovereignty and the principle of self-determination. There are divergent positions among Latin American states on the conflict between these norms, too. Serbin and Pont have observed four divergent tendencies regarding R2P: the "champions" or strong supporters (Argentina, Chile, Guatemala, Uruguay), the "spoilers" or opposers (Cuba, Venezuela and Nicaragua), and the "skeptics" (Ecuador) and "rule entrepreneurs" (Brazil).[24]

The "spoilers" or opposers consider R2P an instrument for strong powers to intervene in the internal affairs of states that do not share the views of the Western powers. They argue that this norm enables the violation of their national sovereignty by stronger powers.[25] On the one hand, R2P contains identitarian elements of Western democratic societies, whose fundamental values are also the basis of the Latin American democracies. On the other hand, the input of Latin American states into the construction of R2P has been limited. These debates included only a few representatives from Latin American states, as we will see in the following description of R2P's construction. Hence, some of these states do not seem to self-identify with the norm due to their limited participation in its construction.[26]

The intellectual and political foundations of R2P can be traced back to the work of Francis Deng and Roberta Cohen, members of the Brookings Institution, in Washington, D.C. In the 1990s, Deng and Cohen developed the concept of "sovereignty as responsibility," in which states are responsible for protecting their own populations.[27] At the beginning of the twenty-first century, then Secretary-General of the UN Kofi Annan demanded that the international community reach an agreement on how to respond to humanitarian crises such as the killing and abuse of civilians perpetrated by militia groups during the civil war in the former republic of Yugoslavia and the systematic murder of Tutsis in Rwanda. In addition, Annan's demand was linked to the crisis in international law caused by the intervention of North Atlantic Treaty Organization (NATO) in the Kosovo conflict in 1999 without a mandate from the Security Council. However, an international response to these crises, like the idea of humanitarian intervention more generally, conflicts with the principles of national sovereignty and non-interference established in Article 2 (7) of the UN Charter.

In 2000, the Canadian government sponsored the establishment of ICISS to develop arguments for and under which conditions the international community should use coercive measures, specifically of a military nature. The ICISS developed R2P, which emphasizes the responsibility of states to protect their populations from genocide, war crimes, crimes against humanity and ethnic cleansing. The Commission's report, published in December 2001, proposed that when a state is not able to or is not willing to fulfill this responsibility, the international community has the responsibility to protect the vulnerable population. The proposal of ICISS includes three pillars of progressive development, focusing firstly on the responsibility of the state to protect its own population; secondly, on the responsibility of the international community if the state is not able or not willing to fulfill it; and thirdly, on the application of coercive measures, including military force, with the approval of the Security Council.

However, the members of ICISS were restricted to a small group of politicians, academics and "friends."[28] From the eleven states that participated, Guatemala was the only representative from the Latin American region. This poor representation belies the diversity of views on R2P among Latin American countries.[29] Most of the Latin American countries that are considered "champions" or "friends" of R2P have contributed to the norm's development since its beginnings, either with representative members of the ICISS (Guatemala) or as members of its Advisory Board (Chile, Mexico and Argentina).[30]

Following the Commission, Kofi Annan requested the establishment of a group of experts and investigators, the High-Level Panel on Threats, Challenges and Change, to further develop these ideas. Out of a total of sixteen members, this Panel included only two national representatives from the Latin American community, an ex-Minister of Foreign Affairs of Uruguay and a former General-Secretary of the Ministry of External Relations of Brazil. Further, the international consultations and workshops took place in Latin American cities on only two occasions out of forty-five: in Rio de Janeiro on March 7 and 8, and in Mexico City on May 17–19, of 2004. By contrast, thirty-three meetings were conducted in Western countries, twenty-one of which were held in the USA.

The High-Level Panel focused on the third pillar of this norm, developing the way the international community should apply R2P following approval from the Security Council.[31] However, most of the Latin American states did not participate in this stage. Those that were not able to build a sense of self-identification with R2P precisely are not in the group of supporters because they did not contribute to its construction. The states that did participate in this stage self-identify with and support R2P; they are classified as "champions" and "friends."[32] These states are Argentina, Colombia, Chile, Costa Rica, Guatemala, Mexico, Panama and Uruguay.

In addition to having participated in its construction, Chile, Argentina, Guatemala and Uruguay appear to have a high level of support for the norm as a reaction to their experiences with violent military dictatorships. Hence, the construction of mechanisms for protecting and implementing human rights are considered important instruments for strengthening these democracies.[33] While the states comprising the skeptics from the "gray zone" and "rule entrepreneurs," such as Brazil, do not necessarily disagree with the principles underlying the norm, they approach it with skepticism. They have seen R2P as a way to legitimize past interventions that have "aggravated existing conflicts, allowed terrorism to penetrate into places where it previously did not exist, given rise to new cycles of new violence and increased the vulnerability of civilian population," instead of providing efficient solutions to the conflicts.[34] As a result, Brazil proposed the concept of "responsibility while protecting" which acknowledges that, although collective responsibility toward foreign populations may require the use of military force, the impact of the intervention must result in less suffering to the civilian population than it already experiences. Nevertheless, "responsibility while protecting" lost its initial positive momentum due both to criticism from the dominating countries and poor continuity in Brazil's subsequent development.[35]

In conclusion, Latin American states lacked opportunities for participation, contribution and discussion in the construction of the norm R2P. This appears to have led to aversion, hesitation and/or rejection of R2P by some Latin American states. The poor dissemination and regionally restricted discussion led to a limited opportunity for internalization and appropriation of the norm within all the Latin American states. In contrast, for states that were involved in this process, their participation appears to have led to self-identification, commitment and acceptance of the normative intentions of R2P's proponents.

The South American divergences on the application of R2P: the cases of Brazil, Colombia and Ecuador in the context of the Libyan conflict

The beginning of the Libyan conflict can be considered an extension of the Arab Spring, which reached Libyan soil on February 15, 2011. Political and popular discontent was manifest in protests against the government of Colonel Muammar el-Qaddafi. In addition to civilians, the protestors included insurgents against whom the dictator reacted with violent repression and air attacks, affecting the insurgents and innocent civilians alike.[36] The international community, represented by the UN, condemned Qaddafi's violent response. The UN Security Council imposed sanctions on the Libyan government, including an arms embargo and asset freeze, and referred the situation to the International Criminal Court (ICC) through Resolution 1970 issued on February 26, 2011. These measures were unanimously adopted by the Security Council on the authority granted by Article VII of the UN Charter. Article VIII determinations, which empowers the Security Council to take appropriate preventive measures, are in accordance with the third pillar of R2P. However, these measures did not have the expected result. The UN's actions increased the number of insurgent groups and the amount of violence. Moreover, the sanctions had no effect on dissuading the Libyan government from responding with violence.

In light of such developments, the Security Council adopted Resolution 1973 on March 17, 2011. The resolution was supported by ten members (Bosnia-Herzegovina, Colombia, France, Gabon, Lebanon, Nigeria, Portugal, South Africa, the United Kingdom and the United States) with five abstentions (Brazil, China, Germany, India and Russia). On March 24, 2011, on the basis of this resolution, NATO was authorized to take action to protect civilians. This authorization empowered NATO to carry out air strikes against the forces of the Libyan government (Querejazu, 2012), which not only debilitated forces loyal to Qaddafi, but also killed an untold number of civilians.[37] As a result of this military intervention, Colonel Qaddafi was killed in October of 2011.

The deliberation surrounding the application of R2P in Libya shows divergent views among Latin American countries. The region's two representatives on the Security Council, Colombia and Brazil, had different views on the application of coercive measures, including military intervention. Additionally, Ecuador, while not on the Security Council, was outspoken in its opposition. Colombia's support for R2P goes back to 2009, at which time its Permanent Representative to the General Assembly, Ambassador Claudia Blum, affirmed support for R2P as an international norm, as well as the use of coercive measures, including military action, that follow from the third pillar. On the one hand, Colombia is a close ally of the United States, the main leader behind NATO operations. Hence, it is reasonable enough to understand Colombia's support for the decisions and actions of a close ally. On the other hand, its identification with the norm and its implementation seems to conflict with its national reality. The Colombian state has not been able to protect its own population from crimes against humanity. For decades, civilians in Colombia consistently had their human rights violated by both the official Colombian military forces and, especially, the Revolutionary Armed Forces of Colombia (FARC), the latter controlling about a third of Colombian territory. Therefore, it is legitimate to ask why Colombia, and the international community for that matter, did not consider the application of R2P in this region if Colombia genuinely supported R2P in Libya.

Colombia's President Juan Manuel Santos announced his country's support of Resolution 1973 and the actions of NATO by stating that, "the Libyan authorities have made a mockery of the resolution and therefore there will be an intervention." Colombia "will always support the positions that favour freedom, democracy and human rights."[38] In September 2011, Ambassador Néstor Osorio Londoño, the Colombian Permanent Representative to the General Assembly at the time, defended President Santos's position by emphasizing that Colombia will continue to back further decisions by the United Nations in Libya following the conclusion of military action. It should be noted, however, that R2P was not created to support the expansion of democracy or the liberal conception of freedom.

The Colombia position on R2P in Libya was not shared by its Latin American counterpart on the Security Council, Brazil, whose criticism took the form of an amended form of R2P. A stronger contrast can be seen, first, by looking to Ecuador's position on the application of pillars two and three in the Libyan conflict. At the World Summit in September 2005, Ecuador rejected the norm altogether. Subsequently, the Ecuadorian position has been cautious and critical of the implementation of pillar three because it would clearly violate established norms of sovereignty and self-determination. In 2009, Ecuador stated that pillar three could only be used "under premises that do not undermine state security and sovereignty," and that the underpinning concepts of pillars two and three should be clarified in order to apply these measures as there was no "precision about the conceptual scope, regulatory parameters and actors."[39]

In the following years, when Resolutions 1970 and 1973 were passed, Ecuador directly opposed the implementation of pillar three and the use of military force against the Libyan government as the means by which the international community would protect civilians. The Ecuadorian government pointed out that there were agitators and insurgents harming civilians, who should also be tackled by the intervening forces. Consequently, Ecuador considered the use of R2P "an excuse for military aggression and further acts that harm the sovereignty of states."[40] Ecuador criticized the international community's handling of the crisis in Libya. The Ecuadorian president, Rafael Correa, often referred to a "double standard" for intervening actors, highlighting that interventions have been made "where there are large natural resources" and where dictatorial governments were not friends of the great powers. Hence, Ecuador rejected NATO's intervention in Libya, but made clear that the country did not support the Libyan government's repression of its own people.

This analysis not only shows Ecuador's position on the implementation and application of R2P, but also its poor self-identification with it. This disapproval continued after the death of Qaddafi. The Ecuadorian representative to the UN, Luis Gallegos, defended Ecuador's opposition to the application of R2P by expressing that "the interference of military forces in other countries never contributes to the stability or to build[ing] democracy, nor to a peaceful life" of the population.[41]

Brazil, as an emergent power, appeared willing to play a strategic role in the debates about the application of pillar three in Libya. Brazil had participated in the construction of R2P and, along with most other Latin American states, approved the norm in the General Assembly in 2005. During the interactive dialogue in 2009, Brazil reaffirmed its support for R2P through its ambassador, Maria Luiza Ribeiro Viotti. Ribeiro Viotti emphasized that "the attribute of sovereignty does not exempt the state from its obligation to protect its population," and that R2P could be conceived as "a powerful political call" for all states to fulfill their responsibilities and legal obligations under the UN Charter of international law.[42] The principle of sovereignty has its limits, according to Brazil, when it is (mis-)used as a shield to commit crimes against humanity. However, the international community should play a more active role in the first pillar of R2P. Principally, it should identify the causes of conflict in order to implement preventive diplomacy. In this context, Brazil proposed developmental cooperation as a way to address what appears to be the primary cause for the outbreak of local and international conflicts, gaps between rich and poor and developed and underdeveloped countries.[43]

Brazil abstained from the vote for Resolution 1973, and so it did not reject outright the use of military force in Libya as a way of fulfilling the third pillar of R2P. Brazil did go on to propose conditions for how military force should be applied. This was later developed into the Brazilian proposal of Responsibility while Protecting (RwP). While Brazilian support for Resolution 1970 and abstention from Resolution 1973 suggests an uncertainty in its position, it can also be understood as a strategic decision to satisfy its BRICS allies, Russia, China and India, who also abstained from the voting process for Resolution 1973.

Nevertheless, Brazil´s tendency to support the application of pillar three became more evident when its Ministry of Foreign Affairs urged Colonel Qaddafi "to respect and ensure the free expression of the protestors" and to seek a peaceful solution to the conflict. Moreover, on February 28, 2011, Ambassador Ribeiro Viotti confirmed Brazil's position in favour of Resolution 1970 by highlighting that Brazil had "publicly and firmly condemned the use of violence and called on the authorities in Libya to uphold and protect the right of freedom of expression of the protesters, as well as to seek a solution to the crisis through dialogue."[44] In addition, Brazilian calls to the international community to use all necessary measures to stabilize the Libyan situation, without excluding the use of force as a last resource, show a clear difference from the unquestionable support shown by Colombia and the outright rejection by Ecuador.

This decision taken by the newly elected Brazilian president Dilma Rousseff to supplement pillar three with more deliberation did not stop NATO's intervention under the Security Council mandate. Nevertheless, President Rousseff highlighted one of the worrying prospects of foreign military interventions that became a reality in Libya: interventions can aggravate conflicts and allow "terrorist infiltration that inaugurate new cycles of violence, multiplying the numbers of civilian casualties."[45] The killing of Colonel Qaddafi, the destruction of state infrastructure and the imposition of an *ad hoc* government created a power vacuum filled by criminal and terrorist groups. Consequently, the civil population was even more unprotected than before the beginning of the conflict. Brazil pointed to this outcome in its argument for RwP.

Moreover, the Brazilian proposal emerged as a critique and alternative to R2P by suggesting that the application of R2P under Resolution 1973 went "far beyond its intention to protect the Libyan population. Instead it had exacerbated insecurity in both the country and the region."[46] In this context, Brazil stressed the importance of preventive diplomacy and peaceful settlement of disputes. This is clear in the post-intervention position on Libya expressed by the Permanent Mission of Brazil to the UN. The use of force, specifically by NATO, "cause[d] greater harm than the one it was supposed to prevent." Going forward, Brazil argued that force must be *unanimously* authorized by the UN Security Council.[47]

The Brazilian proposal clearly obtained sympathy from the "skeptics" and "norm-rejecters" in Latin America. This can not only be understood as a result of the regional and global role Brazil has sought to play, but also because the failure of the intervention in Libya was seen by these countries as an opportunity to question foreign military interventions. RwP has been interpreted as an attempt by Brazil to revise the norm in order to reinforce its position as an independent country, dissuading "any perception that the country is simply following, yet again, a norm created by major powers in the West."[48] Despite Brazil's attempt to develop the South's version of R2P, RwP did not last beyond the debates in the General Assembly. Brazil failed to achieve the changes to R2P it proposed in 2011.

Conclusion

Norms and ethics in IR are not only important for the role normative theory plays when analyzing what international actors ought to do. They also provide insight into the different perspectives within the field to study the ethical behavior of international actors. This chapter has focused on analyzing the construction of the international norm R2P from a Latin American perspective. This investigation has approached these topics by focusing on the role played by normative ideas. In order to do this, it focused on interpreting and analyzing the behavior and positions of Brazil, Colombia and Ecuador in the process of applying R2P in the Libyan conflict. This approach develops answers to the question: "How have ideas about what should be done influenced political behavior?" The chapter has argued that international norms have historically been created for many different purposes, but mainly they have been created without the consultation, participation and influence of those forced to abide by them. The norm recipients mostly have been weaker powers and have not been involved in the process of constructing the norm. Hence, the recipients go on to contest and reject the way the norm is implemented and applied. This can be evidenced in Latin American views on the creation of R2P and its application in Libya. None of the Latin American states that are considered norm rejecters participated in R2P's construction. By contrast, all states that are listed among the so-called "champions" or group of friends of R2P did participate in its construction.[49] Hence, it can be said that states that have poor input in the construction of a norm also have a poor self-identification with it.

Moreover, small states, particularly those that are weak, tend to reject norms that infringe established international norms enabling territorial control and external autonomy, such as the norms of sovereignty and self-determination. This is the case with Ecuador, which rejected the norm from the beginning and has been highly critical of its application in Libya. In contrast, bigger powers, such as Colombia, tend to act in accordance with their closest ally, and great and emergent powers, like the United States or Brazil, tend to act strategically and in their own self-interest. Colombia strongly supported the norm and its implementation through the use of military force, but Brazil was critical about its implementation despite its support of the norm.

Finally, the negative outcomes from Libya challenge the moral motivations behind the stronger powers and those implementing the norms. They call into question whether such norms are primarily instruments of the stronger powers to pursue their own interests, while the purported duties to prevent genocide, war crimes, crimes against humanity and ethnic cleansing are relegated to secondary importance. In this sense, the ideas of humanitarian intervention are weakened instead of strengthened and further developed.

Notes

1 I want to thank Professor Joy Gordon who has provided both encouragement and invaluable advice during the time of writing this manuscript. Thanks are due also to Drew Thompson, who read the drafts and provided feedback.

2 Abram Chayes Abram and Antonia Chayes, "Regime Architecture: Elements and Principles," in *Global Engagement: Cooperation and Security in the 21st Century*, ed. Janne Nolan (Washington, DC: Brookings Institution, 2010), 65.

3 Terry Nardin, "International Ethics," in *The Oxford Handbook of International Relations*, ed. Christian Reus-Smit and Duncan Snidal (Oxford: Oxford University Press, 2010), 594–611.

4 Andrew Hurrell, "Norms and Ethics in International Relations," in *Handbook of International Relations*, ed. Walter Carlsnaes, Thomas Risse, and Beth A. Simmons (London: SAGE Publications, 2010), 137.

5 Paul Viotti and Mark Kauppi, *International Relations Theory*, 5th edn. (New York: Pearson Education, 2012).

6 Chris Brown and Kirsten Ainley, *Understanding International Relations*, 4th edn. (London: Palgrave MacMillan, 2009).

7 Viotti and Kauupi, *International Relations Theory*, 286.

8 Ian Hurd, "Constructivism," in *The Oxford Handbook of International Relations*, ed. Walter Carlsnaes, Thomas Risse, and Beth A. Simmons (London: SAGE Publications, 2010), 137–154.

9 Alexander Barder and Denial Levine, "'The World Is Too Much with Us': Reification and the Depoliticising of *Via Media* Constructivist IR," *Millennium: Journal of International Studies*, 40, 3 (2012): 585–604.
10 Samuel Barkin, "Realist Constructivism," *International Studies Review*, 5, 3 (2003): 325–342; Samuel Barkin, *Realist Constructivism: Rethinking International Relations Theory* (Cambridge: Cambridge University Press, 2010).
11 Hurd, "Constructivism"; Viotti and Kauupi, *International Relations Theory*.
12 Barkin, "Realist Constructivism"; Barkin, *Realist Constructivism*; Patrick Thaddeus Jackson and Daniel Nexon, "Constructivist Realism or Realist-Constructivism?" *International Studies Review*, 6, 2 (2004): 337–341.
13 Viotti and Kauupi, *International Relations Theory*.
14 Barkin, "Realist Constructivism."
15 Jeffrey T. Checkel, "Norms, Institutions, and National Identity in Contemporary Europe," *International Studies Quarterly*, 43, 1 (1999): 83–114.
16 Andrés Serbin and Andrei Serbin Pont, "Latin America and Responsibility to Protect: Divergent Views from the South," *Pensamiento Propio*, 41, 20 (2015): 11–33.
17 Thucydides, *History of the Peloponnesian War*, trans. William Smith (London: Jones & Co., 1831).
18 Chris Brown, Terry Nardin, and Nicholas Rengger, eds., *International Relations in Political Thought: Texts from the Ancient Greeks to the First World War* (Cambridge: Cambridge University Press, 2002).
19 *Ibid.*
20 Alfred Zimmer, *The League of Nations and the Rule of Law 1918–1935* (London: MacMillan, 1936).
21 Bryce Wood and Minerva Morales, "Latin America and the United Nations," *International Organization*, 9, 3 (1965): 714–727.
22 Serbin and Pont, "Latin America and the Responsibility to Protect."
23 *Ibid.*; Raúl Salgado Espinoza, "Responsibility to Protect as a Norm under Construction: The Divergent Views from the South," *LASAFORUM*, 7, 2 (2016): 21–24.
24 Serbin and Pont, "Latin America and the Responsibility to Protect."
25 Carlo Alzugaray, "Cuba and RtoP: A Critical Approach from a Humanitarian Anti-Hegemonic Global-South Powerbroker," *Pensamiento Propio*, 41, 20 (2015): 225–240; Alfred Toro Carnevali, "El Concepto de la Responsabilidad de Proteger: La perspectiva de la República Bolivariana de Venezuela y otros países en desarrollo," *Pensamiento Propio*, 35, 17 (2012): 135–168.
26 Espinoza, "Responsibility to Protect as a Norm under Construction."
27 Alex J. Bellamy, "The Three Pillars of the Responsibility to Protect," *Pensamiento Propio*, 41, 20 (2015): 35–64.
28 Cecile Añaños, "La Responsabilidad de Proteger en las Naciones Unidas y la Doctrina de la Responsabilidad de Proteger," *Anuario Mexicano de Derecho Internacional*, 10 (2010): 199–244.
29 Espinoza, "Responsibility to Protect as a Norm under Construction."
30 Serbin and Pont, "Latin America and the Responsibility to Protect."
31 Bellamy, "The Three Pillars."
32 Serbin and Pont, "Latin America and the Responsibility to Protect."
33 *Ibid.*
34 United Nations General Assembly, *Letter Dated 9 November 2012 from the Permanent Representative of Brazil to the United Nations Addressed to the Secretary-General*, 2011, at http://unbisnet.un.org:8080/ipac20/ipac.jsp?session=N4800AO429971.238010&menu=search&aspect=subtab124&npp=50&ipp=20&spp=20&profile=bib&ri=1&source=%7E%21horizon&index=.UD&term=A%2F66%2F551S%2F2011%2F701&x=0&y=0&aspect=subtab124#focus. A/66/551-S/2011/70, accessed 14/07/2016, 3.
35 Andrés Serbin and Andrei Serbin Pont, "Brazil's Responsibility while Protecting: A Failed Attempt of Global South Norm Innovation?" *Pensamiento Propio*, 41, 20 (2015): 171–192.
36 Roland Paris, "The 'Responsibility to Protect' and the Structural Problems of Preventive Humanitarian Intervention," *International Peacekeeping*, 21, 5 (2014): 569–603.
37 Amaya Querejazu, "Seguridad Internacional y Multilateralismo: Las Organizaciones Internacionales y la Intervención en Libia," *Colombia Internacional*, 76 (2012): 111–136.
38 El Mundo, "Santos Defiende Intervención Militar en Libia," March 19, 2001, https://www.elespectador.com/noticias/elmundo/santos-defiende-intervencion-militar-libia-articulo-257988.
39 Permanent Mission of Ecuador to the UN, *Debate General sobre la Responsabilidad de Proteger*, July 23, 2009, at http://www.responsibilitytoprotect.org/index.php/component/content/article/

35-r2pcs-topics/2493-general-assembly-debate-on-the-responsibility-to-protect-and-informal-interactive-dialogue-#debate.

40 Ministerio de Relaciones Exteriores, Comercio, e Integración de Ecuador, "Agenda de Política Exterior para la Seguridad," Quito, Manthra editores, 2011.

41 Luis Gallegos, "En el Boletín de Prensa No. 1322 durante la 18ª Sesión Especial del Consejo de Derechos Humanos," 2011.

42 Maria Luiza Ribeiro Viotti, "Plenary Meeting of the General Assembly on the R2P," 2009, at http://www.responsibilitytoprotect.org/Brazil_ENG.pdf, accessed on 20/08/2016.

43 *Ibid.*

44 Maria Luiza Ribeiro Viotti, "*Explicação de voto do Brasil na Sessão Especial do Conselho de Segurança sobre a Situação na Líbia*," February 26, 2011, at http://www.itamaraty.gov.br/pt-BR/notas-a-imprensa/2490-explicacao-de-voto-do-brasil-na-sessao-especial-do-conselho-de-seguranca-sobre-a-situacao-na-libia-nova-york-26-de-fevereiro-de-2011; Ministry of Foreign Affairs of Brazil, "Aprovação da Resolução 1973 do Conselho de Segurança da ONU sobre a Líbia," 2011, at http://www.itamaraty.gov.br/pt-BR/notas-a-imprensa/2514-aprovacao-da-resolucao-1973-do-conselho-de-seguranca-da-onu-sobre-a-libia, accessed on 13-05-2016.

45 Dilma Rousseff, "Discurso de Apertura en la Asamblea General de la ONU 21 de Septiembre 2011," 2011, at https://documents-dds-ny.un.org/doc/UNDOC/GEN/N11/ 506/92/PDF/ N1150692.pdf?OpenElement.

46 Alfredo Toro Carnevali, "Has Brazil's *Responsibility while Protecting* Changed Venezuela's Skepticism about the *Responsibility to Protect?*," *Pensamiento Propio*, 41, 20 (2015): 214.

47 Viotti, "*Explicação de voto do Brasil na Sessão Especial do Conselho de Segurança sobre a Situação na Líbia*"; Ministry of Foreign Affairs of Brazil, "Aprovação da Resolução 1973 do Conselho de Segurança da ONU sobre a Líbia."

48 Kai Kenkel, "Brazil and the Responsibility to Protect," *Asia Pacific Centre for the Responsibility to Protect* (2015): 4.

49 Serbin and Pont, "Latin America and the Responsibility to Protect."

6

AGENCY, EXPLANATION AND ETHICS IN INTERNATIONAL RELATIONS

Damian Cox and Michael Levine

Introduction

International affairs involve the actions of both state and non-state actors. Some of these actions appear to be legitimate objects of moral judgement. But what assumptions underlie this judgement? Typically, actors in international relations contexts are not individuals, with individual consciences, but bodies of diverse and distributed decision-makers. Under which conditions, then, does it make sense to attribute moral responsibility to them? This is a particularly important question within international relations scholarship because international relations scholars have generally under-utilized the concept of moral agency. Toni Erskine puts the point this way:

> . . . while, *inter alia*, realist, neorealist, neoliberal institutionalist, and some constructivist approaches rely on the agency of the state, the idea that the state might be a bearer of moral burdens is either precluded or (perhaps most notably in the case of classical realist positions) allowed but unexamined. This combination of an uncritical acceptance of the state as an agent and the rejection, or evasion, of its possible role as a *moral* agent is a puzzling feature of much International Relations scholarship.[1]

Erskine goes on to point out how this tendency is made more problematic by a widespread reluctance within international relations scholarship to acknowledge the moral agency of non-state actors – including organizations such as Al Qaeda, Isis, "coalitions of the willing", non-governmental organizations (NGOs) – in international affairs.

In this chapter, we explore the issue Erskine highlights. We give a general account of the conditions of moral agency and describe the different kinds of moral responsibility that might apply in international relations contexts. There is a rich and important literature in philosophy on the nature of collective agency. This, and allied work within international relations scholarship, is a vital part of the project of understanding the moral responsibility of international actors.[2] However, we do not re-tread this material in our discussion. We take a philosophical step back and ask fundamental questions about the nature of attributions of moral agency as such. We take philosophical accounts of the attribution of moral agency and ask how they can help us understand the responsibility of international actors. The key idea of our account is that moral responsibility is tied directly to satisfactory attributions of agency. A body can only be held morally responsible for its actions if observers can satisfactorily attribute agency to it. And a body can be said to have acted as an agent only if it has acted for reasons. It is a simple idea in outline, but things quickly get complicated. We spend much of the chapter furnishing an account of what it is to attribute agency to state and non-state actors, tying this account in with two important frameworks of international relations theory: realism and constructivism. To begin, however, it is important to get as clear as we can about what constitutes moral responsibility, and what it means to have acted for reasons – that is, what it means to have acted as an agent. Clearly, in order to act as an agent one's reasons need not be rational (even on a broad understanding what rationality might consist in) – let alone morally acceptable. Neither need one's reasons be conscious. If it may at times be difficult to assign responsibility to a single agent, then how much more problematic is it to assign agency and/or responsibility that is spread out among numerous individuals and groups?

Moral responsibility

To hold somebody morally responsible for their actions – in the backwards-looking sense that we take as primary – is to invite either praise or blame, commendation or condemnation, approbation or disapprobation.[3] This is the expressive or reactive core of attributions of moral responsibility, but there is more to it than this. Philosophers have sought to understand what else is involved. Four main approaches have been taken. We label them: consequentialist accounts; attribution accounts; accountability accounts; and answerability accounts. We briefly outline each.[4]

A consequentialist account of moral responsibility ties the practice of assigning praise and blame, and the concomitant practices (when there are any) of reward and punishment, to their utility. The practice of assigning moral responsibility is legitimate only in so far as it is of practical use. It is legitimate to hold a body responsible for their actions only if doing so would, in general, have a salutary effect on their behaviour or function in some other way (for example, as deterrent) to help secure desirable ends.[5] The practice of criticizing nations for their heedless pursuit of national interest over their common interests with others, for example, makes little sense on the consequentialist view if this kind of discourse in general has no good effect – if it is just a pointless sounding-off against organizations that frustrate us and undermine our goals.

Consequentialist accounts contrast with merit-based accounts, in which the concept of desert predominates. Irrespective of whether the practice of assigning moral responsibility to others is of practical use to us, it is legitimate insofar as the object of our judgement in some way deserves our praise or censure. There is a variety of such approaches. Attribution accounts treat the practice as a matter of attribution only. To hold someone morally responsible for an action just is to note a moral success or failure, as if it were an entry in a ledger. It is to judge a case on its merits without necessarily any commitment to acting on the judgement: either making the object of one's judgement accountable for their action in some way, or treating them as if they are answerable for their actions. Assignments of moral responsibility are, at base, merely an observation of the moral status of another.[6] The reactive attitudes – gratitude, blame, resentment, vengefulness, and so on – are not an essential part of the story, but something that may sometimes accompany assignments of moral responsibility and sometimes not.

Accountability theories of moral responsibility equate moral responsibility with accountability: that is, to be held morally responsible for an action is to be a fitting object of reactive attitudes (gratitude, blame, resentment, vengefulness, and so on). Holding another morally responsible for something they have done involves more than merely noting moral success and failure in a virtual ledger, it involves regarding the other as someone who merits praise, blame, reward, vengeance, resentment, and so on.[7] Moral responsibility is essentially an emotional affair.

Answerability theories of moral responsibility restrict assignment of moral responsibility to those in a position to evaluate their actions and thus in principle be answerable for them. Theories of this kind are well represented in the philosophical literature.[8] They appear plausible. It seems, for example, that we don't hold animals, people in a psychotic state, or small children morally responsible for their actions (or rather we should not) because they are not equipped to evaluate themselves and thus answer for themselves. Nonetheless, we argue in the final section of the chapter that answerability theories of moral responsibility are a poor way of understanding moral responsibility within international relations.

Philosophers have wrangled over the best account of moral responsibility, and disagree about what such an account must do, but it is worth keeping in mind the possibility that there are multiple conceptions of it and no single account that does justice to all our intuitions about the legitimate assignment of moral responsibility.[9] Philosophical theories of moral responsibility also tend to focus on individual persons. The question then arises as to how they might extend to non-persons such as institutions and groups. In international affairs, decisions can sometimes properly be assigned to an individual, to a leader, for example, but there are also cases in which decisions are the products of a group process. Can we hold a group morally responsible?

It might seem that moral responsibility is only properly assigned to individual persons because only individual persons have a centre of consciousness and can thus be said to have made a conscious decision to act. Without the decision being made consciously by an individual person, it may seem inappropriate to assign moral responsibility at all. There are, nonetheless, several good reasons for resisting this conclusion. First, it is not at all clear that individual human decisions are a matter of a singular consciousness exercising its powers for decision-making. Individuals often function much more like squabbling committees than authoritative, singular centres of consciousness. We do not restrict assignment of moral responsibility to cases where self-conflict and ambiguity are absent. Second, it is clear from the accounts of moral responsibility outlined above that philosophical theories of moral responsibility do not make essential use of the idea of an individual subject of decision-making.

A consequentialist theory sets store on the question of whether it is of any use to assign moral responsibility and this does not, by itself, preclude holding non-persons responsible for their actions. Attribution theory sets store on the viability of moral ascriptions. Can a non-person (e.g., a government) be said to have acted wrongly (e.g., by ordering the massacre of civilians)? This depends on our theory of moral ascription, but attribution theory does not, by itself, rule out holding non-persons responsible for actions. The same pattern is evident with other philosophical theories of moral responsibility. Whether it makes sense to hold a non-person accountable, in the sense developed by accountability theorists, will depend on our theory of the reactive attitudes. Are reactive attitudes (gratitude, blame, resentment and the like) appropriately directed at non-persons? We know they are directed in such ways, but is it appropriate to do so? It is likely that at least some such attitudes may be. Are non-persons evaluatively capable? Can they reflect upon and evaluate their actions? Can they be made answerable for them? This depends upon the body; but, conventionally understood, the very idea of holding another answerable is not restricted to persons.

The viability of holding non-persons morally responsible is not ruled out by philosophical theories of moral responsibility. The issue will turn on particulars about the case and on one's preferred account of moral responsibility. There is, however, an assumption underlying all philosophical accounts of moral responsibility. Only particular sorts of beings are legitimate objects of moral judgement; only particular sorts can be said to be morally responsible for anything at all. It is not individuality, subjectivity or consciousness, but agency that underpins validity of responsibility assignments. Something can be held morally responsible for what they do only if they genuinely *do* it. Again, something can be held morally responsible for what they do not do only if they are the sort of thing that could *do* it. We do not think a wild dog negligent because it fails to act in a reasonable manner; only creatures that could be reasonable are negligent when they are not. Wild dogs are not morally responsible for what they do or for what they negligently fail to do because they are not agents.

If moral discourse has a serious role to play in discussions of international affairs – beyond the biographical assessment of leaders and individual players – this is because institutions and groups operate as genuine agents. But do they? There are two main approaches we might take to answering this question. One is to develop a theory of agency and see if it applies in various cases. An alternative is to seek an understanding of agency at the very point at which it becomes important in international relations theory: the point at which explanation of events is sought. We discover agency, on this approach, when it forms an ineliminable part of the theoretical explanation of international events and patterns of events. This is the indirect route to understanding agency, and we follow it through in the remainder of this chapter.

Agency and explanatory structure

It is hard to make serious headway in the explanatory tasks central to international relations theory without placing the behaviour of actors centre stage. Actors in international affairs may be nation states, international bodies, sub-state actors, and so on. Anything counts as an actor if it has an enduring identity and is capable of doing something – producing an effect – in response to reasons. This is to say that anything counts as an actor if it behaves over time in a reason-responding way. When an actor evinces reason-responsive behaviour, we say that it acts as an agent.[10] As we discuss in the next section, realist theory and constructivist theory both presuppose a secure basis of agent explanation. Actors must be capable of agency, but not all actor behaviour is reducible to an exercise of agency. It follows that actor behaviour can be explained in agentive and non-agentive ways and we label these two forms of explanation: agent explanation and non-agent explanation, respectively. Agent explanation invokes reasons for action; non-agent explanation does not.

Agent explanation is an extraordinarily powerful explanatory strategy and is at the heart of interpretive social science just as it is at the heart or ordinary common-sense explanation as to why people do things. This does not mean that agent explanation suffices for an understanding of international affairs, merely that it is necessary. A grasp of many things is required for sufficient explanation: non-agentive production of behaviour; the efficacy, power, capability, or luck of actors; the epistemic condition of actors; the material conditions of their actions; unintended consequences of action; systemic and economic forces and that impinge upon and limit actions, and so on. It is in fact these other additional things are crucial to explanation in international affairs even though they may not be necessary in all circumstances. Nonetheless, agent explanation is an important and ineliminable part of the explanatory programme of international relations theory. It is an extension of very familiar patterns of explanation. Let us illustrate the basic form using simple examples drawn from folk psychology. Say that a person drives up to a carwash and lines up behind a sign promising something called "drive-through cleaning." Agent explanation invokes their reasons for doing this in order to explain their doing it. At its simplest, reasons for action are amalgams of beliefs and desires. The person desires their car cleaned as quickly and effortlessly as they can in their present circumstances. They believe that drive-through cleaning does exactly this and the way to get a drive-through cleaning is to line up behind the nearest sign promising one. They thus have a reason to line up their car behind the drive-through cleaning sign, and this reason causes their behaviour. Behaviour explained; mystery, such as it is, solved. Agent explanation of individual behaviour – a core component of what philosophers call "folk psychology" – is generally much more elaborate than this: we may appeal to a wide range of propositional attitudes (beliefs, desires, fears, hopes, intentions, and so on) in an attempt to identify the causes of actions in the most precise available terms. The simple story will suffice for our present purposes, however.

Reasons must be causes if this kind of reason-response interpretation of behaviour is to have explanatory power. Proffered reasons must track actual states of the agent (not hypothetical states) and they must track actual causal pathways leading to action. In agent explanation, actions are portrayed as responses to reasons and explanation succeeds just in case the relevant action really is a response to reasons. Let us alter our example to demonstrate the point. Say we are to pick up an important client, someone it is in our interest to impress and someone who would be distinctly unimpressed by a ride in a dirty car. In one sense, we have a reason to wash the car. In another sense, this reason need not move us at all. We may not have thought about it or we might not care all that much about impressing the client. There is a reason why we should wash the car, but this reason cannot cause our behaviour in the circumstances and so cannot be part of any satisfactory explanation of our behaviour.

Reasons in agent explanation must be causally efficacious, but they need not be entirely good or rational. Desiring to have their car washed, someone lines it up behind a sign that says "Drive-Through Cleaning Available Here" expecting someone to appear and instruct them on what to do. This might be a very bad bit of reasoning – they could wait a long time in the wrong spot, achieving nothing, having interpreted "Here" a bit too literally. They might even be making a mistake they have made many times in the past. Reasons for action aren't necessarily good reasons for action and reason responses can be far from logically perfect or epistemically satisfactory; they are not the same thing as utility-maximizing strategies, for example. Interpretive social science is not committed to a naïvely rationalistic picture of agency simply by dint of the logic of agent explanation.[11] It is an interesting and difficult question, however, just how far reason-response mechanisms can depart from norms of reasoning and remain part of *bona fide* agent explanation. There will come a point – we won't attempt a generic account of it – where the processes generating action are best characterized in non-agentive terms.

Non-agent explanation of everyday behaviour appeals to causes that are not reasons; causes that interact with the cognitive economy of the actor in ways that bypass reason-responding mechanisms. The two modes of explanation co-occur and it is often a mistake to offer explanation wholly in terms of just the one type. Nonetheless, there are cases in which non-agent explanation appears to dominate. For example, habits explain behaviour non-agentively. Most drivers (not all) acquire the habit of indicating when they intend to change lanes; it is something they do as part of an intentional act (lane-changing), but automatically. On a busy road, drivers have a reason to indicate lane-changes (they desire their safety and know that signalling lane changes is important to this safety), but indicating is not caused by these reasons. It is a habitual response to a decision to change lanes. Drivers will sometimes signal lane changes even when no other cars are near. A considerable amount of personal behaviour is best explained non-agentively. Someone slams the door because they are angry. Anger is a propositional attitude (typically, one is angry at someone on account of something), and we explain the door-slamming by citing this propositional attitude. Yet the door-slamming (the anger response) need not be a reason-response and thus need not be amenable to agent explanation. Even though a person is angry for a reason, they might not slam the door as a response to this reason. They might slam the door out of anger; or better, they might slam the door *in* anger. Of course, a person might also slam the door for a reason – say, to make it entirely clear how upset they are. Anger itself, however, does not supply a reason for door slamming and we offer a non-agent explanation of the door slamming when we cite merely the slammer's anger and dispense with any further purpose that might lie behind their door slamming. Consider the decision, made by Donald Trump's administration in 2017, to build a wall between the United States and Mexico. If this happened to be something done in anger, or out of resentment, then it would not be a reason response. It would not be done for a reason or in response to a reason (e.g., that certain people in the United States, or in the US administration, are angry or resentful). It would not be a political calculation as such, but a way of acting out of anger or resentment.

Non-agent explanations of actions do not cite reasons for action. Are we then not responsible for actions which can only be explained non-agentively? No, but the responsibility in such cases is indirect. Moral agents are responsible for what they have done, but also for what they should have done, and didn't. So if non-agent explanation characterizes a moral failing it does so because a reason to act has been negligently (culpably) overlooked. We are negatively responsible for habitual actions – for our acting out of bad habits – if we have negligently overlooked accessible reasons to act. Ignorance is not always a morally acceptable excuse for action if the ignorance itself is inexcusable.

According to psychoanalytic and much other psychological theory, there is a class of action explanation that appears to lie between agent and non-agent explanation. In psychoanalytic explanation of action, reasons translate into action much as they do in agent explanation, but psychoanalytic reasons are largely inaccessible (at least immediately and sometimes permanently) to agents themselves and, if pressed, agents typically disavow them and continue to do so unless therapy, or its equivalent, brings them to lucidity about their actions. Psychoanalytic reasons function within the cognitive economy of an agent in an agent-like way, thus making the agent's behaviour explicable (and inexplicable apart from such reasons). But psychoanalytic reasons do not integrate with the agent's rational self-understanding. Apart from such underlying psychological reasons, an agent's actions remain mysterious. According to psychoanalytic theory, processes of reason formation and maintenance also involve hermeneutical and strategic transformation: one desire is substituted for another; a disavowed belief causes action because it answers to a defensive need of which the agent is largely unaware; and so on.

Psychoanalytic action explanation extends familiar, folk conceptions of the production of reasons for action, but still has the structure of everyday agent explanation. To help clarify this, let us distinguish between accounts of the origin of action and accounts of the origin of reasons. Psychoanalytic action explanation adopts the standard agent-centred account of the origin of action, but adds its own twist to an account of the origin of reasons. (Because it adopts the standard agent-centred account of the origin of action it also integrates with the standard agent-centred account of moral responsibility. See our discussion at the end of the chapter.) Agent explanation is an account of the origin of action—an action becomes explicable because it is found to be caused by reasons. This still leaves unanswered a mountain of questions about reasons themselves. Reasons are sets of propositional attitudes: beliefs, desires, fears, intentions, plans, and so on. Why does an agent possess the propositional attitudes they do? Is the agent fully aware of their propositional attitudes? Do they avow them? Do they endorse them? Do the agent's propositional attitudes form a rational and coherent set? (Explaining them does not entail that they are a rational and coherent set.) Are they fixed by rational or conscious processes? If not, what processes do fix them? Why, in a particular circumstance, does one sub-set of an agent's propositional attitudes cause behaviour and not others? What role might an agent's choice play here? How much agent choice is authentic (that is, brought about by the engaged and reflective decision making activity of the agent)? How much caused by social factors – and in what ways? And so on. Agent explanation cites reasons for action, but it only counts as satisfactory explanation if it is offered in the context of a broad understanding of the nature and production of reasons themselves. We need not have precise answers to the above questions, but we need partial answers to many of them if the appeal to reasons for action is not to be hopelessly shallow.

Agency in realism and constructivism

Agent explanation cites reasons for action; good agent explanation provides a convincing account of the origin and nature of such reasons. How does this play out in international relations theory? Let us illustrate its relevance in terms of the contrast between constructivist and realist forms of explanation in international relations theory. Both realism and constructivism have complex histories within international relations scholarship, and both are developing apace. Nonetheless, we take as our paradigm those forms of realism and constructivism that emphasize a core explanatory project above all else. In realist terms, this is best captured in the neorealist tradition, a theoretical movement which seeks to isolate explanatory projects – for example, how states behave in an anarchic world system – from the moral interrogation of power often undertaken by classical realists and also from classical realist appeals to the virtues of statecraft virtues such as prudence.[12] The exclusive concentration on "scientific" explanation characteristic of neorealism has come under considerable critical scrutiny, but this does not mean that contemporary realists, such as reflexive realists, have dispensed with the explanatory resources of neorealism.[13] Constructivism is another umbrella term that covers a wide variety of approaches to international relations scholarship. Again, we restrict our discussion to constructivism as an explanatory paradigm first and foremost. The work of Alexander Wendt is paradigmatic for our purposes.[14] Recent work in constructivist international relations scholarship has moved away from an exclusive concentration on the explanatory tasks central to Wendt's programme. In particular, it has moved into a deeper engagement with the normative and critical interrogation of international affairs.[15]

Our point is that the core explanatory projects of realism and constructivism are central to the task of understanding the agency, and thus the moral responsibility, of international actors. On this view, realism and constructivism are, essentially, both ways of framing explanation of action by international actors. They share a fundamental assumption that international actors behave in sufficiently coherent and purposeful ways to count as agents for the business of explaining and predicting behaviour. The idea is that within the decision-making systems of states and other international actors there is a process parallel to the reason-responding processes operating within an individual's cognitive system – the processes generating a decision by an international actor are functionally equivalent, broadly speaking, to the reason-responding processes that operate within us all. We think that realists share this explanatory framework with constructivists. Realists and constructivists both assume that international actors act for reasons and the key to understanding their actions is to identify these reasons and track down their origins. If there is a substantial dispute between realists and constructivists, and we think there clearly is, it is about the nature and origin of reasons for action – it is about how to understand the nature and origin of the most significant reasons causing the behaviour of international actors.

Realists emphasize the constitution of reasons for action through abiding, fixed interests of the chief actors. (This is not to deny that, at times, short-term interest or desires predominate over longer-term interests.) The primary interest in all cases is survival. Even self-consciously systemic or game-theoretic forms of realism, such as Waltz's, presuppose the agentive behaviour of actors faced, say, with a security dilemma.[16] Constructivists – at least, those who frame their theories in terms of identity – emphasize the social, reflexive and contingent process of identity formation for international actors and the relativization of reasons for action to identity: what an international actor thinks is in its interests will depend on the identity it operates under. How it pursues its interests, and whether in fact it does pursue them, depends upon the sort of body it understands itself to be. Thus understood, realism and constructivism are contrasting (but not necessarily incompatible) explanatory strategies, based on contrasting ways of understanding state actors. It is, of course, possible (indeed probable) that both strategies are successful: in different ways and in different circumstances. At the same time, they do represent contrasting overarching views of the way international affairs are to be understood. Realists frame explanation of action in terms of the playing out of the constitutive and material interests of actors. (A constitutive interest, by realist lights, is an interest in something necessary for the continued existence and integrity of the actor; a material interest is an interest in the well-being of the actor.) They needn't deny the causal influence of a wide range of other sorts of interests and motives – including those that come about in ways constructivists claim. Realists aren't required to deny such things exist; they deny that non-realist motives are causally crucial and hence they abstract away from such motives. Realist accounts of the international system are idealized models, abstracting away from the great bulk of causal factors to isolate the ones realists think are causally dominant. Realist and constructivists differ in emphasis, but the difference is marked and significant. Realists depart from the truth by simplifying the phenomena they examine. Indeed, they are in the business of doing so. This isn't necessarily a flaw. Realist models of the international system do not *mirror* actual international affairs any more than physical models of ideal gases mirror real gases. Nonetheless, realist models make strong claims about the predominant causal power of certain constitutive and material interests of actors, interests, they claim, that are highly resistant to social re-configuring or re-imagining.

Constructivists, by contrast, think that this is only a partial picture. Sometimes international actors are motivated by constitutive and material interests; sometimes they are motivated in other ways. How they are motivated is not pre-determined by such interests. Reasons for action are a hermeneutic phenomenon: what counts as a reason depends upon the meaning one attributes to one's situation, one's goals, one's identity, the norms one subscribes to, and so on. Hermeneutic phenomena are, at least in part, social, inter-subjective phenomena. They are constructed, not pre-given. Now if this way of framing constructivism is broadly correct, it suggests an interesting way of re-interpreting realism. Realism isn't necessarily a naïve refusal to acknowledge the social and inter-subjective character of identity formation; it is an exercise in the hermeneutics of suspicion. According to realists, the elaborate self-conceptions of international actors hide some brutal truths. The causally dominant motives of international actors come from a slender range of realist options. If an international actor's self-conception is at odds with their realist motives, the realist motives tend to win out and a more or less elaborate cover-story is constructed to deal with the resulting cognitive dissonance. (Constructivists can make a parallel hermeneutical move: an actor's self-conception can win out over avowed realist motives with a similar cover-story erected to deal with cognitive dissonance.) If a nation-state conceives of itself as a good international citizen, as a force for international justice and good order, it may well find its self-conception clashing with its realist motives—and losing out to them. In this case, the realist motives tend to win out and the self-conception protected with blather. For example, the United States' refusal to participate in the International Criminal Court is probably motivated by genuine self-interest (narrowly understood in realist terms), but defence of its refusal tends to go further than acknowledging this self-interest. It tends to aver, instead, to flaws within the ICC or to US exceptionalism.[17] This is *post-hoc* rationalization.

Post-hoc rationalization looks very much like a reason-response, mirrors it in form, but does not cause action. It is a cover story. And it protects the self-conception that the US (both state actors and many ordinary people in the US) have of themselves.

None of this is to suggest that the realists win the argument with constructivists or that there is no prospect of an accommodation of both realist and constructivist insights. The argument, as we see it, is about the predominance of causal influences. International actors act for reasons. To what extent does the production of causally dominant reasons for action answer to constitutive and material interests (as realists claim), interests that will remain motivationally potent no matter how self-conceptions develop and transform? That's a question well beyond the scope of this chapter (and the competence of its authors), but it is a real question, deserving of a real answer. And the answer is by no means obvious. There is, however, a third option, and we want to very briefly highlight it. Realists give us one kind of hermeneutics of suspicion, but there are others. Recall that psychoanalytic explanation of action has two aspects: disavowal of certain beliefs, desires and other action-producing propositional attitudes, and the hermeneutic transformation of the content of these attitudes (so that one belief comes to substitute for another; one desire for another). Realists help themselves to the first of these, but the second may also operate. In this case, actors act for reasons they sincerely disavow, but also for reasons that function in a disguised or substitutive way.[18] For example, the United States invades and subjugates Iraq, not in self-knowing pursuit of its real interests, but in a substitutive defensive gesture. Iraq substitutes for Al-Qaeda; terrorist threats substitute for a symbolic threat to US self-satisfaction. The aim is to act as if one can strike at one's enemies by substituting enemies in search of neurotic satisfaction.[19] So there are at least three ways that agency might play out in international affairs. International actors might operate as sincere agents of identity; as (perhaps insincere) agents of constitutive and material self-interest; or as neurotic agents whose satisfactions are achieved by disavowed, substitutive means. Usually the three are combined albeit with one strand dominant.

Institutional agency, answerability and moral responsibility

Agency through institutions and groups is in play when the best explanation of actions ascribed to them cites reasons operative within the institution or group. These may be shared reason-responses (desires, beliefs, plans, and other attitudes shared by individual members of the group) or systematic reason-responses that emerge from interactions between parts of the group. In the latter case, one part of the organization may set objectives (desires), another develop plans (intentions), another implement them, another review them, another coordinate the other parts, and so on. It might be that no individual element of the whole is fully morally responsible for the actions of the group (though they are likely responsible for the part they play within the group), whereas the group itself, insofar as it is rightly recognized as an agent, is morally responsible for what it has done.

Moral responsibility is a complex phenomenon. Depending upon the account of moral responsibility one finds persuasive or relevant to the case in hand, it involves attributions of moral credit or fault; it elicits appropriate reactive attitudes; it depends upon the evaluative capacities of those held responsible, upon their answerability to us. It makes sense to hold a state or non-state actor morally responsible, from a consequentialist perspective, only if the practice of doing so is overall beneficial: if, in one way or another, the practice improves our lot. The general key is agency. If state and non-state actors are really operating as agents, then they satisfy at least one basic condition upon assignments of moral responsibility: that they are capable of being reason-responsive.

However, answerability accounts of moral responsibility – ones that tie moral responsibility to capacities to be answerable for one's actions – pose a special problem for attributions of institutional responsibility. We are answerable for things that we have the capacity to reflect upon, understand the rights and wrongs of, and respond to others about. But what of dysfunctional institutions whose structures preclude evaluative reflection? Consider an institution of which every part is compelled to act without an understanding, and hence consideration, of the whole. Such an institution doesn't have the capacity to respond to others in a coherent manner. Is the institution to escape moral censure because of this? To do so would be to treat it as a broken piece of institutional machinery, as something that needs fixing or combating, but not morally criticizing. The most effective response to this possibility may well be to reject answerability accounts of moral responsibility. If a body acts on reasons – or fails to act on reasons available to it – then it is morally responsible for what it does. Whether it is capable of responding to moral criticism in the way we would like it to be is another matter altogether. It merits the criticism anyway. What often reinforces this judgement is the view that such broken institutions are themselves responsible for their breakdown.

Rejection of answerability theories of moral responsibility also helps to reconcile moral responsibility with psychoanalytically grounded action. If an institution, or indeed a person, is incapable, as things stand, of understanding the grounds upon which they act – the grounds upon which would be answerable to others – this needn't negate our holding them responsible for what they do. Neurotic self-defence and ideological stupefaction do not turn moral agents into broken machines. Consider the example introduced earlier. The United States invaded and subjugated Iraq in 2003. We suggest that it did so as a neurotic, substitutive gesture; that the real reasons for the invasion were not as announced. It is possible, though we have no grounds for thinking so, that the real reasons for the decision to invade Iraq were inaccessible to the major players (though easily accessible to others trained to know what to look for). Of course, it might well be that the institutions responsible for the decision were perfectly capable of reflecting on the merits of what they were doing, were capable of answering for them lucidly, but choose not to do so for political reasons. Nonetheless, imagine that the stupefaction of substituted desire overwhelms an institution and its leading members. Imagine that it thoroughly undermines the institution's capacity for lucid reflection on the issue. Critics can point to the underlying, disavowed purposes behind its actions, but those answerable for the institution's actions are incapable of appreciating what they say. In such a case, should we concede that neurotic stupefaction absolves the institution of moral responsibility for what it has done? It is better to say that we are, individuals and institutions alike, responsible for what we do irrespective of our capacities to lucidly answer for our actions. If we respond to reasons, we are morally responsible for what we do. If we negligently overlook pressing reasons to act or not act, we are morally responsible for what we do. With agency comes moral responsibility.

Notes

1 Toni Erskine, "Locating Responsibility: The Problem of Moral Agency in International Relations," *Oxford Handbook of International Relations*, edited by Christian Reus-Smit and Duncan Snidal, 2009. 10.1093/oxfordhb/9780199219322.003.0041.

2 For influential philosophical treatments of collective responsibility, see Joel Feinberg, "Collective Responsibility," *Journal of Philosophy*, 65: 674–688, 1968; Peter French, *Collective and Corporate Responsibility*, New York: Columbia University Press, 1984; Margaret Gilbert, *Joint Commitment*, Oxford: Oxford University Press, 2013; Larry May, *The Morality of Groups*, Notre Dame: University of Notre Dame Press, 1987. Examples of the discussion in international relations include Neta Crawford, *Accountability for Killing: Moral Responsibility for Collateral Damage in America's post-9/11 Wars*, Oxford:

Oxford University Press, 2013; Erskine, "'Coalitions of the Willing' and the Shared Responsibility to Protect," in *Distribution of Responsibilities in International Law*, edited by André Nollkaemper and Dov Jacobs, pp. 227–264, Cambridge: Cambridge University Press, 2015.

3 Backwards-looking responsibility (the responsibility bodies have for their past actions) and forward-looking responsibility (the responsibility bodies possess in virtue of being responsible for certain matters in the future) are distinct notions, but they are interconnected. Forward-looking responsibility entails future backwards-looking responsibility. There is no investing a body with ongoing responsibility unless one is also to hold the body responsible, in the future, for success or failure in the discharge of these responsibilities. For discussion of forward-looking responsibility, see the special issue edited by Peter French and Howard Wettstein, "Forward-Looking Collective Responsibility," *Midwest Studies in Philosophy*, 38, 2014.

4 For an overview of current philosophical approaches to moral responsibility, see Andrew Eshleman, "Moral Responsibility," *Stanford Encyclopedia of Philosophy*, 2014. https://plato.stanford.edu/entries/moral-responsibility/

5 Philosophers who defend a consequentialist account of moral responsibility include: Jack Smart, "Free Will, Praise, and Blame," *Mind*, 70: 291–306, 1961; Daniel Dennett, *Elbow Room*, Cambridge, MA: MIT Press, 1984, chapter 7; Joel Kupperman, *Character*, New York: Oxford University Press, 1991, chapter 3; Manuel Vargas, *Building Better Beings: A Theory of Moral Responsibility*, New York: Oxford University Press, 2013, chapter 6.

6 Philosophers who defend an attribution account of moral responsibility include: Joel Feinberg, *Doing and Deserving: Essays in the Theory of Responsibility*, Princeton: Princeton University Press, 1970; Jonathan Glover, *Responsibility*, New York: Humanities Press, 1970; Michael Zimmerman, *An Essay on Moral Responsibility*, Totowa, NJ: Rowman and Littlefield, 1988.

7 Accountability theories of moral responsibility are defended by, among others, R. Jay Wallace, *Responsibility and the Moral Sentiments*, Cambridge, MA: MIT Press, 1994; Gary Watson, "Two Faces of Responsibility," *Philosophical Topics*, 24: 227–248, 1996; John Martin Fischer and Mark Ravizza, *Responsibility and Control: A Theory of Moral Responsibility*, Cambridge: Cambridge University Press, 1998; Stephen Darwell, *The Second-Person Standpoint: Morality, Respect, and Accountability*, Cambridge, MA: Harvard University Press, 2006.

8 The answerability account of moral responsibility is defended by Thomas Scanlon, *What We Owe to Each Other*, Cambridge, MA: Harvard University Press, 1998; and Angela Smith, "Attributability, Answerability, and Accountability: In Defense of a Unified Account," *Ethics*, 1222: 575–589, 2012.

9 On this possibility, see Thomas Nagel, *The View from Nowhere*, New York: Oxford University Press, 1986; Ted Honderich, *A Theory of Determinism: The Mind, Neuroscience, and Life Hopes*, Vol. 2, Oxford: Clarendon Press, 1988; Saul Smilansky, *Free Will and Illusion*, New York: Oxford University Press, 2000.

10 For an account of the current state of play in discussions of reasons for action, see Maria Alverez, "Reasons for Action: Justification, Motivation, Explanation," *Stanford Encyclopedia of Philosophy*, 2016. https://plato.stanford.edu/entries/reasons-just-vs-expl/

11 The commitment we describe here – to the power and ubiquity of agent explanation of action – is weaker than commitment to methodological rationalism. As James Fearon and Alexander Wendt put it, rationalism in international relations refers "variously to formal and informal applications of rational choice theory to IR questions, to any work drawing on the tradition of microeconomic theory from Alfred Marshall to recent developments in evolutionary game theory, or most broadly to any 'positivist' exercise in explaining foreign policy by reference to goal-seeking behavior." Fearon and Wendt, "Rationalism v. Constructivism: A Skeptical View," in Carlsnaes, Risse and Simmons (eds.), *Handbook of International Relations*, London: Sage Publications, 2002, p. 54. Rationalism in the first of the two senses set out here makes claims about the explanatory power of rationality assumptions that go well beyond a commitment to agent explanation as such.

12 Kenneth Waltz is the paradigm example of the realist we have in mind.

13 For a discussion of reflexive realism, see Brent J. Steele, "Eavesdropping on Honored Ghosts: From Classical to Reflexive Realism," *Journal of International Relations and Development*, 10: 272–300, 2009.

14 For example, Alexander Wendt, "Anarchy Is What States Make of It: The Social Construction of Power Politics," *International Organization*, 46: 391–425, 1992.

15 An example is of this ethical turn in constructivist scholarship is Richard Price's edited volume *Moral Limit and the Possibility in World Politics*, Cambridge: Cambridge University Press, 2008.

16 Kenneth Waltz, *Theory of International Politics*, Reading, MA: Addison-Wesley, 1979.

17 Hilary Clinton, for example, speaking in 2005: "the United States has global responsibilities that create unique circumstances. For example, we are more vulnerable to the misuse of an international criminal court because of the international role we play and the resentments that flow from that ubiquitous presence around the world." http://www.amicc.org/docs/Clinton%202_13_05.pdf, accessed 30.5.2012.

18 The disavowal of deeply held reasons for acting implies the fragility and instability of the ego, and the myth of the ego as a self-contained, unified and transparent source of reason. As Ty Solomon argues, the myth of the unified and transparent ego lies behind many explanatory failures of constructivism, in particular, why some identity-conferring constructs are successful over others. Ty Solomon, *The Politics of Subjectivity in American Foreign Policy Discourses*, Ann Arbour: Michigan University Press, 2015.

19 For more on this example, and on psychoanalytic explanation of group behaviour, see Damian Cox, Michael Levine and Saul Newman, *Politics Most Unusual: Violence, Sovereignty and Democracy in the 'War on Terror'*, London: Palgrave Macmillan, 2009, chapters 2 and 7. See also Ty Solomon (2015), and Yannis Stavrakakis and Nikos Chrysoloras, "(I can't get no) Enjoyment: Lacanian Theory and the Analysis of Nationalism," *Psychoanalysis, Culture and Society*, 11: 144–163 for an examination of somewhat similar ideas through a Lacanian lens.

PART II

International relations theory

INTERNATIONAL RELATIONS THEORY

What place for ethics?

Fiona Robinson

Introduction

As the new millennium approached, the journal of the British International Studies Association, *Review of International Studies*, published a special issue called 'The Eighty Years' Crisis'. Referencing E. H. Carr's most famous book, the special issue sought to survey the discipline's development over the eighty years since it was first placed in an academic setting. One of the articles in that special issue is Mervyn Frost's 'A Turn Not Taken: Ethics and IR at the Millennium'. In that article, Frost takes stock of the role of ethical argument in international relations (IR) theory. He is none too pleased with what he sees. Indeed, Frost concludes that, in the main, IR theorists have yet to engage with normative theory properly so called.[1] While Frost blames this primarily on the 'positivist bias in the discipline', he finds that even scholars who question the 'fact/value distinction' still fail to engage in 'detailed normative theorizing about what ought to be done'.[2] While critical theorists believe that so-called 'facts' are always constituted by 'values', their analyses are still largely 'descriptivist'. They fail to tackle the question 'What would it be ethical to do in the circumstances?'[3]

In this essay, I will address some of Frost's claims as part of a general attempt to survey the current role and place of ethics and moral theorizing in IR theory, focusing specifically on the period since the publication of Frost's essay to the present day. I will argue that, in this roughly twenty-year period, there have been significant developments in the field which speak directly both to the role and significance of positivism and to questions of moral judgement and evaluation. Ethics and moral analysis are more important than ever in IR, but it is still the case that only a relatively small group of scholars are in the business of answering the question 'What would it be ethically appropriate to do in these circumstances?' I will suggest that this represents not a failure to engage in 'true' moral analysis, but rather a maturing of the field, and a more astute understanding of the complex relationship between ethics and politics in the global context.

Realism, ethics, and the 'science' of international relations

Despite these developments, however, there still exists a widely held assumption that 'ethics' can be of little or no relevance in the arena of international politics. We can find this view among members of the 'real' world of foreign policy, diplomacy, transnational conflict, and global political economy, as well as in the more traditional corners of 'International Relations' as an academic discipline. Although we can and should assume that the 'real world' and the academy are intimately interrelated—that the latter is informed by the former, and that the former is, in part, constituted by the latter—it is primarily the scholarly field of IR with which this introduction is concerned.

There are two oft-cited explanations for this apparent disjuncture between ethics and IR. The first, pace Frost, points to the dominance of positivism—a methodological approach that upholds the 'fact–value' distinction—and thereby eschews consideration of ethics or moral judgement. The second explanation refers to the discipline's dominant theory—realism—and its position that 'moral judgements have no place in discussions of international affairs or foreign policy'.[4] While both of these explanations have some basis in the existing literature and the development of the field, they both rely on rather narrow definitions—of *realism* and of *ethics*—leading to almost caricatured positions that rely on crude dichotomies rather than complex relationships.

Much criticism in IR has targeted positivism over the past few decades. In 2004, Steve Smith argued that the discipline has been very much focused on providing narrowly defined social science accounts of international relations. An effect of this domination, Smith added, was the 'downplaying' of normative questions, seeing these as in some way lying outside of the realm of 'legitimate' social science.[5] At the source of all of this is 'positivism', which Smith defines as a methodological position reliant on an empiricist epistemology that grounds our knowledge of the world in justification by (ultimately brute) experience.[6] While its proponents argue that this approach leads to the development of testable and value-free social scientific knowledge, critics argue that this dominant method in the mainstream IR academic community is producing a discipline that is marked by 'political assumptions masquerading as technical ones'.[7]

Of all the theories guided by this positivist methodological position, realism has been, by far, the most dominant and pervasive. While there are many varieties of realism—with varying degrees of loyalty to positivism—it has been American neorealism, and later neoclassical realism, which has defined the discipline and been most faithful to value-free theorizing—and thus most hostile to consideration of ethics. Neo-realism—widely associated with the work of Kenneth Waltz—is best characterized as an explanatory theory which shows how the interaction of states generates an (anarchical) structure that constrains them from taking certain actions and disposes them toward taking others. Thus, it explains what it understands as a tendency towards war in the international system, and why 'the style and substance of international politics have remained strikingly constant since the birth of the modern state system in 1658'.[8]

Of course, it should be noted that not all realists subscribe to this economistic understanding of the tradition. The so-called 'classical realism' of Thucydides and Machiavelli engages with moral philosophy and sought to reconstruct an understanding of virtue in light of practice and historical circumstance.[9] Later classical realists such as Hans J. Morgenthau believed that anarchy could be mitigated by wise leadership, and that leaders ignored moral principles in the pursuit of power at their peril.[10] As Brent Steele argues, the works of contemporary realists such as Richard Ned Lebow, Anthony Lang, Jr, and Michael C. Williams have revived some important and obscured ideas from classical realists, thereby 'recovering certain practical ethics proving important for contemporary world politics'.[11]

That said, many US realists in the Waltzian tradition—including John Mearsheimer, Stephen Walt, and Randall Schweller—have regularly and vociferously criticized attempts to bring values or ethics into theorizing international politics. In his contribution to a forum on Andrew Linklater's *The Transformation of Political Community*, Randall Schweller condemns Linklater for arguing by 'fiat' rather than by the weight of hard evidence, and for offering a vision that relies on 'slippery, undefined and unmeasured concepts like globalisation and fragmentation'.[12] In his critique, he outlines clearly his view on why the normative theorist has nothing to offer to the analysis of international politics:

> [T]he task of the normative theorist is to imagine possible, if not entirely plausible, other worlds. Practitioners of international politics, however, understand that foreign policy is too serious a business to entertain utopian ideas about dramatically reconstructed social relations.[13]

It is on this basis that he defends neorealism as the most coherent, elegant, and powerful theoretical perspective that addresses the central issues of the field, *viz*., war and peace, conflict, and cooperation.[14]

Notably, other contributors to this forum, such as R. B. J. Walker, are equally frustrated with Linklater's normative account. Of course, Walker would subscribe neither to Schweller's rather crude account of international politics nor with his suggestions regarding the tools we must use to analyse it. Walker is critical of Linklater's normative analysis, not for its 'utopianism', but rather for its tendency to reproduce the dichotomies between the universal and the particular, the real and the ideal, instead of thinking productively about how to rearticulate the relationship between universality and particularity.[15] For Walker, then, the task is not to replay the same 'tired moves over and over again'. Rather, it is to ask how this set of 'impossible alternatives was set up in the first place'.[16] This critique points to a fissure within critical IR theory regarding the possibility (and dangers) of finding secure ground for moral judgement in international politics.

Values, ethics, and critical theory

If normative moral theory is the antithesis of IR positivism (especially 'realist' positivism), then what is critical IR theory? Where does it fit in this debate between 'value-free' social science and normative theorizing? Even a perfunctory overview of the literature tells us that critical theory exists in its own, separate battle with realism and positivism. Like 'normative theorists', critical theorists point out that the 'moral cartography of realism' has legitimized the evacuation of ethical concerns from international relations; however, they also suggest that this 'moral cartography' has circumscribed the 'ethics and international affairs' literature that seeks to redress the moral lacunae of the field.[17] In this literature, David Campbell and Michael Shapiro argue, the dilemmas of ethical theorizing are generally posed in terms of ameliorating or overcoming, rather than contesting or problematizing, the parameters of anarchy and sovereignty.[18]

Of course, critical theory is a broad church, and different approaches that fall under that wide umbrella would take radically different positions on the nature of ethics, and—in particular—on the possibilities of moral judgement and 'emancipation'. Indeed, the rise of constructivism in IR—especially the literature that explores the role of 'norms' in international politics—can be seen, at least in part, as a response to the dominance of positivism, especially in IR in the United States. But constructivism cannot always be classified as a *critical* theory, since it does not necessarily reject positivism as an epistemological and methodological position, and its interest in norms in IR does not always translate into an explicitly *normative* analysis of the status of those norms. Versions of constructivism that are self-consciously critical, moreover, find that their conclusions reveal tensions between traditional rationalist notions of ethics, on the one hand, and constructivist methodological principles, on the other. As Richard Price asks:

> How does one even approach the task of formulating robust answers to questions of ethics that can respond to charges of subjectivism and relativism when coming out of an intellectual tradition that suggests all such judgements and the complexes of inter-subjective meanings that make them possible are themselves but time- and culture-bound constructions?[19]

This is, in fact, a key epistemological question that goes to the heart of the nature of morality and the status of moral judgement, and which confronts all critical theorists in their engagement with ethics. Thus, we see that Critical Theorists[20] informed by the work of Jürgen Habermas and the Frankfurt School are explicitly and self-consciously 'emancipatory' in their theorizing; Andrew Linklater's work on 'men', 'citizens', and the possibilities for post-Westphalian cosmopolitanism are premised on both an immanent critique of Westphalian citizenship and a faith in the 'force of the better argument' to set out a path towards a cosmopolitan future. Ken Booth's critical theory is also based upon moral universalism; his self-described 'utopian realism' (later renamed 'emancipatory realism') seeks to reclaim Enlightenment ideas in the changing international and global context.[21] Poststructural approaches, by contrast, rely on understandings of ethics in the work of thinkers such as Levinas and Foucault and are much more sceptical about epistemologically secure moral judgement, arguing instead for the need to 'repoliticize' ethical thinking.

As Kimberly Hutchings argues, there is a tension within critical theory between so-called emancipatory or progressive approaches that offer an objective basis for positive transformation and those that question the possibility of any grounded, meaningful judgement at all.[22] Her recent work has also highlighted the hierarchical and exclusive nature of moral reasoning through rationalist–universalist ethics and has pointed to the importance of the postcolonial and decolonial theory in making vulnerable the once-safe position of the moral judge.[23] While Hutchings does not deny the possibility of moral judgement, her critical-theoretical approach entreats the moral theorist to engage with alternative moral imaginaries in ways that 'complicate and expand' her ability to make judgements.[24]

Despite their engagement with 'the ethical', Frost argues that the work of critical theorists (or 'post-positivists') in IR is largely 'sociological' and thus not normative; it has given us 'rich accounts of the complex social structures within which we are constituted and within which we act', and 'stress[es] the important role which normative considerations play in the practices which we study and in our practices of scholarship themselves'.[25] But Frost maintains that, once again, their work fails to take on that most important normative question of all, 'In what would a just world order consist?'[26] One of the contributions of critical theory to ethics in IR, however, lies in revealing the ways and extent to which positivist IR theories, and their so-called 'value-free' accounts of world politics, are themselves laden with normative judgements about what is right, good, and even just.

New paradigms and emerging work

The existence of these many tensions surrounding the place of ethics in IR theory has led to several important developments in the discipline over the past two decades. While many of the same substantive issues tend to dominate—the ethics of war, the moral challenges of poverty and inequality across borders—a combination of rapid change in the nature of these phenomena, combined with theoretical innovations on the relations between ethics and politics in the global context, have resulted in exciting and challenging new work in the field. In this final section, I will focus on three key themes in contemporary ethics and IR: rethinking the ethics of war;

theorizing global justice beyond the distributive paradigm; and understanding the emergence and proliferation of non-liberal or 'alternative' cosmopolitanisms.

Rethinking the ethics of war

Michael Walzer's *Just and Unjust Wars* (1977) revived a centuries-old tradition of theorizing on the ethics of waging and fighting war. It was, explicitly, a response to the moral quagmire that was the Vietnam War—a war that Walzer later described as having been fought 'badly, brutally, as if there were no moral limits'.[27] Vietnam, and Walzer's book, took just war theory (JWT) from the places to which it had been relegated—religion departments and theological seminaries—and into to IR.[28] The book's major argument was also explicitly 'against Realism'—against the general account of war as a realm of necessity and duress.[29]

Recent events in international politics—most notably the end of the Cold War and the 9/11 attacks—have prompted IR scholars to rethink the nature of warfare, as well as the approaches to ethics that must be brought to bear. The result has been not so much another revival of JWT, but rather a rethinking of its relevance in the light of the contemporary world order. In 2003, Neta Crawford asked whether the JWT framework was still useful in the light of the US 'counterterror war'. While she raises a host of conceptual and practical problems that arise at the intersection of JWT and counterterror war, she argues that it remains a useful method of inquiry—if only because it provides a discursive framework for making ethical arguments about a practice that is resistant to the importance of argumentation.[30] Indeed, this claim seems to lie behind a number of recent works on JWT, which address new actors in war,[31] new techniques of warfare,[32] as well as the question of justice after war.[33]

Laura Sjoberg's important book, *Justice, Gender and the Wars in Iraq*, addresses the relationship between feminist perspectives on war and JWT.[34] A key contribution to both feminist IR theory and the literature on the ethics of war, Sjoberg develops a sustained critique of JWT from the perspective of feminism. Unlike some feminist pacifists, Sjoberg does not condemn war as such; rather, she argues for a 'feminist security ethic' as a basis for rewriting the just war tradition to deal with the political conflicts of the twenty-first century.[35] While Sjoberg is clearly attempting to 'trouble' the gendered script of warfare—including 'ethical' and humanitarian warfare—even feminist critics worry that her 'highly demanding criteria' for just war could only actually be met in a world in which the 'gendered discriminations that underpin the legitimation of war were no longer being made'.[36]

To make ethical arguments about war and warfare is to invite criticism: realists will claim that war is immune to ethical argument, and critical theorists will claim that JWT amounts to little more than a justification of war as a means of doing politics. As political violence continues to transform and escalate, however, normative theorists will continue to interrogate the ways in which forms of ethical argumentation can serve not only to justify, but also to limit, that violence.

Justice beyond distribution

Like Walzer's *Just and Unjust Wars*, it is difficult to over-estimate the influence of John Rawls's *A Theory of Justice* on thinking and research on ethics in IR.[37] While it is widely understood that Rawls shaped the direction of contemporary Anglo-American political philosophy, his work was also of great significance in the early literature on ethics and international relations. In *Political Theory and International Relations* (1999), Charles Beitz argued that the demands of distributive justice do not stop at the borders of the nation-state; the basic facts of economic interdependence and the geographical distribution of natural resources are reasons why rational actors in Rawls's 'original position' would recognize the need for *international* distributive justice.[38] After Beitz, there followed a long list of books on global distributive justice in the liberal-cosmopolitan tradition, including Pogge's *World Poverty and Human Rights* (2008) and Simon Caney's *Justice Beyond Borders* (2005).[39]

As Monique Deveaux and Kathryn Walker argue, the distributive approach has been useful in fostering discussion about how to design more just transnational economic and political arrangements, as well as about the duties that citizens of affluent countries should assume. Important as this work has been, however, they point out that the distributive framework has certain limits, including both the focus on North–South redistribution of resources and the side-stepping of questions of gender injustice in the global context.[40] The former limitation means that these accounts of justice, by reinforcing identities of 'Western saviours' and 'Third World victims' often produce and reinforce the relations of domination that they seek to address.[41]

Feminists have been among the most vocal critics of conventional accounts of global distributive justice, pointing out that attention to the gender dimensions of global justice necessarily means challenging the basic assumptions of global distributive justice as a paradigm. For example, as Alison Jaggar has argued, attention to global gender justice requires a rethinking of the domain of justice, to include households and families—thereby recognizing the extent to which they are affected directly by developments at the global level.[42] Feminist approaches to ethics—including the feminist ethics of care—help to reveal aspects of the global political economy which are usually not 'seen' at all: the differing and constantly changing responsibilities for caring work within the household and the community; the global distribution of caring work; and the underprovision for care and of resources for caring work globally.[43]

Critical cosmopolitanisms

Cosmopolitanism is the standard 'ethical' position on international politics—in so far as it is seen to articulate the morally good account of 'one humanity' in contrast to the self-interested statism of 'real' international politics. This view was reinforced at the end of the 'short twentieth century', which was marked by a post-Cold War triumphalism that sought to reassert Western liberalism under the guise of a 'new' cosmopolitanism.[44] In response to this moral universalism, critical thinking on ethics and international relations began moving towards a greater recognition of the complicity of liberal-universalist–rationalist ethics in perpetuating the injustices that lead to inequalities, exclusion, and conflict. Of particular note was the critical thinking on cosmopolitanism—much of it emerging from postcolonial thought—which served as a counterpoint to the liberal cosmopolitanism of the post-Cold War order.

Postcolonial theorist Siba Grovogui argues that, by imagining the world through mere generalizations of 'Western' experiences, some cosmopolitans entertain the fantasy that universal norms and institutions arise solely from Western philosophical systems and ontological categories.[45] In 2007, Vivienne Jabri articulated a convincing alternative to liberal cosmopolitanism based on a political solidarity; she argued that this political cosmopolitanism takes seriously the postcolonial critique of modernity's legacy in the perpetuation of inequality and enables a conception of the universal that is not complicit in such relations.[46] More recently, in 2012, Jabri developed this idea of cosmopolitanism as a normative discourse that serves to enable certain kinds of practices by exploring the relationship between the disciplinary cosmopolitanism of government with the solidarist cosmopolitanism of politics.[47]

James Brassett explores the possibility of a cosmopolitan response to traumatic events like 9/11. While sympathetic to what he calls 'cosmopolitan sentiments', Brasset argues that ethics must be understood as 'embodied social practice that should be understood and engaged via the political question of how we govern'.[48] In a similar rejection of moral rationalism, Renee Jeffrey argues for a 'sentimentalist cosmopolitan ethic' which highlights the indispensable role played by emotions in making moral judgements and motivating ethical actions.[49] Notably, scholars may see Jeffrey's work as part of a wider emerging literature on emotion in IR, which has sought both to explain the absence of emotions in IR theory and to consider particular emotions—fear, guilt, hatred, and (even) love—and the roles they play in the discourses and practices of international politics.[50]

Finally, Anthony Burke seeks to apply a critical cosmopolitanism to the sphere of global security. As part of a larger body of work on 'ethical security studies', Burke's 'security cosmopolitanism' seeks to 'extend and innovate' the body of work in IR on cosmopolitanism to the problems of global security.[51] While still relying heavily on Kantian moral principles, Burke argues that insecurity in the global system 'arises out of' modernity as a function of its histories, choices, powers, relations, and systems.[52]

Conclusion

All IR theories tell us something about the nature and place of ethics in politics. Sustained reflection on the place of ethics in international relations, however, raises questions and reveals tensions. Dominant theoretical perspectives and methodologies in IR seem to discount the role of ethics; this is reinforced by a widespread perception that the world of 'politics'—especially international politics—is either amoral or immoral. The realm of ethics is typically seen as a higher realm of principles that can be 'applied' to politics in order to mitigate the worst excesses of self-interest and power.

This is the view of ethics that informs Frost's telling of the story of ethics in IR. When he castigates positivists, realists, constructivists, and critical theorists for not really 'doing' ethics, he is expressing frustration at the extent to which their theories complicate the place of ethics and the ethical theorist. The ability to answer Frost's question—what would it be ethically appropriate to do in these circumstances?—requires an 'ethics first' approach in which the subjects and objects of ethical theorizing are already set in place. Very often, these categories are constituted through prior notions of gender, and deeply tied to a prior history of conquest and subjugation. The answer to this kind of ethics in IR is not a realist–positivist refusal to engage with morality, but rather a careful interrogation of different social–moral systems at a range of scales—from the local to the global—tied to a deep reflexivity regarding the role of the moral theorist, and of the role of moral and IR theory in shaping world politics.

Notes

1 Mervyn Frost, 'A Turn Not Taken: Ethics in IR at the Millennium,' *Review of International Studies*, 24, no. 5 (1998): 119.
2 Ibid., 123, 129.
3 Ibid., 127.
4 Charles Beitz, *Political Theory and International Relations* (Princeton: Princeton University Press, 1979), 15.
5 Steve Smith, 'Singing Our World into Existence: International Relations Theory and September 11,' *International Studies Quarterly*, 48 (2004): 499–515.
6 Steve Smith, 'Positivism and Beyond,' in *International Theory: Positivism and Beyond*, ed. Steve Smith, Ken Booth and Marysia Zalewski (Cambridge: Cambridge University Press, 1996), 17.
7 Smith, 'Singing Our World into Existence,' 503.
8 Randall Schweller, 'Fantasy Theory,' *Review of International Studies*, 25, no. 1, (1999): 148–149.

9 Tim Dunne and Brian C. Schmidt, 'Realism,' *The Globalization of World Politics: An Introduction to International Relations*, 5th edn., eds. John Baylis, Steve Smith, and Patricia Owens (Oxford: Oxford University Press, 2011), 89.
10 Ibid.
11 Brent J. Steele, '"Eavesdropping on Honored Ghosts": From Classical to Reflexive Realism,' *Journal of International Relations and Development*, 10, no. 3 (2007): 273.
12 Schweller, 'Fantasy Theory,' 147.
13 Ibid., 150.
14 Ibid., 150.
15 Robert B. J. Walker, 'The Hierarchicalization of Political Community,' *Review of International Studies*, 25, no. 1 (1999): 156.
16 Ibid., 154.
17 David Campbell and Michael Shapiro, eds., *Moral Spaces: Rethinking Ethics and World Politics* (Minneapolis: University of Minnesota Press, 1999), viii.
18 Ibid.
19 Richard Price, *Moral Limit and Possibility in World Politics* (Cambridge: Cambridge University Press, 2008), 1.
20 It is customary in IR theory to refer to theorists who rely on the Frankfurt School as 'Critical Theorists' – capital 'C', capital 'T' – in order to distinguish them from the broad range of post-positivist theorists known as 'critical theorists'.
21 Ken Booth, *Theory of World Security* (Cambridge: Cambridge University Press, 2007), 89.
22 Kimberly Hutchings, 'The Possibility of Judgement: Moralizing and Theorizing in International Relations,' *Review of International Studies*, 18, no. 1 (1992): 51–62.
23 Kimberly Hutchings, 'A Place of Greater Safety? Securing Judgement in International Ethics,' in *The Vulnerable Subject: Beyond Rationalism in International Relations*, eds. Amanda Russell Beattie and Kate Schick (London: Palgrave, 2013), 39.
24 Ibid., 37–38.
25 Frost, 1998.
26 Ibid., 129.
27 Michael Walzer, 'The Triumph of Just War Theory (and the Dangers of Success),' *Social Research*, 69, no. 4 (2002): 930.
28 Ibid., 928.
29 Michael Walzer, *Just and Unjust Wars*, 4th edn. (New York: Basic Books, 2006), 4.
30 Neta Crawford, 'Just War Theory and the U.S. Counterterror War,' *Perspectives on Politics*, 1, no. 1 (2003): 21.
31 Eric Heinze and Brent Steele, eds., *Ethics, Authority and War: Non-State Actors and the Just War Tradition* (New York: Palgrave, 2008).
32 Daniel Brunstetter and Megan Braun, 'The Implications of Drones on the Just War Tradition,' *Ethics and International Affairs*, 25, no. 3 (2011): 337–358.
33 See Brian Orend, '*Jus post bellum*,' *Journal of Social Philosophy*, 31, no. 1 (2000): 117–137, and '*Jus post bellum*: The Perspective of a Just-War Theorist,' *Leiden Journal of International Law*, 20, no. 3 (2007): 571–591.
34 Laura Sjoberg, *Gender, Justice and the Wars in Iraq: A Feminist Reformulation of Just War Theory* (Oxford: Lexington Books, 2006).
35 Ibid., 15.
36 Kimberly Hutchings, 'Gendered Humanitarianism: Reconsidering the Ethics of War,' in *Experiencing War*, ed. Christine Sylvester (London and New York: Routledge, 2011).
37 John Rawls, *A Theory of Justice* (Cambridge, MA: Harvard University Press, 1971).
38 Charles Beitz, *Political Theory and International Relations* (Princeton: Princeton University Press, 1979).
39 Thomas Pogge, *World Poverty and Human Rights: Cosmopolitan Responsibilities and Reforms* (Cambridge: Polity Press, 2002); Simon Caney, *Justice Beyond Borders* (Oxford: Oxford University Press, 2005).
40 Monique Deveaux and Kathryn Walker, 'Introduction, Critical Approaches to Global Justice: At the Frontier,' *Journal of Global Ethics*, 9, no. 2 (2013): 111.
41 Margaret Kohn, 'Postcolonialism and Global Justice,' *Journal of Global Ethics*, 9, no. 2 (2013): 193.
42 Alison Jaggar, *Gender and Global Justice* (Cambridge: Polity Press, 2014), 13.
43 See Fiona Robinson, 'Care, Gender and Global Social Justice: Rethinking Ethical Globalization,' *Journal of Global Ethics*, 2, no. 1 (2006): 5–25; and Fiona Robinson 'Global Care Ethics: Beyond Distribution, Beyond Justice,' *Journal of Global Ethics*, 9, no. 2 (2013): 131–143.

44 Mary Kaldor, 'Cosmopolitanism and Organized Violence,' in *Conceiving Cosmopolitanism: Theory, Context and Practice*, eds. Steven Vertovic and Robin Cohen (Oxford: Oxford University Press, 2002), 268–278; David Held, 'Cosmopolitanism: Globalization Tamed,' *Review of International Studies*, 29, no. 4 (2003): 465–480.

45 Siba Grovogui, 'The New Cosmopolitanisms: Subtexts, Pretexts and Contexts of Ethics,' *International Relations*, 19, no. 1 (2005): 103–113.

46 Vivien Jabri, 'Solidarity and Spheres of Culture: The Cosmopolitan and the Postcolonial,' *Review of International Studies*, 33, no. 4 (2007): 715–728.

47 Vivienne Jabri, 'Cosmopolitan Politics, Security, Political Subjectivity,' *European Journal of International Relations*, 18, no. 4 (2012): 625–644.

48 James Brassett, 'Cosmopolitan Sentiments after 9-11? Trauma and the Politics of Vulnerability,' *Journal of Critical Globalisation Studies*, 2 (2010): 12–29.

49 Renee Jeffrey, 'Reason, Emotion and the Problem of World Poverty: Moral Sentiment Theory and International Ethics,' *International Theory*, 3, no. 1 (2011): 143–178.

50 See Neta Crawford, 'The Passion of World Politics: Propositions on Emotions and Emotional Relationships,' *International Security*, 24, no. 4, 2000: 116–156; and Roland Bleiker and Emma Hutchison, 'Fear No More: Emotions and World Politics,' *Review of International Studies*, 34, S1 (2008): 115–135.

51 Anthony Burke, 'Security Cosmopolitanism,' *Critical Studies on Security*, 1, no. 1 (2013): 13–28; and Anthony Burke and Jonna Nyman, eds., *Ethical Security Studies: A New Research Agenda* (New York: Routledge, 2013).

52 Ibid., 19.

7

HUNTING THE STATE OF NATURE

Race and ethics in postcolonial international relations[1]

Ajay Parasram

Introduction

When Phillip Darby and A. J. Paolini described postcolonialism and international relations (IR) as passing each other like "ships in the night," they were referring to how these two intellectual projects avoid engaging one another despite having many overlapping areas of interest.[2] Since then, a significant body of postcolonial IR scholarship has enriched the discipline, both explicitly and implicitly: explicitly in terms of how IR scholars have been producing postcolonial research, and implicitly in terms of how related disciplines have taken up postcolonial IR's issues of concern.[3] As a broad project, postcolonialism has many entry points that contribute to the deconstruction and reconfiguration/orientation of IR's normative assumptions, especially as they pertain to issues of race, gender, nation, heteronormativity, and the epistemic violences associated with how social science has privileged and normalized "Western" ontological assumptions.[4] Postcolonial research has generally emphasized South Asia, Africa, and the Middle East geographically, while the closely related but distinct "decolonial" perspective developed with an area focus on South America.[5] Critical theory emerging from the Marxist tradition informs both projects, and, to a lesser degree, the indigenous resurgence literature in Turtle Island (North America) which, while also taking up normative projects of decolonization, does so in distinction from the Eurocentric textual focus of much postcolonial, decolonial, and IR scholarship.[6]

The textuality of postcolonial research and its emphasis on discursive representation have been among the reasons "hard" IR has been resistant to postpositivist interventions in general and postcolonial ones in particular.[7] Postcolonial research has always been an interdisciplinary project with historical "home bases" in literary studies, cultural studies, as well as art history and historical theory. Its disciplinary entry point into IR has been positioned as part of the postpositivist "third debate" which involved the normative agenda of broadening critical theory of the late 1980s into the 1990s.[8] In this milieu, "postpositivism" offered an opportunity to rethink and diversify what counts as international theory, both in terms of bringing normative questions explicitly back into debates, questioning the stability of core disciplinary concepts like nation, state, and the inter-national, renewing interest in global civil society and transnational movements, resurgent indigenous politics, as well as opening space to rethink the ontological and epistemological starting points of IR theory.[9]

I focus on the normative implications within intellectual projects that can be situated within the broad tent of "postcolonial IR." I argue that postcolonial IR has diversified beyond its initial project of demanding inclusion into a preconfigured and Eurocentric "modern" IR narrative and is increasingly making radical interventions that expose ontological assumptions of modern/colonial IR theory as it relates to questions of land, sovereignty, resources, and the separation of human and nature. Most importantly, recent work is moving beyond deconstruction and exposition and engaging in the decolonizing work of reconstruction, centred around geographical and normative assumptions and knowledge systems that are "other than" or "more than" modern/colonial. In the following section, I survey some scholarship since/within the postpositivist debates, highlighting how the social construction of the "international" has always relied on colonial assumptions about race. Following that section, I draw on the trope of the "state of nature" as a significant and illustrative example of the centrality of race to the normative foundations of IR theory, and world politics more generally. I conclude with a section tracing some contemporary decolonial pathways that exemplify the normative project of (re-)building IR theory on diverse ontological grounds.

Postcolonial international relations and ethics

Postcolonial IR is explicitly normative, meaning that it rejects the idea that people can conceive of politics or ethics separately. This marks it as distinct from a rationalist ethical theory that operates within a normative framework where politics and ethics can be treated separately. A major point of contention for postcolonial ethics and IR rests in the moral universalism implied in rationalist approaches to ethics. In this way, a postcolonial critique of rationalist ethics is closely related to its critique of positivism, in that rationalist and positivist approaches to IR theory both scaffold onto an ontological and cosmological ethical domain that assumes Eurocentric knowledge about the world is universally valid, a point I will return to below.[10] One key distinction within the "post" tradition is that, while postmodernism and poststructuralism are counterdiscourses emanating from within modernism and aimed at moving beyond it, postcolonialism is a counterdiscourse that seeks to destabilize Western cultural hegemony.[11] Thus, even while the postpositivist family shares many methodological and theoretical investments aimed at demonstrating the inseparability of power and discourses of representation, postcolonialism differs in that its first step is to expose the Eurocentricity and cultural domination of modernity.

Within discussions of international ethics and global justice, a binary consideration of relativism or universalism is established, and within this normative framework, postcolonial critiques are grouped into the "relativist" camp. But to pose the question in binary terms that sees relativism as the alternative to universalism commits the ontological violence of naturalizing Eurocentric philosophical assumptions that deny the existence of others. Margaret Kohn's work, bringing postcolonial and global justice literatures into conversation on the question of global ethics, is instructive: "Normative theories of global justice, even ones that are philosophically convincing, may reinforce this sense of moral superiority, which in turn legitimizes potentially oppressive political power."[12] Kohn brings to light the epistemological violence encoded in metaphors, particularly how, over time, the metaphorical basis of an ethical argument is lost and the comparison in question becomes perceived as being truthful. Kohn draws attention to the metaphorical importance of concepts (e.g. "A movie stinks (smell – bad); a big night (size – importance)") and demonstrates how at the scale of colonial history, we require a metaphorical understanding of claims such as "freedom" and "rule of law," which exposes these metaphors as discursive strategies of normalizing the cultural ethic of European supremacy.[13] Said plainly, the metaphorical origins of now-naturalized prejudices about development, the international, race, or gender have been forgotten. We can think of a postcolonial approach to ethics in two steps. First is *remembering* that the discursive rendering of universal "realities" like human development, the state system, race, gender, and heteronormativity is a function of the modern colonial encounter. The second step is delinking from the hegemonic role of Eurocentric ideas about a single reality while theorizing and acting from ontological positions that are other than, or more than only, Eurocentric.

In rejecting the rationalist and positivist binary distinction of universalism or relativism, postcolonial international ethics works to expose the inherently moral decisions that have gone into creating and normalizing the international system and the states that comprise them. For example, Siba Grovogui has shown how the logic of the balance of power which protected the alleged hundred years peace around 1815–1914 was predicated on allowing should-be "failed" European states like Belgium to "succeed" by colonizing African territories.[14] Though there was inter-imperial competition between European empires, late nineteenth-century world politics exhibited a broad imperial consensus in establishing global governance norms and institutions which displaced violence to regions like Africa and Asia.[15] As Grovogui explains:

> Accordingly, the end of European empires through decolonization completed the transformation of the international system into one of fully autonomous states, dependent upon a Western-based political ethos which is encoded albeit imperfectly into the singular regime of sovereignty.[16]

This kind of structural violence does not fit into normalized historical accounts of the nineteenth century, which IR scholars are increasingly looking to as the major critical juncture in the forming of the international system of states rather than the Treaties of Westphalia.[17] More than territory and sovereignty have taken its modern forms through the colonial encounter, temporality itself reflects a Eurocentric orientation. Tarak Barkawi's recent work on the subject of decolonizing war shows how the treatment of war as an "exception" takes for granted Western imperial categories and how a postcolonial understanding of war would be far more everyday.[18]

On the subject of IR's principal agent, the nation-state, Partha Chaterjee's important work shows how the postcolonial nation-state presents an externally homogenous front amidst an internally heterogenous and "fragmented" reality, which speaks to the historical constructions of postcolonial territory as more of "state-nations" via the colonial encounter.[19] Developing the critique of the state further, Shampa Biswas argues that the developmentalist and modernization logic of the nation-state as the inevitable model to aspire to is folly.[20] As Gurminder Bhambra argues, the story of European state formation and the creation of the international system of the nineteenth century ought to be retheorized with reference to how early state theorists like Max Weber understood state formation as an inherently imperial exercise. Extraterritorial control of colonies was understood as the path towards holding one's own within Europe, thus making the project of successful state-building in Europe implicitly a project in imperialism.[21] Similarly, Cristina Rojas demonstrates how regimes of representation through which Europe has been constructed as the source of "progress" has impacted postcolonial national development and justified "regimes of violence" in service to postcolonial national development in nineteenth-century Colombia.[22] Working in more contemporary terms, Giorgio Shani draws attention to the different kinds of spatial and territorial possibilities exhibited by communities of faith internationally, particularly the *Khalsa Panth* and *Umma*, whose strategic exclusion as sources of intellectual knowledge about transterritorial relations give cause to consider non-Western sources of cosmopolitanism in Sikhism and Islam.[23] Also picking up on the problem of the Western-centricity of IR theory, other scholars based outside of the West, like Navnita Behara, have written on and advocated both for (at international scholarly meetings) the need for IR to rethink its orientations and for the teaching of IR in the Global South in particular to avoid replication of the assumptions of Western-centric theoretical concerns.[24]

Geeta Choudhury and Sheila Nair's important edited volume *Power, Postcolonialism and International Relations* brings together a collection of scholars taking up the cognitive authority wielded by mainstream and critical IR theory and how these approaches fail to account for the foundational importance of race, class, and gender to modern IR. The exclusion of these central axis of modern IR represents a concentration of colonial power that artificially narrows the parameters within which IR theorists engage.[25] The project has only deepened and broadened in the decade and a half since this volume was published, with scholars increasingly taking up the project of engaging differently with the past through re-examining international theorists whose ideas were excluded from the canon for reasons of race. The work of W. E. B. Dubois has been central to this, but scholars have increasingly delved vertically into the past and horizontally in the present to identify marginalized intellectual sources that allow us to rethink transatlantic migration, discourses of political economy, and the project of historical writing more generally in a way that delinks from the geopolitical vantage point of the West. In delinking from the West, scholarship can increasingly reorient new histories and broaden theories that take seriously the vantage point of those who have been conscripted as "people without histories" in mainstream social science.[26] This method of delinking, or "border thinking," has been more prominent in Latin America but is on the rise in Anglophone IR scholarship for its potential to expand and improve canonical representations of international theory and ground it in what Walter Mignolo describes as the "colonial matrix of power." The colonial matrix of power refers to the organizing social logics of capitalism, heteropatriarchy, and racism that have been naturalized within a Western-centric understanding of modern philosophy.[27] Most recently, *Race and Racism in International Relations*, edited by Anievas, Manchanda, and Shilliam, challenges IR's constitution on several normative assumptions, focusing in particular on the centrality of race through an engagement with Dubois's international writings. It also includes contributions from scholars challenging how elements of racialized international thinkers like Mohandas Gandhi have been read partially to buttress existing beliefs and ideological projects.[28]

All of these important interventions expose the implications of theorizing from a starting assumption that the history of the "West" is an acceptable starting point for IR. The implications of theorizing otherwise—that is, theorizing from a vantage point that does not privilege European starting assumptions—is that structural power and violence in the ethical framing of the international becomes democratized. It effectively "brings power back in" by demonstrating that power never left in the first place. Told in a different vocabulary of rationalist versus relativist approaches to social inquiry within IR historically, this discussion has created a category of "moderns" who are "knowers" and "traditionals" who are known, though, as I argue throughout, more scholars are challenging this distinction. This position has been central to scholarship in the decolonial tradition, which takes as one of its core objectives exposing the unacknowledged ways that "modern" thought relies upon the interdependent violence of "coloniality," which describes the problematic points of continuities of colonial violence that never "ended" with the achieving of formal institutional independence. The mythology of an endogamous modernity arising within Europe's history without considering the constituent role of genocide and enslavement since 1492 gives rise to what Enrique Dussel has called

"Euro-centrism," and the emphasizing of "ego politics" over the "geo-politics" of knowledge.[29] As Ramón Grosfoguel maintains, the consequences of an Eurocentric and universalistic philosophy is that historically,

> this has allowed Western man (the gendered term is intentionally used here) to represent his knowledge as the only one capable of achieving a universal consciousness, and to dismiss non-Western knowledge as particularlistic and, thus, unable to achieve universality.[30]

Postcolonialism and decoloniality are thus approaches that are both concerned with the making of the modern/colonial world and how Eurocentricity enacts epistemic violence. Postcolonial and decolonial analyses are *not* necessarily concerned with replacing and rebuilding universal theory, because replacing a Eurocentric universal theory with one from elsewhere would be committing the same ethical crime of viewing all existence through a single worldview. In the next section, I explore one aspect of the violence of universal thinking through the coloniality of the "state of nature" trope in IR.

Hunting the state of nature

Assumptions about how humans behaved in the absence of a sovereign have played a pedagogical role in normalizing a Eurocentric ontology of land, nature, and gradual human development that is predicated on racist assumptions about the other-than-European parts of the world, especially those in the Western hemisphere. As Errol Henderson explains, theorizing anarchy in IR derives from

> social contract theorists such as Hobbes, Locke, Rousseau and Kant, whose characterization of the state of nature, which is the hypothetical condition characterized by human interaction prior to the establishment of society, was adopted by IR theorists to conceptualize the global system.[31]

Although the context of Hobbes' writing is the Thirty Year' War, he was also working in the context of one hundred and fifty years of European contact with Latin America. Drawing on Mills, Henderson argues that the state of nature was mobilized in *The Leviathan* as a hypothetical threat or fear of what might befall a more civilized Europe in the absence of a strong sovereign. That fear was abstract for Europe but understood as a literal state of nature in the "new" world.[32] As Cristina Rojas maintains:

> The "state of nature" endorses the ontological distinction between nature and culture by locating certain humans closer to nature and depriving their life of value. On the contrary, moderns are provided with the legitimate right to improvement and the right to destroy those that do not exercise this right, which is seen as equivalent to their failure as humans.[33]

Although the explicit political distinction separating humanity from nature and its implications for territory and sovereignty are most often linked to Hobbes, from a normative perspective it is relevant to consider that the genealogy of this separation can be traced through the Abrahamic traditions to the Book of Genesis (1:26), in which God creates man in his likeness, separates him from nature, and gives him dominion over all other creatures of His creation. As Beate Jahn argues, Europeans "discovering" indigenous peoples in what they perceived as a "real" state of nature provoked philosophical changes in European thought. For Jahn, the blank universality of the state of nature is "itself the product of a particular historical event and hence, already highly charged with cultural, sociological, and ethical meanings waiting to be deciphered."[34] By trying to incorporate difference into a moral explanation of human and natural history, Europeans introduced linear temporality as a universal condition that positioned indigenous people as less developed.[35] The state of nature trope is an ideal example of the geopolitics of knowledge in action, as it privileges the philosophical musings of white European men, informed by their ontological assumptions of creation and, through it, a hypothetical state of nature, out of which structural IR scholars like Kenneth Waltz have built universal theory about "first image" considerations like human nature, "second image" concerns that ignore for sake of parsimony the distinctions between imperial and postcolonial territories, and "third image" behaviours of states within such a metaphorical system.[36] The state of nature trope describes other-than-European worlds as ethically barren and homogenous; they become empty philosophical devices used to explain a problem being faced *within* Europe. The existence of other-than-European places and peoples is thus not an end unto itself, but a means through which to understand Europe: existence by negation. As Frantz Fanon reminds us:

> Native society is not simply described as a society lacking in values. It is not enough for the colonist to affirm that those values have disappeared from, or still better never existed in, the colonial world. The native is declared insensible to ethics; he represents not only the absence of values, but also the negation of values. He is, let us dare to admit, the enemy of values, and in this sense he is the absolute evil.[37]

Hobbes's project was concerned with making sense of the developing context of states and civil war in which he was living, and by appealing to a story that required no empirical evidence to be accepted by his readers, he and subsequent social contract theorists like Jean-Jacques Rousseau and John Locke could render "natives" as irrelevant placeholders, destined to remain mute in a Eurocentric soliloquy. As David Blaney and Naem Inayatullah have argued, following G. W. F. Hegel, freedom is not a condition that exists in the state of nature. Hegel's universal theory of development positions freedom as something that unfolds through human achievement, and ethics becomes a temporal phenomena. Following Blaney and Inayatullah, "Violence and cruelty, kindness and creativity, etc., are not measured against the morality of individuals or groups, but relative to their role in history's deeper purpose – the actualization of freedom as a modern civil society and state."[38]

The state of nature trope thus does not *exclude* race; rather, it relies on a normatively modern, developmentalist reasoning that sees gradual human social evolution linearly, in which Europe and its settler-colonial prodigy are situated at the "end" of historical development. Nineteenth-century race theory, for example, developed all sorts of pseudo-scientific and positivisitic theories about the inherent retarding influence of tropical climates and their tendency to degrade the moral character of people of northern "stock."[39] Late-nineteenth-century globalization *was* colonial imperialism, from the point of view of the other-than-European world, and provided much context for the rise of the discipline in the early twentieth century. The writing of colonials offers insight into the race-based rationality and ethic of civilization that defined the colonial international of the late nineteenth century. Writing from Aotorea (New Zealand), the barrister Coleman Phillips is illuminating:

> By a curious chain of circumstances, we [British] have assumed the position of protectors of native tribes and suppressors of slavery. We are trying to elevate the East Indian; we are appealed to from Africa; and even the inhabitants of Polynesia petition us for protection. It appears as if those races of the human family, inhabiting the tropical lands of the earth, actually required the protection of such a Northern Power as ourselves, not only for the present, but for the centuries to come. . . Not only shall we have to regard their welfare, but also their protection from civilized and uncivilized invasion.[40]

Phillips articulates an entirely common understanding of colonial internationalism in which the gaze remains firmly set on Europe (in this case, England) and the "pre-political savages" held in a state of natural purgatory on account of proximity to the tropics, which darkens their skin as well as their aspirations for a lighter future. Colonial internationalism is, by the late nineteenth century, a moral and pedagogical obligation of the more civilized Northern races.

As Randolf Persaud and R. B. J. Walker explain, it is not that race has been *ignored* in IR; rather, it is that it has been "silenced."[41] To be "ignored" does not carry the same ethical weight as to be "silenced" because the latter requires an active process of rendering quiet and irrelevant and, by implication, treating the racialized consequences of IR as inevitable. In light of the developments in postcolonial IR since Persaud and Walker's intervention, however, it is incumbent on scholars to challenge whether "silencing" is truly the verb to describe this exclusion. If the problem is "silence," then the solution is speech, but speaking within a philosophical, ethical-political, and discursive framework that is constituted on Eurocentric ontological assumptions forces us to consider the violence of universal reason rather than epistemic violence alone. The rise of race science and the modern/colonial constitution and meaning of race as it has played out historically represents ontological violence, because it is only within the modern/colonial universe that race can exist, as we know it historically.[42] Gayatri C. Spivak has long since established the epistemic violence associated with the discursive parameters of scholarship within which the "subaltern cannot speak."[43] This is a particularly important point for dismantling the ontological hegemony of Eurocentrism in IR. As Robbie Shilliam has recently observed in his reinterpretation of the other-than-European cosmopolitan ethics present at the historical Bwa Kayiman gathering that launched the Haitian Revolution, race and justice have meaning beyond the limits of Western European reason that need to be considered alongside if we are to decolonize a sense of global justice:

> Critiquing race only through its own schema is a fundamental failure of our politics and imagination. In doing so we are silencing the response. In the midst of enslavement, of not simply exploitation or oppression but radical dehumanisation and desanctification, literally genocide, shackled, stripped and whipped, the sufferers still remain concerned that their mediation of cosmic forces must be bound by the imperatives of justice for all. Meanwhile, another Jean Jacques – Rousseau – writes that man is born free but everywhere lives in metaphorical chains. Compare. Might those who broke the physical chains have something valuable to say about present-day struggles over global justice? Is it intellectually satisfying to consider anything less?[44]

I will return to ontological violence in the next section, but, working within the framework of silencing, it is relevant to note how even within the less radical critique of "silencing," IR's relative silence on the question of race weakens the discipline. One of the discipline's founding journals, *Foreign Affairs*, was known from 1910 to 1919 as the *Journal of Race Development*, and, as disciplinary historians have noted, "race," "development," and a "racialized and biological understanding of 'development'" was at the centre of the study of world politics at the turn of the twentieth century.[45] Alongside what others have historicized as the "First Great Debate" between "idealism" and "realism" was a silenced non-debate about race at the centre of the making of the colonial international system of the nineteenth and twentieth centuries. Silenced, because racialized theorists of the international like Marcus Garvey, Dubois, Rabindranath Tagore, or Bhagat Singh in the nineteenth and twentieth centuries were writing about and engaging within IR, but their race excluded them from being taken up as qualified intellectuals on the subject of IR. Scholars like Dubois had been explaining in academic texts and international meetings the centrality of the "color line" as early as 1902, and highlighting the interrelatedness of imperial warfare in Africa to bourgeoisie capitalist interest years before V. I. Lenin penned "Imperialism: The Highest Stage of Capitalism."[46] This was not simply an academic concern. As the discipline was taking shape in the early twentieth century, the violent consequences of Western ideas of the "state of nature" intersecting with scientific inquiry and white supremacy worked to justify the kidnapping and public exhibition of Africans in human zoos in the West as "evidence" of missing evolutionary linkages.[47]

The material implications of silencing were multifaceted, and in the Western hemisphere it took the form of *terra nullis*, which defined an early praxis of IR in John Locke's understanding of property rights through which value must be extracted from land to connote ownership.[48] Drawing explicitly from a Christian ontology in which evidence comes from biblical understandings, Locke integrates "Indians" into his ontological framing of land and the separation of humanity from nature by offering a reinterpretation of hunting within this mythological place:

> Though the water running in the fountain be every one's, yet who can doubt, but that in the pitcher is his only who drew it out? His labour hath taken it out of the hands of nature, where it was common, and belonged equally to all her children, and hath thereby appropriated it to himself.[49]

Like John Stuart Mill after him, Locke was more than a philosopher: he was directly invested in the colonization of other-than-European places through his paid employment. As a key contributor to revising the *Fundamental Constitutions of Carolina* (1682) at the same time as writing chapter five of *Second Treatise on Government*, Locke rationalized Indigenous people's "failure" to cultivate land as evidence of their inability to use it properly, thus justifying their dispossession by a more entrepreneurial people.[50]

After Hobbes and Locke, Rousseau also worked on the artificially emptied philosophical category of the state of nature and the problem of hunting. Rousseau's reading of the state of nature and his story about hunters coordinating within the state of nature has been especially influential in structural IR theorizing. Within this scenario emerges the basis for the "security dilemma" based on the "natural" pursuit of self-interest that induces men to "cheat" and abandon their position within the stag hunt to pursue a hare based on short-term self-interest. The problem I seek to highlight in rehashing this familiar story to IR audiences is not the long-debated tension between parsimony and complexity, nor relativism and universalism. I am not concerned with the important differences between how Hobbes, Locke, or Rousseau set up and engaged with the state of nature. My normative concern here is that IR as a discipline has taken the *mythology* of a state of nature as the philosophical inspiration for understanding anarchy and the behaviour of states without relationally considering the empirically observable histories that have gone into forming the state system, including most centrally: genocide, the trans-Atlantic slave trade, and subsequent indentureship which was meant to "improve" slavery. Rethinking IR with a broadly conceived postcolonial ethic in which multiple ontologies exist helps us to see the universal ethics of modern/colonial IR as a broken and severely limiting worldview.

Different ontological starting points for IR theory

The silencing of other-than-modern ontologies and the ethics that extend from them has not prevented the political practising of uninterrupted resistance to colonialism, even if IR has scarcely paid attention to this fact until recently. As Jeff Corntassle observes, the discourse of "rights" over land is itself a normative, Eurocentric ontological imposition, as for many Indigenous people on Turtle Island (North America), it is not a question of a "right" to exploit in the Lockean sense of the word as it is an obligation and responsibility that connects one to the land. The discourse of responsibility more accurately describes and translates indigenous territoriality into colonial/scholarly languages, which long predates and continues alongside the modern/colonial international system.[51] The denigration of indigenous knowledge systems is a consequence—perhaps more accurately, a requirement—of the violence of universalizing Eurocentric values. An ethic and ontology of land as a responsibility or a relationship becomes violently supressed by an historical colonial ontology of land that rationalizes it as a resource to be controlled, owned, and exploited. As Marisol de la Cadena observes, the failure of modern society to perceive the political agency of other-than-human actors has not meant that nature is not active in politics. Drawing on Isabelle Stengers's call to "slow down reasoning," and Jacques Rancière's notion of politics as interruption, de la Cadena urges us to see how the enactments of other "worlds" and ontologies might help to better understand the kinds of "epistemic ruptures" within modern reason that extends from multiple ontologies.[52]

The existence of multiple ontologies, or the "pluriverse," does not suggest that ontologies do not interact. On the contrary, ontologies are always interacting and coming into conflict, out of which new possibilities and trajectories can emerge. Some scholars, not explicitly working in the field of IR, have shown particularly exciting research trajectories. For example, in *Red Skins, White Masks*, Glen Coulthard explains a Dene relational ontology of land using a different kind of hunting story than Locke's or Rousseau's kind. Unlike an abstract and imaginary sense of a state of nature, Coulthard's story comes from an oral testimonial and describes a real-life relation between a human hunter (Edward), a raven, and a moose. Practices of reciprocity between Edward and the raven in hunting a moose helps to articulate that within a Dene ontology of land, one cannot differentiate between the people and a "nature" that is distinct from the people; land is not a "thing" outside of our existence; rather, as Coulthard explains:

> Land is a relationship based on the obligations we have to other people and the other-than-human relations that constitute the land itself. In my book, I refer to this ethical orientation to land and others as "grounded normativity" and it has served as the framework for many of our communities' struggles for self-determination.[53]

Coulthard's grounded normativity is a place-based ontology that has always existed alongside of a Eurocentric, transcendental normativity. The meeting of these ontologically distinct realities illustrates the simultaneous existence of the pluriverse, and at the same time, the historical and empirical implication of ontological conflict on the basis of their irreconcilability.[54] Coulthard draws on the work of Dakota philosopher Vine Deloria, Jr, to develop his argument that indigenous metaphysics takes the centrality of place as its starting point opposite Western metaphysicis which takes linear temporality as its starting point. A Dene ontology and ethic of land, therefore, exemplifies grounded normativity that is praxis-oriented and achievable only through proper relations with the land, instead of abstract normativity such as the kind of reasoning that enabled the trope of the state of nature in the preceding section. Consequently, Coulthard's grounded normativity is necessarily in conflict with a Western understanding of land that takes for granted an ahistorical and abstract separation of nature/land and people that enables land to be "owned" through value-added labour in the vein that Karl Marx and Locke before him describe. Rethinking ontology, then, is an essential step towards decolonizing IR, and grounding it to empirical histories rather than abstract theorizing.[55]

Coulthard's project is not about rethinking IR, but from his work and the work of other indigenous scholars working in the "Indigenous Resurgence" school, rests important implications arising from what IR ought to recognize as multiple ontologies. Long before the making of the modern international system, Indigenous people on Turtle Island had developed sophisticated international relations that operated with indigenous ontological starting points.[56] As Susan Hill observes, writing on the Haudenosaunee Law of Great Peace, this Wampam belt established not only legal treaty amongst five (later six) warring nations, but rather than setting a static legalistic condition of "rights" as we know it in the Western juridical tradition, instead outlines the boundaries for a living legal document. Upon the arrival of Europeans many hundreds of years after the establishment of the Law of Great Peace, the living diplomatic tradition continues to be the basis of IR within Haudenosaunee territories.[57] Wampam diplomacy, as Lynn Gehl explains, is the constitutional history of IR on Turtle Island, within which Europeans initially integrated.[58]

Once ontological starting points are diversified, the kinds of methods and methodology used in the development of epistemology must necessarily follow suit. Another important example of this kind of decolonial ontological starting point can be found in Kwakwaka'wakw scholar Sarah Hunt's juxtaposition of knowledge production in the context of an academic conference in contrast to knowledge cultivation in the form of a potlatch. In the latter context, storytelling and oral history is essential, whereas in the prior, it is the traditional academic format (with which readers of this Handbook will no doubt be familiar).[59] Although positivist (and, arguably, much postpositivist) social science has been methodologically invested in the empiricism of the written word and records, this too is something of a modern, universal inclination. Oral histories have longer traditions and speak not only to the end result of "knowing" an empirical event, but also the processes of exploration and collaboration that go into the cultivation of knowledge. As the Oglala Lakota activist Russell Means explained in a famous speech in 1980:

> The only possible opening for a statement of this kind is that I detest writing. The process itself epitomizes the European concept of "legitimate" thinking; what is written has an importance that is denied the spoken. My culture, the Lakota culture, has an oral tradition, so I ordinarily reject writing. It is one of the white world's ways of destroying the cultures of non-European peoples, the imposing of an abstraction over the spoken relationship of a people.[60]

The world of positivist social science and the worlds of oral historical traditions rely on different ontological premises.

Grounding theorizations of the international in actual empirical events is a better foundation for thinking through IR. My point is not that parables and imaginary situations should not have been used in developing IR theory. I mean only that the imaginary should not replace the empirical because the coloniality of knowledge privileges Eurocentrity and denigrates the knowledge systems of Others. This is particularly important at this juncture in world politics, as the perspectives of other-than and more-than moderns are so badly needed by all. There are real political consequences associated with turning to the imaginary in order to universalize concepts such as "human nature," or the freedom of commercial society, or the merits of promoting global security through regime change and democratic imperialism. By delinking from modern discourses, the ideas, theory, and politics of and by colonized Others become the means through which the modern/colonial world can be understood.

Conclusion

In the last generation, IR and postcolonial theory *have* intervened with increasing frequency, and with increasing sophistication and differentiation within the broad "tent" of postcolonial IR. Even within this chapter's emphasis on the analytical "slice" of race, there has been a growing awareness of the centrality of race to the discipline.[61] The earlier generation (~1980s–2000s) of scholarly interventions have emphasized broadening existing understandings of modernity and history, clearing space for present and future scholars to shape an ethical, postcolonial IR that increasingly reconstrucs and puts into practice other-than-modern knowledge systems that have always existed. The first project, which we might call the "epistemic" project, has been built upon trying to pry open the limited gaze/perspective of modernity, producing "multiple modernities" as a way of bringing a cultural dimension to modernity and acknowledgement that Eurocentricity is not the only way to understand modernity. There are normative political reasons why modernity is usually framed in terms of enlightened philosophy, progress, human rights, and freedom from religious persecution rather than in terms of slavery, genocide, and the immiserization of the European working classes. As Gurminder Bhambra observes, the case for multiple modernities was made to add a cultural dimension and inflection to the processes underscoring universal institutions such as the state and the market. This revision of earlier modernization theory thus sought to escape the charge of cultural relativism by keeping the institutional basis for a universal understanding of modernity, while resisting the Eurodomination of modernity by emphasizing the cultural distinctions of how modernity unfolds in different places.[62] Multiple modernity, then, still implies different perspectives on a materially objective and describable "reality," which is what makes it essentially a concern about inclusion within a pre-existing universal reality. This gives rise to claims of producing and writing "our" modernity within categories and approaches that are part of the modern episteme already.[63] Within postcolonial studies, this would include research aimed at correcting the omissions of the last hundred years of theorizing, but remains largely in the familiar terrain of critique.

The second project, which we might call the "ontological" project, eschews inclusion within a democractized understanding of modernity and applies the logic of putting into practice knowledge systems to theorize anew. This work is less concerned about inclusion within a modern episteme and more concerned about putting what has been exposed through deconstruction into reconstructive practice. Research in the field of "political ontology" is particularly concerned with this, and there is overlap with the decolonial approach more generally.[64] The difference between multiple ontologies and multiple modernities is the centrality of pluriversal politics, in which whole cosmologies, complete with ontological starting points and knowledge cultivated along means that may not be knowable from outside of those worlds, interact.

There is, of course, considerable overlap in the epistemic and ontological projects of postcolonial IR, but I maintain that by thinking through developments in IR theory with these categories in mind, we can best appreciate the exciting vibrancy with which postcolonial IR is both contributing to *and* transcending the parameters of modern normative IR theory. By dwelling upon the trope of the "state of nature" so central to the foundational concept of anarchy in IR theory, I have attempted to demonstrate first the silencing (rather than invisibility) of race to the foundations of international thought, and to illustrate how this particular configuration of race is only possible within a Eurocentric universe of modern reason. This has produced an unspoken ethic of racial domination grounded in the ontological assumption of European ideas being able to represent a universe. I then drew into conversation sources of ontologically distinct theory within shared interdisciplinary intellectual spaces to IR that do not require anchoring itself to the strictures of Eurocentric philosophy, thereby espousing ontologically distinct ethics from which postcolonial IR theory can continue to develop.

In essence, what is happening now in IR is that the project of "exposing" is making way for putting critique into practice and theorizing IR on different ontological terms, arising within tributaries of knowledges delinked from the centrality of Western European thought and put into practice. To "expose," after all, begs the question: To whom are we exposed? Such a representation would only replicate the ego politics of knowledge at the expense of geopolitics of knowledge. That act of exposition—of airing out for others (read: moderns) to see and determine importance reinforces the exclusion of other-than-moderns from the modern narrative, but the politics of "inclusion" is no longer the limit of postcolonial IR research. Pluriversal politics, constituted upon pluriversal ethics, offers exciting directions for twenty-first-century IR theory.

Notes

1 I benefited enormously from participating in twin panels on pluriversal politics at the 2017 ISA conference and the thoughtful critiques offered there by Cristina Rojas, Hans-Martin Jaeger, Esteban Nicholls, Gustavo Morales Vega, and Janet Conway. This chapter also benefited from a related collaboration with Lisa Tilley, and ongoing conversations with Fazeela Jiwa, Gurminder Bhambra, John Munro, Robbie Shilliam, Olivia Rutazibwa, Rosalba Icaza, John Narayan, and Arturo Escobar. I am grateful for the careful editing of Fiona Robinson, Brent Steele, Eric Heinze, as well as the politically astute copy-editing of Stephen Michael Christian.

2 Phillip Darby and A. J. Poalini, "Bridging International Relations and Postcolonialism," *Alternatives: Global, Local, Political*, 19 (1994): 371–397.

3 Robbie Shilliam, Alex Anievas, and Nivi Manchanda, eds., *Race and Racism in International Relations: Confronting the Global Colour Line* (New York: Routledge, 2015); Geeta Chowdhury and Sheila Nair, eds., *Power in a Postcolonial World* (New York: Routledge, 2002).

4 Anna Agathangelou and L. H. M. Lingh, "The House of I.R.: From Family Power Politics to the Poisies of Worldism," *International Studies Review*, 6 (2004): 21–49; Partha Chatterjee, *Nationalist Thought and the Colonial World: A Derivative Discourse?* (Tokyo: United Nations University Press, 1986).

5 Gurminder Bhambra, "Postcolonial and Decolonial Dialogues," *Postcolonial Studies*, 17, no. 2 (2014): 115–121.

6 See Glen Sean Coulthard, *Red Skin, White Masks* (Minneapolis: University of Minnesota Press, 2014).

7 Darby and Poalini, "Bridging International Relations and Postcolonialism," 373–374.

8 Yosef Lapid, "The Third Debate: On the Prospects of International Theory in a Post-Positivist Era," *International Studies Quarterly*, 33 (1989): 235–254.

9 Cf: Fiona Robinson, "Globalizing Care: Ethics, Feminist Theory, and International Relations Theory," *Alternatives*, 22, no. 1 (1997): 113–133; Chandra Mohanty, "'Under Western Eyes' Revisited," *Signs*, 28 (2003): 499–537; "Today We Say Ya Basta! First Declaration from the Lacandan Jungle," *Schools For Chiapas* (December 1993), available online: http://www.schoolsforchiapas.org/library/declaration-lacandona-jungle-2/.

10 I am grateful to Fiona Robinson for helping to clarify this comparison.

11 Pal Ahluwalia, "Out of Africa: Post-Structuralism's Colonial Roots," *Postcolonial Studies*, 8 (2005): 137–154.

12 Margaret Kohn, "Postcolonialism and Global Justice," *Journal of Global Ethics*, 9 (2013): 195.

13 Ibid., 190–192.

14 Siba Grovogui, "Regimes of Sovereignty: Rethinking International Morality and the African Condition," *European Journal of International Relations*, 8, no. 3 (2002): 315–338.

15 Ibid., 318.
16 Ibid., 320.
17 Jordan Branch, "Mapping the Sovereign State: Technology, Authority, and Systemic Change," *International Organization*, 65, no. 1 (2011): 1–36; Andreas Osiander, *The States System of Europe, 1640–1990* (Oxford: Clarendon Press, 1994).
18 Tarak Barkawi, "Decolonising War," *European Journal of International Security*, 1 (2016): 199–214.
19 Partha Chatterjee, *The Nation and Its Fragments: Colonial and Postcolonial Histories* (Princeton: Princeton University Press, 1993).
20 Shampa Biswas, "Deconstructing the 'New Cold War': Religious Nationalisms, Orientalism, and Postcoloniality," in Chowdhury and Nair, eds., *Power in a Postcolonial World*, 184–208.
21 Gurminder Bhambra, "Comparative Historical Sociology and the State: Problems of Method," *Cultural Sociology*, 10, no. 3 (2016): 335–351.
22 Cristina Rojas, *Civilization and Violence* (Minneapolis: University of Minnesota Press, 2002).
23 Giorgio Shani, "Toward a Post-Western IR: The *Umma*, *Khalsa Panth*, and Critical International Relations Theory," *International Studies Review*, 10, no. 4 (2007): 722–734.
24 Navnita Behara, ed., *International Relations in South Asia: Search for an Alternative Paradigm* (New Delhi: Sage, 2008); see also Robbie Shillia, ed., *International Relations and Non-Western Thought: Imperialism, Colonialism, and Investigations of Global Modernity* (London: Routledge, 2010); Amitav Acharya and Barry Buzan, *Non-Western International Relations Theory: Perspectives on and Beyond Asia* (New York: Routledge, 2010).
25 Chowdhury and Nair, *Power in a Postcolonial World*.
26 Walter Mignolo and Arturo Escobar, eds., *Globalization and the Decolonial Option* (New York: Routledge, 2010).
27 Walter Mignolo, *The Darker Side of Western Modernity* (Durham, North Carolina: Duke University Press, 2011); Cristina Rojas, "International Political Economy/Development Otherwise," *Globalizations*, 4, no. 4 (2007): 573–587.
28 Sankaran Krishna, "A Postcolonial Racial/Spatial Order," in *Race and Racism in International Relations*, ed. Shilliam, Anievas, and Manchanda (New York: Routledge, 2015), 139–156.
29 Cristina Rojas, "Contesting the Colonial Logics of the International: Towards a Relational Politics for the Pluriverse," *International Political Sociology*, 10, no. 4 (2016): 378.
30 Ramón Grosfoguel, "The Epistemic Decolonial Turn," *Cultural Studies*, 21 (2007): 213–214.
31 Errol Henderson, "Hidden in Plain Sight: Racism in International Relations Theory," *Cambridge Review of International Affairs*, 26, no. 1 (2013): 79.
32 Ibid., 80.
33 Cristina Rojas, "Contesting the Colonial Logics of the International," 372.
34 Beate Jahn, "IR and the State of Nature: The Cultural Origins of a Ruling Ideology," *Review of International Studies*, 25 (1999): 412.
35 Ibid., 423.
36 Cf: Kenneth Waltz, *Man, The State, and War* (New York: Colombia University Press, 1954); Kenneth Waltz, *Theory of International Politics* (New York: McGraw-Hill, 1979).
37 Franz Fanon, *Wretched of the Earth*, trans. Constance Farrington (New York: Penguin, 2001), 40.
38 David Blaney and Naeem Inayatullah, *Savage Economics* (New York: Routledge, 2010), 125–126.
39 James Duncan, *In the Shadows of the Tropics* (New York: Routledge, 2007).
40 Coleman Phillips (Barrister-at-Law, New Zealand), *British Colonization and British Commerce* (London: Edward Stanford, 1875). British National Library Shelfmark: 8154.e.1(9).
41 Randolf Persaud and R. B. J. Walker, "*Apertura:* Race in International Relations," *Alternatives*, 26, no. 4 (2001): 373–376.
42 I am grateful to Cristina Rojas for this observation.
43 Gayatri C. Spivak, "Can the Subaltern Speak?" in *Marxism and the Interpretations of Culture*, ed. Cary Nelson and Lawrence Grossberg (Basingstoke: Macmillan Education, 1988), 271–313.
44 Robbie Shilliam, "Race and Revolution at Bwa Kayiman," *Millennium: Journal of International Studies*, 45, no. 3 (2017): 23.
45 Errol Henderson, "Hidden in Plain Sight: Racism in International Relations Theory," 73
46 Ibid.
47 "The Man Who Was Caged in a Zoo," *The Guardian* (June 3, 2015), accessed March 31, 2017, https://www.theguardian.com/world/2015/jun/03/the-man-who-was-caged-in-a-zoo.

48 John Locke, *Second Treatise on Government* (1690; Project Gutenburg, 2010), https://www.gutenberg.org/files/7370/7370-h/7370-h.htm#CHAPTER_V.

49 Ibid., Sect. 29.

50 David Armitage, "John Locke, Carolina, and the *Two Treaties of Government*," *Political Theory*, 35, no. 5 (2004): 602–607.

51 Jeff Corntassle, "Re-Envisioning Resurgence: Indigenous Pathways to Decolonization and Sustainable Self-Determination," *Decolonization: Indigeneity, Education and Society*, 1, no. 1 (2012): 92–94.

52 Marisol de la Cadena, "Indigenous Cosmopolitics in the Andes: Conceptual Reflections beyond Politics," *Current Anthropology*, 25, no. 2 (2010): 343.

53 Harsha Walia, "'Land Is a Relationship: In Conversation with Glen Coulthard on Indigenous Nationhood," *Rabble.ca* (January 21, 2015), accessed December 26, 2016, http://goo.gl/bp15ji.

54 Glen Coulthard and Leanne Betasamosake Simpson, "Grounded Normativity and Place-Based Solidarity," *American Quarterly*, 68 (2016): 249–255.

55 Cf.: Mario Blaser, "Ontological Conflicts and the Stories of Peoples in Spite of Europe," *Current Anthropology*, 54, no. 4 (2013): 547–568; Robbie Shilliam, *The Black Pacific* (London: Bloomsbury, 2015).

56 J. Marshall Bier, "Inter-National Affairs: Indigeneity, Globality, and the Canadian State," *Canadian Foreign Policy*, 13, no. 3 (2007): 121–131; Karena Shaw, "Indigeneity and the International," *Millennium: Journal of International Studies*, 31, no. 1 (2002): 55–81.

57 Susan Hill, "Travelling Down the River of Life in Peace and Friendship, Forever," in *Lighting the Eighth Fire: Yhr Liberation, Resurgence, and Protection of Indigenous Nations*, ed. Leanne Simpson (Winnepeg: Arbeiter Ring Publishing, ARP, 2008), 23–46.

58 Lynn Gehl, *The Truth that Wampam Tells* (Black Point: Fernwood, 2014).

59 Sarah Hunt, "Ontologies of Indigeneity," *Cultural Geographies*, 21/1 (2014): 27–32.

60 Russell Means, "Revolution and American Indians: Marxism Is as Alien to My Culture as Capitalism," *Blackhawk Productions*, accessed March 31, 2017. http://www.blackhawkproductions.com/russelmeans.html

61 Benjamin de Carvalho, Halvard Leira, and John Hobson, "The Big Bangs of IR," *Millennium: Journal of International Studies*, 39 (2011): 735–758; Robert Vitalis, *White World Order, Black Power Politics* (Ithica: Cornell University Press, 2015).

62 Gurminder Bhambra, *Connected Sociology* (London: Bloomsbury, 2014), 32–34.

63 Cf. Partha Chatterjee, *Our Modernity* (Dakar: SEPHIS & CODESRIA, 1997).

64 Cristina Rojas, "International Political Economy/Development Otherwise," 573–587.

8

SOCIAL CONSTRUCTIVISM AND INTERNATIONAL ETHICS

Jonathan Havercroft

Introduction: norms as social facts and norms as ethical values

Social constructivist research in international relations (IR) has a complicated relationship with international ethics. As is the case with most academic schools of thought, constructivists define themselves through a series of differentiations from other approaches. These early differentiations closed off possible areas for complementary research by defining some approaches as either implicitly or explicitly not constructivist.[1] In the case of constructivism, the intellectual context in which it emerged in the late 1980s and early 1990s led to three crucial differentiations. First, constructivism was an explicitly idealist approach to IR. This idealism enabled constructivism to differentiate itself from the two dominant materialist approaches in 1980s IR theory—neorealism and historical materialism. The neorealists grounded their explanations of international politics in the material capabilities (often reduced to military power) of states.[2] The historical materialists premised their understandings of world politics in the economic base of the mode of production and took ideas to be part of an ideological superstructure, the content of which was determined by the economic base.[3] In contrast to both positions, second-generation constructivists argue that materiality only acquired its social significance through its ideational interpretation.[4] In Alexander Wendt's famous example, how a state's material capabilities will be interpreted by other states very much depends upon the pre-existing relationship those two states have with each other. The United States will treat a military training exercise by Cuba as threatening, whereas an identical military training exercise by Canada will be interpreted as an ally fulfilling its military obligations under NATO.[5]

Second, constructivism explicitly sets itself up as a social scientific approach that could verify its claims through mainstream positivists' methods. This differentiation was largely made by constructivists contra more explicitly postpositivist IR scholars such as poststructuralists and critical theorists. We can consider here Wendt's distinction between causal and constitutive explanations[6] and Adler's positioning of constructivism as a "middle ground" between positivism and interpretivism[7] as two crucial examples of earlier constructivists positioning constructivism as an explanatory theory whose claims could be recognized as valid by other IR positivists.

Third, second-generation constructivists posit that one of the main contributions of constructivism is overcoming the agent–structure debates that were central to 1980s IR theory. The constructivist argument that agents and structures where co-constituted—that is, that an agent's identity is determined by the structure in which the agent acts, and the social structure is in turn shaped by the actions agents engage in, is shaped via the agent's identity—launched a research agenda in which scholars elucidated this core claim via empirical investigations of how international structures shaped and were shaped by agents' identities.

While these three differentiations were crucial for carving out the early terrain of constructivist research, the consequence of this process of differentiation is that it also closed off alternative paths. In particular, for our purposes in this chapter, how second-generation constructivist scholars positioned themselves with respect to the larger field of IR meant that they explicitly emphasized social constructivism as an explanatory social scientific theory (albeit a constitutive one as opposed to a causal one), and in so doing earlier constructivists closed off the possibility of normative research. The embrace of ideational causes as explanatory for social constructivism meant that research about how ideas shape state behavior became a central research question, whereas the normative question of whether or not a particular idea is a good guide for state conduct was set aside as not scientific—occasionally explicitly so.[8] The positioning of social constructivism as a *via media* between interpretivist and positivist approaches meant that, for the most part, interpretivism was adopted as one possible approach to explanatory social science amongst many, whereas the more explicit normative puzzles explored by interpretivism were set aside. Furthermore, the focus on the co-constitution of structures and agents meant that the responsibility of agents for their actions was often downplayed as part of a larger social process. From a rationalist normative perspective,[9] which requires that agents be responsible for their actions in some shape or form if one is to make a normative judgment about their actions, the focus on structuration foreclosed the possibility of holding agents ethically responsible for their actions.

This early closing off of the normative is perhaps most explicit when we look at how social constructivists handle norms. One of the key axioms of social constructivist research is that the social structures in which agents act are deeply normative. The norms in these structures prescribe what is socially acceptable behavior if an actor wants to be a "good" member of the group. These norms constrain which actions are deemed possible by spelling out social sanctions if one violates the norms of the community.[10] This theory that norms operate according to a "logic of appropriateness"[11] that constrains an actor's behavior, is an explanatory theory. It explains how a norm shapes an actor's identity and how that identity in turn shapes an actor's interests and expected behaviors. In this instance, the norm operates as a social fact. The norm does not have a material basis, but it exists as social more that governs the conduct of actors within the community nonetheless. In order to sustain the core social constructivist axiom that norms constitute identities, expectations, and behaviors of actors, most empirically oriented constructivist scholarship has focused on demonstrating the existence of given norms. So the research has focused on uncovering the existence of nuclear and chemical weapons taboos,[12] human rights norms,[13] and norms around the sovereign status of states.[14] This focus on demonstrating that norms exist and shape the behaviors of states necessarily brackets the international ethics question of whether or not a norm is "good" or "bad," "just" or "unjust."

Part of the reason for this is simply that in making the case for an empirical argument, one cannot spend too much time debating whether or not a given norm is justified. Demonstrating that a norm exists and has social effects is often a challenging enough endeavor for a research agenda. Yet one of the consequences of bracketing the normative in order to pursue the empirical is that a kind of cryptonormativism has crept into constructivist research.[15] By *cryptonormativism*, I simply mean that constructivist scholars often assume or imply that a given norm (such as norms prohibiting weapons use, norms against torture, or norms promoting human rights) is good without fully elaborating the reasons for it.[16] In some cases, social constructivists have fessed up to this cryptonormativism, often arguing that the norms were sufficiently self-evidently good and as such the scholarly focus was more correctly placed on the empirical demonstration of their effects.[17] Yet this assumes that the justification of a norm is self-evident, when often scholars from more critical traditions are quick to point out ways in which norms that are often presumed to be good may have pernicious effects.[18] At the very least, a normative investigation and defense of the ethical validity of norms would address these questions head on.

More generally, the empirical focus on norms means that the study of international norms has fallen into the is–ought problem from philosophy. There are numerous different ways of describing this problem, but for our purposes the cryptonormativism of constructivist research, in so far as these scholars tacitly assume that the norms they study are "good," rests on the mistaken assumption that because a norm is seen as good by a society, it is therefore good. Constructivists have been explicit that they do not think all norms are good.[19] However, in the absence of an explicitly normative research agenda, there is no way (for example) from within empirical constructivism to differentiate between norms of racial superiority in the 18th and 19th centuries that legitimized chattel slavery and the Atlantic slave trade and contemporary norms of racial equality. This gap in social constructivist analysis opened up norms researchers to critique from international ethicists.

The exclusion of the ethical from early social constructivist research

The difficulty that second-generation empirical constructivists have in linking their study of norms to questions of the normative has been an obstacle to the advancement of normative theorizing in their research. In some cases, this lack of normative theorizing is not terribly problematic. For instance, realist scholars contend that the inability to link the normative to the empirical stems from the structure of international politics. Realists contend that, given the state of anarchy that exists between states, any attempt to base political action on a principle other than national interest is irrational and dangerous. Yet in the case of constructivism, the lack of significant normative theorizing is problematic. Constructivist scholarship emerged in the late 1980s in an attempt to show that normative principles do in fact have an effect on the identities, behaviors, and interests of states.[20] Over the subsequent 25-plus years, constructivist scholars have demonstrated that norms have constrained the use of chemical and nuclear weapons, facilitated decolonization, and strengthened human rights, to cite just three examples.[21] Because the role of morality is so central to the constructivist narrative of international society, it is all the more surprising that constructivists have little to say about which norms should be promoted and how different norms should be assessed. Mervyn Frost leveled this critique at constructivist and other constitutive IR scholars when he observed:

> For the task of IR theory according to constitutive theorists is to reveal our global international social order to be a human construct within which are embedded certain values chosen by us and to show how this construct benefits some and oppresses others. . . However, in practice, constitutive theorists have done very little of this kind of theorizing. They do not for the most part tackle the question 'What would it be ethical to do in the circumstances'.[22]

I believe that there are two reasons why this ethical impasse has developed in social constructivism. First, attempts to bring a normative dimension to constructivist scholarship normally involve applying a pre-existing ethical approach to cases within a constructivist research agenda. The problem with this is that the approaches that are most often suggested as possible candidates—Habermasian discourse ethics,[23] Rawlsian political constructivism,[24] and Martha Nussbaum and Amartya Sen's capabilities approach[25]—do not fit with the ontological assumptions of social constructivists. Second, social constructivists who do want to develop the normative implications of their research tend to trip up over the fact–value distinction—that is, the problem of how one develops normative prescriptions from empirical descriptions. As such, to move beyond constructivism's ethical impasse, one must find an approach to ethics that is a good fit with constructivism's ontological assumptions and that has an answer for what meta-ethicists call the is–ought problem.

It is difficult to reconcile constructivist ontological commitments with existing ethical theories. Constitutive social theorists generally engage in thick descriptions of existing social practices to demonstrate how existing social structures emerged contingently. While these analyses often expose a set of social rules that simultaneously enable and constrain human actions, these rules are often so context-specific that it becomes extremely difficult to link them up with broad normative principles developed by political theorists and philosophers. For instance, Christian Reus-Smit argues that neo-Kantian approaches to international ethics—such as those developed by John Rawls[26] and Onora O'Neill[27]—engage in "a form of philosophical inquiry characterized, first and foremost, by logical reasoning from first principles."[28] This approach does not mix well with constructivist scholarship because "'Facts' are chosen selectively to undergird the preferred line of moral reasoning, and often voluminous amounts of relevant empirical research and theory are ignored."[29] The consequence of this is that many approaches to international ethics make moral judgments about general phenomena—such as poverty, war, and human rights—without seeing how particular contexts may make particular courses of action impossible, or perhaps even undesirable.

Kathryn Sikkink is critical of Sen[30] and Nussbaum's[31] pioneered capabilities approach for similar reasons. She critiques Sen and Nussbaum for believing "that they must start from scratch in inventing their central list of rights and capabilities."[32] There is already a dense existing set of international human rights principles, developed over 50 years through the deliberations of over 150 countries and thousands of human rights NGOs. The existing consensus on human rights "provide[s] a more legitimate source of general principles than any I or any other individual or group of researchers could invent."[33] From this perspective, dominant, rationalist ethical theories, in so far as they ignore empirical considerations, appear to be doing little more than reinventing the wheel.

In addition to Reus-Smit's and Sikkink's charges that the existing modes of normative theorizing are insufficiently empirical, constructivists have complained that normative theorizing is often impractical. For instance, Price has been critical of attempts by constructivists to draw on Habermasian discourse ethics[34] because ideal-speech situations "would seem to be empirically rare if not indeed theoretically impossible for some versions of constructivism."[35] None of the dominant approaches in normative theorizing sufficiently incorporate into their approaches analyses of power imbalances and the constraining effects of existing social structures that are the mainstay of constructivist theory. The lack of normative theorizing by constructivists is complemented by the failure of normative theorists to adequately take into account the empirical conditions that govern human action in world politics. Consequently, normatively inclined international relations scholars and empirically inclined social constructivists talk past each other rather than to each other.

Constructivists have difficulty providing ethical foundations for their theories because their commitments and procedures are at odds with many of the dominant theories of international ethics. Constructivists spend much of their time analyzing specific discourses among actors whose normative arguments are deeply embedded in their identities. Power relations between the participants in normative struggles play a significant role in the formulation and resolution of these debates.[36] From this perspective, attempts by liberal rationalists to ground normative theories in original positions or ideal speech situations appear nonsensical.[37] A normative approach to international relations that constructivists might find useful would start from specific normative struggles rather than deduct from first principles. It would be sensitive to the ways that identity and power relations shape possible courses of action. Such an approach would start with normative conditions as they currently exist in the world and propose concrete ways of improving the human condition.

The integration of the ethical and the empirical in social constructivist norms research

In response to these normative theorists' critiques, social constructivists have shifted to ethical research over the last decade. Three works in particular are exemplary of social constructivists' strategies to incorporate normative analysis into their work on global politics. The first of these is Richard Price's edited volume *Moral Limit and Possibility in World Politics*.[38] In this volume, Price invites empirically oriented social constructivists to reflect upon the normative implications of their research. The second is Antje Wiener's recent development of a "bi-focal"[39] approach to the study of norm contestation. Wiener, drawing on recent strands of discourse ethics and agonism in political theory, has developed a set of thinking tools that explicitly call on the scholar to consider the normative and empirical dimensions of international norms simultaneously.[40] The third is Neta Crawford's *Accountability for Killing* that combines just war theorizing with organizational theory to analyze the complicated question of who or what is morally responsible for collateral damage.[41] While there are other works that combine a social constructivist approach to international norms with a normative analysis of global politics,[42] this section will focus on these three examples as they point to three different ways in which constructivist scholars have taken up the ethical challenge in recent years.

The Price volume, in particular, frames itself in part as a response to normative theorists such as Frost who claim that the lack of engagement with the ethical was a significant oversight in social constructivist research. Both Price and Sikkink respond directly to Frost's charge by pointing out that early social constructivist scholarship "was itself a response to the skepticism that moral norms matter in world politics."[43] Similarly, Sikkink writes:

> When I started working on human rights in the late 1980s, the choice of topic alone was a sufficiently normative signal that I felt obliged to spend the rest of my time demonstrating that I was being rigorous in my method and theory.[44]

Early constructivists framed the research agenda as an intervention into debates between neorealists and neoliberals. Neorealists who are skeptical that ideas and moral norms have any impact on world politics dismiss moral speech acts by international actors as "cheap talk." While neoliberals are more sanguine about the possibilities for international cooperation and progress, they ground their explanations in rationalist accounts of state behavior that focused on the logic of consequences. In order to gain a foothold in the debates of the late 1980s and early 1990s, constructivists explicitly bracketed questions of whether a norm was good or bad in order to focus their research on demonstrating that norms have social effects. By the mid-2000s, mainstream IR had widely accepted the main claim of social constructivist research that norms do shape the behavior of international actors, and so now the criticism has shifted terrain. The normative critique of constructivism, however, comes from three different directions. First, more positivist-oriented scholars may have accepted that norms matter in international relations, but they instead now chastise constructivists for promoting norms that are morally good but may have dubious consequences from a pragmatic perspective.[45] Second, international ethicists continue to critique constructivists for not making their normative judgments explicit. Third, critical theorists express deep suspicion about the positive benefits of the (mostly liberal) norms that constructivist scholars study.[46]

Price and the other contributors to the volume framed the normative arguments by defending the virtues of empirical social science. In particular, Price argues that the empirical research of constructivists could assist normative theorists by guiding the ethical question of "what is to be done" with empirical insights into "what one may have some reasonable expectation of working."[47] In his introduction, Price proposes a collaborative partnership between international ethicists, who would work out normative arguments to critique contemporary world politics, and empirical social constructivists, who would analyze what the current international norms are and how the contemporary global political context permits some types of normative theorizing and constrains others. Price argues that social constructivism has six major contributions to make to the study of international ethics. First, social constructivist scholarship naturally occupies a position in the field where it is possible to survey the relationship between the ethical and the empirical. Second, Price contends that the debate between rationalist and social constructivist IR scholars over the nature of agency is significant for normative IR. Recall that rationalists contend that the primary explanation for behavior in international politics is the logic of consequences, whereas for constructivists the primary explanation for behavior in international politics is the logic of appropriateness.[48] A third avenue for constructivist research is through the examination of hypocrisy in world politics. In *Just and Unjust Wars*, Michael Walzer argues that the identification of hypocritical actions in warfare was a good technique for uncovering the moral structures that underpin shared judgments about what is just in warfare.[49] In a similar vein, constructivist scholars have traced cases of hypocrisy by international actors as evidence that an actor is aware a norm exists. Fourth, Price contends that constructivist research offers useful empirical insights into how norms work in practice that might be useful for normative theorists. One key finding of constructivist research is that norms are not simply constraining by prohibiting certain types of actions: norms are also constituting. Norms constitute new identities for actors, and this process of identity constitution in turn constructs new interests. The fifth insight from constructivist scholarship is the relevance of processes of co-constitution of identity for thinking through complicated moral issues of co-optation and complicity. Finally, Price contends that constructivism occupies an ethical middle-ground between poststructuralist approaches to international norms that often argue against putting limits on what is ethically possible in global politics and more realist approaches that believe talk of the normative in global politics is a fruitless exercise.[50]

Some of the participants in the Price project have taken up this call to wed the empirical with the normative in their own research. Consider, for instance, Bahar Rumelili's research, which argues that the EU's projection of integration through the promotion of human rights and democracy within Europe necessarily rests on the construction of other states outside the EU (such as Turkey) as less democratic.[51] Similarly, Helen Kinsella argues that the construction of the civilian within the just war tradition rests in turn on the denigration of non-Christians as heretics who are permissible targets in war.[52] Ann Towns in her research notes that the status of women within a state has been taken as one means of constructing a social hierarchy. However, in the 19th century, Western European states denigrated societies that permitted political participation of women, while celebrating their own exclusionary practices as a mark of civilization.[53] As the status of women in Western European societies shifted in the 20th century, political inclusion of women suddenly became a marker of civilization, yet the use of gender to enforce global hierarchies remained. And I have explored the ways in which the Declaration on the Rights of Indigenous Peoples re-inscribes hierarchies between settler states and their indigenous communities by limiting the recognition of indigenous self-governance under international law.[54] What all these critical analyses reveal is that norms constitute identities, which in turn constitute social hierarchies, and that in many instances social norms that at first glance appear progressive and liberal may rest upon hidden practices of exclusion and domination.

One example of a recently published work of scholarship that draws upon rigorous empirical research methods to examine critically an ethical dilemma is Crawford's *Accountability for Killing: Moral Responsibility for Collateral Damage in America's Post-9/11 Wars*. Crawford argues that "[t]he unintentional killing of civilians is at the root of perhaps the most difficult moral dilemmas that soldiers and their commanders face."[55] While "collateral damage" is legal under the international laws of war, deliberately targeting civilians is not. Sometimes militaries deliberately place civilians next to legitimate targets to dissuade attacks (i.e., "human shields"). Other times militaries have options for fighting in a way that will minimize civilian casualties, but strategic decisions will put soldiers at greater risk (i.e., "force protection") or make the mission more difficult to accomplish. As such, military leaders often have to weigh putting their own soldiers at risk versus putting civilians from the enemy country at risk when developing battle plans. In practice, so long as a civilian is not intentionally targeted, then civilian deaths are legally permitted and even morally excused under just war theory. Crawford argues, however, that this paradigm means that the over 38,000 civilian deaths were counted as collateral damage in its military operations between 2002 and 2012, and that while none of these deaths were intentional, many of these deaths were foreseeable. As a consequence, the central assumption of moral agency that underpins both the laws of war and the just war tradition, the idea of the individual autonomous moral agent, simultaneously "protects noncombatants from deliberate killing [while] allow[ing] unintended killing."[56] Through her critical examination of the laws of war, Crawford uncovers an instance of a dark side of an apparently good norm and then develops an alternative theory of moral agency which she calls "organizational responsibility" to argue that the military as a whole is responsible for minimizing the number of foreseeable (as opposed to simply unintentional) civilian deaths from combat. Because this work empirically investigates the consequences of an existing international norm, critiques the norm, and then develops an account of moral agency that is distinct from the hegemonic model of agency in the just war theory tradition, it is a model of the type of empirical-normative research partnership that Price calls for in his work. The normative argument about organizational agency is only possible because Crawford draws upon organization theory to analyze the causal chain in military decisions that lead to unintentional but foreseeable civilian casualties.[57] The analysis also enables Crawford to make a number of concrete recommendations to military leaders about how foreseeable civilian deaths can be minimized in the future.[58]

In her recently published work, *A Theory of Contestation*, Wiener takes a different approach to integrating international ethics and social constructivism.[59] Whereas Price and his collaborators and Crawford draw upon empirical research techniques to fill in some of the gaps in normative theorizing, Wiener argues that how social constructivists have theorized norms has created an artificial divide between normative and empirical research. Most social constructivist scholarship studies norms from the perspective of compliance. According to this perspective, a norm is legitimate so long as states comply with it, and scholars can demonstrate a norm's existence by demonstrating widespread compliance. Wiener, however, postulates that both the legitimation of norms and the generation of norms come about not via compliance, but via contestation. In order to develop her theory of contestation, Wiener draws upon the public philosophy of

James Tully. Tully's work on democratic constitutionalism and agonistic political philosophy emphasizes the way in which conflict is a form of justice.[60] Whereas other influential approaches to justice, such as Habermas's work on deliberative democracy and Rawls's work on political liberalism,[61] see conflicts in pluralistic societies as problems to be solved through the development of procedures and norms which can achieve consensus amongst all participants, Tully's approach is skeptical about finding such universally acceptable norms as possible or desirable. Instead, the justness of a society should be determined by its capacity to make space for contestation of all norms and procedures, to never seek out a final comprehensive solution, but to treat all norms as always subject to contestation and revision by any and all persons who are affected by them. Wiener brings Tully's political philosophy of contestation into IR debates over norm compliance to argue that disputes and resistance to the implementation of norms is not a problem that IR scholars, international lawyers, and practitioners need to solve. Rather, this contestation of norms (the fact that groups subjected to norms can contest the validity of those norms) is the very mark of their legitimacy. Wiener takes this central insight from Tully's work to critique both liberal and critical varieties of constructivism. Against the liberal constructivists (what she calls 'conventional constructivists'), Wiener argues that Tully's insight that one can demonstrate understanding a norm by going against it has the capacity to explain how contestation can generate norms. Against the conventional constructivists, who draw upon Habermas's distinction between arguing and bargaining to make the case that contestation about norms is appropriate only at the implementation stage,[62] Wiener argues that norms can be contested at any stage in their constitution, reference, or implementation.

In order to develop this theory of contestation, Wiener proposes three "thinking tools": first, the normativity premise; second, the diversity premise; and third, cultural cosmopolitanism. The normativity premise underscores a central tension in the norms literature between sociological approaches that emphasize the ways in which norms habitualize expected behavior (i.e., the ways in which norms normalize behaviors) and legal and philosophical approaches that are concerned with the validity of norms (i.e., the normative dimension of norms). One common critique of conventional constructivists is that in their attempt to develop explanatory theories of norms, they have bracketed questions of whether or not norms are good or bad, just or unjust. This bracketing of the normative means that conventional constructivists often assume that the norms they study are good, thereby potentially ignoring the dark sides of some norms; and they may entirely ignore some norms that are bad (such as those that say a state should protect the interests of private capital over the interests of its least well off citizens). The normativity premise opens the door for a substantial engagement between empirical scholars of norms and scholars of international ethics both to critique existing norms and find sounder normative foundations for international laws. The diversity premise draws upon Tully's critique of Kant and contemporary Kantian political philosophy. According to Tully, one of the problems of Kantian approaches to normative theorizing is that the search for categorical imperatives and universally valid principles can be culturally hegemonic. As such, Tully argues against seeking "end states" in normative deliberations and instead argues that valid norms are those that are worked out through cross-cultural negotiation, premised on mutual recognition, mutual consent, and openness to revision and contestation at a future date. This emphasis on agonistic procedures ensures that diversity is built into the process of norm generation and legitimation. Finally, the principle of cultural cosmopolitanism states that global politics is constituted through cultural practices. Drawing upon Tully once again, Wiener argues that there is an important interaction between practices of contestation and the principle of contestedness. Central to Wiener's argument is that what secures the legitimacy of a norm is if it has been generated through practices open to contestation. Norms that are generated univocally, without making space for challenges from actors who could be affected by that norm are invalid. The principle of contestedness (i.e., the fact that the norm was generated through practices open to contestation, and continues to be open to contestation during referral and implementation) is what makes a norm valid.

The challenges and opportunities in fusing normative and empirical research on international norms

While these moves towards a more explicitly normative constructivism have been well received by international ethicists, there has also been some concern that normative constructivists lack clear evaluative criteria with which to determine if a norm is good or bad. Toni Erskine, in her assessment of the Price volume, makes this argument most forcefully when she writes:

> In other words, this constructivism is able to say that norms matter in a way that is extremely valuable; however, it is less equipped to say why certain norms are more or less just or ethical than others, or why their emergence or transformation constitutes moral progress or regress.[63]

Erskine's critique echoes Matthew J. Hoffman and Nicholas Rengger's respective similar comments that "constructivism lacks a fundamental moral core"[64] and that Price's constructivism is not "clear and explicit about its normative commitments and the reasons it has for them."[65] What all three of these critics are saying is that constructivism lacks a clear moral epistemology. Moral epistemology refers to the metaethical question: How does one *know* if an action is right or wrong?[66] So, the general critique of the constructivists' turn to ethics is that they are lacking a clear set of guidelines by which to determine whether or not a principle is moral.

From the empirical social scientist's perspective, metaethical debates can sometimes seem like arcane philosophical debates about angels dancing on the heads of pins. But for those working in the world of ethics, to accuse a scholar of lacking a moral epistemology is as serious a charge as accusing an empirical researcher of selecting a case on the dependent variable, conflating causation with correlation, confusing the direction of the causal arrow, or lacking a clear hypothesis. Without an account of how one knows whether an action is right or wrong, from the ethicist's perspective, a normative claim is simply an assertion, lacking in any scholarly merit.

Price's response to Rengger's and Erskine's concerns about the lack of a clear moral yardstick is twofold. First, in responding directly to Erskine, Price argues that the primary value of constructivism to normative IR

> is less in extended normative arguments as such grounding general moral commitments. . . and more in offering perspective concerning possibilities for their realization and structural costs, and leverage when brutal trade-offs are confronted between moral commitments that cannot simultaneously be realized.[67]

So the primary contribution of constructivist research to IR scholarship is its use of its empirical discoveries to clarify what is at stake in various normative dilemmas, and thereby clarifying the best possible courses of action. However, Price is not willing to surrender the entire enterprise of defining and defending the evaluative criteria used in normative judgments to international ethicists such as Erskine. After responding to Erskine's charge that a constructivist ethic is inherently conservative because it is dependent upon existing moral norms, Price concludes that "[f]urther development of just how the interpretive analytics of the type [Erskine] seems to champion within normative theory would deal with this would seem to offer one avenue for further conversation."[68] So while Price does not develop a clear moral yardstick, he does concede that this is one gap in the current move towards a normative constructivist research agenda that should (or at the very least could) be filled in.

In addition to addressing the problem of what is social constructivism's moral epistemology, there is also a clear set of academic institutional obstacles to the development of a normative research agenda for social constructivists. To train a scholar to produce publishable knowledge in either international ethics or empirical social constructivist takes years of graduate education. It is rare that university programs happen to have an overlap in scholars in both areas, and rarer still that there are students able to master two very different sets of theories and methodologies all while writing a PhD dissertation that is easily marketable in a very tight job market. When we compound that problem with the challenges scholars face in writing for the two distinct academic audiences of international ethics and social constructivism, there are very strong career disincentives for pursuing a research agenda that combines empirical social constructivist research with normative analysis. As such, one institutional reason for the lack of explicitly normative constructivist research is how the different approaches have incentivized publishing, hiring, and PhD training, thereby making it difficult for scholars to do work that crosses the normative empirical boundary.

More generally, the fact that there have been attempts by both international ethicists and social constructivists to do work at the intersection of these fields indicates that there is at least untapped potential for an explicitly normative social constructivism. Such a research agenda would prod empirically oriented constructivists to move beyond their cryptonormativism by both making their normative commitments explicit and then spelling out the reasons for holding those commitments in a sufficiently philosophically rigorous way so as to answer the concerns of international ethicists such as Erskine, Frost, and Rengger. Simultaneously, international ethicists should be held to greater empirical account when it comes to their normative claims. A greater emphasis should be placed on using existing international law and practice as the starting point for normative theorizing (as opposed to the tendency to begin normative enquiry from abstract first principles), and international ethicists should take seriously the arguments from social constructivists that normative claims should rest on a clear understanding of the causal chains in global politics, and offer prescriptions that are both politically possible and have fully considered the possible trade-offs and moral dilemmas one may confront in implementation. Going forward, a synthesis of social constructivism and international ethics could take two (not necessarily mutually exclusive) paths forward. The first path is collaborative and incremental. It would entail international ethicists partnering with empirical scholars on issue areas of joint concern. For instance, an empirical scholar on the international laws of migration could collaborate with a political theorist working on the ethics of migration on a joint projects that analyzed both what a just migration policy would be, and the political obstacles to implementing such a policy. Crawford's work and the participants in the Price volume are two examples of works that take steps down this path. The second path would involve a larger paradigm shift that would entail rethinking what a norm is so that norms can be analyzed simultaneously from a normative and empirical perspective in such a way that the analysis satisfies both Price's demand for greater empirical rigor and Erskine's call for a clearer moral yardstick with which to assess the validity of norms. Wiener's work on a "bi-focal" approach that considers contestation as a practice of both norm validation and contestation is a step down this path. While it is generally a futile attempt to predict which way an academic discipline will unfold, at the very least recent scholarship points to the possibility for a more productive conversation between international ethicists and social constructivists in the near future.

Notes

1 David M. McCourt, "Practice Theory and Relationalism as the New Constructivism," *International Studies Quarterly*, 60, no. 3 (2016): 476.
2 Kenneth Neal Waltz, *Theory of International Politics* (Reading, Massachusetts: Addison-Wesley, 1979).
3 Robert W. Cox, "Social Forces, States and World Orders: Beyond International Relations Theory," *Millennium: Journal of International Studies*, 10, no. 2 (June 1, 1981): 126–155, doi:10.1177/03058298810100020501.
4 I draw the labeling of constructivism via generations from Brent Steele's recent work. According to Steele's analysis, the first generation of constructivists includes scholars such as Onuf, Kratochwil, and Lapid, who developed their social theories in the context of the Cold War. The second generation emerged in the 1990s and focused primarily on the role of norms in international politics, and upon situating constructivism as a via media between liberalism and realism, and behavioralism and poststructuralism. See Brent J. Steele, "Introduction," *PS: Political Science and Politics*, 50, no. 1 (January 2017): 71–74, doi:10.1017/S1049096516002171; Oliver Kessler and Brent J. Steele, "Introduction: 'Constructing IR: The Third Generation,'" *European Review of International Studies*, 3, no. 3 (2016): 5–19.
5 Alexander Wendt, "Anarchy Is What States Make of It: The Social Construction of Power Politics," *International Organization*, 46, no. 2 (1992): 397.
6 Alexander Wendt, *Social Theory of International Politics* (Cambridge: Cambridge University Press, 1999), 77–89.
7 Emanuel Adler, "Seizing the Middle Ground: Constructivism in World Politics," *European Journal of International Relations*, 3, no. 3 (September 1, 1997): 319–363, doi:10.1177/1354066197003003003.
8 Consider Martha Finnemore and Kathryn Sikkink, "International Norm Dynamics and Political Change," *International Organization*, 52, no. 4 (September 1998): 887–917, doi:10.1162/002081898550789. The article begins by reviewing the long history of normative concerns in IR scholarship before explicitly pivoting towards an empirical analysis of how norms work.
9 I am thinking here of the major texts in international ethics since the publication of Rawls's *A Theory of Justice* such as work by Charles R. Beitz, *Political Theory and International Relations*, revised edn. (Princeton: Princeton University Press, 1999); Thomas W. Pogge, *Realizing Rawls*, 1st edn. (Ithaca: Cornell University Press, 1989), pt. 3; Michael Walzer, *Just and Unjust Wars: A Moral Argument with Historical Illustrations* (New York: Basic Books, 2006). Social scientific accounts that emphasize how structure determines individual actions limit the scope of individual autonomy, and thereby limit individual moral accountability. This of course is not to ignore numerous other interventions in international ethics from more critical and continental perspectives, such as Fiona Robinson, *The Ethics of Care: A Feminist Approach to Human Security, Global Ethics and Politics* (Philadelphia: Temple University Press, 2011); Kimberly Hutchings, *International Political Theory: Rethinking Ethics in a Global Era*, 1st edn. (London; Thousand Oaks, CA: Sage Publications, 2009); Amanda Russell Beattie and Kate Schick, eds., *The Vulnerable Subject: Beyond Rationalism in International Relations* (Houndmills, Basingstoke, Hampshire: Palgrave Macmillan, 2012, 2013); David Campbell and Michael J. Shapiro, *Moral Spaces: Rethinking Ethics and World Politics* (Minneapolis, Minnesota: University of Minnesota Press, 1999).
10 Thomas Risse and Kathryn Sikkink, "The Socialization of International Human Rights Norms into Domestic Practices: Introduction," in *The Power of Human Rights: International Norms and Domestic Change*, ed. Thomas Risse, Kathryn Sikkink, and Stephen C. Ropp (Cambridge: Cambridge University Press, 1999), 8.
11 James G. March and Johan P. Olsen, "The Institutional Dynamics of International Political Orders," *International Organization*, 52, no. 4 (September 1998): 943–969, doi:10.1162/002081898550699.
12 Richard Price, "A Genealogy of the Chemical Weapons Taboo," *International Organization*, 49, no. 1 (1995): 73–103; Nina Tannenwald, "The Nuclear Taboo: The United States and the Normative Basis of Nuclear Non-Use," *International Organization*, 53, no. 3 (1999): 433–468; Richard M. Price and Nina Tannenwald, "Norms and Deterrence: The Nuclear and Chemical Weapons Taboos," in *The Culture of National Security*, ed. Peter J. Katzenstein (New York: Columbia University Press, 1996).
13 Margaret E. Keck and Kathryn Sikkink, *Activists beyond Borders: Advocacy Networks in International Politics* (Ithaca, New York: Cornell University Press, 1998).
14 Jonathan Havercroft, "Sovereignty, Recognition, and Indigenous Peoples," in *Moral Limit and Possibility in World Politics*, ed. Richard M. Price (Cambridge: Cambridge University Press, 2008); Jonathan Havercroft, "Was Westphalia 'all that'? Hobbes, Bellarmine, and the Norm of Non-Intervention," *Global Constitutionalism*, 1, no. 1 (2012): 120–140.

15 I draw the term "cryptonormative" from Habermas's famous critique of Foucault. See Jürgen Habermas and Frederick G. Lawrence, *The Philosophical Discourse of Modernity: Twelve Lectures*, reprint edn. (Cambridge, Massachusetts: MIT Press, 1990), 276.

16 Richard M. Price, "Moral Limit and Possibility in World Politics," in *Moral Limit and Possibility in World Politics*, ed. Richard M. Price (Cambridge: Cambridge University Press, 2008), 4; Paul Kowert and Jeffrey Legro, "Norms, Identity and Their Limits," in *The Culture of National Security: Norms and Identity in World Politics*, ed. Peter Katzenstein (New York: Columbia University Press, 1996), 451–497.

17 Price, "Moral Limit and Possibility in World Politics"; Kathryn Sikkink, "The Role of Consequences, Comparison and Counterfactuals in Constructivist Ethical Thought," in *Moral Limit and Possibility in World Politics*, ed. Richard M. Price (Cambridge: Cambridge University Press, 2008), 83.

18 J. Marshall Beier, "Dangerous Terrain: Re-Reading the Landmines Ban through the Social Worlds of the RMA," *Contemporary Security Policy*, 32, no. 1 (April 1, 2011): 159–175, doi:10.1080/13523260.2011.556857; Kenneth Anderson, "The Ottawa Convention Banning Landmines, the Role of International Non-Governmental Organizations and the Idea of International Civil Society," *European Journal of International Law*, 11, no. 1 (January 1, 2000): 91–120, doi:10.1093/ejil/11.1.91.

19 Finnemore and Sikkink, "International Norm Dynamics and Political Change," 892. Note in particular their argument that slavery from the vantage point of slave owners rested on a norm of racial superiority. Finnemore and Sikkink obviously do not endorse this position, but they also do explain how one should differentiate between good and bad norms.

20 Adler, "Seizing the Middle Ground"; Friedrich Kratochwil, "The Protagorean Quest: Community, Justice, and the 'Oughts' and 'Musts' of International Politics," *International Journal*, 43, no. 2 (April 1, 1988): 205–240, doi:10.2307/40202526; Nicholas Greenwood Onuf, *World of Our Making: Rules and Rule in Social Theory and International Relations* (London: Routledge, 2012); Alexander Wendt, *Social Theory of International Politics* (Cambridge: Cambridge University Press, 1999).

21 Price, "A Genealogy of the Chemical Weapons Taboo"; Tannenwald, "The Nuclear Taboo"; Risse and Sikkink, "The Socialization of International Human Rights Norms into Domestic Practices: Introduction"; Keck and Sikkink, *Activists Beyond Borders*; Finnemore and Sikkink, "International Norm Dynamics and Political Change"; Price and Tannenwald, "Norms and Deterrence: The Nuclear and Chemical Weapons Taboos"; Neta C. Crawford, *Argument and Change in World Politics: Ethics, Decolonization, and Humanitarian Intervention* (Cambridge: Cambridge University Press, 2002).

22 Mervyn Frost, "A Turn Not Taken: Ethics in IR at the Millenium," *Review of International Studies*, 24, no. 5 (1998): 127; see also Matthew J. Hoffmann, "Is Constructivist Ethics an Oxymoron?" *International Studies Review*, 11, no. 2 (June 1, 2009): 231–252, doi:10.1111/j.1468-2486.2009.00847.x; Crawford, *Argument and Change in World Politics*, 427.

23 Jürgen Habermas, "Discourse Ethics: Notes on a Paradigm of Philosophical Justification," in *Moral Consciousness and Communicative Action*, trans. Shierry Weber Nicholsen and Christian Lenhardt (Cambridge, MA: MIT Press, 1990).

24 John Rawls, *A Theory of Justice*, revised edn. (Cambridge, Massachusetts: Harvard University Press, 1999); John Rawls, *The Law of Peoples* (Cambridge, Massachusetts: Harvard University Press, 2001); John Rawls, *Political Liberalism* (New York: Columbia University, 1993).

25 Martha C. Nussbaum, *Women and Human Development: The Capabilities Approach*, new edn. (New York: Cambridge University Press, 2001); Amartya Sen and Martha C. Nussbaum, eds., *The Quality of Life* (Oxford: Oxford University Press, 1993).

26 Rawls, *Law of Peoples*.

27 Onora O'Neill, *Bounds of Justice* (New York: Cambridge University Press, 2000).

28 Christian Reus-Smit, "Constructivism and the Structure of Ethical Reasoning," in *Moral Limit and Possibility in World Politics*, ed. Richard M. Price (Cambridge: Cambridge University Press, 2008), 102.

29 Ibid.

30 Amartya Sen, "Rights and Agency," in *Consequentialism and Its Critics*, ed. Samuel Scheffler (Oxford: Oxford University Press, 1988), 187–223.

31 Nussbaum, *Women and Human Development*.

32 Sikkink, "Consequences, Comparison and Counterfactuals in Constructivist Ethical Thought," 139.

33 Ibid., 141.

34 Thomas Risse, "'Let's Argue!': Communicative Action in World Politics," *International Organization*, 54, no. 1 (January 10, 2000): 1–39, doi:10.1162/002081800551109.

35 Price, "Moral Limit and Possibility in World Politics," 75.

36 Michael Barnett and Raymond Duvall, "Power in International Politics," *International Organization*, 59, no. 1 (January 2005): 39–75, doi:10.1017/S0020818305050010.
37 Raymond Geuss makes a similar critique of this Kantian-influenced form of normative theorizing as being "ethics first" and thereby ignoring the realities of politics and history. See Raymond Geuss, *Philosophy and Real Politics* (Princeton: Princeton University Press, 2008).
38 Richard M. Price, ed., *Moral Limit and Possibility in World Politics* (New York: Cambridge University Press, 2008).
39 Antje Wiener, *A Theory of Contestation*, Springer Briefs in Political Science (Berlin, Heidelberg: Springer Berlin Heidelberg, 2014), http://link.springer.com/10.1007/978-3-642-55235-9.
40 Antje Wiener, *A Theory of Contestation*, Springer Briefs in Political Science (Berlin, Heidelberg: Springer Berlin Heidelberg, 2014), http://link.springer.com/10.1007/978-3-642-55235-9.
41 Neta C. Crawford, *Accountability for Killing: Moral Responsibility for Collateral Damage in America's post-9/11 Wars* (Oxford: Oxford University Press, 2013).
42 Michael N. Barnett and Thomas G. Weiss, eds., *Humanitarianism in Question: Politics, Power, Ethics* (Ithaca, New York: Cornell University Press, 2008); Helen Kinsella, *The Image before the Weapon: A Critical History of the Distinction between Combatant and Civilian* (Ithaca, New York: Cornell University Press, 2011).
43 Price, *Moral Limit and Possibility in World Politics*, 3.
44 Kathryn Sikkink, "Consequences, Comparison and Counterfactuals in Constructivist Ethical Thought," 83.
45 Jack L. Snyder and Leslie Vinjamuri, "Trials and Errors: Principle and Pragmatism in Strategies of International Justice," *International Security*, 28, no. 3 (March 9, 2004): 5–44.
46 Maja Zehfuss, *Constructivism in International Relations: The Politics of Reality* (New York: Cambridge University Press, 2002); Kinsella, *Image before the Weapon*.
47 Price, "Moral Limit and Possibility in World Politics," 7.
48 March and Olsen, "Institutional Dynamics of International Political Orders."
49 Walzer, *Just and Unjust Wars*, 19–20.
50 Campbell and Shapiro, *Moral Spaces*; R. B. J. Walker, *Inside/Outside: International Relations as Political Theory* (Cambridge: Cambridge University Press, 1993), chapter 3.
51 Bahar Rumelili, "Interstate Community-Building and the Identity/Difference Predicament," in *Moral Limit and Possibility in World Politics*, ed. Richard Price (Cambridge: Cambridge University Press, 2008), 253–304; Bahar Rumelili, "Constructing Identity and Relating to Difference: Understanding the EU's Mode of Differentiation," *Review of International Studies*, 30, no. 1 (2004): 27–47.
52 Kinsella, *The Image before the Weapon*.
53 Ann E. Towns, *Women and States: Norms and Hierarchies in International Society* (Cambridge: Cambridge University Press, 2010); Ann Towns, "The Status of Women as a Standard of 'Civilization,'" *European Journal of International Relations*, 15, no. 4 (December 1, 2009): 681–706, doi:10.1177/1354066109345053.
54 Jonathan Havercroft, "Sovereignty, Recognition and Indigenous Peoples," in *Moral Limit and Possibility in World Politics*, ed. Richard M. Price (Cambridge: Cambridge University Press, 2008), 112–138.
55 Crawford, *Accountability for Killing*, 3.
56 Ibid., 7.
57 Ibid., 23.
58 Ibid., chapter 9.
59 Wiener, *A Theory of Contestation*.
60 James Tully, *Public Philosophy in a New Key*: Volume 2, *Imperialism and Civic Freedom* (Cambridge: Cambridge University Press, 2009); James Tully, *Strange Multiplicity: Constitutionalism in an Age of Diversity* (Cambridge: Cambridge University Press, 1995); James Tully, *Public Philosophy in a New Key*: Volume 1, *Democracy and Civic Freedom* (Cambridge: Cambridge University Press, 2009).
61 Habermas, "Discourse Ethics"; Rawls, *Political Liberalism*.
62 Risse, "Let's Argue!"; Nicole Deitelhoff and Harald Müller, "Theoretical Paradise: Empirically Lost? Arguing with Habermas," *Review of International Studies*, 31, no. 1 (2005): 167–179.
63 Toni Erskine, "Whose Progress, Which Morals? Constructivism, Normative IR Theory and the Limits and Possibilities of Studying Ethics in World Politics," *International Theory*, 4, no. 3 (November 2012): 454–455, doi:10.1017/S1752971912000152.
64 Hoffmann, "Is Constructivist Ethics an Oxymoron?," 233.
65 Nicholas Rengger, "Progress with Price?" *International Theory*, 4, no. 3 (November 2012): 476, doi:10.1017/S1752971912000164. Robinson makes a similar point about the volume failing to

reconcile the tension between analysis of the "real world" and the normative question of "how are we to act?". See Fiona Robinson, "Bridging the Real and the Ideal in International Ethics," *International Studies Review*, 11, no. 2 (June 1, 2009): 397, doi:10.1111/j.1468-2486.2009.00866.x.

66 For more on this, see Jonathan Havercroft, *Captives of Sovereignty* (New York: Cambridge University Press, 2011), 214–228.

67 Richard M. Price, "On the Pragmatic and Principled Limits and Possibilities of Dialogue," *International Theory*, 4, no. 3 (November 2012): 487–488, doi:10.1017/S1752971912000176.

68 Ibid., 490.

9

TRUTH AND POWER, UNCERTAINTY AND CATASTROPHE

Ethics in international relations realism

Andrew R. Hom

Introduction

Realism is often understood as an amoral and unethical theory of international politics—a valorization of naked power. As the well-known liberal Joseph Nye asserts, 'in a realist world, morality has little place. Might makes right.'[1] International relations (IR) neorealists agree with him. Kenneth Waltz argued that realism produces necessarily amoral foreign policies.[2] John Mearsheimer explains American antagonism to realism thus: 'realism is at odds with a deep-seated optimism and moralism'; 'utopian moralists' are 'prone to believe that morality should play an important role in politics', a commitment which 'clashes with the realist belief that war is an intrinsic element of life in the international system'.[3] Morality or war, you cannot have both in theory, Mearsheimer insists.[4] Politicians like Henry Kissinger and Condoleeza Rice lend support to these characterizations by authorizing cynical, illegal, and/or violent policies as part of their 'realist' view of politics. In their hands, realism moves beyond amorality to manifest immorality, a 'license to kill, make war, and commit wanton acts of rapine'.[5]

Despite their prevalence and profile, these views of realism misconceive a diverse ethico-political field of inquiry to the point of caricature. The umbrella term 'realism' contains a number of IR theoretical commitments and inclinations, which makes it difficult to pin the entire '-ism' to a single, simplistic moral assessment. More importantly, although they rarely provide easy or satisfying answers, IR realists have long been concerned with normative questions about limiting war, balancing state interests and moral principles, avoiding both radical evil and crusading hubris, the promise and perils of science, and the problem of thermonuclear catastrophe.

Through a historical survey of classical, neo- and reflexive realisms, this chapter traces ethics in realist IR, from its seminal importance, through its attempted purge in the name of 'science', and finally to its contemporary rejuvenation.[6] It shows that classical realists emphasized scepticism and the truth of power in order to confront irreducible moral tensions in foreign affairs. Later, the supposed power of scientific truth helped neorealists subvert and transform classical archetypes into a purportedly 'value-free' theory. However, neorealist science ultimately faltered against the perpetual ethical problem of nuclear war, a demoralized exception that only accentuates the rule of ethics in realism. More recently, reflexive scholars have excavated numerous classical realist writings, recovering and developing their ethical sensibilities and marrying them with social theoretical advances to resharpen realism's critical edge. These efforts bring realism into the 21st century and unlock an issue at the heart of realist ethics: the question of time, and especially the shadow of the future.

Classical realism: the truth of power and the problem of uncertainty

Emerging in the nascent academic field of IR, realism developed from deep anxieties driven by the experience of two world wars, fascism and totalitarianism, and the advent of nuclear weapons.[7] These horrors confounded scholars interested in international politics, who 'too often found themselves emotionally and intellectually unprepared for the event'.[8] Realists diagnosed the problem as resulting from modern pathologies, which placed ill-founded faith in open and representative government, international law, and 'the limitless power of the scientific formula' to cleanly resolve political dilemmas.[9] Despite generating great enthusiasm, such proposals had prevented neither global cataclysm nor the rise of a most appalling politics in Europe. Highlighting this disconnect between wish and fulfilment, realists branded such proposals 'utopian'[10] and 'idealist'[11] because they turned abstract ethical principles and assumptions of harmonized interests into a science of politics, which ignored the concrete particularities and 'the factor of power' that characterized political dilemmas.[12] E. H. Carr and, especially, Hans Morgenthau issued devastating critiques of this vision of science and sought instead to ground IR in a more 'realistic' analysis which distinguished aspiration from analysis, foregrounded power in context, and remained ever sceptical about any promises of clean fixes or scientific control.[13] Theirs was not a *science of politics* but rather a *political science*.

Despite realists' insistence that aspiration and analysis could never be absolutely separate,[14] such claims are commonly misunderstood as denoting a decisive break between realism and ethics. Yet for realists, the root of the problem was not ethical commitments as such but how scholars married them to 'the ideal postulates of abstract reason' and to spurious assumptions about how scientific knowledge influenced human action—all habits that made ethical outcomes *less likely* and, perversely, opened the door to further catastrophes.[15] By clarifying the contingent and imperfect situations through which moral commitments were always 'filtered',[16] classical realists sought in the appreciation of practical context a more reliable path to outcomes reflecting ethical commitments. This had the added benefit of chastening overwrought normative claims, which could *never* be 'independent of politics' because they were 'conditioned and dictated by the social order'.[17] This line of thinking can appear like an embrace of relativism,[18] but when Carr wrote that '[m]orality can only be relative, not universal', he made an empirical point meant to buttress the normative one that immediately followed it: 'Ethics must be interpreted in terms of politics . . . there is no good other than the acceptance and understanding of reality.'[19]

This looks like a rejection of ethics only if we assume that political dilemmas have absolute, optimal solutions and do not require, in any case, a choice between two evils,[20] and if we narrowly construe ethical deliberation as universalistic and rationalistic—as the analytical formulation of an ideal theory, independent of any sociopolitical context, to be applied 'top-down' to political life.[21] Classical realists insisted that political ethics began and ended 'on the ground', where there was no room for abstract ideals rashly applied. Instead, politicians must 'make the best moral choice *that circumstances permit*',[22] and the apex of *political* wisdom was for 'man [sic] to be as good as he can be in an evil world'.[23] Far from dispensing with ethics, classical realists sought to insulate the good from that which too often subverted it—the perfect, 'a source of greater evil' in the twentieth century.[24]

Similarly, classical realism mounted a sustained attack 'on so-called moralism, although not on moral evaluation'.[25] Early realists were not interested in excising ethics but in acknowledging and ensuring that political action would be 'based on a co-ordination of morality and power'.[26] As such, they sought a *modus vivendi*, a way of living with intrinsic tensions between 'utopia' and 'catastrophe', 'exuberance' and 'barrenness',[27] 'altruism' and 'selfishness',[28] 'romance' and 'reality',[29] and 'moral destiny' and 'political nature'.[30] Their overarching ethics involved two commitments: to preserve ethical possibility—the capacity to realize *some* measure of the good (however conceived) in an imperfect world—while avoiding catastrophe—the tendency of international politics to produce the worst outcomes on the widest scales.

Charting a middle course necessarily involves critical and constructive tasks. For Reinhold Niebuhr, this meant sorting out the confusion 'where politics and ethics meet' in order to determine what normative principles could be applied to human collectives.[31] And Carr wrote *The Twenty Years' Crisis* out of a 'passionate desire to prevent war' and to encourage the conditions by which a '*political* utopia' (rather than an abstract utopia) could 'grow . . . out of political reality'.[32] Classical realists understood their critical remit as a matter of unpacking and correcting the sort of intellectual excesses and simplistic principles that had led to the Somme, Auschwitz, and finally the bomb. They embraced this critical task with a gusto, thundering[33] against universalist principles, absolute morality, and abstract ethics. Their polemical and often hyperbolic style makes it possible to misread classical realist critiques of idealism and to cherry-pick aphoristic sentences out of more nuanced wholes in order to paint realism as a denial of *all* normativity, a theory without an ethos.

However, reading beyond and around such aphorisms helps us flesh out classical realism. Carr insisted that 'international politics are always power politics', but he also argued that 'it is an unreal kind of realism which ignores the element of morality in any world order'.[34] For all the talk of realism's pessimistic view of human nature,[35] Niebuhr also found humans naturally endowed with 'a sense of obligation toward the good, . . . a [contentless] principle of action which requires the individual to act according to whatever judgments of good and evil he [sic] is able to form'.[36] Morgenthau declared the 'twilight of international morality', but only by refusing to read his actual article can we interpret its titular metaphor as some triumphalist icon of a postmoral nightfall rather than a lamentation about the decline of 'universal moral rules of conduct' in international politics from vital light to 'feeble rays'.[37] Indeed, the article's purpose was to refute 'the misconception . . . that international politics is immoral, if not amoral, through and through and in any case so thoroughly evil that it is no use looking for ethical limitations'.[38] Morgenthau also insisted that all politics revolves around power, yet he developed realism in his well-cited *Politics among Nations* expressly to identify and develop more reliable ways to 'regulate and restrain the power drives that otherwise would either tear society apart or deliver . . . *the weak to the arbitrary will of the powerful*.'[39] Far from any cool, Thucydidean affirmation that 'the strong do what they will and the weak suffer what they must',[40] Morgenthau's realist classic was written to *prevent* just that sort of Peloponnesian power play.

With a consistency rivalled only by that with which their full comments have been forgotten, classical realists inveighed *not* against moral aspiration or principles *per se*, but against the *universalization* of particular aspirations and the pretence of *certitude* accompanying many ethical claims of their day, both of which could lead to national zealotry and a dangerous 'demonological' interpretation of political dilemmas and actors.[41] Tellingly, when classical realists disagreed with each other, they were quite willing to accuse fellow travellers of being 'utopian[s] of power', of relativism and instrumentalism, or of succumbing to 'the evil game of power politics'—the same charges they faced collectively from non-realist scholars.[42] So in addition to balancing classical realists' potent quotables, a brief look at three of their conceptual pillars—the national interest, the virtue of prudence, and the nature and balance of power,—helps to clarify and underline their moral politics.

The national interest

The idea of different states holding distinct national interests understood 'in terms of power'[43] seems like a relativistic or amoral view of international relations as a contest between egoistic and selfish states pursuing only their own gain. Yet classical realists found in the national interest no fixed content, which was what made it so useful as a heuristic device for 'effective political thinking'.[44] They did, however, find in it important ethical implications. Thinking in terms of national interest provides an epistemic bulwark against universalism. Because we can only ever grasp fully 'our own national interest' and appraise foreign relations through it, we cannot assume 'moral homogeneity'[45] or even 'discernibility' across national boundaries.[46] The national interest thus exposes '[s]upposedly absolute and universal principles' as 'not principles at all, but the unconscious reflexions of national policy'.[47] Far from encouraging pure selfishness, it 'saves' states from 'moral excess and . . . political folly' and enables them to 'do justice to all [nations]' by putting a brake on moralizing rhetoric.[48] In these ways, classical realists constructed an alternative to liberal proposals for checking political power—instead of public opinion, open diplomacy, or international law, the national interest provided a holistic and modest view of state purposes and relations intended to subdue any totalizing objectives and to remove the moral fig leaves from instrumental manoeuvres.[49] The national interest thereby helped temper both moralism and outright cynicism.

The virtue of prudence

In popular discourse, prudence often signifies inaction (think of George H. W. Bush—'It wouldn't be prudent at this juncture') and a way for actors to avoid principled or morally demanded action. Yet classical realist prudence emanated from an ethics of consequences, where outcomes trump intentions.[50] Precisely because outcomes matter most, prudential foresight—'the weighing of the consequences of alternative political actions'—marks 'the *supreme virtue* of politics' because it embraces 'the ineluctable tension between the moral command and the requirements of successful political action'.[51] This is the lynchpin of any 'political morality', for only through such assessment can political actors realize some measure of the good while skirting catastrophe.[52] Prudence complements the national interest by mediating between competing tensions or passions and between the horns of political dilemmas, which rarely admit a clear right or wrong solution.[53] In such situations, rationalistic decision rules, public opinion, and international law might tell us what we can or cannot do (or get away with), but only a 'political wisdom' of prudence can answer the normative question of what we *ought* to do in order to combine 'particular interests' with 'the general interest in peace and order' in a way that might also reflect 'humanity, reason, and justice'.[54]

The nature and balance of power

Classical proponents placed power at the heart of realism, a move usually linked to their pessimistic view of human nature and its *animus dominandi*, or 'desire for power'.[55] IR scholars also frequently misunderstand this to indicate that '[t]he priority of the pursuit of power marginalizes *all* other objectives'.[56] However, such interpretations miss two important points about classical realist power. First, Morgenthau insisted that although power is 'always the *immediate* aim' of international political action, it serves '*ultimate*' aims like freedom, security, prosperity, and 'ethical principles'.[57] He also criticized states, like Nazi Germany, that made power their ultimate aim as immoral and destined for ruin. Such 'naked power' politics could never provide an adequate rubric for understanding or conducting international politics.[58]

Second, although Niebuhr linked power drives to sinful human nature,[59] Morgenthau's power is less about human *nature* or innate drives than it is about the human *condition*, the existential challenge of going on in a dynamic and indeterminate world.[60] Although it may be hypertrophied into relations of domination, our will to power begins well before coercion. As Ulrik Petersen discusses, Morgenthau's *animus* is an epistemic prerequisite, 'an ultimate explanatory principle for whatever there might be' that enables action by imagining our environment as a meaningful 'unity and totality'.[61] Put differently, power expresses 'the ability and the will to discern'.[62] Likewise, *dominandi* indicates that such visions inherently constrain possibilities and provisionally limit other social beings' agency in order to reduce the welter of experience to a manageable level.[63] Rather than simply quoting '*animus dominandi*' or 'a limitless lust for power' and inferring the rest, as many IR scholars do, once again it is helpful to read a sentence or two further. Morgenthau's 'lust for power' does not reduce to a desire to dominate; rather, it expresses 'the mystical desire for union with the universe', a sense of 'transcending' our narrow finitude through acts of imagination that enable orientation and action.[64] This is a very different and more robust notion of power than mere coercion and subordination.

Similarly, classical realism's 'balance of power' has been subject to several different and not necessarily consistent interpretations.[65] Classical realists' enthusiasm for bygone eras of dynastic politics can make 'balance of power' seem like a piece of conservative nostalgia;[66] however, the balance of power originally expressed a theologically inflected conception of a powerful state as a *katechon*,[67] a restraining force that could balance competing interests and thus 'contain disorder', stave off chaos, and 'bracket' war while instituting a concrete order that offered 'meaning and orientation' to international actors.[68] In classical realism, the key contingency to be bracketed was a thermonuclear exchange, the living symbol of Armageddon.

Informed by our re-reading of power, this sort of balance is not just a matter of balancing *against* mighty competitors, it also implies a stability flowing from an epistemically productive organizing principle—a balance *formed of power* that enables orientation and action. In terms of might, classical realists also intended this balance to ensure that the 'the less powerful found themselves relatively guaranteed', 'international law was recognized', and war was 'rapid and limited'.[69] From their perspective, the Cold War balance was too brittle and insulated from any third-party restraining influence, a 'primitive spectacle' inflected with universalizing ideologies where each superpower was 'strong enough to determine with their own weight alone the position of the scales'.[70] Absent a more *empowering* balancing principle, prudent habits, or tempered views of national interest, they feared that the Cold War would descend into rampant power competition, inducing chaos rather than stability—a prospect especially resonant in the early crisis years of the Cold War when classical realists formulated their approach.

The power of truth: neorealism and the problem of nuclear catastrophe

Given the prevalence of ethical and moral concerns running through classical realism, how did realism come to seem amoral or immoral? What process of suppression transformed a strikingly ethical and moral discourse into a caricature of naked power politics?[71] The answer is a neorealist fixation on science, which entailed translating classical realism's moral complexity and nuance into the rhetoric of rigorous, value-free inquiry expunged of ethical content.[72]

From ethical scepticism to a rational science

This process of transformation was a lengthy one, but its main contours are apparent in Kenneth Waltz's early work. From 1957 onward, he sought to develop realism into a *bona fide* social scientific theory that explains the most important facts of international politics in a deductive and generalizable way. While classical realists had identified several important aspects of international politics, they had not settled on a parsimonious theoretical framework. Moreover, Waltz considered their penchant for advocating particular policies and outcomes to be beneath the dispassionate objectivity of a true science. Bluntly, this 'was not scholarship: it was normative policy recommendation'.[73] To present a truly scientific theory, realism would need to be construed more rigorously; it would also need to avoid any inclination toward prescription and, indeed, all normative discourse.

On this understanding of theory, war was neither good nor evil because such *valuations* have no place in a social *science*. War is simply a political phenomenon, and just as natural scientists study earthquakes dispassionately, IR scholars should work toward war's systematic explanation rather than trying to prevent or delimit any particular instance of it.[74] That is, war should be treated as a dependent variable, not an ethical event. Similarly, because scholars derived them scientifically, any foreign policy implications of neorealism were 'neither moral nor immoral'; they embodied 'merely a reasoned response to the world about us'.[75] This denial of morality threw out the baby with the bathwater, turning classical realist scepticism about moralizing language into a rationale for excising normative considerations *per se* from realist inquiry.

Neorealists after Waltz embraced his argument that any and all normative discourse was improper in social scientific inquiry.[76] Philosophers might deliberate values, and wonks could advocate particular policies, but social scientists dealt exclusively with objective truths. Other than contrasting it with realism, Mearsheimer's signature work does not address morality or ethics.[77] Nor does Stephen Walt's *The Origins of Alliances*, except in one empirical quote.[78] Going further, neorealists also argue against the *explanatory* utility of norms in shaping international outcomes.[79] It is not just that ethics have no place in social science; empirically speaking, normative commitments and claims yield to more 'objective', material factors. In this way, neorealism adapts both a reductive and a hypertrophic version of classical realism, diminishing moral and ethical considerations as unscientific while turning philosophical wariness about moralizing claims into an analytical negation of normative import in the face of power politics.

Similarly, neorealist science makes no room for the sort of thinking that preoccupied classical realists, which requires holding opposing concepts in tension or engaging irresolvable antinomies found in international politics.[80] So balancing 'is' with 'ought' becomes a hard distinction: theory is concerned only with what is; ought is for philosophy and other woolly discourses. Likewise, Morgenthau's discussion of the *relationship* 'between political power and ethics' becomes operationalized into a mutually exclusive hypothesis—outcomes are caused by *either* power political *or* normative factors.[81] And classical scepticism about the most feasible means of achieving ethical outcomes mutates into a licence for a hard distinction between liberalism and realism: liberals are optimists; realists are pessimists.[82]

Neorealists thus positioned themselves within wider intellectual currents in American social science of the day, where the cybernetic and behavioural revolutions left little room for philosophical nuance or normative discourse.[83] This effort benefited from a calmer period of the Cold War compared to the rollicking 1950s when classical realism prevailed.[84] In the stabilized bipolarity of the mid-1960s and 1970s, normative deliberations could be pegged to a reified ideological struggle between superpowers. Neorealists could thus focus on turning classical arguments about the importance of 'concrete' contexts into an 'objective' social science based solely on 'material facts', and outright pessimism could replace modulated scepticism without confronting too frequently the inconvenient question of thermonuclear apocalypse.

Realism demoralized

This process translated concepts full of ethical content in classical realism into more social scientific terms. Neorealism turned the modest idea of national interest into generalized self-interest, a variation on the rational actor assumption. Under anarchy, all rational states must be 'self-helpers' and, indeed, self-centred egoists.[85] Rather than providing a heuristic device for analysing different states' positions that also chastened elite claims and the universalizing tendencies of nationalism, rational self-interest flattens out the meaningful differences between state identities and purposes, allowing neorealists to treat 'them like billiard balls of varying size', where the metaphor expresses the varying capabilities with which states all pursue security.[86]

Neorealists also reduced the classical will to power to vulgar power competition by several glosses. First, they attached power drives exclusively to classical realists' comments on human nature,[87] eliminating power's philosophical and epistemic aspects. This enabled one of Waltz's central criticisms, which is that classical realists' 'human nature pessimism' was everywhere and therefore nowhere in theoretical terms—it could explain war in 1914 but not peace in 1910.[88] Second, neorealists narrowed the existential '*struggle* for power'[89] to a straightforward empirical claim about material advantage. Mearsheimer asserts that 'states have an insatiable appetite for power', or what Morgenthau calls 'a limitless lust for power', which means that they constantly look for 'opportunities to *take the offensive* and *dominate* other states'.[90] We have already discussed this passage in Morgenthau, but it is worth repeating that Mearsheimer's reading requires ignoring Morgenthau's immediate elaboration of this lust as the transcendent and 'mystical desire for union with the universe'. Third, neorealists overlook classical ideas about the imaginative foundations of power, linking power instead to empirical observation: the 'will to power . . . pushes each [state] to strive for supremacy'; indeed, their '*ultimate* aim is to gain a position of dominant power over others', measured by military advantage.[91] So 'power', reduced to material capabilities, becomes 'an end in itself'.[92] It is no longer an immediate aim serving other ultimate purposes, which would muddle neorealist efforts to explain power competition as a uniform and rational *behavior* under anarchy.[93] Similarly, and finally, where classical power was the *ultima ratio* or *final arbiter* of political conflicts, neorealism turns all other arbiters into explanatory competitors. A 'scientific' explanation isolates a single, decisive cause, so the final or ultimate arbiter becomes the only factor we care about.

Likewise, neorealism turns the balance of power into a reliable effect specified by parsimonious theory—uniform power drives produce regular balances of power, the polarity of which determines the stability of the system.[94] This lends neorealism its distinctive emphasis on stability, which collapses questions about the *status quo* down to whether powerful states will challenge it or not.[95] It is also more 'equilibrium' than classical 'balance', where the former suggests structurally driven regularities reminiscent of stable economic markets and the latter implies precarity, contingency, and agency. Neorealism's balance of power is no longer an artful technique of statecraft, much less a theologically inflected symbol of *katechontic* restraint. In a particularly clever move, neorealism rationalizes the balance of power as a trans-historical regularity, thus resolving classical anxieties about brittle Cold War balances by theoretical fiat. Any particular balance—even that between overwrought superpowers—represents a single datum; come what may, the international system will eventually return to equilibrium.

As for prudence, neorealism reduces it almost to naught. Waltz's *magnum opus* mentions it twice—once in an economistic allegory for balance of power and once in a quote used as a foil.[96] Mearsheimer's summary statement invokes it only once: under anarchy, 'prudence dictates that [states] behave according to realist logic', which means they 'striv[e] to have as much power as possible *just in case*'.[97] This is no stoic weighing of possible outcomes, much less an ethic of consequences. Instead, neorealism's prudence obeys the ironclad logic-under-anarchy of arming to the teeth, a policy that runs directly *against* the grain of classical prudence.

The failed ethical project of a neorealist social science

Neorealism decisively eliminated moral, ethical, and normative considerations from realism. In doing so, it facilitated a value-free social scientific theory with which scholars could dispassionately grasp the objective truths of international politics. Or so it seems.

However, closer inspection reveals a glaring inconsistency at neorealism's core. As Campbell Craig traces, even as neorealists were establishing their social scientific credibility and disciplinary dominance in the 1970s and 1980s, Waltz changed tack. While he displayed a studied indifference about nuclear weapons in earlier work (claiming that nuclear fears were analogous to earlier panics about balloons or poison-tipped spears), by the 1979 publication of his *Theory of International Politics*, Waltz had adopted an increasingly 'normative view' of nuclear war.[98]

The first normative slide was to move from explaining how bipolarity produces a most stable system to extolling its virtues. Far from some detached object of analysis, Waltz now pitched bipolarity as an effective form of international 'management' that could perpetuate peace and reduce conflict.[99] His moral inclination here was so obvious it hid in plain sight: unlike astronomers who study black holes without caring whether new ones form, Waltz favoured a particular outcome—a balance of power conducive to less war. Second, where he initially downplayed the implications of nuclear weapons, Waltz came to realize that even a most stable bipolar system remained an 'unregulated' competition in which war would still 'occasionally' occur.[100] In the thermonuclear age, this was scientifically true yet morally unthinkable.

These normative concerns produced in Waltz a decisive break with his own formulation of neorealism. Just two years after *Theory of International Politics*, he again tried to argue from the objective facts of international politics to a morally preferred outcome—the prevention of nuclear war. This time, however, he countered the problem of proliferation by arguing that more nuclear states would increase system stability and decrease the likelihood of conflict. To do so, his now (in)famous *Adelphi Paper*[101] turned away from 'third image', systemic constraints and toward a unit-level 'fear of nuclear war', a technologically driven, 'independent causal factor' that not only discouraged nuclear powers from aggressive behaviour but would encourage 'defensive, conservative, and secure states'.[102] This claim shifted the neorealist explanation for war from anarchical structure to individual or collective psychology.[103] Craig argues that Waltz abandoned his own theoretical core because, as the Cold War progressed, his 'great objective' became 'to ascertain how peace can be maintained indefinitely'.[104] Waltz's proliferation thesis is quite provocative. It is also intrinsically and intensely normative.[105] Right at the moment of neorealism's ascent, then, its champion advanced a morally preferred outcome—great-power peace—in a way that was 'theoretically devastating' to neorealism itself.[106]

Yet although this particular theoretical shift sets him apart, Waltz's ethical disposition comports broadly with other neorealists. For all their insistence that values have no place in IR theory, neorealists admit to 'strong moral preferences' and 'deep moral convictions' opposing conflict and war.[107] However, most deny that this influences their analyses of international politics—it is the rare neorealist who insists that scholarship is no matter of 'moral neutrality' but rather the scientific acquisition of facts in service of a 'closet liberal' project.[108] Neorealists *have* purged ethics and morality from their analytical rhetoric. However, an absence of evidence is not necessarily evidence of absence. Neorealists either hold normative commitments but refuse to reflect on how these inflect their purportedly value-free scholarship or, in Waltz's case, they smuggle those commitments in, allowing them to determine the outcomes of supposedly deductive theory and even debasing the theory altogether.[109]

Uncertain truths and the catastrophes of power: ethical reinvigorations of realism

Even with neorealism's normative commitments unmasked, the story of ethics in IR realism so far is not an especially inspiring one. However, over the past two decades, scholars have begun to reinvigorate realism as an intrinsically ethical enterprise. This initially involved re-reading and contextualizing classical realist texts to recover their ethical concerns. Following several efforts in this respect, scholars have also begun to combine classical insights with contemporary social theoretical concerns.[110] We can now identify a third, more 'reflexive' strand of IR realism.[111]

Reflexive realism gained steam at the turn of the millennium, when neoconservative and democratic peace ideologies ran roughshod over US foreign policy, leading to disastrous wars in Afghanistan and Iraq and numerous human rights scandals. This near-constant thrum of hubris, overreach, and catastrophe, as well as the weedy dominance of rationalistic, explanatory, and putatively value-free theory in IR, animated many of realism's rehabilitators. Reflexive realist works coalesce loosely around three overarching themes: the restoration and development of 'principles of agency, prudence, and the recognition of limitations as part of an attempt to provide a practical–ethical view of international politics'.[112]

Reflecting significant advances in social theory, reflexive realists view agency as the finite, anxious, and affective constitution of self-identity, whose efforts produce unintended and often tragic consequences.[113] They also treat scholarship as continuous with politics, a view that demands greater reflexivity about our positionality, political commitments, and the practical implications of our work—in particular, how knowledge might authorize and prop up political power.[114] This move echoes Morgenthau's forgotten vocational argument that 'scholars have a moral responsibility to speak truth to power' and places reflexive realism side by side with critical approaches in IR as a 'subversive force', which should 'stir up the conscience of society', and in doing so, 'challenge the status quo'.[115] It also reunites the normative and explanatory projects estranged by neorealism, for speaking truth to power involves unmasking and explaining its many workings and manifestations in order to question it, highlight its limits, and resist its abuses. On this reading, and contrary to conventional wisdom, IR realism 'can never be . . . a defence of power qua power'.[116] Rather, reflexive realists place scholars in the unenviable but inescapable position of analysing power, challenging it, *and* remaining ready to tell power elites 'what ought to be done'.[117]

Reflexive realists have also re-established the importance of prudence, echoing classical realists but also linking prudence more closely to 'agency' than 'statecraft'.[118] Reflexive realists make two distinct contributions to classical prudence. First, they specify more clearly and carefully two variations: 1) as already discussed, prudence as a matter of deliberating on all possible outcomes before undertaking political action, and; 2) 'prudence-as-stoicism', a *disposition* rather than a calculation, which emphasizes 'rational' (if not rationalist) rather than prickly or crusading responses to uncertainty, surprise, and crisis.[119] Second, although classical realists invoked tragedy with some regularity, reflexive realists have developed a fuller account of the concept of tragedy from Greek thought and connected this with prudence. As Ned Lebow writes, tragedy 'confronts us with our frailties and limits, and the disastrous consequences of trying to exceed them'. This is not meant as mere critique; on Lebow's reading, tragedy is a way to 'balance inference with prophecy and to recognize that the world is full of contradictions that we cannot resolve'.[120] Similarly, tragedy provides the basis of Kamila Stullerova's vigilant realism, which combines a tragic vision with 'human power-aspiration' to understand political action, extend an ethic of consequences, and show why societies must exercise 'summative vigilance' coupled with free expression in order to check political power's 'hubris-prone tendencies, which would otherwise lead to strife and possible annihilation'.[121]

Finally, through a renewed politics of limits, reflexive realists attempt to reconstruct the intellectual resources for an ethos of restraint long absent from mainstream IR and hegemonic foreign policies.[122] As in classical realism, this interest springs from an antinomic concern 'that recognition of the centrality of power in politics does not result in the reduction of politics to pure power, and particularly to the capacity to wield violence'.[123] Reflexive realists therefore develop resources for delimitation, including a 'reasoned understanding of the limits of reason',[124] a renewed emphasis on national self-restraint,[125] and the importance of open dissent as a way to 'cut the national ego down to size' by contrasting soaring promises with concrete realities.[126] Michael C. Williams pushes things a step further by perceptively re-reading a 'politics of limits' as not merely a restrictive ethos but also a productive project—a matter of restraining actors *and* of (re-)constructing political knowledge in a way that fosters 'responsible selves and political orders'.[127]

By reinvigorating realist ethics, reflexive scholars are no doubt living dangerously. First, they explicitly reopen especially thorny dilemmas—foregrounding power without valorizing it,[128] tackling scientific rationalism, considering the case for a world state[129]—which proved insurmountable for past realists. This does not mean, however, that reflexive realists let those dilemmas and their tensions fester. But it does make for harder work than stripped-down explanatory theorizing. Second, by expressly reversing neorealism's expulsion of ethics and morality *per se*, and by embracing the 'nuance and shad[ing]' found originally in classical realism, reflexive realism may not be 'a vision of realism that most realists will recognize'.[130] Yet the thing about recognition is that it depends on both the viewer and the picture. Sometimes the picture itself is fuzzy; sometimes the viewer suffers from cataracts. Far from 'provid[ing] few useful tools with which to explain real-world politics',[131] reflexive realism comports more closely with what most contemporary scholars, hand to heart, will agree is a more realistic view of international politics as a realm without any clean distinctions between scientific facts and moral values, with inextricable links between power and knowledge, and offering uncertainty and contingency as its only enduring factors.

The shadow of the future and realism's enduring antinomy

In addition to these important insights, reflexive realism can push IR theory forward along another line of inquiry—time and temporality.[132] Brent Steele and I have detailed how an 'open' view of time embracing 'contingency and the unknown' distinguishes classical and reflexive realisms from other strands of IR theory, which tend to privilege the certitudes offered by 'closed' interpretations of unilinear progress or cyclical recurrence in international politics.[133] Against these totalizing views of history, an open view understands time as the intrinsically dynamic and indeterminate ground of human experience and meaning. While theological readings of realism might position open time 'under' the moral promise of God, a more radical, Nietzschean realism understands time itself as 'devoid not only of worldly meaning but of any transcendental foundation'.[134] This distinction holds important implications for reflexive realists interested in a more cosmpolitan ethics and those who index all ethics to particular human efforts.[135] The latter involves fraught practical and intellectual efforts 'to imbue human existence with sub-optimal yet beneficial normative vision[s]—an exercise of creative potential meant to responsibly limit excess but not all alternatives'.[136] It also takes on added importance in a thermonuclear age, in which life may 'no longer [be] lived as a coherent and consecutive "whole," with an unfolding history, but rather as . . . a "sensate" and incoherent living from day to day in fragments'.[137]

Radically open time further impels efforts to install limits and prudence as the foundations of a politics balanced between morality and catastrophe. It directs immediate scepticism and scrutiny toward any claims that would foreclose the dynamic diversity of temporal processes, including imputations about universal progress, eschatology, the end of history, the overwhelming pace of events, fluid times that require decisive intervention,[138] or stable recurrence, all of which paper over significant uncertainty with certitudes fuzzily derived and, often, ham-handedly applied.[139] Such temporal presumptions and logics are usually excused from serious interrogation in IR and ethics. A reflexive realism based in open time exposes and resists them as acts of power reflective of a *will to time*—the need to impute an intelligible pattern to complex dynamic processes, which reflects silent, partial, and particular ethical and political commitments.[140] In the tradition of classical realism, these wills to time can only ever be pragmatic proposals adjudicated exclusively through concrete outcomes in the near to distant future, a fact that heightens the political and ethical stakes of their unspoken inner logics.

Thinking about the shadow of the future in two senses clarifies the will to time as an enduring antinomy in realism. First, the future is a limitless and murky expanse into which we peer with at best blurred vision. Second, the future hangs over us like a sword of Damocles, it is the moment when our principles, hopes, and policies may lead to rupture and ruin; when the wages of limited and limiting worldviews underwritten by universalizing certitude will be reckoned. The shadow of the future therefore engenders two understandable responses. The first response is that, as mentioned, we fill it with confident, aesthetic assertions about the arc of history. The second is that we revolt existentially, finding any decision or course of action problematic to the point of enervation. Realist ethics reflects the need to negotiate this antinomy in perpetuity. Precisely *because* these understandable responses to our intrinsically open temporal existence are unresolvably contradictory,[141] they must be held together so that neither can prevail.

The challenges of going on in open time point to long-standing realist concerns. How to develop resources for effective decision-making, to *empower* action without universalizing, moralizing zealotry?[142] How to avoid hubris without reifying the *status quo*?[143] How to ensure dissent without descending into nihilism?[144] How to 'prepar[e] for the worst' without 'paralyz[ing] our capacity to think and act' creatively, and to ensure our existence without collapsing into the drudgery of nuclear deterrence and worst-case scenarios?[145] These sorts of thorny, complex, and insoluble ethical issues are just what IR realism was built for. It is no doubt a delimited ethics—that is the point, after all. *Caveat emptor; caveat actor.* It may not be especially inspirational, yet IR realism constitutes 'an ethos all the same',[146] one committed to progressivism without an ideal, *katechon* without an *eschaton*, and prudence without paralysis, as the means to *continue existing* and to preserve the *possibility of improvement* in the open flow of time.

Conclusion

Realism in IR has never been a doctrine of 'might makes right'. Classical and reflexive realists openly resist this formulation while acknowledging that, in international politics, right will often need might on its side. A more accurate neorealist formulation might be 'might makes safe and sound', but it could not possibly make 'right' since normative evaluation has no place in neorealist 'science'. In any case, this aphoristic perspective on one of the most distinctive and subtle bodies of IR thought does all brands of realism a disservice. It marginalizes any number of ethical and moral themes running through realism from the birth of IR to the present. As neorealism illustrates, it inhibits the complex and careful thinking that international politics demands. And it makes it all too easy to overlook the core truth of IR realism's discourse of power politics. This truth manifests throughout classical realism to all but the most blinkered observers. Neorealist attempts to deny it produce a telling loss of rigour and coherence in neorealism itself, and have driven reflexive reinvigorations of realism into new and productive areas, from intellectual history to the question of time. This truth, simply put, is that the only reliable way to honour IR's basic vocational commitment to delimiting war and forestalling global catastrophe is to hold morality and power *together* in a delicate, reflexive, and never-ending balance.

Notes

1 Joseph S. Nye, Jr, *Understanding International Conflict* (London: Pearson Longman, 2006), 20.

2 Kenneth N. Waltz, *Man, the State and War* (New York: Columbia University Press, 1959), 238.

3 John Mearsheimer, *The Tragedy of Great Power Politics*, updated edn. (New York: W. W. Norton, 2014), 23–24.

4 Critical theorists usually take Mearsheimer and Waltz at their word. Realism 'is about power politics for hegemonic states', a conservative, 'problem-solving' theory that is '"value-free" in its exclusion of moral goals'; see Ching-Chang Chen and Young Chul Cho, 'Theory', in *Critical Imaginations in International Relations*, eds. Aoileann Ní Mhurchú and Reiko Shindo (Abingdon: Routledge, 2016), 249; see also Robert Cox, 'Social Forces, States and World Orders: Beyond International Relations Theory', *Millennium: Journal of International Studies*, 10, no. 2 (1981): 131–132.

5 Robert Gilpin, 'The Richness of the Tradition of Political Realism', in *Neorealism and Its Critics*, ed. Robert O. Keohane (New York: Columbia University Press, 1986), 319.

6 It does not cover neoclassical realism, which adopts neorealism's scientific aspirations and therefore does not explicitly engage ethics; see, e.g., Norrin M. Ripsman, Jeffrey W. Taliaferro, and Steven E. Lobell, *Neoclassical Realist Theory of International Politics* (Oxford: Oxford University Press, 2016).

7 Following recent historiographical critiques of IR's tendency to conflate analytical affinities with actual historical connections, I do not cover political thinkers often considered 'realists' but well beyond the academic field of IR (e.g., Thucydides, Machiavelli, Hobbes, Rousseau); see Brian C. Schmidt, *The Political Discourse of Anarchy: A Disciplinary History of International Relations* (Albany, NY: State University of New York Press, 1998), 27–32. Instead, I begin where IR realism can safely be said to emerge: in the mid-20th-century academy.

8 William T. R. Fox, 'Interwar International Relations Research: The American Experience', *World Politics*, 2, no. 1 (1949): 67.

9 Hans J. Morgenthau, *Scientific Man versus Power Politics* (Chicago: University of Chicago Press, 1946), 104–105; Fox, 'Interwar', 69.

10 Edward Hallett Carr, *The Twenty Years' Crisis, 1919–1939: An Introduction to the Study of International Relations*, second edn. (London: Macmillan, 1946).

11 Morgenthau, *Scientific Man*; Reinhold Niebuhr, *The Children of Light and the Children of Darkness: A Vindication of Democracy and a Critique of Its Traditional Defense* (Chicago: University of Chicago Press, 2011).

12 Carr, *Twenty Years*, 5, vii; Hans J. Morgenthau, *Politics among Nations: The Struggle for Power and Peace*, brief edn. (Boston: McGraw-Hill, 1993), 12; George F. Kennan, *Realities of American Foreign Policy* (London: Oxford University Press, 1954), 14.

13 Morgenthau, *Scientific Man*; Morgenthau, *Politics among Nations*, 12; and Carr, *Twenty Years*, 5–9, whose sociological critique of science uncovered in nascent disciplines the tendency to conflate the appeal of ideas with their truth.

14 Carr, *Twenty Years*, 9.

15 Morgenthau, *Scientific Man*, 104.

16 Morgenthau, *Politics among Nations*, 12.

17 Carr, *Twenty Years*, vi, 89, 7–8, 21, emphasis added; Hans J. Morgenthau, 'The Evil of Politics and the Ethics of Evil', *Ethics*, 56, no. 1 (1945): 18.
18 E.g., Jack Donnelly, 'The Ethics of Realism', in *The Oxford Handbook of International Relations*, ed. Christian Reus-Smit and Duncan Snidal (Oxford: Oxford University Press, 2010), 151.
19 Carr, *Twenty Years*, 21; see also Morgenthau, *Politics among Nations*, 273; 'The Twilight of International Morality', *Ethics*, 58, no. 2 (1948): 96–97.
20 Morgenthau, 'Evil'.
21 In contemporary political theory, this marks an 'ethics first' rather than a 'realistic' approach, a distinction that attests to the durability of classical realist concerns; Raymond Geuss, *Philosophy and Real Politics* (Princeton: Princeton University Press, 2008), 6–7.
22 Arnold Wolfers, *Discord and Collaboration: Essays on International Politics* (Baltimore: Johns Hopkins Press, 1962), 50, emphasis added; see also Ibid., 164–165.
23 Morgenthau, 'Evil', 18.
24 Ibid.; Reinhold Niebuhr, *Moral Man and Immoral Society: A Study in Ethics and Politics* (Louisville, Kentucky: Westminster John Knox Press, 2001), 256; Wolfers, *Discord*, 50–51; Fox, 'Interwar', 68. 'Perfect' here denotes universalized and abstract ideals devoid of concrete content and therefore easily misunderstood as applicable everywhere when in fact they offer practical traction almost nowhere.
25 Wolfers, *Discord*, 164.
26 Carr, *Twenty Years*, 10.
27 Ibid.
28 Niebuhr, *Children of Light*, 21.
29 Kennan, *Realities*, 14.
30 Morgenthau, 'Evil,' 18.
31 Niebuhr, *Moral Man*, 25; Morgenthau, *Scientific Man*, vi.
32 Carr, *Twenty Years*, 8, 10, emphasis added.
33 Morgenthau, *Scientific Man*, 177; Carr, *Twenty Years*, 10.
34 Carr, *Twenty Years*, 145, 235.
35 Waltz, *Man*; Mearsheimer, *Tragedy*; Cox, 'Social Forces', 131.
36 Niebuhr, *Moral Man*, 37–38.
37 Morgenthau, 'Twilight', 96–99.
38 Ibid., 79.
39 Morgenthau, *Politics among Nations*, 219, emphasis added; on realism as against a- and im-morality, see Niebuhr, *Moral Man*, 231–232.
40 E.g., Nye, *Understanding International Conflict*, 20.
41 Morgenthau, 'Twilight', 88; *Politics among Nations*, 13, 7.
42 Hans J. Morgenthau, 'The Political Science of E. H. Carr', *World Politics*, 1, no. 1 (October 1948): 128, 133–134; Niebuhr, *Moral Man*, 233–234; Wolfers, *Discord*, 48.
43 Morgenthau, *Politics among Nations*, 13.
44 Ibid., 10; see Cornelia Navari, 'Hans Morgenthau and the National Interest', *Ethics and International Affairs*, 30, no. 1 (April 2016): 48.
45 Wolfers, *Discord*, 164.
46 Kennan, *Realities*, 103, 36.
47 Carr, *Twenty Years*, 87.
48 Morgenthau, *Politics among Nations*, 13.
49 See ibid., 119; for further discussion, see Donnelly, 'Ethics of Realism', 154; Richard Ned Lebow, *The Tragic Vision of Politics: Ethics, Interests and Orders* (Cambridge: Cambridge University Press, 2003), 33–34, 216–256; Navari, 'Hans Morgenthau', 47.
50 Niebuhr, *Moral Man*, 185–186; Morgenthau, *Scientific Man*, 186–187; and *Politics among Nations*, 16, which reserves special criticism for the 'blunder' of the moral 'fool', who naively enacts principles without considering their likely effects.
51 Morgenthau, *Politics among Nations*, 12.
52 Ibid.
53 Morgenthau, *Scientific Man*, 202.
54 Ibid., 120.
55 Ibid., 192; Niebuhr, *Moral Man*.
56 Donnelly, 'Ethics of Realism', 150.
57 Morgenthau, *Politics among Nations*, 29, 100 emphasis added.

58 Ibid., 32.
59 Niebuhr, *Moral Man*.
60 Morgenthau's realism owes more to Nietzsche than Augustine; see Ulrik Enemark Petersen, 'Breathing Nietzsche's Air: New Reflections on Morgenthau's Concepts of Power and Human Nature', *Alternatives*, 24, no. 1 (1999): 99; Sean Molloy, *The Hidden History of Realism: A Genealogy of Power Politics* (New York: Palgrave Macmillan, 2006).
61 Petersen, 'Breathing Nietzsche's Air', 94–95. Similarly, Carr's 'human *will*' was intimately connected with 'the *vision* of an international order'; Carr, *Twenty Years*, 93.
62 Felix Rösch, *Power, Knowledge, and Dissent in Morgenthau's Worldview* (New York: Palgrave MacMillan, 2016), 60.
63 Andrew R. Hom and Brent J. Steele, 'Open Horizons: The Temporal Visions of Reflexive Realism', *International Studies Review*, 12, no. 2 (2010): 283.
64 Morgenthau, *Scientific Man*, 194; see Rösch, *Power*, 49–74.
65 See Nicolas Guilhot, 'American Katechon: When Political Theology Became International Relations Theory', *Constellations*, 17, no. 2 (2010): 237.
66 Morgenthau, 'Twilight', 98; *Politics among Nations*, 273.
67 This reflects their debt to Carl Schmitt; see Guilhot, 'American Katechon', 226–235.
68 Ibid., 234, 237–238.
69 Hans J. Morgenthau, 'World Politics in the Mid-Twentieth Century', *The Review of Politics*, 10, no. 2 (1948): 162.
70 Ibid., 169, 162.
71 Mearsheimer, *Tragedy*, 23 collects representative quotes.
72 Kenneth N. Waltz, *Theory of International Politics* (Reading, MA: Addison-Wesley, 1979), 63.
73 Campbell Craig, *Glimmer of a New Leviathan: Total War in the Realism of Niebuhr, Morgenthau, and Waltz* (New York: Columbia University Press, 2003), 118.
74 Waltz, *Man*, 1.
75 Ibid., 238.
76 Mearsheimer, *Tragedy*, 23.
77 Ibid.
78 Stephen M. Walt, *The Origins of Alliance* (Ithaca, NY: Cornell University Press, 1987), 26.
79 John J. Mearsheimer, 'The False Promise of International Institutions', *International Security*, 19, no. 3 (1994): 5–49.
80 See Richard K. Ashley, 'The Poverty of Neorealism', in *Neorealism and Its Critics*, ed. Robert Keohane (New York: Columbia University Press, 1986), 264, who argues that neorealists ask classical realists only a few, 'pointed questions' of the 'yes or no' variety.
81 Mearsheimer, 'False Promise', 24; citing Morgenthau, *Scientific Man*, 201.
82 Mearsheimer, *Tragedy*; Waltz, *Man*, 39–41. Scepticism and pessismism, of course, are distinct intellectual perspectives.
83 E.g., Waltz's theoretical shift between *Man* and *Theory*; see Nicolas Guilhot, 'Cyborg Pantocrator: International Relations Theory from Decisionism to Rational Choice', *Journal of the History of the Behavioral Sciences*, 47, no. 3 (June 1, 2011): 279–301.
84 See Craig, *Glimmer*, 140.
85 Waltz, *Theory*.
86 Mearsheimer, 'False Promise', 48.
87 Waltz, *Man*, 16–41; Mearsheimer, *Tragedy*, 418, n32.
88 Waltz, *Man*, 28.
89 Morgenthau, *Politics among Nations*.
90 Mearsheimer, *Tragedy*, 19 emphasis added; discussing Morgenthau, *Scientific Man*, 194; see also Waltz, *Theory*, 116–121.
91 Mearsheimer, *Tragedy*, 19, xv, emphasis added.
92 Ibid., 36; also Waltz, *Theory*, 126–127.
93 This gloss underpins offensive realism: 'if all states have a "limitless aspiration for power" how can there be status quo powers in the world?' Mearsheimer, *Tragedy*, 418–419, n. 35.
94 Walt, *Origins*, 7; Waltz, *Theory*.
95 Mearsheimer, *Tragedy*.
96 Waltz, *Theory*, 107, 119; see also Walt, *Origins*, 69, 175, 179.
97 Mearsheimer, *Tragedy*, 51, emphasis added.

98 Craig, *Glimmer*, 144, 138.
99 Waltz, *Theory*, 112; discussed in ibid., 155.
100 Ibid., 154.
101 Kenneth N. Waltz, 'The Spread of Nuclear Weapons: More May Be Better: Introduction', *The Adelphi Papers*, 21, no. 171 (September 1, 1981).
102 Craig, *Glimmer*, 158–160.
103 Ibid., 161.
104 Ibid., 163.
105 Ibid., 139.
106 Ibid., 165.
107 Mearsheimer, 'False Promise', 48, n. 182; also Russell Hardin and John J. Mearsheimer, 'Introduction to Symposium on Ethics and Nuclear Deterrence', *Ethics*, 95, no. 3 (1985): 412–415.
108 Gilpin, 'Richness,' 319–321.
109 See Ido Oren, 'The Unrealism of Contemporary Realism: The Tension between Realist Theory and Realists' Practice', *Perspectives on Politics*, 7, no. 2 (2009): 283–301.
110 There is no hard distinction here between historiography and theory development; see Brent J. Steele, '21st Century Realism: The Past Is in Our Present', *International Studies Review*, 11, no. 2 (June 1, 2009): 352.
111 Brent J. Steele, 'Eavesdropping on Honored Ghosts: From Classical to Reflexive Realism', *Journal of International Relations and Development*, 10, no. 3 (2007): 272–300; Hom and Steele, 'Open Horizons'.
112 See Steele, 'Eavesdropping', 273.
113 Lebow, *Tragic Vision*; Kamila Stullerova, 'Tragedy and Political Theory: Progressivism without an Ideal', in *Tragedy and International Relations*, ed. Toni Erskine and Richard Ned Lebow (Houndmills, UK: Palgrave Macmillan, 2012), 127.
114 Steele, 'Eavesdropping', 286; Michael C. Williams, *The Realist Tradition and the Limits of International Relations* (Cambridge: Cambridge University Press, 2005), 169.
115 Murielle Cozette, 'Reclaiming the Critical Dimension of Realism: Hans J. Morgenthau on the Ethics of Scholarship', *Review of International Studies*, 34 (2008): 5, 8.
116 Ibid., 10.
117 Ibid.
118 E.g., Lebow, *Tragic Vision*; Williams, *Realist Tradition*, 169.
119 Steele, 'Eavesdropping', 279–280; Anthony F. Lang, *Agency and Ethics: The Politics of Military Intervention* (Albany, NY: State University of New York Press, 2002), 192.
120 Lebow, *Tragic Vision*, 20.
121 Stullerova, 'Tragedy', 127; Vibeke Schou Tjalve, *Realist Strategies of Republican Peace: Niebuhr, Morgenthau, and the Politics of Patriotic Dissent* (New York: Palgrave MacMillan, 2008), 6.
122 Williams, *Realist Tradition*, 131–137.
123 Ibid., 7.
124 Ibid., 40.
125 Steele, 'Eavesdropping'.
126 Tjalve, *Realist Strategies*, 6; Stullerova, 'Tragedy'.
127 Williams, *Realist Tradition*, 169, see also 176.
128 Lang, *Agency and Ethics*, 6.
129 William E. Scheuerman, 'The (Classical) Realist Vision of Global Reform', *International Theory*, 2, no. 2 (2010): 246–282; Craig, *Glimmer*.
130 G. John Ikenberry, review of *The Realist Tradition and the Limits of International Relations*, by Michael C. Williams, *Foreign Affairs* (January 28, 2009), https://www.foreignaffairs.com/reviews/capsule-review/2006-01-01/realist-tradition-and-limits-international-relations.
131 Ibid.
132 Other areas of opportunity include addressing realism's longstanding Eurocentric and gender biases; see J. Ann Tickner, 'Hans Morgenthau's Principles of Political Realism: A Feminist Reformulation', *Millennium: Journal of International Studies*, 17, no. 3 (December 1, 1988): 429–440.
133 Hom and Steele, 'Open Horizons'.
134 Ibid., 280.
135 Ibid., 283–284.
136 Ibid., 285; Williams, *Realist Tradition*, 209.

137 John H. Herz, *International Politics in the Atomic Age* (New York: Columbia University Press, 1959), 229.
138 See Andrew R. Hom, 'Angst Springs Eternal: Dangerous Times and the Dangers of Timing the "Arab Spring"', *Security Dialogue*, 47, no. 2 (April 1, 2016): 165–183.
139 See Hom and Steele, 'Open Horizons', 286.
140 See Andrew R. Hom, 'Timing Is Everything: Toward a Better Understanding of Time and International Politics', *International Studies Quarterly, 62*, no. 1 (March 1, 2018): 73.
141 Lebow, *Tragic Vision*, 20.
142 Williams, *Realist Tradition*, 203.
143 Scheuerman, '(Classical) Realist Vision'; Cozette, 'Reclaiming'.
144 Stullerova, 'Tragedy'.
145 Herz, *International Politics*, 228–230.
146 Steele, '21st Century Realism', 356.

10

ETHICS AND FEMINIST INTERNATIONAL RELATIONS THEORY

Elisabeth Porter

Feminist theory has never fit comfortably within the discipline of international relations (IR). Primarily, this is because feminist theory challenges underlying assumptions about core concepts in IR, such as security, sovereignty, and war, and shows their gendered nature. Throw ethics into the mix—that is, the moral principles that guide our actions and shape the way we live—and the fit becomes more awkward. Part of the reason for this tension is that whereas dominant ethical approaches to IR view the state as the principal actor and thus are concerned with national self-interest and struggles of power, feminist ethical theory explains how international politics affects and is affected by interdependent peoples' ethical decisions in their everyday lives.

This chapter makes four points. First, it briefly traces some key contributions of early feminist theorists to the IR discipline, particularly addressing the silences of women's voices and experiences from the mainstream literature. In providing this background, I highlight unique features of feminist IR theory, such as the use of a gender-lens to reveal gendered inequalities in international politics, and the emphasis on the importance of everyday experiences, reflexive practices, and plural forms of knowledge that realist versions of IR neglect. Not all feminist IR theorists draw explicitly on feminist ethics, so the second point shows how feminist ethical theorists utilize this gender-lens to pay close attention to context, particularities, relationships, life narratives, and diverse differences in explaining the ethical responsibilities that exist within international relations. These theorists understand the nature of being human in relational terms, highlighting the importance of our connections to others, interdependency, and an intersubjective understanding of the political world. The third point demonstrates how feminist ethical theories start with the premise that ethical decisions require choices and practices of responsibility that meet the needs of others. I will explain different theories of a feminist ethics of care and justice to show that the motivations differ from traditional IR theory in seeking to minimize harm and respond in compassionate ways to injustices and suffering, and accepting the responsibilities to care. The fourth point reveals how practical ethical concerns are interwoven into feminist IR theory in interdisciplinary ways. Given the centrality of security to IR theory, one significant example of feminist ethics this chapter discusses is a critical care approach to human security which can assist the building of sustainable, just peace.

Most feminist IR theory is unavoidably concerned with ethics. Matters such as gendered relationships, the plight of refugees, child soldiers, foreign policy, and defence budgets all involve considerations of what is right or wrong and what enhances or undermines well-being.

However, it is important to be aware that not all feminist IR theorists openly use ethical theories. After providing some context of the emergence of feminist IR theory, the focus of the chapter is on feminist IR theorists who explicitly demonstrate a commitment to feminist ethics. My overall argument is that feminist ethical theories provide a significant challenge to orthodox IR theories and to dominant approaches to ethics, containing a potential to instigate positive changes that could lead to a more peaceful, just, and caring world.

Feminist international relations theory

Before explaining the impact of feminist ethics on IR theory, it is necessary to understand how feminist IR theory came about. During the 1980s, scholars of IR began to reflect on why there were so few women in the discipline. For many, the subject matter seemed distant from women's lived experiences, and women were absent from international diplomacy, the military, and foreign policy-making.[1] Cynthia Enloe's 1990 book was path-breaking when she asked the subversive question, "Where are the women?"[2] and showed they are active players on the national and international stages, despite rare glimpses in typical versions of international politics. Many women's political activities are obscured from public view, or they appear in informal or community circles, in addition to slowly increasing numbers in leadership roles. Realist IR concentrates on the state as asocial in an anarchical world, where power, military might, and national self-interest are the chief ideas, but little attention is given to personal experience, gendered inequalities, or ethical dilemmas. The feminist insight that "the personal is political" and "the international is personal"[3] is powerful. It brings together IR, feminism, and gender, and, as Jan Jindy Pettman states, it reveals "that IR *is* gendered, and gendered *male*, in its theory and practice, and that women *are* players in the world that IR seeks to explain."[4] The metaphor of a "gender-lens" grasps this insight because it shows how a gendered focus on international politics influences what we see and what we look at.[5] In particular, the application of a gender-lens brings into view differences in power, in/equality, and women's "unequal social position."[6] Without applying a "gender(ed)-lens," these aspects of international politics are omitted.[7]

Feminists show that IR theory is not ahistorical, but it occurs in specific places, amongst identifiable individuals who connect in distinctive relationships. While feminist theories speak from the experiences of women, they go beyond this positioning to reveal the way that core concepts of the IR discipline, such as global markets, power, state sovereignty, and security, are constituted in part through gendered structures.[8] The end of the Cold War permitted a change in focus from military and national security issues to a more critical scrutiny of IR by feminist scholars. For example, whereas security issues traditionally are analyzed through a structural perspective, feminists tend to critically explore the impact of security on marginalized and disempowered individuals. In doing so, they show that insecurity is not an abstract concept, but it is experienced subjectively as a harmful way of life, a concrete form of daily suffering. As Ann Tickner explains, in thinking about core concepts and in conducting research, most feminists are sceptical of empiricist methodologies based on quantifiable data and instead seek emancipatory, humanistic theories "grounded in everyday experience in conversational, interpretive frameworks"[9] that take social relations as the "central category of analysis."[10] Some feminist IR approaches are post-positivist, a research approach that draws on qualitative data and acknowledges connections between the researcher and what is being researched. Most feminist IR theorists are committed to epistemological pluralism, "with a preference for hermeneutic, historically based, humanistic and philosophical traditions of knowledge accumulation."[11] This rich way to understand the gathering, challenging, and rethinking of knowledge asks what kind of knowledge do we need for whom. As Marysia Zalewski explains, it is about "making sense" of knowledge and particularly "what international (or any) stories become credible[.] Whose lives and what kind of lives count as important?"[12] After outlining this background to the growth of feminist IR theory, we turn now to examine the theoretical basis of feminist ethics.

Feminist relational view of agency

A feminist relational view of agency underlies feminist ethics. What is this agency? Expressed simply, agency refers to the actions and responsibilities of human beings in their social contexts. To answer the question more fully, I highlight four aspects of a feminist view of agency: agency is situated in everyday lives; interdependence is fundamental to being human; our life narratives affect decisions; and there are multiple differences in these narratives.

First, realist IR takes the state and security as starting points for ethical reflection. This contrasts with feminists' stress that active moral agency is situated in everyday, social lives that are complex and contextual. Choices are affected by relationships of power, institutional structures, and gendered differences.[13] This realization can give individuals and groups a voice in challenging the debilitating forces of coercion, control, dependency, and manipulation that block agents from fulfilling their ethical choices. This challenge reinstates the political potential of the ideal and practice of empowerment.[14] Even when people have the capacity to choose between options, they may not be able to use their agency effectively if they are constrained by power barriers, opportunity structures, or living through war. Feminist theorizing about ethics accommodates this complexity of gendered lives, taking into account the obstacles that shape life choices.[15] Choices are affected by the intersections of gender with other markers of identity, such as age, class, education, geographic location, nationality, race, religion, and sexuality. Life opportunities are also influenced by violence and insecurity which often affect women and girls, men and boys, differently. For those living amidst violent conflict, everyday life experiences of bodily danger influence decision-making. This is why Pettman suggests that a comprehensive view of the state and security "begins by asking what, or who, most threatens particular groups of people."[16] This view disrupts traditional notions of national security because oftentimes those supposed to protect women, such as state agents, military personnel, peacekeepers, or male relatives, represent a threat to women's security.

Second, if agency is situated in everyday lives, how do feminists understand the nature of being human? Feminist ontology is based on "social relations that are constituted by historically contingent unequal political, economic, and social structures."[17] Everyday experiences are linked to ways that economic and political power are exercised and affect those living on the margins as well as in the mainstream. Fiona Robinson argues that this relationality goes beyond simply saying that we are social beings, to the claim that both dependency and interdependence are fundamental features of being human.[18] Other feminists offer similiar views of the moral agent. Vivienne Jabri proposes a "critical ethicality" which recognizes the twofold aspect of moral agency located within the self and also influenced by the self's relationship with constitutive others.[19] Selma Sevenhuijsen views moral reflection as a social practice that evaluates different types of moral judgement which affirms agency.[20] So how does this judgement come about? As moral agents, situated in social, yet often fluctuating, settings, we consider various options, often through debating with others before making choices that we believe to be ethical. This reflection does not threaten "the quality of judgment,"[21] but it endorses the importance of connections with others in affecting agents' choices. In contrast, universalist ethics and realist IR theorists view the agent as abstracted from specific circumstances. Beginning to think about IR from the viewpoint of interdependence as basic to being human radically alters the starting point of ethical reflection.

Third, a narrative understanding of the self-in-relationships requires ethical decisions within IR theory and practice to take into account the effect of these decisions on other people, but it is saying more than this. It is declaring that our life narratives and the life stories of those with whom we relate "are a primary way by which we make sense of the world around us, produce meanings, articulate intentions, and legitimize actions."[22] Individuals have complex, changing narratives, as do tribes, clans, communities, states, and regions. Therefore, as Margaret Urban Walker expresses it, "the narrative of 'who I am' (or 'who we are') and the narrative of 'how we have gotten here together' is threaded through by another story, one about 'what this means'."[23] Unless there is an attempt to understand interdependent narratives, meanings can be misinterpreted, and thus ethical decisions made in IR might have devastating consequences on people's lives, livelihoods, human rights, health, and well-being. An intersubjective understanding of the complex political world in which IR operates involves grasping an open, interpretive interplay between differing implications of how political actions affect people's actual lives. This means that ethical judgements on humanitarian aid, foreign policy, refugees, internally displaced persons, and diplomacy, are more likely to fulfil people's practical needs if those making the decisions have access to reliable knowledge that comes through listening to localized accounts of people's life stories.

The fourth aspect of a feminist relational view of agency is the value placed on differences within narratives. This includes appreciating the multiplicity of particular locations that constitute women's lives within families, communities, and the public sphere, all of which are profoundly affected by geographic location in the affluent West, developing nations, internal displacement sites, refugee camps, or war zones. Kimberly Hutchings argues that this assertion of the relevance of particularity draws attention to the way humans differ, so that "the meaning of equality of right may be about the recognition of difference rather than the assumption of sameness."[24] Jacqui True also suggests that feminist alternatives "demand greater historical and cultural contextualization in order to reflect more adequately the complexity and indeterminacy of human agency."[25] Christine Sylvester expresses this recognition of differences starkly: "There are western-middle-class-mother-feminist-peace-activists and Zimbabwean-peasant-mothers-post-colonialist-trade-unionists-ex-guerrillas."[26] Thus, in feminist theorizing on war, the starting point is that of unique individuals who experience war personally, in multiple ways, as violent acts on known bodies.

To summarize this second section, I have shown that a feminist relational view of agency accepts the complexity of everyday, situated lives as the starting point for reflection on ethical decision-making. I have argued that feminist ethics understand moral agents as living in webs of interdependence and building particular life narratives, each one different to others' life stories.

Feminist ethics and IR

Within the global world that IR studies, there are a host of ethical decisions to be made: for example, about minimizing global poverty and allocating resources, improving women's literacy and employment skills, climate change and its effect on the capitalist market, trade with nations that fail to respect human rights, the global refugee crisis, and when/if there should be a military intervention in a state whose government is not protecting its citizens. According to their explanatory theories of world politics, states prioritize their own self-interest since they exist in an anarchical system where the threat of war is always present. This priority highlights the difference between so-called "neutral" theories and normative, ethical theories. There are many normative IR theories that refer to key IR concerns such as humanitarianism, just war, and global justice.[27]

How then do feminists think differently about ethics? Kimberly Hutchings explains two related meanings of ethics as, first, "a set of substantive moral values, beliefs, and practices" about the sorts of distinctions we make every day between what is right and wrong, such as the question we might ask about whether it is ethical to buy fruit that comes from a country with an oppressive regime.[28] Religions, cultures, families, and histories influence these values, which are intermeshed into moral and socio-political life. The second meaning refers to the justification of "our claims about right and wrong," such as asking how we know whether buying this fruit is or is not ethical.[29] Additionally, as Sabina Lovibond states, ethics clarifies what it means to live well, "living a life that, taking one thing with another, we could feel was adequate to our species; a life that would not leave us feeling violated, cheated, ashamed, humiliated, or indeed terminally bored."[30] These accounts highlight the way that ethics is concerned with decisions about what is right and wrong, reasons for our choices, and that ethical decision-making enhances well-being. All normative theorists highlight these points, so what is unique about feminist ethics?

Does bringing ethics, feminism, and IR together really disrupt widely accepted or dominant ways of judging the world? Yes, I believe it does! In many ways, all feminist theorizing is normative and deliberately disruptive because it is constantly applying the gender-lens to question meanings and interpretations in seeking emancipatory forms of gender equality.[31] Through gendering ethics, there is an "opening up of a subject-matter to feminist criticism."[32] This challenges claims of universality that presume that there is only one acceptable idea of what it is to be a moral agent who is capable of reasoning and ethical deliberation. Also, gendering ethics acknowledges the larger feminist project of including differences: everyone should recognize themselves in the proposed model of agency. Feminist ethics brings to the fore questions that are situated in complex lives, querying whose experience theories speak for and to.

One important feminist approach to ethics that is widely used in feminist IR is the ethics of care.[33] This section examines four dimensions of these roots. First, it outlines foundational ideas of early theorists Carol Gilligan and Sara Ruddick. Second, it explains the moral practices of feminist ethical judgement to show why responsibilities to others are paramount. Third, it draws out implications of feminist ethics for research. Fourth, it begins to highlight the impact of feminist ethics on global politics.

First, whilst Carol Gilligan is a social psychologist examining moral reasoning in response to moral dilemmas, her development of the "ethic of care" represents a significant turning point in the development of feminist ethical theory.[34] Gilligan is critical of the idea that moral maturity comes with being able to be emotionally detached from the context of the specific moral dilemma and to make a judgement about what moral rules can be applied in any situation. In contrast, she found that women generally are more likely to make contextual judgements that are influenced by their relationships and patterns of responsibility to others. She concludes that these context-based judgements are not inferior, but different. They reveal socially and culturally based differences in moral views that permit later theorists to talk about the intersectionality between class, colour, ethnicity, race, and sexuality. Feminist ethics keeps asking important questions, like: Who is being represented in IR explanations? Does the portrayal of what is happening include all men and women, only some, or mainly men? Who is the agent under discussion? Whose lives are being debated? Gilligan's care ethic is "tied to feelings of empathy and compassion."[35] Within an ethic of care, personal aspects of life narratives and relationships with others are intrinsic to the moral puzzle, not pushed away, as they are in traditional IR. This is a profound and exciting disruption to dominant views. In making an ethical decision, the moral agent is self-expressive and attentive to the others' emotions, individuality, relationships, histories, and associations of connectedness.

Sara Ruddick's work developed in parallel to Gilligan's work, with a particular concern for peace. She explains that maternal thinking "is a discipline in attentive love" that emerges from the demands of a particular relationship of care, between a mother and her child.[36] Ruddick develops a politics of peace based around the moral orientation that emerges in "maternal thinking" and "preservative love" to reveal "a contradiction between mothering and war," in that mothering preserves life, whereas the military deliberately endangers "bodies, minds, and consciences in the name of victory and abstract causes."[37] Others have criticized Ruddick "for her essentialist association of care with motherhood" that omits power imbalances and paternalistic care-based relationships.[38] However, what she nevertheless shows are ways of thinking and cognitive capacities that emerge from the practices that are required in attentive nurturance, which, I contend, can be seen in nurturant men also. From the standpoint of maternal thinking, ethical judgement builds "on particular experiences of the practice of care to help to identify with and take responsibility for the needs and suffering of others."[39] This sensitivity to the context in which moral dilemmas occur requires ethical judgement that is not simply based on feeling others' suffering, but assuming a responsibility to do something to alleviate their pain. Accepting this responsibility is fundamental to feminist ethical theorists.

Second, in search of richer models of agency that value relationships, feminist ethics of care accentuate "relational moral practices in the everyday lives of people in all settings."[40] These practices include attentiveness and empathetic listening to the particularity of other's needs and "being open to entering another's world,"[41] not avoiding it, as is more typical in the IR discipline. As Robinson reminds us, careful listening to others "means not just hearing the words that are spoken, but being attentive to understanding the concerns, needs, and aims of others in the dialogue."[42] It is by being immersed in daily activities with the relationships of responsibility that the art of listening is best learned, and one is able to make judgements about moral decisions in the light of one's own and also of others' needs. "Effective listening requires learning how to be truly attentive to others, as well as nurturing the virtues of patience and trust," yet there is little emphasis on the moral and political value of effective listening in IR discourse.[43]

These practices of attentive listening prioritize responsibilities to others, actually locating "morality in *practices of responsibility*" so that "the ways we assign, accept, or deflect our responsibilities" express our ethical values.[44] An ethic of care does not only require that individual rights are not infringed, but that the responsibility towards others is recognized.[45] Care ethics can guide ways of thinking about humanitarian intervention, peacekeeping, development and aid, security policy, and human rights protection. For example, examining peacekeeping from a feminist perspective might see a shift from "the right to intervene in a sovereign state to a responsibility to protect citizens who are not being protected by their own state."[46] To avoid paternalism, those providing this protection should consult carefully with local people in order to respond responsibly with culturally sensitive, appropriate care.

Third, feminist ethics lay solid foundations for feminist research in requiring the researcher to be attentive to their own situatedness, to boundaries—incorporating inclusions, exclusions, marginalization, silences—and to "embedded epistemology."[47] This attentiveness to relationships "is concerned with the ways in which social, political, and economic actions are interrelated."[48] The feminist researcher situates herself within the power dynamics of embodied knowledge, moving boundaries, and complex relationships. Sometimes these requirements prompt adjustments to research goals. Megan MacKenzie conducted research in Sierra Leone in 2005 with former female soldiers. She became aware that, despite being profoundly affected by her emotions, she was writing these emotions out of her research in a way that is contrary to feminist IR theory. She maintains that part of researcher reflexivity is an awareness of how emotions can affect the research process.[49] In reflecting on the unedited answers to the question,

"What is the most significant experience you had during the war?" she acknowledges that this leads to random, often messy qualitative results, but ones that are a more "intimate, honest and revealing picture of women's experiences of war."[50] Feminist perspectives on emotions break the gender-based dichotomy between assumed male reason and female emotion, arguing that "connection, compassion and affectivity should be recognized as important sources of moral reasoning."[51]

Fourth, the potential impact of feminist ethics on global politics is immense. I underline three main implications: merging of justice and care; stressing empathy; and using a critical care approach to international politics. First, Gilligan argues that justice and care are "two cross-cutting perspectives" that cut across egoism and altruism.[52] She argues that since we all are vulnerable to oppression and abandonment, two moral visions recur. "The moral injunction not to act unfairly toward others, and not to turn away from someone in need, capture these different concerns" of justice and care.[53] The fear of paternalistic notions of care that dismiss the way that women lose their autonomy and rights when their care work is taken for granted led feminist theorists to develop an ethics of justice, whereby the practices of an ethics of care, such as attentiveness, responsiveness, and responsibility, are integrated with the values connected to justice, such as rationality, rights, and autonomy.[54] As Anna Höglund expresses it, "the best way to care for other people is to respect their rights."[55] In placing her discussion about the ethics of care in a framework of politics and citizenship, Sevenhuijsen formulates "a contextual and situated form of feminist ethics that can accommodate both care and justice arguments."[56] In the public sphere, people meet, identities are shaped through action and interaction, narratives are exchanged, and opinions deliberated, revised, and debated. A principal task of democratic citizenship is judging between good and bad, along with being accountable for choices, even though there may be uncertainty or dissent in citizens' rationale and actual choices. Ethical judgements should be able to deal with deep-rooted differences. As Joan Toronto, in developing the hope of feminist inclusion argues, in a democratic society "all people are responsible for seeing that the care of all is the premise of justice."[57]

A second implication that derives from the potential impact of feminist ethics on global politics is the value placed on empathy. Christine Sylvester presents "empathetic cooperation" as a feminist method.[58] In this "process of positional slippage," one is listening seriously to the concerns of others whilst weighing one's own fears.[59] Empathy comes into play by being willing to engage "in a subjectivity-moving way" that is open "to the stories, identities, and sites that have been bypassed in 'our' field."[60] Traditional IR theory assumes that empathy requires a loss of critical faculties, but Jean Bethke Elshtain argues that empathy helps to create a "robust rather than an anaemic dialogue" on contending ethical positions.[61] Laura Sjoberg suggests that the possible consequences of empathetic cooperation are enormous when dealing with those who are normally seen as opponents, because the motivation is "to understand and feel where others are coming from" in order to "produce mutually satisfactory solutions to political problems."[62] Obviously, these solutions do not always happen because the obstacles between former enemies in conflict zones are formidable. However, the ideal of empathetic cooperation has great potential in breaking down some of the antagonism and mistrust in dealing with opposed groups from differing ethno-religious or ideological backgrounds.

A third far-reaching impact of feminist ethics on global politics lies in what Robinson calls a "critical care approach," whereby she argues that care ethics asks the critical questions about the bases on which care is given and the power relations that lead to inequalities.[63] Robinson does not rely on Ruddick's maternal thinking, but on the importance of care as an everyday practice, embedded in contexts, and contributing to a specific moral orientation. She demonstrates how morality emerges through being responsive to others. Ethical judgement thus is always relational and contextual. Such discernment requires responses of "waiting, listening, focusing attention," as well as responsiveness and responsibility.[64] This attention to people's particular situations "may render their need for care different, or more or less acute."[65] The skills of care ethics: build on the idea that humans exist in relation to others; focus on "responsibility to the needs of particular others as the substance of morality;" commit to addressing moral problems in the contexts of lived experiences; and reconceptualize traditional notions of relationships between the public and private spheres.[66] The critical care approach questions "who is and who is not cared for" and thus "who can and cannot lead a dignified and fulfilled life."[67]

In political terms, Robinson's care ethics "seeks solutions to the problems of the giving and receiving of care that are non-exploitative, equitable, and adequate to ensure the flourishing of all persons."[68] Olena Hankivsky also argues that given care ethics' sensitivity to human differences, it "opens new ways for understanding experiences of discrimination, suffering, and oppression."[69] For example, it grasps the harms associated with globalization, like slave labour, indentured and child labour, and sweatshops. Instead of prioritizing demands of the market or the expertise of the policy expert, an ethic of care prioritizes "the voice of the people, and in particular those vulnerable and at-risk populations" who suffer because of the ruthless market-driven nature of globalization.[70] The explicit focus of an ethic of care is on improving lives through access to health care, education, informal care, and inclusive decision-making.[71] As Robinson argues, there is a "transformative potential" of this ethics that extends to the personal, political, and the global contexts when care ethics are applied to decisions concerning famine, environmental disaster, poverty, HIV, and fair-trade negotiations.[72]

I suggest that there is a possibility for feminist ethics to amend the type of ethical decisions that are made within international relations. An interesting example of this lies with Sweden's 2015 launch of a feminist foreign policy. Its framing is underpinned by normative positions that are committed to "feminist ethical principles of inclusion and human security" and also to "empathetic cooperation" that, like care ethics, stresses the importance of listening and dialogue.[73] Indeed, the policy asks, "Security for whom?"[74] The answer to this question demands a critical scrutiny of patriarchal and Global North power relations and all types of exclusions. Yet, there are pragmatic challenges to fulfilling the expectations of gender-sensitive policies. Karin Aggestam and Annika Bergman-Rosamund offer two examples of notable inconsistencies. First, there is failure to practise inclusivity given the plight of women stuck in refugee camps in the Middle East, a stark contrast to their husbands who have reached Swedish shores. Second, there is a failure to be a consistent advocate of preventive diplomacy, given that Sweden is "one of the world's top ten leading arms exporters" with consequences that harm lives, fuel gender-based violence, and add to the repression of women.[75] The application of feminist ethics to major IR concerns is always difficult, but, I maintain, is worthwhile.

In this section, I have highlighted four main points. I explain the influence of early care theorists in shaping feminist debates on ethics. I show how practices of care lead to and are prompted by responsibilities to care. I clarify the situatedness of research for feminist ethics theorists. Importantly, I argue that there is an enormous potential of feminist ethics to transform IR theory and practice in combining justice and care, being empathetic, and asking critical questions about the nature and quality of care given in ethical political practices in the sphere of international relations.

Feminists rethinking security in building peace

This fourth section revisits ethics in the context of security—a fundamental area of IR theory. As noted above, traditionally, discussions of security stress the role of sovereign, self-interested nation-states, and particular military strategies to protect citizens from external threats. The change of focus from states' preoccupation with militarism to nation-states and people that marked the end of the Cold War gave impetus to feminists in rethinking security as human security, focused on what is required for particular people in different situations to feel secure. Feminists thus ask questions about "who is being secured by security policies."[76] Feminist security theory investigates and problematizes the relationships between women, in/security, peace, and war. As Heidi Hudson explains, human security approaches understand security "comprehensively and holistically in terms of the real-life, everyday experiences of human beings," shifting the focus from "security dilemma of states" to "survival dilemmas of people"[77] that have impact "on life and death."[78]

Defining in/security depends on context. Clearly, there are dangers in generalizations about women from the Global North or South, but Tickner draws attention to the way that many women from the Global South describe insecurity broadly "in terms of the structural violence associated with imperialism, militarism, racism, and sexism,"[79] calling attention to their particular vulnerabilities. Familial, national, and international violence are interconnected through military, economic, and sexual violence. The resulting insecurities are felt deeply and differently in distinctive conflicts. Annick Wibben uses diverse examples of stories that represent these moral problems of insecurity, from prostitution in camp towns in Korea around United States military bases, to the Mayan women of Guatemala whose life stories produce counter-narratives to hegemonic state narratives, to the transformative potential of storytelling about war in Mozambique as a way of making life bearable.[80] Rather than a top-down or structural perspective, these stories are consistent with feminists' "bottom-up approach, analyzing the impact of war at the micro level."[81]

Recall that in traditional security studies, security focuses "on the absence of inter-state political violence," so when the ethical significance "of relations of recognition and responsibility" come into play, meanings of peace and security change.[82] This change is necessary because it shows that war has a massive effect on displacement of populations, the vulnerability of refugees, and on the terrible extent of loss of lives, limbs, dignity, economic livelihoods, and community stability. Rape-in-war demands obvious recognition and appropriate responses. The common feature of systematic rapes in the former Yugoslavia, Rwanda, the Democratic Republic of Congo, and the war between Japan and China, or American soldiers' abuses in Korea and Vietnam with the intention of enforced pregnancy, is part of this ethical analysis. Such acts of violence are cases of injustice, requiring just redress and meaningful, particularized responses to the trauma endured and suffering caused.

As explained in the section above, Robinson's "care-based ethics of human security" permits us to think "critically about how societies—especially societies plagued by endemic violence—think about and value care"[83] and how we live in complex webs of relationships in ethnic and cultural groups, religious associations, tribes, clans, neighbourhoods, communities, and families. This perspective on security is intrinsically critical in revealing relations of power connected to people's insecurities. Robinson uses examples typically hidden from view, including elderly grandmothers in sub-Saharan Africa who are struggling with the care of their children suffering from AIDS, or their grandchildren orphaned by this pandemic, migrant women of colour who work as maids, nannies, or sex workers and have to leave their own children behind, and women struggling to rebuild households after war to find sources of livelihoods to meet family needs.[84] Feminist ethical theorists argue that we have a responsibility to attend to these insecurities with compassionate responses.

Robinson's aforementioned critical care argument relates directly to improving human security. Accepting that humans are "beings-in-relation"[85] with networks of responsibility challenges assumptions about dependency or vulnerability, domination, exclusion, and colonialism, enhances human security in ways that address the daily experiences of insecurities. I am reinforcing the point that ethics in IR is an activity to which care is central. Robinson explains that:

> the widely recognized aspects of human security—freedom from poverty, food security, health care and protection from disease, protection from environmental pollution and depletion, physical safety from violence and survival of traditional cultures—cannot be realized in the absence of robust, equitable, well-resourced relations and networks of care at the household, community, state, and transnational levels.[86]

Considering human security through the lens of feminist ethics of care changes the focus from the state and the absence of violence, to persons experiencing insecurity and needing safety, and thus to the resources needed to realize security in a just, caring fashion. The central component to Robinson's "critical feminist ethics" is the systematic scrutiny of the contextual relationships within global politics. Her point is that ethics in IR is concerned not only with obvious crises such as when ethnic relations break down and erupt into violence, or when barbaric genocide occurs, or when the "coalition of the willing" invades a country. Ethics is also concerned with the quality of "normal" socio-political relations that contribute to processes of marginalization, exclusion, injustices, and powerlessness that prompt structural violence.

In dealing with security, traditional IR theory concentrates on war. For feminist ethics, rethinking security focuses attention on personally felt insecurities and processes that build peace. Violent conflict causes personal injury and serious harms. Minimizing harm fits within concerns for justice, and caring for others comes with "concern for the particular other."[87] This distinction between the principles of universal justice and applied attention to care is significant. In viewing terrible traumas on our nightly news, we may feel sympathy for those who are suffering, but despite goodwill, viewers understandably might feel overwhelmed in not knowing how to assist meeting victims' needs, or remedying the structural violence that caused the suffering.[88] In analysing how a global ethic of care translates, as noted, the central question is: who is in need of care? In her influential early work, Joan Tronto includes compassion as a central value of caring, along with attentiveness, responsibility, nurturance, and meeting others' needs,[89] values that she argues should be applied in a political context.[90] In applying these values, debates on the "ethics of care" broaden into a practical application of a "politics of care" to political decisions that affect international relations. A "politics of compassion" extends this application further, such as generous foreign aid, empathetic immigration policies, and open diplomacy in cases of conflict transformation. Whilst rare, when it exists, there is the understanding of a shared humanity, the idea that we all are vulnerable, therefore we need meaningful care that responds practically to our different and changing needs in ways that protect human dignity.[91] Imagine how different peoples' lives would be if this type of politics became the norm in international relations!

Care ethics and a politics of compassion overlap in their commitment to the particular, contextualized characteristics of care, but differ in their focus of attention. Care ethics is directed toward a known person, whereas applied to the political domain, while a politics of compassion responds to people requiring care who are unknown to politicians, activists, aid workers, peacebuilders, and policy-makers, such as refugees, displaced persons, women and girls raped in war, male victims of sexual torture, HIV/AIDS sufferers, or civilians affected by drones or terrorism. Compassion is demonstrated through responses to alleviate others' suffering.[92] Compassion helps "to reconceptualize a rehumanized view of the other"[93] because it "focuses on people's pain and specific needs," and within a political context, "a struggle for justice and the realization of human rights is part of striving toward a compassionate society."[94] This argument confirms that "compassion is central to the practice of an ethical life and thus compassionate political responses are integral to decent polities."[95] When incorporated into long-term processes of peacebuilding, compassion addresses underlying root causes of conflict, deals constructively with intense forms of suffering in ways that relieve people's pain meaningfully, and re/builds relationships.[96]

A feminist normative framework to security is a solid basis around which to build a sustainable, just peace with caring relationships. This places the aspiration to international peace within a framework that privileges interdependence and the emotional connectedness this involves. Certainly, translating empathy, reciprocity, respect, and understanding in practice in communities that have lived through long-term violence or seeming intransigence appears elusive or unworkable. However, normative frameworks contain goals that are worth striving toward because they have a positive impact on the development of policies, laws, and new institutions within transitional justice processes, even when the practicalities of everyday relationships involved appear unrealistic or agonizingly difficult to achieve.[97]

Conclusion

This chapter shows that despite feminist theory's seemingly uncomfortable fit within IR theory, its contribution to thinking and acting on ethical issues is substantial. I make four main points to the overall argument. First, I show how, through using a gender-lens to explain events in international politics, early feminist IR theorists expose gendered inequalities, injustices, and differences in the ways that people experience political life and make ethical choices. Second, I clarify that not all feminist IR theorists are explicitly committed to feminist ethics. Those who do, typically view moral agency as relational, understanding that all the particular contexts, situations, networks of relationships, and idiosyncrasies that make us different are taken seriously as indispensable to guiding contextually based ethical decision-making. This view of the human agent as being interdependent stands as a stark contrast to the disembodied, abstract individual of traditional IR. Third, I explain how feminist ethics highlight practices of attentiveness, empathy, listening, and responding to particular needs as fundamental to the ethical responsibilities of being an active moral agent and a good citizen. These practices and responsibilities have a considerable influence on global politics in seeking to combine justice with care, in being empathetic, and in integrating critical questioning of power relations into IR theories and practices. Fourth, I contend that suffering caused by insecurities is an ethical dilemma that demands a considerate response. For feminist ethics, this pain prompts a critical care approach to human security and to the hope of creating significant networks of interdependence, and more compassionate, peaceful polities that respond meaningfully to particularized human suffering.

Notes

1 A symposium in 1988 on women in IR led to *Millennium* being the first IR journal to hold a special issue on women in IR. For influential literature that emerged on the topic between 1988 and 1996, see Jill Steans, *Gender and International Relations: An Introduction* (Cambridge: Polity Press, 1998), 184. For the historical background to bringing feminist perspectives into the discipline of IR, see J. Ann Tickner, *A Feminist Voyage through International Relations* (Oxford: Oxford University Press, 2014).

2 Cynthia Enloe's work shows how women are present through sexism implicit in tourism, nationalism, and gendered colonialism, with women living on military bases, in diplomats' lives, as labourers in the workforce, and as domestic servants. See *Bananas, Beaches and Bases: Making Feminist Sense of International Politics* (Berkeley: University of California Press, 1990).

3 Ibid., 195–196.
4 Jan Jindy Pettman, *Worlding Women: A Feminist International Politics* (London: Routledge, 1996), vii.
5 V. Spike Peterson and Ann Sisson Runyan, *Global Gender Issues* (Boulder, Colorado: Westview Press, 1993).
6 Steans, *Gender and International Relations*, 5.
7 Marysia Zalewski argues this is because "they are methodologically skewered when we fail to see through gender(ed) lenses." See Marysia Zelwski, "Feminist International Relations: Making Sense...," in *Gender Matters in Global Politics: A Feminist Introduction to International Relations*, ed. Laura Shepherd (London: Routledge, 2015), 5.
8 J. Ann Tickner, *Gender in International Relations: Feminist Perspectives on Achieving Global Security* (New York: Columbia University Press, 1992), 18.
9 J. Ann Tickner, *Gendering World Politics: Issues and Approaches in the Post-Cold War Era* (New York: Columbia University Press, 2001), 8.
10 Tickner, *Feminist Voyage through International Relations*, 78–79.
11 Ibid., 83. Jacqui True highlights the "feminist commitment to self-reflexivity" as contributing significantly to the study of IR. See Jacqui True, "Feminism," in *Theories of International Relations*, eds. Scott Burchall et al. (Basingstoke: Palgrave Macmillan, 2013), 265. For an account of feminist liberalism, Marxism, socialism, postmodernism, postcolonialism, and critical theory, see Brooke A. Ackerly, Maria Stern and Jacqui True, eds., *Feminist Methodologies for International Relations* (Cambridge: Cambridge University Press, 2006).
12 Zalewski, "Feminist International Relations," 4.
13 Kimberly Hutchings explains how "Post-modern feminists insist on the ethical significance of the fact that all women are not the same," in "Ethics," in *Gender Matters in Global Politics: A Feminist Introduction to International Relations*, ed. Laura Shepherd (London: Routledge, 2015), 58. She states also that there is "always a *political* dimension to ethics," ibid., 59.
14 See Elisabeth Porter, "Rethinking Women's Empowerment," *Journal of Peacebuilding and Development*, 8, no. 1 (2013): 1–14.
15 Annick Wibben, *Feminist Security Studies: A Narrative Approach* (London: Routledge, 2011), 2.
16 Pettman, *Worlding Women*, 105.
17 J. Ann Tickner, "Gendering a Discipline: Some Feminist Methodological Contributions to International Relations," *Signs: Journal of Women in Culture and Society*, 30, no. 4 (2005): 2177.
18 Fiona Robinson, *The Ethics of Care: A Feminist Approach to Human Security* (Philadelphia, Pennsylvania: Temple University Press, 2011), 4.
19 Vivienne Jabri, "Explorations of Difference in Normative International Relations," in *Women, Culture, and International Relations*, eds. Vivienne Jabri and Eleanor O'Gorman (Boulder, Colorado: Lynne Rienner Publishers, 1999), 41.
20 Selma Sevenhuijsen, *Citizenship and the Ethics of Care: Feminist Considerations on Justice, Morality and Politics* (London: Routledge, 1998), 37.
21 Ibid., 59.
22 Wibben, *Feminist Security Studies*, 2. See Chapter 2, "Why Are War Narratives Important?" in Elisabeth Porter, *Connecting Peace, Justice and Reconciliation* (Boulder, Colorado: Lynne Rienner Publishers, 2015).
23 Margaret Urban Walker, *Moral Understandings: A Feminist Study in Ethics* (New York: Routledge, 1998), 113.
24 Kimberly Hutchings, "Ethics, Feminism, and International Affairs," in *Ethics and International Affairs: Extent and Limits*, eds. Jean-Marc Coicaud and Daniel Warner (Tokyo: UN University Press, 2001), 199.
25 True, "Feminism," 256.
26 Christine Sylvester, *Feminist International Relations: An Unfinished Journey* (Cambridge: Cambridge University Press, 2002), 216.
27 See Mervyn Frost, *Global Ethics: Anarchy, Freedom and International Relations* (London: Routledge, 2009); and Richard Shapcott, *International Ethics: A Critical Introduction* (Cambridge: Polity, 2010).
28 Hutchings, "Ethics," 51.
29 Ibid., 51.
30 Sabina Lovibond, "'Gendering' as an Ethical Concept," *Feminist Theory*, 2, no. 2 (2001): 151.
31 See Kimberly Hutchings, "Towards a Feminist International Ethics," *Review of International Studies*, 26, no. 5 (2000): 111.
32 Lovibond, "'Gendering' as an Ethical Concept," 157.

33 Early care ethics theorists who grounded their ideas in the relationships and responsibilities women hold because of their caring practices include: Annette Baier, *Moral Prejudices: Essays on Ethics* (Cambridge, Massachusetts: Harvard University Press, 1995); Eve Browning Cole and Susan Coultrap-McQuin, eds., *Explorations in Feminist Ethics: Theory and Practice* (Bloomington, Indiana: Indiana University Press, 1992); Virginia Held, *Feminist Morality: Transforming Culture, Society, and Politics* (Chicago: University of Chicago Press, 1993); and Elisabeth Porter, *Women and Moral Identity* (Sydney: Allen and Unwin, 1991).

34 Carol Gilligan, *In a Different Voice: Psychological Theory and Women's Development* (Cambridge: Cambridge University Press, 1982).

35 Ibid., 69.

36 Sara Ruddick, *Maternal Thinking: Towards a Politics of Peace* (London: Women's Press, 1989,) 123. This attentive care may also emerge with women in caring roles who are not biological mothers, and with men who are deeply involved in attentive care, particularly through fathering, welfare, and teaching roles.

37 Ibid., 123.

38 Anna T. Höglund, "Justice for Women in War? Feminist Ethics and Human Rights for Women," *Feminist Theology*, 1, no. 3 (2003): 349.

39 Hutchings, "Ethics," 55. Men who nurture others can demonstrate these capacities and virtues.

40 Fiona Robinson, "Methods of Feminist Normative Theory: A Political Ethic of Care for International Relations," in *Feminist Methodologies for International Relations*, eds. Brooke Ackerly, Maria Stern and Jacqui True (Cambridge: Cambridge University Press, 2006), 225.

41 Wibben, *Feminist Security Studies*, 105.

42 Fiona Robinson, "Stop Talking and Listen: Discourse Ethics and Feminist Care Ethics in International Political Theory," *Millennium: Journal of International Studies* 39, no. 3 (2011): 847. For an application of this argument of listening to the risks involved when conflict remains, see Elisabeth Porter, "Risks and Responsibilities: Creating Dialogical Spaces in Northern Ireland," *International Feminist Journal of Politics*, 2, no. 2 (2000): 163–184.

43 Robinson, "Stop Talking and Listen," 856.

44 Walker, *Moral Understandings*, 16; Virginia Held maintains that the ethics of care influences how IR theorists "see the world and our responsibilities in it, and it holds promise for new efforts to improve global relations." See Virginia Held, *The Ethics of Care: Personal, Political and Global* (Oxford: Oxford University Press, 2006), 155.

45 Daniel Warner, *An Ethic of Responsibility in International Relations* (Boulder, Colorado: Lynne Rienner, 1991).

46 True, "Feminism," 260.

47 Brooke Ackerly and Jacqui True, "Reflexivity in Practice: Power and Ethics in Feminist Research on International Relations," *International Studies Review*, 10, no. 4 (2008): 694–696.

48 Ibid., 697.

49 Megan H. MacKenzie, "Their Personal is Political, Not Mine: Feminism and Emotion," *International Studies Review*, 13, no. 4 (2011): 692.

50 Ibid., 693.

51 Sevenhuijsen, *Citizenship and the Ethics of Care*, 12.

52 Gilligan, *In a Different Voice*, 25.

53 Ibid., 20.

54 The concern that abandoning universal moral principles of justice and rights will undermine the possibility of criticism of cultures with norms that devalue women led to articulations of justice ethics, as developed in Seyla Benhabib, ed., *Situating the Self: Gender, Community and Post-Modernism in Contemporary Ethics* (New York: Routledge, 1992).

55 Höglund, 2003, 361.

56 Sevenhuijsen, *Citizenship and the Ethics of Care*, 13.

57 Joan Tronto, *Caring for Democracy: A Feminist Vision* (Utrecht: Universiteit voor Humanistiek, 1995), 18.

58 Sylvester, *Feminist International Relations*, 244.

59 Ibid., 247.

60 Ibid., 256.

61 Jean Bethke Elshtain, "Bringing It All Back Home, Again," in *Global Voices: Dialogues in International Relations*, ed. James Rosenau (Boulder, Colorado: Westview Press, 1993), 106.

62 Laura Sjoberg, *Gender Justice and the Wars in Iraq* (New York: Lexington Books, 2006), 234.

63 Fiona Robinson, "The Importance of Care in the Theory and Practice of Human Security," *Journal of International Political Theory*, 4, no. 2 (2008): 171.
64 Fiona Robinson, *Globalizing Care: Ethics, Feminist Theory and International Relations* (Boulder, Colorado: Westview Press, 1999), 47.
65 Robinson, "The Importance of Care in Human Security," 170.
66 Robinson, *The Ethics of Care*, 29.
67 Robinson, *Globalizing Care*, 31.
68 Robinson, *The Ethics of Care*, 33.
69 Olena Hankivsky, "Imagining Ethical Globalization: The Contributions of a Care Ethic," *Journal of Global Ethics*, 2, no. 1 (2006): 99.
70 Ibid., 102.
71 See Sevenhuijsen, *Citizenship and the Ethics of Care*.
72 Robinson, *Globalizing Care*, 23.
73 Karin Aggestam and Annika Bergman-Rosamund, "Swedish Feminist Foreign Policy in the Making: Ethics, Politics, and Gender," *Ethics and International Affairs*, 30, no. 4 (2016): 326.
74 Ibid., 326.
75 Ibid., 329.
76 Eric M. Blanchard, "Gender, International Relations, and the Development of Feminist Security Theory," *Signs: Journal of Women in Culture and Society*, 28, no. 4 (2003): 1290.
77 Heidi Hudson, "Doing Security as Though Humans Matter: A Feminist Perspective on Gender and the Politics of Human Security," *Security Dialogue*, 36, no. 2 (2005): 163.
78 Wibben, *Feminist Security Studies*, 39.
79 Tickner, *Gender in International Relations*, 54–55.
80 Wibben, *Feminist Security Studies*, 99.
81 Tickner, *Feminist Voyage through International Relations*, 23.
82 Hutchings, "Towards a Feminist International Ethics," 124.
83 Robinson, "The Importance of Care in Human Security," 178.
84 Robinson, *The Ethics of Care*, 8.
85 Ibid., 10. Robinson acknowledges this is close to Carol Gould's concept of individuals-in-relations developed in her *Marx's Social Ontology: Individuality and Community in Marx's Theory of Social Reality* (Cambridge, Massachusetts: MIT Press, 1978).
86 Robinson, *The Ethics of Care*, 59.
87 Karin Marie Fierke, "Who Is My Neighbour? Memories of the Holocaust/*al Nakba* and a Global Ethic of Care," *European Journal of International Relations* online (2013): 2.
88 Nel Noddings suggests that when "one *feels* pity . . . the appropriate response is one of compassion," in *Caring: A Feminine Approach to Ethics and Moral Education* (Berkeley, California: University of California Press, 1984), 211.
89 Joan Tronto, *Moral Boundaries: A Political Argument for an Ethic of Care* (New York: Routledge, 1993), 3.
90 Ibid., 125.
91 Elisabeth Porter, "Can Politics Practice Compassion?" *Hypatia*, 21, no. 4 (2006): 99. Benhabib supports an egalitarian reciprocity that recognizes "the dignity of the generalized other through an acknowledgement of the moral identity of the concrete other," 1992, 164. To this end, the more we seek to identify with another, the greater likelihood we have of being able to understand some of this person's deep needs. As Ruddick argues, the defence of human security can adopt an attitude toward the vulnerable of protective "holding," which minimizes harmful risk, 1989, 78–79.
92 These demonstrations can take many forms, from voting for ethical political representatives, to donating to reliable organizations, raising awareness through writing, or involvement in activism, development aid, trauma counsel, human rights groups, faith-based groups, NGO, and peacebuilding work.
93 Porter, *Connecting Peace, Justice and Reconciliation*, 167.
94 Porter, "Can Politics Practice Compassion?" 106.
95 Ibid., 99.
96 See Elisabeth Porter, *Peacebuilding: Women in International Perspective* (London: Routledge, 2007).
97 See Porter, *Connecting Peace, Justice and Reconciliation*, 174.

11

CRITICAL INTERNATIONAL ETHICS

Knowing/acting differently

Kate Schick

Critical approaches to international ethics stem from a variety of intellectual traditions, but they also have multiple points of commonality. In this chapter, I address some of the tensions between critical and traditional approaches to ethics, highlighting the rationalism that dominates traditional approaches and the alternatives proffered by critical international ethics.

In the first part of the chapter, I argue that critical engagements with international ethics challenge the orthodox approach of seeking abstract universal rules for solving ethical problems. Rationalist rules-based ethics elevate a particular form of knowing that closes off debate and contestation, silences the historical, social, political and economic conditions that create ethical problems, prevents the accommodation of difference, and obscures the self and its place in moral judgement. These approaches pursue 'useful knowledge'[1] that might be wielded to solve global problems, elevating self-mastery and invulnerability in an attempt to shut down insecurity. Critical approaches eschew both the instrumental rationality of traditional ethics and the elevation of security and invulnerability as incontrovertible goods. Instead, they see ethical behaviour as springing from an exploration of relationality and our vulnerable subjectivity.

In the second part of the chapter, I illustrate some of the diverse ways that a critical sensibility enriches our understanding of international ethics by drawing out some key strands of contemporary critical thought and their challenge to moral rationalist hegemony. First, I highlight a different kind of knowing, drawing on radical Hegelian critical theory and its destabilization of epistemic certainty. Second, I explore a different relationship between knower-experts and those who are known, drawing on the recent turn towards autoethnography and its invitation towards reflexivity, vulnerability and contingency. Third, I signal a different kind of political action, drawing on agonistic theories that resist the depoliticization of ethics. I argue that, although a variety of theoretical traditions inform critical engagements with international ethics, they all seek to think otherwise and to refuse the disciplining of messy and precarious lived global experience into tidy and settled theoretical accounts of what has happened and what might be done.

Outside international ethics: problem-solving versus critical theory approaches to ethics in international relations

Rationalist international ethics

International ethics is dominated by a thoroughgoing moral rationalism, which privileges the pursuit of a particular kind of knowledge and a particular approach to ethical problems. Moral rationalism pursues a knowledge that is positivist and rationalist: it focuses on that which can be seen and measured. A central goal of moral rationalism is the accumulation of knowledge, underpinned by the assumption that the more information we have gathered, the more likely we will be able to solve the problems that concern us. According to Hans J. Morgenthau, the pursuit of instrumental forms of knowledge is a central plank of liberal international ethics. Embracing a social scientific view of politics, rationalist liberalism adheres to a belief in 'the power of science to solve all problems and, more particularly, all political problems which confront man in the modern age'.[2] The determined pursuit of 'more facts'[3] goes hand in hand with the belief that a failure to address social and political problems is not due to a lack of understanding, but to a lack of knowledge. The more expert knowledge we have at our disposal, the more efficient and effective targeted solutions we can devise. The type of knowledge privileged by moral rationalism, then, is 'useful knowledge'[4]—knowledge able to be wielded to mitigate global problems.

Moral rationalism's pursuit of instrumental knowledge is inextricably linked with a particular approach to ethical questions that is problem-solving and forward-looking. As noted above, the accumulation of knowledge about global problems is *useful* because it can be wielded to answer the question 'What ought to be done?' Robert Cox famously describes this aspect of liberal rationalism as 'problem-solving theory',[5] saying that formulating solutions to particular global problems leaves deeper political and economic structures intact and fails to address the fractures of the global order that underlie observable manifestations of dysfunction. Problem-solving theory is resolutely forward-looking: it engages with the past and present in so far as it provides knowledge that can be used to develop a vision for the future.

International ethics, then, is dominated by a vision of politics that is resolutely rationalist: it seeks useful knowledge about global problems in order to formulate solutions that might mitigate (or even solve) those problems. The goal of securing the state and/or a particular global order underlies rationalist engagements with global suffering.[6] The question 'What ought to be done?' might more fully be read 'What ought to be done to increase (global/state/human) security?' This privileges security above other goals (such as social justice, poverty relief) in a desire to create a world order marked by stability and predictability. Where changes are enacted, these are reformist changes that leave the (Westphalian, capitalist) *status quo* intact. Mainstream theorizing about international ethics, then, has more in common with traditional positivist international relations (IR) theory than generally acknowledged: they share a rationalist, problem-solving core.

Critical international ethics

Critical theoretical approaches take issue with the rationalist, problem-solving approach that dominates mainstream theorizing about international ethics. Whereas rationalist approaches accumulate knowledge about global problems in order to solve them, critical approaches eschew the pursuit of 'more facts' for instrumental purposes. Instead, they complicate the condition of knowing, maintaining that the pursuit of observable useful knowledge leaves much of what it is to be human in our actually existing world unknown and unquestioned.[7] Cox's distinction between problem-solving theory and critical theory characterizes critical theory as stepping back from global problems and asking questions about the underlying (social, historical, political, and economic) structures and conditions that facilitate global suffering and inequality.[8] Rather than enacting reformist changes that do nothing to challenge the global *status quo*, Cox calls for an interrogation of the patterns of recognition and misrecognition that continue to perpetuate global injustice. Critical approaches desacralize the *status quo*, starting from 'what is'[9] and asking how it might be transformed.

As well as complicating rationalist conditions of knowledge, critical theory also complicates rationalist engagement with ethical problems. Critical approaches maintain that global problems are complex and deeply rooted and cannot be solved by the expert application of technical knowledge. They regard with suspicion ethical prescriptions devised abstractly without reference to actually existing social, historical and political conditions, and seek to destabilize the position of 'expert' knower-theorists in relation to those whose lives they theorize. Critical approaches to international ethics are informed by the turn from classical 'epistemic certainty'[10] towards situated, relational knowledge. Instead of developing blueprints for action that answer the central ethical question 'What ought we to do?', critical approaches advocate a slower interrogation of patterns of power that allows space for contestation and debate and gives voice to the silenced and marginalized.

Raymond Geuss characterizes a critical theoretic approach as falling 'outside ethics'.[11] Refusing moral rationalism's disciplining pursuit of instrumental knowledge in order to determine 'what we ought to do' opens up whole vistas of ethico-political thought and action that fall outside a modern conception of ethics. In what follows, I explore some of the horizons that open up when we step outside moral rationalism's circumscription of knowledge and action. I argue that a critical theoretical approach invites deeper and broader knowledge of global politics that starts with a journey towards (always imperfect and partial) comprehension of situated lived experience.

Thinking ethically: critical theoretical engagements

It is important to note at the outset that critical international ethics is far from uniform: it includes a wide range of theories with diverse philosophical roots (including, for example, Theodor W. Adorno, Hannah Arendt, Judith Butler, Michel Foucault, Carol Gilligan, Antonio Gramsci, Jürgen Habermas, G. W. F. Hegel and Emmanuel Levinas). IR often divides postpositivist theory into two broad categories, referencing their theoretical heritage: Frankfurt School Critical Theory and poststructuralism. However, this division can both obfuscate differences within these traditions and overemphasize differences between them. Within Frankfurt School-influenced critical international ethics, some approaches fall closer to rationalist ethics than others. Habermasian international ethics advocate a more situated and relational epistemology than traditional moral rationalism, but continue to be wedded to a strong version of moral progress and to emphasize rational decision-making. International ethics influenced by first-generation Frankfurt School thinkers (such as Adorno and Walter Benjamin), in contrast, have a much less robust version of moral progress and supplement their critique of instrumental rationality by embracing the *non-identical*: that which cannot be measured or subsumed into known categories or concepts. Like early Frankfurt School approaches, poststructural international ethics are annihilatingly critical of the rationalism of mainstream international ethics and much less sanguine about the possibility of moral progress under conditions of modernity. They, too, are diverse: although poststructural approaches seek to disrupt or invert established hierarchies such as public and private, universal and particular, identity and difference, they respond differently to demands for 'answers' for real-world problems. In what follows, I avoid the rigid categorization of critical international ethics; instead, I highlight the ways critical approaches, broadly conceived, differ from mainstream rationalist approaches rather than from one another.

With these caveats in mind, in the remainder of this chapter I illustrate some of the diverse ways that a critical theoretical sensibility enriches our understanding of international ethics. I necessarily focus on subsections of the critical international ethics literature as I proceed, drawing out some key strands of contemporary critical international ethics by focusing on three interrelated themes: knowing differently, relating differently, and acting differently. First, I highlight critical ethics' fundamentally different approach to knowing, focusing in particular on critical international ethics with a Hegelian sensibility. Hegelian critical theories eschew the forward-looking, problem-solving rationalism of mainstream international ethics, starting with 'what is' rather than 'what ought to be' and drawing attention to our radical relationality. Second, I emphasize the critical unsettling of the relationship between knower and known, focusing particularly on its articulation in the turn to autoethnography. Critical approaches interrogate the privileging of expert knowledge and the silencing of 'other' voices, emphasizing the vulnerability of judgement in the place of self-certainty. Third, I outline critical international ethics' very different relation to political action, particularly as it is expressed in agonistic pluralism. Rather than using abstractly devised ethical theories as a guide to action, critical approaches see the ethical as always already political. They highlight the importance of acting politically in the here and now, taking 'the everyday' seriously as a site of political action.

Knowing differently

Although critical approaches to IR take their theoretical impetus from a variety of sources, many owe a theoretical debt to the philosophy of Hegel, which blazoned the way to a radically different way of knowing. In this section, I outline some of the key dimensions of contemporary (radical) Hegelian thought. Note that I am engaging with a particular reading of Hegel here, which sees his work as an important resource for thinking critically about international ethics. This 'radical' Hegel is quite different to the conservative reading propounded by communitarian thinkers.[12] I argue that where rationalist ethics assumes access to objective, verifiable facts, critical ethics maintains that all knowledge is socially situated and that *knowing* is a process one engages in over time. Furthermore, where rationalist ethics posits the central ethical question 'What ought we to do?',[13] critical ethics insists that we start instead by working towards comprehension of 'what is' in the here and now. These (Hegelian) dimensions of critical international ethics unsettle the confident epistemology of rationalist IR and invite in its place a slower, more difficult journey towards comprehension that tarries with ambiguity, vulnerability and relationality.

Hegelian critical theories challenge the foundationalist epistemology of classical philosophy, with its focus on 'objectivity, representation and truth', and move instead towards historically and socially situated knowledge of the world we inhabit. Against the pursuit of 'epistemic certainty', Hegelian thought emphasizes a journey towards comprehension, one that does not take the world as an '*objectively given* order' but as shaped by social and historical conditions.[14] The Hegelian notion of recognition is a radical concept that encourages a deeper, more holistic understanding of global politics, including our selves and the ways we are implicated in patterns of recognition and misrecognition that marginalize and oppress. The *ongoing* nature of this journey towards knowledge is built into the very structure of the word 're-cognition', with its emphasis on knowing (cognizing) and knowing again (re-cognizing).[15] Rather than having direct access to useful knowledge that we mobilize to solve particular problems, then, a critical theoretic approach maintains that all knowledge is situated in social, historical and political context, and cannot be directly and unproblematically known. Alongside this agonistic approach to knowing, critical approaches also refuse moral rationalism's central ethical question of 'What ought we to do?';[16] instead, they start with *what is*, embarking on a journey towards comprehension of actually existing social and political conditions and the ways that patterns of recognition and misrecognition shape lived experience.[17]

As well as unsettling the rationalist conception of knowledge as positivist and instrumental, critical theoretical approaches also unsettle the position of the knower-theorist, refusing the rationalist conception of the knower as 'an abstract, individuated entity distinct from the object it is trying to grasp'.[18] One of the hallmarks of Hegelian thought is the need to '[unpack] the relation of "I" to its natural condition, to other "I"s, to its social and historical context and to its historically shifting forms of self-understanding in common sense, religion, art and philosophy'.[19] 'I' can only be understood in relational context, and the work of understanding is ongoing; the self is not fully formed and unchanging but always connected and becoming. As a result, we cannot understand ourselves as self-contained, discrete subjects or ask others to recognize us 'as we already are';[20] the very act of engaging in a process of mutual recognition is to 'solicit a becoming, to instigate a transformation'.[21]

An agonistic conception of recognition, then, unsettles our sense of selves as abstract knowers and invites a relational ontology. In critical international ethics, this sensibility is particularly pronounced in some strands of feminist ethics and in the ethics of care. Fiona Robinson maintains that an ethics of care stands in stark contrast to universal prescriptive theories of ethics, saying 'it is a practical philosophy, which starts from the ways in which we experience our ethical lives'.[22] That is, an ethics of care starts with *what is*, drawing attention to patterns of connection, dependence and marginalization. It is attuned to actual relationships and to the particular contexts in which moral problems arise. Eschewing the 'view from nowhere', the relational turn calls our attention not only to relationships between concrete persons but also 'recast[s] issues of difference and exclusion as problems of dominance or subordination in order to disclose the social relationships of power within which difference is named and enforced'.[23] Going back to Cox's characterization of critical theory, an ethics of care steps back from global problems and asks questions about the underlying structures and conditions that facilitate violence and inequality—'not simply by asserting them to be wrong but by understanding how it is that their wrongness is possible'.[24]

The radical shift towards a different way of knowing has profound implications for the exercise of moral judgement in global politics. As we shall see in the discussion of autoethnographic IR below, one of the implications of an Hegelian account of consciousness is to undermine the idea of the 'competent moral agent'[25] making moral judgements on behalf of incompetent others. Against the confident judgement of rationalist theorists, who 'make mistakes' but 'can never be fundamentally wrong',[26] Kimberly Hutchings highlights the 'risky business'[27] of judgement. She argues that being attuned to the *vulnerability* of judgement is transformative, saying

> it is the beginning of a more profound set of arguments in which international ethical and political theorists are obliged to recognize explicitly that they put themselves, as well as those of whom they speak, on the line in the ethical judgements that they make.[28]

As well as unsettling the relationship between knowers and those who are known, the relational turn also unsettles the relationship between givers and those who receive. Fiona Robinson draws our attention to the dangers of paternalism in a global ethics of care, arguing that a 'global ethics of care cannot simply "care about" unfortunate, weak or vulnerable others without critical reflection on the historical and contemporary norms, structures and institutions that shaped the positionalities of these caring relationships'.[29] Recognition of the deeper web of past and present structures and practices that underpin global problems highlights our mutual vulnerability and interdependence and alerts us to our complicity in patterns of power that continue to marginalize and oppress. Highlighting our mutual vulnerability calls us to tolerate ambiguity and risk in the place of self-certainty. As Butler puts it:

> [W]e must recognize that ethics requires us to risk ourselves precisely at moments of unknowingness, when what forms us diverges from what lies before us, when our willingness to become undone in relation to others constitutes our chance of becoming human. To be undone by another is a primary necessity, an anguish, to be sure, but also a chance—to be addressed, claimed, bound to what is not me, but also to be moved, to be prompted to act, to address myself elsewhere, and so to vacate the self-sufficient 'I' as a kind of possession.[30]

Relating/judging differently: unsettling the relationship between knower/known

We have already seen that as well as unsettling the confident epistemology of rationalist international ethics, critical approaches unsettle the relationship between knower-experts and those who are known. In this section, I explore this dimension of critical international ethics with reference to the autoethnographic turn in IR.[31] I argue that autoethnography resists the rationalist discipline of knowledge and foregrounds some key characteristics of the critical project: vulnerable judgement, (self-)reflexivity and relationality. Ethnographic IR takes agency seriously, asking: Whose knowledge counts? Who theorizes global problems and develops blueprints for action? Who enacts them? Whose voices are valued and whose are silenced?

Kimberly Hutchings argues that moral rationalist approaches to international ethics privilege hyper-rationalist expert knowledge and marginalize 'other' voices. Wedded to the exercise of reason and certain of their judgements, ethical theorists reproduce moral hierarchies whereby some voices are valued (those deemed '*rational, knowledgeable*, and *effective*')[32] and others are silenced (those deemed 'the vulnerable, the immature, the wicked, or the incapable').[33]

The autoethnographic turn in critical international theory challenges the rationalist privileging of expert knowledge and unsettles the relationship between academic knowers and those whose lives are observed and written. Autoethnography is alive to the violence scholars do to those whose lives we narrate and encourages a 'reflexive awareness' of our selves as perpetrators of violence. Rather than silencing our selves, autoethnography encourages responsible and responsive scholarship that listens to the lives we narrate and situates ourselves as 'writers, witnesses and participants'.[34] It acknowledges that the discipline of IR is a discipline 'built on the deaths and losses of others',[35] deaths and losses that are observed from a distance and not experienced. The positivist tradition in IR engages with violence and losses as events that can be counted, analysed and theorized, reducing lived experience to data that might be mobilized to produce an account of *what has happened* and *what might be done*. What falls outside the production of 'useful knowledge' is silenced and those whose lives are analysed and written in academic prose are silenced too: 'the informant has no mechanism through which to speak back'.[36]

Elizabeth Dauphinee maintains that she has 'built [her] career'[37] on the life of Stojan Sokolović, her Serbian guide and informant. Her research was radically transformed by his question to her, 'What expert are you?' and his interrogation of the academic endeavour in Bosnia. In her account of their conversation that evening, Dauphinee recounts Stojan Sokolović's words as he communicated his disquiet with the academic endeavour of gathering knowledge in war-torn Bosnia. He observes:

> Violence must be quantifiable in your world. It must count bodies, burned houses, livestock, and graves—lost libraries, churches and synagogues, mosques. It must count the flood of refugees driven across the border from their own fields into those of others—into fields that do not want to shelter them. You have no scale with which to weigh the contents of the heart or soul. And so, you can identify victims—static, immobile entities—but you have not asked yourself about the violence the committer of violence has done to himself, and you have not bothered to theorise about that.[38]

The academic endeavour, as Stojan Sokolović sees it, focuses on quantifying observable violence—it focuses exclusively on that which can be seen and measured, underpinned by the assumption that the more knowledge that we gather (about bodies, graves, refugees, churches and mosques), the better we will be able to understand. He laments the lack of attention to what *cannot be seen*—'the contents of the heart or soul'—maintaining that the academic industry renders victims and perpetrators alike static and immobile. In this endeavour, there is no place for a deeper and broader understanding of those factors that facilitated the violence, and there is no place for recognition of those whose lives are quantified and theorized.

Stojan Sokolović asks, 'What expert are you?' and, in so doing, challenges us to rethink our relationship to our academic writing, to 'those whose lives [we] write'.[39] His question challenges us to think and write differently; it invites self-reflexivity and vulnerability. Dauphinee continues:

> Stojan Sokolović's question is not a question to end questions. It is a question to expand them. It does not ask me to stay silent. It does not ask me to find a way to write that will close all the gaping holes in anything I might say. It does not insulate me against critique, but in fact opens me to it. It makes me vulnerable not just to the colleagues who peer-review my work, but to those whose lives I write, without whom I could not have a career, or a nice office with a big picture window that looks out onto the commons of my university.[40]

As discussed above, epistemic certainty characterizes moral rationalist accounts of global politics. This confident epistemology twins with confident moral judgement: the moral theorist knows herself to be a 'competent moral agent'[41] serving reason and truth as she makes ethical judgements on behalf of those agents incapable of making their own. One of the hallmarks of critical international ethics is a willingness to eschew the rationalist demand for invulnerable judgement and instead acknowledge that 'all moral judgement is unsafe'.[42]

Instead of disciplining data into *knowable* truths, autoethnography invites us to sit with *unknowing*. This 'not knowing' resists silence and despair; instead, it 'requires the articulation of that unknowing, and the reasons for that unknowing, so that the discussion and debate in IR can continue to move in fruitful directions'.[43] Rather than pursuing 'unproblematic truth', then, autoethnographic IR seeks to open scholarly writing to explore wider concerns. In so doing, it seeks to avoid the evacuation of the self, and instead to remain alive to our presence in what we write and to our relationship with those whose lives we narrate.[44] The uncertainty that attends such scholarly endeavour sits in stark contrast to the self-certain projection of expertise that permeates rationalist IR. Dauphinee argues that '[i]f we are willing to show our vulnerability, our uncertainty, our failure, to our students and colleagues, we may become—paradoxically—more generous figures of expertise'.[45]

Acting differently

Critical international ethics *know* differently; they also *act* differently. Where rationalist approaches see ethics as providing a guide for political action, separating ethics and politics, critical approaches see ethics as always already political. In what follows, I interrogate the rationalist separation of ethics and politics, arguing that it depoliticizes both. I then explore critical ethics' very different orientation toward political action through a discussion of agonism and a renewed interest in 'the everyday'. I argue that agonism is attuned to the 'politics of the ordinary'[46] and alive to contingency, vulnerability and risk. It draws our attention to the mundane politics of recognition and misrecognition, and encourages us to take the risk of political action in the here and now by engaging with 'what is' rather than what is to come.

Traditional moral rationalism separates ethics and politics, whereby ethics provides the foundation or ground for politics. In her exploration of the relationship between ethical theories and practical politics, Madeleine Fagan maintains that ethical theories 'do a great deal of work in contemporary political life' in terms of recommending and defending courses of action that might be undertaken in response to political problems.[47] In traditional ethical theories, this work can be understood, at least in part, as 'providing a foundation from which to launch particular political moves or strategies'.[48] That is, moral rationalists begin with ethical theories, devised at a distance from practical politics, and look to those theories for political guidance. Fagan argues that the separation of ethics and politics is driven in part by an 'urge. . . to make politics derivable from something else, something more originary, and so to make it safe and theorisable'.[49] This separation of ethics and politics into neat and tidy categories has profound implications for the place of the ethical in global politics, depoliticizing both ethics and politics. When traditional moral rationalists undertake and defend political engagement on the basis of ethical debates that have already taken place and that have already been resolved, then

> the exact places where difficult, contradictory, unclear and unsecure answers need to be discussed, debated and fought out have already been both occupied and bounded by the very foundations which prior attempts at theorising a judgement or response have put in place.[50]

Critical approaches to international ethics, however, complicate the relationship between ethics and politics, maintaining that one cannot secure the other. Rather than looking to abstractly devised ethical theories for political guidance, critical approaches start with a description of the actually existing social world. They work towards recognition of the inclusions, exclusions and contradictions of political life, and in so doing encourage debate about the ways in which our social norms, practices and institutions foster recognition and misrecognition.[51] Instead of starting with what ought to be, critical approaches start with what there is, a move that recognizes the vulnerability of political judgement and opens space for contestation and debate.

A strand of critical ethics that foregrounds political struggle is agonistic pluralism.[52] Theories of agonism take their name from the ancient Greek concept of the *agon* and emphasize ongoing struggle and debate in democratic discourse. Cognizant of the (inevitable) misrecognitions and marginalization that accompany the organization of democratic space, agonistic pluralism resists the final inscription of guidelines for action. Instead, it emphasizes the need for ongoing contestation, whereby boundaries are always 'contingent, subject to further scrutiny, critique and rearticulation in contentious and widely inclusive democratic spaces'.[53] An agonistic approach to political action encourages subjects to take the risk of acting politically, but is attuned to the vulnerability of political judgement and action. As discussed earlier, one of the hallmarks of a critical approach to political judgement is the willingness to admit that we have got it wrong, a willingness to invite ambiguity and contingency in the place of self-certain judgement.[54] Agonism's ongoing work of the political emphasizes the need to *act*, but is aware that despite our best intentions any action, any boundary drawn, will have unintended consequences and need re-evaluation and re-articulation.

Agonistic politics draws our attention from the ideal to the actual, from the event to the everyday. Drawing on the work of Hannah Arendt, Bonnie Honig highlights her commitment to a

> politics of the ordinary. . . a commitment to the inaugural, even ruptural or revolutionary political powers of daily political practice out of which procedures and other elements of political self-governance may come but by which such daily practice is not always already guided.[55]

A 'politics of the ordinary' calls us to recognize opportunities in our daily lives whereby we might enact love and justice.[56] Instead of reaching for the cosmopolitan ideal of directing love 'immediately to *all* humankind',[57] Honig asks whether we could not instead see universality differently. She draws on Franz Rosenweig's notion of neighbour-love, whereby our neighbour 'presents not a moral problem to be solved. . . but an ethical and political opportunity to be acted upon'.[58] Acting politically in the here and now—performing 'small miracles. . . *one by one*'[59]—starts with 'what there is' and takes the risk of acting politically without waiting for those in power to act on behalf of the marginalized. Thinking through neighbour love in relation to the ongoing misrecognition and insecurity of asylum seekers and refugees, Honig argues that 'taking people in, harboring them, offering them shelter, finding sympathetic agents of discretionary power who are willing to look the other way' means that they 'will not be so dependent on law to position them with more clarity in its network'.[60] She continues that such an approach means that refugees 'will not have to wait for their time to come, and a good thing too',[61] as we cannot trust that those in power will inscribe laws that enact recognition and justice for the profoundly misrecognized and dehumanized.

Enacting an agonistic politics of the everyday challenges the rationalist separation of ethics and politics, whereby political action is guided by ethical ideals. The ethical, on this reading, is found in everyday political practice and is far from ideal. Rather than working towards the future inscription of better law, agonism encourages political risk in the here and now, knowing that 'if [subjects] want power they must take it'.[62] This is not to say that it abandons the universal; however, it stands in different relation to the universal, propounding what might be termed 'aporetic universalism'.[63] Aporetic universalism insists on an approach to the universal that attends to 'the relation between universal and particular, everyone and every "one"'.[64] This dynamic and *political* approach is 'unsettled and unsettling' and 'refuses any beginning or end';[65] it embraces a difficult or aporetic way that refuses to predetermine the outcome of political action. Aporetic universalism emphasizes a 'politics of the ordinary'[66] whereby the struggle is grounded in the everyday, but reaches beyond daily acts of recognition towards a (continually revised and revisable) 'universal or shared notion of justice and the good'.[67]

Conclusion

Critical international ethics has a radically different approach to knowing and acting. It unsettles the confident epistemology of moral rationalism and invites a slower, more difficult journey towards comprehension that starts with 'what is'. It also unsettles the relationship between knower and known, insisting that '[w]e are never independent subjects, but always relational ones',[68] and challenging the privileging of expert knowledge and concomitant silencing of other voices. In the place of self-certain moral judgement, critical ethics acknowledges the vulnerability of judgement; it is willing to embrace uncertainty and the need to 'know again' in the ongoing process of re-cognition of our selves and our relations with others. Critical international ethics also acts differently. It complicates the relationships between ethics and politics, seeing the ethical as always already political rather than as a predetermined and abstractly theorized guide for action that secures political action. An agonistic approach draws our attention from the ideal to the actual, from the event to the everyday, advocating a politics of the ordinary that enacts love and justice in our daily lives whilst also reaching towards the institutionalization of a better justice.

Notes

1 Raymond Geuss, *Outside Ethics* (Princeton, NJ: Princeton University Press, 2005), 3.
2 Hans Morgenthau, *Scientific Man versus Power Politics* (Chicago, IL: University of Chicago Press, 1946), vi.
3 Ibid., 215.
4 Geuss, *Outside Ethics*, 3. Geuss maintains that modern Western ethical thought prioritizes rational knowledge and universal moral guidelines. The type of knowledge that is central to modern ethical thought is 'useful knowledge': knowledge that generates empirically verifiable facts about how the world works and general principles that can be used to make predictions. This technical knowledge influences ethical thought in turn. The central ethical question can be summarized as 'What ought we to do?' The response generates 'some set of universal laws or rules or principles; in particular, a set of universal laws on which 'we' would all agree (under some further specified circumstance)' (p. 3). The 'ought' of 'What ought we to do?' is an abstract, rational ought; it is a generalizable 'ought' that is universally applicable, seeks to restrict subjective judgment, and takes the struggle out of making judgments by prescribing clear guidelines for action. It aspires to motivate change in behaviour by virtue of rational persuasion.
5 Robert W. Cox, 'Social Forces, States and World Orders: Beyond International Relations Theory', *Millennium: Journal of International Studies*, 10, no. 2 (June 1, 1981): 126–155, doi:10.1177/03058298810100020501.
6 The human security literature, for example, promotes a cosmopolitan global order whereby the primary referent is the human being, rather than the state. More generally, broadening the definition of security during the 1990s and 2000s illustrates the primacy that is given to security in IR and global politics: international scholars and actors give heightened attention to global problems when they frame and perceive them as perpetuating insecurity. See, for example, Paris Roland, 'Human Security: Paradigm Shift or Hot Air?', *International Security*, 26, no. 2 (2001): 87–102.
7 It is worth acknowledging here that non-human interactions in international life are even more fundamentally silenced. See, for example, Magdalena Zolkos and Emilian Kavalski, 'Recognizing Nature in International Relations', in *Recognition and Global Politics: Critical Encounters between State and World*, ed. Patrick Hayden and Kate Schick (Manchester: Manchester University Press, 2016), 139–156.
8 Cox, 'Social Forces, States and World Orders'.
9 See below for a discussion about the Hegelian focus on 'what is' rather than 'what ought to be'.
10 Inanna Hamati-Ataya, 'Reflectivity, Reflexivity, Reflexivism: IR's "Reflexive Turn" – and Beyond', *European Journal of International Relations*, 19, no. 4 (2013): 6.
11 Geuss, *Outside Ethics*.
12 For an overview of this interpretation of Hegel, see, for example, Kimberly Hutchings, *Hegel and Feminist Philosophy* (Cambridge: Polity Press, 2003); Judith Butler, *Subjects of Desire: Hegelian Reflections in Twentieth-Century France* (New York: Columbia University Press, 1987); Tarik Kochi, 'Being, Nothing,

Becoming', in *New Critical Legal Thinking: Law and the Political*, by Matthew Stone, Illan Rua Wall, and Costas Douzinas (New York: Routledge, 2012); Kate Schick, 'Re-cognizing Recognition: Gillian Rose's 'Radical Hegel' and Vulnerable Recognition', *Telos*, 173 (2015): 87–105.

13 Geuss, *Outside Ethics*, 3.
14 Hamati-Ataya, 'Reflectivity, Reflexivity, Reflexivism', 6, emphasis in original.
15 Schick, 'Re-cognizing Recognition'.
16 Geuss, *Outside Ethics*, 3.
17 See, for example, Hegel's famous quote in *Elements of the Philosophy of Right*, which maintains that the task of the philosopher is to examine what 'is' rather than what 'ought to be' (see discussion in Hutchings, *Hegel and Feminist Philosophy*, 47). See also the discussion on agonism below in the section on 'Acting differently'.
18 Ibid., 39.
19 Ibid.
20 Judith Butler, *Precarious Life: The Powers of Mourning and Violence* (London; New York: Verso, 2004), 44.
21 Ibid.
22 Fiona Robinson, 'Globalizing Care: Ethics, Feminist Theory, and International Relations', *Alternatives: Global, Local, Political*, 22, no. 1 (1997): 123.
23 Ibid., 127.
24 Kimberly Hutchings, 'Towards a Feminist International Ethics', *Review of International Studies*, 26 (2000): 119.
25 Kimberly Hutchings, 'A Place of Greater Safety? Securing Judgement in International Ethics', in *The Vulnerable Subject: Beyond Rationalism in International Relations*, ed. Amanda Russell Beattie and Kate Schick (Basingstoke: Palgrave Macmillan, 2013), 32.
26 Ibid., 35–36.
27 Hutchings, *Hegel and Feminist Philosophy*, 131.
28 Hutchings, 'A Place of Greater Safety?', 39.
29 Fiona Robinson, 'Paternalistic Care and Transformative Recognition in International Relations', in *Recognition and Global Politics: Critical Encounters between State and World*, ed. Patrick Hayden and Kate Schick (Manchester: Manchester University Press, 2016), 174.
30 Judith Butler, *Giving an Account of Oneself* (New York: Fordham University Press, 2005), 136.
31 See, for example, Morgan Brigg and Roland Bleiker, 'Autoethnographic International Relations: Exploring the Self as a Source of Knowledge', *Review of International Studies*, 36, no. 3 (July 2010): 779–798, doi:10.1017/S0260210510000689; Amanda Russell Beattie, 'Engaging Autobiography: Mobility Trauma and International Relations', *The Russian Sociological Review*, 13, no. 4 (2014): 137–157; Elizabeth Dauphinee, 'The Ethics of Autoethnography', *Review of International Studies*, 36 (2010): 799–818; Elizabeth Dauphinee, *The Politics of Exile* (New York: Routledge, 2013); Roxanne Lynn Doty, 'Autoethnography—Making Human Connections', *Review of International Studies*, 36, no. 4 (October 2010): 1047–1050, doi:10.1017/S026021051000118X; Oded Löwenheim, 'The "I" in IR: An Autoethnographic Account', *Review of International Studies*, 36, no. 4 (October 2010): 1023–1045, doi:10.1017/S0260210510000562.
32 Hutchings, 'A Place of Greater Safety?', 29.
33 Ibid., 35.
34 Dauphinee, 'The Ethics of Autoethnography', 808.
35 Ibid., 802.
36 Ibid., 806.
37 Ibid., 799.
38 Ibid., 800.
39 Ibid., 809.
40 Ibid.
41 Hutchings, 'A Place of Greater Safety?', 32.
42 Ibid., 26.
43 Dauphinee, 'The Ethics of Autoethnography', 809.
44 Ibid., 818.
45 Elizabeth Dauphinee, 'Writing as Hope: Reflections on *The Politics of Exile*', *Security Dialogue*, 44, no. 4 (2013): 358.
46 Bonnie Honig, *Emergency Politics: Paradox, Law, Democracy* (Princeton: Princeton University Press, 2009), xviii.

47 Madeleine Fagan, *Ethics and Politics after Poststructuralism* (Edinburgh: Edinburgh University Press, 2013), 1.
48 Ibid., 2.
49 Ibid., 128. Fagan's comments here are directed towards poststructuralist ethics' (unconscious) reproduction of rationalist binaries, but they apply equally to contemporary moral rationalism.
50 Ibid., 3.
51 Kate Schick, *Gillian Rose: A Good Enough Justice* (Edinburgh: Edinburgh University Press, 2012), 94–95.
52 Prominent theorists of agonistic pluralism include Bonnie Honig, William Connolly, and Chantel Mouffe. See: William E. Connolly, *Identity, Difference: Democratic Negotiations of Political Paradox* (Minneapolis: University of Minnesota Press, 2002); Chantal Mouffe, *The Return of the Political* (London: Verso, 1993); Bonnie Honig, *Political Theory and the Displacement of Politics* (Ithaca, NY: Cornell University Press, 1993). For an excellent overview of these theorists in the context of democratic theory more broadly conceived, see Robert W. Glover, 'Games without Frontiers? Democratic Engagement, Agonistic Pluralism and the Question of Exclusion', *Philosophy and Social Criticism*, 38, no. 1 (2012): 81–104.
53 Glover, 'Games without Frontiers?' 82. There are strong parallels here to a (radical) Hegelian emphasis on recognition. We saw earlier that Hegelian approaches *know differently*, emphasizing the need for an ongoing journey toward comprehension of actuality. They also *act differently*, emphasizing the need to take political risk in pursuit of a better outcome.
54 Hutchings, 'A Place of Greater Safety?'; Schick, 'Re-cognizing Recognition'.
55 Honig, *Emergency Politics*, xviii.
56 See also Alison Phipps' call for a politics of the ordinary in response to the ongoing marginalization and insecurity of asylum seekers and refugees in the United Kingdom. See: Cheryl Cockburn-Wootten, Alison McIntosh, and Alison Phipps, 'Hospitality as Advocacy and Vulnerability', *Hospitality and Society*, 4, no. 2 (June 1, 2014): 111–114, doi:10.1386/hosp.4.2.111_2; Alison Phipps, 'Voicing Solidarity: Linguistic Hospitality and Poststructuralism in the Real World', *Applied Linguistics*, 33, no. 5 (December 1, 2012): 582–602, doi:10.1093/applin/ams054; Alison Phipps, 'Opening My Home to Refugees Has Been Humbling and Eye-Opening', *The Guardian*, September 8, 2015, https://www.theguardian.com/commentisfree/2015/sep/08/hosting-refugees-in-my-home-migration-crisis.
57 Eric L. Santner, *On Creaturely Life: Rilke, Benjamin, Sebald* (Chicago: University of Chicago Press, 2009), 207, emphasis in original, cited in Honig, *Emergency Politics*, 131.
58 Honig, *Emergency Politics*, 131.
59 Santner, *On Creaturely Life*, 207, emphasis in original, cited in Honig, *Emergency Politics*, 130–131.
60 Honig, *Emergency Politics*, 131.
61 Ibid.
62 Bonnie Honig, *Democracy and the Foreigner* (Princeton: Princeton University Press, 2003), 39.
63 Schick, *Gillian Rose*, 81–104.
64 Ibid., 89.
65 Gillian Rose, *The Broken Middle: Out of Our Ancient Society* (Oxford: Blackwell, 1992), 155.
66 Honig, *Emergency Politics*, xviii.
67 Gillian Rose, *Paradiso* (London: Menard Press, 1999), 43. See also the discussion of the everyday by Ty Solomon and Brent J. Steele, which highlights the move away from 'grand theory' towards 'approaches that hold much potential for seeing abstracted global systems and structures through the lenses of lived, embodied and experiential everyday processes'. Ty Solomon and Brent J. Steele, 'Micro-Moves in International Relations Theory', *European Journal of International Relations* (March 7, 2016), 9, doi:10.1177/1354066116634442.
68 Dauphinee, 'Writing as Hope', 356.

PART III

International security and just war

SECURITY AND THE ETHICS OF WAR

Cian O'Driscoll

Introduction

There is a memorable scene in the cult classic movie *The Big Lebowski*, wherein the two primary characters, the Dude, played by Jeff Bridges, and Walter Sobchak, played by John Goodman, are involved in a heated argument at their local bowling alley. The row erupts when Walter alleges that Smokey's strike (Smokey is a member of the rival team) should be discounted on the basis that it had been achieved by foul means. Smokey's foot, Walter charges, had crept over the line before he released the bowling ball, a clear violation of the rules. Smokey contests the charge and insists that the score should stand. The argument escalates and Walter, now irate, takes out a handgun, points it at Smokey's head, and demands that he marks the strike down as a foul. Smokey, visibly rattled, acquiesces. Walter, now ever so slightly bashful, shrugs his shoulders and makes a half-hearted effort to justify his actions: 'This is not 'Nam, Smokey, this is bowling—there are rules.'

While one never needs a justification for quoting *The Big Lebowski*, there is a reason for it in this case. Walter's reference to the Vietnam War belies a pervasive sentiment that the sharp end of international relations, warfare and armed conflict, is a lawless zone, and a realm in which rules of right and wrong have no place or purpose. Can this really be the case? Does ethical reasoning cease when the guns start to boom? Or is Walter's supposition incorrect? This section addresses these questions. It examines the scope of ethical reasoning in respect of what we might term 'power politics'.

This involves two principal areas of focus. The first speaks to what Matt McDonald calls a 'master concept' of international relations, security. The second specifically addresses warfare and armed conflict. The aim in each case is to ascertain how, if at all, ethical reasoning applies to these phenomena, and how this is reflected in the relevant academic literature. Within this, there will be a particular emphasis on the character, purpose, and limitations of ethical reasoning as it pertains to these domains. This agenda ensures that the chapters comprising this Part cover a lot of ground and canvas a lot of disparate ideas. Drawing them together, however, is a commitment, not just to repudiating the notion that the rough and tumble of world politics is not tractable to ethical analysis, but also to expanding our understanding of ethical analysis beyond Walter's reductive association of it with 'rules'.

This chapter's aim is not so much to advance an argument in its own right as to set the scene for the chapters that comprise the substance of this Part. As such, it will be divided into two sections. The first one will lay the groundwork for Seán Molloy's and Matt McDonald's discussions on, respectively, traditional and critical approaches in international relations to the idea of security. The second will introduce the study of the ethics of war, paving the way Rosemary B. Kellison and Nahed Artoul Zehr's, John W. Lango's, and Amy E. Eckert and Caron E. Gentry's chapters on traditional, analytical, and critical approaches to thinking about the morality of armed conflict.

Security

Security has been defined as an 'essentially contested concept'.[1] This means it is the subject of debate and there is little agreement over what the term signifies. A handful of definitions that are prominent within the literature offer a flavour of exactly what is under dispute.[2] Starting us off, Ian Bellamy, writing in 1991, argues that *security* denotes 'a relative freedom from war; coupled with a relatively high expectation that defeat will not be a consequence of any war that should occur'.[3] Prior to this, Arnold Wolfers writes in an essay published in 1962 that 'security, in any objective sense, measures the absence of threats to acquired values, in a subjective sense, the absence of fear that such values will be attacked'.[4] More recently, Peter Hough argues, 'If people, be they government ministers or private individuals, perceive an issue to threaten their lives in some way and respond politically to this, then that issue should be deemed to be a *security* issue.'[5]

It is possible to identify a certain degree of overlap between these definitions, at least at a very abstract level. They all refer in some way or other to the practice or necessity of securing cherished goods or values from any threat of harm. When understood in these broad terms, security seems to be about protection and conservation. As soon, however, as one seeks to get beyond this high level of abstraction, difficulties become apparent. What goods or values are to be secured? From what threats or harms? And to what end? Applying these questions to the definitions cited above, we find that some scholars, for instance, equate the referent object of security (i.e., the value or good that is to be secured) with the state, while others identify it with human life, the environment, or some other such value. Similarly, while some scholars treat war or armed conflict as the principal threat to these goods, others expand their scope to include non-military threats such as climate change and economic deprivation, and other problems. And finally, while there are those who posit the absence of war and armed conflict as the goal of security, others associate it with much broader objectives, such as the advancement of human flourishing or emancipation.

If pinning down an exact definition of security is difficult, it is easier to delineate what we mean by 'security studies'. It comprises the academic study of security. Inclusive of scholars from a wide range of disciplines, including political science and international relations, it encompasses all of the approaches listed thus far, and is animated by the debates between them.

To the degree that security studies has historically been associated with strategic studies and the study of the hard edge of international politics, there has been some reluctance to acknowledge its ethical dimensions. Questions of moral right and wrong, norms, laws, and rules might all have their place and purpose in respect of domestic politics, and perhaps even certain areas of international relations (such as diplomacy, cooperation, and trade), critics claim, but they play no meaningful role when it comes to determining matters of security.[6] When it comes to the protection or conservation of cherished goods and values, they suppose, the only thing that matters is getting the job done. The implication of this is, of course, that worrying about ethics is a luxury that can scarcely be afforded by anybody with a real interest in security.

Recent years have, however, seen this view contested. Two lines of inquiry have been at the forefront of this. On the one hand, certain scholars, such as Molloy, Michael Williams, and Richard Ned Lebow, among others, have cast doubt on the proposition that a traditional or realist focus on security forecloses any ethical dimension.[7] On the other hand, a critical approach to studying security has materialised that variously seeks to highlight, deconstruct, resist, and reorient the ethical claims and commitments built into traditional or realist approaches. The first two chapters of this section treat each of these in turn.

Molloy's chapter tackles the traditional, realist end of security studies. Instead of surveying this entire field, which would be a nigh-impossible task, Molloy opts to focus on one benchmark thinker, Hans J. Morgenthau. Molloy's intent is not to suggest that traditional or realist approaches can be reduced to Morgenthau. He is explicit that the traditional approach is a broad church that encompasses many different voices and contains many disagreements. This, he believes, is both a reflection of its vitality and a part of its charm. Molloy's rationale for focusing his analysis almost exclusively on Morgenthau is, rather, that he is indicative of the intersection between 'classical' security studies and realist approaches to international relations, more generally.

Molloy's approach facilitates a more parsimonious presentation of the relevant ideas than might otherwise be possible to achieve, and Morgenthau is a clever choice. As John A. Vasquez has argued, Morgenthau's writings on international relations were 'the single most important vehicle for establishing the dominance of the realist paradigm' for the study of security-related concerns, among other things.[8] Yet scholars of realism, with Vasquez among them, have also misunderstood (or perhaps just misrepresented) the meaning of Morgenthau's writings ever since.[9]

One of the main areas in which scholars have misconstrued Morgenthau—and, by extension, traditional or realist approaches to studying security—is in respect of their relation to ethical inquiry. Scholars of realism have variously depicted Morgenthau's approach as either amoral or immoral.[10] That is to say, critics often accuse Morgenthau and fellow realist thinkers of advancing a regressive ethical position, overlooking ethical considerations altogether, or pitting their approach in opposition to them. Among those who have asserted these charges, incidentally, is Matt McDonald. I will address his point of view momentarily. In the meantime, what is important to note here is that Molloy rejects these claims. He contends that, in fact, Morgenthau et al. advance a very sophisticated way of thinking ethically about security matters. Rather than promulgate elaborate but ultimately utopian formulae for what constitutes ethical conduct in the international sphere, Morgenthau endorses the more modest goal of establishing (in Molloy's pleasing turn of phrase) 'a working relationship between the requirement of ethics and the necessities of politics'.[11] The key to realising this, however, is to recognise that what counts as ethical conduct is always subtended by the political exigencies of the day.

McDonald's chapter takes the baton from here. Its starting point is the claim that critical security studies (CSS), as it is now widely known, incorporates a broad array of different approaches unified by the belief that 'the assumptions underpinning the [traditional] approach and the implications of the practices it encourages are ethically problematic'. Within this general orientation, there is a difference of approach as to how scholars should engage with the notion of *security* itself. On the one hand, some scholars maintain that its historical connotations have irredeemably tainted it and should therefore be resisted, while others have argued that it may be possible to imbue it with a new set of meanings and, on foot of that, couple it to a new, more progressive agenda. McDonald maps this distinction onto the major cleavages within CSS, thus giving the reader a clear account of what is at stake when, for instance, exponents of the Welsh School turn their fire on the Copenhagen School.

Along the way, he invites the reader to consider his or her own ethical positionality as a security studies scholar. Should one, he challenges, engage in security studies scholarship as a normative project or act of resistance? Does it necessarily entail a normative agenda, or can one study the ethics of security in a purely analytical fashion? And, last but not least, should the security studies scholar assume the status of an objective, disinterested observer, or should he or she engage it as a form of praxis, that is, as a means of acting in (as well as commentating on) world politics? In the final analysis, then, alongside Molloy's chapter, this discussion alerts us to the fact that disagreements over how ethics relates to security are pivotal to the divisions within both CSS and security studies more generally.

War

War is ostensibly a hard case for ethicists. It is a realm of extreme violence where mass killing approximates a form of business-as-usual. Consequently, the prevailing assumption is often that the very idea of speaking about war in terms of ethics is a contradiction in terms. Walter's comment from the bowling alley, with which this chapter opened, captures something of this perspective. War, on this view, is a sphere of human conduct in which rules—and by extension ethics—have no hold. Yet this does not reflect how people experience war. On the contrary, ethics often seems to lie at the very heart of how people encounter and understand armed conflict.

A short vignette illuminates this point. The story is recounted by Karl Marlantes, who is the author of *What It Is Like to Go to War*, and a decorated combat veteran. Marlantes tells of an occasion in Vietnam when his company, having engaged in a vigorous fire-fight with the enemy, found themselves in a position to care for an enemy soldier who was badly wounded, and possibly dying. The question that confronted the commander was what to do with this man. If he was bound to die anyway, there was little point in tasking his men to call in a medevac, thereby compromising the security not only of the unit, but also of the chopper crew. On the other hand, leaving the wounded soldier there to die 'could mean days of agony for the wounded men, and that was really not much different from murder'.[12] In the end, the commander determined that the wounded man was beyond saving. Although the lieutenant believed it was 'certainly wrong' to shoot the man, he also believed this was the only course of action available to him, and so this is what he ordered.[13] The lesson Marlantes gleaned from this experience was not a more definite sense of right and wrong, but the knowledge that 'it's very hard to say when one becomes morally and legally responsible for a prisoner's life, given that such decisions often involve risking the lives of your own people'.[14]

Soldiers as well as observers, then, encounter war not just as a military contest, but also as a series of taxing ethical dilemmas. War, it turns out on further inspection, is freighted with moral meaning. Indeed, to the degree that it is predicated upon a series of ethical distinctions, the very concept of war itself is a normative proposition.[15] War as a form of organised political violence undertaken in the service of a public cause is defined in contradistinction to genocide, massacre, gang crime, and other forms of violence. These distinctions matter in so far as they delineate the boundaries between uses of force that may in certain circumstances be considered legitimate, and those that must always be regarded as beyond the pale. The point here is that, rather than residing beyond the reach of ethics, the very idea of war is itself an ethical category. This is what Michael Walzer calls 'the moral reality of war'.[16]

The literature on the ethics of war is rich and diverse. Interdisciplinary in nature, it is the preserve of religious ethicists, theologians, political theorists, philosophers, lawyers, and military ethics educators, as well as international relations scholars. Although diverse in origin, these constituencies share a common interest in thinking through the moral questions that warfare poses. Three main lines of thought are dominant. The first is pacifism, which supposes that the use of force is never justified. The second is a variant of realism, which supposes that the use of force should always serve the national interest. And the third is just war theory, which, as a *via media* between the first two, submits that war may be justified in certain circumstances, but that its conduct must be limited by ethical constraints. It is also the most interesting approach for present purposes. Not only is it the favoured theory of international relations scholars, it is also frequently invoked by political and military leaders, feeds into how militaries regulate their own actions, informs international law, and inflects popular discourses of war and peace. It is, in sum, the pre-eminent moral vocabulary for how people (in the West, at least) think about the rights and wrongs of war.[17]

What are the main contours of just war theory? It is structured around three principal axes or poles of reasoning. The first one, the *jus ad bellum*, engages the question of when and in what circumstances the recourse to war might be justified. Answers to this question usually turn on the categories or principles of just cause, proper authority, right intention, last resort, and reasonable chance of success. The second one, the *jus in bello*, asks how, once initiated, a war should be conducted. The precepts of proportionality, non-combatant immunity, and necessity dominate this area of inquiry. The third and final pole of just war theory is the *jus post bellum*, which engages questions of post-war justice. In particular, it examines the range of responsibilities that erstwhile enemies have to one another and their respective societies in the aftermath of war.

Tough questions abound within this framework. For instance, what is the proper relation between the requirements of the *jus ad bellum* and those of the *jus in bello*? Is the latter a function of the former, or should they be viewed as independent of one another, such that one could entertain the idea of a just war being waged unjustly and vice versa? And where disagreements arise over how a particular principle should be applied in a given case, how should they be resolved? Should the interested parties look to reason the case out from first principles, or should they instead take guidance from precedent and the weight of the tradition? Finally, must we revise this framework to account for new forms of warfare (e.g., the advent of drone warfare), or can we address them within its current format?

The three chapters gathered here on the ethics of war do not tackle these questions in a direct way. Instead, they seek to lay bare the different approaches that the scholar may take to them. As such, they invite us to think more deeply than we might otherwise about the fundaments of what it actually means to think ethically about war.

The first of these chapters, by Kellison and Zehr, examines what they call 'tradition-based approaches' to thinking about the ethics of war. These approaches are interpretative in character. They encourage scholars to tackle the ethical questions that war raises, not by addressing them from first principles, but by situating them within the traditions of thought that gave rise to them and seeking inspiration therein. If, for example, one wishes to work out where to draw the boundaries of the right of states to national self-defence, advocates of a traditions-based approach advise that the best way to do this is by examining and extrapolating from how one's forebears treated earlier iterations of that question. Kellison and Zehr set out the virtues as well as the vices of these approaches. In the former category, these approaches are sensitive to the religious and cultural sources of ethical reasoning and are amenable to a comparative approach. Indeed, this chapter demonstrates this by setting the tradition of Western just war theorising against its Islamic counterparts. In the latter category, there is room to doubt the critical potential of traditions-based approaches. Harking back as it does to established tradition, they are inclined toward a form of conservatism that reproduces rather than challenges historical precedent.

The second chapter on the topic of thinking ethically about war is by Lango. It adopts a more sceptical attitude toward traditional ways of thinking about the ethics of war. Received wisdoms, Lango ventures, might be part of the problem rather than part of the solution. If so, what is the alternative? Lango provides an excellent analysis of how one might anchor and justify one's ethical thinking about war, not in one historical tradition or another, but conceptually in what he terms the 'abstract principles of moral philosophy'.[18] This *modus operandi*, which is consistent with the general style of analytical political philosophy, has been practised by a wide range of scholars, and has produced very different frameworks, from the 'collectivist' theory of Michael Walzer to the 'individualist' version put forward by Helen Frowe. Lango's chapter focuses primarily on Frowe's individualist theory, which he posits as representative of a larger movement within just war theorising today. He concludes with a critique of Frowe and the proposal of an alternative relational theory. This chapter, then, does not just survey what we might call analytical approaches to just war theory, it also makes a significant contribution to this field.

Last but not least, the final chapter in this section by Eckert and Gentry tackles critical approaches to the ethics of war. This is a particularly interesting area for international relations scholars, as this is the one branch of theorising about the ethics of war where they have led the way. Eckert and Gentry's question is both straightforward and profound: How, if at all, might we construct thinking about the ethics of war as a critical rather than as a problem-solving enterprise? Taking the principle of non-combatant immunity as the focus for their discussion, their analysis connects just war theory and other approaches to a range of philosophical schools, including poststructuralism, Critical Theory, and feminism. In so doing, it both breaks new ground and sets out an agenda for future generations of scholars interested in the ethics of war but dissatisfied by the mainstream approaches that dominate contemporary discourse.

Conclusion

Looking ahead, this collection of essays will serve a useful function by forging a dialogue between, on the one hand, security studies scholars, the heirs of Carl von Clausewitz, and, on the other, ethics of war specialists, the apostles of Saint Augustine. Despite the fact that both camps share a common interest in the sharp end of international relations, there has been to date remarkably little exchange between them. This state of affairs seems downright strange, if not wilfully perverse. This collection of chapters will hopefully lay the grounds for remedying it. Beyond that, this Part demonstrates, I hope, that, contra Walter from *The Big Lebowski*, ethical reasoning can be addressed to the rough and tumble of world politics, and it encompasses so much more than simply the presence of rules and actors' compliance with them.

Notes

1 The idea of an essentially contested concept is derived from W. B. Gallie, 'Essentially Contested Concepts,' *Proceedings of the Aristotelian Society: New Series*, 56 (1956): 184.

2 Alan Collins has very helpfully collated a list of definitions of security in his textbook on the topic. These selections are drawn from that. Alan Collins, 'Introduction: What Is Security Studies?' in *Contemporary Security Studies*, 4th edn., ed. Alan Collins (Oxford: Oxford University Press, 2016), 3.

3 Ian Bellamy, 'Towards a Theory of International Security', *Political Studies*, 29, no. 1 (1981): 102

4 Arnold Wolfers, *Discord and Collaboration: Essays on International Politics* (Baltimore, MD: Johns Hopkins University Press, 1962), 150.

5 Peter Hough, *Understanding Global Security*, 2nd edn. (London: Routledge, 2008), 10, emphasis in original.
6 For a classic examination of this position, see: Stanley Hoffmann, *Duties beyond Borders: On the Limits and Possibilities of International Politics* (Syracuse, NY: Syracuse University Press, 1981).
7 See: Seán Molloy, *The Hidden History of Realism: A Genealogy of Power Politics* (London: Palgrave, 2006); Michael C. Williams, *The Realist Tradition and the Limits of International Relations* (Cambridge: Cambridge University Press, 2005); and Richard Ned Lebow, *The Tragic Vision of Politics* (Cambridge: Cambridge University Press, 2003).
8 John A. Vasquez, *The Power of Power Politics: A Critique* (New Brunswick, NJ: Rutgers University Press, 1983), 17.
9 Seán Molloy, 'Realism: A Problematic Paradigm', *Security Dialogue* 34, no. 1 (2003): 79. Also see: Seán Molloy, 'Truth, Power, Theory: Hans Morgenthau's Formulation of Realism', *Diplomacy and Statecraft*, 15, no. 1 (2004): 1–34.
10 For an example of this, see: Ken Booth, 'Critical Explorations', in *Critical Security Studies and World Politics*, ed. Ken Booth (Boulder, CO: Lynne Rienner, 2005), 7–8.
11 See the Molloy contribution to this Handbook (Chapter 12).
12 Karl Marlantes, *What It Is Like to Go to War* (London: Corvus, 2012), 45–47.
13 Ibid.
14 Ibid.
15 On this, see: Ian Clark, *Waging War: A New Philosophical Introduction*, 2nd edn. (Oxford: Oxford University Press, 2015), 5.
16 Michael Walzer, *Just and Unjust Wars*, 5th edn. (New York: Basic Books, 2015), 1.
17 Michael Walzer, *Arguing about War* (New Haven, CT: Yale University Press, 2004), 3–22.
18 See the Lango contribution to this Handbook (Chapter 15).

12
MORGENTHAU AND THE ETHICS OF REALISM

Seán Molloy

In lieu of any attempt to write a sweeping, general account of 'classical' security studies or realist thought, I propose to investigate the ethical positions taken by a theorist synonymous with both, Hans J. Morgenthau.[1] Despite the still widespread misrepresentation of Morgenthau as an amoral theorist of international relations (IR) or as only minimally interested in ethics, the 'father' of Realism in IR was very clear regarding the importance of ethics in his analyses of international law and international politics: 'The guiding influence. . . as to the ideals, ends, and interests to be pursued by the norms under which a given society lives, emanates from the ethical sphere.'[2] In the course of the chapter, I examine two distinct but linked aspects of Morgenthau's ethical theory: his political-sociological critique of the foundations of post-World War One international society, and his wider, post-1945 project to ground an ethics of the lesser evil firmly within a political framework predicated upon power and necessity.

Exploring Morgenthau's deep and complex ethical theory should go some way toward dispelling two prominent myths that hamper efforts to advance dialogue about ethics in IR as an academic discipline. The first myth is the still persistent notion that realism is a species of ethical void whose adherents eschew considerations of the political that are not predicated solely on the pursuit of power.[3] The second, more sophisticated myth restricts realist ethics to a narrow concern with the welfare of citizens within an individual state.[4] The hope that animates this chapter is that readers whose exposure to realism may have been limited to either of these myths might be inspired to read beyond the strawman representations upon which the dominant ethical theories within IR rely. It is only by moving beyond convenient misrepresentations of realism that the discipline can begin to have the kind of debate that can develop ethical discourse and address the very real ethical challenges that continue to proliferate in global politics.

'A norm is not a wish or an invitation'

Morgenthau's distinctive approach to ethics emerged from his attempts to analyse why the liberal order which was to replace the old system of the balance of power after World War One terminated in the inexorable erosion of its legal, moral, and political foundations.[5]

Morgenthau begins his task through a sociological inquiry into the nature of norms. Genuine norms are prescriptive, according to Morgenthau, and their effectiveness is linked to the sanctions that ensue from their violation.[6] In illustration of the extent to which norms and sanctions are related, Morgenthau presents an ideal type system that 'depends on the recognition by individuals of the legitimacy of the normative order to which the sanctions are attached.'[7] The triad of norms, legitimacy, and sanctions is central to understanding the distinction between what may be described as superficial and deep norms in Morgenthau's work. The fact that this triad rests on and is reliant upon the investment of power complicates it in practice. In the absence of a Leviathan-like figure in international politics, 'authoritative decision is replaced by the free interplay of political and military forces. These factors determine by a competitive contest for power what sociological forces and hence, what rules of international law, shall prevail.'[8] In international relations, the triad relies for its operation on the balance of power—an inherently unstable foundation—which explains why peace remains provisional and fragile.[9] The attempt to replace the balance of power with a system of collective security underwritten by international law through the offices of the League of Nations was undermined by the failure of the architects of the post-World War One normative framework to recognise that

> [t]he rules of international law, at least in so far as they concern international political organization, are only the function, or the reflex, of international politics in the normative sphere. They express in normative terms common or complementary interests of the states to whose activities they apply.[10]

This failure was in part ideological as

> the official ideology of Geneva. . . aimed to substitute political decisions by legal institutions, and therefore attempted, by means of the universality of the League, arbitration, and disarmament, to prevent the breaking up of Europe into antagonistic Power groups and thereby the return of the system of the balance of power.[11]

The crucial test of the victorious powers' normative framework would, however, be a test of legitimacy, rather than legality, and would centre on the efficacy of sanctions. That the League of Nations would fail the test was almost guaranteed by the erosion of its core principle of collective security. The process of wearing down the *superficial* normative commitment to collective security gathered pace after the failure of the sanctions on Italy in the wake of its invasion of Abyssinia but had already started before the ink was dry on the Treaty of Versailles. Morgenthau illustrates the unravelling of the interwar system through the exploration of a contradiction involving the new norm of collective security and the old norm of neutrality. The attempt to square the circle of Swiss membership of the League, and hence under Article 16 a commitment to collective security, with the permanent principle of Swiss neutrality, resulted in the formulation of 'differential' or 'partial' neutrality announced by the Declaration of London in 1920. Under the terms of the declaration, Switzerland was excused from military measures but bound to apply financial and economic sanctions.[12] Hersch Lauterpacht makes clear what the contradiction is for Morgenthau: neutrality and collective security 'are complementary concepts; the more there is of the one, the less there is of the other.'[13] The legal formula of 'differential' neutrality could 'at best create the illusion of solving' but could not 'spirit away' the opposed requirements of collective security ('confederacy, partiality, intervention') and neutrality ('aloofness, impartiality, abstention'). Ultimately, the Swiss, upon participating in the sanctions, realised 'that one cannot at the same time be neutral and partial, join one group of Powers in collective action against another one and still remain aloof from political and military entanglements' and reverted to 'strict' or 'integral' neutrality.[14] Despite unconvincing efforts by the League to argue that Switzerland was a special case, the traditional European neutrals invoked the same 'reasons. . . by which Switzerland justified her request to be freed from the obligations under Article 16' and asserted their right to pursue neutrality in a similar manner while also retaining membership of the League. The superficial norm of collective security had perished on the rocks of the deeper, harder norms of interest. The old normative imperative predicated upon the pursuit of the national interest had reappeared, albeit in different circumstances and within a different constellation of political and ethical possibility than the Concert of Europe.[15]

Morgenthau's account of *why* this collapse occurred is vital to understanding his articulation of a specifically *political* form of ethics. The cause of the failure is rooted in a mistaken mode of thought that proceeds from rational abstraction in both the legal and moral spheres. The dominant conception of international legal theory 'has always laid a strong emphasis on absolute concepts, theoretical generalizations, and systematic constructions,' which in the instance of neutrality, for example, has led to neutrality being 'regarded as an inherent quality of states.'[16] This is an error, as far as Morgenthau is concerned, since neutrality, a calculation of 'temporary political interests,' is distinct from 'natural or fundamental rights' such as sovereignty, independence, or equality that are 'independent of historical developments and native to the very existence of the state.'[17] The 'rights and duties' of neutrality 'result neither from an abstract legal concept called "neutrality" nor from the free will of the state desiring to remain neutral. . . There are no such things as rights and duties of neutrality which would apply everywhere and at all times.'[18] The problem for Switzerland was not 'the legal question whether the belligerent is entitled by a very doubtful rule of international law to oppose a non-military intervention on the part of the neutral by an act of war, but the political problem whether the belligerent is likely to react in this way' regardless of the law itself. The change in the circumstances of Switzerland's deployment of neutrality illustrates Morgenthau's point: from the Treaty of Marignano to the end of World War One, Swiss neutrality was observed because 'the Swiss defense of the Alpine passes against all warring nations was more valuable from the military standpoint than a given successful attack on them by their own armies,' a consideration based on power relations rather than any inherent respect for Switzerland's 'right' to neutrality. Swiss neutrality underwent two quick transformations in response to the 'overwhelming military power which the World War gave to the Western European nations,' which 'meant the end of the European balance of power, on which ultimately rested the neutrality of the small European states.'[19] In this new dispensation, it made perfect political sense for the Swiss to adjust their neutrality to allow them to join the League. When political circumstances changed with the rise of totalitarian states on its southern and northern borders, it likewise made political sense for Switzerland to revert to a strict neutrality because German and Italian 'strategic interest in the joint use of the Alpine passes might prove considerably greater than the fear of having Swiss neutrality violated by France.'[20] Viewing the available options, the Swiss chose to jettison the superficial norms of collective security and differential neutrality in an attempt to secure what they judged to be in their national interest, that is, remaining out of any future war.

The ethics of evil and moral courage

The condition of normative flux during this period demonstrates the primacy of political judgement over legal abstraction and leads to the ultimate question: How can one act ethically in international relations? The first step is to dispense with the '[g]randiose legalistic schemes purporting to solve the ills of the world' and to replace this 'presumptuous exercise' with the 'less spectacular, painstaking search for the actual laws and the facts underlying' social behaviour in the international sphere. 'The social sciences cannot hope to master the social forces,' contends

Morgenthau, 'unless they know the laws which govern the social relations of men.'[21] The first step in this process is to propose, contrary to prevailing liberal ideology, that 'the antithesis is not between power politics, on the one hand, and reason, law, and ethics on the other, but between power politics for evil and power politics for desirable objectives.'[22] Determining what those desirable objectives might be is the task of political thought, that is, the 'history of political thought is the history of the moral evaluation of political power.'[23]

Two key texts, 'The Evil of Politics and the Ethics of Evil' and 'The Twilight of International Morality,' lay the ground for Morgenthau's articulation of Realist ethics in the post-World War Two era. Morgenthau identifies global politics in the nuclear age as even more revolutionary of the normative and ethical constellations of IR than the era of liberal transformation and totalitarian reaction. 'The Evil of Politics and the Ethics of Evil' widens Morgenthau's critique of the predominant ethical theories in IR and continues the search for an ethics that is capable of addressing the challenges of modernity. Having established the inadequacy of liberal ideology in its Wilsonian, legal, and institutionalist guise, Morgenthau clears the ground for realist ethics by addressing the inadequacies of utilitarianism, Kantianism, and—perhaps most significantly—the reason-of-state ethics of Machiavelli and Hobbes.

Morgenthau identifies utilitarianism as the 'prevailing school of thought' of international ethics, in which the aim is 'the attainment of the greatest amount of human satisfaction.' Morgenthau's objection to utilitarianism is at least in part epistemological; he particularly rejects the reduction of ethics to 'anticipating through rational calculation the relation of certain means to certain ends,' an approach in which ethics 'becomes indistinguishable from science, and moral and successful action are one and the same thing.' Utilitarianism has eclipsed traditional morality, either suborning it or treating 'moral scruples and conflicts of conscience' originating from traditional morality as 'a kind of psychotic condition arising from a conflict between the individual and his social environment. . . The discrepancy between the ethical consequences of utilitarian philosophy and traditional ethics is thus overcome by treating the vestiges of the latter as a psychological aberration.' The epistemological requirements of utilitarianism, however, encounter serious ontological and anthropological limits, that is, 'reality is dominated by forces which are indifferent, if not actively hostile, to the commands of reason, an unbridgeable chasm must permanently separate the rules of rationalist ethics from the human reality.' Faced with this insurmountable difficulty, utilitarianism accommodates itself to that reality rather than holding it to moral account, becoming 'the outstanding modern example' of 'a system of ethics which imposes upon adherence' of it the permanent or temporary exchange of the 'sacrifice of successful action for one compatible with successful action. . . they will interpret whatever the letter of the ethical norms may be so as not to make successful action impossible,' in effect reducing ethics to justificatory collusion with politics.[24]

Morgenthau's attitude towards Kantian ethics is complicated. On the one hand, he recognises that the 'test of a morally good action is the degree to which it is capable of treating others not as a means to the actor's ends but as ends in themselves,' clearly echoing the position staked out by Kant in *The Groundwork for the Metaphysics of Morals* and *The Critique of Practical Reason*.[25] This test, however, is inapplicable in a *political* context.[26] A deontological ethic that 'derives from the origin of the action, that is, the intention of the actor,' relies on a 'deceptive harmony and false moral justification.' In this way of thinking, the intention of the actor far outweighs the consequences, such that '[i]f the action resulted in evil, if it brought about war and death and misery for millions, the statesmen are not to blame provided their intentions were good.' In a political environment, the application of Kantian principles, precisely *because* of their perfect rationality, would fall victim to the same forces within human beings that reduce utilitarian ethics to the servile handmaiden of politics.[27]

In what may be a surprising move for those who subscribe to the 'epic' history of realism that incorporates Morgenthau in the same tradition as Machiavelli and Hobbes, Morgenthau firmly rejects the ethical position encompassed by the phrase 'reason of state.'[28] Morgenthau claims that, according to this tradition, 'the state is subject to no rule of conduct but the one which is dictated by its own self-interest.'[29] *Salus publica suprema lex* is as ironclad an ethical rule for the reason of state school of thought as the categorical imperative is morally legislative for Kant. Reason of state solves ethical dilemmas by means of pure expedience: when a 'statesman who is confronted with a choice between two actions, the one ethical, the other not, of which the latter has a better chance of bringing about the desired result, he must choose the latter.'[30] This tradition permits of a duality in which there is a distinction between public and private morality, requiring the politician to conform to ethical standards in his or her private life and relations with other citizens, while being free as a statesman to act by whatever means necessary to ensure the wellbeing of the state. 'No civilization,' argues Morgenthau, 'can be satisfied with such a dual morality; for through it the domain of politics is not only made morally inferior to the private sphere but this inferiority is recognized as legitimate and made respectable by a particular system of political ethics.'[31] Furthermore, the means/ends thinking of both utilitarians and reason-of-state thinkers is bogus:

> The harmony thus achieved between ethical standard and human action is, however, apparent rather than real, ambiguous rather than definite. In order to achieve it, one must weigh the immorality of the means against the ethical value of the end and establish a fixed relationship between both. This is impossible. One may argue from the point of view of a particular political philosophy, but one cannot prove from the point of view of universal and objective ethical standards that the good of the end ought to prevail over the evil of the means.[32]

Morgenthau argues that reason-of-state thinking is too 'ambiguous and relative' as an ethical approach. Identifying a relationship between means and ends is dependent upon the 'social vantage point of the observer' who arbitrarily separates 'a certain chain of actions from what precedes and follows it,' in order to 'attribute to certain actions the exclusive quality of means and ends.' This 'doctrine that the ethical end justifies the unethical means leads to the negation of absolute ethical judgments.'[33] The Machiavellian is the obverse of the Kantian: where the latter cannot accommodate the political within the ethical, the former cannot accommodate the ethical within the political.

The ethics of responsibility and the lesser evil

The establishment of a working relationship between the requirements of ethics and the necessities of politics lies, for Morgenthau, in the Weberian recognition that:

> the political actor has, beyond the general moral duties, a special moral responsibility to act wisely—that is, in accordance with the rules of the political art—and for him expediency becomes a moral duty. The individual, acting on his own behalf, may act unwisely without moral reproach as long as the consequences of his inexpedient action concern only himself. What is done in the political sphere, by its very nature concerns others who must suffer from unwise action. What is here done with good intentions but unwisely and hence with disastrous results is morally defective, for it violates the ethics of responsibility to which all action affecting others and hence political action par excellence is subject.[34]

Such an approach avoids the twin errors of an overly 'optimistic belief in the intrinsic goodness of the rational individual and the pessimistic conviction that politics is the seat of all irrationality and evil.'[35] The issue of evil and how to deal with it, however, *is* of central importance to realist ethics. According to Morgenthau, all action, and particularly political action, is 'at least potentially, immoral' which becomes evident

> when we measure, not one action by another one (e.g., the political by the private) but all actions by the intention in which they originate. Such a comparison shows that our intentions are generally good, whereas our actions generally are not. . . We want peace among nations and harmony among individuals, yet our actions end in conflict and war.[36]

It is at this point that Morgenthau invokes the 'tragic tension between the ethics of our minds and the ethics of our actions,'[37] concluding that the 'very act of acting destroys our moral integrity. Whoever wants to retain his moral innocence must forsake action altogether.'[38] This renunciation of action, however, is not possible in the political sphere, wherein '[w]hatever choice we make, we must do evil while we try to do good: for we must abandon one moral end in favor of another.'[39] In such a situation, 'man cannot hope to be good but must be content with not being too evil.'[40] In addition to the inherently tragic nature of an international society that is predicated upon the necessity of making invidious choices, the presence of the *animus dominandi*, the desire for power, complicates the moral quality of human beings:

> This lust for power manifests itself as the desire to maintain the range of one's own person with regard to others, to increase it, or to demonstrate it. In whatever disguises it may appear, its ultimate essence and aim is in one of these particular references of one person to others.

It is the *animus dominandi*

> which, besides and beyond any particular selfishness or other evilness of purpose, constitutes the ubiquity of evil in human action. Here is the element of corruption and of sin which injects even into the best of intentions at least a drop of evil and thus spoils it.[41]

This double bind of the necessity to make tragic choices and the human, all too human limitation of the *animus dominandi* leads Morgenthau to a particularly strong identification of politics with evil:

> To the degree in which the essence and aim of politics is power over man, politics is evil; for it is to this degree that it degrades man to a means for other men. It follows that the prototype of this corruption through power is to be found on the political scene. For here the animus dominandi is not a mere admixture to prevailing aims of a different kind but the very essence of the intention, the very lifeblood of the action, the constitutive principle of politics as a distinct sphere of human activity. Politics is a struggle for power over men, and, whatever its ultimate aim may be, power is its immediate goal and the modes of acquiring, maintaining, and demonstrating it determine the technique of political action.[42]

The particular challenge of modernity is that the restraints on human behaviour associated with the intellectual and moral traditions of Western civilisation have been eclipsed by political ideologies that elevate the state to the secular equivalent of a God and loyalty to the state a political religion. The state rationalises, justifies, and amplifies the *animus dominandi* beyond the individual to the extent that those tasked with acting evilly in the state's name attach 'a peculiar virtue' to their actions that would be lacking if they acted in such a manner as an individual.'[43] The logical conclusion to this revolution is the point at which

> the lust for power seizes upon the state as the vehicle on which to ride to hegemonial power among the nations. . . absolute corruption follows in the wake of this drive for absolute power. For here the use of all mankind as a means is not wished for in hapless imagination but worked for in actual performance.[44]

Moral courage of the lesser evil

The remainder of realist ethics consists of coming to terms with, *but not surrendering to*, the evil inherent in politics as a distinct sphere of human activity. To act ethically is 'to comprehend the full measure' of the corruption inherent in modern political existence 'and still not destroy the faculty to live and act.'[45] In an age in which 'the evil of power' is 'approaching its consummation' in the lived reality of the Cold War,

> [p]olitical ethics is indeed the ethics of doing evil. . . it must reconcile itself to the enduring presence of evil in all political action. Its last resort, then, is the endeavour to choose, since evil there must be, among several possible actions the one that is less evil.[46]

The 'gulf between ethics and politics has become too wide and too inscrutable for' the 'perfectionists, escapists and the men of the dual standard' only an unflinching 'awareness of the tragic presence of evil in all political action. . . enables man to choose the lesser evil and to be as good as he can be in an evil world.'[47] In contrast to the failed attempts of utilitarianism, reason of state and Kantianism, Morgenthau's ethic of responsibility informed by the standard of the lesser evil combines political wisdom, moral courage, and moral judgement, and thereby 'reconciles his political nature with his moral destiny.'[48] Although this *modus vivendi* is 'uneasy, precarious, and even paradoxical,' it nonetheless is preferable to approaches that 'prefer to gloss over and distort the tragic contradictions of human existence with the soothing logic of a specious concord.'[49]

The twilight of international morality and the articulation of the moral dignity of the national interest

In 'The Twilight of International Morality,' Morgenthau continues to pursue the theme that the contemporary age culminates the process of the erosion of the natural law-inspired universal morality that had, at least in principle, if not always in practice, restrained the activities of statesmen. Morgenthau's contrast of Otto von Bismarck who, 'however ruthless and immoral his particular moves on the chessboard of international politics may have been, rarely deviated from the basic rules of the game which had prevailed in the society of Christian princes,' and Hitler, who 'did not recognize the social framework within whose limitations international politics had operated from the end of the Thirty Years War to his own ascent to power,' demonstrated the extent to which the norms of international society had undergone drastic change in the relatively short period of time that separated their leaderships of Germany.[50] From 1648, with the exception of wars of the French Revolution, the 'moral standards of conduct with which the international aristocracy complied were of necessity of a supranational character. They applied. . . to all men who by virtue of their birth and education were able to comprehend them and to act in accordance with them.' During the course of the 19th century, as bourgeois democratic and republican regimes became more significant and the aristocracy declined, 'the structure of international society and, with it, of international morality underwent a fundamental change. . . [from] a system of moral restraints. . . into a mere figure of speech.' The gradual erosion of 'a formerly cohesive international society into a multiplicity of morally self-sufficient national communities which have ceased to operate within a common framework of moral precepts. . . has weakened, to the point of ineffectiveness, the universal, supranational moral rules of conduct.'[51]

Moral courage in this situation requires acceptance that '[o]nly shreds and fragments survive of this system of supranational ethics. . . [I]t is rather like the feeble rays, barely visible above the horizon of consciousness, of a sun which has already set.'[52] As seen in the first section of this chapter, the international legal rules developed by bourgeois representatives of nationalist and democratic nation-states proved to be inadequate to the task of either replacing the aristocratic standards of previous generations or withstanding the threat posed by the totalitarian states of Italy and Germany. In the contemporary international politics of what would become the Cold War, claims of moral superiority accentuated rather than restrained conflict as '[t]he morality of the particular group, far from limiting the struggle for power on the international scene, gives that struggle a ferociousness and intensity not known to other ages.'[53]

The national interest

The ethical challenge in such an age lies in imbuing the national interest with moral dignity.[54] In a manner similar to his efforts in the 1930s, Morgenthau again poses this problem in terms of interests versus moral abstractions, with the former again preferred to the latter as a source for genuine norms of statecraft and as a means of determining the lesser evil as an ethical imperative. The American political elite, like the statesmen of 1919–1939, was labouring under misapprehensions about ethical conduct in international relations due to the influence of pernicious moral abstractions. The man who became a symbol of the failed system of the interwar period in Europe, Woodrow Wilson, was a product of that same American political elite. The fatal flaw in Wilsonian thinking is that it 'not only disregards the national interest, but is explicitly opposed to it on moral grounds.'[55] Wilsonian thought and the reaction it provoked, isolationism, both fail the requirement of the ethic of responsibility to combine political wisdom, moral courage, and moral judgement. The problem is one of misunderstanding international relations by means of a mistaken antithesis:

> The equation of political moralism with morality and of political realism with immorality is itself untenable. The choice is not between moral principles and the national interest, devoid of moral dignity, but between one set of moral principles, divorced from political reality, and another set of moral principles, derived from political reality.[56]

The decline of international society necessitates the latter as

> [i]n the absence of an integrated international society. . . the attainment of a modicum of order and the realization of a minimum of moral values are predicated upon the existence of national communities capable of preserving order and realizing moral values within the limits of their power.[57]

The issue of limits is vitally important and serves to stake out the essential difference between the realist position and that of the Wilsonians and isolationists. Failing to observe the ethics of responsibility by renouncing action (isolationism) leads to political failure, while Wilsonian exertions predicated upon the harmony of American values and the universal good of mankind, lead to 'moral deterioration through either political failure or the fanaticism of political crusades.'[58] Poised between the Scylla of isolationism failing to meet the limits of the national interest and the Charybdis of Wilsonianism exceeding those limits, realism must chart an ethical path informed by a universal truth of international politics, that is, 'that a nation confronted with the hostile aspirations of other nations has one prime obligation—to take care of its own interests.' Yet although 'there is no other standard of action and of judgment, moral and intellectual, to which a great nation can repair, than the national interest,' how that national interest is articulated is open to interpretation and

> beyond these minimum requirements its content can run the whole gamut of meanings which are logically compatible with it. That content is determined by the political traditions and the total cultural context within which a nation formulates its foreign policy. The concept of the national interest, then, contains two elements, one that is logically required and in that sense necessary, and one that is variable and determined by circumstances.[59]

Morgenthau is anxious to stress once again that a feature of a working ethical system is that it must accept the imperfection of human beings as its starting point. Similar to his work in the 1930s, Morgenthau emphasises that reason is not absolutely legislative, but rather must jostle for position with other forces, such as the *animus dominandi*, that are often inimical to the dictates of reason. Realist ethics, according to Morgenthau, can be directed to improving the world situation, but only if it 'works with those forces, not against them.' The realisation of moral principles is possible in a world of opposing interests, but any such success must be recognised as being 'at best approximated through the ever temporary balancing of interests and the ever precarious settlement of conflicts,' resting on 'a system of checks and balances' that Morgenthau sees as a 'universal principle for all pluralist societies.'[60] Most importantly, and most often ignored by critics of realist ethics, the national interest *does not exist in isolation*:

> the national interest of a nation which is conscious not only of its own interests but also that of other nations *must be defined in terms compatible with the latter.* In a multinational world this is a requirement of political morality: in an age of total war it is also one of the conditions for survival.[61]

Realist ethics then requires *as one of its key principles* the consideration of the interests of other actors.

In this article, Morgenthau makes five points to 'the critics of realism in international affairs,' who he claims disregard 'voluminous evidence' to the contrary and '[pick] a few words out of their context to prove that realism in international affairs is unprincipled and contemptuous of morality.'[62] The first requirement of any attempt to morally evaluate the actions of states is the 'cosmic humility' to recognise that 'states are subject to the moral law is one thing; to pretend to know what is morally required of states in a particular situation is quite another,' only judgement can make a provisional, imperfect effort to accommodate ethical requirements within a political context. Morgenthau's second point is to reiterate the requirement of realist ethics to 'the effectiveness of the restraints which morality imposes upon the actions of states' by guarding against the extremes of 'overrating the influence of ethics upon international politics' or 'denying that statesmen and diplomats are moved by anything else but considerations of material power.'[63] The third clarification emphasises that 'universal moral principles cannot be applied to the actions of states in their abstract universal formulation, but that they must be, as it were, filtered through the concrete circumstances of time and place.'[64] As an example, Morgenthau offers liberty:

> while the individual has a moral right to sacrifice himself in defense of such a moral principle, the state has no right to let its moral disapprobation of the infringement of liberty get in the way of successful political action, itself inspired by the moral principle of national survival.[65]

Key to this filtering of moral principles to particular situations is the key realist virtue of prudence: 'there can be no political morality without prudence, that is, without the consideration of the political consequences of seemingly moral action.'[66] Realist ethics also recognises that

> a moral decision, especially in the political sphere, does not imply a simple choice between a moral principle and a standard of action which is morally irrelevant or even outright immoral. . . The relevant moral question concerns the choice among different moral values.[67]

The realist also has to

> distinguish between his moral sympathies and the political interests he must defend. He will distinguish with Lincoln between his 'official duty' which is to protect the national interest and his 'personal wish' which is to see universal moral values realized throughout the world.[68]

Conclusion: realist ethics beyond the national interest?

In 1945, Morgenthau identified the continuing task of realist ethics as being 'to rediscover and reformulate the perennial problems of political ethics and to answer them in the light of the experience of the age.'[69] By 1954, Morgenthau had identified that '[t]oday all nations have one interest in common which transcends almost all others: the avoidance of a general war.'[70] This universal interest in avoiding war is a result of the revolution in international relations occasioned by the advent of nuclear weapons. Where previously the use of military force had always been a rational policy choice for a state weighing its options in the face of rivals seeking their interests, or as a means to secure advantage by means of the conquest of territory, the

> feasibility of all-out atomic war has completely destroyed this rational relation between force and foreign policy. All-out atomic war, being an instrument of universal destruction, obliterates not only the traditional distinction between victor and vanquished, but also the material objective of the war itself.[71]

In these circumstances, '[a] foreign policy that preserves peace is morally superior to one that leads to limited war, and the latter, in turn, is superior to one which increases the danger of all-out nuclear war.'[72] The profound change in the nature of political existence wrought by the advent of nuclear weapons requires a corresponding change in how we think about political ethics and how the structure of international society might have to change accordingly. 'The refusal to adapt thought and action to radically new conditions has spelled the doom of men and civilizations before,' writes Morgenthau in 'Death in the Nuclear Age,' before ominously concluding, 'it is likely to do so again.'[73]

The threat of the new forced Morgenthau to the conclusion that Western thought faces 'political and moral bankruptcy' due to 'our inability to devise a third alternative' to the options of fighting the Soviet Union in a nuclear war or surrendering to the advance of Communism. Morgenthau's solution to the dilemma is illustrative of his theory's capacity to deal with profound change within the international society:

> [t]he way out. . . is to transcend the two equally unacceptable alternatives of surrendering or fighting a suicidal atomic war, and that means taking nuclear power out of the arsenal of individual nations altogether. . . Not necessarily by multilateral disarmament, but some kind of supra-national agency which we may call world government.[74]

The level of change is so profound that it requires the transcendence of both the nation-state and the politics that had typified international society prior to nuclear weapons: '[a]ny attempt, however ingenious and forward-looking, at assimilating nuclear power to the purposes and instrumentalities of the nation-state is negated by the enormity of nuclear destructiveness,' what is required in these new circumstances is a 'radical transformation—psychologically painful and politically risky—of traditional moral values, modes of thought, and habits of action. . . short of such a transformation, there will be no escape from the paradoxes of nuclear strategy and the dangers attending them.[75] In one of his final writings, Morgenthau stresses the *evolutionary* nature of the national interest in terms of its 'expansion' as a concept after World War Two. The national interest could not be understood in the wake of total war as comprising 'only the interests of a particular nation to the exclusion of all other nations, but certain interests of other nations as well.' This condition of shared national interests extends, in 1980, not only to 'the avoidance of nuclear war and the promotion of nuclear arms control and disarmament' which 'are in the national interest of all nations,' but also to 'the preservation of the natural environment and the availability and distribution of food. . . in our age the content of the national interest in certain respects transcends the limits of a particular nation and comprises the interests of a number of nations similarly situated.'[76] The expansion of the national interest could therefore serve as the basis for a new moral universalism in global politics. Although the era of Morgenthau recedes ever further into the realm of history, the task of realist ethics remains the same now as it was then, that is, 'to rediscover and reformulate the perennial problems of political ethics and to answer them in the light of the experience of the age.'[77]

Notes

1 The process could be repeated, with very different results, for any number of Realist thinkers. See, for example, my treatment of E. H. Carr's ethics in Seán Molloy, 'Spinoza, Carr, and the ethics of *The Twenty Years' Crisis*,' *Review of International Studies*, 39, no. 2 (2013): 251–271, and Seán Molloy, 'Pragmatism, Realism and the Ethics of Crisis and Transformation in International Relations,' *International Theory*, 6, no. 3 (2014): 454–489.

2 Hans J. Morgenthau, 'Positivism, Functionalism, and International Law,' *American Journal of International Law*, 34, no. 2 (1940): 268.

3 I deal with these and similar myths in Seán Molloy, 'Hans J. Morgenthau versus E. H. Carr,' in *Political Thought and International Relations: Variations on a Realist Theme*, ed. Duncan Bell (Oxford: Oxford University Press, 2008), 83–104.

4 See Matt McDonald's chapter in this volume in which he describes the (seemingly singular) ethics of 'traditional' security studies as 'one in which an ever-vigilant nation-state building resources to ensure its continued survival is conceived as the best means of protecting individuals in an anarchic state of nature.' As will hopefully be clear by the end of this chapter, such a representation misunderstands the essence of Realist ethics. Morgenthau, for example, ultimately concludes that state resources, especially nuclear weapons, ought to be administered by a form of world government and that the national interest had to be defined in relation to the interest of other states. The transcending of the nation-state is a consistent theme of Morgenthau's work.

5 The importance of Morgenthau's early work on international law in the development of Realism is explored in Oliver Jütersonke, *Morgenthau, Law and Realism* (Cambridge: Cambridge University Press, 2010).

6 Hans J. Morgenthau, 'Théorie des Sanctions Internationales,' *Revue de Droit International et de Législation Comparée*, 16, no. 3 (1935): 479.

7 Ibid., 503.

8 Hans J. Morgenthau, 'The Problem of Neutrality,' *The University of Kansas City Law Review*, 7 (February 1939): 111.

9 On Morgenthau's complex employment of the balance of power, see Seán Molloy, '"Cautious Politics": Morgenthau and Hume's Critiques of the Balance of Power,' *International Politics*, 50, no. 3 (2013): 768–783.

10 Morgenthau, 'The Problem of Neutrality,' 109.

11 Hans J. Morgenthau, 'The Resurrection of Neutrality in Europe,' *American Political Science Review*, 33, no. 3 (1939): 479.

12 Hans J. Morgenthau, 'The End of Switzerland's "Differential" Neutrality,' *American Journal of International Law*, 32, no. 3 (1938): 559.

13 Hersch Lauterpacht, 'International Studies Conference: La Securité Collective,' (Paris 1936), 441, cited in Morgenthau, 'The Problem of Neutrality,' 112.

14 Morgenthau, 'The End of Switzerland's "Differential" Neutrality,' 561.

15 The return of great power antagonism was not, Morgenthau makes clear, a return to the classical operation of the balance of power in that the 'ethico-legal delimitations of the political sphere itself, especially effective in the nineteenth and early twentieth centuries, have been swept away by the totalitarian political philosophies and practices of recent years,' Morgenthau, 'The Resurrection of Neutrality,' 484.

16 Morgenthau, 'The Problem of Neutrality,' 110.

17 Ibid.

18 Morgenthau, 'The End of Switzerland's "Differential" Neutrality,' 560.

19 Morgenthau, 'Resurrection of Neutrality in Europe,' 481.

20 Ibid., 483.

21 Hans J. Morgenthau, 'Positivism, Functionalism, and International Law,' *American Journal of International Law*, 34, no. 2 (1940): 284.

22 Hans J. Morgenthau, 'Review of R. M. MacIver, *Towards and Abiding Peace*,' *Journal of Political Economy*, 52, no. 1 (1944): 92.

23 Hans J. Morgenthau, 'The Evil of Politics and the Ethics of Evil,' *Ethics*, 56, no. 1 (1945): 1.

24 Ibid., 1–4.

25 Ibid., 14.

26 Morgenthau sees the categorical imperative as a reformulated version of the Golden Rule, both of which gloss over 'the divergence and incompatibility of human aspirations' and are 'appropriate only in an already perfect moral world where nobody wants what could infringe upon anybody else's wants,' Hans J. Morgenthau, 'Justice and Power,' *Social Research*, 4, no. 1 (1974): 168.

27 Morgenthau, 'The Evil of Politics and the Ethics of Evil,' 9–10.

28 Morgenthau's relationship to Hobbes was complicated enough to confuse even a reader as acute as Martin Wight, whose accusation in *International Affairs* that Morgenthau was marking 'an extreme position by endorsing Hobbes's doctrine that outside the state there is neither morality nor law,' prompted Morgenthau to reply that he 'was trying to establish the point, in contrast to Hobbes's, that moral principles are universal and, hence, are not created by the state. I was also trying to establish the point, I think in accord with Hobbes, that moral principles, as applied to political issues, receive their concrete meaning from the political situation within which they are called to operate. Thus, far from endorsing Hobbes, I was really saying that his statement is in error because it is 'extreme,' but that it contains a 'hidden' element of truth.' Hans J. Morgenthau, 'Letter to *International Affairs*,' 35, no. 4 (1959): 502.

29 Ibid., 4–5.
30 Morgenthau, 'The Evil of Politics and the Ethics of Evil,' 4–6.
31 Ibid., 6.
32 Ibid., 8.
33 Ibid., 9.
34 Ibid., 10. There is not enough space to list all the valuable work done on Weber, the ethic of responsibility and Morgenthau, but see, for example, Michael C. Williams, *The Realist Tradition and the Limits of International Relations* (Cambridge: Cambridge University Press, 2005).
35 Morgenthau, 'The Evil of Politics and the Ethics of Evil,' 10.
36 Ibid., 10–11.
37 Ibid., 11.
38 Ibid. See Richard Ned Lebow's excellent treatment of Morgenthau and tragedy in *The Tragic Vision of Politics: Ethics, Interests, Orders* (Cambridge: Cambridge University Press, 2003).
39 Morgenthau, 'The Evil of Politics and the Ethics of Evil,' 11.
40 Ibid., 12.
41 Ibid., 13–14.
42 Ibid., 14.
43 Ibid., 15–16.
44 Ibid., 16–17.
45 Ibid., 17.
46 Ibid. On the lesser evil, see Seán Molloy, 'Aristotle, Epicurus, Morgenthau and the Political Ethics of the Lesser Evil,' *Journal of International Political Theory*, 5, no. 1 (2009): 94–112.
47 Morgenthau, 'The Evil of Politics and the Ethics of Evil,' 17.
48 Ibid., 18.
49 Ibid., 18.
50 Hans J. Morgenthau, 'The Twilight of International Morality,' *Ethics*, 58, no. 2 (1948): 81.
51 Ibid., 88–95.
52 Ibid., 98.
53 Ibid., 99.
54 This theme is explored in most detail in Hans J. Morgenthau, *In Defense of the National Interest* (New York: Alfred A. Knopf, 1951).
55 Hans J. Morgenthau, 'The Mainsprings of American Foreign Policy: The National Interest vs. Moral Abstractions,' *American Political Science Review*, 44, no. 4 (1950): 847.
56 Ibid., 853–854.
57 Ibid., 854.
58 Ibid., 854.
59 Hans J. Morgenthau, 'What Is the National Interest of the United States?,' *The Annals of the American Academy of Political and Social Science*, 282 (1952): 4, 7; 'Another "Great Debate": The National Interest of the United States,' *American Political Science Review*, 46, no. 4 (1952): 972.
60 Morgenthau, 'Another Great Debate,' 962.
61 Ibid., 977, emphasis added.
62 Ibid., 983.
63 Ibid., 984.
64 Ibid., 985.
65 Ibid., 986.
66 Ibid., 986.
67 Ibid., 987.
68 Ibid., 987.
69 Morgenthau, 'The Evil of Politics and the Ethics of Evil,' 1.
70 Morgenthau, 'The Yardstick of the National Interest,' *The Annals of the American Academy of Political and Social Science*, 296 (1954): 83.
71 Hans J. Morgenthau, 'Atomic Force and Foreign Policy: Can the "New Pacifism" Insure Peace?' *Commentary* (January 1, 1957): 502.
72 Hans J. Morgenthau, 'The Demands of Prudence,' *Worldview*, 6, no. 3 (1960): 7.
73 Hans J. Morgenthau, 'Death in the Nuclear Age,' *Commentary* (September 1, 1961).

74 Hans J. Morgenthau et al., 'Western Values and Total War,' *Commentary* (October 1, 1961): 280, 285. Morgenthau continues, '[W]e are living in a political world that has been left behind by technological developments. Nothing short of a political revolution commensurate with the technological revolutions through which we have passed, through which we are in the process of passing, and which are still ahead of us, will solve the problem.' Ibid., 298.

75 Hans J. Morgenthau, 'The Four Paradoxes of Nuclear Strategy,' *American Political Science Review*, 58, no. 1 (1964): 35.

76 Hans J. Morgenthau, 'The Reality of the National Interest,' *Partisan Review*, 47, no. 4 (1980): 580.

77 Ibid.

13
ETHICS AND CRITICAL SECURITY STUDIES

Matt McDonald

It seems relatively uncontroversial to argue that ethical and normative concerns are central to critical security studies. Indeed, to the extent that there is a shared concern underpinning the large body of work that makes up critical security studies, it is built upon recognition of the problematic ethical assumptions and implications of traditional conceptions and practices of security in international relations. Yet the precise nature of the critique of traditional approaches and the contours of the ethical concerns advanced by critical security studies scholars varies significantly across different theorists and 'schools' of critical security studies. This chapter maps both the shared ethical commitments and the key points of difference in this broad tradition, with a particular focus on the 'Aberystwyth' and 'Copenhagen' schools as illustrative of these similarities and differences. It concludes by suggesting that the key difference between them may ultimately be their conceptions of the *politics* of security and the associated question of whether security can be rehabilitated or must be escaped.

Introduction

Ethical and normative concerns are central to critical security studies. While hardly constituting a coherent intellectual project, theorists working in this broad tradition generally ground their analyses in a critique of traditional security conceptions and practices in international relations. The critique here is not that traditional approaches to security are ethics-free. As Seán Molloy notes, there is clearly a rich ethical tradition underpinning 'traditional' security studies: one in which an ever-vigilant nation-state building resources to ensure its continued survival is conceived as the best means of protecting individuals in an anarchic state of nature.[1] Rather, the argument here is that the assumptions underpinning the approach and the implications of the practices it encourages are ethically problematic.

On assumptions *underpinning* traditional security studies, theorists in the critical security studies tradition have pointed to the ways in which the emphasis on the security of states prioritises means over ends, to assumptions about the nature of the international system not borne out by the advance of norms, institutions and practices of cooperation, and to assumptions about the universalisability of a Western image of the liberal democratic nation-state foreign to much of the world and for much of history.[2] Such criticisms clearly range from the analytical to the normative. On the *implications* of adopting a traditional approach, critical security studies theorists have pointed to the ways in which the embrace of a traditional security studies agenda (and associated militarisation) creates opportunity costs, threatens liberal democratic values, breeds distrust, and in some cases directly causes vulnerability, suffering, and harm.[3]

At heart, then, ethical commitments clearly underpin critical security studies scholarship, and theorists share misgivings about the assumptions and implications of traditional approaches to security. Yet it is obviously not the case that these theorists share a unified conception of ethics. At the heart of differences is a different conception of the *politics* of security: of how security (and any claim to it) serves to order social life in particular ways and justifies sets of practices carried out in its name. For some critical studies scholars, the politics of security is inevitably wedded to the nation-state and traditional security discourses, in which claims to security are necessarily means of preserving the interests of the powerful and limiting deliberation and contestation.[4] In this schema, the ethical imperative is to challenge and resist security.

For others, this logic of security is not inevitable. Some claims to security may encourage such practices, but the concept itself may also be reformed to focus explicitly on the vulnerable and their protection or emancipation from structural constraint.[5] For these theorists, rehabilitating security is particularly important because security is high politics: it serves to define priority, attention and funding, and is central to the political legitimacy of key institutions of world politics. As such, it is too important, as Ken Booth argues, to be left to strategists.[6] At its foundation, this distinction is about whether the ethical imperative is to escape or rehabilitate security.[7]

This chapter proceeds in three stages. In the first, I outline both the key contours of critical security studies scholarship broadly and the unifying features of this approach. In the second stage, I illustrate key axes of difference and contestation through a more specific focus on those who endorse emancipation and those who approach the study of security through the securitisation framework. Here, I note the ethical assumptions underpinning these approaches and key points of both agreement and disagreement regarding their vision of the relationship between ethics and security. As noted above, I suggest that different visions of the politics of security are central to this distinction. The conclusion reflects on how this discussion contributes to broader normative political theory, suggesting in the process that it focuses our attention on key questions such as the role of theorists and the extent to which contemporary institutions and practices should be reformed, challenged, or escaped.

The contours of critical security studies

During the heart of the Cold War, the study of security was the study of the threat and use of force.[8] With a handful of exceptions, theoretical approaches and empirical analyses affirming the idea that *security* was about national security, and in particular the preservation of the nation-state from external military threat, dominated the International Relations (IR) subdiscipline of security studies.[9] Of course, the dynamics of broader world politics, especially from the perspective of the US (where the majority of scholars of IR were based), significantly influenced this dominance. From an American perspective, the existential threat of nuclear conflict with the Soviet Union and ongoing participation in proxy wars served to create a context in which security was associated with strategy and the very survival of the state. Profound impediments to any form of international cooperation in the Cold War context also hindered the idea of a focus on a broader security agenda in which transnational challenges to international stability were a genuine object of focus and concern. As Barry Buzan and Lene Hansen note in their historical survey of the study of security, these 'real world' dynamics and processes, especially as experienced in and by the West, were central to the forms of theory and analysis to emerge in the academy.[10]

With the waning and end of the Cold War in the 1980s, however, scholars increasingly contested the dominance (even hegemony) of this conception of security—associated with the territorial preservation of the nation-state from external military threat. A range of voices began pointing to the need to focus our attention at least on a broader range of threats to national security, particularly environmental change.[11] And while less prominent, others still suggested the need to orient towards the security of individuals or the international community as a whole. These positions often reflected their concern with the catastrophic implications of nuclear warfare, with theorists characterising these weapons as a 'common threat' to humankind.[12] By the 1990s, as the possibility of genuine international cooperation and attention to key challenges to a broader community became apparent, it was possible to talk about a 'critical' approach to security.

While we can recognise the emergence and strengthening of dissenting voices on security by the mid to late 1990s, defining *critical security studies* is not a simple exercise. For some scholars, such as Booth, it is an academic project orienting around a critique of traditional approaches to security *and* a concern with the welfare of people rather than states or the institutions that claim to protect them.[13] Columba Peoples and Nicholas Vaughn-Williams see critical security studies less as a project than as an orientation, suggesting a sociological account of critical security studies in academia in which 'the boundaries of "critical" security studies (are) defined by those who frame their work using this label'. [14] Neither of these accounts is uncontroversial. The former risks presenting too unified a purpose for 'critical security studies', excluding researchers whose critique of traditional security studies does not extend to its reimagination in bottom-up or emancipatory terms. The latter, meanwhile, risks excluding those whose work constitutes a fundamental critique of traditional conceptions and practices of security yet avoid the label on the basis of its association with a narrower conception of 'progress' or 'emancipation' of which they are uncomfortable.

Clearly, similar challenges apply when attempting to define *critical security studies* on the basis of epistemology or ontology. Some positivist accounts may be driven by, or at least serve the end of, challenging core claims made by proponents of traditional security studies, such as the relationship between material resources and conflict, for example. In ontological terms, some accounts that focus only on the interests, practices, and politics of states and their militaries do so in ways what advance a critical agenda without necessarily embracing the broad spectrum of referent objects, agents, threats or means that agenda might encourage. And, of course, a range of approaches (including IR's new academic orthodoxy, constructivism) straddle the divide between traditional and problem-solving theories generally, complicating attempts to situate them easily on one side or another.

For the purposes of this chapter, critical security studies is conceived, simply, as a field of study that orients around a critique of traditional conceptions and practices of security. In the process, and relating to the focus of this chapter, approaches and theorists operating in this broad tradition variously interrogate the ethical assumptions of traditional approaches, point to the ethical implications of traditional security practices, and/or advance alternative analytical and ethical accounts of security and security practice. In what follows, I provide a necessarily partial account of the ethics of critical security studies through exploring the manner in which two of its most prominent 'schools'[15] approach security: the Aberystwyth and Copenhagen Schools.

Aberystwyth

For scholars working in the tradition of the Aberystwyth (or Welsh) School, the study of security is underpinned by a concern with emancipation. Drawing on Frankfurt School Critical

Theory, itself drawing broadly on Karl Marx, this approach explicitly embraces an ethical commitment to the emancipation of the most vulnerable from structural constraints that challenge their lives and unnecessarily restrict their life choices.

For Aberystwyth School theorists,[16] the ethical assumptions underpinning traditional approaches to security, and their ethical implications, are indefensible when viewed through the lens of the rights and needs of the most vulnerable. Traditional approaches, for them, legitimate militarisation and the concentration of wealth and power in the hands of powerful people and institutions, drawing our attention away from the most vulnerable and the source of their vulnerability and/or suffering. Indeed, for these theorists, a commitment to national security can directly *endanger* the lives of individuals, as the scale of global refugee populations attest.[17]

At its most fundamental, Aberystwyth School theorists challenge the idea that people should view the state as the referent object of security, pointing out that this involves endorsing the means of security rather than the ends. As Bill McSweeney argues, while realist approaches to security focus on the state as the referent—that in need of securing—the terms of the social contract suggested that states existed to provide for the security and wellbeing of those within the state.[18] As states do not always serve these ends, endorsing this institution in universal terms as the referent object of security is, for McSweeney, analytically misleading and difficult to justify in normative terms. To some degree, we can identify this perspective in the embrace of the Responsibility to Protect, in which the international community only respects a state's right of nonintervention if it protects its own population.[19]

Following the above, a key point of distinction between the Aberystwyth School and much critical security studies scholarship is that the former has a particular idea of what constitutes *real* security. For these theorists, security is emancipation: they are 'two sides of the same coin'.[20] As will be evident through the discussion of the Copenhagen School approach to follow, this is not a view uniformly held across the critical security tradition. Indeed, much of this literature sets out to explore and interrogate the ways in which different political communities come to understand security or at least the content of threats to it. This move to orient towards 'real security', for the Aberystwyth School, is a reflection of the fact that theirs is a deliberate political intervention driven by ethical commitments. It is about correcting the ethical and practical wrongs of traditional approaches to security. We find elements of such an approach in the discourse of human security, at least to the extent that this similarly entails an explicit focus on individuals and a categorical account of what *real* security means. In the most prominent articulation of human security, it is defined in terms of 'freedom from fear' and 'freedom from want', eliciting similar conceptions of the need to orient our concerns towards the rights and needs of people rather than the preservation of institutions.[21]

The above account of the Aberystwyth School suggests a particular conception, not only of security, but also of the role of the theorist. For the Aberystwyth School, this role is to identify and challenge those assumptions and practices that contribute to peoples' insecurity in the first place, and work to correct these challenges and advance the cause of emancipation in the second. As such, while ethical assumptions underpin the concept of security itself, and carrying out practices in its name have ethical implications, those who would theorise about security also have normative and ethical obligations. Richard Wyn Jones's work most directly articulates this, employing the Gramscian notion of 'organic intellectuals' to discuss the ways in which academics should work with progressive civil society forces to advance emancipatory ends.[22]

Among a range of applications, theorists working in the Aberystwyth School tradition have applied the framework to issues and contexts such as regional security dynamics,[23] global health,[24] terrorism,[25] immigration,[26] gender-based violence,[27] popular protests,[28] and environmental change.[29] Each of these varied applications focus on identifying the limits of traditional ways of making sense of contemporary insecurity and/or the limits of practices undertaken to provide security. Each also makes a case for approaching conceptions, dynamics, and practices of security with a focus on the most vulnerable, suggesting that this constitutes a more ethically defensible approach to security.

In my analysis of how an emancipatory framework could help us understand terrorism and the war on terror, I suggested that such a focus would: point to the 'war on terror' as a self-fulfilling prophecy that serves the ends of terrorists through furthering radicalisation and recruitment; emphasise the opportunity costs of the 'war on terror', especially manifestations of this war in Afghanistan and Iraq; interrogate the ways in which state responses limit domestic freedoms and thereby affect the lives of those they exist to protect; and ask first-principle questions about whether claims associated with the threat of terrorism serve to reinforce the primacy of the state and the legitimacy of measures it undertakes. By contrast, practices carried out with a focus on the emancipation of the most vulnerable were more likely to address those threats experienced by those people (e.g., disease, poverty, natural disasters) while providing a stronger basis for preventing future terrorist attacks in promoting dialogue and disrupting cycles of violence and counterviolence. In this sense, and in the context of this example, scholars could view an emancipatory approach as both morally desirable and strategically necessary.[30]

As could be anticipated for an approach that constitutes a radical critique of the *status quo*, is explicitly normative in orientation, and whose key thinkers have been robust in criticism of both traditional and other critical approaches to security,[31] the Aberystwyth School has been subjected to a range of criticisms. Of course, from a traditional perspective, the approach fails the test of policy relevance in a world in which states and their leaders conceive of the ethical limits of security as coinciding with the territorial borders of the state. Expecting key actors to suddenly orient towards the rights and needs of vulnerable populations (especially in other countries) is neither feasible nor (for communitarians) necessarily desirable. And of course, traditional approaches have also challenged the idea that the goal of a security analyst is to build a case for change grounded in normative considerations, rather than 'develop testable theories'.[32]

Aside from these relatively predictable objections to a critical perspective, others have challenged the ethical assumptions and implications of the focus on emancipation. For some, as a universal principle and metanarrative, 'emancipation' risks imposing Western values on other communities or becoming a new orthodoxy that enables violence to be carried out in its name.[33] This might be particularly dangerous in instances of military intervention carried out with the stated aim of freeing others—the risk that progressive ideas are attached to military interventions oriented towards less-than-progressive ends.[34] Indeed, Peoples suggests that advocates of emancipation are less than clear on their conception of violence or the circumstances in which it is permissible.[35]

Scholars have also criticised the approach on analytical grounds, with some raising (in turn) key questions about the ethics of the approach. First, as I have argued elsewhere, the Aberystwyth School does not provide a framework capable of understanding pivotal sociological questions of how and why particular political communities come to understand and practice security as they do.[36] This is an important limitation in that it renders the approach less capable of providing us with resources for understanding how particular political communities might come to view and approach security in emancipatory terms. Second, while advocates of the approach suggest the need to engage security because of its role in designating importance, priority, and funding, engagement with the question of what security actually does in political terms is more limited.[37] Again, this is problematic in normative terms and raises the key question of why we should continue to engage with security to locate a particular conception of progress. If dominant frameworks and practices of security are so problematic—tied as they are to suspicion, militarisation, and a narrow conception of the boundaries of moral community—then why continue to engage with security? Why not locate an ethical vision or even a conception of progress in the language of justice or rights, for example? This, as noted, is a key point of difference across critical security studies, as illustrated by the different conception of the politics of security held by proponents of the Copenhagen School.

Copenhagen

The Copenhagen School framework is particularly distinct from the Aberystwyth School approach in that the former's focus is not on how researchers should define or help realise (true) security, but on how researchers should make sense of the meaning given to security in practice. Central to this is its concept of securitisation. Securitisation refers to the process whereby issues are represented as security threats through a 'speech act' and, if this representation is accepted or endorsed by the relevant constituency,[38] emergency or extraordinary measures are enabled to address that threat. The approach ultimately opens the door to a wider range of threats making up the security agenda while allowing the question of the scope of that agenda to be determined by political practice rather than the position of the researcher. And for proponents of this approach, processes and dynamics of securitisation look different across different 'sectors': arenas entailing particular forms of security interaction, including the military, political, economic, societal, and environmental sectors.

For advocates of the approach, the focus on the way actors give security meaning allows us to engage with security in practice rather than in the abstract. It is a sociological engagement with security, rather than a normative one. And while for some, this questions the extent to which it can be defined as a 'critical' approach,[39] the openness to a broader range of security threats and the focus on the dynamic politics of security constitutes a clear rejection of traditional approaches to security. For advocates, analysts should not be concerned with explaining how states (or other actors) can and should address threats to a security agenda determined by the analyst, but rather analysts should examine how issues come to be defined as threats and the sets of responses subsequently enabled. The process of defining an issue as a security issue is at the heart, for them, of coming to terms with the politics of security.

While the critique of traditional approaches to security suggested here is largely analytical, there is also a normative dimension to the framework, as a range of theorists have suggested.[40] In one of his earliest statements on securitisation, founder Ole Wæver outlined a normative preference for desecuritisation: removing issues *from* the security agenda.[41] This was based on the position that securitisation entails taking an issue out of the realm of 'normal' political practice and debate and treating it with secrecy and urgency. It would therefore normally be preferable, he suggests, to remove issues from the 'panic politics'[42] of security and subject these issues to proper political processes of scrutiny and deliberation. In essence, and while not a central component of the framework itself, this involves endorsing a procedural vision of liberal ethics distinct from the exceptionalist logic of security.[43]

The securitisation framework has been widely embraced in the field of international relations and has been applied to issues such as disease,[44] environmental change,[45] migration,[46] and minority rights.[47] All these applications, albeit in different ways, explore the designation of (non-traditional) issues as security threats, examine the implications of such depictions in terms of the emergency measures enabled, and reflect on the utility of the approach in coming to terms with the dynamics associated with this issue. Indeed, and in part reflecting its role as a framework for exploring the construction of security, it has been more widely taken up and applied than the Aberystwyth School approach.

On the issue of migration in liberal democratic states, the framework has been widely employed and appears to have particular purchase. There is nothing inherent about the arrival of migrants or asylum-seekers that necessitates viewing them as a threat to national security, yet this is precisely what we see in Western states over the past two decades in particular. The example of Australia's approach to asylum-seekers arriving by boat illustrates the framework's utility. In Australia's case, we find statements from political leaders characterising the arrival of asylum-seekers by boat as a threat to the sovereignty and security of the state (speech acts), widespread public support for a strong and more restrictive stance on processing asylum-seekers (audience acceptance), and finally the interception of asylum boats by the military, the excision of Australian land from the migration zone, long-term incarceration of asylum-seekers in offshore detention centres in developing countries, and the refoulement of asylum-seekers and refugees in some instances (emergency/exceptional measures).[48]

This is not an issue that *necessitates* being defined or approached as a security issue: asylum-seeker arrivals could, for example, be defined as a human rights issue. Yet this issue has been viewed through the prism of national security, approaches to boat arrivals have employed the logic of deterrence, and indeed the Department of Immigration—responsible for overseeing Australia's approach to asylum-seekers—has been renamed the Department of Immigration and Border Protection. And if the securitisation framework has purchase here in helping us make sense of the process through which particular exceptional policies and practices have been rendered possible (i.e., through the language of 'security'), it also has normative appeal. In this instance, the language of security has apparently enabled practices inconsistent with international law (in particular, the 1951 Refugee Convention), with the long-term detention of asylum-seekers singled out by UN agencies as a form of 'torture'.[49] Viewed in light of such an example, the push towards desecuritisation appears ethically compelling.

While this example seems to validate both the analytical and normative purchase of the Copenhagen School framework, however, theorists have made a range of criticisms regarding its attempts to come to terms with the construction of security. For some more traditional analysts, it leaves unclear where the boundaries of the study and practice of security should be drawn, potentially enabling a raft of issues better approached and studied through different means.[50] For other critics, it grants too much significance to the role of language (relative to physical action, images, or even silences, for example), it is unclear on the composition or significance of audiences, or it erroneously focuses exclusively on the construction of 'threats' rather than the composition or construction of referents, agents, and means, for example.[51]

On ethical grounds, Booth dismisses the approach (with its general focus on states and political leaders) as conservative,[52] while others suggest that the normative push for 'normal politics' in contradistinction to 'security politics' envisages the latter as a liberal democratic conception of 'normal politics' defined by open political deliberation.[53] This relates directly to the analytical criticism that the distinction made between 'security' and 'politics' is simplistic and binary, ignoring multiple logics of both and the significance of concepts such as risk that seem to operate between these 'poles'.[54]

Yet, to return to a central theme of this chapter, perhaps the key criticism of the framework to note here is regarding its conception of the *politics* of security. This conception ultimately informs its ethical desire to escape security and locate progressive politics elsewhere. For proponents of securitisation, a conception of the meaning of security as ultimately tied to defence and the state,[55] and in particular a conception of the logic of security tied to an illiberal politics of exceptionalism, secrecy, and 'panic politics', drives the inclination towards desecuritisation. As such, while proponents of emancipation attempt to reform security, Copenhagen School proponents incline towards escaping it.

This different vision of whether to escape or engage security is a fundamental distinction between these approaches and is a distinction evident in other approaches that can be located in the broad tradition of critical security studies. For some theorists, it is possible to redefine security and to locate progress through a more progressive conception of security, whether that is emancipation or human security.[56] Indeed, if security is seen as defining political priority and underpinning the political legitimacy of key institutions, it is not simply possible, but necessary. Other theorists, whether working in the poststructural tradition or employing the securitisation framework, are more sceptical. For them, security serves as a master narrative that instils fear, ties individuals to the apparatus of the state, and works to reinforce the power and primacy of already powerful actors at the expense of others.[57]

Yet as a colleague and I have note elsewhere,[58] behind radically different conceptions of the politics of security and the question of whether to engage it are ethical positions that are not wholly incompatible. At least, these orient towards a similar critique of the illiberal and *status quo*-oriented practices carried out in the name of security. At heart, then, the question of whether we can or should escape or reformulate security may be the key question for critical security studies as a whole.

Conclusion: a contribution to normative political theory?

Of course, the above is far from an exhaustive or complete account of critical security studies as a field and its associated ethical commitments. Such a project would need to engage with a wider range of alternative analytical accounts of security that challenge traditional approaches, with recent work focusing on the role of practices and the concept of ontological security, for example.[59] And, more squarely within the broad field of critical security studies, it would need to systematically tackle the normative contributions and claims of feminist approaches (both liberal and poststructural variants), poststructuralism, and postcolonialism, among others. These approaches point to the importance and pathologies of dominant discourses and the ways in which they empower/focus our attention on some actors while marginalising others, though of course do so in a range of different ways. In focusing on the two approaches noted here, I have attempted to touch on some of the core variations within the broad church of 'critical security studies', and use them to illustrate some of the key ethical questions and issues confronting those uncomfortable with the scholarship and practices associated with traditional security studies.

By way of conclusion, however, it is worth reflecting on the contribution these approaches might make to broader normative political theory. Here, I want to focus on two key contributions: the first is attention to the role of the theorist, the second to dilemmas associated with the politics of engagement. Neither of these dilemmas are entirely new to normative political theorists or those engaging with ethics and international relations, but the manner and extent of engagement with these questions in critical security studies can potentially make a broader contribution to normative political theory.

First, scholars in the critical security studies tradition have taken seriously the role of the theorist: not simply as the means through which intellectual light is shed on particular questions, but as potentially consequential political agents. Within the two approaches identified, for example, Aberystwyth School proponents such as Wyn Jones have attempted to build a specific case for viewing academics as organic intellectuals, working with civil society to achieve ethical and practical progress.[60] And Johan Erikson's discussion of the dangers associated with security theorists contributing to securitisation, and subsequent responses, has ensured an ongoing reflection within the Copenhagen School about the political agency of theorists themselves.[61] Both of these interventions, and the broader postpositivism in which their theories are embedded, place the role of academics themselves centre-stage in discussions of ethics. In this sense, work in the tradition of critical security studies particularly encourages us to take account of our own position and reflect on our role in contributing to debates about ethics.

Second, debates within critical security studies raise fundamental questions about the politics of engaging with ethical questions in practical terms. In particular, and to return to the key theme of this chapter, the question of whether to engage or escape security, and in turn whether dominant discourses or institutions can or should be challenged, reformulated, or avoided, are not incidental to critical security studies: they are central to it. The key distinction between the two approaches discussed here over the politics of security is ample illustration of this centrality. And this distinction raises significant questions for normative political theory about whether and how to engage or stand aside from current political arrangements and institutions: to risk co-option or potentially risk irrelevance. Critique of dominant approaches is relatively easy. As debates within critical security studies suggest, the question of whether and how to move beyond critique and to engage existing powerful discourses, institutions, and practices of security is much, much harder. This is a challenge for normative political theory that the dilemmas addressed by, and distinctions apparent in, critical approaches to security serve to illustrate.

Of course, debates about security in international relations are bound to have broader implications for the field of political science and international relations as a whole. Security is a master concept: it underpins the political legitimacy and *raison d'être* of the key institutions of world politics, and for many constitutes the key driver of the behaviour of these institutions. Certainly, claims to security do things politically, making it a site of contestation with potentially significant stakes. Critical approaches to security draw our attention to this politics of security, while raising and confronting key questions about whether or how we should challenge, redefine, or withdraw from 'security'. The absence of consensus in responding to these questions should not be viewed as a limitation, but rather as an inevitable product of the acutely difficult political and ethical challenges these questions raise. In this sense, it is at least a good thing that they are being asked.

Notes

1 See the Molloy contribution to this Handbook (Chapter 12).

2 On these points, see, for example, Bill McSweeney, *Security, Identity and Interests: A Sociology of International Relations* (Cambridge: Cambridge University Press, 1999); Ken Booth and Nicholas J. Wheeler, *The Security Dilemma: Fear, Cooperation and Trust in World Politics* (Basingstoke: Palgrave, 2007); and Anthony Burke, Katrina Lee-Koo and Matt McDonald, *Ethics and Global Security: A Cosmopolitan Approach* (London: Routledge, 2014).

3 On these points, see Ken Booth, 'Security and Emancipation', *Review of International Studies*, 17, no. 4 (1991): 313–326; Ole Wæver, 'Securitization and Desecuritization', in *On Security*, ed. Ronnie D. Lipschutz (New York: Columbia University Press, 1995); Richard K. Ashley, 'The Poverty of Neorealism', *International Organization*, 38, no. 2 (1981): 225–286; Andrew Linklater, 'Political Community and Human Security', in *Critical Security Studies and World Politics*, ed. Ken Booth (Boulder, Colorado: Lynne Rienner, 2005).

4 See, for example, Mark Neocleous, *Critique of Security* (Edinburgh: Edinburgh University Press, 2008).

5 See, for example, Ken Booth, *Theory of World Security* (Cambridge: Cambridge University Press, 2007); Joao Nunes, 'Reclaiming the Political: Emancipation and Critique in Security Studies', *Security Dialogue*, 43, no. 3 (2012): 345–361; Matt McDonald, *Security, the Environment and Emancipation* (London: Routledge, 2012); Paul Roe, 'Is Securitization a Negative Concept?', *Security Dialogue*, 43, no. 3 (2012), 249–266.

6 Booth, 'Security and Emancipation'.

7 On these points, see Christopher S. Browning and Matt McDonald, 'The Future of Critical Security Studies?', *European Journal of International Relations*, 19, no. 2 (2013): 235–255. See also Lee Jarvis and Jack Holland, *Security: A Critical Introduction* (London: Palgrave, 2015), 198–222.

8 For example, Stephen Walt, 'The Renaissance of Security Studies', *International Studies Quarterly*, 35, no. 2 (1991): 211–239. For an introduction to the dominance of this discourse and its historical context, see Karin Fierke, *Critical Approaches to International Security*, 2nd edn. (Cambridge: Polity, 2015), chapter 1.

9 Of course, peace researchers such as Johann Galtung were prominent critics of traditional approaches to security associated with strategic studies. As Buzan and Hansen note, 'Peace researchers of the 1960s and 1970s did not, however, go through the concept of security in launching their critique of Strategic Studies, but through the oppositional concept of "peace".' These theorists ultimately positioned their work outside and separate from 'security', rather than as an engagement with it. Barry Buzan and Lene Hansen, *The Evolution of International Security Studies* (Cambridge: Cambridge University Press, 2009), 102.

10 Ibid.

11 For example, Jessica Matthews, 'Redefining Security', *Foreign Affairs*, 68, no. 2 (1989): 162–177; Norman Myers, 'Environment and Security,' *Foreign Policy*, 74 (1989): 23–41.

12 For example, the 1982 so-called Pale Report coined the concept of 'common security' in response to the nuclear threat. Independent Commission on Disarmament and Security Issues, *Common Security: A Programme for Disarmament* (London: Pan Books, 1982).

13 Ken Booth, 'Critical Explorations', in *Critical Security Studies and World Politics*, ed. Ken Booth (Boulder, Colorado: Lynne Rienner, 2005), 2–3.

14 Columba Peoples and Nicholas Vaughn-Williams, *Critical Security Studies: An Introduction* (London: Routledge, 2010), 1.

15 C.A.S.E. Collective, 'Critical Approaches to Security in Europe', *Security Dialogue*, 37 (2006): 443–487; Rens van Munster, 'Security on a Shoestring: A Hitchhiker's Guide to Security Schools in Europe', *Cooperation and Conflict*, 32, no. 2 (2007): 235–243; Ole Wæver, 'Aberystwyth, Paris, Copenhagen,' paper presented at International Studies Association conference, Montreal, March 2004.

16 Booth, 'Security and Emancipation'; Booth, *Theory of World Security*; Richard Wyn Jones, *Security, Strategy and Critical Theory* (Boulder, Colorado: Lynne Rienner, 1999).

17 Linklater, 'Political Community and Human Security'; Ali Bilgic, *Rethinking Security in the Age of Migration* (London: Routledge, 2013).

18 McSweeney, *Security, Identity and Interests.*

19 See Alex Bellamy, *The Responsibility to Protect: A Defence* (Oxford: Oxford University Press, 2014); Alex Bellamy and Tim Dunne, eds., *The Oxford Handbook on the Responsibility to Protect* (Oxford: Oxford University Press, 2016).

20 Booth, 'Security and Emancipation', 319.

21 United Nations Development Programme, *Human Development Report, 1994* (New York: Oxford University Press, 1994). See also Taylor Owen, ed., *Human Security*, Volume 1 (London: Sage, 2013).

22 Jones, *Security, Strategy and Critical Theory*, 153–159.

23 Pinar Bilgin, *Regional Security in the Middle East: A Critical Perspective* (London: Routledge, 2004); Anthony Burke and Matt McDonald, eds., *Critical Security in the Asia-Pacific* (Manchester: Manchester University Press, 2007).

24 Joao Nunes, *Security, Emancipation and the Politics of Health* (London: Routledge, 2013).

25 Joseph Ruane and Jennifer Todd, 'Communal Conflict and Emancipation: The Case of Northern Ireland', in *Critical Security Studies and World Politics*, ed. Ken Booth (Boulder, Colorado: Lynne Rienner, 2005); Matt McDonald, 'Emancipation and Critical Terrorism Studies', in *Critical Terrorism Studies: A New Research Agenda*, ed. Richard Jackson, Marie Breen Smyth, and Jeroen Gunning (London: Routledge: 2009).

26 Bilgic, *Rethinking Security in the Age of Migration.*

27 Katrina Lee-Koo, 'Security as Enslavement/Security as Emancipation', in *Critical Security in the Asia-Pacific*, ed. Burke and McDonald (Manchester: Manchester University Press, 2007).

28 Ali Bilgic, 'Real People in Real Places', *Security Dialogue*, 46, no. 3 (2015): 272–290.

29 McDonald, *Security, the Environment and Emancipation.*

30 McDonald, 'Emancipation and Critical Terrorism Studies'.

31 The former is particularly true of Aberystwyth School founder Ken Booth, who tended to emphasise the faults/limitations of other critical approaches, despite these apparently sharing similar analytical

or normative positions to his own framework. His sweeping dismissal of both the Human Security approach (*Theory of Security*, 323–326) and the securitisation framework (Ibid., 164–172) are broadly representative of this inclination.

32 Robert O. Keohane, 'International Institutions: Two Approaches', *International Studies Quarterly*, 32 (1998), 393.

33 See, for example, Mohammed Ayoob, 'Defining Security: A Subaltern Realist Perspective', in *Critical Security Studies*, ed. Keith Krause and Michael C. Williams (Minneapolis: University of Minnesota Press, 1997); Mark Neufeld, 'Pitfalls of Emancipation and Discourses of Security', *International Relations*, 18, no. 1 (2004): 109–123; Mark Duffield, *Development, Security and Unending War* (Cambridge: Polity, 2007).

34 This might be applied to the example of military intervention in Iraq in 2003, for example. On these points, see David Chandler and Nik Hynek, 'No Emancipatory Alternative, No Critical Security Studies', *Critical Studies on Security*, 1, no. 1 (2013), 46–63.

35 Columba Peoples, 'Security after Emancipation: Critical Theory, Violence and Resistance', *Review of International Studies*, 37, no. 3 (2011): 1113–1135.

36 McDonald, *Security, the Environment and Emancipation*, 48–51.

37 See Browning and McDonald, 'The Future of Critical Security Studies'.

38 Scholars contest both the nature of audiences and their role in the securitisation process. Thierry Balzacq, for example, argues that we can make a distinction between the speech act as illocutionary or perlocutionary—the former constitutes or *performs* securitisation, suggesting a limited or even non-existent role for 'audiences', while the latter enables securitisation if audiences accept a securitising move. Thierry Balzacq, 'The Three Faces of Securitization', *European Journal of International Relations*, 11, no. 2 (2005): 171–201. On the role of the audiences in the Copenhagen School framework, see also Paul Roe, 'Actor, Audience(s) and Emergency Measures', *Security Dialogue*, 39, no. 6 (2008): 615–635; Matt McDonald, 'Securitization and the Construction of Security', *European Journal of International Relations*, 14, no. 4 (2008): 563–587.

39 See Chandler and Hynek, 'No Emancipatory Alternative, No Critical Security Studies'.

40 Claudia Aradau, 'Security and the Democratic Scene: Desecuritization and Emancipation', *Journal of International Relations and Development*, 7 (2014): 388–413; Lene Hansen, 'Reconstructing Desecuritization', *Review of International Studies*, 38, no. 3 (2012): 525–546; Rita Floyd, 'Can Securitization Theory Be Used in Normative Analysis?', *Security Dialogue*, 42, no. 4–5 (2011): 427–439; Michael C. Williams, 'Words, Images, Enemies: Securitization and International Politics', *International Studies Quarterly*, 47, 4 (2003), 511–531; Jef Huysmans, 'The Question of the Limit', *Millennium*, 27, no. 3 (1998), 569–589.

41 Wæver, 'Securitization and Desecuritization'.

42 Barry Buzan, Ole Wæver, and Jaap de Wilde, *Security: A New Framework for Analysis* (Boulder, Colorado: Lynne Rienner, 1998), 34.

43 See, for example, Williams, 'Words, Images, Enemies'.

44 Stefan Elbe, 'Should HIV/AIDS Be Securitized?', *International Studies Quarterly*, 50, no. 1 (2006): 119–144; Colin McInnes and Simon Rushton, 'HIV/AIDS and Securitization Theory,' *European Journal of International Relations*, 19, no. 1 (2013): 115–138.

45 Thomas Diez, Franziskus von Lucke, and Zehra Wellman, *The Securitization of Climate Change* (London: Routledge, 2016); Rita Floyd, *Security and the Environment* (London: Routledge, 2010).

46 Jef Huysmans, *The Politics of Insecurity: Fear, Migration and Asylum in the EU* (London: Routledge, 2004); 'The European Union and the Securitization of Migration', *Journal of Common Market Studies*, 38, no. 5 (2000): 751–777.

47 Paul Roe, 'Securitization and Minority Rights', *Security Dialogue*, 35, no. 3 (2004): 279–294.

48 On these points, see Anthony Burke, *Fear of Security* (Melbourne: Cambridge University Press, 2008), chapter 6; Don McMaster, 'Asylum-Seekers and the Insecurity of a Nation', *Australian Journal of International Affairs*, 56, no. 2 (2002), 279–290; Matt McDonald, 'Contesting Border Security: Emancipation and Asylum in the Australian Context', in *Contesting Security*, ed. Thierry Balzacq (London: Routledge, 2014); Caroline Fleahy et al., 'Missing the Boat', *International Migration*, 54, no. 4 (2016): 60–73.

49 On this latter point, see Ben Doherty and Daniel Hurst, 'UN Accuses Australia of Systematically Violating Torture Convention', *The Guardian*, March 10, 2015.

50 Daniel Deudney's objection to approaching environmental issues as 'security' issues outlined some similar concerns. While his objection to 'securitisation' was largely on normative rather than analytical grounds, he ultimately endorsed a conception of security as associated with armed conflict in making a case for decoupling environmental issues and security. Daniel Deudney, 'The Case against Linking Environmental Degradation and National Security', *Millennium*, 19, no. 3 (1990), 461–476.

51 On these points, and of an extensive literature, see, for example, Lene Hansen, 'The Little Mermaid's Silent Security Dilemma and the Absence of Gender in the Copenhagen School', *Millennium*, 29, no. 2 (2000): 285–306; Lene Hansen, 'Theorizing the Image for Security Studies', *European Journal of International Relations*, 17, no. 1 (2011): 51–74; McDonald, 'Securitization and the Construction of Security'; Balzacq, 'The Three Faces of Securitization'.
52 Booth, *Theory of World Security*, 64–72.
53 See Williams, 'Words, Images and Enemies'.
54 Rita Abrahamsen, 'Blair's Africa: The Politics of Securitization and Fear', *Alternatives*, 30, no. 1 (2005): 55–80.
55 See Wæver, 'Securitization and Desecuritization', 47.
56 See Booth, *Theory of World Security*; Nunes, 'Reclaiming the Political'; McDonald, 'Contesting Border Security'; Roe, 'Is Securitization a Negative Concept?'; Gunhild Hoogensen Gjørv, 'Security By Any Other Name', *Review of International Studies*, 38, no. 4 (2012): 835–859.
57 Again, see Neocleous, *Critique of Security*.
58 Browning and McDonald, 'The Future of Critical Security Studies'.
59 On security and practice, see, for example, Vincent Pouliot, *International Security in Practice* (Cambridge: Cambridge University Press, 2010). On ontological security, see Brent Steele, *Ontological Security in International Relations: Self-Identity and the IR State* (London: Routledge, 2014).
60 Jones, *Security, Strategy and Critical Theory*, 153–159.
61 Johan Erikson, 'Observers or Advocates? On the Political Role of Security Analysts', *Cooperation and Conflict*, 34, no. 3 (1999): 311–330.

14

TRADITION-BASED APPROACHES TO THE STUDY OF THE ETHICS OF WAR

Rosemary B. Kellison and Nahed Artoul Zehr

Introduction

Among the contemporary debates regarding ethics and international affairs are disagreements not only on the substance of the relevant moral norms—that is, what kinds of practices ought to be considered morally good and therefore legally enforced, and what kinds ought to be discouraged as immoral—but on metaethical questions relating to the source and justification of those norms. When it comes to the ethics of war in particular, there are at least three predominant positions on these issues (with significant overlap between them). The first is liberal political philosophers' and international lawyers' favored human rights-based approach. On this account, the ethical restraints on war derive from the inviolable rights of human beings (whether those rights are understood as natural or as guaranteed by the social contract of international law). Those who take the second approach, including many contemporary moral philosophers, employ logic in an attempt to formulate universally applicable moral principles that can guide the resort to and prosecution of war in any context. Finally, tradition-based approaches to the ethics of war, which are popular among scholars of religion and on which we focus here, involve the identification and reconstruction of particular traditions of moral reasoning on war and the subsequent elaboration of an ethic either in conversation with or explicitly justified by traditional norms.

Because any given moral tradition is rooted in an historical community, ethicists who take a tradition-based approach are much more interested than adherents of the other two approaches in the culture, history, customary practices, and authoritative texts and rituals of specific communities. Indeed, they would argue that moral norms and concepts cannot be understood or justified in isolation from those contexts. Tradition-focused ethicists thus tend to share Alasdair MacIntyre's conviction that "each particular theory or set of moral or scientific beliefs is intelligible and justifiable—insofar as it is justifiable—only as a member of an historical series."[1] For the thinkers described in this chapter, history, especially historical texts and the historical discourse of communities, is therefore foundational. However, the precise role history plays varies among tradition-based projects. As the examples cited in this chapter will show, for some, tracing the historical development of particular moral norms is important primarily because doing so enables greater understanding of the meaning and purpose of those norms. For others, this history is authoritative in that the values and practices produced by earlier communities ought to be adhered to as closely as possible by later heirs of their traditions.

While in very recent years initial forays have been made into scholarship on moral traditions concerning the ethics of war in other cultural contexts, the vast majority of work by Western tradition-focused ethicists of war has focused on the Western Christian just war tradition and, to a lesser extent, the Islamic tradition of moral reasoning about jihad. As explained below, there has also been a concerted effort on the part of a group of scholars to study and investigate these traditions side by side. In this chapter, we too describe examples of tradition-based ethics of war in these two contexts. First, we analyze the work of several thinkers interested in the just war tradition, emphasizing the varying ways in which these thinkers understand the justifying authority of traditional sources. Then, we turn to studies of Islamic ethics of war that focus on the ways in which moral reasoning about jihad has been connected to the development of the jurisprudential tradition of Shariah. Finally, we conclude by considering some of the challenges and potential limitations of the tradition-based approach in comparison with the other approaches mentioned above.

Western tradition-based ethics of war

Tradition-based approaches to the study of ethics of war in the Western context have typically focused on the historical development of what is called the just war tradition. Tradition-focused ethicists distinguish themselves from other just war thinkers by arguing that scholars must describe just war ethics as a tradition rather than as a theory or a set of principles. As the following overview will make clear, there are many variations in the historical moments and thinkers identified by tradition-focused ethicists as constitutive of this tradition. Broadly, however, these ethicists share an interest in the historical roots and development of the notion of just war itself as well as the specific criteria and principles often associated with that concept. Because the majority of the most influential foundational thinkers in this tradition were Christian theologians, the work of tradition-based ethicists (whether they personally identify as Christian or not) tends to include many more references to Christian writings than does that of other contemporary just war thinkers.[2] Another trend common in many tradition-based approaches is the identification of a particular historical period as producing the "classic" statement of the just war idea or the "classic" group of just war thinkers. Finally, when tradition-focused ethicists make normative recommendations regarding the historical or contemporary use of armed force, they tend to justify these arguments with reference to the authority of the just war tradition as they interpret it.

In employing this sort of justification, tradition-focused just war ethicists emulate strategies that many of the thinkers they identify use as significant in this tradition. One example is thirteenth-century theologian Thomas Aquinas, whom nearly all of the ethicists mentioned below cite as a foundational figure in the just war tradition and who was himself an accomplished tradition-focused ethicist. Like his contemporary counterparts, Thomas Aquinas justified his normative conclusions in part by appealing to authoritative traditional figures (including Aristotle, Augustine, and many others) and positioned himself within an historical and ongoing tradition of thought.[3] Other figures also often cited as authoritative representatives of the "classic" just war tradition, such as Francisco Vitoria, Francisco Suárez, and Hugo Grotius, all cited Thomas and built on his contribution. Contemporary tradition-focused ethicists continue to do the same. Thus, their projects simultaneously analyze and critique the just war tradition, appeal to the justifying authority of the tradition, and continue that tradition.

The availability of primary texts, both in their original languages and in translation, and of critical secondary analysis of those texts is essential for the success of tradition-based projects.

Two recent anthologies, both edited by Gregory Reichberg, offer English translations of relevant passages of the writings of a wide variety of historical thinkers.[4] Reichberg has complemented this aspect of his work with secondary scholarship on what he calls the classical thinkers of the just war tradition. Reichberg's writing is typically less explicitly normative than that of some of the other ethicists we discuss here. Instead, Reichberg tends to focus on tracing the historical development of particular concepts and themes within the tradition.[5] Similarly, in his writings on Thomas's ethics of war, Reichberg's focus is on accurate reconstruction and critical analysis of Thomas's arguments more than on the construction of Thomistic responses to contemporary issues.[6]

Alex Bellamy takes a similar approach, though he does not write from an explicitly Christian perspective. Much like Reichberg, Bellamy is interested to track the development of particular ideas and trends through the history of just war writing. Bellamy does not endorse a particular moment or theory as normative for the entire tradition, and grants that historical events will necessarily lead to appropriate changes in just war reasoning over time.[7] However, he does suggest that the "legitimacy" of contemporary arguments can be judged in part based on how well they "balance" what he identifies as three major emphases of just war tradition: realism, positive law, and natural law.[8] Bellamy does not specify what a proper balance would look like. He does, however, offer some examples of failure to achieve that legitimacy, such as Donald Rumsfeld's claim that responsibility for civilian casualties in a just war always rests with those whose unjust actions provoked the war—a claim Bellamy rejects as "counter to the Just War tradition."[9] In doing so, Bellamy comes closer to the practice of many other tradition-focused ethicists who employ their reconstructions of just war tradition in support of normative claims.

Lisa Cahill, for example, identifies two major strands within the broader Christian just war tradition.[10] The first, inspired by Augustine and carried on by Martin Luther, John Calvin, and Reinhold Niebuhr, understands a just war as an act of love. The second, inspired by Thomas Aquinas and carried on in Catholic social teaching, understands just war as motivated not by love but by rational pursuit of the common good. Cahill argues that by rejecting the idea that human wars can enact Christian love, the second of these strands better illuminates the contrast between just war tradition and the Christian pacifist tradition.[11] Therefore, she argues, Christians ought to continue the work of the Thomistic just war tradition and embrace its prioritization of justice over love when it comes to questions of war.[12]

Though Cahill argues for the moral superiority of one strand of just war thinking over another, she does not suggest that either of these strands has a stronger claim to the label of "just war tradition" itself. Several other tradition-focused ethicists who also identify more than one strand within just war tradition do take the step of suggesting that there is among this diversity one "classical" statement of just war tradition. Underlying this move is a claim, sometimes implicit and sometimes stated, that this classical tradition is a normative standard by which contemporary positions on issues of ethics and war ought to be measured. For those who take this approach, it is important not only to get the positions of classical thinkers "right," as Reichberg attempts to do, but also to properly identify which thinkers count as "classical." This task is made more difficult by the reality that there exists a certain tension between the emphasis on tradition and the search for a classical position. That is, given that a tradition necessarily comprises more than one thinker and thus more than one position on any given issue, the identification of one single classical standard is a challenge, if it is even possible. In part for this reason, many of the debates among tradition-focused ethicists have to do with who has correctly identified and interpreted the normative classical opinion. As noted below, whether it is possible to pinpoint one single response to any moral problem as representative of the classical tradition is an open question.

The way most tradition-focused ethicists approach this challenge is by attempting to show continuity in the arguments of several thinkers whose work they identify as part of the classical tradition. This aspect of their scholarship requires close reading of traditional sources (especially the writings of the ancient, medieval, and early modern Christian theologians mentioned above) in order to reconstruct the development of particular concepts and principles. James Turner Johnson has produced more studies in this vein than any other scholar; through his many books, Johnson provides an account of just war thinking as a tradition stretching over centuries. What he calls the "classic just war idea" emerged as the result of the "coalescence" of several different strands of thinking during the medieval period; modern and contemporary examples of just war reasoning can be traced—or at least ought to be able to be traced—back to this classic idea.[13]

Johnson argues that this ability to narrate how an idea developed historically is crucial for a full understanding of that idea.[14] A tradition-based approach provides an inclusive and "unitive" account—a "story"—of a concept rather than a decontextualized single statement, which would inevitably leave out important parts.[15] Especially in his earlier work, Johnson was careful to distinguish a tradition-based approach to ethics from an approach that attempts to isolate one single historical moment or thinker as *the* authoritative one.[16] He instead encourages a consideration of many such moments and thinkers alongside one another, "arraying the results of such analyses like beads on a string."[17] The resulting strand tells a story. Scholars are then to read that story with an eye to both its continuities and its apparent branches and tangents, noting the values and concepts that remain consistent over time as well as those that are contested or rejected along the way. As Johnson summarizes it, scholars ought "to focus upon the original *questions*" that motivated the development of a tradition rather than on what the original answers to those questions were; such an approach allows for inclusive study of all the various responses offered over a tradition's history and of why certain responses were favored or rejected.[18]

Johnson describes several ways in which a tradition-based approach may be useful in the construction of normative moral arguments. First and most obviously, communities may find the just war tradition, as a repository of ethical wisdom, valuable to return to in addressing contemporary issues. Johnson argues strongly that classic just war writings are relevant to many of the moral problems presented by modern war.[19] Enacting the values of those writings in contemporary action is a way of "forging connections with the past" in the construction of moral identity.[20] In his more recent work, Johnson also describes the normative authority of the tradition in a different way: as a kind of standard by which particular acts of war, as well as particular just war arguments, can be judged. As he puts it, "knowing what the historical tradition has actually said provides a basis for nuanced critique of present-day positions that intentionally do not take history into account or use selective or biased understandings of history as their base."[21] In other words, contemporary arguments using the language of just war reasoning can be critiqued based on how well they maintain continuity with the classic statement of that reasoning, which serves as a "compass" pointing in the general direction just war writing ought to go.[22]

As one example of a normative argument of the sort Johnson describes, two scholars have recently critiqued contemporary just war thinkers for their failure to endorse punitive war, which they understand as the paradigmatic just war of classical writing. Nigel Biggar identifies the "early Christian" (roughly, Augustine to Grotius) just war tradition as normative,[23] whereas Oliver O'Donovan's list of "the 'classic' just-war theorists" is somewhat shorter, including only the early modern theologians from Biggar's canon.[24] Both authors interpret these sources as presenting a description of just wars as essentially punitive. Biggar is careful to note the differences between various thinkers' positions on punitive war but concludes that, in spite of these distinctions, "all of the major representatives of early Christian tradition agree that just war is punitive."[25] O'Donovan argues that an understanding of just war as the enactment of a punitive judgment on a law-violating commonwealth was shared by early modern theologians concerned about how to address natural law violations by sovereign states.[26]

In the modern context, both moralists and international law experts have tended to allow only defensive, rather than punitive, justifications for war. The reasons for this shift are many, but two of the most important are the modern conception of states as equal sovereign entities without authority over other states and the fear that punitive wars may be less restrained than defensive ones. O'Donovan and Biggar argue, however, that attempts to reformulate the just war idea without reference to the punitive aspect of the classical just war are often incomplete and incoherent. For example, Biggar argues that, for the early Christian theologians, just war was a way to deal with the reality of human wickedness and to give both wrongdoers and victims of wrong their due; removing punishment from just war thinking leaves it incapable of responding to those initial motivations.[27] O'Donovan suggests that it was in fact the punitive aim of classical just war that put appropriate limits on war by restraining it to only what was deserved; thus, prohibiting punitive war in order to make war more limited is counterproductive.[28] Moreover, O'Donovan argues, the early modern emergence of sovereign states prompted the classical thinkers to formulate the idea of punitive just war as an analogy to law enforcement within states; without punishment, the analogy (and thus the justification for just war thinking) dissolves.[29]

In other words, for some tradition-focused just war ethicists, the problem with many contemporary just war arguments is not best described as a simple lack of faithfulness to the tradition in the sense that these arguments fail to restate classical positions or that they innovate too much. The more substantive critique they are making is that contemporary just war thinkers tend to be selective (to use Johnson's term) in their use of ideas from classical materials and that, in doing so, they sometimes leave behind pieces crucial for coherence. In these cases, thinkers like Johnson argue, the survival of just war reasoning as an effective tool for justly responding to world events is put at risk.

Islamic tradition-based ethics of war

Tradition-based approaches to the study of the ethics of war in the Islamic tradition have, by and large, focused on early Islamic history to deliberate questions related to the just use of force. This is the case in terms of both texts and contexts, as historical discourse on the proper use of force in Islam has referenced the Qur'an, the Hadith traditions, Islamic jurisprudence, and Muslim history as authoritative sources for determining when and how to use force, and for what purpose force ought to be used. Thus, it is useful to explicate these authoritative sources, and how they have worked together in Islamic just war thinking, in broad terms.

In the Islamic tradition, the primary mode for thinking through questions on the ethics of war has been that of Shariah, or Islamic law. Since its beginnings, Islamic law has been a fluid process of interpreting primary texts and traditional narratives with the aim of discerning the divine will. It encompasses a multitude of issues related to marriage, divorce, economics, ritual, politics, social relations, and so on. When Muhammad was alive, he was available to the early community of Muslims to answer questions related to the issues above. As he was deemed God's final emissary, the medium by which the Qur'an was communicated, and the "seal" of the (Abrahamic) prophets, Muslims believe that Muhammad had a unique connection to God. For this reason, his answers to the community's questions, his commentary on a series of doctrinal and ritualistic practices, and his own practice of Islam have been considered authoritative by Muslims both during his lifetime and after his death in 632 CE.

The Muslim community was then tasked with determining how to adjudicate the questions that would inevitably arise as the community grew and developed. Moreover, these questions became increasingly complicated as the territory under the jurisdiction of the Islamic Caliphate grew with tremendous speed and included Spain, North Africa, and parts of India at its height. Islamic jurisprudence began as a grassroots process, by which communities would turn to local figures whom they believed were the most learned in the Qur'an and in the Hadith. The latter were oral narratives, eventually compiled and codified into different collections that captured Muhammad's words, deeds, and behavior, and also those of other figures who knew him most intimately. The topics of these included Islamic belief and ritual (among other things). Muslims consider the Hadith, in light of Muhammad's unique connection to God, to be authoritative and normative models of Islamic piety. Over time, this process of local consultation and deliberation of the sources, while remaining largely local, became more formalized, with "study circles" of those interested in Islamic law developing into established schools of learning that were characterized by geographical context, intellectual leaders, and method.[30]

In Islam, tradition-based thinking on the just use of force is contained primarily within the sections of law that deal with the relations of Muslims with non-Muslims, or Muslims who rebel against Muslim authority. In terms of sources available in English, no figure has added more to our understanding of this component of Islamic law than Majid Khadduri, whose books (published in the 1950s) describe the *siyar*: the Islamic "law of nations."[31] One of the strengths of Khadduri's work is that it describes the development of this branch of Islamic law against the background of Islamic theories of war, peace, and statecraft. One of the theological conceptual foundations of the *siyar* was the *ummah*—the community of Muslims, to which all Muslims belonged. The *ummah* was characterized by "common obligations to a superior divine authority."[32] Muslims need the *ummah*, as both a theoretical and a material political community, as a necessary ingredient to live out the dictates of God. For this reason, Khadduri writes, the classical legal theory came into being with a global mission. Moreover, as he notes, the *siyar* developed during a period in which the Islamic empire was very successfully expanding its territory. Treaties were conducted, but expansion of the geographical territory of the empire, of the territory in which Muslims were in authority, was the goal.[33]

These juristic ideas and positions were developed in the midst of empire. Naturally, then, the fall of the Abbasid Empire, which the sack of Baghdad by the Mongols in 1258 CE epitomizes, and the break-up of Muslim land into a series of (often rival) empires and states led to significant changes in Islamic discourse on the nature of war. By the sixteenth century, the Islamic empire was comprised, by and large, of three separate entities: the Ottoman Empire, Persia, and Central Asia and India under the Mughals. These changes were later accompanied by increasing Western influence and power in Muslim-controlled territory that was mirrored by increasing recognition of Western (Christian) power on the part of Muslim rulers. Europe's post-Reformation shift to a "law of nations" did not originally include Muslim states. Over time, however, and because the Turkish sultans and the changing nature of the Turkish state from religious to national largely initiated it, there was the start of a domino of Muslim nation-states joining and participating in this international order such that Muslim-majority states are full and active members in international legal bodies and treaties.[34]

In the contemporary period, a variety of thinkers have investigated the materials described above to provide a better understanding of the juristic tradition and its positions on war, and also to make normative claims regarding how the Islamic tradition understood justice in war. Interest in these questions was taken up by a group of scholars in the academic study of religion in the late 1980s. John Kelsay and James Turner Johnson, who sought to bring together a group of academics working in both the Western just war tradition and the Islamic jihad tradition, started this work. The hope was to build bridges between the two traditions and to better understand points of similarity and points of difference between their respective historical discourses on the just use of force. The project produced a two-volume collection of essays that provide an early foundation for this work.

The essays focus on a common set of questions, including: Under what circumstances is the use of force justified? What restraints ought to be observed in war? What is the perspective of the tradition on irregular warfare, and how does it define non-combatancy?; and so on. Noteworthy is the fact that the essays stressed the importance of historical context to understanding ideas on warfare produced by these two traditions. Moreover, the essays sought to investigate and describe tradition-based just war ethics in Islam, and also to apply the tradition to contemporary issues and problems in war.

For example, Fred M. Donner asserts the importance of looking outside of the juristic tradition and its opinions for analyzing how Muslims have thought about the just use of force, arguing that the attempt to understand the "attitude" of Islamic civilization towards a "phenomenon as complex and as fundamental to human society as war" requires considering "how the Muslims of a particular time and place dealt with the vital questions of war and peace."[35] Richard C. Martin argues for the importance of the Qur'an and the Hadith (Sunnah) to understanding traditional perspectives on war and peace, but also emphasized the importance of investigating "Muslim worldviews and to social behavior as evinced by Muslims themselves in the course of history" as they seek to deliberate on questions of war and peace.[36] Tamara Sonn's essay seeks to answer why irregular war figures somewhat prominently within current Muslim-majority countries, in spite of the fact that Islam, by and large, prohibits it. She contends that understanding this phenomenon requires taking note of both the high value that Islam places on social and moral goods and that the revival of these values is the goal of many contemporary Islamic movements.[37]

The edited collection demonstrates an approach to the materials that has been maintained in the scholarship of those who have continued to work on tradition-based approaches to the ethics of war in Islam. John Kelsay's first book, *Islam and War*, was especially important in this regard. While certainly Kelsay is interested in international events at the time, particularly the Gulf War, he is more foundationally interested in gaining a perspective on the ethics of war in Islam that went beyond the Gulf War. The hope was to gain an historically grounded understanding of the role of Islam in statecraft, and the role of war within this framework. Importantly, Kelsay uses a comparative method which he described as

> the creation of a kind of comparative dialogue in the mind of the reader. Notions that are familiar (issues connected with the just war tradition) serve as benchmarks in the attempt to understand classical and contemporary Islamic notions of the justification and conduct of war.[38]

This book is interested in determining how the classical tradition described above could help shed light on the Islamic tradition's positions on a variety of issues related to war, including religion as a just cause for war, non-combatant immunity, and irregular wars, and to describe these alongside the same issues in the Western just war tradition. Most of the tradition-based work on Islamic just war ethics employs this approach of investigating the classical tradition in light of, and alongside of, modern problems.

Similar to the Western just war thinkers, those who are interested in tradition-based work on the ethics of war in Islam arrive at divergent positions regarding how people can or should apply the "classic" tradition in Islamic discourse on the use of force to contemporary issues and problems. An excellent example of this point is found in the work of Bassam Tibi and Sohail Hashmi.

Tibi contends that the Islamic tradition on war and peace faces an internal struggle. While, he argues, Muslim countries and institutions have "conformed" to "international standards of law and conduct and acceptance of peaceful relations with non-Islamic countries," they remain committed to "the traditional Islamic belief in the superiority of Islam and the division of the world into Islamic and non-Islamic realms."[39] Such ideas, he argues, run "counter to a pluralist, secular international society."[40] So, while there is "acquiescence" to the current international system of nation-states, there remains no real effort to engage in the type of "cultural accommodation" that, he argues, is a necessary precursor to true acceptance, and not only conformity. What is necessary is a rethinking of the traditional categories such that the tradition can accept a "more universal law regulating war and peace" that would take the place of the classic categories.[41]

Hashmi, on the other hand, responds directly to Tibi's thinking, arguing that his investigation of the classic juristic position on these issues, as well as the way that contemporary Muslim thinkers have thought about them, leads him to a different conclusion. Hashmi contends that the "classic" tradition contains, internally, points of consonance with the norms and laws of the international system.[42] Moreover, thinkers that Tibi refers to as "conformists" have, in fact, demonstrated this point in ways that are much deeper than Tibi recognizes. The discourse on jihad, Hashmi argues, like the international system, is based on the idea that peace is the ideal in regard to conduct between societies. War was to be used only in circumstances in which Islam could not be preached, or, at times, propagated (notably, he mentions that, during the thirteen-year period Muhammad was in Medina, he never advocated for the use of force, not even in self-defense). Moreover, he continues, most Muslims today, including a variety of influential thinkers (he discusses Mohammad Talaat al-Ghunaimi and Muhammad Abu Zahra as examples), reject the idea that Muslims have a duty to propagate Islam (through force if necessary) and contend that war is justified only in self-defense.

Of course, part of the contention is the various ways that tradition-focused thinkers understand what the "tradition" entails. Asma Afsaruddin (2013), in particular, helps draw out this point. As she notes, much of the juristic tradition regarding war or jihad was developed during the Umayyad and Abbasid Empires—empires that were particularly focused on territorial expansion. Those jurists close to the seat of power formed juristic opinions that demonstrate a more military-friendly interpretation of jihad. However, she notes, the consultation of a wider variety of sources demonstrates that "jihad" was a term whose meaning was contested and that the tendency to describe it as armed combat is an interpretation that was certainly not static, but rather subject to contestation and debate. Similar to tradition-focused ethicists in the Western just war tradition, those who work on these issues in Islam do not agree on what constitutes the heart of the tradition.

Limits of the tradition-based approach

Tradition-focused ethicists make a significant contribution to the study of ethics of war, deepening our understanding of the ways these historical traditions of argument have informed and shaped contemporary scholarship and policy-making. Increased knowledge of these historical sources and their contexts enables more critical analysis of contemporary arguments and policies. As many of the authors surveyed above have argued, people may find an understanding of these traditions also useful in justifying contemporary normative positions. There are potential downsides, however, of this strategy, which have led to sometimes contentious debates.

One possible limit of tradition-based ethics of war is that a focus on historical contributions may lead to a tendency to resist change and adaptation in response to new circumstances. The US Conference of Catholic Bishops, for instance, has argued that modern warfare presents a new set of harms (including, especially, nuclear weapons) requiring a new moral response.[43] Similarly, some argue that contemporary trends, including the proliferation of non-state actors using armed force and the use of targeted killing against those actors, require new forms of moral reasoning about authority in war.[44] Johnson responds that the basic facts of human political conflict have not changed, even if technology has, so that traditional just war arguments remain relevant.[45] Those who agree that modern war is morally different from medieval war in one way or another are likely to see tradition-based ethics of war as limited in its applicability to contemporary conflicts. The previously described exchange between Tibi and Hashmi also demonstrates this point. For Tibi, the classic categories are unworkable in the contemporary environment, as they are based on an anarchic understanding of the role of Islam in international affairs. For Hashmi, however, there is more to be mined within those classic categories—such that were the tradition to be investigated from a different perspective, categories and values contained within historical Islamic discourse on the use of force include points of congruence to those of international law and the Western just war tradition.

A second debate has concerned whether tradition-based ethics can successfully ground critique. If justification for moral positions comes from appeal to traditional sources rather than to universal norms, is it ever possible to deem an act or position wrong so long as there is traditional precedent for it? Richard B. Miller raises this question in his critique of Kelsay's work on contemporary Islamist militants. For Miller, it is important to say that when militants target non-combatants, their actions are wrong in a universal sense: as a violation of human rights. Only when equipped with this sort of universal principle of non-combatant immunity can non-Muslims, who do not share the view that the Shariah tradition is authoritative, adequately express their indignation at militant Islamists who target non-combatants.[46] Those seeking a universal ethics of war are likely to find the tradition-based approach unsatisfying.

Finally, ethicists who employ the concept of a "classic" tradition—whether in the Western or the Islamic context—face a particular set of challenges. One issue we have addressed in previous work is the difficulty in identifying one statement, or one school of thought, of just war reasoning as the classic or normative one.[47] There is a paradoxical tension inherent in simultaneously organizing one's studies around the reconstruction of a tradition, which implies a long history of presumably differing arguments and positions, and identifying one particular moment in that tradition as having justificatory authority. This tension can result in reconstructing a moral tradition as a monolith—as a single stream moving in one consistent direction over time, with divergences from that stream seen as deviant, unorthodox, and therefore wrong. In reality, of course, any moral tradition stretching over centuries will be marked by points of confluence as well as points of debate and contestation. The use of the term "classic tradition" can in some cases be used to mask this diversity or to deny that particular thinkers are truly part of the tradition to which they see themselves as contributing.

The idea of a "classic" tradition relates to two other potential downsides to this approach. One is that accounts of the classic statement of any moral tradition, including the just war and jihad traditions, are likely to focus on the writings of elites: highly educated men in positions of social and political favor. The voices of dissenters, of minorities, and of women will often be excluded; tradition-focused ethicists may thus unwittingly reproduce—rather than critically analyze—the structures of authority in the moral communities they study. Additionally, tradition-based ethicists who use arguments of historical elites as their primary source for contemporary arguments will very often be relying on work that was originally produced in support of colonialist or imperialist projects. For this reason, critics like Talal Asad suggest that the concept of "just war," for example, is inherently imperialist; as noted above, given the position of many significant jurists in imperial contexts, the same could be alleged of "jihad."[48]

The second challenge is that disagreements inevitably arise regarding who is getting the normative tradition "right." This difficulty applies first to the question of which thinkers and which historical time periods ought to be considered classical. For example, as described above, Johnson, Biggar, and O'Donovan each present slightly different canons under the label of classic just war tradition. Moreover, even when ethicists agree that a particular figure or group is "classic," they may disagree on how their work ought to be interpreted. So, though ethicists representing many different interests agree that Thomas Aquinas, for instance, ought to be regarded as a classic and traditional just war thinker, there is strong ongoing debate over some of the most basic aspects of Thomas's writings on war. The best known of these controversies regards whether Thomas may be properly said to have endorsed a presumption against war.[49] These inevitable variations in interpretation mean that even those tradition-focused ethicists who share a canon of classic thinkers are likely to disagree on the precise content of that canonical work. In light of contemporary international events, such as the rise of organizations like al-Qaeda and ISIS, there has been an increased level of discourse within the Islamic tradition regarding who is "getting it (the tradition) right." Figures like Khaled Abou El Fadl, for example, argue that "Muslim puritans" (of the Osama bin Laden variety) have hijacked Islam and corrupted the tradition's position on war.[50]

Such contestation is part and parcel of any tradition and has been a feature of both Western and Islamic juridical and interpretive thinking on the use of force (among other issues) throughout their histories. Thus, while the inevitable debate over whose interpretation is most justified might be seen as a limitation of tradition-based approaches, the very fact that moral traditions are so often invoked to justify competing moral claims itself points to the importance of taking tradition seriously. Only with some knowledge of the diversity and development of the tradition can in question can one provide a sufficiently critical account of such claims and their place in the ongoing debates within these communities. Traditions as rich and complex as those of Western and Islamic thinking on the just use of force certainly cannot be truncated to any one position. Quite the opposite, it is the multifarious nature of these traditions that has allowed them to retain their importance and relevance throughout their respective histories.

Notes

1 Alasdair MacIntyre, *After Virtue: A Study in Moral Theory*, 3rd edn. (Notre Dame: University of Notre Dame Press, 2007), 146.

2 This is not to suggest that all Christian just war thinkers take a tradition-based approach. Some prominent recent examples of those who do not include Jean Bethke Elshtain, Paul Ramsey, and the United States Conference of Catholic Bishops, all of whom cited historical figures in their writing, but did not use tradition itself as a primary source of justification for their arguments.

3 For a more thorough analysis of how Thomas employed citation of authoritative figures in his arguments, see: Servais-Théodore Pinckaers, "The Sources of the Ethics of St. Thomas Aquinas," trans. Mary Thomas Noble, in *The Ethics of Aquinas*, ed. Stephen J. Pope (Washington, DC: Georgetown University Press, 2002).

4 The second of these anthologies also includes primary texts from non-Western traditions of the ethics of war. See: Gregory M. Reichberg, Henrik Syse, and Endre Begby, eds., *The Ethics of War: Classic and Contemporary Readings* (Malden, MA: Blackwell, 2006); Gregory M. Reichberg, Henrik Syse, and Nicole M. Hartwell, eds., *Religion, War, and Ethics: A Sourcebook of Textual Traditions* (Cambridge: Cambridge University Press, 2014).

5 See, for example, his discussion of the concept of punishment in classical just war writings: Gregory M. Reichberg, "Culpability and Punishment in Classical Theories of Just War," *Just War: Authority, Tradition, and Practice*, ed. Anthony F. Lang, Jr, Cian O'Driscoll, and John Williams (Washington, DC: Georgetown University Press, 2013).

6 Reichberg explicitly states this self-imposed limit on his writing in the introduction to his article clarifying "classical" just war positions on the moral equality (or lack thereof, as it were) of combatants as well as in his article on whether contemporary Catholic positions on just war continue or break from classical ones (2012, 1974). See: Gregory M. Reichberg, "The Moral Equality of Combatants—A Doctrine in Classical Just War Theory? A Response to Graham Parsons," *Journal of Military Ethics*, 12, no. 2 (2013): 182; Gregory M. Reichberg, "Discontinuity in Catholic Just War Teaching? From Aquinas to the Contemporary Popes," *Nova et Vetera*, 10, no. 4 (2012): 1074. As another example, see: Gregory M. Reichberg, "Thomas Aquinas between Just War and Pacifism," *Journal of Religious Ethics*, 38, no. 2 (2010): 219–241.

7 Alex Bellamy, *Just Wars: From Cicero to Iraq* (Cambridge: Polity Press, 2006), 30.

8 Ibid., 5.

9 Ibid., 180.

10 Lisa Sowle Cahill, *Love Your Enemies: Discipleship, Pacifism, and Just War Theory* (Minneapolis: Augsburg Fortress, 1994).

11 Ibid., 238.

12 Ibid., 238.

13 James Turner Johnson, *The War to Oust Saddam Hussein: Just War and the New Face of Conflict* (Lanham, MD: Rowman & Littlefield, 2005), 16; James Turner Johnson, *Ethics and the Use of Force: Just War in Historical Perspective* (Surrey, Canada: Ashgate, 2011), 15–20.

14 Johnson argues that this historical approach is particularly important in the study of Jewish and Christian ethics, due to the historical nature of values themselves within those traditions: in Jewish and Christian ethics, "moral values have derived from historical experience within the community of faith" and so "ethical guidance comes from the effort to keep one's own reflections and decisions faithful to those of others who have gone before and whose examples are remembered by the believing community as normative ways of doing the will of God." James Turner Johnson, "On Keeping Faith: The Use of History for Religious Ethics," *Journal of Religious Ethics*, 7, no. 1 (1979): 98–99.

15 Ibid., 102, 112.

16 Ibid., 111; James Turner Johnson, "Moral Traditions and Religious Ethics: A Comparative Enquiry," *Journal of Religious Ethics*, 25, no. 3 (1997), 78.

17 Johnson, "Moral Traditions and Religious Ethics," 98.

18 Johnson, "On Keeping Faith," 114; Johnson, "Moral Traditions and Religious Ethics," 98.

19 James Turner Johnson, *Morality and Contemporary Warfare* (New Haven: Yale University Press, 1999), 7.

20 James Turner Johnson, *The Quest for Peace: Three Moral Traditions in Western Cultural History* (Princeton: Princeton University Press, 1987), 284.

21 Johnson, *Ethics and the Use of Force*, 11–12.

22 Ibid., 34; see also: Johnson, *The War to Oust Saddam*, 23–41.

23 Nigel Biggar, *In Defence of War* (Oxford: Oxford University Press, 2013), 151.

24 According to O'Donovan, the early modern just war thinkers built on the "undeveloped" ideas of medieval thinkers like Thomas but adapted those ideas for a context more similar to our own: a world in which sovereign nation-states are the primary actors. Oliver O'Donovan, *The Just War Revisited* (Cambridge: Cambridge University Press, 2003), 11.

25 Biggar, *Defence of War*, 163–164.

26 O'Donovan, *Just War Revisited*.

27 Biggar, *Defence of War*, 11, 140, 256.

28 O'Donovan, *Just War Revisited*, 53, 58.

29 Ibid., 57.

30 As can be generalized from this sketch, Sunni jurisprudence has always been characterized by diversity of juristic opinions regarding how to determine the divine will or commandments. That said, the Islamic legal tradition did develop an interpretive approach called *usul al-fiqh* (sources or roots of jurisprudence). Although the method within usul al-fiqh varies, there is a certain level of agreement regarding which sources are part of Islamic jurisprudence understood in this way. These are the Qur'an, the Sunna or Hadith (described above), Ijma (consensus of the community), Qiyas (a deductive process of analogy by which new rulings, not explicitly discussed in the textual sources, are derived from past events or issues

that are discussed in the Qur'an or Hadith), and Istihsan (a process in which a jurist chooses one ruling over another based on learned preference). The major Sunni schools of law are differentiated, by and large, by the sources that they tend to prioritize in the process of deriving jurisprudence. For sources related to the development of Islamic law, see: Wael B. Hallaq, *An Introduction to Islamic Law* (Cambridge: Cambridge University Press, 2009) and Joseph Schacht, *An Introduction to Islamic Law* (Oxford: Oxford University Press, 1983).

31 Majid Khadduri, *War and Peace in the Law of Islam* (Clark, NJ: The Lawbook Exchange, 2010 [1955]).

32 Ibid., 4.

33 Ibid., Book I, Book II. While these ideas can be assumed to root the work of the classical Islamic jurists on war, it is notable that there was just as much disagreement as agreement on the issue of war. This can be noted when one investigates the different rulings of the jurists on issues related to warfare. Rulings on targeting help demonstrate this point. As Nesrine Badawi demonstrates in the Reichberg edited collection mentioned above, most jurists agreed that there were categories of people that ought not to be killed in war (what we would refer to today as "noncombatants"). There were differences, however, regarding which categories of people were considered to be of the group that could not be intentionally targeted in war. For example, Malik, al-Shaybani, and Ibn Qudama argued that women, children, the elderly, or others unrelated to the hostilities (such as monks) ought not to be targeted. They based their opinion on a series of hadiths in which Muhammad prohibited the slaying of women, children, the elderly, and others who were unable to participate in the fighting. Al-Shafi'i and Ibn Hazm, on the other hand, were of the opinion that all adult males (except for monks) could be targeted and killed intentionally. Moreover, those who were a part of the categories of noncombatants would lose their protected status if they were to participate in the fighting or offer other forms of support. See Nesrine Badawi, "Sunni Islam, Part I: Classical Sources" in Reichberg, Syse, and Hartwell, *Religion, War, and Ethics*, 327–333. The same type of agreement and disagreement is found on a variety of issues related to warfare among the four major Sunni schools of law in the classical period. As noted by Badawi, "there is a general tendency to accept the legitimacy of offensive warfare for the promotion of religion" among the juristic works (2014, 315).

34 For a discussion of these changes, see: Khadduri, *War and Peace in the Law of Islam*, 268–296. For a book-length treatment of the changes in the doctrine of jihad over time, see: Rudolph Peters, *Jihad in Classical and Modern Islam* (Princeton: Markus Wiener Publishers, 1996).

35 John Kelsay and James Turner Johnson, eds., *Just War and Jihad: Historical and Theoretical Perspectives on War and Peace in Western and Islamic Traditions* (Westport, CT: Greenwood Press, 1991), 32.

36 Richard C. Martin, "The Religious Foundations of War, Peace, and Statecraft in Islam," in Kelsay and Johnson, *Just War and Jihad*, 91.

37 Tamara Sonn, "Irregular Warfare and Terrorism in Islam," in *Cross, Crescent, and Sword: The Justification and Limitation of War in Western and Islamic Tradition*, ed. James Turner Johnson and John Kelsay (Westport, CT: Greenwood Press, 1990), 129–147.

38 John Kelsay, *Islam and War: A Study in Comparative Ethics* (Louisville: Westminster/John Knox Press, 1993), 2.

39 Bassam Tibi, "War and Peace in Islam," in *The Ethics of War and Peace: Religious and Secular Perspectives*, ed. Terry Nardin (Princeton: Princeton University Press, 1996), 134.

40 Ibid., 135.

41 Ibid., 140.

42 Sohail Hashmi, "Interpreting the Islamic Ethics of War and Peace," in *The Ethics of War and Peace: Religious and Secular Perspectives*, ed. Terry Nardin (Princeton: Princeton University Press, 1996), 146–166.

43 United States Conference of Catholic Bishops, "The Challenge of Peace" (1983) http://www.usccb.org/upload/challenge-peace-gods-promise-our-response-1983.pdf, accessed August 24, 2016.

44 For example, see: Michael Walzer, "On Fighting Terrorism Justly," *International Relations*, 21, no. 4 (2007): 480–484.

45 Johnson, *Morality and Contemporary Warfare*, 51, 223.

46 Richard B. Miller, *Terror, Religion, and Liberal Thought* (New York: Columbia University Press, 2010), 23–24.

47 Nahed Artoul Zehr, "James Turner Johnson and the 'Classic' Just War Tradition," *Journal of Military Ethics*, 8, no. 3 (2009): 190–201; Rosemary B. Kellison, "Tradition, Authority, and Immanent Critique in Comparative Ethics," *Journal of Religious Ethics*, 42, no. 4 (2014): 713–741; see also: Cian O'Driscoll, "Hedgehog or Fox? An Essay on James Turner Johnson's View of History," *Journal of Military Ethics*, 8, no. 3 (2009): 165–178.

48 Talal Asad, "Thinking about Terrorism and Just War," *Cambridge Review of International Affairs*, 23, no. 1 (2010): 3–24.

49 For those who argue that Thomas did in fact begin his ethics of war with a presumption against the use of violence, see: Alex Bellamy, *Just Wars*, 38; Cahill, *Love Your Enemies*, 197; and Richard B. Miller, "Aquinas and the Presumption against Killing and War," *Journal of Religion*, 82, no. 2 (2002): 173–204. For those who reject that interpretation of Thomas, see: Scott Davis, *Believing and Acting: The Pragmatic Turn in Comparative Religion and Ethics* (New York: Oxford University Press, 2012), 162–174; and Reichberg, "Is There a 'Presumption against War' in Aquinas's Ethics?," in *Ethics, Nationalism, and Just War: Medieval and Contemporary Perspectives*, ed. Henrik Syse and Gregory M. Reichberg (Washington: Catholic University of America Press, 2007), 72–98. Johnson, who also rejects this interpretation, argues that such a presumption cannot be found in any classic just war writings: Johnson, *Ethics and the Use of Force*, 43.

50 Khaled Abou El Fadl, *The Great Theft: Wrestling Islam from the Extremists* (New York: HarperCollins, 2005).

15

HOW SHOULD JUST WAR THEORY BE REVISED?

Reductive versus relational individualism

John W. Lango

Revisionisms

Some wars are just, and some wars are unjust. A goal of just war theorizing is to formulate and support just war principles, by means of which we could determine whether a given war is just or unjust.[1] Usually, principles governing the resort to war (i.e., *jus ad bellum* principles) are distinguished from principles governing the conduct of war (i.e., *jus in bello* principles). Examples of the former are a just cause principle and a last resort principle, and an example of the latter is a noncombatant immunity principle.[2]

The title of this chapter suggests that there is a single received just war theory, but instead there are different received just war theories. Indeed, a historian might write a narrative history about how different persons have theorized morally about wars and construct thereby a historical account of a just war tradition, within which such moral theorizing might be causally or doctrinally interrelated. Further, by means of a historical analysis in search of common elements, this historian might construct an idealized theory, something that no single person ever devised—namely, the traditional just war theory. How should the traditional just war theory be revised?[3]

We might obtain one answer to such a question from a reading of the most influential twentieth-century writing about the ethics of war—namely, Michael Walzer's *Just and Unjust Wars*.[4] Startlingly, Walzer epitomizes his revisionism thus: "Nuclear weapons explode the theory of just war."[5] Noting the word *the* in this quotation, we might construe it as implying that there is a single received just war theory. Helen Frowe classifies Walzer's own theory of just and unjust wars as a collectivist just war theory because it understands war as "a relationship not between persons, but between collectives."[6] How should Walzer's collectivist just war theory be revised?

In the modern world, the primary, or dominant, collectives are states. Arguably, a traditional just war theory today should be a theory about the justice or injustice of wars between states. Similarly, traditional international relations (IR) theory has been state-centric (e.g., the concept of balance of power), as has traditional international legal theory. Arguably, for instance, the only just cause for an interstate war is defense against aggression. Note that the UN Charter acknowledges "the inherent right of individual or collective self-defence if an armed attack occurs."[7] Moreover, a conception of last resort is embodied in the UN Charter, for the use of armed force is permitted only when nonmilitary measures "would be inadequate or have proved to be inadequate."[8] How, in particular, should state-centric just war theories be revised?[9]

In opposition to collectivist approaches to just war theory, several contemporary just war theorists—for instance, Jeff McMahan[10] and Helen Frowe[11]—advocate for an individualist approach. Roughly, according to an individualist, a just war theory should be centered, not on states or other collectives, but on individual human beings. How should an individualist revise either traditional just war theory or Walzer's revisionist just war theory?

Some just war theorists take a historical approach to just war theory.[12] By contrast, in accordance with analytic political philosophy generally, individualist just war theorists take a conceptual approach and often feature a problem of justification—roughly, how can just war principles be grounded, not historically in a just war tradition, but rather conceptually in abstract principles of moral philosophy?[13] The question of whether traditional just war theory should be revised is of great importance, and the intriguing answers by individualists are well worth careful study.

In this brief chapter, I focus on Frowe's individualist just war theory. Her books *The Ethics of War and Peace* and *Defensive Killing* are cogent and illuminating. Her reflective claims about her theory are particularly instructive. For lack of space, I am unable to compare intelligibly her views with the views of other individualist just war theorists. My assumption is that her theory is sufficiently representative of an individualist approach to just war theory.

Preview

To begin with, let me introduce Frowe's "central claim." She claims that "the rules governing killing in war can be reduced to the rules governing defensive killing between individuals."[14] The word *reduced* is significant. Her approach to just war theory is both individualist and reductionist, which she appropriately labels as "reductive individualism."[15] "Reductive individualism is a revisionary approach to just war theory."[16] "The central claim of reductionism [i.e. reductive individualism] is that the moral rules of war are the moral rules of ordinary life."[17] Specifically, "the rules that govern killing in war are reducible to the rules governing interpersonal killing in ordinary life."[18] In summary, I take the central claim of Frowe's reductive-individualist approach to just war theory to be this: We can reduce the moral rules governing killing in war to the moral rules governing interpersonal killing in ordinary life. Note that such reduction is a mode of justification. Instead of being grounded historically in a just war tradition, these moral rules governing killing in war are grounded conceptually in abstract principles of moral philosophy.

Although Frowe's reflective claims about her theory are instructive, they are few in number and brief in content. In this chapter, I attempt to explicate her central claim. What should be meant by the term "reduced"? Also, I attempt to explicate another of her main claims, one that I take to be comparably important—namely, that an "assumption" of her theory is "that there are domestic situations that are relevantly similar to war."[19] What should be meant by the term "relevantly similar"? In general, the following question is explored: What is a reductive-individualist just war theory (briefly, a reductive theory)?

Revealingly, Frowe asserts in *Defensive Killing* that she did not intend "to offer a full reductivist account of just war theory."[20] In explicating her central claim and the other main claim, my purpose is twofold. First, I hope to contribute to the project of developing a fuller reductive theory. Second, as the subtitle of this chapter indicates, I want to outline an alternative individualist account—namely, a relational-individualist just war theory (briefly, a relational theory)—for I would classify my own approach to just war theory as both revisionist and individualist.[21] However, I am skeptical about reductionism. Reductionist projects in philosophy have been problematic (e.g., the reduction of material bodies to sense-data, or the reduction of mental phenomena to brain processes).

Relations matter. The combat between Achilles and Hector in Homer's *Iliad* is not archetypal of modern combats between individual soldiers. A scenario, whether of war or of ordinary life, in which one individual defends against one attacking individual is quite misleading. Additionally, there should be scenarios in which several individuals defend together against several other individuals who attack together. The togetherness of individuals matters. To theorize about such groups of interrelated individuals is not to conceptualize these groups simply as collectives. Therefore, before contemplating abstractly the question of how a reductive theory should be revised, I think that it is helpful to have a concrete illustration of how relations matter. In the next section, I sketch an imaginary, but realistic, combat scenario, in which relations between individual combatants matter. In subsequent sections, this scenario serves to illustrate.

I also find it helpful to utilize, as illustrations of moral rules governing killing in war, some just war principles of last resort. For clarity and simplicity, I formulate these principles briefly and roughly.[22] Readers who are dubious about last resort principles might utilize different moral rules as illustrations, for my main line of argument is mostly concerned abstractly with moral rules generally.

The subject of reductionism versus antireductionism is complex and controversial. In this brief chapter, I am unable to consider various accounts of reductionism, or various accounts of antireductionism (e.g., emergentism). Instead, there is only space for a few general comments. The account of reductionism that I am presupposing is relatively straightforward.

Usually, theory reduction (e.g., the reduction of Kepler's laws to Newton's laws) is distinguished from ontological reduction (e.g., the reduction of substances to events). In a particular reductive-individualist just war theory, there might be both theory reduction and ontological reduction. When critically examining that reductive theory, it is essential to disentangle various reductive claims. In explicating the central claim of Frowe's reductive theory, I distinguish three different reductive claims, which I discuss respectively in three sections below.

In conclusion, let me preview my own central claim: ethicists can derive both the moral rules governing killing in war and the moral rules governing interpersonal killing in ordinary life from universal moral principles governing individual human actions. When a group of individual humans acts, actions of those individual humans are interrelated. Moral constraints on that group action can be derived from moral constraints on the interrelated actions of those individual humans. My approach may be called a derivativist approach. Reductionism and derivationism are different.

A combat scenario of armed humanitarian intervention

I am presupposing that moral rules governing killing in war should be applicable, not only to interstate wars, but also to wars of other types, including armed conflicts within states and armed humanitarian interventions.[23] Frequently, during armed conflicts within states, noncombatants flee combat zones. Paradigmatically, a goal of an armed humanitarian intervention in an internal armed conflict is to establish and defend safe havens for fleeing noncombatants.

As background for my imaginary combat scenario, let me suppose, hypothetically, that genocide is occurring in Host Nation (HN), that a small bands of insurgents is perpetrating this genocide, that these insurgents have various types of weapons (including Toyota pickup trucks armed with heavy machine guns), that HN is unwilling or unable to stop the genocide effectively, that the UN Security Council (SC) authorizes (with HN's consent) a UN peace operation (UNMHN) to intervene in HN, that UNMHN has a Chapter VII mandate from the SC that permits (under specified circumstances) the use of armed force, that a goal of UNMHN is to establish safe havens for fleeing noncombatants, that UNMHN is permitted to use armed force to defend these safe havens, and that UNMHN is supplied with various types of weapons (including surplus US M1 Abrams Army Tanks).

With this background, let me imagine a combat scenario—namely, Abrams tank's defense against an armed Toyota truck's attack: The task of the tank is to defend a remote safe haven. The tank is parked on the safe haven's perimeter. Suddenly, a truck is spotted, speeding toward the safe haven, its heavy machine gun blazing, with the goal of massacring noncombatants. The tank fires, and the truck explodes.

If collectivists understand an interstate war as a relationship between states, they might understand such a combat as a relationship between manned vehicles. Indeed, individualists might object that the scenario is sketched too briefly. Standardly, an Abrams tank has a crew of four: a commander, a driver, a gunner, and a loader. For symmetry, imagine that the armed Toyota truck also has a crew of four (although there is no standard crew size): a driver and a commander in each truck cab and a gunner and a loader in each truck bed, where a heavy machine gun is mounted.

Accordingly, with the same background, let me imagine a revised combat scenario—namely, a defense by the crew members of an Abrams tank against an attack by the crew members of an armed Toyota truck: The tank's crew members are tasked with the defense of the noncombatants residing in a remote safe haven. As the commander has commanded, the driver has driven the tank to the perimeter of the safe haven, and parked it. Suddenly, an insurgent-commanded truck is spotted, its driver speeding it toward the noncombatants in the safe haven, and its gunner (assisted by a loader) firing a heavy machine gun virtually uninterruptedly, with the goal of massacring noncombatants. The tank driver drives the tank quickly to a higher position, the loader quickly loads the main gun, the gunner directs it to the target, and the commander commands the gunner to fire. The truck explodes, killing the crew members.

In this tank-truck scenario, relations matter. Let me make some remarks about the tank crew, but comparable remarks hold of the truck crew. As the definite descriptions that identify them (e.g., "the" commander) implies, the members of the tank crew are interrelated by means of their functions in operating the tank (e.g., the function of commander). These four crew members operate the tank together. Their togetherness matters. The gunner is the proximate human cause of the firing of the main gun, but there is a wider causal network in terms of which it can be said that the four crew members fire the main gun together. Each member of the crew, together with the other crew members, operate the tank, so as to mount a defense against the attacking truck crew, with the goal of defending the noncombatants in the safe haven.

There is a deeper level of analysis. Indeed, the tank's crew members are functionally interrelated, and they are causally interrelated, but they are interrelated also by means of their actions. Each member of the tank crew intentionally performs actions that are interrelated with actions performed intentionally by other members of the tank crew. An intentional action is performed for the sake of a goal. The driver performs the intentional action of driving the tank, with the goal of destroying the truck; the loader performs the intentional action of loading the main gun, with the goal of destroying the truck; the commander performs the intentional action of commanding the gunner to fire, with the goal of destroying the truck; and the gunner performs the intentional action of firing the main gun, with the goal of destroying the truck. Their intentional actions of driving, loading, commanding, and firing are interrelated as means of achieving the goal of destroying the truck. Together, the members of the tank crew intentionally perform interrelated actions that result in the destruction of the truck, for the sake of the further goal of protecting the noncombatants in the safe haven.

A scenario of interpersonal killing in ordinary life

The central claim of a reductive theory is that the moral rules governing killing in war can be reduced to the moral rules governing interpersonal killing in ordinary life. For clarity and simplicity, I discuss particularly a single moral rule that (arguably) governs killing in war—namely, a military last resort principle (briefly, the MLR principle)—which we can formulate (briefly and roughly) as follows: Before resorting to a use of lethal military force, every reasonable nonmilitary measure must be attempted. Correlatively, I discuss particularly a single moral rule that (arguably) governs interpersonal killing in ordinary life—namely, an ordinary-life last resort principle (briefly, the OLR principle)—which we will formulate (briefly and roughly) thus: Before an ordinary person resorts to a use of lethal force against another ordinary person, he or she must attempt every reasonable nonlethal measure. Accordingly, my hypothesis is that, in a reductive theory, the MLR principle can be reduced to the OLR principle.

To test this hypothesis, I propose to compare the tank-truck scenario with the following interpersonal-killing scenario of ordinary life. You are an ordinary person in a well-ordered state. You are not a police officer, nor do you hold any other office that empowers you to use lethal force. But you are licensed to carry a concealed hand gun. Suddenly, an attacker lunges toward you, brandishing a large knife. It is clear that the attacker intends deadly harm. You draw your hand gun. Your defense against this lethal attack is governed by the OLR principle. Is there a reasonable nonlethal measure that you are morally required to attempt? You judge that the attacker is sufficiently distant, that there is sufficient time, and that a reasonable nonlethal measure is to wave your hand gun, fire a warning shot, and shout out, "Drop your knife, or I'll shoot!" (On the other hand, if the attacker were too close, and there were not sufficient time, such a measure would not be reasonable.) The attacker drops the knife and flees. By not shooting, and attempting the nonlethal measure successfully, you satisfy the OLR principle. Let me call this the gun–knife scenario. Such a scenario may be classified as a sufficient-time scenario.

By contrast, we could classify the tank-truck scenario as a rapid-reaction scenario. In that scenario, there is not sufficient time. It is not reasonable for the tank crew to fire a warning shot and shout out on a loudspeaker, "Stop firing your machine guns, or we'll shoot to kill!" Initially, when the truck is speeding toward the safe haven, its heavy machine gun blazing, there is no reasonable nonmilitary measure for the tank crew to attempt. When the main gun is fired by the tank crew—thereby destroying the truck and killing its crew—the MLR principle is satisfied.

In comparing the two scenarios, my purpose is to test the hypothesis that the MLR principle can be reduced to the OLR principle. On the one hand, under the circumstances of the gun–knife scenario, the OLR principle morally prohibits a lethal defense. On the other hand, under the circumstances of the tank-truck scenario, the MLR principle does not morally prohibit a lethal defense. This significant difference between prohibiting and not prohibiting suggests that the hypothesis might be false.

Apparently, the central claim of a reductive theory cannot be readily established simply by comparing war scenarios and ordinary-life scenarios. The particular circumstances of the tank-truck scenario are very different than the particular circumstances of the gun–knife scenario. How can there be such a reduction, if circumstances in war are very different than circumstances in ordinary life?

Three reductive claims

My conjecture is that we need to clarify or rectify the central claim of a reductive theory. An obscure reductive claim might be clarified by analytically subdividing it into a series of clearer reductive claims, or it might be rectified by replacing it with a series of clearer reductive claims. The central claim uses the phrase "killing in war" without distinguishing killing in war by groups from killing in war by individuals. Therefore, I propose to clarify it (or rectify it) by analytically subdividing it into (or replacing it by) three reductive claims, which are stated in the next paragraph. (For my purposes here, my belief is that I do not need to decide whether I am clarifying it or rectifying it.) In summary, my central-claim conjecture is that the central claim of a reductive theory needs to be clarified (or rectified) by means of the following three reductive claims.

First, there is a claim of ontological reduction—namely, that a group can be reduced to its individual members, and that actions of a group can be reduced to actions of its individual members. Second, there is a claim of theory reduction—namely, that moral rules governing actions of killing by a group in war can be reduced to moral rules governing actions of killing by individual combatants in war. Third, there is a second claim of theory reduction—namely, that moral rules governing actions of killing by individual combatants in war can be reduced to moral rules governing actions of killing by individual persons in ordinary life. In the next three sections, these three reductive claims are respectively discussed. I am especially skeptical about the third reductive claim.

My central-claim conjecture involves two different claims of theory reduction. In writing the two sections about these two claims, my plan is to highlight parallels between them, while displaying why they differ significantly. One is a claim about reducing moral rules governing combatants as a group to moral rules governing identically the same combatants individually. (The term "identical" is a technical term. It means numerically identical. For instance, Mark Twain and Samuel Langhorne Clemens are identically the same person.) By contrast, the other is a claim about reducing moral rules governing combatants individually to moral rules governing ordinary persons individually—but these combatants are not identically the same as these ordinary persons. Nevertheless, these combatants and these ordinary persons must still be relevantly similar. Recall Frowe's assumption "that there are domestic situations that are relevantly similar to war."[24]

Can a group be reduced to its individual members?

Is a group nothing but its members? Is a group action nothing but actions of its members? (Compare the reductive claim of resemblance nominalism that a universal is nothing but a set of resembling particulars.) The phrase "nothing but" epitomizes an antirealist approach to the question of the ontological status of groups and their actions. By contrast, according to a realist approach to that question, some groups are real entities that are distinct from their members. These two approaches may be illustrated by means of the tank-truck scenario: an antirealist would claim that the tank crew is nothing but the commander, the driver, the gunner, and the loader; whereas a realist might claim that, in addition to those four individual combatants, there is a fifth real entity—namely, the tank-crew group.

There is an analogous question about the ontological status of molecules: Is a molecule nothing but atoms? For instance, is a carbon dioxide molecule nothing but one carbon atom and two oxygen atoms? A realist about molecules might claim that, in addition to the three atoms, there is a fourth real entity—namely, the chemical compound (i.e., the carbon dioxide molecule) that is produced when the three atoms are combined together by chemical bonds. As related in the scenario, when the four crew members destroy the truck, they are combined together by their interrelated intentional actions.

Analogous to the realist claim about molecules, a realist about groups might claim that, in addition to the members of a group, there is a real entity—namely, the group (i.e., a human compound) that is produced when those members are combined together by their interrelated intentional actions. Analogous to chemical bonds, intentional actions are human bonds. Indeed, a group is derivative from its members, but it is not reducible to them. Let me call this the relational-realist theory of groups.

Critics might object that the concept of a tank-crew-as-a-group is a social construction. Indeed, molecules are natural constructions, whereas human social groups are not. Granted, human social groups are, in a sense, social constructions, but they are not merely mental constructions. The sense in which a human social group is a social construction is this: The members of a human social group are combined together by social relations—namely, relations between the intentional actions of those members. What a human social group is not is a mental construction produced by each member of the group merely thinking of himself or herself as a member of the group. The tank crew is a society of four, and together they socially construct that society, by their interrelated intentional actions.

I am inclined to accept a relational-realist theory of groups, but I have no space to defend it against other objections (e.g., that social groups are supervenient on individuals). Nonetheless, I have to concede that the antirealist project of reducing groups to individuals is not unreasonable. For lack of space, I cannot discuss the difficult and controversial subject of realism versus anti-realism about groups further.

My central-claim conjecture involves the conjecture that we should clarify (or rectify) the central claim of Frowe's reductive theory (which I am assuming to be sufficiently exemplary) by means of this first reductive claim about groups. Let me indicate why this has to be a conjecture. Frowe maintains that "reductive individualism does not deny that there are such things as collectives."[25] But what is not being denied? What is meant by the word "things"? An antirealist about groups might use the word "things" broadly to include sets of human individuals, whereas a realist about groups might use the word "things" narrowly to include groups but not sets.

Can moral rules governing a group be reduced to moral rules governing its members?

Having discussed the first reductive claim in the preceding section, I discuss the second reductive claim in this section. Can moral rules governing actions of killing by a group in war be reduced to moral rules governing actions of killing by individual combatants in war?

For the sake of clarity and simplicity, I want to raise such a question about a particular pair of moral rules. The MLR principle does not distinguish between uses of lethal military force by a group and uses of lethal military force by individual members of the group. I propose to replace it by two last resort principles. On the one hand, there is a moral rule that (arguably) governs killing by a group in war—namely, a group last resort principle (briefly, the GLR principle)—which may be formulated (briefly and roughly) as follows: Before a group of combatants resorts to a use of lethal force against another group of combatants, every reasonable nonlethal measure must be attempted. On the other hand, there is a moral rule that (arguably) governs killing by individual combatants in war—namely, a combatant last resort principle (briefly, the CLR principle)—which may be formulated (briefly and roughly) thus: Before an individual combatant resorts to a use of lethal force against another individual combatant, every reasonable nonlethal measure must be attempted. Can the GLR principle be reduced to the CLR principle?

By means of the tank-truck scenario, let me illustrate how these two last resort principles might be applied. First, there is the question: How is the GLR principle applicable to the combat between the tank-crew group and the truck-crew group? Before the tank-crew group resorts to a use of lethal force against the truck-crew group, the crew must attempt every reasonable nonlethal measure. Let me call this the last-resort constraint on the tank-crew group.

Second, there is the question: How is the CLR principle applicable to the combat between the individual crew members of the tank and the individual crew members of the truck? Indeed, an individualist might object that a combat in war is (primarily) a combat between individual combatants. More exactly, then, the question is: How is the CLR principle applicable to the combat between each individual member of the tank crew and each individual member of the truck crew? Because each crew has four members, there are sixteen different applications of the CLR principle: Before the commander of the tank crew resorts to a use of lethal force against the commander of the truck crew, every reasonable nonlethal measure must be attempted. Before the commander of the tank crew resorts to a use of lethal force against the driver of the truck crew, every reasonable nonlethal measure must be attempted. And so forth. Let me call these the sixteen last-resort constraints on the four tank-crew members.

Utilizing these two applications, we can illustrate the hypothesis that we can reduce GLR principle to the CLR principle as follows: There is a one–many correspondence between the ordered pair <tank-crew group, truck-crew group> and the sixteen ordered pairs <tank commander, truck commander>, <tank commander, truck driver>, and so forth. The following equivalence—which may be classified as a reductive equivalence—holds between the application of the GLR principle and the sixteen applications of the CLR principle: The last-resort constraint on the tank-crew group obtains if and only if the sixteen last-resort constraints on the four tank-crew members obtain. Next, applying the first reductive claim, the following sentence expresses a key step: We can reduce the tank-crew group (and its actions) to the individual tank-crew members (and their actions). Finally, the following concluding sentence illustrates the second reductive claim: Therefore, the last-resort constraint on the tank-crew group can be reduced to the sixteen last-resort constraints on the four tank-crew members.

To establish the second reductive claim, a reductive theory might generalize the reasoning stated in the preceding paragraph: First, ascertain a reductive equivalence between a moral rule governing actions of killing in war by a group and a corresponding moral rule governing actions of killing in war by its individual members. Then, because the group can be reduced to its members, conclude that the former moral rule can be reduced to the latter moral rule. Similar to my concession about the anti-realist project of reducing a group to its individual members, I have to concede that such a reductionist project about moral rules governing war groups is not unreasonable.

Nevertheless, similar to my inclination to accept a relational-realist theory of groups, I am inclined to accept a different individualist theory about group moral rules. Let me summarize that alternative theory: When a group of individual humans acts, actions of those individual humans are interrelated. Moral rules governing that group action can be derived from moral rules governing the interrelated actions of those individual humans. For instance, the GLR principle can be derived from the CLR principle. In particular, the last-resort constraint on the tank-crew group can be derived—by means of the stated equivalence—from the sixteen last-resort constraints on the four tank-crew members. Both this derivation of the GLR principle from the CLR principle and the reduction of the GLR principle to the CLR principle utilize the same equivalence. How is a derivation different than a reduction? This question is addressed below.

My central-claim conjecture involves the conjecture that the central claim of Frowe's reductive theory should be clarified (or rectified) by means of this second reductive claim. Admittedly, however, the subject of reductionism is controversial. Granted, there may be challenges to my presupposed account of reductionism, but I have no space to respond to objections. Conceivably, a reductive theory might utilize an alternative account of reductionism. A main point is this:

Whatever the account of reductionism, what is essential is that a reductive theory should explain adequately how to reduce moral rules governing actions of killing by a group in war to moral rules governing actions of killing by individual combatants in war.

Can moral rules governing combatants individually be reduced to moral rules governing ordinary persons individually?

My central-claim conjecture also involves the conjecture that the central claim of Frowe's reductive theory should be clarified (or rectified) by means of a third reductive claim—namely, that we can reduce moral rules governing actions of killing by individual combatants in war to moral rules governing actions of individual persons killing in ordinary life. In the preceding two sections, I concede that the first and second reductive claims are not unreasonable. However, I am quite skeptical about this third reductive claim.

Recall that, in addition to her central claim, Frowe makes the following main claim: An "assumption" of a reductive theory is "that there are domestic situations that are relevantly similar to war [situations]."[26] In other words, this assumption of a reductive theory is that there are scenarios of ordinary life that are relevantly similar to scenarios of war. In light of this main claim, I propose to explicate the third reductive claim by means of a concept of relevant similarity.

In writing the preceding section and the present section, my plan is to highlight parallels between the second reductive claim and the third reductive claim, while displaying why they differ significantly. The latter involves correspondences between two different scenarios, whereas the former does not. Significantly, the former involves correspondences between groups of combatants (in a war scenario) and identically the same combatants individually (in identically the same war scenario). By contrast, the latter involves correspondences between individual combatants in a war scenario and individual persons in a scenario of ordinary life—but these combatants are not identically the same as, but instead are only relevantly similar to, these ordinary persons. Therefore, a crucial requirement of the latter, but not of the former, is that there are various relevant similarities. Conceivably, for a given actual scenario of war, only imaginary scenarios of ordinary life might be relevantly similar. The second reductive claim and the third reductive claim are significantly different.

What should be meant by "relevantly similar"? Let me summarize my answer to this question: (1) The concept of relevant similarity should be understood in terms of a dyadic relation of relevant similarity (i.e., x is relevantly similar to y). It is not a relation of exact resemblance (which is reflexive, symmetric, and transitive); instead, it is a relation of sufficient resemblance (which is reflexive and symmetric, but not transitive). (2) Given that x is relevantly similar to y, and thus x sufficiently resembles y; it might also be the case that x is non-relevantly dissimilar to y, because x does not exactly resemble y. (3) Let scenario S be relevantly similar to scenario *S. Presumably, the term "relevant" abbreviates the term "morally relevant." Concerning each item in S and each item in *S, there is the question: Is it or is it not morally relevant? There is no mechanical decision procedure for answering such a question. Questions of moral relevance are often complicated and controversial. (4) Morally relevant items in S are interrelated—by the relation of relevant similarity—with corresponding morally relevant items in *S.

My conjecture is that we should explicate third reductive claim by means of this concept of relevant similarity. Can we reduce moral rules governing individual combatants to moral rules governing relevantly similar individual ordinary persons? Again, for the sake of clarity and simplicity, let me raise such a question about a particular pair of moral rules—namely, the CLR principle (about individual combatants) and the OLR principle (about individual ordinary persons). Can the CLR principle be reduced to the OLR principle?

By means of the tank-truck scenario and a relevantly similar scenario of ordinary life, let me illustrate how to possibly apply these two last resort principles. First, there is the question: How is the CLR principle applicable to the combat between each individual member of the tank crew and each individual member of the truck crew? This question is answered in the preceding section, and that answer is presupposed here. Recall that, in the tank-truck scenario, there are sixteen ordered pairs—namely, <tank commander, truck commander> and so forth. The sixteen last-resort constraints on the four tank-crew members may be summarized as follows: Before each individual tank-crew member resorts to a use of lethal force against each individual truck-crew member, every reasonable nonlethal measure must be attempted.

Second, there is the question: How is the OLR principle applicable? Let me suppose, hypothetically, a self-defense scenario of ordinary life, one that is relevantly similar to the tank-truck scenario. Specifically, it is a scenario in which two ordinary persons are defending themselves together against two ordinary persons who are attacking together. Let me call this the duo-defense scenario. Notice that there are four ordered pairs—namely, <first defender, first attacker>, <first defender, second attacker>, <second defender, first attacker>, and <second defender, second attacker>. Accordingly, there are four different applications of the OLR principle: Before the first defender resorts to a use of lethal force against the first attacker, he or she must attempt every reasonable nonlethal measure. And so forth. I call these the four last-resort constraints on the two defenders.

My supposition is that the duo-defense scenario is relevantly similar to the tank-truck scenario. That is, for each morally relevant circumstance in the tank-truck scenario, there is a corresponding relevantly similar morally relevant circumstance in the duo-defense scenario; and conversely. In particular, each defender is relevantly similar to each tank-crew member, and each attacker is relevantly similar to each truck-crew member. Specifically, the morally relevant actions of each defender are relevantly similar to morally relevant actions of each tank-crew member, and the morally relevant actions of each attacker are relevantly similar to morally relevant actions of each truck-crew member. In short, the four individual tank-crew members (and their actions) are relevantly similar to the two individual defenders (and their actions); and the four individual truck-crew members (and their actions) are relevantly similar to the two individual attackers (and their actions).

Utilizing these two applications, the hypothesis that the CLR principle can be reduced to the OLR principle may be illustrated as follows: There is a one–many correspondence between each of the four ordered pairs <first defender, first attacker> and so forth, and the sixteen ordered pairs <tank commander, truck commander> and so forth. The following equivalence—which may be classified as a reductive equivalence—holds between the sixteen applications of the CLR principle and the four applications of the OLR principle: The sixteen last-resort constraints on the four tank-crew members obtain if and only if the four last-resort constraints on the two defenders obtain. Next, applying the concept of relevant similarity, the following sentence expresses a key step: The four individual tank-crew members (and their actions) are relevantly similar to the two individual defenders (and their actions). Finally, this sentence illustrates the third reductive claim: Therefore, the sixteen last-resort constraints on the four tank-crew members can be reduced to the four last-resort constraints on the two defenders.

To establish the third reductive claim, a reductive theory might generalize the reasoning stated in the preceding paragraph: First, ascertain a reductive equivalence between a moral rule governing actions of killing by individual combatants in war and a corresponding moral rule governing actions of killing by relevantly similar individual persons in ordinary life. Then, because the combatants are relevantly similar to the ordinary persons, conclude that the former moral rule can be reduced to the latter moral rule. However, I am skeptical that the third reductive claim can be thus established. The preceding paragraph starts with the phrase "Utilizing these two applications." And, in the preceding section, the fifth paragraph starts with that phrase. In particular, these two paragraphs are written to highlight parallels, while displaying significant differences.

Significantly, the term "relevantly similar" occurs in the first-mentioned paragraph, but not in the next paragraph we consider. Because the tank-truck scenario and the duo-defense scenario are only relevantly similar, they are also non-relevantly dissimilar. For they are only sufficiently similar; their similarity is not an exact resemblance. There is no mechanical decision procedure for determining whether the corresponding morally relevant items are relevantly similar. Questions of moral relevance are often complicated and controversial. In short, especially because the third reductive claim involves a concept of relevant similarity, I am skeptical about it.

Specifically, the first key step—namely, that the tank-crew members and the individual defenders are relevantly similar—is significantly different than the parallel key step—namely, that the tank-crew group can be reduced to the tank-crew members. Significantly, relevant similarity and ontological reduction are quite different. The final sentence in each of the two paragraphs being compared above is flagged by the word *therefore* to signal a conclusion. I am conceding that the conclusion of the first is not unreasonable. By contrast, I am skeptical about the conclusion of the parallel paragraph. In particular, it is quite obscure how the key step about relevant similarity can support this conclusion about reduction.

On the other hand, the key step about relevant similarity might support a weaker conclusion—for instance, that the last-resort constraints on the defenders may help to elucidate, or illuminate, the last-resort constraints on the tank-crew members. But reduction is a mode of justification, whereas elucidation, or illumination, is not.

Admittedly, however, the account of reductionism that I am presupposing might be challenged. Conceivably, a reductive theory might utilize an alternative account of reductionism. A main point is this: Whatever the account of reductionism, what is essential is that a reductive theory should explain adequately how moral rules governing actions of killing by individual combatants in war can be reduced to moral rules governing actions of killing by relevantly similar individual persons in ordinary life. To do this convincingly, the concept of relevant similarity should be clarified adequately.

Reductionism versus derivationism

My aim in this chapter is to critically examine Frowe's reductive theory and to support an alternative relational theory. Instead of a method of reduction, a relational theory utilizes a method of derivation. In this concluding section, I want to indicate why reductionism and derivationism are different.

The reductive method is indirect, in that moral rules of war are obtained indirectly from moral rules in ordinary-life scenarios, through the concept of relevant similarity. By contrast, a relational theory might derive moral rules of war from war scenarios directly. For instance, the CLR principle might be derived directly from the tank-truck scenario and other war scenarios.

Alternatively, a relational theory might utilize a method of deduction: There is a moral principle that (arguably) governs killing both in war and in ordinary life (and under all other circumstances)—namely, a universal last resort principle (briefly, the ULR principle)—which may be formulated (briefly and roughly) thus: Before an individual human being resorts to a use of lethal force against another individual human being, he or she must attempt every reasonable nonlethal measure. Both the CLR principle and the OLR principle can be deduced directly from the ULR principle. These deductions serve to illustrate my own central claim in this chapter—namely, that both moral rules governing killing in war and moral rules governing interpersonal killing in ordinary life can be derived from universal moral principles governing individual human actions.

A reductive theorist might object that this deduction of the CLR principle from the ULR principle is a reduction of the former to the latter, because the method of deduction is a method of reduction. My response is as follows: Instead of being a moral rule governing actions of killing by individual persons in ordinary life, the ULR principle is a moral rule governing actions of killing by individual human beings, including both individual persons in ordinary life and individual combatants in a war. This deduction of the CLR principle might be called a reduction, but it is a reduction that is direct, in that it is neither mediated by a moral rule of ordinary life nor mediated by scenarios of ordinary life. What is most distinctive about reductive-individualist just war theories is absent.

A problem remains. How can the ULR principle be obtained? It might be derived both from ordinary-life scenarios and from war scenarios. It might be derived by a method of deduction from more general principles of morality. It might be derived by a coherentist method (e.g., reflective equilibrium).[27] And so forth. In this chapter, my purpose is only to outline an alternative individualist account. I have no space to explore the difficult and controversial meta-ethical subject of moral derivation further.

Notes

1 While I was revising this chapter, Cian O'Driscoll provided instructive guidance, for which I am very grateful.
2 For an introduction to just war theory, see Steven P. Lee, *Ethics and War: An Introduction* (Cambridge: Cambridge University Press, 2012).
3 For a history of just war theories, see Alex J. Bellamy, *Just Wars: From Cicero to Iraq* (Cambridge: Polity Press, 2006).
4 Michael Walzer, *Just and Unjust Wars: A Moral Argument with Historical Illustrations* (New York: Basic Books, 1977).
5 Ibid., 282.
6 Helen Frowe, *The Ethics of War and Peace: An Introduction* (London and New York: Routledge, 2011), 29, 31.
7 United Nations, *Charter of the United Nations*, October 24, 1945, 1 UNTS XVI, http://www.refworld.org/docid/3ae6b3930.html, Article 51.
8 Ibid., Article 42.
9 For a noteworthy state-centric just war theory, see John Rawls, *The Law of Peoples* (Cambridge, MA: Harvard University Press, 1999).
10 Jeff McMahan, "Just Cause for War," *Ethics and International Affairs*, 19 (2005): 11–12.
11 Helen Frowe, *Defensive Killing* (Oxford: Oxford University Press, 2014).
12 For such an approach, see James Turner Johnson, *Just War Tradition and the Restraint of War: A Moral and Historical Inquiry* (Princeton: Princeton University Press, 1981).
13 For a classic introduction to moral philosophy, see William Frankena, *Ethics*, 2nd edn. (Englewood Cliffs, NJ: Prentice Hall, 1973).
14 Frowe, *Ethics of War and Peace*, 29.
15 Frowe, *Defensive Killing*, 2.
16 Ibid., 15.
17 Ibid., 139.
18 Ibid., 13.
19 Ibid., 124.
20 Ibid., 124.

21 John W. Lango, *The Ethics of Armed Conflict: A Cosmopolitan Just War Theory* (Edinburgh: Edinburgh University Press, 2014). This book is published as a hardback, but it is also published as an Open Access book with a Creative Commons license. E.g., it can be downloaded at no cost from the OAPEN website: http://www.oapen.org/ (accessed February 21, 2017).
22 I discuss the subject of last resort at length in Ibid.
23 Ibid., 12–14.
24 Frowe, *Defensive Killing*, 124.
25 Ibid., 124.
26 Ibid., 124.
27 Lango, *Ethics of Armed Conflict*, 51–56.

16
CRITICAL APPROACHES TO THE ETHICS OF WAR

Amy E. Eckert and Caron E. Gentry

In this chapter, we apply an expansive approach to the critical theory and the ethics of war. We follow the thinking of Chris Brown, who describes critical theory as "a very broad church,"[1] containing within it a collection of theoretical approaches that differ and sometimes even oppose one another. As such, rather than looking at critical theory as a unified endeavor, this chapter deals in multiple critical approaches that are representative of this body of work without claiming that any single approach is solely representative of critical theory.

We begin with a discussion of the difference between "problem-solving" theory and "critical" theory, clarifying that they have differing ontological and epistemological starting points. We continue by introducing the reader to particular critical approaches, the Frankfurt School, poststructuralism, and feminism. Following these considerations, we turn to thinking about how these critical approaches address questions of the ethics of war. Finally, we explore commonalities and differences among these critical approaches by applying them to non-combatant immunity.

Critical theory and problem-solving theory

Despite their differences, there are some commonalities to critical approaches. The critical approaches we consider here are indebted to Robert Cox's "States, Social Forces, and World Orders," which most critical approaches claim as an intellectual ancestor. As Cox argues in his landmark article on critical theory, "theory is always *for* someone and *for* some purpose."[2] Cox distinguishes between "problem-solving" theory and "critical" theory.[3] Problem-solving theory takes the prevailing forms of social organization as a given and works within their confines. It addresses particular issues within the confines of existing social structures but leaves those structures untouched. In this sense, problem-solving theory is a conservative approach. The point of problem-solving theory is to make the existing institutions work and to solve particular issues within their framework.

By contrast, critical theory "allows for a normative choice in favor of a social and political order different from the prevailing order, but it limits the range of choice to alternative orders which are feasible transformations of the existing world."[4] Put differently, critical theory allows for questioning of the prevailing institutions and power relationships—specifically in terms of their origins and the interests that they serve—in a way that problem-solving theory cannot address. Critical theory may address the same issues as problem-solving theory, but it does so in a markedly different manner. The heart of critical theory, then, is the willingness to ask questions about concepts that problem-solving theories treat as off-limits and, implicitly, illegitimate. The willingness to question and challenge elements of political and social structures is something that is shared across critical approaches, even as they differ on particular approaches to doing so.

Problem-solving theory and other "mainstream" traditional approaches are rooted in a foundational ontology (or "what features need explaining"[5]), which holds that the world exists independently of human knowledge of it, and a predictive or explanatory epistemology (or "what counts as explanation"[6]) that emulates scientific approaches[7] which claim a value-free and neutral positivist methodology. In contrast, critical theory begins with an anti-foundationalist ontology, holding instead that the world is socially and discursively constructed. It is more concerned with empirical, not empiricist, frameworks.[8] Epistemologically, it holds that "[s]ocial phenomena do not exist independently of our interpretation of them, rather it is this interpretation/understanding of social phenomena which affects outcomes."[9] This works with multiple postpositivist methods, where nothing is value-free or neutral, but most things are evidence of a knowledge–power nexus.[10] Within critical security studies, these anti-foundational and postpositivist approaches lead to the "widening and deepening" of how we understand security and the issues that comprise security.[11] While a mainstream approach may only hold a neorealist viewpoint that states are the primary actor in security studies, and states are the only actor that can wage war, a critical approach looks at other actors, such as individuals, sub-state groups, and other organizations, in addition to the state, as well as expanding security and war to include interpersonal forms of violence[12] or how a threat to security comes into being, that is, the process of securitization.[13]

Critical approaches

We focus here on three key critical approaches: the Frankfurt School, poststructuralism, and feminism. While these three approaches by no means exhaust the range of approaches that fall into the broad category of critical theory, these critical approaches are both important in their own right and make important contributions to the study of ethics and war. Additionally, each embodies key features of a broad critical approach that calls into question the origins, purposes, and consequences of theory.

Frankfurt School

A narrow construction of "Critical Theory" arguably refers to the Frankfurt School. As such, "Critical Theory" refers (for purposes of this chapter) specifically to the Frankfurt School rather than to critical approaches or theories more broadly. The origins of this body of thought, which draws on the philosophies of Immanuel Kant, G. W. F. Hegel, and Karl Marx, date back to the founding of the Institute for Social Research in the early 20th century. Scholars within the Frankfurt School question the prevailing social order by means of immanent critique, a search for contradictions in the present social order that can open up possibilities for the future.

Unlike some of the other critical approaches we consider here, which are neutral among normative positions, the Frankfurt School has an explicit normative commitment to the emancipation of individuals. In Max Horkheimer's famous definition, Critical Theory is "an indissoluble moment in the historical effort to create a world which satisfies the needs and powers of human beings."[14] This stands in contrast to the traditional focus of theory on the accumulation of knowledge.

We can associate two "generations" of scholars with the Frankfurt School. The first, beginning in the 1930s, includes Horkheimer as well as Theodor Adorno, Herbert Marcuse, Walter Benjamin, and others. The second, which originated in the 1970s, was led by Jürgen Habermas, who is for our present purposes perhaps the most influential of those associated with the Frankfurt School. Neither of these generations of Frankfurt School scholars engaged with international relations in a meaningful way, but Habermas's theory of communicative action would be imported into international relations by critical theorists including Cox, Richard Ashley, and Andrew Linklater. Cox's discussion of problem-solving and critical theories owes an obvious debt to the Frankfurt School and its recognition that the prevailing social order is not an objective reality independent of human agency, but instead the product of social forces and the interests guiding them.

Habermas's influence on critical theorists of international relations (IR) stems largely from his discussion about types of knowledge-constitutive interests, which he describes as practical, technical, and emancipatory.[15] These knowledge-constitutive interests address very different facets of human endeavors. The technical interest aims at an understanding of the natural world and is exemplified by the natural sciences and those aspects of social sciences that emulate them. The practical interest relates to the conduct of life and is the knowledge necessary to understand things like the use of language. The emancipatory interest is, in the words of critical theorist Ashley, about securing freedom from unacknowledged constraints, relations of domination, and conditions of distorted communication and understanding that deny humans the capacity to make their future through full will and consciousness.[16]

This focus leads critical theorists to reflect on possibilities for emancipation within the international system.[17] Because of the explicit normative commitment to emancipation, critical theorists approach questions of war and security in a manner that inverts some of the conventional assumptions of security studies, beginning with shifting the focus from security of the state to the security of humanity. The sovereign state is not understood as an obstacle to achieving security rather than as the referent of security. Because of this focus on individuals, critical formulations of security are often closely tied to individual autonomy. At a minimum, autonomy requires an absence of threats. As Ken Booth notes, we can view security and emancipation as "two sides of the same coin."[18]

Obstacles to individual autonomy may be the focus of securitization, a process by which issues of public health or environmental quality come to be characterized as linked with the concept of security.[19] This concept presents the issues in question as existential threats requiring the same urgent response and allocation of resources more conventionally reserved for issues of national security.[20] The process of securitization, which poststructuralism further developed, is directly indebted to the Frankfurt School and Habermas's communicative action.

Poststructuralism

In contrast to problem-solving theory, poststructuralism is more interested in developing critique than building theory. Influenced strongly by the work of Michel Foucault, poststructuralism came into IR in the 1980s from literary criticism through the work of IR theorists like Ashley and R. B. J. Walker. Poststructuralists emphasize the role of discourse, which examines the power of words to construct and reify political and social structures. This clearly extends Foucault's claim that knowledge is power, as mentioned above. Jens Bartelson's *A Genealogy of Sovereignty* exemplifies this approach. Bartelson argues that, in the absence of a "proper mode of knowledge to render it intelligible, sovereignty cannot exist, [sic] and loses its power to organize political reality."[21] As poststructuralists have approached war and conflict over the past 30 years, there have been multiple "turns" in discursive approaches and understandings of how the field of IR and beyond construct security, threat, and war. The first turn, one of the most prominent poststructural approaches to security, and therefore war, is the theory of securitization. The second turn is "emotion," and the greater inclusion of emotion in the study of conflict and war. The final turn is the aesthetic turn, looking at the awe-inducing manifestation of the violence from conflict.

Securitization theory examines how a particular form of discourse is used to construct a threat and therefore elicit an exceptional response to the threat. Securitization is based upon a trilogy of a speech act, an actor, and an audience. An actor (most often a state in IR) with some influence, power, and credibility makes a speech act establishing that a referent object (the territorial integrity of the state, the government's legitimacy, or a group's identity) is at perilous risk. This risk is often "existential"—it promises annihilation or to be such a significant threat as to completely undermine and destroy the reference object. From this, the actor proposes extraordinary measures, or measures outside of normalized routines, thus breaking rules and norms to deal with the existential threat. If the audience "buys" the threat, the situation has been securitized.[22]

One example of a successful securitization is how the George W. Bush administration built the case for both the war in Afghanistan and Iraq and the overarching "War on Terror." The Bush administration used the events of 9/11 to discursively construct an existential threat of radical Islamist terrorism to the safety and security of the United States. Utilizing scholarship that had captured the attention of Washington policy-makers, such as Samuel Huntington's "clash of civilizations" and Robert Kaplan's "new barbarism" thesis, the Bush administration's Manichean discourse pitted the "West" against radical Islamism (if not all of Islam).[23] This existential, civilizational threat sold the War on Terror and its "policies" of illegal detention, torture, and domestic surveillance in the PATRIOT Act to the American people.

The second turn is the "introduction" of emotion into the study of IR broadly, but with a focus on security and war more specifically. In 2000, Neta Crawford[24] wrote a seminal article in which she argued that emotion is threaded throughout the study and activity of international relations, yet most scholars and practitioners would deny its importance (or even that emotions are present at all). Crawford argued that the incorporation of emotion into the study of security has three implications. [25] First, it would allow international relations and security studies to "shift from regarding actors as primarily rational, removing neo-realist and positivist tendencies to rely on the rational actor model," such as seen in Waltz's argument for global nuclear proliferation.[26] Second, "it might be more accurate, as the early realists did, to attribute fear as the engine of the security dilemma;" Crawford continues by stating that "[f]ear and other emotions are not only attributes of agents, they are institutionalized in the structures and processes of world politics."[27] Finally, the recognition of emotion would aid in "diplomacy, confidence building, and postconflict peacebuilding."[28] Crawford's article, cited 442 times according to Google Scholar, opened the doors to other critical scholars to begin such an incorporation and recognition.

Within poststructuralist work, the starting point is often to differentiate between affect and emotion. Affect is, for lack of a better word, a precursor to emotion. Ty Solomon holds that affect is an "'indeterminate' stat[e] of mood that remain[s] outside of discourse."[29] Linda Åhäll and Thomas Gregory associate affect with internal "influence" and "sensation."[30] Emotions are the discursive, limited articulation of affect; affect becomes a "discursive reality" when people articulate it via "recognizable emotional signifiers," or communally shared ways of identifying what is being felt.[31] Since discourse does something—it is performative, constructive, and powerful—putting affect into the communally shared discursive constructions of emotions does something as well.[32] According to philosopher Martha Nussbaum, emotions are not irrational (as opposed to the Western line of thought that holds emotions in binary opposition to rational, logical thought), but, as Emma Hutchison adds, emotions are "part of the perceptive tools that individuals use to make sense of the world and to situate themselves."[33] Therefore, this notion of communal and relational is important to emotions in critical security studies as humans use emotions to construct the Self and Self-same group in opposition to the Other.[34] This can be seen in how the US constructed the terrorist threat after 9/11;[35] how people respond to terrorism through fear and anxiety;[36] and how self-martyrdom (or suicide bombings) are related to humiliation.[37]

The emotional turn is significantly related to the aesthetic turn, which was largely introduced by Roland Bleiker (as well as Alex Danchev, although for these purposes he did not identify as a poststructuralist). Aesthetics helps IR scholars interpret and "offer alternative insights into" their subject.[38] Specifically, it is an alternative to the dominance of neopositivist scholarship, one where hierarchies and structures can be revealed, critiqued, and dismantled.[39] This happens because art and aesthetics are moral and ethical explanations for social and political events; as Alex Danchev argues, art "articulates a vision of the world that is insightful and consequential."[40] This vision of aesthetic IR converges with poststructuralism's emphasis on revealing and dismantling power structures.

Bleiker wrote rather powerfully about encountering the sublime—as "excitement," "astonishment," "awe," and "fear, and pain"[41]—in the 9/11 attacks. 9/11 has become a narrativized event, something that has changed or at least dominated IR scholarship and global politics, but the aesthetic dimension offers alternative insights.[42] As "[a]esthetics is neither good nor bad," it functions by:

> [A]dd[ing] a different dimension to our understanding of the political, and, by consequence, to the ethical discourses that are central to waging political debates. . . [A]esthetics can expose political practices who problematic dimensions are no longer recognized because years of habit have turned them into common sense.[43]

Thus, the 9/11 attacks as an encounter with the sublime allows scholars, artists, and other individuals to grapple with some of the silences that a mainstream approach to IR did not allow—it allows us to continue the discussion of emotion or the importance of art as an intervention in ways not previously (necessarily) allowed by foundationalist and/or neopositivist approaches.[44]

Feminism

Feminism enjoys an affinity to critical theory because of the willingness of some feminists to question the gender bases of political systems within states and within the international system. Feminist approaches to the study of IR began in the 1980s, often by asking the question, "Where are the women?"[45] This question is often seen within the remit of liberal feminism, arguing that women's participation (or lack thereof) offers a different perspective to IR and asks different questions. Feminists look for women's participation in government, diplomacy, and the military. As feminism in IR has evolved, "standpoint" feminism began to question the gender binary between masculinity and its association with men and femininity and its association with women.[46] Feminism and gender studies more generally argue that masculinity is associated with characteristics such as logic, rationality, aggression/assertiveness, and sovereignty, and femininity's traits are in opposition, thus, emotionality, irrationality, passivity, and dependency.[47]

Arguing that gender is a social construction dependent upon discursive hierarchies, this form of feminism began to cohere with poststructuralism. The question, "Where are the women?"

evolved into, "How are women and men socially constructed?" and thus queried how the actors in IR are gendered to replicate the masculine/feminine binary. This has led to recent work that argues the international system (and IR itself) is a gendered hierarchical structure that, for "success" as defined by power and hegemony, demands that actors, particularly states, reify and exhibit masculine behaviors.

Cynthia Enloe's *Bananas, Beaches and Bases* is a pioneering work of liberal feminism, which sought to call attention to the often overlooked role that women play in the international system. Empirical feminism also takes issue with the implicit assumption that the more visible male experience adequately represents the reality of international relations. Beyond this, however, it leaves social constructions of gender and gender relationships untouched. This is similar to another key early text on feminism and war: Jean Bethke Elshtain's *Women and War*, in which she argues that the gender roles women and men are expected to play in war time also determine how their citizenship is conceived.[48] Men are meant to be the "Just Warriors," the chivalrous warriors sent into a righteous war to protect homeland and home; women are the "Beautiful Souls" left behind, tending the home and hearth.[49] Citizenship is directly linked to fighting in war—meaning that women are left out of the citizenship equation.

Lately, however, some liberal "feminisms" has fallen into a quantitative trap—where a statistical analysis outweighs a critical one. This can be seen specifically in those who adhere to the "feminization" argument. Feminization theorists argue that women's social, political, and economic insecurity are directly tied or statistically correlated to a state's economic development and its internal and regional security.[50] This feminization argument works with the decline-of-violence thesis, which asserts that death in war is declining, which will ultimately lead to the triumph of a liberal democratic peace. In particular, Valerie Hudson et al.'s work on feminization correlates women's personal security with regional security. They found that in societies where women's rights and security are stable, then there is also state and regional stability. Thus, these texts argue for the expansion of women's rights, mainly in the developing world, in order to solve regional security. Due to the reliance upon statistical evidence and positivist methodology, this work is critiqued for failing to critically analyze how gender operates as a social structure.[51]

Standpoint feminism extends this concern with women in the international system by questioning the gendered underpinnings of the international system. Ann Tickner's work argues that concepts that may seem gender-neutral—like security and citizenship—are in fact gendered.[52] Tickner takes issue with the Hobbesian conception of the state and the international system that underlies realism. The experience of the state of nature that comes from Hobbes, for instance, is a society that is doomed to extermination within a single generation, as it provides no space for reproduction. Likewise, citizenship idealizes the concept of sacrifice for the country through military service, an experience long denied to female citizens. In questioning of apparently neutral concepts like security and citizenship, as poststructural feminism questions the discursive structuring of gender hierarchies it exemplifies critical approaches to international relations.[53]

In regards to thinking specifically about war, poststructural feminist Christine Sylvester's starting point in the 1990s was very similar to Tickner's. She argues that, due to the masculine construction of the state and the international system, IR needs a feminist perspective in order to be more empathetic.[54] To be empathetic meant "taking on board rather than dismissing, finding in the concerns of others borderlands of one's own concerns and fears."[55] This foreshadows her more recent work on experiencing war. Finding that IR has abstracted war so much that it fails to take on board and theorize individuals' experience of war, Sylvester argues that deabstraction can only happen when IR scholars grapple with the sights, smells, fear/terror, and annihilation that can only come from a person's experience of war.[56]

Ultimately, Tickner, Sylvester, and Elshtain's work, alongside V. Spike Peterson, Ann Sisson Runyan, and others, argues that gender is not an empirical category (as Steven Pinker and Hudson use it) but an analytical one—where gender is not just a way of describing the socially constructed differences between men and women but also as a way of hierarchically structuring international relations. Thus, Laura Sjoberg's *Gendering Global Conflict*[57] builds upon this work, as well as Raewyn Connell and James Messerschmidt's hegemonic masculinity theory,[58] when she seeks a different answer from Kenneth Waltz's question, "What is the cause of war?"[59] Instead of accepting anarchy as the permissive cause of war, Sjoberg finds that gender hierarchy is the permissive cause of war. As masculinities are in constant competition with each other, this competition, when it is unbalanced, leads to war and conflict. Thus, the international state structure is best explained by the gender hierarchical nature of state competition.

Critical approaches and the ethics of war

The just war tradition constitutes our "predominant moral language" for thinking about the ethics of warfighting.[60] Based on the foregoing, it should be unsurprising that the critical approaches we consider in this chapter are skeptical about aspects of what can be a rather conservative intellectual tradition. As such, we will consider these critical approaches in relationship to the just war tradition, but also in connection with broader treatments of the ethics of war.

Critical approaches to non-combatant immunity

Non-combatant immunity is the centerpiece of both legal and ethical thinking about the conduct of wars. In the modern formulation, this principle mandates that civilians are non-combatants who actors should spare the horrors of war as far as possible. While non-combatant immunity is often associated with the protection of innocent life, the practice of non-combatant immunity does not necessarily correspond to individual intent.[61] This is so in part because the individuals who are the target of this norm have no real role in the decision to go to war.[62] Even in a democracy, the role of individual citizens is "occasional, intermittent, limited in its effects."[63] Rather than intent, the principle of non-combatant immunity extends to individuals based on their relationship to the state. For many on both sides of the divide, their status may be at odds with their intent. Many combatants did not choose to fight in any real sense, but their obedience to their state places them in a different position. Michael Walzer argues that soldiers, by virtue of fighting, gain rights as combatants and, potentially, as prisoners, but they lose the other rights that they held as civilians—including the rights to life and liberty—even though they themselves may have committed no wrong.[64] Because they take part in combat, soldiers may legitimately be killed, while non-combatants retain their rights, which stems from their "moral standing independent of and resistant to the exigencies of war."[65] This is so even for non-combatants who support the war in a political sense.

For those non-combatants who support the war in a material sense, the protections afforded to them under this principle may be more complex. A. J. Coates observes that even activities far removed from the fighting of war, such as maintaining a supply of oil, can be crucial to the success of a war.[66] He suggests that war brings about transformations in civilian enterprises, such as an increase in production and proposes that "the distinction [between combatants and non-combatants] needs to be modified" in recognition of these wartime transformations.[67] Walzer also acknowledges that "workers must be mobilized before an army can even appear in the field," but he distinguishes among them based on how direct their contributions to the war effort are.[68] Civilian workers in a munitions factory and workers in a food processing plant are distinguishable in terms of their contribution, even though they both contribute to the war effort in some capacity.[69] While the former may legitimately be the target of attack because their contribution to the war effort is substantially more direct, Walzer argues, necessity still comes into play and they may not be attacked when their work can be stopped in some other way.

In summary, the principle of non-combatant immunity is intended to shield those designated as non-combatants from the harm that war entails. However, the meaning of this term is neither natural nor obvious. Instead, it is the product of social and political structures and, as such, lends itself to scrutiny by the critical approaches that we consider in this chapter.

The Frankfurt School and non-combatant immunity

The Frankfurt School seeks to promote human liberation and minimize harm to individuals, but non-combatant immunity may not be adequate to this task, in part because of the changing nature of harm. The critical focus of the Frankfurt School is helpful to understanding potential inadequacies of the principle of non-combatant immunity because of its recognition that the transnational system includes more than states. Andrew Linklater draws upon, but extends, insights from the English School for this purpose. He notes the English School's focus on institutions as a means of reducing harm among states and also, by extension, for individuals as well. Likewise, the English School's incorporation of dialogue opens up possibilities for a universal communication community like the one Habermas envisions.[70]

Linklater introduces a key distinction between international harm and transnational harm, which is blurred by conflict between states and consequences for civilians. International harm, or harm between states, stands in contrast to transnational harm, which can extend to the individual members of transnational society. Nevertheless, Linklater notes that "attempts to harm states. . . harm individuals by exposing them to fear and insecurity."[71] The ability of states to harm individuals in the course of harming other states—whether this harm is intentional or not—has only grown with the industrialization of war. Nonetheless, Linklater argues that the recognition of the principle of non-combatant immunity, embraced by states, implies a recognition that there remains an important distinction between international and transnational harm.

In keeping with the Frankfurt School's focus on individuals as the appropriate locus of security rather than states, Linklater observes that, in parts of the world, transnational harm has overtaken international harm as the primary source of insecurity for individuals. He notes that "citizens may feel more threatened by their state's decision to co-operate with firms to import waste products which can endanger health than by the danger of inter-state warfare."[72] When considering human rather than national security, the harm posed by something like environmental pollution can be indistinguishable in its effects from more conventional forms of armed conflict, though the principle of non-combatant immunity does not extend to these contexts. The principle of non-combatant immunity extends some protections to civilians, but to the extent that it only addresses harm to individuals within a limited context, it is inadequate for purposes of securing human emancipation.

Poststructuralism and non-combatant immunity

Because poststructuralism looks at discursive processes that produce and reify particular structures, a poststructural approach to both just war and non-combatant immunity would seek to trouble how words and definitions focus attention, prioritizing what we look at, what we see as legitimate, and what we see as permissible.[73] Thus, in looking at the just war tradition, several questions might be posed: Why do we believe states are legitimate actors within war and others are not? Why do just war theorists see state-affiliated combatants as lawful combatants while sub-state actors are not (or might not be)? And how might we expand or contract who is included in a definition of combatant, thus making them targetable?

For instance, Tarik Kochi's *The Other's War* argues for a new epistemic vision in IR's approach to war. According to Kochi, the just war is a particular, Western moral vision of war that delegitimizes non-Western and terrorist violence. Therefore, in order to disrupt the knowledge/power praxis of the just war tradition, we might ask what gives "legitimacy" to "the state and international law," question "differing accounts of individual and group rights," such as those that prioritize the protection of state-affiliated combatants and deprioritize those perceived to be "terrorist" agents.[74]

Looking more specifically at non-combatant immunity, poststructuralism focus on discourse easily troubles the US's use of drone strikes against "terrorist" actors in Pakistan, Afghanistan, Somalia, and Yemen. According to the Bureau of Investigative Journalism's Drone Warfare database, there have been 2,262 confirmed strikes since January 2004. As a result of these strikes, the US has killed somewhere between 6,263 and 9,049 people. Of this number, the US killed an estimated 736 to 1,394 civilians, including 242 to 307 children. Yet the definition of *combatant* in regards to drone strikes and targets is expansive; the US has even changed the definition of *civilian* in order to expand individuals targeted in the strikes.[75] Furthermore, drone operators identify people on the ground with algorithms that Lauren Wilcox shows to be imprecise at best[76] and dependent upon biases that become encoded in a proposition that actually violates the mutuality of death and risk that is implicit in the good functioning of the just war tradition.[77] Thus, if we only view the US as a state as *always* legitimate, we fail to recognize when they might be committing war crimes and breaching the just war tradition. Going further, if we always see the US as a state as legitimate, then when it begins a drone strike war to protect their combatants and expansively redefine who is a combatant, then we fail to recognize that war crimes might be happening. Poststructuralism helps us to query what might be seen as legitimate and acceptable by troubling the discourses that sustain particular hierarchies, such as states as legitimate and the definition of "combatant" as uncontestable.

Feminism and non-combatant immunity

Feminist approaches to the ethics of war mirror other critical approaches in questioning the construction of the principle of non-combatant immunity and identifying inadequacies that fail to protect all individuals from harm. Feminists add to this critical focus the unique role played by gender in the construction of concepts like "civilians" and their treatment. In her work, Sjoberg notes the tension between the strong norm of non-combatant immunity and the failure to protect civilians, sometimes by deliberately targeting them as strategy.[78] One specific form that intentional victimization of civilians can take is sexual violence, despite the fact that this practice violates the widely recognized prohibition of harming civilians. The strategy of deliberately targeting civilians through intentional sexualized violence is fueled by influential gender tropes that drive the construction of the non-combatant immunity principle itself: that men are "just warriors" tasked with defending vulnerable feminine "beautiful souls."[79]

Conclusion

The task of critical approaches is to question what problem-solving theory takes as given. Because of widespread moral consensus, often reflected in international law, the ethics of war contains a number of core principles that have come to be viewed as fixed, given, and unquestionable, including the principle of non-combatant immunity. Critical approaches to the ethics of war inquire about the origins of these principles and the politics of their construction. In this sense, there is a possibility for dialogue between the critical perspectives we consider and a relatively conservative body of thought like the just war tradition. Indeed, while much of the work that constituted critical theory is heavily philosophical in nature, Devetak rightly reminds us of the importance of historical and material thought to critical theory.[80] Such emphasis was particularly relevant to Cox and other "first generation" critical theorists, he notes.[81]

The lens of historical development has been particularly useful in analyzing a principle like non-combatant immunity, which often suffers a presentist treatment that strips it of its historical origins and limitations. Although it is safe to say that non-combatant immunity is now recognized (in principle, if not in practice) as an absolute, inquiring into the historical construction of this principle reveals a very different truth regarding the initially limited categories of people entitled to protection, and the gradual extension of protection to all civilians. This historical perspective lends credence to some critical theorists' allegations that the protection extended by an "absolute" principle is in fact often limited, leaving the most vulnerable to suffer the consequences of both war and other types of violence.

Notes

1 Chris Brown, "Theory and Practice in International Relations," in *International Relations Theory Today*, ed. Ken Booth and Toni Erskine (Cambridge: Polity, 2016), 46.
2 Robert W. Cox, "Social Forces, States and World Orders: Beyond International Relations Theory," *Millennium: Journal of International Studies*, 10, no. 2 (1981): 128, emphasis in original.
3 Ibid.
4 Cox, "Social Forces, States and World Orders: Beyond International Relations Theory," 130.
5 Tim Dunne, Milja Kurki, and Steve Smith, eds., *International Relations Theories* (Oxford: Oxford University Press, 2013), 9.
6 Ibid.
7 David Marsh and Gerry Stoker, eds., *Theory and Methods in Political Science* (London: Palgrave: 2010).
8 J. Ann Tickner, "What Is Your Research Program? Some Feminist Answers to International Relations Methodological Questions," *International Studies Quarterly*, 49, no. 1 (2005): 1–22.
9 David Marsh and Paul Furlong, "A Skin Not a Sweater: Ontology and Epistemology in Political Science," in *Theory and Methods in Political Science*, ed. David Marsh and Gerry Stoker (London: Palgrave, 2002), 26.
10 Michel Foucault, *Discipline and Punish: The Birth of the Prison* (London: Penguin, 1991).
11 See Barry Buzan, Ole Wæver, and Jaap de Wilde, *Security: A New Framework for Analysis* (Boulder, CO: Lynne Reinner, 1998).
12 See Rachel Pain, "Everyday Terrorism: Connecting Domestic Violence and Global Terrorism," *Progress in Human Geography*, 38, no. 4 (2014): 531–550; Alexandria J. Innes and Brent J. Steele, "Spousal Visa: Law and Structural Violence: Fear, Anxiety and Terror of the Everyday," *Critical Studies on Terrorism*, 8, no. 3 (2015): 401–415.
13 Buzan, Wæver, and de Wilde, *Security*.
14 Max Horkheimer, *Critical Theory: Selected Essays*, trans. M. J. O'Connell et al. (London: Bloomsbury Academic, 1972), 245.
15 Jürgen Habermas, *Knowledge and Human Interest* (New York: Beacon Press, 1972), 168.
16 Richard K. Ashley, "Political Realism and Human Interests," *International Studies Quarterly*, 25, no. 2 (1981): 227.
17 Andrew Linklater, *Beyond Realism and Marxism: Critical Theory and International Relations* (London: Palgrave Macmillan, 1990).
18 Ken Booth, "Security in Anarchy: Utopian Realism in Theory and Practice," *International Affairs (Royal Institute of International Affairs 1944–)* (1991).
19 Steven C. Roach, *Critical Theory of International Politics: Complementarity, Justice, and Governance* (London: Taylor & Francis, 2013), 121.

20 Barry Buzan, Ole Wæver, and Jaap de Wilde, *Security: A New Framework for Analysis* (Boulder, CO: Lynne Rienner, 1998), 26.
21 Jens Bartelson, *A Genealogy of Sovereignty* (Cambridge; New York: Cambridge University Press, 1995).
22 See Buzan, Waever, de Wilde, *Security*, 25–26; Lene Hansen, *Security as Practice: Discourse and the Bosnian War* (London: Routledge, 2013), part 1.
23 See Dag Tuastad, "Neo-Orientalism and the New Barbarism Thesis: Aspects of Symbolic Violence in the Middle East Conflict(s)," *Third World Quarterly*, 24, no. 4 (2003): 591–599; Richard Jackson, *Writing the War on Terrorism: Language, Politics, and Counter-Terrorism* (Manchester: Manchester University Press, 2005); Lee Jarvis, *Times of Terror: Discourse, Temporality and the War on Terror* (London: Palgrave MacMillan, 2009).
24 Neta C. Crawford, "The Passion of World Politics: Propositions on Emotion and Emotional Relationships," *International Security*, 24, no. 4 (2000): 116–156.
25 Ibid., 119.
26 Scott Douglas Sagan and Kenneth Waltz, *The Spread of Nuclear Weapons: An Enduring Debate* (New York: W. W. Norton, 2012).
27 Crawford, "The Passion...," 119.
28 Ibid., 119.
29 Ty Solomon, "'I Wasn't Angry, Because I Couldn't Believe It Was Happening': Affect and Discourse in Responses to 9/11," *Review of International Studies*, 38, no. 4 (2012): 907–928, 918.
30 Linda Åhäll and Thomas A. Gregory, "Security, Emotions, Affect," *Critical Studies on Security*, 1, no. 1 (2013): 117–120, 118.
31 Solomon, "I Wasn't Angry," 909, 918.
32 See Sarah Ahmed, *The Cultural Politics of Emotions* (Edinburgh: Edinburgh University Press, 2014).
33 Martha C. Nussbaum, *Upheavals of Thought: The Intelligence of Emotions* (Cambridge: Cambridge University Press, 2003); Emma Hutchison, "Affective Communities as Security Communities," *Critical Studies on Security*, 1, no. 1 (2013): 127–129.
34 See Hutchison, "Affective Communities as Security Communities."
35 See Solomon, "I Wasn't Angry."
36 Caron E. Gentry, "Anxiety and the Creation of the Scapegoated Other," *Critical Studies on Security*, 3, no. 2 (2015): 133–146; Jenny Edkins, "Forget Trauma? Responses to September 11," *International Relations*, 16, no.2 (2002): 243–256.
37 Khaled Fattah and Karin M. Fierke, "A Clash of Emotions: The Politics of Humiliation and Political Violence in the Middle East," *European Journal of International Relations*, 15, no. 1 (2009): 67–93.
38 Roland Bleiker, *Aesthetics and World Politics* (New York: Routledge, 2009), 2.
39 Ibid, 2.
40 Alex Danchev, *On Art and War and Terror* (Edinburgh: Edinburgh University Press, 2009), 4.
41 Bleiker, *Aesthetics and World Politics*, 5, 15, 70.
42 Bleiker, *Aesthetics and World Politics*, 67–68, 50–51, 72–73.
43 Ibid., 11.
44 Ibid., 51, 70–71.
45 Cynthia Enloe, *Bananas, Beaches, and Bases: Making Feminist Sense of International Politics* (Berkeley: University of California Press, 2014).
46 See, for instance, Jill Steans, *Gender and International Relations*, 3rd edn. (London: Polity, 2013), 97–99.
47 Ibid., 9–13.
48 Jean Bethke Elshtain, *Women and War* (Chicago: University of Chicago Press, 1987).
49 See also Kimberly Hutchings' piece on how war constructs masculinity and masculinity constructs war. Kimberly Hutchings, "Making Sense of Masculinity and War," *Men and Masculinities*, 10, no. 4 (2008): 389–404.
50 Valerie M. Hudson et al., *Sex and World Peace* (New York: Columbia University Press, 2012); Nicholas D. Kristof and Sheryl WuDunn, *Half the Sky: Turning Oppression into Opportunity for Women Worldwide* (New York: Vintage Books, 2010); Steven Pinker, *The Better Angels of Our Nature: The Decline of Violence in History and Its Causes* (London: Penguin, 2011).
51 Jacqui True, "Winning the Battle but Losing the War on Violence," *International Feminist Journal of Politics*, 17, no. 4 (2015): 554–572.
52 J. Ann Tickner, *Gender in International Relations: Feminist Perspectives in Achieving Global Security* (New York: Columbia University Press, 1992).
53 Steans, *Gender and International Relations*, 32.

54 Christine Sylvester, "Empathetic Cooperation: A Feminist Method for IR," *Millennium: Journal of International Studies*, 23, no. 2 (1994): 315–334.
55 Ibid., 317.
56 Christine Sylvester, *War as Experience* (London: Routledge, 2012).
57 Laura Sjoberg, *Gendering Global Conflict* (New York: Columbia University Press, 2012).
58 Robert W. Connell and James W. Messerschmidt, "Hegemonic Masculinity: Rethinking the Concept," *Gender and Society*, 19, no. 6 (2005): 829–859.
59 Kenneth Waltz, *Man, the State, and War* (New York: Columbia University Press, 1959).
60 Anthony F. Lang, Jr and Cian O'Driscoll, "The Just War Tradition and the Practice of Political Authority," in *Just War: Authority, Tradition, and Practice*, ed. Anthony F. Lang Jr, Cian O'Driscoll, and John Williams (Washington, DC: Georgetown University Press, 2013).
61 A. J. Coates, *The Ethics of War* (Manchester: Manchester University Press, 1997), 234.
62 Colm McKeogh, *Innocent Civilians: The Morality of Killing in War* (New York: Palgrave, 2002), 6.
63 Michael Walzer, *Just and Unjust Wars: A Moral Argument with Historical Illustrations*, 3rd edn. (New York: Basic Books, 2000), 301.
64 Ibid., 136.
65 Ibid., 135.
66 Coates, *The Ethics of War*, 238.
67 Ibid.
68 Walzer, *Just and Unjust Wars: A Moral Argument with Historical Illustrations*, 145.
69 Ibid., 146.
70 Andrew Linklater, "Towards a Critical Historical Sociology of Transnational Harm," in *Historical Sociology of International Relations*, ed. Stephen Hobden and John M. Hobson (Cambridge: Cambridge University Press, 2002).
71 Ibid., 169.
72 Ibid., 170.
73 Jacob L. Stump and Priya Dixit, eds., *Critical Terrorism Studies: An Introduction to Research Methods* (New York: Routledge, 2013), 7–8.
74 Tarik Kochi, *The Other's War: Recognition and the Violence of Ethics* (New York: Routledge, 2009), 28.
75 Chris Woods, "Analysis: Obama Embraced the Redefinition of 'Civilian' in Drone Wars," *Journal of Investigative Reporting*, May 29, 2012, https://www.thebureauinvestigates.com/opinion/2012-05-29/analysis-obama-embraced-redefinition-of-civilian-in-drone-wars, accessed 4 May 2017.
76 Lauren Wilcox, "Embodying Algorithmic War: Gender, Race, and the Posthuman in Drone Warfare," *Security Dialogue*, 48, no. 1 (2017).
77 Sebastian Kaempf, "Post-Heroic US Warfare and the Moral Justification for Killing in War," in Caron E. Gentry and Amy E. Eckert, *The Future of Just War: New Critical Essays* (Athens: University of Georgia Press, 2014).
78 Laura Sjoberg, *Gendering Global Conflict: Toward a Feminist Theory of War* (New York: Columbia University Press, 2013).
79 Elshtain, *Women and War.*
80 Richard Devetak, "A Rival Enlightenment? Critical International Theory in Historical Mode," *International Theory*, 6, no. 3 (2014).
81 Ibid.

PART IV

Justice, rights and global governance

ETHICS AND INSTITUTIONS

Anthony F. Lang, Jr

Law, justice, and rights frame political discourse in liberal democracies.[1] The role of those liberal democracies in shaping the global order in the twentieth century has resulted in a global realm similarly constituted by these normative ideals. Global institutions such as the United Nations, World Trade Organization, and International Criminal Court, along with regional organizations such as the European Union and Council of Europe, seek to promote the rule of law, international criminal justice, and human rights. The ability of either liberal democracies or global institutions to promote and protect those ideals is, of course, open to debate. But it is clear that the global order draws upon a discourse shaped by these ideals.

Admittedly, rights and justice can be advanced without formal institutions and outside of legal frameworks through practices of contestation and debates around recognition and identity. Indeed, many who wish to contest the dominance of the neoliberal economic and political order that unfairly distributes power and wealth have resisted the liberal framing of the current order. Examples of these sites of resistance include indigenous rights claims to deploy the law to advance restorative justice;[2] the emergence of a right to recognition in opposition to (or sometimes in alliance with) institutionalized human rights discourses;[3] coalitions of NGOs whose advocacy has shaped the creation of institutions such as the International Criminal Court;[4] and the global Occupy movements and World Social Forum that have sought to disrupt existing global economic arrangements. Interestingly, though, as they reject the existing formal institutions at both domestic and international levels, many of these efforts frame their responses through the ideals of justice, rights, and law.[5] In so doing, they demonstrate that, while institutions designed to promote such norms can become corrupted, the norms themselves provide a basis through which contestation and dialogue takes place.

Indeed, the combination of liberalism and contestation reveal why a focus on institutions can provide new insights into ethics and international relations. As this Handbook demonstrates, there is a diversity of ways in which one might engage ethics in international relations. Global institutions are sometimes seen as embodying the best possible outcomes in global politics. Because of the anarchic nature of international affairs, no global authority can coerce states and leaders to act in conformity with human rights or global justice. International institutions provide a halfway house of sorts, where international actors can slowly achieve global norms and make a better world possible. Yet we need to interrogate those institutions through moral frameworks in order to ensure that they do truly advance moral goods for all people. More importantly, not just the formal institutions, but the very norms themselves—rights, justice, law—need to be subject to constant critical scrutiny or they will become settled as the only possible "goods" worth pursuing at the global level. So while liberal ideas manifest in global institutions might provide one set of standards for how the world should be, the contestation and critique to which they are constantly subject is not only the result of political dynamics, but can itself be an important moral good. That is, both institutions and the contestation to which they are subject must be a focus of international ethical inquiry.

Ethics and institutions, in other words, can be understood in a diversity of ways. The four chapters in this section provide theoretical insight and empirical examples of this diversity. This short introduction addresses three themes that cut across all four chapters in this section: institutions, liberalism, and contestation.

Institutions

Institutions can be understood as either state-created formal bureaucratic structures to advance interests and normative agendas or informal political practices that seek to voice the interests and normative agendas of various local, national, and global constituencies. We can evaluate both formal and informal institutions through ethical frameworks, seek to advance ethical agendas, and provide spaces for contesting ethical standards.

There is a large body of literature in international relations (IR) on institutions and institutionalism.[6] Much of this work avoids explicit normative reflection, though ethical reflection has been part of some of the most important works on international institutions. For instance, Robert Keohane, a leading liberal IR theorist, concludes his 1984 book *After Hegemony* by reflecting on the ethical implications of cooperation through institutions. Using a cosmopolitan ethical standard, Keohane argues that such institutions might benefit individuals in advanced states, but that individuals in poorer states do not benefit from the existence of such regimes. He qualifies this slightly by noting some forms of cooperation might be possible through informal networks and negotiations. He also notes that, in terms of self-interest, it is unlikely that powerful states will abandon such institutions because they do not benefit the poorest. Yet he does conclude, "This conditional acceptability of international economic regimes, however does not relieve citizens of the advanced industrialized countries of the obligation to seek to modify the principles on which these institutions are based."[7] This obligation parallels the efforts of political philosophers such as Thomas Pogge who propose reforms of international institutions in order to benefit the poor.[8]

The existence of institutions, then, is not necessarily a moral good for all persons. But all institutions at the global level create outcomes and enable practices that have moral implications. As the contributors to this section demonstrate, then, a focus on ethics and institutions does not mean celebrating specific institutions but rather investigating how they function and evaluating whether or not they advance good outcomes.

Liberalism

The institutions that dominate the international order largely arise from liberal principles. Liberalism is a difficult tradition to define. This is in part because it is not a moral theory like deontology or even a clearly defined political theory such as Marxism. International liberalism raises further complexities, for it arises less from theories and more from political efforts to change the international order, such as late-nineteenth-century Anglo-American efforts to legalize international relations and eighteenth- and nineteenth-century theories of political economy that sought to overcome mercantilism.

Michael Joseph Smith suggests that one of the defining features of international liberalism is an effort to reform the global political order. He notes that international liberalism has proposed "ideas of limiting arbitrary power and protecting individual freedom in a milieu in which such freedom is regularly violated with impunity."[9] The fruits of those efforts have been international institutions and legal structures that define the landscape of global politics, though they soon succumb to the same pathologies of power that existed when states act in unfettered ways.

In her contribution to this Handbook, Beate Jahn provides more nuance for this liberal internationalism in her chapter on historical contexts. Her analysis points to how these ideas arose from particular states and their assumptions about good governance, but also, and more intriguingly, how this international liberalism intersected with assumptions about science and progress. The intersection of science and politics resulted in assumptions about scholarly inquiry which both sustained and was also disrupted by normative inquiry. When a more formal "normative" international relations agenda emerged in the second half of the twentieth century, the liberal theory of John Rawls revived the liberalism which animated these early twentieth-century efforts to create international institutions.[10] In his contribution, Antonio Franceschet highlights Rawls's influence in his chapter on justice, though Franceschet also emphasizes the diverse reactions to Rawls's efforts. Rawls's influence on international theories of liberalism is less the result of his own reflections and more from how it arises from the efforts of those who sought to reinterpret his ideas for a global community, such as Charles Beitz and Thomas Pogge. These figures have not only written important works on global justice: they have also proposed specific ways to reform the global realm, reinforcing Smith's point that international liberalism is animated by a strong reformist agenda (Beitz 1999).[11]

This international liberalism provides a normative foundation to many existing international institutions. As Patrick Hayden describes in his contribution to the Handbook, the international human rights system, composed of UN institutions and legal documents, reflects the liberal ideals of dignity, equality, freedom, and solidarity. In her contribution, Andrea Birdsall highlights how contemporary international legal norms, while originating in a distinctly non-liberal society of states, today reflect a more cosmopolitan liberal agenda, with some going so far as to identify a global constitutional order as its most recent variation (Lang and Wiener 2017).[12]

Liberalism, then, forms an important starting point for considering the ethics of international institutions. But while the contemporary international system is defined in part by key liberal norms, those norms remain subject to continuous evolution and contestation, as described across all four contributions to this Part of the Handbook.

Contestation

Unlike natural law or realism, both of which assume a timeless reality that emerges from either a divine source or the nature of the human person, liberalism assumes change and evolution. This evolution, though, is very much a progressivist one, mirroring the theoretical assumptions of one of the most important liberal political philosophers, Immanuel Kant.[13] Instead of a liberal progressivism, however, the international system displays a more contested character, one that has shaped and reshaped the supposedly settled norms of liberalism noted above.

Antje Wiener argues that contestation is at the heart of global politics. Contestation takes place around norms and practices and within institutions, both formal and informal. The contributors to this section of the Handbook highlight these contested practices. Jahn's account suggests that rather than a unified political science resting on shared liberal norms, the history of ethical reflection on international relations has led to more fragmentation than unity. While this fragmented order can lead to confusion about universalism and a challenge to singular standards, it also gives space for more diversity and plurality.

Franceschet suggests that one of the central political principles, justice, has been subject to more critique than consensus in recent years. This critique, though, is not something that has led to a collapse of the international order, but to an emergence of new perspectives and ideas. Hayden's chapter on human rights explores similar dynamics, pointing to the ways in which supposedly settled rights are constantly being remade and recast by the political activism of different groups and individuals around the globe. Demands of recognition and political action in pursuit of rights both re-inscribe certain liberal norms and also result in new ideas about who or what we count as a subject of our attention in global politics. Birdsall finds similar patterns in international law. Her emphasis on both critical legal theorists and feminist legal theory suggest how contestation is not simply a species of liberalism but can be a full-fledged attack on liberal assumptions, revealing how liberalism can be simply a device by which powerful actors protect their privileges through the control of global rule-making.

Contestation emerges out of liberal assumptions of change and progress. But the institutions that are the focus of these chapters demonstrate how contestation and critique define the international institutional order more than settled assumptions about liberalism. This Part of the Handbook demonstrates how a focus on international institutions from an ethical perspective need not result in an embrace of liberal norms as the only possible way of imagining our world. Instead, they point to how critical, creative, and contested ideas are just as ethical and important for creating a just and peaceful world order.

Notes

1 Thank you to the four contributors to this Part of the book for their feedback on this introduction.
2 S. James Anaya, *Indigenous Peoples in International Law*, 2nd edn. (Cambridge: Cambridge University Press, 2004).
3 Patrick Hayden and Kate Schick, eds., *Recognition and Global Politics: Critical Encounters between State and World* (Manchester: Manchester University Press, 2015).
4 Michael Struett, *The Politics of Constructing the International Criminal Court: NGOs, Discourse, and Agency* (New York: Palgrave, 2008).
5 Anthony F. Lang, Jr, "Global Constituent Power: Protests and Human Rights," in *Protecting Human Rights in an Age of Uncertainty*, ed. Aiden Hehir and Robert Murray (London: Routledge, 2017).
6 Lisa Martin, "Neoliberalism," in *International Relations Theories: Discipline and Diversity*, ed. Tim Dunne, Milja Kurki and Steve Smith (Oxford: Oxford University Press, 2016).
7 Robert Keohane, *After Hegemony: Cooperation and Discord in the World Political Economy* (Ithaca: Cornell University Press, 1984), 256–257.
8 Thomas Pogge, *World Poverty and Human Rights: Cosmopolitan Responsibilities and Reforms*, 2nd edn. (Cambridge: Polity Press, 2008).
9 Michael Joseph Smith, "Liberalism and International Reform," in *Traditions of International Ethics*, ed. Terry Nardin and David Mapel (Cambridge: Cambridge University Press, 1992), 201–202.
10 John Rawls, *A Theory of Justice* (Cambridge, MA: Harvard University Press, 1971).
11 Pogge, *World Poverty and Human Rights*; Charles Beitz, *Political Theory and International Relations*, 2nd edn. (Princeton: Princeton University Press, 1999).
12 Antje Wiener, *Theory of Contestation* (Heidelberg: Springer Publishers, 2014).
13 Immanuel Kant, "Idea for a Universal History from a Cosmopolitan Point of View," [1784] in Immanuel Kant, *Political Writings*, edited and introduced by Hans Reiss, translated by H. B. Nisbet (Cambridge: Cambridge University Press, 1991).

17
HISTORICAL CONTEXT

Beate Jahn

Introduction

Opening a textbook on ethics in international affairs today, one tends to find chapters on a variety of issues. What should we do about poverty, terrorism, human rights violations, or migration?[1] Such issues, however, are not a standard feature of international relations (IR) literature during much of its history. Ethical questions are, hence, subject to historical change. First, ethical problems are the product of historical development. Nuclear weapons or drones, for example, had to be invented before they could be perceived as raising particular ethical challenges. And whether or not, and by whom, such weapons are perceived as a particularly pressing issue also varies over time. Today, for example, nuclear weapons rarely (if at all) feature in ethics textbooks. Second, the way in which we formulate and approach ethical questions changes over time and takes a variety of different forms. Ethics is embedded in the very project of studying international relations as a separate field or discipline; it plays a crucial role in determining the subject matter of this field and the theoretical and methodological approaches we apply to this subject matter. The development of the discipline itself is thus intimately tied to changing perceptions of, and approaches to, ethical questions.

In this chapter, I will therefore tell a history of the discipline in terms of its ethical concerns and approaches, focusing particularly on institutions, law, and rights. Yet I will locate this disciplinary history in the broader context of the development of the modern sciences, on the one hand, and the political context, on the other. The first section briefly outlines the intellectual and political beginnings and the early years of the discipline. The second section describes the development of international thought and its ethical concerns from World War II to the Cold War, and the third section from the 1980s to the post-Cold War period. In the conclusion, I will briefly take stock of the current state of the discipline and its implications for ethics.

Origins and early years

Identifying the origins of particular historical phenomena is always a question of interpretation and choice. As a modern field of study, however, IR has its origins in the nineteenth century in the context of the development of modern academic disciplines in general. Revolutions and the breakup of empires at the end of the eighteenth century undermined not only conventional forms of politics but also its intellectual foundations. This crisis gave rise to a new episteme, that is, a new structure of thought, that established the internal nature of individual phenomena and hence severed them from their context. This way of thinking led to a fragmentation of the field of knowledge and the constitution of a variety of new disciplines like economics, politics, law, history, and sociology. Each of these fields was defined in terms of its internal functions that in turn required specialist methods for their study.[2] Accordingly, the subject matter of the new field of political science was the sovereign state understood in terms of the relationship between government and society.[3] This hierarchical relationship, however, could not account for the horizontal nature of relations between such sovereign states and thus ultimately gave rise to the 'discourse of anarchy' and hence the discipline of IR.[4]

Historically, relations between states became a pressing issue towards the end of the nineteenth century in the context of imperialism. Shifting power relations between major states led to competition for colonies; colonial powers were confronted with indigenous resistance; and demographic change appeared to threaten the superiority of the white over other races—an issue particularly pertinent for multiracial entities like the United States and the British Empire. Addressing these dangers, scholars highlighted growing economic interdependence and held it up as the basis for (potential) cooperation between major states.[5] Norman Angell, for example, argues that states depending for their material wellbeing on industrial production and international trade had nothing to gain, but everything to lose, from war.[6] The ethical desire to prevent conflict between major states and between races thus drove early research into colonial administration, race relations, and interdependence—even while it served to uphold racial and political inequality.

The outbreak of World War I radically undermined these optimistic assumptions that growing interdependence would lead to the obsolescence of war. The scale and horrors of that war provided the impetus for the establishment of the first Chair of International Politics at Aberystwyth in 1919, and thus the first step to the institutionalization of IR as an independent field of study. The remit of this chair was unequivocally ethical: to find ways of preventing (especially major) wars in the future. In this spirit, the first generation of IR scholars analysed the causes of the Great War and identified aggressive tendencies of autocratic governments, on the one hand,[7] and the institutional structure of the international system—especially secret diplomacy and alliance politics—on the other.[8]

Based on these analyses, they developed models for an alternative organization of the international system.[9] Thus Woodrow Wilson famously advocated for democracy, self-determination for European minorities, and collective security arrangements like the League of Nations in his 'fourteen points' speech. International organization and the rule of law played an important role in these models.[10] John Hobson's solution to the problem of imperialism was to internationalize it—with clear parallels to the mandate system of the League of Nations.[11] Paul Reinsch studied 'public international unions',[12] and Leonard Woolf strongly criticized European imperialism (even while he denied colonized Africans the ability to govern themselves).[13]

Early IR scholars, in short, were motivated by the ethical goal to prevent war and conflict and did so by promoting a proactive liberal internationalism in which the development of international law, international institutions facilitating cooperation and rights like self-determination played a crucial role.[14] The latter was supported also by the political commitments of late-nineteenth-century liberalism—a gentler, more community- and welfare-oriented type of liberalism than its classical predecessor—inspired by the work of G. W. F. Hegel.[15] Early IR scholars, in short, were searching for a basis of cooperation and found it in the promises of social science and technological innovation.[16]

World War II and the early Cold War

This early liberal phase of the IR discipline came to an end with the failure of the League of Nations, economic crisis, and ultimately the outbreak of World War II. Realists held the 'liberal idealists' or 'liberal utopians' responsible for the political failure of their projects—for advocating an approach to international politics based on 'abstract principles' and wishful thinking that had no connection with the 'historic processes as they actually took place'.[17] The solution to this problem lay in providing an analysis of 'what is' rather than of 'what ought to be' as a starting point and then prudently work within the given forces for a 'lesser evil' rather than an 'absolute good'.[18] And yet the realist project is itself explicitly an ethical project. Realists saw the very purpose of the disciplines of political science or IR as the ethical desire to 'cure the sicknesses of the body politic' and advocated for the analysis of objective laws of politics as a more promising approach for achieving this goal.[19] Both classical realists and liberal internationalists agreed on the ethical purpose of the discipline and assumed that science was a promising means to achieve such ethical ends: 'Political thought is itself a form of political action.'[20] Classical realists, in fact, set out to rescue the liberal project, to put it on a more realistic footing, rather than to bury it.[21] Hence, ethical concerns determined the development and choice of theoretical approaches.

Classical realists thus tried to identify the objective forces that govern international politics. Crucially, in contrast to domestic politics, there was no overarching power in the international sphere. Consequently, each state had to pursue its national interest through the accumulation of power. Yet, such policies simultaneously presented a potential danger to other states, and thus generated a security dilemma.[22] War was therefore always a possibility, but states could avoid it through successful balancing policies. In most situations, an alliance that would make war too costly could deter would-be aggressors. Such power politics was, however, not devoid of morality. It was, rather, a morality specifically suited to international conditions. The moral obligation of the state lay in the protection of the population. And the pursuit of power and the national interest was the most effective and prudent way to discharge this obligation.

This preponderance of realist approaches fit the political context of the early Cold War period well.[23] Looking over the shoulder of statesman, as Hans Morgenthau suggests,[24] confirmed the bipolar structure of the international system and developed policy advice within these parameters. Managing the standoff with the Soviet Union and developing strategies for dealing with a potential nuclear war thus constituted a major preoccupation of IR scholars at the time. But it also generated critical reflections, again on ethical grounds. Thus, Stanley Hoffmann argues that IR had become an American social science precisely because the desire to influence political practice drove its practitioners—and hence they placed themselves too close to the 'kitchens of power'.[25] Looking over the shoulders of American statesmen meant overlooking the perspectives and interests of other, particularly weaker, actors in the international system. It also entailed accepting the practitioners' understanding of the problems and challenges of world politics rather than to provide them with alternatives. Hoffmann thus argues that science could only fulfil its ethical promise if IR scholars sufficiently distanced themselves from practice, both in time and space, to develop alternative conceptions of international politics.

A second substantive theme that preoccupied IR scholars—together with economists, political scientists, and sociologists—after World War II was the specter of decolonization. There was considerable continuity here, since the question of colonialism had played a crucial role in the constitution and development of IR since the end of the nineteenth century. World War I had already given the resistance and independence movements in many colonies a boost, and the mandate system of the League of Nations essentially acknowledged that the days of Western domination were numbered—even if it managed to extend its lifeline in practice. World War II weakened the old colonial powers further, strengthened independence movements in the colonies, and catapulted two at least formally anti-imperialist superpowers to the top of a bipolar international order. Decolonization had the potential to lead to conflict and war in cases where colonial powers resisted, and it presented the latter with the challenge of safeguarding their economic interests tied up in the resources, labour, and markets of former colonies. With the onset of the Cold War, moreover, both sides vied for the integration of the newly independent states into their sphere of influence.

Modernization theories and the English School took up these challenges. The former developed strategies for integrating these newly independent countries into the liberal capitalist camp through economic aid and political (including at times military) pressure.[26] The latter explored the possibility of expanding an international society hitherto based on European/Christian culture and political institutions into one based on much more basic, and hence universally valid, principles of social life—the protection of life, truth, and property.[27] Moreover, Martin Wight explored the potential of constitutionalism through his research on the legislative council in British colonial government.[28]

Despite the preponderance of realist approaches after World War II, moreover, the earlier preoccupation with international organization also continued into the post-World War II period. David Mitrany had early on argued that scientific and technological advances provide the means to govern a complex international order.[29] His work remained important after World War II and inspired the neofunctionalism of authors like Ernst B. Haas, who explored regional integration.[30] The political developments in the 1960s provided the backdrop against which this type of work moved to the centre of the discipline. The first détente undermined the realist focus on military power, which was further weakened by the experience of the Vietnam War; meanwhile, regional integration in Europe and the oil crisis of the 1970s highlighted the importance, and the complexity, of economic interaction as well as the role of transnational and private actors in international affairs, and it ultimately led to the notion of 'complex interdependence'.[31] Just like the liberal work of the interwar period, the ethical desire to identify means of international cooperation that could then be used to develop a more peaceful international order drove all these approaches. To this end, they analysed a rich variety of technical, legal, institutional forms of cooperation between state and non-state actors.

Finally, nuclear weapons presented a huge ethical challenge that played a key role in shaping the discipline during that period. Nuclear weapons, as their use by the United States against Japan at the end of World War II demonstrated, had destructive powers that radically surpassed conventional weapons. The nuclear arms race between the capitalist camp, led by the US, and the communist Warsaw Pact seemed to bring the annihilation of humanity distinctly into the realm of the possible. This challenge provided the impetus for the development of strategic studies and for peace research. Both were motivated by the aim to prevent a deliberate or accidental nuclear war. The former developed rationales and strategies for 'safely' managing this danger. The doctrine of mutually assured destruction (MAD), for example, held that the ability of both parties to completely annihilate the other side would act as a deterrent for aggression. Stockpiling sufficient nuclear weapons was consequently advocated as a way of preventing nuclear war.[32] Peace researchers, meanwhile, tended to advocate for balanced or even unilateral disarmament. But they too spent much of their time counting weapons and publicizing their findings in the hope that relatively accurate information would lower the risk of war.[33]

But it was not only political developments that influenced the IR field and its ethical motivations. Disaffection with 'idealism' had already materialized in philosophy at the beginning of the twentieth century. New analytic philosophers like Bertrand Russell and G. E. Moore attacked

British idealism for its metaphysical speculation. Analytical philosophers argued instead for a commitment to common sense, clarity, and an openness, particularly to the natural sciences.[34] In IR, though, the realists had insisted on studying 'what is' rather than 'what ought to be', their methodologies, combining historical narrative, philosophical speculation, and anecdote, did not quite live up to this scientific standard. Their work lacked systematic empirical support and was accused of being vulnerable to abuse by totalizing ideologies like communism and fascism.[35]

IR scholars, particularly in the United States, therefore, called for the introduction of more rigorous scientific methods into the discipline—many of them imported from other disciplines, including the natural sciences. Correlation and regression, game theory, and hypothesis testing were all developed in other disciplines and imported into IR.[36] Hence, the ethical desire to produce 'nonideological' knowledge led to new developments in the field. These included systematic data-collection as in J. D. Singer's Correlates of War project,[37] cybernetics and modelling in Karl Deutsch's work,[38] mathematical modelling and game theory in the work of Thomas Schelling,[39] and the 'scientific' reformulation of existing theories in the works of Morton Kaplan[40] and Kenneth Waltz.[41]

Again, however, it was because of ethical concern that conventional methods produced less than 'objective' knowledge, and therefore also questionable political outcomes, that motivated the introduction of these new methods. And it was the same ethical concerns that inspired other scholars to resist these developments and defend a wider range of approaches to international politics.[42] Yet, while the choice of method may have been driven by ethical considerations, both realism and behaviourism assume that excluding normative commitments from the inquiry itself enables science to establish objective knowledge—and hence ethical concerns were, during the early Cold War period, largely relegated to the choice of research topic and method.

The late Cold War period and its aftermath

The onset of the second Cold War, the oil crisis, and European integration led, on the one hand, to a new and this time more 'scientific' formulation of realism by Kenneth Waltz—one that discards assumptions about human nature and provides a systemic explanation for state behaviour instead.[43] Yet the political context also highlighted the continuing importance of the world economy and of international organization and cooperation reflected in turn in neoliberal institutionalism. The 'Neo–Neo debate' thus characterized the 1970s and 1980s.[44] Despite the new methods, however, in substantive terms neorealism did not differ much from classical realism, just as the core ideas of neoliberal institutionalism had been around since the end of the nineteenth century. Neither of these approaches, moreover, seemed to provide answers to the inequalities, economic crises, wars, and human suffering that continued to characterize the international order. This dissatisfaction provided the background for more radical challenges within the discipline.

Critics accused neorealism and neoliberalism of being complicit in maintaining a violent and unjust international order.[45] It was, critics argued, their epistemological commitment to positivism broadly defined that stood in the way of more critical and emancipatory analyses. As Robert Cox famously argued, 'theory is always for someone and for some purpose'[46]—and mainstream theories were seen to reflect the interests of powerful states, classes, and genders. This critique provided the basis for the introduction of a range of new approaches into the discipline.

These included Marxist work that focused on the reproduction of material and political inequality in the international system—from Wallerstein's word systems theory[47] through neo-Gramscian analyses of hegemony[48] to classical Marxist reinterpretations of international relations.[49] Inspired by the second wave of feminism and gender studies, feminists began to investigate the place of women in the international order and identified gender inequalities not only as constitutive of core features of international politics but also of the core concepts of international relations theories.[50] Inspired by Jürgen Habermas, Critical Theorists explored the possibility that the European Union represented a new, post-Westphalian or postnational form of politics and hence a model of political organization conducive to the realization of universal norms.[51] The introduction of Michel Foucault, Jacques Derrida, and other poststructuralist authors allowed IR scholars to highlight the power/knowledge nexus within the discipline as well as in world politics and to explore the performative role of international theories in constituting an unequal and violent world order.[52] Inspired by Edward Said, Homi Bhaba, and Gayatari Spivak, these critical approaches were followed in the 1990s by postcolonialism that investigated the operation of gender, race, and class in the reproduction of unequal power relations between postcolonial and Western states and peoples.[53]

The ethical desire to address and rectify particular forms of injustice within the international system motivate all these approaches—from economic inequalities through the suppression of women and the violation of human rights to racism and neoimperialism. All of them are also inspired by developments in other fields of knowledge. Yet arguably the most important development for ethics and IR occurred in the field of political theory/philosophy with John Rawls's publication of *A Theory of Justice*[54] that constituted an explicitly normative form of theorizing. Inspired by analytical philosophy, Rawls provided a systematic account of the principles by which a just society could be established—and he did so explicitly by abstracting from concrete people or circumstances. Rawls thus paved the way for a conception of normative theory independent of, and indeed constituted in direct opposition to, the assumption that ethical possibilities were determined by the way things 'really are'. Charles Beitz first introduced this approach into the discipline of IR when he adopted it to develop principles for international distributive justice.[55]

The introduction of this type of theorizing into IR led to the establishment of normative theory as a separate subfield of the discipline. Scholars explicitly explored the place and function of norms in international affairs and passionately debated the most promising approach.[56] Originally, cosmopolitanism, inspired by the work of Rawls, was pitched against communitarianism that took its lead, among others, from Michael Walzer's *Spheres of Justice* and *Just and Unjust Wars*.[57] Soon, however, normative theorists began to branch out and explore the implications of classical authors like Kant and Hegel,[58] as well as contemporary alternatives such as Richard Rorty.[59] This body of normative theory in turn also engendered more analytical approaches that explored the constitutive role of normative theories in and for international politics throughout history.[60]

However, the establishment of a separate field of normative theory was also subject to the fragmentary dynamics of modern knowledge in general: that is, it led to internal fragmentation and specialization. Following the original argument that ethical concerns required an approach in their own right within the discipline and the debate between normative theorists over the strengths and weaknesses of different types of normative theory, many scholars devoted their attention to particular ethical challenges—to the development of ethical principles explicitly designed to address particular injustices.

The problem of material inequality was already taken up in the 1970s by Peter Singer who argued on utilitarian grounds that the rich owe the poor a duty of assistance.[61] It was further developed by Charles Beitz, who applied Rawls's principles of justice to the international sphere.[62] More recently, Thomas Pogge identifies the institutional mechanism of the international system that reproduce poverty and thus violate moral principles.[63]

The political organization of the international order constitutes another area for ethical debate. The disjuncture between state-based political organization and the transnational nature of international politics has led to calls for reform. These range from David Held and Daniele Archibugi's model of cosmopolitan democracy through John Dryzek's project of transnational democracy to Allen Buchanan's more conventional state-based attempts to democratize the international order.[64]

Human rights also play a crucial role in normative international theory. The experience of World War II and the Holocaust made it clear that the protection of human rights was not just a matter of domestic politics and led to the Universal Declaration of Human Rights. Yet which rights are to be considered 'human' or basic rights, who has the obligation to protect these rights, and by what means, is highly contested.[65]

One of the core concerns of the discipline—war—has given rise to long-standing debates about the ethics of the use of force. Traditional just war theory has been imported into the discipline and is variously applied to contemporary cases—even while its applicability to contemporary actors, cases, and weapons is contested.[66] The question of Cold War interventions, and in particular the Vietnam War, motivated Michael Walzer's *Just and Unjust Wars*. Jean Elshtain used just war criteria to legitimate the Afghanistan war following the 9/11 attacks.[67] Just war theory also plays an important role in the justification as well as the critique of the theory and practice of humanitarian intervention and the Responsibility to Protect.[68]

Normative theorists, in addition, explore whether and to what extent (international) law provides the means to further ethical goals,[69] what rights and obligations refugees and states have in relation to each other,[70] as well as the ethical implications of environmental challenges.[71] Normative theory, in sum, is a vibrant subfield of IR that explicitly identifies and addresses ethical challenges. Like other fields of study, however, it is also subject to the fragmentary dynamics of modern knowledge. The proliferation of courts, for example, has led to concerns about fragmentation in international law. Such concerns, however, are intimately linked to the normative assumption of a coherent global legal system that only became possible after the end of the Cold War. Against this background, fragmentation can be understood as the struggle against the hegemony and universal aspirations of particular political and legal logics and principles—even while that struggle itself is fought in the name of universality and thus entails 'imperial' aspirations.[72] In a similar vein, normative IR theory—by separating, first, ethical from analytical approaches and, second, particular ethical challenges from others—fails to provide an integrated account of ethics and international politics.

Ethics and IR today

Ethical concerns are embedded within the very constitution of IR as an independent field of study and constitute an integral element of all its theoretical approaches, methodologies, and epistemologies as well as its substantive studies. What is more, ethical commitments have played a crucial role for the dynamic development of the discipline. It was the failure to prevent war that inspired the realist case for new ontologies, the desire to pre-empt abuse by totalitarian ideologies that motivated the introduction of new methodologies, and the goal to establish a just world order that engendered the import of new epistemologies. Ethics thus plays a crucial and pervasive role in IR.

As an integral dimension of the discipline, however, it is also subject to and affected by the latter's general developments. The recent debate on 'the end of IR theory'[73] has shown that the discipline is today characterized by two features: theoretical, methodological, and issue area pluralism, on the one hand, and the almost complete absence of debate between these different approaches, on the other. [74] This picture of the discipline as a whole is also reflected in its normative or ethical subfield. The latter rests on theoretical approaches borrowed from other disciplines, particularly political theory and philosophy. It started out as an explicit critique of conventional theories like realism in IR and quickly led to a vibrant debate between different normative approaches. Theoretically inconclusive, this debate resulted in the coexistence of a variety of normative approaches in the field. And these approaches are now variously applied to a wide range of concrete ethical challenges (or issues) in international politics. Ethics is thus clearly subject to the same dynamics of knowledge-production as other dimensions of the field.

At the core of these dynamics lies fragmentation—the establishment of a plurality of different theoretical approaches and issue areas, each analysed in terms of its own internal nature and thus separated from others. The ethics of war, for example, differs from the ethics of human rights, which is in turn different from green ethics. This fragmentation limits the practical relevance of ethics to its particular issue area. And by doing so, it also leaves unaddressed the ethical dimension of the current international system as a whole—and hence contributes to its reproduction.

This fragmentation in turn undermines one of the historical functions of ethical commitments for the discipline: that of identifying the complicities of IR in constituting an unjust world order and of engendering alternative developments. While partial ethical approaches speak to their particular issue area, they do not offer a general account of the ethical dimensions of knowledge production *per se* and its link to international politics. Consequently, they do not any longer provide a challenge to existing conceptions of the discipline and its dominant approaches.

Neither the fragmentation of the discipline nor a disjointed ethical world order indicate an end of history—and therefore also not an end of theory or of ethics. They do, however, raise the questions of whether and how it can or should address its own increasingly fragmented condition.

Notes

1 Duncan Bell, ed., *Ethics and World Politics* (Oxford: Oxford University Press, 2010).
2 See Michel Foucault, *The Order of Things: An Archeology of the Human Sciences* (London: Tavistock, 1970); Michel Foucault, *The Archeology of Knowledge* (London: Tavistock, 1972); and for a summary with particular attention to IR, see Beate Jahn, 'Theorizing the Political Relevance of International Relations Theory,' *International Studies Quarterly*, 61, no.1 (2016), doi: 10.1093/isq/sqw035.
3 Brian C. Schmidt, *The Political Discourse of Anarchy: A Disciplinary History of International Relations* (Albany: SUNY Press, 1998), 44; James Farr, 'Political Science,' in *The Cambridge History of Science*, ed. T. M. Porter and D. Ross (Cambridge: Cambridge University Press, 2008), 306–328.
4 Schmidt, *Political Discourses*.
5 David Long and Brian C. Schmidt, 'Introduction,' in *Imperialism and Internationalism in the Discipline of International Relations*, ed. by David Long and Brian C. Schmidt (Albany: SUNY Press, 2005), 14; Robert Vitalis, *White World Order, Black Power Politics* (Ithaca: Cornell University Press, 2013).
6 Norman Angell, *The Great Illusion: A Study of the Relation of Military Power in Nations to their Economic and Social Advantage* (London: Heinemann, 1910).
7 Woodrow Wilson, President Wilson's Message to Congress, January 8, 1918, Records of the United States Senate, Record Group 46, National Archives, accessed October 18, 2016.
8 Paul S. Reinsch, *Secret Diplomacy: How Far Can It Be Eliminated?* (London: George Allen and Unwin, 1922), 178.
9 See Schmidt, *Political Discourse*, especially chapters 5 and 6; as well as David Long and Brian C. Schmidt, eds., *Imperialism and Internationalism in the Discipline of International Relations* (Albany: SUNY Press, 2005).
10 Alfred Zimmern, *The League of Nations and the Rule of Law* (London: Macmillan, 1936).
11 John A. Hobson, *Imperialism: A Study* (London: James Nisbet, 1902).
12 Paul S. Reinsch, *Public International Unions, Their Work and Organization: A Study in International Administrative Law* (Boston: Ginn and Co., 1911).
13 Leonard Woolf, *Mandates and Empire* (London: League of Nations Union, 1920).
14 Long and Schmidt, *Introduction*, 19.

15 See, for example, David Boucher and Andrew Vincent, *British Idealism and Political Theory* (Edinburgh: Edinburgh University Press, 2000).
16 Jan Stefan Fritz, 'Internationalism and the Promise of Science,' in *Imperialism and Internationalism in the Discipline of International Relations*, ed. David Long and Brian C. Schmidt (Albany: SUNY Press, 2005), 141–158.
17 Edward H. Carr, *The Twenty Years' Crisis 1919–1939* (London: Macmillan, 1939), 7, 8; Hans J. Morgenthau, *Politics among Nations: The Struggle for Power and Peace* (New York: Alfred A. Knopf, 1948), 3, 4.
18 Carr, *Crisis*, 5; Morgenthau, *Politics*, 3–4.
19 Carr, *Crisis*, 3; Morgenthau, *Politics*, 4.
20 Carr, *Crisis*, 5.
21 Michael C. Williams, 'In the Beginning: The International Relations Enlightenment and the Ends of International Relations Theory,' *European Journal of International Relations*, 19, no. 3 (2013).
22 John H. Herz, *Political Realism and Political Idealism: A Study in Theories and Realities* (Chicago: University of Chicago Press, 1951).
23 Reinhold Niebuhr, *Moral Man and Immoral Society* (New York: Charles Scribner's, 1932); George Kennan, *American Diplomacy* (New York: New American Library, 1952).
24 Morgenthau, *Politics*, 5.
25 Stanley Hoffmann, 'An American Social Science: International Relations,' *Daedalus*, 106, no. 3 (1977): 49.
26 Edward L. Morse, *Modernization and the Transformation of International Relations* (New York: The Free Press, 1976); Walt W. Rostow, *The Stages of Economic Growth: A Non-Communist Manifesto* (Cambridge: Cambridge University Press, 1971); Robert A. Packenham, *Liberal America and the Third World: Political Development Ideas in Foreign Aid and Social Science* (Princeton: Princeton University Press, 1973); M. E. Latham, *Modernization as Ideology: American Social Science and 'Nation Building' in the Kennedy Era* (Chapel Hill: University of North Carolina Press, 2000).
27 Hedley Bull, *The Anarchical Society: A Study of Order in World Politics* (Basingstoke: Macmillan, 1977), 5, 13.
28 Anthony Lang, Jr, 'Global Constitutionalism as a Middle-Ground Ethic,' in *Ethical Reasoning in International Affairs: Arguments from the Middle Ground*, ed. Cornelia Navari (Basingstoke: Palgrave, 2013), 116.
29 Fritz, 'Internationalism,' 156.
30 Ernst B. Haas, *The Uniting of Europe: Political, Social, and Economic Forces, 1950–1957* (Stanford: Stanford University Press, 1958).
31 Robert O. Keohane and Joseph S. Nye, eds., *Transnational Relations and World Politics* (Cambridge, MA: Harvard University Press, 1971); and Robert O. Keohane and Joseph S. Nye, *Power and Interdependence: World Politics in Transition* (Boston: Little, Brown, 1977).
32 Mark Trachtenberg, *History and Strategy* (Princeton: Princeton University Press, 1991); Morton Kaplan, ed., *Strategic Thinking and Its Moral Implications* (Chicago: University of Chicago Press, 1973); Thomas C. Schelling, *The Strategy of Conflict* (Cambridge, MA: Harvard University Press, 1960).
33 The Peace Research Institute Oslo (PRIO) was founded in 1959, the Stockholm International Peace Research Institute (SIPRI) in 1966, and the Peace Research Institute Frankfurt (PRIF) in 1970, to mention but a few.
34 Colin Bird, 'Ethics and Analytical Political Philosophy,' in *Ethics and World Politics*, ed. Duncan Bell (Oxford: Oxford University Press, 2010), 18.
35 Thomas Biersteker, 'Critical Reflections on Post-Positivism in International Relations,' *International Studies Quarterly*, 33, no. 3 (1989): 266.
36 Mary S. Morgan, 'Economics,' in *The Cambridge History of Science*, ed. T. M. Porter and D. Ross (Cambridge: Cambridge University Press, 2008), 282–283, 300.
37 The Correlates of War Project, http://correlatesofwar.org, accessed October 7, 2016.
38 Karl W. Deutsch, *Nationalism and Social Communication: An Inquiry into the Foundations of Nationality* (Cambridge, MA: The MIT Press, 1953); and Karl W. Deutsch, B. Fritsch, H. Jaquaribe and A. S. Markovitz, eds., *Problems of World Modeling: Political and Social Implications* (Cambridge, MA: Ballinger, 1977).
39 Thomas C. Schelling, *Arms and Influence* (New Haven: Yale University Press, 1966).
40 Morton A. Kaplan, *System and Process in International Politics* (New York: John Wiley and Sons, 1957).
41 Kenneth W. Waltz, *Theory of International Politics* (New York: McGraw-Hill, 1979).
42 See Morton A. Kaplan, 'The New Great Debate: Traditionalism vs. Science in International Relations,' *World Politics*, 19, no. 1 (1966): 1–20; Hedley Bull, 'International Theory: The Case for the Classical Approach,' *World Politics*, 19, no. 3 (1966): 361–377; Nicolas Guilhot, *The Invention of International Relations Theory* (New York: Columbia University Press, 2011).

43 Waltz, *Theory.*
44 David A. Baldwin, ed., *Neorealism and Neoliberalism: The Contemporary Debate* (New York: Columbia University Press, 1993).
45 Richard K. Ashley and R. B. J. Walker, 'Speaking the Language of Exile: Dissident Thought in International Studies,' *International Studies Quarterly*, 34, no. 3 (1990): 259–268.
46 Robert W. Cox, 'Social Forces, States, and World Orders,' *Millennium: Journal of International Studies*, 12, no. 2 (1981): 128.
47 Immanuel Wallerstein, *World Systems Analysis: An Introduction* (Durham: Duke University Press, 2004).
48 Robert W. Cox, 'Gramsci, Hegemony, and International Relations: An Essay in Method,' *Millennium: Journal of International Studies*, 12, no. 2 (1983), 162–175.
49 Justin Rosenberg, *The Empire of Civil Society: A Critique of the Realist Theory of International Relations* (London: Verso, 1994).
50 Cynthia Enloe, *Bananas, Beaches and Bases: Making Feminist Sense of International Politics* (London: Pandora, 2001); Fiona Robinson, *Globalizing Care: Ethics, Feminist Theory and International Relations* (Boulder, CO: Westview Press, 1999); J. Ann Tickner, 'You Just Don't Understand: Troubled Engagements between Feminists and IR Theorists,' *International Studies Quarterly*, 41, no. 4 (1997), 611–632.
51 Andrew Linklater, *Men and Citizens in the Theory of International Relations* (Basingstoke: Macmillan, 1982); Andrew Linklater, *The Transformation of Political Community: Ethical Foundations of the Post-Westphalian Era* (Cambridge: Polity Press, 1998); Mark Hoffmann, 'Critical Theory and the Inter-Paradigm Debate,' *Millennium: Journal of International Studies*, 16, no. 2 (1987), 231–250; Mark A. Neufeld, *The Restructuring of International Relations Theory* (Cambridge: Cambridge University Press, 1995).
52 David Campbell, *Writing Security: United States Foreign Policy and the Politics of Identity* (Minneapolis: University of Minnesota Press, 1992); Jenny Edkins, *Post-Structuralism and International Relations: Bringing the Political Back In* (Boulder, CO: Lynne Rienner Press, 1999); Ashley and Walker, *Dissident Thought.*
53 Roxanne L. Doty, *Imperial Encounters: The Politics of Representation in North–South Relations* (Minneapolis: University of Minnesota Press, 1997); Sanjay Seth, ed., *Postcolonial Theory and International Relations: A Critical Introduction* (London: Routledge, 2012); Robbie Shilliam, *The Black Pacific: Anticolonial Struggles and Oceanic Connections* (London: Bloomsbury Academic Press, 2015).
54 John Rawls, *A Theory of Justice* (Cambridge, MA: Harvard University Press, 1971).
55 Charles R. Beitz, *Political Theory and International Relations* (Princeton: Princeton University Press, 1979).
56 Charles R. Beitz, Marshall Cohen, Thomas Scanlon and A. John Simmons, eds., *International Ethics* (Princeton: Princeton University Press, 1985); Stanley Hoffmann, *Duties Beyond Borders: On the Limits and Possibilities of Ethical International Politics* (Syracuse: Syracuse University Press, 1981); Hugh C. Dyer, *Moral Order/World Order: The Role of Normative Theory in the Study of International Relations* (Basingstoke: Macmillan, 1997); Chris Brown, *International Relations Theory: New Normative Approaches* (New York: Columbia University Press, 1992).
57 Michael Walzer, *Spheres of Justice: A Defense of Pluralism and Equality* (New York: Basic Books, 1984); Michael Walzer, *Just and Unjust Wars: A Moral Argument with Historical Illustrations* (New York: Basic Books, 1977).
58 Kimberly Hutchings, *Kant, Critique and Politics* (London: Routledge, 1996); Kimberly Hutchings, *Hegel and Feminist Philosophy* (Cambridge: Polity Press, 2003); Mervyn Frost, *Towards a Normative Theory of International Relations* (Cambridge: Cambridge University Press, 1986).
59 Molly Cochran, *Normative Theory in International Relations: A Pragmatic Approach* (Cambridge: Cambridge University Press, 1999).
60 David Boucher, *Political Theories of International Relations: From Thucydides to the Present* (Oxford: Oxford University Press, 1998); Beate Jahn, ed., *Classical Theory in International Relations* (Cambridge: Cambridge University Press, 2006).
61 Peter Singer, 'Famine, Affluence, and Morality,' *Philosophy and Public Affairs*, 1 (1972): 229–243.
62 Beitz, *Political Theory.*
63 Thomas Pogge, *World Poverty and Human Rights* (Cambridge: Polity Press, 2002).
64 David Held, *Democracy and the Global Order: From the Modern State to Cosmopolitan Governance* (Cambridge: Polity Press, 1995); Daniele Archibugi, *The Global Commonwealth of Citizens: Toward Cosmopolitan Democracy* (Princeton: Princeton University Press, 2008); John Dryzek, *Deliberative Global Politics: Discourse and Democracy in a Divided World* (Cambridge: Polity Press, 2006); Allen Buchanan and Robert O. Keohane, 'The Preventive Use of Force: A Cosmopolitan Institutionalist Perspective,' *Ethics and International Affairs*, 18, no. 1 (2004): 1–22.

65 Henry Shue, *Basic Rights: Subsistence, Affluence, and US Foreign Policy* (Princeton: Princeton University Press, 1980); Onora O'Neill, *Bounds of Justice* (Cambridge: Cambridge University Press, 2000); Jack Donnelly, *Universal Human Rights in Theory and Practice* (Ithaca: Cornell University Press, 2003).

66 Nicholas Rengger, *Just War and International Order: The Uncivil Condition in World Politics* (Cambridge: Cambridge University Press, 2013).

67 Jean B. Elshtain, *Just War against Terror: The Burden of American Power in a Violent World* (New York: Basic Books, 2003).

68 Nicholas J. Wheeler, *Saving Strangers: Humanitarian Intervention in International Society* (Oxford: Oxford University Press, 2000); Alex Bellamy, *Responsibility to Protect: The Global Effort to End Mass Atrocities* (Cambridge: Cambridge University Press, 2009); Anthony F. Lang, Jr, *Agency and Ethics: The Politics of Military Intervention* (Albany: SUNY Press, 2002).

69 Cecilia Lynch and Michael Loriaux, eds., *Law and Moral Action in World Politics* (Minneapolis: University of Minnesota Press, 2000).

70 Arash Abizadeh, 'Citizenship, Immigration and Boundaries,' in *Ethics and World Politics*, ed. Duncan Bell (Oxford: Oxford University Press, 2010), 358–376.

71 Matthew Humphrey, 'Green Political Theory,' in *Ethics and World Politics,* ed. Duncan Bell (Oxford: Oxford University Press, 2010), 181–199.

72 Martti Koskenniemi and Päivi Leino, 'Fragmentation of International Law? Postmodern Anxieties,' *Leiden Journal of International Law*, 15, no. 3 (2002): 559, 562, 574, 578–579.

73 Colin Wight, Lene Hansen and Tim Dunne, 'The End of International Relations Theory?' *European Journal of International Relations*, 19, no. 3 (2013): 405–425.

74 Christine Sylvester, 'Experiencing the End and Afterlives of International Relations/Theory,' *European Journal of International Relations*, 19, no. 3 (2013): 609–626.

18

JUSTICE

Constitution and critique

Antonio Franceschet

Introduction

The idea of justice is many things. The idea is represented in countless paintings and sculptures of Lady Justice.[1] Typically blindfolded and holding scales high in one hand, she carries a sword in her other hand. Sometimes she stands firmly on a serpent, preventing it from doing harm. Justice is supposed to be impartial, enforceable, and morally praiseworthy. We approximate justice by integrating these features into interactions with others, and by ensuring them in our social institutions.

Since the early 1970s, debates about international justice and global justice—a domain that encompasses yet transcends interstate politics—have influenced the research of key topics.[2] As this volume attests, we can assess war and security, humanitarian intervention, economics, the environment, and health, among other issues, from a justice perspective. Moreover, concern with justice and injustice has brought critical attention to issues such as gender, the environment, and nonhuman species. Putting justice at the center of discussion in international ethics makes sense. As John Rawls famously argued: "Justice is the first virtue of social institutions, as truth is of systems of thought."[3] Even for those more skeptical about universal truth claims and reified "systems of thought," justice motivates contestation over the fairness and legitimacy of global political life. In recent years, resistance to neoliberalism, global economic institutions, and growing global inequalities is framed as the "global justice movement."[4]

This chapter argues that justice is at the crossroads of two key aspects of international ethics: the constitution and critique of politics. By "constitution," I refer to the persistent role of ideas about justice in reasoning about moral agency, choice, and outcomes across intersocietal boundaries. The concept of "critique" points to the practice of standing apart from hegemonic political assumptions and rules, and evaluating them from a standpoint of justice.[5] Rather than treat justice as a single, substantive, and fixed essence, the ensuing discussion highlights the shifting, intersubjectively shared (and contested) senses of what is due to others, particularly among individuals, groups, and societies in international politics.

This chapter has two sections. First, I question the conventional wisdom that domestic, intrasocietal politics is the foundational source of the concept and experience of justice. Instead, I show that justice's meaning is derived very directly from international political issues. Such issues include how different societies treat outsiders, and the responsibilities of those with power and authority to enforce and punish violations of moral and legal rules. Rather than being devoid of justice, international politics are an indispensable crucible through which the concept's connotation has been continually reshaped.

The second section examines the unique role of liberalism in reshaping justice and international politics. Beginning in the eighteenth century, liberalism's chief influence has been at two related levels: ideas and fundamental institutions. At the level of ideas, liberal theory has altered the discussion of justice, from a focus on the interactions among agents to the coercive and distributive nature of social institutions. At the level of institutions, liberal ideas about procedural justice have shifted power to contractual international law and multilateralism, reconstituting the international system, and thereby creating new opportunities for justice at the global level. Yet some liberals and many radical critics of liberalism contest how the translation of its ideas into institutions has sustained and created numerous global injustices.

Constituting justice

Justice concerns what is fair and what is due to individuals, peoples, states, and, more recently, to other beings or entities such as animals and the natural environment. International politics is traditionally viewed as a special case of justice. Many presume that the international domain provides little or no opportunity for impartial, enforceable, and ethical action. Insecurity, competition, and the tendency for partiality (or an in-group bias) thwart the reliable fulfillment of the Lady Justice's iconic virtues.[6] A realist tradition of international ethics is deeply skeptical about moral obligations to treat others justly, or the need to comply with international institutions.[7] Other traditions, such as natural law, cosmopolitanism, and liberal internationalism, are more positive and hopeful, while each still presumes that a higher standard of justice is achievable *within* political communities.[8] For these traditions, international politics needs to be reined in, either by encouraging leaders to behave ethically or by domesticating such politics through enforceable principles. Justice creates general obligations that travel across borders. At the same time, justice is not first born and then perfected in domestic isolation. Rather, its meaning has been constructed through international confrontations, violations, and recognitions among collective selves and others.[9]

Philosophers have long assumed that justice has various preconditions, including what Rawls called a "sense of justice," or a basic capacity for reciprocity.[10] The specific manifestations of this sense vary in different historic contexts. Ancient scholars wondered whether the capacity for justice is inherent and natural or rooted in a person's particular moral education. For Plato, justice had an underlying form and can be expressed through rational speech.[11] Moreover, justice could be understood in fairly exacting terms, compared to what the poets and Sophists offered. Yet Plato suggested that, in actual cities, perfect justice was impossible; it could only be achieved in degrees. Moreover, political justice relies on a city of individuals who possess harmonious souls, constituted by desire, reason, and spirit.[12] Aristotle compared and categorized different Greek constitutions, but like Plato, he presumed that justice is an adjective attached to the virtuous individual, acting moderately and treating others fairly.[13] Ultimately, as a discourse spanning more than two and a half millennia, the canon on justice has not determined whether the most important source of justice is philosophic knowledge, membership in a just city, or simply a basic and human sense of justice that can be encouraged and cultivated with the right set of institutions.

A value of a constitutive approach to international politics and justice can be illustrated through a critique of the previous paragraph's silences. The standard entry point for conceptualizing justice is to note that the ancient tendency to attach justice to the individual agent is largely *passé* and has been supplanted by a modern concern with "the justice or otherwise of social institutions."[14] But to dive into an abstract discussion of the principles of just social institutions would elide certain major assumptions and exclusions in the canon. Merely shifting the discussion *from* an individual person's sense of justice *to* social institutions leaves unchallenged the gendered and sexist presumptions pervading the entire philosophical discourse. Plato and Aristotle presumed that men and women have unequal capabilities *vis-à-vis* cultivating justice and, for that reason, play different roles in society.[15] Equally significant, the canon is often presented as a straight line from ancient Greece, to the European Enlightenment, to the liberal present, without leaving the West. Amartya Sen's *The Idea of Justice* corrects the tendency towards Western parochialism:

> [S]imilar—or closely linked—ideas of justice, fairness, responsibility, duty, goodness and rightness have been pursued in many parts of the world. . . [Yet] the global presence of such reasoning is often overlooked or marginalized in the dominant traditions of contemporary Western discourse.[16]

The contents of Confucian, Islamic, and Buddhist traditions, among others, raise the need both to be "just" about the concept of justice and to give what is due to different global formulations of the same basic ideal. Critiques of leading narratives and conceptions of justice feed into the possibility of *re*-constituting accepted notions of which agents are capable of a sense of justice, how that sense is expressed, and how legitimate variations among societies emerge from different epistemic, cultural, and political contexts. Indeed, repressing such variation is an unjust and often violent form of domination to be critiqued. Inter-societal violence and domination are key themes in long-standing narratives through which international politics and justice are mutually constitutive.

In much of the canon, domestic politics is treated as a higher, ethically superior realm. But rather than reflecting a given reality, international politics is constituted not by the *absence* of justice, but by its continuously assumed *presence* as an ideal. Martin Wight's famous "Why Is There No International Theory?" reaffirms this narrative.[17] In response, R. B. J. Walker critiques the historically contingent and unstable inside/outside dichotomy that animates (received interpretations of) the Western tradition.[18] A constitutive account of justice holds that, in practice, there is no international politics without the concept of justice. Justice's content has been fashioned through repeated, institutionalized, historic encounters between international selves and others.

Plato's *Republic* discusses how a just city requires a guardian class educated in justice, not least to know how best to defend insiders from attack.[19] Plato and Aristotle each question whether a just city limits its appetites for more power and domination over others.[20] For the philosophers, these questions must be dealt with comprehensively and critically. Therefore, Plato's Socrates rejects the notion that justice is simply the "advantage of the stronger," as the Sophist Thracymachus puts it.[21] Rather, Socrates holds that injustice is simply wrong and is therefore wrong in relations within and among cities.[22] Plato and Aristotle use dialectical rationality in order to invent ethical standards with a direct application to politics *qua* politics, and not simply domestic politics. Moreover, in ancient Athens and other cities, internal strife, upheavals, and injustices within the political community were regular, widely known occurrences. Aristotle's *Politics* diagnosed how various actual cities, as unique selves, could be compared and critically judged in relation to the others. Although no city was perfectly just, some were singled out for being more or less just or moderate in all things. Among different cities, moral judgments among collective selves and others shaped the meaning of politics generally, not just domestic politics.

To what extent does justice depend on the faithful adherence of enforceable rules of reciprocity? This question frames the discussion differently than positing a harmony of the parts of the individual soul or city. If among separate communities there is no functional integration between the self and others, but only mere "relations" such as trade, alliances, and war, then there is no substantive *good* implied by justice. Equally important, if there is nothing but ignorance and distrust about distant threats, what degree of reciprocity is possible? Here, the notion of a sense of justice is less idealized. What matters is how we should treat the other and strangers.

Such questions raise two contrasting narratives about international justice as articulated by Thucydides's in *The History of the Peloponnesian War*.[23] The first is that having a common sense of justice does not prevent injustices. The situation of anarchy and war eliminates any real ethical choice. Moreover, the possibility of reciprocity among unequal powers is questionable, particularly in times of war. Notoriously in the *History*, Athens dictates to the weaker Melian people that they can either capitulate or face merciless slaughter and subjugation.[24] The Athenians also insist that, if the situation were reversed, the Melians would behave no differently. Some realists see this episode as affirming the timeless truth that power and survival trump justice.[25] Michael Walzer resists this form of realism and argues that a common morality, found in the just war tradition, inserts a sense of justice in even the most extreme situations of violent conflict.[26] For Walzer, there is *always* ethical discourse and moral choice, and even where there are major power asymmetries, the strong and weak are obligated to observe basic norms of reciprocity rooted in widely recognized standards of justice. Thucydides reports on the Melian episode as a detached observer, and therefore some modern readers infer his acceptance of Athens's cynical position.[27] However, Athens is eventually wracked by internal dissension and external defeat, the causes and conditions of which were connected to having defied the Greek gods and moral conventions.[28] The second narrative from Thucydides's account is that when the powerful act without *any* regard for international justice, they typically suffer corrosive and damaging domestic injustices.[29]

Powerful actors are never entirely free from the constraints of justice. As Walzer argues, "moral talk is coercive, one thing leads to another."[30] Discourse about justice reflects ideas about the possibility and necessity of punishing international actors for wrongdoing. Historically, wrongs invite varying responses, secular and religious. From infamy to eternal damnation, from reprisals to criminal trials, a sense of justice is enacted in various forms of punishment.[31] Lesser forms of punishment include moral criticism and infamy, and are often viewed as a price worth paying, particularly if, as the Athenians claimed, injustices are simply a brute reality, "as the world goes."[32] Many realists argue that justice is an insubstantial constraint when a community is faced with existential threats to survival. After all, even Walzer's "moral talk" becomes hushed when he famously outlines a concept of "supreme emergency" as a necessary but temporary suspension of justice, permitting the deliberate slaughtering of enemy civilians.[33] But Walzer's explanation is that, even when otherwise decent actors are forced to do evil (by an unjust enemy), justice remains audible and is commanding. Lady Justice's virtues remain to oversee social reality, providing a sense of limits to the extent of injustice that a state might be forced to commit while resisting evil. Walzer's example of such evil is the Nazis.[34] In invading, colonizing, enslaving, and liquidating populations, the Nazis illustrated no capacity for a sense of justice. Destroying the Nazi regime is a constitutive moment in modern politics. In this case, we see that, by nature, justice that cannot be automatically associated with life *within* an exclusive domestic political community. To the contrary, justice requires an international community with the will and power to coercively impose a wider, collective sense of justice to defeat a racially defined misconception of justice. This coercive dimension of international justice is discussed further below.

Deep misconceptions of justice are difficult to correct through international political means alone. Walzer's work is again illustrative. He suggests that the just war tradition grounds a pre-existing moral consensus brought to bear in modern international laws on protecting sovereignty and outlawing aggression.[35] If everyone adopts the same basic justice framework, and outliers (like the Nazis) are checked and punished, then, for Walzer, politics is playing its proper role. But by recalling that the just war tradition has roots in natural law theory, we see that political power does not always relate to justice so neatly, and that blaming politics for the commission of injustices would miss the point. Going back to the Crusades and the so-called discovery of the Americas, horrible injustices were committed from *within* the same, basic moral framework. Individuals and entire civilizations were constituted as deficient and lacking in the sovereign capacities required of a sense of justice.[36] Indeed, a shared European and putatively Christian conception of justice was used to authorize a right of conquest and punishment of non-believers. The realist critique of discourses of international justice is a critique of such fervent moralism.[37]

A constitutive account of justice highlights its fraught, multiple relationships to power and international politics. On the one hand, justice requires enforcement powers. Lady Justice carries a sword. On the other hand, the ideal of justice is used and abused by those with power, claiming a moral authorization to violate and dominate others without restraint. When power is overly shaping justice, it is not always an "equal opportunity" language. That is, the coercive talk of morality—to paraphrase Walzer—is asymmetrically distributed in favor of dominant actors and their interests. Interestingly, the Athenians never claimed to the Melians that Athens had the gods or natural laws on its side, but only material power resources. Yet at the same time, the Melians responded that honor was at stake in their resisting Athens's injustice. Weaker groups have nearly always expressed and mobilized resistance through the concept of justice.[38]

Liberalism, justice, and international ethics

This section argues that, starting in the eighteenth century, liberal ideas contributed to a shift in hegemonic conceptions of international justice. Focusing on the similarities of two key liberal justice theorists, Immanuel Kant (1724–1804) and Rawls (1921–2002), we see how justice becomes a matter of coercive and distributive features of social institutions and not as it was for the ancients, a moral virtue of agents. Additionally, both thinkers formed a distinctly modern idea that the moral legitimacy of institutions depends ultimately on individual rights. Such rights are the basis for establishing and reforming institutions to be more just or fair, and to critique and reject incorrect principles of justice, such as those based entirely on tradition, religious precept, or ensuring the harmonious functioning of the political community.

Liberalism is a complex, diverse tradition with a common concern for the individual person's moral interests. These interests are typically discussed in terms of the rights of "man," of citizens, and, by the twentieth century, human rights. Not all liberals see the need to situate rights in a systematic theory of justice. In arguing that rights claims need to be grounded in institutions, Kant and Rawls each set an influential standard. As Brighouse writes, most contemporary philosophers assume that justice concerns "how we relate to other people through social institutions."[39] Based on ideas within Kant and Rawls, a reconstitution of international justice means going beyond classical forms of ethical reasoning found in both the ancient and the natural law traditions. Moreover, we can critique and reform existing international practices that have institutionalized unjust outcomes including war, colonialism, racial discrimination, and human rights abuses. For each thinker, individual liberties matter but are only consistent with justice when grounded in specific institutional forms, located both within and among states.

Kant divides ethical virtues from political justice. He starts by arguing that the categorical imperative is the underlying principle of ethics. Moral agents need to test their proposed actions against this principle's requirements of universalizability and respect for humanity.[40] Moral action is for its own sake rather than for any positive feelings or anticipated benefits. In contrast to the classical tradition, Kant argues that the precondition of justice is not virtuous individuals. Rather, justice is a property of broader systemic interactions among agents.[41] Thus, when it comes to the ownership of property, obedience to a society's laws, criminal punishment, and questions of war and peace, justice concerns the underlying institutional order that constrains all agents' choices. For this reason, Kant argues that justice requires the sovereign state to coercively ensure consistent domains of external freedom.[42] He even writes, "[A]s difficult as it may sound, [justice] is a problem that can be solved even for a nation of devils (if only they possess understanding)."[43] This is a bold claim: even rational egoists would recognize that they are better off with systemic constraints on their choices. Even for devilish individuals, there is a sufficient sense of justice to motivate compliance with a social order based on equal rights. Once the state's institutions are established, individuals have trust in an enforced constitutional order rather than in specific men, be they kings or religious authorities.

The logical extension of Kant's theory of justice is a global social contract, a universal sovereign, with centralized coercive restrictions of all human beings. But Kant rejects the idea, claiming that a global state would undermine the morally legitimate independent states already in existence.[44] Instead, Kant argues that states have obligations to eventually submit to a coercive order when their peoples are ready to take that step. In what one might see as a precursor to the European Union, he claims that states could gradually move towards a unified system justice rather than having it imposed on them. At the same time, Kant did not foresee the need to deterritorialize sovereign powers through multilevel governance. Instead, individuals have cosmopolitan rights to hospitality and to visit other societies, with political citizenship being firmly anchored in a particular set of constitutional arrangements.

Ultimately, Kant treated the elimination of war as the most urgent international justice issue. War is unjust because it resolves conflicts through violence rather than law. Moreover, Kant diagnosed war as the symptom of unjust domestic conditions, where absolutist rulers imposed the costs and risks of foreign adventures on their subjects—and without their consent. A just international order would replace war with arbitration and diplomacy and would see international society band together to enforce peace against aggressors. Here, Kantian liberalism intersects with a modern form of just war thinking, discussed further below. Unjust enemies are those "whose publicly declared will (be it through words or deeds) betrays a maxim which, if it were made into a general rule, would make peace among the peoples impossible and would instead perpetuate the state of nature."[45] Kant clarifies that such deeds constitute a "breach of public contracts" rather than arbitrary and irrelevant characteristics of the state, such as regime type, religion, or internal political and social practices.

Kant's theory of international justice is significant for two key reasons. First, his philosophy provides the basis for a radical, liberal critique of pre-existing ideas and practices of his day. That today his critique seems relatively conservative is a function of how liberalism has come to dominate modern conceptions of justice. Second, Kant's liberalism reflects a modern reconstitution of how international society institutionalizes justice. Contemporary society's key post-eighteenth-century features mirror the gist of Kant's arguments that states ought to relate to each other through trust and legal procedures that protect each other's sovereignty, and, in the process, the fundamental rights of individuals.

Social constructivist theorists Alexander Wendt and Christian Reus-Smit each show how, in practice, the international system has changed to reflect Kantian precepts. For Wendt, international anarchy among states is not static; it reflects the underlying distribution of state ideas and conceptions about self and other.[46] Rather than anarchy being an empty given, as in neorealist theory, anarchy is constituted by states through repeated interactions. Wendt's social theory of international politics supports the idea that states view each other through a justice lens. Justice has a role in different historically specific anarchies, each constituted by distinctive sets of shared judgments. These judgments vary along a continuum of Hobbesian, Lockean, and Kantian ideals.[47] In a Hobbesian anarchy, states regard each other as enemies who cannot trust each other to act justly. Lockean anarchy relaxes such insecurity; states view each other as rivals who can "live and let live" without harm. Finally, in Kantian anarchy, states view each other as friends; they rely on each other to ensure their mutual security, and by internalizing a sense of obligation and trust. To Wendt, the post-World War II institutional order among states in the Western security community reflects a Kantian, liberal anarchy.[48] Although imperfect from the standpoint of Kant's ideal ethical theory, Wendt's narrative of progressive change reflects an institutional approximation of international justice. Indeed, Wendt's social theory forecasts the development of a world state that goes beyond Kant's hopes for collective security.[49]

A liberal order among states is also the product of more specific institutional practices. Reus-Smit's account of modern international society also dovetails with Kantian justice.[50] The sovereign state's "moral purpose" is constituted from social interactions, both within and among societies. Reus-Smit argues that, beginning in the late eighteenth century, the state's purpose shifted away from upholding a divinely sanctioned, natural order among absolutist monarchs. In place of that role, the state's moral purpose shifted to augmenting the individual person's potential and possibilities as an autonomous agent.[51] At the same time, international society's norm of procedural justice is modernized and liberalized. In this norm, all states affected by institutional rules ought to be included in rule-formation. Reus-Smit shows how the modern, liberal purpose of the state, and its legislative ideal of procedural justice, shaped international society's two fundamental institutions: multilateral diplomacy and contractual international law.[52] Both institutions are ultimately grounded by a purposive ideal of respect for individual persons and in processes meant to replace violence with generalized procedures based on the consent of the governed. In this respect, multilateralism and international law reflect a working real-world form of Kantian liberalism, even if they sustain outcomes that fall short of an ideal theory of justice.[53]

As Brighouse writes, "[a]ll theorizing about justice in the English language . . . operates within a framework set by Rawls."[54] There is no need here to sketch Rawls's entire, complex theory, which includes much of the conceptual language and methodology of contemporary liberal political philosophy. Overall, Rawls echoes Kant's idea of justice as a matter of systematic constraints on freedom, but he pushes this vision in a specific direction.[55] His concept of "justice as fairness" generates moral responsibilities related to designing and reforming the social institutions with the power to distribute benefits and burdens to different individuals.[56] These institutions include national constitutions, political institutions, property rights, and the market.[57] Remarkably, Rawls's 1971 magnum opus *Theory of Justice* paid scant attention to justice beyond the state's borders, producing a gap that he filled in his 1999 *The Law of Peoples*.[58] In the interim, however, a new generation of global politics scholars emerged from within the intellectual space created by Rawls's focus on justice and institutions.

By the 1970s, political philosophers began to grasp the significance of international interdependence and globalization. Rawls's focus on justice emerged from a particular historic and national context, namely the New Deal and Great Society efforts to reshape American society.[59] But the issue of distributive justice could apply globally, to any situation where people's lives are shaped by regular social interactions and institutions. The global capitalist economy, the ongoing legacies of colonial rule, the international legal order that recognizes sovereign authority, all of these institutions have distributive effects. Moreover, with the globalization of information technologies, public officials, scholars, and citizens have greater awareness about the effects of such institutions. Onora O'Neill, Peter Singer, Charles Beitz, and Thomas Nagel, among others, brought attention to the effects of global politics on poverty and inequality.[60] Globalization had created a set of mutual vulnerabilities on a planetary scale, and thereby brought renewed attention to a cosmopolitan ethical vision. Although Rawls brought fairness and distributive questions to the table, compared to Kant, until he published *The Law of Peoples*, he seemed incurious about justice beyond borders.

Liberal ideas about justice also play a significant role in reconstituting the just war tradition. According to Nicholas J. Rengger, liberalism's ambivalent attitude towards war accounts for fundamental shifts in how the tradition is understood and applied.[61] To see this ambivalence, we can refer back to Kant, Walzer, and Rawls. As discussed above, the natural law conception of justice ties righteous warfare to traditional authorities, religious and monarchic. Liberalism's view is that justice must be institutionalized in a system of clear, coercively enforceable rules based on consent of the governed. Unsurprisingly, Kant condemned war and the natural lawyers who justified it.[62] Nonetheless, he also developed a uniquely liberal conception of just war based on the idea that all states, especially republics, must follow rules restricting the use of force.[63] Such rules connect with Walzer's discussion of the legalist paradigm codified in part by the UN Charter.[64] And Rawls's *Law of Peoples* situates the just war tradition's criteria within a similarly secularized code that all "reasonable" states would accept.[65] For each thinker, war and intervention are unjust and illiberal, except for self-defense and in exceptional cases.[66] To return to Wendt's language, liberal rules institutionalize states as friends rather than as enemies or rivals. International society has a duty to impose justice through force only when "outlaws" or "unjust enemies" challenge that friendship through aggression or massive human rights violations.

Liberal ideas about justice both ground and spark various critiques of international institutions and the hegemonic interests that they serve. Numerous contemporary cosmopolitan liberals critique the limited application of justice to world politics. Some critique the intellectual limits built within the liberal tradition by the foundational system-builders Kant and Rawls. Kant is viewed as having taken an essentially Hobbesian and absolutist conception of state sovereignty as a limit on cosmopolitan institution-building.[67] Rawls is criticized as also having taken an unnecessarily conservative position on global distributive justice.[68] A new generation of justice theorists critique current international institutions for being a major *cause* of—rather than the *solution* to—global injustices.[69] Among other issues, global poverty, inequality, women's subordination, the perilous effects of climate change, and crimes against humanity and genocide, have all been permitted—and in some cases, facilitated—by international institutions. Nevertheless, most cosmopolitan critiques from within liberalism take for granted the possibility of reforming existing institutions. And if these institutions end up being completely closed to reform, some invoke a right to resist global injustices.[70]

Beyond liberalism, calls for resistance inform more radical critiques of international institutions. Adopting what Rainer Bauböck calls a "dark view of political power,"[71] numerous critical approaches cast doubt on the universalism of liberalism and its cosmopolitan offshoots. Whether radical scholars work within various feminisms, poststructuralisms, postcolonialisms, or Marxism, they point to domination practices being legitimated and implemented through the liberal constitution of justice. From such perspectives, either justice should be rejected as a dubious, elitist concept, or it should be reconceptualized as a tool for counter-hegemonic, anti-domination struggles from outside of the institutions of global politics.[72] From this more radical perspective, justice matters as something to be *fought for* rather than as a fixed reality aligned with prevailing power structures. Additionally, radical critiques of liberal justice have changed the substantive focus of international ethics. As Patrick Hayden's chapter in this volume shows, there is increasing focus on recognition and identity rather than only legal equality or the redistribution of resources.[73] In pursuing new formulations of justice, radical scholars have challenged liberalism's hegemonic constitution of international politics.

Conclusion

This contribution challenges a conventional presumption that justice is a distant afterthought to global political life. Instead, the concept's meaning has been continually formed and refashioned in relation to intersocietal and global questions. These questions include what is owed to insiders versus outsiders, and how principles of fairness, respect, and reciprocity govern the use of power among diverse peoples. The second main point from this discussion is that liberalism has had a powerful role in critiquing and reshaping how justice is conceived and practiced in global politics. Liberal theories that have grown out of Kant and Rawls make justice a matter of coercive and distributive social institutions, rather than the moral virtues held by individual persons, whether state leaders or citizens. At the same time, liberalism has evolved to become a self-critical tradition; a new generation of cosmopolitan liberals has critiqued the way ostensibly liberal institutional structures have permitted and caused various global injustices. Standing outside of the liberal hegemonic order, radical critics have questioned whether justice is achievable using the ideas and institutions of powerful and exclusionary forces in global politics.

In sum, justice sits at the intersection of the constitution and critique of international politics. And at this intersection, justice pushes and expands the limits of what is necessary, possible, and desirable. For this reason, justice comes with many forms and adjectives. For example, Aristotle distinguished between general and particular, distributive and corrective justice, with an example of each within.[74] In today's world, one could make important distinctions between retributive and distributive justice and thereby contrast the former with restorative justice, and as a core purpose of transitional justice. Such analysis is beyond the scope of this chapter. Yet for all the various guises in which justice appears, the ideal has important limitations. There are only so many positive, morally praiseworthy properties that we can associate with the concept, and—in the real world—they cannot always be accomplished together. Even the iconic Lady Justice has only two hands for her sword and scales, and although she is impartial, her blindfold prevents her from seeing manifold injustices in the world.[75] Theorizing justice requires attention to the many trade-offs among different justice-related values and interests such as order, peace, freedom, fairness, equality, and rights. Moreover, the great justice theorists throughout history have struggled with the problem of political feasibility in light of human beings, as they are, and the non-ideal conditions blocking institutional change.[76] The idea of justice is many things, and while it cannot be all things, without it, there is no prospect of relating to each other ethically.

Notes

1 The image is sometimes labelled the Goddess of Justice. See Cathleen Burnett, "Justice: Myth and Symbol," *Legal Studies Forum*, 11 (1987): 79–94.

2 On global justice, see also the contributions in this volume by Kok-Chor Tan and Puneet Dhaliwal.

3 John Rawls, *A Theory of Justice*, revised edn. (Cambridge, MA: Belknap Press, an imprint of Harvard University Press, 1999), 3.

4 Donatella Della Porta et al., *Global Justice Movement: Cross-National and Transnational Perspectives* (New York: Routledge, 2015).

5 Of course, the meaning of critique is contested, see Michael Kelly, ed., *Critique and Power: Recasting the Foucault/Habermas Debate* (Cambridge, MA: MIT Press, 1994).
6 See the discussion in Stanley Hoffmann, *Duties beyond Borders: On the Possibilities and Limits of Ethical International Politics* (Syracuse, NY: Syracuse University Press, 1981), chapter 1.
7 See Stephen Forde, "Classical Realism," in *Traditions of International Ethics*, ed. Terry Nardin and David R. Mapel (Cambridge: Cambridge University Press, 1993), 62–84.
8 See Terry Nardin and David R. Mapel, eds., *Traditions of International Ethics* (Cambridge: Cambridge University Press, 1992); and Antonio Franceschet, *Kant and Liberal Internationalism: Sovereignty, Justice, and Global Reform* (New York: Palgrave Macmillan, 2002).
9 The word "international" has a more recent, modern lineage, even if it points to something more general. See Hidemi Suganami, "A Note on the Origin of the Word 'International,'" *British Journal of International Studies*, 4, no. 3 (1978): 226–232.
10 John Rawls, "The Sense of Justice," *The Philosophical Review*, 72, no. 3 (1963): 281–305; Rawls, *Theory of Justice*, 397–471.
11 Plato, *The Republic of Plato*, trans. Allan Bloom (New York: Basic Books, 1991). See especially Book I.
12 Ibid., sec. 435b, 113.
13 Aristotle, *Aristotle's Politics*, 2nd edn., ed. Carnes Lord (Chicago: University of Chicago Press, 2013), books II, IV, VII; Aristotle, *Nicomachean Ethics*, revised edn., ed. Roger Crisp (Cambridge; New York: Cambridge University Press, 2014), book V.
14 Harry Brighouse, *Justice* (Cambridge: Polity Press, 2004), 2.
15 Susan Moller Okin, *Women in Western Political Thought* (Princeton, NJ: Princeton University Press, 1979), parts I and II.
16 Amartya Sen, *The Idea of Justice* (Cambridge, MA: Harvard University Press, 2009), xiv.
17 Martin Wight, "Why Is There No International Theory?," in *Diplomatic Investigations: Essays on the Theory of International Politics*, ed. Herbert Butterfield and Martin Wight (London: Allen and Unwin, 1966), 17–34.
18 R. B. J. Walker, *Inside/Outside: International Relations as Political Theory* (Cambridge: Cambridge University Press, 1993).
19 Plato, *The Republic*, books II and II.
20 Ibid., sec. 373e, 50; Aristotle, *Politics*, sec. 1324, 397.
21 Plato, *The Republic*, sec. 338c, 15.
22 Ibid., sec. 335d, 13.
23 Thucydides, *History of the Peloponnesian War* (Auckland, NZ: The Floating Press, 2008).
24 Ibid., 564–575.
25 Forde, "Classical Realism," 69–73.
26 Michael Walzer, *Just and Unjust Wars: A Moral Argument with Historical Illustrations* (New York: Basic Books, 1977), xiv.
27 Ibid., 5.
28 Peter Karavites, *Capitulations and Greek Interstate Relations: The Reflection of Humanistic Ideals in Political Events* (Göttingen: Vandenhoeck & Ruprechtin, 1982), 51.
29 Forde, "Classical Realism," 73.
30 Walzer, *Just and Unjust Wars*, 12.
31 Anthony F. Lang, Jr, *Punishment, Justice, and International Relations: Ethics and Order after the Cold War* (New York: Routledge, 2008).
32 Thucydides, *History of the Peloponnesian War*, 566.
33 Walzer, *Just and Unjust Wars*, 251.
34 Ibid., 253.
35 Ibid., 58–65.
36 Antony Anghie, "Finding the Peripheries: Sovereignty and Colonialism in International Law," *Harvard International Law Journal*, 40 (1999): 1–80.
37 Duncan Bell, "Political Realism and the Limits of Ethics," in *Ethics and World Politics*, ed. Duncan Bell (Oxford: Oxford University Press, 2010), 99–101.
38 Howard Caygill, *On Resistance: A Philosophy of Defiance* (London: Bloomsbury Academic, 2013), 12.
39 Brighouse, *Justice*, 12.
40 Immanuel Kant, *Groundwork of the Metaphysic of Morals*, trans. H. J. Paton (New York: Harper Torchbooks, 1964).

41 Immanuel Kant, "Metaphysics of Morals," in *Toward Perpetual Peace and Other Writings on Politics, Peace, and History*, ed. Pauline Kleingeld (New Haven: Yale University Press, 2006), 111–112.
42 Ibid., 112; Thomas W. Pogge, "Kant's Theory of Justice," *Kant-Studien*, 79, no. 4 (1988): 407–433.
43 Immanuel Kant, "Toward Perpetual Peace: A Philosophical Sketch," in *Toward Perpetual Peace and Other Writings on Politics, Peace, and History*, ed. Pauline Kleingeld (New Haven: Yale University Press, 2006), 90.
44 Ibid., 80.
45 Kant, "Metaphysics of Morals," 144.
46 Alexander Wendt, *Social Theory of International Politics* (Cambridge: Cambridge University Press, 1999), 6, 21.
47 Ibid., 249.
48 Ibid., 297–307.
49 Alexander Wendt, "Why a World State Is Inevitable," *European Journal of International Relations*, 9, no. 4 (December 1, 2003): 521–523.
50 Christian Reus-Smit, *The Moral Purpose of the State: Culture, Social Identity, and Institutional Rationality in International Relations* (Princeton: Princeton University Press, 1999).
51 Ibid., 7.
52 Ibid., 132.
53 Reus-Smit's more recent work shows how modern international institutions developed in part through resistance to European imperial powers, and on the basis of claims by colonists and colonial subjects for individual rights; see *Individual Rights and the Making of the International System* (Cambridge: Cambridge University Press, 2013).
54 Brighouse, *Justice*, 8.
55 Rawls, *Theory of Justice*, 221–227; John Rawls, "Kantian Constructivism in Moral Theory," *The Journal of Philosophy*, 77, no. 9 (1980): 524.
56 Rawls, *Theory of Justice*, 6–10.
57 Ibid., 47–52.
58 Ibid., 7, 332–335; John Rawls, *The Law of Peoples* (Cambridge, MA: Harvard University Press, 1999).
59 Michael P. Zuckert, "On Constitutional Welfare Liberalism: An Old Liberalism Perspective," *Social Philosophy and Policy*, 23, 1 (2007): 271.
60 Onora O'Neill, "Lifeboat Earth," *Philosophy and Public Affairs*, 4, no. 3 (1975): 273–292; Peter Singer, "Famine, Affluence, and Morality," *Philosophy and Public Affairs*, 1, no. 3 (1972): 229–243; Charles R. Beitz, "Justice and International Relations," *Philosophy and Public Affairs*, 4, no. 4 (1975): 360–389; Thomas Nagel, "Poverty and Food: Why Charity Is Not Enough," *Global Justice: Seminal Essays*, vol. 1, ed. Thomas Pogge and Darrel Moellendorf (St. Paul, MN: Paragon House, 2008), 49–60.
61 Nicholas J. Rengger, "On the Just War Tradition in the Twenty-First Century," *International Affairs*, 78, no. 2 (2002): 356.
62 Kant, "Toward Perpetual Peace," 80.
63 Brian Orend, *War and International Justice: A Kantian Perspective* (Waterloo, Canada: Wilfrid Laurier University Press, 2000).
64 Walzer, *Just and Unjust Wars,* 61–65.
65 Rawls, *Law of Peoples*, 37, 89–94.
66 Kant, "Toward Perpetual Peace," 70; Rawls, *Law of Peoples*, 80.
67 Franceschet, *Kant and Liberal Internationalism.*
68 The critiques of Rawls's *The Law of Peoples* are too numerous to cite, but see: Andrew Kuper, "Rawlsian Global Justice: Beyond the Law of Peoples to a Cosmopolitan Law of Persons," *Political Theory*, 28, no. 5 (October 1, 2000): 640–674; and Allen Buchanan, "Rawls's Law of Peoples: Rules for a Vanished Westphalian World," *Ethics*, 110, no. 4 (2000): 697–721.
69 Thomas Pogge, "Divided against Itself: Aspiration and Reality of International Law," in *The Cambridge Companion to International Law* (Cambridge: Cambridge University Press, 2012), 373–397; Allen Buchanan, *Justice, Legitimacy, and Self-Determination: Moral Foundations for International Law* (Oxford: Oxford University Press, 2004).
70 Simon Caney, "Responding to Global Injustice: On the Right of Resistance," *Social Philosophy and Policy*, 32, no. 1 (September 2015): 51–73.
71 Rainer Bauböck, "Normative Political Theory and Empirical Research," in *Approaches and Methodologies in the Social Sciences: A Pluralist Perspective*, ed. Donatella Della Porta and Michael Keating (Cambridge: Cambridge University Press, 2008), 50.

72 See, for example, Michael Hardt and Antonio Negri, *Empire* (Cambridge, MA: Harvard University Press, 2001).
73 See, for example, Nancy Fraser, *Justus Interruptus: Critical Reflections on the "Post-Socialist" Condition* (New York: Routledge, 1997); and Nancy Fraser, *Scales of Justice: Reimagining Political Space in a Globalizing World* (New York: Columbia University Press, 2009).
74 Aristotle, *Nicomachean Ethics*, book V.
75 On the concept of injustice as not simply the opposite of justice, see Eric A. Heinze, *The Concept of Injustice* (New York: Routledge, 2013).
76 Brighouse, *Justice*, 19–20, 28.

19

THE ETHICAL TERRAIN OF INTERNATIONAL HUMAN RIGHTS

From invoking dignity to practising recognition

Patrick Hayden

Introduction

It is now commonplace to declare that we live in an age of rights.[1] Indeed, it is fair to say that the global popularity of human rights has reached the point where, as Alan Gewirth phrases it, many people regard them as fundamental to the "civilizing and moralizing of human life".[2] However, while no topic arguably is as vital to international ethics, questions remain about what our rights are, who is entitled to claim certain rights, and how these rights should be implemented and enforced. The purpose of this chapter is to provide a guide to the intricate relations between the institutional development of international human rights, the central ethical principles offered to support human rights norms, and the politics of human rights. To this end, I draw inspiration from recent attempts to understand the making of rights claims as performative social and political practices. On this understanding, I propose that, for us to attend properly to the political significance of claiming rights, we should approach human rights and dignity as the achievements of generative struggles for recognition. In the first section, I offer a brief account of the translation of the idea of human rights into international legal norms and political institutions, focusing on the International Bill of Human Rights. In the middle section, I bring analytical attention to bear upon the ethical underpinnings of international human rights, characterized in terms of the four pillars of dignity, liberty, equality, and solidarity. Finally, I offer some reflections on the ways by which rights claims are positioned, in performative terms, as emergent political struggles to achieve reciprocal recognition, equal status, and human dignity.

The international human rights system

Human rights are, by definition, universal in scope. This is because they are supposed to be the rights that persons have simply by virtue of being human, thereby extending to all human beings in all times and all places.[3] Although the current idea of human rights derives from earlier philosophical and religious sources—most prominently the natural law and natural rights traditions that inspired the European Enlightenment and the revolutions of the eighteenth century—the contemporary human rights system and associated body of international law is a product of the second half of the twentieth century.[4] There were some complementary exceptions of course, such as the various treaties to abolish the slave trade (1862, 1885, 1890) and the Geneva (1864, 1899, 1907) and Hague (1899, 1907) Conventions setting out the obligations of states to allow for the provision of humanitarian assistance to sick, wounded, and captured soldiers. In addition, the International Labour Organization was established following the First World War to develop labour regulations intended to protect workers' rights, and the League of Nations introduced limited measures to protect ethnic, linguistic, and religious minorities in parts of Europe.[5] Yet there was little effort by governments to adopt a formal system of internationally recognized human rights. This situation changed dramatically in the wake of the mass atrocities perpetrated by the Nazi government and the subsequent establishment of the United Nations and its affiliated agencies. The decolonization movement of the 1950s and 1960s also contributed to the historical circumstances inspiring the formation of human rights law in international affairs.

The contemporary human rights regime that developed concurrently with and under the auspices of the United Nations system constitutes a set of norms, institutions, and procedures that most states now accept as binding to some degree.[6] The Preamble to the UN Charter states that the fundamental objectives of the UN are partly to "reaffirm faith in fundamental human rights, in the dignity and worth of the human person, in the equal rights of men and women and of nations large and small". Article 1 of the Charter states that the UN is also intended to achieve international cooperation in "promoting and encouraging respect for human rights and for fundamental freedoms for all without distinction as to race, sex, language, or religion".[7] Although the Charter refers to human rights in several places, it does not define what those rights are. Thus, one of the first tasks the UN assumed was to draft a document that would specify consensually agreed human rights norms, a task delegated to the Commission on Human Rights (CHR) chaired by Eleanor Roosevelt.[8] The work of the CHR resulted in the Universal Declaration of Human Rights (UDHR), which according to its Preamble serves as a "common standard of achievement for all peoples and all nations".[9] The UDHR was unanimously adopted by the UN General Assembly on 10 December 1948. Because the UDHR is a resolution and not a treaty, it is not legally binding. However, over time the majority of the provisions of the UDHR have come to be accepted as part of customary international law.[10] In addition, the UDHR has been supplemented by two treaties that, when ratified by signatory states, give human rights binding force in international law, both of which were adopted by the General Assembly in 1966 and entered into law in 1976: the International Covenant on Civil and Political Rights (ICCPR), and the International Covenant on Economic, Social, and Cultural Rights (ICESCR). States parties to these and other human rights treaties assume primary responsibility for protecting and enforcing the rights of individuals within their jurisdiction, under the supervision of the UN as well as numerous regional and intergovernmental bodies, while individuals and NGOs have secondary responsibility to critique state practices when these violate or fail to promote human rights.[11] Indeed, one of the primary concerns of international human rights law is to encourage states to reform their political-legal systems in order to achieve the domestic guarantee of basic rights and freedoms. When differences between national and international standards do exist, the latter are supposed to supplement the former and in that way secure the same rights for all persons even though they live within different domestic jurisdictions. Since the adoption of the UDHR, the human rights system has expanded enormously, evolving new conceptions of rights and a multitude of declarations, conventions, and Charter-based and treaty-based human rights bodies. Two notable developments include the creation of the position of UN High Commissioner for Human Rights in 1993 and coordination of the Universal Periodic Review process—which monitors each member state's fulfilment of its human rights obligations and commitments in a four-year cycle—by the Human Rights Council (successor to the Commission on Human Rights) since 2008.[12]

At the heart of the human rights system remains what is known as the "International Bill of Human Rights", which consists of the UDHR together with the ICCPR and ICESCR. Both covenants proclaim that states must undertake to respect and ensure the following rights: to life and personal integrity and security; to freedom from torture and cruel, inhuman, and degrading treatment or punishment; to freedom from coercion, slavery, and forced labour; to due process of law and to a humane and working penal system; to freedom to travel within and outside one's country; to freedom of thought, conscience, religion, expression, assembly, and association; and to take part in the conduct of government and public affairs (including the right to vote and be elected). The dominant themes in the ICCPR are equality (equal treatment, equal protection of the law, equality of opportunity) and non-discrimination on the bases of race, colour, sex, language, religion, opinion, origin, birth, and status. In connection with non-discrimination, members of minorities within states also are granted the rights, in community with other members of their group, to enjoy their culture, practise their religion, and use their language.[13]

According to the ICESCR, states are supposed to take steps "individually and through international assistance and cooperation . . . to the maximum of their available resources . . . with a view to achieving progressively full realization"[14] of the following rights: to work; to just and favourable conditions of work, including leisure; to join trade unions and to strike; to social security; to social protection of the family, mothers, and children; to an adequate standard of living, including adequate food, clothing, housing, medical care, and social services; to the highest possible standards of physical and mental health; to education and training; and to take part in the cultural life of the community and benefit from any scientific progress therein. Again, the themes of equality and non-discrimination are dominant in this Covenant.

According to the standards established by the International Bill of Human Rights, human rights are to be both international and universal, applicable to all persons within and across states. In addition, basic or fundamental human rights are thought to be inviolable individual entitlements; in other words, they are supposed to work as superior norms, generally having priority when in conflict with other weighty norms, values, or goals (e.g., the greater good), and resistant to cost–benefit trade-offs.[15] The rights articulated in the International Bill are also viewed as interdependent and protective of a range of fundamental moral and public goods.[16] Interdependent human rights embody aspects of both "negative" rights and "positive" rights. Negative rights are principles not to impede or coerce other individuals from participating in securing, protecting, and promoting the conditions in which they may exercise their rights. Positive rights are principles to aid and cooperate with other individuals in securing, protecting, and promoting the conditions in which they may exercise their fundamental rights and liberties. Civil and political rights are sometimes characterized as negative rights in so far as they entail the freedom of individuals from governmental interference. Economic, social, and cultural rights are frequently characterized as positive rights in so far as they require the promotion of governmental policies designed to create the social conditions that enable individuals to exercise their rights and freedoms effectively. It is clear, though, that effective enjoyment of civil and political rights often requires state assistance providing for the basic socio-economic rights of individuals—such as food, education, health, and shelter—while the progressive realization of economic, social, and cultural rights requires safeguards against the possible abuse of supporting civil-political rights—such as the right to life, freedom of speech, due process of law, and political participation—by the actions of government.[17] Furthermore, a concern with community and cultural pluralism is expressed in the UN human rights framework: the International Bill recognizes a number of human rights that must be exercised by individuals as members of different racial, ethnic, economic, and religious groups, in the understanding that membership and participation in those groups are essential to a life of dignity. Thus, the right of individuals in a community with others to practise and observe their religion is an integral part of freedom of religion and might forbid establishing measures on the part of the state whose effects are the impairment of that right. Of special importance are the cultural rights of minority cultures within multinational states; thus, Article 27 of the ICCPR ensures to members of those cultures in community with others the right to preserve their distinctive language, religion and, ultimately, their "way of life".[18]

The human rights system continues to develop and change over time in response to various social, cultural, political, and economic concerns while retaining its aspiration of mitigating injustice and abuses of state power. The International Bill is now complemented by a number of "core" human rights treaties that address, *inter alia*, the elimination of racial and gender discrimination, protection against torture and forced disappearance, and the rights of women, children, migrants, and persons with disabilities; each core treaty has its own committee of experts to monitor implementation of treaty obligations by its states parties. The core human rights treaties have been joined by numerous declarations of emerging entitlements, which may eventually become codified as legally binding conventions. Most recently, the United Nations Declaration on the Rights of Indigenous Peoples was adopted by the UN General Assembly on 13 September 2007. Human rights norms also have penetrated into cognate areas of global politics that bear on individuals' rights to be treated with humanity, including refugees and internally displaced people, and those affected by genocide, forced labour, human trafficking, climate change, and global poverty. Thus, despite lacking strong enforcement mechanisms and sanctioning powers, the human rights system has not remained static. It is constantly changing, with states constructing new conceptions of the nature and content of rights, and devising new mechanisms for the promotion and protection of international standards in response to shifting global circumstances.[19]

The moral architecture of international human rights

The previous section established that since the end of the Second World War, the promotion and protection of human rights has rapidly assumed increased global salience. It is no exaggeration to suggest that the UDHR has become "the moral touchstone for all claims at the international level".[20] Indeed, in the Final Declaration and Programme of Action produced at the 1993 World Conference on Human Rights in Vienna, more than 170 states endorsed the universality and indivisibility of human rights first articulated in the UDHR, confirmed the legitimacy of the global human rights regime, and reaffirmed the idea that "it is the duty of States, regardless of their political, economic and cultural systems, to promote and protect human rights and fundamental freedoms".[21] Consequently, there is today "not a single nation, culture or people that is not in one way or another enmeshed in human rights regimes".[22] Despite the troubling gaps that exist between human rights rhetoric and human rights abuses, a significant body of human rights law now occupies a prominent place in world politics. Human rights, however, are not only institutionalized legal standards. Such rights are properly called "human" rights because they furnish us with a critical vision of what it means to be human in society with others. Consequently, they are not simply a functional scheme for coherence of the international order but also possess their own normative content and potent trajectory.

Aside from demonstrating the expansive role played by human rights at the international level, as well as indicating how claims for human rights have mushroomed since 1948, the most important issue in the contemporary rights framework is the search for a shared understanding of the normative foundation(s) for human rights. This project has been surrounded by controversy, however, as the standards professed in the UDHR were conceived first and foremost as a set of practical norms amenable to political consensus between diverse peoples from all over the world. International human rights are, as Charles Beitz points out, a "public doctrine" arising from a "collective political enterprise".[23] The collection of rights contained in the International Bill is not expressly associated with any specific religious faith, metaphysical theory, or philosophical worldview, so that the list of rights in principle can be associated with and interpreted from a variety of traditions and perspectives.[24] Attempts to ground human rights theoretically—that is, to provide justifiable reasons for why there are human rights at all, and why they should be prized so highly—are thus characterized by philosophical heterogeneity and extrinsic tensions, but by considerable overlap as well. The vast and ongoing philosophical argument about the adequate grounds for human rights—ranging widely across "foundationalist" and "non-foundationalist" approaches—is beyond the scope of this chapter.[25] Such debates are crucial nonetheless to providing the dynamic for the continuing development of how human rights are both conceived and practised, and demonstrate that there are, in fact, several possible bases to justify rights morally (which may also help prevent human rights from simply becoming a matter of dogma). While acknowledging the complexity of mediating among different justifications, this section will briefly set out a propositional grounding for human rights as provided by the French jurist René Cassin, one of the main drafters of the UDHR. Cassin compared the Declaration to the portico of a temple resting on four cornerstones corresponding to "dignity, liberty, equality, and brotherhood".[26] Cassin's simple imagery of the architecture of the UDHR yields four interlocking principles that can be broadly agreed to underpin all categories of human rights, and which encapsulate the aspirations of people throughout history who have struggled against domination and for fundamental interests they deem vital for a properly human life.

The first cornerstone of the human rights doctrine is the concept of human dignity.[27] Most influentially, the Preamble to the UDHR states that "recognition of the inherent dignity and of the equal and inalienable rights of all members of the human family is the foundation of freedom, justice and peace in the world". Article 1 reiterates the first principle that "all human beings are born free and equal in dignity and rights".[28] The idea of dignity adopted in the UDHR reflects a characteristically modern understanding of the intrinsic, inalienable worth of the individual as a human being. While the origin of the English term is found in the Latin word *dignitas*, meaning nobility of status attached to a role, rank, or office, the concept has been formulated in different ways throughout its intellectual history.[29] In the classical natural law tradition, dignity designated a hierarchical distinction between what is worthy and unworthy, whether referencing a privileged aristocratic elite or certain types of conduct considered to be morally superior. Thus, some people (e.g., a monarch or religious leader) and actions (e.g., donating to charity) merit "worthiness", while others (e.g., profiting through deceit) do not. An important feature of this view is that it correlates dignity with morally obligatory duties, rather than to anything to which a person has a right as such. Yet the concept of dignity underwent a pivotal symbolic shift between the fifteenth and eighteenth centuries under the influence of Renaissance humanism, coming to signify equal human worth attributed to all persons as opposed to unequal social rank bestowing superiority on some and inferiority on others.[30] Immanuel Kant (echoing Cicero) played a key role in this metamorphosis with his deontological injunction to treat "humanity" always "as an end, never merely as a means".[31] Kant's account emphasizes that all human beings have an intrinsic moral worth entirely independent of their position in a social hierarchy, which should never be violated by treating them as if they are potentially usable means to an end. The Kantian idea of respect for human dignity became the central insight behind the modern natural rights tradition—namely, that the inviolability of human dignity correlates to the inviolability of a person's moral rights—before then informing the human rights discourse to the point that the two concepts now are seen to be inseparable.[32] On the one hand, to respect a person means to respect their human rights while, on the other hand, to violate a person's rights is to violate their human dignity; rights violations, in other words, connote a sense of indignation, humiliation, or degradation in particularly egregious cases of mistreatment.

This connection between human dignity and human rights is reiterated in the ICCPR and ICESCR. The Preambles to both Covenants affirm that "the equal and inalienable rights of all members of the human family . . . derive from the inherent dignity of the human person".[33] Importantly, then, the notion of dignity as treating each human being with the respect they deserve serves not only as the principal normative justification for all human rights but, further, as a yardstick against which to set the relevant conditions whereby everyone may enjoy civil and political as well as economic, social, and cultural rights. One such essential and defining condition is equality.[34] The principle of equality implied by statements equating equal worth with equal rights contains two elements: the formal and the substantive (or material). Formal equality follows from the non-discrimination provision in Articles 2 and 7 of the UDHR, which affirms that everyone is entitled to human rights without distinction of any kind, such as nationality, race, religion, age, gender, sexual orientation, economic background, or disability. Formal equality thus concerns itself with ensuring that legal and political processes provide equal protection to all citizens, prohibiting discriminatory policies that arbitrarily deny the rights of some or accord special treatment to the rights of others. The value of formal equality lies, in part, in the way it draws our attention to the prevalence of differences between people in society, and supports the contention that respect for human rights means all rights-holders ought to be treated equally. Substantive equality reflects the fact that social conditions exhibit systemic patterns of inequality that persist over time, which may arbitrarily disadvantage some individuals by undermining their prospects for exercising rights in a manner that is meaningfully equal to those with greater material advantages. Many international human rights instruments therefore promote positive duties on the state to remedy pre-existing disadvantages, provide equality of opportunity, and uphold a cluster of interrelated rights meant to establish minimum conditions needed to achieve a dignified human existence, including primary education, adequate subsistence, basic health care, fair remuneration in employment, and social security.[35] Formal and substantive equality sometimes overlap and sometimes compete within human rights discourse and practice, of course, suggesting that equality remains a fragile and contested norm. Liberal and socialist theorists, for instance, have frequently (and often unproductively) debated the relative priority of formal and material equality, and many countries adopting neoliberal market-based economic policies oppose the redistributive consequences implied by socio-economic rights.[36]

The third cornerstone of liberty associates dignity and rights with the human capacity to freely choose what to do and to be in the autonomous conduct of our lives, a capacity deemed by many to be central to the moral status of personhood.[37] The principle of liberty reflects an image of "the ideal of free human beings", as expressed in the Preambles to the ICCPR and ICESCR.[38] The appeal to liberty as a condition to which all humans are entitled is one of the most compelling claims within human rights discourse, regularly serving as a powerful, and indeed revolutionary, platform for social struggles against innumerable forms of subordination and domination; historically, the right to liberty repeatedly appears as the right to liberation or emancipation.[39] The moral demand of respect for individual freedom comprises both negative and positive liberty. On the one hand, it means being free from unwarranted external constraints on or coercive interference with our life plans, choices, beliefs, and goods. Being free from slavery, torture, and arbitrary arrest, detention, or exile represents basic negative liberties. But, on the other hand, liberty also requires being free to pursue possible courses of action, to exercise powers of choice, and to achieve preferred goals or ends to which one aspires, provided such actions are compatible with the equal liberties of others.[40] The kind of liberty at issue in the human rights framework also has a dual aspect, looking simultaneously to the private and the public freedoms of all persons. Hence the rights enumerated in the International Bill include freedom of thought, conscience, and religion, as well as freedom of movement, freedom to organize politically, freedom of speech and press, and freedom to vote and take part in government. Taken together, the negative and positive, and the private and public, facets of liberty ground a cluster of rights that aim to secure both freedom from oppression as well as the means and opportunities for exercising self-transforming activity (whether individually or in association with others).[41]

The final cornerstone of the human rights structure is controversial and elusive, yet it has proved indispensable to widening the idea of human rights in general. "Fraternity" entered the lexicon of rights with the French Revolution of 1789, and subsequently inspired widespread demands for social inclusion in the spirit of human unity. This universalist vision of unity amongst the peoples of all countries on the basis of common concerns, goals, or activity—popularized in the nineteenth century by the motto "*Unus pro omnibus, omnes pro uno*" ("One for all, all for one")—was later taken up by Article 1 of the UDHR, which declares that all human beings "should act towards one another in a spirit of brotherhood".[42] The idea of universal "brotherliness" is now usually embodied in the language of solidarity.[43] Solidarity has often been regarded as an arbitrary affective force in contemporary political thought, one that is either too weak to promote the constitutional juridification of rights, or that, in its emotive volatility, is a threat to stable social cohesion.[44] There can be little doubt that the great rallying cry of solidarity has a certain revolutionary allure capable of inspiring fierce antagonism towards political and economic systems regarded as gross affronts to human dignity. Nevertheless, the quest for solidarity is predominantly empowering; it can motivate sentiments of togetherness conducive to political action between people who are situated differently in the world and foster collective commitments to progressive social transformation that may advance the cause of justice—even across territorial boundaries.[45] Solidarity's international or transnational role in human rights is seen in Article 28 of the UDHR: "Everyone is entitled to a social and international order in which the rights and freedoms set forth in this Declaration can be fully realized."[46] By incorporating solidarity as an essential entitlement for the achievement of a suitably just world society, normative human rights discourse identifies solidarity as a two-way street: states should not only think of human rights in terms of costs and benefits for themselves but also in larger terms of collective goods applied to the world as a whole. States therefore should choose to work with each other—assuming shared responsibility for cooperative human rights schemes—in order to achieve outcomes ultimately beneficial to humanity as a whole. The 1986 Declaration on the Right to Development, for example, holds that states "have the duty to co-operate with each other . . . to promote a new international economic order based on sovereign equality, interdependence, [and] mutual interest".[47] Similar concerns for reciprocal normativity animated decolonial struggles for independence and the right to self-determination, and continue to stimulate transnational movements for post-imperial social justice linking the Global North and South.[48] Solidarity, then, may be interpreted as not only a right in itself but as one of the social conditions supporting the realization of all other human rights.

Struggles for dignity and the politics of rights recognition

The moral edifice of the international human rights system rests upon the main pillars of dignity, freedom, equality, and solidarity. In political terms, however, the challenge for human rights is not simply to presume a dignity intrinsic to the self but to make oneself recognized by others.

Political struggles for human rights exploit precisely this ambiguity: they might articulate a perfectly intelligible claim to dignity in the abstract, but the key is to gain public recognition and acknowledgement from a community of others of what in practice turns out to be palpably concrete identities—often based on a combination of intersecting characteristics—and particular situations of grievance. Although formally an assertion of antecedent moral principles, the politics of human rights points to the fact that rights claims are performative acts whereby the claimant opens up a public scene of persuasion, negotiation, and diffusion through which rights themselves are engendered, practised, and, when successful, accepted by those to whom the claims are addressed.[49] The notion of performativity has its conceptual origins in the speech-act theory of J. L. Austin, according to which the performance of linguistic utterances (such as rights claims) is a species of action.[50] On the performative position, rights-claiming practices have the potential to disrupt and transform conventional understandings of self, other, and community—in other words, to shift prevailing meanings of who we are as plural human beings, thereby foregrounding questions of inclusion and exclusion.[51] A performative understanding of the activity of rights claiming thus sees rights, as well as human dignity, as intersubjective political achievements between people rather than subjective possessions within them. These achievements should be regarded as only ever provisionally settled, however, and always subject to "complex processes of public argument, deliberation, and exchange through which universalist rights claims are contested and contextualized, invoked and revoked, posited and positioned throughout legal and political institutions, as well as in the associations of civil society".[52]

Human rights claims, therefore, are not simply invocations of a priori norms but performative utterances of particular normative meanings and beliefs within the relational contexts of social co-existence. On this view, rights morph from being fixed objects possessed by essential subjects to being dynamic social practices through which rights and the subjects who claim them are mutually constituted.[53] Revisions of our moral-political identities go hand in hand with ongoing refigurations of the normative values of dignity, liberty, equality, and solidarity. Consider how myriad members of racial, religious, sexual, or ethnic minorities deemed of unequal worth and standing have rhetorically reshaped understandings and practices of equality through particular deployments of human rights language across space and time, re-positioning themselves from "outside" to "inside" humanity. Hence mutual recognition between different individuals as subjects with rights to be respected, protected, and fulfilled within political communities is, I suggest, the first political step toward the active realization of human dignity. The dynamic process of mutual recognition, in other words, underscores how practices of making (and, for that matter, unmaking) the value and status of human dignity are pervasive features of our political lives with others.

Performative theory points us towards paying closer attention to how speech-acts accomplish, rather than merely represent, the core principles of dignity, liberty, equality, and solidarity on which human rights rely. In so doing, it challenges two recurring assumptions in the history of thinking about human rights: first, that rights are "free-floating" values that operate external to social, symbolic, and institutional contexts; and second, that once rights claims have been established, they will remain permanently fixed or securely perpetuated over time. Neither assumption does proper justice to the extent to which successful rights claims emerge out of and are shaped by concrete historical struggles—whether it be against racism, sex and gender discrimination, economic exploitation, or oppression—and the degree to which they remain relatively effective only when re-articulated and re-positioned by future socio-political interventions. Emphasizing how achieving human rights and the situated struggles for dignity, equality, liberty, and solidarity are intertwined highlights the way in which the concept of "recognition" is at the heart of the political dimension of human rights. One of the advantages of rooting human rights in social processes of recognition is that it frames the condition of being human, and therefore of human dignity, as a political status, that is, as an achievement of existing experience rather than a mere natural object.

Taking its cue from Hegel's famous depiction of the master–slave dialectic in the *Phenomenology of Spirit*,[54] the model of social recognition posits that the identity and agency of the subject is established in the context of intersubjective relations with others. Herein, not only is consciousness and identity shaped through dialectical mediations of self and other, but our sense of self-worth is tied to the ways in which others recognize us and how we recognize others. This implies that the freedom and dignity of both self and other arises through reciprocal affirmation of symmetrical claims to equal recognition and respect. The broader point is that the type of egalitarian relationship necessary for enacting and enjoying human rights claims presupposes empowering individuals as equal peers in political representation, participation, and decision-making.[55] The "vital human need" for recognition, as Charles Taylor puts it,[56] thus extends to acknowledging not only the presumed equal worth of individuals but even more so to what Joel Feinberg refers to as their "recognizable capacity to assert claims" regarded as socially meaningful or institutionally legitimate.[57] Axel Honneth contends that rights are "depersonalized symbols of social respect".[58] What this means is that human rights express a general public recognition that particular human beings are deserving of—that is, entitled to—the political and legal status of rights-bearers; this is another way of rendering Hannah Arendt's notion of the "right to have rights".[59] Arendt's point is that the subject of human rights, as an agent capable of enacting rights claims, does not exist in the abstract but as a fellow person acknowledged as such by others within a shared web of legal and political practices that implement equality. Thus, the performance of due recognition of equal status is an action indispensable to individuals developing a sense of self-respect as responsible political agents. As Honneth argues, public recognition constitutes an experience in which "one is able to view oneself as a person who shares with all other members of one's community the qualities that make participation" possible.[60]

This brings us to another crucial insight regarding the relationship between recognition and rights, centred on the problem of political inclusion and exclusion. While social recognition denotes the positive experience of reciprocally extending due respect to the equal status, dignity, and rights of others, it also implies the negative experience of misrecognition, to wit, the failure to value individuals and their rights or to recognize them only in a way that ignores, distorts, or devalues their social, political, and personal experiences. Honneth identifies three pivotal experiences of asymmetric misrecognition or "disrespect": abuse, torture, and other violations of physical integrity; denigration of individual or collective ways of life and cultural practices; and denial of equal rights and of equal standing as a fully fledged member of a political community.[61] Misrecognition is most injurious to socially vulnerable individuals and groups: the poor and destitute; racial, ethnic, and religious minorities; women and children; the disabled; and gay, lesbian, bisexual, and transgender people (as well as to those who may be several of these simultaneously). Those who are not recognized in terms of dominant identities often are regarded as inferior, defective, threatening, or of being otherwise essentially constituted in a way that makes them less deserving of equal respect and status. In contrast, a critical recognition approach argues that possessing human rights is not "a matter of being constituted in a certain way" but "of being afforded a certain sort of social recognition" that acknowledges our constitutive differences as being compatible with establishing political equality.[62] This is because any attempt to specify the underlying generic properties of what it is to be a human being will almost inevitably exclude "some groups of humans [who] fail to meet the criteria".[63] One of the most important insights that Honneth offers is that the experience of misrecognition can inaugurate resistance and social movements demanding the expansion of relations of mutual recognition and political inclusion. The search for recognition is an irrepressible motivational impetus for the subordinated and excluded to challenge hierarchical deprivations of dignity and rights by means of the very act of claiming to be equal.[64]

An example of the pivotal importance of this performative moral grammar of struggles for recognition—which is another way of describing the demand for equal humanity and equal rights by the excluded themselves—can be seen in the fight for access to essential anti-retroviral medicines by South Africa's Treatment Action Campaign (TAC). TAC emerged in 1998 as part of both the transnational movement for universal health care justice and the human right to health, and the grassroots campaign for access to adequate medical treatment and essential medicines on behalf of HIV-infected individuals in South Africa.[65] Combining rights-based public interest litigation with assorted performative devices such as symbolic positioning, ethical-political narratives, and publicly engaged argumentation, TAC mounted a compelling drive for the production of and importation into South Africa of affordable generic medicines.[66] By positioning itself as a successor to the antiapartheid struggle, TAC invoked a powerful narrative that recollected a defiant people united in solidarity against social injustice and political subordination. Moreover, they also portrayed those needing anti-retroviral drugs as concurrently embodying the basic principles of "human dignity, equality and freedom" applicable to all citizens under the new South African Constitution,[67] as well as the distinctive vulnerabilities of specific communities of people living with HIV/AIDS, such as pregnant women and homeless children. Finally, out of a belief that structural change, such as expanding the scope of health-care delivery, is unlikely to be achieved without also affecting "hearts and minds", TAC deployed rhetorical devices, such as when Nelson Mandela famously wore a TAC T-shirt at one of their demonstrations in 2002, dramatizing the figurative transformation of racist, sexist, homophobic, and other discriminatory stereotypes. With the help of these performative acts, TAC provided a significant material and symbolic connection with the public that enabled a stigmatized section of South African society to repudiate an imposed sense of inferiority as to their status in society and move forward as equal human rights-bearing agents in the political realm.

Such examples can be multiplied in many other contexts and from various different perspectives: India's Dalits leveraging an international network of solidarity NGOs to challenge local and national caste-based discrimination;[68] San farm workers in Namibia asserting labour and housing rights against institutional attempts to anchor their group identity to a traditional hunting and gathering lifestyle;[69] LGBTQIA activist coalitions in all world regions, including South-East Asia, contesting multiple forms of "heteronormative" exclusion and violence on the basis of sexual orientation and gender identity;[70] Colombian activists using "people's tribunals" to publicize peasant land dispossession and violence against indigenous communities committed by state-linked paramilitaries and multinational corporations;[71] and more than 200 NGOs helping to create a Women's Court in Sarajevo, giving women a public space to talk about their experiences of rape and sexual violence during the wars in the former Yugoslavia throughout the 1990s, thereby empowering them as legal and political right-holders and not simply passive victims.[72] The striking resonance with the politics of recognition as an enactment of equal human status, dignity, and rights is clear. Each of these struggles for rights and recognition was at pains to show that rights violations also should be seen as lived experiences of misrecognition that demonstrate a lack of respect and concern for the dignity of those affected. Hence, misrecognition involves a symbolic devaluation of the very idea of shared humanity. The performative features of the search for recognition illustrate, therefore, that successful recognition of equal human rights depends, however precariously, upon reciprocal acknowledgement of equal and inclusive belonging between self and other.[73] In this way, recognition amounts to a social practice which brings into existence the very rights the act of claiming aspires to achieve.

Conclusion

Because of their discursive elasticity and pragmatic availability, human rights claims have been expanded into the social, political, and legal entitlements of previously excluded individuals and groups since the end of the Second World War. This chapter has sought to clarify that human rights function simultaneously as an institutional-legal scheme, a moral-normative stance, and a social-political struggle. In all these forms, the prominence of the contemporary quest for human rights is attributable to the degree to which it has affected not only the domestic and international conduct and policies of states, but also the practices and influence of a constantly expanding range of non-governmental organizations, advocacy groups, and social movements committed to an assortment of human rights causes. At the same time, I have underscored that the strength and effectiveness of any human rights ascription depends on performative practices of seeking and extending reciprocal recognition of equal human status. In many ways, human rights represent performative figurations for portraying what it means to live a dignified human existence or, conversely, what it means to suffer unacceptable dehumanizing indignities in our relations with others. Rather than signalling a single, unchanging human nature untouched by the realities of social co-existence, human rights embody ethical and political practices that human beings constantly work out for accepting and engaging with one another on equal terms. For this reason, analyses of human rights also must reckon with the fact that the normative, political, and institutional elaborations of rights will always exceed their empirical manifestations; struggles in support of particular human rights will always be confronted with strong countertendencies and outright refusals, and will never yield a final, straightforward triumph. From the perspective offered here, however, the power of human rights is less a matter of definitive success than the pervasive capacity of subjects to undertake continually evolving practices of declaring, negotiating, and recognizing their specific claims to liberty, equality, solidarity, and dignity.

Notes

1 Norberto Bobbio, *The Age of Rights* (Cambridge: Polity, 1996).
2 Alan Gewirth, "Duties to Fulfill the Human Rights of the Poor", in *Freedom from Poverty as a Human Right: Who Owes What to the Very Poor?*, ed. Thomas Pogge (Oxford: Oxford University Press, 2007), 236.
3 Jack Donnelly, *Universal Human Rights in Theory and Practice*, 2nd edn. (Ithaca: Cornell University Press, 2003), 1.
4 See Samuel Moyn, *The Last Utopia: Human Rights in History* (Cambridge, MA: Harvard University Press, 2010).
5 Mark Mazower, "The Strange Triumph of Human Rights, 1933–1950", *The Historical Journal*, 47 (2004): 379–398.
6 Roger Normand and Sarah Zaidi, *Human Rights at the UN: The Political History of Universal Justice* (Bloomington: Indiana University Press, 2008).
7 Charter of the United Nations (26 June 1945), http://www.un.org/en/charter-united-nations/.
8 Mary Anne Glendon, *A World Made New: Eleanor Roosevelt and the Universal Declaration of Human Rights* (New York: Random House, 2001).
9 Universal Declaration of Human Rights (10 December 1948), http://www.un.org/en/universal-declaration-human-rights/index.html.
10 Roozbeh B. Baker, "Customary International Law in the 21st Century: Old Challenges and New Debates", *European Journal of International Law*, 21 (2010): 173–204.
11 Charles Beitz, *The Idea of Human Rights* (Oxford: Oxford University Press, 2009), 115.
12 See Hilary Charlesworth and Emma Larking, eds., *Human Rights and the Universal Periodic Review: Rituals and Ritualism* (Cambridge: Cambridge University Press, 2014).
13 International Covenant on Civil and Political Rights (16 December 1966), http://www.refworld.org/docid/3ae6b3aa0.html.

14 International Covenant on Economic, Social and Cultural Rights (16 December 1966), Art. 2(1), http://www.refworld.org/docid/3ae6b36c0.html.
15 The International Bill sets out, however, circumstances in which certain limitations on and temporary derogations of rights are permissible, such as during national or international emergencies.
16 The Vienna Declaration and Programme of Action, adopted by the 1993 UN World Conference on Human Rights, emphasizes that human rights are treated as "indivisible and interdependent and interrelated". The World Conference of Human Rights, Vienna Declaration and Programme of Action, ¶5, July 12, 1993, http://www.refworld.org/docid/3ae6b39ec.html.
17 See Henry Shue, *Basic Rights: Subsistence, Affluence, and U.S. Foreign Policy*, 2nd edn. (Princeton: Princeton University Press, 1996); and James W. Nickel, "Rethinking Indivisibility: Toward a Theory of Supporting Relations between Human Rights", *Human Rights Quarterly*, 30 (2008): 984–1001.
18 International Covenant on Civil and Political Rights, Art. 27, http://www.refworld.org/docid/3ae6b3aa0.html.
19 See Christian Reus-Smit, *Individual Rights and the Making of the International System* (Cambridge: Cambridge University Press, 2013).
20 Thomas Franck, *Nation against Nation* (New York: Oxford University Press, 1985), 232.
21 Vienna Declaration and Programme of Action, ¶5, http://www.refworld.org/docid/3ae6b39ec.html.
22 Johannes Morsink, *The Universal Declaration of Human Rights: Origins, Drafting, and Intent* (Philadelphia: University of Pennsylvania Press, 1999), x.
23 Beitz, *The Idea of Human Rights*, 102–103.
24 Johannes Morsink, *Inherent Human Rights: Philosophical Roots of the Universal Declaration* (Philadelphia: University of Pennsylvania Press, 2009).
25 For a survey of these approaches, see Guglielmo Verdirame, "Human Rights in Political and Legal Theory", in *Routledge Handbook of International Human Rights Law*, ed. Scott Sheeran and Nigel Rodley (London: Routledge, 2013), 25–48.
26 René Cassin, "*La Déclaration universelle et la mise en oeuvre des Droits de l'homme*", *Recueil des cours de l'Académie de droit international*, 79 (1951): 278.
27 Patrick Capps, *Human Dignity and the Foundations of International Law* (Oxford: Hart Publishing, 2009).
28 Universal Declaration of Human Rights, Preamble and Art. 1, http://www.un.org/en/universal-declaration-human-rights/index.html.
29 Jeremy Waldron, "Citizenship and Dignity", in *Understanding Human Dignity*, ed. Christopher McCrudden (Oxford: Oxford University Press, 2013), 327.
30 See Jeff Malpas and Norelle Lickiss, eds., *Perspectives on Human Dignity* (Dordrecht: Springer, 2007); and Michael Rosen, *Dignity: Its History and Meaning* (Cambridge, MA: Harvard University Press, 2012).
31 Immanuel Kant, *Groundwork of the Metaphysics of Morals* (Cambridge: Cambridge University Press, 1997), 38.
32 Jürgen Habermas, "The Concept of Human Dignity and the Realistic Utopia of Human Rights", *Metaphilosophy*, 41 (2010): 464–480.
33 International Covenant on Civil and Political Rights, Preamble, http://www.refworld.org/docid/3ae6b3aa0.html; International Covenant on Economic, Social and Cultural Rights, Preamble, http://www.refworld.org/docid/3ae6b36c0.html.
34 See Ronald Dworkin, *Taking Rights Seriously* (Cambridge, MA: Harvard University Press, 1977), and Allen Buchanan, "The Egalitarianism of Human Rights", *Ethics*, 120 (2010): 679–710.
35 The human rights emphasis on substantive equality is deeply implicated in the 2000 Millennium Development Goals and the 2015 Sustainable Development Goals.
36 Paul O'Connell, "On Reconciling Irreconcilables: Neoliberal Globalization and Human Rights", *Human Rights Review*, 3 (2007): 483–509.
37 James Griffin, *On Human Rights* (Oxford: Oxford University Press, 2008). Some critics contend that this belief is a peculiarly modern and Western conceit.
38 International Covenant on Civil and Political Rights, Preamble, http://www.refworld.org/docid/3ae6b3aa0.html; International Covenant on Economic, Social and Cultural Rights, Preamble, http://www.refworld.org/docid/3ae6b36c0.html.
39 Costas Douzinas, *The End of Human Rights: Critical Legal Thought at the End of the Century* (Oxford: Hart, 2000).
40 Alan Gewirth, *Human Rights: Essays on Justification and Applications* (Chicago: University of Chicago Press, 1982).
41 Carol C. Gould, *Globalizing Democracy and Human Rights* (Cambridge: Cambridge University Press, 2004), 33–34.

42 Universal Declaration of Human Rights, Art. 1, http://www.un.org/en/universal-declaration-human-rights/index.html.
43 Hauke Brunkhorst, *Solidarity: From Civic Friendship to a Global Legal Community* (Cambridge, MA: MIT Press, 2005), 1–2.
44 Lawrence Wilde, "The Concept of Solidarity: Emerging from the Theoretical Shadows?", *British Journal of Politics and International Relations*, 9 (2007): 171–181.
45 Carol C. Gould, "Transnational Solidarities", *Journal of Social Philosophy*, 38 (2007): 148–164.
46 Universal Declaration of Human Rights, Art. 28, http://www.un.org/en/universal-declaration-human-rights/index.html.
47 Declaration on the Right to Development (4 December 1986), Art. 3(3), http://www.refworld.org/docid/3b00f22544.html.
48 See Roland Burke, *Decolonization and the Evolution of International Human Rights* (Philadelphia: University of Pennsylvania Press, 2010).
49 Seyla Benhabib refers to this dynamic of public claims-making as the "jurisgenerative" potential of rights; see *Dignity in Adversity: Human Rights in Troubled Times* (Cambridge: Polity, 2011), 125.
50 J. L. Austin, *How to Do Things with Words* (Oxford: Oxford University Press, 1961).
51 Karen Zivi, *Making Rights Claims: A Practice of Democratic Citizenship* (Oxford: Oxford University Press, 2012), 16–19, 46–47.
52 Benhabib, *Dignity in Adversity*, 16.
53 See Andrew Vincent, *The Politics of Human Rights* (Oxford: Oxford University Press, 2010), 180ff.
54 G. W. F. Hegel, *The Phenomenology of Spirit*, trans. A. V. Miller (Oxford: Oxford University Press, 1977), 114–117.
55 Nancy Fraser, *Scales of Justice: Reimagining Political Space in a Globalizing World* (Cambridge: Polity, 2008), 28–29.
56 Charles Taylor, "The Politics of Recognition", in *Multiculturalism: Examining the Politics of Recognition*, ed. Amy Gutmann (Princeton: Princeton University Press, 1994), 26.
57 Joel Feinberg, *Rights, Justice, and the Bounds of Liberty* (Princeton: Princeton University Press, 1980), 151.
58 Axel Honneth, *The Struggle for Recognition: The Moral Grammar of Social Conflicts* (Cambridge: Polity, 1995), 118.
59 Hannah Arendt, *The Origins of Totalitarianism* (New York: Schocken Books, 2004), 376–377.
60 Honneth, *The Struggle for Recognition*, 120.
61 Ibid., 131–135.
62 Derrick Darby, *Rights, Race, and Recognition* (Cambridge: Cambridge University Press, 2009), 132.
63 Anne Phillips, *The Politics of the Human* (Cambridge: Cambridge University Press, 2015), 40.
64 Axel Honneth, *Disrespect: The Normative Foundations of Critical Theory* (Cambridge: Polity, 2007).
65 For more information on the history of TAC and its various campaigns, consult the group's website at http://www.tac.org.za/.
66 Mark Heywood, "South Africa's Treatment Action Campaign: Combining Law and Social Mobilization to Realize the Right to Health", *Journal of Human Rights Practice*, 1 (2009): 14–36.
67 The Constitution of the Republic of South Africa provides that "[e]veryone has the right to have access to health care services" and that "[n]o one may be refused emergency medical treatment". South Africa Const. § 27.
68 Clifford Bob, "'Dalit Rights Are Human Rights': Caste Discrimination, International Activism, and the Construction of a New Human Rights Issue", *Human Rights Quarterly*, 29 (2007): 167–193.
69 Renee Sylvain, "Class, Culture, and Recognition: San Farm Workers and Indigenous Identities", *Anthropologica*, 45 (2003): 105–113.
70 Anthony J. Langlois, "Human Rights, 'Orientation,' and ASEAN", *Journal of Human Rights*, 13 (2014): 307–321.
71 Lara Montesinos Coleman, "Struggles over Rights: Humanism, Ethical Dispossession and Resistance", *Third World Quarterly*, 36 (2015): 1060–1075.
72 Janine Natalya Clark, "Transitional Justice as Recognition: An Analysis of the Women's Court in Sarajevo", *International Journal of Transitional Justice*, 10 (2016): 67–87.
73 See Judith Butler, *Precarious Life: The Powers of Mourning and Violence* (London: Verso, 2004).

20
INTERNATIONAL LAW AND ETHICS

Andrea Birdsall

Primarily, international law is the 'law of nations'; it is the law between states that they create and obey or disobey. It constitutes a system of rules and principles that are regarded as binding on states and which prevail over national laws. Its main focus is on rights and duties of states and the relations between them. It was initially established by states to bring some order into the relations between them, while at the same time preserving their independence as sovereigns.

International law does not have the same features that characterise domestic legal systems (e.g., enforcement mechanisms such as courts or police forces), and it is therefore sometimes criticised for not being 'law' in the strict sense, but rather a set of moral statements that express general political obligations for states. H. L. A. Hart, one of the most prominent legal philosophers of the twentieth century, argued that in order to determine whether or not certain rules can be considered to constitute 'law', it is important to look at their functions and conditions on the international level. He argued that:

> [i]t is clear that in the practice of states certain rules are regularly respected even at the cost of certain sacrifices; claims are formulated by reference to them; breaches of the rules expose the offender to serious criticism and are held to justify claims for compensation or retaliation. These, surely, are all the elements required to support the statement that there exist among states rules imposing obligations upon them. The proof that 'binding' rules in any society exist, is simply that they are thought of, spoken of, and function as such.[1]

Though international law is not 'soft' law—it provides more than just guiding principles in a complementary fashion—it has no independent powers of enforcement and is therefore reliant on states' political will to cooperate. International law is not imposed on states, but decentralised and founded on consensus. It is based on reciprocity, which means that states see it as in their mutual interests to obey the established rules. Most norms of international law are non-controversial, as they confirm powers that states already exercise, such as sovereignty over their territory. Other norms, such as justice and human rights, are more problematic, however, because they are based on differing cultural or moral values, and because there is no clear agreement on their content. International law is created in one of two ways: it is either formulated as treaty law in international agreements that create rules that are binding on all signatories, or it is created by state practice (customary law) that is recognised by the international community as providing rules that have to be complied with.[2]

Traditionally, debates in the legal studies literature have focused on discussions surrounding the nature of international law, focusing on divisions between positive law and natural law. Natural law is based on the idea that there is a kind of perfect justice given to man by nature and that man's laws should conform to this as closely as possible. This includes a strong moral element in theorising law and a belief in 'God-given' principles of higher values mankind should aspire to. On the other side, positive law is the body of law imposed by states; the empirical focus of this approach is on existing law and on what *is* rather than what it *ought* to be. In terms of a positive law approach, law is seen as separate from morality.

Debates in international law have changed in recent years to shift away from its state-centrism towards an increased focus on individuals as well as moral and ethical considerations. Debates have therefore moved away from the natural/positive law division to focus more on issues such as human rights in constitutional law, domestic and international humanitarian law, and so on. As Ruti Teitel, for instance, argues:

> The emerging legal order addresses not merely states and state interests and perhaps not even primarily so. Persons and peoples are now at the core, and a non-sovereignty-based normativity is manifesting itself, which has an uneasy and uncertain relationship to the inherited discourse of sovereign equality.[3]

Such an increased focus on individuals and their rights led to a so-called 'turn to ethics' in international law discourse, opening up new ethical and moral agendas that are reflected in more recent debates in the legal field. The remainder of this chapter will look at four such developments. Firstly, this chapter will look at the idea of global constitutionalism that allows for the integration of politics, law, and ethics. Constitutionalism focuses on legal and institutional structures of certain norms (such as rights, rules, and responsibilities). Global constitutionalism is based on the idea that a global constitutional order exists that includes international norms and rules that enable and constrain international actors. Secondly, this chapter will examine institutions that develop to take account of the increased importance of the individual in global politics, using the idea of cosmopolitanism to frame these developments. This tradition of thought not only puts the individual at the centre of its arguments, but also bases this on a belief in universalism of the normative substance of law. Cosmopolitan theorists advocate notions of a universal morality, universal human rights, and so on. The third section will include a discussion of critical legal theory, which is sceptical about notions of such 'universal' values of justice and human rights in the international community. Critical legal theorists argue that international law is embedded in a specific context that reflects and reinforces existing power relations between states that has been developed in international politics over the past decades. And finally, the chapter will look to how feminist perspectives also challenge underlying power relations and normative assumptions of international law.

Global constitutionalism

Constitutions include norms, principles, and practices that organise political life and can be understood as an operating system behind political decisions. To follow Hans Kelsen's distinction between constitutions in material and formal senses, a constitution in a material sense can be seen as 'those rules, procedural or substantive, that regulate the creation of general legal norms establish organs, and delimit their powers'.[4] In a formal sense, constitutions are written texts that can only be changed according to special procedures that are designed to make changing those norms difficult. 'The formal constitution serves to safeguard the norms determining the organs and procedure of legislation (the core features of the material constitution).'[5] Constitutions include checks and balances that are aimed at preventing the abuse of power by individual institutions.

Constitutionalism sits at the intersection between law and politics. It is 'a political theory that protects individuals from arbitrary exercise of power through the rule of law and a system of checks and balances'.[6] Constitutionalism assumes that political power is used by political actors through law and institutions that are enabling as well as constraining: it enables the creation of institutions and laws but at the same time limits those who lead those institutions and execute those laws. This is achieved through principles of the rule of law, the protection of fundamental rights, the separation of power, as well as constituent power (i.e., giving a voice to those affected by the constitution).

Domestically, constitutions create institutions that balance power and (at the same time) protect rights. Global constitutionalism takes this further by looking at such norms and rules beyond the state level, analysing international law and how it affects international actors. It assumes the existence of a global constitutional order and involves the study of changing norms that are important for international relations between states. Global constitutionalism can therefore be understood as a theoretical framework that brings together law, politics, and ethics, based on the idea that a constitutional order at the global level exists. It is concerned with implementing the rule of law on a global level, but it is more than that: it focuses on individuals as the ultimate constituent power and not just states, and is therefore concerned with the protection of individual human rights.

Global constitutionalism takes into account that even though international law has no overarching enforcement mechanism (such as a global police force that enforces law between and among states consistently), governance structures exist that are relevant to actors and influence their choices of action. Global constitutionalism can be used as a reference frame to establish questions of legitimacy of international laws that are then not dependent on a state-like government or governance structure in the international sphere. As Martti Koskenniemi argues: 'What is important is the use of the constitutional vocabulary to express a fundamental critique of the present politics.'[7] The universalising focus of constitutionalism allows

> extreme inequality in the world to be not only shown but also condemned. . . . individual suffering [is transformed] into an objective wrong that concerns not just the victim, but everyone. If calculation is needed, then 'all' must be counted as cost.[8]

One instance that is brought forward as evidence for the importance of global constitutionalism,[9] is the so-called *Kadi* case that was decided by the European Court of Justice (ECJ) in 2008. In short, following a UN Security Council Resolution to deal with terrorism in the aftermath of 9/11, Yassin Kadi, a Saudi national, was placed on a list of individuals suspected of having links to Al Qaeda. Being placed on that list resulted in freezing most of his assets and restricting his abilities of free travel. Article 103 of the UN Charter sets out supremacy of UN Chapter VII resolutions over any other legal obligations. The EU was therefore required to adopt the UN resolution without any alteration. The resolution impinged on some of Kadi's fundamental human rights, however, such as a right to be heard, respect for the rights of the defence, and the right to effective judicial protection. Such rights of due process are fundamental rights, which means that they are part of the European constitutional order and enshrined as such in EU law. According to the UN resolution, however, Kadi had no right to challenge being placed on the list and being subject to the imposed sanctions. The case therefore involved a conflict between different legal orders: European, national, and international law.

Kadi brought his case before the ECJ and won on appeal. The ECJ decided that '[t]he European Union may not impose restrictive measures on Mr Kadi, without evidence to substantiate his involvement in terrorist activities'.[10] The ECJ ruled that Kadi's rights to a fair trial and due process had been violated and that it could not uphold the UN resolution. In terms of global constitutionalism, this case is instructive, as the ECJ 'highlighted the constitutional dimension that results from the interaction between different political and legal arenas in the global system'.[11] The existing order is based on the UN having the 'final normative authority',[12] but the ECJ in this case emphasised the rule of law and the protection of human rights over that order. The ECJ ruling was therefore hailed by constitutionalists as having 'promoted the constitutionalisation of the global system'.[13] The case is important in showing how human rights in international law are affected by the interaction between different legal systems and thereby raises constitutional questions beyond the state on a global level.

This is in line with global constitutionalism's idea that individuals are the primary agents in the international order and that their rights need to be protected. This approach is similar to cosmopolitanism, which makes an even stronger case for the link between law and universal morality as well as the central role individuals play in the global order.

Cosmopolitanism

Ideas of cosmopolitanism are based on individuals being citizens of the cosmos, citizens of the world, regardless of their belonging to particular states. It is also based on a belief in a universal morality, universal values, and a normative substance of law. Other chapters in this Handbook focus on cosmopolitanism more generally, but in this chapter the focus is on how this framework relates to international law and legal principles such as *jus cogens*. Cosmopolitanism is a move even further away from the traditional state-centric view of international law towards a greater recognition of human beings as the ultimate subjects of that law.

Cosmopolitanism is (broadly) characterised by three concepts.[14] First is *individualism*, which means that individual persons are the ultimate units of concern. Second is *universality*, which is based on the idea that this 'status of ultimate concern is attached to every human being equally—not merely to some subset'.[15] Third is *generality*, which means that this special status that is attributed to individuals has global force and is not just confined to fellow nationals, likeminded individuals, or such like. 'In short, cosmopolitanism emphasizes the *moral worth* of persons, the *equal* moral worth of *all* persons and the existence of derivative *obligations to all* to preserve the equal moral worth of persons.'[16]

Undoubtedly, there have been developments in international law that can be seen as expressions of this cosmopolitan ideal. Some principles exist that are regarded to be so fundamental and important for the international community as a whole that they supersede all other norms in international law. These norms have *jus cogens* status and become peremptory norms that constitute obligatory law and are binding on all states. *Jus cogens* norms are seen as being fundamental to the interests all states. They are given special status in international law by imposing obligations on every state to assist in the trial and punishment of those offences. *Jus cogens* crimes 'may be punished by any state because the offenders are common enemies of all mankind and all nations have an equal interest in their apprehension and prosecution'.[17] Such a commitment is found in international legal provisions such as the Torture Convention, the Genocide Convention or the definition of crimes against humanity, where a link to all states in international society exists through the notion of common humanity. This can then be seen as an expression of cosmopolitanism in international law, because in that sense 'all human beings form a single moral community, and . . . they owe each other certain obligations just in virtue of their being members of that single community'.[18]

Jus cogens norms are special because they are binding on all states and allow no exceptions or contradiction by other treaty provisions or customary law. They constitute a new way of perceiving relations between states and individuals, because 'for the first time, the international community has decided to recognize certain values . . . that must prevail over any other form of national interest'.[19]

Offences against *jus cogens* norms create the possibility of universal jurisdiction by individual states. Universal jurisdiction means that crimes can be punished by any state, regardless of where they have been committed. Such procedures are then based, not on nationalities of those involved, but on the idea of a common morality. The crime is punished because of a moral wrong that has been committed against humankind, regardless of state borders. Universal jurisdiction does not presume a world government or a world court, but it relies on national court systems to administer justice; it requires national systems to do the morally 'right' thing.

Such *jus cogens* norms have also found their way into independent international institutions such as the International Criminal Court (ICC), which has jurisdiction over genocide, crimes against humanity, and war crimes. Even though the ICC's jurisdiction is not truly universal,[20] its Statute and ability to act still recognise that individuals have rights and duties under international law independently of states.

Despite being able to find such cosmopolitan ideas in international law, a number of criticisms can be brought forward. One of the most important criticisms regards the question of universal enforcement: even though individual states (or particular institutions) have a *right* to punish *jus cogens* crimes, it does not necessarily mean that this will actually happen. Any exercise of jurisdiction (nationally or through an international court) is based on political cooperation and will. Critics would argue that states would only ever act to protect universal moral values if it would also serve their national interests.[21] States would never act altruistically and solely motivated by ideas of a common morality. Such criticisms speak to a realist conception of international law which is very sceptical of law in the international sphere. Realists see law as a tool and as only serving the powerful. They argue that because international law is based on states voluntarily consenting to it, states will only accept those laws that serve their own interests. Realists argue that state power and national interests are the ultimate aspects when trying to understand state behaviour and compliance—not questions of universal moral values.[22]

Cosmopolitanism also does not deal sufficiently with the difficult tension between moral unity (i.e., universal values and rights), on the one hand, and institutional fragmentation, on the other. Moral ideas need to be translated into rights and duties of individuals that can be protected by institutions. This is also linked to difficult questions of whether moral unity actually exists in international law. Are references to 'universal' values not just reinforcing existing power structures? It is important to recognise that cosmopolitanism is situated in its own context, and it can be debated whether it is truly based on 'common' values and interests. Considerations like these are being discussed in critical legal theory.

Critical legal theories

Critical legal theorists argue that appeals to universal, shared values and a 'common morality' in international legal discourse are in fact just disguised self-interested actions, used by the most powerful to maintain their own position in the global order. As Anthony Carty, for instance, argues:

> The crucial question is simply whether a positive system of universal international law actually exists, or whether particular states and their representative legal scholars merely appeal to such positivist discourse so as to impose a particularist language upon others *as of if it were a universally accepted legal discourse.*[23]

Critical legal theory sees law not as a distinctive and concrete discipline but as being interlinked with other issue areas such as politics and sociology, and as being dependent on morality. Critical legal theorists, such as David Kennedy and Koskenniemi, are sceptical about notions of 'universal' values of justice and human rights in the international community, however. They argue that international law is embedded in a specific context that reflects and reinforces existing power relations between states developed in international politics over the past decades. These relations, they argue, contain elements of imperialism and suppression of weaker states.[24]

Koskenniemi, for instance, asserts that there is a danger that, by claiming to act in the name of universal values and the international community as a whole, international law can be distorted to reflect only the interests of the most powerful but, at the same time, claim to be based on universality. He argues that 'law is a surface over which political opponents engage in hegemonic practices, trying to enlist its rules, principles and institutions on their side, making sure they would not support the adversary'.[25] He asserts that 'universal values' and 'international community' can only be expressed through a state or international organization, and therefore only embody *one* certain view of international law, because 'the whole' cannot be represented without at the same time representing a particular.[26]

One example that illustrates difficulties attached to actions based on 'universal' values is that of humanitarian intervention (i.e., intervention by one of more states in another state's internal affairs to protect the human rights of individuals that are not of the interveners' nationality). Such an intervention is then said to be based on ideas of common morality and doing 'the right thing' in the face of serious human rights abuses. Critical legal theorists argue that applying international law to justify such intervention is problematic because motivations for actions are ultimately dominated by *political* considerations of the most powerful states rather than by universal ethics norms. Koskenniemi argues that this 'turn to ethics' has 'often involved a shallow and dangerous moralisation which, if generalised, transforms international law into an uncritical instrument for the foreign policy choices of those whom power and privilege has put into decision-making positions'.[27]

Kennedy similarly criticises the hidden power politics in such human rights language and argues against using human rights norms as justifications for interventions. He argues that 'humanitarians are conflicted—seeking to engage the world, but renouncing the tools of power politics and embracing a cosmopolitan tolerance of foreign cultures and political systems. These conflicts have gotten built into the tools—the United Nations, the human rights movement, the law of force—that humanitarians have devised for influencing foreign affairs.'[28] Similar to Koskenniemi, he asserts that the states of the centre employ the language of human rights to justify their decisions against states of the periphery. This language then constitutes a vehicle for imperialism and reinforces existing power imbalances by referring to universal values that are in fact only based on the values of the most powerful. Kennedy sees humanitarians as misguided in their belief that humanitarian ideas and institutions are absolute virtues that can excuse any state action whereas, in reality, they are likely to be used to disguise other intentions. He argues that, by relying primarily on humanitarian justifications, the issues that motivated humanitarian intervention are fudged: too much attention is placed on justifying actions in human rights terms even when the main motivating factors were entirely different.[29]

Critical legal theorists argue that the law is inherently political and that the application of objective and general international legal provisions only takes place selectively. They doubt that international legal provisions can resolve conflicts and ambiguities, because their vagueness opens up the possibility of self-serving interpretations. Values such as 'morality' or 'justice' are always interpretative rather than objectively 'given'. International law, for instance, provides some threshold criteria when it comes to the protection of human rights, but borderline cases persist which then leads to the selective enforcement of international legal provisions.

Arguably, due to the lack of independent enforcement mechanisms, international law is always dependent on some form of agency—one or more states need to be willing to act in the face of serious human rights abuses. If they do so, it is because they focused on one particular situation and called it a 'crisis' that warrants intervention, but this can then hardly be called an action in the name of the international community as a whole. It is much rather action by one or more states that chose to act independently in particular circumstances, but still claim to act in line with the appropriate enforcement of universal principles of international law. This difficulty is evident, for instance, in recent cases of humanitarian intervention in Libya that included references to a common responsibility to protect human beings from the most serious human rights abuses. Whilst the international community decides to take action in this particular situation, a very similar human rights catastrophe in Syria does not lead to similar interventions to protect civilians.

Critical legal theorists are concerned that 'the more international lawyers are obsessed by the effectiveness of the law to be applied [in situations defined as] 'crises', the less we are aware of the subtle politics whereby some aspects of the world become defined as 'crisis', whereas others are not.'[30] Such a decision is ultimately a political act, however much it is justified in terms of ethics. Establishing 'universal' standards of human rights that legitimise intervention poses problems, because 'human rights often excuses government behavior by setting standards below which mischief seems legitimate. It can be easy to sign a treaty and then do what you want.'[31]

The selectivity that arises from such 'crisis' language is problematic because it normalises and justifies all other conduct that falls short of being called an 'atrocity'. The difficulty lies in devising criteria that are flexible enough but also encompass all situations on an international level. In the domestic context, formal rules work well; occasional injustices can be tolerated because of the 'bigger picture' resulting from the need to honour the formal validity of the law. In the international context, however, 'an injustice caused by the law immediately challenges the validity of a legal system that calls for compliance even against self-interest'.[32] Establishing criteria in international law that can encompass *all* cases is near impossible because such criteria are likely to be either over- or under-inclusive. Establishing criteria also provides a permission, it provides a threshold until no action needs to be taken. For instance, a criterion for humanitarian intervention could be set as 'at least 500 civilians being killed'. This would mean that 499 killed civilians would (justifiably) trigger no response from the international community or individual states, and would signal to the human rights abuser that his or her actions are legitimate.

Critical legal theory is concerned about the danger that exists when actions that are based on *individual* states' morality and ethics are used as precedents for the 'rightful' application of international law that are then incorporated into that law as 'objective' principles said to reflect international society as a whole. Such selectivity and situational interpretation of a 'crisis' does not lead to a consistent and universal application of international law and also reinforces existing power relations between states. Similar to critical legal theory, but moving from the state level to individual actors, feminist approaches are also concerned about inherent power relations in international law that exclude and disadvantage women.

Feminist approaches to international law and ethics

Feminist legal theory is linked to critical legal theory, but it is 'much more focused and concrete . . . and derives its theoretical force from immediate experience of the role of the legal system in creating and perpetuating the unequal position of women'.[33] It is not a single school (there are various strands of feminism, such as liberal, radical, and other forms), but it aims to give voice to diverse experiences women have in different parts of the world. Feminist legal theory can be seen to be more a set of questions rather than a set of answers; it is a particular perspective, a mode of analysis and an approach to life.

Feminist scholars argue that 'international law is a thoroughly gendered system'.[34] They claim that women's voices are silenced because of international law's organisational as well as its normative structure. Firstly, in terms of organisational structure, states are the principal subjects of international law, with international organisations also becoming increasingly more important. Feminists criticise the fact that women play only marginal roles in both—they are under-represented in decision-making processes and hold very few positions of power (within states and other organisations). For instance, for many years, women have not had prominent roles in important international legal institutions such as the International Law Commission, or featured highly among the judges' benches of the International Court of Justice. Feminists therefore argue that issues that are most relevant to women (rather than to men) are often ignored. Secondly, in terms of its normative dimension, a presumption exists that international legal norms that are directed at individuals are neutral and universally applicable, even though in reality they may affect men and women differently.[35]

A feminist critique of international law argues that its normative and institutional structures are committed to masculinist and imperial power. 'The absence of women in the development of international law has produced a narrow and inadequate jurisprudence that has among other things, legitimated the unequal position of women around the world rather than challenged it.'[36] Feminists argue that women are disadvantaged and subordinated in a number of areas in the international sphere: socially, politically, and culturally. Existing international institutions are seen as disadvantageous to women, and even if (formal) equality exists, discrimination occurs.

Feminist legal theorists argue that international law, and particularly human rights thinking, are based on a political conception of the division of life into private and public spheres, and that international law is seen as reflective of a gendered international order.[37] International law prioritises public institutions over the private sphere. This means that rights are particularly associated with the public sphere (e.g., right to freedom of speech, right to vote, and rights that protect individuals from arbitrary state interference). Rights have been more associated with activities engaged in by men and generally offer little protection from dangers characteristically faced by women. Historically, women have been systematically excluded and been confined to the private sphere, which is where women need protection (and rights). Feminists argue that protection is needed from other individuals rather than the state; women experience violations of their rights from husbands and other family members which are not covered by the international human rights regime.

> The law has always operated primarily within the public domain; it is considered appropriate to regulate the workplace, the economy and the distribution of political power, while direct state intervention in the family and the home has long been regarded as inappropriate.[38]

Some parts of international human rights law are being revised to respond to this critique. For instance, it is acknowledged that rape can be a war crime and that it can be used as a weapon of war; or in refugee law, it is acknowledged that women can constitute a social group subject to persecution. Even though these are positive developments to advance rights for women, they do not go far enough in addressing more structural problems that would require a more radical rethinking of international institutions that are linked to international law.[39] Feminist international legal theorists call for *structural* changes to the international legal system as a whole. As Hilary Charlesworth argues:

> Feminist analysis of international law has two major roles, one deconstructive, the other reconstructive. Deconstruction of the explicit and implicit values of the international legal system means challenging their claims to objectivity and rationality because of the limited base on which they are built.[40]

This approach challenges ideas of 'universal' morality and values that are based on gendered assumptions. Deconstructing such notions of universality have transformative potential. The second role of feminist analysis in international law, the idea of reconstruction, 'requires rebuilding the basic concepts of international law in a way that they do not support or reinforce the domination of women by men'.[41] This would then lead to an overall more inclusive and ultimately fairer system.

Conclusion

Debates in international law have moved in recent years from discussions about sources of law towards questions of ethics and the role of individuals as the ultimate subjects of the law. As this chapter has shown, a number of theoretical approaches address issues that cross disciplines of law, ethics, morality, and politics. The theoretical approaches explored here were chosen as illustrations of different aspects of debates in current international legal thinking. Global constitutionalism looks to different constitutional structures and how they interact beyond the state level, whereas cosmopolitanism focuses on the role of the individual and ideas of a common morality. Challenging some of these normative assumptions of international law, critical legal theory and feminism question some of the more structural and underlying ideas of international law and call for radical transformations of the system.

Notes

1 H. L. A. Hart, *The Concept of Law*, 2nd edn. (Oxford: Clarendon Press, 1994), 231.
2 For discussions on the distinction between treaty law and customary law, see, for instance, Peter Malanczuk, *Akehurst's Modern Introduction to International Law*, 7th edn. (London, New York: Routledge, 1997); or Antonio Cassese, *International Law* (New York: Oxford University Press, 2001).
3 Ruti Teitel, 'Humanity Law: A New Interpretive Lens on the International Sphere,' *Fordham Law Review*, 77, no. 2 (2008): 667–668.
4 Jean L. Cohen, 'Constitutionalism beyond the State: Myth or Necessity? (a Pluralist Approach),' *Humanity: An International Journal of Human Rights, Humanitarianism, and Development*, 2, no. 1 (2011): 130.
5 Ibid.
6 Anthony F. Lang, Jr, 'Global Constitutionalism as Middle Ground Ethic,' in *Ethical Reasoning in International Affairs: Arguments from the Middle Ground*, ed. Cornelia Navari (London: Palgrave, 2014), 109.
7 Martti Koskenniemi, 'Constitutionalism as Mindset: Reflections on Kantian Themes about International Law and Globalization,' *Theoretical Inquiries in Law*, 8, no. 1 (2007): 35.

8 Ibid.
9 See, for instance: Antje Wiener et al., 'Global Constitutionalism: Human Rights, Democracy and the Rule of Law,' *Global Constitutionalism*, 1, no. 1 (2012); Anthony F. Lang, Jr, 'Global Constitutionalism as Middle Ground Ethic,' in *Ethical Reasoning in International Affairs: Arguments from the Middle Ground*, ed. Cornelia Navari (London: Palgrave, 2014); and Cohen, 'Constitutionalism beyond the State,' 127–158.
10 Court of Justice of the European Union, 'Judgment in Joined Cases C-584/10 P, C-593/10 P and C-595/10 P,' news release, July 18, 2013, http://curia.europa.eu/jcms/upload/docs/application/pdf/2013-07/cp130093en.pdf.
11 Wiener et al., 'Global Constitutionalism,' 1.
12 Ibid.
13 Ibid.
14 See Thomas W. Pogge, 'Cosmopolitanism and Sovereignty,' *Ethics*, 103, no. 1 (1992).
15 Ibid., 48.
16 Roland Pierik and Wouter Werner, 'Cosmopolitanism in Context: An Introduction,' in *Cosmopolitanism in Context: Perspectives from International Law and Political Theory*, ed. Roland Pierik and Wouter Werner (Cambridge: Cambridge University Press, 2010), 3.
17 Ben Chigara, 'Pinochet and the Administration of International Criminal Justice,' in *The Pinochet Case: A Legal and Constitutional Analysis*, ed. Diana Woodhouse (Oxford; Portland, Oregon: Hart Publishing, 2000), 118.
18 Neil Walker, 'Making a World of Difference? Habermas, Cosmopolitanism and the Constitutionalization of International Law' (working paper, EUI Working Paper Law, European University Institute, 2005), 4.
19 Antonio Cassese, *Human Rights in a Changing World* (Cambridge: Polity Press, 1990), 168.
20 The ICC can take action if the crime occurred on a state party's territory or if it was committed by a state party's national. It can also exercise jurisdiction if the UN Security Council refers a situation to it under Chapter VII of the UN Charter. 'True' universal jurisdiction would not require any nationality tie to the crime or the individuals involved.
21 Alex J. Bellamy, 'Humanitarian Intervention and the Three Traditions,' *Global Society*, 17, no. 1 (2003).
22 Ibid.
23 Anthony Carty, 'Critical International Law: Recent Trends in the Theory of International Law,' *European Journal of International Law*, 2, no. 1 (1991): 1, emphasis in original.
24 David Kennedy, 'International Humanitarianism: The Dark Sides,' *International Journal of Not-for-Profit Law*, 6, no. 3 (2004).
25 Martti Koskenniemi, 'International Law and Hegemony: A Reconfiguration,' http://www.helsinki.fi/eci/Publications/Koskenniemi/MHegemony.pdf.
26 Ibid.
27 '"The Lady Doth Protest Too Much": Kosovo, and the Turn to Ethics in International Law,' *The Modern Law Review*, 65, no. 2 (2002): 159.
28 Kennedy.
29 Ibid.
30 Koskenniemi, 'The Lady Doth Protest Too Much,' 173.
31 Kennedy.
32 Koskenniemi, 'The Lady Doth Protest Too Much,' 169.
33 Hilary Charlesworth, Christine Chinkin, and Shelley Wright, 'Feminist Approaches to International Law,' *American Journal of International Law*, 85, no. 4 (1991): 613.
34 Ibid., 615.
35 David Weissbrodt, Fionnuala Ni Aolain, Frank C. Newman, and Joan Fitzpatrick, *International Human Rights Law, Policy, and Process*, 4th edn. (London: LexisNexis, 2009).
36 Hilary Charlesworth and Christine Chinkin, *The Boundaries of International Law: A Feminist Analysis* (Manchester: Manchester University Press, 2000), 1.
37 See, for instance: Hilary Charlesworth, Christine Chinkin, and Shelley Wright, 'Feminist Approaches to International Law'.
38 Ibid., 627.
39 Christine Chinkin, 'Feminist Interventions into International Law,' *Adelaide Law Review*, 19 (1997): 61.
40 Hilary Charlesworth, 'Feminist Critiques of International Law and Their Critics,' *Third World Legal Studies*, 13 (1994): 3.
41 Charlesworth and Chinkin, *Boundaries of International Law.*

PART V

International intervention

ETHICS AND INTERNATIONAL INTERVENTION

James Pattison

On the face of it, humanitarian intervention appears paradoxical. It is, in effect, waging war to save lives, but it almost always leads to civilian casualties, refugee flows, and damage to vital infrastructure. The devastation caused by military intervention seems to render it an inappropriate measure to save lives. Nevertheless, on occasion there arise situations where a state or rebel movement is unwilling to halt the mass violation of basic human rights unless there is external military intervention. As a result, prominent individuals and groups have often called for military intervention, such as in Darfur in response to the killing and violence by the *Janjaweed*, and in Syria in response to mass atrocities by the Assad regime and ISIS. States have sometimes heeded these calls—they have engaged in several instances of humanitarian intervention since 1989. These include intervention by the Economic Community of West African States (ECOWAS) in Liberia in 1990 and Sierra Leone in 1997 to restore law and order; the US-led intervention in Somalia in 1992 to open up humanitarian corridors; NATO's interventions in Bosnia in 1995 and Kosovo in 1999; Australian-led intervention in East Timor in 1999; French-led intervention in Côte d'Ivoire in 2003 and 2011; NATO-led intervention in Libya in 2011; and potentially the ECOWAS action in Gambia in early 2017.

These cases have often been controversial, given the potential for humanitarian intervention to both tackle and cause the violation of human rights. Indeed, humanitarian intervention raises a series of central moral questions for international relations (IR), international law, and political philosophy. These include the moral import and meaning of state sovereignty, whether states possess obligations to those beyond their borders, to what degree military intervention can be deemed 'humanitarian', and the utility of military force. These in turn raise issues for thinking about humanitarianism, and humanitarian action more generally, including humanitarian aid by non-governmental organisations (NGOs) and states.

The debates on these issues have been important beyond the narrow issue of the permissibility of humanitarianism. They have also been important more generally for the development of the fields of international ethics and international relations. For instance, humanitarian intervention provides the clearest challenge to realist approaches that are often viewed as denying the possibility of international ethics. In short, if, as some realists claim, states are only interested in increasing power or security, why do they engage in military operations to save lives? To that extent, humanitarian intervention has been a central example used by constructivists in the development of constructivism in IR. For instance, the work of Martha Finnemore and

Nicholas J. Wheeler provides influential accounts of why states engage in these interventions and, more generally, of constructivism and the notion that states are concerned not simply with their narrow material interests.[1] Realists have struggled to respond, often offering weak, ill-conceived, or implausible accounts of humanitarian intervention and why states intervene.[2]

Similarly, humanitarian intervention has been a central example used by cosmopolitans to defend their approach and to repudiate statism, nationalism, and communitarianism. The cosmopolitans claim that we have duties to those beyond our borders and state sovereignty/nationality/community are not independently morally valuable.[3] Thus, they claim, if there is another Rwanda-style situation, it would be morally wrong to stand by, when we have the military capacity to tackle genocide. The point has been a powerful one, and has helped lead to notable statists, communitarians, and nationalists appearing to shift their views (e.g., Walzer 2002) and new, more moderate forms of statism, communitarianism, and nationalism that concede much ground to cosmopolitanism.[4]

Thus, these are debates that constructivists and cosmopolitans have largely won. The debates have since shifted on, away from the issues of *why* states intervene and *what is permissible* of the humanitarian intervention. A key moment was the adoption at the 2005 UN World Summit, with over 150 heads of state in attendance, of the 'Responsibility to Protect' (R2P) doctrine. The R2P originated in the 2001 report by the International Commission on Intervention and State Sovereignty (ICISS), which argues that sovereignty implies *responsibility*—the responsibility to protect human rights. If a state is unable or unwilling to fulfil its responsibility to prevent or tackle mass atrocities, there exists a remedial responsibility on the part of the international community to react. This may, on occasion, necessitate humanitarian intervention. The agreement reached at the 2005 World Summit differed somewhat from the original ICISS report.[5] Yet the central tenets of R2P remain: state sovereignty necessitates responsibility and the international community has a moral obligation to stop mass atrocities.[6] This was fleshed out in 2009 by the then UN secretary general Ban Ki-moon in terms of three pillars.[7] The first pillar concerns the protection responsibilities of states—states are morally obliged to look after their own populations. The second pillar concerns 'international assistance', that is, that states are morally obliged to assist other states in helping them realise their domestic responsibilities to tackle mass atrocities. The third pillar is 'timely and decisive response'. This concerns action to persuade and coerce states that are manifestly failing to prevent or tackle mass atrocities. Most of the focus of pillar three is on humanitarian intervention, but R2P advocates are keen to emphasise that it involves much more than this. There are a variety of non-military measures, ranging from economic sanctions to non-violent resistance, which can be used to help fulfil R2P.[8]

R2P is now the predominant framework for discussing the issue of humanitarian intervention. Debates surrounding humanitarian intervention are now typically framed in terms of R2P, in academia and beyond. For instance, the 2011 intervention in Libya was widely discussed in terms of this doctrine. Indeed, the R2P doctrine has become the main focus of debate. Perhaps the most contested issue is whether R2P has had any real effect or is just empty rhetoric.[9] As we will see, the question of whether the R2P is efficacious concerns, in particular, the notion of an international remedial responsibility to protect. Key sceptics—such as Aidan Hehir, writing in this volume—deny that states widely endorse the key aspect of this *international* responsibility (for instance, they note that the notion of international responsibility is generally absent from the resolutions of the UN Security Council that cite R2P).[10] They also claim that, even when it is cited, R2P is not influential—there are other reasons for state intervention (e.g., in Libya) that are not to do with R2P.

The defenders of R2P, however, point to the explicit endorsement of the international responsibility to protect, the criticism of inaction (which shows that R2P exerts an expected standard of behaviour), and evidence of influence of R2P in decision-making.[11] They also point to developing 'habits of protection', whereby the international community now at least attempts to do *something* in response to mass atrocities. Thus, key figures on R2P, Alex Bellamy (Director of the Asia-Pacific Centre for the Responsibility to Protect) and Jennifer Welsh (the former UN Special Representative on R2P), argue that there is now an accepted 'duty of conduct'/'responsibility to try' to prevent and tackle mass atrocities and, importantly, that this is a norm.[12] That is, it is widely accepted that there is an international, remedial responsibility to address mass atrocities and, moreover, this exerts influence on states.

Although the sceptics and advocates on R2P are often seen as significantly opposed, their positions are in fact fairly close.[13] Key figures appear to accept that norms matter in international politics, that narrow material self-interest is sometimes more important in states' decision-making than R2P, and that R2P at best can only make a relatively small difference to state behaviour. The current debate is, in fact, really only about how much difference R2P makes. To put it colloquially, it is whether R2P makes a bit of a difference or none.

The chapters in this Part concern several key issues in these debates about humanitarian intervention and R2P. In Chapter 24, the world-renowned scholar on humanitarian intervention Fernando R. Tesón focuses on the issue of right intention. This is one of the trickiest issues facing the ethics of humanitarian intervention. Many sceptics of intervention claim that it is self-interested and so morally problematic. Moreover, it is vital to understand whether humanitarian intervention has a right intention in order to grasp whether an intervention is a 'humanitarian' intervention or not. If it has another intention, such as self-interest, it cannot be properly classified as an instance of *humanitarian* intervention—it would rather be another form of intervention, such as imperialistic intervention or intervention for purposes of self-defence. The 2003 war in Iraq, for instance, might be viewed as a case of self-interested action, to the extent to which the US-led alliance was focused on removing the threat from Saddam Hussein's alleged weapons of mass destruction, as well as seemingly more nefarious motives, such as securing access to oil. More recently, the bombing campaigns against ISIS in Syria and Iraq might be viewed as a counterterror operation, rather than humanitarian intervention, given that the predominant aim is to weaken, contain, and ultimately defeat ISIS, rather than tackling the egregious human rights violations faced by Syrian and Iraqi civilians.

Tesón calls this issue 'the question of categorization'. He argues that the distinction between wars of self-defence and humanitarian dimension 'is illusory', since it is *not* 'necessary first to categorize a war and then inquire whether or not it is justified'. According to Tesón, then, the issue of categorisation is redundant, since what matters is whether the war is *justified*, not how we *categorise* it. To be sure, for Tesón, the justification depends on right intention. Tesón goes on to offer the most detailed typology of potential intentions in humanitarian intervention (and war) to date in the literature. He draws distinctions between 'pure intent', 'conditional intent', 'ulterior motive', 'pure side effect', and 'evil intent'. The first three—pure intent, conditional intent, and ulterior motive—meet the requirements of right intent, he argues, but evil intent doesn't. Central to his account is the difference between intention—which 'covers the contemplated act, what the agent wills to do'—and motive—which is a further goal that one wishes to accomplish with the intended act. This is a very helpful distinction and is central to criminal law, but is often missed on account of the ethics of self-defence and war (and intervention). As long as the intervener *intends* the just cause, say to tackle the mass violations of basic human rights, even if they have an ulterior motive, such as the pursuit of oil, this is still sufficient for their intervention to meet the requirements of right intention. Of course, it is a further question whether the intervention is *all-things-considered* justifiable—this will depend on other considerations such as proportionality. Interestingly, though, cases of evil intent, where the intervener intends to tackle mass atrocities but does so for highly problematic motives, Tesón thinks do *not* meet the requirements of right intention.

Tesón offers, then, a highly thoughtful and stimulating response to one of the central questions of intervention, which surround its permissibility, that is, the *right* to intervene. In his chapter for this volume, Luke Glanville, one of the leading scholars on the history of political thought and intervention, considers one of the other central set of questions, that is, around the *duty* to intervene. To do this, he focuses on the Swiss diplomat and jurist Emer de Vattel. He criticises the undue focus on Kant in much of the writing on the ethics of intervention, suggesting instead that Vattel is far more relevant, given that Kant highly circumscribes international duties, largely to a duty only to respect asylum-seekers. By contrast, Vattel, Glanville argues, offers a much richer and more helpful account in thinking through the ethics of humanitarian intervention. Indeed, Vattel offers guidance to two of the central issues for humanitarian intervention. The first concerns the relationship between individuals and state sovereignty, and the need to maintain a principle of non-intervention in order to maintain order in the international system, but also the need to be able to redress abuses of human rights. The second concerns the relative weight that should be given to international duties *vis-à-vis* domestic duties, that is, states' duties towards their own citizens. If the latter are viewed as unduly weighty, humanitarian intervention would not be permissible, unless fully self-interested.[14] But it does seem still that states have obligations to prioritise the interests of their own citizens.

Vattel offers interesting and helpful answers to both questions, Glanville notes. To start with, Vattel defends a duty of collective defence to help a neighbouring nation facing unjust attack. Vattel also posits a duty to assist in cases of humanitarian crises, including in non-coercive ways. This reflects, Glanville argues, much of the content in the R2P doctrine, which under pillar two requires international assistance to ensure that they can meet their protection requirements (and under pillar three too). Although Vattel recognises the importance of non-intervention, he also, Glanville highlights, accepts that humanitarian intervention is permissible on occasion. This is 'in instances where governmental oppression was so extreme as to destroy the relationship between ruler and people, extinguishing the very political community that once enjoyed the privileges of liberty and independence'.

In response to the second question, Glanville notes that Vattel warns that the first priority must be to care for 'the nation who has committed herself to his care'. Yet, on the other hand, the need for prudence does not justify neglecting others. Vattel calls nations to recognise a duty not only to contribute to the urgent needs of others in times of crisis but also to engage in routine efforts to contribute to the capacities of others to avert or effectively respond to emergent crises themselves. More specifically, nations are under a duty to assist when there is 'little inconvenience' to themselves. This reflects the mainstream view in the ethics of war and defence that there are humanitarian duties to assist others providing that one can do so at a *reasonable* cost. As Glanville nicely puts it, 'a state should not hesitate to sacrifice its interests a little in order to help others a lot'. Interestingly, Glanville notes, Vattel also justifies this in terms of a form of enlightened self-interest, whereby nations recognise the 'ideational benefits that they would derive from contributing to the perfection of others'. This is in somewhat similar vein to the constructivist accounts of intervention noted above.

One of the central themes of Glanville's chapter is that Vattel anticipates much of the central notions in the R2P doctrine, from the emphasis on consensual, preventive, and non-violent measures, to the acceptance of international duties, to the highlighting of a general principle of non-intervention that can occasionally be overruled. In his chapter, Aidan Hehir focuses more specifically on the contribution of R2P. Hehir is one of the most renowned scholars on R2P and undoubtedly the leading sceptic of its significance. As noted above, the R2P has become the central *framework* for considering the case for humanitarian intervention and responses to mass atrocities. Yet measuring the *impact* of R2P is extremely difficult, given its multifaceted and normative nature. It would clearly be difficult, for instance, to design a large-number quantitative study to test this. The upshot is that we need to look to other ways of considering whether R2P has had an impact. One might consider the number of mass atrocities since R2P was accepted in 2005, but this is a dubious measure, given the numerous factors involved in mass atrocity crimes. Could one say that any potential fall in mass atrocities was really the result of R2P, rather than, say, other factors, such as economic growth or human rights movements? And if there is a particular mass atrocity, such as in Syria, how can one really say that this shows that R2P is ineffective? After all, the mass atrocities in Syria seem to stem from fairly intractable factors, such as the long history of intra-ethnic tensions in the region, the Russian support to Assad, and the military capabilities of the Assad regime, which a norm such as R2P would be hard-pressed to resolve. As noted above, defenders of R2P highlight, on the contrary, that R2P at least gets mass atrocities onto the international agenda, and at least states are *trying* to redress them, even if this is not always possible. To put this another way, R2P is seen as only (at best) a norm and still maintains the expected standard of behaviours that states don't engage in mass atrocities and that other states react to them.

What becomes crucial for this argument is the extent to which there *are* these expected standards of behaviour. One of the central determinants is seemingly the rhetoric of states and the extent to which they invoke R2P. The defenders of R2P often highlight that states invoke R2P frequently. If this is right, then it *might* be the case that R2P is a norm that informs the decision-making of states, even if they can't necessarily react to all decisions. Hehir, however, strongly challenges this. He argues that, although states often invoke R2P, this is *not* in its crucial, value-added element. This concerns the *international* responsibility to protect. As noted above, what makes R2P stand out from notions of human rights and the previous doctrine of humanitarian intervention concerns the acceptance that there is a remedial, *international* responsibility to respond to mass atrocities. Standing by is not an option. Hehir argues that states do acknowledge that they have domestic responsibilities to look after their own populations, but this is nothing new; crucially, he claims, they do not invoke their *international* responsibility. In his words, 'simply focusing on the number of times R2P has been invoked positively, and the scale of state support for R2P-related campaigns, is a highly superficial means by which to judge the concept's efficacy and future potential'.

More specifically, Hehir argues that there are three arguments presented by defenders of R2P to claim that it has an influence—the consensus on R2P, the number of UN Security Council resolutions which mention R2P, and support from groups and campaigns. Against this notion, he posits that the ascendancy of R2P has been accompanied by a decline in respect for human rights. Although he admits that the proliferation of R2P might make it more difficult for states to justify inaction, he questions whether this can really be viewed as 'progress' or as anything 'new'. Crucially, the support given is only really for pillars one and two, he argues, and includes the backing from disreputable states such as Bahrain, Sudan, and Qatar. Crucially, he posits, support for pillar three is sorely lacking. In his words:

> In none of the 69 Security Council Resolutions passed to date that mention R2P is there any direct reference to Pillar III or intimations that the Security Council can – through R2P – take action to prevent or halt the commission of one or more of the four crimes within a particular state.

Chapter 22 in this Part moves beyond the issue of military intervention, to consider humanitarian aid. This could be one potential measure under R2P to help tackle mass atrocities.[15] Of course, however, humanitarian aid can be given in other cases as well, where mass atrocities are not ongoing or likely, where states are simply struggling to meet the basic socio-economic rights of their populations. Although not as contentious as major intervention, humanitarian assistance still, however, raises several vexing ethical issues. These are discussed by Hugo Slim, who is a celebrated scholar of humanitarian ethics and has recently taken up the post of Head of Policy at the International Committee of the Red Cross (ICRC). Slim documents the ethical commitments that drive humanitarianism, but that can also lead to several notable problems.

More specifically, Slim highlights the size of the humanitarianism sector, with huge transnational organisations such as Oxfam and Save the Children and a global spend of over $28 billion. He charts how humanitarian action emerged from the remnants of World War II and grew rapidly at the end of the Cold War. A crucial part of this is movement has been the propagation of international humanitarian law (IHL), which aims to limit the horrors of war and is defended by the ICRC at great lengths. Slim notes how four central principles—humanity, impartiality, neutrality, and independence—have become a touchstone of humanitarian action. Yet he also notes that these principles do not mean that humanitarianism is carried out well. Potential problems with humanitarianism abound, Slim notes, including worries that, like for military intervention, it is unduly influenced by power politics, with states using humanitarian aid to advance their own interests. 'Localisation'—giving locals more control—appears a straightforward answer, but Slim highlights that locals might simply not have sufficient ability and that local actors might be morally problematic themselves, such as by restricting their aid to one side or by being implicated in the conflict. Other issues include those surrounding paternalism, how much humanitarianism should aim to redress long-term causes rather than providing quick solutions, and the dangers posed to humanitarian workers in the field, ranging from traffic accidents to infectious diseases and their deliberate killing by armed actors. Slim concludes by highlighting that the rise of the BRICS—Brazil, Russia, India, China, and South Africa—is likely to provide a shake-up for humanitarian action, as they may have different views of how to conduct humanitarianism than the Western model.

The chapters in this section, then, provide exceptionally helpful and insightful accounts of intervention and humanitarianism by the leading figures in the field.

Notes

1 Martha Finnemore, *The Purpose of Intervention: Changing Beliefs about the Use of Force* (Ithaca: Cornell University Press, 2004); Nicholas J. Wheeler, *Saving Strangers: Humanitarian Intervention in International Society* (Oxford: Oxford University Press, 2000).

2 E.g., Robert Pape, 'When Duty Calls: A Pragmatic Standard of Humanitarian Intervention', *International Security*, 37, no. 1 (2012): 41–80.

3 E.g., Simon Caney, *Justice beyond Borders: A Global Political Theory* (Oxford: Oxford University Press, 2005); Fernando R. Tesón, *Humanitarian Intervention: An Inquiry into Law and Morality*, 3rd edn. (New York: Transnational Publishers, 2005).

4 E.g., David Miller, *National Responsibility and Global Justice* (Oxford: Oxford University Press, 2007).

5 See James Pattison, *Humanitarian Intervention and the Responsibility to Protect: Who Should Intervene?* (Oxford: Oxford University Press, 2010), Ch. 1.

6 As Alex J. Bellamy highlights, despite the wariness of some states to be legally bound to intervene militarily, the 2005 agreement still emphasises international responsibilities to assist states and to use non-military means. See: Alex J. Bellamy, 'The Responsibility to Protect Turns Ten', *Ethics and International Affairs* 29, no. 1 (2015): 169.

7 Ban Ki-moon, *Implementing the Responsibility to Protect*, UN doc A/63/677 (2009).

8 I assess these in detail in James Pattison, *The Alternatives to War: From Sanctions to Nonviolence* (Oxford: Oxford University Press, 2018).

9 See, e.g., Alex J. Bellamy, *The Responsibility to Protect: A Defense* (Oxford: Oxford University Press, 2015); Alex J. Bellamy, 'Responsibility to Protect Turns Ten'; Luke Glanville, 'Does R2P Matter? Interpreting the Impact of a Norm', *Cooperation and Conflict*, 51, no. 2 (2016): 184–199; Aidan Hehir, 'Assessing the Influence of the Responsibility to Protect on the UN Security Council during the Arab Spring', *Cooperation and Conflict*, 51, no. 2 (2016): 166–183; and Hehir's contribution to this Handbook (Chapter 23).

10 See: Aidan Hehir, 'The Responsibility to Protect: "Sound and Fury Signifying Nothing"?', *International Relations*, 24, no. 2 (2010): 218–239; Aidan Hehir, *The Responsibility to Protect: Rhetoric, Reality and the Future of Humanitarian Intervention* (London: Palgrave Macmillan, 2012); Aidan Hehir, 'The Permanence of Inconsistency: Libya, the Security Council, and the Responsibility to Protect', *International Security*, 38, no. 1 (2013): 137–159; Hehir, 'Assessing the Influence of the Responsibility to Protect'; and Justin Morris, 'Libya and Syria: R2P and the Spectre of the Swinging Pendulum', *International Affairs*, 89, no. 5 (2013): 1265–1283.

11 Bellamy, *The Responsibility to Protect*; Glanville, 'Does R2P Matter'; Jennifer M. Welsh, 'Implementing the "Responsibility to Protect": Catalysing Debate and Building Capacity', in *Implementation and World Politics: How International Norms Change Practice*, eds. Alexander Betts and Phil Orchard (Oxford: Oxford University Press, 2014), 124–143.

12 Bellamy, *The Responsibility to Protect*; Bellamy, 'Responsibility to Protect Turns Ten'; Jennifer M. Welsh, 'Implementing the Responsibility to Protect'. See also: James Pattison, 'Mapping the Responsibilities to Protect: A Typology of International Duties', *Global Responsibility to Protect*, 7, no. 2 (2015): 190–210. Here, I consider what an account of the *'duty of conduct'* / *'responsibility to try'* should mean.

13 This is true, I think, of the following: Bellamy, *The Responsibility to Protect*; Glanville, 'Does R2P Matter?'; Hehir's contribution to this Handbook (Chapter 23); Theresa Reinhold, 'The Responsibility to Protect: Much Ado about Nothing?', *Review of International Studies*, 36, no. S1 (2010): 55–78; Welsh, 'Implementing the Responsibility to Protect'; and perhaps, Morris, 'Libya and Syria'.

14 See, for a very helpful discussion: Allen Buchanan, 'The Internal Legitimacy of Humanitarian Intervention', *Journal of Political Philosophy*, 7, no. 1 (1999): 71–87.

15 See: Pattison, *The Alternatives to War*.

21

HISTORICAL THINKING ABOUT HUMAN PROTECTION

Insights from Vattel

Luke Glanville

So much theorizing about international ethics today proceeds on the assumption that Immanuel Kant—or at least an idealized "Kantianism" —can be understood as setting the terms of debate and that there is little need to grapple with the ideas of philosophers, jurists, and theologians that preceded him.[1] Kant has thus largely succeeded in his effort to supplant earlier natural law theorists and to position himself as one who transcended his historical, regional, and political context and provided a timeless, universal, and pure framework for moral reasoning.[2] Building on John Rawls's landmark "Kantian" theory of justice, scholars have developed a wide range of "Kantian" theories of *global* justice over the last forty years, ranging from Charles Beitz's cosmopolitan theory to Rawls's own internationalist theory.[3] In doing so, however, many have derived from Kant not only arguments that he did not conceive of making, but also arguments that were well known to him that he deliberately chose not to make.

This is particularly so with respect to theorizing about humanitarianism and humanitarian intervention. Numerous scholars have relied on Kant—or at least "Kantian" reasoning—to develop theories about the international ethics of assisting and protecting strangers beyond borders.[4] But Kant himself refrained from positing duties of international humanitarian assistance or humanitarian intervention. Indeed, he suggested a strict duty of non-intervention. He did so, it seems, not because the idea of caring for strangers did not occur to him. After all, he knew well the works of numerous earlier theorists who had posited demanding duties to assist and protect strangers beyond borders. Rather, preoccupied as he was with the problem of war, Kant asserted that morality required not the establishment of a "friendly" community of nations, but merely a "peaceful" one. Thus, while he accorded to nations stringent negative duties to refrain from interfering in each other's affairs, the positive duties that states were said to bear in their relations with each other in his ideal "cosmopolitan constitution" were remarkably minimal. "Cosmopolitan right shall be limited to conditions of universal *hospitality*," he claimed, and this involved merely "the right of a foreigner not to be treated with hostility because he has arrived on the land of another."[5]

Present-day Kantians seeking to explain why states might have duties to care for the vulnerable beyond their borders tend to derive such duties from Kant's foundational principles and maxims. In doing so, they are compelled to either ignore or awkwardly explain away the fact that Kant himself implicitly rejected these duties. As fruitful as some of this present-day work is, we would surely be well served by also re-engaging with pre-Kantian theorists who gave careful consideration to the ethics of assisting and protecting people beyond borders and who Kant may have been too quick to dismiss.

This chapter focuses on the thinking of the Swiss diplomat and jurist Emer de Vattel (1714–1767).[6] Vattel was a particularly influential pre-Kantian theorist who not only embraced rights and duties to assist and protect strangers beyond borders but also gave sustained attention to the nature, scope, and implications of these rights and duties. In his treatment of the ethics of human protection, Vattel grappled with the tension between the rights of sovereign states to manage their own affairs and the rights of others to ensure the wellbeing of the people within these states. This is a topic that remains politically fraught today, as heated United Nations Security Council (UNSC) debates on the appropriate international responses to crises in Burundi, South Sudan, Syria, and elsewhere make clear.[7] Much ink has been spilled in recent decades by theorists seeking to resolve this tension between sovereignty and interference, including several works that have sought insights from the history of ideas.[8] We will see that Vattel's proposed resolution finds a middle ground between those who defend an unconditional, non-interventionist understanding of sovereignty that shields tyranny, and those who seek to dilute the rights of sovereigns in ways that facilitate abusive interventions by the powerful against the weak.

Crucially, however, Vattel realized that a tension that was equally in need of consideration was that between the duties of states to help others and their duties to help themselves. As present-day advocates for more consistent and effective international responses to grave suffering realize, sovereignty is not the only obstacle to the protection of the vulnerable. Indeed, in many instances, such as when states consent to the provision of humanitarian, peacekeeping, or peacebuilding assistance, sovereignty poses no obstacle at all. Rather, it is the unwillingness of capable states to accept and act upon duties to care for those beyond their borders that is the problem. This problem seems to be worsening as I write, with the governments of several powerful states acquiescing to, and in some cases actively encouraging, populist calls to focus exclusively on duties to their own citizens, to reduce foreign aid, to close borders, and to disengage from distant and complex crises. Vattel's detailed treatment of the tension between duties to others and duties to oneself emphasizes the need for prudence while also insisting that states should be willing to make sacrifices for the sake of outsiders. Confronted as we are today with humanitarian catastrophes, civil wars, and mass atrocities that have cost the lives of hundreds of thousands and generated the displacement of 65 million more, Vattel's ideas demand renewed attention.

The first two sections of the chapter examine Vattel's discussion of this tension between duties to distant strangers and duties to one's own people. The next two sections then detail his arguments about the permissibility of assisting or rescuing others in the absence of sovereign consent. The chapter concludes by considering how Vattel's work can make a valuable contribution to our thinking about the ethics of human protection today.

The duty to "perfect" strangers

In the second of the four books of his influential work, *The Law of Nations* (1758), Vattel expounded a wide range of duties that nations owed to others and considered how they should be weighed against duties to themselves.[9] Vattel's model for working through this tension was grounded in a notion of "perfection," which he took from the natural law writings of Gottfried Wilhelm Leibniz (1646–1716) and Christian Wolff (1679–1754). All states have a duty to contribute to the perfection and preservation of other states, he claimed, in so far as they can do so without neglecting their duties toward themselves. The perfection of other states was said to involve providing for their necessities and conveniences, helping them to secure peace and justice, and contributing to their capacities to achieve these things for themselves—tasks that are central to the humanitarianism, peacebuilding, and Responsibility to Protect (R2P) agendas today.

Vattel began by outlining the "general principle of all the mutual duties of nations": "One state owes to another state whatever it owes to itself, so far as that other stands in real need of its assistance, and the former can grant it without neglecting the duties it owes to itself." He framed this principle in terms of a duty to perfect others for their own sake, but he also founded it upon considerations of self-interest. It is the inability of individuals to supply all their wants and to preserve and perfect themselves on their own that obliges them to extend to each other mutual aid and assistance. And those same duties that individuals owe to each other are, in a way, also owed by nations to each other, he explained. However, he offered two observations to relieve those readers "who might be alarmed at this doctrine, as totally subversive of the maxims of sound policy":

1. Social bodies or sovereign states are much more capable of supplying all their wants than individual men are; and mutual assistance is not so necessary among them, nor so frequently required . . .
2. The duties of a nation towards itself, and chiefly the care of its own safety, require much more circumspection and reserve, than need be observed by an individual in giving assistance to others.[10]

Nevertheless, despite these two considerations, Vattel proceeded to outline a range of ways in which states ought to discharge their duty to preserve and perfect others. He outlined a duty to take up arms to aid a neighboring nation unjustly attacked by an aggressive enemy, like many before him had done. In response to those who might object that a ruler should not expose the lives of his soldiers for the sake of a foreign nation if not treaty-bound to do so, he replied that the ruler was justified in doing so because, "in giving energy to the spirit and disposition to afford mutual aid," the ruler's actions increased the likelihood that others would come to his own nation's assistance in time of need.[11]

But, in a break from earlier theorists who tended to focus on such duties to resort to arms, he added that nations ought also to provide non-coercive assistance to others afflicted with "famine or any other calamities":

> if a nation is afflicted with famine, all those who have provisions to spare ought to relieve her distress, without however exposing themselves to want . . . To give assistance in such extreme necessity is so essentially conformable to humanity, that the duty is seldom neglected by any nation that has received the slightest polish of civilization.[12]

He cited the example of Henry IV of France, whom he (somewhat misleadingly) indicated as having facilitated the supply of food to "obstinate rebels who were bent on his destruction" during his Siege of Paris in 1590.[13]

"Whatever be the calamity with which a nation is afflicted," Vattel declared, "the like assistance is due to it." He invoked the example of "little states in Switzerland" who ordered public collections to succor villages of neighboring countries that had been ruined by fire, "the difference of religion proving no bar to the performance of so humane a deed." He likewise endorsed the "noble generosity" of England whose parliament responded to the Lisbon earthquake of 1755 by voting for the provision of one hundred thousand pounds' worth of assistance, half in money and half in ships laden with food, clothing, and tools, for the relief of the suffering people of Portugal. Protestant England's generosity, he claimed, convinced the Catholic Portuguese that "an opposition in belief and worship does not restrain the beneficence of those who understand the claims of humanity."[14] The obligations to perform these "offices of humanity," he explained, were "solely founded on the nature of man." No nation can refuse them to another on the grounds of difference of religion. Rather, "to be entitled to them, it is sufficient that the claimant is our fellow creature."[15]

Crucially, Vattel added that a nation is bound not only to contribute to the perfection of other nations by providing for their necessities and conveniences and helping them to secure peace and justice. It is also obligated to "occasionally, and according to its power," contribute to the capacities of these nations so that they can better procure such things for themselves. Thus, for example, if a nation should seek instruction in the sciences or in wise laws, a learned nation ought not to refuse these things. The "offices of humanity," then, are not owed only in times of crisis. Rather, they should be discharged whenever possible, so that nations may be made more capable of preventing or responding to crises themselves.[16]

Such a claim is echoed today in calls from scholars and practitioners of humanitarianism, peacebuilding, and R2P for more substantial and effective international efforts to strengthen the capacities of states and societies so that they might be better able to prevent the emergence of humanitarian crises, the descent into civil war, and the occurrence of mass atrocities.[17] Such calls push against a tendency to conceive of duties beyond borders as being generated by crises. It is relatively easy to articulate an urgent duty and therefore to mobilize political will for international action in response to crises that have already erupted. It is more difficult to expound an ordinary and ongoing duty and motivate international action to build capabilities and resilience and to empower societies so that they are better able to prevent such crises from occurring in the first place. More attention is given to the need for states to respond to cases like Libya (2011) in which atrocities are already occurring than to cases like Kenya (2007–2008) and Guinea (2009–2010) in which international actors can play a significant role in preventing possible atrocities, or to a range of other cases in which international actors can engage in ongoing action, empowering locals and helping to strengthen governance, enhance security, and promote justice, such that future crises might not emerge.[18] While practices of capacity-building and prevention are in many instances just as complex and precarious as forcible intervention, they are usually much less costly in terms of blood and treasure and much less destabilizing at local, regional, and international levels. States would do well to heed Vattel's call to recognize a duty not only to contribute to the urgent needs of others in times of crisis, but also to engage in routine efforts to contribute to the capacities of others to avert or effectively respond to emergent crises themselves.

Weighing duties to strangers against duties to one's own population

Vattel insisted that nations must always retain the right to judge for themselves what they can and cannot contribute to the preservation and perfection of others. While every nation has a right to ask another for assistance, the nation that receives the request for its kind offices has "a right of judging whether the case really demands them, and whether circumstances will allow her to grant them consistently with that regard which she ought to pay to her own safety and interests." A nation that refuses to perform such duties without good reason "offends against equity . . . but thereby no injury is done." Consequently, the offending nation should not be subject to compulsion.[19]

He also emphasized that nations need to exercise prudence when considering what they can do for others. After all, the law of nature does not oblige good nations to become "the dupes and prey of the wicked," nor does it command that they strengthen enemy nations who have intentions of "plundering and oppressing" them. Likewise, a prince should be careful not "to obey without reserve all the suggestions of a noble and generous heart impelling him to sacrifice his own interests to the advantage of others." The prince's first priority is to care for "the nation who has committed herself to his care."[20]

But Vattel did not thereby let states off the hook. While he noted that states were not rightly subject to compulsion for the performance of their duties to others, he insisted that they were still morally culpable for violating them. And while they needed to exercise prudence when weighing their moral obligations, this in no way justified unreasonably neglecting the needs of others. He suggested, by way of example, that Russia had recently carried out a "prudent performance" of its duties in that she "generously assisted Sweden when threatened with a famine," but refused to allow other nations to purchase corn that she needed for her own people. He offered a similar suggestion when he turned to discuss the duty to admit refugees. He recommended that, while states should exercise prudence when contemplating what this duty demanded of them in a given instance, "this prudence should be free from unnecessary suspicion and jealousy" and a nation ought "never to lose sight of the charity and commiseration which are due to the unhappy."[21]

Moreover, he made clear that, while a state should pay attention to its own safety and interests, it should nevertheless be willing to bear some cost and inconvenience for the sake of the vulnerable beyond its borders. Certainly, a state was under no obligation to contribute to the welfare of another if this would require doing "an essential injury to herself."[22] But it ought not to refuse to aid others out of fear of "a slight loss, or any little inconvenience: humanity forbids this; and the mutual love which men owe to each other, requires greater sacrifices."[23] While states should weigh their duties to others against their duties to themselves, it was by no means the case that the national interest should simply trump the good of others: "a nation ought on all occasions to regulate her conduct by reasons proportioned to the advantages and necessities of others, and to reckon as nothing a small expense or a supportable inconvenience, when great good will thence result to another nation."[24] It is instructive to compare this sentiment with the Dutch theorist Hugo Grotius (1583–1645), who had earlier proposed a much more restrictive conception of duties beyond borders, recommending that sovereigns come to the defense of friends who are unjustly attacked only if such aid "can be rendered easily and without loss."[25] Vattel elaborated on his theme of self-sacrifice in powerful terms:

> A nation is under many obligations of duty towards herself, towards other nations, and towards the great society of mankind. We know that the duties we owe to ourselves are, generally speaking, paramount to those we owe to others; but this is to be understood only of such duties as bear some proportion to each other. We cannot refuse, in some degree, to forget ourselves with respect to interests that are not essential, and to make some sacrifices, in order to assist other persons, and especially for the greater benefit of human society: and let us even remark, that we are invited by our own advantage, by our own safety, to make these generous sacrifices; for the private good of each is intimately connected with the general happiness. What idea should we entertain of a prince or a nation who would refuse to give up the smallest advantage for the sake of procuring to the world the inestimable blessings of peace?[26]

Having made this point clear, Vattel was, as always, willing to supplement his arguments about assisting others for their own sake with an appeal to the long-term utility derived from providing such assistance. The "sacrifices" that states were required to make for the sake of others were not contrary to their interests, he insisted, since "it is natural to think that others will behave in the same manner in return; and how great the advantages that will result to all states from such a line of conduct!"[27]

However, Vattel took this argument about utility one step further, arguing that nations can work towards "perfecting" themselves in an important ideational sense by contributing to the perfection of others. He claimed that a nation is bound not only to seek to benefit others when it is in a position to do so. Rather, for a nation to truly perfect itself, it should strive to cultivate ever greater capacity to promote the perfection and happiness of others.[28] Nations, then, are not called to simply weigh their duties to others against their duties to themselves as if they are mutually exclusive. Rather, their perfection of others should be understood as in some way constitutive of the perfection of themselves. This idea was borrowed from Leibniz, who had urged individuals to recognize that they would derive enduring happiness from pursuing the perfection of others, and in so doing they would further their own perfection. The "true interest" of individuals, Leibniz insisted, lay not in the pursuit of material utility but in the pursuit of happiness and perfection—understood in the Thomist sense of completeness or wholeness—and this happiness and perfection was advanced by contributing to the good, wellbeing, and perfection of others.[29] Vattel thus applied Leibniz's argument about individuals to states. He by no means rejected the pursuit of material utility as a motivation for right action. Indeed, as we have seen, he endorsed material utility as the grounds for sociability among states. But he encouraged states to recognize not only the material advantages but also the ideational benefits that they would derive from contributing to the perfection of others and suggested that this should motivate them to not only give of their existing resources but to strive to cultivate ever greater capacity to give.[30]

Today, at a time in which many nations appear increasingly unconvinced by arguments in favor of the material benefits of caring for vulnerable people beyond their borders and are instead turning inwards, Vattel's Leibnizian appeal to the ideational benefits of contributing to the needs of those beyond borders may well be worth reinserting into public debate. Indeed, German Chancellor Angela Merkel's efforts in 2015 to encourage the German people to recognize the "happiness" and "pride" that could be derived from bearing a measure of vulnerability and sacrifice in order to assist refugees fleeing the Syrian crisis arguably represents an example of such a Leibnizian appeal to the ideational benefits of performing the "offices of humanity."[31]

No right to impose perfection on unwilling others

While a nation has a duty to promote the perfection of others in so far as it can, such perfection ought never to be forcibly imposed against the wishes of the recipient nation, Vattel declared. To thrust one's good offices on an unwilling nation and compel them to receive assistance would constitute a violation of their natural liberty and independence. He admonished those "ambitious Europeans who attacked the American nations, and subjected them to their greedy dominion, in order, as they pretended, to civilize them, and cause them to be instructed in the true religion." The Europeans' pretext for war was "equally unjust and ridiculous."

He supplemented this rejection of the right to impose perfection with a scathing critique of Grotius's notion that sovereigns have a right to punish grave violations of the natural law wherever they may occur:

> But we have shewn that men derive the right of punishment solely from their right to provide for their own safety; and consequently they cannot claim it except against those by whom they have been injured. Could it escape Grotius, that, notwithstanding all the precautions added by him in the following paragraphs, his opinion opens a door to all the ravages of enthusiasm and fanaticism, and furnishes ambition with numberless pretexts?[32]

Vattel supplemented these arguments with a more general rejection of the right of states to interfere in each other's affairs. From the liberty and independence of nations flow a right of each to govern itself as it thinks proper, Vattel insisted, and this sovereign right is one that others "ought the most scrupulously to respect, if they would not do her an injury." Even if a sovereign should treat his subjects with severity, no outsider may oblige him to alter his conduct. The Spaniards had violated this law when they acted as judges of the Inca ruler, Atahualpa, he claimed. Had Atahualpa injured the Spaniards, they would have had a right to punish him. But he was not accountable to them for the crimes of human sacrifice and polygamy of which they accused him.[33] However, this strict principle of non-intervention, which Vattel was among the first to articulate, was not absolute.

Intervention against tyranny is permissible

Upon expounding the sovereign right to freedom from interference and intervention, Vattel immediately offered a crucial exception:

> But if the prince, by violating the fundamental laws, gives his subjects a legal right to resist him, - if tyranny becoming insupportable obliges the nation to rise in their own defence, - every foreign power has a right to succour an oppressed people who implore their assistance.

Like others before him had done, he offered James II of England as an example of such a tyrant, who sought "to overthrow the constitution, and to destroy the liberties and the religion of the people." The nobility and patriots of England, having determined to resist the tyrant, appealed to the United Provinces for assistance, and William of Orange was right to respond to their plea in 1688: "for when a people from good reasons take up arms against an oppressor, it is but an act of justice and generosity to assist brave men in the defence of their liberties." Vattel indicated that such interference did not constitute a violation of the liberty and independence of the state because, in such instances, "the bands of the political society are broken, or at least suspended, between the sovereign and his people." In such instances, it remains for other states to judge for themselves whether the sovereign or the people have justice on their side and to grant their assistance accordingly.[34]

Vattel thus sought to offer a reasonable middle ground between those who too cautiously defended an unconditional understanding of the right of sovereign states to freedom from external intervention and those who too rashly supplied pretexts for powerful states to undertake predatory interventions against the weak. His proposition was that intervention was permissible only in instances where governmental oppression was so extreme as to destroy the relationship between ruler and people, extinguishing the very political community that once enjoyed the privileges of liberty and independence. This echoed arguments offered by earlier theorists such as Alberico Gentili (1552–1608) and Samuel Pufendorf (1632–1694). It finds parallels today in the tentative defense humanitarian intervention offered by Michael Walzer, who suggests that "when a government turns savagely upon its own people, we must doubt the very existence of a political community to which the idea of self-determination might apply."[35]

Certainly, Vattel's willingness to permit intervention against tyranny constituted a significant exception to his principle of non-interference. This exception aside, however, he tended to prioritize the need to respect the liberty and independence of states.[36] His willingness to allow states to judge for themselves whether they have just grounds for intervention in a given instance may strike us as troubling today. For all their faults, we have good reasons to embrace the regional and international multilateral procedures that we now have in place for authorizing the resort to force.[37] Nevertheless, we can at least note that the principles that Vattel outlined to guide states in their decision-making about when and where to intervene set quite a high bar to intervention.[38] He detailed a demanding set of duties to preserve and perfect the vulnerable beyond borders, but for the most part, he recommended that these duties be discharged without resorting to force. While he called for the provision of non-coercive and consensual assistance to the vulnerable, he largely rejected efforts to forcibly remake the world. The values of state liberty and independence, and the interests of international peace and security, were to be prioritized over the desires of powerful states to set themselves up as judges of weaker others and to seek to civilize or convert them without their consent. Only if others were willing to receive aid and assistance, should a state discharge its duty to perfect. Given what we increasingly understand about the difficulties of achieving good rather than harm via non-consensual military intervention,[39] the Swiss jurist's model of mutual duties of consensual assistance can reward renewed consideration today.

Conclusion

For all the distance between him and us, Vattel's treatment of the rights and duties of assistance and protection contains several insights that can help us as we think about the ethics of helping the vulnerable today. I will conclude by highlighting three ideas in particular that may fruitfully inform or challenge some of the parameters and assumptions of present-day debate. The first is his claim that states are obligated not only to contribute to the perfection of others in time of crisis, but also to seek to build the capacities of others so that they are better able to care for themselves and to prevent crises from emerging. This idea is remarkable for its prescience, and is increasingly well understood by theorists of humanitarianism, peacebuilding, and R2P. But, in practice, international society can still do much more to implement the kind of routinized programs for capacity-building in weak and fragile states (in addition to routine responses to attention-attracting crises) that Vattel recommends.

The second relates to his suggestion that states should be willing to bear a measure of sacrifice for the sake of vulnerable outsiders. Political leaders today commonly emphasize that their engagement with global duties needs to conform to their national interests. When they discharge duties that do not seem to advance their short-term interests, they tend to emphasize the gaining of longer-term benefits, noting that grave suffering, injustice, and instability in one part of the world can have global consequences. Consider, for example, President Barack Obama's insistence that, in a globalized world, it is in the interests of all to have concern for "the plight of the powerless, the plight of refugees, the plight of the marginalized."[40] While Vattel certainly endorsed such an "enlightened" understanding of self-interest, he also went further and appealed to states to be willing to sacrifice their interests to a degree for the sake of vulnerable outsiders, so long as in discharging their duties to others they did not do an "essential injury" to themselves. Such a claim is echoed in Merkel's appeal to Germans to embrace the element of self-sacrifice involved in opening up Germany's borders in 2015, declaring that "Germany is a strong country—we will manage."[41] Vattel insisted that states are not bound to help others only in those instances when they can do so without trouble and inconvenience. Rather, the care of one's own interests should be in proportion to the needs of others, and a state should not hesitate to sacrifice its interests a little in order to help others a lot.

The third idea worth highlighting regards Vattel's conceptualization of the relationship between the duties that states owe to others and the duties they owe to themselves. As we have seen, Vattel suggested that a state's perfection of others should be understood as constitutive of its own self-perfection. Rather than simply helping states to work through the tension between cosmopolitan duties and statist duties—between other-perfection and self-perfection—Vattel encouraged states to recognize that the cultivation of greater ability to contribute to the perfection of others should be understood as a fundamental aspect of their own perfection. We perhaps hear echoes of such a claim in Obama's suggestion that we are in some sense "diminished" when "ethnic cleansing is happening somewhere around the world and we stand by,"[42] but it is otherwise a sentiment little explored today. Vattel's claim entails more than an appeal to recognize the long-term material utility derived from serving others. It is an appeal for states to appreciate that they are unavoidably united with each other in the "great society" of humankind and, as such, the ends of others are, in some ultimate and non-material sense, inseparable from their own.

Notes

1 Onora O'Neill highlights the importance of distinguishing Kant's own ideas from present-day "Kantianism." Onora O'Neill, *Bounds of Justice* (Cambridge: Cambridge University Press, 2000), 65–80.

2 See Ian Hunter, *Rival Enlightenments: Civil and Metaphysical Philosophy in Early Modern Germany* (Cambridge: Cambridge University Press, 2002).

3 Charles R. Beitz, *Political Theory and International Relations* (Princeton: Princeton University Press, 1979), 9; John Rawls, *The Law of Peoples* (Cambridge, MA: Harvard University Press, 1999), 10.

4 See, for example, Garrett Wallace Brown, *Grounding Cosmopolitanism: From Kant to the Idea of a Cosmopolitan Constitution* (Edinburgh: Edinburgh University Press, 2009); Heather M. Roff, *Global Justice, Kant and the Responsibility to Protect: A Provisional Duty* (London: Routledge, 2013).

5 Immanuel Kant, *Practical Philosophy*, ed. Mary J. Gregor (Cambridge: Cambridge University Press, 1996), 6.352, 8.357, emphasis in original.

6 My analysis of Vattel draws on Luke Glanville, "Responsibility to Perfect: Vattel's Conception of Duties beyond Borders," *International Studies Quarterly*, 61, no. 2 (2017): 385-395.

7 See, for example, UN Docs S/PV.7752 (UNSC meeting on Burundi, July 29, 2016), S/PV.7754 (UNSC meeting on South Sudan, August 12, 2016), S/PV.7784 (UNSC meeting on Syria, October 8, 2016).

8 See, for example, Stefano Recchia and Jennifer M. Welsh, eds., *Just and Unjust Military Intervention: European Thinkers from Vitoria to Mill* (Cambridge: Cambridge University Press, 2013); Luke Glanville, *Sovereignty and the Responsibility to Protect: A New History* (Chicago: University of Chicago Press, 2014).

9 Vattel tended to use the terms "nation" and "state" interchangeably.

10 Emer de Vattel, *The Law of Nations*, ed. Béla Kapossy and Richard Whatmore (Indianapolis: Liberty Fund, 2008), II.1.3.

11 Ibid., II.1.4.

12 Ibid., II.1.5.

13 In fact, the military strategy deployed by the Duke of Parma against Henry allowed Paris to receive the food supplies. Archer Jones, *The Art of War in the Western World* (Urbana, IL: Illinois University Press, 2001), 207.

14 Vattel, *The Law of Nations*, II.1.5.

15 Ibid., II.1.15.

16 Ibid., II.1.6.

17 See, for example, Serena K. Sharma and Jennifer M. Welsh, eds., *The Responsibility to Prevent: Overcoming the Challenges of Atrocity Prevention* (Oxford: Oxford University Press, 2015).

18 For critical reviews of the Kenyan and Guinean cases of atrocity prevention, see chapters by Sharma and Naomi Kikoler in Sharma and Welsh, *The Responsibility to Prevent*. For critical reviews of a range of international peacebuilding projects, see Oliver P. Richmond, ed., *Palgrave Advances in Peacebuilding: Critical Developments and Approaches* (New York: Palgrave Macmillan, 2010).
19 Vattel, *The Law of Nations*, II.1.9–10.
20 Ibid., II.1.16–17.
21 Ibid., II.1.9, I.19.231.
22 Ibid., Prelim. §14.
23 Ibid., II.10.131.
24 Ibid.
25 Hugo Grotius, *De Jure Belli ac Pacis Libris Tres*, vol. 2, ed. Francis W. Kelsey (Oxford: Clarendon Press, 1925), II.25.5.
26 Vattel, *The Law of Nations*, II.18.332.
27 Ibid., II.10.131.
28 Ibid., II.1.13.
29 Gottfried Wilhelm Leibniz, *Political Writings*, ed. Patrick Riley (Cambridge: Cambridge University Press, 1972), 83, 197.
30 Vattel offered a detailed defense of Leibniz's argument about self-perfection in an "Essay on the Foundation of Natural Law" (1746), found in Vattel, *The Law of Nations*, 747–771.
31 For discussion, see Luke Glanville, "Self-Interest and the Distant Vulnerable," *Ethics and International Affairs*, 30, no. 3 (2016): 335–353.
32 Vattel, *The Law of Nations*, II.1.7.
33 Ibid., II.4.54–55.
34 Ibid., II.4.56. See also II.4.62. For further discussion, see Jenifer Pitts, "Intervention and Sovereign Equality: Legacies of Vattel." In *Just and Unjust Military Intervention*, ed. Recchia and Welsh, 132–153.
35 Alberico Gentili, *De Jure Belli Libri Tres*, vol. 2, trans. John C. Rolfe (Oxford: Clarendon Press, 1933), 77–78; Samuel Pufendorf, *De Jure Naturae et Gentium Libri Octo*, vol. 2, ed. C. H. Oldfather and W. A. Oldfather (Oxford: Clarendon Press, 1934), VIII.6.14; Michael Walzer, *Just and Unjust Wars: A Moral Argument with Historical Illustrations*, 4th edn. (New York: Basic Books, 2006), 101.
36 A further exception to the principle of noninterference that Vattel permitted was the right of war against those beastly rulers and mischievous nations, both from within Europe and beyond, who disturb the peace, trample on justice, and willingly disregard the law of nations. Such monsters do an injury to all nations, he claimed. Therefore, nations may rightly form a coalition to chastise them and deprive them of their power. Vattel, *The Law of Nations*, II.4.53, 5.70, III.3.34, IV.2.5. See also Walter Rech, *Enemies of Mankind: Vattel's Theory of Collective Security* (Leiden: Martinus Nijhoff, 2013).
37 Stefano Recchia, "Authorising Humanitarian Intervention: A Five-Point Defence of Existing Multilateral Procedures." *Review of International Studies*, 43, no. 1 (2017): 50–72.
38 Simone Zurbuchen, "Vattel's 'Law of Nations' and the Principle of Non-Intervention," *Grotiana*, 31, no. 1 (2010): 69–84.
39 For some analysis, see Matthew Krain, "International Intervention and the Severity of Genocides and Politicides," *International Studies Quarterly*, 49, no. 3 (2005): 363–387; Taylor B. Seybolt, *Humanitarian Military Intervention: The Conditions for Success and Failure* (Oxford: Oxford University Press, 2007).
40 Barack Obama, "Remarks by President Obama to the United Nations General Assembly," New York, September 28, 2015, www.whitehouse.gov/the-press-office/2015/09/28/remarks-president-obama-united-nations-general-assembly.
41 BBC News, "Migrant Crisis: Merkel Warns of EU 'Failure,'" August 31, 2015, http://www.bbc.com/news/world-europe-34108224.
42 Quoted in James Pattison, *Humanitarian Intervention and the Responsibility to Protect: Who Should Intervene?* (Oxford: Oxford University Press, 2010), 177, n. 6.

22
THE GLOBAL ETHICS OF HUMANITARIAN ACTION

Hugo Slim

Humanitarian action has achieved extraordinary critical mass in international relations in the last thirty years to become a major field of applied global ethics. Humanitarian issues and operations are routinely discussed at the UN Security Council as an essential part of its discussions on international peace and security. Humanitarian principles are repeatedly called for in UNSC resolutions on specific conflicts. The UN General Assembly debates and agrees resolutions on humanitarian policy each year, and many governments and UN agencies have major humanitarian budgets. Humanitarian organizations and their field operations have expanded exponentially—more and more people and organizations are trying to apply the principles of humanitarian action in today's wars and disasters.

The purpose of this chapter is to examine the fundamental ethical commitments that drive international humanitarian action and describe their elaboration into the laws, operational principles, institutions, and ethical problems that shape international humanitarian action today. The first part of the chapter gives some historical context to the development of applied humanitarian ethics in modern international relations, especially the development of specifically values-based humanitarian organizations.[1] The second part looks more precisely at the principles upon which humanitarian action is based and the particular ethical problems that arise in the dominant practices of international humanitarian action today.

Humanitarian boom

There has been a humanitarian boom in the last thirty years. There are more global humanitarian organizations active in the world today than ever before, and their scale and reach is bigger than at any time in history. Individuals and groups of very different convictions across the spectrum of international society have found common cause in the fundamental ethical ambition of humanitarian action. Religious groups of all kinds, secularists, liberals, conservatives, and radicals have all recognized and valorized the core principle in humanitarian action that we should protect and assist other people when they suffer calamity of various kinds, even if we do not know them and they are far away.

Peoples and parties with different ideological perspectives may argue over humanitarian details of how, where, when, and how much we should do for so-called "distant others"—and who precisely should do it—but the great majority still recognize the moral claim of extreme suffering and the obligation to respond. Even religious ideologies that see human suffering as righteous judgment, or secular ideologies that see violence and destruction as politically necessary for a greater transformation, may still recognize the importance of human compassion within the context of divine censure or political revolution. Humanitarian conviction does not always hold firm, particularly in armed conflicts, but it is usually and universally there somewhere on the ground.

The boom in formal international humanitarian action, coordinated around UN efforts, has been largely driven by Western states and Western publics, who have financed the great part of its growth and diversification. Growth in UN agencies has been accompanied by an extraordinary expansion in the number and size of NGOs driven by a global humanitarian commitment to respond to universal human suffering and to save and protect the lives of people in armed conflict and disaster. Many of these organizations have also been entrepreneurs of humanitarian norms and practices. They have advocated for new international laws, policies, and institutions to protect and assist people in armed conflict and disasters. They have pioneered new forms of treatment and response in emergency health, nutrition, food security, livelihoods, water supply, and protection.

Several of these organizations, like Save the Children, Oxfam, IRC, CARE, Islamic Relief, and World Vision, are now large transnational organizations with global bureaucracies and reach. Their business models and organizational cultures are now closer to transnational corporations than to the amateur organizations of their founding ancestors.[2] Their church cousins like CARITAS, ACT Alliance, and LWF are just as big, but are more rooted in religious communities and local church governance around the world. MSF is also a large transnational organization today, but its refusal to take much government money, its exceptional reliance on independent financing, and its stubborn retention of a radical and rebellious organizational culture makes it rather different. The International Red Cross and Red Crescent Movement (RCRC) has also grown dramatically during the boom years and retains its place as the world's largest humanitarian network.

In 2015, the global spend on international humanitarian action rose to a new peak of $28 billion.[3] This is not much compared to the annual global chocolate market, which is expected to reach $132 billion in 2019, or global military spending, which was $1.57 trillion in 2016, but it is still bigger than any time since records began.[4] Diaspora remittances to countries affected by disaster and conflict are also increasingly significant, and often greater than formal humanitarian budgets in some countries. The World Bank estimates that remittances to low-income countries in 2016 was about £440 billion—most of this is sent directly to families, but an increasing amount is structured as informal emergency aid to affected communities.[5]

What comes next in the formal humanitarian sector—more boom or gradual bust—will be determined by the financing decisions of investor states and the potential backlash against today's expeditionary and interventionist model of humanitarian action by recipient states enduring war and disaster. Much will also depend on if and how the consensus on internationalism is sustained as nationalism rises around the world and liberal internationalism is profoundly challenged.

The emergence of humanitarian organizations

The field of humanitarian action itself is an ancient one. It would be very wrong to say that humanitarian action was invented in modern times and in the West. Religious organizations, philanthropic individuals, local communities, and benign monarchs have long engaged in organized efforts to respond to plague, earthquake, drought, and the ravages of war in all cultures of the ancient and modern worlds. But it was in the modern world and alongside the rise of liberal internationalism that international and institutionalized humanitarian action found new form and structure as a global norm and practice in formal international relations, with much of it paid for by North American and European powers and populations.

The ICRC and the wider RCRC movement began to develop its distinct humanitarian mission and global movement in 1859, when it was founded with a focus on armed conflict and the suffering of wounded soldiers. In World War I, the Spanish Civil War, the Sino-Japanese War, the Italian invasion of Ethiopia, and World War II, the ICRC diversified and began responding to the needs of prisoners of war and the civilian population as a whole. With each step, it worked carefully with states to formalize state conduct in war and ICRC's practice in international law. This resulted in the various Geneva Conventions and their Additional Protocols which have emerged over the last 154 years. This gradual development of a body of modern international humanitarian law (IHL) and formal humanitarian practice has determined the legal framework and practices of humanitarian action in armed conflict. In the process, the role, influence, and international recognition of the ICRC, a private Swiss humanitarian organization, remains one of the most masterful examples of sustained norm entrepreneurship in modern international relations.

The ICRC were by no means alone in the first half of the twentieth century. The Quakers, the churches, and the huge US humanitarian operations of Herbert Hoover's American Relief Administration (ARA) were leaders amongst many other humanitarian actors working to bring aid to the battlefields, internal displacement camps, and devastated civilian communities of World War I. At the end of the war, Save the Children was founded by a group of well-connected British liberals with support from the Miners' Union. Their immediate purpose was to stop children starving to death from the effects of the victorious Allies' blockade of Germany and Austria. Save the Children then went big for the first time in 1921 with their major famine relief operation in post-revolutionary Russia, where ARA was also active. The UN's predecessor, the League of Nations, launched its refugee agency because of the millions of people displaced by World War I, with Fridtjof Nansen as its first and high-profile High Commissioner.[6] Between the wars, many NGOs and churches also continued their leading roles as the charitable and missionary face of empire and colonialism.

The 1930s saw the creation of the International Rescue Committee (IRC) by Albert Einstein and others—rescuing people from Nazi persecution and resettling them in the USA. World War II saw CARE, OXFAM, and the Norwegian Refugee Council (NRC) founded to provide aid to war-torn Europe. CARE was set up in 1945 and carried out massive airlifts with US funding, and it delivered the famous "CARE parcels" throughout Europe at the end of the war. Oxfam was much smaller. Their small founding group of English academic liberals, businessmen, Anglicans, and Quakers worked with the ICRC to send food and clothing parcels to civilians in Nazi-occupied Greece and campaigned to lift the Allied blockade of occupied Europe. In 1947, the Quakers were awarded the Nobel Peace Prize for their silent work for peace and for the decades of practical relief action to aid people in war.

After World War II, the newly established UN launched a range of Specialized Agencies, like UNICEF, WHO, UNHCR, and the World Food Programme, which have become the major players in UN humanitarian action. A new era of global expansion in humanitarian action then began. After playing a significant and pioneering humanitarian role in Europe's two brutal and devastating world wars, Western international humanitarian action began to formalize and spread throughout the world, often along previously imperial lines, to engage in former colonies as an ethical response to the many problems of postcolonial state-formation. Many struggled with neutrality in conflicts between European power and liberation movements.[7] In the process, humanitarian action often found itself working alongside two close relations—international development and human rights. UN and NGO humanitarian agencies made roles for themselves in niches of different kinds on various sides of the wars of liberation to end colonial rule.[8] They worked in refugee and IDP camps or in wider projects to support children, health, and education. New NGOs, like World Vision, Handicap International, Médecins Sans Frontières (MSF), Concern, and Action Contre le Faim (ACF), were born during this period in conflicts in Korea (World Vision), Nigeria and East Pakistan (MSF and Concern), Cambodia (Handicap International), and Afghanistan (ACF).

Fierce communist–capitalist proxy wars followed independence in many new states. These brutal conflicts dominated and destroyed the lives of millions of people in Africa, Asia, and Latin America during the 1970s and 1980s. In Africa, in particular, these conflicts often combined with drought and famine to kill millions of people in countries like Ethiopia, Sudan, Mozambique, Angola, and Uganda. The end of the Cold War saw humanitarian action pushed much more into the center of armed conflicts like the civil wars in the Balkans, West Africa, Sri Lanka, and the Horn of Africa. With no more great power competition over these wars, the space for humanitarian action opened up, funding increased, and there was new consensus in the UN Security Council to try to address these conflicts with a combination of humanitarian action, peacekeeping, and post-conflict reconstruction.[9]

The story of the rise of international humanitarian action in the Western world is really one of two parallel paths: a Red Cross and Red Crescent path that stayed firmly humanitarian with a limited ethic of prevention, rescue, repair, and political neutrality; and a UN and NGO path that merged with the much wider ethics of poverty eradication, international development, social justice, and human rights. UN agencies were always charged with a dual mandate of some kind that gave them joint humanitarian and development responsibilities. As they engaged over time in the conflicts of Europe, Africa, Asia, and Latin America, many NGOs became more concerned with the root causes of suffering and embraced much wider ethical missions. In the jargon of the sector, the RCRC path stuck firmly with a "single mandate" or limited "Dunantist" ethics, after the founder of the ICRC, Henry Dunant. Many on the UN and NGO path became "multimandate" in their multiple ethical commitments, and were said to have "Wilsonian" vision, after President Wilson of the USA, who was a key mover in the modern liberal internationalist movement and its transformative ambition for world order. NGOs like MSF, IRC, and NRC followed the narrow RCRC path of a limited humanitarian ethic in war and disaster, while others, like Save the Children, Oxfam, CARE, and World Vision, travelled the wider path of global ethics. Yet, most of the time, these multimandate organizations have pinned their humanitarian commitments to the RCRC model when operating in humanitarian mode in war and disasters.

So, what is this essential humanitarian tradition in Western thinking, and how has it developed into the modern ethical framework that we have today in international relations?

The evolution of humanitarian terminology

The word *humanitarian* is a word of the European Enlightenment. Behind it lies the noun *humanity* and a sense that we—the human race—share a common humanity and are united in bonds of what Adam Smith called "fellow feeling" and reciprocal responsibility.[10] Throughout the Enlightenment, people and policies were humanitarian if they focused on alleviating the suffering of others. Humanitarian did not tend to describe kindness towards intimate others like family and friends. It would sound odd to thank your mother or father for being humanitarian to you when you were in bed with flu. Instead, humanitarian was more a term of political ethics that grew with ever-widening Enlightenment notions of social reform, responsible government, and international society. So, your mother might not be humanitarian to you, but she would be humanitarian the moment she campaigned against the slave trade, organized adult literary classes for the poor, or lobbied to reduce the working hours of children. Such humanitarianism was also known as *philanthropy*—the Greek word doing a more explicit job of describing a love of humanity than its Latinate counterpart.

Between the seventeenth and early twentieth centuries, the word "humanitarian" kept this wide sphere of reference and its link to progressive social causes and reforming government. Humanitarian work covered the whole array of activities intended to create a more humane and better world—usually by a benevolent middle class towards an impoverished working class, which is why Marx and Engels derided the term in their *Communist Manifesto*.[11] In the twentieth century, this Latinate word fell out of use in the more Protestant and Anglo-Saxon societies of Britain and the US, which reverted to simpler terms like *good works*, *charity*, *reform*, and *relief*. The Anglo-Saxon world retained this more practical vocabulary, while the French-speaking world of Switzerland and France maintained the term "humanitarian" and developed a more specific philosophy and legal framework to support it. This tradition applied humanitarianism in an increasingly narrow sense after World War II and began to brand it firmly with immediate and limited relief to people affected by war and administered by a politically neutral and impartial body of some kind.[12] Meanwhile, in Britain and the US, government agencies and NGOs like World Vision, Oxfam, IRC, and Save the Children described their work as relief or emergency aid.

With the Somalia conflict and the Bosnian War in the 1990s, all this began to change as Anglo-Saxon NGOs reached out for a clearer ethical and legal justification for their work in the middle of armed conflicts. They began to take a more active interest in the Geneva Conventions and the fundamental principles of the RCRC movement. In reaching out, they found the highly developed ethical and legal schema of the ICRC and took it up. British and American emergency departments became humanitarian departments, and relief workers became humanitarian workers, and all of them began to align with international humanitarian law and humanitarian principles. A similar shift in principles and nomenclature happened in UN circles. The "master narrative" of the RCRC movement dominated, and in 1991 UNGA Resolution 46/182 formally adopted the principled approach to humanitarian aid.[13] NGOs worked with the RCRC movement to develop their own Code of Conduct in 1994. In 1997, at the front of their new SPHERE humanitarian standards, they placed a Humanitarian Charter to guide and justify their operations. The French language had won for once because it came with principles and not just pragmatism.

Humanitarian law and humanitarian principles

The ethical and legal schema for humanitarianism that developed with states and the RCRC movement has now moved center stage. The Geneva Conventions and humanitarian principles have become the touchstone for the definition, practice, and institutional development of humanitarian action as an expanding field of international relations, so consolidating a global ethic of humanitarian action for armed conflict and disasters. This ethical and legal basis to humanitarian action is best described by summarizing key principles in international humanitarian law, and exploring the structure and intent of humanitarian principles.

Principles in international humanitarian law

International humanitarian law (IHL) is clearly defined by the ICRC:

> IHL is a set of rules which seek, for humanitarian reasons, to limit the effects of armed conflict. It protects persons who are not or are no longer participating in the hostilities and restricts the means and methods of warfare.[14]

These rules form part of international law which governs relations between states and so are contained in treaties and conventions, in customary rules and in general principles. Importantly, IHL is concerned with conduct in armed conflict—*ius in bello*—and not with the laws and principles concerning the right to go to war—*ius ad bellum*. The legality of going to war is governed by a distinct part of international law set out in the United Nations Charter.

Inherent to the Geneva Conventions and other areas of IHL, like the Hague Conventions, is the fundamental ethical principle of *humanity*. This principle puts great value on individual human life—every human life—and so the principles and rules of IHL aim to make the conduct of war as humane as possible in a context in which states are using violent force. As they fight and try to win, IHL requires states and other parties to the conflict to find a balance between humanity and "military necessity" —the term used in the Geneva Conventions to preserve the right of states to be as forceful as they need to be to achieve their legitimate military objectives.

Ethically, therefore, IHL is essentially about finding a balance between humanity and military necessity in a range of different situations on and around the battlefield. This fundamental ethical concern in IHL is expressed in certain key humanitarian principles in IHL which guide its specific rules and require interpretation and application in the conduct of armed conflict. Many of these rules are about ensuring as much *protection* as possible for combatants and non-combatants alike and are captured in the ICRC's overall campaigning slogan that "even war has limits."

The first key principle in IHL is the principle of *distinction* which requires military forces always to distinguish between combatants and non-combatants in their military strategy and operations. This principle generates important rules about protecting and assisting civilians and those military personnel who may be *hors de combat* as wounded or prisoners. The principle of *precaution* requires that civilians and non-combatants must be protected from harm as much as possible and significant precautions must be taken to warn them of impending attacks, protect them from hostilities and in military actions avoid them during combat. *Proportionality* is another fundamental principle which requires that military force is only used in proportion to the threat posed against it or the military objective that is being targeted. This principle affirms that the means and methods of warfare are not unlimited—parties to conflict cannot fight in any way they like, with any weapons they like, and using as much force as they like. This is a principle which protects combatants and non-combatants alike. The prohibition of *cruel, inhuman, and degrading treatment* runs through IHL as another key principle that generates rules against murder, rape, and torture, as well as rules about necessary standards of conditions in detention. Finally, the principle of *assistance* as the provision of relief recognizes the necessarily material nature of humanitarian action in supporting food, shelter, water, health, livelihood, and family contact that sustains a dignified human life in armed conflict.

These principles are manifest in the many rules and practices established in the Geneva Conventions, their Additional Protocols, and other instruments of IHL. These laws impose obligations on states to respect and ensure respect for IHL in international armed conflicts (IAC) and in non-international armed conflicts (NIAC)—more commonly referred to as civil wars. It is the parties to conflict that have the responsibility to see that wars are fought in this way, but all states who have ratified the Geneva Conventions, as the High Contracting Parties, also have a continuous responsibility under Common Article One of the Conventions to "ensure respect" for the Geneva Conventions.

First principles in humanitarian action

As humanitarian action developed in practice around the world after World War II, the RCRC movement recognized the need to formulate its own principles more precisely. In 1965, the movement agreed to seven Fundamental Principles. Jean Pictet, the distinguished ICRC lawyer, led the drafting of the principles and later wrote the first commentary on the principles in 1979, having already written a pioneering commentary on the Geneva Conventions between 1952 and 1959.[15]

The first four RCRC principles—humanity, impartiality, neutrality, and independence—have deeply influenced the wider humanitarian sector of government departments, UN agencies, and NGOs engaged in humanitarian aid, and have also been taken up as key principles in UN policy at the UNGA and UNSC. The last three principles of voluntary service, unity, and universality are particular to Red Cross and Red Crescent societies and embody the main rules of belonging to the movement.

The first principle of humanitarian action is *humanity* itself. Humanity is the simple goal of all humanitarian action, and Pictet formulated the principle as the fundamental purpose of the RCRC Movement as follows: "to prevent and alleviate human suffering wherever it may be found. Its purpose is to protect life and health and to ensure respect for the human being." This sets out clearly that humanitarian action has no wider goals than the protection of the human person. Humanitarian action is a teleology of person, not politics. Humanitarian action is an urgent and limited ethics of protection and assistance *in extremis*. There is no wider political or social project: not peace; not democracy; not religious conversion; not socialism, liberalism, conservatism, or political Islam; just human life itself and the dignity of the human person. The defining goal of humanitarian action is to save and protect individual human lives so that they may have the opportunity to flourish. It is not to determine how they should flourish and to organize this flourishing.[16]

The second principle of humanitarian action is *impartiality*. This too is a fundamental value and includes within it a universalist commitment to everyone. The classic RCRC formulation declares that humanitarian action "makes no discrimination as to nationality, race, religious beliefs, class or political opinion. It endeavours only to relieve suffering giving priority to the most urgent cases of distress." This principle elaborates the principle of humanity's universal claim by affirming a radical equality of all people and distinguishes between them only on the basis of their urgent needs.[17]

After setting out these two values as the goal and purpose of humanitarian action—the prevention and alleviation of suffering and non-discrimination and respect for every human being—the next two principles see humanitarian ethics having to find a reasonable and practical way to achieve this everywhere, even in the fiercest and most partisan armed conflicts. To do this, humanitarian ethics adopts a political posture of neutrality and independence. This discreet and apolitical approach is seen as its best bet to achieve entry and access into armed conflicts and a natural complement to its universal and non-discriminatory values.

This means that the RCRC movement's third principle is *neutrality*, which is elaborated as follows: "in order to enjoy the confidence of all, the Red Cross and Red Crescent may not take sides in hostilities or engage at any time in controversies of a political, racial, religious or ideological nature." Here, the prohibition on "taking sides" includes both material support and ideological support. The fourth principle of *independence* follows naturally from neutrality and impartiality to ensure operational autonomy so that humanitarian action may remain free to make its own decisions and direct its own resources without undue influence from parties to the conflict. This principle requires the RCRC movement and humanitarian action must "always maintain their autonomy so that they may be able at all times to act in accordance with the principles."

Neutrality and independence are primarily prudential principles. They see humanitarian ethics moving from establishing the moral ends of humanity and impartiality to the moral means of achieving them on the ground: from what is good to do, to how it is best and wisely done. The operational posture of neutrality and independence is a role morality, like that of a referee in a football match, and represents the best way to be inside an armed conflict without being caught up in it, compromised, restricted, or attacked.[18]

Secondary principles in humanitarian action

Being humane, impartial, neutral, and independent is an essential and practical way to frame humanitarian action but it does not tell you how to deliver humanitarian action well. A humanitarian organization could embody all four of these first principles but still deliver a poor quality health program or run a food program in a way that treats people badly. Humanitarian ethics must also be about the ethics of care and respect, and in the 1990s the RCRC movement worked with international NGOs to lead a further development in the ethics of humanitarian action. This produced a Code of Conduct for adoption by the humanitarian sector as a whole. This Code was largely designed for disaster relief rather than humanitarian action in armed conflict but most of its principles are recognized as important guides to doing humanitarian action well in conflict too.

The Code of Conduct largely endorsed the "core four" principles of the RCRC movement in the first four of its ten principles, but it then went further to set out wider principles of dignity and stewardship to guide how humanitarian organizations and other actors should manage humanitarian aid ethically and in the best interests of those who need it.[19] The Code put people more firmly at the center of humanitarian ethics. There is a clear focus on the dignity of people as victims and an important recognition of people as agents in their own survival and recovery. Articles 5 commits to respect the culture, customs, and structures of the communities of the countries and communities in which humanitarian action is engaged. Article 6 sets out to build humanitarian response on local capacities and working with and through local organizations and local government wherever possible. In Article 7, people's participation in humanitarian programs is then recognized as fundamental to people's dignity and to successful program design. Article 10 then makes clear the importance of portraying people with dignity in the marketing material of humanitarian agencies, and so avoiding the misrepresentation and degradation of what has been called "disaster pornography" in the simplistic representation of people as starving, helpless, and incapable in much humanitarian advertising.

Articles 8 and 9 of the Code focus on humanitarian organizations' responsibilities of humanitarian stewardship. Article 8 recognizes the importance of humanitarian action having a lasting impact on individuals and communities wherever possible and so being a sustainable good, so that it "reduces future vulnerabilities as well as meeting basic needs". This ethical commitment to a sustainable impact in people's lives is complemented by a commitment to deliver aid in an environmentally responsible way, as much as possible, so preserving the ecology of the planet too in a consideration of humanitarian aid's environmental footprint. Article 9 affirms an ethical concern for the proper management and accountability of financial and other resources given on trust by governments and the public for the effective delivery of humanitarian action.

The people-centered ethical principles of the Code of Conduct were soon developed still further in the elaborate standard setting for humanitarian action that was led by the Sphere Project—a consortium of humanitarian agencies that has set a detailed range of minimum standards for humanitarian action. These standards combine a focus on key technical standards in areas like health, water, and nutrition with important social standards of how best to work with people and respect their agency and dignity.[20]

Moral problems in humanitarian action

Humanitarian action is not easy. Most individuals and organizations who do it are soon faced by a variety of ethical problems as they try to do it well and in line with its elaborate principles and standards. The work of humanitarian organizations in armed conflicts and disasters has thrown up three main areas of moral problem: political challenges; professional problems of quality and rationing; and issues of personal security.[21]

Politics

The political problems in humanitarian action focus on power and consequences. The first power risk most commonly observed by critics of humanitarian action is the ethical distortion that arises from the Western dominance of formal international humanitarian action.

As it has come to be constructed over the last hundred years, international humanitarian action has a neocolonial character that is proving hard to transform into a more ethical form of global solidarity. The generosity and humanitarian intent of large amounts of money and resources that flow from rich to poor countries is clear, but there is still an expeditionary logic to much humanitarian action that sees a Western elite controlling humanitarian aid and setting out to poorer lands to put things right. This is not necessarily a bad thing in itself, depending on the levels of popular consent, genuine cooperation, and alignment with humanitarian principles involved in such a global humanitarian project. Much good can come of it, with many lives saved. But the power dynamics are troubling.

The neocolonial problem has resulted in a strong push back against Western "interference" by some G77 states and a drive for the "localization" of humanitarian aid by these states, their civil society, and by progressive Western NGOs and the RCRC movement. Developing greater localization of humanitarian action would be a fulfillment of much of the Code's ambition to build national capacity and ensure people's participation in humanitarian action as the subjects not objects of aid. Certainly, this is the logic of Western states themselves in the development of strong government welfare services, civil defense structures, well-resourced Red Cross and Red Crescent humanitarian auxiliaries, and an empowered civil society in their own states. In a major disaster or armed conflict, Western states would expect any expeditionary humanitarian action from other countries to work with them on their humanitarian response rather than to take over this response.

Localization is right but not as ethically simple as it sounds, and it usually requires two qualifications—one of capacity and another of principle. First, many countries enduring protracted armed conflict—like South Sudan, Syria, and Yemen today—are quite simply overwhelmed by it in certain parts of their government and civil society capacity. Government and voluntary structures have been destroyed, or their key staff have dispersed and fled. This makes it very difficult not to engage in some form of direct substitution of local services by international capacity in the disastrous interim of widespread devastation. It is hard for some form of international action not to "take over" and substitute for local power and capacity in some way. The elephant of corruption also sits quietly in the room whenever localization is discussed. Many localized humanitarian projects have been profoundly compromised by corruption and theft in societies where these things are a norm of business dealings and kinship networks. Ethically, therefore, the challenge of localization is about how best to manage international substitution and control by always focusing on the double objective of life-saving and institution-building. An international humanitarian effort may not always be able to localize fully but it must always be localizing as much as is possible and prudent.

The second qualification to localization is one of humanitarian principles, especially in armed conflicts. Not all localized humanitarian action is able or willing to be principled. Many national and local institutions and organizations who may be able to carry out humanitarian action may be party to the conflict or deeply compromised in their choices by the parties. As we will see, this is true of international humanitarian action too and is not just a local agency problem. Local and national organizations may be biased and restrict their aid to one side or use it to leverage their war aims in some way by encouraging population displacement away from enemy areas or using hunger as a weapon of war by deliberately limiting food programming. Sometimes principled local actors face real personal dangers of arrest and persecution if they try to stand up against the partisan politics around them to deliver aid impartially and neutrally. In such situations, where principled local action is limited, then well-recognized and highly principled international action, like that of the ICRC, may be an essential complementary strategy to localization.

Political manipulation and obstruction is a generic risk for all humanitarian actors, whether local, national, or international. Humanitarian actors have soft power rather than hard power. They must usually negotiate their way into a role in armed conflicts and disasters, developing their access to affected populations by the consent of authorities and suffering communities alike. All too often, authorities will not agree with this access, but instead will deny, delay, or obstruct it in line with their own political aims rather than with an objective and impartial view of humanitarian needs. The rich states who pay for much humanitarian action may also be swayed by political priority. They will tend to focus on armed conflicts where they have a political stake and where aid may add value to their goals to contain a crisis or win the hearts and minds of a contested population. All these factors lead much humanitarian ethics to be preoccupied with the risk of politicization and instrumentalization, which would breach the fundamental principles of the humanitarian endeavor.

The struggle to understand and mitigate the possible consequences of assistance and protection are as routine in humanitarian ethics as in all other fields of ethics. The wider consequences of humanitarian action are a constant source of concern for humanitarian actors. It is not always easy to predict how humanitarian programming will be played by political, military, and economic actors. This has led to a constant ethical ambition to "do no harm" in humanitarian programming and a duty of care not to make a bad situation worse.

The concern for consequences may be economic—a proper ethical concern to ensure that the delivery of large amounts of food aid does not disastrously reduce market prices for people with something to sell or barter, so impoverishing people still further. The problem of unintended consequences affects health decisions too. For example, a worry that attracting people into badly serviced humanitarian camps will increase death rates from infectious diseases. And there are legitimate concerns about escalating violence too. Will a food or cash distribution encourage armed thieves or armed forces to attack, rob, and kill people as they leave the distribution? The risk of political consequences is constant too. Will humanitarian work with a political authority that violates IHL and human rights in some way increase their repressive power and control, or will it influence them to the contrary and encourage more law-abiding behavior? Here, the moral risks of wrongful association, and even complicity, with maleficence run real in humanitarian action.

Professionalism

The quality of humanitarian action is a constant concern in humanitarian ethics. The great majority of humanitarian workers recognize that it is not enough simply to try to help people. One must help them professionally and well. As a result, there has always been a considerable effort put into standard-setting, professional guidelines, training, and competence. In the process, there have been major improvements and innovations in humanitarian action across many areas like health, water, gender, livelihoods, and protection that have professionalized the humanitarian sector. The greater commitments to respectful behavior, people's participation and localization have also reduced—but not eradicated—a culture of paternalism that always hovers around ambitions to help in human society. All in all, the determination to set high standards for humanitarian action has been good. It must be right to do things as well as possible even in extremely difficult circumstances.

The professionalism of humanitarian action has therefore brought considerable improvements, but has also brought with it a new moral risk of bureaucratization and distance in the humanitarian encounter. Many humanitarians rightly worry that the spirit of compassion and the simple solidarity of voluntarism is being lost in an increasingly systematic and digitally driven modern profession. A lot of humanitarian workers never see the people they care about and only ever work on screens. Modern humanitarian action resembles the modern military in which the back office has become much bigger than its frontline forces.

Rationing

Even if humanitarian workers are trying to do things well, they usually cannot do everything that is needed. In most situations, humanitarian organizations are faced with rationing problems—difficult choices about exactly who they can help and what they can do. With limited resources and typically widespread need, organizations have to focus. To focus responsibly means finding a need that one's agency is good at meeting—this may be health, food, or protection—and maximizing their programs in some way so that as many people benefit as possible. But still the cruel necessity of some form of triage is often inevitable in humanitarian action. As in all areas of ethics, the necessity of an incomplete action requires some form of mitigation strategy. So, if an agency cannot do all that needs doing, it should try to attract others who can, and work very deliberately in a collective action strategy of some kind that tries to cover gaps. If this is impossible, and it often is in the worst moments of war and disaster, then humanitarian workers have to live with the difficult emotions of knowing that they could not do everything, that they were not solely responsible, and that terrible things happened that were beyond their powers to stop.

Ethical limits—relief and development?

One major concern of humanitarian ethics is uncertainty about the limits of its ethical ambitions. Is humanitarian action only a quick fix? Or does it bear a responsibility to work longer term with people to set them on a path to sustainable recovery, and even address the root causes of their suffering? Most humanitarians agree that they are not development organizations. Humanitarian ethics, with its urgent and neutral emphasis on the prevention and amelioration of suffering wherever it may be found, does not have a political ideology of the perfect society. It does not hold to a particular politics of progress.

Humanitarian ethics and humanitarian law have no political eschatology but function as an interim ethics of prevention, protection, and assistance. And yet, it is often morally impossible to help people meet their basic needs and then stop short of accompanying these same people and local authorities as they seek to develop more resilient systems of health, food security, water, and sanitation which will ensure that they can keep on meeting their needs. This is particularly true in protracted conflicts where the same communities may be continuously rendered desperate and vulnerable by wars that last for decades. But even when humanitarian action does work long term with individuals, communities, and authorities, it can remain impartial and neutral, focused only on a moral project of meeting basic needs and not some wider and partisan political program of liberalism, socialism, nationalism, jihadist Islamism, or conservatism. Instead of being driven by a particular political ideology, the humanitarian ethic responds on the basis of need alone in line with humanitarian law and the principle of humanity.

Personal security

One final area of humanitarian ethics that is often uppermost in the minds of humanitarian workers in armed conflict is the level of risk they are prepared to accept for themselves and their teams as they try to help others at risk. Humanitarian workers like soldiers, policemen, and firefighters may genuinely expect to suffer and die in pursuit of their duty. Humanitarian workers have often died while doing their jobs—most usually from infectious diseases or traffic accidents. They are also deliberately killed as humanitarian workers by armed actors of various kinds. The ethics of personal risk in humanitarian action is not discussed publicly very much in order to maintain the moral and legal taboo on killing humanitarian workers. But, in reality, many humanitarian workers decide to put their lives at risk every day. To do so responsibly means balancing risks against results—how important is it to deliver this convoy today? It also means working with a strong duty of care towards one's staff and with their full and informed consent when it comes to engaging in risky operations. Coercion in such cases would be wrong because voluntarism—an informed desire to help others—is at the moral root of humanitarian action, not obedience.

What next for humanitarian ethics?

Today's geopolitical world is becoming more genuinely multipolar, with various poles of power emerging as stronger and more distinctly different cultures of power. China, India, other parts of Asia, Africa, the Middle East, and Latin America are now in a position to challenge the previously dominant view of humanitarian ethics described in this chapter. These powers have ancient cultures of humanitarianism, and many have no missionary or expeditionary tradition of international aid. These different powers need no longer accept that there is one way of helping people suffering in armed conflict and war—their own or other citizens'. It is highly likely that they will either engage independently with distant human suffering or encourage changes in the predominantly Western model. This greater variety of approaches could bring innovation, cooperation, and contest to global humanitarian norms and international practice. A shake-up may be on the cards.

Notes

1 I am particularly grateful to Dr. Eleanor Davey at Manchester University, one of the great pioneers of humanitarian history, for advising me on the historical section and alerting me to several important articles. Any historical errors remain my own.

2 Heike Weiters, "Reinventing the Firm: From Post-War Relief to Humanitarian Agency," *European Review of History*, 23, nos. 1–2 (2016): 116–135; Kevin O'Sullivan, "Humanitarianisms in Contexts: Non-State Actors from the Local to the Global," *European Review of History*, 23, nos. 1–2 (2016): 1–15.

3 Development Initiatives, "Global Humanitarian Assistance 2016," June 7, 2017, at http://www.globalhumanitarianassistance.org/report/gha2016/.

4 Markets and Markets, "Cocoa Market Worth $2.1 Billion & Chocolate Market Worth $131.7 Billion by 2019," at http://www.marketsandmarkets.com/PressReleases/cocoa-chocolate.asp; IHS Markit, "2016's $1.57 Trillion Global Defense Spend to Kick off Decade of Growth," December 12, 2016, at http://news.ihsmarkit.com/press-release/2016s-15-trillion-global-defence-spend-kick-decade-growth-ihs-markit-says.

5 Ade Darami, "Remittances Are Three Times Greater Than Aid: How Can They Go Even Further?" Guardian Global Development Professionals Network, May 11, 2016 at https://www.theguardian.com/global-development-professionals-network/2016/may/11/remittances-three-times-greater-aid-sdgs.

6 Claudena M. Skran, *Refugees in Inter-War Europe: The Emergence of a Regime* (Oxford: Clarendon Press, 1995).

7 Andrew Thompson, "Humanitarian Principles Put to the Test: Challenges to Humanitarian Action during Decolonization," *International Review of the Red Cross*, 97, nos. 897–898 (2015): 45–76.

8 On African liberation wars, see Christina Bennet, Matthew Foley, and Hanna B. Krebs, eds., "Learning from the Past to Shape the Future: Lessons from the History of Humanitarian Action in Africa," HPG Working Paper, October 2016, London.

9 Boutros Boutros Ghali, "Agenda for Peace," UN, 1992.

10 Adam Smith, *The Theory of Moral Sentiments* (London: Penguin, 2009).

11 Karl Marx and Friedrich Engels, *The Communist Manifesto*, ed. David McLellan (Oxford: Oxford University Press, 1998).

12 Amanda Alexander, "A Short History of International Humanitarian Law," *European Journal of International Law*, 26, no. 1 (2015): 109–138.

13 Katherine Davies, "Continuity, Change and Contest: Meanings of 'Humanitarian' from the 'Religion of Humanity' to the Kosovo War," HPG Working Paper, London, August 2012.

14 International Committee of the Red Cross, "What Is International Humanitarian Law?," December 31, 2014, at https://www.icrc.org/en/document/what-international-humanitarian-law.

15 See Pictet's commentary: Jean Pictet, "The Fundamental Principles of the Red Cross: Commentary," International Committee of the Red Cross, at https://www.icrc.org/eng/resources/documents/misc/fundamental-principles-commentary-010179.htm.

16 For a full discussion of the principle of humanity, see Hugo Slim, *Humanitarian Ethics: A Guide to the Morality of Aid in War and Disaster* (London: C. Hurst & Co., 2015), 45–55.

17 For a full discussion of impartiality, see: Ibid., 56–64.

18 For a fuller analysis of neutrality and independence, see: Ibid., 65–73.

19 For a commentary on these six principles of the Code of Conduct, see: Ibid., Chapters 4 and 5.

20 For the Sphere Standards, see: The Sphere Project, http://www.sphereproject.org.

21 For a fuller treatment of persistent ethical problems in humanitarian action, see Slim, *Humanitarian Ethics*, 183–230.

23

THE RESPONSIBILITY TO PROTECT

The evolution of a hollow norm

Aidan Hehir

Introduction

Since first advanced in 2001 by the International Commission on Intervention and State Sovereignty (ICISS), the Responsibility to Protect (R2P) has garnered a vocal body of supporters who have argued that it holds the key to a better world; indeed, some described it as 'the only show in town for those serious about preventing future Kosovos and future Rwandas'.[1] Numerous academics, think tanks, and NGOs have come to focus exclusively on promoting the concept, so that today R2P can boast an impressive array of allies and advocates. But R2P has also achieved more than this; it is today widely referenced at the highest levels of international politics and a concept that states routinely affirm. Those who believe in R2P, therefore, can point—as they invariably do—to solid evidence that their vision of a future world order made more responsive to human suffering is not utopian.

The statement given by Simon Adams—Executive Director of the Global Centre for the Responsibility to Protect—at the 2016 UN General Assembly Informal Interactive Dialogue on the Responsibility to Protect is illustrative of the line of reasoning that has come to characterise R2P advocacy. Adams declared that the consensus on R2P 'is as strong as it is undeniable', and as evidence, noted the increased use of the term in Security Council Resolutions, the increased number of states that had joined various R2P organisations, and the unwillingness of any state to reject the basic principles underlying the concept. These facts proved, he argued 'that R2P is not just an idea, but a practical guide to action'.[2]

These sentiments may come as something of a surprise to many who have watched aghast as the world has recently experienced a remarkably precipitous decline in respect for human rights and a dramatic upsurge in intra-state oppression, civil war, and mass atrocity crimes. Yet nothing Adams said is actually wrong; there *has* been a dramatic increase in references to R2P in Security Council Resolutions, states *have* increasingly joined R2P-related groups, and instances when states have publicly rejected R2P *are* very rare. There is, therefore, clearly something of a paradox; R2P's ascent has been accompanied by a decline in respect for the principles it enshrines. Why?

I argue that, while the evidence presented by Adams and others is incontrovertible, simply focusing on the number of times R2P has been invoked positively, and the scale of state support for R2P-related campaigns, is a highly superficial means by which to judge the concept's efficacy and future potential. To explain the paradox, I argue, one must analyse the *manner* in which R2P is invoked rather than the frequency. To this end, I engage with literature on the efficacy of norms which highlights that norms can be co-opted whilst being proliferated. As a consequence, their original aims can be diluted and/or obscured whilst they appear to be generating more and more 'support'. In fact, the proliferation of a norm need not actually constitute a positive development if it has been manipulated to cohere with pre-existing dispositions and practices antithetical to the ethos underpinning the norm.

The first section provides an overview of the context in which debates about R2P's efficacy are taking place and the divisive nature of the claims made about R2P's impact. The subsequent section outlines the arguments extoling the virtues of R2P; here, I highlight that R2P's transformative impact is invariably portrayed as imminent as opposed to extant. The notion of 'progress' is thus central to the narrative supporting R2P, and this is predicated on the three claims discussed in the third section below relating to R2P's history to date. The final section argues that, while the concept has undeniably garnered widespread state support, the nature of this support is shallow, and thus ultimately of little significance. In fact, the proliferation of R2P—in a particular circumscribed form—can actually be deemed to constitute a negative development, cohering as it does with the retrogressive agenda of certain states.

'Many grounds for optimism about the future of R2P'?

While many supporters of R2P have offered measured analyses which acknowledge R2P's limitations as well as its added value, others have engaged in more superlative-laden—and polarising—exhortations.[3] Indicatively, Adams declared that R2P has made 'tremendous progress'[4] and claimed that proponents of R2P 'have won the battle of ideas',[5] while Alex Bellamy, Director of the Asia-Pacific Centre for the Responsibility to Protect, asserted that 'R2P has begun to change the world'.[6] Likewise, Gareth Evans—co-chair of the ICISS panel—claimed there are 'many grounds for optimism about the future of R2P over the next decade and beyond'.[7]

Of course, this tendency to engage in such effusive rhetoric is in certain cases understandable; those who work for organisations solely dedicated to promoting R2P are naturally inclined to 'talk up' the value of the concept that sustains them. Likewise, those whose careers or reputations are largely built around the 'success' of R2P are understandably reluctant to acknowledge its limited influence. Of course, a simpler explanation is that they genuinely believe what they say about R2P.

Either way, since 2014, a series of reports and statements from NGOs, think tanks, and UN agencies—such as the UN High Commissioner for Refugees,[8] the Uppsala Conflict Data Program,[9] Human Rights Watch,[10] Amnesty International,[11] the International Crisis Group,[12] Freedom House,[13] and the International Committee of the Red Cross[14]—have highlighted two depressing trends; an upsurge in violence/oppression committed by states against their citizens, and a growing inability/unwillingness on the part of the 'international community' to take preventative or remedial action. Indeed, Ban Ki-moon's 2016 report on R2P criticised the international community for having 'fallen woefully short' in its response to intra-state crises, and lamented that the 'frequency and scale of atrocity crimes have increased'.[15] In light of these trends—exemplified by the conflict in Syria and the refugee crisis in Europe—it is not surprising that many have questioned the relevance and efficacy of R2P.[16]

The 'look at the evidence, R2P isn't working' argument, however, is generally rejected as short-sighted. Those who support R2P and continue to believe in its utility invariably argue that its efficacy should not be judged solely on the basis of its contemporary influence. This is not to suggest that defenders of R2P's efficacy do not claim it has had real-world influence; R2P is credited by some as having proved its influence during the international response to, among others, Côte d'Ivoire,[17] Kenya,[18] Kyrgyzstan,[19] Libya,[20] and the Central African Republic.[21] Yet the primary basis for the claims made regarding R2P's worth invariably orientate primarily around its growing prominence and *future* potential.

Progress by numbers?

To appreciate R2P's efficacy, we must, it is claimed, look to the signs of its *growing* influence rather than its *actual* influence now.[22] To this end, many reflections on R2P's ten-year anniversary in 2015 focused in particular on the *progress* made to date and the bright future ahead.[23] The arguments made about R2P's progress and potential rest on three claims: first, that there is no longer any major disagreement amongst states regarding the principles inherent in R2P; second, that this absence of disagreement has manifest in practice in the increased use of the term in official discourse; third, consensus around R2P has resulted in a growing number of states joining R2P-related groups and campaigns. Each are discussed in turn below.

The consensus on R2P

The obvious starting point for claims made about the consensus on R2P is the 2005 World Summit. Despite the summit occurring at a time of pronounced international division and acrimony—largely as a result of the invasion of Iraq and the 'War on Terror'—a version of R2P was endorsed by all states, manifesting as Paragraphs 138 and 139 of the Outcome Document. While, for some, the version of R2P recognised in 2005 was a dilution of the ICISS formulation, the recognition undeniably gave R2P an 'official' status.[24]

The publication of the Outcome Document did not mean, however, that R2P had created a new binding law: Paragraphs 138 and 139 were not in any sense a legal innovation. Rather, as noted by the vast majority of R2P's supporters, the Outcome Document constituted the consolidation of a number of existing laws and principles under the R2P umbrella.[25]

Paragraph 139 of the World Summit Outcome Document recognised 'the need for the General Assembly to continue consideration of the responsibility to protect populations from genocide, war crimes, ethnic cleansing, and crimes against humanity and its implications'. In keeping with this commitment, in July 2009 the General Assembly convened the first official meeting on implementing R2P; this has now become an annual event. A feature of the eight annual General Assembly debates held to date—routinely highlighted by R2P's supporters—has been that states have overwhelmingly expressed their support for R2P at these events.[26] Only very rarely has a state openly questioned R2P, and there have been no explicit rejections of the concept. On the basis of the statements given since 2009, therefore, many have declared that there exists a strong consensus on R2P amongst states. This has been presented as the foundation upon which the implementation of R2P can begin.[27]

Therefore, having 'won the battle of ideas',[28] as ostensibly evidenced by the consensus amongst states, the task now is to 'implement' R2P. Naturally, this notion of the evolution to an implementation phase, by definition, concedes that R2P is not as yet fully respected. Hence, the various derogations from R2P still evident today are cast as regrettable but inevitable at this point in the life-cycle of R2P.[29] The point is, these derogations will ostensibly diminish in time as R2P's influence grows on the back of the consensus it now commands.[30]

Security Council resolutions

In the five years after the recognition of R2P at the 2005 World Summit, the Security Council mentioned the concept in only four resolutions. Naturally, this lack of engagement with R2P suggested it was being ignored. Yet on February 26, 2011, the Security Council employed the term in Resolution 1970 on Libya, and did so again less than a month later when sanctioning a no-fly zone over Libya in Resolution 1973. Since February 2011, the Security Council has passed sixty-four resolutions which mention R2P.

This dramatic increase has, unsurprisingly, been widely heralded as key evidence by those advancing the 'R2P is making progress' argument.[31] Additionally, this increased use of R2P by the Security Council happened, many have noted, after Libya had allegedly sounded R2P's death knell. Naturally, supporters of R2P argued that R2P could not be 'dead', or even just divisive or contested, at the same time as it was being increasingly invoked in the official statements of the UN's most important body.[32] Additionally, this increased usage of the term by the Security Council has not been unique; both the General Assembly and the Human Rights Council—as well as a number of regional organisations—have increasingly evoked the term, thereby—so it is claimed—further demonstrating R2P's progress.[33]

Support for R2P groups and campaigns

The third foundation upon which the 'R2P is making progress' argument is based, is the increased willingness of states to join R2P groups and campaigns. Again, the empirical evidence supporting these claims is clear and irrefutable. During September 2010, the Global Centre for R2P launched the 'R2P Focal Points' initiative with the support of Denmark and Ghana. Six years later, fifty-five states had formally appointed an R2P Focal Point. Likewise, at the time of writing, fifty states have joined the 'Group of Friends of R2P'. Additionally, the 'Restrain the Veto' campaign has attracted the support of one hundred and fifteen states. This campaign stems from the ICISS report's recommendation that the Security Council commit to a code of conduct whereby they agree not to veto draft resolutions aiming to prevent or halt mass atrocity crimes.[34]

Not unreasonably, the increase in numerical support for R2P groups and campaigns is regularly touted as evidence that R2P is gaining momentum. Proponents of this view also point to the fact that this state support is diverse; in countering the charge that R2P is a 'Western' concept, supporters point out that membership of these groups includes 'countries in all regions of the world',[35] as evidence of R2P's truly global appeal.

Explaining R2P's popularity

There are, therefore, undeniably numerous facts the 'R2P is making progress' argument can proffer in its defence. R2P is today unquestionably 'part of the world's diplomatic language',[36] and a concept that states have invariably, and increasingly, evoked in positive terms at official international meetings. The increase in both references to the term and membership of R2P-related campaigns and groups certainly gives empirical weight to the 'progress' narrative.

Yet while R2P's popularity amongst states has grown, its influence on state behaviour remains in some doubt. Given both the scale of human suffering evident across the world today, and the rancour and division that so often impedes the international community's response to intra-state crises, the rise in state support for R2P seems curiously inconsequential. How can it be that R2P's popularity has soared at the same time as there has been a dramatic deterioration in respect for the principles it embodies? The following subsections seek to explain this paradox.

A 'norm'?

Given that R2P is not a law, its influence on state behaviour has invariably been premised on its putative status as a 'norm'.[37] The role of norms has become an increasingly popular research field within international relations in recent years and, certainly within academia, R2P's efficacy has been explained through this constructivist framework. Indeed, norms, according to Bellamy, are 'the stuff of R2P'.[38]

Literature on norms certainly suggests that state behaviour can be shaped without the need for punitive legal codes. Though they lack formal legal expression, 'norms'—usually defined as 'a standard of appropriate behaviour for actors with a given identity'[39]—exert a controlling influence over state behaviour. Throughout history, ideas regarding appropriate standards of behaviour have come to be promulgated by certain states; these 'norm entrepreneurs' have then promoted this behaviour in such a way that, over time, other states have become socialised into accepting this as the appropriate way to behave.[40]

Research on norms also demonstrates that the existence of a norm is not contingent on it being universally and consistently respected; norm violations can occur without the norm itself 'dying'.[41] Indeed, the violation of a norm can actually serve to prove its currency, provided the violation is widely condemned. Therefore, while R2P has clearly not been universally and consistently respected, these derogations are portrayed as typical of norm emergence and adoption.

The history of R2P certainly coheres with the key elements of Martha Finnemore and Kathryn Sikkink's norm 'life-cycle' model,[42] comprising as it does initial norm entrepreneurs, a 'tipping point', and then a 'norm cascade'. The problem is, while the life-cycle model explains R2P's emergence as a popular and routinely avowed term, it fails to account for the fact that R2P's ascendency has been accompanied by a decline in respect for human rights; a decline that is so widespread it cannot reasonably be portrayed as an aberration. In theory, R2P has worked perfectly; in practice, it has failed.

R2P's fate does not, of course, call into question the efficacy of norms more generally. What it does show, however, is that understanding how norms emerge and effect change is more complicated than some have suggested. The literature on norms—particularly postpositivist accounts—has noted that, while certain terms and phrases go through the archetypal life-cycle model, they nonetheless fail to meaningfully influence state behaviour.[43] This is a function of a number of factors that determine both the influence, and indeed the content, of norms. First, there exists a key distinction between constitutive and regulative norms. Only the latter actually change the behaviour of states, as they constitute norms that have been internalised; the former merely constitute principles that states have affirmed without necessarily having implemented changes.[44] Additionally, the emergence, proliferation, and ascendancy of a norm need not be a process exclusively controlled by the original norm entrepreneurs. At times, the initial emergence of a norm can be followed by the co-optation of the norm by actors keen to dilute or blunt its impact.[45] In these respects, the norm is allowed to proliferate only in a circumscribed way which coheres with pre-existing preferences. Thus, while superficially the norm may appear to have begun to command international consensus, in fact the nature of the norm has been denuded to the point where it is in effect so vague as to be meaningless or, even worse, come to be manipulated so that it actually reaffirms the disposition it sought to change. The following subsections highlight aspects of R2P's evolution and status which appear to cohere with this form of norm proliferation.

Who wouldn't affirm R2P?

In the course of the speech delivered at the 2016 General Assembly debate on R2P, Simon Adams asked the audience of state ambassadors, 'Who here believes that governments should simply ignore genocide occurring within sovereign borders? That states should be permitted to commit war crimes if they deem it militarily necessary?'[46] No one raised their hands. While Adams no doubt took this to constitute proof of the consensus around R2P, how much can we really infer from this reluctance by states to publicly admit that they support indifference to genocide or commit war crimes? Does the fact that states do not publicly admit to holding these beliefs necessarily translate into 'proof' that they do not actually harbour these beliefs? The evidence suggests otherwise.

An analysis of the myriad reports detailing the perilous state of global respect for human rights and increased frequency of atrocious crimes clearly suggests that many states have little compunction about either committing mass atrocities against their own people or tolerating it when their allies commit atrocities internally. The fact that states do not admit this publicly, and in fact routinely disavow such behaviour, is clearly not in itself a true reflection of their disposition. Indeed, it is worth noting that, if states genuinely meant what they said in public forums, then there would never have been any need for R2P; all four crimes under R2P's remit were proscribed by states long before the 2005 World Summit. Since (at least) the end of World War II, states have routinely declared their support for human rights, their revulsion at genocide, and their commitment to stand against war crimes and crimes against humanity. Yet historically there has been, as Thomas Weiss noted, 'a dramatic disconnect between political reality and pious rhetoric'.[47]

This is not to suggest, however, that states *always* lie, or that what states say is meaningless; clearly, if a state expresses a commitment to a particular principle then its subsequent derogation from this principle can be critiqued on the basis that the state is violating a principle it previously affirmed, rather than an abstract moral principle contrived by others. And so the proliferation of R2P may possibly be credited with making it more difficult for states to overtly justify engaging in the four crimes or inaction in the face of others doing so.[48] But in reality, this is quite a modest achievement; can we really say we have made 'progress' if those committing mass atrocity crimes deny they are doing so? Additionally, is this really something new? Since at least 1945, states have been reluctant to openly admit to engaging in mass atrocity crimes, and yet they have often done so. In this sense, that R2P makes it difficult—though clearly not impossible—to legitimise committing mass atrocities is hardly revolutionary.

The disjuncture between the rhetorical commitment of states to R2P and the behaviour of states is further enabled by the ambiguity surrounding R2P. In his 2009 report, UN Secretary General Ban Ki-moon outlined the three 'Pillars' of R2P: Pillar I is 'the enduring responsibility of the State to protect its populations'; Pilar II is 'the commitment of the international community to assist States in meeting those obligations'; and Pillar III is 'the responsibility of Member States to respond collectively in a timely and decisive manner when a State is manifestly failing to provide such protection'.[49] Therefore, rather than constituting one norm, R2P is better understood as a bundle of norms commanding varying degrees of consensus.[50] As a result, when states issue statements declaring their support for 'R2P', one must examine to which aspect of R2P they are referring.

The evidence suggests that state support for R2P is primarily for Pillars I and II; these pillars encapsulate principles predicated on state consent.[51] In this sense, when states affirm Pillars I and II, they are essentially asserting that states should prevent, and not engage in, the four crimes, and that the international community can 'assist' states in so doing. While this is not inherently problematic, it coheres with the self-regulatory nature of international human rights law, which has long been deemed weak.[52] In this sense, to declare support only for Pillars I and II is to affirm the *status quo*. Given that it was the problematic nature of the *status quo* that led to the emergence of R2P, contriving a new means by which to affirm it is naturally of questionable added value. This can be seen in practice through the support afforded to R2P by certain states routinely cited as having engaged in one or more of the four crimes. If Bahrain, Sudan, and Qatar are happy to declare their support for a particular interpretation of R2P, then we must surely question the utility of the concept.

Additionally, the 'support' ostensibly afforded to R2P by certain states has at times been questionable. Indicatively, according to Bellamy, North Korea's statement on R2P in 2014 was 'its most positive statement' to date and evidence that it 'has engaged reasonably constructively in dialogue on R2P'.[53] The (brief) statement itself, however, appears, if anything, to be quite negative; it asserts that R2P should only be implemented with the host state's consent, that intervention 'should not be allowed', and that more time should be spent discussing R2P because '[t]he definition is not clear and there is a very risky element of misinterpretation regarding this element'.[54] That a statement such as this can be construed as 'positive' arguably casts some doubt on the veracity of the claims regarding the 'consensus' on R2P.

In terms of Pillar III, it is widely acknowledged that consensus on this aspect of R2P is minimal.[55] This is hardly surprising given that this is the aspect of the concept that deals with the permissibility of external intervention. While many of R2P's proponents have (rightly) been at pains to note that R2P—and indeed Pillar III—is about far more than 'humanitarian intervention', suspicions persist that affirming this pillar will facilitate Western-led military interventions. This aversion to Pillar III has increased in the wake of the intervention in Libya in 2011, which has been routinely cited since as evidence of the perils of R2P interventions.[56]

While there are clearly reasonable grounds for being cautious about supporting a principle that—in theory—can be used to legitimise military intervention, without Pillar III, R2P is deprived of an essential element; the capacity to punish those who wilfully violate the proscription against committing the four crimes. Without Pillar III, therefore, R2P is more obviously a reaffirmation of the pre-existing self-regulation system. As Bellamy stated in an address to the General Assembly in 2012, 'without the use of force in the RtoP toolkit, the international community would effectively need to rely on the perpetrators to deliver protection'.[57] In this sense, the significance of state 'support' for R2P is diminished; without the prospect of incurring censure for derogating from R2P, *why would* states *not* affirm a circumscribed rendering of the concept?

The dark side of R2P

The fact that R2P is now widely used and subject to widespread state affirmation is not necessarily positive. As with all putative norms, the manner in which R2P is employed—rather than the scale of its use—more accurately determines its worth. An analysis of the way R2P is used in fact highlights two negative trends.

First, references to R2P by the Security Council have been consistently orientated to Pillar I. Each of the 59 Resolutions passed since 2011 which mention R2P do so in the context of reiterating that the host state is primarily responsible for intra-state affairs. Thus, when Resolutions have been passed mentioning R2P in the context of the crises in Libya,

South Sudan, Democratic Republic of the Congo, Côte d'Ivoire, Mali, Liberia, Syria, Central African Republic, Yemen, and Somalia, the wording has always emphasised that the particular government has 'the primary responsibility to protect'. In none of the 69 Security Council Resolutions passed to date that mention R2P is there any direct reference to Pillar III or intimations that the Security Council can – through R2P – take action to prevent or halt the commission of one or more of the four crimes within a particular state. This was the case even in Resolution 1973 which did mention R2P and authorise intervention in Libya; the reference to R2P read, 'Reiterating the responsibility of the Libyan authorities to protect the Libyan population', while the basis for authorising action was later noted as being Chapter VII of the Charter. In this respect, R2P was not then, nor has it ever been since, presented as the basis for action taken without the consent of the host state. It has been used only to reaffirm the legal principle—which predates R2P—that states have the primary responsibility to prevent or halt atrocities crimes within their territory.[58]

This is significant because it highlights two things, one obvious the other more speculative. First, Security Council Resolutions by definition require the consent of the P5. China and Russia's position on R2P has, since its inception, been that the principle should only be employed with host state consent. The fact that the fifty-nine Security Council resolutions passed since 2011 that mention R2P do so only in relation to the host states' responsibility thus suggests that the Chinese and Russian position has not changed and that they have consistently succeeded in limiting R2P's scope. Naturally, this has profound implications for the notion that R2P is making 'progress'; if anything, it suggests the concept's evolution has stalled.

Second, this willingness to use R2P in a highly circumscribed way could be interpreted as a strategy to deflect responsibility away from the Security Council. Even before the post-2011 proliferation of references to R2P by the Security Council, some had worried that R2P was being, quite paradoxically, employed by certain P5 members to evade responsibility, a point made most forcefully by Bellamy with respect to the UK's statements on the situation in Darfur.[59] Referring to R2P in this way, therefore, lends a degree of moral legitimacy to inaction; R2P is thus presented as a principle that must be respected and concomitantly one that frees the Security Council from any responsibility to act. Evoking R2P, therefore, enables the Security Council to present itself as both receptive to ethical concerns and engaged, whilst actually facilitating its inertia.

In addition to the problematic nature of the Security Council's use of R2P, questions must be asked about the motivation driving certain states to affirm R2P. As noted previously, the 'consensus' on R2P widely touted as evidence of the concept's progress and looming influence is predicated on the willingness of states to date to iterate their support for R2P, especially at General Assembly meetings. Yet, like the manner in which the term is employed in Security Council Resolutions, the interpretation of R2P affirmed is in many cases quite narrow and potentially evidence of the manipulation of the concept to cohere with a retrogressive notion of sovereignty. As noted by Jennifer Welsh, many states have expressed their support for R2P precisely because it can be interpreted in such a way that it does not disturb either the *status quo* or threaten their freedom of action. R2P has become popular with states, she emphasises, 'precisely because it was not seen as transformational'.[60] In fact, Welsh warns that many consciously use R2P—in its Pillar I and II formulations—as a way to preserve 'legal egalitarianism', which is a means by which the principle of sovereign inviolability is reaffirmed.[61] Only a circumscribed rendering of R2P is thus avowed, and this is then proliferated to legitimise behaviour that is actually antithetical to R2P's ethos. Clearly, R2P was not established as a means by which to cement the notion that states have the exclusive right to determine what happens within their own territory, and yet this is precisely how it is being used by many states.

Conclusion: 'It cannot fail'

In his statement to the General Assembly in 2016, Adams accepted that the many crises still raging around the world mirror 'a collective failure to adequately protect vulnerable populations'. He argued, however, that this should not be taken as evidence of the failure of R2P because it 'does not possess independent agency and it cannot fail'.[62] The idea that R2P 'cannot fail' is certainly debatable; it may not have 'independent agency', but must it? Many ideas, ideologies, and norms are deemed to have failed. If a prescription is advanced as a means to change prevailing behaviour, but the behaviour continues unabated, surely the prescription has failed? If we follow Adams's logic about independent agency, then we must accept that communism did not fail; a manifestly absurd notion.

Yet, as noted earlier, that people such as Adams—whose careers depend on R2P—should maintain a narrative of 'progress' and 'success' despite all evidence to the contrary is hardly either a surprise or particularly interesting. What *is* interesting about the fate of R2P, however, is the nature of the disjuncture between its proliferation and its impact; R2P provides great insight into the role of norms in international relations.

The contemporary hollow nature of R2P also points, however, to the role global civil society can play in facilitating the unacceptable behaviour of states by virtue of a determination to maintain the perceived efficacy of their campaigns. By way of example, during the 2016 General Assembly debate on R2P, Qatar proudly announced it had been chosen to host the 2017 meeting of the 'R2P Focal Points'. This was welcomed by R2P related groups—particularly the Global Centre for R2P which established the Focal Point initiative—yet by any standards Qatar is a curious choice. In September 2016, the Group of Friends of R2P issued a statement in which they declared that '[w]idespread and systematic abuses or violations of human rights often serve as early warning signs of potential genocide, war crimes, ethnic cleansing and/or crimes against humanity'.[63] Yet Qatar exhibits precisely these characteristics; numerous human rights organisations have criticised the Al Thani monarchy for an array of systemic domestic human rights violations, including torture, the abuse of foreign workers, discrimination against women and homosexuals, judicial corruption, and heavy restrictions on civil liberties.[64] Additionally, in March 2015, Qatar joined a Saudi Arabian-led coalition that has since been widely condemned for indiscriminately targeting civilians, with Ban Ki-moon denouncing their bombing of hospitals and schools.[65] The campaign has contributed to a 'severe humanitarian crisis' involving the displacement of two and a half million people, and the death of more than three thousand civilians, including over seven hundred children.[66]

Though hypocritical, that Qatar would declare itself to be committed to the promotion and protection of human rights is hardly surprising. What *is* surprising, however, is that the Global Centre for the Responsibility to Protect has supported Qatar in presenting itself as a fulsome supporter of R2P and enthusiastic host of the Focal Points. Given episodes like this, it is not hard to conclude that the determination to preserve R2P's image has led to compromises being made, and inconvenient facts overlooked, that enable obviously oppressive states to add their names to a list of 'R2P supporters', so that this growing list can then be proffered as 'evidence' that R2P is making 'tremendous progress'.

Notes

1 Alex Bellamy, 'The Responsibility to Protect after the 2005 World Summit', policy brief no. 1 (2006), Carnegie Council on Ethics and International Affairs, 15.
2 Simon Adams, 'Statement of the Global Centre for the Responsibility to Protect at the 2016 UN General Assembly Informal Interactive Dialogue on the Responsibility to Protect', 6 September 2016, http://www.globalr2p.org/media/files/2016-gcr2p-r2p-interactive-dialogue-statement.pdf.
3 Adrian Gallagher, 'The Responsibility to Protect Ten Years on from the World Summit: A Call to Manage Expectations', *Global Responsibility to Protect*, 7, no. 3 (2015): 254–274; Christopher Hobson, 'Responding to Failure: The Responsibility to Protect after Libya,' *Millennium: Journal of International Studies*, 44, no. 3 (2016): 433–454; Mark Kersten, 'The Responsibility to Protect Doctrine Is Faltering. Here's Why', *The Washington Post*, December 8, 2015, https://www.washingtonpost.com/news/monkey-cage/wp/2015/12/08/the-responsibility-to-protect-doctrine-is-failing-heres-why/.
4 Simon Adams, 'The Responsibility to Protect: Ten Years On', OpenCanada, May 8, 2015, https://www.opencanada.org/features/the-responsibility-to-protect-10-years-on/
5 Simon Adams, 'R2P at Ten', E-International Relations, March 29, 2015, http://www.e-ir.info/2015/03/29/r2p-at-10/.
6 Alex Bellamy, *The Responsibility to Protect: A Defence* (Oxford: Oxford University Press, 2015), 111.
7 Gareth Evans, 'R2P: Looking Back, Looking Forward', keynote address, Phnom Penh, Cambodia, February 26, 2015, http://www.gevans.org/speeches/speech568.html.
8 UNHCR, 'World at War: UNHCR Global Trends', 2015, http://unhcr.org/556725e69.html, 3–5.
9 Uppsala Conflict Data Program, 'Organized Violence in the World 2015,' http://www.pcr.uu.se/digitalAssets/61/61335_1ucdp-paper-9.pdf, 1.
10 Human Rights Watch, *World Report 2015*, www.hrw.org/sites/default/files/wr2015_web.pdf, 1.
11 Amnesty International, 'Annual Report 2014/2015', https://www.amnesty.org/en/latest/research/2015/02/annual-report-201415/.
12 Jean-Marie Guéhenno, 'The World's Fragmenting Conflicts', International Crisis Group: The Future of Conflict, October 26, 2015, https://medium.com/the-future-of-conflict/the-world-s-fragmenting-conflicts-7d9c2eac98d6.
13 Freedom House, 'Freedom in the World: 2016', https://freedomhouse.org/report/freedom-world-2016/overview-essay-anxious-dictators-wavering-democracies.
14 International Committee of the Red Cross, 'World at a Turning Point: Heads of UN and Red Cross Issue Joint Warning', October 30, 2015, https://www.icrc.org/en/document/conflict-disaster-crisis-UN-red-cross-issue-warning.
15 Ban Ki-moon, 'Mobilizing Collective Action: The Next Decade of the Responsibility to Protect', report of the Secretary-General, A/70/999–S/2016/620, July 22, 2016, 3.
16 Gabriele Lombardo, 'The Responsibility to Protect and the Lack of Intervention in Syria: Between the Protection of Human Rights and Geopolitical Strategies', *International Journal of Human Rights*, 19, no. 8 (2015): 1190–1198; Justin Morris, 'The Responsibility to Protect and the Use of Force: Remaking the Procrustean Bed?', *Cooperation and Conflict*, 51, no. 2 (2016): 200–215.
17 Gareth Evans, 'R2P: The Next Ten Years', in *Oxford Handbook of the Responsibility to Protect*, ed. Alex Bellamy and Tim Dunne (Oxford: Oxford University Press, 2016), 3.
18 Adams, 'R2P at Ten'.
19 Eduard Luck, 'The Responsibility to Protect at Ten: The Challenges Ahead', Stanley Foundation, policy brief, May 2015, 4.
20 Bellamy, *The Responsibility to Protect*, 94.
21 Thomas Weiss, 'Military Humanitarianism: Syria Hasn't Killed It', *The Washington Quarterly* 37, no. 1 (2014): 7.
22 Bellamy, *The Responsibility to Protect*, 61; Jennifer Welsh, 'Norm Contestation and the Responsibility to Protect,' *Global Responsibility to Protect* 5, no. 4 (2013): 395; Alexander Betts and Phil Orchard, 'Introduction: The Normative Institutionalization-Implementation Gap', in *Implementation and World Politics: How International Norms Change Politics*, ed. Alexander Betts and Phil Orchard (Oxford: Oxford University Press, 2014), 1; Weiss, 'Military Humanitarianism: Syria Hasn't Killed It'.
23 Evans, 'R2P: The Next Ten Years'; Adams, 'R2P at Ten'; Bellamy, *The Responsibility to Protect*, 70.
24 Thomas Weiss, *Humanitarian Intervention* (London: Polity, 2007), 177.
25 Ban Ki-moon, 'Implementing the Responsibility to Protect', UN Secretary General Report, A/63/677, January 12, 2009. http://responsibilitytoprotect.org/implementing%20the%20rtop.pdf, 2; Bellamy, *The Responsibility to Protect: A Defence*, 15; Jennifer Welsh, 'Conclusion: The Evolution of Humanitarian

Intervention in International Society', in *Humanitarian Intervention and International Relations*, ed. Jennifer Welsh (Oxford: Oxford University Press, 2006), 210; Carsten Stahn, 'Responsibility to Protect: Political Rhetoric or Emerging Legal Norm?', *American Journal of International Law*, 101, no. 1 (2007): 120.

26 Evans, 'R2P: The Next Ten Years', 2; Adams, 'R2P at Ten'; Ban Ki-moon, 'A Vital and Enduring Commitment: Implementing the Responsibility to Protect', report of the Secretary-General, A/69/981–S/2015/500, July 13, 2015; Jess Gifkins, 'R2P in the UN Security Council: Darfur, Libya and Beyond', *Cooperation and Conflict*, 51, no. 2 (2016): 148–165; Global Public Policy Institute, 'Effective and Responsible Protection from Atrocity Crimes: Towards Global Action', Policy Paper, April 2015, http://www.globalnorms.net/fileadmin/user_upload/Publications/GlobalNorms_2015_Effective_and_Responsible_R2P.pdf.

27 Ban Ki-moon, 'A Vital and Enduring Commitment', 3–4.

28 Adams, 'R2P at Ten'.

29 Luke Glanville, 'Does R2P Matter? Interpreting the Impact of a Norm', *Cooperation and Conflict*, 51/2, 2016: 184–199; Nicole Deitelhoff and Lisbeth Zimmermann, 'Things We Lost in the Fire: How Different Types of Contestation Affect the Validity of International Norms', Peace Research Institute, Frankfurt, Working Paper 18, 2013; Gregor Hofmann, 'Ten Years R2P: What Doesn't Kill a Norm Only Makes It Stronger?', Peace Research Institute, Frankfurt, Report 133, 2015, 29.

30 Evans, 'R2P: The Next Ten Years', 2; Adams, 'R2P at Ten'; Ban Ki-moon, 'A Vital and Enduring Commitment'; Gifkins, 'R2P in the UN Security Council: Darfur, Libya and Beyond', 148–165.

31 Gifkins, 'R2P in the UN Security Council: Darfur, Libya and Beyond'; Adams, 'The Responsibility to Protect: Ten Years On'; Bellamy, *The Responsibility to Protect: A Defence*, 26; Tim Dunne and Katherine Gelber, 'Arguing Matters: The Responsibility to Protect and the Case of Libya', *Global Responsibility to Protect*, 6/3, 2014, 326–349; Glanville, 'Does R2P Matter?', 184–199; Global Public Policy Institute, 'Effective and Responsible Protection from Atrocity Crimes: Towards Global Action', 10.

32 Adams, 'The Responsibility to Protect'; Weiss, 'Military Humanitarianism'.

33 Ban Ki-moon, 'A Vital and Enduring Commitment', 4.

34 International Commission on Intervention and State Sovereignty, *The Responsibility to Protect* (Ottawa: International Development Research Centre, 2001), 51.

35 Global Centre for the Responsibility to Protect, 'R2P Focal Points Factsheet', 2016, http://www.globalr2p.org/media/files/r2p_focalpoints_factsheet.pdf.

36 Welsh, 'Norm Contestation and the Responsibility to Protect', 378.

37 Bellamy, *The Responsibility to Protect*, 72; Luke Glanville, 'Does R2P Matter?' 184–199; Jennifer Welsh, 'Implementing the Responsibility to Protect: Catalyzing Debate and Building Capacity', in Alexander Betts and Phil Orchard, eds., *Implementation and World Politics: How International Norms Change Politics* (Oxford: Oxford University Press, 2014), 125; Dunne and Gelber, 'Arguing Matters: The Responsibility to Protect and the Case of Libya'; Cristina Badescu and Thomas Weiss, 'Misrepresenting R2P and Advancing Norms: An Alternative Spiral?', *International Studies Perspectives*, 11/4, 2010: 354–374.

38 Bellamy, *The Responsibility to Protect: A Defence*, 59.

39 Peter Katzenstein, 'Introduction: Alternative Perspectives on National Security', in Peter Katzenstein, ed., *The Culture of National Security* (New York: Columbia Press, 1996), 5.

40 Martha Finnemore and Kathryn Sikkink, 'International Norm Dynamics and Political Change', *International Organization*, 52/4, 1998, 895.

41 Amitav Acharya, 'How Ideas Spread: Whose Norms Matter? Norm Localization and Institutional Change in Asian Regionalism', *International Organization*, 58/2, 2004: 239–275; Freidrich Kratochwil and John Ruggie, 'International Organization: A State of the Art on an Art of the State', *International Organization*, 40/4, 1986, 753–775; Vaughan Shannon, 'Norms Are What States Make of Them: The Political Psychology of Norm Violation', *International Studies Quarterly*, 44/2, 2000: 293–316; Wayne Sandholtz, 'Dynamics of International Norm Change', *European Journal of International Relations*, 14/1, 2008, 101–131; Diana Panke and Ulrich Petersohn, 'Why International Norms Disappear Sometimes', *European Journal of International Relations*, 18/4, 2011, 719–742.

42 Martha Finnemore and Kathryn Sikkink, 'International Norm Dynamics and Political Change', *International Organizations*, 52/4, 1998, 887–917; see also, Jeffrey Checkel, 'Norms, Institutions, and National Identity in Contemporary Europe', *International Studies Quarterly*, 43/1, 1999, 83–114.

43 Antje Wiener, 'Enacting Meaning-in-Use: Qualitative Research on Norms and International Relations', *Review of International Studies*, 35/1, 2009, 175–193; Amitav Acharya, 'The R2P and Norm Diffusion: Towards a Framework of Norm Circulation', *Global Responsibility to Protect*, 5:1, 2013, 466–479; Alan Bloomfield and Shirley Scott, *Norm Antipreneurs and the Politics of Resistance to Global Normative Change* (Oxon: Routledge, 2016); Mona Lena Krook and Jacqui True, 'Rethinking the Life Cycles of

International Norms: The United Nations and the Global Promotion of Gender Equality', *European Journal of International Relations*, 18/1, 2010, 103–127; Kees Van Kersbergen and Bertjan Verbeek, 'The Politics of International Norms', *European Journal of International Relations*, 13/2, 2007, 217–238.

44 Katzenstein, 'Introduction: Alternative Perspectives on National Security', 5.

45 Jack L. Goldsmith and Eric A. Posner, 'Introduction', *Journal of Legal Studies*, XXXI, 2002, 104.

46 Adams, 'Statement of the Global Centre for the Responsibility to Protect at the 2016 UN General Assembly Informal Interactive Dialogue on the Responsibility to Protect'.

47 Thomas Weiss, 'Halting Genocide: Rhetoric versus Reality', *Genocide Studies and Prevention*, 2/1, 2007, 7.

48 Justin Morris, 'The Responsibility to Protect: A Long View', in Aidan Hehir and Robert W. Murray, eds., *Protecting Human Rights in the 21st Century* (London: Routledge, 2017).

49 Ban Ki-moon, 'Implementing the Responsibility to Protect', 8–9.

50 Bellamy, *The Responsibility to Protect: A Defence*, 72; Glanville, 'Does R2P Matter?', 184–199; Welsh, 'Implementing the Responsibility to Protect', 125.

51 Morris, 'The Responsibility to Protect and the Use of Force', 200–215; Aidan Hehir, 'Assessing the Influence of the Responsibility to Protect on the UN Security Council during the Arab Spring', *Cooperation and Conflict*, 51, no, 2 (2016): 166–183.

52 Louis Henkin, 'Compliance with International Law in an Inter-State System', Academie de droit international, Recueil des cours 1989 (Dordrecht: Martinus Nijhoff, 1990).

53 Alex Bellamy, 'A Chronic Protection Problem: The DPRK and the Responsibility to Protect', *International Affairs*, 91, no. 2 (2015): 229–230.

54 'Democratic People's Republic of Korea's Statement at the General Assembly Dialogue on the Responsibility to Protect', 2014, http://www.globalr2p.org/media/files/dprk.pdf

55 Ban Ki-moon, 'A Vital and Enduring Commitment: Implementing the Responsibility to Protect', 12–13; Justin Morris, 'Libya and Syria: R2P and the Spectre of the Swinging Pendulum', *International Affairs*, 89, no. 5 (2013): 1265–1283; Roland Paris, 'The "Responsibility to Protect" and the Structural Problems of Preventative Humanitarian Intervention', *International Peacekeeping*, 21, no. 5 (2014): 1–35.

56 Natalie Nougayrède, 'Interview with Kofi Annan: "On Syria, It's Obvious, We Haven't Succeeded"', *Le Monde*, July 7, 2012, http://www.lemonde.fr/proche-orient/article/2012/07/07/kofi-annan-sur-la-syrie-a-l-evidence-nous-n-avons-pas-reussi_1730658_3218.html; Andrew Garwood-Gowers, 'The BRICS and the Responsibility to Protect: Lessons from the Libyan and Syrian Crises', in *Responsibility to Protect in Theory and Practice*, ed. Vasilka Sancin and Maša Kovič Dine (Ljubjana: GV Založba, 2013), 310; Ramesh Thakur, 'R2P after Libya and Syria: Engaging Emerging Powers', *Washington Quarterly*, 36, no. 2 (2013): 61–76.

57 Alex Bellamy, 'Remarks to the General Assembly Informal Interactive Dialogue on the Responsibility to Protect', New York, September 5, 2012, http://responsibilitytoprotect.org/Alex%20Bellamy.pdf.

58 Simon Chesterman, '"Leading from Behind": The Responsibility to Protect, the Obama Doctrine, and Humanitarian Intervention after Libya', *Ethics and International Affairs*, 25 (2011): 279–285.

59 Alex Bellamy, 'Responsibility to Protect or Trojan Horse? The Crisis in Darfur and Humanitarian Intervention after Iraq', *Ethics and International Affairs*, 19, no. 2 (2005): 45.

60 Welsh, 'Norm Contestation and the Responsibility to Protect', 373.

61 Ibid., 394.

62 Adams, 'Statement of the Global Centre for the Responsibility to Protect at the 2016 UN General Assembly Informal Interactive Dialogue on the Responsibility to Protect'.

63 Statement by the Group of Friends of the Responsibility to Protect in Geneva at the HRC 33 General Debate Item 10 – 'Technical Assistance and Capacity-Building', September 29, 2016, http://www.globalr2p.org/resources/1100.

64 Freedom House, 'Qatar', *Freedom in the World*, 2016, https://freedomhouse.org/report/freedom-world/2016/qatar; Office of the High Commissioner for Human Rights, 'Qatar', Human Rights by Country, 2016, http://www.ohchr.org/EN/Countries/MENARegion/Pages/QAIndex.aspx; Amnesty International, 'Qatar', 2016, https://www.amnesty.org/en/countries/middle-east-and-north-africa/qatar/; Human Rights Watch, 'Qatar', Country Reports, 2016, https://www.hrw.org/world-report/2016/country-chapters/qatar.

65 Ban Ki-moon, 'Secretary-General's Address at Event Co-organized by the United Nations Association of the United Kingdom and Chatham House', February 5, 2016, https://www.un.org/sg/en/content/sg/statement/2016-02-05/secretary-generals-address-event-co-organized-united-nations.

66 Amnesty International, 'Yemen: The Forgotten War', 2016, https://www.amnesty.org/en/latest/news/2015/09/yemen-the-forgotten-war/.

24
RIGHT INTENT IN HUMANITARIAN INTERVENTION

Fernando R. Tesón

In this chapter I examine the requirement that a humanitarian intervention, to be justified, must be accompanied by the right intent. My thesis is that current views on right intent are too simplistic and do not do justice to the complexities of the relationship between intention and permissibility of action. The plain requirement that the intervener must have the right intent is highly ambiguous. The assertion "P has the intent to do X" has multiple meanings. There are many ways in which an agent may intend an action or a result. These several meanings of intention may imply permissibility of action in a broader range of cases that it has been traditionally assumed. The upshot of my analysis is that there are several ways in which the intervener's intent entails the permissibility of the intervention (provided that the other conditions for the justification of war are present).

Humanitarian intervention is a war characterized by a specific cause: saving persons from attack by their government or other groups in their territories. This raises the question of right intent: must those who start a humanitarian war *act on* the humanitarian motive for the war to be justified? Traditional just war theory has required right intent, that is, an appropriate mental state on the part of the intervener. Here is Thomas Aquinas: "For it can happen that even if war is declared by a legitimate authority and for a just cause, that war may be rendered unlawful by a wicked intent."[1] Similarly, Alex Bellamy claims that right intention is pivotal for the permissibility of intervention.[2] The idea is that a necessary condition for the justification of humanitarian intervention is that the intervener act out of humanitarian reasons, at least in part. This condition helps "orient military action toward justice rather tan revenge, bloodlust, or mere expansionism."[3] On the traditional view, if a government's pre-eminent reasons or motives are non-humanitarian, the intervention will not be humanitarian, and should not be evaluated under the doctrine of humanitarian intervention, even if the doctrine is accepted. The use of force will be something else (self-defense, for example), and it should be judged accordingly. The International Commission on Intervention and State Sovereignty (ICISS) Report concluded, more realistically, that mixed motives in state action are a fact of life, and therefore they are not enough to disqualify an otherwise legitimate intervention, provided that the primary purpose is to halt or avert human suffering.[4]

The issue was hotly debated during the wars in Iraq and Afghanistan. Many thought that George W. Bush, for example, did not really intend to liberate Iraq from Saddam Hussein but rather to achieve something else, such as destroying the elusive weapons of mass destruction, or even worse, grabbing Iraq's oil. Because any of those motives revealed the real intent of the intervener, the invasion of Iraq, it was thought, could not possibly *count* as humanitarian intervention.[5] As I anticipated, I believe that this view is too simplistic and does not do justice to the complexity of the relationship between intention and permissibility of action.

Categorization and justification

Before tackling intent, I address a question that has received muddled treatment in the literature (including from the present writer). This is the question of categorization. When ascertaining whether a given military action could be justified as humanitarian, writers often start with asking whether such action is a proper *candidate* for humanitarian intervention. They ask first: "Is this really a humanitarian intervention?" The idea is that humanitarian intervention is a species of the genus war, so before addressing whether or not a war is justified, we should preliminarily ascertain whether this particular war exhibits the attributes of a humanitarian intervention. To simplify, let us suppose that a humanitarian war is justified when it meets two conditions: (1) the war's goal is to rescue persons from severe tyranny (or massacre, genocide) and (2) the war is proportionate, that is, it will (predictably) not cause excessive damage. The second condition, proportionality, is common to all wars. So a determination that the war qualifies as a humanitarian intervention is a determination that the war satisfies the first condition: that it aims at rescuing people from violence. If the war does not satisfy the first condition, then it will not be a humanitarian intervention. However, it could still be a justified war—for example, if the war's goal is to repel an aggression.

This approach treats humanitarian intervention and national self-defense as two *essentially* distinct types of war. On this view, humanitarian intervention is an offensive war because it is not in response to aggression. The intervener has not been attacked; therefore, he cannot permissibly wage war. Say that the government of state A is committing atrocities against its own citizens. On the traditional view, this is of course terribly wrong, and one would hope that the victims would have the wherewithal to resist. But the wrongness of the atrocities does not generate a permission for foreign armies to intervene, because in that case state B, the intervener, would be attacking state A without B's having itself suffered any attack by A. The war waged by A, then, would be a presumptively impermissible offensive war. On this view, a humanitarian intervention is much harder to justify than a war of national self-defense because such justification must defeat the justificatory reasons that the target state has for exercising *its* self-defense.

Both critics and supporters of humanitarian intervention treat these two types of war as essentially different. Cécile Fabre defines humanitarian intervention as "a humanitarian war against a sovereign political community" over which that agent lacks jurisdiction.[6] The implication is that humanitarian intervention differs *in kind* rom national self-defense. In national self-defense, persons fight for their own rights; in humanitarian intervention, they fight for the rights of others. Similarly, David Rodin writes that humanitarian intervention is antithetical to self-defense:

> if there is a right of humanitarian intervention, then it is because the moral basis of the right of national defense can in certain circumstances be justly overridden, not because the right of humanitarian intervention is, in some sense, an application of those moral considerations.[7]

Michael Walzer is particularly firm: states are the arenas of self-determination from which in principle foreign armies are excluded.[8] And Allen Buchanan thinks that while institutions should make room for humanitarian intervention, what he calls the Just War Norm, that is, the norm that authorizes war only in response to aggression, should be preserved.[9]

However, the distinction is illusory. It is not necessary first to categorize a war and then inquire whether or not it is justified. This is because *all* wars have the same justification, namely to defend persons and their rights from unjustified attacks. A war in self-defense is a war to defend myself and my compatriots against foreign aggression. A humanitarian intervention is a war to defend persons and their rights *in their territory* against attacks by their government or other groups.[10] All justified wars, in short, are *defensive* wars, wars to defend persons. If this is correct, then the only question is whether a particular war is justified. One should simply ask whether the two conditions, just cause and proportionality, have been satisfied. When critics of the Iraq war say it was not a humanitarian intervention, they mean it did not satisfy the *first* condition, that is, it did not have a just cause.[11] There is no issue of categorization. There is only the issue of justification.

Just cause and intent

Now of course, the problem of right intent remains. We say there is objectively a just cause for war when the massacre is taking place. But we want to say that a commander, to justify the harm of an invasion, must aim at realizing the just cause and must realize it. This still leaves us in the dark about intent and motives. The requirement of success (that the just cause be realized) is fairly straightforward. But the requirement that the commander must *aim at* (intent, will) the realization of the just cause is obscure.

To see why, assume regime A is perpetrating a massacre and B, the leader of a neighboring state, is contemplating an intervention to stop it. Assuming B has a just cause, stopping the massacre, what kind of intention must B form to make the intervention permissible? There are a number of possibilities.

1) *Pure intent*: B starts a war to prevent massacre in A, and this is an *end in itself.* This is a pure case where the agent directly wills the just cause. NATO's 1999 intervention in Kosovo may be such a case. It is hard to see in that incident motives other than stopping Serbia's ethnic cleansing of Kosovo.[12]
2) *Conditional intent*: B intends to deter A's future aggression, and militarily defeating A is the way to achieve that. B foresees that defeating A will also end the ongoing massacre. She decides to invade *on the condition* that the massacre stops.[13] An example could be World War II. The Allies fought Germany in order to neutralize Germany's military power and end its aggressive behavior. Stopping the Third Reich's humanitarian crimes was not the goal. Yet, plausibly, the Allies proceeded on the condition that those crimes stop.
3) *Ulterior motive*: B intends to stop A's massacre *as a means* to achieve regional hegemony. B directly intends the just cause, ending the massacre, but only as a means to achieve another end, regional hegemony, which by itself would not have justified the war. Perhaps the 1971 intervention of India in East Pakistan exemplifies this case. India saved the Bengalis from genocide (arguably) as a means to gain hegemony over Pakistan in the Indian peninsula.[14]
4) *Pure side effect*: B invades A to recover a part of B's territory unlawfully annexed by B. All B's commander needs to achieve that goal is military victory. She also *foresees* that the massacre will stop as a side effect. However, she does not care one way or the other: she would start the war and recover the territory even if there was no massacre or, if one was afoot, it could not be stopped. Perhaps the Falklands/Malvinas war is, *mutatis mutandi*, an example. Margaret Thatcher wished to respond to the Argentine Junta's unlawful occupation of the

islands. She started a successful war with that goal, but the British victory also ended the Junta's repressive regime and brought back human rights and democracy to Argentina. Thatcher did not care about that one way or the other: she would have proceeded with the war regardless of these humanitarian effects on Argentine society.

5) *Evil intent*: B intends to stop the massacre in A as a means of imposing B's own tyrannical rule over A's territory for years to come. She can predict, however, that such rule will be a lesser evil than allowing A to consummate the massacre. A possible example may be the 1979 Vietnamese invasion of Cambodia, where the intervener's intention was to secure tyrannical domination.[15] Vietnam surely would have secured domination whether or not it entailed the demise of the murderous Pol Pot regime. The overthrow of Pol Pot was *obliquely* intended by the Vietnamese invader, who could foresee that the Pol Pot regime would fall as a result of the invasion, but the humanitarian goal was not a condition of Vietnamese action. Worse, the Vietnamese goal was "wicked," as Aquinas would have said.

This surely incomplete classification reveals the complexity of intent.[16] An intervener can have several goals, and the just cause may occupy various alternative places in the intentional structure attached to his action. For example, assume the just cause in 2003 would have been the overthrow of Saddam Hussein at an acceptable cost. The coalition arguably had several aims: finding weapons of mass destruction; securing Iraq as an ally in the region; making a post-9/11 demonstration of power to avoid loss of prestige, and so on. These several objectives do not disqualify the presence of the just cause as a trigger for permissibility in the complex intentional structure of the intervener. Critics of the Iraq War are on much better footing when they condemn the war for having violated the proportionality condition.[17]

In my view, the requirement of right intent can be satisfied in (1), (2), and (3) but not in (5). Case (4), where the realization of the just cause is the pure side effect, is harder. I think (2), conditional intent, is sufficiently close to (1), pure intent, to satisfy the right intent requirement.

In case (3), the intervener directly intends the just cause as a means to a non-just-cause goal. I think the intervention is permissible in those kinds of cases. Following John Stuart Mill, I distinguish between *intention* and *motive*. Mill wrote:

> The morality of the action depends entirely upon the intention—that is, upon what the agent wills to do. But the motive, that is, the feeling which makes him will so to do, when it makes no difference in the act, makes none in the morality: though it makes a great difference in our moral estimation of the agent, especially if it indicates a good or a bad habitual disposition—a bent of character from which useful, or from which hurtful actions are likely to arise.[18]

Intention covers the contemplated act, what the agent wills to do. Suppose you see a person in distress and decide to rescue him. You commit to do it and then do it. The action is an act of rescue. Intention covers the willed act and the willed consequences of the act. Intention, then, implies not only your desire to do something but your commitment to doing it. This involves believing that the act is under your control.[19] If you intended to rescue someone but failed to do so, say because you did not put enough effort into it, or you were clumsy or otherwise mistaken in your choice of means, then I could say, perhaps, that yours was not an act of rescue. In the case of humanitarian intervention, this requirement translates into the reasonable prospects of victory. The intervener must reasonably believe that he can succeed in stopping the massacre. To intend X implies a direct connection between willing X, committing to doing X, and doing X.

It is generally believed, however, that your mental state can confer greater or lesser moral value to your act of rescue. Suppose you rescue the victim because you believe that is the right thing to do. In that case, you have *no further motive*. Yours is a pure act of rescue, as it were. But suppose you rescue the person because you want to appear as a hero in the local newspaper (or worse: you condition the rescue to your victim's payment of ten thousand dollars). In this case, your act of rescue is not pure because *you have a further motive*. *Motive*, therefore, must be distinguished from *intention*. It is a further goal that one wishes to accomplish with the intended act. In this case, you rescued the victim for a further (in this case selfish) motive.

This motive is not part of the class of actions called "acts of rescue"; only the intention is. Yet it is widely accepted that motives matter, and that your self-interested act of rescue has lesser value than the unselfish act of rescue, even if in both cases you saved the person's life. It makes sense for me to say that your act of rescue was good (it saved a life), but that you are not a particularly admirable person, since your motive was self-interested, not altruistic. In introducing this distinction, Mill showed that intention is more important than motive in evaluating *action* (as opposed to evaluating *persons*). The concept of intention fulfills a double role: it allows us to characterize the act, to say that the act belongs to a class of acts, such as acts of rescue; and it allows us, correspondingly, to praise or criticize the act under the moral principles that apply to that class of acts, acts of rescue.

The upshot is that someone may will X as *an end in itself or as a means to another end Y*. If stopping a massacre is an independent just cause for war, then it is justified to start a war that would stop the massacre, even if the intervener has a further motive Y (say, grabbing oil). It is not against usage to say that the intervener intended X: he intended X as a means to achieve Y. The Iraq War may have been unjustified for a number of reasons, but not because the coalition lacked the intent to liberate Iraq. The coalition *willed* the overthrow of Saddam Hussein, probably not as an end in itself but in pursuit of other ends. In the worst scenario, the coalition intended to liberate Iraq as a means to achieve some other non-just-cause-related purpose. So when the agent intends the just cause (defending the victims of massacre) as a means to achieving a further motive (securing economic benefits), the act of saving the victims is justified, even if the intervener's motive may be such that it alone would not have justified the war. As Mill pointed out, the existence of a questionable motive may be a reason to criticize the *agent*, but not a reason to criticize his *act*. This is the sense of intent used in the criminal law: juries are called to determine the *mens rea*, that is, whether the accused had the intent of committing the crime. This is the Millian sense of intent. For the criminal law, too, the motive for the crime (say, the criminal's rage of jealousy or his desire to feed his family) rarely excuses the crime.[20]

So far, the just cause is intended, either as an end in itself, a condition for action, or a means to a further end (which itself could not be a just cause). Cases (2) and (4) above are those where the intervener does not intend the just cause either as means or as an end, but simply foresees it. However, there is an important difference between them. In *conditional intent*, the intervener acts on condition of the foreseen just cause. Francis Kamm has argued that war may be justified in these kinds of cases. She writes that starting a war might be justified even if one does not intend the just cause, even as means, provided the intervener knows the just cause will be realized, and acts on condition that it will be realized:

> [T]he intention to act for the sake of a factor that constitutes a just cause is, in itself, unnecessary from a deontological perspective in order for starting a war to be morally *permissible*, at the very least, if the factor that could be a just cause is or will be present regardless of one's intention, one knows this, and one acts on condition that the factor is or will be present.[21]

For Kamm, then, starting a war can be justified even if the warrior does not intend the just cause but simply knows that the factor (the realization of the just cause) will be present and acts on condition that it will be present. This case differs from (3), *ulterior motive*, where the intervener intends the just cause as a means to some further end. The difference is that in *ulterior motive* the intervener presumably would have pursued his ulterior motive (regional hegemony) if he could have done so without stopping the massacre. In (2), *conditional intent*, the intervener acts on condition of stopping the massacre, even if that is not his goal. This makes (2) closer to (1), *pure intent*, because the just cause figures more prominently in the intentional structure of the agent. Still, as I suggested, in (3), *ulterior motive*, the intervention is permissible.

Consider an intervention by NATO against ISIS. The intervention would fall under (1), *pure intent*, if NATO rescues the victims of ISIS and seeks no further goal. The intervention would fall under (2), *conditional intent*, if NATO seeks to secure oil in the region, foresees that the defeat of ISIS will result in the end of ISIS' atrocities, and intervenes on condition that those atrocities end. The intervention would fall under (3), *ulterior motive*, if NATO directly intends rescuing the victims, but as a means to secure oil in the region, an ulterior motive. Characteristically, in (3) securing the humanitarian benefits is *causally necessary* for the intervener to secure the non-humanitarian ulterior motive. Stopping ISIS' atrocities is a causally necessary condition for NATO's securing oil in the region.

The differences between (1), (2), and (3) are not crucial with respect to humanitarian intervention. I would say that in the three cases the intervener *intends* the just cause. In the three of them, the intervener performs the act of defeating ISIS, which includes saving the victims. This act is intended, not as an end in itself, but as a means to the further motive of the coalition's securing oil. In (2) and (3), NATO intends securing oil but knowingly brings about saving the victims, either as a foreseen side effect or as a necessary condition of ISIS' defeat, and thus a necessary condition of the coalition's securing the oil. In all three cases, the intervention is permissible.[22]

A harder case is (4), *pure side effect*. The intervener pursues a non-just-cause goal such as securing oil, the just cause obtains as a foreseeable side effect, but the intervener does not care. She would intervene to secure oil whether or not the just cause, ending a massacre, comes to pass. In such a case, the just cause is further removed, as it were, from the core of the intervener's intentional structure. Consider the 1982 Falklands/Malvinas War. The United Kingdom started a war to recover the islands from a bloodless but forcible seizure by the military Junta that then governed Argentina.[23] The United Kingdom quickly defeated Argentina, and as a result, democracy and human rights returned to that country. Was the war permissible? This case is complicated by the fact that the United Kingdom arguably had another just cause available: responding to Argentine aggression. Setting that aside, the actual war did not qualify as humanitarian intervention under (3), because Margaret Thatcher did not intend to liberate the Argentines *as a means* to recover the islands. Nor did the intervention qualify under (2), because Margaret Thatcher did not fight the war *on the condition* of ending tyranny in Argentina.

This case falls under (4), *pure side effect*. But if so, then the war would have been impermissible had there not been Argentine aggression, that is, had Thatcher invaded for a goal that is not a just cause, such as grabbing the oil in the islands' continental shelf, even if tyranny in Argentina would have ended as a side effect. Here, we must apply the analysis of *conditional causes*. A conditional cause is a cause that would not have justified a war (say, oppression of women) but that arguably the intervener could pursue once it intervened for a just cause (say, genocide).[24] In these kinds of cases, the intervener cannot permissibly start the war because *ex hypothesi* she does not have a just cause. In the Falklands/Malvinas War, Margaret Thatcher neither knew that human rights restoration would ensue nor did she act on condition that human rights restoration would ensue. That humanitarian benefit could or could not have ensued, and Margaret Thatcher did not know or care one way or the other.[25] This means that the Falklands/ Malvinas War is not really a good example of (4), because the United Kingdom had available a separate just cause: responding to aggression. My intuition, and quite a tentative one at that, is that a military intervention aimed at something else where the just cause, ending tyranny, is removed from the intervention itself and where the intervener does not care about its occurrence, is impermissible (unless, of course, that something else is a different just cause).

What about (5), where the intervener has a really evil (not merely selfish) motive? An evil motive is worse than a self-regarding motive. A self-regarding motive would be rescuing the victims to gain access to oil. An evil motive would be rescuing the victims to torture or kill them. We saw that Aquinas condemns wars, even if they have a just cause, when the intervener's motive is wicked. Likewise, John Stuart Mill thinks that an evil motive destroys the nature of the act:

> I submit, that he who saves another from drowning in order to kill him by torture afterwards, does not differ only in motive from him who does the same thing from duty or benevolence; the act itself is different. The rescue of the man is, in the case supposed, only the necessary first step of an act far more atrocious than leaving him to drown would have been.[26]

Kamm gives the example of an intervener who really wishes to kill a few civilians, but this evil action requires the intervener to stop a massacre.[27] Proponents of the doctrine of double effect will condemn this war even if it realizes the just cause, because under that doctrine it is never permissible to intend evil. Kamm disagrees. She thinks that the war is permissible despite the evil intention, if the massacre will be stopped, the intervener knows this, and acts on the condition that it the massacre is stopped, *and* if the killing of these persons is proportionate to ending the massacre. The intervener would be doing the right thing for an evil reason. Notice that in this example, the killing of civilians, which the intervener *directly wills*, would have been the same killing that would have been permissible *as a side effect* under the doctrine of double effect.

This situation can be quite common in practice. The most notorious example, already mentioned, is the 1979 intervention of Vietnam in Cambodia. That intervention put an end to the massacre perpetrated by the Pol Pot regime, but at the same time it started two decades of tyrannical rule in Cambodia, albeit with no massacres. The intent of the Vietnamese interveners was to impose their own tyrannical rule. Under Mill's analysis, this was their *motive* (Kamm would say their *intent* was to impose tyrannical rule). The case could fall under (3), where stopping Pol Pot's massacre was the means to impose their rule. The difference is that the motive is evil, and not just self-regarding. Was this a justified case of humanitarian intervention? If one thinks that it is never permissible to intend evil, then Vietnam's intervention was unjustified, notwithstanding the fact that it prevented Pol Pot from committing further crimes. In contrast, if, following Kamm, one relaxes that condition, then Vietnam's intervention was permissible if: (1) the just cause, stopping Pol Pot's crimes, was realized and (2) the principles of proportionality are satisfied. In that case, it does not matter if (1) is accompanied by an evil intention (imposing tyranny in Cambodia) which is, furthermore, implemented (since, *ex hypothesi*, that is a permissible cost of stopping Pol Pot). All that matters is that the agent knew that (1) was the case and acted on condition of (1)—because (1) necessarily accompanied or was necessary to the achievement of the intervener's bad aim. So, if stopping Pol Pot's crimes was a just cause of war *and* the harm of Vietnam's domination was proportionate to the realization of the just cause (Pol Pot's crime-ending), then, for Kamm, the intervention was justified.

I confess that I hesitate to follow Kamm here, although I do not have a conclusive argument against her position. Since Kamm relies on her intuitions on the matter, I will consult my own intuition: an action that simultaneously causes good and bad effects can be so tainted by evil intent that it ought to be impermissible even if that action would, as a side effect, produce a good result that *would* justify the bad result *if* the action carried an altruistic or neutral intent. After all, humanitarian intervention is concerned with *freeing* persons from harm, that is, restoring in some sense their freedom. If this is so, then the intent to wield tyrannical power for the foreseeable future seems, in some sense, to contradict the realization of the just cause. Put differently: perhaps the just cause of ending a massacre is not an isolated factor that should be considered divorced from broader liberty concerns. As Mill argued, someone who rescues a person in danger only to inflict new suffering to the victim has not performed an act of rescue. Similarly, perhaps the act by the Vietnamese government of rescuing the Cambodians from Pol Pot was not an act of humanitarian intervention, given that the Vietnamese inflicted their own tyrannical rule. The idea is that a self-regarding motive such as securing oil is not in tension with ending tyranny, but establishing a less severe tyranny *is* in tension with ending the more severe tyranny. This means that humanitarian interveners should be held to a higher standard on the question of intending evil. We have, then, an important dichotomy with respect of right intent. As I argued in this chapter, the just humanitarian intervener need not have the *just cause* at the core of his intent. But this is different from allowing an intervener to *directly intend evil.* The latter, but not the former, is incompatible with the justice of humanitarian intervention.

Still, Mill's analysis is of dubious application here, because in Mill's example the harm visited by the evil rescuer is equal or worse than the harm from which the person was rescued. In the Vietnam–Cambodia case, it is possible to argue that the tyrannical rule established by the Vietnamese was a significantly lesser evil than Pol Pot's killing fields. These kinds of cases resemble the ticking-bomb torture cases, where even the prospect of a massacre is not enough to convince us of the permissibility of torturing the person who has the information that will allow us to prevent the massacre. I find the issue excruciatingly hard. All in all, I endorse the Doctrine of Double Effect's prohibition of intending evil and hesitantly err on the side of condemning governmental wickedness in war, even in those rare cases where such wickedness avoids an even greater evil.

Conclusion

The analysis here affirms the traditional view that intentions matter for the permissibility of action. However, on the matter of the justification of humanitarian intervention, it rejects the simplistic binary view that any time interveners exhibit self-interested motivations, their action will be automatically disqualified as humanitarian intervention. It also rejects the less simplistic view that humanitarian motives must somehow predominate over other motives in other to make the action permissible. Rather, the article recognizes that the intentional structure of an agent can be quite complex in the sense that the humanitarian rationale may show various degrees of intensity. Several of those situations entail the permissibility of acting. Finally, my analysis does not enlarge the class of permissible military interventions in any significant way. This is because humanitarian interventions, like all wars, are subject to double constraint of the *existence* of the just cause and, crucially, the requirement of proportionality. Right intent is entirely parasitic on the first requirement. And the second requirement, that humanitarian interventions not cause excessive damage, is quite difficult to satisfy.

Notes

1 Thomas Aquinas, *Political Writings* (Cambridge: Cambridge University Press, 2002), 241.

2 Alex J. Bellamy, "Motives, Outcomes, Intent, and the Legitimacy of Humanitarian Intervention," *Journal of Military Ethics*, 3, no. 3 (2004): 227. See also George R. Lucas, Jr, "From Jus ad Bellum to Jus ad Pacem: Rethinking Just War Criteria for the Use of Military Force for Humanitarian Ends," in *Ethics and Foreign Intervention*, ed. Deen K. Chaterjee and Don E. Scheid (Cambridge: Cambridge University Press, 2003), 87.

3 C. A. J. Coady, "The Ethics of Armed Humanitarian Intervention," The Institute for Peace, 2002, at http://www.usip.org/publications/the-ethics-armed-humanitarian-intervention, 19.

4 R2P Report, 35–36.

5 I discuss the issue of categorization in Fernando R. Tesón, "Ending Tyranny in Iraq," *Ethics and International Affairs*, 19 (2005): 1–20. Helen Frowe also thinks that the issues of categorization and permissibility are different. Helen Frowe, "Judging Armed Humanitarian Intervention," in *The Ethics of Armed Humanitarian Intervention*, ed. Don Scheid (Cambridge: Cambridge University Press, 2014), 96.

6 Cécile Fabre, *Cosmopolitan War* (Oxford: Oxford University Press, 2012), 166.

7 David Rodin, *War, Aggression, and Self-Defence* (Oxford: Oxford University Press, 2003), 131. See my reply, Fernando R. Tesón, "Self-Defense in International Law and Rights of Persons," *Ethics and International Affairs*, 18 (2004): 87–91.

8 Michael Walzer, "The Moral Standing of States: A Response to Four Critics," *Philosophy and Public Affairs*, 9 (1980): 209–229.

9 Allen Buchanan, "Institutionalizing the Just War," *Philosophy and Public Affairs*, 34 (2006): 2–38.

10 I develop this unified theory of just cause in Fernando R. Tesón and Loren Lomasky, *Justice at a Distance: Extending Freedom Globally* (Cambridge: Cambridge University Press, 2015), chapter 8; and in Fernando R. Tesón and Bas van der Vossen, *Debating Humanitarian Intervention* (Oxford: Oxford University Press, 2017), chapter 2.

11 See, e.g., Kenneth Roth, "Was the Iraq War a Humanitarian Intervention?," *Journal of Military Ethics*, 5 (2006): 84–92.

12 See Tesón, *Humanitarian Intervention*, 374–390.

13 See F. M. Kamm, *Ethics for Enemies: Terror, Torture, and War* (Oxford: Oxford University Press, 2011), 124–128.

14 A discussion of the Bangladesh war can be found in my *Humanitarian Intervention*, 242–253.

15 See Nicholas Wheeler, *Saving Strangers: Humanitarian Intervention in International Society* (Oxford: Oxford University Press, 2000), 78–110.

16 Because of this complexity, I do not endorse James Pattison's requirement that an intervener "must have the predominant *purpose* of preventing, reducing or halting actual or impending loss of lives and human suffering, whatever the underlying *reasons* or motives, for doing so." Pattison, *Humanitarian Intervention and the Responsibility to Protect: Who Should Intervene?* (Oxford: Oxford University Press, 2012), 161 (emphasis in the original). How predominant the purpose is will vary, as the typology in the text shows.

17 For a discussion, see Fernando R. Tesón and Bas van der Vossen, *Debating Humanitarian Intervention: Should We Try to Save Strangers?* (Oxford: Oxford University Press, 2017), appendix to Part I.

18 John Stuart Mill, *Utilitarianism*, ed. Roger Crisp (Oxford: Oxford University Press, 1998), 65.

19 Here, I follow Michael Ridge, "Mill's Intention and Motives," *Utilitas*, 14 (2002): 54.

20 Pattison disputes my claim that the coalition in Iraq had a humanitarian intent, namely the intent of removing Saddam; Pattison, *Humanitarian Intervention and the Responsibility to Protect*, 173–176. But this overlooks my definition of intent, which is the intent to perform an action even if that is as a *means* to bring about something else. On this definition, it is plain that the Coalition intended to overthrow Saddam as a means to whatever else they wanted to achieve. Pattison's argument, it seems to me, is different, and it has nothing to do with intent. He does not (and cannot) really question that the coalition intended to remove Saddam. Rather, to him, removing Saddam was not a just cause. See especially page 175. My defense of the war in Iraq can be found in Fernando R. Tesón, "Ending Tyranny in Iraq," *Ethics and International Affairs*, 19 (2005): 1–19.

21 Kamm, *Ethics for Enemies*, 119–120. Notice that Kamm's standard is stronger than (c) above, because it says that the agent act on condition that the just cause will occur. As Kamm says, there is a difference between oblique intention (knowledge and foresight but not direct intention) and oblique intention *plus* the agent's acting *on condition* that the just cause occur. The difference between the two is that in one case the side effect, while foreseeable, is not a condition of acting, while in the other case the side effect is a

condition of acting. I do not treat this case separately because I think it falls between (b) and (c) above, and can be assimilated to either.

22 Kamm distinguishes between the goal of an action and the condition of an action. That someone acts on condition of X need not mean that he acts with the intention of bringing about X. The object of his intent may be Y. But, as Kamm puts it, the condition of an action "can provide a nongoal reason to act because it defeats a potential defeater of an act undertaken for a reason that is a goal." Ibid., 126.

23 A recent account of the events, largely from the British side, can be found in Martin Middlebrook, *The Falklands War* (Barnsley, UK: Pen and Sword, 2012). For an Argentine perspective, see Rosana Gruber, *¿Por qué Malvinas? De la causa nacional a la guerra absurda* (Mexico City: Fondo de cultura económica, 2013).

24 A full analysis of conditional causes can be found in Tesón and Van der Vossen, *Debating Humanitarian Intervention*, chapter 2.

25 This is consistent with saying (1) that the war could be justified as self-defense and (2) that Margaret Thatcher unwittingly rendered a great service to Argentina. Kamm discusses cases like this one, where the occurrence of the just cause is more radically divorced from the intervener's intent. Kamm, *Ethics for Enemies*, 128–130.

26 Mill, *Utilitarianism*, 6.

27 Kamm, *Ethics for Enemies*, 122–123.

PART VI

Environment, health and migration: the ethics of vulnerability

THE ETHICS OF VULNERABILITY IN INTERNATIONAL RELATIONS

Debra L. DeLaet

Introduction[1]

Notions of vulnerability are at the center of conversations about ethics in international relations. The discipline's focus on issues of war, peace, and security, the global economy and poverty, and international law and human rights inevitably involve ethical considerations. Whether or not global ethics are explicitly identified as a central concern, the study of international relations raises fundamental questions about obligations to protect populations from physical violence, duties to mitigate global poverty, and mechanisms for pursuing justice in response to various forms of violence in the international system. Ethical inquiry in the field of international relations (IR) is grounded in constitutive assumptions about the groups in particular need of protection and the actors with the capacity and obligation to protect. In this way, vulnerability—a concept framed by some scholars as a condition of liability to harm[2]—becomes central to considerations of ethics in IR. Indeed, global ethics have involved, to a large extent, efforts to delineate categories of the vulnerable and to prescribe appropriate responses to conditions of vulnerability.

Examinations of the ethics of war focus on questions connected, either implicitly or explicitly, to the concept of vulnerability. In just war theory, for example, the protection of innocent life is a fundamental criterion that needs to be met for a war to be considered just. The just war tradition also requires that wars be conducted in a manner that distinguishes between combatants and non-combatants and that minimizes disproportionate harm to civilian life and institutions. The contemporary Responsibility to Protect Doctrine, likewise, asserts both that states have the responsibility to protect their populations from genocide, war crimes, ethnic cleansing, and crimes against humanity, and that institutions within the United Nations system also have a responsibility to protect. In the context of wartime violence and mass atrocity, attributions of innocence and civilian status tend to be associated with presumed vulnerability, conceived as a state in which designated individuals or populations (e.g., the innocent, civilians) are particularly susceptible to unjustifiable harm from violence. Sociocultural factors, such as race, ethnicity, and gender, fundamentally determine whether innocence and vulnerability are attributed to specific populations facing violence. The widely used trope of "innocent women and children" in discourses on war throughout much of human history is a prominent case in point.[3]

IR scholarship on global economics also reflects assumptions about the presumed vulnerability of specific territories and populations. IR has historically relied on hierarchical categorizations of the global economy (e.g., First, Second, and Third Worlds; developed versus developing countries; high-income, middle-income, and low-income countries; the Global North and the Global South). Such categorizations tend to locate the responsibility for ethical action in centers of power and wealth, and to identify the populations in need of remediation and aid as existing at the periphery. As in the case of war and mass atrocity, ethical inquiry in IR commonly has unacknowledged underpinnings in assumptions about a gendered and racialized political order, with predominantly white, wealthy actors in high-income states "acting ethically" on behalf of "the vulnerable" (typically non-white populations, with women often serving as the ultimate signifiers of vulnerability) outside of global centers of political and economic power and wealth. Postcolonial critiques reveal the racialized nature of global development aid and traditional conceptualizations of vulnerability in the global economy.[4]

Questions related to global ethics also are at the core of scholarship on human rights in international relations. At the most basic level, human rights invoke moral and legal claims that are universal in nature; the idea that fundamental rights belong to all human beings infers the unquestionably universal nature of such claims. Indeed, widespread global consensus about the universality of human rights exists, as evidenced by the 1993 Vienna Declaration on Human Rights stating that "[t]he universal nature of these rights and freedoms is beyond question."[5] Despite widespread agreement about the universality of human rights in the abstract, the interpretation and implementation of these universal human rights is filtered through particular sociocultural frameworks, which helps to explain the significant gap between universal legal claims and disparate human rights outcomes. As in the case of ethical inquiry on war and the global economy, the contested nature of human rights reveals the way in which notions of vulnerability are shaped by race, ethnicity, and gender. The disparate treatment of female genital cutting and male genital cutting under international human rights law, even when comparing cutting practices that involve comparable degrees of physiological invasiveness and that are driven by similar cultural rationales, reveals that constructions of vulnerability remain central to ethical considerations in human rights scholarship.[6]

As these brief examples suggest, the study of ethics in international relations—while sometimes viewed as being wholly distinct from power-based perspectives in the discipline—remains linked in significant ways to socio-economic and political power structures. Furthermore, the claim that explicit investigations of ethics in international relations serve as a corrective to purportedly non-normative approaches in the field elides the reality that the distinction between ethical and "rational" or empirical approaches in the discipline is not clear and bright. All theoretical and methodological approaches to the study of international relations involve normative assumptions and frameworks. Likewise, the study of ethics in international relations has been fundamentally shaped by power dynamics and sociocultural factors, acknowledged or otherwise.

Ethical frameworks applied to the central concerns of international relations—war and peace, wealth and poverty, rights, law, and justice—may unintentionally replicate the systems of power and wealth that they seek to investigate with a critical eye. In both scholarship and practice, the ethical obligation to act (or not) in response to violence, global poverty, human rights violations, and other global issues remains the prerogative of the powerful and the privileged. The intended beneficiaries of policies formulated within a global ethics framework are presumed to be the innocent, the poor, the marginalized—the vulnerable. Shaped by dichotomous distinctions between the powerful and the vulnerable, much of the scholarship on ethics in international relations treats vulnerability as a given. Accordingly, ethical inquiry in IR often starts from the premise that the key consideration is examining the obligations that certain actors (the powerful, the wealthy, the privileged) have to address and rectify the vulnerability of others. However, the concept of vulnerability itself can be subjected to ethical interrogation. A growing body of scholarship in vulnerability studies indicates that vulnerability is a contested concept rather than a given condition. Critical evaluations of the uses and potential misuses of an ethics of vulnerability reveal the ways that the concept of vulnerability can actually reinforce violent power structures, socio-economic inequities, and systemic injustices.

This Part of the Handbook critically investigates the ethics of vulnerability as a framework for understanding a range of global issues, including migration, global health, the environment, and climate change, that have fundamental implications for the longevity and quality of human life and for the health of the planet. In examining the genuine challenges to human security and wellbeing arising from transnational migration, globalized health disparities, and global climate change, this section also considers economic, political, and social construction of vulnerability. The chapters in this Part examine the ways in which vulnerability is perceived and experienced based on constructions of vulnerability around markers of race/ethnicity, gender, socio-economic class, age, and geopolitical space. Taken together, the chapters in this Part reveal how an ethics grounded in the concept of vulnerability may itself produce or entrench categorical distinctions between "the vulnerable" and "invulnerable" in ways that mask or perpetuate the underlying causes of violence, inequity, and injustice across the globe. The chapters also challenge characterizations of marginalized populations as passively dependent on ethical action by powerful external actors for mitigation of their vulnerability. Instead, the chapters show that populations characterized as vulnerable play an active role in challenging conditions of vulnerability and exhibit substantial resilience in the process.

Constructing vulnerability, constructing ethics

A brief overview of the emergence of an ethics of vulnerability framework reveals the contested and constructed nature of vulnerability as a concept. Much of the work on vulnerability has been done in the field of moral philosophy and political theory. It also has been a major focus of discussion in feminist theory, especially in work on dependency and care ethics, and bioethicists and legal theorists also have devoted significant attention to the concept of vulnerability.[7] Despite the fact that notions of vulnerability fundamentally connect to core issues in the discipline, IR scholars have only recently begun robust investigations into the concept of vulnerability and its applicability to understanding global ethics.[8]

The contested meaning of vulnerability

At the most fundamental level, vulnerability can be defined as a susceptibility or liability to harm.[9] Defined in this way, vulnerability can take many forms and has a range of causes. Catriona Mackenzie, Wendy Rogers, and Susan Dodds suggest a taxonomy of vulnerability that identifies three primary sources of susceptibility to harm. *Inherent* vulnerability is an intrinsic feature of the human condition grounded in human corporeality and our inherent existence as part of basic social structures of care and dependence. *Situational* vulnerability describes susceptibility to harm stemming from particular economic, environmental, political, and social contexts. Finally, *pathogenic* vulnerability describes entrenched susceptibility to harm that is embedded in dysfunctional social relationships or systemic patterns of exclusion and inequity that place certain people in persistent risk of serious harm.[10]

Although threats of harm may take either physical or emotional forms, much of the literature on vulnerability stresses the embodied nature of susceptibility to harm. In this conceptualization, "the capacity to suffer that is inherent in human embodiment" is a defining feature of vulnerability.[11] Alasdair MacIntyre,[12] Martha Fineman,[13] Bryan Turner,[14] and others prominently stress the corporeal nature of human vulnerability. For these theorists, the inherent susceptibility of the human body to harm indicates that vulnerability is a universal human condition. Judith Butler also emphasizes the corporeal nature of vulnerability but diverges from other scholars in her treatment of vulnerability as a condition that implies not exclusively a liability to harm but also broader susceptibility to change via social relationships. Butler's broad conception of vulnerability contrasts with her concept of precariousness, more narrowly focused on the inherent fragility of life and the susceptibility to harm from the actions of others. In contrast to this conception of precariousness focused on harm and risk, vulnerability has indeterminate effects that can include an openness to being positively affected and changed by others as well as harmed. In Butler's view, vulnerability also encompasses the potential for agency and resilience rather than passive acceptance of the risks of harm.[15] Erinn Gilson builds on Butler's broadened conception of vulnerability by explicitly delineating the positive values and potential benefits that stem from an acknowledgment of universal, shared vulnerability.[16]

Whether conceptualized in negative or positive terms, the concept of vulnerability provides the possibility of reorienting prevailing discussions about how to respond to political violence, structural inequity, and human rights violations in the international system.[17] The emphasis on vulnerability as a universal condition is more likely to point to cooperative, shared responses to global challenges. Accordingly, an ethics of vulnerability challenges the prevailing conceptual emphasis on autonomy, sovereignty, self-interest, and power in much of the scholarship on international relations.[18]

Tensions between vulnerability and security as frameworks for understanding global issues

The concept of vulnerability contrasts with the concept of security as a framework for understanding and responding to global issues. In the IR field, the concept of security has been broadened from a narrow state-centric vision of national security to a broad, individualized conception of human security that encompasses almost every realm of human experience and has been applied to a wide range of global issues, including terrorism, international migration, health, human rights, and the environment. Discursive frameworks that emphasize security (either conceptualized as national or human security) have constitutive effects that sustain threat-based conceptions of politics and governance that are more likely to generate militarized policy responses. The securitization of global issues, in turn, shifts public resources towards militarized actors and risks reinforcing exclusionary politics that produce discrimination, stigma, and paternalistic policies towards marginalized populations.[19] Whereas preoccupations with security can produce zero-sum approaches to global challenges, an emphasis on shared vulnerability points to the possibility of cooperative, positive-sum responses to these challenges.

The tension between security and vulnerability as conceptual frameworks for understanding and responding to global issues is evident in the field of global health. Global health initiatives, both in historical and contemporary contexts, typically involve efforts to contain communicable diseases via policies and regulations that reinforce and strengthen territorial and socio-economic borders. Statist approaches to global health challenges emphasize the threat that communicable illnesses pose to the security and stability of states and, accordingly, emphasize efforts to contain health threats through measures intended to regulate the movement of people, goods, and, thereby, germs across borders. In contrast, a vulnerability framework emphasizes solutions that address the root causes of global health challenges and prioritize serving the populations most immediately threatened by disease. (See Elizabeth Mills in Chapter 26.)

In a similar vein, global responses to economic, political, and social challenges stemming from migration vary depending on whether they are grounded in a security or vulnerability framework. Securitized responses to international migration fundamentally depict migrants as potential threats to security. Thus, a security framework prioritizes statist responses that involve the regulation and control of territorial borders. Conversely, a vulnerability framework focuses on the factors that drive international migration and is more likely to identify the potential benefits as well as the potential costs of migration in ways that blur the presumed rigidity of territorial and socio-economic borders. (See Michele L. Statz in Chapter 25.)

In regards to global environmental challenges, likewise, a vulnerability framework is more likely to point in the direction of shared, cooperative solutions than a security framework. A security approach to global environmental challenges is most likely to emphasize statist responses to environmental threats. Given the distribution of power in the international system, statist dynamics will reflect the interests and preferences of the most powerful states. Instead, a vulnerability framework stresses the ways in which all people share vulnerability to global environmental threats. Although such an approach does not guarantee global cooperation, it points to the need for and possibility of cooperative, positive-sum responses. (See Chapters 27 and 28, by Tabitha M. Benney and Carol Farbotko, respectively.)

The inequitable distribution and social construction of vulnerability

Although vulnerability is a universal human condition and feature of social life, not all human beings experience its effects equally. Some populations are *more* vulnerable to the actions of others because prevailing global political and economic structures produce heightened risks of susceptibility to harm from political violence, economic inequity, social exclusion, and environmental threats for marginalized populations.[20] Robert E. Goodin recognizes the uneven distribution of vulnerability and refers to such forms of vulnerability as socially conditioned. Because he views vulnerability as relational, he argues that humans have special responsibilities to protect those who are especially vulnerable to their actions.[21] Similarly, Butler distinguishes precariousness—the fragility and insecurity inherent in human life—from precarity, the politically conditioned experience of precariousness. All human life exists in a state of precariousness, but we are more likely to recognize the precariousness of the lives we value more.[22]

A recognition of the uneven distribution of vulnerability helps to draw attention to the political and socio-economic structures that produce it. In this way, a relational, social view of vulnerability helps to illuminate its causes and to clarify the ethical responsibilities of actors whose actions place other groups of people at heightened risk of susceptibility to harm. However, placing the uneven distribution of vulnerability at the center of ethical analysis also risks reproducing or exacerbating the very conditions that place some populations in harm's way. Fineman, for example, argues that the classification of certain populations as particularly vulnerable can lead to the identification of these groups with "victimhood, deprivation, dependency, or pathology."[23] In turn, such characterizations can elicit discriminatory, stigmatizing, and paternalistic responses and the attendant harms that typically accompany such exclusionary politics. Further, narrow applications of vulnerability to certain populations can inappropriately divert attention from the structural causes of violence and inequity and can perpetuate entrenched, economic, political, and social hierarchies.[24]

At the macro level, Ian Clark identifies global society as one of the key international determinants of what he refers to as social vulnerability. Clark identifies ideational structures and global norms themselves as a primary cause of the heightened risk of harm experienced by some populations in international society. He argues that global society's framing of and responses to global problems affect the relative distribution of susceptibility to harm in the international system. To this effect, "international society is not always the author of the underlying problem but, in the way that it intervenes, it certainly becomes the author of its moral consequences."[25] Even when motivated by seemingly altruistic intentions, powerful actors in global society are implicated in the production of vulnerability for other actors in the international system.

According to Clark, an ethics of vulnerability provides an integrative framework for understanding a range of global issues with seemingly disparate causes and implications. War, climate change, transnational migration, and global health represent distinct policy arenas linked by common dynamics in which the framing of particular groups as vulnerable heightens their likelihood of being exposed to harm.[26] Global norms governing the legitimate use of violence reflect the values and interests of the most powerful actors in the international system and render certain populations more liable to harm from legitimated forms of violence.[27] The international legal regime on climate change has institutionalized a dichotomy between powerful actors and vulnerable populations that does not recognize the most powerful actors in the international system as the primary source of susceptibility to harm from climate change.[28] In the case of international migration and refugees, the international laws that codify the refugee as a legal category of persons deserving of protection ultimately defer to sovereignty and the right of states to regulate their territorial borders via exclusionary national laws.[29] Likewise, international norms governing global health have legitimated an uneven distribution of vulnerability through an emphasis on efforts to regulate health problems that are perceived as significant threats to powerful actors rather than the challenges that pose the greatest risks to human health across the globe.[30]

In seeking to establish regimes of protection in these various policy areas, international society simultaneously creates, reinforces, and legitimates patterns of vulnerability.[31] Notably, significant linkages across these global issues exist. Thus, increases in the susceptibility to harm in one area simultaneously amplify the risks in other areas.[32] International society's construction of vulnerability—representing an ostensible effort to prioritize ethics—actually reveals and replicates the power dynamics of more traditionally statist, rationalist understandings of international relations.

Erinn Gilson's recent work, grounded in feminist theory and social and ethical philosophy, offers a potential corrective to the constitutive dynamics that, to date, have shaped the ethics of vulnerability in international relations. Gilson cautions against models of vulnerability that "fail to account for how peoples' vulnerabilities can be exacerbated by the very mechanisms designed to protect or aid them."[33]

Gilson contests a negative conception of vulnerability that associates it exclusively with susceptibility to harm. Conceived in purely negative terms, vulnerability denotes "injury, weakness, dependency, powerlessness, incapacity, deficiency, and passivity."[34] A negative understanding of vulnerability identifies invulnerability as the desired state. In so doing, it projects vulnerability onto other people and groups as a form of renunciation and self-protection. In turn, the pursuit of invulnerability prevents the kind of openness and awareness required for actors to broaden their sense of ethical responsibility towards others.[35]

In contrast to this negative formulation, Gilson argues for a recognition of the positive features of vulnerability, including care and dependency, as inherently valuable conditions in social life. Gilson reconceives vulnerability as a pervasive, immanent condition inherent in everyday life that produces potential benefits as well as potential harms. Rather than being a marginal condition, vulnerability is an essential part of human experience, for everyone. This positive conceptualization, according to Gilson, helps to create an ethical disposition that intentionally embraces vulnerability as a tool for challenging inequitable power relationships and structural injustices.[36] Drawing on Butler's work, Gilson imagines vulnerability as a universal, shared condition that can generate an openness to an expanded sense of community that, in turn, undergirds a broadened sense of ethical responsibility towards others.[37]

This brief overview of the ethics of vulnerability reveals larger tensions at stake in this approach to ethics in international relations. On the one hand, the concept of vulnerability draws attention to patterns of violence and deep-seated structural inequities in global politics. As a result, an ethics of vulnerability framework can be used to mobilize support for the idea that actors with the capacity to redress these challenges have an ethical responsibility to do so. On the other hand, the concept of vulnerability risks reinforcing deficit views of populations at heightened risk of harm from violence and inequity. It further risks creating, sustaining, and reproducing exclusionary politics that amplify the voices, viewpoints, and preferences of powerful and wealthy actors at the expense of populations with less political, economic, and social power. In doing so, an ethics of vulnerability risks underestimating the resilience of populations that have been characterized as vulnerable and undermining their agency. Indeed, recent feminist work on vulnerability suggests that genuinely ethical responses to the challenges at stake in these discussions require recognizing and enabling marginalized populations' capacities for autonomy rather than reinforcing a dichotomous view of autonomy versus vulnerability that assumes that ethical action is primarily the purview of the powerful and the privileged.[38]

Overview of theme

A conceptual shift from a primary focus on sovereignty, autonomy, and power to vulnerability, dependency, and care necessarily reorients the lens through which scholars examine ethical issues in international relations. However, with the prominent exception of Clark's work, scholars working within the disciplinary traditions of IR and political science have not engaged as broadly or deeply with the concept of vulnerability as scholars in other disciplines, including philosophy, legal studies, and anthropology. Thus, an investigation of the ethics of vulnerability in international relations requires attention to work on vulnerability in other disciplines. Accordingly, the chapters in this section represent a variety of disciplines, including political science, anthropology, and cultural geography. The incorporation of diverse disciplinary perspectives and work from scholars from different regions of the world strives to ensure that this examination of the ethics of vulnerability includes viewpoints representing populations that have been characterized as vulnerable rather than only the perspectives of powerful actors deemed as primarily responsible for ethical action. Ultimately, this decentering of an ethics of vulnerability framework itself represents an effort to be attentive to the ethical issues involved in scholarly inquiry.

With this goal in mind, this section critically examines the processes by which the scholarly treatment of presumed vulnerabilities can be constitutive and can reproduce violence, human insecurity, and socio-economic inequities when the perspectives of scholars and practitioners from relatively privileged populations drive scholarly dialogues and policy discussions. To avoid such exclusionary dynamics, the chapters for this Part have been authored by scholars from diverse disciplinary backgrounds and emphasize the perspectives of populations that have been characterized as vulnerable.

The section's first chapter, by Michele L. Statz, explores transnational migration and vulnerability. Writing from the perspective of sociocultural anthropology, Statz focuses on the vulnerabilities experienced by—and assigned to—global youth in the context of transnational migration. Today, there are more than 244 million international migrants, a 41% increase since

2000. Of this population, an estimated 53 million individuals are under the age of 25. Though the transnational migration of children and youth is not a new phenomenon, it commands a great deal of policy and media attention owing to these migrants' age and corresponding presumptions of vulnerability. Firmly acknowledging the *simultaneity* of transnationalism—i.e., that the daily life of transnational migrants simultaneously incorporates and responds to multiple states and social institutions—Statz's chapter calls for a nuanced recognition of the simultaneous forms of vulnerability migrant youth experience, encounter, and embody. It does so by turning to more pervasive and decontextualized designations of vulnerability, namely occasions when young migrants are framed in policy and media discourse as exclusively dependent children and as victims of political processes, state abandonment, kin, or culture. To accentuate the victimhood of a young person in this way raises necessary questions about the ethics of vulnerability in the context of transnational migration. For one, is there such a thing as "ordinary ethics" when a young migrant's vulnerability must be sufficiently—or selectively—amplified to elicit attention, sympathy, and political action? What does this reveal about other "explicitly ethical" questions, including those of citizenship and bare life, rights and protection, security and care, age, disaster, and displacement? And finally, what are the consequences, both intimate and international, of prioritizing the language of vulnerability?

In exploring answers to these questions, Statz calls for a re-imagining of transnational migration and the presumptions of vulnerability associated with it. Such a re-imagining requires a recognition of the multiplicity of territories, identities, needs, goals, and obligations that shape the experiences of migrant youth. It further requires scholars and practitioners to critically consider the uses and misuses of a discourse of vulnerability as applied to youth. The chapter ultimately suggests that uncritical assignations of vulnerability to global youth divert attention from other vulnerabilities that can be masked through discourses of "care" and "rights." Statz concludes that an ethics of vulnerability, properly framed, must recognize that global youth, and other populations that have been designated as vulnerable, have a multitude of experiences that involve challenges that have come to be associated with the concept of vulnerability but that also reflect their resilience and agency in the face of these challenges.

Grounded in the discipline of medical anthropology, Mills's chapter on global health and vulnerability in the era of AIDS explores vulnerability as a corollary of global health. Her chapter draws on critical scholarship that focuses on the fragile consensus among global health scholars that a commitment to improved and equitable health for all represents a fundamental principle of research and practice in the field. Drawing on recent work in the field of vulnerability studies, particularly linked to and extending Judith Butler's notion of precarity and Clark and Gilson's critiques of (in-) vulnerability, this chapter situates twelve months of ethnographic research on HIV in South Africa and Brazil alongside the evolution in critical global health studies. Through detailed accounts drawn from visual and participatory research methods, Mills describes calls made by study participants in South Africa and Brazil for policymakers and scholars to understand how global institutions can work more effectively to ensure improved and equitable health for all. The ethnographic accounts highlighted in Mills's chapter demonstrate how global institutions are, themselves, implicated in people's embodied vulnerability. The chapter also draws attention to the intersecting forms of inequality, linked to race, class, and gender that undermine improved and equitable health—with a focus on access to AIDS medicines—across the scale from the molecular to the global.

Drawing on this ethnographic research in South Africa, alongside qualitative and secondary research in Brazil and India, this chapter situates current debates in global health in light of the networked threads that weave HIV-positive women's embodied vulnerability into the governance of biomedical technologies and the technologies of governance. Mills's chapter challenges static, dichotomous conceptions of vulnerability that draw a distinct line between the vulnerable and invulnerable and that treat the condition of vulnerability as a given. On the one hand, Mills's research shows that a range of actors that regulate access to life-sustaining medicines, including national governments and international organizations, contribute to the vulnerability of HIV-positive women. At the same time, the active engagement of study participants in her fieldwork reveals that "the vulnerable" play an active role in advocating for access to essential medical therapies. In the process, the women featured in this chapter demonstrate agency and resilience in the face of vulnerability.

Tabitha M. Benney, a political scientist, highlights the constructed nature of vulnerability in her chapter on climate change and sustainable development. Noting that a disproportionate share of the effects of climate change are experienced by some of the most vulnerable countries and populations, Benney indicates that the primary ethical challenges related to the global environment are the inequitable distribution of the negative effects of climate change and the lack of resources necessary to adapt. Benney's chapter also underscores that the burdens of climate change are especially challenging for the most vulnerable populations because of their intrinsic connections to global economics and other sociopolitical issues.

As such, ethical responses to global environmental challenges cannot be disentangled from ethical considerations related to economic development, global health, and other global issues related to human wellbeing. Because of the interconnected nature of these global challenges, sustainable development is an appropriate framework for exploring potential solutions to a range of global issues. To this end, Benney uses an ethics of vulnerability framework to explore the complex linkages that characterize the environmental, social, and economic effects of climate change policies on vulnerable populations in countries pursuing economic development. Benney's chapter examines the real vulnerabilities faced by disadvantaged populations. At the same time, the chapter highlights the ways in which vulnerability is constructed along racialized and gendered lines and, thus, serves to reproduce inequities in international relations.

In her chapter, Carol Farbotko, a cultural geographer, explores the vulnerability, agency, and resilience of island populations in the face of climate change. Island populations contribute negligible amounts to global greenhouse gas emissions, yet the effects of climate change are likely to be significant in small island states, compounding existing development challenges. This widely acknowledged inequity for island populations has been ineffectively addressed in international climate change agreements, although leaders of small island states have pursued early and deep engagement in the climate change negotiations, spurred by the prospect of sea level rise rendering their territories uninhabitable. With international climate frameworks dominated by fossil-fuel-intensive nation-states, the concerns of small island populations have remained marginal. In particular, the question of future uninhabitable territory has not been answered, in part due to the focus on mitigation by small island state leaders themselves.

When addressed in terms of international policy, uninhabitable territory has been framed largely as an issue of migration, with broader political and legal issues such as sovereignty often neglected. The focus on migration, moreover, raises questions about the agency of potentially affected island populations, who recognize the vulnerability of their territory but tend to question proffered solutions based on protection for "climate refugees." Grassroots activism on climate change in small island states is vibrant, however, suggesting significant cultural and political resilience specifically tuned to the challenge of future uninhabitable territory among small island populations.

Notes

1 I would like to express my gratitude to Brent Steele and Eric Heinze for their vision and leadership in coordinating this project. The October 2015 workshop at the University of Utah that they organized for section editors of this Handbook was a rich and engaging scholarly experience, and I am grateful to have had the opportunity to participate. I also want to express my gratitude to the University of Utah and to the Hinckley Institute of Politics at the University of Utah for their support of the workshop. I would like to thank Patricia and Daniel Jorndt for their great generosity in creating the David E. Maxwell Distinguished Professorship in International Affairs at Drake University. With support from this professorship, I was able to attend the February 2017 conference on Vulnerability and the Politics of Care at the British Academy in London, a conference that significantly expanded my understanding of the ethics of vulnerability in international relations. Finally, I am grateful to the contributors for their thoughtful, engaging scholarship. I have learned a great deal from each of you.

2 Ian Clark, *The Vulnerable in International Society* (Oxford: Oxford University Press, 2013), 3.

3 Jean Bethke Elshtain, *Women and War* (Chicago: University of Chicago Press, 1995), 3–13; R. Charli Carpenter, *'Innocent Women and Children': Gender, Norms and the Protection of Civilians* (New York and London: Routledge, 2006).

4 Siba N. Grovogui, "A Hermeneutics of Race in International Theory," *Alternatives*, 26 (2001): 425–448; Paulette Goudge, *The Whiteness of Power: Racism in Third World Development and Aid* (London: Lawrence and Wishart, 2003); Robert Vitalis, *White World Order, Black Power Politics* (Ithaca and London: Cornell University Press, 2015).

5 World Conference on Human Rights, *Vienna Declaration and Programme of Action*, June 25, 1993, http://www.ohchr.org/EN/ProfessionalInterest/Pages/Vienna.aspx.

6 Robert Darby and J. Steven Svoboda, "A Rose by Any Other Name? Rethinking the Similarities and Differences between Male and Female Genital Cutting," *Medical Anthropology*, 21, no. 3 (2007): 301–323; Debra L. DeLaet, "Framing Male Circumcision as a Human Rights Issue?: Contributions to the Debate over the Universality of Human Rights," *Journal of Human Rights*, 8, no. 4 (2009): 405–426; Richard A. Shweder, "The Goose and the Gander: The Genital Wars," *Global Discourse*, 3, no. 2 (2013): 348–366;

7 Catriona Mackenzie, Wendy Rogers, and Susan Dodds, eds., *Vulnerability: New Essays in Ethics and Feminist Philosophy* (Oxford: Oxford University Press, 2014), 2.

8 Clark, *Vulnerable in Global Society*.

9 Robert E. Goodin, *Protecting the Vulnerable: A Reanalysis of Our Social Responsibilities* (Chicago: University of Chicago Press, 1985), 110; Clark, *Vulnerable in Global Society*, 3.

10 Mackenzie, Rogers, and Dodds, *Vulnerability*, 7–9.

11 Ibid., 4.

12 Alisdair MacIntyre, *Dependent Rational Animals: Why Human Beings Need the Virtues* (Chicago: Open Court, 1999).

13 Martha A. Fineman, "The Vulnerable Subject: Anchoring Equality in the Human Condition," *Yale Journal of Law and Feminism*, 20, no. 1 (2008): 1–23.

14 Bryan S. Turner, *Vulnerability and Human Rights* (University Park, Pennsylvania: The Pennsylvania State University Press, 2006).

15 Judith Butler, *Precarious Life: The Powers of Mourning and Violence* (London: Verso, 2004); Judith Butler, *Giving an Account of Oneself* (New York: Fordham, 2005); Judith Butler, *Frames of War: When Is Life Grievable?* (New York: Verso, 2009).

16 Erinn C. Gilson, *The Ethics of Vulnerability: A Feminist Analysis of Social Life and Practice* (New York: Routledge, 2014).

17 Fineman, "Vulnerable Subject"; Goodin, *Vulnerability and Human Rights*, 1.

18 Mackenzie, Rogers, and Dodds, *Vulnerability*, 4.

19 Debra L. DeLaet, "Whose Interests Is the Securitization of Health Serving?" in *The Routledge Handbook of Global Health Security*, ed. Simon Rushton and Jeremy Youde (New York and London: Routledge, 2015): 339–348.

20 Judith Butler, "Performativity, Precarity and Sexual Politics," *AIBR. Revista de Antropología Iberoamericana*, 4, no. 3 (2009), ii, http://www.aibr.org/antropologia/04v03/criticos/040301b.pdf.

21 Goodin, *Protecting the Vulnerable*, 109–117.

22 Butler, *Frames of War*, 22–30.

23 Fineman, "The Vulnerable Subject," 8.

24 Mackenzie, Rogers, and Dodds, *Vulnerability*, 16; Erinn C. Gilson, *The Ethics of Vulnerability*, 31–39; Susan Dodds, "Inclusion and Exclusion in Women's Access to Health and Medicine," *International Journal of Feminist Approaches to Bioethics*, 1, no. 2 (2008): 58–79; Florencia Luna, "Elucidating the Concept of Vulnerability: Layers Not Labels," *International Journal of Feminist Approaches to Bioethics*, 2, no. 1 (2009): 121–139.
25 Clark, *Vulnerable in International Society*, 5.
26 Ibid., 6–8.
27 Ibid., 39–40.
28 Ibid., 77–78.
29 Ibid., 86–89.
30 Ibid., 117–126.
31 Ibid., 26.
32 Ibid., 154.
33 Gilson, *Ethics of Vulnerability*, 29.
34 Ibid., 5.
35 Ibid., 75–85.
36 Ibid., 11.
37 Ibid., 55.
38 Catriona Mackenzie, "The Importance of Relational Autonomy and Capabilities for an Ethics of Vulnerability," *Vulnerability: New Essays in Ethics and Feminist Philosophy*, ed. Catriona Mackenzie, Wendy Rogers, and Susan Dodds (Oxford: Oxford University Press, 2014), 33–59.

25

TRANSNATIONAL MIGRATION AND THE CONSTRUCTION OF VULNERABILITY

Michele L. Statz

Introduction: the vulnerable child migrant

"No wonder the children cry," begins a 2015 article on Hungary's closure of its border with Serbia. "They're thousands of miles from home, wandering from country to country, sleeping on the ground. They have no toys. Some lost their shoes. . ."[1] Entitled "Children Suffering: A True Picture of Europe's Migrant Crisis," the article next describes the closure of its border with Serbia, and follows the above excerpt with a description of the "proportionate police force" used to drive back individuals attempting to cross into Hungary at Horgos, Serbia. The border closure blocked tens of thousands of people from entering the European Union, the article states, most of whom were "fleeing violence in the Middle East."[2] After detailing the tear gas and water cannons police used on migrants, the piece closes with a photo gallery that first warns the viewer of graphic images. Here, we see the bodies of very young migrant children—one photograph depicts a child alone on a vast beach, cradled by a helpless adult, in a coffin. The story is at once devastating and bewildering, unbearably intimate and, yet, hopelessly vague.

"It's hard for anyone to feel alone in the world," begins another news article.[3]

> For children it should be unimaginable. But as Europe's leaders squabble over what should be done about the recent influx of refugees. . . some of the most vulnerable are slipping through the net. The number of children seeking asylum in Europe has gone up almost 74%.[4]

While much could be written about the collapse of historical, political, and socioeconomic context—let alone individual agency—when a migration pattern is so swiftly explained as "fleeing violence in the Middle East," this chapter instead focuses on a more central, though no less complex, image: the vulnerable migrant child. In the above and so many other media and policy reports,[5] the figure of a suffering child is portrayed as wholly representative—the "true picture"—of a migration crisis. It is likewise a critique, signaling the devastating elusiveness of individuals who "slip through the net" of failed international efforts to coordinate, care, and control. It motivates the reader to care, and perhaps also to donate. At its most base interpretation, it sells. Somehow, the figure of a hapless, nameless, and even genderless[6] child explains more, or more powerfully, what it means to migrate. There is little need for context.

What these images also reveal is that the figure of the young migrant—or more specifically, the figure of *the vulnerable child migrant*—does, and arguably *must*, communicate something besides her or his own individual experience. To accentuate the victimhood of a young person in this way raises necessary questions about the ethics of vulnerability in the context of transnational migration. Is there such a thing as "ordinary ethics"[7] when a young migrant's vulnerability must be sufficiently—or selectively—amplified to elicit attention, sympathy, and political action? What are the consequences, both intended and unexpected, when perceptions and designations of "vulnerability" overshadow considerations of rights or resistance?

Image, language, body: the ethics of vulnerability and global youth

As this chapter demonstrates, vulnerability is powerfully implicated in the image of, the language around, and the actual embodiment of global youth. Following Martha Fineman,[8] the characterization of young migrants as inherently vulnerable is a consequential one: by pathologizing a young person's mobility—and, in many ways, the young person herself—as abnormal, the necessarily "sympathetic" response reifies prevailing views of humanitarianism and national sovereignty. It also denies and exacerbates the more complex vulnerabilities young migrants experience over time and across diverse socio-political spaces.[9] Unsettling these processes reveals much about structural inequity and exclusionary politics, and also about responsibility, autonomy, and age.

Image

When considered through the ethics of vulnerability, the process detailed above, namely the circulation of images of young migrants—or specifically, images of very young migrants—both illuminates and unsettles the requirements of humanitarian intervention. In these photos, complex lives and histories are represented as "pure victims in general,"[10] with intervention by humanitarian bodies presumed to be "outside politics" a necessary good. The implicit corollary, that a young im/migrant who needs or receives humanitarian assistance is by extension apolitical, is, of course, extremely political. So long as the youth is depicted as appropriately weak, dependent, and passive, complex questions of individual rights, international relations, and state responsibility can be eclipsed through *charity*. The mechanisms designed to protect or provide aid thus exacerbate the vulnerability[11] put into play by the failed ideals of supranational "inalienable" rights.

Language

As Ian Clark points out,[12] an ethics of vulnerability also illuminates the intersecting discourses of policy and practice that both mitigate and compound an individual's exposure to harm. In the context of transnational migration, for instance, international laws codify individuals' "deservingness" of protection through legal categories such as refugee—yet international law ultimately defers to a state's sovereignty and exclusionary laws.[13] Seen in sharp relief today, these national laws render young migrants even more susceptible to harm, exacerbating the stress of im/migrant precarity in new and often unexpected ways. Adding dimension to these processes through the language of childhood and children's rights, this chapter focuses on the protections put forth in the Convention of the Rights of the Child (CRC). While the CRC establishes children's rights as protection against the exercise of state power, there emerges in the space of youth mobility a power-filled disconnect between the international language of rights, on the one hand, and the everyday, discretionary realization of youths' political agency and legal entitlements, on the other. Also detailed here, these arbitrary or contingent understandings of age and mobility are often reified through scholarship and broader institutional discourses that present youth migration as an outcome of either circumstance or independence—but rarely both.

Body

As discussed in this chapter, it is the body of the young migrant—diminutive and implicitly dependent, larger and unsettlingly independent—that is both utilized and potentially undermines broader efforts aimed at explaining, publicizing, and mobilizing around global migration crises. Recognizing that embodiment is a universal feature of vulnerability in its inherent susceptibility to harm,[14] it is necessary to underscore the corporeal nature of vulnerability in the context of transnational migration. Whether documented and circulated or largely and critically unnoticed, the corporeal risks many young migrants experience comprise dangerous migration passage, violence (including sexual or gender-based violence), insufficient or unavailable health and social services, and even death. Yet building on Judith Butler's more expansive conception of vulnerability, in which vulnerability encompasses a liability to harm as well the indeterminate and positive effects of change via social relationships, the young migrant's body also signals power and potential. Here, the actions of others have the potential to render a transnational youth susceptible to harm *but also* to open new possibilities for agentive and resilient change.[15] As this chapter demonstrates, if we are to meaningfully conceive of vulnerability, it must include that simultaneously experienced by, assigned to, and mediated by global youth across life courses—or stages of embodiment—and diverse social fields.

Global youth

To outline the contemporary contours of transnational migration, scholars and policy experts generally detail rising numbers of refugees worldwide; new and renewed questions about immigrant integration, human rights, and asylum; changing geographies of international migration; rapid internal displacement of people by conflict, violence, and natural disasters; the near-doubling of victims of forced labor over the past decade; an increase in migrant fatalities; and an ever-increasing structural reliance on migrant labor and the exponential growth of remittances.[16] Today, there are more than 244 million international migrants, a 41% increase since 2000. Of this population, an estimated 53 million individuals are under the age of 25.[17] While this latter figure commands a great deal of public attention, it is important to underscore that the transnational migration of young people is not new.[18]

Why and how an individual youth migrates has changed, of course—and as this chapter explores, so also has the language surrounding global youth. Historical studies of states' roles in facilitating and even promoting the migration of youth often underscore the marked *absence* of vulnerability discourse around this mobility, particularly as children were often viewed as vital cargo or units of labor.[19] Today, however, public and institutional discourses persistently frame youth mobility as somewhat more extraordinary. Young people are often depicted as exclusively "left behind" by parents who migrate, as "on their own" owing to natural disasters, family breakdown, famine, or war, or as "unaccompanied children."[20] These frameworks illuminate the very real vulnerabilities that youth experience in the context of migration, including disrupted family relationships,[21] developmental trajectories,[22] care and care-giving,[23] and educational attainment;[24] heightened exposure to harsh labor or living conditions,[25] abuse or abandonment;[26] and inadequate institutional interventions.[27] At the same time, however, research on global youth often fails to critically consider the complexity of migration decisions, age, relatedness and belonging;[28] the fluidity of households over time;[29] and youths' agency as social and political actors who powerfully shape and redefine transnational families, communities, and institutions.[30]

While insufficient, the surmised either/or binary that emerges here is a powerful one. Either global youth are children who are victims and helpless, their migration the *outcome* of circumstances, or they are resilient, independent young people who exercise power both here and there—and who may even *choose* to migrate. Each of these depictions reveals much about the ethics of vulnerability. That they simultaneously exist reveals even more.

An extra/ordinary ethics

Firmly acknowledging the *simultaneity* of transnationalism—namely, that the daily life of transnational migrants simultaneously incorporates and responds to multiple states and social institutions[31]—this chapter likewise calls for a nuanced recognition of the simultaneous agency and vulnerabilities that global youth embody, encounter, wield, and are designated. By asking why there is no conceptual space for this simultaneity in media and political discourse, and what the consequences are of prioritizing certain constructions of vulnerability, we can begin to understand how an "extraordinary ethics" becomes ordinary.

"[T]he 'ordinary,'" writes Michael Lambek, "implies an ethics that is relatively tacit, grounded in agreement rather than rule, in practice rather than knowledge or belief, and happening without calling undue attention to itself."[32] In a sense, then, it is its implicit ambiguity that makes this ethics "ordinary." It is both "what we say when" and that which exceeds or escapes specific words or acts. It is not premised on an objectively agreed-upon idea of the common good, but a moral striving that in its uncertainty is simply a dimension of everyday life.[33] When ethics becomes explicit, adds Lambek, it is generally in respect to its breaches—those occasions when the right thing to do is unknown or powerfully contested. Accordingly, "today the subject of 'ethics' is more closely connected to law and regulation, with respect to such matters as professional conduct, human rights, refuge and citizenship."[34]

As demonstrated here, constructions of vulnerability are premised on explicit ethics—passionately disputed and troubling questions about human rights, mobility, violence, age, and the responsibilities of governments and citizens. In the context of transnational migration, these issues are imagined and depicted as immediately "ethical" in their exceptionality, a not-impossible task when complex regional histories are commonly dismissed and the individual agency of migrants diminished. Yet in centering on the figure of "the vulnerable child migrant," we see the ordinariness of the exceptional. "Because [the] understanding of the human rights victim is so fundamental," writes Sally Engle Merry, "advocates and even victims tend to define themselves in these terms. They do this even when they are not as helpless and vulnerable as the image of victim requires."[35]

Mobility "outside politics"

Whether characterized as "illegal," irregular, refugees, unauthorized, or undocumented, arguably all im/migrants who appeal to human rights activism and humanitarian intervention[36] must be reframed as vulnerable in order to elicit help. Without a bureaucratically legible right to membership, these individuals are in a sense depoliticized bodies, reduced to "bare life."[37] That they lack the right to have rights[38] exposes the failed ideals of supranational "inalienable" rights, as well as fears about national sovereignty and legitimacy made manifest in zealously guarded borders.[39] It also reveals a shift toward humanitarianism, a moral and political project promoted largely through the widespread development of—and reliance upon—transnational non-governmental organizations (NGOs).[40] In their efforts to protect the "bare life" of displaced people, these international organizations implicitly recognize—and, in a sense, reify—a broader shift, one in which complex political questions of immigrant rights are reconfigured into a focus on *charity*.[41] This is what Liisa Maalki calls the process of bureaucratized humanitarian intervention: here, the specificities of individuals, including their circumstances and particular historical experiences, are reconstituted as "pure victims in general."[42] The process is further facilitated by the assertion that human rights activism and humanitarianism are inherently "neutral," that is, this work is motivated by the protection of suffering individuals regardless of their political leanings. While this presumed neutrality may legitimize intervention, it comes at a significant cost.

Framing humanitarianism as "outside politics" implies that an im/migrant who needs or receives assistance is by extension apolitical—the "universal displaced person." Yet this presumption is arguably its own form of violence, one that further depoliticizes an individual by depicting her or his political agency and legal entitlements as uncertain at best, destabilizing at worst. What results is *silence*—visual rather than voiced accounts of suffering, and images of anonymous and often dead bodies. Not only do these representations deny more vast socio-political inequities and individual particularities, but they also contribute to a sustained and intimately destabilizing truth: in the humanitarian regime, "[t]he immigrant loses some level of predictability and entitlement and gains the possibility of compassion."[43]

Of course, that compassion is (just) a possibility underscores its inherently discretionary nature. Who is deemed *deserving* of compassion thus emerges as a critical dimension of vulnerability in the context of transnational migration. That many im/migrants are excluded from a political community, and also deemed unworthy of the attention and investment of a *moral* community,[44] both explains and reinforces their perceived silence.

Vulnerability, childhood, and the nation

Perhaps nothing is more "ordinary" in this context than the figure of the child migrant. Indeed, the inherent neediness and "less-ness"—toyless, shoeless, homeless, and, above all, helpless—of this figure is arguably so common as to no longer reliably evoke sympathy. Consider this excerpt, from "World Shrugs as New Photos of Dead Children Highlight Horror of Migrant Crisis":

> Almost 40 people drowned. . . when a boat taking migrants to Greece capsized after hitting rocks. Among the dead were at least 10 children and the photographs of their lifeless bodies. . . again served as a reminder about the ever-rising death toll of the tragedy that has been engulfing Europe. The photos recalled that of 3-year-old Aylan Kurdi, whose death that was captured on film brought global attention to the crisis. Global attention, however, seems to be elsewhere now.[45]

The article concludes with a photo captioned "Bodies of migrant children and a woman are washed up on the beach in Canakkale's Bademli district."[46]

The beginning of this chapter discusses the relative "utility" of the figure of child migrant: it represents or even *explains* a migration pattern or migration crisis, it signals failed state efforts, and it incites compassion and perhaps also giving. More subtly, of course, this image is powerfully tied up in complex understandings of childhood and citizenship. As Sharon Stephens points out, when coupled with the spread of the "universal child" model put forth by international NGOs, the popular imagery of disappearing, lost, or stolen childhoods perpetuates a compelling imaginary of the childhood domain as threatened or invaded by adult worlds.[47] This imagery is rife in so many media and policy portrayals, whereby young migrants are generalized—and sensationalized—as "unusually vulnerable children" whose opportunities for "normal" childhood are threatened by violence, poverty, unstable families or home countries.

In modern discourses of childhood, the concept is at times contingent on nationhood and at others in opposition to it. On the one hand, each is constructed[48] or "imagined."[49] Both are worthy of care, respect, and protection, and the stability of one presumably depends on that of the other. At the same time, however, children are often viewed as a largely apolitical social group. Prefiguring further tensions, Kristin Cheney writes that "[w]e continue to think of childhood as an apolitical social space, while those classified as 'youth'—another ambiguous category usually referring to teenagers—are merely seen as social problems."[50] In a sense, this both reifies and complicates the "corporeal nature of vulnerability"[51] discussed in the introduction to this section. While any human body is susceptible to harm and therefore vulnerable, there often appears to be something more "inherently" vulnerable about a smaller human body and, to many, something more innocent.[52]

The popularity and power of the vulnerable child migrant image thus relies upon an assumption that childhood is at once a time of stability and rootedness, a nostalgic social space, and "protected" (versus excluded) from the political realm. Not only are these views historically and regionally contingent, but they often infer that a nation is itself stable and "rooted." When someone does not experience this version of childhood, a relative likelihood amidst today's widespread political and socioeconomic instability, the category of "child" becomes something of a burden, a central trope in the discourse of a nation's development or its failure.[53]

In the meantime, young people are further excluded from political engagement (though are no less political actors, discussed below) in that advocacy is usually directed to youths' "moral" rather than "political" rights. Indeed, it is far more common to discuss a young migrant's care, protection, and best interests than it is her or his rights as a citizen and a social actor. This is not to imply that youth are not granted political rights: while national policies certainly differ, international human rights law presents an unequivocal approach to the rights of youth. Officially, everyone is entitled to the rights and freedoms set forth in the Universal Declaration of Human Rights (UDHR) without distinction such as social origin or birth.[54] The Convention on the Rights of the Child (CRC), a legally binding international human rights treaty, grants further specificity to the UDHR's general acknowledgment of children's rights as human rights. "If the UDHR laid the foundation for acceptance of [youths'] human rights vis-à-vis the state," writes Jacqueline Bhabha, "then the CRC, albeit cautiously, added the platform for these children to assert their human rights vis-à-vis their families, their teachers, and their communities."[55]

Yet while the CRC establishes children's rights as protection against the exercise of state power and promotes them in international migration and social welfare policy, it cannot guarantee that these rights are effectively enforced. Consider, for instance, the particular implications of this for unaccompanied minors in the United States.[56] Just one of two nation-states to not ratify the CRC, the US has only limited obligation to bring domestic law into conformity with the convention. Thus, despite the CRC's expectation that comprehensive guardianship and legal representation be provided to unaccompanied minors, undocumented youth in the US are not guaranteed the right to counsel. This illustrates a discrepancy, not only between the rights guarantees of international law and the domestic realization of access to rights, but also between the substantive and procedural rights of documented versus undocumented youth in the US. More simply still, we find that the language of rights, like that of vulnerability, proves discretionary in the context of transnational youth migration.

Presenting and resisting vulnerability

In this context, we may begin to understand the multiple vulnerabilities that young migrants skillfully navigate. As many scholars note, this is often an explicitly *agentive* process: to be "entitled" to human rights and humanitarian relief, an individual must be defined—and likewise self-present—as extraordinarily worthy of that care. Im/migrants thus actively shape identities as appropriately powerless and compliant,[57] isolated, marginal, and "traditional,"[58] and motivated to migrate by coercion rather than for "rational" economic and social reasons.[59] Emerging scholarship that focuses on global youth in particular is perhaps even more destabilizing, most notably when one considers all the innocence, rootedness, and apoliticalness childhood is believed to signify. Many young migrants strategically appeal to limited legal and humanitarian aid frameworks by prioritizing real accounts of suffering or by self-identifying as victims of family, culture, or nation—even as they confront more immediate but less "pitiable" vulnerabilities, including the absence of safe, secure, or lawful employment in communities of destination.[60] These youth simultaneously maintain and transform kin, peer, and political networks through their transnational physical and technological mobility.[61] Young migrants likewise navigate and forge experiences of belonging in the very institutional spaces—the courtroom, the detention center, and so on—that engender their exclusion.[62]

Yet while state and non-governmental actors are certainly witnesses to, and at times complicit in, youths' skilled maneuvering, it often goes unacknowledged. To do so would arguably demand a broader admission: amidst hierarchies and anxieties of power, race, and gender,[63] widespread assumptions of the universalizing potential—versus universal validity—of rights,[64] and the "securitization" of humanitarian aid and intervention,[65] the figure of the vulnerable migrant remains necessary to legitimate human rights and aid protocols' own "worthiness." As a result, though an anti-trafficking initiative or new funding project may in some way aim to preserve the agency of vulnerable individuals, it too often results in "an ongoing lie: a misleading image of victims and a false set of expectations for those who feel called to protect the needy rather than to respect the active resisters."[66]

And what of these resisters? Within the context of care and control, global youth are often imagined as moving in one of two impossible trajectories—either that of victimhood and dependence, or of delinquency, deportability, and danger to a nation's economy and safety.[67] Rather than be vessels for global sympathy and generosity,[68] the youth in the latter "trajectory," most of whom are portrayed as teenagers, and typically as young men, are pathologized as unaware perpetrators and extensions of state propaganda;[69] as embodying a violence that is an innate characteristic of the regions from which they migrate—rather than produced by complex historic and sociopolitical factors;[70] and as threats to the stability of a nation's economy and well-being. Though they illuminate the aforementioned link between childhood and nationhood, these portrayals at once obscure the conditions that spur migration, fail to recognize youth as themselves political, resistant, and gendered actors, and meaningfully neglect that young people's motivations, responsibilities, and lived and assigned vulnerabilities change across space and *age*.[71] What this means at a practical level is that some young migrants in detention centers may have access to legal relief and specialized services, while their counterparts do not.[72] Some may be depicted as "neutral" subjects of concern, while others are targeted as "radicalized."[73]

Some may be characterized as "trafficked," while others are simply "economic migrants."[74] That young migrants' vulnerabilities are viewed, not as simultaneous and fluid, but as something for which to select, exclude, prioritize, and even pathologize, is not care but violence. In terms of ethics, the ordinariness of this process now renders it explicit—only in a way that too few people recognize, or admit.

Conclusion

As this chapter demonstrates, young people's vulnerability in the context of transnational migration is both lived and performed, experienced and assigned. Perhaps most important, it is at once compounded and resisted as youth age and move across diverse social, political, and geographic spaces. To be sure, much of this vulnerability is acute and relatively explicit. Many young migrants will encounter restricted or denied access to legal relief, safe migration passage, work-related rights and protections, transnational kin and community networks, education, or health and social services. Some will deal with risks associated with sexual and reproductive health, and others with intersecting forms of discrimination based on age, gender, migration status, ethnicity, or religion.

What is as critical, though less considered, is that these very real vulnerabilities are often exacerbated by vulnerability *language*. Without diminishing the sustained and consequential exclusion experienced by youth who are imagined as too violent, old, or political to be vulnerable, it is necessary to underscore the consequences of "successful" vulnerability claims. As evidenced in this chapter, constructions of global youth as dependent, non-agentive children implicitly ignore the multidimensional expectations and transnational "simultaneity" of global youth. Not only does this deny—and thus, compromise—youths' meaningful efforts to maintain kin and community networks, meet long-term financial commitments, and successfully transition to adulthood, but it powerfully forecloses opportunities for youth to be public and political actors—and to move public and political discourse from "deservingness"[75] to "entitlement." It likewise reveals and implicates international research and policy efforts that fail to recognize the role of power, privilege, and subjectivity—both young people's and adults'—in those practices that shape and define childhood and migration.

What remains, then, is a call for a necessary re-imagining of transnational migration and the vulnerabilities experienced by—and assigned to—global youth. These efforts require an acknowledgment that youths' social fields may combine several national territories (versus movement back and forth between nation-states and national identities); attention to practices of transnational being and/or belonging; and new modes of incorporation, integration, and connection. Perhaps more uncomfortably, they require an urgent, ongoing, and critical consideration of what the figure of the "vulnerable child" is used for, and why.

This question exists amidst so many others in the context of transnational migration—questions of citizenship and bare life, rights and protection, security and care, age, labor, disaster, and displacement. Yet, as this chapter demonstrates, "the vulnerable child" largely underlies and illuminates these tensions. In this way, it is perhaps the most *explicitly ethical* question raised here. Indeed, only until we critically interrogate the imagined and assigned vulnerability of global youth can we meaningfully address so many other vulnerabilities masked through the language of "care" and even "rights."

Acknowledging the simultaneity of vulnerability demands a more nuanced appreciation of global youths' culturally situated and legally and developmentally contingent needs, goals, obligations, and political participation "on the move."[76] Instead of arguing for a discursive alternative to vulnerability, such as invulnerability,[77] we must consider the possibilities inherent in more fully recognizing global youths' multiple, ongoing, and embodied experiences of vulnerability—experiences that exist simultaneously with "intentional" passivity[78] and agentive expressions of resilience and resistance.

Notes

1 Ralph Ellis and Gul Tuysuz, "Children Suffering: A True Picture of Europe's Migrant Crisis," *CNN*, September 18, 2015, accessed September 13, 2016, http://www.cnn.com/2015/09/17/europe/migrant-children/.
2 Ibid.
3 Katya Adler, "Exploited and Abandoned: A Child's Journey to Europe," *BBC News*, September 15, 2015, http://www.bbc.com/news/world-europe-34286458.
4 Ibid.
5 See, among others, Francis Robles, "Wave of Minors on Their Own Rush to Cross Southwest Border," *New York Times*, June 4, 2014, http://www.nytimes.com/2014/06/04/world/americas/wave-of-minors-on-their-own-rush-to-cross-southwest-border.html?_r=0#; United Nations High Commissioner for Refugees, *Children on the Run: Unaccompanied Children Leaving Central America and Mexico and the Need for International Protection*, 2014, http://www.unhcr.org/56fc26d27.html; UNICEF, "Children on the Move," 2016, http://www.unicef.org/emergencies/childrenon themove/.
6 A photo of a toddler crawling across a floor is captioned, "A migrant child looks on as it sits on the ground at an improvised temporary shelter." Larisa Epatko, "Photos: Children Are Most Vulnerable in the Refugee Crisis," *PBS Newshour*, October 2, 2015, http://www.pbs.org/newshour/updates/photos-children-vulnerable-refugee-crisis/.
7 Michael Lambek, *Ordinary Ethics: Anthropology, Language, and Action* (New York: Fordham University Press, 2010).
8 Martha Fineman, "The Vulnerable Subject: Anchoring Equality in the Human Condition," *Yale Journal of Law and Feminism*, 20, no. 1 (2008): 8.
9 Erinn Gilson, *The Ethics of Vulnerability: A Feminist Analysis of Social Life and Practice* (New York: Routledge, 2014).
10 Liisa Malkki, "Speechless Emissaries: Refugees, Humanitarianism, and Dehistoricization," *Cultural Anthropology*, 11, no. 3 (1996): 377–404.
11 Gilson, *The Ethics of Vulnerability*, 29.
12 Ian Clark, *The Vulnerable in International Society* (Oxford: Oxford University Press, 2013), 6–8.
13 Clark, *The Vulnerable in International Society*, 86–89.
14 Catriona Mackenzie, Wendy Rogers, and Susan Dodds, eds., *Vulnerability: New Essays in Ethics and Feminist Philosophy* (Oxford: Oxford University Press, 2014), 4.
15 Judith Butler, *Precarious Life: The Powers of Mourning and Violence* (London: Verso, 2004); Judith Butler, *Giving Account of Oneself* (New York: Fordham, 2005); Judith Butler, *Frames of War: When Is Life Grievable?* (New York: Verso, 2009).
16 United Nations, Department of Economic and Social Affairs, Population Division, "Trends in International Migrant Stock: The 2015 Revision," 2015, http://www.un.org/en/development/desa/population/migration/data/estimates2/estimates15.shtml; Cati Coe et al., eds., *Everyday Ruptures: Children, Youth, and Migration in Global Perspective* (Nashville: Vanderbilt University Press, 2011); Craig Jeffrey and Jane Dyson, eds., *Telling Young Lives: Portraits of Global Youth* (Philadelphia: Temple University Press, 2008).
17 UN, "Trends in International Migrant Stock."
18 See, e.g., John Boswell, *The Kindness of Strangers: The Abandonment of Children in Western Europe from Late Antiquity to the Renaissance* (Chicago: University of Chicago Press, 1988); Michele Statz, "Between Children and Transnational Economic Actors: The Discounted 'Belongings' of Young Chinese Migrants," *PoLAR: Political and Legal Anthropology Review*, 39, no. S1 (2016): 4–18.
19 Bernard Bailyn, *Voyagers to the West: A Passage of the Peopling of America on the Eve of the Revolution* (New York: Knopf, 1986); Paula Fass, "Children in Global Migrations," *Journal of Social History*, 38, no. 4 (2005): 937–953; Lauren Heidbrink, *Migrant Youth, Transnational Families, and the State: Care and Contested Interests* (Philadelphia: University of Pennsylvania Press, 2014).

20 Lauren Heidbrink and Michele Statz, "Parents of Global Youth: Contesting Debt and Belonging," *Children's Geographies* (2017): 1–13.
21 Yang Gao, Liping Li, Jean Kim, and Sian Griffiths, "The Impact of Parental Migration on Health Status and Health Behaviours among Left Behind Adolescent School Children in China," *BioMed Central Public Health*, 10, no. 1 (2010): 1–10.
22 William Perez, *Americans by Heart: Undocumented Latino Students and the Promise of Higher Education* (New York: Teachers College Press, 2015).
23 Lan Anh Hoang and Brenda Yeoh, "Sustaining Families across Transnational Spaces: Vietnamese Migrant Parents and Their Left-Behind Children," *Asian Studies Review*, 36, no. 3 (2012): 307–325; Frieda McGovern and Dympna Devine, "The Care Worlds of Migrant Children: Exploring Inter-Generational Dynamics of Love, Care and Solidarity across Home and School," *Childhood*, 23, no. 1 (2015): 37–52.
24 Victor Cebotari and Valentina Mazzucato, "Educational Performance of Children of Migrant Parents in Ghana, Nigeria and Angola," *Journal of Ethnic and Migration Studies*, 42, no. 5 (2016): 834–856.
25 Iman Hashim, *The Positives and Negatives of Children's Independent Migration* (Brighton: Development Research Centre on Migration, Globalisation and Poverty, 2010).
26 Olga Byrne, *Unaccompanied Children in the United States: A Literature Review* (New York: Vera Inst. Justice, 2008), http://www.vera.org/download?file=1775/UAC%2Bliterature%2Breview%2BFINAL.pdf; Carola Suarez-Orozco and Marcelo Suarez-Orozco, *Children of Immigration* (Cambridge, MA: Harvard University Press, 2001).
27 Kathryne Farr, *Sex Trafficking: The Global Market in Women and Children* (New York: Worth Publishers, 2005); Alcinda Honwana, *Child Soldiers in Africa* (Philadelphia: University of Pennsylvania Press, 2011); Catherine Panter Brick, "Street Children, Human Rights, and Public Health: A Critique and Future Directions," *Annual Review of Anthropology*, 31 (2002): 147–171.
28 Elana Caneva, "Children's Agency and Migration: Constructing Kinship in Latin American and East European Families Living in Italy," *Childhood*, 22, no. 2 (2015): 278–292; Marta Moskal and Naomi Tyrrell, "Family Migration Decision-Making, Step-Migration and Separation: Children's Experiences in European Migrant Worker Families," *Children's Geographies*, 14, no. 4 (2015): 453–467; Jason Pribilsky, "Nervios and 'Modern Childhood': Migration and Shifting Contexts of Child Life in the Ecuadorian Andes," *Childhood*, 8, no. 2 (2001): 251–273; Allen White et al., "Children's Roles in Transnational Migration," *Journal of Ethnic and Migration Studies*, 37, no. 8 (2011): 1159–1170.
29 Lorraine Young, "Journeys to the Street: The Complex Migration Geographies of Ugandan Street Children," *Geoforum*, 35, no. 4 (2007): 471–488; Hoewook Chung, "Korean Temporary Migrant Mothers' Conceptualization of Parent Involvement in the United States," *Asia Pacific Journal of Education*, 33 no. 4 (2013): 461–475.
30 Joanna Dreby, "Children and Power in Mexican Transnational Families," *Journal of Marriage and Family*, 69 (2007): 1050–1064; Shao-hua Liu, *Passage to Manhood: Youth Migration, Heroin and AIDS in Southwest China* (Stanford: Stanford University Press, 2010); Gail Mummert, "Siblings by Telephone: Experiences of Mexican Children in Long-Distance Child-Rearrangements," *Journal of the Southwest*, 51, no. 4 (2010): 503–522.
31 Peggy Levitt and Nina Glick Schiller, "Conceptualizing Simultaneity: A Transnational Social Field Perspective on Society," *International Migration Review*, 38, no. 145 (2004): 595–629.
32 Michael Lambek, *Ordinary Ethics*, 2–3.
33 Stanley Cavell, *Conditions Handsome and Unhandsome: The Constitution of Emersonian Perfectionism*, The Carus Lectures, 1988, Vol. 19 (Chicago: University of Chicago Press, 1990).
34 Michael Lambek, *Ordinary Ethics*, 2–3.
35 Sally Engle Merry, "Introduction: Conditions of Vulnerability," in *The Practice of Human Rights: Tracking Law between the Global and the Local*, ed. Mark Goodale and Sally Engle Merry (Cambridge: Cambridge University Press, 2007).
36 While human rights activism and humanitarianism are certainly distinct, I move somewhat interchangeably between the two terms in this chapter. Both focus on vulnerability, employ a historically "neutral" stance, and grant primacy to suffering victims, as opposed to political persons. The influence of humanitarianism (as a way of dealing with injustice) on human rights work is likewise well documented (Merry, "Introduction," 198).
37 Giorgio Agamben, *Homo Sacer: Sovereign Power and Bare Life* (Stanford: Stanford University Press, 1998).
38 Hannah Arendt, *The Right to Have Rights* (New York: Harcourt Brace Jovanovich, 1973); see also Didier Fassin, "Another Politics of Life Is Possible," *Theory, Culture, and Society*, 26 (2009): 44–60.

39 Miriam Ticktin, "Where Ethics and Politics Meet: The Violence of Humanitarianism in France," *American Ethnologist*, 33, no. 1 (2006): 33–49.
40 Miriam Ticktin, "Transnational Humanitarianism," *Annual Review of Anthropology*, 43 (2014): 273–289.
41 Merry, "Introduction," 197.
42 Liisa Malkki, "Speechless Emissaries: Refugees, Humanitarianism, and Dehistoricization," *Cultural Anthropology*, 11, no. 3 (1996): 377–404.
43 Merry, "Introduction," 197.
44 Miriam Ticktin, "Migration, 'Illegality,' and Health: Mapping Embodied Vulnerability and Debating Health-Related Deservingness," *Social Science and Medicine*, 74 (2012): 805–811.
45 Daniel Politi, "World Shrugs as New Photos of Dead Children Highlight Horror of Migrant Crisis," *Slate*, January 30, 2016, http://www.slate.com/blogs/the_slatest/2016/01/30/new_photos_of_dead_children_highlight_horror_of_refugee_crisis.html.
46 Ibid.
47 Sharon Stephens, *Children and the Politics of Culture* (Princeton: Princeton University Press, 1995), 9.
48 Philippe Aries, *Centuries of Childhood: A Social History of Family Life* (New York: Random House, 1962).
49 Benedict Anderson, *Imagined Communities: Reflections on the Origin and Spread of Nationalism* (New York: Verso, 1991).
50 Kristen Cheney, *Pillars of the Nation: Child Citizens and Ugandan National Development* (Chicago: University of Chicago Press, 2007), 13.
51 See the DeLaet contribution to this Handbook.
52 Jean Bethke Elshtain, *Women and War* (Chicago: University of Chicago Press, 1995), 3–13; R. Charli Carpenter, *"Innocent Women and Children": Gender, Norms and the Protection of Civilians* (New York and London: Routledge, 2006).
53 See, e.g., Cheney, *Pillars of the Nation*.
54 UN General Assembly, "Universal Declaration of Human Rights," 1948, http://www.un.org/en/universal-declaration-human-rights/, art. 2.
55 Jacqueline Bhabha, "Arendt's Children: Do Today's Migrant Children Have a Right to Have Rights?" *Human Rights Quarterly*, 31 (2009): 410–451, 420.
56 Unaccompanied children are individuals under the age of 18 who have no lawful immigration status in the United States and who have no parent or legal guardian to provide care and custody.
57 Susan Berger, "(Un)Worthy: Latina Battered Immigrants under VAWA and the Construction of Neoliberal Subject," *Citizenship Studies*, 13, no. 3 (2009): 201–217.
58 Jean Jackson, "Rights to Indigenous Culture in Colombia," in *The Practice of Human Rights: Tracking Law between the Global and the Local*, ed. Mark Goodale and Sally Engle Merry (Cambridge: Cambridge University Press, 2007), 204–241.
59 Emily Ryo, "Deciding to Cross: The Norms and Economics of Unauthorized Migration," *American Sociological Review*, 78, no. 4 (2013): 574–603.
60 Statz, "Between Children and Transnational Economic Actors."
61 Lotta Frändberg, "Temporary Transnational Youth Migration and Its Mobility Links," *Mobilities*, 9, no. 1 (2014): 146–164; Glynda Hull, Amy Stornaiuolo, and Urvashi Sahni, "Cultural Citizenship and Cosmopolitan Practice: Global Youth Communicate Online," *English Education*, 42, no. 4 (2010), 331–367; Craig Jeffrey, "Geographies of Children and Youth, II: Global Youth Agency," *Progress in Human Geography*, 36, no. 2 (2012), 245–253; Statz, "Between Children and Transnational Economic Actors."
62 Lauren Heidbrink, "Criminal Alien or Humanitarian Refugee: The Social Agency of Migrant Youth," *Children's Legal Rights Journal*, 33 (2013): 133–190.
63 Heather Hindman, "The Hollowing Out of Aidland: Subcontracting and the New Development Family in Nepal," in *Inside the Everyday Lives of Development Workers: The Challenges and Futures of Aidland*, ed. Anne-Meike Fechter and Heather Hindman (Sterling, VA: Kumarian Press, 2011), 169–191; Ann Stoler, "Rethinking Colonial Categories: European Communities and the Boundaries of Rule," *Comparative Studies in Society and History*, 31, no. 1 (1989): 134–161.
64 Martin Chanock, "'Culture' and Human Rights: Orientalising, Occidentalising and Authenticity," in *Beyond Rights Talk and Culture Talk: Comparative Essays on the Politics of Rights and Culture*, ed. Mahmood Mamdani (Cape Town: The Rustica Press, 2000), 15–36.
65 Sara De Jong, "False Binaries: Altruism and Selfishness in NGO Work," in *Inside the Everyday Lives of Development Workers: The Challenges and Futures of Aidland*, ed. Anne-Meike Fechter and Heather Hindman (Sterling, VA: Kumarian Press, 2011), 21–40; Mark Fathi Massoud, *Law's Fragile State: Colonial, Authoritarian, and Humanitarian Legacies in Sudan* (Cambridge: Cambridge University Press, 2013).

66 Merry, "Introduction," 203; see also Jyoti Sanghera, "Unpacking the Trafficking Discourse," in *Trafficking and Prostitution Reconsidered: New Perspectives on Migration, Sex Work, and Human Rights*, ed. Kamala Kempadoo, Jyoti Sanghera, and Bandana Pattanaik (Boulder, CO: Paradigm Publishers, 2005), 3–24.

67 Lauren Heidbrink and Michele Statz, "Parents of Global Youth."

68 David Rieff, *A Bed for the Night: Humanitarianism in Crisis (*New York City: Simon & Schuster, 2002).

69 Karen Depuy and Krijn Peters, *War and Children: A Reference Handbook* (Santa Barbara, CA: Praeger Security International, 2010); David Rosen, "Social Change and the Legal Construction of Child Soldier Recruitment in the Special Court for Sierra Leone," *Childhood in Africa,* 2, no. 1 (2010): 48–57.

70 Estella Carpi and Chiara Diana, "Child Protection or Security Agendas? NGOs Address the Syrian Refugee Crisis in Lebanon," *Youth Circulations*, March 1, 2016, http://www.youthcirculations.com/blog/2016/2/26/child-protection-or-security-agendas-ngos-address-the-syrian-refugee-crisis-in-lebanon.

71 Leisy Abrego, "Legitimacy, Social Identity, and the Mobilization of Law: The Effects of Assembly Bill 540 on Undocumented Students in California," *Law and Social Inquiry*, 33, no. 3 (2008): 709–734; Roberto Gonzales, "Learning to Be Illegal: Undocumented Youth and Shifting Legal Contexts in the Transition to Adulthood," *American Sociological Review*, 76, no. 4 (2011), 602–619.

72 Greta Lynn Uehling, "The International Smuggling of Children: Coyotes, Snakeheads, and the Politics of Compassion," *Anthropological Quarterly*, 81, no. 4 (2008): 833–871.

73 Carpi and Diana, "Child Protection or Security Agendas?"

74 Statz, "Between Children and Transnational Economic Actors."

75 Carol Sargent, "'Deservingness' and the Politics of Healthcare," *Social Science and Medicine*, 74 (2012): 855–857.

76 Paolo Boccagni, Jean-Michel Lafleur, and Peggy Levitt, "Transnational Politics as Cultural Circulation: Toward a Conceptual Understanding of Migrant Political Participation on the Move," *Mobilities*, 11, no. 3 (2015): 1–20; Peggy Levitt, "Transnational Migrants: When 'Home' Means More Than One Country," *Migration Policy Institute*, 2004, http://www.migrationpolicy.org/article/transnational-migrants-when-home-means-more-one-country.

77 Robert Gooden, *Protecting the Vulnerable: A Reanalysis of Our Social Responsibilities* (Chicago: University of Chicago Press, 1985).

78 Veena Das, "Voices of Children," *Daedalus*, 118, no. 4 (1989): 262–294.

26
AT A CROSSROADS
Health and vulnerability in the era of HIV

Elizabeth Mills

Introduction

The contemporary modern age is marked less by relations that take place within national borders and far more by those that transcend these frontiers.[1] Not only are more people crossing these borders than ever before, but 'things'—like ideas, technologies, behaviours—are moving through virtual and real spaces, reconfiguring the 'edges' of temporal and spatial boundaries. It is perhaps, then, no coincidence that this global recognition of our increasingly interconnected world has run alongside an escalation in international efforts to contain—through development initiatives and public health programmes, for example—the spread of epidemic diseases.[2] This interconnection has, according to John Agnew,[3] resulted in the phenomenon of 'time–space compression',[4] and it has fostered the emergence of what Castells describes as the 'network society';[5] together, these phenomena point to the extent to which the local is tied into the global. Put differently, the global movement of pathogens has foregrounded the extent to which individual lives are intricately connected, from the molecular to the global. Further, as discussed in this chapter, not only are individual lives connected through their shared vulnerability to disease, but this vulnerability is unevenly distributed, as some individuals are less able to access vital health care than others.

Engaging with recent work on ethics, vulnerability, and health, this chapter situates ethnographic research on HIV in South Africa and Brazil alongside a literature in international relations (IR). Through detailed accounts drawn from visual and participatory research methods, the people with whom I worked in South Africa and Brazil called for policymakers and scholars to not only understand how global institutions can work more effectively to ensure improved and equitable health for all; they also highlighted both how global institutions are themselves implicated in people's embodied vulnerability and how they draw attention to the intersecting forms of inequality, linked to race, class, and gender, that undermine improved and equitable health—with a focus on access to AIDS medicines—across the scale from the molecular to the global. Drawing on this ethnographic research in South Africa, alongside qualitative and secondary research in Brazil and India, this chapter situates current debates in global health in light of the networked threads that weave HIV-positive women's embodied vulnerability into the governance of biomedical technologies and the technologies of governance.

International relations and the politics of global health

Although the concept of 'global health' entered scholarly circulation only in the last two decades, there has been a longstanding concern to contain and, where possible, curtail diseases of the 'other', principally through international health regulations and the application of biomedical interventions.[6] Early attempts to limit the spread of disease across borders in the late 1800s were followed by greater efforts to advance the health of citizens through science-based interventions within the nation's borders in the mid to late twentieth century. However, the limitations to the application of science became increasingly apparent in the late twentieth century, and this precipitated an increased sense of vulnerability—by citizens, nations, and international agencies.[7] This chapter suggests that vulnerability cannot be understood as residing in the individual body, or in the body of the population, a national government, or international agencies. Instead, and as discussed in the sections below, vulnerability links and implicates all of these groups as their respective boundaries 'have become increasingly eroded and redefined, resulting in new forms of social organization and interaction across them'.[8]

Sara Davies develops a typology to describe two prevailing approaches within IR to health, insecurity, and vulnerability.[9] Each perspective offers a unique framing of the threat, response, and ethos of global health, and each holds a different set of actors accountable for generating insecurity or alleviating vulnerability. The 'statist perspective' aligns most closely with the normative framework, in which IR scholars focus on the threat of infectious disease to a state's economic and political stability; the language of 'health security' is used by 'statist' scholars, and their principal referent is the state. In contrast, scholars of the 'globalist perspective' focus on those who are most vulnerable to disease; the principal referent is therefore the individual. The 'statist' response to a threat to the state is to strengthen institutions that can protect the state system, under an ethos that the state is the most appropriate actor to manage health threats (along with other actors that can assist the state's ability to respond). The 'globalist' response to an individual's vulnerability is to identify any number of actors or institutions that are most likely to alleviate the impact of disease; this follows an ethos that anyone who can alleviate this vulnerability is best placed to do so.

Leading scholars, notably Obijiofor Aginam and Paul Farmer in health, and Solomon Benatar in IR, have argued against the statist perspective and have called for greater focus on the structures that have generated vulnerability and therefore warrant reform.[10] Like Fineman and Clark, who call for a recognition of the global actors that play a role in constructing the nature of vulnerability, Aginam and Farmer have demonstrated, through their ethnographic research on tuberculosis, malaria, and HIV, that international economic and political actors are crucial in deciding who is treated for what, where, when, and for how much.[11]

In contrast to the statist perspective, whereby the state is the main actor, the globalist perspective includes a wide array of actors including: individuals, the state, donor states, neighbouring states, international organizations, private donors, multinational corporations, and civil society organizations (CSOs). The language of human security (not health security) is used by globalist scholars, and the principal referent is the individual (and not the state). Despite their many significant differences, security features strongly in the statist and globalist perspectives, although at different scales: the security of the state is the principal concern of 'statists', and the security of the individual is the principal concern of 'globalists'.[12] Taking heed of Davies's warning to resist the logic of securitization, I turn to look at security's corollary: vulnerability.[13]

The political and ethical dimensions of vulnerability

Scholars in IR, such as Jennifer Prah Ruger (2006), and feminist researchers like Brooke Ackerly and Jacqui True (2008), have called for a robust theoretical framework that can address uneven forms of vulnerability by engaging with the ethical challenges facing the global health community.[14] Drawing Aristotle's political theory together with Amartya Sen's capability approach, Ruger explores why global health disparities are morally problematic and seeks to understand why efforts to reduce them are justified.[15] In place of speaking about the inter-relatedness of human life, Ruger calls for a (related) recognition of the inter-relatedness of health and other social ends. She argues that deprivations in people's health is a form of vulnerability; this approach echoes Butler's notion of precarity as 'the politically induced condition in which certain populations . . . become differentially exposed to . . . violence'.[16] Deprivations, Ruger goes on to write, are unjust because they undermine individual capabilities to assert agency and flourish in life.[17]

Approaching vulnerability from a feminist and philosophical stance, Butler presents a case for the political and ethical importance of vulnerability in *Dispossession* and *Precarious Life*.[18] Across these publications, Butler details the conditions that create vulnerability and articulates the ethical importance of recognizing our 'common' corporeal vulnerability as a new basis for humanism. There are two significant components of Butler's theorization of vulnerability that I introduce in this section and go on to discuss more fully in the ethnographic accounts below. First, Butler emphasizes that the body is the site of common corporeal vulnerability. Second, as a form of ontological embodiment, vulnerability is both common (shared by all individuals) and relational (created through inherent sociality): vulnerability exists as a fundamental part of our lived worlds, and it takes shape through our relationship with other individuals in these worlds.

In her subsequent writing on precarity and precariousness, Butler articulates a shift towards thinking about the conditions that generate vulnerability, that threaten one's life and are beyond one's control.[19] Extending the concept of common corporeal vulnerability, Butler argues that precariousness is an existential concept, a result of our embodiment and a characteristic of the inherent vulnerability in all human life; it is thus evenly distributed.[20] Precarity, on the other hand, is more specifically political and therefore unevenly distributed.[21] Where Butler's theorization of common corporeal vulnerability speaks to the ethics of vulnerability—our responsibility to one another, to ourselves—her theorization of precarity foregrounds the politics of vulnerability.[22]

Scholars in related fields, like anthropology, have adopted precarity and precariousness to mean very specific—and yet related—things. In medical anthropology, physician and anthropologist Didier Fassin writes that 'from the etymology, *precarious* does not correspond to the static description of a condition, it involves a dynamic relation of social inequality.'[23] The centrality of relationality, as asserted by Didier Fassin in his description of precariousness, corresponds with Butler's discussion of common corporeal vulnerability as it comes into play through people's relationships with one another.[24] Approaching vulnerability in the field of IR, and moving out from anthropology's focus on the individual and their society, Ian Clark considers relationality and the ethical dimensions of vulnerability at a global level. His approach highlights the construction of vulnerability and the role that global actors play in framing global problems and therefore in shaping the uneven distribution of susceptibility to harm by individuals and populations across the globe.[25]

Similarly, as Debra L. DeLaet writes in the theme's introduction with reference to Clark's discussion on ethics and global society, while vulnerability is a universal condition and an ontological dimension of social life, global political and economic structures generate heightened risks of susceptibility to harm that affect some populations more than others.[26] According to Goodin, this uneven form of vulnerability, which Butler describes as precarity, is socially and politically conditioned.[27] There is value, on the one hand, in recognizing that some populations are more susceptible to harm than others; as I discuss below, the recognition that HIV-positive people living in conditions of poverty are less likely to be able to access life-saving treatment in the private sector than wealthier people has prompted a global reconfiguration of regulations that govern the development and distribution of essential medicines.

On the other hand, as DeLaet discusses in the theme's introduction with reference to Fineman's classification of vulnerability, there is a risk that recognizing the unevenness of vulnerability might further marginalize—and pathologize—vulnerable individuals and groups.[28] This connects, too, to Clark's notion of an ethics of vulnerability in which he calls on global actors to recognize that their construction of global problems and corresponding responses can (actively or inadvertently) reproduce uneven susceptibility to vulnerability. I have observed this dynamic in my own research in the early 2000s, when public health interventions assigned the term 'high risk' to groups that were believed to be more likely to be at risk to contract and transmit HIV, including sex workers, truck drivers, or intravenous drug-users. The aim of assigning the label 'at risk' to these groups was to ensure that public health practitioners actively worked to access these groups and to provide them with health resources (like condoms) that could minimize their vulnerability to HIV. However, by assigning vulnerability to these groups, public health interventions fuelled stigmatizing behaviours in communities where these groups were already socially, economically, and politically marginalized.[29]

In the ethnographic sections that follow, I discuss access to antiretroviral (ARV) treatment for people living with HIV in Brazil and South Africa, and I consider some of the ethical and political dimensions of vulnerability generated by their ability, or inability, to access these life-saving medicines. I draw on this ethnography for three reasons. First, I aim to show how global health actors—detailed in the section on globalist and statist perspectives—engender vulnerability that is embodied in the lives of the people with whom I worked in Brazil and South Africa. In this respect, these accounts connect most closely with Butler's theorization of precarity. Second, I recount individual stories alongside the role of global gatekeepers in order to reflect the construction of vulnerability, and the extent to which socio-economic inequalities shape the way that individuals in South Africa experience this vulnerability unevenly. In this respect, these accounts reflect Clark's call for a recognition of vulnerability as constructed and contingent on the framing of global problems by international actors.[30] Finally, I draw on this ethnography to demonstrate the limits of framing vulnerability in exclusively negative terms. These accounts resonate most strongly with Gilson's approach to vulnerability in light of feminist theory and ethical philosophy. As noted in the theme's introduction, if the negative formulation of vulnerability is flipped on its head, it becomes more possible to see how the construction of 'invulnerability' itself undermines the positive ethics of care, connection, and dependency that emerge from a proactive recognition of the value of vulnerability.[31]

HIV and embodied vulnerability

The multi-sited ethnography underpinning my research was configured to explore and link the political and embodied dimensions of accessing AIDS biomedicine as a life-sustaining technological intervention. I conducted fieldwork in South Africa for ten months and in Brazil for two months. Through my fieldwork in South Africa, I researched women's embodied experience of AIDS biomedicine and their political engagement with the state; and through my fieldwork in Brazil, I located my findings on women's embodied experiences of precarity in South Africa within a matrix of networks that moved between the molecular and the global, and drew a range of global health actors into view.

Ethics approval was secured from the University of Sussex's Cross-Schools Research Ethics Committee. In addition to following the guidelines entailed in this formal ethics approval, such as ensuring consent, confidentiality, and anonymity, my approach to ethnography, and therefore the data, was informed by a commitment to conducting ethical research that foregrounds recognition of shared humanity (and vulnerability) between myself and the people with whom I worked.

I have written elsewhere on the importance of addressing broader socioeconomic inequalities alongside the provision of ARVs, and the value of engaging with intersecting forms of inequality that are discussed across the following sections.[32] In order to delimit the scope of this chapter, however, I focus on HIV as the principal global health concern, on national, local, and international actors as the principal 'gatekeepers' in this global health terrain, and on access to ARVs as the primary means through which HIV-positive people can manage their embodied vulnerability, linked to HIV-related illnesses and ARV-related side-effects.

'On the other side of the road, no ARVs': the uneven terrain of vulnerability

Many of the women you will hear from in the sections below strategically utilized their 'assigned' vulnerability—as poor, HIV-positive women—to draw attention to the social and economic inequalities that characterized much of their lives, including their ability to access essential AIDS medicines. Through their assertion of embodied vulnerability, and through collective action as activists, these women called on the government to provide better 'care' for their citizens in post-apartheid South Africa. These accounts resonate with Gilson's argument that a positive conceptualization of vulnerability can create an ethical disposition through which structural inequalities can be more effectively highlighted and disrupted. The section starts with a vignette from my research, and it introduces Miriam—her everyday life, and her search for healing as a woman living with HIV in South Africa.

> The shebeen's corrugated iron walls were the same blue as the brutal skies that arch over Khayelitsha in winter.[33] In this part of Khayelitsha, called Nkanini, homes were built on top of the sand. Like the shebeen, their windowless walls were made from cardboard posters and sheets of corrugated iron. One of the shebeen's three co-workers had painted larger-than-life bottles of beer along the rippled wall with painstaking precision. Each bottle a bright rendition of the real thing that, along with the pumping bass beating in my body, brought Nkanini's residents in to drink. We walked on, under snaking electricity wires, around Nkanini's single tap and over the muddy veins that leaked down the dusty road.
>
> 'This way sana, remember?' said Miriam as she looped her arm through mine.[34] We turned left after the tap and shuffled along a short alley, our bodies bumping into each other and the shack walls and wire fences that lined our route; against our sturdy bodies, these markers of home felt fragile. We turned right, left, and finally right into her garden. I sat down in Miriam's sitting room, my shoes resting on the linoleum floor that kept out the fine beach sand that covers the Cape Flats: an impoverished peri-urban area that stretches across the barren land between the Cape Peninsula's two oceans in South Africa. Miriam is one of 7.06 million people who live with HIV in South Africa.[35] A translucent line had been walked into the linoleum floor; like a thin

membrane, it linked the kitchen to the bedroom and broadened out around the single-seat couch where Miriam sat. In the adjacent bedroom, next to the hand-held mirror on her dressing table, were a cluster of white tubs. Each tub held one third of a triple combination of antiretroviral therapy (ART). Miriam was on the third antiretroviral combination and on the second line of treatment, along with her twelve-year-old daughter, Nena. Nena started life on the brink of death, compelling Miriam to move to Cape Town in search of health care that could decipher and heal her dying child's body. Through this move, and in the face of the government's obdurate AIDS denialism, Miriam entered the Médecins Sans Frontières (MSF) trial in 2001. She is one of the first people to start ARVs in South Africa's public sector.

Months later, after spending the morning in a clinic with the women I worked with (who handcrafted bowls with Miriam) as they waited for their monthly supply of ARVs, I went to a workshop with MSF on South Africa's patent laws. The meeting was held in a high-security complex in Obs, a former 'whites-only' area with houses built from bricks, resting on foundations sunk into fertile earth. Obs is spatially buffered by the M5 highway from the violent poverty in the former 'non-white' areas of the Cape Flats. My phone rang as I left MSF's offices. It was Miriam. She wanted to know if I had taken her question to MSF in asking whether there were options for third-line ARVs when she developed resistance to second-line treatment. I told her that, as far as I understood, third-line treatment had been developed, was effective, and was available in the world. But at that time—in 2011—it was not available in South Africa's public sector. We both knew what lay beneath my words: that for Miriam—when intersecting subjectivities like HIV-positive, poor, woman become salient—her life would end when her HI virus had mutated sufficiently to outwit her second-line medicines; medicines held in tubs on her dressing table, provided by the state through her clinic, embodied as she moved through Nkanini's maze of homes into her own.[36]

During my fieldwork in South Africa, I witnessed a tension among the women I came to know: like Miriam, most of them had learned they were HIV-positive in the late 1990s and had struggled to survive without ARVs. Their inability to access these life-saving medicines through the public health sector confounded their—indeed most South Africans'—belief that the democratically elected government would prioritize the care of the most vulnerable, particularly those people who had been made vulnerable through centuries of discrimination during the colonial and apartheid eras.

As noted above, with respect to Gilson's call for a positive configuration of vulnerability, I learned that these women's inability to access ARVs for themselves, or to prevent the transmission of HIV to their children, had prompted them to take action and join the Treatment Action Campaign (TAC) and call on the government to provide 'care' to its citizens.[37] TAC was a powerful national CSO that, at the time of these women's activism (between 1999 and 2009), exemplified Davies's conception of the 'globalist' perspective.[38] TAC worked nationally to mobilize South Africans to call on the state to provide ARVs, and they worked transnationally with other activist organizations (in Brazil and Thailand, for example), with national governments (including Brazilian politicians), and international humanitarian organizations (like Médecins Sans Frontières).

In contrast to the 'statist' perspective that emphasizes the role of the state in addressing the vulnerability of its citizens, TAC formed a global coalition of actors that could place pressure on the national government to provide essential AIDS medicines to its citizens. Therefore, not only did individuals assert their embodied vulnerability to AIDS-related illnesses through their activist engagement with TAC, but activist organizations like TAC also asserted a form of collective vulnerability to act on the national government and on international gatekeepers, like the World Trade Organization. The ethics of vulnerability—and the assertion of vulnerability as fundamentally unequal—underpinned the actions taken by both individuals and activists as an organization: in both cases, the history of apartheid South Africa was brought into the present as individuals and activist organizations demonstrated the links between structural inequality, poverty, and the inability of the majority of black South Africans to pay for medicines that could save their lives.

Former President Mbeki's period of leadership (1998–2009) was most strongly characterized by his government's obdurate assertion of the toxicity of ARVs and its failure to provide these medicines through the public health sector.[39] Over this time, hundreds of thousands of South Africans died each day of AIDS-related illnesses that could have been prevented had the post-apartheid government made ARVs available to its citizens (Chigwedere, 2008).[40] Responding to the unfolding health crisis in South Africa, MSF set up an ARV trial in Khayelitsha in 2001, three years before the government started to (sluggishly) roll out ARVs through the public health sector. It was through this trial—and the actions of MSF within the global health terrain—that Miriam was able to access ARVs for herself, and for Nena, her daughter.

Gilman (1988) suggests that global health paradigms—the ones that look at health at a national or regional level—run the risk of dislocating 'disease' from the socio-spatial contexts that play a role in engendering vulnerability.[41] Put differently, where people live—and how they live—is important, especially in countries with high levels of socioeconomic inequality, like South Africa and Brazil.[42] As described in the vignette above, South Africa's history is etched into the organization of space, with places like Khayelitsha separated out from former 'whites only' areas, like Obs. Class and race remain closely tied in South Africa's socioeconomic landscape, and this intersection is reinforced by the provision of resources that continue to privilege those living in former 'whites only' areas and disadvantage those living in former 'coloured' or 'African' areas. Intersecting forms of inequality engender precarity when people—like Miriam—are made vulnerable by the absence of state resources, like education and health care.

While Khayelitsha remains a poignant illustration of the extent to which precarity persists over time, and across government regimes, the introduction of ARVs by MSF both alleviated and generated new forms of vulnerability for people living with HIV in South Africa. As Lilian's account below illustrates, access to these life-saving medicines through the MSF trial was spatially circumscribed—available only to those people living in Khayelitsha.

The logic of public health care provision in post-apartheid South Africa relies on the principle of 'catchment areas' in which people in geographically demarcated areas are referred to corresponding community health centres. Lilian, Lihle, and Nomfundo became close friends following their pregnancies with their first children in 2000. Lilian, at that time, lived in Langa, whereas Lihle and Nomfundo lived in Khayelitsha. When MSF started to provide HIV testing and treatment in Khayelitsha in 2001, Nomfundo was able to test for HIV and receive treatment to prevent vertical transmission to her baby. Lilian, however, was required to attend her local clinic in Langa for antenatal care. As a result, she was not tested for HIV. Further, even if she had been tested positive, she would not have been able to access biomedicine to prevent her child from contracting HIV because the government refused to provide resources for prevention of mother-to-child transmission (PTMCT) through the public health system at that time, and because MSF could not provide treatment to those living outside the designated catchment area. Although Lihle lived in Khayelitsha, she chose to go to a clinic in a different area.

In the quote below, Lilian captures the embodied vulnerability that she and Lihle experienced because ARVs were not provided to all those in need of this treatment at the time of their pregnancies. She said:

> I don't know what drove Lihle to go for antenatal care somewhere else but not in her own area because she would have also gotten AZT if she had gone to MSF [in Khayelitsha]. But she didn't. And as a result both our children were born HIV-positive. . . Nomfundo's baby was born negative. It's the same year, but on the other side of the road, no ARVs. And on the other side, there was MSF dishing out AZT and women were giving birth to HIV-saved children.[43]

Lilian's account of 'living on the wrong side of the road' draws attention to the spatialization of her pregnant friends' vulnerability. Because she was 'on the wrong side of the road' and unable to access PTMCT through her clinic, Lilian's daughter was born with HIV and died a few months after birth. Both Nomfundo and Lihle's children were twelve years old at the time of my fieldwork. Although their children are both alive, Lihle's child is HIV-positive and struggles with the accumulative impact of a life characterized by persistent illness. Lilian's account points to the embodied ramifications of the government's failure to provide ARVs; in this particular instance, and in line with Fineman's classification of differential vulnerability, the vulnerability that was generated by the government was unevenly distributed across its citizens based on their class, race, and gender.[44] Lilian, Nomfundo, and Lihle were all African women who, as a result of apartheid's discriminatory education system, had received inadequate formal education and were far more dependent on the post-apartheid state's resources for care than, for instance, their white male counterparts, who had been actively shielded from potential vulnerability by the apartheid (and colonial) government. Lilian's account also speaks to an ethics of care implicit in MSF's provision of essential medicines at a time when the state refused to do so.

While the provision of ARVs through MSF's trial does speak to an ethics of care as a counterpoint to the state's generation of vulnerability among HIV-positive South Africans at the time, there is a further dimension to the ethics of vulnerability that warrants critique. As noted above, the dimensions of vulnerability itself are constructed. Clark, for example, traces the role that global actors play in delineating the nature of a 'global problem' and, through this delineation, determining the corresponding course of action to ameliorate the issue.[45] In directing attention to a particular problem, like HIV for example, there is a risk that this attention will generate further forms of vulnerability. The visibility of HIV in Khayelistha, at the time of my fieldwork, was a driver and a product of international attention and health funding. Over the course of my fieldwork in 2010–2011, and indeed in the decade preceding this time, I had observed a broader issue around the injection of funding into Khayelitsha at the cost of funding development initiatives in the other under-resourced areas. This dynamic is highlighted by Lilian, in the excerpt below:

> Not everything should be about Khayelitsha and Soweto. Other areas should get the same services that we're given. . . [O]nly people from Khayelitsha benefited. Women from other places never benefited. . . . If we put resources in one place then others on the other side of the road will feel cheated. This is the same for me. I feel cheated. There were no ARVs where I went.[46]

Lilian's assertion speaks to the complex interplay of government responsibility, on the one hand, to ensure the provision of services, with the role of NGOs like MSF, on the other hand, who move in to provide resources, like ARVs, when the government fails to do so. This account resonates with Prince's (2012) ethnography in Kisumu, Kenya, where residents referred to their city as 'NGO city', a cynical reflection on the injection of health funding into vertical HIV programmes. Implicit in this reference to their 'NGO city' is a critique that mirrors Clark's discussion of the construction of vulnerability by global actors through their framing of global problems and corresponding responses to these problems.[47] Similarly, in South Africa the rush of funding for HIV into sites like Khayelitsha where HIV had been made most visible by global and local actors, there was a risk that the government would transfer its responsibility for providing basic resources to its citizens onto NGOs, and therefore distance itself from its constitutional obligations to citizens in less visible and poorly resourced areas.

The tension between the global actors and national government's constitutional commitment to its citizens emerged as a strong theme in my fieldwork. As I discuss below, I found that the ability of HIV-positive citizens to manage their embodied vulnerability was not only contingent on their government's response to 'caring' for them through the public sector; it was more broadly contingent on their government's ability to engage strategically with international actors that moderate the development and distribution of essential medicines.

Global health gatekeepers and embodied vulnerability

Like Miriam, the women with whom I worked in South Africa are on first- or second-line ARVs, and, for the moment, these medicines are working effectively to limit their susceptibility to secondary infections. However, over time and through contact with different viral strains, HIV becomes adept at mutating to resist older ARVs. This new horizon of embodied vulnerability will become more salient as people develop resistance to second-line ARVs and, with limited access to third-line biomedicines, they will face death because they cannot afford to purchase life and buy these essential drugs through the private sector. Therefore, a principal avenue for addressing health-related vulnerability among people like Miriam lies in creating sustainable processes that enable medicines to move from pharmaceutical laboratories and factories, across and within the borders of countries, through government-funded public health systems into clinics, and into people's bodies.

In this section, I explore three national actors (Brazil, South Africa, and India) that function within a regional and international global health network (through BRICS and with the European Union). I suggest that these national, regional, and international actors function as gatekeepers, shaping and responding to complex international laws that govern the development and distribution of essential medicines like ARVs—thus fundamentally shaping the nature of vulnerability as it is experienced by individuals and populations living with HIV. This section therefore highlights what João Biehl and Adriana Petryna describe, with reference to Fidler, as 'an "open-source anarchy" around global problems—a policy space in which new strategies, rules and distributive schemes, and the practical ethics of . . . care are being assembled, experimented with, and improvised by a wide array of deeply unequal stakeholders'.[48]

At the first meeting of BRICS health ministers, UNAIDS Executive Director Michel Sidibé affirmed the 'intimately connected' relationship between people's embodied precarity and the role of BRICS in the global AIDS response:

> [T]he five BRICS countries are bringing a new voice, a new perspective and new solutions to today's global challenges. It is a voice with incredible economic, technological and innovative strength behind it, and at the same time, a voice intimately connected to the needs and interests of the developing world. . . . The geopolitical future is being shaped by yourselves and the alliances you are building.[49]

As identified by the BRICS ministers of health at this meeting, this entails transforming complex and expensive processes that prohibit the development and distribution of medicines, like

ARVs, from reaching people in developing countries. Four principal challenges to the sustainable provision of essential medicines were identified at this meeting. The first challenge relates to a country's ability to use TRIPS flexibilities. Unless ARV-producing countries like India, Brazil, and South Africa make use of TRIPS flexibilities, they are unable to import or export these medicines at a reasonable price. The second, third, and fourth challenges relate to the pressure placed on national countries to amend the legislative infrastructure governing the development, importation, and exportation of biomedical technologies. This includes the push for countries to amend their intellectual property rights legislation to include TRIPS plus provisions, like Patent Term Extension and Data Exclusivity.

The history of India and Brazil for challenging restrictive international provisions makes BRICS a powerful global actor in the network that enables ARVs to move from the laboratory, over borders, and into people's bodies. This history also places pressure on these countries to balance neoliberal reforms with democratically established rights to life and health, due to their government's express commitment to rapid economic growth as emerging economic powers. This, in turn, increases the appeal for governments to bow to international pressure in order to secure free-trade agreements, such as the one under negotiation with the European Union and India at the time of my research.

India's ability to reverse-engineer active ingredients has earned it the title of 'Pharmacy of the Developing World', and it is through competition stemming from Indian generics that the cost of first-line ARVs has dropped from more than $10,000 per person per year in 2000 to approximately $150 per person per year in 2012.[50] By producing low-cost medicines through reverse engineering, India has become the largest supplier of antiretroviral medicines to low- and middle-income countries, providing 80% of all donor-funded ARVs to low-income countries.[51] The technological capacity to identify and reverse-engineer active ingredients relates to the national government's legislative infrastructure that has historically protected its domestic pharmaceutical market, and which has very recently been challenged by the World Trade Organization (WTO) and the European Union. Significantly, India's production of generic AIDS medicines has—through competition—driven down the price of brand-name medicines.[52]

Both India and Brazil have made use of TRIPS flexibilities in order to produce ARVs, but at different points in relation to South Africa's history. Brazil signed onto TRIPS in 1996, almost a decade before India. Like India (although on a smaller scale) and South Africa, Brazil has a domestic pharmaceutical industry, and in 2000 it started producing generic ARVs.[53] Brazil's capacity to provide ARVs was facilitated through its domestic production of some AIDS medicines alongside its active negotiation with global health actors, including pharmaceutical companies and the WTO.[54]

Leena Menghaney, manager of MSF's Access Campaign in India, encapsulates the ethical implications of the relationship between individuals' embodied precarity and global health gatekeepers that govern ARV development and distribution, in the following quote: 'The threat to the developing world is real—millions of people rely on affordable drugs from India. If patents are granted more easily in India, patients across the world will see their supply of life-saving drugs dry up.'[55] For instance, in April 2013, India's Supreme Court delivered a landmark judgement that rejected Novartis's 1998 Indian patent application for a beta-crystalline form of a drug called Gleevac that is used to treat chronic myeloid leukaemia.[56] In countries where Novartis has obtained a patent for Gleevac, the drug is sold for $2,600 per patient per month; in India, the generic version of this drug is sold for less than $200 per patient per month.[57]

In MSF's 2017 Briefing Paper, it notes that the global production of HIV medicines is in decline as donor funding and attention have diminished.[58] They argue that the World Health Organization's pending report on the shortages of medicines and vaccines should include an assessment of the intellectual property barriers that restrict market access for pharmaceutical suppliers. The impact of these barriers on people's embodied vulnerability is, in many cases, a matter of life or death. For instance, in 2015, Abbvie, the pharmaceutical company that holds the patent on an ARV (called lopinavir/ritonavir), was unable to meet the demand for this medicine in South Africa; because it held a patent on the drug, local generic suppliers were barred from providing this essential medicine to the South African health department. As a result, HIV-positive patients were turned away from health facilities without their AIDS medicines for over six months (MSF, 2017).[59] In their most recent briefing paper, MSF calls for countries like South Africa to be better supported in navigating international intellectual property laws, in order to alleviate potential stock-outs and shortages that place HIV-positive people at even greater risk of developing resistance to first- and second-line ARVs.[60] The cases of Brazil, India, and South Africa's struggle for affordable medicines illustrate the extent to which vulnerability is constructed at a global level, and foregrounds the role that international actors play in both creating *and* addressing embodied vulnerability across the scale from the global to the molecular level.[61]

Conclusion

The diverse set of actors that shaped the evolution of South Africa's and Brazil's response to HIV highlight the extent to which individuals, activist organizations, and policymakers interact in the global health terrain to co-construct health policy through these networks of governance and the governance of health technologies. This challenges binaries such as citizen/state and unidirectional assumptions of biopower.[62] James Ferguson similarly questions the usefulness of concepts such as 'civil' and 'local', suggesting that international NGOs (like MSF) have, in some African countries, come to take on a 'state-like' shape. He writes, 'The globalization of politics is not a one-way street. If relations of rule and systems of exploitation have become transnational, so have forms of resistance.'[63]

Recognizing the importance of tracing embodied vulnerability to a network of global health actors, Comaroff similarly asks,

> [J]ust how useful, in confronting these issues, is the concept of bare life, spoken of in terms of pure subjection and gross biopolitical being, meaningful only as a sign of sovereign power? The question is crucial if we are to take seriously Agamben's own exhortation to engage in a politics that recuperates civic being. More immediately, it is consequential if we are to make sense of the various ways in which HIV has been politicized and politics biologised.[64]

To this end, I argue that the possibility of life or the threat of death not only exposes the ethics of vulnerability underlying the biopolitical relationship between citizens and the state; it calls attention to a global health network into which their vitality is woven, rendering the body of the state and the state of the body both porous and precarious.

This conception of the ethics of vulnerability relates to both the statist and globalist perspectives on health: for globalists, the individual body is vulnerable and subject to both remedial and harmful actions of a range of actors; and, for statists, the vulnerable body of the individual calls attention to the role of the state in mitigating against this vulnerability and, in this case, against the risk of secondary illnesses and potential death in the absence of access to essential HIV medicines. Further, while this chapter has explored the range of actors that are implicated in the embodied vulnerability of the people with whom I worked, it has also offered another narrative—in line with Gilson—that challenges these two prevailing approaches to health in IR:

the accounts of activists in both Brazil and South Africa demonstrate that people do not simply embody vulnerability in different ways because they are acted 'on' by global actors, like national governments or international organizations that regulate a country, and therefore a citizen's access to life-sustaining medicines.[65] Instead, by making their vulnerability visible through transnational activist coalitions, people in both Brazil and South Africa engaged with this network of global health actors in order to bring ARVs out of laboratories and factories in places like the United States and India, into their country, into their public health systems, and into their bodies. Demonstrating Gilson's call for a recognition of the value of vulnerability to encourage an ethic of care, and reflecting on Comaroff's observation above, it is perhaps, then, the people within this global health network, and not the virus, who have generated 'a new sense of the nature and possibilities of the political'.[66]

Notes

1 Alan Scott, 'Risk society or angst society? Two views of risk, consciousness and community,' *The Risk Society and Beyond: Critical Issues for Social Theory* (2000): 33–46; Barbara Adam, Ulrich Beck, and Joost Van Loon, *The Risk Society and Beyond: Critical Issues for Social Theory*. London: Sage Publications, 2000.

2 Johanna Hanefeld et al., 'Why do medical tourists travel to where they do? The role of networks in determining medical travel,' *Social Science and Medicine*, 124 (2015): 356–363; Julio Frenk, Octavio Gómez-Dantés, and Suerie Moon, 'From sovereignty to solidarity: a renewed concept of global health for an era of complex interdependence,' *The Lancet*, 383, no. 9911 (2014): 94–97.

3 John Agnew, 'The new global economy: time–space compression, geopolitics, and global uneven development,' *Journal of World-Systems Research*, 7, no. 2 (2015): 133–154.

4 Cf. David Harvey, 'Time–space compression and the postmodern condition,' *Modernity: Critical Concepts*, 4 (1989): 98–118.

5 Manuel Castells, 'Toward a sociology of the network society,' *Contemporary Sociology*, 29, no. 5 (2000): 693–699.

6 Mark Zacher and Tania J. Keefe, *The Politics of Global Health Governance: United by Contagion*. New York: Springer, 2008; Tim Brown, '"Vulnerability is universal": considering the place of "security" and "vulnerability" within contemporary global health discourse,' *Social Science and Medicine*, 72, no. 3 (2011): 319–326.

7 Brown, 'Vulnerability is universal.'

8 Lee Kelley, *Health Impacts of Globalization: Towards Global Governance*. London: Palgrave Macmillan, 2003, 21.

9 Sara E. Davies, 'What contribution can International Relations make to the evolving global health agenda?' *International Affairs*, 86, no. 5 (2010): 1167–1190.

10 Obijiofor Aginam, *Global Health Governance: International Law and Public Health in a Divided World*. Toronto: University of Toronto Press, 2005; Paul Farmer, 'On suffering and structural violence: a view from below,' *Daedalus*, 125 (1996): 261–283; Paul Farmer, *Pathologies of Power: Health, Human Rights, and the New War on the Poor*. Oakland: University of California Press, 2005; Solomon R. Benatar, *Global Health: Where to Now?* Center for Global Health Studies, Seton Hall University, 2008.

11 Aginam, 'Globalization of infectious diseases;' Farmer, *Pathologies of Power*; Martha Albertson Fineman, 'The vulnerable subject: anchoring equality in the human condition,' *Yale JL and Feminism*, 20 (2008): 1; Ian Clark, *The Vulnerable in International Society*. Oxford: Oxford University Press, 2013; Sara E. Davies, 'What contribution can International Relations make to the evolving global health agenda?' *International Affairs*, 86, no. 5 (2010): 1167–1190.

12 Sara E. Davies, 'What contribution can International Relations make to the evolving global health agenda?' *International Affairs*, 86, no. 5 (2010): 1167–1190.

13 Sara E. Davies, 'What contribution can International Relations make to the evolving global health agenda?' *International Affairs*, 86, no. 5 (2010): 1167–1190.

14 Jennifer Prah Ruger, 'Ethics and governance of global health inequalities,' *Journal of Epidemiology and Community Health*, 60, no. 11 (2006): 998–1002; Brooke Ackerly and Jacqui True, 'Reflexivity in practice: power and ethics in feminist research on international relations,' *International Studies Review*, 10, no. 4 (2008): 693–707.

15 Amartya Kumar Sen, 'Development as capability expansion,' *The Community Development Reader*, 2nd edn., ed. J. DeFilippis and S. Saeger (1990): 319–327; Ruger, 'Ethics and governance of global health inequalities.'
16 Judith Butler, 'Performativity, precarity and sexual politics,' *Antropólogos Iberoamericanos en Red*, 4, no. 3 (2009): 1.
17 Ruger, 'Ethics and governance of global health inequalities.'
18 Judith Butler and Athena Athanasiou, *Dispossession: The Performative in the Political*. New York: John Wiley & Sons, 2013; Judith Butler, *Precarious Life: The Powers of Mourning and Violence*. New York: Verso, 2006.
19 Butler, *Performativity, Precarity and Sexual Politics*.
20 Butler and Athanasiou, *Dispossession: The Performative in the Political*.
21 Butler, *Performativity, Precarity and Sexual Politics*.
22 Butler, *Precarious Life*.
23 Didier Fassin, *Humanitarian Reason: A Moral History of the Present*. Oakland: University of California Press, 2011, 265.
24 Ibid.; Butler, *Precarious Life*.
25 Ian Clark, *The Vulnerable in International Society*. Oxford: Oxford University Press, 2013.
26 See the DaLeat contribution to this Handbook; Clark, *The Vulnerable in International Society*.
27 Butler, *Performativity, Precarity and Sexual Politics*; Robert E. Goodin, 'Vulnerabilities and responsibilities: an ethical defense of the welfare state,' *American Political Science Review*, 79, no. 3 (1985): 775–787.
28 See the DaLeat contribution to this Handbook; Clark, *The Vulnerable in International Society*; Martha Fineman, 'The vulnerable subject: anchoring equality in the human condition,' *Yale JL and Feminism*, 20 (2008): 1.
29 Elizabeth Mills, 'From the physical self to the social body: expression and effect of HIV-related stigma in South Africa,' *Journal of Community and Applied Social Psychology*, 16 (2006): 498–550; G. M. Herek, J. P. Capitanio, and K. F. Widaman, 'Stigma, social risk, and health policy: public attitudes toward HIV surveillance policies and the social construction of illness,' *Health Psychology*, 22, no. 5 (2003): 533.
30 Clark, *The Vulnerable in International Society*.
31 See the DaLeat contribution to this Handbook; E. Gilson, *The Ethics of Vulnerability: A Feminist Analysis of Social Life and Practice*. New York: Routledge, 2013.
32 Elizabeth Mills, 'From the physical self to the social body'; Mills, '"When the skies fight": HIV, violence and pathways of precarity in South Africa,' *Reproductive Health Matters*, 24, no. 47 (2016): 85–95; Mills, 'Biopolitical precarity in the permeable body: the social lives of people, viruses and their medicines,' *Critical Public Health*, 27, no. 3 (2017): 350–361.
33 A name for (legal and illegal) pubs in South Africa.
34 An isiXhosa word meaning 'dear'.
35 Statistics South Africa, 2017. *Mid-Year Population Estimates*. P0302. Pretoria: South Africa.
36 Personal fieldnotes, 2011.
37 Gilson, *Ethics of Vulnerability*.
38 Sara E. Davies, 'What contribution can International Relations make to the evolving global health agenda?' *International Affairs*, 86, no. 5 (2010): 1167–1190.
39 Mark Heywood, 'Preventing mother-to-child HIV transmission in South Africa: background strategies and outcomes of the treatment action campaign case against the Minister of Health,' *South African Journal on Human Rights*, 19 (2003): 278.
40 Nicoli Nattrass, 'AIDS and the scientific governance of medicine in post-apartheid South Africa,' *African Affairs*, 107, no. 427 (2008): 157–176; Pride Chigwedere, George R. Seage III, Tun-Hou Lee, and M. Essex, 'Efficacy of antiretroviral drugs in reducing mother-to-child transmission of HIV in Africa: a meta-analysis of published clinical trials,' *AIDS Research and Human Retroviruses*, 24, no. 6 (2008): 827–837.
41 Sander Gilman, *Disease and Representation: Images of Illness from Madness to AIDS*. Ithaca, New York: Cornell University Press, 1988.
42 J. Biehl, *Vita: Life in a Zone of Social Abandonment*. Berkeley: University of California Press, 2005; Mark Hunter, *Love in the Time of AIDS: Inequality, Gender, and Rights in South Africa*. Bloomington: Indiana University Press, 2010; Fabian Cataldo, 'New forms of citizenship and socio-political inclusion: accessing antiretroviral therapy in a Rio de Janeiro favela,' *Sociology of Health and Illness*, 30, no. 6 (2008): 900–912.
43 Personal fieldnotes, 2011.
44 Fineman. 'The vulnerable subject: anchoring equality in the human condition.'

45 Clark, *The Vulnerable in International Society.*
46 Personal fieldnotes, 2011.
47 Clark, *The Vulnerable in International Society.*
48 David P. Fidler, 'A theory of open-source anarchy,' *Indiana Journal of Global Legal Studies*, 15, no. 1 (2008): 259–284; João Biehl and Adriana Petryna, eds., *When People Come First: Critical Studies in Global Health.* Princeton: Princeton University Press, 2013, 410.
49 Michel Sidibe, 'BRICS: seizing a leadership role in global health,' UNAIDS, 2001.
50 Hans Lofgren, ed., *The Politics of the Pharmaceutical Industry and Access to Medicines: World Pharmacy and India.* London: Taylor & Francis, 2017; Ellen 't Hoen, 'A victory for global public health in the Indian Supreme Court,' *Journal of Public Health Policy*, 34 (2013): 370–374.
51 Brenda Waning, Ellen Diedrichsen, and Suerie Moon, 'A lifeline to treatment: the role of Indian generic manufacturers in supplying antiretroviral medicines to developing countries,' *Journal of the International AIDS Society*, 13, no. 1 (2010): 35.
52 Jacob Bor, 'The political economy of AIDS leadership in developing countries: an exploratory analysis,' *Social Science and Medicine*, 64, no. 8 (2007): 1585–1599; K. Jayaraman, 'India flouts patent for blockbuster biologic,' *Nature Biotechnology*, 31 (2013): 9; Waning et al., 'Lifeline to treatment;' J. Wouters et al., 'Some critical issues in EU–India Free Trade Agreement negotiations,' *European Law Journal*, 20, no. 6 (2014).
53 Amy Nunn et al., 'AIDS treatment in Brazil: impacts and challenges,' *Health Affairs*, 28 (2009): 1103–1113.
54 Ibid.; Matthew Flynn, 'Public production of anti-retroviral medicines in Brazil, 1990–2007,' *Development and Change*, 39 (2008): 513–536; N. Ford et al., 'Sustaining access to antiretroviral therapy in the less-developed world: lessons from Brazil and Thailand,' *AIDS*, 21 (2007): S21–S29.
55 Please see above.
56 Patralekha Chatterjee, 'India's patent case victory rattles Big Pharma,' *The Lancet*, 381, no. 9874 (2013): 1263; Jayaraman, 'India flouts patent for blockbuster biologic;' S. Chaudhuri, 'The larger implications of the Novartis-Glivec Judgment,' *Economic and Political Weekly*, 48 (2013): 11.
57 Ibid.
58 Please see above.
59 Please see above.
60 Médecins San Frontières, 'Addressing the global shortage of medicines and vaccines' (executive report, 2017), https://www.msfaccess.org/sites/default/files/EB%20140%20briefing%20on%20Stockouts_Agenda%20Item%208-3.pdf.
61 Clark, *The Vulnerable in International Society.*
62 Foucault's concept of biopower concerns the biological existence of human beings and the mechanisms through which humans become an object of political intervention and strategy. Biopower refers to the 'techniques of power' that manage and control the bodies of individuals (anatomopolitics) and the life of the population (biopolitics).
63 James Ferguson, *Global Shadows: Africa in the Neoliberal World Order.* Durham, NC: Duke University Press (2006), 109.
64 Jean Comaroff, 'Beyond bare life: AIDS, (bio)politics, and the neoliberal order,' *Public Culture*, 19 (2007): 209.
65 Gilson, *Ethics of Vulnerability.*
66 Comaroff, 'Beyond bare life,' 198.

27

CLIMATE CHANGE, SUSTAINABLE DEVELOPMENT, AND VULNERABILITY

Tabitha M. Benney

Introduction

The issue of climate change is complex in many ways. It is scientifically difficult to measure. At the same time, it includes dynamically coupled human and natural systems, which may interact in ways that we simply do not yet understand. Perhaps the hardest aspect of climate change is its ethical side, because the impacts of climate change do not accrue fairly throughout the world. In fact, a disproportionate number of those impacts will fall upon some of the most vulnerable countries, people, and environments on our planet. The burdens of climate change are particularly tough for regions facing the harsh realities of development because environmental issues, such as climate change, are clearly linked with economics (e.g., global finance and trade) and other sociopolitical issues (e.g., development, health).

From an international ethics perspective, any well-thought-out solution to the problem of sustainable development in an era of climate change raises fundamental questions about obligations to identify and protect vulnerable populations from physical and economic hardship and the mechanisms for pursuing justice in response to climate-related impacts in the international system. While approaches to sustainable development have advanced dramatically since the issue was first tackled in the 1980s, solutions to the problem have become entrenched, thus shaping, for better or worse, the notions of vulnerability that exist in the international system. Clarifying the role of vulnerability, and developing the theoretical and methodological approaches to study vulnerability, are essential for improving our understanding of the environmental, social, and economic effects of climate change policies on vulnerable populations facing economic development. This chapter will use the ethics of vulnerability framework to explore these complex linkages.

To explore these connections, this chapter begins with an overview of climate change, sustainable development, and vulnerability. Here, I illustrate how climate change impacts vulnerable populations within developing regions. In examining the real vulnerabilities faced by disadvantaged populations, the chapter will summarize the key debates in this area. Next, the chapter lays out various definitions of vulnerability as they apply to the topic. I also highlight the ways in which the very notion of vulnerability is constructed and serves to reproduce inequities in international relations. Critical examples explored in this chapter include racialized and gendered constructions of vulnerability and their impacts on important outcomes in sustainable development. After a review of these important topics, the chapter concludes with some key events that are challenging and shaping the field into the future.

The ethics of vulnerability and sustainable development

While the study of ethics in international relations (IR) broadly defines *vulnerability* as a condition of liability to harm,[1] the term becomes infinitely more complex when the immense issues of climate change and sustainable development are considered together. Research on vulnerability and sustainable development in an era of climate change faces an important challenge: to model socioeconomic transformation and its interactive relationship with climate change. Vulnerability assessment, therefore, must account for multiple dimensions: the physical–environmental impact of changed climate; a region's capacity to recover from extreme events and adapt to change over the longer term; and the degree to which international trade, aid, and health are used regionally to further aspects of economic development. This complexity helps to explain the broad range of definitions found in the field.

According to Hallie Eakin and Amy Lynd Luers, the various definitions for vulnerability are drawn from three academic traditions: risk and hazard studies, political economy, and ecology.[2] The concept of vulnerability in the field also tends to have a more scientific orientation. For instance, the IPCC argues that "[v]ulnerability is dynamic and context specific, determined by human behavior and societal organization, which influences for example the susceptibility of people (e.g., by marginalization) and their coping and adaptive capacities to hazards."[3] However, defining vulnerability can also be extremely political. Attributing vulnerability to climate-related impacts is a contentious issue because of the implications relative vulnerability has for apportioning international funds.[4]

Despite the complexities of defining vulnerability in this context, it is clear that climate change, development, and vulnerable populations share a fundamental linkage. They are inextricably linked through ecology, economics, and sociopolitical norms and behavior. To account for these complex linkages, the concept is commonly framed using the Three Pillars of Sustainable Development: environmental protection, social development, and economic growth.

The Pillars of Sustainable Development heuristic was first put forward at the 2005 World Summit on Social Development to reflect the lessons learned since the 1992 Earth Summit held by the UN Conference on Environment and Development (UNCED).[5] While the Earth Summit aimed to move the sustainable development agenda forward by forging a pact between the developed and developing world and by linking environmental and developmental concerns, it was not until 2005 that the trinity of sustainability was explicitly conceptualized. What makes the final concept unique from the past is that the Three Pillars of Sustainability acknowledge that social development, like environmental protection and economic considerations, is interdependent. Hence, in the long run, any attempts at sustainable development under the conditions of climate change cannot be successful without all three elements.[6]

Vulnerable populations and sustainable development in an era of climate change

Within the confines of the international community, broad linkages interconnect vulnerable populations to sustainable development and climate change in a variety of ways. In particular, differential vulnerability among populations of the world are often a result of the locations where populations reside, the resilience of a given population's physical environment, and the disproportionate access to resources, which are necessary for adaptation.[7] As a result, much of the scholarship on ethics in international relations tends to treat vulnerability here as a given. However, as Debra L. DeLaet points out in the introduction to this section, "[s]uch categorizations tend to locate the responsibility for ethical action in centers of power and wealth and to identify the populations in need of remediation and aid as existing in the periphery."[8] In reflection of this, how we delineate these groups should be based on more than just the criterion used to define them, the types of vulnerabilities they face, and how they react to their circumstances. The following is an overview of these key issues.

Who is considered vulnerable?

A common perception throughout much of the developed world is that climate change is something that may impact us in the near future. Yet if one moves the attention to developing countries, this problem has already arrived. As Carol Farbotko illustrates in her chapter on the vulnerability, agency, and resilience of small island populations,[9] rising sea levels are already causing large-scale evacuations in the islands around Fiji, yet the concerns of small island populations have remained marginal.

> While rich countries still debate the proper mitigation efforts, perhaps slowly moving towards measures of adaptation and resilience, the poor countries in the world focus on justice in damage compensations and controls, and restorations efforts—a debate that potentially involves burden sharing with a special responsibility of the rich countries since their lifestyles mainly caused the problem in the first place.[10]

When considering who the most vulnerable populations are, several factors come into play. In general, vulnerable populations are comprised of racial and ethnic minorities, low-income women, children, and elderly persons, and other economically disadvantaged or marginalized sections of society including those with chronic physical health, immunodeficiency (e.g., HIV),[11] and mental health issues. Vulnerable populations may also include rural residents, who often encounter barriers to accessing health care and other critical resources, or coastal communities that are vulnerable to storm surges, drought, and sea level rise. In addition, the vulnerability of these individuals is enhanced by race, ethnicity, age, sex, and factors such as income, access to clean water and sanitation, air and other forms of pollution, macroeconomic volatility, corruption, and civil unrest.[12] Finally, all these factors may also intersect with social factors, including housing, poverty, and inadequate education.

At the international level, such considerations tend to focus on the most vulnerable countries. In particular, developing states are the most vulnerable to climate change impacts because they have fewer resources with which to adapt to climate change. In addition, climate change has greater impacts on the sustainable development of developing countries where the burdens from adaptation may take away from other critical national goals such as poverty reduction or education. What is worse is that vulnerability to climate change does not accrue equally within countries, communities, or households.[13] For instance, women tend to be impacted more by climate change, and they also tend to have less access to the resources necessary to deal with such impacts. Despite this, it is difficult to account for such nuances in the broad definitions used to conceptualize vulnerable populations.

What criteria are generally used to determine vulnerability?

It is difficult to determine, with any real accuracy, who and what may be vulnerable to climate change. Since the 1990s, greater efforts to measure and assess vulnerability have taken place, but progress has been slow.

> Nevertheless, appropriate measurement of poverty remains complex and controversial. This is particularly true in developing countries where (i) the stakes with respect to poverty reduction are high; (ii) the determinants of living standards are often volatile; and (iii) related information bases, while much improved, are often characterized by significant non-sample error.[14]

In addition, according to the CARE Poverty, Environment, and Climate Change Network, current approaches to assessing vulnerability for the purpose of allocating adaption funds do not accurately capture the actual differences within countries "and therefore risk excluding the very people that adaptation resources must benefit if they are to be used effectively."[15]

In order for adaptation efforts to be successful, vulnerability assessment must go beyond identification of vulnerable countries.

> Processes for vulnerability analysis and adaptation planning must involve all relevant stakeholders, including local communities and in particular the most vulnerable members of those communities. These processes must examine the social, economic and political drivers of vulnerability in order to identify the most vulnerable people within countries and communities and ensure that their needs, priorities and aspirations are reflected.[16]

This enables policymakers and adaptation practitioners to target resources and interventions where they are needed most.

What vulnerabilities do disadvantage populations face?

The vulnerabilities faced by disadvantaged populations are various and numerous. These vulnerabilities differ by region and state, and can include dangers posed by the changing landscape (e.g., erosion, desertification), rising sea levels, extreme weather, or even disruptions over traditional ways of life. As a result, individuals may be challenged by resettlement, a reduction in the means of production, or the loss of critical resources.

One unfortunate example of the vulnerabilities faced by such populations can be found in the high mountain regions of the Himalayas. Here, production processes throughout the region create black carbon deposits that interact with rising global temperatures and exacerbate large-scale glacial melting, which in turn cause changes in water and other natural resources. Water resources in the high mountain regions are particularly important because water is used for energy production, agriculture, ground water remediation, and waste management for local populations. When the natural balance of this key resource is shifted through excessive melting, it can also lead to dangerous hazards such as landslides, food shortages, and glacial lake outburst floods (GLOF). The GLOFs in particular can be exceptionally detrimental to local populations because the glacial lakes have been part of the local geography for literally hundreds of years. However, once melting reaches a tipping point, the entire lake disappears permanently, often washing entire towns from the mountainside and destroying the basic livelihood of the traditional societies that remain in the area.[17]

Furthermore, when vulnerable individuals are impacted by climate change, the problem is often compounded by a cascade of additional disruptions; yet, they lack the resources needed to adapt. In the Himalayan case, communities disrupted by GLOFs are also further cut off by the destruction of infrastructure these events cause. This creates further disruptions, as these isolated communities then face forest depletion, lack of access to health care and medicine, and reduced access to education and other important resources.

> For the most vulnerable people in many communities, access to and control over resources such as agricultural, forest lands and water sources is an essential determinant of vulnerability. When people do not have secure access to these critical livelihood resources, their options are limited and they are less able to act on adaptation.[18]

How do vulnerable populations respond to the vulnerabilities caused by climate change?

When faced with the vulnerabilities caused by climate change, a range of responses are possible, but in the developing world these options are much more limited. How people respond to these issues will depend largely on their different abilities to cope with climate change impacts. People who live in poverty, for instance, will have a difficult time coping with changes. These populations have limited financial resources to cope with heat, relocate, or respond to increases in the cost of food (as the United States Global Change Research Program, or USGCRP, notes).[19] More importantly, when the things that people value contribute to their sense of well-being, their loss may be significant in ways that vulnerability assessments cannot capture.

Differing worldviews, captured by individualism, egalitarianism, materialism, and fatalism, influence how people may respond to both the drivers and consequences of climate change.[20] While each country is unique, many regions of the developing world share characteristics that can affect their ability to prepare for, respond to, and cope with the impacts of climate change. For instance, it is not uncommon for traditional communities to count on the surrounding environment and natural resources for food, cultural practices, and income.[21] Since much of the developing world still relies on the local environment in ways that we are no longer accustomed to in the West, these conditions must be accounted for in adaptation and mitigation responses.

As Karen O'Brien and Robin Leichenko rightly point out:

> [i]ndividuals and communities faced with both rapid change and increasing uncertainty are challenged to respond to climate change in new ways that protect their social, environmental, and human rights, and that empower them to respond through both mitigation and adaptation.[22]

Because populations undergoing economic development may have additional limitations, the vulnerabilities produced by climate change may, at times, be inappropriately defined as a form of weakness or deficiency, and individual actors may be portrayed as powerless or passive. This perception may further prevent actors from responding in a meaningful or ethical manner. As Erinn Gilson states:

> When vulnerability is regarded as weakness and, concomitantly, invulnerability is prized, attentiveness to one's own vulnerability and ethical response to vulnerable others remain out of reach goals.[23]

The end perspective then is largely reliant upon how vulnerability is defined in the international system.

On a positive note, there is a surprisingly important and under-emphasized point about vulnerability in this literature that is often missed. In this case, vulnerability can be seen as a fundamental human condition that both calls for ethical response and enables moral agency.[24] Extending from Gilson's broadened conception of vulnerability: because we share this planet, we should be able to point to the positive values and potential benefits that stem from an acknowledgement of this universal and shared vulnerability.[25] In doing so, it may be possible to re-focus the emphasis on vulnerability as a universal condition, which should encourage cooperative, shared responses to the challenges climate change poses for our planet and humanity as a whole.

Vulnerability and the Pillars of Sustainable Development

Since the 1980s, approaches to sustainable development have advanced dramatically, yet many of the issues highlighted above help to illustrate how a seeming moral theory of vulnerability may still be lacking. Even in the literature on ethics in IR, the concept has remained stagnant, and only recently have postmodernist conceptions highlighted the impacts of such epiphenomena. To shed light on some alternatives, several critical examples have emerged to demonstrate the racialized and gendered constructions of vulnerability that exist and their impacts on important outcomes. Despite this, solutions to the problem of sustainable development in the context of increasing anthropogenic global warming have become entrenched, thus shaping, for better or worse, the notions of vulnerability that exist in the international system.

To illustrate this concern, one need only return to the Three Pillars of Sustainable Development heuristic. While useful in its goal of simplifying a complex topic, the Three Pillars have broadly shaped the field in three additional ways. First, they illustrate and explain how vulnerability is structured in this area of IR. Second, since 2005, the heuristic has been adopted widely in the research on sustainable development and has served to identify who and what has been studied in the field, which in turn shapes the criteria used to identify and classify vulnerability. Finally, the Three Pillars have also helped to frame global climate governance and with it the development policies and practices used in the international arena. Subsequently, the trinity has helped redefine how we approach development and its associated vulnerabilities at the international level. So, for better or worse, the Three Pillars of Sustainable Development heuristic helps to explain the structural context in which the notion of vulnerability has emerged and evolved over time in IR.

As with all structural determinates, using the Pillars of Sustainability as the logical and ethical standard by which to operate at the international level has helped to focus the lens of vulnerability in this area of IR. In some ways, the heuristic has served to improve the inequalities associated with climate-related vulnerability and economic development. For example, variations of this heuristic have been adopted by most of the world's international organizations (IOs) (e.g., the United Nations, World Bank, World Trade Organization), and, as a result, the Three Pillars have positively influenced numerous sustainability standards and policies from the fair-trade alliance certifications of the coffee industry[26] to the millennium development goals (MDGs) that emerged from the UN General Assembly's summit of world leaders in 2000.

Although the Three Pillars heuristic reflects the state of the field and is considered an important advancement since the issue first gained traction in the 1980s, the sheer complexity and scale of the problem means that some epiphenomena have also resulted. For instance, as the realities of climate change have become increasingly apparent, the international community has established multiple institutions and systems that can be stagnant and inflexible, thus inadvertently perpetuating differential vulnerability to environmental disasters among developing states and populations. By exploring critical, racialized, and gendered perspectives on sustainable development, it becomes clear that the Three Pillars approach may also serve as a means to reproduce or perpetuate inequalities in IR. The following is a brief overview of these perspectives and how each constructs the notion of vulnerability in this area of IR.

Critiques of vulnerability in sustainable development

While advancements in the field of development have largely improved the livelihood of people around the world, the sheer notion of development has a long history of contention. Despite the rise of emerging and developing economies, it is clear that much of the critical literature on climate change and development still perceives international economic relations as fundamentally unfair. The basis of this argument is that the industrialized countries, because of their dominance in the production and consumption of pollution-creating goods, are responsible for environmental problems and should bear the responsibility for any solution to those problems generally. These beliefs are reflected broadly in the policy responses and negotiated strategies developing states take while undergoing development.

The classic example of this dilemma as it relates to development was the belief that, as a country develops, support for sustainable development grows as well. This hypothesis was put forth by the work surrounding the environmental Kuznets Curve.[27] However, critical theorists have more recently demonstrated that improved environmental outcomes in post-industrial states are more likely the result of exporting high-polluting industries to lesser developed states.[28] This is only one way that the structural fixtures of the past have served to perpetuate ongoing inequality and create distrust around this issue in the developing world. As a result, many developing countries argue that industrialized countries in the Global North must adopt more sustainable consumption and production patterns and significantly reduce the use of natural resources and fossil fuels before the South follows suit. However, this notion is clearly missing from the Three Pillars of Sustainable Development.

Now, as the concept of sustainable development has been adopted as a policy goal by the major governments, IOs, and non-governmental organizations (NGOs) of the world, careful scrutiny of the Three Pillars concept has produced a wealth of critiques. In particular, as the Three Pillars concept has gained popularity for its generality, critical theorists point out how this should create alarm as well. Because the concept is somewhat fluid and dynamic, it allows the international community to reinterpret it for their particular purposes and varying situations.[29] John Drexhage and Deborah Murphy, for example, argue that the innate flexibility of the Three Pillars concept should be seen as a liability because the various interpretations have led to confusion and compromised implementation—often with dire consequences for those it claims to protect.[30] Jacobus du Pisani, likewise, contends that sustainable development is a complex, but contradictory term because true development is at odds with sustainability.[31]

A direct example of this issue has already emerged with the successful implementation of the MDGs, which were produced from the Millennium Assembly held in September 2000 by the UN General Assembly. The MDGs are a set of development goals aimed at "addressing extreme poverty in its many dimensions—income poverty, hunger, disease, lack of adequate shelter, and exclusion—while promoting gender equality, education, and environmental sustainability."[32] In a relatively short period, the MDGs have become highly respected, primarily in development circles, but increasingly in related trade and finance spheres. Many developing countries and IOs have also adopted the MDGs as their framework for international development cooperation. As a result, these partnerships have resulted in sound progress in some areas, and some of the targets have been reached in advance of their target dates.

Despite some early success, some believe that the implementation of the MDGs has served to drive the flows of aid and finance in the international community away from important environmental concerns. This has resulted because the MDGs are a large part of the overall UN agenda, and most international aid programs have traditionally focused on the economic and social development pillars of sustainable development. In response to this, many environmental regimes have tried to show how their priorities are in fact aligned with the MDGs so that they will continue to receive attention within the larger development agenda.

If international actors merely aim for a means to justify continued growth that is only mildly more sensitive to social and environmental concerns, is this truly progress? "One has to ask if it is possible to have an increase in economic activity (growth) without having increases in the rates of consumption of non-renewable resources. If so, under what conditions can this happen?"[33] Such concerns also have ramifications for how notions of vulnerability are formed in the international system. As Ian Clark demonstrates, if we continue to stand behind exogenous standards in regards to how "vulnerability is to be diagnosed, and its remedial requirements addressed",[34] we ignore the moral theoretical foundations of vulnerability. In short, the desire to conceptualize the concept takes priority over the true purpose of establishing an ethics of vulnerability to begin with. As a result, it becomes clear that the Three Pillars approach may also serve as a means to reproduce or perpetuate inequalities in IR.

Racial constructs of vulnerability

In addition to critiques of the sustainability concept itself, further debate in the field stems from the racialized constructions of vulnerability. For instance, environmental justice theory often points to explicit forms of environmental racism because it recognizes how discrimination and marginalization involve expropriating resources from vulnerable groups and exposing these communities to the ecological harms that result from use of those resources. William E. Rees and Mathis Wachernagel, for example, argue that constructs like the "ecological footprint" help to hide the process by which wealthy and predominately white populations are able to live beyond their means by appropriating biocapacity from poorer populations.[35] Likewise, Jeffery Sachs contends that marginalized populations, which are generally based on race and poverty, "serve 'locations of enrichment,' safely removed and largely in the North, with resources, while becoming 'danger zones' for climate change, pollution and global resource price fluctuations elsewhere."[36]

However, environmental racism comes in many shapes and forms. In tandem with the blatant hegemonic forms so often cited are the implicit and less-recognized forms of environmental discrimination, which are simply glossed over by the generalities of the Three Pillars heuristic. A great example of this is the work by Malin Ideland and Claes Malmberg, who analyze Education for Sustainable Development (ESD).[37] In their work, they explore how the textbooks used in the study of sustainable development in Sweden, while well-meaning, substantiate the colonial histories of white societies and their role in development. In doing so, they illustrate how this process discursively constructs and maintains differences between "us" and "them." Not only do such approaches illustrate how racism is perpetuated in the system, but they define how ecological racism is defined as dirty, uncivilized, or bad.

Another way that works on racialized constructs of vulnerability are exposed is through the use of visual images of individuals already impacted by climate change. For example, in the work of Chris Methmann, he analyzes 135 images collected from publications, newspapers, and websites on climate-induced migration.[38] Through this analysis, Methmann demonstrates how the climate migrant/refugee appears as a racialized figure, a passive and helpless victim of global warming, which is portrayed as an erratic threat that impacts large parts of the global population. Together, these constructs weaken the concept of vulnerability in this area because it "depoliticizes the issue of global warming, makes those affected by it responsible for their own survival, reinstates them as the dangerous 'Other' and so bars them from crossing the global 'life-chance divide.'"[39] As a result, the international community needs only to teach such populations how to be resilient as a means to secure them and is, therefore, able to shed the blame of responsibility for climate change itself. Visually securitizing climate-induced migration in this way not only provides a subtle image of "white supremacy," but also depoliticizes the issue of climate change and makes those affected by it responsible for their own survival.[40]

A final area where racialized approaches are able to illustrate how mainstream constructs, such as the Three Pillars of Sustainable Development, may actually perpetuate the problems of vulnerability in this area of IR is through the study of spatiality. Spatiality is the layering of "relations between social space and society."[41] The landscapes created by this layering, according to David Delaney,

> are formed when race-centered ideologies combine with other ideological elements such as those centered on public-private, ownership, sexuality, citizenship, democracy, or crime, and with other axes of power to produce the richly textured, highly variegated, and power-laden spatialities of everyday life.[42]

Because the mainstream approach to vulnerability in this area of IR is centered on social, political, and economic impacts on the environment, they tend to ignore those issues that exist outside of this context. Thus, when solutions are proposed, they are not as "holistic" as presumed. However, by excluding race from such solutions, the *status quo* is maintained and only partial solutions are produced. In short, a key aspect of vulnerability is ignored in how vulnerability is conceptualized.

Gendered constructions of vulnerability

Like racialized constructs, gendered perspectives of vulnerability also provide important insights into how mainstream notions of vulnerability may perpetuate inequalities in international relations. More specifically, feminist approaches in this area highlight how constructs, such as the Three Pillars of Sustainable Development (with its focus on economic, social, and environmental factors), can be still be exclusionary, thus further marginalizing those it is expected to help. What makes this approach different from racialized conceptions of development is the recognition that the vulnerabilities faced by women are different from those of men, which creates a unique set of issues. Subsequently, the literature on ecofeminism, feminist environmentalism, and feminist poststructural approaches have continued to grapple with the impacts such populations face and the epiphenomena that result from how sustainable development is conceptualized and explained in IR.

Interestingly, while the Three Pillars heuristic acknowledges a need to focus on social issues, especially those relating to women and children, the acceptance of gender-related differences based on biology has often served to portray women as weak and captive to such environments. This greatly ignores the ingenuity, strength, and sacrifice made by women in such circumstances. For example, Dianne Rocheleau, Barbara Thomas-Slayter, and Esther Wangari:

> suggest that there are real, not imagined, gender differences in experiences of, responsibilities for, and interests in 'nature' and environments, but that these differences are not rooted in biology per se. Rather, they are derived from the social interpretation of biology and social constructs of gender, which vary by culture, class, race and place and are subject to individual and social change.[43]

Thus, the acceptance of gendered differences ignores the underlying social constructs that perpetuate forms of power and thus the notion of vulnerability.

Another consideration that gendered approaches point to in the literature is how vulnerable populations are unequally impacted by climate adaptation techniques in especially gendered ways that can be easily glossed over through generalized utilitarian approaches that put the state above the individual. This approach consistently impacts women disproportionately. For instance, in her work on the Lesotho Highlands Water Project, Yvonne Braun uses an ethnographic approach to demonstrate how this large-scale project serves to reorganize and commodify rural resources for the benefit of the nation-state in gendered ways, with women disproportionately "subsidizing this international project with their environmental resources, labor, money, and, in some cases, their nutritional status."[44] So while the mainstream approaches would highlight the need for balance between the Three Pillars of Sustainability, such harmony is rarely ever achieved in practice. This research helps to illustrate how vulnerable populations can be conceived of in very general terms in an effort to achieve the appearance of balance between the three policy areas. Even if women are extremely disadvantaged by the development project, true equality is acceptably forgone in an effort to achieve the desired trinity of sustainable development.

Another issue that arises from the acceptance of biological differences between the sexes is that, in doing so, women are often portrayed as less valued than men. This issue may be more obvious in the developing world, where woman are more impacted by development practice, access to natural resources, and traditional societal roles. However, such frames have important consequences throughout the world because "the growing literature on environmental justice argues that those people and communities that are most poor or undervalued, are most likely to be exposed to environmental hazards."[45] While this also has consequences for racial and ethnic minorities, women (due to long life spans, their being single mothers, and other factors) are more likely to be poor than their male counterparts—regardless of race, sexual orientation, or ethnicity—and also make up a disproportional part of poor communities. This is a critical point because, despite mainstream efforts to acknowledge women, the social, political, and economic structures of the international system are still centralized around a system of international capital, without which women remain disadvantaged.

Understanding the linkages between the Three Pillars of Sustainable Development is key to understanding the advancement of notions of vulnerability as they relate to sustainable development in an era of climate change. As the linkages between the climate and development have evolved, so have the boundaries of the field, and there is much still to be gained through research and work in the field. However, by exploring critical, racialized, and gendered perspectives on sustainable development, it becomes clear that the Three Pillars approach may, at times, serve as a means to reproduce or perpetuate inequalities in IR.

Looking toward the future

While the overall findings of this chapter remain somewhat pessimistic, there remain at least two important areas of optimism to consider when looking toward the future. First, in an era when power in the global system has become increasingly diffused, the importance of regional hegemons should not be underemphasized. Not only are these countries the future drivers of international policies, but they are also essential to the solutions for a broad range of issues at the international level. As these states experience the hardships of development and emerge to positions of power at the international level, they will increasingly serve to shape the outdated structures that perpetuate vulnerability and inequality.

A second but also important consideration for the future is the possible role that developing economies may play in the transition to renewable energy. Nowhere is the question of energy more important than in the developing world. As these economies have gained autonomy, their influence in this area has grown. Because variance in fossil fuel prices can lead to volatility within the economy, for countries undergoing transition, these impacts can seriously undermine development efforts. Due to the rural and underdeveloped status of many emerging economies, renewable energy can serve as a particularly suitable solution for these states. For example, in rural and remote areas, transmission and distribution of energy generated from fossil fuels can be difficult and expensive. Producing renewable energy locally can offer a viable, sustainable, and affordable alternative, especially as countries transition through the industrialization process.

While it seems clear that countries can reduce the impacts of climate vulnerability by promoting more efficient, competitive, and sustainable energy resources, other benefits can also be garnered from cleaner forms of industrialization. Along with reducing carbon dioxide emissions, deploying renewables delivers co-benefits, including reduction of other pollutants, improved energy security, reduced fossil-fuel imports, and community-based economic development. The challenge, then, is to design creative renewable policy regimes that are effective and cost-efficient but also take into consideration existing and planned infrastructure in order to minimize adverse effects. Consequently, efforts to support renewable energy in the developing world may help to undercut the impacts of vulnerability in the long run.

The goal of this work is to further understand how the ethics of vulnerability framework provides valuable insights into the theoretical and policy-based arguments that lay the foundation of logic in the field of international relations. This, in turn, helps IR scholars to understand the context in which actor behavior is embedded and provides a useful explanation of the normative implications of this behavior in the international system. By exploring the issue of sustainable development and vulnerability from an international ethics perspective, some positive findings can be identified. Despite this, the critical literature on the subject raises important concerns about how the notion of vulnerability is defined and perpetuated in the international system. Hence, solutions to the problem have become entrenched, thus shaping, for better or worse, the notions of vulnerability that exist in the international system. Clarifying the role of vulnerability and developing the theoretical and methodological approaches to study vulnerability are essential for improving our understanding of the environmental, social, and economic effects of climate change policies on vulnerable populations facing economic development.

Notes

1 Ian Clark, *The Vulnerable in International Society* (Oxford: Oxford University Press, 2013), 3.
2 Hallie Eakin and Amy Lynd Luers, "Assessing the Vulnerability of Social-Environmental Systems," *Annual Review of Environment and Resources*, 31 (2006): 365–394.

3 Michael Oppenheimer et al., "Emergent Risks and Key Vulnerabilities," in *Climate Change 2014: Impacts, Adaptation, and Vulnerability, Part A: Global and Sectoral Aspects.* Contribution of Working Group II to the Fifth Assessment Report of the Intergovernmental Panel on Climate Change, ed. C. B. Field et al. (Cambridge: Cambridge University Press, 2015), 1045.
4 Megan Rowling, "Apples, Oranges and Climate Vulnerability Indices," Thomson Reuters News Foundation, October 11, 2011.
5 United Nations General Assembly, *2005 World Summit Outcome*, Resolution A/60/1, September 15, 2005. http://www.un.org/womenwatch/ods/A-RES-60-1-E.pdf.
6 John Morelli, "Environmental Sustainability: A Definition for Environmental Professionals," *Journal of Environmental Sustainability*, 1 (2013).
7 W. Neil Adger and P. Mick Kelly, "Social Vulnerability to Climate Change and the Architecture of Entitlements," *Mitigation and Adaptation Strategies for Global Change*, 4 (1999): 253, 253–266.
8 See the DeLaet contribution to this Handbook.
9 See the Farbotko contribution to this Handbook.
10 Thomas Potthast and Simon Meisch, eds., *Climate Change and Sustainable Development: Ethical Perspectives on Land Use and Food Production* (Wageningen, Netherlands: Wageningen Academic Publishers, 2012), 17.
11 See the Mills contribution to this Handbook.
12 Lu Ann Aday, "Who Are the Vulnerable?," in *At Risk in America: The Health and Health Care Needs of Vulnerable Populations*, 2nd edn. (San Francisco, CA: Jossey-Bass, 2001), 1–15.
13 CARE Poverty, Environment and Climate Change Network, "Understanding Vulnerability to Climate Change," 2011, CARE website, www.careclimatechange.org/files/adaptation/CARE_Understanding_Vulnerability.pdf.
14 Channing Arndt and Finn Tarp, *Measuring Poverty and Wellbeing in Developing Countries* (Oxford: Oxford University Press, 2017).
15 CARE, "Understanding Vulnerability to Climate Change," iii.
16 Jane A. Bullock, Damon P. Coppola, George D. Haddow, and Kim S. Haddow, *Living with Climate Change: How Communities Are Surviving and Thriving in a Changing Climate* (New York: Auerbach Publications, 2015), 257.
17 Samjwal Ratna Bajracharya, Pradeep Kumar Mool, and Basanta Raj Shrestha, *Impact of Climate Change on Himalayan Glaciers and Glacial Lakes: Case Studies of GLOF and Associated Hazards in Nepal and Bhutan* (Kathmandu, Nepal: International Centre for Integrated Mountain Development, 2007).
18 CARE, "Understanding Vulnerability to Climate Change," 5.
19 U.S. Global Change Research Program (USGCRP), "Impacts of Climate Change on Human Health in the United States: A Scientific Assessment," in A. Crimmins et al., eds. (Washington, D.C.: U.S. Global Change Research Program, 2016).
20 Timothy O'Riordon and Andrew Jordan, "Institutions, Climate Change and Cultural Theory: Towards a Common Analytical Framework," *Global Environmental Change*, 9 (1999): 2, 81–93.
21 USGCRP, "Impacts of Climate Change on Human Health in the US."
22 Human Development Report Office, *Human Development Report 2007/2008*, International Public Document (New York: United Nations Development Programme, 2008), http://hdr.undp.org/sites/default/files/hdr_20072008_summary_english.pdf, 23.
23 Erinn Gilson, *The Ethics of Vulnerability: A Feminist Analysis of Social Life and Practice* (New York: Routledge, 2014), 6.
24 Sturla J. Ståsett, "The Ethics of Vulnerability, Social Inclusion and Social Capital," *Forum for Development Studies*, 34, no. 1 (2011): 45–62.
25 Gilson, *Ethics of Vulnerability*.
26 Juliance Reinecke, Stephan Manning, and Oliver von Hagen, "The Emergence of a Standards Market: Multiplicity of Sustainability Standards in the Global Coffee Industry," *Organization Studies*, 33, 5–6 (2012).
27 Simon Kuznets (1955), "Economic Growth and Income Inequality," *American Economic Review*, 49 (1955): 1–28; A. Ansuategi, E. B. Barbier, and C. A. Perrings, "The Environmental Kuznets Curve," in *Theory and Implementation of Economic Models for Sustainable Development*, ed. J. C. J. M. van den Bergh and M. W. Hofkes (Dordrecht: Kluwer, 1998).
28 Matthew A. Cole, "Development, Trade, and the Environment: How Robust Is the Environmental Kuznets Curve?" *Environment and Development Economics*, 8 (2003): 557–580; David Stern, "The Rise and Fall of the Environmental Kuznets Curve," *World Development*, 32, no. 8 (2004): 1419–1439; V. Suri

and D. Chapman, "Economic Growth, Trade and Energy: Implications for the Environmental Kuznets Curve," *Ecological Economics*, 25 (1998): 195–208.

29 R. W. Kates, T. M. Parris, and A. Leiserowitz, "What Is Sustainable Development? Goals, Indicators, Values and Practice," *Environment: Science and Policy for Sustainable Development*, 47, no. 3 (2005), 8–21.

30 John Drexhage and Deborah Murphy, "Sustainable Development: From Brundtland to Rio 2012," *United Nations Headquarters, First Meeting by the High Level Panel on Global Sustainability* (New York: United Nations, 2010).

31 Jacobus A. du Pisani, "Sustainable Development: Historical Roots of the Concept," *Environmental Sciences*, 3 (2006): 2, 83–96.

32 Millennium Project, "What They Are," Millennium Project Webpage, 2017, http://www.unmillenniumproject.org/goals/.

33 Albert Bartlett, "Reflections on Sustainability, Population Growth, and the Environment," *The Future of Sustainability* (Dordrecht: Springer, 2006), 27.

34 Ian Clark, *The Vulnerable in International Society* (Oxford: Oxford University Press, 2013), 13.

35 William E. Rees and Mathis Wackernagel, "The Shoe Fits, but the Footprint is Larger than Earth," *PLoS Biology*, 11, no. 11 (2013).

36 Jeffrey Sachs, "Institutions Don't Rule: Direct Effects of Geography on per Capita Income" (working paper, National Bureau of Economic Research, 2003), 8–9.

37 Malin Ideland and Claes Malmberg, "Our Common World Belongs to 'Us': Constructions of Otherness in Education for Sustainable Development," *Critical Studies in Education*, 55, no. 3 (2014), 369–386.

38 Chris Methmann, "Visualizing Climate-Refugees: Race, Vulnerability, and Resilience in Global Liberal Politics," *International Political Sociology*, 8 (2014): 4, 416–435.

39 Ibid., 418.

40 Ibid., 420.

41 Laura Pulido, "Rethinking Environmental Racism: White Privilege and Urban Development in Southern California," *Annals of the Association of American Geographers*, 90, no. 1 (2000): 17.

42 David Delaney, "The Space That Race Makes," *The Professional Geographer*, 54, 1 (2002): 4.

43 Dianne Rocheleau, Barbara Thomas-Slayter, and Esther Wangari, *Gender and Environment: A Feminist Political Ecology Perspective* (London: Routledge, 2016), 3.

44 Yvonne A. Braun, "Selling the River: Gendered Experiences of Resource Extraction and Development in Lesotho," in *Nature, Raw Materials, and Political Economy*, ed. Paul S. Ciccantell, David A. Smith, and Gay Seidman, vol. 10 (Bingley, UK: Emerald Group Publishing, 2005), 374.

45 Susan Buckingham-Hatfield, *Gender and Environment* (London: Routledge, 2000).

28
CLIMATE CHANGE AND ISLAND POPULATIONS

Carol Farbotko

Introduction

The possible rendering, by climate change, of entire islands as uninhabitable has been a matter of significant concern in small island states (and other island locations) since the identification of sea level rise risk for these types of geographic sites in climate science in the early 1990s.[1] Sea level rise and other climate change impacts, such as changing rainfall and extreme weather patterns, compound existing development challenges in small island states, such as limited natural resources and remoteness. Livelihoods, many of which are subsistence-based, are at risk, as are water and food security, health, indigenous knowledge, and cultural identity.[2] Whole island and coastal communities, and entire nations in the case of low-lying atoll states such as Kiribati and Tuvalu, face increased pressure to relocate—in some cases due to environmental conditions, but also as alarmist rhetoric circulates and policy decisions about sites of future risk are implemented.[3]

The Intergovernmental Panel on Climate Change (IPCC), which is the international body for assessing the science related to climate change, states that, '[g]iven the inherent physical characteristics of small islands, [there is a] high level of vulnerability of small islands to multiple stressors, both climate and non-climate', but also that diversity in human attributes means that climate change vulnerability on islands is also highly variable.[4] The nonclimate stressors faced by small islands, it should be noted, are profound; lacking economic bargaining power, small island states have typically emerged from colonial rule and into the era of neoliberal globalization with a reliance on aid. Climate change exacerbates and further complicates these existing challenges.

While the vulnerability of physical geography in small islands is undeniably important, island populations have also typically been perceived as somehow inherently socially vulnerable to climate change. In other words, despite the IPCC's conclusion that vulnerability is variable because of diversity in human attributes, there is a widely assumed causal relationship between physical vulnerability, and the emergence of a new class of vulnerable, climatically impacted people, so-called 'climate refugees'.

This type of thinking allows very little space for consideration of resilience. By way of illustration, the most severe of the climate change risks—loss of habitability of some low-lying islands and forced migration—has, in popular discourse attributable largely to foreign journalists, documentary-makers, and environmental organizations, become the *sole* focus.[5] And yet, for inhabitants of such low-lying islands, such a scenario (while widely known in island communities as a scientific prediction and accepted as a valid policy issue) remains almost existentially untenable. The result is a discursive and political paradox, whereby it is largely external actors who posit wholesale migration of island populations as a problem, while the purported future migrants themselves largely do not—culturally, spiritually, or philosophically—countenance the possibility of life without a homeland to live in or return to.[6] In this respect, vulnerability discourse helps to create, reinforce, and legitimate patterns of vulnerability in global politics, in line with Ian Clark's insight, as discussed in DeLaet's introductory chapter to this section, that ideational structures and norms in global society are a primary determinant of social vulnerability.[7]

For island populations, reduced emissions of greenhouse gases globally and adaptation to climate change *in place* therefore remains the most important way to address climate change vulnerabilities. Policy, at both international and national scales, is only beginning to grapple with such issues. Migration and relocation are officially considered options of last resort, for example, in Kiribati and Tuvalu.[8] Island populations, in short, see themselves as both vulnerable and yet also resilient. They are typically closely attuned to an exceedingly complex politics of climate, people, and place, and they construct their vulnerability in multiple ways: as a threat to indigenous cultures, identities, and connections to land and sea; as impacting livelihoods and daily life; and as a risk to self-determination and human rights.[9] Questions of ethics of vulnerability abound in the contentious political landscape of small islands and their potentially mobile, climate-impacted population, and it is through such issues of climate change and mobility for populations of small islands that the ethics of vulnerability is explored in this chapter.

Small islands and climate governance

Among governments of small island states, concern about climate change, commencing in the late 1980s, was channelled into concerted and long-term lobbying in the context of the United Nations Framework Convention on Climate Change (UNFCCC). Island leaders have made a consistent argument at successive UNFCCC conferences of parties, primarily for global reductions in greenhouse gas emissions, in order to reduce risk of sea level rise and other climate change impacts. They have also made the argument for international assistance in building an adaptive capacity to facilitate in-place adaptation to climate change. To support their arguments, island leaders draw attention to the unique contribution made by island cultures to global cultural diversity, and the need for the international community to ensure protection of rights to self-determination, territory, and identity.

A position of 'emissions innocence' is at times invoked by leaders of small island states on behalf of their populations in international climate change governance. Their intent is to provide ethical weight to their arguments for greenhouse gas reductions and, increasingly, more resources for adaptation globally. 'Emissions innocence' can be understood in terms of the negligible contributions by small island populations to global greenhouse gas emissions; on this basis, responsibility for the cost of harm minimization and risk management should, it is posited, largely be in the domain of big, industrialized states, yet such reductions are beneficial to all, since climate change is a global challenge, albeit with regionally differentiated impacts. Within an emissions-innocence discourse, climate change is sometimes invoked as a form of terrorism against island populations, again by their political leaders.[10] This is terrorism by omission: by failing to act on climate change, larger nation-states are said to be committing a terrorist act.

Such arguments have been only moderately successful. The international climate negotiations have been dominated by fossil-fuel-intensive nation-states protecting their economic interests, while the development of alternatives, such as renewable energy industries, has been sluggish. The concerns of small island states have remained marginal. The question of future uninhabitable sovereign territory has not been satisfactorily answered. There is no international law addressing the question of sovereign territory, and related issues of self-determination, made uninhabitable by climate change. Furthermore, the integration of climate change into wider international governance on development, human rights, and so on, is in its infancy. Conversely, the UNFCCC does not deal with broader structural issues that shape overall vulnerability. Currently, focus is on place-based adaptation measures, such as building sea walls and relocating coastal settlements.

Small islands and 'climate change migration'

Meanwhile, often pushed by non-islander advocates, the issue of 'climate change migration' has enjoyed a relatively lively debate in some arenas of policy, media, and research. Little, however, has been achieved by way of formal governance of the phenomenon of 'climate migration'. Few states have amended their immigration laws, for instance, to accommodate recognition, or provision for facilitation of, climate migration, although there is rhetoric suggesting movement in such a direction. For example:

> Fiji has offered to give a permanent home to the populations of two of our closest neighbours—Kiribati and Tuvalu—in the event that current scientific projections are realised and the rising seas envelop them altogether. We will naturally need the assistance of the global community to carry out that mass movement of people when the time comes, and help them adapt to new lives in Fiji.[11]

Islanders are typically imagined, in much international debate, in terms of existing power relations: people often perceive Australia and New Zealand, for example, as wealthy and larger and therefore more able to accommodate climate change migrants from small Pacific islands, regardless of whether or not such a 'solution' is within the cultural and political rights and aspirations of islanders themselves. This example illustrates Clark's notion that the construction of vulnerability in international society actually reveals and replicates the prevailing power dynamics in global politics.[12]

However, there is no institutionalized mechanism for individual or collective categorization of climate migrants under international law. Indeed, 'climate migrant' remains a largely abstracted analytical category, rather than an identity—or legal marker—for particular individuals or communities. Legally, to date, climate migrants do not exist. Anyone who is displaced within or across national borders when an island (or any other territory) becomes unliveable cannot be identified by application of an instrument of international law, as with those displaced by political persecution or war.

The vulnerability of inhabitants of islands is only partially shaped by absence of legal protections in the context of exposure to climate risk, and there is a broad geopolitics of knowledge, global capital, mobility, and international governance at work. For example, even if a legal framework recognizing and assisting climate migrants was developed, it could exclude the most vulnerable of all: those who experience climate-related immobilities are known to be particularly vulnerable.[13]

The rhetoric, and sometimes sensationalism, surrounding climate change, 'disappearing islands', and 'climate refugees' is arguably of as much interest as the lack of a policy framework, as a discourse with effects on the populations named as potentially vulnerable.[14] Certain accounts, characterized by hyperbole, paradox, and sometimes unsubstantiated research, have cemented as truths about climate change migrants, with an apocalyptic imaginary underlying much representation, across academia, popular science, and policy.[15] In the context of a risky physical geography (i.e., low-lying islands susceptible to rising sea levels), there is often a language of bodily vulnerability: inundation, even drowning. The logical 'solution' is that inhabitants of low-lying islands must be viscerally removed from watery danger, even though the science suggests that the insidiousness of the rising seas is more likely to influence livelihood decline over time than corporeal security *per se*.

This inundation imagery all too easily reduces the question of indigenous territory disappearance away from islanders and their territory and onto the 'generous neighbour' who 'opens its borders to those named as climate refugees, in the process denying more complex subjectivities, and a future more open to the possibility of self-determined physical and emotional safety'.[16] In other words, complex issues of self-determination, political agency, ancestral ties to place, and cultural identity are deflected, while a question of mobile bodies crossing international borders becomes a racialized matter of welcoming or denying 'climate refugees'. In a world 'where movement across international borders is tightly regulated and border politics of fear deploys considerable power, the term climate refugee must also be recognised as politically charged'.[17]

In short, the political agency of (possible future) climate migrants is often far too simplistically 'reduced to the question of "to stay or to go"; to live or to die';[18] within this binary, the 'rational' response is typically assumed to be to go, on any terms, rather than stay and die (an assumption explored in more detail below). Yet climate migrants in the international order, post-displacement, are also imagined to be out of place. This is an ambiguous moral geography that renders climate migrants at once *placeless* and yet somehow sufficiently *emplaced* to be encroaching upon the borders of large, wealthy states. The often implicit positioning of populations, or even humanity at large, as fundamentally sedentary is at work here, failing to take into account the fact that mobility (and immobility) can reflect both long-standing customs and traditions, along with new opportunities and challenges in a globalized world. What is often ignored is that whether mobility associated with climate change feels like uprootedness, opportunity, or, more likely, a complex mixture of both for those involved will always depend on context. Mobility, even among indigenous populations, does not necessarily indicate a pathological condition of uprootedness and the necessary creation of 'refugees'.[19] On the other hand, place attachments among indigenous people can be of utmost importance. Such considerations mean that understandings of vulnerability and resilience are complex.

There are multiple politics at work, shaping resilience or lack thereof. Firstly, there is the assumption that mobile populations are harder to govern than sedentary ones; mobility (particularly of the poor) is regarded as contrary to a 'stable' world order. Secondly, that a North–South axis of security, where the supposedly rational and reasonable North is positioned hierarchically in relation to 'chaotic' Southern states, with sovereignty in the Global North thereby under threat. It is deeply embedded as common sense that the North reproduces the South as 'subject to surveillance, development and management in Northern terms'.[20] There is thus a received wisdom that climate migrants present a 'security risk' to receiving states. On the other hand, arenas for mobilized populations in a changing climate to articulate and negotiate their interests remain almost nonexistent, and are certainly typically outside institutions of the state or international order. Yet migrants (and possible future migrants) can participate in their own risk management and build resilience by self-organizing and forming new types of peaceful, mobile sociopolitical groups, perhaps advancing new forms of citizenship and self-determination.[21]

Climate migrants are estimated to be forming in very large numbers globally. Predictions about the number of climate migrants emerging in the future cannot be disproved but are circulated with sufficient frequency that they have become institutionalized truths. For example, twenty-five million to one billion climate migrants by 2050 is estimated in the United Nations High Commissioner for Refugees' report, *The State of the World's Refugees* (2012), with no indication of sources or methodologies supporting the figures. Simultaneously, climate migrants are empirically elusive. Climate migration is typically theorized as a complex nexus of economic, social, cultural, and political—as well as environmental—factors that contribute to mobility associated with climate change. Locating actual climate migrant populations, at least in the present, remains an almost impossible project.[22] Much anticipated climate migration has not happened yet: it is currently a projection, a scenario, a statistical probability—these technologies of science are very difficult to pin to real people and events.[23] The elusiveness of climate migrants is also partly due to highly varied mobility trajectories, as these can involve anything from circular rural-urban household migrations to international individual labour and education mobilities to planned, top-down locally relocating communities (O'Brien, 2013).[24] Mobility trajectories may be away from, or even towards, spaces of environmental risk, depending on other circumstances such as political unrest.[25]

The empirical elusiveness of 'climate migrants', combined with 'climate migration' as a young, emergent policy issue, means that there is a certain ease of appropriation of the *climate migrant* subject into very different agendas: the climate migrant seems to be at once both a vulnerable Other; a source of 'enormous potential for disorder and disruption on the planet';[26] and a resilient economic and political agent who might influence institutional change.[27] Climate migration should not strictly be understood as an observable 'real-world' phenomenon but as emergent in practices, including (especially) institutional and political practices that attempt to know and govern a set of subjects called 'climate migrants'. Indeed, it is arguable that climate migration from small island origins is enacted not so much in the daily lives of migrants or possible future migrants, but in the research, policies, documentaries, and media reports that attempt to make climate migration visible and knowable.[28]

Climate migrants have been subjects of proposed radical new international legal frameworks for *ex-situ* sovereignty:

> A status that allows for the continued existence of a sovereign state, afforded all the rights and benefits of sovereignty amongst the family of nation-states, in perpetuity. It would protect the peoples forced from their original place of being by serving as a political entity that remains constant even as its citizens establish residence in other states. It is a means of conserving the existing state and holding the resources and well-being of its citizens—in new and disparate locations—in the care of an entity acting in the best interest of its people. In practice, this would require the creation of a government framework that could exercise authority over a diffuse people.[29]

Climate migrants have been named as deserving recipients of international hospitality, inspiring compassion and 'climate justice' on a global scale.[30] From this largely external perspective, vulnerability equates, not with victimhood, but with humanitarianism and justice. As peaceful advocates for climate change mitigation and adaptation efforts, particularly through performance arts and non-violent direct action, this external perception is reinforced by future climate migrants themselves, who focus on issues of justice and peace in their advocacy work.[31] For example:

> Pacific Climate Warriors network is an inspiring group of young Pacific Islanders who are re-envisioning Pacific futures by resisting narratives about the future demise of their homelands and people as well as re-casting historical patriarchal figures (warriors) in new ways. The Pacific Climate Warriors network has used solidarity and symbolism to convey a collective identity and message that is ultimately about fighting for their survival.[32]

Steiner explains how Pacific islanders in various artistic performances using song and dance have 'the rich environmental heritage that their islands have nurtured, they have expressed what it would mean to lose that heritage and those islands, and they have called on all the world to work together to prevent further loss'.[33] Steiner goes on to argue that:

> there is a world of difference between viewing Islanders as climate-change victims in a far and rising sea and viewing them as a sea of warriors with the power to rise up against climate change. The first emphasizes helplessness and victimization, while the second acknowledges Islanders' agency and ability to work together . . . to make their voices heard and to effect change.[34]

Generally, future possible climate migrants wish to be viewed as resilient subjects, 'proactive, self-determining, and active agents of change'.[35] They do not wish to be identified as vulnerable victims or 'climate refugees'.[36] And yet while future climate migrants can be agents of their own economic destinies in the face of considerable environmental risk,[37] Felli provides an important counterargument to the idea of labour-mobility producing individual 'resilient' subjects, namely that these are also subjects who are useful in the neoliberal world order, as sources of mobile labour for capitalist expansion.[38]

Further, while some external observers see a need for compassion and justice for *vulnerable mobile subjects*, others construct vulnerability elsewhere, and it is the mobile subjects who themselves present a security risk: the integrity of national borders and 'ways of life' are deemed vulnerable and in need of defence. Climate migrants are frequently imagined as potential perpetrators of cross-border violence, often on the basis of dubious data.[39] They have been assigned a position in lists of security threats to the Global North, conveniently conjured in security reports that often simply furthered the interests of private defence contractors and anti-immigration lobbyists.[40] Other external groups appropriate the idea of *host-destinations as vulnerable* for various other political projects beyond national security. Some climate change campaigners, for example, see political potential in mobilizing a climate refugee 'threat' to prompt populations into action to reduce greenhouse gas emissions to prevent climate change, in an interesting alignment of conservative and environmentalist agendas.[41] For other (often white) environmentalists, climate migrants are heroes, able to instruct non-indigenous peoples on how to live more 'traditionally' in 'harmony with nature', even in the face of evidence that consumerism presents as much of a problem in places of extreme climate risk as it does elsewhere.[42] Climate migrants are considered by still other environmentalists as expendable in the pursuit of proof of climate change that their displacement might offer to climate sceptics.[43]

Climate migration as a security threat

Climate migrants have been constructed as a security threat, which in turn constructs assumed destination states as vulnerable, an argument that continues to have significant purchase, and hence is examined in more detail here. According to Barnett (2003), this security approach places 'solutions' to environmental migration within the realm of the military and the protection of sovereignty, rather than as a global commons problem and an issue for foreign policy.[44] MacGregor offers a useful summary of the main elements of the security approach:

> There has been growing interest in recent years in presenting climate change as a serious threat to national and global security. . . Conflicts in some regions of the developing world are attributed to climate change . . . These are seen to have knock-on effects for affluent countries such as the influx of environmental refugees from impoverished countries. The security threats posed by climate related mass migration are met with calls for the tightening up of borders and the increasing of aid budgets.[45]

In short, there is a fear that, collectively, migration associated with environmental decline will exacerbate tensions over resources and thus lead to conflict. While there is some evidence to support this position, there is also substantial criticism of its weaknesses. It depends for much of its persuasiveness on alarmism and fear, since articulations of the 'threat' posed by environmental migration are frequently unsubstantiated by rigorous data and analysis.[46] The conflation of development and the military is an element of defence policy that helps to justify a security response to environmental migration.[47] The Global North–South geopolitical divide is closely linked to development narratives that 'blame the victims' for being vulnerable—poor rural farmers.[48] Pacific populations specifically have been victim-blamed for presuming to inhabit hazardous environments.[49] Placing agency for these processes largely with the rural poor excludes consideration of structural political and economic forces such as lack of land reform and commercial agriculture, over which small-holder and subsistence farmers often have little control.[50] A further problematic underlying logic is that environmental problems can be mitigated through institutional redesign and technological innovation. Such solutions are apparently less likely in the Global South due to lack of wealth and expertise.[51] Therefore, as Hartmann notes:

> while it is commonly assumed that scarcity can lead to institutional and technological innovation in more affluent countries, just the opposite is assumed for poor people in less affluent countries. Scarcity renders them into [mobile] victims/ villains, incapable of innovation or livelihood diversification and naturally prone to violence.[52]

Climate change migration framed as a security issue purports to derive at least part of its authority and legitimacy from climate change science, including the Intergovernmental Panel on Climate Change.[53] The oft-cited scientist Norman Myers has produced work that typifies an alarmist approach to environmental migration in need of a security response, positioning the racialized 'Other' as a bringer of disease, disorder, and incompatible cultural differences which may lead to conflict and political breakdown.[54] Tellingly, research that supports a counterframe, for example, of traditional conflict resolution institutions successfully managing and reducing conflict over resources, is much less widely circulated.[55] There is also a problematic conflation of scale in linking migration and resource conflict in research that is more alarmist than balanced. According to Bettini, most existing databases on the occurrence of (apparently resource-related) conflicts do not provide disaggregate information on different scales of conflict: 'a quarrel for a loaf of bread is not the same as an armed conflict opposing States'. Kelly argues that a host of divisions accompany the national security approach to climate change migration, with nationalism providing the emotive geopolitical weaponry with which to continue to draw on old, deeply problematic, racialized distinctions between 'us' and 'them', 'citizen' and 'foreigner', and 'friend' and 'enemy'.[56]

Understanding the security frame fully involves contemplation of alternative narratives that are rarely given an airing within its alarmist rhetoric. For example, the chief ways in which climate change migrants are imagined to be able to self-organize is into organized violence, while portrayals of new types of peaceful socio-political groupings and networks, building new forms of citizenship and self-determination, are rare.[57] The many possibilities for non-violent organization by climate change migrants needs attention and publicity as a counter to imaginings of the climate change migrant as inherently prone to violence. One useful approach is that of the Government of Kiribati, under the Tong administration (2003–2015), which explicitly viewed planned migration as a viable, although not highly desirable, long-term response to island inundation by sea level rise. President Tong imagined and pioneered a policy for migrating with dignity in a changing climate.[58] Integrated with broader climate change adaptation, the strategy was to prevent forced migration when possible, and to manage migration to promote human security when migration was not avoidable: (gradual) economic and education-based international migration would be key. This Migration with Dignity policy, as it became widely known, offered opportunities for voluntary circular migration and involved negotiation of bilateral agreements with Australia and New Zealand (such as nursing scholarships for i-Kiribati students in Australian universities), but it also built on long-established labour mobility patterns established across the population, particularly among those employed as commercial seafarers.[59] The building of resilience was thus explicitly operationalized—both place-based and mobile adaptation to climate was deemed to be possible, through building skills of value both at home and in international markets.

Enviroracism

The security framing of environmental migration dovetails with an approach to population and climate change among some environmental groups: there is a synergism between some extreme green and border-tightening narratives. 'Climate refugees' have been used to draw attention to the human consequences of climate change, including potential pressures for migration, with the aim of fostering political action on climate change.[60]

For some, decreased population growth is seen as the solution to environmental pressure, achieved through reduced migration. For others, a way of achieving reduced greenhouse gas emissions in the Global North is to mobilize an external, imminent climate refugee 'threat'.[61] Some environmental groups single out ethnic groups with high birth rates as targets for exclusion through migration channels.[62]

Further, there are fairly clear ideological links to the reception of other, non-climate political migrants and refugees in, for example, Australia:

> The imagined trajectories of climate refugees, who cannot (yet) be found in detention centres or boats headed towards Australian shores, form both a strange projection from, and an ominous shadow of, the politics of asylum seekers in Australia. Inhabitants of low-lying islands are not drowning *en masse*, yet there is an anticipation, a disturbingly performative expectation, that they will do so in the near future, like boat people [have] before them.[63]

Perera argues that, in Australia, climate change anxieties have manifested in terms of enviroracism, leading to a shift in official policy from 'sovereignty to sustainability': a shift in emphasis from defending borders against incursions on national sovereignty by asylum seekers in small boats in the war on terror, to defending the sustainability of the island continent by limiting migration.[64] Underlying such a shift is a search for continued justifications for keeping borders closed, at least partly based on racialized stereotypes of 'dark-skinned, over-breeding, dangerous poor'.[65]

Immobility

There is an ostensibly deeply compassionate, humanitarian impulse—across some sectors of policy, activism, and research—to help potentially mobile climate-vulnerable populations. Here, as explained above, the question of bodily safety is often paramount. Imagined in terms of 'saving' islanders from drowning, questions of upskilling for participation in international labour markets, ancestral ties to place, cultural identity, political agency, and *ex-situ* sovereignty have less urgency, although this has been changing in recent years.[66] First and foremost is a perceived need to guide or transfer vulnerable bodies to a place of physical safety. Following that is the question of economic and social support. Culture, politics, and identity are deemed, not necessarily consciously, to be of less importance. But priorities may be different for the affected people. An individual sense of bodily safety or socioeconomic support, it seems, can be less important than the maintaining of spiritual, cultural, and historical ties to an island, and perhaps the declaration of collective political agency in the face of a future shaped significantly by outsider greenhouse gas emitters. The camps and detention centres that too often shape the experience of displaced populations loom large in the policy gap here, yet are rarely discussed in climate change migration discourse. According to Angela Oel's application of Giorgio Agamben, when the governing of the displaced is carried out outside state borders, it is necessary to be wary of spaces of exception where lives might be saved but political voices are silenced.[67]

When mobility is assumed to be necessary in order to protect vulnerable human life, is there—and should there be—space for voluntary immobility? What types of protection should be prioritized at the mobility/immobility interface: corporeal, political, psychological, legal, or cultural? If even a minority of indigenous people seek voluntary immobility, what ethical and political spaces are open to them? If articulations of voluntary immobility occur, what tools are available to ethically interact with the voluntarily immobile in a deteriorating environment? Are the voluntarily immobile displaying their own understanding of resilience? An important case—allegorical or otherwise—of voluntary immobility, related by a young Pacific climate activist, to other Pacific islanders:

> Two decades ago, a foreign scientist visited a small Pacific island. He was a climatologist, and he spoke to the people there. His message was frightening and clear. On the eve of the new millennium, he said, the island would sink under the sea forever. The scientist left the island after that, never to be seen there again.
>
> On the night of the new millennium, the people of the island dressed in white. They gathered together on the beach. They sang hymns and prayed, waiting for the sea to rise up. They wanted to stay with their God, their land, their ancestors, and their ocean.
>
> The people waited on the beach till dawn. The island was still there, and the sea was no higher than usual. The people went back to their homes and thanked God for saving their island.[68]

This story, about Tokelau, tells us little about climate change as a biophysical phenomenon. It does suggest low levels of scientific responsibility: the unknown scientist seemed to be engaged in a rogue science. His certainty of prediction—which turned out to be false—has no role in respectable science, where only probabilities of events in complex systems are possible. Here is a rare, but nevertheless important, account of voluntary immobility in the face of climate risk. Immobility in the face of climate risk can be shaped not only by economic disadvantage or by a particular political climate that reduces agency, but by a distinct choice to prioritize ancestral ties to place, a collective identity, and religion.

The certainty of the islanders about their place and identity at the moment when the islands were to become uninhabitable is vital to the story. The plan formulated by the Tokelau people provided a grassroots answer to a question that has vexed policymakers: How to govern the forced mobility of populations affected by environmental decline? The difficult question of where islanders will go, and the seemingly unanswerable question of who they will be (politically and legally) once islands become uninhabitable, was answered simply, and utterly tragically: they will stay on their island, and they will accept death as the 'solution'. Crucially, the islanders did not leave at the moment when sea level rise was expected to swamp their home. They did not exercise their legal right, as inhabitants of a territory of New Zealand, to leave Tokelau for New Zealand's shores. Nor, it seems, did they agitate for their island to be protected, perhaps through building a sea wall. Nor did they seek any form of financial compensation or assistance. What they did do was decide among themselves on a plan. They wanted to stay on the island and accept the fate that was said to be coming that night. The Tokelau islanders wanted to face the ocean as it rose to claim them and their island. They would do so peacefully, in white, in prayer, together and—possibly most importantly—on their own terms. While the story ends happily—the islanders were not taken by the sea that night—a deeply unsettling issue remains: the islanders apparently chose to face death rather than leave the island.

The story resonates with similar emotionally charged narratives about disappearing islands that have been encountered in Tuvalu, where some people express a preference to die on their islands rather than to leave as climate change impacts become severe.[69] One woman, for example, in tears, stated: '[I]f the worst comes to the worst, I think I would rather just stay here and die. I don't want to leave my country.' At the Kyoto climate negotiations, the then Prime Minister of Tuvalu stated: 'Unless urgent actions are taken against climate change, in 50 years' time the world would just come and collect our bodies in the sea.' Allegorical or otherwise, voluntary immobility issues have received little policy or scholarly attention to date. Such articulations become ethically complex when a humanitarian discourse is taken into account, positing an international obligation to assist climate-vulnerable populations to migrate. In such a discourse, there is no room for a preference to perish or to categorize such a decision as resilience. But the questions remain: How should voluntary immobility narratives be interpreted? Can and should the international community attempt to govern a climate-vulnerable population who declare a right to die in the face of climate change—with dignity, identity, culture, and sense of place intact? Are the voluntarily immobile vulnerable or resilient? Given that 'equitable climate change governance requires greater openness to emotions, values, mobilities and spaces',[70] it seems likely that new conceptual and policy arenas are needed in which emotional, affective, and nonstatic attachments to place are taken seriously. Perhaps most importantly, the political space of climate migrants should not be 'reduced to the question of "to stay or to go"; to live or to die' in the first place.[71]

For governments of low-lying island states slated for possible disappearance in a warming world, emissions innocence, adaptive agency, global cultural diversity, and rights to self-determination, territory, dignity, and identity have framed responses to anticipated lost home islands, and yet such calls have largely been silenced in the international climate negotiations. There is the very real possibility that articulations of a preference to die rather than migrate indicate that the complex concerns of islanders are falling on deaf ears. Rather than a voluntary immobility, in other words, can we interpret the willingness to face death on an island as a resistance to being defined by mobility? If so, perhaps a paradigm shift is required. The most important issues, according to those who resist mobility, are not 'where will we go?' or 'how will we survive?' but 'how do we self-identify and collectively consider and build pathways to a self-determined, resilient future?'

Voluntary immobility needs to be taken seriously by the research and policy communities concerned with climate change and the ethics of vulnerability. It should not be dismissed as irrelevant to policy because of its emotional intensity and ethical complexity. Rather, articulations of a preference to die on a disappearing island raise a number of important questions that have received little research or policy attention to date. Do the vulnerable have a right to die in the face of climate change—with dignity, identity, culture, and sense of place intact, on their terms? Or must they conform to a deeply compassionate humanitarian impulse to save their bodies, even against their wishes, and subject them, at best, to an international 'protection' system that often deals poorly with the displaced? What is the more significant risk here? The disappearing island home, or an unknown, possibly dispersed and displaced future when they may not only have little political traction but would be considered a security risk? And who gets to decide? These questions deserve a great deal of thought and discussion.

Conclusion

A 'successful' inhabitant of the current neoliberal world order is a resilient, skilled risk manager, identifying, analysing, prioritizing, and acting on specific risks. Populations in small islands typically have highly precarious livelihoods and bear significant climate change-related and other kinds of risks. According to Ulrich Beck's risk society thesis, however, risk itself is essentially noncalculable while omnipresent, meaning the risk society citizen exists in a fundamentally uncertain state, knowing that risks abound but that they are ultimately impossible to control. In this sense, then, resilience is somewhat elusive. However, islanders are reflexive about climate risks and mobility, emphasizing that soft risks, such as threats to culture, identity, and agency, are as important to them as the hard risks typically associated with environmental change and mobility, such as damage to life and property. While such 'soft' risks, such as silencing of a political voice due to statelessness, are not sufficiently taken into account in climate change governance, grassroots activism suggests that communities are building resilience to the soft risks that they perceive are important. Island populations are responding to the challenge of climate change by both recognizing their vulnerabilities, and the changing ways in which they are, and will be, resilient to climatic and associated social and structural risks.

Notes

1 John C. Pernetta and Danny L. Elder, 'Climate, Sea Level Rise and the Coastal Zone: Management and Planning for Global Changes', *Ocean and Coastal Management*, 18, no. 1 (1992): 113–160; Peter Roy and John Connell, 'Climatic Change and the Future of Atoll States', *Journal of Coastal Research* (1991): 1057–1075.

2 L.A. Nurse et al., 'Small Islands', in *Climate Change 2014: Impacts, Adaptation, and Vulnerability*. Part B: *Regional Aspects*. Contribution of Working Group II to the Fifth Assessment Report of the Intergovernmental Panel on Climate Change, ed. V. R. Barros, C. B. Field, D. J. Dokken, M. D. Mastrandrea, K. J. Mach, T. E. Bilir, M. Chatterjee, K. L. Ebi, Y. O. Estrada, R. C. Genova, B. Girma, E. S. Kissel, A. N. Levy, S. MacCracken, P. R. Mastrandrea, and L. L. White (Cambridge and New York: Cambridge University Press, 2014), 1613–1654; J. Campbell, 'Climate-Induced Community Relocation in the Pacific: The Meaning and Importance of Land', in *Climate Change and Displacement: Multidisciplinary Perspectives*, ed. J. McAdam (Oxford: Hart Publishing), 191–219.

3 Michael Green, 'Contested Territory', *Nature Climate Change*, 6, no. 9 (2016): 817–820.
4 Nurse et al., 'Small Islands', 1616.
5 W. Kempf, 'Representation as Disaster: Mapping Islands, Climate Change and Displacement in Oceania', *Pacific Studies*, 38, no. 1/2 (2015): 200–228.
6 Ibid.; C. Farbotko, C. E. Stratford, and Heather Lazrus, 'Climate Migrants and New Identities? The Geopolitics of Embracing or Rejecting Mobility', *Social and Cultural Geography*, 17 (2016): 1–20.
7 Ian Clark, *The Vulnerable in International Society* (Oxford: Oxford University Press, 2013), 26.
8 'Relocation', Office of the President Government of Kiribati, http://www.climate.gov.ki/category/action/relocation/; Te Kaniva: 'Tuvalu Climate Change Policy 2012', Government of Tuvalu, 2012, http://www.sprep.org/attachments/Climate_Change/Te_Kaniva_Tuvalu_Climate_Change_Policy_2012_Eng_Translation.pdf.
9 'On the Road to Paris #COP21 Milañ Loeak Republic of the Marshall Islands', M. Loeak, 2015, https://tewhareporahou.wordpress.com/2015/10/06/on-the-roadto-paris-cop21-milan-loeak-republic-of-the-marshall-islands/; 'The Human Face of Climate Change', M. Tiimon, 2011, http://compassreview.org/spring11/5.pdf.
10 ABC News, 'Tuvalu Prime Minister Enele Sopoaga says climate change 'like a weapon of mass destruction'', *Australian Broadcasting Corporation*, August 15, 2014, http://www.abc.net.au/news/2014-08-15/an-tuvalu-president-is-climate-change-27like-a-weapon-of-mass-/5672696; K. Seneviratne, 'South Pacific Seeks Action to Solve Climate "Terror" not of its Making', *Solomon Star*, May 20, 2016, https://www.indepthnews.net/index.php/sustainability/global-partnerships/416-south-pacific-seeks-action-to-solve-climate-terror-not-of-its-making; S. Sopoanga, 'Statement by The Honourable Saufatu Sopoanga OBE, Prime Minister and Minister of Foreign Affairs ofTuvalu', 58th United Nations General Assembly, September 24, 2003, http://www.un.org/webcast/ga/58/statements/tuvaeng030924.htm.
11 The Fijian Government, 'Hon PM Baimimarama's Remarks at the Side Event—Commitments and Opportunities to Implement the Nansen Initiative Protection Agenda—Turkey, 5/24/2016, http://www.fiji.gov.fj/Media-Center/Speeches/HON-PM-BAINIMARAMA-S-REMARKS-AT-THE-SIDE-EVENT---C.aspx?feed=news.
12 Clark, *Vulnerable in International Society*.
13 R. Black et al., 'Migration, Immobility and Displacement Outcomes Following Extreme Events', *Environmental Science and Policy*, 27 (2013): S32–S43.
14 C. Farbotko and H. Lazrus, 'The First Climate Refugees? Contesting Global Narratives of Climate Change in Tuvalu', *Global Environmental Change*, 22, no. 2 (2012): 382–390; E. Marino and H. Lazrus, 'Migration or Forced Displacement?: The Complex Choices of Climate Change and Disaster Migrants in Shishmaref, Alaska and Nanumea, Tuvalu', *Human Organization*, 74, no. 4 (2015): 341–350.
15 G. Bettini, 'Climate Barbarians at the Gate? A Critique of Apocalyptic Narratives on "Climate Refugees"', *Geoforum*, 45 (2013): 63–72; Kempf, 'Representation as Disaster'.
16 E. Stratford et al., 'Reading Suvendrini Perera's Australia and the Insular Imagination', *Political Geography*, 30, no. 6 (2011): 329–338.
17 Farbotko and Lazrus, 'The First Climate Refugees?'
18 C. Methmann and A. Oels, 'From "Fearing" to "Empowering" Climate Refugees: Governing Climate-Induced Migration in the Name of Resilience', *Security Dialogue*, 46, no. 1 (2015): 51–68.
19 L. Malkki, 'National Geographic: The Rooting of Peoples and the Territorialization of National Identity among Scholars and Refugees', *Cultural Anthropology*, 7, no. 1 (1992): 24–44.
20 S. Chaturvedi and T. Doyle, 'Geopolitics of Fear and the Emergence of "Climate Refugees": Imaginative Geographies of Climate Change and Displacements in Bangladesh', *Journal of the Indian Ocean Region*, 6, no. 2 (2010): 206–222.
21 M. Burkett, 'The Nation Ex-Situ: On Climate Change, Deterritorialized Nationhood and the Post-Climate Era', *Climate Law*, 2, no. 3 (2011): 345–374; A. Mountz, 'Where Asylum-Seekers Wait: Feminist Counter-Topographies of Sites between States', *Gender, Place and Culture*, 18, no. 3 (2011): 381–399.
22 A. Baldwin, 'Orientalising Environmental Citizenship: Climate Change, Migration and the Potentiality of Race', *Citizenship Studies*, 16, no. 5–6 (2012): 625–640; A. Baldwin et al., 'Securitizing "Climate Refugees": The Futurology of Climate-Induced Migration', *Critical Studies on Security*, 2, no. 2 (2014): 121–130; C. Methmann, 'Visualizing Climate-Refugees: Race, Vulnerability, and Resilience in Global Liberal Politics', *International Political Sociology*, 8, no. 4 (2014): 416–435.
23 Baldwin, 'Orientalising Environmental Citizenship'; Baldwin et al., 'Securitizing Climate Refugees'.
24 H. Ransan-Cooper, 'The Role of Human Agency in Environmental Change and Mobility: A Case Study of Environmental Migration in Southeast Philippines', *Environmental Sociology*, 2, no. 2 (2016):

132–143; Campbell, 'Climate-Induced Community Relocation in the Pacific'; L. O'Brien, 'Migrating with Dignity', A Study of the Kiribati-Australia Nursing Initiative (KANI), University of Kansas (2013).

25 A. Geddes et al., 'Migration, Environmental Change, and the "Challenges of Governance"', *Environment and Planning, C: Government and Policy*, 30, no. 6 (2012): 951–967.

26 Methmann, 'Visualizing Climate-Refugees'.

27 H. Ransan-Cooper et al., 'Being(s) Framed: The Means and Ends of Framing Environmental Migrants', *Global Environmental Change*, 35 (2015): 106–115; R. Felli, 'Managing Climate Insecurity by Ensuring Continuous Capital Accumulation: "Climate Refugees" and "Climate Migrants"', *New Political Economy*, 18, no. 3 (2013): 337–363.

28 Kempf, 'Representation as Disaster'; Farbotko and Lazrus, 'The First Climate Refugees?'

29 Burkett, 'Nation Ex-Situ', (2011), 346.

30 S. Klepp and J. Herbeck, 'The Politics of Environmental Migration and Climate Justice in the Pacific Region', *Journal of Human Rights and the Environment*, 17, no. 4 (2016): 54–73; N. Clark, 'Acquiescence: Fluid Realities and Planned Retreat', *Reading Room: A Journal of Art and Culture*, 4 (2010): 42–59.

31 C. E. Steiner, 'A Sea of Warriors: Performing an Identity of Resilience and Empowerment in the Face of Climate Change in the Pacific', *The Contemporary Pacific*, 27, no. 1 (2015): 147–180.

32 McNamara and Farbotko (2017).

33 Steiner, 'A Sea of Warriors', 171.

34 Ibid., 149.

35 T. Dreher and M. Voyer, 'Climate Refugees or Migrants? Contesting Media Frames on Climate Justice in the Pacific', *Environmental Communication*, 9, no. 1 (2015): 58–76.

36 K. E. McNamara and C. Gibson, '"We Do Not Want to Leave Our Land": Pacific Ambassadors at the United Nations Resist the Category of "Climate Refugees"', *Geoforum*, 40, no. 3 (2009): 475–483.

37 McNamara et al. (2015); Ransan-Cooper, 'Human Agency in Environmental Change and Mobility'.

38 R. Felli, 'Managing Climate Insecurity by Ensuring Continuous Capital Accumulation: "Climate Refugees" and "Climate Migrants"', *New Political Economy*, 18, no. 3 (2013): 337–363.

39 Bettini, 'Climate Barbarians at the Gate?'; François Gemenne, 'Why the Numbers Don't Add Up: A Review of Estimates and Predictions of People Displaced by Environmental Changes', *Global Environmental Change*, 21 (2011): S41–S49.

40 B. Hartmann, 'Rethinking Climate Refugees and Climate Conflict: Rhetoric, Reality and the Politics of Policy Discourse', *Journal of International Development*, 22, no. 2 (2010): 233–246; M. Aufrecht, 'Rethinking "Greening of Hate": Climate Emissions, Immigration, and the Last Frontier', *Ethics and the Environment*, 17, no. 2 (2012): 51–74.

41 R. Black, 'Environmental Refugees: Myth or Reality?', working paper, New Issues in Refugee Research, UN High Commissioner for Refugees, 2001; Stratford et al., 'Reading Suvendrini Perera's Australia'.

42 C. Farbotko, '"The Global Warming Clock Is Ticking so See These Places while You Can": Voyeuristic Tourism and Model Environmental Citizens on Tuvalu's Disappearing Islands', *Singapore Journal of Tropical Geography*, 31, no. 2 (2010): 224–238.

43 C. Farbotko, 'Wishful Sinking: Disappearing Islands, Climate Refugees and Cosmopolitan Experimentation', *Asia Pacific Viewpoint*, 51, no. 1 (2010): 47–60.

44 J. Barnett, 'Security and Climate Change', *Global Environmental Change*, 13, no. 1 (2003): 7–17.

45 S. MacGregor, 'A Stranger Silence Still: The Need for Feminist Social Research on Climate Change', *The Sociological Review*, 57, no. s2 (2009): 124–140.

46 Hartmann, 'Rethinking Climate Refugees and Climate Conflict'; R. Nordås and N. P. Gleditsch, 'Climate Change and Conflict', *Political Geography*, 26, 6 (2007): 627–638.

47 Hartmann, 'Rethinking Climate Refugees and Climate Conflict'.

48 Ibid.

49 J. Barnett and J. Campbell, *Climate Change and Small Island States: Power, Knowledge, and the South Pacific* (New York: Routledge, 2015).

50 Hartmann, 'Rethinking Climate Refugees and Climate Conflict'.

51 R. Reuveny, 'Climate Change-Induced Migration and Violent Conflict', *Political Geography*, 26, no. 6 (2007): 656–673.

52 Hartmann, 'Rethinking Climate Refugees and Climate Conflict'.

53 Chaturvedi and Doyle, 'Geopolitics of Fear'; Nordås and Gleditsch, 'Climate Change and Conflict'.

54 E. Kelly, 'A Rough Climate for Migration', *Alternate Routes: A Journal of Critical Social Research*, 23 (2012): 59–84.

55 Hartmann, 'Rethinking Climate Refugees and Climate Conflict'.

56 Kelly, 'Rough Climate for Migration'.
57 Cf. Burkett, 'Nation Ex-Situ'; Mountz, 'Where Asylum-Seekers Wait'.
58 K. E. McNamara, 'Cross-Border Migration with Dignity in Kiribati', *Forced Migration Review*, 49 (2015): 62.
59 C. Farbotko, Stratford, and Lazrus, 'Climate Migrants and New Identities?'
60 Felli, 'Managing Climate Insecurity by Ensuring Continuous Capital Accumulation'.
61 Stratford et al., 'Reading Suvendri Perera's Australia'.
62 Aufrecht, 'Rethinking Greening of Hate'.
63 Stratford et al., 'Reading Suvendrini Perera's Australia'.
64 S. Perera, 'From "Sovereignty" to "Sustainability": The Loops and Lineaments of Exclusion, 2001–2010', in *Enter at Own Risk? Australia's Population Questions for the 21st Century*, ed. S. Perera, G. Seal, and S. Summers, 1–28.
65 Hartmann, 'Rethinking Climate Refugees and Climate Conflict'.
66 Ransan-Cooper et al., 'Being(s) Framed'.
67 A. Oels, 'Saving Climate Refugees as Bare Life? A Theory-Based Critique of Refugee Status for Climate-Induced Migrants', working paper, ESF-ZiF-Bielefeld Conference on Environmental Degradation and Conflict: From Vulnerabilities to Capabilities, Center for Interdisciplinary Research, Bielefeld, Bad Salzuflen, Germany, 2010; see also Methmann and Oels, 'From "Fearing" to "Empowering" Climate Refugees'.
68 Paraphrased from Pacific Climate Warrior address to Tuvaluan community in Brisbane, 2014. Tuvalu Brisbane community church hall, attended by author.
69 Farbotko, Stratford, and Lazrus, 'Climate Migrants and New Identities?'
70 Farbotko and Lazrus, 'The First Climate Refugees?'
71 Methmann and Oels, 'From "Fearing" to "Empowering" Climate Refugees'.

PART VII

Ethics and the global economy

INTERNATIONAL POLITICAL ECONOMY AND THE ETHICS OF A GLOBAL ECONOMY

James Brassett

Introduction: the politics of a global economy

Recent years have seen a growth in popular and critical awareness of the instability that accompanies a global economy. Rising personal and public debt, excessive financial risk-taking by banks (and questions about regulation), and flexible production practices, with their attendant effects on job security and working conditions, have combined to generate a wide constituency of market resistance in the Global North. Popular movements like Los Indignados, Occupy, Podemos, and Momentum have enjoyed a rare period of acceptability and growth, as the idea of a smooth-functioning global economy is set against the effects of its instabilities, inequalities, and a wider set of values in the public sphere. Indeed, a commitment to sound money, financial stability, and transparency—the hallmarks of macroeconomic fiscal rectitude—have been forcibly questioned and critiqued throughout events like the United States bank bailouts and the European debt and currency crises.

In this context, the critique of a global economy is no longer the fringe activity of sandal-wearing malcontents on the Left but has become a mainstream concern of popular discourse. This mood holds *across the political spectrum*: witness the rise of popular movements on the Right like the Tea Party and UKIP, with the growing politicisation of transnational production practices, the bank bailouts, and economic immigration. Of course, awareness of such issues in the Global North is only an addendum to the wider, more challenging experience of the global economy in the Global South. When thought about in parallel with poverty, malnutrition, fluctuating commodity prices, food riots, and corporate land grabs, the vast inequalities associated with modern forms of global 'development'—between urban and rural, male and female, propertied and peasant, tourist and hotel worker—the politics of a global economy is more complicated than the reform compromise of 'tax-and-spend' welfare on a state-by-state basis. Historical contingencies of empire, statehood, property, language, human rights, gender rights, and more all underline the fact that the global economy is itself a political construct, situated within power relations that produce and constrain agency. In short, *it is a political economy*.

Beyond economics: history, power, agency

International political economy (IPE) as a discipline and field of inquiry has long been marked out by a set of analytical and methodological concerns that resonate with this current conjuncture.[1]

An overriding question about the interrelationship between politics and economics, or between states and markets over time, has led scholars from different theoretical traditions to highlight the deep imbrications between public and private systems of governance and authority in the global economy.[2] The idea of a divergence between economics as the study of a global economy with a set of independent logics and political science as the study of discrete sovereign state entities is fundamentally problematised. Indeed, for Susan Strange (1970), the 'point' of IPE was to end the tradition of mutual neglect between economics and political science; to emphasise *the entwined nature of their object*.[3] As Penny Griffin's contribution to this theme (Chapter 31) highlights, IPE can therefore undermine one important image of the global economy provided by economics that conceives of markets as a 'natural' occurrence.[4]

For economics as a discipline, the complexity of the object—a global economy—can (and, indeed, should) be pared down by appeal to certain basic assumptions about markets and the people who inhabit them. Such 'economism' is an incredibly powerful logic that envisages self-interested individuals coming together to maximise their utility through the free exchange of goods and services as part of *a human nature* to 'truck and barter', compete, and 'enjoy'. On this view, the emergence of a global economy is part of a progress of rationalisation—*everything in its right place*—whereby the complicating matters of politics are gradually removed from the day-to-day activities of market life. In neoliberal visions, of course, this natural emergence of economic logics can also be rephrased as an *objective aim* of politics: to scale back the state, letting the 'magic of the market' benefit us all by allowing the price mechanism to direct scarce resources most efficiently.[5]

This is a vision of liberty and beneficence that has captured the imagination of many policymakers and thought leaders throughout the second half of the twentieth century and early part of the twenty-first century. As a 'claim to reality', however, the neoliberal worldview can be fundamentally problematised and across a range of IPE approaches that question the veracity of state–market dichotomies, the disingenuous absence of power, and (consequently) the two-dimensional view of politics established. Taken together, this amounts to a common proposition in numerous IPE courses and textbooks that politics and economics are fundamentally co-constitutive.[6]

The idea that economics is always-already political promotes a degree of reflexivity to the relationship between theory and practice in IPE (Cox, 1981).[7] There is no area of economic activity that does not rest upon and (re-)produce forms of power, authority, and governance. For example, the ordering processes of any large corporation rely upon (political) norms of leadership, rules, and a set of negotiated limits to competitive practice. Equally, there are few areas of political activity that do not involve or affect the economy in some way, not least since states and public-sector organisations are major market players with purchasing power. States provide infrastructural support through roads, education, and *increasingly* by marketing the opportunities for trade and investment.[8] Finally, I would note, there is a glaring paradox in the neoliberal vision of a free-functioning global economy, which is that it has become a political project *per se*; as bound up with the interests of certain parties and politicians as it is any underlying 'nature'. Thus, different visions of the global economy persist because they are argued for, agreed, or contested, and compromises are struck.

So how might we think about the global economy from an IPE perspective? First, we must place the emergence of the global economy in an *historical perspective*. The neoliberal idea of a gradual progress towards a seamless global economy both ignores the previous historical examples of global economic interactions—most notably during the *Pax Britanica* and the Gold Standard—and erases the role of states in promoting that interconnectivity.[9] Think of the work of the state in the promotion of travel, communications, and the Internet through the provision of education, support for national champions, and funding for science. More fundamentally, the political context required for a globalisation of economic activity involves an absence of political restrictions and a norm of encouraging trade and competition. Realists and liberals diverge over their explanations of these different historical examples, emphasising either the role of great powers in promoting the stability necessary for trade to take place or the importance of a normative consensus in favour of trade and the evolution of institutions that can support it. However, the point remains the same: the global economy must be understood as a political contingency of history, not the straightforward or natural endpoint of modernisation.

Secondly, and related to this observation of contingency, we must develop an analytical conception of *power* in the global economy. Indeed, for authors like Susan Strange, an understanding of power in IPE was a fundamental prerequisite for answering some of the more ethical questions of politics: *who gets what, why, and how might it be changed?* Developing from the awareness of historical contingency above, this has led some in IPE to focus on the role of *state power* in the promotion and success of a global economy. For instance, while many of Adam Smith's anecdotes about the possibilities of market society have been retroactively used by neoliberals to justify the inevitability of the Industrial Revolution, an IPE perspective might point to the power of the *imperial* British state: slavery, cheap resources, and vast market access as important elements.[10] More contemporary arguments have looked to the role of the United States in promoting global trade through international agreements like the North American Free Trade Agreement (NAFTA), the World Trade Organization (WTO), and now the Transatlantic Trade and Investment Partnership (TTIP). On this view, a global economy does not simply 'emerge', but is actively shaped, promoted, and enforced through the will of powerful states with a particular 'interest' in opening overseas markets, namely: *they and their companies can profit from it.*

While sensitivity to the role of powerful states is an important critical reflex in the armoury of IPE scholarship, it should be noted that this was never the neorealism of international relations (IR). Quite the opposite, in fact, when we consider two important thinkers for IPE scholarship: Susan Strange and Friedrich List. For authors in this tradition of IPE realism, power can emerge from/be based within a number of social structures—financial, productive, knowledge-based, and more—and often the role of the state is to nurture and *protect* social capital through the support of education and infant industries.[11] On this view, a global economy is not a straight power-grab by—and for—the powerful states but represents the emergence of overlapping structures of power with their own attendant possibilities and limits.

Finally, and drawing these points together, an IPE perspective can emphasise the role of *agency* in negotiating the ethics and politics of the global economy. Refusing both the methodological individualism of economics, on the one hand, and the structural determinism of neorealism, on the other, a wide spectrum of IPE scholarship emphasises the political agency of states, civil society, or individuals to change or contest the global economy. From John Ruggie, who emphasised the role of ideas and ideational actors in fostering the post-war embedded liberal compromise of social welfare, to the neo-Gramscian work on the anti-globalisation movement, agency is a central concern of IPE. This assumption of ethicopolitical agency permits a questioning of the assumed common sense of a global economy—the TINA logic ('there is no alternative') or 'austerity'—and allows scholarship to reflect on the diversity of ways of inhabiting the global economy that might exist. This has promoted sensitivity to how economic relations are more or less *embedded* within a set of social norms of justice/welfare, and how the agency of workers, the marginal, and intellectuals can be understood as a potential counter movement to trends of marketisation.[12]

Taken together, a focus on *history, power, and agency* suggests that the global economy is made and remade in a political manner. On this view, the global economy is not straightforwardly 'good' or 'bad', ethical or unethical. Instead, it represents a complex social arena, experienced differently depending upon where you stand and how you come to know it. This is because the very idea of a global economy is itself a construction, a discourse, or, in neoliberal terms, a progressive rationality. Thus, at least a part of the politics of the global economy is in understanding how questions of ontology are not just a quaint theoretical concern, but represent an arena of political contest. As Marxists have long argued, the very assumption of a separation between politics and economics and between states and markets permits a host of political actions while restricting others. This ontological politics is only magnified when thinking about the global political economy.

Two ontologies of IPE

Drawing these points together, IPE can provide a critical perspective on the ethics of a global economy.[13] This is because thinking about a global economy from an IPE perspective foregrounds the question of power and politics. This might entail questions about the role of great powers in orchestrating global economic governance according to particular interests or cultural assumptions about the proper form of markets. Think about the rolling out of particular norms of financial accounting on a global scale or the role of certain conceptions of property (and life) involved in the incorporation of intellectual property within the WTO.[14] Or such a perspective might promote a focus on social structures—for example, production, finance, race, or gender—and how they enable or constrain certain forms of agency within the global economy. Here, we might consider how *being male, white, educated,* or *urban* can overlap with the historical availability of credit, or the social form of governance in private companies to privilege certain individuals or groups over others. However, while the substantive focus of IPE can offer important insights on the ethics of the global economy, the academic discipline has tended to treat ethics as a separate issue, suitable for discussion only once the hard-nosed politics of globalisation have been addressed and understood.[15] In order to address this lacuna, this thematic section proposes a shift from a 'theories and issues' approach to IPE to a focus on 'ontology' in the discussion of the ethics of a global economy.

Rather than provide an analysis of IPE by means of a 'theories and issues' template, whereby certain theories articulate issues in particular ways (e.g., a realist approach to trade, a liberal approach to global economic governance), this theme's introduction and subsequent chapters do something slightly different and are *potentially* more open to ethical conversation. This introduction will typify and engage the ethics of a global economy via two broad ontologies of IPE: *systemic* and *everyday*. The reason for this is to try and set up a move away from a tradition of theorising in IPE—and indeed international relations more broadly—that presents theory as a 'once and for all' choice, encouraging students down a path of ever more refined assumptions, questions, and arguments. On this view, you are a realist, a liberal, a Marxist, or a feminist, and every new empirical issue or political dilemma is taken as a quandary *for theory* to adapt to, or to explain, rather an important political emergence in its own right. In pragmatic terms, my suggestion is that different theories can do different things, highlighting the importance of order and stability in some areas, and galvanising critical energies for change in others. They are part of a repertoire of political engagement: *tools, not ends.*

On the one hand, IPE has been marked by a tradition of theorising the global economy according to certain *systemic* properties. A system of states, a system of production, a system of domination, or a system of rational self-interest realised through particular and benign institutions like the market, property, and governance organisations. This 'large' view of what IPE 'is' assumes that the 'stuff of the world' can be taken as a straightforward background against which we can locate particular issues and debates. In particular, I would associate systemic ontologies of IPE with the first generation of the discipline that sought to place knowledge about economy in a specifically *international* context—of states, or institutions, or capitalism. For such approaches, IPE can be understood to locate around certain specific issue areas—trade, finance, and production—and the ethics of the global economy can be thought of in terms of the distribution of opportunities between wealthy and poor, powerful and powerless, rule-makers and rule-takers. On the other hand, an emergent tradition of IPE seeks to promote the importance of the *everyday* and cultural elements of a global economy.[16] Everyday market subjects may be poor or lower class, and/or they might be 'outside' the normal terms of reference for a global economy (e.g., people who take out payday loans, or who consume sustainably or locally). But for scholars of everyday and cultural political economy, it is precisely these 'small' practices of market life that go together to make up what we have come to 'know' as the global economy.

From an everyday perspective, decisions to save or invest, whether to own or rent, how networks emerge or fall apart, can all have a cumulative impact on the life of the global economy. This approach intuitively steers away from a view of settled issue areas that develop and change towards a more dynamic understanding of how multifaceted practices of market life emerge, combine, change, and affect the broader contours of IPE. In other words, agency is performative. However, while some scholars within this tradition seek to ascertain how everyday non-elite actors combine to produce the possibilities and limits of the global economy,[17] certain cultural political economists are concerned to decentre their research entirely from a systemic account.[18] Here, the key questions relate to contingent practices of market life, how market rationalities are culturally known or narrated, and how market subjects take up or rephrase such logics.[19] On this view, the idea of a global economy *can never* serve as an 'unproblematic' background assumption, but it must be taken as a contingent rationality whose meaning is in a process of change that is actively produced *and contested* by market subjects.[20]

While we might wish to engage in a discussion over 'the soul of IPE', asking whether or not each ontology fits with, upholds, or diminishes the political stakes of IPE as a discipline—as per the divide between critical and problem-solving approaches, and (more recently) between the American and British Schools of IPE—I want to suggest a pragmatic approach.[21] The consequences of this ontological divergence within IPE for how we think about the ethics of the global economy are important and hold distinctive implications for the kinds of political agendas that might emerge. But this is not so much an 'either–or' dilemma, as a 'both–and' possibility for ethical conversation. Different traditions of IPE simply have different things to say about the ethics of the global economy and about how IPE might engage more productively with other traditions of political ethics (e.g., democracy, justice, postcolonialism).

A systemic approach to IPE can proffer important ethical dilemmas and questions along the lines of *institutional reform*, whether it be by identifying large ethical 'bads' in the global economy such as differential incomes, levels of life expectancy, or access to systems of education or healthcare. Equally, systemic approaches have an important facility to highlight the ethical concerns of inclusion and exclusion via an analytical sensitivity to structural hierarchies within the global economy.[22] On each account, common lines can be drawn with the concerns of global justice theorists, deliberative or radical democrats, and various human rights agendas on gender and race.[23] More critically, those Marxist- or neo-Gramscian-inflected accounts of domination might rephrase the political objectives of global ethics away from piecemeal reforms like fair trade or redistribution via development aid and towards the mobilisation of affected classes or constituencies.[24] On this view, systemic accounts of IPE might be understood as (more easily) commensurate with traditional normative approaches to the global economy.

Everyday and cultural approaches to IPE arguably develop a *more critical* set of ethical questions by focusing attention upon *how* particular ideas about a global economy have been normalised, what is silenced, and how alternatives are thought or licensed. The crucial point to retain here is that such ideas are not 'imposed' upon us (e.g., by 'America' or 'capitalism'), but that everyday actors and practices work to produce such possibilities. Here, we might think about the common components of markets—e.g., property, labour, capital, and money—as *social constructs*. A quantity like labour, or the idea that someone is a worker, cannot be understood outside of a cultural history of knowing and disciplining workers in particular ways. Equally, the consumer is a diverse and variegated subject whose interests and desires are actively cultivated in different directions at different times. Understanding when and how consumption choices expand, contract, and change tack is not just a trick for marketing executives to master, for it also holds implications for the way we understand ideas like justice. What is an acceptable level of consumption on a global scale? How do we judge appropriate consumption patterns between people, ages, cultures? What do these changing norms do to the environment, our concept of time, place, and community?

More fundamentally, I would argue that a turn to everyday and cultural approaches allows for an inclusion of poststructural and postcolonial approaches that problematise the politics of ethics in more *resistant* tones. For instance, the ethics of labour are clearly problematic when placed in the context of colonial rule, the promotion of slavery, and the differential access to property, credit, and the rights of marriage and dwelling that follow over time. Yet from a cultural political economy perspective, the redress of these violent histories is not as straightforward as the equalisation of rights, since this ignores the way that colonial patterns of 'knowing the other' are part of the normal functioning of the global economy. This understanding of hierarchy sees power *as a component of social practice*, rather than as a distribution. Thus, we might begin to think about the racial feminisation of particular sectors of the global economy like the garment industries and post-Fordist patterns of production that actively target the low-waged, poorly regulated employment patterns of non-Western countries.[25] On this view, the car we drive, the clothes we wear, the phones we use, and other commodities we consume, are all part and parcel of systems of knowing, dividing, and disciplining the global economy.[26]

The ethics of the global (political) economy

Understood as a political construct, the global economy—as an idea and as a lived experience of market life—presents a number of ethical challenges. From a systemic point of view, structures of inclusion and exclusion appear asymmetric and violent: inequalities of wealth and power bear out statistics on infant mortality, life expectancy, poverty-related malnutrition, and highly exploitative practices of low-wage or debt-bonded labour. Neatly encapsulated in the campaign mantra of 'the 99%', there is a suggestion that inequality is a/the defining feature of the global economy, which has implications for opportunity, autonomy, and choice. On this view, a systemic ontology tends to point to the ethical reform of global governance as an important pre-requisite for ethical discussion in the global economy.[27] However, locating the centre(s) of governance in such a system has often implied one of the big three global economic institutions—the IMF, the World Bank, or the WTO—and it is here that privileging of a particularly economistic view of the global economy is greatest.[28] After decades of resistance to and critique of structural adjustment and trade liberalisation—that is, the Washington Consensus—it can be fairly argued that reform has been modest, and even then highly contested by developing states. While global policymakers have made positive noises on ideas like a 'New International Financial Architecture', the Doha Development Round, or the Millennium Development Goals, the continuing pre-eminence of the goals of economic growth and liberalisation seem to undermine the rhetoric. Alternatives, such as there are, tend to run up against the traditional sovereign rivalries of international negotiation—witness the death of Doha and the relative silence on financial reform in Europe—and the growing realisation amongst powerful states that a strong position within the organisations of global economic governance does not insulate a national economy from global instabilities. Systemic visions of ethics tend to be limited to vague and often piecemeal victories like the rise of corporate social responsibility or the evolving systems for setting ethical standards rather than any 'systemic' shift in the politics of the global economy.

Therefore, I would argue, the ethical dimensions of a global economy are relatively straightforward to identify, if hard to address from a systemic view. Firstly, we need to understand the dynamics of economic (in-)justice in the global economy. Secondly, we need to promote reflection on the possibility of democratising globalisation at multiple levels. This generally amounts to a mapping exercise of political contingency in the global economy and has tended to promote a mixture of cosmopolitan and global radical democratic alternatives, while nevertheless problematising this Eurocentric approach with the promotion of non-European voices and values in the reform of that global economy.[29] Thus, numerous accounts have pointed to the intensification of economic injustice on a global scale: cosmopolitan theorists have often pitched this as a North–South dynamic, or more accurately a sovereign logic of wealthy states and poor states. And critical responses have included mixtures of reformism—the promotion of redistribution, debt alleviation, patterns of fair trade including geographical indicators, and more—to more ambitious agendas to rescale political welfare locally, regionally, and globally. Of course, arguments for global justice go hand in glove with the governance question, and here IPE has been rather more active, if focused on the limits of democratising globalisation. Here, research emphasises the historical (and colonial) divides between rule-makers and rule-takers, the continued dominance of sovereign and corporate interests in governance reform, and the comparatively weak and poorly coordinated nature of global civil society.[30] However, for all that debates about global ethics can benefit greatly from an engagement with the systemic ontology of IPE, especially in relation to gaining a better understanding of the political strategies that might exist, there is more that can be said. Everyday approaches to IPE can provoke a different and arguably more challenging set of ethical dilemmas. This is, in part, a critical reflex *against* the potential for a totalising universalism in systemic approaches—that reproduce questions of global scale and notions of ethics which might themselves be placed in question. Yet it is also possible to conceive of a different notion of political and ethical engagement.

Everyday and cultural approaches to IPE can offer some creative ideas about how to conceive of agency.[31] From an everyday perspective, the ethical challenges of a global economy are quite distinct and can be couched in terms of the lived experiences of global market life. Practices of knowing the global economy, the promotion of subject positions, and the curtailment of alternatives are understood as ongoing processes. These processes might, for instance, give us purchase on how legitimate social relations are negotiated through particular norms of home ownership, for example.[32] Or else, by identifying the manner and the mode of producing norms of market life, everyday and cultural approaches can also provide a set of insights on how there might be *other ways* of living *otherwise*. Questions that might be addressed include: How do we narrate the global in systemic terms (whether it be a universe of states and/or a universal market)? What patterns of accumulation, consumption, and borrowing are taken as essential in public discourse? What frameworks of knowing markets permit the reduction of options to capital movement, skills, and growth? How do we think of the market subject? Why is it always a poor black African face that adorns the charity posters of Amnesty and Live Aid?[33] How do gender norms promote a particular vision of justice in market life—as embedded, stable, and productive? On this view, ethics is not something that can be 'added-on' to a global economy, like a doctor might prescribe a medicine to a patient. Instead, ethics is *a part of* the performative politics of market life whereby frameworks of knowing 'right' and 'wrong', 'good' and 'bad', are intrinsic to the legitimation of particular settlements. On these terms, two broad areas of inquiry stand out as important for understanding how global market life is produced and how alternatives might be thought. First, by denaturalising the global economy and understanding it as a social construction, we might ask: *What rationalities are doing the work?* And second, assuming an everyday ontology is involved in the reproduction of such rationalities, we could also ask: *How are particular subjects of a global economy performed?*

Phrased in terms of rationalities of global market life, we might, for instance, question the pervasive and expansionary logic of financialisation, how it seemingly translates to all aspects of human existence with little clarity on how to question it politically or ethically.[34] Or else, the idea of development and how it has been woven to particular economistic ideals of growth and technology has virtually occupied certain areas of ethical discourse such that development and justice can be thought of as analogous. The point of this is not to recreate such rationalities as a new 'systemic' account of the global economy, but rather it is to think through how such rationalities are inhabited and produced by certain subjects of a global economy. Here, we might think about notions of human capital, how a skills agenda has been supplemented by moves to responsibilise the market subject—credit rating, investment for pensions (or 'privatised Keynesianism'). People partake in these exercises, refract them, and perform them in new ways, as illustrated by the rise of the quantified self-movement or the promotion of forms of ethical investment or consumption. On this view, the challenge is to identify alternative economies as both a form of resistance, and a way of making new global economies possible.

Each of the chapters in this Part engage with the ethics of the global economy in their own manner, albeit with a set of specific references back to the problematics identified in this introduction. What comes across in all four chapters is the way everyday and systemic ontologies of the global economy blur. From Brassett, Richardson, and Smith's inquiry into the way global governance is often enacted by small everyday processes of reflexive administration, to Griffin's critical engagement with how systemic visions of finance-as-natural rely upon particular instantiations of the everyday in gendered and racial terms, ethics is mobilised as both a question *and a problem*. Nowhere is this more acute than in Dhaliwal's critique of global justice, which, he argues, implicitly reveals its colonial dimensions by failing to acknowledge the historical emergence of certain global institutions and economic practices on the back of a Western experience of colonial supremacy. This use of ethics as a supplement or legitimation device for power is echoed in the chapter by Clarke, who points to the entwinement between ethics and everyday practices of financialisation. This crossing of ethics with positive accounts of 'alternative finance' has allowed for a realm of finance that seems to arrive insulated from ethical critique. Indeed, a similar argument in Brassett et al.'s chapter suggests that a normative goal like 'sustainability' can all too easily segue into a form of legitimation for market-making on a global scale. While critical in tone, these chapters orient to the discussion of ethics and the everyday in a manner that reflects what Griffin calls 'a curious and enabling mindset . . . generative of creative thinking and writing about who and what matters in and to world politics.'[35] In this sense, questioning the ethics of ethics might be an important first step in engaging the possibilities and limits of a global economy.

Notes

1 A. Broome, *Issues and Actors in the Global Political Economy* (New York: Palgrave, 2014).
2 R. B. Hall and T. J. Biersteker, eds., *The Emergence of Private Authority in Global Governance* (Cambridge: Cambridge University Press, 2002).
3 S. Strange, 'International Economics and International Relations: A Case of Mutual Neglect', *International Affairs*, 46, no. 2 (1970): 304–315.
4 See the Griffin contribution to this Handbook (Chapter 31).
5 Wendy Brown, *Undoing the Demos: Neoliberalism's Stealth Revolution* (Cambridge, MA: MIT Press, 2015).
6 A. Broome, *Issues and Actors in the Global Political Economy* (New York: Palgrave, 2014); R. O'Brien and M. Williams, *Global Political Economy* (New York: Palgrave, 2010).
7 R. Cox, 'Social Forces, States, and World Orders: Beyond International Relations Theory', in *Millennium: Journal of International Studies*, 10, no. 1 (1981): 126–155.
8 P. Cerny, 'Paradoxes of the Competition State: The Dynamics of Political Globalisation', in *Government and Opposition*, 32, no. 2 (1997): 251–274.
9 P. Hirst and G. Thompson, *Globalisation in Question*, 3rd edn. (Cambridge: Polity, 2009).
10 Ha-Joon Chang, *Kicking Away the Ladder: Development Strategy in Historical Perspective* (London: Anthem Press, 2002). See also: B. Buzan and G. Lawson, 'The Global Transformation: The Nineteenth Century and the Making of Modern International Relations', *International Studies Quarterly*, 57, no. 3 (2013): 620–634.
11 Chang, *Kicking Away the Ladder.*
12 V. Birchfield, 'Contesting the Hegemony of Market Ideology: Gramsci's "Good Sense" and Polanyi's "Double Movement"', *Review of International Political Economy*, 6, no. 1 (1999): 27–54.
13 M. Andreu and J. Brassett, 'Anti-Globalization 2.0: International Political Economy and the Contested Ethics of Globalization', CSGR working paper, 2017.
14 Valbona Muzaka, 'Developing Countries and the Struggle on the Access to Medicines Front', *Third World Quarterly*, 30, no. 7 (2009): 1343–1369.
15 See the Dhaliwal contribution to this Handbook (Chapter 30).
16 J. Hobson and L. Seabrooke, eds., Everyday Politics of the World Economy (Cambridge: Cambridge University Press, 2007).
17 Ibid.
18 J. Best and M. Paterson, eds., *Cultural Political Economy* (New York: Routledge, 2010).
19 P. Langley, 'The Uncertain Subjects of Anglo-American Financialization', *Cultural Critique*, 65 (2007): 66–91.
20 James Brassett, 'British Comedy, Global Resistance: Russell Brand, Stewart Lee, and Charlie Brooker', *European Journal of International Relations*, 22, no. 1 (2016): 168–191
21 J. Brassett, 'British Irony, Global Justice: A Pragmatic Reading of Chris Brown, Banksy, and Ricky Gervais', *Review of International Studies*, 35, no. 1 (2009): 219–245.
22 R. Higgott, 'Contested Globalisation: The Changing Context and Normative Challenges', *Review of International Studies*, 26 (2000): 131–153; C. Murphy, 'Global Governance: Poorly Done, Poorly Understood', *International Affairs*, 76, no. 4 (2000): 789–803.
23 See the Dhaliwal contribution to this Handbook (Chapter 30).
24 S. Gill, 'Toward a Postmodern Prince? The Battle in Seattle as a New Moment in the Politics of Globalisation', *Millennium: Journal of International Studies*, 29, no. 1 (2000): 131–140.
25 J. Elias, 'Stitching-Up the Labour Market: Recruitment, Gender and Ethnicity in the Multinational Firm', *International Feminist Journal of Politics*, 7, no. 1 2005: 90–111.
26 R. Kremers and J. Brassett, 'Mobile Payments, Social Money: Everyday Politics of the Consumer Subject', in *New Political Economy* (2017), online first.
27 D. Held, *Cosmopolitanism: Ideals and Realities* (Cambridge: Polity, 2010); J. A. Scholte, *Globalization: A Critical Introduction* (New York: Palgrave, 2005).

28 Higgott, 'Contested Globalisation'.
29 J. A. Scholte, 'Re-Inventing Global Democracy', *European Journal of International Relations*, 20, no. 1 (2014).
30 Murphy, 'Global Governance'.
31 Brassett, 'British Comedy, Global Resistance'.
32 L. Seabrooke, 'What Do I Get? The Everyday Politics of Expectations and the Subprime Crisis', *New Political Economy*, 15, no. 1: 51–70.
33 Brassett, 'British Irony, Global Justice'.
34 See the Clarke contribution to this Handbook (Chapter 29).
35 See the Griffin contribution to this Handbook (Chapter 31).

29

THE ETHICS OF ALTERNATIVE FINANCE

Governing, resisting, and rethinking the limits of finance

Chris D. Clarke

Finance has long been a site and subject of ethical and moral discourse. Questions about the morality of money and debt, who gets what and why because of how finance is governed, or how the international, domestic, or local organisation of credit affects daily life, all encourage debate about the ethical concerns and moral dilemmas of finance. For many people the financial crisis of 2007–2008, the subsequent debt crisis, and the recessionary era were pivotal episodes calling for a ratcheting up of the scrutiny of the ethics of finance in general. These experiences produced a renewed intensification of moralising discourses surrounding the significance of finance to contemporary economy and society, even from mainstream economists.[1] Crucially, the crisis also fostered interest in, and reinvigorated existing pursuits of, 'alternative' ways of thinking and practising finance. Some of these alternatives emerge from, and indeed raise further, fundamental questions about what finance 'is' and what it 'does' across and within national borders, including how it affects—and how it is *produced by*—the normativity of everyday life.

The post-crisis era, if it can be called that, has witnessed a series of responses that can be read through the lens of a concern for the ethics of finance. What forms of politicisation of the ethics of finance exist? How are different ethically oriented practices of finance pursued or refused? In what ways are trends in finance implicitly or explicitly appealing to ethical imaginaries of finance? Using this lens, the (re-)politicisation of finance can be characterised along at least three lines.

First, at the level of (global) *governance*, efforts have been made to reform the architecture of global finance in a sense at least echoing the tradition of embedded liberalism, even if weak in application. Renewed emphasis has been placed on issues like stability and growth, transparency and accountability, and a new macroprudential policy shift.[2] Here much attention focuses on the flaws in the 'system' of global finance, so that policy interventions can be made to improve or reform it, at least implicitly in morally desirable ways, and to make that system more 'resilient'.[3] For instance, the desire to ensure that bank failure does not come at the cost of ordinary citizens has been at the heart of efforts to boost bank capital ratios. Governance agendas such as those driven by the IMF have also involved new efforts to combat tax evasion, especially after a number of high profile campaigns highlighted the injustices apparent in the global financial system and the moral outrage fuelled by the release of the Panama Papers.

A second wave of politicisation of finance comes from a broad array of activities that might be understood as *resistance* to formal sites of financial governance. For instance, anti-elite movements such as the Indignados and Occupy, among other positions, represent a rejection of the unequal system of finance and its governance, which were blamed for the crisis and its aftermath. Such forms of resistance to the dominant financial architecture build on critique of the inequalities and injustices of global finance, mobilising metaphors such as global banks like Goldman Sachs as 'vampire squids' who suck value out of the productive economy and extract rents from ordinary people's labour.[4] Resistive efforts in this sense have a clear moralising agenda to politicise, and politically challenge, the place of the elite financiers who were responsible for the crash, as well as the governments (particularly in the Global North) who were heavily involved in the production and maintenance of a crisis-prone and unequal financial system.

A third form of politicisation of finance goes beyond a systemic reading. It involves what might be termed an everyday or cultural *rethinking* of the relationality of finance and seeks to encourage critical reflection about what it means to have a relationship with 'it'. How is the normativity of everyday life tied to finance, and how does it (re-)produce 'finance', *per se*? For instance, the subprime crisis marked in a very real sense how the normative aspects of everyday life, such as the desirable 'good' attached to owning one's home through mortgage debt, mean that huge parts of Anglo-American populations in particular constitute and reproduce finance after a particular image. Yet the complex entanglements between ordinary life and finance under neoliberalism lead some people to attempt to think and enact this relationship differently. Examples might include efforts to resist foreclosure, occupation, collective debt cancelation, platform cooperativism, and avoiding use of traditional financial institutions. These everyday politicised practices of finance have clear links with more overt forms of resistance indicated above, and they are not completely divorced from governance strategies either. An everyday or cultural engagement with the ethics of finance goes beyond a neat governance/resistance, inside/outside divide. In short, this third form of politicisation is about people questioning whether finance constitutes a 'system' at all and, perhaps, seeking ways to transform or refuse their financial subjectivity in light of ethical concerns about finance.

This chapter seeks to situate these three forms of politicisation of finance, briefly sketched here, within a particular set of debates about the 'turn' to the alternative in the current financial conjuncture. This allows for a consideration of the ethics of alternative finance, indicating where the limits and possibilities of 'alternatives' in finance might be drawn. For the purposes of this chapter, ethical–political perspectives will be heuristically outlined as 'responses' to 'the crisis', even though in many respects they overlap with each other and of course date back much further than the late 2000s. It is also important to be attentive to how the crisis itself was performed as an 'event' with particular 'consequences' that are themselves ethically loaded.[5] Nevertheless, perspectives on crisis prove a useful starting point to investigate the ethics of this turn to the alternative.

The chapter is divided into three parts. First, the themes of *governing*, *resisting*, and *rethinking* finance in the context of the crisis are developed. How are the ethics of finance performed in each of these variants of politicisation? Second, the ways in which these perspectives prefigure particular alternatives will be scrutinised. In particular, the key trends associated with alternative circuits of monies/payments and platform economies will be outlined. Finally, a case discussion of the rise of online peer-to-peer (P2P) lending will help demonstrate, on the one hand, the problematic nature of the tendency to think that 'finance' can be 'fixed' with a particular turn to one set of ethical alternatives, while, on the other, that it is still a useful experiment in *rethinking* the ethical relationality of finance.

Perspectives on 'post-crisis' finance

Governing finance

To what set of financial practices or circumstances are responses to the crisis calling for an alternative? At the level of governance, the ethics of financial practices during the build-up to the crisis are usually discussed in terms of singling out forms of discrete 'unethical' behaviour to be juxtaposed with a notion of the smooth running of morally neutral finance. Predatory lending, bank mismanagement, credit rating conflicts of interest, Madoff-style Ponzi schemes, Libor-rigging, and so on, are generally held to be either explicitly or implicitly morally undesirable practices that threatened the ordinary benevolent functioning of the financial system. Mobilising a sense of a 'bad apples'-type analysis, illustrated in the documentary *Inside Job*, particular individuals and institutions are considered to be a threat to the financial system, which is held to be essentially desirable and part of the 'normal' workings of a (global) market economy.

To the extent that governance agendas focus explicitly on questions of the ethics of finance, they tend to use the concept of 'moral hazard'. This term is used to refer to the particular circumstance in which individual financial actors behave with little or no regard for the wider social consequences of their actions because ultimately the state will step in to save the institution for which they work if their actions result in large financial losses.[6] During the run-up to the crisis, the implicit government deposit guarantee granted to licensed banks is deemed to have created a situation of moral hazard whereby there was no cost to an individual for morally reckless behaviour. In other words, in economistic terms, the state was at fault for 'incentivising' the wrong type of financial activity. This type of analysis relies on a broader set of liberal governance claims, which essentially rest on the premise that as long as the state gets the broad institutional configuration correct, it can remove itself from the 'economic realm' and allow self-interested individuals to pursue their own ends in a functioning market economy. This is the morality of the market in simplest terms.

Governance-level appeals to and endorsements of 'alternative' ways of organising finance should be understood within this context. To be sure, there have been some moves towards 'fixing' the global financial system using morally charged language.[7] The moral appeal of unwinding some of the excesses of the post-Bretton Woods era has been recognised in terms of protecting populations from the consequences of leveraged financial losses, but this does not necessarily involve altering in any fundamental sense the drivers of financial behaviour themselves. Concrete measures tend to focus on large banking institutions. For instance, across a number of national contexts, in order to remove the need for the taxpayer to pick up the bill of a failing bank, Glass–Steagall-type 'Chinese walls' have been mandated, liquidity ratio requirements have been increased, and new rules for banking conduct have been written. However, a predominantly neoliberal worldview structures the scope and willingness to pursue genuine reform after what has been called a 'status quo crisis'.[8]

Some international institutions and national governments have sought to rethink how finance is governed. The macroprudential policy agenda is often flagged as important because it directs policy to the systemic whole of finance, as opposed to the individual operations of banks and other financial institutions. As part of this turn, conceptual mappings of finance as a 'complex ecosystem' have become influential and the necessity of building 'resilience' has been recognised.[9] Notably in terms of alternatives, these trends mean that new and ostensibly innovative financial business models have received a largely warm welcome from governing elites at the state and international level. For instance, states, regulators and central banks have called for a diversification of the financial system so that new 'challenger' banks and nontraditional lenders, such as credit unions, community banks, and online lenders, can increase competition in the retail sector.[10] This has come in the face of one of the key outcomes of the crisis being the concentration of the banking sector, such as rescue takeovers in the US or the destruction of the *cajas* in Spain.

While important in themselves, what is most interesting from the perspective of thinking through how ethical claims have been made about the alternative in finance is that these post-crisis governance agendas in a certain way help to *legitimise* those firms and organisations that style themselves as a new alternative to 'mainstream' bank-based finance. For instance, along with the challenger banks that have benefitted from changes to banking licence laws, 'digital financial innovation' and 'FinTech' have been actively embraced by governing elites, particularly in the US and the UK.[11] The relationship between financial centres like Hong Kong, New York, and London and states has become highly politicised in the last decade or so as politicians and regulators have, at least in public, sought to distance themselves from the immorality of financial elites. This opens the door for 'the alternative' to be actively endorsed by the state, even by those same actors and institutions that make up the global financial 'system'.

Post-crisis financial governance has thus been flavoured by the ostensible appeal of those operating using alternative financial business models. The key point is that diversification is seen as desirable because this helps to counter the perceived homogeneity of large bank finance that led to the crisis. A diversity of financial firms and activities is thought to be to the good of the ordinary consumer, in governance terms equitable to the citizen. Essentially, alternative financial providers are often championed as part of an ostenstibly 'disruptive' financial moment.

Resisting finance

Coordinated forms of resistance garnered by the financial crisis have taken a number of forms. Perhaps the most visible of these are the anti-austerity movements that have influenced party politics and election outcomes, especially in some European states experiencing the harshest forms of state restructuring. A notable dynamic is the association of EU institutions with the mechanisms of global finance and large international financial institutions, such that blame for austerity is laid at the door of EU officials, ruling national governments, and international financiers and banks. Some of the most acute protests against the imposed austerity agenda in Greece, for example, have been flavoured with a distinct nationalistic character as anger is directed at 'creditor' EU member states. The discourses mobilised by governing elites tend to come in the form of morality tales that put the blame for national indebtedness at the door of Greek people themselves.[12]

For many, resistance to this reading of crisis and its governance response comes in the form of a scaling back or in a sense a *rejection* of finance. The concerns about moral hazard, for instance, coming as they do from a restrictive and economistic interpretation of financial behaviour, do not go far enough in terms of an engagement with the ordinary experiences of finance, which are often highly class-based, gendered and racialised. On this view, concepts like individual or institutional 'moral hazard' serve to exclude much of the ethical content that is at stake in an analysis of the crisis. When a broader lens on the crisis is brought into view, the relationship between finance and society is shown to be deeply political and of ethical concern. Anti-austerity campaigns tend to focus on a limiting or unwinding of some of the key tenets of financialisation. This often revolves around efforts to improve wages and working conditions and halt the retrenchment of public services and support. It also tends to privilege certain areas of economic activity over others. While finance is castigated for having destroyed wealth and wellbeing, more traditionally understood 'productive' activities such as manufacturing are stressed as morally desirable by comparison.

There is also a 'localist' flavour to these calls, whereby an alternative economy with a reduced financial system would depend on more focussed connections between ordinary savings and productive investments, not between flows of footloose capital and speculative investments. While such idealised images are hard to pursue, a number of campaigns are organised around getting money out of the big banks and into productive investment, as if the two can be coherently and neatly separated. They might also involve the various anti-free trade agendas involved in campaigns around multilateral trade agreements, giving some resistive efforts a protectionist flavour.

The turn to the alternative from such a perspective tends to coalesce around two key trends. The first might be characterised as the search for alternative *economies* in general, as opposed to looking for alternative *finance per se*. In this more radical frame of reference, the roles of credit and debt in economy are questioned, such that forms of economic interaction are pursued that reduce the presumed *need* for debt itself. Examples might include forms of barter economy, neighbourhood-swap schemes, not-for-profit platform exchanges, and so on. The agenda is one of *de*-financialisation. A second is that which stresses the need for financial services like lending and payments in a more 'just' vision of economy but articulates alternatives that can reduce the power attached to those who provide them. Key examples here would include the Positive Money campaign, which seeks to remove from banks the power to 'create' money when issuing a loan, and support for cryptocurrencies based on blockchain technologies, such as Bitcoin and Etherum. Notably, these initiatives have an anti-elite ethos in the sense that they attempt to undermine the institutional power of large financial institutions, on the one hand, and central banks and national governments, on the other. Resistive efforts here, such that they turn to and support the alternative, are in a sense 'outside' the current system of finance and provide an important point of reference for understanding different types of alternative finance.

Rethinking finance

A set of deeper questions about rethinking finance comes from an array of people and groups in the post-crisis moment. These include positions spanning across governance and resistive efforts, at the interstitial spaces between the academy and activism, and in the often mundane and everyday practices that serve to reproduce finance in daily life. For the purposes of this chapter, what unites the particular line of questioning under consideration is a certain cultural disposition towards problematising the inside/outside distinction in finance. How is it possible to live 'outside' of finance in a neoliberal financialised economy? Is 'debt-free' living morally desirable in the current conjuncture? Instead of refusing it, how can finance be performed *differently*? Rather than fetishise 'alternative finance' as a remedy that will fix all of the problems of contemporary capitalism, those practices that represent an experimentation with finance suggest a more complex relationship between the everyday and the performance of finance.[13] Finance is neither granted the status of a totalising force, legitimised as a natural and inevitable part of contemporary life, nor is it assumed that it is straightforward to intervene within, change, or resist 'it'. To go beyond such dichotomies, a repurposing of finance can be identified along a number of lines that raises three central points.

First, a key set of drivers of such experimentation has developed out of the energy produced by an everyday frustration with finance. While Occupy at the street level lasted for a number of months, over six years later there are still a number of activities undertaken by the people and groups involved, as well as those whom it inspired. For instance, growing directly out of

Occupy, Loomio, a cooperative that builds open-source software for collaborative decision-making, was established in 2011 and ran a successful international crowdfunding campaign in 2013. It now has raised additional capital and runs as a successful social enterprise. Another example would be the Strike Debt campaign as a form of debt-based collectivism, which ran a crowdfunding campaign to buy and then cancel student debt in the US.[14]

Second, and related to the first point, another trend can be identified in forms of financial experimentation coalescing around an ostensible theme of 'social' or 'relational' finance.[15] Emerging forms of finance here in a sense mobilise the inherent social relations of finance in order to produce, harness, and market 'the social' itself. Such mobilisations of the social are never unproblematic, loaded as they are with issues related to seeing the social as conceptually separate and ethically separate-*able* from 'the market'. Likewise, the valorisation of social ties is not without moral dilemmas, such as precisely how they are monetised and who owns the outputs.

Third, the ethos of some emerging forms of finance nevertheless suggest a different way of conceiving 'the alternative'. The theme is experimentation, tinkering, and 'hacking', not outright rejection of finance.[16] As opposed to the notion of alternative as in opposition to a 'dominant force', this conception of alternative is closer to Bill Maurer's suggestion that it can be understood as 'an alternation in phase over time'.[17] Everyday practices and experiments may at times weave into established systems of finance, while at other times they may produce different spaces for interaction. The point is to not foreclose the outcome. As Taylor Nelms points out, '[w]hile we frequently hear about 'disruption' and 'innovation' from London and Silicon Valley, this corporate rhetoric too often occludes the radical experiments taking place all the time, all around us'.[18] Drawing these points together, it is possible to see how an attentiveness to the everyday practices that perform finance helps to show how active attempts—and refusals—are shot through with normative concern, especially when they perform finance differently.

Emerging alternative financial practices

This section outlines two developments in financial practice that are often associated with the post-crisis turn to the alternative: monies/payments, on the one hand, and platform economies, on the other. The aim of this section is not to give a definitive account of each, but rather to begin to think through how they can be understood through the lenses of the three themes outlined above: governing, resisting and rethinking finance. Each of these contains a number of ethical implications that can be explored through a discussion of the practices themselves. The argument developed is that the turn to the alternative should be treated with caution in ethical terms, concerning both the novelty and desirability of the practices involved, and the extent to which finance can be reimagined in the current conjuncture.

Monies/payments

Alternative currencies are not new. To some degree, it makes more sense to think about all currency as making 'alternate' and competing claims to social legitimacy.[19] Money is what we make of it, in a certain sense, and it is only shared faith in a particular currency that gives it 'value' in use. However, the recent emergence of cryptocurrencies is a particularly interesting trend in terms of thinking about the ethics of alternative finance. Such currencies make use of blockchain technologies to establish forms of 'digital cash' that can be used as an alternative to state-based fiat currencies. The best-known example is Bitcoin, but there are many others. In short, three basic aspects of cryptocurrencies are important for this discussion. First, they are alternative in the sense that they do not rely on a system of formal governance beyond the blockchain itself. Simply put, the creation ('mining') of 'Bitcoins', for instance, happens when computer processing power solves mathematical puzzles (called 'proof of work'), which essentially confirms previous transactions in the 'chain' (think ledger). Second, while in theory cryptocurrencies like Bitcoin are celebrated for being 'trust-free' forms of money dependent purely on the security and stability of machine code, in practice they actually work much more in terms of a form of sociality whereby Bitcoin communities are pivotal to the whole success of the currency *in use*.[20] Third, the similarities between the blockchain and a ledger system of past transactions have led some to argue that rather than as a straightforward currency, cryptocurrencies such as a Bitcoin are better thought of as emerging forms of payment systems.[21] In other words, cryptocurrency is more akin to a payments 'rail' for a financial transaction than a unit of account, *per se*. This is why it is important to think about changes in monies and payments at the same time.

In terms of the ethical potential and limits that are established by cryptocurrency, one of the major issues is the way in which it contains an active avoidance of the state. Advocates usually stress the political and ethical desirability of this feature. It thus represents something of a fusion of leftist–anarchist thinking with right-wing libertarianism. The Snowdon generation is suspicious of state surveillance, and the blockchain as a means of breaking the shackles of sovereign abuse of citizens thus becomes available for support.[22] For governments and regulators, cryptocurrencies are often castigated for their facilitation of illegal (and immoral) activities beyond the state. For instance, Bitcoin has been associated with activities like the illegal trade in drugs and human trafficking through websites such as Silk Road (which has been closed down).[23] National authorities have also raised substantial concerns about how they can be used to facilitate tax evasion and money laundering. However, for those seeking to resist the workings of mainstream financial circuits, the very fact that blockchain technologies avoid state regulation and policing represents an advantage. On this view, the morally unacceptable uses to which cryptocurrencies are put are not built into the technology itself but only come as a result of the ways in which people deploy agency when using them. Bitcoin, for instance, has been defended against charges of being 'evil' through an insistence that it is 'ethically neutral'.[24]

That being said, perhaps the more significant point is that there are major established financial institutions rushing to embrace blockchain technologies with full state encouragement and this is changing the nature of the associated financial practices themselves. The security enhancements that the blockchain can provide are usually cited as the major reason why banks and governments get behind cryptocurrencies. However, the result is that blockchain technologies have also witnessed increasing forms of *enclosure*. In short, there has been a recent growth in private permissioned ledgers, which runs against the radical open ethos of the blockchain.[25] This presents a fundamental challenge for those seeking more deep-seated change in finance through the promise of the blockchain. At the time of writing, blockchain experimentation remains contested and uncertain, with the apparent struggle between more collaborative and more purely capitalist agendas producing ambiguous outcomes in ethical terms.

Platform economies

Beyond the blockchain, online digital technologies more broadly are changing the way people conceive of and interact with finance. Trends associated with the 'platform economy' ostensibly offer new ways of organising and funding financial services. However, it is important to be attentive to what kinds of economic interaction are occurring in platform economies in general, before thinking through how this might apply to financial practices specifically.

There are fierce debates around the nature of 'sharing' and 'gig' economies in which people use online and mobile digital technologies to coordinate economic interactions. One reading is that the rise of the online platform has created a new world of efficiency, flexibility, mobility, speed, and so on. Another critical reading suggests that it benefits certain groups over others, such the same set of dynamics produces extraction of rents, vulnerability, precarity, and further inequality. Is the share economy really about *sharing*? Or is it more about the leasing out of owned assets for the extraction of rents? Is the platform economy about harnessing digital technologies to enhance consumer-producer interaction and efficiency? Or is it more about a platform using a fee-based system to extract surplus while not taking on any risk or responsibility for the activity or transaction involved?

The popular fascination with the rise of 'platform capitalism' has not gone unnoticed by governing elites.[26] The economic realms where digital technologies have served to 'disrupt' existing business organisation—such as ride sharing with Uber, accommodation with Airbnb, and so on—have become something of a blueprint for how the digital disruption of finance can be fostered. One of the pressing moral dilemmas concerning the liberal orientation of some of the platform operations is that (the attempt) to remove an element of government regulation from economic interaction often concomitantly produces an augmentation of the power that corporations have in the organisation of that economic activity. As Paul Langley and Andrew Leyshon point out, '[p]revailing explanations cast digital economic circulations as horizontal, networked exchange relations between users which are new and different because of their disintermediated, collaborative, and even democratising qualities'.[27] Such accounts are problematic, they argue, 'because they render platforms largely invisible in the understandings that they offer of the digital economy'.[28] Indeed some of the largest firms in the world are at the heart of the so-called FinTech wave, including 'an alliance of technology leaders' involving Amazon, Apple, Google, Intuit, and PayPal.[29] In a recent report, this alliance (called Financial Innovation Now [FIN]) argues that while technology firms are often thought to have fewer regulations surrounding their conduct compared to traditional financial institutions, in reality the sector is 'heavily regulated'.[30] Despite representing some of the largest firms in the world, FIN aims to inform policymakers of how the current regulatory compliance requirements constitute a 'significant market barrier for any new entrant in financial services'.[31] This is rather ironic but also important because online platforms have the potential to create new forms of Internet monopolies: 'Acting to make market networks as what we might call infrastructural intermediaries, platforms necessarily "standardise" the circulations in which they specialise, whether these be ideas, knowledge, labour, or use rights for otherwise idle assets'.[32]

Individuals and groups seeking to rethink how platform organisation could more fundamentally change economy and society often do not address finance specifically, but debates about platform economies in general are informative. Those calling for more cooperative platform models, for instance, ask such questions as: 'What if Uber was owned and governed by its drivers? What if Airbnb was owned and governed by its hosts?'[33] Existing examples of successful platform co-ops include Fairmondo, a cooperative online marketplace where sellers on the platforms are its owners, Peerby, a neighbour-to-neighbour goods sharing platform, and Loomio, as previously mentioned above.[34] While platforms of this type operate across a range of spheres of activity, the relationship between platform cooperatives and the state is a problematic one. In short, a number of activities that constitute and help support platform 'commoning' are often criminalised, thus disciplining people to avoid such types of economy and reproduce market economy norms. In addition, the value that commoning creates through such platforms is not easily recognised by the state and society, such that it becomes difficult for commons-based organisations to sustain themselves.[35] As with debates about future applications of the blockchain, platform-based commoning and platform capitalism remain largely undecided sets of practices in ethical terms.

Drawing these points together, the ethics of the turn to these alternatives can be read in relation to the three key themes of governing, resisting, and rethinking finance after the crisis. On the governance side, the 'digital disruption' that alternative finance presents in the form of blockchain technologies and platform economies has effectively been championed by major Western governments. While there are some initial concerns surround the promotion of 'immoral' forms of behaviour beyond the state, the fact that large commercial firms are heavily invested into the future of the blockchain and the platform economy means that states are largely following in step. In the name of diversification and (market-competitive) disruption to the ostensible benefit of the consumer citizen, alternative finance is deemed a morally progressive force. In relation to resistive efforts, there are opposing views that stress concern over the growing commercialisation and privatisation of the blockchain and platform economies, such that much of their radical anticapitalist potential is thought to have been lost. Those involved in an everyday and cultural rethinking of finance still see pockets of potential within alternative finance, but, as the last section seeks to develop in relation to peer-to-peer (P2P) lending in particular, the extent to which finance can be made alternative *from within* is always an ethically ambiguous process that just as often ends in failures as successes.

P2P lending and the ethics of the alternative

From social to direct lending

Over the last decade, the emergence of online P2P lending has posed a series of ethically interesting questions concerning the turn to alternative finance. Can the matching of investor 'surplus' with borrower 'need' be coordinated in a fairer and more equitable process than through mainstream banking? Does the direct matching of savers with borrowers remove the systemic risk associated with causing harm to broader society (in the form of threat of economic downturn)? Can the formation of online 'peer' communities foster a deeper 'ethicality' to economic interaction and exchange? If so, can we learn about and rethink finance based on this?

The founding of online P2P lending is usually associated with the establishment of the platform Zopa (an acronym for Zone of Possible Agreement) in 2005. It introduced a website that connected borrowers and investors directly online using a reverse-auction system to allocate investor funds with potential borrowers. In other words, individual borrowers and small businesses listed their requirements for a loan online and lenders would then 'bid' with loan offers to make them a loan. In this sense platforms brought together 'ordinary' people online to establish trust and facilitate credit assessment in something approximating an interactive community of 'peers'. The sums involved were unsecured and tended to be in the realm of what is usually thought of as 'microcredit', albeit without a specific development focus. Early studies of P2P lending were interested in the potential 'peer community' that such a platform based credit system could instantiate. For example, Hulme and Wright talked about how 'notions of the individual within community, transparency and broader ethicality are fundamental to Social Lending schemes'.[36] Markedly, in the early years, P2P lending was sometimes referred to as 'social lending' to designate not a necessarily social *purpose* to the loans, but a kind of social basis to the *process* of intermediating loans. Such an ethos was ostensibly in contrast to the asocial and facelessness of financial intermediation undertaken through banks. In fact, at one leading

P2P lending industry conference a CEO of a major platform insisted that their model allowed for at least some kind of 'equality' between capital providers and borrowers, framed in terms of both sides of the creditor-debtor relation benefitting from the supposed 'efficiency' gains of the platform model. As another commentator put it, this is not 'shadow' but 'sunlight' banking.

The story of the development of online P2P lending since the mid-2000s can in part be understood through reference to the changing terminology use around the sector. So while the sector was originally given a 'social' designation and appeared to offer an alternative form of credit based on bringing 'small' economic actors (that is, individuals) directly together online, the growth in volume and operations has caused quite dramatic change. Particularly in the US, but across other contexts as well, increasingly P2P loans have been produced as a new investor asset class.[37] As part of this trend, institutional money has moved into the sector as more and more loans are funded by traditional investors searching for (a relatively attractive) yield in a globally low interest rate environment. Thus, in some quarters the 'peer' label has been dropped altogether in favour of the notion that this is a 'marketplace' for loans in the sense that platforms provide a means through which *any* investor (of any size) can invest and match loans using a 'purer' market ideal than that which banks offer. The development of secondary markets (i.e., the securitisation of loans) has also been quite substantial, which is typically interpreted as a sign the 'industry' is 'maturing'. 'Online direct lending' still constitutes a fraction of retail and small business lending globally, but most commentators suggest it is here to stay in its current form. With growth, the ideal of interaction between lenders and borrowers has effectively long been jettisoned. Instead, platforms claim to be facilitating 'direct' lending in that investor funds are transferred (by the platform and using *their* credit decision processes) to borrowing customers. In other words, platforms claim to only lend out the funds that they have coming in so there is no 'leveraging' or anything close to the fractional reserve lending model on which most traditional banks rely.

Governing and resisting peer finance

From a governance perspective, the apparent simplicity of the practice and the direct matching of loan funds are the primary reasons why P2P lending is welcomed as a form of alternative finance that does not pose a 'systemic' risk to society. Indeed, the former regulator Adair Turner talks about the sector's 'simplicity and transparency'.[38] While small compared to other forms of unsecured consumer credit and small business lending, there continues to be a 'warm glow' around the P2P lending sector from a regulatory respective.[39]

The regulatory regime in the UK is held up as a global standard setter in terms of allowing the industry to flourish. This is perhaps not all that surprising given that the UK-based platforms were collectively able to bargain for their own set of relatively mild consumer standards to be formally recognised by the Financial Conduct Authority.[40]

To return to the key agendas of diversification and challenging bank monopoly, P2P lending in a sense can do no wrong in the eyes of the state and regulators: it is currently relatively small scale so cannot pose systemic risk; it matches invested funds with deposits so raises no real questions around deposit protection or leverage; and it suits an agenda of fostering diversity (and as such resilience) within the retail lending sector, even if tiny in scale compared to bank lending. However, thinking through the ethics of alternative finance, to the extent that P2P lending even constitutes 'an alternative' these features are incredibly conservative in ambition. It speaks to discourses of financial disruption, diversification, and antisystemic risk, but does it really change any of the practices of finance? Does it *do* finance differently?

From a normative perspective interested in removing the institutional power attached to lending credit to 'oil the wheels' of a functioning market economy, there is some promise, again, in the fact that P2P lending is built on a model that matches invested funds with borrowing need without leverage. Yet, crucially, the purposes to which loan money is put are never part of the lending equation. This is not even social 'impact' investing. The fact that P2P borrowers in the main use their loans to refinance their student loans, buy cars on credit, or restructure existing debts, means that the lending model does not really change anything in terms of debt-fuelled models of growth or the ability of everyday people to finance or meet social provisioning needs.

Rethinking finance without rethinking capitalism

P2P lending platforms have used explicitly normative language to differentiate themselves from banks, just as much as they have used the language of market competition and consumer choice. Indeed, inside the industry, many practitioners (perhaps rightly) believe that they are part of a systemic rethinking of how finance operates post-crisis and in turn its relationship with society. Peer lending speaks to localism, consumer empowerment, and democracy, not to globalism, institutional power, and monopoly. Advocates even stress the links with the 'genuine' production of value as opposed to a delinked financialised pattern of speculative accumulation.

However, two key dynamics limit the extent to which P2P lending can speak to those seeking a 'rethinking' of finance in meaningful terms. The first involves issues of inclusion. Essentially, the P2P lending industry sees financial inclusion as an unquestionably desirable end in itself. As such, the ways in which platforms offer loans to people and businesses rejected by banks is celebrated with little questioning, as is the incorporation of an ever-greater number of borrowing customers at whatever cost. Thus, while P2P lending is not exactly involved in some of the well-documented excesses of payday lending, it contains within it a logic of an ever-expanding set of borrowers, even though it might on the surface be relatively prudent in its lending decisions. Furthermore, on the lender side, those involved in P2P lending are made up of an exceptionally privileged set of investors in relative terms. They are more likely to be male, old, and with a background in finance than any other characteristic. Put simply, any attachment to a notion of rethinking the ethics of finance through an equal 'peer' status is thrown into doubt when one looks at who is lending what to whom.

Secondly, the specificities of the technology deployed by P2P lending platforms in making their lending decisions cannot go ignored. On the one hand, the fact that P2P lending involves firms that are just as much 'tech' firms as they are 'finance' firms is usually celebrated as bringing benefits to the consumer. However, on the other hand, what this also brings is a certain disposition towards the ends to which that technology can be employed, *on its own terms*. Put simply, inside the industry, there is a particular obsession with the collection, use, and manipulation of mobile and digital *data sources*. If a platform can lend through a website, it can track internet usage. If a platform can lend through a mobile phone in Sub-Saharan Africa, it can track purchase history and credit use through that mobile phone (in order to score credit and offer more products). This is a new world of credit-scoring that builds on and extends previous faith placed in objective credit data for making credit decisions.[41] Crucially, as loans are extended to those at the limits of formal finance, the disciplinary effects of standardising and sorting populations gets increasingly intense. While a relatively understudied area at present, if anything P2P lending is reshaping the retail finance sector by forcing it to engage in a new technological utopia of big data, machine learning, and automated credit decisions. Class, gender, and race are *produced* just as much as they are 'objectively ignored' in such practices.

Overall, in terms of efforts to genuinely *rethink* finance, it is difficult to see beyond the issues of, first, unequal incorporation within P2P lending networks and, second, beyond the (perhaps) dangerous and essentially 'asocial' obsession with new data analytics. On these terms, practices of alternative finance appear to get mediated by established financial norms and the ethical imperatives of 'traditional' forms of finance. This is not to say there is nothing new about these financial practices: only a very structural reading of capitalism could expunge alternative finance of any diversity in practice whatsoever. More productively, it is interesting to think about how those involved in 'the industry' are using the means, funds, and discourses of neoliberal finance to turn it back on itself, to think of ways of rethinking (albeit in small ways) how lending could be performed differently. To this extent there is still an ethic of rethinking and performing finance on alternative terms.

Conclusion

Crypto- and local currencies, peer lending, local banking, debt forgiveness, and as well as campaigns to scrutinise tax havens all suggest a critical dimension to the 'democratisation' of finance in recent years. There is certainly not a lack of 'alternatives' in the current financial(ised) conjuncture. Perhaps what is lacking in the mainstream is an ethical vocabulary to understand emerging practices. What this chapter has sought to highlight are the possibilities and limits contained within thinking about governing, resisting and rethinking finance in light of the crisis and the production of alternatives. More appropriately than assuming that 'alternatives' to the 'bad' world of a financial 'system' in crisis exist and are therefore better, forms of governance, resistance and rethinking finance have been indicated to suggest that it is not really a question of what is more or less 'ethical' in design, but more that finance should be always already conceived of as a site of ethical contestation.[42] In this sense, 'alternative' presents nothing new, merely a set of sites, provocations, and practices that need and call for further thinking, from within and without of finance, about how 'it' and 'us' could made otherwise.

Notes

1 Malcolm Campbell-Verduyn, 'Moral Economese of Scale? Crisis, Discursive Change and the Varying Authority of Economists', *Global Society*, 30, no. 4 (2016): 507–530.

2 Andrew Baker, 'The New Political Economy of the Macroprudential Ideational Shift', *New Political Economy*, 18, no. 1 (2012): 112–139.

3 James Brassett and Chris Holmes, 'Building Resilient Finance? Uncertainty, Complexity, and Resistance', *British Journal of Politics and International Relations*, 18, no. 2 (2016): 370–388.

4 Matt Taibbi, 'The Great American Bubble Machine', *Rolling Stone*, April 5 (2010). Available online: http://www.rollingstone.com/politics/news/the-great-american-bubble-machine-20100405 [last accessed 18/09/17].

5 James Brassett and Chris Clarke, 'Performing the Sub-Prime Crisis: Trauma and the Financial Event', *International Political Sociology*, 6, no. 1 (2012): 4–20.

6 Financial Crisis Inquiry Commission, *The Financial Crisis Inquiry Report: Final Report of the National Commission on the Causes of the Financial and Economic Crisis in the United States* (Washington, DC: Financial Crisis Inquiry Commission, 2011), 61.

7 Adair Turner, *Between Debt and the Devil: Money, Credit, and Fixing Global Finance* (Princeton: Princeton University Press, 2015).

8 E. Helleiner, *The Status Quo Crisis: Global Financial Governance after the 2008 Meltdown* (Oxford: Oxford University Press, 2014).

9 Brassett and Holmes, 'Building Resilient Finance?'.
10 Mark Carney, 'The Promise of FinTech – Something New under the Sun?', speech at the Deutsche Bundesbank G20 Conference on Digitising Finance, Financial Inclusion and Financial Literacy, Wiesbaden, 25 January 2017. Available online: http://www.bankofengland.co.uk/publications/Documents/speeches/2017/speech956.pdf [last accessed 30/07/17].
11 Chris Rogers and Chris Clarke, 'Mainstreaming Social Finance: The Regulation of the Peer-to-Peer Lending Marketplace in the UK', *British Journal of Politics and International Relations*, 18, no. 4 (2016): 930–945.
12 Marion Fourcade, 'The Economy as Morality Play, and Implications for the Eurozone Crisis', *Socio-Economic Review*, 11, no. 3 (2016): 620–627; Wolfgang Streeck, 'The Construction of a Moral Duty for the Greek People to Repay Their National Debt', *Socio-Economic Review*, 11, no. 3 (2013): 614–620.
13 Rob Aitken, *Fringe Finance: Crossing and Contesting the Borders of Global Capital* (New York: Routledge, 2015).
14 Rob Aitken, 'Everyday Debt Relationalities: Situating Peer-to-Peer Lending and the Rolling Jubilee', *Cultural Studies*, 29, no. 5–6 (2015): 845–868.
15 Chris Clarke and Lauren Tooker, 'Social Finance Meets Financial Innovation: Contemporary Experiments in Payments, Money and Debt', *Theory, Culture and Society*, forthcoming.
16 Brett Scott, *The Heretic's Guide to Global Finance: Hacking the Future of Money* (London: Pluto Press, 2013).
17 Bill Maurer, 'Resocializing Finance? Or Dressing It in Mufti?', *Journal of Cultural Economy*, 1, no. 1 (2008): 65–78.
18 Taylor C. Nelms, 'Alt.economy: Strategies, Tensions, Challenges', *Journal of Cultural Economy*, 9, no. 5 (2016): 7.
19 Nigel Dodd, *The Social Life of Money* (Princeton, NJ: Princeton University Press, 2014).
20 Nigel Dodd, 'The Social Life of Bitcoin', *Theory, Culture and Society*, forthcoming.
21 Bill Maurer, Taylor C. Nelms, and Lana Swartz, '"When Perhaps the Real Problem Is Money Itself!": The Practical Materiality of Bitcoin', *Social Semiotics*, 23, no. 2 (2013): 261–277.
22 Primavera De Filippi and Benjamin Loveluck, 'The Invisible Politics of Bitcoin: Governance Crisis of a Decentralised Infrastructure', *Internet Policy Review*, 5, no. 3 (2016).
23 Lawrence Trautman, (2014), 'Virtual Currencies: Bitcoin and What Now after Liberty Reserve, Silk Road, and Mt. Gox?', *Richmond Journal of Law and Technology*, 20, no. 4 (2014).
24 James J. Angel and Douglas McCabe, 'The Ethics of Payments: Paper, Plastic, or Bitcoin?', *Journal of Business Ethics*, 132, no. 3 (2015): 603–611.
25 Robert Herian, 'Anything but Disruptive: Blockchain, Capital and a Case of Fourth Industrial Age Enclosure', *Critical Legal Thinking*, 18 October 2016. Available online: http://criticallegalthinking.com/2016/10/18/anything-disruptive-blockchain-capital-case-fourth-industrial-age-enclosure-part/ [last accessed 19/09/17].
26 Paul Langley and Andrew Leyshon, 'Platform Capitalism: The Intermediation and Capitalisation of Digital Economic Circulation', *Finance and Society*, published as *Early View*, 2016.
27 Ibid., 3.
28 Ibid.
29 Financial Innovation Now, 'Examining the Extensive Regulation of Financial Technologies', July 2016: 1. Report available online: https://financialinnovationnow.org/wp-content/uploads/2016/07/Examining_the_Extensive_Regulation_of_Financial_Technologies.pdf [last accessed 19/09/17].
30 Financial Innovation Now, 'Examining the Extensive Regulation of Financial Technologies', 2.
31 Ibid.
32 Langley and Leyshon, 'Platform Capitalism', 9.
33 Cat Johnson, '11 Platform Cooperatives Creating a Real Sharing Economy', *Shareable.net*, 18 May 2016. Available online: http://www.shareable.net/blog/11-platform-cooperatives-creating-a-real-sharing-economy [last accessed 19/09/17].
34 Ibid.
35 David Bollier, 'State Power and Commoning: Transcending a Problematic Relationship'. Report available online: https://cdn8.commonsstrategies.org/wp-content/uploads/2016/07/State-Power-and-Commoning.pdf [last accessed 19/09/17].
36 Michael Hulme and Collette Wright, *Internet-Based Social Lending: Past, Present and Future* (London: Social Futures Observatory, 2006), 7.
37 Rob Aitken, *Fringe Finance: Crossing and Contesting the Borders of Global Capital* (New York: Routledge, 2015), 212.

38 J. D. Alois, 'Lord Adair Turner: Direct Lending May Make the Financial System More Stable', *Crowdfund Insider*, 11 October 2016. Available online: https://www.crowdfundinsider.com/2016/10/91121-lord-adair-turner-direct-lending-may-make-financial-system-stable/ [last accessed 30/07/17].

39 Bank for International Settlements and Financial Stability Board, 'FinTech Credit: Market Structure, Business Models and Financial Stability Implications'. Report prepared by a Working Group established by the Committee on the Global Financial System and the Financial Stability Board, 2017. Available online: http://www.fsb.org/2017/05/fintech-credit-market-structure-business-models-and-financial-stability-implications/ [last accessed 30/07/17].

40 Rogers and Clarke, 'Mainstreaming Social Finance'.

41 Andrew Leyshon and Nigel Thrift, 'Lists Come Alive: Electronic Systems of Knowledge and the Rise of Credit-Scoring in Retail Banking', *Economy and Society*, 28, no. 3 (1999): 434–466.

42 Chris D. Clarke, *Ethics and Economic Governance: Using Adam Smith to Understand the Global Financial Crisis* (London and New York: Routledge, 2016).

30
DECOLONIAL GLOBAL JUSTICE
A critique of the ethics of the global economy

Puneet Dhaliwal

Introduction: the coloniality of global justice theory

From its emergence in the 1970s, global justice theory has matured into a prominent field in contemporary political philosophy, populating a host of academic publications, department syllabi, and research programmes. Indeed, political theory today is now replete with all manner of arguments on global wealth distribution, international trade, the world environment, migration policy, and even the global arms trade. Yet despite its initially progressive appearance, much of this scholarship fails to adequately address what is perhaps the definitive instance of injustice on a global scale, namely imperialism. The imperial power relations that emerged during the age of European empire, and which continue to shape the present global order, should arguably be a central problematic in discussions of the ethics of a global economy.[1]

The oppressive relationships erected through European colonial expansion—beginning in the late fifteenth century and later consolidated under the aegis of Western imperialism in subsequent centuries—did not simply wither away following formal processes of decolonization in the nineteenth and twentieth centuries, but survived, evolved, and even strengthened through informal means of indirect rule that continue to this day.[2] The present world is profoundly shaped by imperial power, which requires attention from global justice theorists. As this chapter argues, however, mainstream global justice theory—grounded, as it is, in abstract analytical political philosophy—cannot properly apprehend or critique such imperial power relations. Indeed, the dominant paradigm of global justice theory, I argue, ultimately functions to uphold imperial power, either by implicitly accepting that status quo or, more subtly, by 'serving as the language of governance and administration of the [imperial] system'.[3]

Prior to advancing this argument, we must specify the parameters of global justice scholarship under consideration here. The contemporary enterprise of global justice theory spans almost five decades and encompasses a diverse range of topics and political standpoints that are not easily generalized. This chapter makes no claim to comprehensiveness in its treatment of global justice scholarship, but it instead focuses on key debates and theories within the field that serve as an indicative basis of the coloniality of mainstream global justice theory. It begins with an overview of the extensive debates about the appropriate scope of principles of distributive justice and whether theories of justice should apply beyond national borders to the realm of international politics.[4] Although such debates arose in the 1970s, they have remained a preoccupation for political philosophers and therefore constitute a significant aspect of contemporary global justice theory. The chapter then moves on to discuss two influential theories of global justice that, in distinct ways, ostensibly provide more direct and robust responses to the injustices of imperial power relations. The first is Simon Caney's ideal theory of global egalitarianism, which presents a forward-looking account of a just international distribution of resources.[5] The second is Daniel Butt's theory of global distributive justice for the non-ideal conditions of colonialism and its pernicious legacy, which underwrite extensive material reparations from developed nations to former colonies.[6] In so far as political philosophers approach global justice—whether in ideal or non-ideal conditions—primarily as a matter of 'applied ethics', they largely prioritize ascertaining the just 'design' or 'reform' of global institutions and policies, as well as individual and collective moral duties.[7] Accordingly, political philosophers typically theorize global justice in a predominantly moral realm of justice and duties that is considerably abstracted from a critical analysis of the actual operation of the aforementioned imperial power relations. As the introduction to this Handbook theme suggests, global justice theorists rely upon a relatively systemic vision of the global economy, within which they then seek to address or ameliorate certain instances or circumstances of (in)justice.[8] This chapter will argue that the historical contingency of that system should become a subject of justice.

It is important to be precise here about the link between the abstract nature of analytical political philosophy and the coloniality of global justice theory, particularly since theorizing about politics invariably entails some degree of abstraction about social realities. The problem in analytical political philosophy is not so much abstraction *per se* but rather a highly *idealized* form of abstraction—or in, Charles W. Mills's formulation, 'idealization to the exclusion, or at least marginalization, of the actual.' This idealized abstraction is particularly egregious in so far as it can either downplay 'relations of structural domination, exploitation, coercion, and oppression', or invoke idealized understandings of political institutions and economic structures 'with little or no sense of how their actual workings may systematically disadvantage' marginalized groups.[9] Importantly, such shortcomings are evident throughout mainstream global justice scholarship, including across the putative ideal-theory–non-ideal-theory spectrum. The protracted debates about the proper scope of ideal principles of justice, for example, operate at a level of abstraction that effectively marginalizes from consideration many of the unjust features of imperial power relations, such as Western military interventions in weaker and poorer countries or corporate land grabs and resource exploitation across peripheral regions of the world economy. Large parts of the system of imperial power are thereby tacitly accepted and left in place in much of the contemporary literature on global justice, even in theories that advocate the global application of relatively demanding principles of justice.[10] Despite the progressive gloss of theories of global justice, then, their idealizing suppositions lead them to operate, in a perhaps unintended role, as coopted discourses that uphold imperial power. The conclusion of this chapter will identify some important and emerging work on decolonial theories of justice that seek to license the everyday agency of non-Western subjects, subaltern campaign agendas, and alternative visions of economy.

Informal imperialism and global injustice

The overwhelming majority of global justice scholarship upholds imperial power, not in an explicit manner, but implicitly by simply neglecting to address it. Much academic discussion about global justice is of a highly abstract nature, revolving around a fairly narrow set of concerns regarding the international applicability of principles of justice, which were typically assumed to be broadly Rawlsian in character.

In broad terms, Rawlsian principles of justice refer to a liberal egalitarian position that prioritizes the defence of equal basic liberties, equal opportunities, and distributive arrangements that are to the benefit of the least-advantaged in society. Global justice debates begin with John Rawls's theory of justice and his complementary argument for demarcating domestic and international justice, with principles of distributive justice being restricted to nation-states.[11] However, many commentators note an inconsistency, arguing that, since one's nationality and place of birth are morally arbitrary facts that would be concealed behind the veil of ignorance in the original position, Rawls's theory of justice should also apply at the global level.[12]

Subsequently, accounts of global distributive justice have spawned a wealth of literature dedicated to ascertaining which institutions are relevant in triggering duties of justice. In broad terms, right-institutionalists deny the existence of substantive international duties of distributive justice on the grounds that such duties only arise within a shared coercive legal system that invokes the will of its members in the formation of public policy. Whereas nation-states are characterized by a 'centralized and hierarchic' basic structure, they argue, global politics comprises institutions and structures that are comparatively 'decentralized and anarchic'.[13] Left-institutionalists, by contrast, contend that claims of distributive justice need not rest upon coercion but may arise on the basis of a shared cooperative system whose members are collectively associated through ties of interdependence and reciprocity. On this view, the global economic system constitutes an international basic structure that is sufficiently interconnected for certain distributive obligations to apply beyond national borders.[14] Although political philosophers have moved on to address other aspects of global justice, the question of the relevant scope of principles of distributive justice has occupied a central place in global justice scholarship, and so warrants our attention when critiquing the overarching field of global justice theory.

The debate on the global scope of justice is important for this chapter because its interlocutors exhibit the same basic limitation. That is to say, many global justice scholars *focus primarily* on the conceptual matter of determining the scope in which principles of distributive justice apply. By contrast, many of the deep-seated injustices that characterize the actual global order receive scant attention. To be sure, global justice scholars are very mindful of the extent of poverty and inequality across the world, yet they respond to such issues 'in a vague or promissory way' rather than by treating 'systematic oppression' as the central concern of their theories.[15] Accordingly, mainstream global justice theory rests upon idealized assumptions about the nature of the global order, presupposing either the absence of structural injustices that are amenable to the demands of justice or the claim that any such injustices will be resolved in due course by given proposals for international distributive justice.[16] As a result of such idealization, large parts of contemporary global justice scholarship implicitly accept, and therefore leave intact, many oppressive imperial power relations as background conditions for theories of justice.

In the case of right-institutionalists, this shortcoming is plain to see. At its most stringent, right-institutionalism denies the existence of any demands of justice beyond nation-states since the international community lacks a 'coercively imposed collective authority.'[17] While we may nonetheless have some humanitarian obligations to prevent starvation and the like, these duties are of a moral character rather than the result of claims of distributive justice that can be coercively enforced. Even in its more moderate inflection, right-institutionalism stipulates only rather modest requirements of international distributive justice. In general, such redistribution does not apply to international trade and other economic activity, and is instead restricted to minimal duties of assistance to ensure that the interstate system remains well ordered and peaceful.[18] Whether adopting a stringent or more moderate stance, right-institutionalists therefore focus almost exclusively on conceptualizing the nature of coercive legal authority and denying its existence at the level of international politics. Accordingly, such theorists approach global justice by abstracting away from all manner of economic stratification and political hierarchy within the global order, which consequently remains largely unchanged according to such theories of global justice.

On the face of it, left-institutionalists are better placed to address a broader and deeper set of global injustices, in so far as they advocate the application of principles of justice beyond nation-states to the modern system of global governance. Specifically, such theorists argue that international trade and transnational political and economic institutions together constitute an international basic structure—understood as a site of interdependent cooperation—to which principles of distributive justice ought to apply. Charles Beitz and Thomas Pogge, for instance, argue that Rawls's difference principle should apply globally, with international institutions being reformed in such a way that the inequalities they generate would be justified only if they benefit those who are worst off.[19] In a similar vein, Pogge has himself developed a proposal for a Global Resources Dividend (GRD) on the basis of the existence of a 'shared institutional order' comprising the interstate system and world economy.[20] According to this view, global distributive justice requires that governments 'share a small part of the value of any resources they decide to use or sell', with this dividend being directed towards a fund for eradicating global poverty.[21] From what has been said so far, left-institutionalism seems to entail relatively far-reaching changes to the present global order, both in terms of redistributing resources and restructuring international institutions in more egalitarian and democratic directions. For example, the implementation of a global difference principle and GRD may substantially redress the current power imbalances in international trade deals and international organizations like the World Trade Organization (WTO), not to mention the disparities of wealth between the 'Global North' and 'Global South.' In what sense, then, do such theories of global justice buttress, rather than challenge, imperial relationships of inequality, domination, and so on?

While left-institutionalist accounts of global justice may conceivably have some progressive impact on the present global order, it is important to note that such theories also rest upon idealized assumptions about the world. Despite acknowledging the existence of global injustices like poverty and wealth inequality—and even going so far as to identify their structural roots in international institutions, which are, in part, the legacy of European colonialism—theorists like Pogge ultimately labour under the illusion that the requirements of global justice can be discharged with rather modest reform proposals. As Pogge himself admits, the GRD is intended as a 'moderate proposal' for institutional reform that can 'sustain itself in the world as we know it.'[22] Global justice, on this view, is therefore anchored in the underlying structural makeup of the present global order, which is accepted as a background condition for the realization of principles of justice. Although Pogge adopts this position for reasons of pragmatism, this manoeuvre has the effect of placing a host of oppressive features of the global order beyond consideration and redress by theories of justice. As James Tully presciently notes of such theorists who claim to present progressive alternatives to the present world, 'what they present as an alternative is often another aspect of imperialism they did not foreground in their criticism but left unexamined in the background.'[23] Importantly, these neglected aspects of imperialism are not some historical curiosity, but structural features of the present global order.

According to critical scholars like Tully, imperialism did not end with formal processes of decolonization but continued through 'informal' means, such as the threat and practice of Western military intervention, installing a dependent local governing class, and structurally adjusting weaker countries in order to open their resources, labour, and markets to free trade dominated by Western powers. Imperial power of this kind is most immediately visible in the hegemony of the United States, its G8 allies, and multinational corporations operating through the WTO, IMF, and World Bank—and it is precisely this 'complex web of imperial relationships' that remains unchallenged in global justice scholarship, even in its more progressive strands like left-institutionalism.[24]

Indeed, this theoretical distance from the reality of imperial power is particularly acute in Pogge's politically naïve insistence on the progressive impact that his views on justice could have on the world, when he asserts that 'moral convictions can have real effects even in international politics.'[25] If we were to rely, like Pogge, on the moral mobilization of citizens in the West and the goodwill of the United States and European Union—both of which are deeply imbricated in imperial relationships—then we would be waiting a long time for the resolution of global injustices. Large parts of mainstream global justice scholarship, then, are ill-equipped to address the breadth and depth of global injustices, which are considerably obscured by the idealized assumptions that inform discussions about the scope of principles of justice.

The imperial horizons of global justice theory

The current field of global justice scholarship now incorporates theories that postulate extensive demands of justice that, on the face of it, seem to mitigate the most egregious aspects of imperial power relations. Two theories from this literature serve as exemplars of far-reaching philosophical proposals for global justice, spanning the ideal- theory–non-ideal-theory spectrum.

First, let us consider Caney's espousal of a cosmopolitan ideal of global egalitarianism. In broad terms, Caney rejects particularist arguments for confining duties of distributive justice to the institutional framework of nation-states, arguing that the 'internal logic of the standard theories of distributive justice generates cosmopolitan principles of distributive justice' that apply beyond national borders.[26] The theoretical basis for this claim is a commitment to moral universalism, whereby every human deserves equal moral recognition and treatment regardless of their nationality and position within the world, so that moral principles apply universally and not just to specific contexts. Accordingly, Caney effectively circumvents the abstract debates about what does and does not constitute a basic structure and whether that triggers international demands of justice. Instead, he establishes an account of global distributive justice on the basis of our shared moral humanity and proposes four related principles of global distributive justice: a human right to subsistence; equal opportunities, regardless of nationality; equal pay for equal work; and a prioritarian concern with benefiting those who are worst off. Taken together, these principles endorse a substantial reconfiguration of the present global order, particularly in negating many of the world's deep structural inequalities and hierarchies. Global wealth disparities, for instance, would be lessened, severe deprivation and impoverishment eliminated, and the stratified international division of labour radically restructured. To be sure, Caney's cosmopolitanism does not entail a strict equality of outcome in terms of resources, but it nonetheless seems sufficiently robust in its egalitarianism to produce a significant progressive impact upon imperial power relations.

While Caney's ideal account of global distributive justice seems to stand in contradiction to imperialism, at least in principle, it does not necessarily follow that the same is true for his proposed means of operationalizing these principles of justice. In fact, it is in the process of implementing global egalitarianism that the coloniality of Caney's theory becomes apparent. We therefore need to unpack his account of just political structures involved in the realization of global egalitarianism. In general terms, Caney suggests that some kind of 'global political authority' is necessary to ensure that people actually adhere to fairly demanding principles of global distributive justice that call for the transfer of wealth from the affluent to the impoverished.[27] As regards the specific character of this political structure, Caney's view largely dovetails with that of cosmopolitan democrats like Daniele Archibugi and David Held, who propose a multilevel system of governance incorporating national states alongside substate and suprastate decision-making bodies and institutions.[28] From this perspective, just global political institutions are those that protect human rights—including that of democratic self-determination—in addition to implementing global principles of distributive justice.

Importantly, Caney's characterization of this cosmopolitan political structure as one that is just rests upon highly idealized assumptions about the actual workings of its constituent political institutions and economic structures. Broadly speaking, this political structure is presumed to amount to a 'democratic framework' that enables people to 'hold to account the powerful economic and social forces that determine their rights and fundamental interests.'[29] For example, this would entail greater popular influence through the United Nations and democratic oversight of the WTO, IMF, and World Bank. Such institutions, of course, are deeply undemocratic in their present configuration, and it is the cosmopolitan's belief that they can be democratized through their proposals. In other words, Caney's global egalitarianism invokes a view of the present system of global governance as one that, although highly stratified and hierarchical at present, is amenable to internal democratic reform. Yet it is not clear that liberal cosmopolitans are justified in adopting this view, which rather optimistically treats 'the existing distribution of power as a resource to be utilized for cosmopolitan ends rather than as a problem in itself.'[30] The thought here is that the overarching framework of global governance employed by Caney's global egalitarianism does not exist in isolation from imperialism, but, to the contrary, is itself deeply inscribed with imperial power relations.

Specifically, many of the aforementioned international political and economic institutions, or their precursors, were created at the end of World War II by European imperial powers and the hegemonic United States. The intention in doing so was to curb destructive wars of inter-imperial competition and to form an international system of laws that would facilitate the continued penetration of the natural resources and labour force of former colonies, which would be integrated in a global market dominated by imperial powers. Moreover, Western powers continued to exercise their influence over weaker states through the imposition of structural adjustment programmes in addition to direct and indirect military interventions.[31] Given all this, it seems highly dubious to claim that global egalitarianism could effectively be established through the present system of global governance unless, of course, we were to abstract it away from its imperial character. As Tully notes of liberal cosmopolitans like Caney, they typically 'disregard the depth and breadth of informal imperialism' such that 'they do not ask if the post-Second World War institutions on which their proposals for global governance and cosmopolitan democracy are built are not themselves institutions of continuing informal imperialism.'[32] Accordingly, even fairly demanding ideal theories of global justice, as articulated by mainstream liberal cosmopolitan scholars, may serve to uphold the present system of imperial power, not through lack of trying to redress global injustices, but by indirectly providing a normative language that enables the continued administration of that imperial system.[33]

At this stage, we may reasonably wonder whether political philosophers could avoid this shortcoming of Caney's model by theorizing global justice in closer methodological connection to the unjust conditions of the present imperial system. This form of 'non-ideal' theorizing, of course, may be conducted in various ways, but the basic idea is to start with the imperfect world as it currently exists and to develop normative principles of justice to govern our conduct accordingly. This approach stands in contrast to simply positing an ideal account of how the world should be, and so ostensibly offers a way of theorizing global justice without unwittingly accepting the imperial character of the present world. In order to explore this possibility at its strongest, this chapter now turns to discuss Daniel Butt's account of global distributive justice for the non-ideal conditions of colonialism and its pernicious legacy that continues to this day. Broadly speaking, he conceptualizes global justice with reference to contemporary 'obligations of compensation and restitution' to repair the damage rooted in historic wrongdoing, particularly that associated with European colonialism.[34]

It is important to note here that, although Butt distances himself from ideal theory, there is nevertheless a foundational methodological continuity between Caney's and Butt's approaches to global justice that is relevant to the argument developed below. As we have seen, Caney sketches an account of global justice by asserting a set of normative principles, and then suggesting a set of institutions through which they might be realized. Butt, by contrast, proposes principles of justice to guide the present repair of historical injustices that shaped the present world, yet he nonetheless theorizes global justice under the auspices of some kind of ideal. As he himself notes, '[r]ectificatory justice is not free-standing—it can only be properly articulated and examined with implicit or explicit reference to an understanding of justice in a broader sense. Of particular importance to the questions of the rectificatory project is distributive justice.'[35] This broader ideal in question, for Butt, is an image of a counterfactual world that is characterized by 'consensual and cooperative' productive interactions between 'different political communities' rather than colonial domination by some over others.[36] Both Caney and Butt, then, theorize global justice principally in the realm of ethics, with some reference to a universal normative ideal, from which principles of justice, proposals for just institutions, and duties of justice are directly or indirectly derived. So how does Butt employ this methodological framework to develop a theoretical account of global justice, and how does it fare in responding to the injustices of imperialism?

In brief, his argument proceeds as follows. European imperialism undoubtedly generated countless injustices in the form of genocide, slavery, plunder, torture, displacement, and exploitation, which generate immediate 'duties of rectification' on the part of the colonizer to 'repair the harm which her [sic] action has caused to the victim.'[37] This general picture, of course, is somewhat complicated by the passage of time to the point where the original wrongdoers and victims no longer remain. Against those who insist that bygones be bygones, Butt endorses an account of global justice with a 'significant backward-looking context' such that 'the actions of previous generations make a difference to the entitlements of persons in the present.'[38] In order to establish the existence of reparative duties today, Butt then makes several theoretical manoeuvres. First, he argues that injustice may extend beyond the initial harms of colonial interactions. In the event that the original obligations are not discharged, Butt argues, the harm is compounded and 'the bearers of the obligations are themselves the perpetrators of a fresh injustice against the victims of the original act of injustice.'[39] Second, according to Butt, these outstanding reparative duties may persist and pass down to future generations within a national community. This contention rests on the normative claim that nations can bear collective responsibility for the actions of their leaders in conjunction with the conceptual claim that a shared national identity endures over the course of multiple overlapping generations. On this basis, historical reparative obligations continue to exist centuries after the moment in which they arose. Finally, present-day citizens of former colonial powers may come to bear these obligations in so far as they benefit from the 'unjust enrichment' that many developed nations enjoy as a result of colonialism.[40] By the same token, these reparative duties, Butt argues, are owed to contemporary descendants of the victims of colonialism since they today suffer from this unjust enrichment, at least relative to how the world would look according to the counter-factual ideal of consensual and cooperative interaction between societies.

Drawing together these various threads, Butt therefore concludes that many developed nations that were once colonial powers hold extensive reparative duties 'to correct the distributive distortion caused by both the initial wrongdoing and the subsequent failure to fulfil rectificatory obligations.'[41] The descendants of colonized peoples are thus owed substantial compensation, whether in the form of resource transfers, debt relief, or development assistance. Given this argument in support of extensive reparations to formerly colonized nations, it may seem counterintuitive to suggest that there is any colonial dimension in Butt's account of global justice. Unfortunately, as with Caney's ideal model, Butt's non-ideal theory rests upon certain idealized assumptions that mask a darker side to his account of global justice. In particular, his argument for rectificatory transfers implicitly appeals to the supposedly well-functioning institutional mechanisms of the interstate system, through which reparations may, in principle, be paid from Western states to formerly colonized nations.[42] This institutional system, however, is at present compromised as a means of implementing global justice, primarily because of the structural influence that dominant Western states hold over weaker postcolonial states through the burden of debt and the imposition of capitalist development programmes. That is, former colonies' legal and political institutions—themselves fashioned in the image of Western models—are typically organized so as to surrender local control of resources and to strengthen relations of dependency between core and peripheral regions of the capitalist world economy.[43]

Accordingly, even if Western states were prepared to jeopardize their dominant position in the global order by paying reparations to former colonies, Butt's theory of global justice has little to say about the importance of structural impediments to resource transfers actually remedying the injustices of colonialism. Importantly, this concern is echoed in the discourse of contemporary reparations movements, with pan-Afrikan activist Cecil Gutzmore expressing reservations over Caribbean governments pursuing hasty or miscalculated reparations claims that do not serve the cause of Afrikan emancipation.[44] To be sure, Butt does not wholly neglect realistic constraints on the implementation of reparations, but they play a minimal role in informing his theorization of global justice. For instance, he acknowledges that affluent states will not likely pay reparations in the short term but then leaves such matters aside, emphasizing the 'theoretical' nature of his argument, which concentrates on determining 'what modern-day distributive rights and obligations are entailed by historic colonial practices.'[45] Butt's theorization of global justice, then, ultimately remains a fairly abstract exercise in positing universal normative principles, with a view to them later influencing interest groups, the media, and policymakers. While these principles are derived with reference to non-ideal conditions, these conditions are themselves not critically analysed as ongoing relations of informal imperialism, which remain largely unchallenged in Butt's theorization of global justice.

Taking stock of the argument so far, we have identified significant limitations on the utility of mainstream global justice theory in responding to the injustices of imperial power relations. Even in Caney's relatively demanding model of global egalitarianism and Butt's argument for extensive reparations, their accounts of global justice were shown to rest upon idealizations that abstracted away from the breadth and depth of informal imperialism. Accordingly, mainstream global justice scholars implicitly accept a wide array of imperial power relations that would consequently be upheld even with the implementation of their proposed global principles of justice. Undoubtedly, political philosophers that theorize global justice will object to this unflattering depiction of their work and argue that it is unfair to criticize their philosophical accounts of justice with reference to political criteria regarding their actual implementation. The thought here is that theorists of global justice are engaged in a highly specialized task of clarifying concepts and articulating normative principles that can later guide political conduct in manifold ways. The aforementioned conceptions of global justice, then, serve as only one component in what Adam Swift and Stuart White characterize as a 'collaborative division of labour' between political theorists, on the one hand, and social scientists and practitioners of politics, on the other.[46]

On this view, the global justice theorist may serve as a 'democratic underlabourer' who offers 'arguments to the democratic process' and thereby aids fellow citizens and policymakers in making political choices.[47] In the case of Caney's model of global egalitarianism, for instance, it may be the case that his ideal theory serves as an appropriate benchmark for the reform of international institutions like the WTO.[48] If, in the actual process of such reform, imperial power is simply recomposed and consolidated through such institutions, why is that a flaw in the ideal theory rather than those engaged in its enactment? Similarly, as regards Butt's theory of global justice, his arguments are intended to be of use to 'protagonists in [the] real world debate' who 'seek to have an effect upon policy outcomes in the real world.'[49] While such a policy may not always effectively challenge imperial power relations, this need not necessarily reflect negatively on the general case for reparations in the abstract. So if we envisage some kind of methodological division of labour between theory and practice, this might remove some of the sting from the foregoing critique of mainstream global justice theory. Indeed, that is surely part of the intuition behind handbooks that seek to bring together ethics and IR, or ethics and a global economy more broadly.

The problem with this response, though, is that the division-of-labour metaphor does not adequately capture the relationship between mainstream global justice theorists and the full range of political practitioners, particularly campaigns and movements against global injustices. In fact, the 'theoretical' component in the putative division of labour often shapes and colours the 'practical' component in such a way that marginalizes such grassroots practitioners, or minimizes their significance, in our understanding of global justice. Needless to say, a collaborative division of labour, properly understood, would integrate differentiated tasks that broadly cohere in the construction of some common end. So the various tasks—roughly, intellectual and political—would be complementary rather than in tension with one another. Yet it is precisely this collaborative relationship that does not bear out in mainstream global justice scholarship. Analytical political philosophers are primarily engaged in articulating 'historically invariant' normative principles of justice that, despite being derived from the philosopher's own intuitions, are taken to be universally applicable.[50] Accordingly, global justice theory, at least when conducted by analytical political philosophers, is by and large an instance of what Tully characterizes as 'elite political theory,' in which 'the theorist is elevated above the *demos*.' The elite theorist, for Tully, envisages 'universal normative principles' and then aims to 'study these unchanging principles,' before advocating their application to the real world.[51] By enacting this methodological distance between theory and practice, though, political philosophers relinquish any claim to be engaged in a collaborative division of labour with the vast majority of political practitioners engaged in grassroots campaigns and popular movements from below.

Mainstream global justice scholars routinely marginalize the perspectives and practices of such agents and instead narrowly conceive the practical relevance of their theories in terms of influencing state-based policymaking and top-down institutional design. Indeed, it is quite telling that mainstream global justice scholarship has had little to no engagement with actual struggles against global injustices, such as the 1970s Third World revolt, IMF riots in subsequent decades, and the broader alterglobalization movement beginning in the 1990s. Caney's theory of global justice, for instance, explicitly foregrounds the realization of global egalitarianism through the present imperial framework of global governance, and neglects to engage with the perspectives and practices of existing struggles for global justice. The colonial character of his theory, then, is not simply something that emerges anew in its practical implementation, but is a flaw that is internal to the theory itself. As for Butt's theory, while it establishes a conclusion that seems important for reparations movements, it displays a similar methodological distance from such movements, whose perspectives and practices are not employed in his theorization of global justice. For example, Butt neglects the view—articulated by various pan-Afrikan activists—that reparations must be pursued from the bottom-up perspective of individuals and collectives committed to self-repair and self-empowerment as preconditions for effective reparation. Without engaging with such perspectives, Butt effectively confines his argument for reparations to justifying resource transfers from former colonial powers to privileged sections within the dominant social, legal, and political establishment in postcolonial states. The division-of-labour rejoinder, then, does not refute this paper's argument about the coloniality of mainstream global justice scholarship.

Global justice theory and decoloniality

As we have seen, the current state of global justice scholarship leaves a lot to be desired. The protracted debates about the scope of principles of justice demonstrate that many political philosophers are more concerned with restricting, rather than advancing, responses to manifest injustices in the global order. It is not only those of a nationalist or statist bent, however, who propose inadequate theories of global justice. Liberal cosmopolitans, who advocate the application of principles of justice beyond nation-states, tend to propose, in practice, institutional designs that are either too modest to disrupt imperial power relations or are simply modifications of the existing imperial system of global governance that upholds Western hegemony. In effect, global justice theorists typically focus on the realm of ethics and justice to the exclusion of a critical analysis of existing power relations, which are consequently left in place in many theories.

The imperial character of the present world, the historical depth of imperial power relations, and their extension over the world-economy and interstate system, for example, are all profoundly undertheorized by mainstream global justice scholars. Even when explicitly anchoring their accounts of global justice in the non-ideal conditions associated with European colonialism and its pernicious legacy, political philosophers do not engage in any meaningful analysis of the unjust, non-ideal situation in question. Instead, global justice is theorized in terms of abstract normative principles, without attending to a proper analysis of the actual operation of imperialism and how it may be meaningfully contested. On this basis, mainstream global justice scholarship may be said to have a colonial character on account of its limited ability to apprehend and critique imperial power today. Global justice theory, then, is itself in need of being decolonized, or divorced from this coloniality. By way of conclusion, this paper ends by sketching two broad ways of moving forward with a decolonial approach to global justice. These proposals are intended, not as a firm model for global justice scholarship, but as tentative suggestions for shifting the terms of discussion in theoretical work on global justice today.

Firstly, global justice theorists ought to take as their conceptual starting point the oppressive and unjust nature of the present world with respect to its imperial character. This paper has touched upon various aspects of imperial power today largely by drawing upon the important work of James Tully, though there is much valuable critical scholarship to which we might turn in developing our understanding of contemporary imperial power relations. Of particular note is the Latin American intellectual and political project of 'decoloniality', which conceptualizes the contemporary global order in terms of a 'colonial matrix of power' that was instituted through European colonial expansion and survived formal processes of decolonization. This global system of coloniality encompasses a host of global hierarchies: a racialized international division of labour, an interstate system dominated by Western nation-states, heterosexist and patriarchal gender hierarchies, and an epistemic hierarchy that privileges Western knowledge over other forms of knowledge.[52]

A decolonial approach to global justice theory, then, may begin from a critical analysis of the inner workings of such power relations and how they are experienced as oppressive by marginalized subjectivities, particularly across the postcolonial world. It is important to note here that, although we are technically taking the 'non-ideal' as the starting point, this is not understood as merely a deviation from some preordained ideal. Rather, the non-ideal is taken to be important *in itself* for theorizing global justice for two reasons. First, since imperial power relations underpin many deep-seated injustices on a global scale, global justice theorists need to understand the way in which such relations persist and may be transformed. Second, those marginalized groups that are systematically excluded by imperial relations have a particular phenomenological experience of injustice that is valuable in theorizing the contestation and alteration of imperial power relations. As Mills notes, 'concepts crystallize in part from experience, rather than being a priori,' such that 'it may be that the non-ideal perspective of the socially subordinated is necessary to generate certain critical evaluative concepts in the first place, since the experience of social reality of the privileged provides no phenomenological basis for them.'[53]

The second decolonial proposal for global justice theory follows from this point. Once we recognize that political philosophers and the knowledge that they produce are contextually situated in this manner, we can see their theories of global justice for what they really are: an articulation of certain moral intuitions that have, over time, become formalized as common principles within academic philosophy, a profession dominated by middle-to-upper-class white males. The principles of global justice that regularly emanate from university institutions, then, are not universal normative truths delivered from some transcendental 'view from nowhere,' but are instead reflective of an ideology of 'political whiteness' that is commonplace in analytical political philosophy.[54] It is for this reason that mainstream global justice theory privileges Eurocentric institutional forms over legal and political pluralism, Christian charity instead of Third World resistance, and the assertions of white philosophers over and above the rooted knowledge of socially subordinated groups that are engaged in struggles against injustices. A decolonial approach to global justice theory, by contrast, would challenge the epistemic authority of analytical political philosophers and relate normative theorizing about global justice more closely to the perspectives and practices of subaltern groups.[55] In doing so, we may theorize global justice in a manner that critically interrogates the complex web of imperial power relations in which principles would be enacted, rather than implicitly accepting them as background conditions for theories of justice. Our understandings of the notion of global justice, moreover, would extend beyond the anodyne register of moral duties and obligations on the part of Western citizens and states, and instead accentuate everyday forms of political agency beyond Eurocentric horizons.

Casting our attention back to the field of global justice scholarship with these two proposals in mind, it is evident that decolonizing global justice theory is a vast intellectual and political undertaking. Thankfully, the discipline does include some critical scholars, who are prepared to challenge orthodoxies and, for example, theorize global justice in closer relation to the political agency necessary to bring about a just world.[56] Much of this thinking is still somewhat embryonic, of course, and does not yet directly engage in the decolonization of global justice theory outlined above. Nonetheless, it is a promising sign that the nature of contemporary global justice scholarship is not set in stone and may be reoriented in more theoretically critical and politically radical directions.

Notes

1 The nature of imperialism is a matter of considerable contention, with scholars debating the conceptual and empirical aspects of imperial power, in both historical and contemporary periods. A detailed survey of literature on imperialism is beyond the scope of this chapter, which instead focuses on the central normative aspect of imperialism that any plausible approach to global justice should be able to critically address, namely the 'deep-seated global relationships of oppression—of inequality, dependency, domination, exploitation and environmental damage' that govern the lives of people across the world. See: James Tully, *Public Philosophy in a New Key, Volume II: Imperialism and Civic Freedom* (Cambridge: Cambridge University Press, 2008), 127.

2 Aníbal Quijano, 'Coloniality of Power, Eurocentrism, and Latin America,' *Nepantla: Views from the South*, 1, no. 3 (2000): 533–580.

3 James Tully, 'The Struggles of Indigenous Peoples for and of Freedom,' in *Political Theory and the Rights of Indigenous Peoples*, ed. Duncan Ivison, Paul Patton, and Will Sanders (Cambridge: Cambridge University Press, 2000), 43.

4 Brian Barry, 'Humanity and Justice in Global Perspective,' in *Contemporary Political Theory: An Anthology*, ed. Robert Goodin and Philip Pettit (Oxford: Wiley-Blackwell, 2005); Charles Beitz, *Political Theory and International Relations* (Princeton, NJ: Princeton University Press, 1979); Thomas Pogge, *Realizing Rawls* (Ithaca, NY: Cornell University Press, 1989).

5 Simon Caney, *Justice beyond Borders* (Oxford: Oxford University Press, 2005).

6 Daniel Butt, *Rectifying International Injustice: Principles of Compensation and Restitution between Nations* (Oxford: Oxford University Press, 2009).

7 Raymond Geuss, *Philosophy and Real Politics* (Princeton, NJ: Princeton University Press, 2008).

8 See the contribution by James Brassett to this Handbook.

9 Charles W. Mills, '"Ideal Theory" as Ideology,' *Hypatia*, 20, no. 3 (2005): 168–169.

10 This problem is arguably less apparent in more far-reaching theories of global justice, such as Caney's global egalitarianism, in which many of the injustices associated with imperial power relations are, almost by definition, negated. Nevertheless, the coloniality of Caney's theory emerges in his proposals for implementing principles of justice through transnational institutions that, in practice, would be structured so as to privilege the interests of hegemonic Western powers. A similar difficulty also arises in Butt's argument for material reparations, according to which such redistributive transfers would be made from developed nation-states to the governments of formerly colonized nations. Since this argument for reparations is purely normative, it makes no reference to the ways in which such redistribution would, in fact, be circumscribed by the informal structural influence that Western nation-states hold over postcolonial states in virtue of their differential power in the interstates system.

11 John Rawls, *A Theory of Justice* (Cambridge, MA: Harvard University Press, 1971); John Rawls, *The Law of Peoples* (Cambridge, MA: Harvard University Press, 1993).

12 Beitz, *Political Theory and International Relations*; Pogge, *Realizing Rawls*; Thomas Pogge, 'An Egalitarian Law of Peoples,' *Philosophy and Public Affairs*, 23, no. 3 (1994): 195–224.

13 Kenneth Waltz, *Theory of International Politics* (Reading: Addison-Wesley, 1979), 88; Mathias Risse, 'What to Say about the State,' *Social Theory and Practice*, 32, no. 4 (2006): 671–698; Michael Blake, 'Distributive Justice, State Coercion, and Autonomy,' *Philosophy and Public Affairs*, 30, no. 3 (2001): 257–296; Thomas Nagel, 'The Problem of Global Justice,' *Philosophy and Public Affairs*, 33, no. 2 (2005): 113–147.

14 Darrel Moellendorf, 'Cosmopolitanism and Compatriot Duties,' *The Monist*, 94, no. 4 (2011): 535–554.

15 Mills, '"Ideal Theory" as Ideology,' 168–169.

16 Ideal theorists, of course, may remark that we require some ideal theory of justice in the abstract to diagnose present injustices in the first place. This view, however, largely acts to derail discussion of manifest

injustices in the here and now. Moreover, ideal theorists neglect the importance of phenomenological experiences of oppression in reaching a deeper understanding of injustices. See Ibid.; Amartya Sen, *The Idea of Justice* (Cambridge, MA: Harvard University Press, 2009).

17 Nagel, 'The Problem of Global Justice,' *Philosophy and Public Affairs*, 33, no. 2 (2005): 140.
18 Samuel Freeman, 'The Law of Peoples, Social Cooperation, Human Rights, and Distributive Justice,' *Social Philosophy and Policy*, 23, no. 1 (2006): 29–68; Rawls, *Law of Peoples*.
19 Beitz, *Political Theory and International Relations*; Pogge, *Realizing Rawls*.
20 In his later work, Pogge has reached such conclusions on the basis of negative rights and duties to refrain from harming, rather than to assist the poor. On this account, the shared institutional order is designed by wealthier nations (who were beneficiaries of colonialism) for their benefit, and in a manner that reproduces poverty and radical inequality, which violates the human rights of the global poor. See: Pogge, *World Poverty and Human Rights: Cosmopolitan Responsibilities and Reforms* (Cambridge: Polity, 2002).
21 Thomas Pogge, 'Eradicating Systemic Poverty: Brief for a Global Resources Dividend,' *Journal of Human Development*, 2, no. 1 (2001): 66.
22 Ibid., 66.
23 Tully, *Public Philosophy in a New Key, Volume II*, 130.
24 Tully, 'The Struggles of Indigenous Peoples for and of Freedom,' 130.
25 Pogge, 'Eradicating Systemic Poverty,' 72.
26 Caney, *Justice beyond Borders*, 121.
27 Ibid., 160.
28 Daniele Archibugi and David Held, eds., *Cosmopolitan Democracy: An Agenda for a New World Order* (Cambridge: Polity, 1995).
29 Caney, *Justice beyond Borders*, 161–162.
30 Rahul Rao, *Third World Protest: Between Home and the World* (Oxford: Oxford University Press, 2010), 68.
31 Ibid.; Tully, *Public Philosophy in a New Key, Volume II*.
32 Tully, *Public Philosophy in a New Key, Volume II*, 138.
33 Costas Douzinas, *Human Rights and Empire: The Political Philosophy of Cosmopolitanism* (Oxford: Routledge, 2007). Critical scholars commonly identify the ways in which (liberal) cosmopolitanism is philosophically and politically intertwined with imperialism. See, for example: Walter Mignolo, *Local Histories/Global Designs: Essays on the Coloniality of Power, Subaltern Knowledges and Border Thinking* (Princeton, NJ: Princeton University Press, 2011).
34 Butt, *Rectifying International Injustice*, 2.
35 Ibid., 32.
36 Daniel Butt, 'Repairing Historical Wrongs and the End of Empire,' *Social and Legal Studies*, 21, no.1 (2012): 239.
37 Daniel Butt, 'Nations, Overlapping Generations, and Historic Injustice,' *American Philosophy Quarterly*, 43, no. 4 (2006): 358.
38 Daniel Butt, 'Repairing Historical Wrongs and the End of Empire,' 5.
39 Butt, 'Nations, Overlapping Generations, and Historic Injustice,' 360.
40 Butt, 'Repairing Historical Wrongs and the End of Empire,' 6.
41 Ibid., 13.
42 Butt, *Rectifying International Injustice*.
43 Tully, *Public Philosophy in a New Key, Volume II*; I. Wallerstein, *World-Systems Analysis: An Introduction* (Durham, NC: Duke University Press, 2004).
44 Cecil Gutzmore, 'Preparation before Slavery Compensation,' *The Voice*, February 12, 2014, http://www.voice-online.co.uk/article/preparation-slavery-compensation.
45 Butt, 'Repairing Historical Wrongs,' 3–4.
46 Adam Swift and Stuart White, 'Political Theory, Social Science and Real Politics,' in *Political Theory: Methods and Approaches*, ed. David Leopold and Marc Stears (Oxford: Oxford University Press, 2008).
47 Ibid., 50, 54–56, 68.
48 Simon Caney, 'Cosmopolitan Justice and Institutional Design: An Egalitarian Liberal Conception of Global Governance,' *Social Theory and Practice*, 32, no. 4 (2006): 725–756.
49 Butt, *Rectifying Injustice*, 6–9.
50 Geuss, *Philosophy and Real Politics*, 7.
51 Tully, *Public Philosophy in a New Key, Volume I: Democracy and Civic Freedom* (Cambridge: Cambridge University Press, 2008), 9.

52 Quijano, 'Coloniality of Power, Eurocentrism, and Latin America;' Mignolo, *Local Histories/Global Designs*; R. Grosfoguel, 'A Decolonial Approach to Political-Economy: Transmodernity, Border Thinking and Global Coloniality,' *Kult*, 6 (2009), 10–38; María Lugones, 'Toward a Decolonial Feminism,' *Hypatia*, 25, no. 4 (2010): 742–759.

53 Mills, '"Ideal Theory" as Ideology,' 177.

54 Santiago Castro-Gómez, *La Hybris del Punto Cero: Ciencia, raza e ilustración en la Nueva Granada (1750–1816)* (Bogota: Universidad Javieriana, 2005); Charles W. Mills, *Blackness Visible: Essays on Philosophy and Race* (Ithaca, NY: Cornell University, 1998), 125.

55 For example, see: Boaventura de Sousa Santos, *Epistemologies of the South: Justice against Epistemicide* (New York: Routledge, 2014).

56 Lea Ypi, *Global Justice and Avant-Garde Political Agency* (Oxford: Oxford University Press, 2012).

31

GENDER, NATURE, AND THE ETHICS OF FINANCE IN A RACIALISED GLOBAL (POLITICAL) ECONOMY

Penny Griffin

Introduction

Discussions of global finance often foreground ethics as an end game, an icing of sorts on an otherwise perfectible, if currently flawed, cake of human behaviour. If finance can be reformed, it might better support ethical distributions of wealth, capital, capability, and risk. If financial crisis can be moderated or better managed, certain 'gendered outcomes' might be prevented, including the reproduction of systemic vulnerabilities for certain social groupings, or the problematically elitist concentration of wealth and privilege.

In the approaches that have emanated from dominant financial, regulatory, and governance sources (international organisations, epistemic communities and networks, governments and national regulators, central banks, and so on), systemic improvements should, and can, be made. Here, the 'ethics' of finance lives somehow outside of finance itself; as externalisable, monitorable, and regulatable, rather than intrinsic to the everyday practices that make financial capitalism possible. In light of this regulatory (artificial) separation of ethics from financial practice, this chapter sets out to locate the ethical content of financial activity as inherently significant to understanding global finance. To do this, it outlines and critiques the everyday gendered and racialised practices that naturalise, and thereby render unremarkable, the 'ethics' of finance, considering the possibilities offered by thinking about financial activity in terms of the ordinary, cultural locations of economic systems, social behaviour, and 'ethical' financial practice.

Looking at the assumptions, norms, and discursive limits embodied in the ethics of finance, mainstream or 'alternative', this chapter seeks to understand how the authority located in financial discourse (to define people, places, things, and to undertake or circumscribe particular financial actions) is constructed through knowledge and representations that are both racialised and gendered. The chapter argues that a turn to 'alternative' arrangements and 'everyday' local and global social practices is not a resolution or panacea to global economic ills; rather, it is a call to engage the contested, messy, and often contradictory 'ethics' of market life. This carries uncertainties, risks, and possibilities for alternative finance. Looking closely at the everyday politics of Islamic finance, the chapter considers how these are sites of struggle for thinking about alternative visions of finance, as much as any other. Especially in the context of the global financial crisis and the massive bank bailouts that have led to increasing public-sector austerity in the West, the widening of the divergence between ideas about financial success and everyday practices of social care is important and has been widely noted.[1] At the same time as corporate, philanthrocapitalist, alternative, and even governance approaches to 'systemic' failures have sought to incorporate, and make profitable, 'everyday' practices, the gap between the financially privileged and underprivileged continues to widen, not least for those trapped in the volatile markets that their securitised indebtedness exposes them to.

The ethics of finance

As James Brassett's contribution to this Handbook notes, and much like financial discourse itself, traditions of thought in international political economy (IPE) have repeatedly classified the world as ontologically divided: as *either* realist or liberal, profitable or unproductive, critical or poststructural, private or public, American or British, or systemic or everyday. Students and scholars have been pushed to make singular choices where they might more usefully have benefited from thinking about the 'both–and', where the different things that diverse traditions and practices have to say are in conversation with each other and themselves. As Barkin and Sjoberg have noted (2015), rarely, in terms of method and methodology, are mainstream and non-mainstream approaches to world politics feasibly separable. A mythology of methodology has arisen across international relations (IR) and IPE, resulting in totalising, 'once and for all' universalisms that cannot do justice to the big, less big, and sometimes very small ways people live, and are able to live.[2] Consideration of ethics, gender, and nature in relation to global financial activity requires a particularly 'pragmatic', rather than uniform and universal, approach to these layers of real life.

Why the 'everyday' makes the financial world go around

IR and IPE have not been particularly good, so far, at engaging consistently with the 'everyday'. While they can (to a point) understand how world politics might impact everyday life, they are less effective in showing how everyday life itself constitutes world politics. IPE is growing more interested in how political economy is 'enacted and performed at the local level, by non-elites and via various cultural practices'.[3] Scholars have increasingly emphasised 'the role of everyday social relations, actions, and the perspectives of nonelite groups and actors in the making of the global political economy'.[4] Yet 'regulatory' approaches still dominate IPE, where positivist scholars are to be found 'engaged in identifying the sources of governance and regulation in the global economy', or critical scholars are found reifying 'the significance of capitalist structures in their understanding of the global political economy'.[5] Even work that is otherwise open to alternatives has often excluded particular voices, particularly feminist and non-Western voices, exhibiting a particular tendency 'to ignore the social relations of gender'.[6]

The regulatory perspective is, perhaps unsurprisingly, 'top-down' in its approach: this is not to say 'that a focus on international institutions, world orders, or the mechanisms of capitalist hegemony are not important issues for IPE', rather that 'these are not the only issues, and a focus on the regulatory at the expense of the everyday results in us losing sight of some important questions'.[7] Such questions might include how apparently 'top-down' processes are mediated, shaped, and even made possible by those 'below', or how informal mechanisms, regimes, norms, and actors are created by everyday actors (ibid.).[8] Importantly, 'governance', across world politics, today and historically, emanates not only from formal mechanisms of state and legislature but from the everyday, gendered processes and practices of, for example, labour and employment, education, healthcare, the media, and numerous private and informal mechanisms of socioeconomic reproduction.

Interpretive approaches to world politics (not all of which would describe themselves as 'belonging' to the disciplines of IR and IPE and are perhaps more comfortable in sociology, social anthropology, or cultural studies) have instead started at the bottom, so to speak, to focus on how crucial practices of interpretation are invariably carried out on an 'everyday' level in world politics. Not many people understand what they see, hear, touch, smell, and taste about the world through anything other than intimate, personal, and subjective cognitive moments or events. Some people might like to believe that they process the world at a higher level, but the emotionality of living demands that our reactions, our psychological responses, and our sorting through of what is happening, occur somewhere just beyond our control. As Bleiker notes, many social scientists remain sceptical about approaches 'whose nature and understanding of evidence do not correspond to established scientific criteria'.[9] Boundaries are, however, what have kept feminist IR in place.[10] Boundaries, though they offer comfort, exist to be violated. Approaches that foreground the everyday are particularly noteworthy because they make space for emphasising resistance and agency: they might, and do, highlight relations of power, desperation, and exploitation, but at the same time, by highlighting avenues for creative thinking *and* doing, they enable a certain *hopefulness*. They also enable, rather than constrain, the possibilities for hearing and centralising potentially powerful 'other' voices in IR and IPE, challenging the persistent androcentricity and Eurocentricity of much IR and IPE scholarship.

Since the initial rumblings of global financial crisis in 2007 and 2008, the emergence of a number of discourses seeking to reconfigure finance have been noteworthy, arising in part from what are perceived to be financial capitalism's 'ethical' failures, and issuing from organisational, governmental, private, and also academic sources. Firstly, the emergent discourse of 'philanthrocapitalism' (philanthropic capitalism) has sought to make from poverty reduction and social welfare 'profitable business ventures', as Kish and Leroy articulate.[11] This discourse reveals in stark extreme the polarities through which global financial activity and its everyday constituents are believed to exist, particularly as philanthrocapitalist ventures gain increasing prominence in their attempts to 'marry finance capital with a moral commitment to do good', often in the form of the financialisation of public services in the form of 'social impact bonds' (SIBs).[12] Second, the emergent discourse of 'alternative' finance, often under the guise of so-called 'ethical finance' has promoted, especially in terms of banking, a number of social, alternative, civic, and sustainable banking arrangements and is ostensibly concerned with the social, environmental, and governance impacts of investments and loans.[13] Third, a focus on the possibilities afforded by Islamic finance has been evident across governance and corporate sources. Islamic finance has become, according to the International Monetary Fund (IMF), 'one of the fastest growing segments of the global financial industry', worth at least $820 billion by the end of 2008.[14] The largest Islamic banks are located in the countries of the Gulf Cooperation Council (Bahrain, Kuwait, Oman, Qatar, Saudi Arabia, and the United Arab Emirates). Over the past decade, Robertson notes, citing IMF and World Bank data, 'Sharia-compliant assets have grown at double-digit rates annually, from about $200 billion in 2003 to an estimated $2 trillion today'.[15] A substantial sector of the financial market already, Islamic finance is largely welcomed and invested in as a *sine qua non* of ethical finance, seemingly embodying (for some, but of course not all, financial actors) a superior approach to distributive and social justice and a capacity to bridge ethical and cultural 'divides' in the global economy.

Entailing different products and consumer choices, it is not clear how differently 'alternative' or 'ethical' financial discourses embody the relationship between provider and consumer.

Their products, although not traditional financial products, are bought and sold in much the same ways as in conventional financial activities, rendering valuable what (and who) was once considered valueless in ways that do not necessarily challenge the problematically gendered and racist assumptions and practices that lie at the heart of the financialisation of everyday, human life. Rather, such discourses combine the systemic and the everyday, and it is this that makes them seem 'alternative'. They do this by seeking to widen the reach of global finance's profit motive, quantifying and making profitable 'everyday' practices and social relations rather than, say, challenging existing hierarchies, privileges, and problematic practices. Islamic finance, on the other hand, embodies a relationship between provider and consumer that *is* fundamentally different to that found in Western financial institutions. It is for this reason perhaps that Islamic financial practice has been articulated by some as an alternative model to the failures of Western finance, a means to ease some of the ethical expectations of the more information-rich financial consumers. Posited as an 'alternative' to neoliberal financial capitalism, this view, however, has the potential to fix Islamic finance, in essentialising and universalising ways, as financial capitalism's non-Western 'Other', ignoring the ways in which Islamic finance constitutes a site of struggle in and of financial thinking. This chapter aims to show how different ways of thinking, involving the 'both–and' of the possible conversations between diverse traditions and everyday practices might do better justice to the big, less big, and small of global financial activity, including Islamic finance.

Financial capitalism as (always) human, ethical behaviour

This chapter asks what ethical possibilities global finance enables and how these possibilities can be understood as gendered and racist. It takes as its starting point that ethical positions are already embedded in financial practices. Asking ethical questions of finance is, then, less about measuring the prevalence of poor or fraudulent practice, which has often been the go-to for systemic, governance approaches that are determined to advocate for market behaviour as perfectible. Rather, understanding how global finance is complicit in reproducing particular understandings of the world, and thus 'natural' behaviours, practices, and outcomes in the financial sphere, necessitates engaging with how the financial industries have constructed and supported particular social forces, human behaviours, and economic rationalities.

As Mazzucelli and Fargnoli note, 'the political sphere is never devoid of moral questions'.[16] All politics is human behaviour, and all human behaviour is socially, culturally, historically, and morally constituted. We are our choices, or the choices made available to us. Nowhere in recent years has human behaviour come under closer scrutiny than in consideration of the financial services industry, its practices, and the widespread perception that financial services are somehow more *unethical* than other domains. The 'crimes' for which five senior bankers and one prominent investor were jailed in Iceland in 2015 point especially to 'ethical', systemic lapses in financial practice, including insider trading, fraud, money laundering, misleading markets, breach of duties, and lying to the authorities.[17]

Global finance touches everyone directly and profoundly. This is not only because it is a massive endeavour, although the scale of financial activity is undeniably impressive: by 2015, personal remittances alone exceeded $601 billion US.[18] In Australia, a country of only 22 million people, the size by market capitalisation of the banking system exceeds the Eurozone, Japan, Britain, and China (making it the second largest in the world, representing more than 8 per cent of the world banking industry by market value).[19] Australian household debt sits at a whopping 123 per cent (July 2016): only Denmark and Switzerland exceed this figure (Spain and Greece, for example, sit at 66.9 and 61.7 per cent, respectively).[20] Global finance is big, but it is also intimate, with human behaviour, possibilities, and outcomes implicated at each stage of financial activity. How and where people labour, what they produce, save, and spend, or whether, indeed, they create financial policy, consume financial products, or regulate financial practices.

There is, as Steve Smith has powerfully argued, 'no possibility of a neutral observation of the world of international relations'. All engagement, whether by student, scholar, or practitioner, is necessarily partial, carrying with it 'a set of ethical consequences that rest, in the final analysis, on violence'.[21] Smith asserts that simply to study a phenomenon is to render ethics an implicit (but not often centralised) consideration.[22] His point is that the theories of and approaches to world politics that social scientists and policymakers construct and apply do not stand aside as power relations are written across actual people's lives. Rather, these theories and approaches, and the understandings and actions they generate, have supported, and continue to reproduce, specific social forces; 'quietly, unquestioningly', and (often) 'innocently' taking sides 'on major ethical and political questions'.[23] By learning about and studying global affairs, students, scholars, and practitioners enable the existence of a world that makes possible certain international events and which normalises particular social inequalities, elevating certain 'natural' economic practices, and, indeed, making financial crises possible. Whether the global political economy's scholars and practitioners choose to admit it or not, what they do and do not see in the world, and what they know and do not know about the social relations that drive it, are ethical positions: moral principles that guide action, governing how they research; what they know; who they talk to; how, where, and to whom they teach, and so on. This is no less true for those who craft financial policy, who regulate the financial system, and who are engaged, every day, in making financial decisions. There are foundations, ethical foundations, to the possibilities, common-sense assumptions, modelling techniques, regressive analyses, and decisions about profitability that drive financial practice, and thus shape its outcomes. These, this chapter argues, are gendered.

The pursuit of value-neutral practices (analysis, process, research design, modelling techniques, dissemination of research, policy-design and policymaking, and so on) has often, as Smith also notes, obscured the ethical positions and questions that underlie a great deal of knowledge about, and for, the world.[24] The search for value-neutrality has enabled IR and IPE to recreate 'a world of international relations that has quietly supported the views, and ultimately the interests, of specific forms of social power'.[25] IR has effectively been a 'handmaiden' to the rise and preternatural dominance of Western rationality, derived of and reproduced through historically and culturally specific relations of power. Global finance, driven by the uniformity and dominance of modern finance theory, is a palpable creature of this rationalism. In the global economy, a particular constellation of financial practices have arisen from the development and centralisation of modern finance theory, and, particularly, financial actors' training in neoclassical formalism. While economic thinking is, of course, neither homogenous nor closed, the rise of neoclassicism and the 'cliometrics revolution'[26] in modern finance has made modern physics a model for economics, and heterodox traditions of Marxian economics and Keynesianism have been entirely eclipsed by the uptake of the equilibrium framework.[27] This plays out in the deployment of highly abstract frameworks and methods that may seem, on the surface, 'value-neutral' because they have proved so effective at, figuratively and literally, removing any hint of the human body from economic analysis and practice (as in, for example, a focus on 'financial coordination', financial 'regulation' and 'adjustment', 'excessive risk-taking', the build-up of 'financial imbalances', the accumulation of 'vulnerabilities', 'fiscal stabilisers', and so on).

Ethics, gender, and finance

The discourses that create the 'natural groups' that possess 'women' and 'men' are a powerful source of compulsion and prohibition, forcing bodies and minds 'to correspond, feature by feature, with the idea of nature that has been established for us'.[28] Neoliberalism constitutes a specific and dominating constellation of discursive practices and normative articulations that make the individual intelligible in particular, culturally specific ways. Rarely explicit in neoliberal discourse, gender constitutes the social norms on which depends, as Butler articulates, the viability of our individual personhood.[29]

For many gender and postcolonial scholars, meaning is not fixed, pre-given, or guaranteed in nature; rather, it is a process and an outcome, generated by the ways in which 'nature' is represented in 'culture'. The development of modern financial, capitalist practices is not 'natural' or 'inevitable' but has been built from particular gender and racial hierarchies, to particular effect. Discussing neoliberalism as a discourse dependent on social relations and practices, gender and postcolonial scholars have shown how neoliberal discourse, and the practices it has instituted, can only be understood well by considering explicitly their historical development as 'solutions' to economic 'crisis'. Attuned to the patterns of gendered and racialised power that reside behind the production and distribution of goods, gender and postcolonial scholars have troubled existing notions of 'naturalness' or normality in capitalist practices, including how the categories of sex and gender have often been collapsed, such that masculinity has come to signify the male body, femininity the female. Highly attendant to historically constituted social relations of power and their changing forms, they have shown how the imposition of crude binaries has led to artificial but powerful separations in ideas about production and consumption in relation to gender and sex, compelling the organisation of labour according to existing or prevailing logics about how, and for what, men and women labour (for example, the notions that men produce and women consume, that 'femininity' is subservient and domestically located, 'masculinity' authoritative, wage-earning, and responsible, and in post-Fordist societies that all options and possible social configurations are commodifiable).

Queer approaches seek to subvert the apparent naturalness of the 'straight' authorities, hierarchies, and discourses residing in the socioeconomic systems that govern us. Here, gender, sex, and heterosexuality are social, political, and economic constructs, not the pre-given basis for human interaction that they are made to seem. As such, 'truth', 'nature', and 'fact' are not (contrary to conventional wisdom) universally valid, but are instead discursive constructions. Studies in heterosexist bias and the reproduction of heteronormativity have a significant intellectual heritage in historical analyses of the means and functions of mechanisms of social control over the body.[30] The effects of constituting sexual difference as 'fundamental to culture', assumed by the body and not assigned to it according to a variety of cultural practices, are the fundamental 'naturalness' that underlines neoliberal agents' understanding, and manipulation, of human bodies, such that they can assume, 'naturally', that there exists one set of traits for characterising men and one for women. To conceive of gender as constitutive of the very processes that drive the beneficiaries of international economic interaction is to ask, however, how and where the construction of gender takes place. The compulsion to become 'man' or 'woman' does not come from 'sex' but from the setting of 'certain limits to analysis'.[31]

To talk of gender as something owned and conveyed by the human body is to fail, then, to see the power that gender brings to our everyday understandings, and especially to our understandings of economic 'common sense'.[32] Rather than reflective of some kind of inner biological 'core', gender is a composite part of the relations of power that drive systems of economic development and growth, global financial flows, and systems of manufacturing and production.[33]

'Natural' actors in finance

Neoliberal discourse and rational 'economic man'

Neoliberal discourses, of which modern finance theory and practice are devolved, understand 'rational' action where it is centred on the primacy of capital acquisition, private property rights, and the socially distributive mechanism of the market. The assumption that people everywhere adhere to the rule of the market renders neoliberalism a powerful model for human interaction and behaviour, and very few areas of the world exist today without some relationship to the desirability of market growth and development.[34] Neoliberalism is, however, a cultural, ethical model of human action, produced from centuries of Western liberal ideology and rhetoric naturalising the binding power of certain acts, including the essentiality of trade, the accumulation of capital, and the centrality of economic growth through the liberal 'free market'.[35] These acts are made possible through assumptions about the appropriate mechanisms of socioeconomic exchange and distribution, based on the assumed 'natural fact' and inevitability of economic liberalisation, integration, and market growth, and the actors native to this realm. This can be denaturalised to reveal particular, gendered, and racist, assumptions about who is expected to 'act' in the global economy (states, governments, market participants, classes, men, and so on).

For example, assumptions about who 'acts' shape the 'facts' of neoliberal discourse, without which much economic theorising would not make sense: the single model of individual behaviour (the rational economic choice model), value neutrality (economic modelling as intrinsically objective), the idea that actors in markets are functionally individualistic (responsible only for themselves), the belief that a market is fully functioning only when it is said by economists to be 'competitive', and the sense that a well-functioning competitive system is 'naturally' efficient. These 'facts' are not often questioned in conventional economic theory and are beyond question in modern finance theory. They are pertinent here because they depend on but also reproduce highly gendered assumptions of behaviour, embodied, in particular, in the 'natural fact' of *homo economicus*, or economic man.

Economic man is a founding figure of modern finance theory, both universal and highly masculinised. The norms of human economic behaviour that he embodies include assumptions about the centrality of profit-motivated behaviour, 'competitive' performance, human 'rationality', fiscal 'responsibility', and so on. Modelled on the white, elite, and (economically) liberal masculinity of European colonisers and, more recently, transnational businessmen, this (masculinised) human subject is deployed so widely in economic discourse as to be considered a natural fact in and of himself, although he is no accident of historical development.[36] Economic man represents a gendered, ethnocentric, and always ethical (in his normative and purposive content) decision about what people are and what they do, based on a model of human activity derived from the privileging and experiences of certain men, 'globalised' through Western economic rationality's ongoing colonisation of 'Other' worlds, peoples, and practices.

Economic man has been represented in many contemporary and historical forms: he is embodied in Adam Smith's competitive but respectful and cooperative economic actor, in the scoundrels and rogues of eighteenth- and nineteenth-century European and US 'speculative' capitalisms, in the 'gentleman banker' of Philip Augar's famous (2001) analysis of London's merchant banking sector in the 1970s, in the ambitious US financier with little respect for hierarchy and conservatism à la Gordon Gekko in the 1980s, and in the rise of 'transnational business masculinity' in the 1990s that placed the 'power of transnational corporations' strategically in the hands of particular groups of white men.[37] The discursive limits of neoliberal discourses have developed historically and have been culturally bounded by the experience of white, elite men's actions in the economic sphere. While economic models and assumptions use economic man as an approximation of the human actor, and the actor in the market is not gender-distinguished (or, indeed, distinguished in any particular way, since economic actors are assumed in neoclassical economic theory to be functionally similar), the position of economic man is not easily disentangled from his historical development as the substantive person in economic theory and practice, derived of times when men *were* the only assumed actors in the market.

Human bodies *learn* how to function correctly in the global marketplace; they do not intrinsically know this, nor are they born programmed with the attributes of 'rational' behaviour. Ethical, social, political, and cultural 'truths', including the core principles, logics, and rationales of financial 'success', are inscribed upon the human body and performed by that body, and as bodies labour, produce, and reproduce, they become complicit in the viability of neoliberal finance. The construction of neoliberalism's appropriate human subject, rational economic man, is a powerful normalising principle throughout the social practices instituted by neoliberal discourse. Economic man is neoliberalism and global finance's 'intelligible gender', and his discursive role is to maintain the coherence, logic, and continuity of economic theory and practice.

The Smithsonian 'nature' of economic man was, for example, intrinsically competitive and territorial, but it was also essentially cooperative, with bonding instincts where like-minds were found.[38] Importantly, Adam Smith's early description of human nature, which extended only to the white, middle-class male (wise, self-restraining, and able to restore peace and order), would come to define the parameters of the economic actor to the modern day, evident in the noble and civilised credentials of financial 'professionalism' across the Western, liberal world. The more ruthlessly aggressive character of neoliberal economic man, achieving prominence during the widespread 'structural adjustments' of the late 1970s onwards, would create different incentives for competitiveness, territoriality, and promiscuity among market actors, interacting with local gender orders in various, often troubling, ways. Although by the 1980s, women presented an increased percentage of the business classes, the climate of aggressive corporate masculinism that sustained financial capitalism was so strong that women's only hope of advancement would be to play 'like men' in the corporate power-houses of the business world.[39]

In failing to recognise or act upon the prevalence of economic man in their formulations and policy prescriptions, the neoliberal thesis and its advocates (including individual policy-makers, governments, organisations, networks, and epistemic communities) reproduce norms and standards in the global political economy, especially those related to standards of appropriately responsible, competitive, profitable, and rational economic behaviour, that are culturally specific, evolved from historically and culturally elitist, racist, and sexist decisions about who holds, or should hold, authority. These are, in effect, the limits of normalised, 'natural', and acceptable human behaviour; the biased inscription on bodies of what should and can be done, represented as 'universal' standards against which real bodies are measured. As Pin-Fat argues, claims to universality are political and ethical practices, providing foundations that identify particular desirable, and thus undesirable, 'features of reality (and being human)'; foundations that are, therefore, exclusionary.[40] It is less important that financial services are dominated by men (they are, but only at senior levels) than that global finance is governed by dominant models of behaviour that have become, subsequent to the concentrating of historical privilege in the hands of white men, associated with masculine subjectivities. The prescribed legibility of neoliberal global finance, made possible through the gendered regulation of bodies, is an ethical practice, entwined in politics of privilege, exclusion, and historical myopia. On this view, a systemic vision of IPE is always already a partial summary of contingent market hierarchy.

'Rational economic woman', 'womenomics', and the turn to women's leadership

The rise of the so-called 'rational economic woman' in and across development discourse has heralded the targeting of poor women as beneficiaries and agents of development schemes and lending across the world.[41] Women are recruited into neoliberal financial activity, however, 'not because they are considered universally capable market actors', but because 'as nurturers and carers of the household, women are considered less likely to display men's "risk-taking" behaviour'.[42] In effect, women achieve 'rationality' because they are somehow 'outside' the formal, normalised economy, and, because they 'are considered essentially reproductive, care-giving and domestically situated', they are described as 'more responsible, reliable and trust-worthy'.[43] Where the neoliberal market is not quite producing equitable outcomes, women have become a 'solution' to policies based fundamentally on achieving economic growth and efficiency, but where questions of social justice are pushing at agents' and agencies' of development profit line.

This essentialised, and essentialising, development discourse, ostensibly 'for' (but really about regulating) poor women, finds its parallels in governance efforts during and after the global financial crisis and the notable 'turn to women' in governance responses to the crisis. As True notes, perceptions and responses to the crisis have frequently been 'shaped by the turn to women's leadership', despite the crisis triggering 'the intensification of gendered inequalities and the co-optation of feminist discourses', causing 'deleterious consequences for many groups'.[44] It is also not clear, notwithstanding the introduction of quotas and active recruitment strategies aimed specifically at women, that the masculine privilege embedded in, and embodied by, global finance has fundamentally been challenged since the crisis.[45] Yet increasingly, multilateral and financial institutions are seeking to recognise and tap into women's economic 'potential', with claims that, for example: 'intervention' (rather than quotas) 'really makes sure that you're meeting targets' (Macquarie Bank chairman Kevin McCann, February 2014, in Yeates 2014),[46] a 'much faster reduction in gearing [debt to equity relationship]' occurred 'at companies with women on the board as the financial crisis and global slowdown unfolded',[47] or gender discrimination is bad for economies and for business and that countries with 'incentives' for women to work do better on the Gini coefficient.[48]

In 2012, the World Bank famously released a World Development Report (WDR) dedicated to 'Gender Equality and Development', a document that intersected smoothly with, as Roberts and Soederberg demonstrate, Goldman Sachs's framework of 'womenomics'.[49] Womenomics frames 'gender equality and poverty alleviation as smart economics', assuming that, as women are driven to enter the workforce, they 'raise the productivity and consumption rates of a country', simply by virtue of being women.[50] Women are here driven by rational self-interest, as per economic man, but their inherently different, domestic, and nurturing qualities mean that their formal economy efforts will also lift their children and families out of poverty. This is especially the case, as the WDR argues, once 'determinants of inequality' (e.g., lack of market access, legal restrictions, and so forth) and gendered outcomes are addressed (by appropriate development actors and policymaking initiatives) such that 'optimal conditions will be present to achieve equal opportunities for both sexes in the global South'.[51]

Goldman Sachs is, of course, one of the world's best known and most powerful investment banks, a Goliath of global neoliberal finance. It is no coincidence that the corporation should be centralised by the Bank, a leading proponent of public–private 'partnerships' across development. The turn to women's leadership post-global financial crisis has been backed by the use of data showing an apparently positive correlation between companies with women on their boards and their financial success.[52] Women are especially praised for making 'efficient' choices, for being intrinsically less 'corrupt', more likely to invest in health and education, likely to have higher savings, more productive investments, a better use and repayment of credit, and less nepotism and corruption in the boardroom than men.[53]

Women in Islamic finance

It is worth noting that, while the Western financial services industry reports the highest gender pay gap and is exhibiting a *drop* of women on boards (from 41.7% in 2013 to 39.7% in 2014), gendered employment and recruitment in Islamic financial institutions is increasing. Two of Malaysia's sixteen Islamic lenders, for example, are *run by* women and three of the eleven-member central bank Sharia Advisory Board are female. McAughtry goes so far as to suggest that women are 'an increasingly powerful force, both in terms of industry talent and client targets', citing figures from the Kuwait Financial Center that hint at women's net worth across the GCC growing 'up to 15 per cent to US$258 billion by 2023'.[54]

This is not, however, an even process, and the prominence of women in Malaysian institutions makes this example something of an outlier across both conventional and Islamic institutions. Despite its regional dominance in terms of women's representation in finance, women in Malaysia are also 'still hugely under-banked or unbanked'.[55] More conservative countries, such as Saudi Arabia, employing stronger religious and social constraints on women's labour force and economic participation (such as requirements for male guardianship, prohibitions against women driving, proscriptions against women and men mixing in public spaces, including the work environment, and so on), render the picture yet more inconsistent.

This is not, however, stopping Islamic institutions from targeting women, in some cases aggressively and consistently. Standard Chartered, Noor Islamic Bank, and Islamic Financial Services have each in recent years run advertorials exclusively depicting or aimed at women (often mimicking Western neoliberal assumptions about women's 'value', where women are shown as homemakers, shoppers, and workers in the caring professions and service industries). *OIC Today* argues that Islamic banks can 'leverage' their female work force 'to promote participation of those financially excluded women through mobilisation of savings and easier access to credit', which brings them into 'the formal banking net' and tackles 'financial exclusion issues'.[56] *OIC Today* suggests that the 'ladies' branches' that have proven to be 'successful' in Saudi Arabia can be emulated elsewhere:

> The proposed ladies branches may also provide a full package of banking, beauty and health services so as to meet the requirements and needs of women customers. The Dubai Islamic Bank (in the United Arab Emirates) has targeted this niche area by developing Johara banking for ladies and has gone a step further by offering women-focused financial products such as beauty, health and shopping benefits. The ladies only branches can also house children nurseries for the working women, an area that is bound to be extremely profitable in a country like Malaysia.[57]

Such newfound enthusiasm for women does not quite tell the whole story, of course, and, as for Western finance, the turn to women is not well matched with universally high levels of representation and access. 'Women have virtually zero representation at board level in Islamic banks and very little at senior management', notes Harris Irfan, Managing Director of the European Islamic Investment Bank (speaking at the KPMG launch of the Women in Islamic and Ethical

Finance Forum (WIEFF) in July 2015): if little changes, 'the culture of Islamic finance will be little different to the culture of conventional finance'. [58]

As the global political economy transforms the body into a profit-producing global resource, it does so through social structures, ethical choices, cultural expectations, and historical precedent (including expectations around physical and virtual availability, the presence of technology, the desirability of flexibilisation, the background noise of unpaid reproductive labour, and so on). These structures and expectations prescribe femininity's and masculinity's roles in the successful growth of the global market, as 'natural' market actors (men), as pseudo-rational actors (working women), or as outsiders (those who are not officially productive or who are located only in the reproductive sphere, which does not 'count' in official economic statistics).

Global finance and neoliberal financial practice may be pervasive, but they are not necessarily accessible. Institutions, governments, and industries have expended no small effort in seeking to 'mystify' finance in the twentieth century: simultaneous to administrative endeavours to incorporate working-class and 'everyday' populations in spaces of 'popular finance', 'capital' has often also been represented, popularly and academically, as 'an implacable kind of force' and the financial world as 'an unknowable and, importantly, undoable centre of power and domination'.[59] Financial elitism and inscrutability has significant ethical repercussions, especially for the underprivileged many.

Contesting Western rationality? The 'natural' actor in Islamic finance

Rational actors are prerequisites, not only for mainstream finance, but also for alternative forms of finance, including Islamic but also so-called 'ethical' financial activities. It would be a mistake, however, to assume that finance can easily be separated into various divisions of differing ethical content: to see finance as either ethical or unethical, systemic or everyday, is to miss how the language of finance depends widely on questions of positionality, privilege and so-called 'choice' (often described in terms of consumers of finance making better choices, but rarely approached as the choices the global financial industry takes to sustain itself).

Some have suggested that Islamic finance's different formulation of financial activity insulated Islamic financial institutions during and following the global financial crisis. This is largely because Islamic banks had not traded in the 'toxic' assets that characterise Western financial accumulation.[60] The 'smaller investment portfolios' and 'lower leverage' of Islamic banks, which precluded them 'from financing or investing in the kind of instruments that have adversely affected their conventional competitors', the IMF argues, 'helped contain the impact of the crisis on Islamic banks'.[61] Subsequent 'weaknesses in risk management practices in some Islamic banks' after 2008, however, 'led to a larger decline in profitability compared to that seen in conventional banks' and so the evidence for Islamic banking strength vis-à-vis conventional banking is not clear.[62] Thus, despite 'the higher profitability of Islamic banks during the pre-global crisis period (2005–07)', their average profitability during 2008 to 2009 'was similar to that of conventional banks'.[63] The IMF does suggest that Islamic banks showed 'better cumulative profitability', 'higher pre-crisis profitability' and credit and asset growth 'at least twice as high as that of conventional banks'.[64] The Fund's analysis also suggests 'that large Islamic banks fared better than small ones, perhaps as a result of better diversification, economies of scale, and stronger reputation'.[65]

Sharia-based finance operates according to particular assumptions and prohibitions, as does Western finance, but in different ways. Importantly, and as previously noted, Islamic finance is often considered to embody a relationship between provider and consumer that is different in important ways to that of Western financial institutions. In particular, the assumption that the risks and rewards of financial activity must be shared equitably between lender and recipient marks Islamic finance from Western, neoliberal finance, which has, particularly since the rise of structural adjustment policymaking in the late 1970s, effectively evacuated from Keynesian ideas about the mutuality of debt and fiscal responsibility. Unlike Western finance, Sharia finance's major prohibitions and principles concern paying or receiving interest, profiting from uncertainty, production and the sale of haram (forbidden) goods and services (including alcohol, firearms, tobacco, and pornography). The concept of partnership (*mudarabah*) dominates Islamic business, as it has done for centuries, while the concept of interest has found little application in day-to-day transactions. While in Western banking, only minimal reserves of people's deposit-based assets are held (meaning that in times of crisis, the possibility of a consumer losing everything is palpable), the Islamic system requires that loans made by banks should be equity-based. Trade agreements, rather than direct lending, establish loans.[66] According to Islamic jurisprudence, that which is not explicitly prohibited is permissible.

The principles of Sharia that shape 'Islamic' economic philosophy centre on sharing risk, while also achieving more equitable social outcomes.[67] They are not, however, as fixed and predetermined as they are often portrayed, in Western discussions especially, depending as they do on the recurrent interpretation of religious principles. As Pollard and Samers point out, Islamic finance is 'a project under construction, underpinned by a host of definitional, language and doctrinal debates'.[68] As with all Islamic thought, the concepts of Sharia that shape Islamic finance are contested both in terms of jurisprudence and the ways in which they are implemented in various contexts.

As Rethel notes, dominant Western discourse views Islamic finance as rooted in religious doctrine rather than as a product of a specific historical, economic, and industrial context.[69] Here, the question of ethics is implicated automatically in considerations of Islamic finance, since Islamic finance is considered by Western sources as fundamentally and primarily based on specific ethical and moral considerations. Across Islamic finance, both the economic viability of a project and its moral character are considered, and, as such, economic activity is committed to 'achieving a socially embedded financial system that includes—if not actively promotes—ethical and moral dimensions for productive purposes'.[70] This contrasts with the 'efficient market model of conventional finance theory' such that Islamic finance 'contrasts sharply with the proliferation of financial claims increasingly detached from the real economy that are a root cause of the current global financial crisis'.[71]

If Islamic actors are driven primarily by religious doctrine, they become, at least according to Anglo-Saxon economic doctrine, fundamentally *irrational*. In effect, *homo Islamicus* 'differs from *homo economicus* by preferring a moral economy over pragmatic benefits'.[72] Even where Islamic actors behave 'according to universal motives, such as interest maximisation', and although liberal systems 'can be founded even without liberal participants', assumptions that Islamic actors are different to other economic actors because they are driven (apparently) by religious doctrine, rather than self-interested utility, retain a substantial place in existing literatures on Islamism, Demiralp and Demiralp argue.[73]

Islamic finance cannot, despite the best efforts of dominant Western discourse, 'be abstracted from developments in the wider political economy', including 'an increasingly affluent Muslim middle class, the explosion of oil revenues, and a reorientation towards cultural-religious values'.[74] Consequently, 'increasing efforts' are expended 'to structure Sharia-compliant financial products, to develop and institutionalize Islamic capital markets and above all, to make Islamic finance acceptable (and thus investable) to the mainstream'.[75] Throughout the 1990s and 2000s, the Gulf states, in particular, sought to integrate themselves more thoroughly in the logics of global financial markets, particularly through involvement of major multinational banks.

As Rethel remarks, Islamic international regulatory organisations, such as the Islamic Financial Services Board, prioritise integration into mainstream markets and 'the emerging regulatory framework for Islamic finance reproduces existing governance structures rather than offering an ethical alternative'.[76] Many financial services professionals working in Islamic institutions are also trained primarily in the methods and practices of modern finance theory, indeed many undertake their training in Western institutions. According to the Shah Foundation, they therefore 'lack the requisite vision and conviction about the efficiency of the Islamic banking'.[77] In a similar vein, the Institute of Islamic Banking and Insurance notes that:

> [T]he one key contributory factor that is currently affecting the growth of the Islamic financial services industry is the lack of available expertise of people who are well conversant with Islamic and insurance operations and with the principles and objectives of Islamic economics and the Shari'ah requiring them to be wholly committed both materially, and more so morally, to the implementation of the products and services.[78]

As Islamic finance is made both 'acceptable' and more investible within mainstream understandings of 'legitimate economic activity', it becomes increasingly entangled in the (re-)production of the Western, masculinised knowledges that underpin contemporary international financial system. As Islamic financial systems look to profit, and sediment themselves, globally, and as Islamic finance grows and moves towards the mainstream, its ethical principles will likely become increasingly challenged.[79] Importantly, Sharia-compliant is not necessarily Sharia-based. The emergence of 'secularized Islamic finance' reproduces conventional finance with a few cosmetic changes, Islamic largely only in name. Sharia finance becomes largely restricted to procedural understandings of legitimacy, namely the Sharia compliance that is to be ensured by Sharia boards. While a Sharia-compliant financial system is not unattainable and a more equitable economic order may still be possible, as it stands, Islamic finance, for all its 'otherness' and irrationality, will likely serve 'to reproduce, to legitimize, and thus to further entrench current financial structures' through frameworks 'originally devised by mainly Western elites and only made Sharia-compliant in hindsight'.[80]

Conclusions: everyday finance, gender, and ethics

In line with a focus on the everyday production and performances of a global political economy, this chapter has shown how a certain ethics of nature—or naturalness—is ushered into the ontological status of finance, indeed global markets more broadly. By considering the global political economy an everyday social structure, this chapter has asked upon what kinds of naturalised assumptions about and forms of gendered and racialised agency financial activity depends.

A long line of critical thought on financial discourse has highlighted the role of metaphors of nature in its discursive construction: from ideas of crisis as a global hurricane/earthquake/tsunami, to highly ethnocentric, gendered discussions of the excessive masculinity of bankers and the need for a more feminine ethics of compassion and nurturing finance, global finance is almost invariably represented as a 'natural', and therefore somehow implacable and predictable, force. Sadly, there is little at the moment to suggest that 'alternative' financial frameworks, such as 'ethical' and Sharia-compliant finance, and also philanthrocapitalism, challenge this.

Highlighting the everyday, gendered practices of finance, however, reveals how global and financial processes are constituted *most powerfully* at local and social levels, rather than assuming that economic power, behaviour, and possibility are imparted somehow magically only from above. The financialisation of the world economy has depended on deeply gendered and racialised processes, categorising human bodies and their behaviours as valuable and valueless according to restrictive categories of gendered and racial identity. These processes have often been hidden or obscured, because they are too small, too intimate, or too physical to matter to the 'big', abstract politics of financial governance and reform. So too have systemic, governance-based approaches depended, even where they have tried to account for the everyday, upon essentialist and universalising assumptions. These have included positing whiteness as aspirational, and women as inherently, and naturally, different, domestic, and nurturing. This has rendered such approaches at once hegemonic in and blind to the emergence of truly alternative visions of political economy.

Taking the everyday seriously, on the other hand, calls for the application of a curious and enabling mind-set to world politics, generative of creative thinking and writing about who and what matters in and to world politics. Such a focus is capable, this chapter argues, of challenging the eurocentrism and androcentrism of IR and IPE, emphasising resistances and agency in world politics as sources of power and meaning-making. An 'everyday' approach to interrogating the gendered ethics of global finance engages with how pictures (including stories and narratives) of the world are created as sequences of isolated events unrelated to everyday practices of social and cultural reproduction, and how this might be different. Taking the frivolous and insubstantial politics of the everyday seriously, this research agenda shows how the everyday locations of political and economic activity are, in all their dimensions, core components of world politics, including their corporate capitalist content, its legitimations, dominant narratives, practices, and sources of support and subversion. To see how world politics really works, it is necessary to engage fully with its otherwise marginal considerations and constituents, becoming more attentive to everyday world politics by recognising that the world rarely happens simply 'out there'. The function of gender and race in neoliberal discourse has long been obscured by practices of apparently value-neutral 'good governance' and economic development. The possibility, then, that attention to everyday world politics might make obvious their constitutive role, undoing some of IR and IPE's powerful, and power-laden, constructions of 'legitimate' knowledge, is worth struggling for.

Notes

1 See, e.g., Brigitte Young, Isabelle Bakker, and Diane Elson, eds., *Questioning Financial Governance from a Feminist Perspective* (London: Routledge, 2011); P. Ashton, '"Troubled Assets": The Financial Emergency and Racialized Risk', *International Journal of Urban and Regional Research*, 36, no. 4 (2012): 773–790; James Heintz and Radhika Balakrishnan, 'Debt, Power, and Crisis: Social Stratification and the Inequitable Governance of Financial Markets', *American Quarterly*, 64, no. 3 (2012): 387–409; Shirin. M. Rai, Catherine Hoskyns, and Dania Thomas, 'Depletion: The Cost of Social Reproduction', *International Feminist Journal of Politics*, 16, no. 2 (2014): 86–105; Penny Griffin, 'Crisis, Austerity and Gendered Governance: A Feminist Perspective', *Feminist Review*, 109 (2015): 49–72; Johnna Montgomerie and Daniela Tepe-Belfrage, 'Caring for Debts: How the Household Economy Exposes the Limits of Financialisation', *Critical Sociology*, 43, 4–5 (2016); Juanita Elias and Adrienne Roberts, 'Feminist Global Political Economies of the Everyday: From Bananas to Bingo', *Globalizations*, 13 no. 6 (2016): 787–800.

2 J. Samuel Barkin, and Laura Sjoberg, 'Calculating Critique: Thinking outside the Methods Matching Game', *Millennium*, 43, no. 3 (2015): 852–871.

3 Juanita Elias and Adrienne Roberts, 'Feminist Global Political Economies of the Everyday: From Bananas to Bingo', *Globalizations*, 13, no. 6 (2016): 787.

4 Juanita Elias, 'Locating the "Everyday" in International Political Economy: That Roar which Lies on the Other Side of Silence', *International Studies Review*, 12 (2010): 603.

5 Ibid., 604.

6 Elias, 'Feminist Global Economies of the Everyday', 788.

7 Elias, 'Locating the Everyday in International Political Economy', 604.

8 Ibid.
9 Roland Bleiker, *Aesthetics and World Politics* (Basingstoke: Palgrave Macmillan, 2009), 44.
10 Marysia Zalewski, *Feminist International Relations: Exquisite Corpse* (New York: Routledge, 2013), 127.
11 Zenia Kish, and Justin Leroy, 'Bonded Life: Technologies of Racial Finance from Slave Insurance to Philanthrocapital', *Cultural Studies*, 29, nos. 5–6 (2016): 630.
12 Ibid.
13 For example, focused on sensible investments and long-term decisions, see: Anthony Murray, 'What Is Ethical Finance?', *Co-Operative News*, 22 October, 2014, https://www.thenews.coop/91000/sector/what-is-ethical-finance/, last accessed April 2017.
14 Ananthakrishnan Prasad, 'Global Aspirations', *Finance and Development*, 52, no. 3 (2015), http://www.imf.org/external/pubs/ft/fandd/2015/09/prasad.htm, last accessed October 2017.
15 Holly Robertson, 'How Malaysian Women Are Making Waves in Islamic Finance', *Southeast Asia Globe*, 9 February, 2016, http://sea-globe.com/malaysian-women-in-islamic-finance/, last accessed April 2017.
16 Colette Mazzucelli and A. Nicholas Fargnoli, 'Ethics and International Relations in Today's Classrooms without Borders', *Carnegie Council*, 14 July 2010, https://www.carnegiecouncil.org/education/001/ethics/0004/:pf_printable, last accessed April 2017.
17 See, e.g., Ian Birrell, 'Iceland Has Jailed 26 Bankers, Why Won't We?', *The Independent*, 15 November 2015, http://www.independent.co.uk/voices/iceland-has-jailed-26-bankers-why-wont-we-a6735411.html; Edward Robinson and Omar Valdimarsson, 'Welcome to Iceland, Where Bad Bankers Go to Prison', 1 April 2016, http://www.smh.com.au/business/banking-and-finance/welcome-to-iceland-where-bad-bankers-go-to-prison-20160331-gnvn68.html, last accessed October 2017.
18 World Bank, *Migration and Remittances Factbook 2016*, 3rd edn. (Washington, D. C.: World Bank, 2016).
19 See: David Uren, 'BIS Warns Australia's Finance Sector Is Too Big for Our Economy', *The Australian*, August 20, 2012, http://www.theaustralian.com.au/business/opinion/bis-warns-australias-finance-sector-is-too-big-for-our-economy/news-story/adf7ac9ab0e819d9f723b2241e6e70fb, last accessed October 2017.
20 Trading Economics, 'Australian Households' Debt to GDP, 1977–2017', 2017, http://www.tradingeconomics.com/australia/households-debt-to-gdp, last accessed April 2017.
21 Steve Smith, 'Singing Our World into Existence: International Relations Theory and September 11', *International Studies Quarterly*, 48, no. 3 (2004): 405.
22 Smith, 'Singing Our World into Existence'.
23 Ibid., 500.
24 Ibid., 504, 513–515.
25 Ibid., 514.
26 The cliometrics revolution, otherwise known as 'new economic history', is based on the combination of neoclassical theory and econometric methods, or the quantification of history through the application of formal, mathematical models.
27 Amin Samman, 'Making Financial History: The Crisis of 2008 and the Return of the Past', *Millennium: Journal of International Studies*, 42, no. 2 (2014): 315–316.
28 Monique Wittig, 'One Is Not Born a Woman', in *Feminisms*, ed. S. Kemp and J. Squires (Oxford: Oxford University Press, 1997), 220–226.
29 Judith Butler, *Gender Trouble: Feminism and the Subversion of Identity* (New York: Routledge, 1990), 2.
30 Penny Griffin, 'The Role of *Power* in Hetereosexism', in *Encyclopedia of Power*, ed. Keith Dowding (London: Sage, 2011).
31 Butler, *Gender Trouble*, 12.
32 Penny Griffin, *Gendering the World Bank: Neoliberalism and the Gendered Foundations of Global Governance* (Basingstoke: Palgrave Macmillan, 2009), 6.
33 Penny Griffin, 'Gender, Governance and the Global Political Economy', *Australian Journal of International Affairs*, 64, no. 1 (2010): 100.
34 Griffin, *Gendering the World Bank*, xv.
35 Penny Griffin, 'Poststructuralism and IPE', in *Critical International Political Economy: Debate and Dissensus*, ed. I. Bruff, H. Macartney, and S. Shields (Basingstoke: Palgrave Macmillan, 2011), 43–58.
36 Raewyn W. Connell, 'Masculinities and Globalization', *Men and Masculinities*, 16, no. 1 (1998): 3–23; Griffin, *Gendering the World Bank*.
37 Philip Auger, *The Death of Gentlemanly Capitalism: The Rise and Fall of London's Investment Banks* (London: Penguin, 2001): Connell, 'Masculinities and Globalization', 15.

38 See: Penny Griffin, 'Masculinities and Financial Capitalism', in *Masculinities and Literary Studies: Intersections and New Directions*, ed. A. Carabí (New York: Routledge, 2017).
39 See: Melissa S. Fisher, *Wall Street Women* (Durham, NC: Duke University Press, 2012).
40 Veronique Pin-Fat, '(Im)possible Universalism: Remarks on the Politics and Ethics of Grammar', *e-International Relations*, 2016, http://www.e-ir.info/2016/07/29/impossible-universalism-remarks-on-the-politics-and-ethics-of-grammar/, last accessed April 2017.
41 See: Katharine. N. Rankin, 'Governing Development: Neoliberalism, Microcredit, and Rational Economic Woman', *Economy and Society*, 30, no. 1 (2001): 18–37.
42 Griffin, *Gendering the World Bank*, 76.
43 Ibid.
44 Jacqui True, 'The Global Financial Crisis's Silver Bullet: Women Leaders and "Leaning In"', in *Scandalous Economics: Gender and the Politics of Financial Crises*, ed. Aida A. Hozić and Jacqui True (Oxford: Oxford University Press, 2016), 55.
45 E. Prügl, 'If Lehman Brothers Had Been Lehman Sisters', *International Political Sociology*, 6, no. 1 (2012): 21–35; Elisabeth Prügl, '"Lehman Brothers and Sisters": Revisiting Gender and Myth after the Financial Crisis', in *Scandalous Economics: Gender and the Politics of Financial Crises* (Oxford: Oxford University Press, 2016), 21–40.
46 C. Yeates, 'Gender Balance: Finance Chiefs Want Women to Move Up within Their Firms', *Sydney Morning Herald*, 5 February 2014, http://www.smh.com.au/business/banking-and-finance/gender-balance-finance-chiefs-want-women-to-move-up-within-their-firms-20140204-31z8o.html, last accessed April 2017.
47 Credit Suisse, *Gender Diversity and Corporate Performance* (Zurich: Credit Suisse, 2012), 14.
48 World Bank, *Women, Business and the Law* (Washington, D.C.: World Bank, 2015).
49 Adrienne Roberts and Susanne Soederberg, 'Gender Equality as Smart Economics? A Critique of the 2012 World Development Report', *Third World Quarterly*, 33, no. 5 (2012): 949–968.
50 Ibid., 950–951.
51 Ibid., 950–951.
52 For companies with greater female participation in boards less likely to be hit by governance scandals, see: Credit Suisse, *Gender Diversity and Corporate Performance*.
53 World Bank, *Women, Business and Law*.
54 Lauren McAughtry, 'The Importance of Being Equal: How Women Are Winning in Islamic Finance', *Islamic Finance News*, August 26, 2015, http://www.womenieff.org/Resources/Documents/v12i34a%201-5.pdf, last accessed April 2017.
55 OIC Today, 'Women Empowerment through Islamic Banking and Finance', n.d., http://oictoday.biz/Women_Empowerment.html, last accessed April 2017.
56 Ibid.
57 Ibid.
58 Women in Islamic and Ethical Financial Forum (WEIFF), 'Women in Islamic and Ethical Finance Successfully Launched on 30th July 2015', Press Release, 20 August 2015, http://www.womenieff.org/Press-Releases, last accessed October 2017.
59 Rob Aitken, 'Performativity, Popular Finance and Security in the Global Political Economy', in *International Political Economy and Poststructural Politics*, ed. M. de Goede (Basingstoke: Palgrave Macmillan, 2006), 78–80.
60 Seda Demiralp and Selva Demiralp, 'The Rational Islamic Actor? Evidence from Islamic Banking', *New Perspectives on Turkey*, 52 (2015): 5.
61 International Monetary Fund, 'IMF Survey: Islamic Banks: More Resilient to Crisis?', *IMF Survey Online*, 4 October 2010, http://www.imf.org/external/pubs/ft/survey/so/2010/res100410a.htm, last accessed April 2017.
62 Ibid.
63 Ibid.
64 Ibid.
65 Ibid.
66 Demiralp and Demiralp, 'The Rational Islamic Actor?', 4
67 Lena Rethel, 'Whose Legitimacy? Islamic Finance and the Global Financial Order', *Review of International Political Economy*, 18, no. 1 (2011): 79.

68 Jane Pollard, and Michael Samers, 'Islamic Banking and Finance: Postcolonial Political Economy and the Decentring of Economic Geography', *Transactions of the Institute of British Geographers*, 32, no. 3 (2007): 315.
69 Rethel, 'Whose Legitimacy?'
70 Ibid., 81–82.
71 Ibid.
72 Ibid., 81.
73 Demiralp and Demiralp, 'The Rational Islamic Actor?', 11–12.
74 Rethel, 'Whose Legitimacy?', 76.
75 Ibid., 75.
76 Ibid., 89.
77 Shah Foundation, 'Islamic Banking: Problems and Prospects', n.d., http://www.shahfoundationbd.org/hannan/article10.html, last accessed April 2017.
78 Institute of Islamic Banking and Insurance, 'Training', n.d., http://www.islamic-banking.com/training.aspx, last accessed April 2017.
79 Rethel, 'Whose Legitimacy', 81–82.
80 Ibid., 89.

32

BIOFUELS AND THE ETHICS OF GLOBAL GOVERNANCE

Experimentalism, disagreement, politics

James Brassett, Ben Richardson and William Smith

Introduction: the everyday ethics of global governance

As the introduction to this thematic section suggests, critical thinking about the global economy is often rendered according to either *systemic* 'or' *everyday* ontologies of international political economy (IPE).[1] Within global ethics, a similar divide between the *universal* and the *particular* basis of moral reasoning has often accompanied debates about global justice, human rights, and cosmopolitan democracy.[2] However, also pronounced in existing global ethics debates is a tendency to adopt 'middle-way' positions; that is to say, even the most ardent cosmopolitan approach to global governance is willing to foreground the role of states and the importance of community in practice.[3] Likewise, theorists of communitarian ethics are keen to explore the possibility of speaking beyond the 'cave', as it were.[4]

When thinking about the ethics of the global economy, such middle-way approaches point to a more practical set of questions about how universal moral principles are realised through everyday practices: campaigns, law-making, and the evolving spheres of global governance. One important variant of this turn to practice in global ethics can be found in the rise of experimentalism.[5] Neither a cosmopolitan nor a communitarian 'model' of global governance, experimentalism engages a more pragmatic ethical tradition of everyday problem-solving under conditions of uncertainty. In particular, experimentalist governance is oriented to the practical dynamics of bureaucratic expansion, change, and contest associated with globalisation.[6] On this view, an experimentalist approach questions how complex and technocratic forms of governance can also be an everyday basis of ethical growth. A political logic is identified whereby a combination of normative uncertainty in any given policy area combines with peer group surveillance, and regulatory revision, to provide a (potentially) productive arena for the emergence of democratic rule.[7]

While sympathetic to many of the pragmatic and democratic commitments of experimentalism, this chapter will identify important limits relating to the difficulties of reconciling moral disagreement at a global level. We do this by developing a case study of one important policy area in the field of environmental ethics, namely: the regulation of biofuels.

Our argument proceeds in three sections. The first section defines *experimentalism* as an ethical approach to global governance. Experimentalist governance is typified by a concern with deliberative polyarchy, stakeholder inclusion, and democratic destabilisation.[8] In these ways, it seems to carry certain advantages over rival 'models' of ethical global governance, like cosmopolitanism, that can privilege a systemic vision of ethics and the global economy from the outset. Here, an important element in experimentalism is the emergence of a concern with finding 'experimental pathways' that seek to harness contingent possibilities for recursive learning, adaptation, and innovation. In short, experimentalism purports to be both critically engaged in the practice of global governance and reflexive to everyday ethical contests over the substance and direction of such practice.

The second section surveys the emergence of European Union (EU) standards of biofuels regulation. Biofuels are an interesting test case of experimentalism because the architecture of regulation emerged in precisely the unpredictable, 'experimental' fashion that might tend towards pluralist learning. Normative uncertainty appears to be a core feature of biofuels regulation whereby the 'universal' ethical goal of sustainability is read into their status as renewable, low-carbon energy. However, to date, the everyday politics of biofuels regulation has been marked by a pronounced moral disagreement over the attractiveness of biofuels in practice, a lack of effective central sanction, and highly variegated forms of peer review between roundtabling bodies.[9] Thus, we find that, while there are important elements of NGO inclusion, peer review, and experimental patterns of regulation, the capacity for forum shopping seems to combine with policy drift to license major stakeholders to behave in ways that push, or even contradict, the goal of sustainability.

There is an important politics to global environmental ethics that seems to exceed experimentalist logics. Well-reasoned normative agendas for reducing carbon emissions have entailed (unintended) knock-on effects such as spikes in commodities prices, as well as covert (and sometimes overt) practices of land-grabbing. Potential advantages, like the widespread inclusion of critical NGOs and modest attempts to feed back critical perspectives to governance agencies, are undermined by a weak locus of formal sanction or a clear set of normative ends that can be easily communicated for industry uptake.[10] Thus, in the third section, we revisit the critical potential of experimentalism to both expose democratic fragilities in global governance and provide pragmatic reflections on new directions in this area. Ethical attachments to a goal of sustainability have combined with the expansion of global governance to legitimate wider processes of market-making. By foregrounding this paradox, we hope to promote deeper practices of recursive learning within environmental ethics.

Experimentalist governance

Experimentalism has developed as a framework for analysing innovative forms of rule-making in national, transnational, and global contexts. Unlike much of the literature on public–private regulation and 'hybrid' governance, it is not concerned with the (re-)location of authority *per se*.[11] Rather, the framework defends complex governance architectures that promote processes of provisional goal-setting, then revision, based on comparison of alternative approaches to advancing such goals in everyday contexts. There are several elements to experimentalist governance. Here, we focus on three core tenets that best illustrate its normative value: deliberative polyarchy, stakeholder inclusion, and democratic destabilisation. Accepting that any policy area will be guided by a basic normative goal, these are treated as emergent, but by no means fully realised, properties of a number of regulatory regimes in global contexts.[12] Indeed, the concept of *experimental pathways* is proposed here as a framing device for further developing the critical potential of experimentalism.

Deliberative polyarchy

For experimentalists, a key feature of modern governance is that rule-makers only have access to loosely specified goals, such that 'actors have to learn what problems they are solving and what solutions they are seeking through the very process of problem solving'.[13] The idea of 'deliberative polyarchy' is therefore presented as a means of *discovering* collective goals and monitoring their realisation.[14] It is 'deliberative' in the sense that 'questions are decided by argument about the best ways to address problems, not simply exertions of power, expressions of interest, or bargaining from power positions on the basis of interests'.[15] It is a 'polyarchy' because of 'its use of situated deliberation within decision-making units and deliberative comparisons across those units to enable them to engage in a mutually disciplined and responsive exploration of their particular variant of common problems'.[16]

The governance architecture recommended by deliberative polyarchy involves 'central' and 'local' units setting provisional goals and methods to achieve these goals. The local units are given a significant degree of discretion to pursue these goals, but should undergo an ongoing process of peer review, performance auditing, and comparison with agents pursuing similar goals. The goals and methods are then revised in the light of the outcomes of this review process.[17] The pooling of information between units facilitates a process of *social learning*.

Stakeholder inclusion

The participation of stakeholders contributes to processes of social learning through the sharing of relevant information and the weighing of competing arguments. In terms of the democratic dimensions of experimentalism, inclusion signals that participation is a possible and important component of governance. The participation of everyday stakeholders with local interests contributes to the anticipated end that decentralised units will take the lead in implementing policy goals. According to Joshua Cohen and Charles Sabel, 'direct participation helps because participants can be assumed to possess relevant information about the local contours of the problem and can relatively easily detect both deception by others and unintended consequences of past decisions'.[18] The participation of stakeholders with specific and fragmented interests can also provide some protection against the possible danger that experimentalist regimes are hijacked by powerful actors. This strategy can only succeed if central and local units guarantee more-or-less equal opportunities for agenda-setting and policy evaluation. Thus, the institutional design of experimentalism should aim for 'a multi-polar distribution of power [such] that no single actor can impose her own preferred solution without taking into account the views of others'.[19] This multipolarity has a capacity to foster democratic destabilisation.

Democratic destabilisation

The process of peer review establishes a contest between competing sources of technocratic authority that undercuts the threat of rule by policy elites. The establishment of new administrative units also has the democratising effect of triggering inclusive processes of reason giving between and within affected publics.[20] Importantly, this process can be driven by external actors who publicise or engage with emerging governance structures. Cohen and Sabel suggest that a progressive deepening of global administration across an expansive policy agenda – including trade, security, environment, health, and education – can contribute to the emergence of a 'global public'.[21] Indeed, it is argued that a growing awareness of, and participation in, this administrative structure on the part of affected publics could mean that 'dispersed peoples might come to share a new identity as common members of an organized global populace'.[22]

Evaluating experimentalism

Of course, the practical realisation of experimentalist governance is complicated by certain dynamic tensions. For instance, consider the issue of ethical or political disagreement. The experimentalist ideal emerges in contexts where there is broad stakeholder agreement over governance goals but considerable disagreement (or uncertainty) about the best means to pursue those goals. An excess of disagreement would stymie efforts to get stakeholders to collaborate on problem-solving, whereas an excess of agreement among decision-makers would stymie efforts to broaden stakeholder participation and collective learning. The upshot is that 'experimentalist governance seems to progress in a "Goldilocks Zone" – where there is neither too much nor too little agreement, and the balance, like the temperature of Goldilocks' porridge, is "just right"'.[23] In a similar vein, consider again the process of democratic destabilisation. This process is necessary in order to open up governance networks to democratic scrutiny, thus undercutting the threat of rule by bureaucrats. However, there are limits to the extent that the process of destabilisation can be taken before it is seen as a simple impediment to governance. An emergent governance regime might be placed under considerable strain, then, if criticism from external actors cannot be fed back into ongoing processes of social learning without *antagonising* other stakeholders.

Both of these tensions can be read through our case study of biofuel regulation in the following section where disagreement among actors over the *very idea of achieving sustainability through biofuels* means that the balance between democracy and governance is hard to strike. In the past, we have argued that the experimentalist possibilities of global Roundtables make for an impressive forum for including and engaging multiple voices in the formation of standards for certification.[24] However, any such process of experimental inclusion must be seen as contingent upon a range of questions, such as: *How open is the normative goal? How easy or difficult is it for competition amongst rival certification bodies? What are the possibilities and limits for external critique, e.g., by consumers or affected landholders?* Such questions and the wider contingency of how certification regimes evolve in different areas – e.g., first movers, public influence, industry capture, and so forth – mean that the concept of 'pathways' has become an important element in the experimentalist literature.

Pathways are a means of identifying trajectories toward more robust forms of experimentalist governance and the mechanisms that drive this. For example, Christine Overdevest and Jonathan Zeitlin have argued that, through the diffusion of multistakeholder certification schemes and multilateral procedures which require reflexive engagement between trade partners, various forms of experimental and transnational forestry sector governance emerged within the EU. Moreover, the Forest Stewardship Council certification schemes and the EU Forest Law Enforcement Governance and Trade legislation have interacted to the extent that they have formed a kind of 'regulatory assemblage', now converging with timber regulation acts in the US through mutual influence and formalised information exchange.[25] These regimes are said to have combined to such an extent that they now contribute to 'the de facto emergence of a joined-up transnational experimentalist regime for sustainable forestry and control of illegal logging, which blurs and may ultimately efface standard distinctions between public and private regulation'.[26] This account chimes with other governance literature that has identified situations in which states and international organisations have pursued policy objectives at arm's length by 'orchestrating' novel governance schemes through directive or facilitative means.[27]

In a different fashion, Steven Bernstein and Benjamin Cashore (2012) have sought to delineate how complex forms of global governance can influence *domestic policy* through international rules, international norms, market exchange, and direct access to the policy-making process.[28] In this sense, they reverse the previous line of enquiry and ask how the activities of transnational experimentalist governance might expand the openness and accountability of states. This pays greater attention to the experimentalist property of democratic destabilisation and implies that an element of indirect influence should be included in the evaluation of experimentalism, since its value might be realised in part via its contribution to improving or advancing existing governance arrangements. For us, these *experimental pathways* show how architectures of social learning might be used as a pragmatic resource for the critique and substantive democratisation of rule-making; a theme we return to in the third section.

Transnational EU biofuels regulation

In ideal terms, then, experimentalism suggests a way of thinking about the ethics of the global economy that takes certain normative goals as the *beginning* of a process that draws upon everyday practices of implementation and disagreement to draw out new techniques of governance. From an experimentalist point of view, the use of standards to certify commodities or products can – through the inclusion of multiple stakeholders and the emergence of (more or less effective) peer review – lead to the globalisation of governance in a plural, inclusive, and potentially democratising manner. The systemic and everyday are blurred. At its best, experimentalist governance may produce normative improvements across issue areas and geographical boundaries without recourse to traditional state-centric forms of sovereign authority (i.e., imposition). With successful cases such as the Forest Stewardship Council (FSC) as an example, we might therefore suggest that similar possibilities might be entailed within the EU regulation of biofuels via Roundtables that certify according to sustainability criteria.

This section reviews the emergence of transnational biofuels regulation and identifies certain experimentalist elements within it, namely an open-ended normative goal of sustainability as well as a pluralistic and largely inclusive form of participation. Our case is based upon the EU, which, by virtue of its large import volumes and formal commitment to sustainability, extends further into the territories of other sovereign states when compared to other bodies of biofuel regulation. Yet while experimentalist elements can be discerned within this architecture, the substantive differences over the normative content of sustainability and the relative impasses in governance that have emerged, lead us to reflect on the limits of 'effective' biofuel governance.

Biofuels in the EU: fertile ground for experimentalism?

Biofuels are not a new class of commodity. The use of vegetable oils (processed into biodiesel) or grains and sugar (into ethanol) to power internal combustion engines was explored by Henry Ford as far back as the early twentieth century. Later, in the 1970s and in the economic context of debt crisis and oil price spikes, Brazil developed a national programme for petroleum substitution, establishing the agroindustrial basis and energy-transport infrastructure for what is now the 'greenest' vehicle fleet in the world in terms of renewable energy use.

What has made this commodity of increasing interest to scholars of *global* regulatory governance is the adoption of biofuel programmes in the EU and US, each of which have expanded the production of biofuels and had sizeable cross-border impacts. In both cases, government mandates for the use of biofuel have spurred domestic consumption such that, by 2010–2012, the share of biofuel in the EU's transport system was 4.5% of petrol usage and 5.2% of diesel usage, and for the US, 8.4% of petrol and 1.4% of diesel. Because of the size of their fuel markets, this meant they collectively accounted for 55% of world ethanol consumption and 71% of world biodiesel consumption across the same period.[29] However, what differentiates the EU and makes it particularly apposite as a case study of transnational experimentalism is: (1) its import dependence, (2) its sustainability requirements on biofuel, and (3) its regulatory architecture that operationalised 'localised' units in the form of member states and private sustainability schemes to meet and monitor the EU's Renewable Energy Directive.

Biofuels were introduced to the EU policy debate as a measure to help meet the emission-reduction goals of the Kyoto Protocol. In a 1997 white paper on energy, the European Commission noted how the transport sector contributed around one-fifth of all greenhouse gas emissions in the EU and suggested that renewable fuel consumption should be doubled to try and reduce this.[30] With support from a coalition of farmers and crop processors, biotech and oil companies, and initially Green parties and NGOs as well, a range of EU-wide policies followed in the early 2000s. These included billions of Euros for research funding into green technologies, tax breaks for companies that sold renewable fuels, indicative targets set for biofuel consumption, and border tariffs erected to help European-based producers. When it became clear in the mid-2000s that the EU as a whole would not reach this target, the Commission began to promote the idea of having increased *mandatory* targets. This was realised in the 2009 EU Renewable Energy Directive that stipulated 10% of transport energy must come from renewable sources by 2020.

Importantly, this policy was born of a concerted effort to create a market for biofuels; industrial policy for the green economy, if you will. The economic sustainability of biofuel, that is, the ability of the (EU-based) industry to continue in the absence of state support, has never been far from policy-makers' minds.[31] That said, for practical and legal reasons – that is, limits on the availability of European crops and the opportunity for protectionism under international trade law – it was always anticipated that some biofuel feedstock would be imported. Indeed, by 2010 an extra-European 'land holding' of 2.4 million hectares was supplying agricultural crops to the EU biofuel market, spread across countries including Argentina, Indonesia, Brazil, the US, Canada, and Ukraine.[32] Data from 2013 confirms the EU as the biggest net importer of biofuels and the inextricably international dimension of its biofuel policy.

Table 32.1 Net biofuel trade of major importing and exporting countries, 2010–2012 average

	Ethanol, used as petrol substitute (million litres)	*Biodiesel, used as diesel substitute (million litres)*	*Total net trade (million litres)*
EU-27	–1669	–2723	–4392
Japan	–877	N/A	–877
Canada	–349	–71	–420
Philippines	–297	0	–297
Mexico	–132	N/A	–132
US	1624	244	1868
Brazil	1823	–4	1819
Argentina	–157	1740	1583
Indonesia	38	1012	1050
South Africa	177	0	177

Source: FAO-OECD (2013), pp. 260–261.

Another distinctive aspect of the EU case has been the rhetorical attachment to the concept of 'sustainability'. More so than in Brazil and the US, the justification for biofuels was tethered to the need to 'green' European energy production and meet carbon emissions targets under the UN Kyoto Protocol, as opposed to quickly cutting the oil import bill, boosting agroindustrial profits, or providing energy security.[33] Thus, without discounting the commercial interests of groups like oil companies, vehicle manufacturers, and rapeseed farmers, debates in the EU about the legitimacy of biofuels have tended to be framed in terms of their sustainability in respect to lowering total greenhouse gas emissions from the transport sector.

While such trends might be read as an unambiguous positive – reduce reliance on oil and carbon emissions, and reduce the threat of global warming – the record is more mixed. As the production of biofuels grew, so did concern about their 'true' socio-ecological impact.[34] Two lines of argument criticised the huge transfer of crops into the biofuel market. One focused on increased food prices and how these had aggravated hunger and food riots amongst the global poor.[35] Another focused on changes in land-use caused by biofuels production, as rainforest or grassland was converted to farmland in order to fill the agricultural supply gaps. Added to the fossil fuel energy used in their very production, it was argued that land conversion meant that many biofuels were actually *harming* the environment, both in terms of biodiversity loss and increased greenhouse gas emissions.[36]

To quell growing opposition, public authorities recognised the need to better define and monitor sustainable biofuel production.[37] Thus, in the 2009 Renewable Energy Directive, alongside mandatory targets, the EU also required that all biofuels sold in the EU, including those imported from outside the bloc, meet high environmental standards. These were that biofuels must provide at least 35% greenhouse gas emission savings compared to fossil fuels and *not* come from crops cultivated on land with a high biodiversity value or high carbon stock (the savings target in the US, by contrast, was 20%). So as to avoid legal action under the rules of the World Trade Organization, it was agreed that failure to meet these criteria would not mean that biofuel could not be sold in the EU, only that it would not count against member states' binding energy targets nor qualify for tax relief.[38] Nevertheless, to the extent these remained incentives, the sustainability criteria effectively constituted a *de facto* market access requirement.[39]

The final differentiating characteristic of the EU relates to its innovative governance architecture. This architecture follows the experimentalist logic of a central agent establishing a common framework to guide the pursuit of a shared policy goal, while delegating to local units the responsibility to pursue that goal. So under the Renewable Energy Directive, it was the responsibility of the national governments of member states to meet the biofuel target. In addition, anticipating the problem of weak enforcement of the new sustainability criteria the European Commission licensed a variety of non-state schemes to come up with their own standards and ways of checking compliance. The license was contingent on the scheme's own standard meeting the EU's 'meta-standard'[40] and proof that they had robust systems in place to prevent lax monitoring. Biofuel would be certified at source by any licensed scheme and then tracked right through the supply chain to prevent double-counting, all of which would be paid for by the businesses involved.[41]

This system contrasted with the more statist approach taken in the US, which relied on inspections carried out by national public agencies and more closely resembled the 'transnational experimentalist regime' described by Overdevest and Zeitlin in relation to forestry.[42] Indeed, the Roundtable of Sustainable Biofuels was explicitly designed with the model of the FSC in mind.[43] Since conditions and compliance checks applied to biofuel produced inside and outside of the EU, scholars such as Jolene Lin (2011) argue that this was a form of 'regulatory outsourcing' that blurred both the public–private divide *and* the national–international

Table 32.2 Sustainability criteria for biofuels in the EU's 2009 Renewable Energy Directive

Carbon criteria	*Environmental criteria*	*Social criteria*
Biofuels must save 35% greenhouse gas emissions compared to fossil fuels, rising to 50% by 2017, and, for those installations built after this date, 60%.	Biofuel shall not be made from raw material obtained from land that from January 2008 had high biodiversity value – including primary forest, protected areas, and highly biodiverse grassland. Biofuel shall not be made from raw material obtained from land that from January 2008 had high carbon stock – including wetlands and continuously forested areas. Biofuel shall not be made from raw material obtained from land that from January 2008 was peatland.	No compulsory criteria

Source: European Parliament and the Council of the European Union 2009: Article 17.

divide.[44] Reflecting on the unprecedented level of scrutiny this applied to the production of a primary commodity, the European Commission exuberantly declared its transnational biofuel governance to be '*the most comprehensive and advanced binding sustainability scheme of its kind anywhere in the world*'.[45]

Civil society criticism of biofuel governance

Ambitious as the EU regulation of biofuels according to sustainability might be, the governance record has been mixed, especially so from the point of view of civil society and environmental NGOs. Two major concerns have been raised with the efficacy of this innovative governance system. The first relates to the levelling down of more ambitious sustainability standards to the benchmark set by the Commission, and the second to the absence of control. Levelling down applied to both standards set by member states as well as standards set by the non-state certification schemes. The more ambitious of these had already been established by multistakeholder 'Roundtables' comprised of mainly businesses and NGOs that were seeking to promote best practices in commodity sectors such as palm oil, soybean, sugar cane, and biofuels.[46] As a result of their particular constituency and mandate, their sustainability standards were much wider and more transparent in how they were managed. In comparison, the sustainability standards that sprang up in response to the Commission's Renewable Energy Directive were less ambitious and more instrumental. These were developed primarily by businesses and/or government environmental agencies and were being designed to meet rather than exceed minimum EU requirements. Further, while the Roundtables' certification has been based upon more rigorous auditing practices such as on-site field visits, the industry-led schemes made extensive use of company self-declaration and desk audits based on paper trails.[47]

This uneven rigour of different certification schemes and their respective standards has created an incentive for 'forum shopping' (or even 'forum creation') as biofuel producers with contentious land claims or highly polluting levels of pesticide use, for instance, would be able to opt for certification schemes with weaker standards. Indeed, the dilemma that this creates for the Roundtables has been openly recognised by the Roundtable on Sustainable Biomaterials (RSB, formerly the Roundtable on Sustainable Biofuel):

> How do we make compliance with RSB standards practical and cost-effective for companies while addressing complex issues such as biodiversity, food security or land rights? In other words, how can the RSB cope with fierce competition from a number of emerging schemes offering cheap and simple alternatives, while at the same time remaining true to its aspirations of comprehensively addressing sustainability?[48]

Table 32.3 EU-licensed certification schemes as of December 2013

Institutional design	*Certification system*	*Geographical focus*	*Certificates issued*
Industry-led	Abengoa RED Bioenergy Sustainability Assurance (RBSA)	Spain	76
	Biomass Biofuels Sustainability voluntary scheme (2BSvs)	France	665
	Ensus	UK	Unknown
	Greenergy	Brazil	Unknown
	NTA 8080	Netherlands	0
	REDcert	Germany	1904 (of which 757 are RED compliant)
	Red Tractor	UK	Unknown
	Scottish Quality Farm Assured Combinable Crops (SQC)	Scotland	Unknown
Government-led	Biograce GHG Calculation Tool	International	Unknown
Roundtable or multistakeholder	Bonsucro[a]	Brazil	33 (of which 30 are RED compliant)
	International Sustainability and Carbon Certification (ISCC)	International	4,401
	Roundtable on Responsible Soy (RTRS)[a]	Argentina, Brazil	32
	Roundtable on Sustainable Biomaterials (RSB)[a]	International	10 (all RED compliant)
	Roundtable for Sustainable Palm Oil (RSPO)[a]	Indonesia, Malaysia	621 (of which 1 is RED compliant)

Source: Certification scheme websites. Note: not all certificates are issued for farms and processors; most are for intermediaries.

a Featured WWF as a founder member.

This trade-off is reflected in the number of certificates issued by approved EU schemes detailed below. The ISCC, which dominates the regulatory marketplace, has been placed in the multi-stakeholder category thanks to the participation of the WWF, although it is important to note that these came on board after the standard was already devised and is less integral to its management. In Stefano Ponte's words, it was a case of *ex-post* roundtabling.[49]

Reaction to the problem of levelling down varied among civil society groups. Unsurprisingly, as a founder member of most of the Roundtables, the WWF called for the EU to require a multi-stakeholder approach for all approved schemes, make voluntary reporting requirements around the other socio-ecological impacts of biofuel production mandatory, and implement a monitoring system to assess whether certification schemes are themselves doing an effective monitoring job.[50] Meanwhile, in light of the mounting evidence that EU biofuel policy was leading to practices of 'land-grabbing' in developing countries related to the renewed demand for agricultural crops, Oxfam called for social sustainability criteria for biofuels to be made a mandatory part of the RED rather than just a reporting requirement on the part of the Commission.[51] For their part, NGOs with a more antagonistic relationship to the biofuels industry actually took the Commission to court for failing to provide information on why particular schemes had managed to gain approval.[52] Moreover, some NGOs argued that Roundtable certification systems were ineffective tools of governance. Friends of the Earth argued that such schemes are

> unable to solve indirect issues such as rising commodity prices or displacement effects [i.e., indirect land-use change]. . . . The new plantation could be certified as 'sustainable' but if it has simply pushed other farming activities into sensitive areas then this makes a mockery of any certification scheme. This is a major failing that is unlikely to ever be solved by certification schemes.[53]

For instance, it is no coincidence that as more of the European rapeseed crop has been diverted into the biodiesel market, increased amounts of palm oil has been imported from Indonesia for use in the vegetable oil market.[54] This is an example of indirect land-use change stretching across continents and crop sectors, a causal effect impossible to prove and extremely contentious to model. Determined to strike a blow to the seemingly ceaseless growth of biofuels, many of the NGOs cited above coalesced around this effect of indirect land-use change as a means to criticise the ungovernability of biofuels and to call for a slowdown in their adoption, if not outright abandonment.[55] From this more radical position, food-based biofuels were off the agenda and the case made that climate change imperatives in the transport system instead be addressed through investment in mass transit, electric vehicles, and better urban planning.[56]

So, notwithstanding the sustainability criteria and monitoring mechanisms introduced in the Renewable Energy Directive, opposition was still being directed toward EU biofuel policy. In response, the European Commission organised consultations and commissioned studies around how best to factor in indirect land-use change to the greenhouse gas savings of various biofuels, seeking to find a consensus point on this technically complex matter (or perhaps more cynically, stalling for time).[57] In 2012, the Commission proposed that just 5% of its 10% renewable energy target should be met with biofuels from food crops, with the remainder supplied by so-called 'second-generation' biofuels produced from non-food sources like grass and straw.[58]

However, despite pressure from NGOs to factor in indirect land-use change –which would likely mean that most biodiesel, including European rapeseed, would fail to meet the 35% minimum[59] – this was only added as a non-binding reporting requirement.[60] This fudging left few satisfied. The European biofuels industry complained that this constituted 'a wholesale withdrawal of political support from the Commission' and would deter investment in the sector;

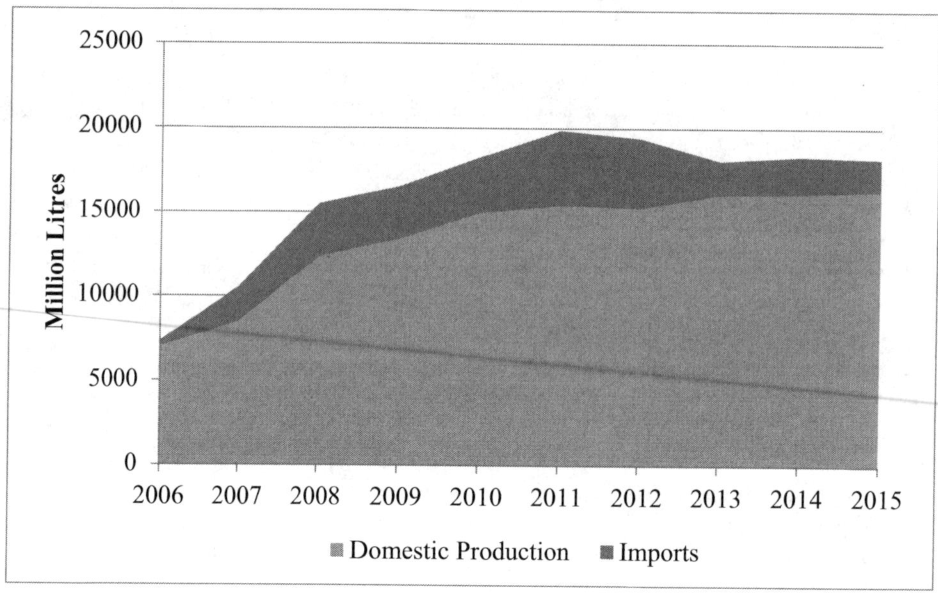

Figure 32.1 EU biofuels supply, 2006–2015

Source: USDA Foreign Agricultural Service (various years) EU Biofuels Annual.

Note: 2013 is an estimate; 2014 and 2015 are forecasts.

NGOs countered that even with a lowered production ceiling in place, conventional biofuels would continue to cause upward pressure on food prices and land conversion.[61] The chart below supports this account of a stalled but still significant biofuel supply to the EU.

Finally, although it was not an issue pushed by civil society critics, the ability of the EU to govern as a 'central' unit was also brought into question. This is important for our analysis since numerous examples of successful experimentalist governance depend upon the possibility of sanctions or 'penalty defaults'.[62] However, many member states were slow to transpose the EU Renewable Energy Directive fully into national legislation, meaning that inadequate checks were put in place to ensure the sustainability of biofuel in their countries.[63] Indeed, just 57% of total biofuel consumption in the EU was certified as sustainable in 2012.[64] The Commission has responded to this by sending 'reasoned opinions' to 19 countries for failing to inform them about their transposition of the Directive and proposing at least four of these be fined by the European Court of Justice for further refusal to properly implement EU law.[65] In addition, the major incentive for member states to certify biofuels in the first place is so that they will count against their national targets for renewable fuel use.[66] However, the resolve of the Commission to actually punish member states who fail to meet the 10% target by 2020 remains untested (a target that looks unlikely to be met given the stalling of biofuel supply).[67]

The everyday politics of environmental ethics

Elements of an experimentalist agenda are at work in the governance of biofuels, especially via the leeway afforded to member states to reach the EU's 10% renewable energy target and the decentralised and (partially) participatory non-state organisations charged with monitoring regulation. Interestingly, this form of experimentation has also led to a close interaction with public opinion (both for and against), meaning that regulation has been imbued with a normative component that goes beyond the goal of sustainability and incorporates values such as inclusion, deliberation, and transparency. However, there are equally strong indications that the democratic substance arising from this normative component has led to instability, wherein government support for this 'politically instituted' industry has wavered and the investment climate worsened.[68] On the other side of the coin, certain civil society actors regard the very idea of regulating biofuel markets as problematic for sustainability, highlighting the pressure placed on existing patterns of land-use and the concentration of agricultural production on non-food markets.

Indeed, critics of the regulation of biofuels through certification schemes have pointed to a particular issue in the complexity of deliberation produced by Roundtables *per se*. For instance, Ponte posits that the RSB is marked by an extravagant and complex organisational structure with initially eleven chambers and then seven chambers representing the interests of farmers, industrial biofuel producers, retailers and blenders, rights-based NGOs, smallholders and indigenous groups, environmental NGOs, and international organisations.[69] The effect of such an organisational structure has been to make deliberation cumbersome at best. At worst, Schleiffer argues that the particular discourse that has emerged has been collapsed into power struggles and interest-bargaining that represent a form of 'deliberation failure'.[70] In this context, it might be tempting to reach back to the example of the FSC and its ability to influence the wider assemblage of certification schemes to provide inspiration. Could the more ambitious, if slightly more cumbersome, standard of the RSB provide normative guidance (indeed pressure) for the ISCC to improve its own standard? Again Ponte suggests reasons to be sceptical:

> It is unlikely that the RSB will be able ride the normative wave that helped the FSC to remain commercially relevant and that led to improvements in the features of its competitors: RSB did not enjoy the FSC's head start over competitors; biofuels are mixed with regular fuel making consumer boycotts difficult to carry out; and following the food crisis of 2007/2008, some social movements and NGOs have argued that sustainability certification of biofuels should be avoided.[71]

On numerous points, then, EU attempts to regulate biofuels according to sustainability criteria *can be read as something of a failed experiment* where existing strategies appear to be either unworkable or undesirable. Aspects of this failure relate to the substance of the goal of sustainability: there is just serious and credible doubt as to whether biofuels are a good mechanism for achieving sustainability (whether in terms of GHG reductions or wider issues of land-use and biodiversity). Aspects of this failure relate to governance. For us, the lack of an effective central sanction, that is, the EU, is a key problem. For critics of the RSB, it is in the complex nature of governance and – when push comes to shove – the entrenched attitudes of certain NGOs. What cannot be denied is that the combination of these weaknesses is a boon for questionable practices in biofuel production/import and that pathways are urgently required. However, while certain environmental NGOs may see the certification of biofuels as a constitutive element of the problem of sustainability *per se*, we would argue that part of the challenge of experimentalism is to accept and engage with such ambiguity. In the context of failure, what pathways forward can be discerned for the governance of biofuels?

Experimental pathways

While the capacity for the RSB to influence the ISCC directly may be hindered for the reasons given above, this does not exhaust the range of governance solutions that might be developed.

In the first instance, peer review between the certification schemes could become a requisite for licensing. While there are some *ad hoc* practices of benchmarking that happen at present – for example, studies undertaken by the WWF[72] – there is currently no response required from those schemes assessed. By having these local units engage in a formalised process of review and reason-giving, then pressure could be created to avoid some of the weaker auditing practices. For instance, lest an individual scheme become discredited and potentially have their licence revoked by the Commission. In ambitious terms, again with appropriate central sanction, licensing could be made conditional on such benchmarking, or indeed – as would likely emerge from such a process – *the disclosure of biofuel certification audits for public oversight*. Such a move could provide much-needed transparency to a system of governance that is perhaps so divisive for environmental NGOs because so little is known about the land-use and biodiversity effects of biofuel production. Indeed, member state government agencies responsible for implementing the Renewable Energy Directive could be encouraged to engage in similar practices of peer review. While there is already government reporting of both the requirements in place and various studies commissioned on the effectiveness of national legislation in respect to biofuels, they function very much in a 'hub and spoke' manner, with information flowing into the European Commission, but with seemingly little deliberation *between* the member states themselves.[73] Again, the role of the EU and member states in providing a locus of sanction is crucial.

Legislation in the Renewable Energy Directive states that the European Commission was obliged to report every two years on the environmental and social sustainability of the EU's biofuel policy. The first of these reports was two years late and was immediately branded as a 'whitewash' and an exercise in wilful ignorance by campaigners.[74] In the same way that the Commission organised consultations around indirect land-use change, it could also solicit submissions around the effects of its biofuel policies on land and labour rights, food prices, and biodiversity to signal the intrinsic importance of inclusion. Alongside this single centralised response, forums could also be organised, which better reflect the constituencies of biofuel production and thereby widen the pool of competing argument. Although a European Sustainable Biofuels Forum designed to share information and build cooperation among stakeholders does currently exist, it is mainly comprised of industry associations and other business. And perhaps one issue that would need to remain at the centre of such forum debate is the extent to which biofuels are indeed moving the transport sector in a low-carbon direction, given that fossil fuel consumption in the EU has continued to increase despite the additional consumption of biofuel.[75]

Other experimental pathways exist in the form of 'event-notification systems'.[76] These are designed to alert the central unit to major incidents, which are then co-investigated with the local unit in question, resulting in new prevention procedures put in place and communication to other local units warning of potential threats to their own operation.[77] In our context, this could take the shape of an ombudsman who receives complaints from civil society groups or affected people outside the EU about major legal violations linked to biofuel exports. Again, much of this argument relates to the combination of wider transparency and an effective locus of central sanction. It does not call for a final arbitration of the attractiveness of biofuels themselves.

Joined-up governance

As suggested in the first section, one of the vectors of further research in experimentalism relates to its effects beyond the issue area by which it was initially bound (hence the language of regulatory assemblage and so on). Similarly, in biofuels, there have been opportunities for spillover that could be revisited and extended. One of these relates to the trade in biomass – namely, wood pellets burned like coal in power stations – which are also classed as a renewable energy and promoted under EU directives. Despite the concern that these wood pellets are increasingly being produced from freshly cut trees rather than wood waste, and that those trees are not replaced within sustainably managed woodland, the European Commission demurred on applying mandatory environmental criteria on biomass in the same way it did for biofuel. Instead, it has deferred to member states to put in place their own (non-discriminatory) requirements which are being met by the industry through standards and processes being developed by the Sustainable Biomass Partnership, which are explicitly modelled on existing certification schemes, namely the Forest Stewardship Council and Programme for Endorsement of Forest Certification. In other words, the same trajectory that timber and biofuels have already mapped out is being taken, suggesting that more effective and EU-wide environmental regulation is not just plausible but perhaps even imminent in this area.

Another possibility is to extend the standards to which biofuels are held to other fuels and agricultural commodities, requiring local reporting on the conditions in which these are produced. In this respect, there is a curious disconnect at present between the Renewable Energy Directive and the Fuel Quality Directive that could be bridged. The former requires that 10% of transport fuel be from renewable sources by 2020, and the latter stipulates that a 6% reduction in the greenhouse gas intensity of all transport fuel across the board by 2020. To reach this 6% reduction, member states can promote the use of biofuels and electric vehicles, but also promote the use of less-polluting 'cleaner' fossil fuels. Yet the methodology to calculate the greenhouse gas emissions associated with fossil fuels took five years to agree and settled on a very crude assessment supported by the oil industry.[78] Moreover, neither are there any land-use change criteria or biodiversity reporting requirements attached to fossil fuel production. In short, even though they are covered by the same piece of legislation, the standards and scrutiny applied to the environmental properties of oil and gas fuels are ultimately much weaker than those attached to biofuels.

There is also a regulatory paradox as far as other agricultural commodities are concerned. If, say, palm oil produced in Indonesia is sold into the EU as biofuel, then it is subject to environmental sustainability criteria. However, if that same palm oil is sold as vegetable oil, then it can be linked to all types of destructive activity without consequence. In this light, a case could be made for the EU and/or member states to instigate reporting requirements on the sustainability of commodities clearly affected by the price changes induced by its biofuel policy. While this monitoring and evaluation would not necessarily have to be done via certification schemes (nor carry the threat of trade sanction, thus avoiding WTO dispute), it is notable that business associations in Belgium, France, Germany, and the Netherlands, and government departments in the UK, have all made pledges towards using certified palm oil, again suggesting the utility of this mode of governance in transnational supply chains. Indeed, palm oil is something of a special case in standards due the current emergence of an industry-wide commitment to zero net deforestation. Here, we might consider whether possibilities for recursive learning might extend the other way? Whether biofuels producers might be persuaded to improve their own standards as a market-oriented device to improve their own sustainability criteria without first waiting for certification?

Finally, another experimental pathway might be to join 'across scale' rather than across issue-area. For example, various sets of indicators for sustainable biofuels have been developed at the global level – most notably by the G8-sponsored Global Bioenergy Partnership (GBEP), an organisation launched in 2005 encompassing national governments, international organisations, and industry associations – although these twenty-four 'sustainability indicators' remain guidelines only. The experience of the EU shows that transnational regulatory architecture can be erected without excessively antagonising national sovereignty, suggesting that forums such as GBEP could, and should, explore ways to make effective their collectively agreed standard in such a way that trade partners can legitimately impose import duties if they have not been followed. Again, certification by GBEP-licensed global certification schemes would be one way to do this. Another would be to accept national implementation of the sustainability indicators on the condition that they are subject to benchmarking and peer review under the auspices of an independent authority like the UN's Intergovernmental Panel on Climate Change. Of course, this brings no guarantees that efforts to address the GBEP indicators would be sufficient, but in stimulating processes of comparison and encouraging a contextual treatment of sustainability (rather than the often contentious uniform standards emanating from the West), it would at least begin to foster oversight of the sector.

Conclusion

This chapter has developed a critique of transnational biofuel regulation. This emerging governance structure is too imperfect to be treated as a functioning experimentalist regime, but our analysis has diagnosed its failings *and* suggested democratic pathways towards a more effective, reflective, and inclusive governance system. In this way, a turn to everyday practices of governance can inform and transform the wider ethics of a global economy. There are many difficult issues confronting stakeholders responsible for constructing enhanced regulatory regimes for biofuel production and consumption. Not least of these is the fundamental civil society concern that pursuing sustainability through biofuels, rather than more far-reaching social and economic transformations, is counter-productive. In this light, we argue, the critical dimension of experimentalist governance should not be downplayed. Experimentalist governance is a theory that both diagnoses and explains empirical developments in public administration. But there is also a normative dimension, which defends a certain vision of how opaque forms of governance can be opened up through the democratising values of inclusion, deliberation, and accountability. Acknowledging the genuine ambiguities of the normative goal of sustainability might therefore allow for a process of social learning that leads to new experiments in joined-up governance across issue-areas.

Notes

1 See the Brassett contribution to this Handbook. See also: John M. Hobson and Leonard Seabrooke, eds., *Everyday Politics of the World Economy* (Cambridge: Cambridge University Press, 2007).

2 Chris Brown, *International Relations Theory: New Normative Approaches* (New York: Columbia University Press, 1992); Molly Cochran, *Normative Theory in International Relations: A Pragmatic Approach* (Cambridge: Cambridge University Press, 1999).

3 Owen Parker and James Brassett, 'Contingent Borders, Ambiguous Ethics: Migrants in International Political Theory', *International Studies Quarterly*, 49, no. 2 (2005): 233–253.

4 Toni Erskine, 'Qualifying Cosmopolitanism? Solidarity, Criticism, and Michael Walzer's "View from the Cave"', *International Politics*, 44, no. 1 (2007): 125–149.

5 Charles Sabel and Jonathan Zeitlin, 'Experimentalist Governance', in *The Oxford Handbook of Governance*, ed. David Levi-Faur (Oxford: Oxford University Press), 169–186.

6 Ibid.

7 James Brassett, Ben Richardson, and William Smith, 'Private Experiments in Global Governance Primary Commodities Roundtables and the Politics of Deliberation', *International Theory*, 4, no. 3 (2012): 367–399.

8 Ibid.

9 Ponte (2013).

10 P. Schleifer, 'Orchestrating Sustainability: The Case of European Union Biofuel Governance', *Regulation and Governance*, 7, no. 4 (2013): 533–546.
11 S. Ponte and C. Daugbjerg, 'Biofuel Sustainability and the Formation of Transnational Hybrid Governance', *Environmental Politics*, forthcoming.
12 Brassett, Richardson, and Smith, 'Private Experiments in Global Governance Primary Commodities Roundtables'.
13 Joshua Cohen and Charles Sabel, 'Global Democracy?', *NYU Journal of International Law and Politics*, 37, no. 4 (2006): 774.
14 Joshua Cohen and Charles Sabel, 'Directly Deliberative Polyarchy', *European Law Journal*, 3, no. 4 (1997): 313.
15 Cohen and Sabel, 'Global Democracy?,' 779.
16 Ibid., 780.
17 Sabel and Zeitlin, 'Experimentalist Governance'.
18 Cohen and Sabel, 'Directly Deliberative Polyarchy', 326.
19 Sabel and Zeitlin, 'Experimentalist Governance'.
20 Cohen and Sabel, 'Global Democracy?', 780.
21 Ibid., 795.
22 Ibid., 796.
23 Gráinne de Búrca, Robert Keohane, and Charles Sabel, 'New Modes of Pluralist Global Governance', *NYU Journal of International Law and Politics*, 45 (2013): 781–782.
24 Brassett, Richardson, and Smith, 'Private Experiments in Global Governance Primary Commodities Roundtables'.
25 Christine Overdevest and Jonathan Zeitlin, 'Assembling an Experimentalist Regime: Transnational Governance Interactions in the Forest Sector', *Regulation and Governance*, 8 (2014): 22–48.
26 Ibid., 29.
27 See: Kenneth Abbott and Duncan Snidal, 'Strengthening International Regulation through Transnational New Governance: Overcoming the Orchestration Deficit', *Vanderbilt Journal of Transnational Law*, 42, no. 2 (2009): 501–578; Stephen Bell and Andrew Hindmoor, 'Governance without Government? The Case of the Forest Stewardship Council', *Public Administration*, 90, no. 1 (2011): 144–159.
28 Steven Bernstein and Cashore Benjamin, 'Complex Global Governance and Domestic Policies: Four Pathways of Influence', *International Affairs*, 88, no. 3 (2012): 585–604.
29 Organisation for Economic Co-operation and Development and Food and Agriculture Organization, *FAO-OECD Agricultural Outlook 2013–2022* (Paris: Organisation for Economic Co-operation and Development, 2013), 260–261.
30 Commission of the European Communities, 'Energy for the Future: Renewable Sources of Energy', *White Paper for a Community Strategy and Action Plan*, COM (97) 599 (November 26, 1997).
31 The Commission is quoted here as saying: 'Given the rising demand for biofuels, the Commission is seeking the appropriate development of both EU domestic production and enhanced import opportunities for biofuels and their feedstocks *and to develop their economic viability*' (italics added): Commission of the European Communities, 'An EU Strategy for Biofuels', *Communication from the Commission*, COM (2006) 34 (February 8, 2006).
32 Countries are cited here in descending order of importance. CEC (2013): 11; Ecofys (2012).
33 Commission of the European Communities, 'Energy for the Future: Renewable Sources of Energy'; Mark Harvey and Sarah Pilgrim, 'The European Political Economy Impasse for Renewable Transport Energy', *New Political Economy*, 18, no. 3 (2013): 373.
34 Mairon G. Bastos Lima and Joyeeta Gupta, 'The Policy Context of Biofuels: A Case of Non-Governance at the Global Level?', *Global Environmental Politics*, 13, no. 2 (2013): 46–64.
35 Oxfam International, 'Another Inconvenient Truth: How Biofuel Policies Are Deepening Poverty and Accelerating Climate Change', *Oxfam Briefing Paper*, 114 (2008).
36 Joseph Fargione et al., 'Land Clearing and the Biofuel Carbon Debt', *Science*, 319, no. 5867 (2008): 1235–1238.
37 Renewable Fuels Agency, *Gallagher Review of the Indirect Effects of Biofuels Production* (St. Leonards-on-Sea, East Sussex: Renewable Fuels Agency).
38 The same did not apply to human rights and labour standards attached to biofuel production, which the European Commission essentially vetoed from the outset. Even the legality of the environmental process and production methods required of biofuels is not entirely straightforward and Argentina, Indonesia and Malaysia have registered their concern that their biofuel exports are unfairly discriminated against

by the Renewable Energy Directive (see WTO, 2013). That said, a formal complaint has not been lodged and Ponte and Daugbjerg (2014) for one suggest that the EU's environmental criteria can be considered exempt to the extent it is 'no more trade-restrictive than necessary to fulfil a legitimate objective': Ponte and Dugbjerg, 'Biofuel Sustainability and the Formation of Transnational Hybrid Governance'; World Trade Organization, 'Concerns Raised over Trade Restrictions on Dairy Products, Biofuels, Cars and Seafood', *WTO News Items*, October 18, 2013, http://www.wto.org/english/news_e/news13_e/good_18oct13_e.htm.

39 See Ponte (2013).

40 See Ponte (2013).

41 See Ponte (2013).

42 Although the EU RED also requires that member states set up a national system through which companies can show that they comply with the sustainability requirements for biofuels, non-state certification has been preferred. Companies can thus choose to follow national systems or certification schemes, but since national standards can differ between member states and each national system is normally only valid in the member state where it was set up, certification schemes have the advantage of being 'trade-enabled': Overdevest and Zeitlin, 'Assembling an Experimentalist Regime'.

43 Ponte (2013).

44 Jolene Lin, 'Transnational Environmental Law in Action: The European Union's Sustainable Biofuels Experiment', University of Hong Kong Faculty of Law Research Paper, 2013/034 (2013).

45 Commission of the European Communities, 'Communication from the European Commission on Voluntary Schemes and Default Values in the EU Biofuels and Bioliquids Sustainability Scheme', *Official Journal of the European Union*, 160, no. 1 (2010), 1.

46 Brassett, Richardson, and Smith, 'Private Experiments in Global Governance Primary Commodities Roundtables'.

47 P. Schleifer, 'Orchestrating Sustainability: The Case of European Union Biofuel Governance', *Regulation and Governance*, 7, no. 4 (2013): 533–546, at 9.

48 RSB (2012): 1.

49 Five new schemes were approved during 2014, all led by industry associations. Full list available at: http://ec.europa.eu/energy/renewables/biofuels/doc/sustainability_schemes/voluntary_schemes_overview.pdf

50 World Wildlife Fund Deutschland, *Searching for Sustainability: Comparative Analysis of Certification Schemes for Biomass Used for the Production of Biofuels* (Dusseldorf, Germany: WWF), 8.

51 Oxfam International, 'The EU Must Urgently Fix Biofuels Policy Driving Scramble for Land in Poor Countries', news release, September 29, 2011, *Blogactive.eu*, http://oxfameu.blogactiv.eu/2011/09/29/the-eu-must-urgently-fix-biofuels-policy-driving-scramble-for-land-in-poor-countries/.

52 ClientEarth (2011). Experience in regulating carbon offset projects through independent audits suggests that scepticism is warranted. The Executive Board of the UN's Clean Development Mechanism have recently suspended two of the leading auditing firms involved for failure to properly assess that a minimum amount of GHG emissions are being saved. See: J. Scott, 'The Multi-Level Governance of Climate Change', in *The Evolution of EU Law*, ed. P. Carig and P. and G. de Búrca (Oxford: Oxford University Press, 2011), 805–835.

53 Bebb, cited in ICTSD (2008).

54 International Council of Clean Transportation, 'Vegetable Oil Markets and the EU Biofuel Mandate', briefing, February 2013, http://www.theicct.org/sites/default/files/publications/ICCT_vegoil_and_EU_biofuel_mandate_20130211.pdf

55 Les Levidow, 'EU Criteria for Sustainable Biofuels: Accounting for Carbon, Depoliticising Plunder', *Geoforum*, 44 (2013): 211–223.

56 Jos Dings, 'Open Letter to Gunther Oettinger, EU Energy Commissioner', petition, September 25, 2012, http://www.foeeurope.org/sites/default/files/news/letter_oettinger_iluc_sep2012.pdf.

57 In its public consultation on indirect land-use change in 2010, the Commission received five submissions from citizens, 18 from public authorities, and 120 from 'private' authorities (chiefly national or EU-wide business associations, international social and environmental NGOs, and multinational companies). See: Commission of the European Communities, 'Communication from the European Commission on Voluntary Schemes and Default Values in the EU Biofuels and Bioliquids Sustainability Scheme', *Official Journal of the European Union*, 160/01 (2010).

58 CEC (2012). As it passed through the EU policy-making process, this target was raised to 6% by the European Parliament and then to 7% by EU energy ministers. The proposal was due to return to the European Parliament for a second reading in late 2014.
59 Annex II of the Commission's RED amendment proposal and Annex V of the Fuel Quality Directive set additional emissions values linked to indirect land-use change. They were 12g CO^2 equivalent per MJ for cereal-based biofuel, 13g for sugar cane/beet-based biofuel, and 55g for oilseed-based biofuel. These values were based on four studies requested by the Commission from the International Food Policy Research Institute and its own Joint Research Centre; they were immediately contested by the European Biodiesel Board.
60 This decision was taken by the European Parliament, which debated the Commission's proposals in 2013. The Parliament did make emissions from indirect land-use change binding in the context of the Fuel Quality Directive – which requires a 6% reduction in lifecycle greenhouse gas emissions for all fuels by 2020 – but this is arguably less relevant to the regulation of biofuels *per se*.
61 Nelson (2012). Perhaps the one interest group that was left happy were the biotechnology companies involved in the development of biofuels from non-food sources, and which benefit from the shifting of incentives from first- to second-generation biofuels.
62 Ponte (2013).
63 Commission of the European Communities, 'Renewable Energy: Commission Refers Poland and Cyprus to Court for Failing to Transpose EU Rules,' press release, March 21, 2013, European Union, http://europa.eu/rapid/press-release_IP-13-259_en.htm, 11.
64 EurObserver'ER, 'Biofuels Barometer', July 2013, *Energies-renouvelables.org*, http://www.energies-renouvelables.org/observ-er/stat_baro/observ/baro216_en.pdf.
65 As above.
66 There may be an independent national interest in increasing the consumption of biofuels, of course, separate from the obligation to meet the EU Renewable Energy Directive.
67 Ponte (2013).
68 Harvey and Pilgrim, 'The European Political Economy Impasse for Renewable Transport Energy'.
69 Ponte (2013), 7.
70 P. Schleifer, 'Let's Bargain! Setting Standards for Sustainable Biofuels', working paper, Robert Schuman Centre for Advanced Studies, Global Governance Programme, 148.
71 Ponte (2013), 10.
72 In so far as the WWF is a member of many of the Roundtable certification schemes, their benchmarking exercise also functions as a kind of internal review. See: WWF Deutschland, 'Searching for Sustainability'.
73 Commission of the European Communities, 'Renewable Energy Progress Report', report, COM (2013) 175, March 17, 2013.
74 ActionAid, 'ActionAid's Reaction to the EC's Analysis of the Social Impacts of its Biofuels Policies', press release, March 27, 2013, http://www.actionaid.org/news/reaction-actionaids-reaction-ecs-analysis-social-impacts-its-biofuels-policies; Oxfam International, 'Oxfam Reaction to European Commission's Report on Impact of EU Biofuels Policy on Food and Land Rights', press release, March 27, 2013, http://www.oxfam.org/en/eu/pressroom/reactions/european-commission-report-impact-eu-biofuels-policy-food-land-rights.
75 In 2000, the EU road transport sector used the equivalent of 279 million tonnes of oil; in 2010, this had increased by a further 20 million tonnes, of which 13 million tonnes came from biofuel. See: European Union, *EU Transport in Figures: Statistical Pocket Notebook* (Luxembourg: Publications Office of the European Union, 2012); EurObserver'ER, 'Biofuels Barometer'.
76 Ponte (2013).
77 Sabel and Zeitlin, 'Experimentalist Governance'.
78 Commission of the European Communities, 'Executive Summary of the Impact Assessment on the Calculation Methods and Reporting Requirements . . . Relating to the Quality of Petrol and Diesel Fuels', working paper, October 6, 2014.

PART VIII

Religion and international ethics

THE SIGNIFICANCE OF RELIGIOUS ETHICS IN INTERNATIONAL POLITICS

Cecelia M. Lynch

It is almost a truism that "religion is back" in international relations. Those of us concerned with religion and international ethics, however, have worked to expose and interrogate the barely hidden anxieties and ethical assumptions that continue to underpin this return and shape scholarship. In international relations, these anxieties revolve around two main issues, which demonstrate built-in ethical assumptions: 1) that religion is anachronistic and dangerous in the modern world, and therefore religious identities inevitably promote exclusivist views of belonging, resulting in violence towards non-religious or differently religious "others," and 2) that religion is incompatible with the form of government that *should* rule the world, that is, democracy. As a result, numerous studies have examined the connection between religion and violence, with some moving towards opposite (but potentially problematic) assertions that religion *a priori* promotes peace instead. Still others examine the possibility of combining different levels of religious acknowledgment with forms of democratic governance. Increasingly, however, groups of scholars are moving beyond these debates to explore interesting questions and issues about religion, ethics and ontology/methodology, religion, ethics and race, different kinds of "religious worlds," indigenous and post-colonial practices, and new ways of conceptualizing and understanding the ethical implications of religious experience. This section of the Ethics and International Relations Handbook sets out parameters for important components of this innovative work, while also recalling aspects of ongoing debates that require continued or further excavation and examination.

Many scholars have argued that the preoccupations about connections between religion *vis-à-vis* violence/peace and religion *vis-à-vis* democracy are valid, but only up to a point, and that the very reasons for their persistence – the *ethics* at stake – need interrogating as much as the substantive questions that emanate from them.[1] Below, I discuss some of the important issues and questions that can be opened up with a broader focus. It is important to recognize that, too often still, assumptions about religious ethics in international politics continue to reflect the concerns of the "secularization thesis," which asserted for decades that modernization, and hence progress, could only occur with the "progressive" secularization of states and societies around the world. While this thesis has largely been debunked, including by some of its original authors (especially Peter Berger in his 1999 volume[2]), its assumptions and legacies continue to shape the study of religion and ideas about religious ethics in powerful ways.

As a result, this Handbook provides an excellent and timely space to articulate a strong argument that religion in international relations (IR) can be best approached precisely by studying religious ethics in ways that both help us understand these anxieties and point out how to move beyond them. But what are the best ways to interrogate a) the topic of religion and ethics, b) the residual power of the secularization thesis, and c) the many facets of religious/spiritual practice *and* belief that are beginning to be examined, or that have not yet been examined in IR, but should be? Accomplishing these tasks will go a fair way towards achieving the twin objectives of this volume: to provide both a state-of-the-art understanding of the positioning of religious ethics in the field, and to be forward-looking in pointing to cutting-edge themes and debates.

Given these two goals, there are several ways to cut into the topic of "religious ethics." One that immediately comes to mind is to compare and examine the ethics of different "religions" or "religious traditions": Buddhist, Hindu, Jewish, Muslim, Christian, Rastafarian, Zoroastrian, Wicca, African Religious, Sikh, and Shinto among many, many others, perhaps also tracing the trajectory of new work on reformists, fundamentalists, and instances of syncretisms among a number of these traditions. Such an endeavor would tell us much about the "common good" that each of these traditions seeks to accomplish, and allow us to compare and contrast whether and what kinds of good are "common" among religions.[3] It could also expose some of the tensions within traditions themselves.

Such a project would be an important endeavor for any study of comparative religions. This Part of the Handbook, however, takes a different path – one that uses this opportunity to begin to historicize pressing ethical questions for religious traditions in different parts of the globe. This path also incorporates tensions, reform, and syncretic movements, it but does so with a different objective and in a different manner. Instead of repeating debates engendered by the problematic assumptions of the secularization thesis, this path interrogates the complex intersections of religion and politics in different eras and parts of the world, and integrates political economy, race, and emotion. I assert that this path is more productive for the task at hand, for a number of reasons.

First, a comparison of religious traditions soon runs into numerous problems. One simple issue is that there are simply too many religions to do a fair accounting and comparison. Moreover, they each have their own divisions and further subdivisions, with some adherents believing that their own sect exemplifies "truth" and a radical departure from the beliefs of adherents of other sects, but with others less concerned with differentiating themselves from "co-religionists." In other words, there is no one Christian (or Buddhist, or Islamic) identity or "ethics." Examples of difference and variety abound in each of the above religious traditions, and are very easy to see in Christianity, Islam, Buddism, Hinduism, and Judaism. Many Catholics consider themselves the original (and therefore most authentic) Christians, while many Evangelicals (despite an overlap in guidelines regarding sexual ethics) do not even consider Catholics to be Christian. Catholics and "mainline" Protestants such as Lutherans, Methodists, and Presbyterians, among others, along with Anglicans/Episcopalians (who some consider to be a combination of Catholic and Protestant) have ethical similarities on some issues, for example just war, which differ from the more nationalist sentiments of more recent Evangelical and Pentecostal sects. Islamic sects include not only Sunni and Shi'a, but also Wahabi Sunni versus the Muslim Brotherhood versus those who consider themselves more progressive or mainstream Sunni, the more mystical Sufi sects (which include, in Senegal alone, for example, numerous "brotherhoods" with important political roles), but also the Amadiyyas and syncretic offshoots such as the Alawis whose roots are challenged by some co-nationals. Similar subdivisions and ethical differences exist in Hinduism, regarding caste for example, and Buddhism; while Reform, Conservative, and Orthodox Jews also demonstrate both overlaps and differences in ethical positions. Even the existence of sacred texts helps only minimally in deriving ethical standards for particular religious traditions that are important for international relations. This is because texts such as the Torah, the Bible, and the Qu'ran (to name a few) are each extremely complex, and each have motivated hermeneutic practices that have themselves become longstanding traditions characterized by vociferous debates among schools of thought. So, while one can distill some core beliefs in each religious tradition, the different interpretations of the ethics of putting them into practice make it not entirely helpful to approach the task in that way.

Second, the interdisciplinary study of religion over the past two decades, including those concerned with religious ethics in IR, has foregrounded the question of whether "religion" is even an appropriate term for understanding socially interpreted ethical guidelines in different parts of the world. Following the argument of Talal Asad (1993) that the very term "religion" is an historical construct that emerged out of the Early Modern era and the Enlightenment, many scholars have pointed out that this term was constructed in relation to an alleged opposite, "secularism," and that the twin reifications of both terms over time was part of a mostly European, liberal politics that attempted to normalize secularism while redefining religion as anachronistic, anti-modern, and irrational. As a result, it is not only "religious" ethics that need interrogation, but also "secular" ones. Focusing on well-known religious traditions alone does not allow us to understand the symbiotic relationships and development of religion/s and secularism/s (in particular, the constitutive nature of Western Protestant Christianity and liberal secularism), the power of secularist assumptions and faith in secularization processes, or the nature of secularist and/versus religious commitments in non-Western parts of the world.

It is important for a handbook on ethics to acknowledge the continued dominance of the *Europeanist* construction of the terms "religion" and "secularism," while also keeping open the investigation of the political meanings and implications for international relations of other constructions (or, in Wittgensteinian terms, "family resemblances") both temporally and spatially.

Third, people do not always identify with only one religious or spiritual tradition, and even when they do, their religious practices may embody various forms of hybridity or syncretism. While some anthropologists, such as Hirschkind, note the partially problematic nature of terms such as "syncretism," many people "on the ground," not exclusively but perhaps most evidently in post-colonial societies, combine what comparative religion observers might identify as more than one religious tradition. Even when such identifications are not explicit or self-aware, religious actors can engage in practices that transcend a particular religious tradition, as Schwarz[4] has shown in her study of the Taizé community and its practice of chanting. And as William Ackah points out in his chapter on the implications of race for African diasporic peoples and their interaction with Christianity, the very deployment of African modes of spirituality could both strengthen and undermine then contemporary Christian commitments. Taken together, this body of work challenges received views of "what counts" as religion, as well as providing new ontological and methodological paths for analyzing the practice/belief composite.

While there is not space in this volume to address, for example, whether Buddhist, Hindu, or Confucian social ethics might incorporate similar distinctions (see, however, Ashis Nandy versus Rajeev Bhargava, or Lily H. M. Ling, on this point[5]), we begin by examining the "religious" origins of Enlightenment economic thought, as a way to problematize easy notions of separation between the "religious" and the "secular" at the same time as we acknowledge the movement and fluidity of ethics in a changing economic and political context. David Blaney's work on the Scottish Enlightenment philosopher and economist Adam Smith (1723–1790) provides an important window into the complex ethics of Enlightenment economics and their connections with religious concerns, and especially the tensions they bring to the fore.

In Chapter 33, Blaney relates to the task of approaching religious ethics through historicizing pressing ethical questions for religious traditions in different historical times and places. He does not directly answer a closely related debate about whether secularism is symbiotically related to Christianity, and specifically Protestantism (a task that is not possible within these pages), instead emphasizing the point that the ethics embodied in Enlightenment philosophy and Smith's "invisible hand" need to be dissected and interrogated in ways that do not ignore the religious problematics at stake. Regarding liberalism, some scholars have taken the position that it is indistinguishable from Protestantism, both in its historical construction and in its eventual focus on individualism, in terms of earning merit as well as access to God, which also, essentially, ties liberalism and Protestantism symbiotically to secularisms of various kinds today (see, for example, the work of Saba Mahmood or Talal Asad, among others[6]). Such a focus points out how the development of Protestant sects such as Calvinism and Puritanism co-constituted historical forms of capitalism, as Max Weber famously argued,[7] with continuing ethical repercussions today. Blaney, however, approaches the ethical tensions involved through a detailed exploration, or immanent critique, of the moral economies and dislocations of Smith's context, and his consequent method of addressing the problem of "theodicy." In particular, Blaney points out that while Enlightenment philosophers, including Kant, are known for their alleged "secularism," few of them rejected God, and most worried about how to address the existence of evil in the world. Smith's "invisible hand" is one method of "performing theodicy," that is, finding a mechanism by which evil may exist in the short term, but is put into the perspective of a longer-term plan. That plan may be either deist or – in Smith's case – methodological in nature, but the teleology and belief in a triumph over "evil," including poverty, continues in the field of international political economy to this day. Just as Smith accorded government some regulatory role when market forces produced great inequalities in the short term, contemporary political economy views the creation of "rational" incentives as necessary for encouraging the kinds of collaborative behavior that will, in its view, increase prosperity in the longer term. In both cases, God might be displaced as the creator of ultimate good, but the concerns, motivations, and ethical tensions in early Protestant thought remain.

Similarly, Mustapha Kamal Pasha's chapter on the Arab Muslim historian Ibn Khaldun (1332–1406), Chapter 37, challenges received notions about this prominent Islamic philosopher. Taking us back before the Reformation to another part of the world, yet one symbiotically related to "the West" through religious and political opposition as well as accommodation, Pasha also explores Ibn Khaldun's views on political economy in order to examine the ethics of wealth creation and "the materialist foundations of civilization." Khaldun is well known for his civilizational theory, but Pasha employs Khaldun to lessen the binary between medieval and "modern" worlds and ethics. This chapter also moves the center of power – and the center of debates about the history of religion – to the Middle East and North Africa, while enabling a comparison of the "oikonomia" of an historically "Islamic zone" that borders Europe.

Both Blaney and Pasha re-situate our understanding of international ethics by examining thinkers who navigated the terrains of religion, law, and economy in terms of their own civilizational worlds, and who established modes of thought that traversed the religious/secular binary and continue to reverberate in the complex of religion, ethics, and international relations today.

Similar challenges posed by forms of immanent critique to the complex of religion/secularism and ethics run throughout other contributions to this Part. The contributions acknowledge that we are writing this Handbook in an era when some religious traditions are seen as more irrational, anti-modern, anachronistic, or even dangerous than others, that is, more prone to violence and/or more incompatible with democracy, in the terms outlined above, whether or not such assumptions have any strong evidentiary basis (most do not). Mostly, these are labels used in the West to describe Islam, although many in academia apply them to conservative

Christianity as well. Thus, it is important to keep a space open for understanding some of the particularities and situatedness of different traditions in the present time.

However, Chapter 34, by Mona Khanwal Sheikh, directly embraces rather than attacking or dismissing the alleged irrationality of religion, by looking at how emotion plays a central role in religious adherence. This chapter also returns us, implicitly at least, to the question of belief. Unlike the Enlightenment era, which was supposed to dispense with religious passion in favor of reason and rationality, Sheikh argues that the emotions and passions excited by religious commitment include not only fear but also what we might consider positive emotions such as affection and love. Recent work in international relations that focuses on emotion rejects robotic rationalism and argues that scholarship that avoids emotion misses out on the very links between commitments and behavior.

In her study of the Pakistani Taliban as well as in this chapter, Sheikh confronts how and why actors who self-identify as religious draw from their interpretations of religious traditions and their political contexts the perceived necessity of emotive acts of affection that may include violence. Islam, more than other religions, has been "securitized," despite its numerous variations and the wide range in beliefs and practices of its adherents. Yet, in challenging this securitization, part of the import of Sheik's chapter is to show the importance of problematizing the preoccupation with the religion/violence nexus and its focus on Islam, without romanticizing any assumptions that all religious adherents – including but not limited to Muslims – are inherently peaceful, either. Sheikh's research on the emotional aspects of the Pakistani Taliban's articulation of its ethics distills both the complexity and contradictions within the ethical stances of groups labeled "extremist," while it also demonstrates the centrality of emotions to any genuine conceptualization of ethics.

Chapter 35, by Erin K. Wilson, explores critique through an analysis of ongoing displacements of people moving across the globe – movements operating at the contemporary intersection of religious ethics, debates about the secular/religious binary, and debates about justice. Wilson's prior work on religion and global justice has, like the other work in this Part, contextualized how contemporary religious actors view poverty, egalitarianism, and human dignity.[8] In this chapter, however, she addresses this complex of issues while re-evaluating and reconceptualizing the ontological basis of the religion/secularism/ethics triad, arguing for the more inclusive framework of "multiple ontologies." Just as William Ackah demonstrates the injustices perpetuated by hypocritical religious and secular ethical pronouncements for enslaved peoples in the past, Wilson interrogates the need for greater ontological "justice" to enable the capacity to understand the multiple religious ethics and practices constitutive of the movement of peoples in the present. In particular, Wilson argues, secularist frames that conceptualize religion in narrow ways commit an "ontological injustice," which needs to be rectified by uncovering the problematic nature of secularist assumptions regarding refugee issues, as well as the multiple manifestations of religious ethics at issue in "welcoming the stranger."

Chapter 36, by William Ackah, also moves out of the Europeanist religio-secularist trajectory, but also (like the contributions of Pasha and Sheikh) without being able to leave it entirely. Ackah's contribution considers how race has been and continues to be implicated in the transnational diffusion of religion, and particularly Christianity, across Africa and the Americas through colonization and chattel slavery. Instead of the securitization that is continually reproduced *vis-à-vis* Islam, Ackah details the racialized hierarchies that underpinned both colonialism and ongoing post-colonial anxieties. At the same time, slaves in the New World navigated their own ethical conundrums, including whether and how to salvage aspects of colonialist Christianity and reformulate them – often along with African religious ethics – into something that could be sustaining and liberating in the midst of great cruelty. The Haitian Revolution and its aftermath act as a prominent example in demonstrating the ability of slaves and former slaves to enact a new ethics, while at the same time starkly showing the severe limits of Enlightenment Christian promises of self-realization and fulfillment. In other words, the new United States and post-Revolutionary France were proclaiming human rights while attempting to crush the Haitian revolution. Ackah's chapter, in sum, not only demonstrates the problematic nature of the religious/secular "model" put forward by Western actors from the colonial era to the present, but it also introduces new conceptualizations of ethics and syncretic religious practices that enable resistance to racialized hierarchies (on the part of indigenous religious practitioners of all kinds). Such ethics and syncretisms are little understood by scholars who assume fixed boundaries for the dominant "world religions" (in Weberian terms). The implications of Ackah's chapter show us just how necessary it is to move beyond such fixed boundaries to understand religion and ethics today as well as in the past. This chapter, finally, also discusses the work done by a transnational movement of scholars and religious figures, the Transatlantic Roundtable on Religion and Race (TRRR), which brings race centrally back into the social analysis of religion, and up-ends ethics and international relations by putting reparations centrally on the agenda. Again, historicized immanent critique is necessary to draw out the ethical problems exposed and possibilities articulated by such religious movement(s).

Taken together, these chapters provide an extremely exciting entrée into the worlds of religion and ethics in international relations, worlds that delve much deeper and broader than many conventional studies of international relations, or even ethics and IR, allow. Each of these chapters challenges the lack of ontological depth of conventional studies of religion and international relations; each proposes new ways of cutting into religious/secular worldviews and imaginaries, and each provides novel empirical material to chew on as we reflect on the complex of religious traditions, beliefs, and practices extant in the world, historically and today. Most also confront the problematic ethics that have been inherent in religio-secular political practices, and the ways in which belief has been interpreted to justify them. In confronting these issues and proposing new ways of understanding the intersection – and symbiotic nature – of religion, ethics, and international relations, they help point the way forward to a new generation of productive research, as well as ethically minded steps to take to move away from racial, ontological, and liberal injustices.

Notes

1 Schwarz, Tanya B., and Cecelia Lynch, forthcoming, "Religion in International Relations," in William Thompson, ed., *Oxford Research Encyclopaedia of Politics.* Oxford and New York: Oxford University Press; Schwarz, Tanya B., 2018, *Faith-Based Organizations in International Politics: What Are We Missing?* London: Rowman and Littlefield.

2 Berger, Peter L., ed., 1999, *The Desecularization of the World: Resurgent Religion and World Politics.* Grand Rapids, MI: William B. Eerdmans.

3 Lynch, Cecelia, 2009, "A Neo-Weberian Approach to Religion in International Politics," *International Theory*, 1 (3): 381–408.

4 Schwarz, Tanya B., 2018, *Faith-Based Organizations in International Politics: What Are We Missing?* London: Rowman and Littlefield.

5 Nandy, Ashis, 1999, *Traditions, Tyranny and Utopias: Essays in the Politics of Awareness*, Oxford: Oxford University Press; Bhargava, Rajeev, 2010, *The Promise of India's Secular Democracy*, Oxford: Oxford University Press; Ling, Lily H. M., 2014, *The Dao of World Politics: Towards a Post-Westphalian, Worldist International Relations.* London: Routledge.

6 Mahmood, Saba, 2016, *Religious Difference in a Secular Age: A Minority Report.* Princeton: Princeton University Press; Asad, Talal, 1993, *Genealogies of Religion: Discipline and Reasons of Power in Christianity and Islam.* Baltimore: Johns Hopkins University Press.

7 Weber, Max, 2002, *The Protestant Ethic and the Spirit of Capitalism, and Other Writings.* London: Penguin.

8 Wilson, E. K., and Manfred Steger, 2013, "Religious Globalisms in the Post-Secular Age," *Globalizations*, 10 (3): 481–495.

33

ADAM SMITH'S AMBIGUOUS THEODICY AND THE ETHICS OF INTERNATIONAL POLITICAL ECONOMY

David L. Blaney

When feeling in need of ethics, international relations (IR) largely resorts to Enlightenment figures, especially Kant and his intellectual descendants. Scholars tend to see the ethical legacy of the Enlightenment as secular, despite Kant's own writings on rational religion and theodicy. My interests and expertise run along the different pathways laid down by political economy; for me, the key Enlightenment figure is Adam Smith. Carl Becker places Smith in that Enlightenment movement that "demolished the Heavenly City of St. Augustine only to rebuild it with more up-to-date materials." Human life still appears as a "significant drama"—as a theory of orderly progress that replaces classical cyclical theories or Christian eschatology.[1] More precisely, Cassirer argues that the key intellectual problems engaging Enlightenment thinkers are "fused with religious problems," none more troubling than how to reconcile a vision of creation as simple and harmonious with the disorderly "facts of human experience," a problem of theodicy to which "they recur untiringly."[2]

In his assessment of the Enlightenment legacy for social theory, Neiman argues that it is eighteenth-century thinkers who effect a "radical" separation of "what earlier ages called natural from moral evils," thereby making central the idea that humans share responsibility with God for "the state of the world."[3] In the simplest terms, thinkers could separate the perfection of the natural world, which cannot and should not be altered, from those moral evils for which human action offers an explanation and, perhaps, a solution. Adam Smith shares this distinction with his Enlightenment peers, but gives the laws of natural order much greater weight. Consistent with the invisible hand metaphor, Smith tends to invert the source of our Enlightenment optimism: it is Nature guiding human action towards unintended consequences that is the source of most human advancement and our conscious efforts at reform that produce much of the evil. It is interference in the "natural course of things"—the "obvious and simple system of natural liberty" or "perfect liberty"—that produces genuine moral evil.[4]

This shift from theology to political economy might seem abrupt, though Carl Schmitt famously argues that all the concepts of modern political theory "are secularized theological concepts."[5] But it is Agamben who draws our attention more directly to an "economic theology:" "from the beginning," he notes, "theology conceives of divine life and the history of humanity as *oikonomia*." The *oikos* appears, first, as the domain of "administration," but over time emerges as *oikonomia*—an eschatological space, where salvation emerges in the "fullness of time."[6] *Oikonomia*, Agamben explains, remains fractured between God's design for salvation and the order of creation, which operates imperfectly without God's continuous and active administration.[7] For Agamben, this formulation prefigures Smith's eighteenth-century political economy, where the tension between natural order/disorder and active administration is finessed by locating an invisible hand through which an emergent order unfolds in nature.[8] The necessity *and* impossibility of such moves is indicated in the next section, which review's Leibniz's Enlightenment theodicy as a prelude to exploring Smith's own, albeit complicated, theodicy.

If Smith's political economy embraces Providentialist themes, contemporary international political economy (IPE) claims, by contrast, to build on the explicitly disenchanted imaginings of neoclassical economists, who eschew ethics in the name of secular science and a hard-headed (and -hearted) pragmatism.[9] Yet, as Boucoyanis notes, the IPE "[u]tilitarians" draw on the edifice of economics to "imagine a world in which harmony is possible."[10] In this respect, as I argue in the final section, IPE still bears the mark of Enlightenment theodicy: it turns ethically indifferent motives into ethically marked outcomes, however much practitioners of IPE suppress any explicit normative content.

Adam Smith offers a far deeper analysis. In the middle section of this paper, I deploy Smith to complicate the complacency attendant on many liberals' assumption of harmony. Smith does deploy a theodicy, however secularized, to show the necessity of social evils and moral failing to the successes of advanced commercial societies. In this way, he establishes a moral template for justifications of the "natural order" of market societies and, by extension, a global society ordered on a market pattern. But Smith's theodicy remains incomplete. At certain points, he turns to the state to directly administer *oikonomia* to redress its moral limits. At other points, he refuses to face some failures of the "system of natural liberty" to secure moral and material advance or social harmony, but, rather than justifying these evils as necessary to progress or accepting interventions that would impair the system of natural liberty, Smith acts *as if* such evils are not present, however evident they appear to a critical reader. In this way, and consistent with later economists and their acolytes in IPE, Smith both produces and represses theodicy at key moments in his political economy.

In the end, I argue that reading Smith might inspire us to a different economic theology: one that owns the costs of market society, facing honestly the evils accompanying the productive advances and moral consequences of market society, and cautioning us against the temptation to wash these evils away with salutary stories of progress or harmony.

The symbolic structure of theodicy

Theology becomes theodicy when focused on the problem of pervasive and inexplicable suffering and evil in a creation that God saw as "very good."[11] For many thinkers, Augustine, Bishop of Hippo (354–430) stands in for the Christian tradition of theodicy,[12] but it is Leibniz, building on Augustine, who coined the term in *Theodicy* (1710), and crafted a theodicy closer to modern political economy.[13] In *Theodicy*, Leibniz takes on the challenge of evil directly.[14] He insists that nothing escapes God's will yet simultaneously denies that God is "the author of sin" and "misery;" God "simply permits it." But how can God's creation admit of evil? Leibniz quickly separates God from creation and, by extension, from evil.[15] As an emanation of God's will, creation cannot be identical to God and therefore suffers a "privation" or is "limited in its essence," leading to additional privations, including chains of choices and actions that result in evil and suffering. Though God's creation, including free will, was good, it is humans who have chosen sin and brought suffering into the world.[16]

This solution leaves irremediable problems: it creates a fissure that both makes possible and casts doubt on God's identity as all-knowing, all-powerful, and all-goodness.[17] We wonder how human beings, as a good creation, exercise free will to choose evil. Since good cannot cause evil, an ontological gap now opens between God and creation, but Leibniz cannot leave this issue so tenuously resolved. In Žižek's terms, Leibniz covers this "immanent crack or impossibility" by working to characterize evil as only an apparent anomaly, one that plays a central, though often mysterious, role in creation's harmony.[18] Leibniz sees creation as uniting "a variety of things into a pleasing whole,"[19] as God the wise and good architect brings together diverse elements in "the most fitting plan."[20] Though each element appears as a "finite instantiation" and, therefore, limited and less perfect in form than we might desire, the whole, Leibniz assures us, is the best possible. By "optimizing" the highest values—"richness in variety in phenomena, and simplicity of laws"—God's creation expresses a harmony of laws and rules, "nature and grace," and past and future that are consistent with and can be apprehended by the highest reason. [21]

Here, Leibniz updates earlier theodicies with a language inflected by modern notions of (natural) order and recognizable to contemporary economists. As Rescher argues, Leibniz treats the problem of creative perfection as a maximization problem and endows the "divine mind" with the calculating capacity to produce the most perfect whole with the largest amount and diversity of parts in their most harmonious conjunction.[22] Leibniz thereby assures Early Modern thinkers that what some might perceive as "disorder in the part is order in the whole."[23] And, even limited human beings can observe the "objectivity of goodness" present in creation, the same "harmony and regularity" that allows "the universal laws in the world" to be discernible by scientists.[24] These harmonies, Blumenfeld stresses, create the greatest happiness, since it is the capacity to appreciate and live according to the harmonies of regular laws that produces happiness for God's creatures. [25]

Leibniz also holds onto the divine plan for redemption *in time*. The continuing presence of evil and suffering requires an act of divine balancing and redemption that unfolds in history.[26] Thus, suffering in the present appears as disorder or disharmony only if we fail to see it "as a penalty owing to guilt" and as a "means," guiding individuals by example and contributing to a "greater perfection" and exemplifying a "pre-established harmony."[27] Here, in a "cosmic melioration," short-run evils produce a beneficial final result.[28] The ontological gap is given a temporal solution; the very fracturing of the social order—the presence of evil—appears as the cause of a plan for redemption, and evil appears as truly evil only from a limited point of view.

In the same way, the "invisible hand" entices us with promises of a harmonious domestic and global social order, built principally on the unfettered operation of the laws of the market or market-like transactions, where active administration of the economy is minimized. But preserving the harmony of this natural/market order requires placing evil and suffering at a distance, so they do not confront the goodness of social order as an *internal* antagonism. The invisible hand operates as theodicy by turning (apparent) evil into the good, revaluing morally limited motives as desirable, and conceiving various social ills and failings variously and simultaneously as harmony or perhaps optimality. And the worst social evils are given a temporal melioration in promises of progress. But social ills and moral failings remain immune to complete revaluation or smoothing by the invisible hand in the present or in some future state. We are drawn thereby to acts of denial or disavowal of social evil.

Adam Smith's complicated and incomplete theodicy

However illusive Smith's actual religious beliefs, much recent scholarship supports reading Smith's work as theodicy.[29] Harrison argues that Smith operates "within a providentialist and teleological framework,"[30] including, as Evensky notes, the idea that "the progress of humankind rests ultimately on . . . the existence of a benevolent deity as the designer of the universe."[31] More strongly, Hill writes that "Adam Smith's social and economic philosophy is inherently theological and that its Providentialist underpinnings cannot be removed without impairing his theory of social order."[32] Informed by the "complacent, providentialist suggestion" that things would be worse if subject to "human contrivance," Smith leans towards a relative political quietism.[33] Tilley explains that theodicy is often thought to perform this function: in order to restore the "spotless hands" of the creator/creation, Enlightenment "theodicies" distance us from suffering and leave us "oblivious to the commitment, practical wisdom and constancy needed to counteract some evils."[34]

Smith seems to distance natural order from suffering precisely as Tilley suggests; he describes the Stoics in an approving fashion in *The Theory of Moral Sentiments*. The "ancient stoics" saw the cosmos as a domain "governed by the all-ruling providence of a wise, powerful, and good God, [where] every single event ought to be regarded, as making a necessary part of the plan of the universe, and as tending to promote the general order and happiness of the whole." The plan of the universe includes the necessity of "the vices and follies of mankind," so that nature displays that "eternal art which *educes good from ill*."[35] Later in the text, and much like Leibniz, Smith assures us that the "great disorder in our moral sentiments," including "hatred and contempt," are often turned to the good, and we may "admire the wisdom of God even in the weakness and folly of men."[36] Smith insists that the "passions" that drive human beings tend to produce, though without intending, the "beneficient ends which the great Director of nature intended to produce by them."[37] Thus, as Smith argues, "wise and virtuous" men should remember that God as a "benevolent and all-wise being can admit into the system of government no partial evil which is not necessary for the universal good."[38]

Yet, just after educing good from ill, Smith warns that we should *not* confuse vice and virtue. Though he reworks classical understandings of virtue somewhat for a commercial era, Smith insists that any such "speculations" about nature's plan do not "diminish our natural abhorrence for vice, whose immediate effects are so destructive, and whose remote ones are too distant to be traced by the imagination."[39] Here, Smith indicates that our natural moral sentiments allow us to discern those imperfections of the natural order that remain, those where providence does not make vice into virtue and nature doesn't invariably educe good from ill in its "remote" effects. Educing good from evil does not eliminate the need for a moral vocabulary of virtue necessary to evaluate the goods and evils of social life and does not remove completely the need for human responsibility to recognize and right social wrongs.

It is already clear that Smith's theodicy exhibits and he readily admits the impossibility of closure. I believe Smith's theodicy resists closure in four respects. First, like Leibniz, he uses the invisible hand in *Wealth of Nations* and *Theory of Moral Sentiments* to educe the good from evil, but he refuses to grant evil full play: he re-values individual self-love as a relative moral good, attempting to cover the fracture between virtue and vice he fears has opened in the market order. Second, Smith acknowledges a deeper fracture in the order of nature. Reversing contemporary economic thinking, where a Leibniz-like Pareto-optimal outcome secures the collective and individual good simultaneously, Smith not only de-links the social good from individual desire and happiness, he sets them in opposition. Third, and contrary to the initial presumption of complete natural harmony, he acknowledges the presence of some social ills that require governance of the *oikonomia* by the visible hand of administration for the common good of society, lest these *moral* evils undercut the good of the system of "natural liberty." Finally, in the face of the impossibility of covering the fractures in natural order with a theodicy, Smith performs acts of denial or disavowal, where his thinking exposes serious social ills that he treats *as if* they were simply not present.

Smith's most famous use of the "invisible hand" seems to vindicate the principle that good may be educed from ill. In *Wealth of Nations*, Smith warns of the dangers of governmental intervention in commerce, particularly in foreign trade.[40] Since individuals "endeavor" to achieve returns of the "greatest value," each "necessarily labours to render the annual revenue of the society as great as he can," though he "neither intends to promote the public interest, nor knows how much he is promoting it. . . . . and he is in this, as in many other cases, led by an invisible hand to promote an end which was no part of his intention." Smith seems clear: the good of society is educed from acts of little virtue aimed at individual gain by an automatic mechanism that, operating as a law of nature without the conscious intention of the actors, produces agreeable effects.

Though often treated as exhaustive of his views, Smith does not simply vindicate amoral behavior with the invisible hand; rather, this self-regarding behavior, when seen from a deeper vantage point, appears closer to virtue. He begins *Theory of Moral Sentiments* by stressing that "sympathy," *not self-love*, is the starting point of moral psychology:

> How selfish soever man may be supposed, there are evidently some principles in his nature, which interest him in the fortune of others, and render their happiness necessary to him, though he derives nothing from it except the pleasure of seeing it.[41]

Smith suggests that how we imagine the feelings of others, including how we imagine they view us, is key to the plan of the "all-wise Author of Nature."[42] That is, we *naturally* learn to consider the situation and viewpoint of others in "a candid and impartial light," and this capacity shapes our moral perspective and our behavior.[43]

Our sensitivity to the gaze of others also produces less salutary consequences, though these too may be turned to the good. Smith explains that we naturally sympathize "more entirely with joy than with sorrow," and this explains why we "make parade of our riches, and conceal our poverty." Fortunately, "it is chiefly from this regard to the sentiments of mankind, that we pursue riches and avoid poverty," though Smith doubts that vanity-driven gains in material wealth contribute much *directly* to human satisfaction. Happiness, says Smith, does not result from the assiduous calculation of every "saving or gain" or the passion for acquiring some object as for the maximizers of the *Principles* textbook, since such objects are "in the highest degree contemptible and trifling."[44] Here, Smith opens a gap between material progress and human happiness that today's theorists of *oikonomia* rule out.

Smith closes this gap somewhat where he recommends general rules of moderate behavior—the modulation and refinement of appetites and vanity with the virtue of "self-command."[45] Instead of giving free rein to the passion for gain, Smith recommends "the steadiness" of "industry and frugality."[46] Yet, Smith finds human beings less consistently capable of rational pursuit of well-being than his self-proclaimed descendants presume.[47] Just as in Leibniz, creation puts these weaknesses of the flesh to good use. For Smith, though "the desire of bettering our condition" that "comes with us from the womb" may be "violent and difficult to restrain," resulting in a kind of "profligacy," nature gradually guides enough individuals to more "calm and dispassionate" desires, prompting them "to save and accumulate" to the benefit of society as a whole.[48]

Via these "means most vulgar" and "obvious," Smith claims that frugality comes to "predominate very greatly" in human behavior, so that these individual acts of prudent self-seeking produce "the natural progress of opulence"[49] and corresponding changes (generally, improvements) in institutions, laws, and manners.[50] Though individual acts may not be especially virtuous or prudent, *oikonomia* is given a universal history that serves as "a repository of exemplars, for good or for evil."[51]

Smith's theodicy seems to tie things up—mostly. Despite human frailties and moral failings, nature works towards the good. What appears as human vice may, on closer consideration, appear as a kind of virtue. And where virtue fails, the natural order rescues humanity by educing social good from individual vice, including a redemptive outcome of material progress.

Yet doubts about the benefits of material progress for individuals lurk deeply in Smith's work, found particularly in *Theory of Moral Sentiments*, where he resorts to what we might read as parables. The first parable begins with the "unfeeling landlord," who imagines that he can consume the entire harvest from his fields without regard to the needs of others. Since his direct consumption is limited by the size of his stomach, he turns his produce into high living and "baubles and trinkets." In the process, "he is obliged to distribute" much of his produce to those who provide him services or goods, securing "that share of the necessaries of life, which they would in vain have expected from his humanity and his justice." Smith immediately invokes the invisible hand. The "natural selfishness and rapacity," of the rich, "though they mean only . . . the gratification of their own vain and insatiable desires, are led by an invisible hand" to "divide with the poor the produce of all their improvements."[52]

While the landlord is gratifying only "vain" and "insatiable" desires, the common people's happiness is even less certain. Smith underscores his doubts about the materialist's path to happiness with his parable of the "poor man's son, whom heaven in its anger has visited with ambition." His admiration for the rich leads him to despise his own condition and imagine the happiness of possessing all the accouterments of wealth. In pursuit of "superior rank," he subjects himself to "more fatigue of the body and more uneasiness of the mind than he could have suffered through the whole of his life from want of" such conveniences. In order to bring his talents forward, "he makes his court to all mankind; he serves those whom he hates, and is obsequious to those whom he despises." Smith's punch-line is dramatic: "Through the whole of his life he pursues the idea of a certain artificial and elegant repose which he may never arrive at, for which he sacrifices a real tranquility that is at all time in his power." [53]

But all is not lost. Though often futile for individuals, great effort in the pursuit of wealth and power is not wasted by nature. Because the "pleasures of wealth and greatness," however wrongly, "strike the imagination as something grand and beautiful and noble," we are led to much "toil and anxiety" in their pursuit. "And," Smith assures us, "it is well that nature imposes upon us in this manner," a "deception which rouses and keeps in continual motion the industry of mankind." Without this deception, man would not have cultivated or built, founded cities and countries, or developed arts and sciences, all of "which have entirely changed the whole face of the globe." [54] But Smith cannot assure us that the unintended social good will produce the happiness of each individual; indeed, nature builds on misalignment of individual and social good.

Perhaps such moral costs must be borne by many. Smith remains "haunted" by such "moral shortcomings in commercial society," despite general confidence in the natural machine.[55] Though he usually works to sustain the Providentialist narrative, he explicitly departs from this dominant theme when he discusses justice and the division of labor, invoking the *visible hand* of the state—the power of government to intervene and restore harmony in the national *oikonomia.*

As we saw above, Smith promises that spending by the rich will provide the poor with an adequate share. Smith holds commercial society to this standard where, he admits, we find "indigence": "Wherever there is great property, there is great inequality. For one very rich man, there must be at least five hundred poor, and the affluence of the few supposes the indigence of the many."[56] Smith knows well that indigence creates "misery and distress" for those who fall below the level of social respectability.[57] Though admittedly a social failure and a danger to social order, Smith observes that humans possess a natural "disposition to admire, and almost to worship, the rich and the powerful," so that nature turns great inequality to partial advantage as the *very basis of* social stability and justice.[58] As he puts it, "Nature has wisely judged that the distinction of ranks, the peace and order of society, would rest more securely upon the plain and palpable difference of birth and fortune, than upon the invisible and often uncertain difference of wisdom and virtue." Since the "great mob of mankind" can easily identify wealth but lacks the capacity to discern virtue and wisdom, the undue deference shown to wealth and power appears as part of "the benevolent wisdom of nature."[59]

Despite this natural softening of potential class resentment and violence, Smith cannot trust the preservation of social order simply to the sentiments of humankind and calls for active administration of *oikomonia*. The "central task of civil government" is to hinder us "from hurting our neighbor,"[60] or, in striking comments in his *Lectures on Jurisprudence*, Smith argues that, where there is great inequality, "it is necessary that the arm of authority . . . [make] permanent laws or regulations" to secure "the property of the rich from the inroads of the poor, who would otherwise continually make incroachments upon it." And the punch-line: "Laws and government may be considered in this and every case as a combination of the rich to oppress the poor."[61] Less than fully self-correcting, natural order requires the visible hand of sovereign power.

The division of labor offers an additional and telling example. In *Wealth of Nations*, Smith delivers a startling and famous condemnation of commercial society. With an extensive division of labor, most individuals lose the opportunity to "exert [ ] understanding, . . . generally becom[ing] as stupid and ignorant as it is possible for a human creature to become." Working men become "incapable of relishing or bearing a part of any rational conversation" or "of conceiving any generous, noble, or tender sentiment, and consequently of forming any just judgment concerning many even of the ordinary duties of private life," and even less capable of considering "the great and extensive interests of his country."[62] From this, it is hard to discern what advantages a commercial society has for common people. The sober consequence is that, "in every improved and civilized society this is the state into which the laboring poor, that is, the great body of the people, must necessarily fall."[63]

So worried is Smith that he calls upon the state to provide public education and diversions. If the state does not provide such counter-measures, warns Smith, "all the nobler parts of the human character may be, in a great measure, obliterated and extinguished in the great body of the people."[64] In stark contrast to his quietist sensibilities born of a trust in the ultimate goodness of the automatic tendencies of a system of natural liberty, Smith advocates government intervention lest commercial society destroy the very thing it advances—ennobling and civilizing wealth. Complacency in the face of Providence gives way to intended and urgent social reform.

Finally, and at his worst, Smith seemingly ignores the deep failings of market society that his careful analysis brings to the surface. I read his practice as a form of disavowal of elements at once necessary to *and* incompatible with the goodness of natural order—as evidence of the necessary incompleteness of a symbolic order that theodicy attempts to redeem. In the usual pattern, Smith begins by embracing the division of labor as a natural mechanism that matches the varied goods produced to the individuals who need them, particularly the workman who achieves the steady assistance of others via a set of bargains, where he offers an equivalent in exchange.[65]

However, when he examines the allocation of the country's revenues in more detail, he shows that, in fact, some must die in order to secure the function of *oikonomia* because they cannot offer an equivalent in exchange. Smith recognizes, like Marx, that the amount of the total produce the workers receive "depends every where upon the contract made between those two parties, whose interests are by no means the same."[66] Bargains are ordinarily struck to the disadvantage of the laborers, who, as Smith recognizes, are more easily compelled since they are unable to provide their own subsistence.[67] Smith assures us that this is the "ordinary" condition: masters combine to keep wages at their minimum level—the cost of labor or subsistence—or even "to sink the wages of labour below this rate." Workmen respond, as Smith says, "with the folly and extravagance of desperate men, who must either starve, or frighten their masters into an immediate compliance with their demands." Fortunately, "the civil magistrate" puts this "most shocking violence and outrage" to rest.[68]

Lest we become anxious that society might fall into this kind of disorder, Smith comforts us with the thought that the great machine of nature offers an automatic solution, assuring that wages stay near the natural (subsistence) level. Smith's account involves population dynamics, or a "necro-economics," in which, as Montag bluntly puts it, "life itself" is rationed.[69] Vibrant growth seems to keep the demand for labor high, pushing wages above subsistence for some time, until the higher wages encourage higher fertility and an increase in the supply of workmen.[70] But where the economy stagnates or owners exercise their clout, the wages of labor are "sunk" below the amount required to support a family. Where wages fall, fewer children survive until adulthood, thereby decreasing the supply of labor and forcing wages back to subsistence,[71] "an equilibrium or harmony productive of life that is paradoxically created and maintained by the power of the negative, of death."[72] In this respect, people are no different than other commodities: "It is in that manner that the demand for men, like that for any other commodity, necessarily regulates the production of men; quickens it when it goes too slowly, and stops it when it advances too fast."[73] But this "intricate harmony" appears, and here Montag invokes Leibniz, "as a kind of austere and awful beauty, a self-regulating system, not the ideal perhaps, but the best of all possible systems."[74]

Smith is less frank about the "necro-economics" of corn duties, resorting to what Montag calls "a gesture of theoretical/historical denial."[75] Smith defends free markets in the face of calls for government intervention in staples, such as subsidizing grain prices or restricting exports when grain prices increase. Grain traders, not the government, are the heroes of Smith's story, because they assure "that the daily, weekly, and monthly consumption, should be proportioned as exactly as possible to the supply of the season." If traders raise prices too high, consumption will drop, leaving them with excess supplies of a commodity that will drive prices down further when the new crop arrives. If they set prices too low, hungry people will consume at a level that exhausts supplies before the next crop comes in.[76] The market effects a "disciplining of the hungry" that, Smith asserts, will preserve grain supplies throughout lean seasons, vindicating the natural operation of *oikonomia*.[77]

Smith uses an analogy of trader and ship captain, who rations provisions on board when they run short, to illustrate this harmonious working of the market. It is worth quoting Smith at length:

> Without intending the interest of the people, [the trader] is necessarily led, by a regard to his own interest, to treat them, even in years of scarcity, pretty much in the same manner as the prudent master of a vessel is sometimes obliged to treat his crew. When he foresees that provisions are likely to run short, he puts them upon short allowance. . . [,] yet all the inconveniences of which his crew can thereby suffer are

> inconsiderable, in comparison of the danger, misery, and ruin, to which they might sometimes be exposed by a less provident conduct. Though from excess of avarice, in the same manner, the inland corn merchant should sometimes raise the price of his corn somewhat higher than the scarcity of the season requires, yet all the inconveniences which the people can suffer from this conduct, which effectually secures them from a famine in the end of the season, are inconsiderable, in comparison of what they might have been exposed to by a more liberal way of dealing in the beginning of it. [78]

But Smith's analogy radically misleads, because it misses effective buying power. The ship captain rations to each seaman equally (or perhaps according to rank); seamen do not depend for their provisions on their effective demand. The market, by contrast, rations provisions according to ability to pay; some can afford higher prices and maintain something like normal consumption levels. Others are forced to consume less and less, or even forced out of the market altogether to glean, or eat next year's seeds, or dig barely edible roots. The price mechanism of a free market may well assure that grain supplies last a season, but does not assure that the masses of hungry people survive the season. Studies of famine confirm that people starve not because improper price signals have emptied the local or international markets of grain, but because they are poor and priced out of the market and have no political clout to alter government policies.[79] The integrity of the market may be preserved, but many individuals are sacrificed to its "austere and awful beauty," and Smith's theodicy works only because attendant social evils—the rationing of life and death by the market—are barely acknowledged.

IPE: a theology of harmony and denial

Contemporary neoclassical economists appeal, often by name, to something like Smith's invisible hand. They begin with self-regarding individuals—"all motivated to seek the highest level of satisfaction of [ ] wants . . . available to [them]"—and the assumption that individuals can readily compare "competing goods to satisfy (if to different degrees) the same desire," because "acts of consumption of different goods all provide a common result: the satisfaction or utility of the consumer."[80] The market provides the space where bargains are struck and these "voluntary transactions between individuals enhance their well-being." And "[g]iven an initial endowment . . ., voluntary transactions will take place among individuals to the extent that they improve the well-being of each individual and will, thereby, improve the well-being of the group." It is in this Pareto-optimal sense alone that neoclassical economists can speak of the "welfare of the . . . whole."[81] This account of a self-adjusting and mutually beneficial natural mechanism suggests the continuing Providential or idealistic faith element in their thinking.

This is a tight system, appearing closer to Leibniz's optimal world than Smith's more complicated assessment of natural order. Even where we, like Smith, may be tempted to speak of social suffering or evils or moral loss, it is difficult to do so in the neoclassical *oikonomia*. In neoclassical economics strictly understood, there are no needs—only preferences, or perhaps desires. By maximizing one's gains through voluntary exchange, each individual achieves as much of that mysterious substance "utility" as is possible given their initial endowments and society's supply curve. Having one's *insatiable desires* only partly fulfilled is the human condition; it does not entail existential loss even for those with few resources. There can be no morally meaningful loss—by definition. Smith would insist, by contrast, that deprivation of *needs* due to uneven bargaining power entails suffering or loss, being denied something necessary to one's humanity or one's flourishing as a physical *and* social being. And though Smith generally minimizes concerns about inequality, he does recognize the psychological costs to those who fall below a standard of reputability. Such costs associated with invidious comparison are difficult to speak about if, as for today's economists, an individual's relative position in enduring social relations *cannot* be at stake where exchange is modeled in a timeless space among socially unmarked individuals. At most, the individual's social position can be treated as a unit trait, exogenous to the economic model, but not produced by the operations of economic processes themselves. In short, economists want Smith's invisible hand theodicy, but they foreclose the complexities and moral evaluation central to it.

IPE, at least in its rationalist variants, embraces similar formulations, including the theodicy of the invisible hand, rendered without Smith's complications.[82] As Krasner explains, the "market" serves as "a powerful metaphor for many arguments . . . in international relations." The assumption of a "world of atomized, self-seeking egoistic individuals" (perhaps states) drives claims that international institutions "derive from voluntary agreements among juridically equal actors."[83] A "long term harmony of interests" results, because, as Gilpin describes the view, "trade and economic interdependence are a source of peaceful relations among nations."[84] Deborah Boucoyannis puts a fine pint on it: the IPE "[u]tilitarians are the real radicals" in the discipline. By assuming that "all preferences have a common denominator," individual rationality, and that "a bargaining space always exists, within which solutions can be found to reconcile initially competing demands, we can imagine a world in which harmony is possible." More precisely:

> [t]he concept of an indifference curve—whereby one good can be substituted for another—represents the measurable expression of this idea (with the important substitution of measurable preferences for utility). These principles lead to the expectation, if not of a harmony of interests, at least of a possible bargain. [85]

The global political economy appears as harmonious: an outcome of bargaining that disadvantages some relative to others, in that they may find their preferences or demands less well fulfilled, but without any real moral loss.

This intellectual edifice also makes possible a dynamic account of harmony unfolding in time. For liberal IPE, a minimally governed, market-like space of international relations provides "incentives for cooperation," including attempts by egoistic units to overcome "market failures,"[86] which, for Keohane, comprises the central dynamic of institutional creation and change.[87] As Caporaso notes, any adequate account of institutional evolution must attend to asymmetrical "bargaining or relative capabilities" beyond the presumed formal equality of actors in market models, yet the global *oikonomia* retains a harmonious character, since "progressive institutions [that] could benefit society as a whole" depend on "privileged groups" which, benefitting the most, commit their superior resources to such regimes.[88] Without such action by privileged groups, bargaining processes fall far short of Pareto-optimality, where the whole gains without loss to any actor. For example, Caporaso identifies the creation of rules governing property rights and exchange as key to promoting optimal market performance by gradually reducing uncertainties and transaction costs.[89]

Any convincing version of this theory, Caporaso explains, adopts an evolutionary perspective that assumes institutions and structures are "adaptive outcomes" produced by "selection pressure" that lead over time to a "fit between individual and institutional environment."[90] Here, institutions are treated as "functional" or "adaptive (efficient)," where the "idea of efficiency . . . provides the central mechanism by which economic history acquires its direction" or eschatology: a propulsion to progress. "Without such a dynamic," Caporaso stresses, "history would amount to a series of hapless founderings, with no resultant goal or directional drift."[91]

Though IPE scholars might protest their ethical neutrality and eschew any teleological implication of their thinking, we find Keohane and Nye describing regime analysis in progressive terms as a "theory of learning,"[92] and, as we have seen above, identifying a functionalist evolutionary logic in their account of demand-driven regime change. Similarly, after assuring us that consistent liberals eschew teleology, Moravscik works to demonstrate that "taking preferences seriously" allows us to model the micro-foundations of institutional change as an evolutionary process, embracing Kant's Enlightenment dialectic alongside contemporary theorizations of democratic peace.[93] Finally, in a broad assessment of liberal political economic theory, Keohane assesses its strengths as "a belief in the possibility of ameliorative change facilitated by multilateral arrangements," its emphasis, as in Smith, on "the moral value of prudence" and "holding out the prospect that we can affect, if not control, our fate," encouraging "both better theory and improved practice."[94]

Yet, Caporaso warns, claims about a progressive or ameliorative directional drift identified by IPE may favor group survival, but IPE often ignores the costs to individuals.[95] Consistent with Smith, there may be species or societal advance accompanying institutional change, but no claim of Pareto-optimality need follow, since some individuals adapt successfully and others don't. Here, Caporaso seems as clear-eyed as Smith about the implications of competitive processes. It is not only institutions that are competitively winnowed: some individual and groups suffer and die from their maladaption. Yet the language of suboptimality hardly seems to capture the problem when markets or market-like processes ration life and death.

Thinking with Smith's theodicy gets us a bit further. Like Newton, from whom he draws inspiration, Smith can be placed in a potent tradition of "scientific natural theology" in which identifying creation's "lawful regularities" is taken to reveal God's purposes. Apparent irregularities found in the world require somewhat different treatment; they may reveal some hidden purpose or they might require redress by God's active intervention.[96] Thus, for Smith, the harmonies of the invisible hand coexist with forms of suffering that necessitate the visible governing *oikonomia*. In IPE, by contrast, such suffering seems necessary to social order, but made difficult to see in the parsimonious models with their indifference curves that assure us optimal, or at least good, outcomes without moral loss. Though Smith himself often can't face fully the suffering essential to natural order, something difficult for all of us who have benefitted from the material wealth produced by modern capitalism, his openness to acknowledging moral loss should shame a modern economist or political economist, for whom denial seems a professional imperative. To his credit, Smith reveals that markets ration life and death, not only greater and lesser utilities, a hard truth that economists deflect and we must face. And, instead of offering us a valueless universe that resists facing these issues, Smith forestalls the moral flattening that neoclassical economists perform, even where he works to turn vice into virtuous social outcomes. We might do well to return to Smith to restore some heart to the heartless imaginings of liberal IPE.

Notes

1 Carl L. Becker, *The Heavenly City of the Eighteenth-Century Philosophers* (New Haven and London: Yale University Press, 1932), 123–126.

2 Ernst Cassirer, *The Philosophy of the Enlightenment* (Princeton, NJ: Princeton University Press, 1951), 143–148.

3 Susan Nieman, *Evil in Modern Thought: An Alternative History of Philosophy* (Princeton, NJ: Princeton University Press, 2002), 4.

4 Adam Smith, *The Theory of Moral Sentiments*, ed. D. D. Raphael and A. L. Macfie (Indianapolis, IN: Liberty Fund, 1976), 208.

5 Carl Schmitt, *Political Theology: Four Chapters on the Concept of Sovereignty*, trans. George Schwab (Cambridge, MA: MIT Press, 1985), 36.
6 Giorgio Agamben, *The Kingdom and the Glory: For a Theological Genealogy of Economy and Government* (Stanford: Stanford University Press, 2011), 3, 17–23.
7 Ibid., 88–93, 111–114, 140.
8 Ibid., 1, 283–284.
9 Benjamin J. Cohen, "Are IPE Journals Becoming Boring?" *International Studies Quarterly*, 54 (2010): 887–891.
10 Deborah Boucayannis, "The International Wanderings of a Liberal Idea, or Why Liberals Can Learn to Stop Worrying and Love the Balance of Power," *Perspectives on Politics*, 5, no. 4 (2007): 709.
11 Genesis 1:31.
12 David Ray Griffin, *God, Power, and Evil: A Process Theodicy* (Philadelphia: Westminster, 1976).
13 Freiherr von Gottfried Wilhelm Leibniz, *Theodicy* (Bibliobazaar.com., 2007). Also see Donald Rutherford, *Leibniz and the Rational Order of Nature* (Cambridge: Cambridge University Press, 1995), 18.
14 Leibniz, *Theodicy*, 63.
15 Ibid.,139, 144–146, 161.
16 Ibid., 218–219, 306. See also Griffin, *God, Power, and Evil*, 57–59.
17 Griffin, *God, Power, and Evil*, 60–66.
18 Slavoj Žižek, "The Spectre of Ideology," in *Mapping Ideology*, ed. Slavoj Žižek (New York: Verso, 1994), 21.
19 Rutherford, *Rational Order*, 13–14.
20 Leibniz, *Theodicy*, 168.
21 Ibid., 160, 261, 344–345.
22 Nicholas Rescher, *Leibniz: An Introduction to His Philosophy* (Totowa, NJ: Rowman and Littlefield, 1979), 39–40.
23 Leibniz, *Theodicy*, 204.
24 David Blumenfeld, "Perfection and Happiness in the Best Possible World," in *The Cambridge Companion to Augustine*, eds. Elenore Stump and Norman Kretzmann (Cambridge: Cambridge University Press, 1995), 383, 394.
25 Ibid., 398–399. See also Leibniz, *Theodicy*, 192.
26 Terrence W. Tilley, *The Evils of Theodicy* (Eugene, OR: Wipf and Stock, 2000), 125–130, and Griffin, *God, Power, and Evil*, 70–71.
27 Leibniz, *Theodicy*, 140, 166.
28 Blumenfeld, "Perfection and Happiness," 404–405.
29 Douglas G. Long, "Science and Secularization in Hume, Smith and Bentham," in *Religion, Secularization, and Political Thought*, ed. James E. Crimmins (New York and London: Routledge, 1989); Brendan Long, "Adam Smith's Theodicy," in *Adam Smith as Theologian*, ed. Paul Oslington (New York: Routledge, 2011), 98–105, 129–131; Ingrid A. Merikoski, "The Challenge of Material Progress: The Scottish Enlightenment and Christian Stoicism," *The Journal of the Historical Society* II, no. 1 (2002), 55–76; and Paul Oslington, "Introduction: Theological Readings of Smith," *Adam Smith as Theologian*, ed. Paul Oslington (New York: Routledge, 2011), 3–5.
30 Peter Harrison, "Adam Smith, Natural Theology, and the Natural Sciences," in *Adam Smith as Theologian*, ed. Peter Oslington (New York: Routledge, 2011), 77.
31 Jerry Evensky, "Adam Smith's Moral Philosophy: The Role of Religion and its Relations to Philosophy and Ethics in the Evolution of Society," *History of Political Economy*, 30, no. 1 (1998): 18.
32 Lisa Hill, "The Hidden Theology of Adam Smith," *European Journal of the History of Economic Thought*, 8, no. 1 (Spring 2001): 1.
33 Donald Winch, *Riches and Poverty: An Intellectual History of Political Economy in Britain, 1750–1834* (Cambridge: Cambridge University Press, 1996), 64.
34 Tilley, *The Evils of Theodicy*, 231–234.
35 Adam Smith, *The Theory of Moral Sentiment*, ed. D. D. Raphael and A. L. Macfie (Indianapolis, IN: Liberty Classics, 1976), 36.
36 Ibid., 253.
37 Ibid., 78.
38 Ibid.
39 Ibid., 36; see also Charles L. Griswold, *Adam Smith and the Virtues of Enlightenment* (Cambridge: Cambridge University Press, 1999), 7–20.

40 Adam Smith, *An Inquiry into the Nature and Causes of the Wealth of Nations*, ed. Edwin Cannan (Chicago, IL: University of Chicago, 1976), I, 477–478.
41 Smith, *Theory of Moral Sentiments*, 9.
42 Ibid., 16, 20, 22–26, 129–130.
43 Ibid., 22, 26, 120–130.
44 Ibid., 172–173, 183.
45 Ibid., 28–29.
46 Ibid., 215.
47 Smith, *Wealth of Nations*, i. 17, ii, 324–325.
48 Ibid., ii, 362–363.
49 Ibid., i, 400.
50 Christopher Berry, *Social Theory of the Scottish Enlightenment* (Edinburgh: University of Edinburgh Press, 1997), 93–99, 180–181.
51 Knud Haakonssen, *Natural Law and Moral Philosophy: From Grotius to the Scottish Enlightenment* (Cambridge: Cambridge University, 1996), 6.
52 Smith, *The Theory of Moral Sentiments*, 184.
53 Ibid., 181.
54 Ibid., 183–184.
55 Richard E. Teichgraeber, *'Free Trade' and Moral Philosophy: Rethinking the Sources of Adam Smith's Wealth of Nations* (Durham, NC: Duke University Press, 1986), 168.
56 Smith, *Wealth of Nations*, ii, 232.
57 Smith, *The Theory of Moral Sentiments*, 50–51.
58 Ibid., 50, 61.
59 Ibid., 226.
60 Ibid., 80–81.
61 Adam Smith, *Lectures on Jurisprudence*, ed. R. L. Meek, D. D. Raphael, and P. G. Stein (Indianapolis, IN: Liberty Fund, 1978), 208.
62 Smith, *Wealth of Nations*, ii, 302–303.
63 Ibid., ii, 303–304.
64 Ibid., ii, 303.
65 Ibid., i, 15, 18.
66 Ibid., i, 73–74.
67 Ibid., i, 74–75.
68 Ibid.,, i, 75.
69 Warren Montag, "Necro-Economics: Adam Smith and Death in the Life of the Universal," *Radical Philosophy*, 134 (2005), 15.
70 Smith, *Wealth of Nations*, i, 76–80.
71 Ibid., i, 88.
72 Montag, "Necro-Economics," 16.
73 Smith, *Wealth of Nations*, i, 89.
74 Montag, "Necro-Economics," 16.
75 Ibid., 15.
76 Smith, *Wealth of Nations*, ii, 30.
77 Montag, "Necro-Economics," 15.
78 Smith, *Wealth of Nations*, ii, 31.
79 Amartya Sen, *Poverty and Famine: An Essay on Entitlement and Deprivation* (Oxford: Oxford University Press, 1981).
80 James A. Caporaso and David P. Levine, *Theories of Political Economy* (Cambridge: Cambridge University Press, 1991), 80.
81 Ibid., 83.
82 Benjamin J. Cohen, *International Political Economy: An Intellectual History* (Princeton, NJ: Princeton University, 2008), 17–20.
83 Stephen D. Krasner, "Structural Causes and Regime Consequences: Regimes as Intervening Variables," in *International Regimes*, ed. Stephen D. Krasner (Ithaca, NY: Cornell University Press, 1983), 6–7, 11.
84 Robert Gilpin, *The Political Economy of International Relations* (Princeton, NJ: Princeton University Press, 1987), 30–31.
85 Boucayannis, "The International Wanderings of a Liberal Idea," 709.

86 Krasner, "Structural Causes and Regime Consequences," 11.
87 Robert O. Keohane, *International Institutions and State Power: Essays in International Relations Theory* (Boulder, CO: Westview, 1989), 108–110.
88 James A. Caporaso, "Microeconomics and International Political Economy: The Neoclassical Approach to Institutions," in *Global Changes and Theoretical Challenges: Approaches to World Politics for the 1990s*, ed. Ernst-Otto Czempiel and James M. Rosenau (New York: Macmillan, 1989), 147, 150–151.
89 Ibid., 144–146.
90 Ibid.
91 Ibid., 150–152.
92 Robert O. Keohane and Joseph S. Nye, *Power and Interdependence*, 2nd edn. (New York: HarperCollins, 1989), 267.
93 Andrew Moravcsik, "Taking Preferences Seriously: A Liberal Theory of International Relations," *International Organization*, 51, no. 2 (1997): 513–553, 521, 530, 543–548.
94 Robert O. Keohane, "International Liberalism Reconsidered," in *The Economic Limits to Politics*, ed. John Dunn (Cambridge: Cambridge University Press, 1990), 194.
95 Caporaso, "Microeconomics," 152–155.
96 Harrison, "Natural Theology," 85–86.

Bibliography

Agamben, Giorgio, *The Kingdom and the Glory: For a Theological Genealogy of Economy and Government* (Stanford: Stanford University Press, 2011).

Becker, Carl L., *The Heavenly City of the Eighteenth-Century Philosophers* (New Haven and London: Yale University Press, 1932).

Berry, Christopher, *Social Theory of the Scottish Enlightenment* (Edinburgh: University of Edinburgh Press, 1997).

Blumenfeld, David, "Perfection and Happiness in the Best Possible World," in Elenore Stump and Normal Kretzmann (eds.), *The Cambridge Companion to Augustine* (Cambridge: Cambridge University Press, 1995), 382–410.

Boucayannis, Deborah, "The International Wanderings of a Liberal Idea, or Why Liberals Can Learn to Stop Worrying and Love the Balance of Power," *Perspectives on Politics*, 5, no. 4 (2007): 703–727.

Caporaso, James A., "Microeconomics and International Political Economy: The Neoclassical Approach to Institutions," in Ernst-Otto Czempiel and James M. Rosenau (eds.), *Global Changes and Theoretical Challenges: Approaches to World Politics for the 1990s* (New York: Macmillan, 1989), 135–160.

Caporaso, James A., and David P. Levine, *Theories of Political Economy* (Cambridge: Cambridge University Press, 1992).

Cassirer, Ernst, *The Philosophy of the Enlightenment* (Boston, MA: Beacon Press, 1955).

Cohen, Benjamin J., "Are IPE Journals Becoming Boring?" *International Studies Quarterly*, 54 (2010): 887–891.

Evensky, Jerry, "Adam Smith's Moral Philosophy: The Role of Religion and Its Relations to Philosophy and Ethics in the Evolution of Society," *History of Political Economy*, 30, no. 1 (1998): 17–42.

Gilpin, Robert, *The Political Economy of International Relations* (Princeton, NJ: Princeton University Press, 1987).

Griffin, David Ray, *God, Power, and Evil: A Process Theodicy* (Philadelphia, PA: Westminster Press, 1976).

Griswold, Charles L., *Adam Smith and the Virtues of Enlightenment* (Cambridge: Cambridge University Press, 1999).

Haakonssen, Knud, *Natural Law and Moral Philosophy: From Grotius to the Scottish Enlightenment* (Cambridge: Cambridge University Press, 1996).

Harrison, Peter, "Adam Smith, Natural Theology, and the Natural Sciences," in Peter Oslington (ed.), *Adam Smith as Theologian* (New York: Routledge, 2011), 77–91.

Hill, Lisa, "The Hidden Theology of Adam Smith," *European Journal of the History of Economic Thought*, 8, no. 1 (2001): 1–29.

Keohane, Robert O., "International Liberalism Reconsidered," in John Dunn (ed.), *The Economic Limits to Politics* (Cambridge: Cambridge University, 1990), 165–194.

Keohane, Robert O., *International Institutions and State Power: Essays in International Relations Theory* (Boulder, CO: Westview, 1989).

Keohane, Robert O. and Joseph S. Nye, *Power and Interdependence*, 2nd edn. (New York: HarperCollins, 1989).

Krasner, Stephen D., "Structural Causes and Regime Consequences: Regimes as Intervening Variables," in Stephen D. Krasner (ed.), *International Regimes* (Ithaca, NY: Cornell University Press, 1983), 1–21.

Leibniz, Freiherr von Gottfried Wilhelm, *Theodicy* (Bibliobazaar.com., 2007).

Long, Brendan, "Adam Smith's Theodicy," in Paul Oslington (ed.), *Adam Smith as Theologian* (New York: Routledge, 2011), 98–105.

Long, Douglas G., "Science and Secularization in Hume, Smith and Bentham," in James E. Crimmins (ed.), *Religion, Secularlization and Political Thought: Thomas Hobbes to J. S. Mill* (New York and London: Routledge, 19891), 90–110.

Merikoski, Ingrid A., "The Challenge of Material Progress: The Scottish Enlightenment and Christian Stoicism," *The Journal of the Historical Society* II, no. 1 (2002): 55–76.

Montag, Warren, "Necro-Economics: Adam Smith and Death in the Life of the Universal," *Radical Philosophy*, 134 (2005): 7–17.

Moravcsik, Andrew, "Taking Preferences Seriously: A Liberal Theory of International Relations," *International Organization*, 51, no. 4 (1997): 513–553.

Nieman, Susan, *Evil in Modern Thought: An Alternative History of Philosophy* (Princeton, NJ: Princeton University Press, 2002).

Oslington, Paul, "Introduction: Theological Readings of Smith," in Paul Oslington (ed.), *Adam Smith as Theologian* (New York: Routledge, 2011), 1–16.

Rescher, Nicholas, *Leibniz: An Introduction to His Philosophy* (Totowa, NJ: Rowman and Littlefield, 1979).

Rutherford, Donald, *Leibniz and the Rational Order of Nature* (Cambridge: Cambridge University Press, 1995).

Schmitt, Carl, *Political Theology: Four Chapters on the Concept of Sovereignty*, trans. George Schwab (Cambridge, MA: MIT Press, 1985).

Sen, Amartya, *Poverty and Famine: An Essay on Entitlement and Deprivation.* Oxford: Oxford University Press, 1981.

Smith, Adam, *An Inquiry into the Nature and Causes of the Wealth of Nations*, ed. Edwin Cannan (Chicago and London: University of Chicago Press, 1976).

Smith, Adam, *The Theory of Moral Sentiments*, ed. D. D. Raphael and A. L. Macfie (Indianpolis, IN: Liberty Fund, 1976).

Smith, Adam, *Lectures on Jurisprudence*, ed. R. L. Meek, D. D. Raphael, and P. G. Stein (Indianapolis, IN: Liberty Fund, 1978).

Teichgraeber, III, Richard E., *'Free Trade' and Moral Philosophy: Rethinking the Sources of Adam Smith's Wealth of Nations* (Durham, NC: Duke University Press, 1986).

Tilley, Terrence W., *The Evils of Theodicy* (Eugene, OR: Wipf and Stock, 2000).

Winch, Donald, *Riches and Poverty: An Intellectual History of Political Economy in Britain, 1750–1834* (Cambridge: Cambridge University Press, 1986).

Žižek, Slavoj, "The Spectre of Ideology," in Slavoj Žižek (ed.), *Mapping Ideology* (New York: Verso, 1994), 1–33.

34

RELIGION, EMOTIONS AND CONFLICT ESCALATION

Mona Kanwal Sheikh

Introduction

The contemporary interest in studying *religion* in international relations (IR) is particularly important, because it can offer insight into the exact characteristics that led to its exclusion from IR in the first place. These characteristics are its appeal to what most people instinctively would describe as the 'irrational', more specifically to emotions, and their ability to infuse a high degree of passion and devotion into a political cause. This chapter deals with the relationships between religion, emotions and conflict escalation. I show that *collective emotions* are interlinked with cognitive processes and representational practices in which religious ethics, or conceptions of right and wrong, good and evil, play a role. Collective emotions – sometimes also referred to as higher-order, cognitive or moral emotions – are of particular value for understanding justificatory practices embraced by violent religious movements and the dynamics of conflict escalation.

Dealing with religious affection and the concept of emotion appears to be a methodological challenge for a field like IR, where concepts such as interest and rational choice have been central to explaining the dynamics of international relations. As Hutchison and Bleiker put it, emotions have been taken for granted and 'seen as a phenomena that rational policy makers deal with or react against', which points to the difficulties for the field of IR to access emotions.[1] Perhaps one of the explanations for this void is the foundational assumption that emotions refer to abstract inner states, and that they are isolated from more relevant behaviors that have a 'rational' explanation. Even the allegedly 'softer' side of IR, which addresses the construction and impact of ideas and culture, has not dealt explicitly with the emotive dimensions of politics and violence.

This chapter challenges the assumption that emotions belong unambiguously to an irrational category, in line with some of the recent contributions on collective emotions and IR.[2] In this context, I argue specifically for the significance of considering collective emotions in the analysis of religion and conflict escalation/de-escalation. The point I seek to make by linking religion, emotions and conflict escalation is threefold.

First, I argue that religion is particularly interesting for IR, not only because of its instrumental relevance, or even because of its significance for identity and culture. Based on empirical research on militant religious movements, I assert that aside from fear, moral emotions - strongly held convictions about right and wrong – can guide behavior and have an enormous mobilizing capability.

Second, I illuminate why a focus on what sociological studies have labelled collective emotions (which overlap the ideas of moral, higher order, and cognitive emotions only stressing the social aspect) is relevant for conflict studies in general. This part of the chapter also highlights the link between ethics, which is the thematic focus of this volume, and collective emotions. The argument is that the type of emotions that are often cultivated in conflicts has an ethical frame of reference that requires a higher degree of cognitive processing than other types.

This leads me to the third part of my argument, where I outline how a focus on collective emotions can add to the theory of securitization, and thereby to our understanding of how conflicts escalate or de-escalate. I show that a focus on collective emotions can both add breadth to the theory's conception of the securitizing actor, as well as depth to its conception of the audience. Taken together, such a focus can illuminate the premises on which a successful securitization can take place. This part will also elaborate on why the study of representation can remain the methodological entry point to study the 'emotional climate' of successful securitization.

The X-factor of religion

In spite of the fact that emotions are under-theorized in IR, they still have an implicit role in some of the core ideas and theories of the field. Most notably, fear – one of the emotions that psychologists would describe as basic and instinctive - is a human emotion that is part of the foundation of conflict escalation theories, such as the dynamics driving a security dilemma.[3] Anger, indignation, revenge and resentment of certain actions or values in the literature on conflict are also drawn into the equation, though more sporadically, in order to explain patterns of conflict behavior (Hutchinson and Bleiker 2014).

The classical realism of Hans Morgenthau acknowledged the importance of emotions in international politics and shows that emotions have not been completely marginalized in IR thinking (Ross 2013).[4] Going further back, the political philosophies of Hobbes and Machiavelli, which inspired much of the development in modern IR each emphasized fear and passion as important drivers of the political. Even Aristotle was preoccupied with the persuasive influence of a powerful orator's identification of danger as well as representations of both the subjects and objects of threat. In many of these conceptions the power of emotions becomes an almost invisible hand that can incite the masses and justify policies and political acts, without becoming the center of analytical attention. Hence, on one hand, emotions have gained relatively little notice in modern elaborations of IR theory due to their being viewed as abstract inner states that are not easily observable, while on the other hand, many of the analyses that underpin IR are based on the idea that human beings are driven by emotions such as the lust for power, the fear of losing territory, identity, and status, or the drive for revenge.

My task here is to link these instinctive ideas about the power of emotions to debates about the relevance of studying religion and ethics in IR, and to propose a framework in which we can analyze the dynamics of religion, emotions and conflict. Religion brings into the picture not only 'negative feelings' (anger, resentment, fear etc.), but positive ones as well, such as commitment, passion or affection for particular values or visions of society. One of the paradoxes and characterizing features of religious violence is precisely that there is a strong linkage between positive feelings of commitment and affection to religion and the negative feelings of resentment and anger that can result in violence.[5]

In the growing body of literature on religion and IR it has been argued that one of the main reasons religion was exiled from the social sciences was its conceptualization as something irrational and non-verifiable; as belief and superstition in contrast to science. Like the case of religion, Craig Calhoun has described how emotions fall on the 'wrong' side in a number of dichotomies in western thought, such as body/mind, nature/culture, male/female, public/private (Calhoun 2001).[6] IR, shaped by a dominant enlightenment discourse, placed both religion and emotions on that side of these boundaries, which was regarded as non-scientific and non-rational for decades (Sheikh 2012).[7] These dichotomies, the secular ethos of the field, and the disregard of religion were however strongly questioned after 2001 by scholars of IR, motivated by the fact that religion was suddenly making headlines in news about international politics and terrorism (Philpott 2002).[8] The debate within the field quickly moved from being focused on whether religion matters at all (as more than a strategic instrument or a rhetorical gloss over something 'more real'), to becoming a debate about exactly how religion matters for the field, and the methodological repercussions of including religion *as religion*. The last type of literature on how religion matters has made a convincing case for considering cognitive, cultural, and interpretational aspects of religious thinking and doctrines as motivational forces.[9]

The work of Mark Juergensmeyer, in particular, shows how religious imagery and visions of the just society are part of the political aspirations of violent religious groups.[10] Transgressing the boundaries of religious traditions and sub-traditions, some shared patterns in the justification of violent religious movements include the vision of doing good, creating just societies, fighting a just war, and being wronged by an aggressor. These patterns also apply to the Pakistani Taliban, which I have studied for the past decade. Two observations in particular stand out, with relevance for the topic of religious ethics.

First, like much of the literature on comparative religious violence shows, the Taliban frame their violence in terms of both a defensive battle and a more offensive one, which is about pursuing their vision of the just society in which only the Almighty is given the mandate to define laws. While the fear that religion or Islam will be eradicated is a dominant part of their narrative, so is their affection for religion and particular religious doctrines. The Pakistani Taliban frame themselves as do-gooders who are motivated by their vision of the just society, with a well-functioning justice-infrastructure. They also see themselves as resisting the assault on Islam by the West and its allies, which in this case is the Pakistani government and army. They frame their violence as justified, with many similarities to the western just war discourse in their discussion of issues of proportionality, necessity, intentionality, sufficiency, legitimacy and efficiency (Sheikh 2016).[11] The core proposition of the corpus of just war discourse is the idea that, under the proper conditions, states have moral justification for resorting to armed force. The idea of the 'higher purpose' that justifies violence is in the Taliban's case related to their religious imagery.

The second observation that stands out is the Taliban's reference to a mythic past and apocalyptic future, and the ability of their religious imagery to reinforce the strength of their commitment and motivation. The widespread use of religious imagery and myth adds a transcendental layer to the explanation of jihad and thus also ascribes to it a special spiritual significance. Among the themes I have identified in the constitution of the Taliban jihad is the willingness to sacrifice oneself for religion, which is framed as a specifically pious trait that enhances one's religious standing in the eyes of God (Sheikh, 2016). The willingness to sacrifice oneself for religion, with the particular meaning that legitimizes undertaking a suicide mission, is framed as a sign of devotedness to God. While it is relatively easy to describe the content of the imagery that they draw upon in justifying violence and their apocalyptic vision through an analysis of their narratives and communication materials, the religious experience that is 'felt' or reflected in the imagery, and the effects of the jihadi anthems on the actual mobilization of violence is more difficult to explore using these strategies. It is important to recognize that the emotional mobilization is intimately tied up with the belief and imagery that are cultivated through anthems and legendary myths, which in turn are shared at social gatherings. This religious passion is difficult to capture if one only looks at narratives and framings without considering how they are linked to emotions. This challenge is described by Goodwin et. al, who argue that, that science tends to be the dominant language of legitimation, which makes us overlook the significance of feelings. As they write, regardless of whether a movement defines itself as secular or religious, 'science not feeling is the dominant language of legitimation and persuasion. . . . measurable costs and benefits, atmospheric data. . .work well' (Goodwin et al 2001, 15).[12]

The challenge is that the justificatory narratives and framings that are linked to a particular moral code and ethics (e.g. a particular ethics of just war) are typically approached as purely cognitive phenomena without consideration of the emotional dimensions of mobilization. This tendency has also been dominant in the field of cultural sociology where the attempts to approach the individual through frames, narratives, and discourses have generally been silent about emotions (Goodwin et al 2001, 6). The reason why this void requires attention is that frames, narratives and discourses that avoid including emotions can end up gaining too much explanatory power. In addition, the absence of attention to emotions reinforces the tendency to focus on leaders and their way of framing events or manipulating the masses, leaving out the all-important issue of the social dynamics of the masses and their receptiveness to particular framings.

The emotional or affective dimension that accompanies the framings and discourses of the religious movements is what I call the 'x-factor of religion,' the special thing which makes religion a sui generis phenomenon. Today, some aspects of religion are studied in IR under the rubric of culture, identity, ethics, or organization, without including 'religious' as a qualifying adjective (Sheikh 2012). As I have argued elsewhere, while the field of IR is surely concerned with the functionalist interest in the effects (on peace, war, and order for instance) produced by religious commitments, their ability to affect behavior, legitimacy, and conflict dynamics simultaneously require a better sense of the sui generis aspects of religion, particularly the affective. This requires taking into consideration how different religious traditions interpret, legitimize or condemn acts such as terrorism within the same faith community. Analyzing these interpretations and traditions can point to particular ethical considerations about the common good, including what constitutes a just war, which are concerns at the heart of IR theory. As Lynch (2009) has pointed out, one of the characteristics (or definitions) of religious actors is that they act out of ethical considerations about the common good. This focus on the ethics inherent in different interpretations of religious tradition, however, also requires a similar insight into the collective emotions that lead to actual action on behalf of the ethical stances.

Studying cases of religion and religious violence can add important insights to the study of emotions and conflict. Such cases highlight the fact that it is not only negative emotions such as hatred, fear or humiliation that can lead to conflict, but that 'positive' ones such as religious commitment, affection or love for particular values and figures of authority can reinforce commitments that lead to violence as well. This resembles what Michael Young (2001) describes as 'affective' emotions in his analysis of evangelical Protestants and their view on slavery: the change from embracing slavery as part of a Christian vision to framing it as a sin was possible because it resonated with a broader pattern for affective commitments unique to evangelicals born after the American Revolution. [13]It is worth noting that affective emotions that could also fall under the category of being moral emotions, because they are related to other human beings or visions of society, do not necessarily have what we consider to be a 'morally acceptable' outcome. The wish to see the enemy suffer can be based on a moral emotion, for example, but would not result in a 'moral' act.

Collective emotions and conflict

Having argued that the emotional dimension of religion is one of the essential elements of the x-factor that makes religion particularly interesting to study in its own right, I elaborate here on the questions of why and how emotions can be brought into IR.

Goodwin, Jasper and Polletta, authors of *Passionate Politics* (2001), have shown how emotions are central for social movement theorists who study politics and conflict. This compilation of essays demonstrates that emotions are intimately involved in the processes by which people come to join social movements, emphasizing the cultivation of affective feelings through rituals, songs, heroes, denunciation of enemies and folktales. This recent focus on emotions in sociology, which is also relevant for IR, treats emotions as a crowd-based phenomenon, in contrast to Freudian approaches that deal with emotions as interior to the human psyche. A basic assumption is that a member of a society, group or movement shares collective emotions, not necessarily because of some direct personal experience that is shared with others who have experienced exactly the same thing, but because of identification with the society, group or movement as a collective. Hence, by dealing with emotions as a social rather than individual phenomenon, one acknowledges that all collective identities have an emotional element, which upholds the identification. In line with this notion, Randall Collins describes how pride is a central emotion of strong social bonds.[14] The process of developing a collective emotional orientation can reflect shared norms or common experiences. Aside from being an aspect of collective identity, another reason why a focus on collective emotions is relevant for conflict studies is that the dynamics of the group can amplify or even transform the initial feeling into something stronger. Collective attention to a particular issue can, for example, strengthen feelings of outrage.

One part of the social science literature on collective emotions is focused on the transformation from individual to collective emotions, as if the development of emotions always moves in that direction (e.g., Hutchington and Bleiker 2014, who theorize the processes through which individual emotions become both collective and political). Another part of the literature looks at how social interaction and expectations can shape emotions, also in predictable ways, which challenges the idea that emotions are always instinctive, irrational and undisciplined. For the field of IR, it makes sense to adopt the social perspective on emotions where interaction and not methodological individualism is the starting point. This does not mean that emotions cannot be individual or internal, but rather that the social or moral emotions, those that are responsive to the situation of other human beings, are relevant for the study of the political. One of the assumptions behind studying emotions as a collective/social phenomenon is that affect constitutes social networks and social networks constitute affect. The inside/outside dichotomy between the internal and the social is dissolved.

At the same time, the focus on collective emotions also challenges the idea that there are radical differences between emotions and cognition or emotions and rationality.[15] Instead, some emotions require more cognitive processing than others, since they strongly depend on our understanding of the events around us. In contrast to instinctive emotions, the more processed emotions are less immediate, and this points to a link between framing or discourse analysis and emotions. As Calhoun argues, it is important to bring the relationships between cognition, emotion and perception to the forefront because emotional response, and not cognitive agreement alone, results in action.

The kind of emotions that are particularly relevant for conflict studies and IR are moral emotions like indignation or pride. As Goodwin, Jasper and Polletta (2001, 34) put it:

> Moral outrage over feared practices, the shame of spoiled collective identities or the pride of refurbished ones, the indignation of perceived encroachment on traditional rights, the joy of imagining a new and better society and participating in a movement toward that end – none of these are automatic responses. They are related to moral institutions, felt obligations and rights, and information about expected effects. . .

Here, ethics enters the picture, because moral emotions depend on possessing certain kind of beliefs. The adherents of a movement like the Pakistani Taliban have clear directions to do what they find mandatory for Muslims – to fight what is unjust and defend religion whenever it is attacked. At the same time, they are driven by a particular vision of the just society where, as I was told, 'A woman could walk all the way to Herat [a city in western Afghanistan], and nobody would even dare to look. You could have a briefcase full of dollars, and no one would try to rob you' (Sheikh 2016).

The communication and recruitment materials of the Taliban movement also include information about 'the expected effects' of their violent activism: namely, the transformation of injustices into a just society with no crime or hierarchy among human beings. The study of the framings and discourses of violent religious actors are hence not irrelevant to the study of collective emotions. However, frames and discourses should be deployed to explain why and how the emotions of indignation or outrage, or the passion of religious belief, can be so strong.

Connecting emotions to securitization

The idea of securitization was both a contribution to the conceptual debate on how to understand security among a range of options, but it also developed into a theory about why the survival of some objects gain prominence and calls for extraordinary measures more than others.[16] It can also be applied to conflict theory, since it deals with the escalatory dynamics of speech acts. This section looks at the intersection between collective feelings and the process of securitization and conflict escalation. Religious violence can reflect successful securitization, understood as the process by which a powerful actor (the securitizing actor) manages to convince an audience that some dimension of religion is existentially threatened, and extraordinary means are therefore necessary in order to avert the danger.[17]

Securitization theory is relevant in this context because of its insight that the securitization of particular dimensions of religion (its doctrines, material manifestations or legal dimensions) mobilizes conflict behavior. I have argued elsewhere (Sheikh 2014) that this general dynamic, which is applicable in a variety of contexts, requires sensitivity to the multiple ways that religious communities can be conceptualized, in order to avoid ethno-centric concepts of the 'religious' (and the 'political'). Ethno-centrism should be avoided because it can lead to problematic conclusions about how to de-escalate conflicts with religious dimensions.[18] Similarly, when approaching emotions, it is important to acknowledge that culture, ethics and norms have an impact on emotional expressions.[19]

Securitization theory (ST) has described three elements necessary for securitization: the successful framing of an issue as a security challenge that demands extraordinary measures, a securitizing actor and object that is claimed to be threatened, and an audience that accepts the claim of the securitizing actor. Again, however, these three elements do not sufficiently explain what mobilizes audience actions or makes an act of securitization successful.

I suggest that the emotional climate is also critical to analyze. Emotional climate is a term that can be mounted to securitization analysis as a way of conceptualizing the audience, as it 'refers to the predominant collective emotions generated through the social interaction of a group's members in a particular milieu'.[20] The social sharing of emotional experiences constructs convergence and similarity and reinforces the emotions, as do collective rituals.

Though the founders of securitization theory have chosen to blackbox actors' psyches due to the theory's particular interest in speech acts and their effects, I argue that collective emotions are a major part of the explanation of why a securitization process is successful. This is not a radical challenge to the theory but an elaboration of why securitization can take place. Looking into the dynamics of collective emotions could illuminate what characteristics and abilities the securitizing actor has, and what the requirements for securitization and escalation for the recipients of the discourse of threat might be.

Successful securitization requires that the securitizing actor is able to convince the audience being addressed that the emergency situation requires extraordinary measures and that 'normal' behavior is insufficient to face the threat. For states that are democracies, the audience is the state's population, but for militant movements opposed to the state, the audience comprises co-ideologists and potential recruits. Successful securitization in the latter case – measured by, for example, the mobilization capability of a militant religious movement – reflects the resonance of the framing narrative among the target audience. Consequently, it also reveals something about how deeply rooted is the audience's attachment to the referent object the actor is claiming to defend.

ST has previously been criticized for being too silent about the cultural context in which the audience is situated, instead attributing too much power to the speech-act of security. According to Balzacq, ST usually describes security both as a self-referential process and as an inter-subjective process. He argues that effective securitization remains audience dependent and that successful securitization only occurs when the securitizing agent and the audience reach a common, structured perception or interpretation of an ominous phenomena/the threatening nature of the referent object.[21] This implies that the analysts must take into consideration the psycho-cultural disposition of the audience and the power that both the speaker and listener bring to the interaction, in addition to the discourse of the securitizing actor. The ability of securitizing actors to identify with the audience's feelings, needs and interests or to capture the *Zeitgeist* based on collective memory, social views, trends and ideological and political attitudes is thus important because these elements constitute the cultural context in which the audience is situated. Hence, contextual and non-linguistic factors need to be incorporated, that is, the social field in which the rhetorical game takes place.

In their analysis, Cox and Wood point to the importance of group leadership in the processes through which emotions are collectivized.[22] By having the ability to frame the danger and the appropriate response, Cox and Wood describe the characteristics of a group leader/securitizing actor. However, they add that the group leader also displays an emotion, which can have an effect on observers when they identify with the actor and share the same cultural dispositions. This means that an act of securitization can only be successful if the actor manages to frame the danger and response in a way that is in concordance with the emotional climate in which the audience is situated.

Snow and Benford (1992) focus on the process of mobilization to protest movements, which is also relevant to the study of religious violence. They assert that during recruitment, an organization and potential recruits align their frames, thereby achieving a common definition of a social problem and a common prescription for solving it.[23] Again, similar to securitization theory, they describe how a diagnosis of the situation that needs to be acted on, a prognosis about the appropriate strategy, and the expected output of the action (e.g., the transformation of society, aversion of danger, etc.) are prerequisites for mobilization. But they also add a motivational component, which draws the crowd into the activities that are proposed by the recruiters or securitizing actors. The last element demands a closer inspection into how cognitive meanings, classifications and frames are linked to feelings.

Securitization is a good entry point to study the relationship between collective emotions and conflict escalation because it is focused on representation. In light of the above, representational practices not only create emotional climates, but they are also reflective of emotional climates. Representation is also the process through which emotions become political (see Hutchington and Bleiker 2014, 506).

Concluding remarks: the study of ethics is also a study of emotions

The debate about whether ethics is primarily a matter of reason or emotion is an ancient philosophical one. Increasingly, scholars from various disciplines have embraced the idea that emotions play a role in ethical decision-making, hence also in motivating action. Studies of religious violence show that ethical judgments can often be highly emotional acts, reflected in the fact that militants sometimes express their strong approval or disapproval of various ideas or visions of society through violent means.

This chapter has called for integrating a focus on collective emotions, on one side, and studies of discourses, framings and representational practices, on the other. For instance, fear involves the belief that bad things will occur and that one is not fully in control of warding them off – unless action is taken. Fear is thus both a feeling but also a speech-act that can be studied through a focus on how the fear is represented.

An important implication of conceptualizing emotions as part of the rational/cognitive realm is the idea that changes in the relevant beliefs entail changes in emotion: one who learns that danger is not an 'objective' fact will, for example, cease to fear. This opens the door to thinking about de-escalation through changing cognitive patterns or representational practices. Anthropologists have stressed the role played by social norms in shaping the emotion-categories of different societies. These accounts raise questions about the extent to which an emotional repertoire is malleable; if we see that emotions transform with the learning of social norms and ethical standards, then a fruitful area for conflict studies could be to look for ways to transform the emotional climate that enables securitization to occur and conflicts to escalate.

Notes

1 Emma Hutchinson and Roland Bleiker, 'Theorizing Emotion in World Politics', *International Theory*, 6:3 (2014), 491–514.

2 E.g., Jonathon Mercer, 'Feeling Like a State: Social Emotion and Identity', *International Theory*, 6:3 (2014), 515–535; Ty Solomon, '"I Wasn't Angry, Because I Couldn't Believe It Was Happening": Affect and Discourse in Responses to 9/11', *Review of International Studies*, 38:4 (2012), 907–928; Andrew A. G. Ross, *Mixed Emotions: Beyond Fear and Hatred in International Conflict* (Chicago: Chicago University Press, 2014); Lloyd Cox and Steve Wood, '"Got Him": Revenge, Emotions, and the Killing of Osama bin Laden', *Review of International Studies*, 43, part 1 (2016), 112–129.

3 Within the discipline of international relations, a security dilemma traditionally refers to a situation wherein states are drawn into conflict over security concerns, even though none of the states actually desire conflict. The security dilemma occurs when states fear for their security vis-à-vis other states, and as each state acts to make itself more secure, the other states interpret its actions as threatening. A cycle of unintended provocations emerges, resulting in an escalation of the conflict. John H. Hertz, 'Idealist Internationalism and the Security Dilemma', *World Politics*, 2 (1950), 2.

4 A. A. G. Ross, 'Realism, Emotion, and Dynamic Allegiances in Global Politics', *International Theory*, 5:2 (2013), 273–299.

5 Mark Juergensmeyer and Mona Kanwal Sheikh, 'A Sociotheological Approach to Understanding Religious Violence,' *The Oxford Handbook of Religion and Violence* (Oxford: Oxford University Press, 2013).

6 Craig Calhoun, 'Putting Emotions in Their Place', in Jeff Goodwin, James M. Jasper, and Francesca Polletta (eds.), *Passionate Politics: Emotions and Social Movements* (Chicago: University of Chicago Press, 2001).

7 Mona Kanwal Sheikh, 'How Does Religion Matter? Pathways to Religion in International Relations', *Review of International Studies*, 38:2 (2012), 365–392.

8 Daniel Philpott, 'The Challenge of September 11 to Secularism in International Relations', *World Politics*, 55 (2002), 66–95. Other important contributions have been made arguing that the global resurgence of religion challenges hegemonic Western concepts and thought patterns of IR by showing how the 'constructedness' of the religious/secular division affects established theoretical approaches to understanding international relations, for example, Scott M. Thomas, *The Global Resurgence of Religion and the Transformation of International Relations: The Struggle for the Soul of the Twenty-First Century* (New York: Palgrave Macmillan, 2005); Elizabeth Hurd, *The Politics of Secularism in International Relations* (Princeton, NJ: Princeton University Press, 2007); 'Theorizing Religious Resurgence', *International Politics*, 44 (2007): 647–665. See also Pavlos Hatzopoulos and Fabio Petito (eds.), *Religion in International Relations: The Return from Exile* (New York: Palgrave Macmillan, 2003).

9 See, for example, Cecelia M. Lynch, 'A Neo-Weberian Approach to Religion in International Politics', *International Theory*, 1:3 (2009), 381–408.

10 Mark Juergensmeyer, *Terror in the Mind of God: The Global Rise of Religious Violence*, revised edn. (Berkeley: University of California Press, 2003); Mark Juergensmeyer, *Global Rebellion: Religious Challenges to the Secular State, from Christian Militias to Al Qaeda* (Berkeley: University of California Press, 2008); Cynthia K. Mahmood, *Fighting for Faith and Nation: Dialogues with Sikh Militants.* (Philadelphia: University of Pennsylvania Press, 1996); Michael Jerryson, *Buddhist Fury: Religion and Violence in Southern Thailand* (New York: Oxford University Press, 2011).

11 Mona Kanwal Sheikh, *Guardian of God: Inside the Religious Mind of the Pakistani Taliban* (Delhi: Oxford University Press, 2016).

12 Jeff Goodwin, James M. Jasper, and Francesca Polletta, 'Why Emotions Matter', in *Passionate Politics: Emotions and Social Movements* (Chicago: University of Chicago Press, 2001).

13 Michael P. Young, 'A Revolution of the Soul: Transformative Experiences and Immediate Abolition', in Jeff Goodwin, James M. Jasper, and Francesca Polletta (eds.), *Passionate Politics: Emotions and Social Movements* (Chicago: University of Chicago Press, 2001).

14 Randall Collins, 'Social Movements and the Focus of Emotional Attention,' in Jeff Goodwin, James M. Jasper, and Francesca Polletta (eds.), *Passionate Politics: Emotions and Social Movements* (Chicago: University of Chicago Press, 2001).

15 Interestingly, modern neuroscience suggests that emotion and cognition are inextricably fused. See Todrov Fiske Prentice, *Social Neuroscience: Toward Understanding the Underpinnings of the Social Mind* (Oxford: Oxford University Press, 2011).

16 Ole Wæver, 'Securitization and Desecuritization', in *On Security*, ed. Ronnie D. Lipschutz (New York: Columbia University Press, 1995), 46–86. Barry Buzan, Ole Wæver, and Jaap De Wilde, *Security: A New Framework for Analysis* (Boulder, CO: Lynne Rienner Publishers, 1998).

17 Mona Kanwal Sheikh, 'The Religious Challenge to Securitisation Theory', *Millennium: Journal of International Studies*, 43:1 (2014), 252–272.

18 The critique I raise in reaction to the Copenhagen School theorization of religion in an article in a special issue of *Millennium* published in 2000 (Carsten Bagge Laustsen and Ole Wæver, 'In Defence of Religion: Sacred Referent Objects for Securitization', *Millennium: Journal of International Studies*, 29, 3 (2000): 705–739). This critique is important, I argue, because of its repercussions for the thinking on de-securitization, and because the applied definitions of religion and religious securitization create a challengeable theoretical link between religion and violence.

19 Daniel Bar-Tal, Eran Halperin, and Joseph de Rivera, 'Collective Emotions in Conflict Situations: Societal Implications', *Journal of Social Issues*, 63, 2, 441–460.

20 J. De Rivera and D. Páez, 'Emotional Climate, Human Security, and Cultures of Peace', *Journal of Social Issues*, 63 (2007), 233–253.

21 Thierry Balzaq, 'The Three Faces of Securitization: Political Agency, Audience and Context', *European Journal of International Relations*, 11, 2 (2005): 171–202.

22 Lloyd Cox and Steve Wood, '"Got Him": Revenge, Emotions, and the Killing of Osama bin Laden', *Review of International Studies*, 43, part 1 (2016), 112–129.

23 D. A. Snow and R. D. Benford, 'Master Frames and Cycles of Protest', in A. D. Morris and C. M. Mueller (eds.), *Frontiers in Social Movement Theory* (New Haven: Yale University Press, 1992), 133–155.

35

SOLIDARITY BEYOND RELIGIOUS AND SECULAR

Multiple ontologies as an ethical framework in the politics of forced displacement

Erin K. Wilson

Introduction

Displacement is one of the major challenges facing the global community in the 21st century. Described by some as a 'refugee crisis', others have argued that this narrative represents a mislabeling and attempted misdirection by political leaders unwilling to acknowledge their own failure to adequately prepare and respond to the inevitable outcomes of ongoing intractable conflicts in places such as Syria, Eritrea, the Democratic Republic of Congo, Myanmar, to name but a few. In other words, rather than a 'refugee crisis', the current moment represents a crisis of leadership,[1] a crisis of solidarity[2] and/or a crisis of humanity.[3]

Questions of ethics and justice are central to the debates and dilemmas that policymakers, activists, scholars and people presently experiencing displacement are dealing with. These dilemmas range from large-scale collective questions regarding which countries and organizations should be primarily responsible for meeting the immediate survival and protection needs of people experiencing displacement, how we identify what those needs are, the duration of the responsibility for meeting those needs, how to ensure long-term protection, to smaller personal issues such as, in some cases, which family members flee and which ones remain? What possessions should be taken in the moment of flight? Where and how are food and shelter to be obtained along the way? What are the best and safest ways for people to seek protection – through processing at refugee camps, despite years-long waits, or through irregular migration via dangerous land and sea routes?

Religious and secular dynamics and actors are an integral part of displacement, though far greater attention has been paid to the impact of religious worldviews than to secular.[4] This chapter attempts to rectify this gap. Building on the critiques of humanitarianism more generally by Ager and Ager, Barnett and Stein, Lynch and others,[5] the chapter argues that secular ways of knowing and being in the world dominate the politics of forced displacement, constituting a form of ontological injustice. Drawing on literature from cultural anthropology, the chapter demonstrates how secular ontological assumptions about 'what exists' influence prevailing approaches from intergovernmental, governmental and non-governmental actors responding to the so-called refugee crisis, contributing to the exclusion of religious and spiritual ontologies.

The result is that displacement – what it is, what it means, how it is experienced and how it should be responded to – are understood primarily through the lens of secular ontologies. As such, alternative non-secular interpretations and experiences, many of which characterize the way people presently experiencing displacement understand the world, are excluded. The chapter develops a multiple ontologies ethical framework as a response to conflicts between religious and secular ways of being in the world. The framework aims to generate greater space for dialogue and solidarity across ontologies and empower people currently living the displacement experience.

While multiple factors shape and influence the processes and actors entangled in the displacement crisis at various levels, recently it has been questions of religion, and particularly Islam, which have garnered most attention. Arguably, however, this somewhat unbalanced attention that is given to religious, and especially Islamic, worldviews and actors in the context of migration is at least in part attributable to the implicit dominance of secular ontologies,[6] or as Stacey Gutkowski refers to it, secular *habitus* in the discourses and policies surrounding forced migration.[7] Secular worldviews insist that there is something clearly distinguishable that we can identify and label as 'religion', which possesses specific characteristics that make it different from, and implicitly subordinate to, the secular.

This chapter contributes to broadening and deepening knowledge on the impact of secular ontologies on global political issues in general, and displacement in particular. Specifically, the chapter argues that secular ways of being dominate the politics of forced displacement, thereby constituting a form of ontological injustice. In the first section, the chapter outlines specific features of the current displacement crisis, noting particularly the significance of 'religion', and especially 'Islam' in discourses and policy. Following this, the chapter sketches developments in the study of secularism in international relations that have enabled the identification of secularism as a worldview, ideology and specific ontology,[8] rather than the neutral universal arbiter of public reason it has long been assumed to be. Building on these insights, with the assistance of literature from cultural anthropology, the chapter argues that secularism constitutes a specific kind of ontology that dominates global institutions with regard to migration and that this dominance of secularism in turn constitutes an ontological injustice. Secular ontological assumptions about 'what exists' influence prevailing approaches from intergovernmental, governmental and non-governmental actors responding to the so-called refugee crisis, contributing to the exclusion of religious and spiritual ontologies.

The chapter concludes by developing an ethical framework for decision-making and public discussion that draws on both political ontology[9] and deep equality[10] in an attempt to address this ontological injustice in dealing with displacement. The goal is to generate greater space for dialogue and solidarity across ontologies and empower people currently living through the displacement experience.[11] The chapter also engages with the challenges posed by the emergence of so-called 'post-truth politics', since this phenomenon is bound up with discourses around migration, religion (especially Islam) and violence.

The 'refugee crisis' and secular assumptions

According to the United Nations High Commissioner for Refugees (UNHCR), as of the end of 2016, 65.5 million people were displaced globally at a rate of 20 per minute.[12] This is the largest number of displaced people ever recorded.

The scale and speed of displacement has resulted in mass overcrowding in refugee camps in countries surrounding the conflict zones,[13] meaning that the majority of the world's refugee population (84%) are hosted in developing countries, where infrastructure is poor and resources are scarce.[14] This statistic means that only 16% of the global population of people who are displaced are hosted in developed countries.

Another effect of current displacement levels is increasing flows of irregular migration to Europe, North America and Australia, and, in connection with this, increased numbers of deaths on deadly land and sea routes.[15] On 23 December 2016, UNHCR announced that, with the drowning of another 100 people the day before, the annual death toll from drownings in the Mediterranean had reached over 5,000 – 'the worst annual death toll ever seen', and over 1,200 more than in the whole of 2015.[16] As a result of the EU–Turkey deal and crackdowns in Italy and Libya, fewer migrants are now attempting the crossing to Europe, but the death rate amongst those who do attempt the crossing has doubled.[17]

There is, however, an additional factor that is exacerbating the already serious consequences of the size and speed of the displacement crisis, namely the lack of political will across multiple contexts to accept refugees and displaced persons. In some cases, this is simply the result of practicalities – many neighbouring developing countries are already overwhelmed with refugees and simply do not have the capacity to accept any more.[18] This, however, is not the case for developed countries. As the Organisation for Economic Co-operation and Development (OECD) noted in 2015 with regard to Europe, it is not the numbers of refugees generating this 'crisis', since Europe has the capacity and experience to deal with large movements of people.[19] 'Crisis' also implies an event that has happened suddenly and unexpectedly. As several commentators have noted, the current situation has been developing over several years and can hardly be said to have caught policy-makers unawares.[20] European Union leaders' failure to formulate joint, coherent responses is also a crucial factor in the generation of the so-called crisis.[21] Despite priding itself on its commitment to humanitarianism, human rights, democracy and cosmopolitan ideals of international citizenship, with few exceptions (notably Germany and Sweden), the European response has been to implement increasingly hard-line migration policies and deploy harsh exclusionary rhetoric.[22] European countries are not the first to resort to such measures, however. In the early phases of the European crisis, European leaders explicitly highlighted the deterrence-driven Australian model of mandatory detention, offshore processing and third country resettlement as a serious policy option for the European context.[23]

Arguably, the principal catalyst for these increasingly harsh immigration policies and growing exclusionary discourses is the question of 'religion', and in particular, 'Islam'. Religion has become the primary characteristic by which refugees are conceptualized. Alexander Betts has labelled Islam 'the elephant in the room', the primary reason why states are unwilling to accept refugees generated by the Syrian conflict in particular, though they are unwilling to admit that this is the case.[24] Kenneth Roth, Executive Director of Human Rights Watch, has argued that right-wing opposition to accepting refugees is ultimately not about employment, social welfare or management: 'What it is really about is that they are Muslim'.[25] Some Eastern European states have openly acknowledged this, declaring that they will only accept Christian refugees from Syria.[26] Similar statements emerged early in the 2016 US presidential campaign, and were also voiced by the Abbott and Turnbull governments in Australia.[27] These stances are fuelled by numerous assumptions about the nature of 'religion' in general, of 'Islam' in particular, and the relationships between categories of 'religion', 'Islam', 'violence' and 'refugees'. However, they are also the result of the assumed 'secular' nature of Euro-American states and the perceived incompatibility of 'religion', especially 'Islam', to peacefully co-exist within and alongside secular political values. These assumptions are not new, but have been part of the emergence of secularism as a political ideology and model of statecraft since the Enlightenment.[28] Further, it is not just one small group within society that expresses these assumptions, but a wide range of political leaders, media commentators, business elites and members of the general public.

The desire to stress the difference between supposedly secular Euro-American societies and the refugees and migrants arriving from the Middle East and North Africa encourages an over-emphasis on religious identity in the context of the displacement crisis. Over-emphasizing the religious identity of refugees contributes to a predominant conclusion that because a majority of refugees are from countries where Islam is the dominant religion, they must therefore be Muslim. Yet while many refugees do identify as 'Muslim', many also do not. Many are Christian, atheist, Baha'i, Druze, Yazidi, amongst many others. To characterize or assume that all refugees are 'Muslim' is therefore misleading.

Second, while many refugees do identify as 'Muslim', being 'Muslim' can mean any number of different things. Saba Mahmood observes that some Coptic Christian leadership in Egypt have at times identified themselves as 'Muslim by country and Christian by religion', implying that 'Muslim', just like 'Christian' or 'Buddhist' or 'Hindu' and so on, can operate as a political and cultural identity as well as a 'religious' one.[29] Muslim, like Christian, can mean highly observant, but also lapsed, and all the various stages in between; Muslim can mean Sunni, Shi'a, Alawi, to name but a few, all with multiple variations in terms of beliefs and practices. Assuming that all refugees are 'Muslim', and are all 'Muslim' in the same way, can lead to erroneous judgements regarding what the most important and pressing needs for refugees are when they arrive in a resettlement country.[30] Over-emphasizing religious identity can make it more difficult for refugees to resettle and be accommodated in their new country.

Further, presenting all refugees as 'Muslim', with little or no nuance concerning what it actually means to be 'Muslim', contributes to the unnecessary securitization of migration, because of the way the words 'Muslim' and 'Islam' have become erroneously entangled with 'terrorism' in parallel discourses surrounding violent extremism. Islam is not singular. Indeed, there is a vast diversity of practices and beliefs associated with what are known as Islamic religious traditions across different geographic, historical, political and cultural contexts. Yet this diversity and nuance is absent from the violent extremism narrative. The prominence accorded to the 'violent extremism' discourse and to the 'refugee crisis' discourse has resulted in a complicated entanglement amongst the terms 'refugee', 'Muslim' and 'terrorist' in public conversations and consciousness. Muslims have become suspect as potential terrorists, refugees are assumed to be Muslim, and consequently refugees are also assumed to be potential terrorists. This entanglement contributes to increasingly securitized approaches to forced migration.[31] This is not to say that religion should be completely ignored. Leaving religion out of discussions and analysis of displacement is equally problematic.[32] The challenge is to develop approaches that allow for the nuanced consideration of 'religion' as a category without making it the sole explanatory factor.

It is not only around questions of Islam that 'religion' has become entangled with policy and public discourses on the refugee crisis. In recent years, the UNHCR, for example, has sought to develop its 'religious literacy' through greater engagement with faith leaders and more nuanced understanding of local faith communities. Examples of this drive include the 2012 High Commissioner's Dialogue on Protection and the 2014 Note on partnership with faith-based organizations and local faith communities.[33] Long before the present crisis moment, religious civil society organizations were crucial providers of assistance and support to refugees and asylum seekers, often stepping in to fill the gaps left by the increasing privatization of state services.[34] Religious organizations continue to be key service providers in the present context. Further, 'religion' and 'faith' are important dynamics that shape and are shaped by the lived experiences of people who are displaced. Yet this interaction occurs in complex ways that often defy the dominant categorizations of 'secular' and 'religious', and their associated assumptions that scholars and policy-makers frequently seek to apply to the lives of refugees and migrants. All of these dynamics point to the need to rethink our approaches to 'religion' and its relationship with the 'refugee crisis', which, I suggest, are dominated by secularist assumptions and world-views, constituting an ontological injustice.

Conceptualizing ontological injustice

The idea of ontological injustice remains largely under-developed in academic theorizing. The term has been applied in criminal psychology[35] and spatial sciences,[36] but appears rarely in other social science and humanities literature. When it does,[37] it is often utilized without explanation. In developing a concept of ontological injustice, I draw on this existing literature, but especially Mario Blaser's work on 'political ontology', as part of the recent so-called 'ontological turn' in cultural anthropology.[38]

Ontological injustice is entangled with both material and epistemological injustices.[39] Where epistemological injustice may be described as the exclusion of alternative views of the world, ontological injustice is concerned with the exclusion of views of alternative worlds.[40] It is not simply that we must acknowledge that different people view the world differently, but rather that we must be open to the possibility that different people inhabit different worlds. It is not that we assume that there is a 'real', 'factual' world 'out there' that is simply interpreted differently (and incorrectly) by people who do not think 'like us', but rather that we consider the possibility that their world is in fact different.[41] For example, an ontology that views states as the main actors in global politics would provide a completely different analysis and thus policy response to questions of forced migration than an ontology that has no conception of states, or indeed of global politics or 'forced migration', and instead views communities, villages, families, corporations, warlords or religious actors as the key actors relevant to the decision-making processes that influence their lives and enable them to remain in one place or move to another to ensure their survival.

Further, it is not just that the worlds are different, but that they are differently and unequally valued. This is a crucial contribution from political ontology, where 'politics' is understood as 'power differences' and 'ontology' is understood as the 'the power of difference'.[42] Following this line of reasoning, ontological injustice is concerned with the power differences that exist amongst visions of different worlds, which begin in the subordination of particular realities to others and are entangled with and contribute to material and epistemological power differences. The dominance of secularism may then be argued to constitute an ontological injustice because it excludes, or at the very least subordinates, worlds where gods, spirits and ancestors, for example, are real actors with power, agency and influence that impact on daily life as well as societal and political institutions and structures. Similar to the way in which Daley has argued that, from a Marxist perspective, capitalism is an ontological injustice because it prevents people from becoming fully human by emphasizing their labour as the key aspect of their identity,[43] secularism may be considered a form of ontological injustice because it attempts to privatize, minimize and exclude ways of understanding and living that do not conform to the assumptions of secular ontologies.

Venkatesan provides a lucid explanation of the problem on which ontological injustice focuses: 'Ontologies, theories of being and reality, have histories (and genealogies). They are also not necessarily transcontextually stable.'[44] Ontologies – which can be held by individuals, communities, groups, constituted along various lines of belonging – possess specific assumptions about what exists – what the world is, what human beings are, their fundamental characteristics, their relationship to one another, nature, the divine or supernatural (if it exists), and to themselves. Yet these assumptions are contextually specific, and do not necessarily make sense from one context to another. In relation to forced migration and displacement, where people find themselves in unfamiliar places, often suddenly and with little time to adjust; where global institutions and non-governmental actors are operating in line with understandings of the world that may be vastly different from those of the context in which they are working as well as the displaced people they are serving, a multiple ontologies framework is essential. Only through acknowledging the existence of these different ontologies can we endeavour to build understanding across them.

'Religious' and 'secular' approaches to the foundations for 'rational' enquiry provide an example of the kinds of ontological differences that are being referred to here. For secular thinkers, rational enquiry must focus on things that can be observed and for which significant tangible 'scientific' evidence is available to support their existence. Thus, for example, secular rational enquiry cannot acknowledge God's existence because accepting the existence of God must, at some point, occur on the basis of faith, or on the basis of certain kinds of evidence that secular enquiry finds unreliable.

From certain non-secular/religious/cosmological perspectives, however, acknowledging the existence of God or of a higher being is foundational for the search for truth. Both Pope John Paul II[45] and Pope Benedict XVI[46] articulated this view: any rational search for truth and reason must begin and end with God. The argument is based on the belief that God is omnipotent. Therefore, it is only through knowing God that humans can begin to understand and know themselves and the world they live in. Faith and reason are not mutually exclusive, but rather complement and complete one another. Christian theologians have also long argued that God's existence is revealed through various aspects of 'general revelation' – the complexity of the natural world, the fact that individuals have a conscience – and thus the existence of God can be logically derived from these phenomena.[47]

In these diverging approaches, there are different understandings of what constitutes acceptable 'evidence', as well as what is an acceptable starting point for 'rational' enquiry. These are not simply different views of the world, but different worlds, one where the existence of God is the foundation of everything, and one where the existence of God is barely relevant, if at all. We may profoundly disagree with one or both of these views, but ontological justice requires that we take both seriously on their own terms and allow them to articulate their perspectives and arguments through their own language and frameworks.[48] Failing to do this contributes to marginalization, inequality and exclusion in contemporary global politics.

Multiple ontologies should not be understood simply as a modified version of cultural relativism, or the reification of difference for the sake of difference. It is not a question of just 'believing' or accepting visions of alternative worlds, when they are fundamentally opposed to our own. The disagreement over whether God or the supernatural or spirits exist or not is an ongoing one, unlikely to ever be solved, and indeed resolving this disagreement is not the point. It is not a matter of simply accepting that some people believe and others do not, though this is important to acknowledge. To just accept or 'believe' the view of an alternative ontology, when it fundamentally contradicts what one 'knows' from the perspective of one's own ontology does not do justice to either viewpoint.[49] What is at stake in the disagreement over the existence of God/gods/the spiritual and supernatural is not whether such things exist or not, but the different understandings of these things *and* of their relationship to human beings and the nature of human beings themselves that leads some people to believe God does exist and others not. It is these issues, and especially the different understandings of what human beings themselves are, which are crucial in discussions on the global displacement crisis, and where the dominance of secularism may be said to constitute an ontological injustice.

Secularism as ontological injustice in international relations and the global displacement crisis

By now, the argument that secularism is itself a particular, culturally embedded worldview has been well rehearsed by many eminent scholars working at the intersection of religious studies, international relations, law, philosophy, anthropology and sociology.[50] As an ideological and ontological formation, secularism has come to subtly influence the ways in which we think about the nature of religion itself, as well as its relationship with politics and religion's proper place relative to public life.[51]

Analysis of religion and global politics was, for a long time, dominated by the assumptions of secularization theory, which viewed religion as becoming increasingly irrelevant and therefore unnecessary to analyse. This view has shifted in the last decade or so, however, to be replaced by an overarching narrative of 'good religion/bad religion' – religion is still present and relevant in global politics, but manifests in either 'good religion', which is tolerant and inclusive and can make an important contribution to peace, human rights and prosperity; or 'bad religion', which is reactionary, exclusionary and seeks to disrupt and, in some cases, destroy public order.[52] While this narrative may seem to create greater space for religion in discussions on politics and public life, it does so on the terms of the secular, leaving the concepts of secular and religious intact, and implicitly aligning 'good religion' with the secular. Thus, secularism is still the dominant overarching framework.

In the context of displacement and forced migration, both of these modes of secularist dominance are evident. It is only since the early 2000s that religion has been explored as a relevant component of these issues, and there again, we can see the influence of the good religion/bad religion narrative. Good religion is a source of comfort and support for people on the move, either in their personal spiritual life or through the work of faith-based organizations. Bad religion, on the other hand, is a source of persecution and flight, or a potential security threat, as we see in the discourses where categories of 'Muslim', 'refugee' and 'terrorist' are entangled.

Yet the assumptions of secular ontologies that permeate and underpin much discussion and analysis of public issues does not simply effect how we understand 'religion'. It also affects how we understand societal organization, the relationship between religion and various issues in politics and public life, even the forms of knowledge that are privileged and the voices that are acknowledged and excluded. These assumptions can be summarized as follows:

a) 'religion' is something tangible and identifiable, that *can* be clearly distinguished, defined and separated from the 'secular', which can also be clearly defined. Not only that but
b) 'religion' *should* be clearly distinguished and separated from other areas of human activity, such as politics, economics, law, education and so forth, that are grouped under the 'secular',[53] because
c) 'religion' is highly subjective, particular, individual and irrational (Hurd 2008; Wilson 2012), as opposed to the 'secular' which is neutral and universal; and,
d) 'religion' is what people will disagree about more frequently and violently than anything else,[54] thus 'religion' is the fundamental cause of violence, intolerance and chaos; therefore

e) 'religion' must be kept out of the 'public' sphere and relegated to the 'private' to preserve order and peace,[55] meaning that the distinction between 'religion' and the 'secular' is managed through the existence of 'public' and 'private' spheres (that are equally as unstable, shifting and problematic as the categories of 'religion' and 'secular'). Finally,

f) 'religion' is always subordinated to the 'secular', in that, even if 'religion' is viewed as something that can positively contribute to politics and public life, its interventions should still be regulated by so-called 'secular' authorities and institutions (what Kuru refers to as 'passive secularism', and Hurd as 'Judeo-Christian secularism').[56]

This is not to suggest that secularism is monolithic, homogenous or exclusively 'Western'. Like 'religion', 'secularism' is not a singular entity. It is diverse, shifting, changing, unstable and contextually specific.[57] Rather, what I posit is that these shared assumptions constitute 'family resemblances' that characterize secular ontologies across their different manifestations.

It is also important to note that these assumptions are not necessarily exclusively secularist. Indeed, secularism is so entangled with discourses of modernization, Enlightenment, development, colonialism and liberalism that it is in many respects difficult to determine what, if anything, is attributable exclusively to secularism, other than what they relate specifically and exclusively to 'religion'. Nonetheless, secular assumptions form an important part of knowledge and power regimes in contemporary politics that affect how the world is interpreted and responded to by global institutions that have been established out of the predominantly European (and consequently modern, liberal, secular) state system, the issues that are perceived as important and the voices and approaches that are considered the best or most effective for responding to those issues.[58] The migration sector is a case in point, as I explore further below.

The recognition of these dimensions of secularism leads to a further realization that secularism is not just about the judicial and political arrangements for managing religion's relationship with politics, but is underpinned by an ideological agenda that makes assumptions about the worth of religious belief and practice in relation to other human pursuits, about the existence and value of immanent and transcendent realms, about the very nature of religion itself. These assumptions, as noted above, impact the way in which states engage with religious actors, with other states where 'religion' is perceived to be far more central than it is in Western secular worldviews, and how states carry out their policies. These assumptions also underpin global governance structures and frameworks aimed at addressing issues of injustice, including (but not limited to) displacement. Secular assumptions are deeply embedded within these global governance frameworks and are internalized and reproduced by actors that self-identify as 'religious' and as 'secular' alike. 'Religious' actors, in trying to challenge the secular agenda's exclusion of them, by, for example, highlighting how their religious traditions 'fit' with a human rights agenda, or the 'added value' that a religious approach can bring, unintentionally reinforce the secular/religious binary, at the same time as they try to resist it.

Foucault's concepts of governmentality and counter-conducts are useful here to make sense of the complex relationship between secularism and religion. His understanding of power as a procedure, a set of mechanisms and, importantly, that these mechanisms exist within all political, economic and societal relationships enables an analysis of religion and secularism that recognizes the dynamism in the two concepts and their interconnection.[59] In the relationships that exist between religion, politics, society and culture, there are not co-existent mechanisms of power. Rather, the mechanisms of power are constitutive of the relationships that exist across these concepts themselves. As such, the secular/religious binary can be understood as a relationship of power in which complex dynamics of exclusion and resistance operate and affect multiple areas of politics and public life. At the same time that both secularism and religion try to resist one another, they in turn reinforce one another's power and re-constitute the narrow, specific conceptions we have of both.[60] As such, this also highlights the almost inescapable logic of secularism in contemporary politics and the need to explore alternative ways to think about dimensions of immanence and transcendence, sacred and profane, in contemporary global politics. For this reason, I suggest that thinking of the dominance of secularism as a form of ontological injustice may be a helpful analytical tool in endeavouring to develop alternative frameworks for ethics and solidarity beyond the categories of 'religion' and 'secular'.

Within displacement and protection, 'secular' ontologies are not only dominant over religious/spiritual/cosmological ontologies, but any encounters between the two are automatically interpreted by states, intergovernmental actors and many humanitarian NGOs through the lens of the secular. Whilst there are a number of international and intergovernmental bodies tasked with dealing with issues related to migration, the UNHCR bears primary responsibility for areas of forced migration, though what constitutes 'forced' migration is becoming increasingly contested.[61] In regard to the UNHCR's approach to religion, the UNHCR has been cooperating with religious actors since its foundation, but it is only since 2012 that it has been more conscious and directive about this. The 2012 United Nations High Commissioner for Refugees' Dialogue on Protection Challenges specifically focused on the issue of Faith and Protection, part of what the UNHCR described as a 'journey of mutual discovery with faith-based organizations'.[62] Despite the fact that the UNHCR has been working with faith-based organizations since 1950, this was the first formal multi-faith dialogue the UNHCR had ever engaged in,[63] highlighting that it is not necessarily that religion has become more prevalent in the politics of migration, but rather that so-called 'secular' actors are increasingly recognizing the importance of proactively engaging with religious actors. It represents a shift from the dominance of secularization theory to the good religion/bad religion narrative, but nonetheless the dominance of secularist ontologies.

During this dialogue, the High Commissioner called for the development of a code of conduct for faith leaders working in contexts of forced displacement. This raises the immediate question of why there is a need for a code of conduct specifically for faith leaders. Arguably, this relates to the frequently raised concern that faith leaders and faith-based organizations may take advantage of people in vulnerable situations such as displacement and attempt to manipulate them to convert to their religion, or worse, may actively deny them protection or even participate in their persecution if they are not from the same religion. Whilst this is indeed a legitimate and worrying concern, it ignores the possibility that secular organizations also attempt to 'convert' people in displaced contexts to adopt secular worldviews, values and approaches,[64] and that the secular can also be 'a site of domination, isolation, violence and exclusion'.[65] It singles religion out and, in doing so, reinforces the assumptions of secularism – that 'religion' is something clearly identifiable, sufficiently different from the 'secular', that it requires an entirely separate and new code of conduct for faith leaders that does not apply to secular leaders; that religion and religious actors are dangerous and that they are or should be subordinated to the secular.

Such a stance also makes no attempt to try to understand such religious actors on their own terms. The assumption is that organizations that endeavour to convert people in vulnerable situations are doing so 'self-interestedly', desiring more followers. It ignores the possibility that, from the ontological worldview of these faith-based organizations, they are not fulfilling their duty of care towards people who are displaced if they do *not* introduce them to their faith or attempt to convert them, because they are not only concerned about their immediate physical survival, but also about their eternal metaphysical survival. I am not at all condoning organizations that take advantage of people on the move in attempts to convert them. I am, however, suggesting that if we attempted to engage with and understand faith-based organizations and actors that do engage in such practices on their own terms, we may have a greater capacity for discussing and debating with them and potentially encouraging them to desist in such practices.

In 2014, the UNHCR published its *Partnership Note on Faith-Based Organizations, Local Faith Communities and Faith Leaders*, a document designed to give guidance to UNHCR staff about how to reach out to and engage with this diverse group of religious actors. The partnership note contains numerous examples of the ways in which secular worldviews dominate current approaches to displacement. First, the partnership note makes a clear delineation between religious and secular actors, without explaining either category. Thus, the *a priori* division of the world into secular and religious, public and private, is simply assumed, not explained or justified. This sets up an automatic, though arguably implicit, oppositional division between religious and secular actors. Second, notions of who or what constitute 'religious' actors contained in the partnership note privilege ideas of 'faith', a primarily cognitive activity of choosing to commit to certain beliefs. The idea of 'faith' assumes that the actions of 'religious' actors follow on from and are secondary to beliefs, that beliefs are the primary catalyst for action. Not only does this privilege the cognitive aspect of religion over its experiential dimensions,[66] but also represents a highly Christian, and indeed specifically Protestant, way of understanding what 'religion' and 'faith' are.[67]

A further example of implicit secular assumptions within the UNHCR approach concerns the emphasis on 'building capacity' amongst their faith-based partners. In connection with the increasing influence of neoliberal globalization, several scholars have noted recently how the language of professionalization, such as words like 'capacity building', are to an extent associated with increasing secularization by religious actors. This is in part because so-called 'professionalization' requires the implementation of procedures and practices designed to be efficient, 'logical', 'rational' and transparent, which are in turn underpinned by assumptions about what types of knowledge and practice are most suitable or appropriate for professionalized settings, particularly in the humanitarian aid sector, where neutrality is so highly valued. This is a highly complex and challenging way in which the division between secular and religious is reinforced.[68]

Another recent example of the influence of secular assumptions on policies and approaches to forced and irregular migration comes from the European response to the Mediterranean migration crisis. Much of the political rhetoric and media reporting on the migration crisis in the Mediterranean has pointed to various dimensions of religion. For example, former Italian foreign minister (later prime minister) Paolo Gentiloni, in an interview with the BBC in February 2015, talked about the risk of terrorists from Islamic State (IS) infiltrating Europe through irregular migration across the Mediterranean.[69] Far-right political representatives, such as former UKIP leader Nigel Farage, have also made this link.[70] Newspaper and television news reports emphasize the rise of Islamic State in Syria and Iraq as a multidimensional factor in the migration crisis: on the one hand, a potential security threat, using migration as a means for terrorists to infiltrate Europe; on the other, fostering migration through persecution of religious minorities. Other incidents of religious persecution in Libya, Nigeria, Pakistan and Eritrea, amongst others, have also made headlines in recent months, connected to the migration crisis. Yet when the EU issued its statement from the 23 April 2016 special meeting held in response to the crisis, there was no mention of IS, religious persecution, or any other factors related to religion. Four key points were made:

> *Our immediate priority is to prevent more people from dying at sea.*

- Strengthening presence at sea
- Fighting traffickers
- Preventing illegal migration flows
- Reinforcing internal solidarity and responsibility

Despite the significant presence of religion in the public discourses on the migration crisis, it did not feature at all in the policy announcements. This suggests, firstly, that a secular view of religion as irrational, chaotic and irrelevant is being reinforced in this approach. Secondly, it suggests that politicians in the EU hold a highly instrumentalized view of religion, happy to utilize it to gain public support, but viewing it as of little practical policy relevance.[71] It further suggests that while religion may be considered relevant outside of the formal sphere of policy-making, it is still excluded when decision-making occurs. This fits with the implications of the secular worldview outlined above. The motivations of people seeking asylum and refuge are assumed on the basis of secular rationalist thought and thus the main priorities for addressing the movement of people are to reduce the number of pull factors. Other potential factors that could be driving people's decisions to migrate – the duty to seek asylum if one's life is at risk, for instance, that has been identified within some Islamic traditions,[72] spiritual frameworks, whereby people believe their destiny is being driven by another unseen force; along with others that are neither secular nor religious, such as the lack of safe legal pathways for migration, and the untenable nature of life in contexts of intractable poverty and conflicts – are ignored in the dominant policy frameworks, arguably because the views of those who are displaced have not been adequately considered.

Perhaps the most significant influence of the ontological dominance of secularism that is evident here is the universality of the reasons and thought processes that people go through when fleeing, and the one-size-fits-all approach to policy-making in an attempt to respond to the crisis of displacement. Secularism positions itself as the universal arbiter of reason, as the only means for providing a neutral space in which to discuss and decide appropriate policy responses, because it creates the space in which universal common reason can be exercised. Yet it has been amply demonstrated across multiple disciplines in recent years that there is no such thing as universal reason; that what is referred to as universal reason is a product of the European Enlightenment and is in fact culturally specific and particular.[73] Overcoming the dominance of secularist ontologies in displacement thus requires learning lessons from anthropology, sociology, philosophy and religious studies, and engaging with the specific, particular experiences of individual displacement to understand its diversity and develop equally appropriate diverse policy responses.

Multiple ontologies as an ethical framework

In this final section, I explore the possibilities offered by the so-called 'ontological turn' in anthropology to develop an alternative 'multiple ontologies' ethical framework for addressing issues of ontological injustice in response to the global crisis of displacement. The key goal is to develop mechanisms for understanding and solidarity across ontological divides, in this case specifically to move beyond the entrenched 'secular/religious' divide, whilst at the same time not reducing ontological differences to cultural relativism, or worse, to 'alternative facts' or contributing to the so-called 'post-truth' environment that has been observed by journalists and analysts in the context of the Brexit vote in the UK and the 2016 US presidential election. Multiple ontologies is not 'postmodern' in the sense of denying the existence of truth. It does not ask that we see all ontologies as equally right and correct, or that we have to agree with the views and arguments of different ontological perspectives. It does, however, ask that we take all ontologies seriously on their own terms, that we actively and deeply engage with other ontologies and understand them, not just dismiss them without bothering to appreciate their foundations. It means, in some ways, that we must undertake two seemingly contradictory acts at the same time. Firstly, we must hold fast to our values and convictions and be prepared to argue for them and defend them; second, however, we must do so with an attitude of humility and always keep open the possibility that we may in fact be wrong. We must believe and doubt at the same time.

Another possibility for describing what I am attempting to outline here is Beaman's model of deep equality. For Beaman, deep equality is not a policy platform or programme, but a practice that is enacted and experienced by ordinary people in their everyday lives as a way to navigate difference.[74] Drawing inspiration from these everyday practices provides a means for circumventing the assumed universality of the secular, by learning from and utilizing the everyday and the particular. Beaman notes that governments (and, I would argue, intergovernmental agencies) have the capacity to create situations in which difference becomes accentuated and highlighted or in which it is minimized. By combining the deep equality framework with the multiple ontologies framework, it is possible to generate a context in which different ways of being are taken seriously and valued, but where their differences are neither over- nor under-emphasized. They are acknowledged and discussed as important, but not as insurmountable obstacles to equality, justice, respect and acceptance of others – if there is willingness on both sides to achieve this.

This approach is helpful not only in the context of navigating between ontologies grounded in secular assumptions and other ways of being that do not see 'religion' as a distinct separate entity, but is, I suggest, a useful approach for dealing with the rise of populism and the post-truth environment. As Katharine Murphy writing in *The Guardian Australia*, states:

> this doesn't mean white-washing or excusing [statements] that are intolerant, bigoted or discriminatory. It means looking [people] in the eye, comprehending them and acknowledging their fears for the future, which are entirely reasonable and rational.[75]

While Murphy is here writing about the rise of right-wing national populism, it is a sentiment that could be equally applicable to engaging with the arguments and justification provided by groups such as IS for their terrorist activities. Simply dismissing the views of these extreme and marginalized populations only aggravates their sense of injustice. Taking their views seriously without condoning them or their actions is a key challenge for 21st-century politics, and it is a crucial component of how we respond to the crisis of displacement, given the ways in which all three are entangled in contemporary political discourse. What is required, then, is a co-mingling of grassroots practices of navigating difference on a daily basis, as Beaman highlights, combined with a conceptual, philosophical and political commitment to taking differences seriously – not dismissing them as antiquated, pre-modern, irrational, conservative, and so on – but genuinely endeavouring to understand and appreciate them on their own terms.

Notes

1 F. Giustra (2016). 'A Crisis of Leadership', *The Huffington Post*, 21 June. Available at http://www.huffingtonpost.com/frank-giustra/a-crisis-of-leadership_1_b_10268584.html; accessed 27 September 2017.
2 B. Ki-moon (2016). 'A Crisis of Solidarity', *Handelsblatt Global*, 13 May. Available at ttps://global.handelsblatt.com/opinion/a-crisis-of-solidarity-518274; accessed 27 September 2017.
3 B. Evans and Z. Bauman (2016). 'The Refugee Crisis Is Humanity's Crisis', *The New York Times*, 2 May. Available at https://www.nytimes.com/2016/05/02/opinion/the-refugee-crisis-is-humanitys-crisis.html; accessed 27 September 2017.
4 See, for example, E. Gozdziak and D. Shandy (eds.) (2002). *Journal of Refugee Studies*, Special Issue on Religion and Forced Migration, 15, 2; E. Fiddian-Qasmiyeh (ed.) (2011). *Journal of Refugee Studies*, Special Issue on Faith-Based Humanitarianism in Contexts of Forced Displacement, 24, 3.
5 A. Ager and J. Ager (2011). 'Faith and the Discourse of Secular Humanitarianism', *Journal of Refugee Studies*, 24, 3, 456–472; A. Ager and J. Ager (2015). *Faith, Secularism and Humanitarian Engagement: Finding the Place of Religion in the Support of Displaced Communities*. New York: Palgrave Macmillan; M. Barnet and J. Gross Stein (eds.) (2012). *Sacred Aid: Faith and Humanitarianism*. Oxford and New York: Oxford University Press; C. Lynch (2011). 'Religious Humanitarianism and the Global Politics of Secularism', in C. Calhoun, M. Juergensmeyer, and J. Van Antwerpen (eds.), *Rethinking Secularism*. New York: Oxford University Press, 204–224.
6 I choose to utilize the word 'ontologies' or the phrase 'secular ways of being', rather than 'worldview' or 'ideology'. Ontologies is not a perfect word, and it is potentially too embedded in academic jargon. However, ontologies is the closest word I can for now arrive at that captures not only the cognitive differences but also the lived, experienced, embodied dimensions and practices of 'religious' and 'secular' ways of being. 'Worldview' and 'ideology' still retain a focus on the cognitive dimensions of the ways we understand and live in the world. I am also trying to draw attention to the unconscious, visceral, embodied, and emotional dimensions of this. I am grateful to Jonathan Chaplin for this insight.
7 S. Gutkowski (2014). *Secular War: Myths of Religion, Politics and Violence*. London: I. B. Tauris.
8 S. Mahmood (2016). *Religious Difference in a Secular Age: A Minority Report*. Princeton: Princeton University Press; E. K. Wilson (2017). '"Power Differences" and "the Power of Difference": The Dominance of Secularism as Ontological Injustice', *Globalizations*. Available at http://www.tandfonline.com/doi/full/10.1080/14747731.2017.1308062; accessed 27 September 2017.
9 M. Blaser (2013). 'Ontological Conflicts and the Stories of Peoples in Spite of Europe: Towards a Conversation on Political Ontology', *Cultural Anthropology*, 54, 5: 547–568.
10 L. Beaman (2014). 'Deep Equality as an Alternative to Accommodation and Tolerance', *Nordic Journal of Religion and Society*, 27, 2, 89–111.
11 Throughout the chapter, I deliberately refrain from using the terms 'refugees', 'migrants', 'asylum seekers', and instead use phrases such as 'people on the move' or 'people experiencing displacement'. This is for two reasons. Firstly, 'refugee', 'migrant', 'asylum seeker' have become pejorative terms with multiple, usually negative connotations. Secondly, using these words reduces people to a category, obfuscating multiple other dimensions of their identity and personhood.
12 UNHCR (2017). *Global Trends Report: Forced Displacement in 2016*. Available at http://www.unhcr.org/5943e8a34.pdf; accessed 20 June 2017.
13 P. Dobbs (2016). 'Burundians Continuing to Flee the Country One Year after Crisis Began', *UNHCR*, 22 April. Available at http://www.unhcr.org/news/briefing/2016/4/5719f0119/burundians-continuing-flee-country-year-crisis-began.html; accessed 13 June 2016; C. McDonald-Gibson (2013). 'Syrian Refugees Find Discomfort and Unrest in Bulgaria', *Time*, 16 November. Available at http://world.time.com/2013/11/16/syrian-refugees-find-discomfort-and-unrest-in-bulgaria/; accessed 13 June 2016.
14 UNHCR 2017, *op cit.*
15 International Organization for Migration (2016). 'Mediterranean', *Missing Migrants Project*. Available at https://missingmigrants.iom.int/mediterranean; accessed 23 January 2017.
16 UNHCR, 2016. 'Mediterranean Sea: 100 People Reported Dead Yesterday, Bringing Year Total to 5000', 23 December. Available at http://www.unhcr.org/news/briefing/2016/12/585ce804105/mediterranean-sea-100-people-reported-dead-yesterday-bringing-year-total.html; accessed 23 December 2016.
17 M. Townsend (2017). 'Mediterranean Death Rate Doubles as Migrant Crossings Fall', *The Guardian*, 4 June. Available at https://www.theguardian.com/world/2017/jun/03/mediterranean-refugees-migrants-deaths; accessed 27 September 2017.

18 Dobbs, *op cit.*

19 OECD (2015). 'Is This Humanitarian Migration Crisis Different?' *Migration Policy Debates*, September. Available at https://www.oecd.org/migration/Is-this-refugee-crisis-different.pdf; accessed April 2016.

20 Patrick Kingsley, Mark Rice-Oxley, and Albert Nardelli (2015). 'Syrian Refugee Crisis: Why Has It Become So Bad?' *The Guardian*, 4 September. Available at https://www.theguardian.com/world/2015/sep/04/syrian-refugee-crisis-why-has-it-become-so-bad; accessed 13 June 2016; *The Guardian* editorial (2015). 'The Turmoil of Today's World: Leading Writers Respond to the Refugee Crisis', *The Guardian*, 12 Septembe. Available at https://www.theguardian.com/books/2015/sep/12/the-turmoil-of-todays-world-leading-writers-respond-to-the-refugee-crisis; accessed 13 June 2016.

21 Kenneth Roth (2016). 'A Way for Europe to Remove Chaos from the Migration Crisis', *Human Rights Watch*, 1 February. http://www.hrw.org/news/2016/02/01/way-europe-remove-chaos-migration-crisis; accessed 26 March 2016.

22 Janet Daley (2016). 'Why the Migration Fiasco Spells Doom for Project Europe', *The Telegraph*, 30 January. Available at http://www.telegraph.co.uk/news/newstopics/eureferendum/12130589/janet-daley-eu-migrant-crisis-brexit.html; accessed 11 June 2016.

23 Sara Davies and Phil Orchard (2015). 'Would Australia's Asylum Seeker Policy Stop Boats to Europe?', *The Conversation*, 23 April. Available at https://theconversation.com/would-australias-asylum-seeker-policy-stop-boats-to-europe-40645; accessed 11 June 2016; Zam R. Ionel (2015). 'Asylum Policy in Australia: Between Resettlement and Deterrence', European Parliamentary Research Services, October. Available at https://epthinktank.eu/2015/10/16/asylum-policy-in-australia-between-resettle-ment-and-deterrence/; accessed 11 June 2016.

24 Alexander Betts (2016). 'The Elephant in the Room: Islam and the Crisis of Liberal Values in Europe', *Foreign Affairs*, 2 February. https://www.foreignaffairs.com/articles/europe/2016-02-02/elephant-room; accessed 31 March 2016.

25 Quoted in Rick Lyman (2015). 'Eastern Bloc's Resistance to Refugees Highlights Europe's Cultural and Political Divisions', *The New York Times*, 12 September. Available at http://www.nytimes.com/2015/09/13/world/europe/eastern-europe-migrant-refugee-crisis.html?_r=0; accessed 11 June 2016.

26 BBC (2015). 'Donald Trump Urges Ban on Muslims Coming to US', 8 December. Available at http://www.bbc.co.uk/news/world-us-canada-35035190; accessed 5 June 2016.

27 Anna Henderson and Chris Uhlman (2015). 'Syrian Migrant Crisis: Christians to Get Priority as Abbott Faces Pressure to Take in More Refugees', *Australian Broadcasting Corporation (ABC) News*, 8 September. Available at http://www.abc.net.au/news/2015-09-08/christians-to-get-priority-in-syrian-refugee-intake/6757110; accessed 11 June 2016; J. Burnside (2017). 'The Leaked Transcript of Turnbull's Call with Trump Shows Him at His Worst', *The Guardian*, 5 August. Available at https://www.theguardian.com/commentisfree/2017/aug/05/the-leaked-transcript-of-turnbulls-call-with-trump-shows-him-at-his-worst; accessed 27 September 2017; G. Miller, J. Vitkovskaya, and R. Fischer-Baum (2017). 'This Deal Will Make Me Look Terrible': full transcripts of Trump's calls with Mexico and Australia', *The Washington Post*. Available at https://www.washingtonpost.com/graphics/2017/politics/australia-mexico-transcripts/?utm_term=.1d4ec4de9075; accessed 27 September 2017.

28 T. Asad (2003). *Formations of the Secular: Christianity, Islam, Modernity*. Stanford: Stanford University Press; J. Casanova (2011). 'The Secular, Secularizations, Secularisms', in *Rethinking Secularism*, ed. C. Calhoun, M. Juergensmeyer, and J. Van Antwerpen. Oxford: Oxford University Press, 54–74.

29 Mahmood (2016), *op cit.*

30 L. G. Beaman, J. Selby, and A. Barras (2016). 'No Mosque, No Refugees: Some Reflections on Syrian Refugees and the Construction of Religion in Canada', in L. Mavelli and E. K. Wilson (eds.), *The Refugee Crisis and Religion: Secularism, Security and Hospitality in Question*. London: Rowman and Littlefield International, 77–96.

31 E. K. Wilson and L. Mavelli (2016). 'The Refugee Crisis and Religion: Beyond Conceptual and Physical Boundaries', in L. Mavelli and E. K. Wilson (eds.), *The Refugee Crisis and Religion: Secularism, Security and Hospitality in Question*. London: Rowman and Littlefield International, 1–22.

32 Ager and Ager (2011), *op cit.*

33 UNHCR (2012). *Report of High Commissioner's Dialogue on Faith and Protection*. Geneva: UNHCR. Available from: http://www.unhcr.org/50aa5b879.pdf; accessed 17 April 2016; UNHCR (2014). *Partnership Note on Faith-Based Organizations, Local Faith Communities and Faith Leaders*. Geneva: UNHCR. Available at http://www.unhcr.org/539ef28b9.html; accessed 18 February 2015; Ager and Ager (2015), *op cit.*

34 J. Eby, E. Iverson, J. Smyers and E. Kekic (2011). 'The Faith Community's Role in Refugee Resettlement in the United States', *Journal of Refugee Studies*, 24, 3, 586–605; C. Lynch (2011), *op cit.*; E. K. Wilson (2011). 'Much to be Proud of, Much to be Done: Faith-Based Organizations and the Politics of Asylum in Australia', *Journal of Refugee Studies*, 24, 3, 548–564.
35 P. Gray (2007). 'Youth Justice, Social Exclusion and the Demise of Social Justice', *The Howard Journal*, 46(4): 401–416.
36 John Calvelli (2011). 'Experiments in Correlative Ontography: The Visualization of Environmental and Ontological Injustice', in S. Caquard et al. (eds.), *Mapping Environmental Issues in the City: Arts and Cartography Cross Perspectives*, Lecture Notes in Geoinformation and Cartography, DOI 10.1007/978-3-642-22441-6_12, © Springer-Verlag, Berlin Heidelberg.
37 See, for example, J. Daly (2000). 'Marx and Justice', *International Journal of Philosophical Studies*, 8, 3, 351–370.
38 Blaser (2013), *op cit.*; E. Viveiros de Castro (2013). 'The Relative Native', *HAU: Journal of Ethnographic Theory*, 3 (3): 473–502.
39 E. K. Wilson (2017), *op cit.*
40 E. Viveiros de Castro (2013), *op cit.*
41 Blaser (2013), *op cit.*, 552–553.
42 Martin Holbraad, Morten Axel Pedersen, and Eduardo Viveiros de Castro (2014). 'The Politics of Ontology: Anthropological Positions', *Cultural Anthropology* website, 13 January. https://culanth.org/fieldsights/462-the-politics-of-ontology-anthropological-positions.
43 Daley (2000), *op cit.*
44 Soumhya Venkatesan (2008). 'Debate: Ontology Is Just Another Word for Culture – Introduction', *Critique of Anthropology*, 30, 2, 154.
45 Pope John Paul II (1998). 'Fides et Ratio (Faith and Reason)', *Encyclical Letter of the Supreme Pontiff John Paul II to the Bishops of the Catholic Church on the Relationship between Faith and Reason*. Available at http://www.vatican.va/holy_father/john_paul_ii/encyclicals/documents/hf_jp-ii_enc_15101998_fides-et-ratio_en.html; accessed 8 January 2007.
46 Zenit Catholic News Service (2007). 'Angelus: On the Faith-Reason Synthesis – A Precious Patrimony for Western Civilization', *Zenit – The World Seen from Rome*, 28 January. Available at http://www.zenit.org/english Code: ZE07012804; accessed 29 January 2007.
47 G. C. Berkouwer (1959). 'General and Special Divine Revelation', in Carl Henry (ed.), *Revelation and the Bible: Contemporary Evangelical Thought*. London: The Tyndale Press, 14, 16; Millard J. Erickson (1998). *Christian Theology*, 2nd edn. Grand Rapids, Michigan: Baker Books, 177–223. See also Bruno Latour's (2010) essay on fetishes and 'factishes', highlighting similarities between the construction of both, yet while fetish-worshippers are aware that fetishes are human-made, 'facts' have taken on a new universal, 'other-worldly' quality in the modern ontology.
48 Viveiros de Castro (2013), *op cit.*
49 Ibid., 494–495.
50 See, for example, Asad (2003), *op cit.*; Hurd (2008), *op cit.*; Casanova (201), *op cit.*; C. Lynch (2003). 'Dogma, Praxis, and Religious Perspectives on Multiculturalism', in Fabio Petito and Pavlos Hatzopoulos (eds.) (2003). *Religion in International Relations: The Return from Exile*. New York: Palgrave Macmillan, 55–78; L. Mavelli and F. Petito (2012). 'The Postsecular in International Politics: An Overview', *Review of International Studies*, 38, 5, 936; L. Mavelli (2012). *Europe's Encounter with Islam: The Secular and the Postsecular*. London: Routledge.
51 Hurd (2008), *op cit.*; Casanova (2011), *op cit.*
52 E. S. Hurd (2015). *Beyond Religious Freedom: The New Global Politics of Religion*. Princeton: Princeton University Press.
53 Talal Asad (2002). 'The Construction of Religion as an Anthropological Category', in M. Lambek (ed.), *A Reader in the Anthropology of Religion*. London: Blackwell, 116.
54 William T. Cavanaugh (2009). *The Myth of Religious Violence*. Oxford: Oxford University Press.
55 Charles Taylor (2009). 'The Polysemy of the Secular', *Social Research*, 76, 4, 1143–1166; E. K. Wilson (2012). *After Secularism: Rethinking Religion in Global Politics*. Basingstoke: Palgrave.
56 Ahmed T. Kuru (2007). 'Passive and Assertive Secularism: Historical Conditions, Ideological Struggles, and State Policies Toward Religion', *World Politics*, 59, 4, 568–594; Hurd (2008), *op cit.*
57 Anila Daulatzai (2004). 'A Leap of Faith: Thoughts on Secularistic Practices and Progressive Politics', *International Social Science Journal*, 567.
58 Gutkowski (2014), *op cit.*, 6.

59 M. Foucault (1978), *Security, Territory, Population: Lectures at the Colleges du France, 1977–78*. New York: Picador, 2007, 2.

60 R. McCutcheon (2007). '"They Licked the Platter Clean": On the Co-Dependency of the Religious and the Secular', *Method and Theory in the Study of Religion*, 19, 3, 173–199.

61 Alexander Betts (2013). *Survival Migration: Failed Governance and the Crisis of Displacement*. Ithaca, NY: Cornell University Press.

62 UNHCR (2014), *op cit.*, 6.

63 Ibid., 6, 8.

64 Ager and Ager (2011), *op cit.*

65 Mavelli and Petito (2012), 931.

66 L. Mavelli (2012). 'Postsecular Resistance, the Body, and the 2011 Egyptian Revolution', *Review of International Studies*, 38, 5, 1057–1078.

67 Asad (2003), *op cit.*

68 Lynch (2011), *op cit.*; My Ngo (2015). *Religious Space, Transnational Space, Humanitarian Space: Case Study of a Faith-Based Organisation on the African Migration Route*, unpublished PhD thesis, Swinburne University, Melbourne, Australia.

69 Neil Arun (2015). 'Militants, Migrants and the Med: Europe's Libya Problem', *BBC News*, 24 February. Available at: http://www.bbc.com/news/world-middle-east-31584236; accessed 27 September 2017.

70 Eleanor Rose (2017). 'Nigel Farage Says EU Leaders Caused Terror Attacks by Letting People from "Different Cultures and Religions" Live in Their Countries', *The Standard*, 18 August. Available at https://www.standard.co.uk/news/uk/nigel-farage-says-eu-leaders-caused-terror-attacks-by-letting-people-from-different-cultures-and-a3614501.html; accessed 27 September 2017.

71 Azza Karam (2012). *Religion, Development and the United Nations*. Social Science Research Council Report. New York: Social Science Research Council. Available at http://www.ssrc.org/workspace/images/crm/new_publication_3/%7Beb4b29c9-501d-e211-bb1a-001cc477ec84%7D.pdf; accessed 13 August 2015.

72 Sadia Kidwai (2014). 'The Rights of Forced Migrants in Islam'. Islamic Relief Worldwide.

73 C. J. Eberle (2002). *Religious Conviction in Liberal Politics*. Cambridge: Cambridge University Press, 314.

74 Beaman (2014), *op cit.*, 96.

75 Katherine Murphy (2016). 'Comprehending Pauline Is Not the Challenge: Engaging Constructively with Hansonism Is', *The Guardian Australia*, 14 September. Available at https://www.theguardian.com/commentisfree/2016/sep/14/comprehending-pauline-is-not-the-challenge-engaging-constructively-with-hansonism-is?CMP=soc_567; accessed 23 January 2017.

36
ETHICS FROM THE UNDERSIDE

William Ackah

The ethical principles expressed in the major national and international documents that have shaped national and international relations are profound statements. The constitution of the United States, the Charter of the United Nations, the Universal Declaration of Human Rights, and others are towering moral and ethical documents that have provided humanity with road maps to a progressive, equitable, and peaceful world.[1] The highest ideals of rational thought emanating from these Enlightenment-influenced documents have had a major impact on the political, social, and economic fabric of the world, particularly in the 19th and 20th centuries. Yet for all the ideals that the West has bequeathed to the world, such as democracy, rule of law, and human rights, African descendants' rights have been trampled upon by Western nations and others as the latter have pursued profits and their own interests.

In this chapter, I want to explore how people of African descent have responded to the disregard of their humanity by nation-states and international bodies whose foundational statements and charters appear to be based on high ethical and moral values. This chapter also seeks to outline what the ethical and spiritual response of African peoples across the globe has been to the abuse of their human rights and dignity. An ethics from the underside of history. This ethics from the underside moves discussion of ethics from that of abstract theory to that which is shaped by the lived realities of marginalized and oppressed peoples. This framework also posits an ethic of elevation for marginalized and oppressed peoples, an ethics that champions the dignity, integrity, and particularity of people who have suffered from discrimination and oppression, and who have been forced to exist on the margins of the political, economic, and social systems of the world. Finally, I advocate for an ethics of repair, a recognition and acknowledgement of the impact of past injustices, and a determination to repair what has been broken. Such an ethics poses profound challenges to the field of ethics, as well as studies of religion, in international relations.[2]

Towards an ethics of deeds

As Tom Paine was setting out his liberal ethical statement on the rights of man,[3] and other European Enlightenment thinkers were advancing ideas of individual liberty, freedom, and justice,[4] Africans were being shackled in chains and shipped across the Atlantic in horrific conditions and circumstances.[5] As the ethical dimensions of life, liberty, and the pursuit of happiness were being framed, Africans were being denied their basic rights. Even worse, they were not deemed capable or worthy of having the same rights as the rest of humanity. They were deemed to be cargo; goods to be bought, sold, traded, and abused as their 'owners' saw fit. The same Enlightenment thinkers who were laying the groundwork for what would become the foundations for international ethics also provided intellectual justification for racism and enslavement, as Cornel West outlines:

> The intellectual legitimacy of the idea of white supremacy, though grounded in what we now consider marginal disciplines. . . was pervasive. This legitimacy can be illustrated by the extent to which racism permeated the writings of the major figures of the enlightenment. . . Montesquieu and Voltaire of the French Enlightenment, Hume and Jefferson of the Scotch and American Enlightenment, and Kant of the German Enlightenment not merely held racist views; they also uncritically – during this age of criticism – believed that the *authority* for these views rested in the domain of naturalists, anthropologists, physiognomists, and phrenologists.[6]

African-descended people resisted this depiction of themselves in a multitude of ways from outright armed resistance, economic sabotage, to a cultural resistance centred on countering efforts to dehumanize and strip African descendants of their humanity and cultural and spiritual identities.[7] Enslaved Africans developed spiritual, cultural, political, and social resources to challenge and overcome enslavement. The source materials for this resistance were a mix of fragments of African ideals and values remembered and translated from home, a nuanced critique of Western ideals and values being lived out in transatlantic contexts, and an ongoing religious and racialized identity born out of their lived experience, historical memories, and an ethic of striving towards freedom and dignity for the people.[8] It is within this context that one can find an alternative set of ethics at work that have relevance for how people, communities, and nations relate to each other in the contemporary moment.

For African descendants, an ethical and lived reality that has stemmed from the experiences of enslavement, colonialism, Jim Crow in the United States, apartheid (officially in South Africa, but also operating elsewhere), and other encounters with white supremacy is that pious proclamations and ethical principles are meaningless if they are not lived up to. A rather simple truism but with profound implications for African descendant relations with the international community is that the 'White' man's word can't be trusted; deeds and actions are what count. African descendants have a complex and intimate relationship to ethics and ideals emanating from Europe, particularly religious-inspired ethics.[9] From African continental elites educated in missionary schools, to enslaved and free Africans in the diaspora who have embraced Christianity, knowing it was the predominant faith of the slave masters and white supremacists, the ethics of biblical scripture were appealing, whilst the actions of many 'White Christians' were anything but. Hence there emerges an ethical call from the voices of African descendants from enslavement to contemporary times that names the hypocrisy and calls on the West to live up to the ideals it thought it had 'bequeathed' to African descendants.[10] This call was given voice in the spirituals of enslaved Africans[11] who saw the contradictions between the masters' proclaimed faith and their actual deeds, with notable lines such as 'Everybody talking about heaven ain't going there'.[12]

Thinkers of African descent have called upon the West to live up to its ethical pronouncements and have produced some powerful ethical statements of their own in doing so. Figures such as Frederick Douglass,[13] Henry Highland Garnett,[14] Bishop Henry McNeal Turner,[15] Sojourner Truth,[16] and Edward Blyden,[17] writing and speaking at the intersection of enslavement, segregation, and colonization in the 18th and 19th centuries, challenged Western governments, religious institutions, and persons of influence operating in these spheres to recognize that it was hypocritical and unethical to deny African descendants equal rights and dignity of personhood. These thinkers and others of the era were influenced by their belief in God to pursue justice for their communities. Most had deep familiarity with the religious traditions and wider philosophical thought of the people who had oppressed them, and many actually believed these ideals had merit, but that they needed to be applied to the person and not viewed as abstract principles.

Abstract principles by themselves were mere hypocrisy. David Walker, the prominent 19th-century abolitionist speaker and writer, exemplified this wave of thought in his 1829 *Appeal in Four Articles; Together with a preamble to the Coloured Citizens of the World, but in particular, and very expressly, to those of the United States of America.*[18] In his pamphlet, he castigates the hypocrisy of American Christians who send missionaries to foreign lands to convert the so-called 'heathen' yet engage in atrocities against 'coloured' people worshipping God at home. He asserts that if the nation does not address its immoral actions in enslaving Africans, then they will face the wrath of God's Judgement. In a powerful statement, he contrasts the ideals as set out in the Declaration of Independence (the 'all men are created equal' excerpt) with the treatment of African descendants:

> *Compare your own language above, extracted from your Declaration of Independence, with your cruelties and murders inflicted by your cruel and unmerciful fathers and yourselves on our fathers and on us—men who have never given your fathers or you the least provocation!!!!!!*[19]

A point to note from Walker's appeal here is the characterization of the Declaration of Independence as 'yours' and not his or ours. Enslaved people had no obligation to be beholden to principles to which they were not party and which were framed within a broader context of ideologies and policies that denied them their liberty and undermined their dignity. The ethics of white supremacy, the ethics underpinning imperialism, the ethics of continued exploitation and marginalization of peoples of African descent across the globe, exposes the hypocrisy of abstract idealism.[20] African descendants in their various contexts have sought to expose this hypocrisy and have exhorted their fellow white citizens to live up to the nation's espoused ideals. In the United States, the espoused ideals of the nation were and are immersed in a combination of religious and secular-leaning Enlightenment ideals.[21] African American activists, from Ida B. Wells[22] in her tireless campaign against lynching to Martin Luther King Jr's letter from a Birmingham jail[23] exhorting US religious leaders to act, have used the language, thought, and spirit of religious ideals to challenge society to put idealism into practice. Their words and actions are examples of a thread that runs through the history, thought, and practice of people of African descent after their encounter with white supremacy and is an important facet of an ethics from the underside of history. Ethics need to be applied, and need to be relevant to the lived experiences of marginalized peoples. Those in positions of privilege, power, and responsibility need to stand up and live out the ethical principles of their nations and religious and secular institutions internationally. Too often, unfortunately, in the case of African descendants, they have failed to do this.

The treatment of Haiti by Western nations is a powerful case in point. Here, enslaved Africans drew on the highest ideals of the French Revolution—liberty, fraternity—and combined these with their spirit of resistance, creativity, and resilience to break the shackles of French tyranny and create the first independent black republic in the Western hemisphere.[24] It was the best and most powerful example of Enlightenment ideals come to fruition in the so-called new and old worlds, a truly landmark event.[25] And it was led by a formerly enslaved

African, Toussaint L'Ouverture, who, as C. L. R. James outlines, went on to produce in his declaration of freedom one of the great statements of liberation of the era:

> Soldier and administrator above all, yet his declaration is a masterpiece of prose excelled by no other writer of the revolution. . . . Toussaint, uninstructed as he was, could find the language and accent of Diderot, Rousseau, and Raynal, of Mirabeau, Robespierre, and Danton and in one respect he excelled them all. . . . . Toussaint could defend the freedom of blacks without reservation, and this gave to his declaration a strength and a single-mindedness rare in the great documents of the time.[26]

One would think that the Haitian revolution would be lauded in the same way as the French Revolution or the United States' fight for independence. It has not, however, been afforded its rightful place among the pinnacles of freedom and liberation, neither at the time nor subsequently. Rather than respect and acknowledge the freedoms of these diasporic Africans, European powers fought to re-enslave them in the early 1800s. When this failed, they economically strangled the fledgling nation, refusing to bring it into the international community. Subsequently, the United States colonized the Haitians, and the French demanded and obtained reparations from them as compensation for their losses. These actions fatally damaged the greatest freedom project of the latter part of the 18th century, and the legacies of these actions impact the lives of Haitians today.[27] The instability of their governance arrangements, the myriad of international interventions, and the ecological and environmental disasters that have laid the country low and from which they continually struggle to recover can be traced back to the Western hypocritical response to the birth of this new nation. The disparity between the ethical ideals that would promote independence, freedom from tyranny, and the rights and dignity of the individual person and the actual treatment that Africans have received at the hands of the nations that espouse these ideals is glaring. Haiti is but one example of the repeated failure of the West to promote and protect the human rights of African descendants.

The fact that African descendants, in spite of their appeals to the highest ideals of Western ethical thought, are still, in the 21st century, on most objective measures, amongst the poorest, most discriminated against, having the poorest health outcomes, increased chance of becoming victims of violence, and higher vulnerability to ecological and environmental disasters, shows that even the greatest appeals from key moral and ethical protagonists to the West have in actuality had at best partial impact. Even when African descendants and other people of colour fought valiantly in both world wars for the preservation of European democracies and against fascism, discrimination, and tyranny, they returned to their homes to the same denials of their freedom and dignity that they had been fighting against. Instead of experiencing liberation, they returned to continued colonization, segregation, discrimination, and second-class citizenship. They were not deemed worthy of the ethical ideals for which they fought.

These inconsistences between ideals and experience as outlined leads to a logical conclusion that one cannot just appeal to the West to live up to its existing ethical ideals in relation to African descendants and other marginalized peoples. It is one prong that has been used, but by itself it is not enough. The legacies of enslavement, colonialism, and the ideologies of racism and white supremacy on which they were carried have had a more powerful impact on the lived realities of Africans than have political and economic arrangements based on international ethics. Hence, there is a need for a different kind of ethics to buttress and deepen existing ethical arrangements. A set of ethical principles that will address legacies of injustice and lift up those groups who have been marginalized and who in practice have had their rights trampled upon within the existing framework of 'Western ethical values'.

African descendants, in their religious and cultural rhetoric and their continued search for economic and political liberation, require something more nuanced, principles that reflect the realities of their lived experience in the world of the last five hundred years, and which point to a flourishing and renaissance of African personality and identity in the world in the next five hundred.

Towards an ethics of elevation of African descendants and other marginalized communities

Black Lives Matter has been a 21st-century clarion call, bringing critical attention to the ways in which black bodies have been routinely dehumanized by the US prison industrial complex, which in its most egregious manifestations has led to the shooting of unarmed men and women by US police officers.[28] The call, which has turned into a movement, has echoed around the globe into a sisterhood of movements. The movement has importance even beyond its immediate concerns. It is important because African descendant women are at the core of the movement and have infused it with womanist philosophies and intersectional understandings of race, gender, class, sexual orientation, disability, and religion. They have led the movement and brought into focus what an embodied, liberationist, spirit-filled ethic might look like.[29]

They have also brought to the fore an important intervention that points to the sacred nature of particular identities that have been brutalized, marginalized, and oppressed in societies, regardless of the ethics that purport to protect their rights. Black Lives Matter points to an important ethical principle, that African lives and the lives of other marginalized and oppressed groups are sacred and need to be elevated and revered in the public imagination. That these bodies should to be valued as humans with particular ethical as opposed to only an ethnic value. Over the past five hundred years, with the ascent of Western Europe and her Atlantic descendants to political and economic dominance of global affairs, we have witnessed a relegation of African descendant spirituality and cultures, and those of other indigenous people and marginalized people, to little more than ethnic or cultural specificities. In contrast, Western cultural values are deemed to be of universal importance.[30]

Alongside the relegation of non-white cultures, religions, and practices to the underside of world history and experience, the people who produced these cultures and religions have been subjected to colonization, enslavement, and genocide. The economic, political, and cultural subjugation of non-white peoples has gone hand in hand. To correct this, there is a need to ethically elevate the cultures of marginalized communities. In this chapter, the focus is on African descendants, but this elevation would apply to Native Americans, Aboriginal peoples, and other indigenous or marginalized peoples who have faced dehumanization and the attempted eradication of their cultures. African descendant cultures need to be given an ethical elevation to remove the stain of racism that continues to demean and undermine the value of African lives wherever African descendant peoples are found across the globe. It is evident that wherever African descendants reside, racism, discrimination, under-development, and marginalization follow them. And this, I would argue, is because of a history that continues to have an impact on the present. Hence, there is a need for a concerted ethical endeavour to create a change in these circumstances. An ethical elevation should recognize the sacred nature of these cultures and communities, and the tremendous value that they could bring to the world of knowledge, science, arts, and of the spirit. Sacred because in diverse religious traditions, one is admonished to take care of the least of these, to have a heart for marginalized and oppressed people, and sacred because it is in the realm of the spirit, in ethics of community and of love and sustainability, that African traditional cultures and other indigenous cultures still have much to teach the world.[31] Elevating the cultures of the marginalized and recognizing their contribution to the planet ultimately means repositioning the ethical and moral authority of the West from that of the superior to that of an equal. In this new ethical dispensation, no one tradition would assume dominance in the name of all, and no tradition, spiritual or otherwise, would be relegated to the margins of world history and experience.

One of the tragedies of our era is that in recognizing the cultural contributions of marginalized communities to world civilization, these cultures are fetishized, with Aboriginal art sold for millions of dollars and African artefacts housed in museums and credited for influencing arts, fashions, and music across the globe, whilst the producers of the culture remain impoverished. The same occurs in the world of technologies; the precious metals on which the world of mobile technologies revolves emerges out of African soil, yet the people of that soil live in precarious conditions of poverty, conflict, and disenfranchisement. Hence, a cultural elevation of African descendants needs to be an embodied elevation, where the lives not just the culture matters.

There have been historical efforts by African descendant thinkers and activists to elevate the concept of the special nature and importance of African cultures and to bring the spirit and genius of Africanity to the wider world. For instance, the Negritude movement, which brought together African descendants from French colonies in Africa and the West Indies to 1930s Paris.[32] These thinkers were educated in the French system, which exposed them to the ways in which the elites and wider educated French society viewed them and their cultures. They were viewed as backward and as having nothing of value to contribute towards French and European civilization. Colonization was regarded as bringing civilization to the so-called 'dark continent' and its people of African descent scattered across the globe.

The Negritude thinkers recognized the incongruity between their knowledge and experiences of their homes and peoples and how Europe viewed them, and decided to challenge this negative conception, with positive, poetic, and philosophical visions of African descendant lives and cultures.[33] They contrasted the militaristic, technocratic, secular, impersonal industrial expanses of Europe bent on conquest and destruction with a view of African peoples as communal, loving, at home with their environment, with a rich and spiritually informed culture built on an ethic of community. Leopold Senghor, a future President of Senegal, and Aime Cesaire, a future Mayor of Martinique, were key figures in this movement (although they had differing conceptions of the term/movement). It was critiqued at the time and later as being essentialist and propagating idealized and romantic versions of African communities, but it did help to underpin alternative discourses of African experiences and ideals in the world, which were part of a catalyst to give Africans dignity and purposeful reference points in struggles against colonialism and racism. Particularly in the articulations of Senghor, there was the idea that Africans were a people with a spiritual essence and that this essence traversed the continent and the diaspora and was a value in and of itself and potentially to the world.[34]

Kwame Nkrumah, the first President of Ghana, also shared some of these ideals with his concept of the African Personality. Here, he was articulating a philosophical vision of being African in the world that would be an alternative to the Capitalism of the West and the Communism of the East.

> An important aspect of Pan-Africanism is the revival and development of the 'African Personality'. . . It finds expression in a re-awakening consciousness among Africans and peoples of African descent of the bonds which unite us—our historical past, our culture, our common experience and our aspirations.[35]

Africans could forge their own way in the world, based on their own traditions and values but with modern application. Hence the African Personality was not a rigid religious or ethical system, but rather a way of being that sought to elevate the status of Africans in the world via a reassertion of their dynamic history and culture; in that sense, as Nkrumah asserts, it is a spiritual project.

> I was determined, soon after independence had been achieved in Ghana, to take practical steps to revive the cultural and spiritual unity of the African people, and to promote research into every aspect of our heritage, so that the African personality would become a driving force within the African revolution, and at the same time become a factor to be reckoned with in international affairs.[36]

The idea of an independent African ethical tradition taking route in the world did not get off the ground, as fledgling African nations got caught up in the crossfire of Cold War politics, and the struggle to survive politically in a neo-colonial economic and political environment. Nkrumah's dream of Pan-Africanism, of a unified political and economic African continent where the African Personality could develop, was a bold vision but has not been realized in practice. African states have come together to form continental institutions, foremost being the African Union. The AU, however, despite its high rhetoric, including making the powerful resonating gesture of making the diaspora one of its regions, has not provided the space for the elevation of African lives and culture in any long-term, sustainable sense.[37]

It has been the civil societies of African descendant communities on the continent and in the diaspora, where the articulation of an ethic of African elevation is closer to being realized. I have already touched on the Black Lives Matter movement, but in Latin and Central America, African descendant communities are increasingly protesting the discrimination they face and are fighting the marginalization and denigration of the African aspects of their cultural heritage. The increasing advancement of woman rights within this civil society space in the diaspora and on the continent has added layers of nuance and an intersectional lens that disrupts the essentialization of African experience in these contexts. The Circle of Concerned African Women Theologians (Circle), founded by Ghanaian theologian Mercy Oduyoye in Ghana in 1989, is an example of this emanating from the realm of formalized religion.[38] Religious institutions have been at the heart of African civil society, and women have been the core agents in their success and durability, even whilst suffering marginalization and exclusion at the highest levels in many of these institutions. The activities of the Circle by bringing to the fore the untold stories of women in religious communities and by drawing attention to issues of gender justice, HIV/AIDS, and doing so across the continent, utilizing African frames of reference, is in some ways a philosophical, spiritual, and practical embodiment of an anti-essentialist elevation of Pan-African identities, focusing on the 'least of these'.[39] The critique is that it is still a Christian-dominated grouping and does not have enough input or representation from women of other religions and spiritual orientations. Time will tell if this will change.

Another Pan-African effort to utilize the burgeoning power and ubiquity of African descendant spirituality for social justice purposes has been the nascent work of the Transatlantic Roundtable on Religion and Race (TRRR). Formed in 2010 by a group of academics from South Africa, the United Kingdom, and the United States, the TRRR is an emerging network of scholars, community activists, and religious leaders (again predominantly Christian) who through conferences, campaigns, and publications seek to advance the cause of social justice for African descendants and others who have suffered oppression and marginalization.[40]

The TRRR focuses on the role that religious and spiritual communities can play in bringing about equity and justice. As part of its activities in 2013, it launched a petition to end black enslavement, and in it articulated an ethics of the sacredness of black lives:

> *We the undersigned call on international organizations and sovereign nation states to focus their collective will and resources toward eradicating practices and policies that are contributing to the continued dehumanization and modern-day enslavement of African peoples in many parts of the world. . . .*
>
> *We also call on these international institutions and national governments to consciously develop deeper level strategies to ensure that the dignity and sacredness of the lives of African-descended peoples are upheld and that their human rights are realized and protected alongside those of their fellow citizens around the world.*[41]

The language of the petition ties an intersectional perspective on justice with an appeal to international institutions to uphold the dignity of African descendants. The petition uses theological language to posit its ethic of elevation of people of African descent. It recognizes that the lives of imperilled African descendants have intrinsic value, but that it needs the global community to embrace the ethical imperative, that Black Lives, Black Space, and Black Cultures matter.

The fact that African descendant lives have been undervalued and marginalized by Western nations and the international community in the past does shape the present, and it is to this that our focus now turns.

Towards an ethics of repair

A deep frustration in thinking about the legacies of enslavement and colonialism is the lack of acknowledgement from Western nations that they were deeply culpable in the undermining of the development of African peoples across the globe and that they have a moral and ethical responsibility to make amends and repair what they damaged in African descendant economies, polities, and cultures. Some, including very well-meaning religious and ethical figures, have advocated racial reconciliation as a way of healing divisions between groups.[42] This appears to be the dominant ethical and moral framework of our age in relation to dealing with conflict related to 'race', ethnicity, and religion. It was exemplified in South Africa with the truth and reconciliation commission, and variations of this framework were used in Northern Ireland and Rwanda. This process, however, as we see in South Africa, for example, has left perpetrators of gross injustices with their freedom and resources intact, having paid no penalty for their immoral and unethical actions. The West has had a long history of these actions, from illegally occupying the lands and nearly wiping out indigenous populations in North, Central, and South America, and Aboriginal peoples in Australasia. By enslaving millions of Africans and, by colonial conquest, illegally occupying vast swathes of the world, Western nations have a sad and sorry history of exploitation, brutalization, and subjugation of people of colour across the globe. And in most instances, they have not had to pay any penalty for their crimes and have resisted the idea that their conquering, exploitative activities were immoral and illegal. In certain cases, they have even been compensated when they had to stop their nefarious activities, as in the case of British slaveholders, who were given lavish compensation payments by the British state, whilst the Africans they had enslaved received nothing.[43] Movements that have and are attempting to hold Western nations to account on these issues have struggled to gain traction for their cause, but that is changing. The movement for reparations, which has been community-led in the Caribbean, North America, and Europe, and for a time has had some powerful protagonists such as a former Nigerian head of state, has now been joined by nation-states that comprise the regional grouping for the Caribbean, CARICOM.[44] In 2013, they established a reparations commission (Caricom Reparations Commission, CRC) to lead the way in seeking restitution from the governments and institutions of Europe that were engaged in the enslavement of African people. The justification for their claim is outlined below.

> *THE CRC ASSERTS THAT EUROPEAN GOVERNMENTS:*
>
> *Were owners and traders of enslaved Africans instructed genocidal actions upon indigenous communities*
>
> *Created the legal, financial and fiscal policies necessary for the enslavement of Africans*
>
> *Defined and enforced African enslavement and native genocide as in their 'national interests'*
>
> *Refused compensation to the enslaved with the ending of their enslavement*
>
> *Compensated slave owners at emancipation for the loss of legal property rights in enslaved Africans*
>
> *Imposed a further one hundred years of racial apartheid upon the emancipated*
>
> *Imposed for another one hundred years policies designed to perpetuate suffering upon the emancipated and survivors of genocide*
>
> *And have refused to acknowledge such crimes or to compensate victims and their descendants.*[45]

The process initiated by CARICOM does provide a mechanism for Western nations to acknowledge their wrongdoing and to make amends. It sets out in clear and precise language the ethical, moral, political, and economic rationale for reparatory justice. It makes clear that it is in obtaining justice for the victims of enslavement that one finds a more genuine route to reconciliation. Some African descendant religious reparations activists have used the example of Zacchaeus to urge religious institutions to embrace the cause.[46] Zacchaeus, according to the biblical narrative of Luke Chapter 19, was a tax collector who, after meeting Jesus, acknowledged that he had cheated people of their resources and that he had participated in a system of inequity and injustice. In acknowledging his complicity in wrongdoing, he took a further step and stated that he would make amends:

> *But Zacchaeus stood up and said to the Lord, 'Look, Lord! Here and now I give half of my possessions to the poor, and if I have cheated anybody out of anything, I will pay back four times the amount.'*

And Jesus says to Zacchaeus in response:

> *'Today salvation has come to this house, because this man, too, is a son of Abraham. For the Son of Man came to seek and to save the lost.'*
>
> *(Luke 19: 8–10, New International Version)*

The ethical call for justice that stems from this model links the idea of reconciliation to that of repair and justice for victims. In order to forge better local, national, and global relations between peoples of differing ethnicities, religions, ideological outcomes, past injustices need to be acknowledged, dealt with fairly and ethically, with a view towards achieving equity of outcome for groups disadvantaged by that injustice.

Conclusion

In this chapter, I have attempted to set out an ethics from the underside. It is based on a need to acknowledge the circumstances of the past five hundred years that has led to African descendants being victims of colonial exploitation, enslavement, and racism and the impact that this has had on these communities' development and standing in the world. It has been argued here that in order for African descendants to experience equity and dignity in international relations, Western nations should live up to their own ethical standards and confront the racism that still lingers and impacts their ability to treat African descendants as equals. Secondly, due to the dehumanization of African experience caused by the inculcation of racist ideals into Western thought, it is argued that international organizations and states need to promote an ethic of African elevation, whereby African cultures, values, and ways of being are valued and appreciated. Thirdly, we can't expect to live in the world without an acknowledgement that past immoral and illegal actions done to African descendants do have consequences, and that Western nations need to face up to these and be made to repay and repair what they have damaged. This calls for the worlds of international relations and ethics to look beyond the rational and the abstract and to acknowledge and engage in the lived realities and communal and spiritual connections of African descendants, for the good of all humanity.

Notes

1 Ian Shapiro and Joseph Lampert (eds.), *Charter of the United Nations: Together with Scholarly Commentaries and Essential Historical Documents* (New Haven: Yale University Press, 2014).
2 Hans Kung, 'A Global Ethic in World Politics: The Middle Way between "Real Politics" and "Ideal Politics"', *International Journal of Politics, Culture and Society*, 13, 1 (1999): 5–19.
3 Thomas Paine, *Rights of Man* (London: Penguin, 1984) (originally published 1791).
4 Jean Jacques Rousseau, *On The Social Contract* (New York: Dover, 2003) (originally published 1762).
5 David Eltis and David Richardson, *Atlas of the Atlantic Slave Trade* (New Haven: Yale University Press, 2015).
6 Cornel West, *Prophecy Deliverance: An Afro-American Revolutionary Christianity* (Philadelphia: Westminster Press, 1982), 61.
7 Gayraud Wilmore, *Black Religion and Black Radicalism: An Interpretation of the Religious History of African Americans* (New York: Orbis, 2006), 52–57.
8 W. E. B. DuBois, 'Of the Faith of the Fathers', in *The Souls of Black Folk* (New York: Penguin, 1983) (originally published 1903), 210–225.
9 Kelly Brown Douglas, *What's Faith Got to Do with It? Black Bodies/Christian Souls* (New York: Orbis, 2005).
10 Tony Martin, 'Some Reflections on Evangelical Pan-Africanism, or Black Missionaries, White Missionaries and the Struggle for African Souls 1890–1930', in *The Pan-African Connection from Slavery to Garvey and Beyond* (Dover: Majority Press, 1983), 31–46.
11 James H. Cone, *The Spirituals and the Blues: An Interpretation* (New York: Seabury Press, 1971).
12 James Newman, *Go Down Moses: Celebrating the African American Spiritual* (New York: Clarkson Potter, 1998), 133.
13 Frederick Douglass, *Narrative of the Life of Frederick Douglass: Written by Himself* (New York: Dover, 2016) (originally published 1845).
14 Joel Schor, *Henry Highland Garnett: A Voice of Black Radicalism in the Nineteenth Century* (Westport: Greenwood, 1977).
15 Stephen Ward Angell, *Bishop Henry McNeal Turner and African American Religion in the South* (Knoxville: University of Tennessee, 1992).
16 Nell Irvin Painter, *Sojourner Truth: A Life, a Symbol* (New York: W. W. Norton, 1998).
17 Edward W. Blyden, *Christianity, Islam and the Negro Race* (Baltimore: Black Classic Press, 1994) (originally published 1887).

18 David Walker, *David Walker's Appeal to the Coloured Citizens of the World, but in particular, and very expressively, to those of the United States of America* (Baltimore: Black Classic Press, 1993) (originally published 1829).
19 Ibid., 95.
20 Kelly Brown Douglas, *Stand Your Ground: Black Bodies and the Justice of God* (New York: Orbis, 2015).
21 Charles W. Mills, *The Racial Contract* (Ithaca: Cornell University Press, 1999).
22 Ida B. Wells, *On Lynchings* (New York: Dover, 2014).
23 Martin Luther King, Jr, 'Letter from Birmingham Jail', in Martin Luther King, Jr, *Why We Can't Wait* (New York: Signet, 2000), 85–112.
24 David P. Geggus (eds.), *The Impact of the Haitian Revolution in the Atlantic World* (Columbia: University of South Carolina Press, 2001).
25 C. L. R. James, *The Black Jacobins: Toussaint L'Ouverture and the San Domingo Revolution* (London: Allison & Busby, 1991).
26 Ibid., 198.
27 Laurent Dubois, *Haiti: The Aftershocks of History* (New York: Metropolitan, 2012).
28 Keeanga-Yamahtta Taylor, *From #BlackLivesMatter to Black Liberation* (Chicago: Haymarket, 2016).
29 Katie G. Cannon, Emilie M. Townes, and Angela D. Sims (eds.), *Womanist Theological Ethics* (Louisville: Westminster John Knox, 2011).
30 Stuart Hall, 'The West and the Rest: Discourse and Power', in Stuart Hall and Bram Gieben, *Formations of Modernity* (Cambridge: Polity, 1992), 275–320.
31 Dwight N. Hopkins and Marjorie Lewis (eds.), *Another World Is Possible: Spiritualities and Religions of Global Darker Peoples* (London: Equinox, 2009).
32 Siba N. Grovogui, *Beyond Eurocentrism and Anarchy: Memories of International Order and Institutions* (New York: Palgrave Macmillian, 2006).
33 Lilyan Keseltoot, *Black Writers in French: A Literary History of Negritude*, translated by Ellen Conroy Kennedy (Philadelphia: Temple University, 1974).
34 Sylvia Washington Ba, *The Concept of Negritude in the Poetry of Leopold Sedar Senghor* (Princeton: Princeton University Press, 1973).
35 Kwame Nkrumah, *Revolutionary Path* (London: Panaf, 1973), 205.
36 Ibid., 205.
37 Mammo Muchie, Phindil Lukhele-Olorunju, and Oghenerobor Akpor (eds.), *The African Union: Ten Years After* (Pretoria: Africa Institute of South Africa, 2013).
38 Isabel A. Phiri, 'The Circle of Concerned African Women Theologians: Its Contribution to Ecumenical Formation', *The Ecumenical Review*, 27, 1 (2005): 34–41.
39 Dora Rudo Mbuwayesango, 'The Circle's Contribution to HIV Discourse on the Global Level', *Journal of Feminist Studies in Religion*, 28, 2 (2012): 145–147.
40 William Ackah, 'Mapping the Religious Expressions and Spirituality of African Descendant Communities', in William Ackah, Jualynne Dodson, and R. Drew Smith (eds.), *Religion and Spirituality in Africa and the African Diaspora* (London: Routledge, 2017), 1–19.
41 religionandrace.org/campaigns.
42 Desmond Tutu, *No Future without Forgiveness: A Personal Overview of South Africa's Truth and Reconciliation Commission* (London: Rider and Co., 1999).
43 Catherine Hall, Nicholas Draper, Keith McClelland, et al., *Legacies of British Slave-Ownership: Colonial Slavery and the Formation of Victorian Britain* (Cambridge: Cambridge University Press, 2014).
44 Hilary McD. Beckles, *Britain's Black Debt: Reparations for Caribbean Slavery and Native Genocide* (Kingston: University of the West Indies, 2013).
45 caricomreparations.org/caricom/caricoms-10-point-reparation-plan
46 Leonara Tubbs Tisdale, *Prophetic Preaching: A Pastoral Approach* (Louisville: Westminster John Knox, 2010).

37

IBN KHALDUN AND THE WEALTH OF CIVILIZATIONS

Mustapha Kamal Pasha

Received scholarship often recognizes Ibn Khaldun (1332–1406) as a major Islamic philosopher of history preoccupied with the rise and fall of civilizations.[1] His profound reflections on civilizational cycles serve as an indispensable *medieval* contrast to *modern* accounts commonly available in Spengler, Gibbon or Toynbee. Less appreciated in standard historiography is Ibn Khaldun's status as a political economist seeking answers to the secret of wealth creation and the materialist foundations of civilization. The boundary between the medieval and modern worlds produces not only the fiction of cultural incommensurability, but also reveals the implicit hierarchy undergirding teleological thinking. This essay seeks to recover Ibn Khaldun's contributions to political economy as an attempt to rebuild bridges between the two worlds that are traditionally separated by time and culture. The task of reconstruction relies on a critical reading of Ibn Khaldun's Introduction (the *Muqaddimah*) to his magnum opus, the *Kitāb al-'Ibar* or 'Book of Lessons,' as well as an engagement with scholarly commentaries sheltering interdisciplinary horizons. The essay is also based on a refusal to embrace rigid binaries between religious and secular worlds. Ibn Khaldun's work melds the two worlds without succumbing to analytical paralysis.[2]

Introduction

Abd al-Rahman Ibn Muhammad Ibn Khaldun al-Hadrami (1332–1406), known to posterity simply as Ibn Khaldun, is well recognized as the pre-eminent Islamic thinker associated with the science of civilization ('*umran*). His status as the precursor of several 'modern' disciplines such as the philosophy of history, sociology,[3] and (dynamic) civilizational analysis provides an important 'decentering' counterpoint to Eurocentric renditions of knowledge production and its global dispersal.[4] While Ibn Khaldun's rich contribution is no longer peripheral to a more globalized story of modernity, key parts of his corpus addressing the inextricable nexus between political economy and civilization have received inadequate attention.[5] Nearly four hundred years before the publication of Adam Smith's *The Wealth of Nations* (1776) and the emergence of classical political economy as a distinct Western discipline of academic inquiry, another *magnum opus* appeared on the horizon, laying the foundations of 'modern' sociology, philosophy of history, political economy, and the study of civilizations. With *Kitāb al-'Ibar* and its unprecedented breadth and depth of civilizational analysis, Ibn Khaldun rightly emerged, to paraphrase

Toynbee, as one of the greatest thinkers humanity has produced.[6] Receiving lesser attention in modern intellectual circles is his remarkable contribution to economic thought, which is traditionally seen principally as a Western discipline.[7]

Surprising to many interlocutors is Ibn Khaldun's ability to transcend cultural limitations drawn from assumed adherence to an unrelenting Faith unwilling to entertain any lay comprehension of the mysteries of either the Creator or the created world. Hence, for Gibb: 'The true originality of Ibn Khaldun's work is to be found in his detailed and objective analysis. . . that constitute(s) the "new science" which he claims to have founded.'[8] That a thinker from the Islamic world could present a *world* picture seems anomalous; rather, he would necessarily reflect the biases and constrictions of his cultural and religious inheritance.[9]

Against the stubborn image of Western rationalism as a secular project, Ibn Khaldun remains an enigmatic figure. How could his philosophy of history emerge from an essentially religiously tainted world and serve Reason? The bifurcation of thought into Faith and Reason as rival templates in the history of ideas is well entrenched to exclude thinkers of Ibn Khaldun's temperament. Either he is a religious heretic who found cover as a Maliki judge, or he is plainly agnostic, pursuing his science of civilization as a secular enterprise on one track while confirming his religiosity only parenthetically. This enigma haunts intellectual history, one founded on the rational fundamentalism of a gulf separating the religious and the secular. Denying its own religious roots with continued presence of the theological in its constitution, rationalism denies Reason in religious others. Those seeking harmony, reconciliation or coexistence between *human* affairs and affairs of the Divine, on this view, are neither true representatives of their particular civilizational milieu, nor entirely original. Ibn Khaldun's fate at the hands of most of his commentators mirrors the pathology of the Great Separation.[10] Refracted into the past, this separation between the religious and the secular discriminates the West and Islam. Despite Ibn Khaldun's considerable achievements, therefore, he is unable to rise above his cultural filiations. Conversely, his 'science of civilization' is essentially a secular enterprise fully consistent with the modern sociological imagination.[11] Signifying Ibn Khaldun's alleged secularity, for instance, a notable contemporary scholar of Islamic economics writes:

> Being the science of culture, the shari'ah was interpreted by Ibn Khaldun as the universal law for all shades of belief and regional contexts. This interpretation of the shari'ah as the science of culture endowed Ibn Khaldun's interpretation of the philosophy of history, and the dynamics of civilization as a claimed universal theory. Yet for all this, Ibn Khaldun's philosophy of history remained a materialist interpretation of historicistic change and transformation of civilization.[12]

Those seeking to situate Ibn Khaldun into a secularist camp would countenance strong affinity with Choudhury's verdict that 'Ibn Khaldun could not provide the historistic legacy of the moral values that induce predominant influence in the shaping of civilization in its human form'.[13] For Choudhury, Ibn Khaldun deviated to a reckless degree from an Islamic conception of the cosmic order and its dynamics. Relying on a 'new science of civilization', Ibn Khaldun constructed a parallel theoretical universe in which religious cosmology was under-represented. Similar reservations have been recited in other important studies, questioning Ibn Khaldun's religiosity. In fact, it is religion's assumed absence in his philosophy of history that elevates his stature as a rationalist and proto-modern thinker. Discounted in received imaginings is the possibility, if not necessity, of Faith as a precondition for reflexive knowledge. Once liberated from the mundane by Faith, the thinker can pursue the mundane without fear or favor.

On the other side of the debate, a common strategy to deny Ibn Khaldun originality is to stress his Hellenistic background,[14] mostly at the expense of his Arab intellectual wellspring with Islam as its centerpiece. At the other extreme, some elect to emphasize principally his Arab ethos and outlook; he is confined to his own world: 'Ibn Khaldun's theory of history is deeply embedded in an appreciation of the contexts of human actions and their highly pragmatic consequences, rather than some stratospheric vision of cyclical social movements.' Rosen's choice of 'stratospheric vision' *particularizes* Ibn Khaldun's writings. Hence, 'his way of both considering and finessing the role of individual leaders,' Rosen asserts, 'is consonant with the orientation of one coming from an *Arab* (perhaps especially North African) background.' These observations give Rosen the confidence to adjudicate that 'the Western tendency to emphasize the similarities between the historiography of Ibn Khaldun and that of many Western analysts obscures the distinctive style of his own form of theorizing.'[15] Yet Rosen, like many other commentators, recycles an Orientalist prejudice[16] in dismissing Ibn Khaldun as 'very characteristically Arab' in his thinking, since 'the self, in Arab culture, was not envisioned as fractionated—through religious, cultural, or political history—into a set of roles, reinforced as extant and natural as drama, theology, or conceptions of time and space.'[17]

The tussle between those who recognize Ibn Khaldun's originality and those who underscore mostly his Hellenistic or Arab roots springs largely from an inability to read the religious and secular domains as *unified* components of the Islamic intellectual firmament. For Ibn Khaldun and several other notable Muslim thinkers, the production of knowledge is sanctioned by God-given reflexive capacity. The presence of the Divine is accentuated in one instance more than another, but never absent. This becomes evident in Ibn Khaldun's reflections on political economy centering on the pursuit of wealth but delimited by religiously ordained ethical constraints. Similarly, in the realms of philosophy or politics, sociology or history, the inseparability of the religious and the secular repudiates anticipations of modern secularity or assumed irreconcilable philosophical conflicts between Hellenism and Islam.[18] Ibn Khaldun may be applauded for conceiving his own variant of Tönnies's *Gemeinschaft* and *Gesellschaft*,[19] but it is more important to accord his conceptual apparatus the originality that it deserves.

Ibn Khaldun inherits multiple philosophical currents, but Faith rarely sits apart from his thinking. As Gibb convincingly shows:

> Ibn Khaldun was not only a Muslim, but as almost every page of the *Muqadimma* bears witness, a Muslim jurist and theologian, of the strict Maliki school. For him religion was far and away the most important thing in life—we have seen that he expressly calls his study a thing of subsidiary value—and the *Sharia* the only true guide.[20]

Ibn Khaldun

> uses the term religion in two different senses. On the one hand is religion in the true or absolute sense, when the whole will of man is governed by his religious conviction and his animal nature is held in check. Opposed to this is 'acquired' religion, a second-hand and relatively feeble thing, which saps his manhood and fails to control his animal impulses.[21]

This essay offers a synoptic picture of the confluence of the religious and the secular in Ibn Khaldun's reflections on political economy in the *The Muqaddimah*. The principal aim here is to resist a bifurcated reading, one that assigns distinct intentions to different passages. Beginning with a rather condensed summary of Ibn Khaldun's cosmology, the remaining discussion focuses on Ibn Khaldun's philosophy of history and political economy, but especially the ethical considerations that attend wealth creation. Needless to say, the current exercise here misses detailed analysis that Ibn Khaldun's corpus ineludibly demands.

Cosmology

Gibb offers a succinct précis of the religious background to Ibn Khaldun's thinking. Tackling the problem of 'reconciling the ideal demands of the Sharia with the facts of history,' Ibn Khaldun repeatedly 'drives home the lesson, over and over again, that the course of history is what it is because of the infraction of the Sharia by the sin of pride, the sin of luxury, the sin of greed.' Ibn Khaldun, according to Gibb, extends his analysis even to the realm of economic life that can yield prosperity 'only when the ordinances of the Sharia are observed.' The main inference is that, since human beings are imperfect, they 'will not follow the Sharia.' Hence, they are 'condemned to an empty and unending cycle of rise and fall, conditioned by the "natural" and inevitable consequences of the predominance of the animal instincts.' Gibb's conclusion is that, in this context, 'Ibn Khaldun may be a 'pessimist' or 'determinist,' but his pessimism has a moral and religious, not a sociological, basis'.[22] The primacy of religious law retains Ibn Khaldun's location squarely within a theological framework unhindered by sociological deviance.

Ibn Khaldun's complex theoretical structure is multi-layered. For analytical reasons, he classifies 'the world of existing things,' but a world that is interwoven:

> It should be known that the world of existent things comprises pure essence, such as the elements, the things resulting from their influence, and the three things that come into being from the elements, namely, minerals, plants, and animals. All these things are connected with the divine power. . . It also comprises actions proceeding from living beings, that happen through their intentions, and are connected with the power that God has given them. Some of their actions are well arranged and orderly. Such are human actions. Others are not well arranged and orderly. They are the actions of living beings other than man.[23]

Classification itself, however, does not furnish the key toward unlocking the 'science of civilization.' Ibn Khaldun finds the answer in *causation*, the organizing principle of his design. Causation is both a sign of the existence of God and the ephemeral character of human existence. Accepting this principle means to embrace both Eternity and Finitude, the former linked to the Divine, the latter to Creation:

> It should be known that the things that come into being in the world of existing things, whether they belong to essences or to either human or animal actions, require appropriate causes which are prior to (their coming into being). They introduce the things that come into being into the realm dominated by custom, and effect their coming into being. Each one of these causes, in turn, comes into being and, thus, requires other causes. Causes continue to follow upon causes in an ascending order, until they reach the Causer of causes, Him, who brings them into existence and creates them, Praise be He, there is no God but Him.[24]

For Ibn Khaldun, 'there are two basic categories of things: that which stems from the divine, and that which stems from the beings created by the divine.' This hierarchy also marks other 'spheres of knowledge—that of the knowable, concerned with the actions of man (and, to a lesser extent, of other beings), and that of the impenetrable, of ultimate causes and divine influence.'[25]

Ibn Khaldun recognizes Divine Will as the foundation of historical causation, but gives *asabiyya*[26] a defining role in the rise and decline of civilizations. In turn, *asabiyya* is inextricably tied to economic processes, notably the division of labor, its expansion, the generation of wealth, and the formation and consolidation of the State (*dawla*).[27] On a superficial reading, Ibn Khaldun erects a secular theoretical edifice, but a close reading of his *magnum opus* would help dispel this error. The sanctity of labor, the distinction between legitimate and illegitimate sources of wealth creation, the ends of State, and advancement of the Golden Mean in human affairs—all point toward Ibn Khaldun's embeddedness in a religious milieu that links conduct in commerce or government with Divine principles.

Despite the fatalistic tenor[28] of his philosophy of history which recognizes rise, decline, and fall of civilizations as an historical necessity, albeit conditioned by particular circumstance and local factors, Ibn Khaldun is not a nihilist. Life has a sacred purpose:

> The purpose of human beings is not only their worldly welfare. The entire world is trifling and futile. It ends in death and annihilation. God says: 'Do you think that we created you triflingly?' The purpose (of human beings) is their religion, which leads them to happiness in the other world, 'the path of God to whom belongs that which is in heaven and that which is on earth.' Therefore, religious laws have as their purpose to cause (human beings) to follow such a course in all their dealings with their God and their fellow men.[29]

Devotion to Divine principles does not efface human freedom. A core element in Ibn Khaldun's framework is his recognition of God-given human attributes, notably thinking capacity: 'God distinguished man from other animals by an ability to think which He made the beginning of human perfection and the end of man's noble superiority over existing things.'[30] In this connection, Ibn Khaldun advances a sophisticated theory of consciousness that melds Divinity, (human) reflexivity, and material forces. In the domain of political economy proper, for example, trades and crafts have a conditioning effect on cognitive processes. They are the result of different ways of making a living. For Ibn Khaldun, humankind is separable from other parts of the Creation. What defines human distinctiveness is, to reiterate, thinking capacity. Ibn Khaldun illustrates the manifestations of this capacity in a poignant passage:

> We say that man is distinguished from other living beings by certain qualities peculiar to him, namely: (1) The sciences and crafts which result from that ability to think which distinguishes man from other animals and exalts him as a thinking being over all creatures. (2) The need for restraining influence and strong authority, since man, alone of all animals, cannot exist without them . . . (3) Man's efforts to make a living and his concern with the various ways of obtaining and acquiring the means of (life). . . (4) Civilization. This means that human beings have to dwell in common and settle together in cities and hamlets for the comforts of companionship and for the satisfaction of human needs, as a result of the natural disposition of human beings toward co-operation in order to be able to make a living. . .[31]

Philosophy of history

While Ibn Khaldun remains a committed believer, he does not depend upon metaphysical answers to explain human affairs. Ibn Khaldun's abiding belief in God-given human faculties for knowledge, reflexivity, and intuition allows him to probe causality. For Ibn Khaldun, there is a nexus between the cosmic order and order in the created world. History has a causal structure. In probing this structure, Ibn Khaldun, in Aristotelian fashion, recognizes the distinction between 'essential' and 'accidental' causes. Only the essential causes ensure a deeper understanding of societal phenomena. It is this ability to theorize connections among phenomena, rather than depend only on pure observation, that sets him apart from his peers.

In short, what distinguishes Ibn Khaldun from traditional Islamic scholars of his time is a self-conscious effort to connect logic and history. His 'science of civilization' captures the durable patterns in history, but as a series of dynamic processes. Observing the decline and collapse of societies around him provided Ibn Khaldun a keen insight into the changeability of events.[32] What is the referent theoretical object in accounting for historical change?

Ibn Khaldun's enterprise focuses on *'umran*, loosely translated as 'civilization.' An underlying source of *'umran* is wealth creation. The dynamics of this process and its institutional effects occupy the bulk of Ibn Khaldun's meditations on political economy. In broader context, unlike previous Islamic chroniclers, Ibn Khaldun's novelty lies in seeking deeper truths of civilizational dynamics. Events history is insufficient; history must rely upon philosophy to make sense:

> The inner meaning of history. . . involves speculation and an attempt to get at the truth, subtle explanation of the causes and origins of existing things, and deep knowledge of the how and why of events. (History), therefore, is firmly rooted in philosophy. It deserves to be accounted a branch of (philosophy).[33]

The challenge for Ibn Khaldun is to understand the 'inner meaning of history' in a universe of fluidity and flux. Ibn Khaldun's profound reflections are based upon his keen awareness of civilizational decline, an irreversible process in human evolution. These reflections are not restricted to late 14th-century North Africa or simply the spatial worlds of a once-glorious Arab-Islamic civilization, but reach out into other worlds, both past and future. On the one hand, Ibn Khaldun needs to recognize the changeability of things:

> It should be known that the world of the elements and all it contains comes into being and decays. This applies to both its essences and its conditions. Minerals, plants, all the animals including man, and the other created things come into being and decay, as one can with one's own eyes. The same applies to the conditions that affect created things, and especially the conditions that affect man. Sciences grow up and then they are wiped out. The same applies to crafts, and to similar things.[34]

To resolve the tension between the laws of historical change and events history, Ibn Khaldun recognizes two aspects of history: external and internal. The exterior only provides mere information about battles or past dynasties. On the inside, Ibn Khaldun sees speculation, verification, interpretation, and deeper knowledge as crucial elements in identifying the true causes of events. This quest inevitably directs inquiry into the rise and decline of civilizations. Recognizing two ideal-typical social formations—*'umran badawi* and *'umran hadari*—each reflecting the manner in which material life is produced, Ibn Khaldun advances a philosophy of history that in modern parlance approximates determinism. As Ibn Khaldun posits, 'the goal of civilization is sedentary culture and luxury. When civilization reaches that goal, it turns toward corruption and starts being senile, as happens in the natural life of living beings.'[35]

Political economy

The principal foundation of political economy for Ibn Khaldun lies in the human need for cooperation: As soon as human beings, with their God-given power of thinking, begin to co-operate with each other and to form some kind of social organization, *umran* results.[36] Human purpose, for Ibn Khaldun, can be realized only as a social quest. The state of nature is unnatural to human beings; society is indispensable for survival and flourishing:

> The existence and persistence of the human species can materialize only through co-operation of all men in behalf of what is good for them. It has been established that a single human being could not fully exist by himself, and even if, hypothetically, it might happen as a rare exception, his existence would be precarious.[37]

A solitary life is an impossibility. Cooperation ensures human survival. Social life, however, is dynamic, characterized by growth, development, and decay. For Ibn Khaldun, without this cooperation, a human being is unable to obtain food and nourishment and, therefore, cannot survive because of the need for God that God has instilled in his life. It is not only the need for food that necessitates cooperation. There is also the elementary question of security. A human being cannot defend himself without weapons, and thus falls prey to beasts. He soon perishes before his natural death. Hence, cooperation allows food for survival, weapons for defense, and thus realizes God's will of preserving the human species. In short:

> Social organization is necessary to the human species. Without it, the existence of human beings would be incomplete. God's desire to settle the world with human beings and to leave them as His representatives on earth would not materialize. This is the meaning of civilization.[38]

The need for cooperation is a recurrent theme in *The Muqaddimah*. Ibn Khaldun, however, does not curtail his thinking on cooperation to bare survival but considers it as a source of wealth expansion. The mechanism for that expansion is the division of labor since 'what is obtained through co-operation of a group of human beings satisfied the need of a number many times greater (than themselves).'[39]

Umranic activity, as Hasan notes, 'is basically an economic activity, and the 'umranic process is a process of socio-economic development. Wealth creation is the lynchpin of 'umran and labor is its primary source.' Relying on Quranic verses, Ibn Khaldun stresses the abundance of resources God provides 'to operate as His representative on the planet Earth.' God's design ensures that 'resources were created that they would yield to human intelligence, creativity and effort to produce for him the means of sustenance and facility.' Although 'life on earth started with men and resources,' they are merely 'a contributory element; human effort (*labour*) must be combined with them for wealth creation.' Ibn Khaldun appreciates the process of development in which the confluence of labor and instruments enhances productivity and produces profit. Ultimately, for profit is a part of the product as well as the result of human labor.[40]

Ibn Khaldun sees two fundamentally distinct domains in which all human cooperation takes place and the forms of sociability evolve: desert life and sedentary life. The engine of social evolution is the production of surplus. Originally, people are concerned with meeting their basic necessities. This endeavor gives birth to the social type, *'umran badawi*. With greater division of labor, there is increase in surplus which facilitates the transition to *'umran hadari*. A basic feature of *'umran hadari* is the production of luxury goods. The former is characterized principally by agricultural labor; the latter consists of industrial and commercial labor. Greater differentiation between the two intensifies the difference between town (*harar*) and country (*badu*). Not only are these physical worlds, but each spawns a different mental and ethical state.[41]

Once the ethical dimension of political economy in Ibn Khaldun is acknowledged as the secret to the riddle of the rise and decline of societies, the religious and the secular terrains can be bridged. If it is the creation of wealth that drives societies in their transition to statehood, this process can also be corrosive. Societies ultimately move toward becoming polities, but it is the nature of how wealth is produced that accounts for differences in social formations. The presence or absence of oppression can be pivotal in hastening decline or rise. In noticing linkages between labor and value, supply and demand, and development and civilization, Ibn Khaldun anticipates much of modern economics, but he eschews a utilitarian horizon.

Human survival and flourishing depend upon cooperation and political authority. Concentrating here on economic life, the system of economic relations for Ibn Khaldun is a total system with multiple layers. Central to this system is labor, or more accurately, the division of labor. Economic life, for Ibn Khaldun, is a semi-autonomous zone, albeit linked to the political and ideational spheres. What is distinctive about economic life is its historicity, the possibility for flux, change, and transformation. Notwithstanding Ibn Khaldun's reputation as a cultural theorist, it is the *dynamic* character of the economy that gives the Khaldunian system its defining properties. It is in this context that Ibn Khaldun's mediations on the wealth of civilizations remains, perhaps, his finest contributions to human thought. Yet, in the same context, Ibn Khaldun repels traditional explanations for the rise and decline of civilizational orders.

As noted, the production of economic surplus is at the heart of the development of *'umran*; it is labor, in the final analysis, that is the source of value. Nevertheless, no civilization can rely entirely on material development. Economic activity must be imbued with religious purpose, or *asabiyya*, to ensure social cohesion. Binding the social process in various phases is *asabiyya*, a dynamic socio-political phenomenon. The ultimate destination of *asabiyya* is the establishment of a state, hence the movement from *'umran badawi* to *'umran hadari*. In turn, the state cannot survive with coercion alone. An expanded *asabiyya* is required to ensure the consolidation of state power.

Ibn Khaldun's political economy is unimaginable without ethical content. This becomes expressly manifest in his distinction between 'natural' and 'unnatural' ways of making a living. Conceding the reality of 'unnatural' ways in the economic process, Ibn Khaldun fully recognizes the concept of *exploitation*. The essence of exploitation is the gain or surplus without the exertion of labor. Ibn Khaldun identifies not only the need for *asabiyya* to bind society and state, but the necessity of justice in economic life. 'Among the most oppressive measures, and the ones most destructive of 'umran,' Ibn Khaldun stresses, 'is to force the subjects to work without remuneration or justification.' Exploitation 'leads to the ruin and collapse of 'umran.'[42] Furthermore, Ibn Khaldun links economic activity, especially the labor process, to hope—the anticipation of a better life. The decline in *'umran* is directly connected to an attrition in hope. This insight further recasts Ibn Khaldun not as an economic determinist, but as a thinker cognizant of the relation between material and mental dimensions of social and economic life. This is also confirmed with his astute awareness of the concept of prestige (*jah*) as an important dimension of social class. The aspiration to acquire prestige through wealth conjoins materiality with symbolic aspects of economic life.

The economy is not a neutral sphere of human activity for Ibn Khaldun, but a space imbued with ethical content. Ibn Khaldun is particularly sensitive to the notion of oppression (*zulm*). He sees a direct relation between oppression and illegal confiscation:

> Injustice should not be understood to imply only the confiscation of money or other property from the owners, without compensation and without cause. It is commonly understood in that way, but it is something more general than that. Whoever takes someone's property, or uses him for forced labour, or presses an unjustified claim against him, or imposes upon him a duty not required by the religious law, does an injustice to that particular person. People who collect unjustified taxes commit an injustice. Those who infringe upon property (rights) commit an injustice. Those who take away property commit an injustice. Those who, in general, take property by force, commit an injustice. It is the dynasty that suffers from all these acts, in as much as civilization, which is the substance of the dynasty, is ruined when people have lost all incentive.[43]

Wealth is a double-edged sword for Ibn Khaldun. Translated into luxury, it corrupts the character. Again, the ethical dimension is a paramount consideration, since a consequence of luxury is that 'the soul acquires diverse kinds of evils and sophisticated customs.'[44] But it is ultimately the exploitation of labor that engages the force of Ibn Khaldun's ethical commitments:

> One of the greatest injustices and one which contributes most to the destruction of civilization is the unjustified imposition of tasks and the use of subjects for forced labor. This is so because labor belongs to the things that constitute capital. . . Gain and sustenance represent the value realized from labor among civilized people. All other efforts and all their labors are (means) for them (to acquire) capital and (to make a) profit. They have no other way to make a profit except (through) labor.[45]

For Ibn Khaldun, the wealth of civilizations depends on the value realized in human labor; it the availability of available labor that is the source of profit, and hence, wealth. Similarly, the expansion of the market increases wealth:

> Thus, when a city has a highly developed, abundant civilization and is full of luxuries, there is a very large demand for those conveniences and for having as many of them as a person can expect in view of his situation. This results in a very great shortage of such things. Many will bid for them, but they will be in short supply. They will be needed for many purposes, and prosperous people used to luxuries will pay exorbitant prices for them, because they need them more than others. Thus, as one can see, prices come to be high.[46]

While labor is critical to Ibn Khaldun's ethical reflections on political economy, he also recognizes the linkage between unlawful seizure of property and civilizational decline. Hence, in addition to the exploitation of labor:

> [A]n injustice even greater and more destructive of civilization and the dynasty than (the one just mentioned) is the appropriation of people's property by buying their possessions as cheaply as possible and then reselling the merchandise to them at the highest possible prices by means of forced sales and purchases.[47]

In sum, Ibn Khaldun's analysis sees the civilizational process as the production of basic necessities of life towards the production of conveniences and luxuries. In similar vein, the development of the economy is intertwined with urbanization and the production of wealth of nations. Central to wealth generation is surplus labor, itself the result of the division of labor. As wealth increases, it enhances the size of the population upon which prosperity then depends.

Conclusion

The interlinkages between wealth creation, civilization, and ethics recast Ibn Khaldun in a new light. Liberated from secularist readings, his 'science of civilization' does not appear at odds with the ethos of high Islamic culture. Conventional interpretations of Ibn Khaldun as a theoretical heretic divert focus away from that culture's rich inheritance. More significantly, perhaps, these accounts embellish the gulf dividing the premodern and the modern worlds, one religious, the other secular. Naturalizing this divide, a permanent wedge is created between cultures belonging to either side. Reclaiming Ibn Khaldun's ethics helps to disturb some entrenched biases. Ibn Khaldun's achievement lies not merely in anticipating the horizon of modern knowledge production, but in simultaneously crystallizing and transcending the intellectual temper of his spatio-temporal worlds. Recognizing this achievement may help broaden the cultural myopia that lies at the source of modernity's self-image.

Notes

1 For a background on Ibn Khaldun, see Yves Lacoste, *Ibn Khaldun: The Birth of History and the Past of the Third World* (London: Verso, 1984). A broader context of Ibn Khaldun's philosophical terrain can be found in Oliver Leaman, *An Introduction to Medieval Islamic Philosophy* (Cambridge: Cambridge University Press, 1985).
2 Duncan Black Macdonald, *The Religious Attitude and Life in Islam: Being the Haskell Lectures on Comparative Religion delivered before the University of Chicago in 1906* (Chicago: University of Chicago Press, 1909).
3 Mahmoud Dhaoudi, 'Ibn Khaldun: The Founding Father of Eastern Sociology,' *International Sociology*, 5, no. 3 (September 1990), 319–335.
4 Natalie Zemon Davis, 'Decentering: Local Stories and Cultural Crossings in a Global World,' *History and Theory*, 50, no. 2 (2011), 188–202.
5 Ameer Ali and Herb Thompson, 'The Schumpeterian Gap and Muslim Economic Thought,' *The Journal of Interdisciplinary Economics*, 10 (1999), 31–49.
6 Robert Irwin, 'Toynbee and Ibn Khaldun,' *Middle Eastern Studies*, 33 (July 1997), 461–479.
7 Ali and Thompson, 'The Schumpeterian Gap,' op. cit. Also see Joseph J. Spengler, 'Economic Thought of Islam: Ibn Khaldun,' *Comparative Studies in Society and History*, 6, no. 3 (April 1964), 268–306.
8 H. A. R. Gibb, 'The Islamic Background of Ibn Khaldun's Political Theory,' *Bulletin of the School of Oriental and African Studies*, 7, no. 1 (February 1933), 25, 23–31.
9 White, Hayden, 'Ibn Khaldun in World Philosophy of History,' *Comparative Studies in Society and History*, 2 (October 1959), 110–125.
10 Mark Lilla, *The Stillborn God: Religion, Politics and the Modern West* (New York: Alfred Knopf, 2007).
11 Masudul Alam Choudhury, 'Ibn Khaldun's Political Economy,' *Islam Ekonomisi Finansi Dergisi* (Journal of Islamic Economics and Finance), 2 (2016), 1–23.
12 Ibid., 2.
13 Ibid., 14.
14 Stephen Frederic Dale, 'Ibn Khaldun: The Last Greek and the First Annaliste Historian,' *International Journal of Middle East Studies*, 38, no. 3 (August 2006), 431–451. Also see Muhsin Mahdi, *Ibn Khaldun's Philosophy of History: A Study in the Foundation of the Science of Culture* (Chicago: University of Chicago Press, 1957).
15 Lawrence Rosen, 'Theorizing from within: Ibn Khaldun and His Political Culture,' *Contemporary Sociology*, 34, no. 6 (November 2005), 596, 596–599.
16 Mohammad R. Salama (ed.), *Islam, Orientalism and Intellectual History* (London: I. B. Taurus, 2011). ProQuest EBook Central.
17 Gibb, op. cit. 598.
18 G.E. Grunebaum, *Islam and Hellenism: Essays in the Nature and Growth of a Cultural Tradition* (Menasha, Wisconsin: American Anthropological Association, 1955).
19 Ferdinand Tönnies, *Community and Society (Gemeinshaft und Gesellschaft)*, trans. Ed. Charles P. Loomis East Lansing Michigan, 1957).
20 Gibb, 'The Islamic Background,' op. cit., 28.

21 Ibid., 29. Also see Miya, Syrier, 'Ibn Khaldun and Islamic Mysticism,' *Islamic Culture*, 21, no. 3 (1947), 264–302.

22 Ibid., 31.

23 *The Muqaddimah*, vol. II, 413–414.

24 *The Muqaddimah*, vol. III, 34.

25 Briton Cooper Busch, 'Divine Intervention in the "Muqaddimah" of Ibn Khaldun,' *History of Religions*, 7, no. 4 (May 1968), 317–329.

26 *Asabiyya* is the pivot around which Ibn Khaldun's theoretical project revolves. Translated variously as 'group feeling,' the force that binds a community, or the animating spirit that drives historical change, the concept is best understood in dynamic and dialectical terms: a social force that confers cohesion and purpose to a community but evolves both spatially and temporally. No static definition does justice to this vital Khaldunian concept. For a Durkheimian reading of *asabiyya*, see Ernest Gellner, *Muslim Society* (Cambridge: Cambridge University Press, 1981).

27 As Ibn Khaldun reasons: 'However, the power of the individual human being is not sufficient for him to obtain (the food) he needs, and does not provide him with as much food as he requires to live. Even if we assume as absolute minimum of food—that is, food enough for one day, (a little) wheat, for instance—that amount of food could be obtained only after much preparation such as grinding, kneading, and baking. Each of these three operations requires utensils and tools that can be provided only with the help of several crafts, such as the crafts of the blacksmith, the carpenter, and the potter. Assuming that a man could eat unprepared grain, and even greater number of operations would be necessary in order to obtain the grain: sowing and reaping, and threshing to separate it from the husks of the ear. Each of these operations requires a number of tools and many more crafts than those mentioned. It is beyond the power of one man to do all that, or (even) part of it, by himself. Thus, he cannot do without a combination of many powers from among his fellow beings, if he is to obtain food for himself and for them. Through cooperation, the needs of a number of persons, many times greater than their own (number), can be satisfied.' *The Muqaddimah*, vol. I, 89-90.

28 B. A. Mojuetan, 'Ibn Khaldun and His Cycle of Fatalism: A Critique,' *Studia Islamica*, no. 53 (1991), 93–108.

29 *The Muqaddimah*, Vol. I, 386.

30 *The Muqaddimah*, vol. II, 411.

31 *The Muqaddimah*, vol. I, 84.

32 Nathaniel Schmidt, *Ibn Khaldun: Historian, Sociologist and Philosopher* (New York: Columbia University Press, 1930).

33 *The Muqaddimah*, vol. I, 6.

34 *The Muqaddimah*, vol. I, 278.

35 *The Muqaddimah*, vol. II, 296.

36 'Umran (translated here as 'civilization') is one of the key terms in Ibn Khaldun's system. It is derived from the root which means 'to build up, to cultivate,' and is used to designate any settlement above the level of individual savagery.' Rosenthal, *The Muqaddimah*, vol. I, lxxvi. Also see Mahmoud Dhaoudi, 'The Ibar: Lesson of Ibn Khaldun's Umran Mind,' *Contemporary Sociology*, 34, no. 6 (November 2005), 585–591.

37 *The Muqaddimah*, vol. II, 329.

38 *The Muqaddimah*, vol. I, 90–91.

39 *The Muqaddimah*, vol. II, 271.

40 Zubair Hasan, 'Labour as a Source of Value and Capital Formation: Ibn Khaldun, Ricardo, and Marx—A Comparison,' *JKAU: Islamic Economics*, 20, no. 2 (2007), 47–48, 39–50. Cf. *The Muqaddimah*, vol. II, 311.

41 Rosenthal, *The Muqaddimah*, vol. I, lxxvii.

42 *The Muqaddimah*, vol. II, 107–108.

43 *The Muqaddimah*, vol. II, 106–107.

44 *The Muqaddimah*, vol. I, 341.

45 *The Muqaddimah*, vol. II, 108–109.

46 *The Muqaddimah*, vol. II, 277.

47 *The Muqaddimah*, Vol. II, 109.

38

THE FUTURES OF ETHICS AND INTERNATIONAL RELATIONS

Dan Bulley

Even a cursory glance through the many excellent chapters contained in this volume reveals one thing for sure: the study of ethics and international relations (IR) has no future; it has several. From its contested history, superbly summarised by Kimberly Hutchings, to its disputed present, the chapters demonstrate the plethora of approaches, foci, methodologies and ontologies that now comprise this burgeoning field. And this is without considering those approaches and issues that were not included in this volume (such as a focus on disability[1] or a contribution from Queer theory[2]). Editing is unavoidably violent and exclusionary, after all; summarising a field is necessarily a 'falsification in process'.[3] What is particularly encouraging is that throughout this volume, there is little trace of the cosmopolitanism versus communitarianism framing device that became so influential in the 1990s.[4] Whilst the motivating tension between universalism and particularism remains, it no longer stifles a field which, as Beate Jahn's chapter points out, is characterised by fragmentation rather than unity. This diversification and absence of overarching and limiting frames is a sure sign that the health of, and widespread interest in, the field of ethics and international relations is here to stay. The ethical 'turn' is one that has certainly been taken, but in a variety of directions.

Eric A. Heinze and Brent J. Steele note in their editor's Introduction that 'the same diversity that enriches the field of Ethics and IR also makes it a difficult one to characterize'. Equally, this diversity makes the field's futures impossible to forecast. And as theoretical physicist Niels Bohr is said to have observed, prediction is always very difficult, especially when it's about the future.[5] Not only are predictions susceptible to unexpected events in international politics, disciplinary changes can emerge through unforeseen cross-pollinations from other fields of study. Most importantly, predictions are always personal and political, reflecting what the forecaster *fears* or *wants* to occur. With this in mind, I point in this chapter to three foci and challenges that I believe will grow, or become more urgent, over the coming years. They are also areas I would like to see become more influential. These issues – the environment and non-human, the decolonial challenge and unexceptional slow violence – will be examined in turn, but they are also linked in key ways, and each takes its lead from certain contributions to this volume. I begin with the environment, as this is often presented as the most urgent and catastrophic challenge to life itself.

Environment, climate change and the non-human

It is normal practice to commence any writing on the environment and climate change with a set of scary statistics. These are not difficult to find. Every day brings a fresh news story about the deadly and potentially catasrophic effects of the damage humans have been doing to the environment for the last two centuries. According to the Lancet Countdown on Health and Climate Change, an international research collaboration that tracks 40 key indicators and publishes its findings each year in *The Lancet*, the threats to human life posed by this damage are now potentially irreversible.[6] It has already led to 125 million more people made vulnerable to heatwave events between 2000 and 2016, a 46% increase in weather-related disasters between 2000 and 2013, and 24 million more undernourished people than in 1990. Both confirming and contesting Carol Farbotko's chapter in this volume (which noted that 'climate migrants are empirically elusive' and almost impossible to locate in actuality, if often the subject of many dire predictions), the Lancet Countdown confidently reports that 'climate change alone has directly forced at least 4,400 to migrate and over 1 billion people may be at risk of migration by the end of the century'.[7] In spite of this, people remain largely unmoved by the ethical or political urgency of the situation, a problem reflected in the headline of the *New Scientist*'s article on the 2017 Lancet report – 'Climate change will kill millions but you knew that already'.[8]

Environmental degradation and climate change are challenges to which international ethics must respond, and yet beyond Green theory it is unsurprising that it has yet to do so in a convincing or sustained way. Other than Benney, Farbotko and Brassett, Richardson and Smith's chapters, there is little in this volume to suggest an imminent change in this regard. And yet there is plenty of potential in each theme of the present volume. The philosophical foundations of international ethics in Joy Gordon's theme could be turned to the issues of collective and differential responsibilities for environmental damage, as well as the anti-egalitarian, unjust nature of its outcomes. IR theory could take more account of Green theory, which is inherently critical, normative and cosmopolitan in its approaches and recommendations.[9] Critical security studies in its various hues has been engaging with environmental security since the 1990s,[10] and with its recent turn to the Anthropocene is well ahead of international ethics in this regard.[11] The role, and current failure, of international institutions in any response to climate change appears inevitable, while the impasse posed by state sovereignty on the potential for intervention is a perennial issue. Whether or not Responsibility to Protect (R2P), a prominent topic in James Pattison's theme in intervention and sovereignty, could be part of any reaction must be doubtful: this emerging norm has proven incapable of reformulating to cope with refugees fleeing the atrocities it was designed to deal with;[12] there can be little hope of it providing for the protection of climate refugees who have no status in international law (see Chapter 28). The imbrication of the environment with issues of vulnerability and political economy are well recognised already in this volume, but the role of religions and their various relationships to the non-human could be a source of further work.

Perhaps this general myopia is a sign that ethics and IR still remains too wedded to the staples of the international system: state sovereignty and the mitigation of anarchy. Climate change could be taken as an opening to begin debates in ethics and IR that are more fundamental and ontological, such as what duties of care we owe to the non-human that co-constitute our world, making it liveable and breathable.[13] It also generates questions involving different conceptualisations of time and space: do we need to look to alternative spaces, often ignored by IR, such as islands made vulnerable by ecological change? What about global cities as the command and control nodes from which these changing ecologies are directed? After all, cities such as London and New York direct the flows of finance that can strip rural populations of their land in the Global South, turning it over to agribusiness interests that pollute and destroy local environments.[14] Such cities are largely dependent for their very material existence on the populations they helped expel and to whom they outsourced their most polluting industry, with up to 80% of London's food imported from outside the UK[15] – does this incur particular obligations of responsibility, care or justice? What responsibilities do current individuals, communities and populations owe to future generations who will live with the choices made, or avoided, now? How do we deal with the contingency of this future, and how is such uncertainty helping to construct our present? Can those in the Global North who were not directly responsible for the damage of past industrialisation, but continue to experience the benefits of it, be held accountable to vulnerable populations in the present day? Should we be discussing issues of reparation, as noted by some of the literature discussed in Puneet Dhaliwal's chapter in the context of colonialism, or do we need something more structural and far-reaching, as he implies? Are the philosophical foundations outlined in this volume by Matthew Lindauer, Kok-Chor Tan and David Atenasio able to address these questions? Are conventional IR theories even able to think them?

In confronting the challenge of man-made ecological transformation, however, the turn to ethics and IR needs to avoid positing itself as the source of solutions or motivations for changed behaviour. Madeleine Fagan has pointed to the way that such a simple narrative tends to reproduce a particular vision of the ethical subject (the individualised, non-relational liberal subject of later modernity who is capable of collective action) and its civilisation (made up of businesses, airports, infrastructure and power stations) which is to be saved.[16] This is not only depoliticising, it also limits our ethical imagination whilst re-entrenching the 'very modernist project that has arguably brought us to this point in the first place'.[17] What is perhaps needed is a more intricate vision of the ethical subject as co-constituted in relation with the non-human – as inter-species as well as international. Outlined by Donna Haraway, this vision involves thinking of ourselves as a co-shaped species, emerging in a 'knot' with microbes and genus of all varieties, 'in layers of reciprocating complexity all the way down'. The point for Haraway is 'not to celebrate this complexity but to become worldly and to respond', building a wider vision of the cosmopolitical that includes the non-human in a web of contingent obligation and care.[18] Such a conception would offer no solutions to climate change, but opens the possibility of thinking responsibilities outside the frame of human exceptionalism that currently limits ethics and IR. Regardless of how the problem is faced and from which angles, the challenge of climate change and relations to the non-human is an area with which ethics and IR will need to wrestle, both now and in the future.

The decolonial and postcolonial challenge

One way of approaching this problem is hinted at in Ajay Parasram's brilliantly provocative contribution to this volume. Illustrating the coexistence of alternative ontologies made visible from a postcolonial framing, Parasram finds inspiration in the indigenous North American Dene ontology of land relayed by Glen Sean Coulthard in *Red Skins, White Masks*. For the Dene, human and non-human are not considered separable entities, society is not opposed to nature and land is not an external background but a *relationship* based in obligations towards the human and non-human alike. Such a 'grounded normativity' is posed by Parasram as an alternative to the abstract reasoning of Eurocentric 'state of nature' theorising. But it also illustrates the fact that different ethico-ecological ontologies and accounts of co-existential subjectivity have existed for centuries *outside* what Robbie Shilliam calls the 'European-modern'. This external status has ensured its practitioners have been excluded as unworthy interlocutors in ethical inquiry policed by the Western academy.[19]

The post- or decolonial challenge is therefore the second issue that ethics and IR will increasingly need to confront. This language of 'challenges' and 'confrontation' between international ethics and post-/decolonialism is obviously profoundly problematic, as it implies these are two separate and internally homogenous fields of inquiry, encountering each other only now on level terrain. On the one hand, this is clearly false: the diversity of ethics and IR has already been stressed and the critical chapters of Parasram, Puneet Dhaliwal, William Ackah and Mustapha Pasha in this volume demonstrates how the field encompasses this challenge; meanwhile postcolonialism and decolonialism are marked by different spatial, temporal and intellectual origins and concerns, as well as internal differences.[20] And yet, on the other hand, the post- and decolonial critiques remain marginalised contestations because of the way they point to the Eurocentric foundations (Parasram), abstract methods of reasoning (Dhaliwal) and constitutive exclusion of colonial violence and peoples (Ackah) that grounds and legitimises the majority of international ethical thought. Dhaliwal and Ackah, in different ways, call attention to the coloniality of power relations that remain infused within our understandings of global justice, cosmopolitanism, human rights, empowerment and emancipation.

It is partly for this reason that Louiza Odysseos cautions against a rush to translate the decolonial into the 'familiar ethical languages and approaches' of the Western academy. Her stress on retaining decolonial ethics precisely as a challenging *question* is 'not a prohibitive move but one that encourages a fundamental questioning of the language, praxis and figures of ethics',[21] upon which many contributions to this volume rely. In this way, then, decolonising international ethics remains a challenge we *all* must confront, rather than being simply an alternative approach, an exotic form of cosmopolitanism we choose whether or not to engage alongside more accustomed forms. For example, could the just war tradition and critical security studies, the focus of Cian O'Driscoll's section in this volume, explore their problematic entanglements with Western modernity and colonial violence by adopting the 'perspective of subjects who inhabit its [modernity's] underside', as Nelson Maldonado-Torres does in *Against War*?[22] Can the ethics of international institutions stand up to historical inquiries which reveal their consciously erased origins in the perpetuation of colonial domination, as provided by Peo Hansen and Stefan Jonsson's investigation of the EU in *Eurafrica*?[23] Would the norms of intervention, sovereignty and humanitarianism look different if interrogated not just from the perspective of contemporary Latin American states (as in Raúl Salgado's chapter), but also according to the vision of the neo-liberal, depersonalised, non-relational 'human' they seek to 'protect' within an historically particular understanding of the Western state?

As the decolonial challenge has swept through the arts, humanities and social sciences, it becomes harder for ethics and IR not to engage it more fully. Yet there is an important caveat to stress with regard to the mode of that present and future engagement. Just as scholars would do well to follow Oddyseos in not seeking to 'translate' decoloniality into accepted forms of ethics, they should also avoid attempts to mine colonial experience for alternative ontologies which could in some sense 'save' Western civilisation, whether ecologically, morally or politically. Seeking to instrumentally draw out and export the Dene ontology of land, for example, would be to reprise the extractive power relationships of coloniality once again. Rather, the decolonial critique and its gradual decolonisation of ethics and IR could be seen as a multiplicity of challenges and questions which strive for new, hybrid and potentially revolutionary forms of knowledge and practices of being human-in-relation.[24]

The unexceptionality of complex violence

Ackah's passionate defence of an 'ethics from the underside' in this volume points to a crucial aspect of the decolonial critique of the international system, noting that the precarious conditions, poverty and disenfranchisement of African peoples goes hand-in-hand with the fetishisation and commodification of Africa's culture and its natural resources that produce mobile technologies. In doing so, decolonialism signals precisely the unexceptional, everyday ways in which injustice, exploitation and irresponsibility are practised in a depersonalised, market-driven global economy. While this 'everydayness' of injustice is a major emphasis of the themes on 'International Political Economy' and 'Vulnerability' in this volume, strongly flagged up in their thematic overviews by James Brassett and Debra L. DeLaet, many other contributions also highlight, in one way or another, the chronically uneven spread of suffering and how it is perpetuated by quixotic ways of being a modern, international subject.

There will always be a need for ethics and IR to maintain a focus on preventing and mitigating exceptional events, such as war, humanitarian disasters, genocide and ethnic cleansing. But the critical insights of feminists and post-Marxists have ensured that the greater complexity of unexceptional, structural violence within the global economy and international system has gained increasing traction in recent times, striated as it is by divisions including race, class and gender. The trend towards the unexceptional will, I would suggest, continue in the coming years; there is still some way to go in this regard, however, as a tendency remains in much of ethics and IR to focus on exceptional events, on abstract theorising and grand solutions, leaving everyday injustice to feminists, decolonialists and political economists. This is highlighted by a quick review of the journal *Ethics and International Affairs* and its recent issues. Here, an overwhelming preference becomes clear to favour international norms, human rights law, theorisations of global justice and attempts to plug holes in just war theory, more often than not written from the perspective of white, Western men.

An example of the sidelining of unexceptional violence is demonstrated by exploring the similarities and differences of two major events which took place in global cities – London and New York – creating terrible suffering and injustice. The first event, the attack on the World Trade Center in New York on the 11 September 2001, is deeply familiar to everyone. This exceptional occurrence prompted the prouncement of a global war on terror which resulted in hundreds of thousands of deaths across the world, as well as countless books and articles. Many of these publications emerged in the field of ethics and IR, perhaps the most prominent early example being Jean Bethke Elshtain's extraordinary defence of the invasion and occupation of Afghanistan.[25] In contrast, the second event is perhaps less familiar to many. When the Grenfell Tower burned down in London on 14 June 2017, killing at least 71 people in one of the worst preventable disasters in UK history, there was almost no comment at all from scholars of ethics and IR (or IR in general), either on conventional or social media platforms. As Jenny Edkins will point out in a forthcoming book, the events bore key similarities, such as the horror of the intense fire in a high-rise building, with people seen in the windows seeking rescue; people forced to jump to their deaths; survivors and onlookers helplessly speaking by phone to their loved ones trapped inside; as well as a confused emergency response and the pulling together of a local community in solidarity.[26] Yet the reaction to the two events has been markedly different: the victims of 9/11 were held up as national heroes, appropriated by the state despite their diverse international origins to support wars of retribution; the victims of Grenfell were treated with pity and charity in most quarters, or as the undeserving poor with uncertain immigration status in others.

There are several elements that account for the silence of ethics and IR on Grenfell, but I will draw out two that illustrate the need to engage the unexceptionality of complex international violence. First, whilst both events happened at the heart of global cities, 9/11 was undeniably 'international', with a global terrorist network accepting responsibility and placing the blame on US foreign policy. Grenfell appeared a more local, at best a national tragedy, with no 'evil' hand directing it. It was more easily left to other disciplines, such as sociology, law, urban geography and city planning. The fact that it seemed the result merely of poor everyday local planning and governance meant it was effortlessly marginalised from IR. And yet the Grenfell tower victims, and many survivors, came from all over the world, from Italy to the Philippines, including Syrian refugees and Lebanese nursery officers.[27] The reasons for the deadliness of the blaze are not yet fully known, but they appear equally international. The recent renovation of the tower had involved a complex array of subcontractors and imported goods, including a French-owned project management firm, a German ventilation system, low-grade American-made cladding which many have blamed for the speed with which the fire spread, and a Qatari-owned gas network.[28] Meanwhile, the cost-cutting that led to this sub-standard renovation was blamed by the local council and the independent management organisation it employed – Kensington and Chelsea Tenant Management Organisation (KCTMO) – on the austerity measures imposed by the global financial crisis.[29]

A second reason for IR's silence on issues like Grenfell is perhaps that the violence which led to it was so mundane, the responsibility complex, diffused and difficult to determine. In contrast to the sudden, unexpected and spectacular violence of the 9/11 attacks, Grenfell was the result of what Edkins calls a slower, more silent violence, the outcome of years of neglect, inequality and discrimination.[30] The links between Kensington and Chelsea as one of the UK's most internationally diverse and socio-economically unequal boroughs and the rise of London as a centre of global finance are obvious, but difficult to trace precisely. Meanwhile, the ideologically inspired hollowing-out and privatisation of local government provision, the neo-liberal deregulation of social housing from the 1980s, the resultant outsourcing and cost-cutting of renovation, all generated an unresponsive, undemocratic Tennant Management Organisation (the KCTMO) which could shift responsibility for the fire to the material choices and design decisions of architects and subcontractors. The problem here is that the ethics and politics of such local organisation and bureaucracy is dull, unexceptional and appears divorced from the more abstract, spectacular concerns of global justice and genocide. The perpetrators of such slow violence are not evil terrorists or genocidal warlords; they are an assemblage of private companies, planning and building regulations, economic and political decisions taken at all levels over many years. But these are precisely the same neo-liberal management techniques that have spread to more traditional areas of international ethics in recent decades, including the organisation of humanitarian aid and provision for refugees, victims of war and famine.[31] It is within these mundane governmental assemblages that people's everyday lives (and deaths) are decided globally. If ethics and IR is to deal with issues of international responsibility, care, accountability and justice in the future, it will need to turn its focus much more to dealing with the slow violence that led to Grenfell *as well as* the quick, unexpected violence of 9/11. And it will need the conceptual and methodological tools to track and trace the unexceptionality of these more everyday, gradual forms of injustice.

Conclusion

This volume has done an incredible job of showcasing the plurality and vibrancy of ethics and IR as a field that has a range of futures. What I have tried to do in this concluding chapter is offer suggestions for certain directions that I see those futures taking. Other scholars will, of course, see very different future trajectories, and these may turn out to be much more accurate predictions. But I have focused on the areas – the environment, the decolonial and the unexceptional – that are already signposted in this volume, and which I see as the most pressing concerns, those that most urgently need to be addressed. What links all these future directions most prominently perhaps is the need for ethics and IR in the future to deal more explicitly with the issue of power: the exercise of power in the discipline regarding *what counts* as ethics and IR, or IR more broadly; and the exercise of material, socio-economic and normative power internationally which decides *who counts* as worthy of recognition as subjects of ethical regard, as well as *when* and *where* the lines will be drawn. Whatever the future holds for the field, there must be an acknowledgement that practices of ethics and IR, as well as their theorisation, necessarily involve the use of power – without exercising power, nothing can be done, no one can be saved, nor anything achieved.[32] But equally, the traditional language of humanitarianism, human rights and justice, as well as security and resilience, have been adopted by states, international organisations and NGOs as means for shaping and governing people's behaviour globally.[33] These concepts are now just as much tools of government and control as they are inspirations and means of emancipation and empowerment. So how do we deal with the ambivalence of ethics and IR that is always *both* oriented to incorporation/freedom *and* marginalisation/government, in ever more complex ways? This is a broad and intricate problem for the present and the future of international ethics.

Notes

1 See Helen Meekosha and Russell Shuttleworth, 'What's so "critical" about critical disability studies?', *Australian Journal of Human Rights*, 15(1), 2009, pp. 47–75.

2 Cynthia Weber, 'Why is there no Queer International Theory?', *European Journal of International Relations*, 21(1), 2015, pp. 27–51.

3 Jacques Derrida, in Jacques Derrida and Bernard Stiegler, *Echographies of Television: Filmed Interviews* (Oxford: Polity Press, 2002), p. 50.

4 Chris Brown, *International Relations Theory: New Normative Approaches* (Hemel Hempstead: Harvester Wheatsheaf, 1992).

5 Alan G. Mencher, 'On the Social Deployment of Science', Educational Foundation for Nuclear Science, December 1971, *Bulletin of the Atomic Scientists*, 27, 10: 37.

6 The Lancet Countdown, *The 2017 Report of the Lancet Countdown*, available at http://www.lancetcountdown.org/the-report/ (accessed 18 December 2017), indicators 1.2–1.7.

7 *Ibid.*, indicator 1.8.

8 Andy Coghlan, 'Climate change will kill millions but you knew that already', *New Scientist*, 30 October 2017.

9 Peter Christoff and Robyn Eckersley, *Globalization and the Environment* (Lanham: Rowman and Littlefield, 2013).

10 Matt MacDonald, *Security, the Environment and Emancipation: Contestation over Environmental Change* (London: Routledge, 2011).

11 See Simon Dalby, 'Biopolitics and climate security in the Anthropocene', *Geoforum*, 49, 2013, pp. 184–192.

12 Dan Bulley, 'Shame on EU? Europe, RtoP, and the politics of refugee protection', *Ethics and International Affairs*, 31(1), 2017, pp. 51–70.

13 See Donna Haraway, *Staying with the Trouble: Making Kin in the Cthulucene* (Durham and London: Duke University Press, 2016).

14 Saskia Sassen, *Expulsions: Brutality and Complexity in the Global Economy* (Cambridge: Harvard University Press, 2014).

15 Jenny Jones, Green Party Member of the London Assembly, *Edible London: Why London Needs to Grow More Food.* Report for the London Assembly (2008). Available at: file:///C:/Users/pisp115638/Downloads/assembly-members-jonesj-docs-secure_food%20(1).pdf (accessed 12 December 2017).

16 Madeleine Fagan, 'Who's afraid of the ecological apocalypse? Climate change and the production of the ethical subject?', *British Journal of Politics and International Relations*, 19(2), 2017, pp. 233–235.

17 *Ibid.*, p. 237.

18 Donna J. Harway, *When Species Meet* (Minneapolis: University of Minnesota Press, 2008), pp. 41–42.

19 Robbie Shilliam, 'Decolonising the grounds of ethical inquiry: a dialogue between Kant, Foucault and Glissant', *Millennium: Journal of International Studies*, 39(3), 2011, p. 650.

20 For a brief summary of the differences between postcolonial and decolonial theory, see Gurminder K. Bhambra, 'Postcolonial and decolonial dialogues', *Postcolonial Studies*, 17(2), 2014, pp. 115–121.

21 Louiza Odysseos, 'Prolegomena to any future decolonial ethics: coloniality, poetics and "being human as praxis"', *Millennium: Journal of International Studies*, 45(3), 2017, p. 471.

22 Nelson Maldonado-Torres, *Against War: Views from the Underside of Modernity* (Durham and London: Duke University Press, 2008), p. 2.

23 Peo Hanssen and Stefan Jonsson, *Eurafrica* (London: Bloomsbury Academic, 2014).

24 See Odysseos's reading of Sylvia Wynter and the praxis of being hybridly human, 'Prolegomena to any future decolonial ethics', pp. 464–471. See also Robbie Shilliam, *The Black Pacific* (London: Bloomsbury Academic, 2015).

25 Jean Bethke Elshtain, *Just War against Terror: The Burden of American Power in a Violent World* (New York: Basic Books, 2003).

26 Jenny Edkins, *Memory, Security, Politics* (Manchester: Manchester University Press, 2018).

27 A 'full' list of the victims (the number is still doubted by many) is available at: https://www.theguardian.com/uk-news/2017/jul/13/grenfell-tower-fire-victims-dead-missing-identified-named-so-far (accessed 1 December 2017).

28 See Naomi Rovnick, 'Grenfell Tower: the cladding, the contractors and the chain of confusion', *Financial Times*, 29 June 2017 (https://www.ft.com/content/b8bb72d2-5c1a-11e7-b553-e2df1b0c3220); Robert Booth, Amelia Gentleman and Mustafa Khalili, 'Grenfell Tower gas pipes left exposed, despite fire safety expert's orders', *The Guardian*, 27 June 2017 (https://www.theguardian.com/uk-news/2017/jun/27/grenfell-tower-gas-pipes-left-exposed-despite-fire-safety-experts-orders); Rob Davies, 'Complex chain of companies that worked on Grenfell Tower raises oversight concerns', 16 June 2017 (https://www.theguardian.com/uk-news/2017/jun/15/long-builder-chain-for-grenfell-a-safety-and-accountability-issue). All accessed 15 November 2017.

29 Seraphima Kennedy, 'When I worked at KCTMO I had nightmares about burning tower blocks', *The Guardian*, 16 June 2017 (https://www.theguardian.com/commentisfree/2017/jun/16/worked-kctmo-nightmares-burning-tower-blocks). Accessed 15 November 2017.

30 Edkins, *Memory, Security, Politics.*

31 See Suzan Ilcan and Anita Lacey, *Governing the Poor: Exercises of Poverty Reduction, Practices of Global Aid* (London: McGill-Queen's University Press, 2011); Mark Duffield, *Development, Security and Unending War* (Cambridge: Polity Press, 2007).

32 Dan Bulley, *Migration, Ethics and Power: Spaces of Hospitality in International Politics* (London: Sage, 2017), pp. 10–11.

33 See Didier Fassin, *Humanitarian Reason: A Moral History of the Present* (Berkeley: University of California Press, 2012); Bal Sokhi-Bulley, *Governing (Through) Rights* (London: Hart, 2016); William Walters, 'Foucault and frontiers: notes on the birth of the humanitarian border', in Ulrich Bröckling, Susanne Krasmann and Thomas Lemke (eds), *Governmentality: Current Issues and Future Challenges* (New York: Routledge, 2011), pp. 138–164; Ilcan and Lacey, *Governing the Poor*; Duffield, *Development, Security and Unending War.*

INDEX